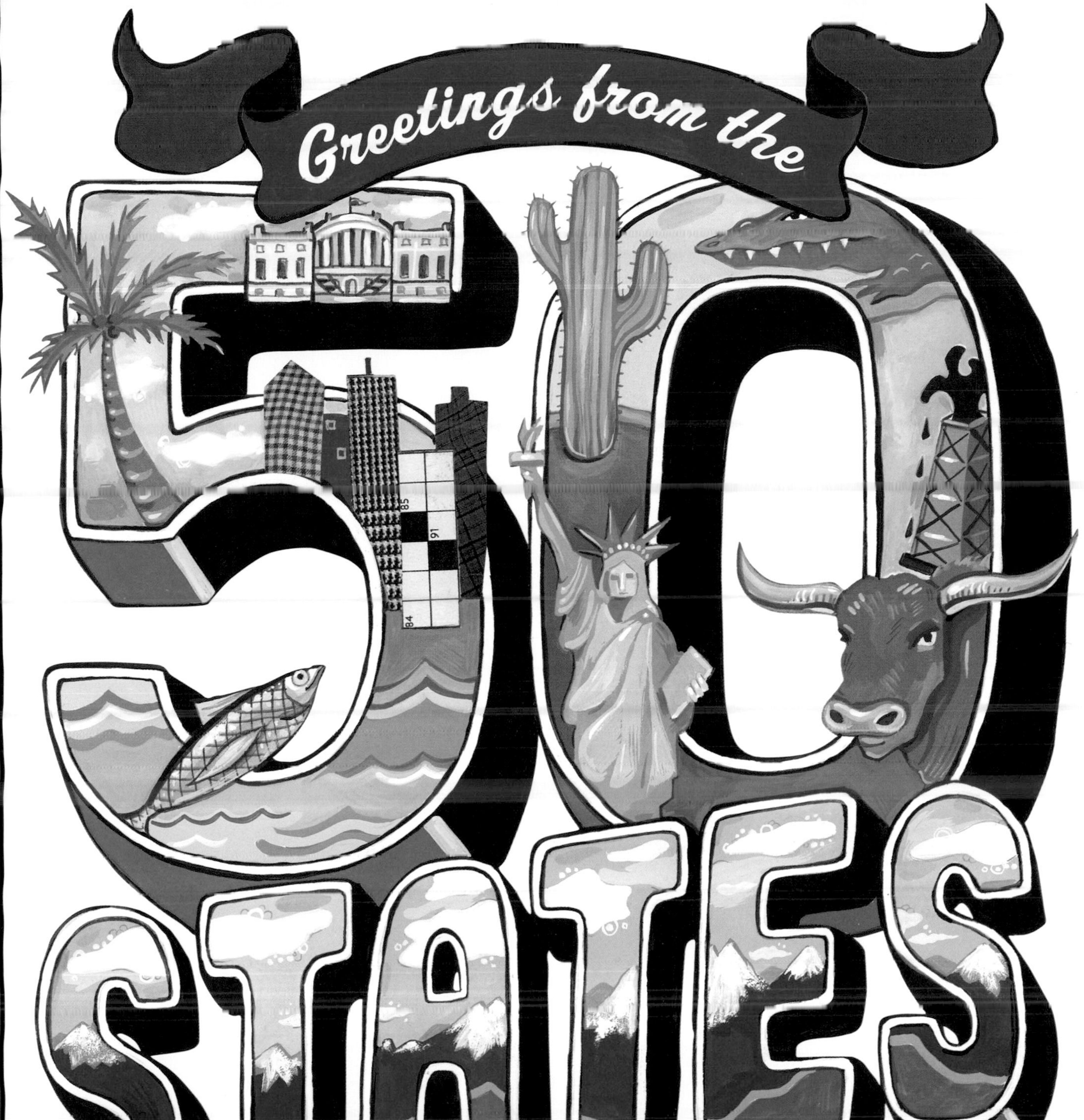

Greetings from the 50 STATES

How They Got Their Names

By Sheila Keenan

Illustrated by Selina Alko

For Kevin: On the road again, I just can't wait to get on the road again . . .

Many thanks to Kate Waters for yet another wonderful editorial enterprise;
to Brenda Murray for her unflagging enthusiasm and help with this book; to
Erin Black for pitching in; to Becky Terhune and Kay Petronio for the beautiful
design work; and to Selina Alko for the cool, cool geography visuals! —S.K.

To Sean, Isaiah, and Ginger, with love; and to Ben, Kay, and the group for
guiding me on my journey of self-discovery here in the United States. —S.A.

Library of Congress Cataloging-in-Publication Data Available

ISBN-13: 978-0-439-83439-1
ISBN-10: 0-439-83439-2

10 9 8 7 6 5 4 3 2 1   8 9 10 11 12 13/0

Printed in Singapore   46
First printing, September 2008
Book design by Kay Petronio

Contents

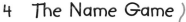

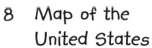

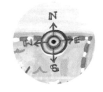

The Name Game

It could have happened.

These are names once used for New Jersey, Hawaii, New York, and Nevada. Whose idea was that? Try a British King, an English sea captain, a Dutch trading company, and a miner who may have read *The Hunchback of Notre Dame*.

To find out how our 50 states and the District of Columbia were named, you have to time travel through American history, going back more than 500 years to when the full-scale European exploration of our country began. These explorers, settlers, missionaries, and entrepreneurs came looking for (choose one or more):

○ a passage to China and the Indies

○ *gold*

○ a good place for a colony

○ *gold*

○ souls to save

○ *gold*

○ fish, fur, and timber

○ Did we mention *gold*?

Of course, the United States wasn't one big blank map waiting for the Europeans to come fill in the missing names and borders. There were millions and millions of Native Americans living in North America when Columbus arrived in 1492. That's a lot of people who already had words for themselves, their cities, settlements, hunting grounds, mountains, plains, rivers, and streams. This explains why 27 state names come from Native American words . . . or at least what the Spanish, French, English, Portuguese, or Dutch *thought* they heard the Indians say. Tribal names were often spelled phonetically by Europeans using their own languages. Then as English-speaking people spread across the country, they often respelled place names in their language and *voilà!* — you end up with 24, maybe even 80 different spellings of Kansas, for example.

What *else* was in play in the name game *besides* tribal languages? Royalty, red, and romance.

Romance?

Yup! Our third largest state may be named after a mythical place in a Spanish romance novel. Two other states are named for the color red. And as for royalty? Say you wanted to get in good with your king or queen so they'll keep financing your expeditions or set you up with a colony. Wouldn't they just love it if you or your trusty representative sailed over to America, "discovered" and claimed a huge chunk of land (ignoring the tribes who were already there), and gave the place their royal name?

You bet they would; in fact, sometimes the monarchs spelled it out in writing: Name the place after me. Seven states can give themselves royal airs over their names. Oddly enough, that's six more than are named after a U.S. president.

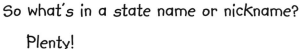

Behind each state's name is a story of how Americans felt about the land they settled in, how they connected to its history and geography, how they recognized its unique character, how proud they felt of themselves and their state. That's true for a state's nickname, too.

Well, it's usually true.

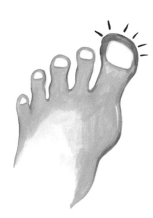

Okay, sure, who wants to say they're from the Mosquito State or the Web-footed State or the Mud-waddler State or the Stub-toe State? Luckily, those aren't the *official* nicknames for New Jersey, Oregon, Mississippi, and Montana; they all have perfectly respectable other nicknames. Many states have more than one nickname, some official, some unofficial but widely used.

So what's in a state name or nickname?

Plenty!

Let's go on a cross-country trip to find out where all those big names on our map came from.

Things to Know Before You Go . . . deeper into this book.

⭐ The 50 states are arranged alphabetically; Washington, D.C., follows at the end. Each entry includes information about the state's name, nickname, and the year it was granted statehood.

⭐ Historically, there were many different ways to spell the same place name. The most common spellings are used here.

⭐ Quoted material is from the primary source mentioned in an entry. That's the beauty of the Internet: you can go online and read the *Charter for the Province of Pennsylvania* and see exactly what "CHARLES the Second by the Grace of God King of England, Scotland, France and Ireland" had to say to "Our Trustie and wellbeloved Subject WILLIAM PENN" in 1681. Some good Web sites: The Avalon Project at Yale Law School, www.yale.edu/lawweb/avalon; Library of Congress, www.loc.gov; National Archives and Records, www.archives.gov.

⭐ The full history of a state and its original native inhabitants could never fit in a book this size. That would be like writing your life story on a postcard. So when you get to the last page, check the list of Web sites to find out where you can read more about the great states of our United States.

9

Alabama

Capital Montgomery

Alabama became our 22nd state on December 14, 1819.

Sweet Home Alabama. Or is that Alebamon? Allibamou anyone?

There are 31 different spellings recorded for this southern state. It all depended on which Spanish, French, or British explorer or settler was taking the notes.

The name was first recorded by three gentlemen who traveled with the Spanish conquistador Hernando de Soto. In 1540, de Soto came tromping through Alabama with his horses, dogs, herd of pigs, and gold-hungry, plundering army. One gentleman's written account tracked the expedition through *Alibamu;* the other man penned *Alibamo.* De Soto's secretary was even more geographically creative: He wrote *Limamu* in his diary.

No matter how you spell it, Alabama isn't a European name anyhow. The resident Choctaw probably called their farming neighbors the Alabama from the Choctaw *alba* for "plants" or "vegetation" and *amo* for "gatherer." The Alabama River got its name from the tribe; the state got its name from the river. (And the movie got its name from the song!)

You'll find "Heart of Dixie" on everything from souvenir T-shirts to Alabama license plates. Dixie is a nickname for the South or for the Confederate states. The word may have come from old $10 bills called dixies, which were used before the Civil War.

MT. McKINLEY

midnight sun

Arctic OCEAN

RANGE
MOUNTAIN

RUSSIA

SEWARD
PENINSULA
Teller

oil   GOLD

"we were many, now we are few"

BERING
Sea

KING SALMON

ALASKA PENINSULA

NATION
PARK

JUNEAU

500
miLes to
U.S.
mainland

ALáXsXaQ

PACIFIC

OCEAN

Alaska

Capital Juneau

Alaska became our 49th state on January 3, 1959.

Alaska has 34,000 miles of shoreline. No wonder it got its name from *aláxsxaq*, the Aleutian word for "shore" or "that toward which the sea is directed." The Aleut are one of the native peoples of Alaska. At first, their word and others like it — *agunalaksh, al-ak-shak*, or *al-ay-ek-sa* — were used only for the Alaskan peninsula that juts into the chilly Bering Sea. Russians and Americans who migrated and took over former tribal lands in the 18th and 19th centuries began to use the word *Alaska* for the whole 586,400 square miles of what became our 49th state.

Seward's Folly. Seward's Ice Box. Icebergia. The Polar Bear Garden. Alaska's early nicknames were a joke. That's because many people thought U.S. Secretary of State William H. Seward was a fool to pay Russia $7,200,000 in gold in 1867 for the vast, frozen, unexplored wilderness it owned in the far north. The territory was so remote, it wasn't even connected to the U.S. mainland.

Then in the 1880s, prospectors struck gold in Alaska. Nobody was laughing at Seward anymore, especially since he'd only paid 2.5 cents an acre for the whole gigantic state!

Alaska's modern nicknames, the Last Frontier or the Land of the Midnight Sun, honor the northern state's beautiful, rugged landscape, and long — *really long* — Arctic summer days.

2.5¢
Last Frontier State

13

14

Arizona

Capital Phoenix

Arizona became our 48th state on February 14, 1912.

Once there was a small spring out west called *Alehzon* by the Pima who lived near it. The Spaniards came exploring in the 16th century and eventually called these Pima tribal lands *Arizonac*, a variation on native words.

At least, that's the most common explanation. Others say "the place of the small spring" might have been called *Ali-Shonak*. Or Arizona may have come from Spanish words for "arid place."

Wet or dry, the name *Arizona* took. And a silver miner helped make it official.

Charles D. Poston was a mining entrepreneur who loved the place: "The valleys of Arizona are not surpassed for fertility and beauty by any that I have seen, and that includes the whole world." In 1862, Poston went to Washington, D.C., chatted up President Lincoln, threw a lovely oyster dinner for some congressmen who wanted to move out west to help the "galoots" (and their own flagging careers), and got a bill passed officially recognizing the Arizona Territory.

In 1867–1868, Lieutenant Joseph Ives led an expedition for the U.S. War Department. He surveyed parts of the American West, including some of what is now Arizona. Lieutenant Ives reached the southern rim of the Grand Canyon. He predicted no other party would come to visit this "profitless locality," which he declared "altogether valueless . . ."

Altogether WRONG!

Today, nearly 5,000,000 people a year come to the Grand Canyon State to see one of the natural wonders of the world.

Grand Canyon State

Arkansas

Capital Little Rock

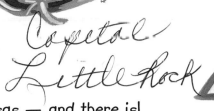

Arkansas became our 25th state on June 15, 1836.

There oughta be a law about Arkansas — and there is!

In the 19th century, you'd probably say you were from ARKanSAW, but your fellow Americans would claim you hailed from ArKANSAS. Even Arkansas's two U.S. senators couldn't agree on where they came from.

Phonics and spelling saved the day! In 1881, the state legislature passed a bill that declared the state's name would be spelled Arkansas, but pronounced "Arkansaw."

The original confusion shows what happens when French-speaking explorers tangle with tribal names. In the 17th century, the French met up with native people who lived west of the Mississippi River. They called themselves the Ugakhpa or "those going downstream"; Quapaw was also used; and Algonquian-speakers called them Arkansas, meaning "south wind." The explorers wrote down the Indian names as they heard them — and of course, they were writing in French. At one time, there were around 70 variations, from Aksansea to Acansa.

It's had two pronunications, so why not two official nicknames? The Land of Opportunity was adopted in 1947 to encourage businesses and tourism. In 1995, the Arkansas legislature decided the Natural State was a better way to promote the state's "unsurpassed scenery" and "abundant wildlife."

OZARK mountains

Natural State

17

18

California

Capital Sacramento

In the early 16th century, Spanish adventurers — looking for treasure as usual — sailed to what they thought was an island. The explorer Hernán Cortés called it California.

He probably got the name out of a book.

Las Sergas de Esplandián (*The Adventures of Esplandian*), written by García Ordoñez de Montalvo, was a very popular Spanish novel of the time. It was filled with romance, chivalry, and fantastic tales of California, the "strangest island of the world." This legendary California was paradise: It was laden with gold and strewn pearls; it was inhabited only by brave, beautiful women, who harnessed wild beasts and galloped around waving golden weapons. (Ordoñez de Montalvo would have loved Hollywood!)

Mapmakers started labeling the "island" on the Pacific coast *California*. The name stuck even though later explorers and missionaries proved the "island" was a pensinsula, now Baja California in Mexico, and that the rest of California was on the mainland.

The Spaniards weren't the only ones looking to get rich quick in California. Thousands of people rushed there after precious nuggets of gold were discovered in 1848. The fevered California Gold Rush tops the list of what makes this the Golden State.

Golden State

19

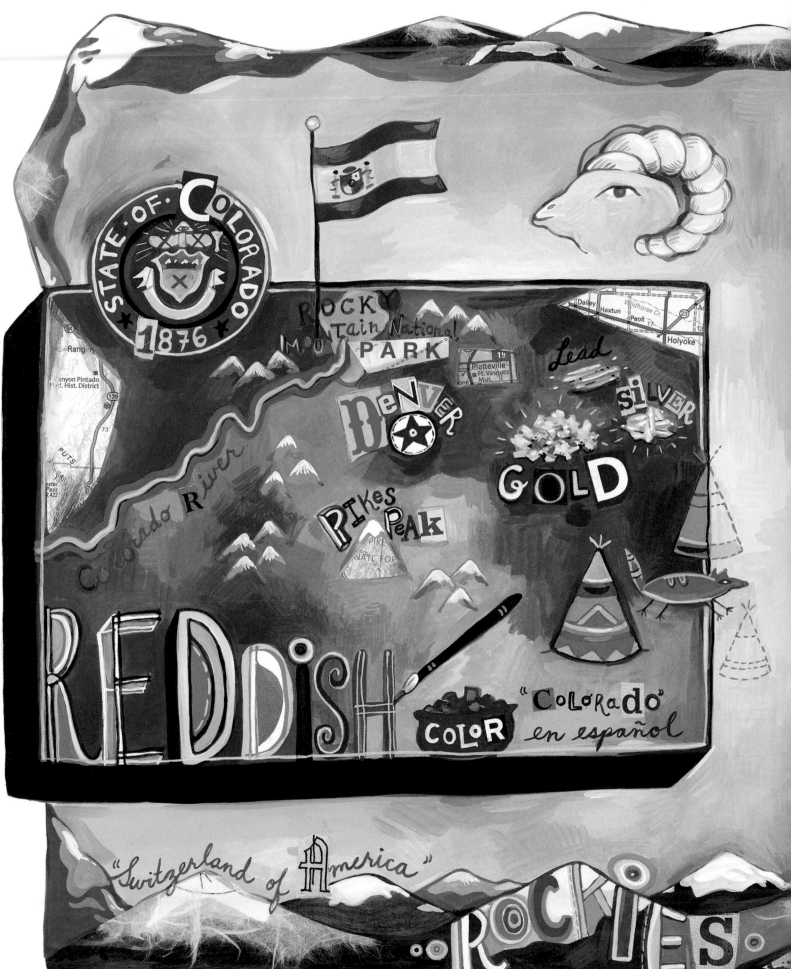

Colorado

Capital
Denver

Colorado became our 38th state on August 1, 1876.

Who's in favor of naming this place Idaho?

No, that's a coined word.

Jefferson?

Okay, but, it's a temporary thing only.

Colorado?

Si! That's a great name for a state.

The Spanish were the first Europeans to reach this western state; they got here in the 16th century. *Colorado* means "reddish color" in Spanish. It was a good, descriptive name for the area because of the warm, earthy color of its land and river.

Over the next 200 years, trappers and settlers eventually pushed out the native peoples. New geographic names such as Osage, Colona, and Idaho were considered and rejected. From 1859 to 1861, Colorado temporarily organized itself as the Territory of Jefferson. But gold, not red, became the name of the game.

Gold was discovered near what is now Denver; the mountains were full of silver and lead, too. The rush was on!

The boom territory soon wanted to be part of the Union. Congress was happy to officially recognize such a rich region as the Colorado Territory in 1861.

Colorado's nickname, the Centennial State, shows good timing. It became a state in 1876, the same year the United States celebrated the hundredth anniversary of the signing of the Declaration of Independence. It's also called the Switzerland of America. Colorado's Rocky Mountains have more than 1,000 peaks that top 10,000 feet.

Centennial State

21

The Constitution State

We, the People

410 miles

MA

OYSTERS

1st hamburger

HARTFORD

Connecticut River

INDUSTRY

Mohegans

QUoneHtacut

LONG · ISLAND · Sound

the Turtle

N

22

Connecticut

Connecticut became
our 5th state on
January 9, 1788.

If you were in a spelling bee and were asked to spell the word from which we got Connecticut, you could win with *Quinnehtukqut* . . . or *Quinnihticut* or even *Quonehtacut*.

No matter how it is written in English, this Mohegan word means "beside the long tidal river." The native people used the word as the river's name; in the 1600s, European explorers and colonists used it to mean the area that became the state.

The *Quonehtacut* or Connecticut River is indeed long: At 410 miles, it's the longest river in New England and flows through or passes by four states: New Hampshire, Vermont, Massachusetts, and Connecticut. Maritime history was made on its waters. In 1776, David Bushnell launched an amazing invention on the Connecticut: the *American Turtle*, a submarine!

Because of the river, Connecticut became a thriving manufacturing state. Industry made Connecticuters famous for their — what else? — industriousness. People called the state the Land of Steady Habits.

Nearly 150 years before our Constitution was written, settlers in Connecticut adopted The Fundamental Orders. This 1639 document declared Connecticut would govern itself by "the free consent of the people." This is sometimes called the first written constitution in history. And in Connecticut, they agree: It's officially the Constitution State.

Unofficially, it's the Nutmeg State. A nutmeg looks like a nut, but is actually a very, very hard fruit seed that's used as a spice. Colonial Connecticut "nutmeggers" peddled these seeds; some customers didn't realize you had to grate them and thought they had been sold wooden goods.

Nutmeg State

GREAT SEAL OF THE STATE OF DELAWARE
1793 · 1847 · 1907

1st State

horseshoe crab

Delaware River

ZAP!

ATLANTIC OCEAN

DOVER

DELAWARE BAY

Dover Air Force Base

Lord BARON De La WAR Jr.

1982 Square MILES

Rehoboth Beach

Shaft Ox Corner   Frankford
Pepperbox
Gumboro
Selbyville

24

Delaware

Capital Dover

Our tale opens with a terrible storm.

In 1610, the English explorer Samuel Argall was on a mission to bring supplies to the desperate, starving colonists in Jamestown, Virginia. Bad weather blew him off course into an unfamiliar bay. Captain Argall named the bay and the river that flowed into it Delaware, after Lord De La Warr, the English colonial governor of Virginia. The governor, who was waiting in Virginia, was no doubt honored. But he was probably even happier when Argall and his boatload of goods got back on course.

The Delaware River and Delaware Bay lap at the coastline of the state that eventually inherited the same name.

Delaware may be the second smallest state, but it's the proud First State. That's because on December 7, 1787, Delaware became the first state to ratify the U.S. Constitution.

Just because you're a small state that's not quite 2,000 square miles, doesn't mean you're not big enough for *several* nicknames. Delaware is also called the:

DIAMOND STATE

You won't get rich hunting diamonds here. This nickname comes from Thomas Jefferson. The founding father and president said that Delaware was a small, valuable jewel because of its important location on the East Coast.

BLUE HEN STATE

Sounds like a cute name from a heartwarming animal story, right? Probably not. It may refer to chickens used in game fights that were popular with Revolutionary War soldiers. The Blue Hen Chicken was a scrappy fighter and a winning breed, so some Delaware soldiers took to calling themselves after the bird. However, no one's really sure where the nickname comes from.

Blue Hen State

OKALOOSA
EGLIN A.F.B.
Niceville
Valparaiso
Ocean City

WALTON

TALLAHASSEE

the SUNSHINE

PONCE de León

THE Fountain of Youth

PASCUA FLORIDA

GULF OF MEXICO

Calusa People

ATLANTIC OCEAN

West Park
Pembroke Park
Miami Gardens
Miami North

Manchineel Tree

ORANGES

Miami Beach

Miami

EVERGLADES National PARK

26

State Florida

Capital Tallahassee

Florida became our 27th state on March 3, 1845.

The 16th century Spanish explorer Juan Ponce de León was looking for the mythical fountain of youth whose magical waters were said to make you stay forever young.

He found Florida — and death.

Ponce de León landed on the northeast coast of the state on April 2, 1513. As explorers are apt to do, he claimed the whole place and then gave it a name: Florida.

Pascua florida was the Spanish feast of the flowers held at Eastertime. April was Eastertime. The newfound land was lush with flowers, trees, shrubs, and blooming vines; *florida* also means flowery, so Ponce de León figured he had picked the perfect name.

Alas! Plants were his undoing.

In 1521, Ponce de León and his men were scouting good locations for a Spanish colony in Florida. They were attacked by a band of Calusa who already lived there. The Calusa dipped their arrows in sap from the manchineel tree. This tree is so poisonous that if a raindrop slides down a manchineel leaf and then drips onto your skin, you'll get burning blisters. When Ponce de León was pierced by a Calusa's poison arrow, he didn't stand a chance.

Pick up a travel brochure for Florida and you'll see white sandy beaches, sunny blue skies, palm trees. Tourism is one of Florida's main businesses, hence the official nickname: the Sunshine State.

Then there's the fun nickname, the Alligator State. Spanish explorers called them *largatos* (lizards). Gators live in just about any body of freshwater in Florida: rivers, lakes, swamps, marshes, and the state's unique Everglades. There were once so many alligators in Florida, an 18th-century writer said you could cross a river on their heads, "had the animal been harmless."

Alligator State

STATE OF GEORGIA · CONSTITUTION · JUSTICE · 1776

13th British Colony

THE GOOBER STATE

ATLANTA

n-guba

Tailor

Carpenter

Savannah

King George II

Baker

DEBT

Columbus

Okefenokee Refuge

James Oglethorpe

ATLANTIC

Georgia

Capital
Atlanta

This state is named after a rich English king who wished to "relieve the wants of our . . . poor subjects."

Of course, there was something in it for His Highness, too.

In 1732, King George II of England granted a charter to James Oglethorpe, a British philanthropist, for what became the 13th British colony in America. The King spelled out the name of the new colony in this charter: Georgia, in honor of . . . himself. King George II hoped that Georgia, once settled, would "increase the trade, navigation and wealth of our realms." It would also help prevent its British colonial neighbor, South Carolina, from being overrun by Spanish colonists from Florida.

Originally, Oglethorpe planned Georgia as a place where poor people could resettle instead of suffering and dying in British prisons because of their debts. It was a noble idea, but there were plenty of people outside jail willing to head for America. Oglethorpe set sail on November 17, 1732, with 115 men, women, and children. They included carpenters, tailors, a baker, a basketmaker, a heelmaker, and one William Little, who "understands flax and hemp."

There were no debtors.

Peaches or peanuts? Take your pick. Georgia is called the Peach State or the Goober State because these are the state's big cash crops.

Goober is another word for peanut. It comes from the African *n-guba*, a word used in several Bantu tribal languages. The word and the nuts came to North America with enslaved Africans. Georgia produces more than two billion pounds of peanuts a year — not to mention the world's largest peach cobbler, a tasty dessert that uses 250 pounds of sugar, 300 pounds of flour, and 75 gallons of peaches.

Peach State

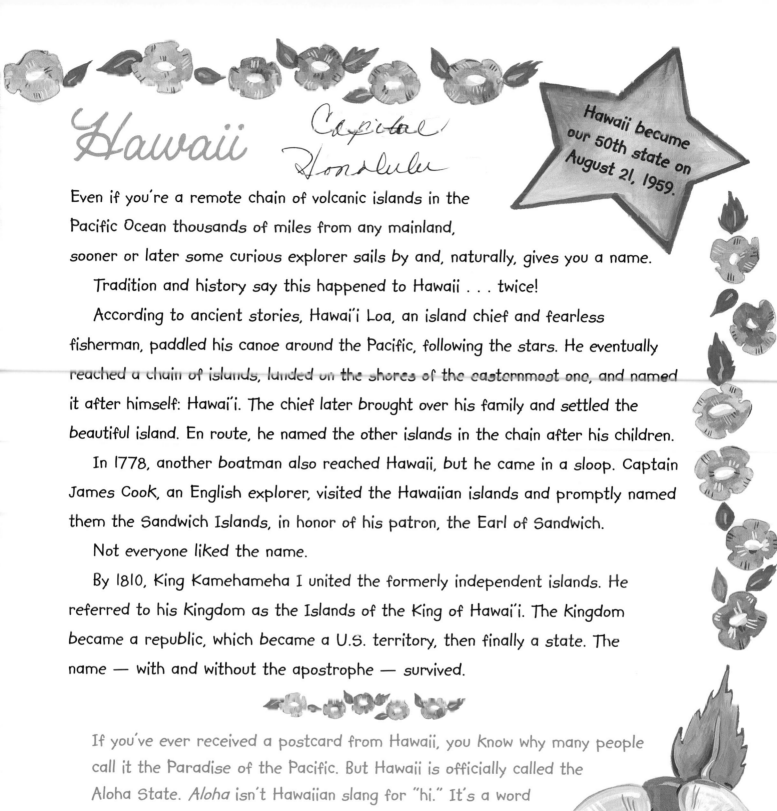

Hawaii

Capital Honolulu

Hawaii became our 50th state on August 21, 1959.

Even if you're a remote chain of volcanic islands in the Pacific Ocean thousands of miles from any mainland, sooner or later some curious explorer sails by and, naturally, gives you a name.

Tradition and history say this happened to Hawaii . . . twice!

According to ancient stories, Hawai'i Loa, an island chief and fearless fisherman, paddled his canoe around the Pacific, following the stars. He eventually reached a chain of islands, landed on the shores of the easternmost one, and named it after himself: Hawai'i. The chief later brought over his family and settled the beautiful island. En route, he named the other islands in the chain after his children.

In 1778, another boatman also reached Hawaii, but he came in a sloop. Captain James Cook, an English explorer, visited the Hawaiian islands and promptly named them the Sandwich Islands, in honor of his patron, the Earl of Sandwich.

Not everyone liked the name.

By 1810, King Kamehameha I united the formerly independent islands. He referred to his kingdom as the Islands of the King of Hawai'i. The kingdom became a republic, which became a U.S. territory, then finally a state. The name — with and without the apostrophe — survived.

If you've ever received a postcard from Hawaii, you know why many people call it the Paradise of the Pacific. But Hawaii is officially called the Aloha State. *Aloha* isn't Hawaiian slang for "hi." It's a word with several spiritual and emotional meanings. According to the 1959 state law that established Hawaii's popular name, "Aloha Spirit" is "the coordination of mind and heart within each person."

Aloha State

ROCKY Mountains

IDAHO

Columbia River

GEM of the MOUNTAINS

STAR GARNET

boise

Salmon river

IDAHO FALLS

gold

Snake river

GREAT SEAL OF THE STATE ☆ OF IDAHO

ESTO PERPETUA

32

Idaho

Capital
Boise

George M. Willing, a 19th century mining lobbyist, had a way with words. He claimed Idaho was an Indian term that meant "gem of the mountains."

He didn't say which Indians.

Idaho was the perfect name for a booming Rocky Mountain territory, Willing suggested, especially one that included the rich mining area Pikes Peak. People in the area, even Congress, were willing to go along . . . until they found out Idaho wasn't really a Native American word. It wasn't even really a word; Willing had invented it himself. The U.S. Senate called the territory Colorado instead.

Meanwhile, "Idaho" traveled to the Northwest. In the 1860s, a steamboat named *The Idaho* chugged up and down the Columbia River. Towns like Idaho Springs sprang up. Gold was discovered in the area, and people rushed to what were soon called the Idaho mines. In a few short years, no one cared about where the word came from, it suited where they were just fine. In 1863, Congress went with Idaho when it designated the territory that became our 43rd state.

Gem of the Mountains stuck. It's true Idaho is known for its rare purple gem, the star garnet. But it's even more famous for another underground prize: spuds. Idaho, the Potato State, grows more of this crop than any other state. We're talking 13.8 billion pounds of spuds a year!

Potato State

Illinois

Illinois became our 21st state on December 3, 1818.

In the 17th century, French explorers reached part of the homeland of the Illinois, a confederacy that included about 12 or 13 independent tribes. The Illinois shared many things in common, including the Algonquian language. As was often the case, not everything translated clearly between native peoples and newcomers. The Illinois, for example, called themselves "inoca."

Father Jacques Marquette, one of the first European explorers to reach Illinois, wrote in 1674 that the name of the people, which he transcribed as *Ilinois*, meant "the men," and was intended to elevate the Illinois above other native peoples. Illinois has also been translated as "warrior" or "tribe of superior men." The French commonly used it for the Native Americans they met within this area. So it made sense to French explorer René-Robert Cavelier, Sieur de La Salle, to use it on his river journey in 1679. La Salle called the waterway he sailed on the Illinois River. He built Fort Crèvecoeur, which means "Heartbreak," on the river, near present-day Peoria, Illinois. From there, La Salle and his crew of Frenchmen and Native Americans hopped in canoes and paddled downstream on into the Mississippi River.

But that's another story — Louisiana's story, actually!

Tall grass and a tall president gave this state two nicknames. Informally, Illinois is called the Prairie State, after the wide swaths of flatland filled with tall, coarse grasses and other prairie plants.

Officially, Illinois is known as the Land of Lincoln in honor of the state's favorite adopted son, President Abraham Lincoln. Lincoln moved to Illinois as a young man. There he worked his way up from clerk to congressman.

The rest is history.

Land of Lincoln

Indiana

*Capital
Indianapolis*

In 1800, Congress passed a resolution that created a new U.S. territory. The act, approved and signed by President John Adams, created a new territory out of what is now Indiana, Illinois, Michigan, Wisconsin, and part of Minnesota. Congress declared this region "shall be called the Indiana Territory."

Indiana. Land of the Indians.

Indiana Territory was indeed home to many tribal groups: the Miami, the Potawatomi, the Kickapoo, the Mascouten, the Delaware (Lenni-Lenape), and the Shawnee.

The Indiana territorial government wanted people to come settle the area. They encouraged people to buy farmland on credit. Meanwhile, most Native Americans moved or were removed from Indiana Territory. The name remained.

Indianans are proud to be from the Hoosier State. But where "hoosier" comes from, nobody knows for sure. Hoosier could be a contraction of "Who's yere?," a common reply if you knocked on a cabin door during Indiana's pioneer days. Or it could come from "husher," slang for tough brawling Indiana riverboat men who hushed up their foes by beating them in fights.

IOWAY
fur pelts
GRANT WOOD
Iowa River
Sioux City
FARM Land
DesMoines
pie
eggs
MIDLE of America
milk
bread

Iowa

Capital, Des Moines

It's all about geography and history, with a little bit of spelling thrown in.

The state of Iowa is named after the Iowa River. The river was named after the native peoples living near its banks. Here's where spelling comes in.

French explorers called the tribal people they met in the river area the Ayuwha. By the 1700s, the Ayuwha and French traders were doing business. Bartering brought European goods like glass beads, iron knives, and gun parts to the Indian villages; the French took away valuable fur pelts. By the 1800s, British entrepreneurs and American colonists had moved in. They called the tribe they traded with the Ioway or Iowa.

White settlement of Iowa began in earnest in 1833. The Ioway, like other Native American groups in the United States, were soon pushed off their lands. Iowa became home to more pioneer Iowans than Native American Ioways.

The most common nickname for Iowa is the Hawkeye State.

But why Hawkeye?

One claim is that it's in honor of Chief Black Hawk, a courageous Sauk war chief. Black Hawk and his people had been forced to give up their land in Illinois and move to Iowa. In 1832, the chief fought back . . . he lost. Six years later, editor James G. Edwards named his newspaper the *Burlington Hawk-eye*. Edwards and his friend, Judge David Rorer, promoted the name in honor of the man who had tried to save his land and people.

Others say the name honors Natty "Hawkeye" Bumppo, the fearless scout in James Fenimore Cooper's popular American novel *The Last of the Mohicans* (1826).

CHIEF BLACK HAWK

Hawkeye State

GREAT SEAL of the STATE of KANSAS · 1861 ·

THE

KAW

SOUTH wind

tornados

Kansas River

Hamlin
Hiawatha
Iowa Point
Brown S.F.I.
Highland
Fanning DONIPH
Leona
Troy

TOPEKA

GREAT
PLAINS

Mulvane Art Mus. S.
WASHBURN UNIV.
Big Shunga Park
Warren Park
TOPEKA

CAN
KENISER
Escanzaques

KANZE

Bleeding Kansas

40

Kansas

Capital Topeka

KaNze, the word source of this state's name, looks like it could be a hip-hop label. Actually, it's a Native American tribal word, which may mean "south wind."

It's easy to see how KaNze became Kansa or Kansas when the French explorers who crossed the great plains of this state and floated down its waterways started taking notes and drawing maps.

As more European explorers and then American settlers headed west and spelled things *their* way, the confusion about the name increased. Some sources say there could be as many as 125 different spellings of this tribe's name, from Can to Keniser to Escanzaques.

The Kansas, who are also commonly called the Kaw, were buffalo hunters who maintained villages near what came to be called the Kansas River. Eventually the region also became known as Kansas. The Kansas-Nebraska Act of 1854 helped standardize the spelling. It also led to Kansas's historical nickname. The congressional act said that the people of the territories Kansas and Nebraska could decide for themselves whether or not to allow slavery within their borders. Since the territories wanted to apply for statehood, what the Kansans and Nebraskans decided would affect the entire Union. Pro-slavery and antislavery forces rushed into Kansas. These settlers wanted to sway the vote — and they didn't just stick to the ballot box. Violent clashes broke out across "Bleeding Kansas."

Modern Kansas has a cheerier nickname, the Sunflower State. Bright yellow wild sunflowers grow like weeds across Kansas. The 1903 law that made *Helianthus annuus* the official state flower praised the sunflower as "richly emblematic of the majesty of a golden future."

Sunflower State

41

Kentucky

Capitol

Kentucky came from words in any one of several Native American languages. Interpretations of these tribal word sources vary from "prairie" to "great meadow" to "land of tomorrow." Land of opportunity is how many people looked at this central state bounded by rivers and mountains on three sides.

Kentucky was traditionally a rich hunting ground for several major Native American groups, including the Shawnee, the Chickasaw, and the Cherokee. It was a political bargaining chip for the Spanish, French, and English who each made claims on it in the 17th and 18th centuries. Colonel Richard Henderson tried to buy a big chunk of it from the Cherokee in an enterprising, but illegal, real-estate trade in 1775. He offered 10,000 English pounds worth of guns, blankets, clothes, rum, and other trading goods. A group of Cherokee leaders agreed to sell him 20 *million* acres of land. Virigina, which claimed Kentucky itself, nixed the deal. And let's not forget Daniel Boone and all the pioneers who followed him down the Wilderness Road and settled Kentucky.

The grass is greener in the Bluegrass State. Kentucky bluegrass really has green blades, but its buds are blue-purple, hence the name. Bluegrass seeds came along with the pioneers and their grazing animals. As the people spread out, so did the grass, growing what Native Americans called white man's tracks. Bluegrass is also a form of stringed American country music, popularized by Kentucky's own mandolin-playing Bill Monroe, the late great "Father of Bluegrass Music."

Bluegrass State

43

Louisiana

Capital
Baton Rouge

Gumbo is a spicy Louisiana stew that mixes a French base with a dash of Spanish, a dollop of African, and a pinch of American flavors.

This state is just like its famous stew.

Louisiana was home to many Native American peoples, including tribes of the Choctaw, Caddo, and Natchez nations. Then the Europeans came along and claimed huge parts of the Mississippi Valley.

Hernando de Soto explored the region and staked a claim for Spain in 1541; the Spanish pretty much left it at that. The intrepid French explorer, René-Robert Cavalier, Sieur de La Salle, started at the Great Lakes and traveled on down the entire Mississippi River. Along the way, he claimed the whole area for France in 1682. La Salle dubbed the river valley Louisiana, after the flamboyant French king Louis XIV.

For the next 121 years, European nations passed the Louisiana territory around like a big bowl of gumbo. France gave part of it to Spain; Great Britain snagged another section; Spain returned the colony to France; the French ruler Napoleon Bonaparte finally sold the Louisiana Territory to the United States in 1803 for $15,000,000. Nine years later, a portion of it became the state of Louisiana.

Louisiana is called the Pelican State because there once were so many of these cool birds flapping about. The brown pelican, which is the largest web-footed bird in the world, nearly died out in Louisiana because of pollution, but state conservation efforts have helped bring back pelican colonies.

Pelican State

Maine

Capital
Augusta

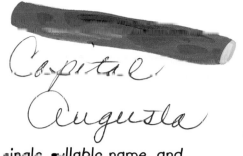
Maine became our 23rd state on March 15, 1820.

Maine is the only state with a single syllable name, and it's a pretty simple name at that. Finding out what it means is a lot more complicated.

There's the "land, ho!" explanation. Maine may come from "the main," Meyne, or Mayne, words that signified the mainland, as opposed to the more than 3,000 islands off the state's coast. French explorers, fishermen, and sailors like this explanation.

There's also the "I'm the King and I said so" explanation. In 1622, an English charter granted land it called "the province of Maine" to Sir Ferdinando Gorges and Captain John Mason. Mason spun off New Hampshire from this grant. In a 1639 charter, King Charles I made it clear to Sir Gorges what he was to do with his share: ". . . the Mayne Lande and Premises aforesaide shall forever hereafter bee called The Province or Countie of Mayne and not by any other name or names whatsoever."

Sir Gorges didn't get to pick a name for his landholding, but he was entitled to everything Maine had to offer, from lumber and fish to the "Wrecks of Shipps or Merchandize" that might wash up on its shores. Not a bad deal when you're talking around 3,500 miles of coastline.

Maine, the Pine Tree State, has 17 million acres of forest. How else would they be the leading producer of wooden toothpicks?

The official state tree, the white pine, is the largest conifer in the Northeast. No wonder colonial shipbuilders hewed them down and hauled them up as masts.

Pine Tree State

QUEEN MARY

Henrietta Maria

Lord BALTIMORE

D.C ANNaPOLIS

Bay

CRESCENTIA

Chesapeake

O SAY CAN YOu See

SCVTO BONA VOLVNTATIS TVE CORONASTI NOS

1632

ATLANTIC

Maryland

Capital
Annapolis

Maryland became our 7th state on April 28, 1788.

Remember studying compound words? Remember underlining the small words inside the big word to make the meaning clear? Try it now.

Mary land. Got it. But who's Mary?

Maryland was named for Queen Henrietta Maria — Queen Mary for short — the wife of the English king Charles I. King Charles I granted the Maryland charter to Cecilius Calvert, the second Lord Baltimore, on June 20, 1632.

Lord Baltimore's father, George Calvert, had started the process of getting a colony from the king. The first Lord Baltimore thought Crescentia was a lovely name. Perhaps it was inspired by the crescent-shaped Chesapeake Bay that divides Maryland in two. But wisely the lord left the decision up to his lord; the king proposed *Terra Mariae,* Maryland. The king promised not to impose taxes on the residents of the Baltimores' colony, but in the charter, he did ask for a fifth of any gold or silver that might be unearthed and "Two Indian Arrows of these Parts, to be delivered at the said Castle of Windsor, every Year, on Tuesday in Easter Week."

You'll see Chesapeake State on some Maryland license plates, but it also has two historical nicknames, the Old Line State and the Free State.

General George Washington is said to have called Maryland the Old Line State in recognition of the bravery of Maryland's troops, the Maryland Line, during the Revolutionary War.

In 1923, a congressman from Georgia railed against Maryland as a traitor to the Union for not passing state laws to enforce the national Prohibition amendment banning alcohol. Hamilton Owens, a Maryland newspaper editor, ironically suggested that Maryland then just be its own Free State.

Old Line State

1620

ATLANTIC

Puritans

mayflower

MASSACHUSETTS

blue Hills

SALEM

BOSTON

MASSACHUSETTS BAY

Cape Cod BAY

PLYMOUTH

Cape Cod

Mus. of Antique Autos
Princeton
Lancaster
Sterling
Clinton

Sharon
Mansfield
Easton
North Attleboro
Norton

MARTHA'S VINEYARD

SIGILLUM · REIPUBLICAE · MASSACHUSETTENSIS ·

Massachusetts

 Capital Boston

Massachusetts became our 6th state on February 6, 1788.

Before the Puritans and the Pilgrims; before the French and Spanish cod fishers; before Leif Eriksson and his Norsemen; *long* before the Red Sox, there were "the people of the great hills," the Massachuset.

There are several ways to interpret the tribal name Massachuset, but they all pretty much include the same ideas: "near," "by," "great," "mountain," or "hill." Makes sense. This Native American group lived in and around the Blue Hills, a chain of 22 rises, including the 635-foot high Great Blue Hill near Boston. Their territory also extended south to Plymouth and north to Salem.

The Massachuset were few in number, made fewer by diseases brought over by European explorers and traders who sailed the Atlantic coast. Smallpox had wiped out 90% of the tribe's roughly 3,000 members by the time the Pilgrims arrived in 1620. When the Puritans established the Massachusetts Bay Colony several years later, only 500 or so Massachuset were still alive. As a separate tribe, the Massachuset did not survive their own name, which was given to the bay, the colony, and ultimately this New England state.

Massachusetts is nicknamed the Bay State (do the geography). It's also called the Baked Bean State. Puritans were strict about no cooking — pretty much no *anything* — on the Sabbath. So Puritan women whipped up hot baked beans on Saturday, which meant warm *baked beans* on Sunday morning . . . after church, of course.

Baked Bean State

Michigan

Capital: Lansing

Michigan is surrounded by great lakes, four of them to be exact. Its name is connected to its unusual geography.

French explorers and traders first visited Michigan in the early 1600s. Their journals, letters, and early maps sometimes referred to place names already in use by the Native Americans who lived in the region. Many historians and linguists say Michigan comes from *michi-gama*, an Algonquian word that means "large lake" or "large body of water." A good name for a state washed by the waters of four of the five Great Lakes: Lake Michigan, Lake Superior, Lake Huron, and Lake Erie.

Other sources stay on dry land. They say Michigan comes from *majigan*, a Chippewa word for a clearing on the western side of the Lower Peninsula.

A wolverine is a fierce relative of the weasel, but a lot bigger and badder. They have large paws, sharp claws, and can chew through a cabin wall a foot thick.

So why would you nickname your state the Wolverine State?

A. There were a lot of wolverines wandering around Michigan. (Scientists and historians are still arguing about this.)

B. During the 1830s, Native Americans may have compared the settlers gobbling up their land to wolverines gobbling their food.

C. Michigan and Ohio were fighting over some land. Ohioans claimed the Michiganers were like bloodthirsty wolverines.

D. Any, all, or none of the above.

No one is sure where this unofficial nickname came from. So could we just use the other nickname instead? The Great Lake State sounds so much nicer.

Wolverine State

SEAL OF THE STATE OF MINNESOTA

L'ÉTOILE DU NORD

CANADA

the DAKOTA

WATER that REFLECTS the SKY

"Minisota"

lake ITASCA

LAKE SUPERIOR

WiNTER Carnival

ice Sculptures

Mississippi

Twin Cities

Minneapolis

110 111

ST. PAUL

Minesota river

River

VOYAGEURS NATL PARK

KABETOGAMA STATE

N
W E
S

Minnesota

Capital St. Paul

Minnesota became our 32nd state on May 11, 1858.

This midwestern state was traditionally home to the Dakota. They called one of the major rivers that flowed through their tribal lands *minisota*, "water that reflects the sky."

In the mid-1800s, thousands of European and American pioneers moved in and staked out their claims to timber-rich forests and tillable farmlands. The U.S. government forced the Dakota and other tribal people to give up their lands to make room for the new settlers.

By the late 1840s, the non-native people were clamoring for their own territory. A group of concerned citizens met in a store in Stillwater in 1848 to figure out how to get this territory recognized. Of course they also had to figure out what to call it. They considered presidential names like Washington or Jackson and tribal names like Chippewa or Algonquian. Itasca was suggested. The headwaters of the Mississippi River flow from Minnnesota's Lake Itasca. The name was coined by an American geologist from *veritas caput*, Latin for "truth" and "head."

The Stillwater delegates settled on a name already commonly used, added an "n" to change the pronunciation, and petitioned Congress to recognize the Minnesota Territory. Within a decade, Minnesota — still with two n's — became a state.

Minnesota is the Land of 10,000 Lakes — give or take a few lakes. The state actually has 11,842 lakes (the ones smaller than 10 acres don't count) and 6,564 streams and rivers, including the mighty Mississippi. All this water creates 90,000 miles of shoreline.

No wonder one out of six Minnesotans owns a boat.

Land of 10,000 Lakes State

Mississippi

Capital Jackson

Quick! How many *s*'s and *p*'s are there in Mississippi?

This southern state, which is named after the famous Mississippi River that runs through it, is always a tough one to spell. Maybe it would have been easier if some of the original Native American names had been used instead.

Messipi, a name from the Algonquian language, means "great water." The Chippewa called the Mississippi *mici zibi*, meaning "great river" or "gathering in of all waters." That's certainly true: The Mississippi is joined by the Illinois, Missouri, Ohio, Arkansas, and Atchafalaya Rivers.

The Spanish and French who sailed and paddled along the Mississippi River in the 16th and 17th centuries, used a variety of names for the waterway, some based on Native American words. The French explorer, René-Robert Cavelier, Sieur de La Salle, may have been the first to put the name Mississippi on a map . . . literally. He labeled the river as such on a map made in 1695.

More than one hundred years later, Congress organized the Mississippi Territory, naming it after the river whose source is in Minnesota and mouth is in Louisiana.

Mississippi is called the Magnolia State after the state's official — and fragrant — state tree and state flower. Mississippi schoolchildren made this choice when they voted for the magnolia flower in 1900 and the magnolia tree in 1935.

Magnolia State

MISSOURI PEOPLE

PEKITANOUI

missouri River

Mississippi River

Kansas City

JEFFERSON CITY

PEOPLE with the DUGOUT CANOES

YOU HAVE got to SHOW me

Congressman VANDIVER

I'm from MISSOURI

Missouri

Capital Jefferson City

Show me how to use Missouri three times in a sentence:

Missouri is named after the Missouri River, which is named after the Missouri.

The Missouri people were a small tribe whose name meant "people with the dugout canoes." They were among the Native Americans who were living in our 24th state when the Europeans arrived.

In 1673, the French explorer Louis Jolliet and the French missionary Father Jacques Marquette paddled their birch-bark canoe along the Mississippi River. They passed the mouth of a river: "So great was the agitation, that the water was very muddy, and could not become clear," Marquette later wrote in his journal.

That's why Native Americans called the river *pekitanoui*, which means "muddy water." Marquette, however, called this waterway the Missouri River on a map he made in 1673. This really muddied the waters and for a long time people misinterpreted the word *Missouri*. They mixed up the meaning of *pekitanoui* with the meaning of *Missouri*.

Ever drive behind a car with a Missouri license plate and wonder what they want you to show them? There are several different explanations for the state's unofficial nickname, the Show Me State. The most widely known one says it shows Missourians can't be fooled easily. Or as Missouri congressman Willard Duncan Vandiver put it at a dinner speech in 1899, ". . . frothy eloquence neither convinces nor satisfies me. I am from Missouri. You have got to show me."

Show Me State

Montana

Capital Helena

Montana became our 41st state on November 8, 1889.

Montana has more than 50 mountain ranges, including the magnificent Rocky Mountains. The word *montaanus* means "mountainous" in Latin; one Latinate form of this word is *montana*.

Montaanus. Montana. Get it?

Apparently Congress didn't.

A congressional committee met in February 1863 to discuss creating and naming a new western territory. James M. Ashley, a Republican representative from Ohio, suggested Montana. A senator didn't believe Montana was a real word; a Latin dictionary was produced as proof. Some congressmen wanted to use a Native American word, but couldn't think of the right one. Others played politics with the name: Democrats suggested Jefferson, after the third president and founder of their party; Republicans voted nay to that idea.

The name game ranged from Shoshone to Abyssinia until finally Congress reached an agreement. They settled on Ashley's original suggestion, Montana.

Montana's two main nicknames come from the earth below and the sky above. "Big Sky Country," found on the state's standard license plates, celebrates its wide-open spaces and wide-angle views. The phrase was inspired by A. B. "Bud" Guthrie, Jr.'s *The Big Sky*, a 1947 historical novel about the fur trade and the movement west.

Montana is also known as the Treasure State because of the rich gold, silver, and copper deposits that lured miners and mineral companies eager to strike it rich.

Treasure State

otoe

U of Nebraska

OmAHa
"Ni-ubthatka"
"SPREADING WATER"

Nebrathka
"FLAT WATER"

Lieutenant Frémont

PLATTE River

DUNDY
61
Rock Creek Lake
St. Rec. Area
Parks
34   24

LINCOLN

Omaha

RICHARDS
Salem
8
Falls City

F · O · L · A · T

tree PLANters StATE

Nebraska

Capital ~ Lincoln

Nebraska is flat . . . in more ways than one.

The name of this Great Plains state comes down to us from its largest river and several languages. The Otoe called this 310-mile river *nebrathka*, meaning "flat water." French explorers and fur traders of the early 18th century used the Omaha name for the river, *ni-ubthatka*, which means "spreading water." They also gave it a French name, Platte River. Flat again.

Along comes Lieutenant John C. Frémont. He's on a mission for the U.S. government. The United States needs to get some pioneers settled out west before other countries, like England, take over the place. In 1842, Frémont explored the plains and Rocky Mountains with an eye toward opening it up for expansion. He wrote about the Platte River, using its Indian name. Frémont's report was the first time Nebraska appeared in print. Two years later, when the government was organizing this part of the country into a U.S. territory, the Secretary of War recommended it be called Nebraska because of the big, broad, and flat river that flowed through it.

Arbor Day started here in 1872, which made tree-planting an annual national activity and led to one of Nebraska's nicknames, the Tree Planters State.

Officially, Nebraska is the Cornhuskers State, after its state university football team and the old-school way of harvesting corn.

Corn-huskers State

Nevada

Capital
Carson City

Nevada became our 36th state on October 31, 1864.

"¡Mira la sierra nevada!"

Spanish sailors checking out the scenery may have helped name our 36th state. As they sailed the Pacific from the Philippines to Mexico in the 1600s and 1700s, they spied whitecapped mountains along the way. *Sierra* means "saw-toothed mountain range," and *nevada* means "snow-covered" in Spanish. In 1776, Father Pedro Font, a member of a Spanish expedition, became the first to use the name on a map. The Sierra Nevada are technically in California; then again, before it became its own territory in 1861, Nevada had once belonged to California, as well as to Mexico and to Utah.

At a Nevada territorial convention in 1863, the delegates argued over what name to use when applying for statehood. The odds were against Nevada at first. The State of Washoe was a good bet. This name, which came from a local tribe, was popular with voters. Humboldt was proposed. So was a county name, Esmeralda. *Esmeralda* means "emerald" in Spanish; it's also the name of a female character in a popular French novel, *The Hunchback of Notre Dame*. In the end, the delegates chose Nevada.

Nevada was admitted to the Union toward the end of the Civil War, earning it the nickname the Battle Born State. It's also been called the Silver State. Nevada's famous Comstock Lode deposit yielded $400 million in silver and gold ore between 1859 and 1878. Comstock miners focused on digging for the gold at first and ignored the gray gunk that stuck to their shovels . . . until folks figured out that that gray was silver!

Silver State

SEAL of the STATE of NEW HAMPSHIRE · 1776 ·

CANADA

PELTS

Captain John MASON

VERMONT

MAINE

ENGLAND

HAMPSHIRE

WHITE MOUNTAINS

Timber

Concord

Keene

CONCORD

ATLANTIC

MASSACHUSETTS

66

New Hampshire
Capital Concord

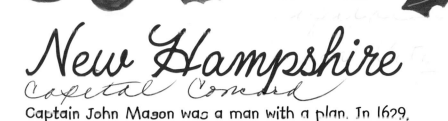

Captain John Mason was a man with a plan. In 1629, the Londoner received a land grant for "makeing a plantation" on 60 miles of land in an area first called North Virginia by the explorer John Smith (Pocahontas's pal), then renamed New England by King James I (who clearly outranked Smith). Mason called his property New Hampshire, after Hampshire county in his native England.

Mason advertised for settlers and sent people over to start a fishing colony. New Hampshire isn't called the Mother of Rivers for nothing. The sources of five great New England rivers flow from its mountains. There were plenty of fish, not to mention fur pelts and timber.

Captain Mason spent a fortune on his investment in the wilderness. He had lands cleared, buildings erected, and intended to visit his "plantation." But his plans went awry: Mason died before he ever sailed for New Hampshire.

The little colony was later embroiled in some big boundary disputes. Massachusetts claimed part of New Hampshire; New Hampshire claimed most of Vermont; there was a land spat with New York and a border brouhaha with Quebec. Luckily for mapmakers, by 1842 New Hampshire's borders had finally been settled . . . except for a modern day quarrel with Maine, which the U.S. Supreme Court ruled on in 2001.

New Hampshire is called the Granite State because there is so much of that igneous rock there. New Hampshire granite was used to build everything from curbs to the Library of Congress — where there's more than 30,000 tons of it!

Granite State

New Jersey

New Jersey became our 3rd state on December 18, 1787.

New Jersey was a hand-me-down. First it was home to the Lenni-Lenape. Then Dutch and Swedish settlers moved in, followed by the English, who took over.

In 1664, King Charles II of England passed along all the land between the Hudson and the Delaware Rivers to his brother James, the duke of York. The duke granted it to his two good friends, Lord John Berkeley and Sir George Carteret. The duke's charter called the place "New Caeserea or New Jersey." But Carteret came from the Isle of Jersey, a little island off the coast of England. He named his new lands in honor of his old home, where he had once been governor.

Berkeley and Carteret divided their land grant in half. Berkeley's "half" was almost twice as big as Sir George's share. No surprise: Some surveyors of the boundaries worked at night, when it's hard to see clearly and accurately; they used flaming tar barrels as markers. The noblemen owed the Duke of York 40 beaver skins and 20 gold coins rent a year for their New Jersey grant.

New Jersey officially became the Garden State in 1954, when the state legislature passed a bill adding it to car license plates. There are several interpretations of the nickname, but all of them have to do with New Jersey farms supplying food. (Beats the Clam State, a nickname tied to the Jersey Shore.)

Garden State

69

New Mexico

Capital
Santa Fe

You can trace this state's name all the way back to the Aztecs.

New Mexico is named after "old" Mexico. Mexico, the country south of the United States, got its name from Tenochtitlán, the capital city the Aztecs built in 1325. The Aztecs referred to themselves as Mexicas after the war god Mexitli. Their city was an amazing place built on an island. By the time Hernán Cortés first arrived there in 1519, Tenochtitlán was larger than any city in Europe at the time, with between 100,000 and 300,000 inhabitants. The Aztecs renamed their powerful capital Mexitli, in honor of the Aztec god of war. Mexico comes from Mexitli.

Spanish missionaries on an expedition in 1582 looking for Native Americans to convert are thought to be the first to have used *la Nueva Mejico* for what became our 47th state. Having a name inspired by a war god is fitting. Native Americans, Spanish conquistadors and settlers, the Mexican army, the U.S. army, Texans, cattlemen, and sheepherders all clashed over land, boundaries, and governance at one time or another in New Mexican history.

New Mexico officially became the Land of Enchantment on April 8, 1999. But the nickname has been around since 1935, when the tourist industry started using it to promote New Mexico's natural beauty. It was coined by author Lilian Whiting, who wrote *The Land of Enchantment*, a book about the region published in 1906.

Land of Enchantment State

King James II

DUKE OF YORK

Peter Stuyvesant

Nieuw-Amsterdam

N

FuR!

VERMONT

ADIRONDACKS

Niagra FALLS

Syracuse

ONONDAGA IND. RES.

A

Buffalo

ALBanY

$24

CATSKILLS

MASS.

Hudson River

HENRY HUDSON

CT

60

MANHATTES

guilders

NY

Long Island Sound

ATLANTIC

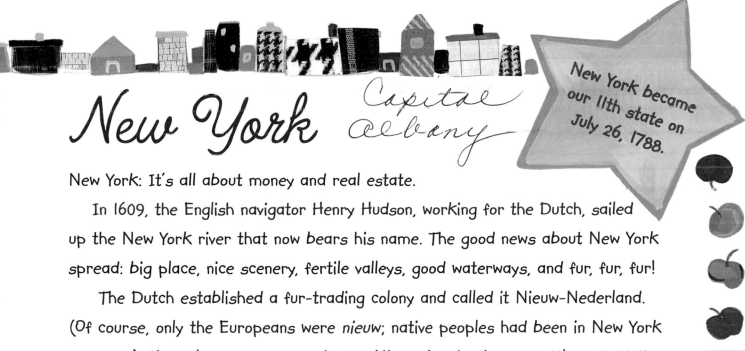

New York

Capital Albany

New York: It's all about money and real estate.

In 1609, the English navigator Henry Hudson, working for the Dutch, sailed up the New York river that now bears his name. The good news about New York spread: big place, nice scenery, fertile valleys, good waterways, and fur, fur, fur!

The Dutch established a fur-trading colony and called it Nieuw-Nederland. (Of course, only the Europeans were *nieuw*; native peoples had been in New York for ages.) The colony was governed from Nieuw-Amsterdam, a settlement at the mouth of the Hudson. In 1626, Nieuw-Amsterdam's governing official, Peter Minuit, made the real estate deal of the century — make that centuries! He bought Manhattan, an island owned by native people of the same name, for 60 guilders ($24). Upriver, the Dutch cleared big farms and opened a thriving trading post at Fort Orange, now Albany.

The Dutch ruled for almost 50 years. Then the English decided that everything between the Connecticut and Delaware Rivers belonged to them. Four heavily armed British ships sailed into Nieuw-Amsterdam harbor in August 1664. The English offered a deal: Give up, we'll rule, you go about your business. Peter Stuyvesant, the peg-legged Dutch governor, was hopping mad; everybody else pretty much shrugged. The English took over without a shot and renamed the colony New York, in honor of their Duke of York, who later was crowned King James II.

From 1785 to 1790, New York City was the temporary capital of the new United States. George Washington is said to have called it "the seat of the Empire." The Empire State worked for New Yorkers.

Empire State

1st flight
WRIGHT BROTHERS

KING CHARLES IX

Greensboro

GREAT SMOKY MOUNTAINS

RALEIGH

NORTH

Asheville

Wilmington

Croatan

South

Kings CHARLES

ATLANTIC OCEAN

II

I

North Carolina

Capital Raleigh

Three Kings, two states, one name: Carolina.

Carolina is from *Carolus,* a Latin form for the name *Charles.* In 1562, French explorer Jean Ribaut reached the coast of the Carolinas and named the whole place in honor of Charles IX, the boy-King of France.

The French didn't get a colony going, but in the 1580s, the British tried to. By 1587, they had established a small settlement on Roanoke Island. But by 1590, this "lost colony" had vanished, leaving only a mysterious clue: the word CROATAN carved on a tree.

Just because it was the kind of place where people disappear didn't mean the British were willing to give up their territorial claim. In 1629 and again in 1663, English Kings bestowed royal charters on some of their faithful noblemen, granting them rights to Carolina. Luckily, both these Kings were called Charles (I and II), so no change of name was required.

Carolina was divided in 1710; by 1729, it was officially two British colonies: North Carolina and South Carolina.

In the 19th century, North Carolina, the Tarheel State, was a big producer of sticky tar and smelly turpentine. According to legend, during a fierce Civil War battle, while other troops fled, a North Carolina regiment bravely stood its ground and won. They later joked that their fellow soldiers needed to put some North Carolina tar on their heels, so they'd stay put in the next fight.

Tarheel State

North Dakota

Capital Bismark

For hundreds of years, the great Northern Plains in this midwestern state were home to millions of buffalo and the Native American peoples who hunted them. The Dakota were one of these tribal groups. *Dakota* means "friend" or "ally." When American settlers and soldiers started moving into the area in the 19th century, they called their new-claimed territory Dakota because of the original inhabitants. They also slaughtered the buffalo and changed the Dakota tribal way of life forever.

Congress formally recognized the territory in 1861 and admitted both North Dakota and South Dakota as states in 1889.

North Dakota is one of the few states that every once in a while — say 1947, 1989, 2001 — considers changing its name. Some enterprising Dakotans think North says "too chilly," and that maybe more people would be tempted to move to the state if it was just called Dakota. So far, the measure hasn't passed.

In 1957, the state legislature officially made North Dakota the Peace Garden State. The International Peace Garden straddles the border between North Dakota and Manitoba, Canada. The beautiful garden—with its trees, groves, lakes, and 150,000 flowers—celebrates the friendly relationship between the United States and Canada. The garden was the botanical brainstorm of a Canadian plant scientist, Dr. Henry J. Moore. It opened in 1932.

Peace Garden State

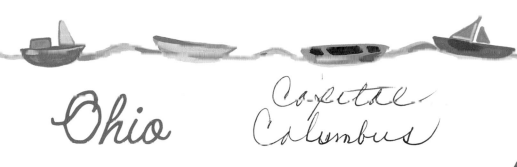

Ohio

Capital Columbus

The Ohio River flows through American history. In 1669, it brought in René-Robert Cavelier, Sieur de La Salle, the first European to see what he called *la belle rivière*, the beautiful river. Later, the Ohio served as a watery (but temporary) dividing line between encroaching settlers and Native American homelands.

The Ohio River flows through or along the borders of six states: Pennsylvania, West Virginia, Ohio, Kentucky, Indiana, and Illinois, connecting to other important tributaries along the way. In the early 19th century, it was a choice route for pioneers headed west. It was a lot easier to float yourself, your loved ones, and all your stuff on the river than it was to haul it over the Appalachian Mountains. As the territories around the river were settled, the Ohio became an important commercial route for crops and other goods. The river was also the border between slave states and free states. Making it across the Ohio could mean freedom for an escaped slave.

A river this important to this many different people is bound to have more than one name. In fact there are 59 various names or spellings for the 981-mile river. *Ohio* is thought to come from an Iroquois word for "large," "beautiful," or "great river."

Great name for a state, too.

The Buckeye State is named after a tree whose nut looks like a deer's eye. In the 1840 presidential campaign, a newspaper called candidate William Henry Harrison of Ohio a country bumpkin. The down-home idea worked for his campaign; pictures of buckeye-wood canes and cabins became Harrison's symbols. He won.

Buckeye State

Oklahoma *Oklahoma City*

Oklahoma became our 46th state on November 16, 1907.

"O-O-O-O-O-Oklahoma, where the wind comes sweepin' down the plain!" is the opening line from the title song of Rodgers and Hammerstein's famous 1943 musical, *Oklahoma!* Lots of people came sweepin' down the plain in this state.

Oklahoma was part of the Indian Territory Congress established in 1830 as a homeland for tribal peoples being pushed off their ancestral lands elsewhere. Cherokee, Chickasaw, Choctaw, Creek, and Seminole peoples were forced to move there; thousands died along this "Trail of Tears." Sixty-seven tribes lived in the territory.

After the Civil War, illegal settlers urged the federal government to officially open up these lands to non-Indian settlers. Instead of traditional tribal rule, a territorial government for the Native American area was proposed. During one meeting about this, Reverend Allen Wright, a New York-educated Choctaw Presbyterian minister, suggested the redefined territory be called Oklahoma. *Okla* in Choctaw means "people"; *huma* (or *humma*) means "red."

The land didn't stay unassigned.

On April 22, 1889, 50,000 cowboys, farmers, laborers, entrepreneurs, and other hopefuls lined up for the first of several Oklahoma land rushes. They came in wagons and buggies. They rode horses, ponies, and mules. When the starting shot cracked, they raced off in a whirlwind of noise and dust to stake their claims in what became our 46th state.

The Sooner State gets its nickname from eager pioneers who jumped the gun, snuck into Oklahoma, and staked land claims "sooner" than land rush rules allowed.

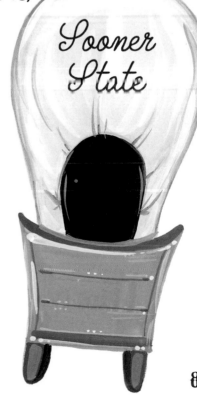

Sooner State

Columbia River

oil

Salem

Ouragon Ourigan

Cascades

Ooligan

Vitamin A

Vitamin C

Travels Through the Interior Parts of North America

766 767 768

smelt fish

Oregon

Capital
Salem

This is the oil,

that came from the fish,

that swam in the river,

that flowed through the northwest,

that gave Oregon its name . . . maybe.

No one knows for sure where the word *Oregon* came from. In 1765, Major Robert Rogers, an enterprising English army officer, wrote of an expedition he proposed to "the River called by the Indians Ouragon." King George II refused to pay for the trip; Major Rogers tried again seven years later with a different spelling, Ourigan. Historians still differ on how and where the officer heard these tribal words and what they mean.

In 1778, Captain Jonathan Carver, an associate of Major Rogers, published a bestseller called *Travels Through the Interior Parts of North America 1766, 1767, and 1768.* He followed Roberts's lead, but reworked the spelling to the River Oregon. Mapmakers went with Oregon when they were labeling what's now the Columbia River.

Recently, two anthropologists have offered a hotly debated new idea. They suggest that the name *Oregon* is linked to *ooligan*, a fish grease Native Americans got from an oily little smelt swimming around in the Northwest. Ooligan was a valuable all-purpose golden oil: you could eat it (Vitamin A! Vitamin C!), light a lamp with it, slather it on as medicine, and barter it.

Castor canadensis, the thick-pelted, tail-slapping, tree-gnawing American beaver, drew fur trappers and traders to Oregon and gave the state its nickname.

Beaver State

Pennsylvania

Capital
Herrisburg —

Pennsylvania became our 2nd state on December 12, 1787.

It pays to have a king owe you money.

England's King Charles II had borrowed money from a trusted admiral, Sir William Penn. Penn senior's death meant the king owed his son, William Penn, £16,000.

William Penn, a Quaker, wanted to create what he called a Holy Experiment in the New World, a colony where people could worship freely and participate in their government. King Charles II wanted to expand his empire — and retire his debt at the same time. The royal charter of 1681 solved everything. It gave Penn a large tract of land, which the king decreed should be called Pensilvania, in honor of Admiral Penn. *Sylvania* comes from the Latin word for woods; *Pennsylvania*, as it came to be spelled, means "Penn's woods."

Dutch and Swedish settlers had already moved onto some of the lands that now belonged to William Penn, not to mention all the Native Americans who lived there, too. Penn arrived to establish his new, enlightened colony in 1682. He struck a bold and at the time unusual bargain: Although he held a royal charter for Pennsylvania, Penn and his followers didn't settle it until they had met with tribal leaders and paid the Indians for their land claims. Dealing with his fellow European colonizers was tougher. Penn had to defend his colony against border disputes with Maryland, Delaware, and New Jersey.

A keystone is the essential middle wedge in an arch that holds the whole curve together. The true meaning of Pennsylvania's nickname, the Keystone State, is unknown, but it probably refers to the key position Pennsylvania held as a political, commercial, and geographic center of the 13 American colonies.

Key-stone State

ROODTEYLNDT
RED + ISLAND

Greece
RHODES

PRoViDENCE

State of Rhode Island & the PRoViDENCE PLaNTaTioNS · 1636 ·
HOPE

SILVERWARE

West Warwick
116
117
Anthony
Washington
Quidn
33
Nathanael
Greene
Homestead
3
Tiogue
Lake

NARRAGANSET BAY

Newport

cLamS

N

Verrazano

Block Island Sound

BLoCK ISLaND

ATLANTIC OCEAN

Rhode Island

Rhode Island became our 13th state on May 29, 1790.

In 1524, the Italian navigator Giovanni Verrazano sailed north from New York. He spied "an Ilande in the forme of a triangle . . . about the bigness of the Ilande of the Rhodes." Rhodes is an island in Greece.

In 1614, Adriaen Block, an intrepid Dutch explorer and fur trader, also explored the region. He named Block Island, the largest of 35 islands in Rhode Island's waters, after himself. When he sailed into the Narragansett Bay, he noted the "fiery aspect" of its red clay shoreline and wrote *Roodt Eylandt* (red island) on his charts.

Here's where tracking this state's name gets tricky.

Verrazano was actually talking about Block Island; Block may have been talking about Rhode Island. Then in 1636, Roger Williams fled Puritan-controlled Massachusetts. The clergyman bought some land from the Narragansett and called his new home Providence as thanks to his god. *Plantations* was added because that's an old English word for colony. Williams thought Verrazano's Rhodes reference was to Aquidneck Island, another part of the growing new colony. Aquidneck became Rhode Island in 1644.

By 1663, what is now our smallest state had its really big name: The State of Rhode Island and Providence Plantations. That's what it was called in the royal charter granted by England's King Charles II. It guaranteed Roger Williams's dream: There would be "full libertie in religious concernements" in Rhode Island.

Rhode Island, the Ocean State, has only 1,045 square miles of land, but 384 miles of shoreline along the Atlantic Ocean and Narragansett Bay. That puts all its residents about 30 miles, or a half-hour away, from the water — not counting summer beach traffic!

Ocean State

South Carolina

Capital
Charleston

South Carolina became our 8th state on May 23, 1788.

Native Americans, Spanish explorers, French soldiers and sailors, British noblemen, immigrants from Barbados and Virigina, even pirates, all wanted a piece of the action in what became two adjoining southern states: North Carolina and South Carolina.

The Carolinas were once one big territory called Carolina in honor of a French and then two British Kings, all named Charles. Thousands of Native Americans already called the place home before the Europeans arrived in the 16th century. The Spanish sailed in first, followed by the French. Each got to first base in the colonial game: claim and name. It was the English who scored. A British royal charter of 1663 spelled out their claim to all land, coast, and waterways in the geographic area between 36 and 31 degrees northern latitude — not to mention the "whales, sturgeons, and all other royal fishes in the sea" there.

Like the French, the British called the region Carolina after their monarch. But unlike their European competitors, the English moved in and stayed. One British settlement became a thriving port and the colony's capital. It too got the royal treatment when it came to names: Charles Town (now Charleston).

How to become a state nickname:
1. Grow some palmetto trees.
2. Cut down these trees.
3. Use the palmetto wood to build a fort on Sullivan's Island to protect Charleston.
4. Get attacked by British warships on June 28, 1776, during the Revolutionary War.
5. Win the battle because the fort's palmetto tree walls aborbed the shock of cannonballs and held.
6. Become the Palmetto State.

Palmetto State

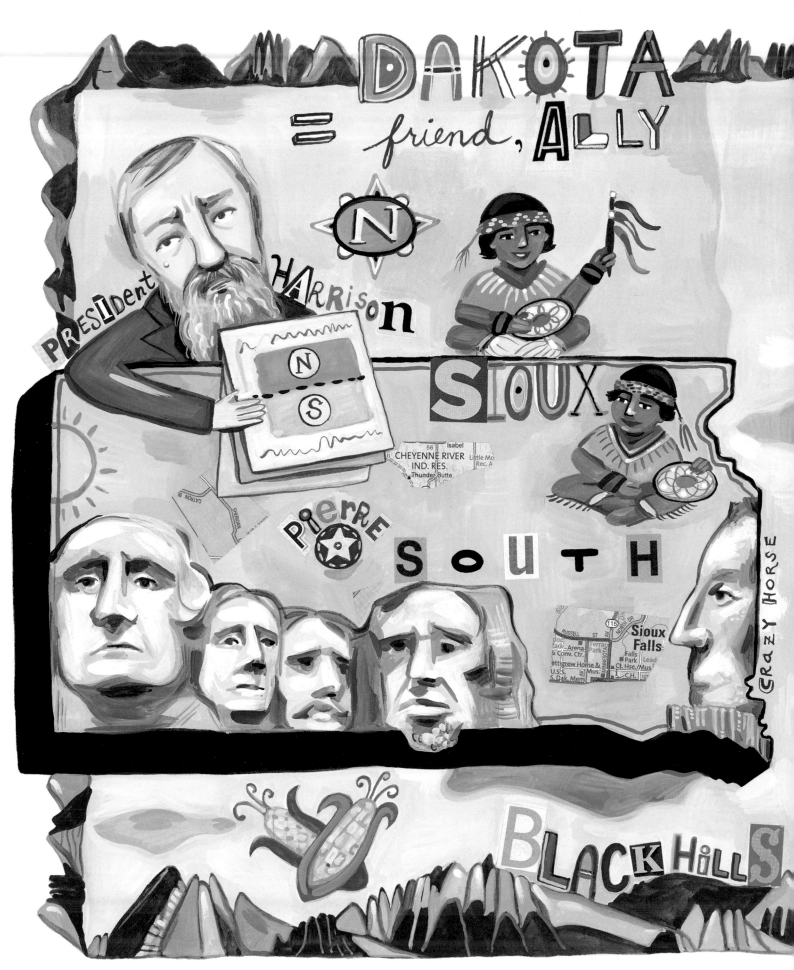

South Dakota

Capital Pierre

Dakota is a tribal word for "friend" or "ally." But when it came to statehood, the north and south parts of the Dakota Territory were more like feuding twins.

In 1883, the settlers in southern Dakota were outraged when the territory's capital shifted from Yankton to Bismarck, which was in the northern part of the territory. The north was more populated. Folks up there thought the capital should go where the people are. There had already been talk of breaking up the Dakota Territory into two; now the rumbling, grumbling, and politicking to recognize South Dakota got really loud.

A congressional bill in 1889 created the states of North Dakota and South Dakota. Once President Benjamin Harrison signed the documents, the 39th and 40th states would join the Union. There was just one big, politically loaded question: North or south, who would be admitted first?

President Harrison wisely asked his Secretary of State to shuffle the papers so he couldn't see which he was signing. Both North Dakota and South Dakota became states on November 2, 1889.

Nobody knows which twin was born first. (The Dakotas are numbered based on alphabetical order.)

You can't miss the namesake for this state's nickname, the Mount Rushmore State. Five hundred feet up a mountain face in the Black Hills are sculptures of George Washington, Thomas Jefferson, Theodore Roosevelt, and Abraham Lincoln. Each presidential head carved on Mount Rushmore is 60 feet high.

Mount Rushmore State

Tennessee

Capital
Nashville

"The U.S. Territory South of the River Ohio" is a little long to stamp on license plates or print on Key chains, coffee mugs, and baseball caps. Of course, there were no cars or souvenir stands in 1790, when this name was in use. But lucky for today's tchotchke manufacturers, by the time this territory became our 16th state, its citizens were using a shorter name: Tennessee.

Everyone agrees that Tennessee comes from a Native American word, but no one is quite sure how, when, or where. Captain Juan Pardo, a Spanish explorer, reached an Indian village called Tanasqui in 1567. A couple of centuries later, settlers ventured near two neighboring Cherokee river villages, Tanasqui or Tanase. People started calling the waterway the Tennessee River. Next thing you Know, in the 1750s, James Glen, the governor of nearby South Carolina, is penning letters referring to the region as Tennessee.

It's easy to hear how Native American words like *Tansqui* or *Tanasi* glide into Tennessee. But what these tribal words meant to their original speakers is lost in history.

When duty called, Tennesseans answered. That's why it's nicknamed the Volunteer State. During the War of 1812, volunteer soldiers from this state marched on down to help General Andrew Jackson trounce the British in the Battle of New Orleans.

Volunteer State

93

Texas

*Capital
Austin*

Texas became our 28th state on December 29, 1845.

Howdy! Welcome to the state whose motto is friendship and whose name means nearly the same thing.

Texas comes from *taysha,* a Caddo word for "friend," or "ally." The Caddo were a confederacy of native peoples who lived and farmed the river valleys of parts of Texas, Louisiana, Arkansas, and Oklahoma. When Spanish explorers first trekked through these Caddo lands and into Texas in the 16th century, they were impressed with the confederacy's organization and civilization — and with the fact that these tribes were less hostile than other native peoples they encountered. The Spanish called the Caddo the "great kingdom of Tejas," their interpretation of the "friend" word, and named their first mission in the area San Francisco de los Tejas in 1690. Eventually, the name *Tejas* evolved into *Texas.*

After that, Texas was pretty much called Texas, right on into statehood.

The Lone Star State gets its nickname from the Texan flag. The single, or lone, star on this flag is said to represent Texans' stand-alone struggle for independence. Single stars appeared on various flags of the Republic of Texas and waved at many a battle, including the decisive Battle of San Jacinto in 1836. The Texan army led by General Sam Houston defeated General Antonio López de Santa Anna's Mexican army. Texas then became independent of Mexican rule.

*Lone
Star
State*

THE GREAT SEAL OF THE STATE OF UTAH

INDUSTRY

1847

1896

INDUSTRY

GREAT SALT LAKE

SALT LAKE CITY

Uinta Mountains

WASATCH-CACHE NATL. FOR.

UINTA MTS.

ASHLEY NATL FOR.

MORMONS

CHURCH of the LATTER DAY SAINTS

BOOK OF MORMON

Hunters & gatherers

the UTE Bands

Utah

Capital
Salt Lake City

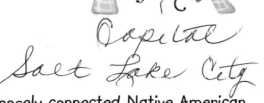
Utah became our 45th state on January 4, 1896.

The Ute, a group of 12 loosely connected Native American bands, were hunters and gatherers whose traditional lands stretched across what is now Colorado and Utah. *Ute* is interpreted to mean "land of the sun" or "high-up." It's a reference to the often mountainous areas the Ute inhabited or hunted in. From Ute came Utah — literally, once settlers started displacing these native peoples.

In 1847, members of the Church of Jesus Christ of Latter-Day Saints, seeking religious freedom, began moving to Utah in large groups. These pioneers were commonly called Mormons; they settled in Ute lands.

The Mormons quickly cleared and planted farmlands and built thriving communities. In a few short years, they were ready and eager for statehood. In fact, they organized their own Territory of Deseret. *Deseret* comes from the religious text, the *Book of Mormon*; it means honeybee. The Mormon pioneers were a close-knit society that valued cooperation, hard work, and shared goals and values. They often used a beehive as a metaphor for themselves or their beliefs.

The Mormons petitioned Congress to be admitted as the Territory of Deseret in 1849. Congress approved the territorial request in 1850, but as the Territory of Utah.

There are two giant bronze beehives with buzzing bees at the steps of Utah's State Capitol Building. That's because Utah is the Beehive State. You'll see dome-shaped beehives, the symbol of industriousness, all over Utah on buildings, road signs, ads, the state flag, police cars, even on the doorknobs in the Capitol building.

Beehive State

Samuel Champlain

LAKE Champlain

GREEN MOUNTAINS

MONTPELIER

NEW Connecticut...

State of Vermont

1777

Ethan Allen

& the GREEN MOUNTAIN BOYS

Vermont

Capital Montpelier

Vermont became our 14th state on March 4, 1791.

In July 1609, French explorer and geographer Samuel Champlain and his party of nine Frenchmen and 60 Huron and Algonquian sailed into a big beautiful lake. He named it after himself, Lake Champlain, and claimed all he saw for France, including the mountain range in the distance, *les Verts Monts* . . . the Green Mountains.

Call it like you see it, Sam.

More than 150 years later, the colonies of New Hampshire and New York both laid claim to the region Champlain visited, which was by now called the New Hampshire Grants. Feisty local citizen Ethan Allen formed his famous Green Mountain Boys to fight off the "Yorkers" they feared would overrun the region's original settlers.

In 1777, delegates from the New Hampshire Grants met and declared the region a republic called New Connecticut. Dr. Thomas Young, a Philadelphia scholar and statesman, and friend of Ethan Allen's, urged New Connecticut to join the other 13 American colonies that had declared independence. Young suggested New Connecticut write a state constitution and change its name to Vermont, in honor of the mountains and the boys. The idea got the *vert* light; the republic became Vermont on June 30, 1777.

Vermont, the Green Mountain State, is nicknamed after:

○ The mountain range that's made of green-colored shale and runs most of the length of the state.

○ The state and Revolutionary War heroes Ethan Allen and the Green Mountain Boys.

○ Both

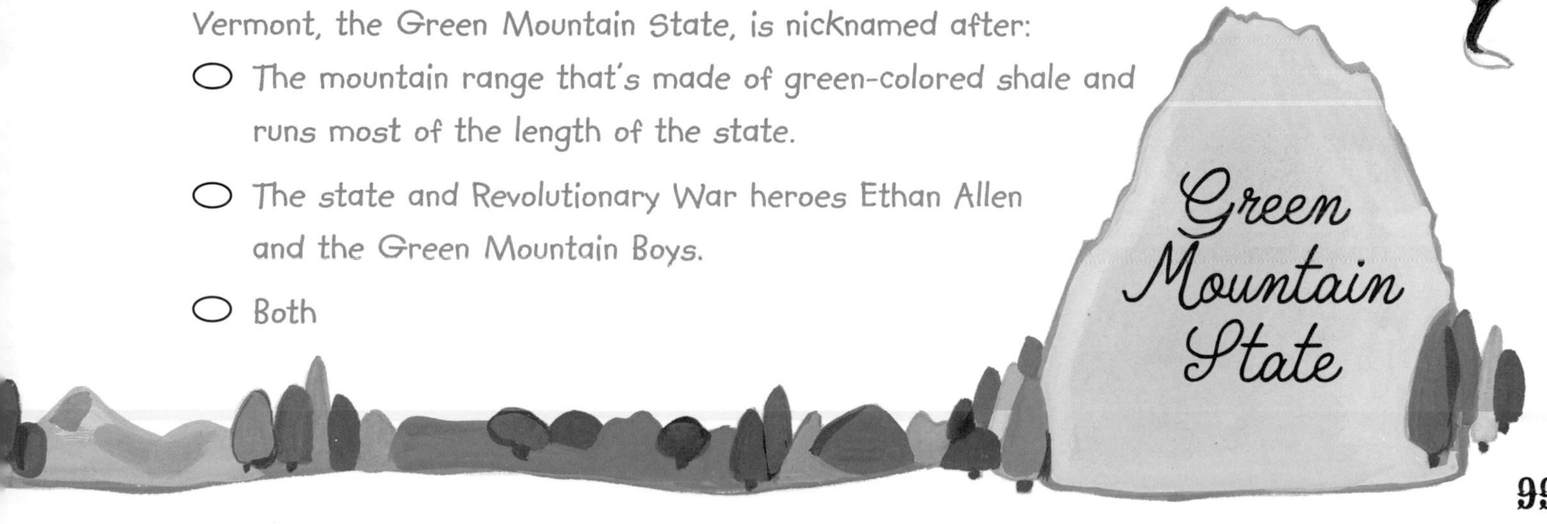

Green Mountain State

Virginia

Capital Richmond

Once upon a time there was a brilliant 16th-century British queen named Elizabeth I. Since she was unmarried, everyone called her the Virgin Queen. One of Elizabeth's favorite members of her court was the pirate-fighting, poetry-writing, dashing soldier and explorer Sir Walter Raleigh.

Raleigh dreamed of gold, silver, and a thriving English colony in the "New World." His queen liked the idea of expanding her empire to the American continent. More fame! More riches! A chance to beat out her royal rivals in Spain and Portugal!

On March 25, 1584, Elizabeth signed a charter giving Raleigh the right "to discover . . . and view such remote . . . and barbarous lands . . . not actually possessed of any Christian Prince." In other words, he should lay claim to anything the Spanish and Portuguese hadn't already snatched up. (Of course, there already were thousands of native peoples living in these supposedly "barbarous lands.")

Between 1585 and 1587, Raleigh, along with several other noblemen and merchants, sponsored three expeditions to America. The ships reached what is now the coast of North Carolina. Raleigh claimed and named the whole region Virginia, in honor of his queen.

Raleigh's Roanoke colonies failed, but the name Virginia stayed on the map.

Dominion means complete ownership of a place. Virginia is the Old Dominion because England's King Charles II thought so highly of his colony that sometime around 1663, he added it to his shield, making Virginia the equal of France, Ireland, and Scotland. It's also known as the Mother of Presidents, since 7 of the first 12 U.S. presidents came from there.

Old Dominion State

The Seal of the STATE of WASHINGTON

1889

PUGET SOUND

trout

SEATTLE

MT. SAINT HELENS

OLYMPIA

red apples

CASCADES

ROCKIES

Columbia River

MT. RAINIER
Sunrise Visitor Ctr.
Mt. Rainier
Ht. in Wash.
14,411
NATL.
PARK
Paradise
123
CLOSED

PIONEERS

COLUMBIA territory

OREGON

Universit Place
Steilacoom
Steilacoom Tribal Cultural Ctr.
FT. LEWIS MILITARY RES.
Lakewoo
Lakewold Garden
Estates
American Lake

Kirkland
Bainbridge Island
Silverdale
Seattle
Bremerton
Port Orchard
KITSAP
Burien
Seattle-Tacoma Intl. Arpt.
SeaTac

Washington

Capital
Olympia

In the 1850s, this state was part of the vast Oregon Territory (think Oregon, Washington, Idaho, and part of Montana, put together!). The territory was just a little too big and unwieldy for its northernmost citizens.

On August 29, 1851, 27 disgruntled pioneers who lived north of the Columbia River met at Cowlitz Landing. They wrote a petition to Congress, complaining that it was cheaper to travel all the way from St. Louis, Missouri, to Boston, Massachusetts, than it was for North Oregonians to head on down south and see a clerk or judge in the government seat of their own territory. The pioneers wanted to carve out a new region with a separate government; they called it Columbia Territory.

Congress considered the petition. They were okay with the idea of splitting the Oregon Territory, but the name? It could be confusing, since there already was a District of Columbia. Washington Territory was substituted, so there would be "a sovereign State bearing the name of the Father of his Country." The bill passed on February 10, 1853, making Washington the only state named after a U.S. president . . . and the only one that has to keep adding "state" after its name.

There already was a Washington, too.

Charles Tallmadge Conover was a real-estate entrepreneur in Seattle, Washington, at the turn of the 20th century. He also chaired the publicity committee of the Chamber of Commerce. Conover nicknamed Washington the Evergreen State after its richly forested lands.

Evergreen State

West Virginia *Capital Charleston*

West Virginia became our 35th state on June 20, 1863.

The Civil War that divided the nation also divided Virginia.

Up until 1861 Virginia and West Virginia were one big but not-so-happy state. East Virginians tended to be slaveholding owners of large plantations. West Virginians owned smaller properties, if they owned land at all; slavery was not as widespread. State government, tax and voting rules, and services usually favored East Virginia.

In 1861, the Civil War broke out, and Virginia voted to secede from the Union. The western part of the state voted to secede from Virginia. Delegates met at a constitutional convention on December 3, 1861, and agreed their new state should remain part of the Union. They didn't agree on what to call it. The top contenders:

Kanawha

Pros

- It's an Indian word for "place of white stone," which refers to local salt deposits.
- States name themselves after rivers and there are two Kanawha Rivers here.
- It's got a soft and musical sound.

Cons

- The post office will get confused: There already is a Kanawha County.
- Voters hate it.

Allegheny

Pros

- Nice, scenic mountain range in the state.

Cons

- What about the places that aren't near the mountains?

West Virginia

Pros

- Love the name, love its history, and westerners have a right to it, too.
- Already a familiar name.

Cons

- Doesn't sound like a clean break.

The vote? Allegheny, 2; Kanawha, 9; West Virginia, 30.

Pretty much all of West Virginia is mountainous, hence its nickname, the Mountain State.

Mountain State

Wisconsin

Capital Madison

Wisconsin became our 30th state on May 29, 1848.

Our 30th state is named after a river that not even two Frenchmen on the same expedition spelled the same way.

The Wisconsin River flows for 430 miles; it's the largest river in the state. In 1673, the fur-trapper Louis Jolliet and the missionary Father Jacques Marquette paddled along exploring what Marquette called the Meskousing in his journal; he also wrote *Miskous* in another reference. Meanwhile, his partner Jolliet inked in *Miskonsing* on a map he drew a year later.

Fast-forward nine years and another French explorer, René-Robert Cavelier, Sieur de La Salle, claims the local native peoples call the river Ouisconsing, or Misconsing. Ouisconsing was in pretty common use until the 19th century, when the Americans moved in, especially when there was a lead mining rush in 1825. They slowly "Americanized" the name and officially organized the region as the Wisconsin Territory in 1836. But free-form spelling didn't die. Various newspaper editors and even the territorial governor liked Wiskonsan better, so they used it.

Depending on how you pronounce it or spell it, Wisconsin may come from tribal words meaning "red stone river" or "great stone river."

The Badger State is named after an animal, but a two-footed one. In the 1800s, lead miners tunneled through southwest Wisconsin. They even dug out caves to sleep in. People called the miners "badgers," after the fierce, furry, burrowing mammal with 2-inch claws that could dig a hole and disappear in minutes.

Wyoming

Capital Cheyenne

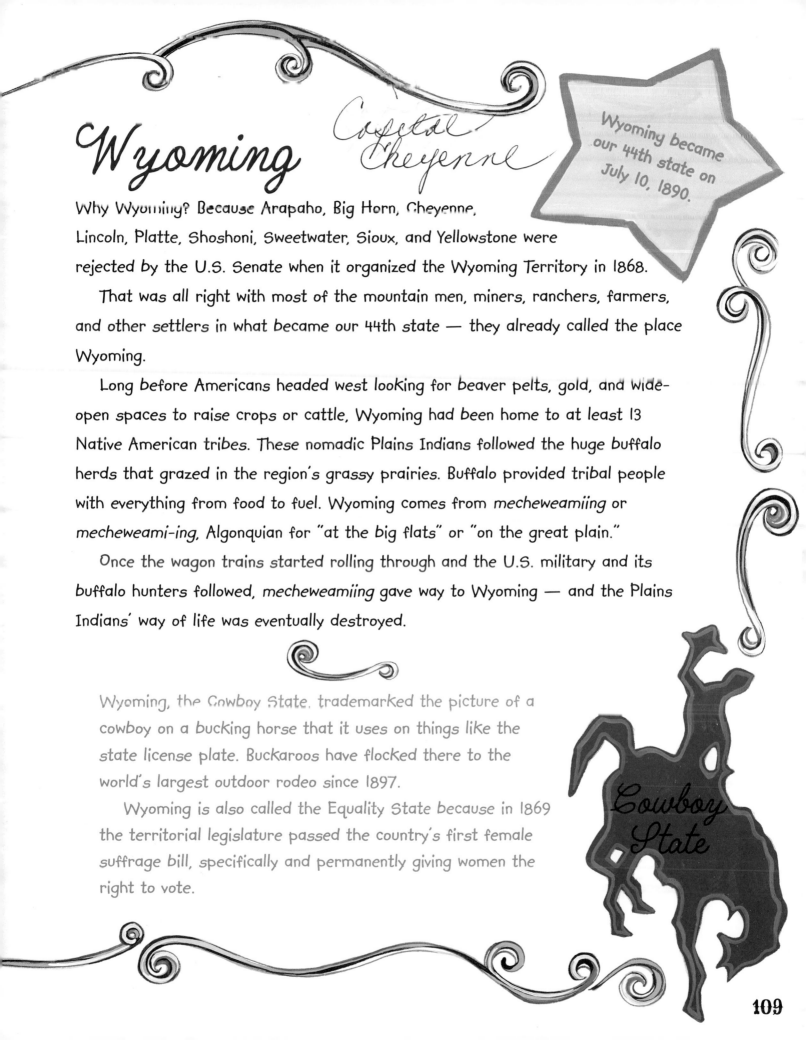

Wyoming became our 44th state on July 10, 1890.

Why Wyoming? Because Arapaho, Big Horn, Cheyenne, Lincoln, Platte, Shoshoni, Sweetwater, Sioux, and Yellowstone were rejected by the U.S. Senate when it organized the Wyoming Territory in 1868.

That was all right with most of the mountain men, miners, ranchers, farmers, and other settlers in what became our 44th state — they already called the place Wyoming.

Long before Americans headed west looking for beaver pelts, gold, and wide-open spaces to raise crops or cattle, Wyoming had been home to at least 13 Native American tribes. These nomadic Plains Indians followed the huge buffalo herds that grazed in the region's grassy prairies. Buffalo provided tribal people with everything from food to fuel. Wyoming comes from *mecheweamiing* or *mecheweami-ing*, Algonquian for "at the big flats" or "on the great plain."

Once the wagon trains started rolling through and the U.S. military and its buffalo hunters followed, *mecheweamiing* gave way to Wyoming — and the Plains Indians' way of life was eventually destroyed.

Wyoming, the Cowboy State, trademarked the picture of a cowboy on a bucking horse that it uses on things like the state license plate. Buckaroos have flocked there to the world's largest outdoor rodeo since 1897.

Wyoming is also called the Equality State because in 1869 the territorial legislature passed the country's first female suffrage bill, specifically and permanently giving women the right to vote.

Cowboy State

Washington, D.C.

Washington, D.C., the capital of the United States, is both the city of Washington and the District of Columbia.

In the early days of the nation, Congress met in eight different cities: Philadelphia, Baltimore, Lancaster, York, Princeton, Annapolis, Trenton, and New York. But some legislators had a capital idea: Let's establish a real, permanent capital.

Maryland and Virginia ceded lands along the Potomac River to Congress; the 10 square miles were first called Federal City. On July 16, 1790, Congress declared the city of Washington in the District of Columbia the permanent capital of the United States. The city was officially named Washington on September 9, 1791, in honor of George Washington, the hero of the Revolutionary War and the unanimously elected first president of the nation. The District of Columbia's name comes from a Latin word form related to the explorer Christopher Columbus.

Its nickname? What else? D.C.

Web Sites

Official State Sites

All 50 states have their own Web sites; so does Washington, D.C. These sites usually have general information about the history and geography of the state, its symbols, flag, motto, and official designations. They also have links to other important sites, such as the state library or historical society and official tourism sites.

Alabama
www.alabama.gov/

Alaska
www.state.ak.us/

Arizona
www.az.gov/

Arkansas
www.state.ar.us/

California
www.ca.gov/

Colorado
www.colorado.gov/

Connecticut
www.ct.gov/

Delaware
www.delaware.gov/

Florida
www.myflorida.com/

Georgia
www.georgia.gov/

Hawaii
www.hawaii.gov/

Idaho
www.state.id.us/

Illinois
www.illinois.gov/

Indiana
www.in.gov/

Iowa
www.iowa.gov/

Kansas
www.accesskansas.org/

Kentucky
www.kentucky.gov/

Louisiana
www.louisiana.gov/

Maine
www.state.me.us/

Maryland
www.maryland.gov/

Massachusetts
www.mass.gov/

Michigan
www.michigan.gov/

Minnesota
www.state.mn.us/

Mississippi
www.mississippi.gov/

Missouri
www.mo.gov/

Montana
http://mt.gov/

Nebraska
www.nebraska.gov/

Nevada
www.nv.gov/

New Hampshire
www.nh.gov/

New Jersey
www.state.nj.us/

New Mexico
www.newmexico.gov/

New York
www.ny.gov/

North Carolina
www.ncgov.com/

North Dakota
www.nd.gov/

Ohio
http://ohio.gov/

Oklahoma
www.ok.gov/

Oregon
www.oregon.gov/

Pennsylvania
www.state.pa.us/

Rhode Island
www.state.ri.us/

South Carolina
www.sc.gov/

South Dakota
www.state.sd.us/

Tennessee
www.state.tn.us/

Texas
www.state.tx.us/

Utah
www.utah.gov/

Vermont
www.vermont.gov/

Virginia
www.virginia.gov/

Washington
http://access.wa.gov/

West Virginia
www.wv.gov/

Wisconsin
www.wisconsin.gov/

Wyoming
http://wyoming.gov/

Washington, D.C.
www.dc.gov/

SHACKLETON

THE ANTARCTIC CHALLENGE

E.H.Shackleton

SHACKLETON
THE ANTARCTIC CHALLENGE

∾

Kim Heacox

NATIONAL
GEOGRAPHIC

WASHINGTON, D.C.

CONTENTS

*The Antarctic icescape, pages 2-3, was integral to the life and spirit
of explorer Ernest Shackleton, here pictured in the anorak he wore south.*

The Greatest Leader

Ernest Shackleton was the grandfather I never knew.
In 1922 he died, aged 47, whilst leading his third expedition
to the Antarctic. My father, aged ten, had had little time
to get to know him, whilst I had none at all. How should
Ernest Shackleton be viewed? It is not possible to separate the
man from his achievements. He was a dedicated Antarctic
explorer and a unique leader of men. One of the
Nimrod expedition, James Boyd Adams, described him thus:
"The greatest leader who ever came on God's earth, bar none."

Alexandra Shackleton with a portrait of her grandfather, and the Bible he abandoned on the ice

If one were to list Shackleton's qualities, he appears to be a mass of contradictions. This was a man romantic yet practical; visionary yet pragmatic, a man of action, yet able to display sustained patience; a strong leader, who—uniquely for the time—involved his men in decision-making; a man who enjoyed the limelight, but was modest withal.

It would be tempting to assume that what might be described as Shackleton's less showy qualities acted as a brake on his others, tempering them. I do not believe that this was the case; in fact I believe that the clue to his superb leadership lies in the fact that these less showy qualities were outstanding in their own right. Shackleton was a romantic man who both quoted and wrote poetry, and had metaphorically laid his first Antarctic expedition at the feet of his bride. At the same time, he was an extremely practical, hands-on leader who was capable of performing any task, however menial, that an expedition required. He was a visionary, seeking glory, who told his little sister, "You cannot imagine what it is like to walk in places where no man has walked before." Yet when the *Endurance* was crushed in the ice and his dreams with her, he simply noted in his diary, "A man must shape himself to a new mark directly the old one goes."

A man naturally swift to action, he showed exemplary patience during the long, dark months of waiting before the breaking-up of the ice released the expedition. He made sure all of the members were fully occupied, supervised their diet, and produced carefully timed treats. There was no discord and no scurvy. Shackleton was an essentially strong leader, but he made a point of getting to know each man and listening to his views. Everyone knew he was valued for what he could do, regardless of his official ranking. Plans were made for every contingency; Capt. Frank Worsley, in describing the grueling journey of the lifeboat *James Caird,* wrote: "He inspired one with a feeling that he would find some way of easing the hardship." When fame came to Shackleton, he frankly enjoyed it, but it was noticed that his own books played down his achievements, and on the lecture platform he never said "I," only "We." His men always came first.

Alexandra Shackleton

"Tongue and pen fail in attempting to describe the magic...."

ERNEST SHACKLETON

NIMROD EXPEDITION • JANUARY, 1908

PINK PASTELS OFFER A DECEPTIVELY WARM WELCOME, COMPELLING
EXPLORERS DEEPER INTO THE ANTARCTIC FREEZER WHERE CONDITIONS
CAN SUDDENLY CHANGE AND LOCK A SHIP IN TIGHT PACK ICE.

SHACKLETON'S *ENDURANCE*, BESET IN THE ICE OF THE WEDDELL SEA, IS FRAMED IN A RARE COLOR IMAGE BY CREW PHOTOGRAPHER FRANK HURLEY, WHO DESCRIBED THE SHIP AS A "BRIDE OF THE SEA."

IN THE TRADITION OF ADVENTURE ENGENDERED BY SHACKLETON,
A DIVER DISCOVERS A NEW ANTARCTIC REALM: CLUSTERS OF STARFISH
IN THE INKY SHALLOWS BENEATH A BLUE DOME OF SEA ICE.

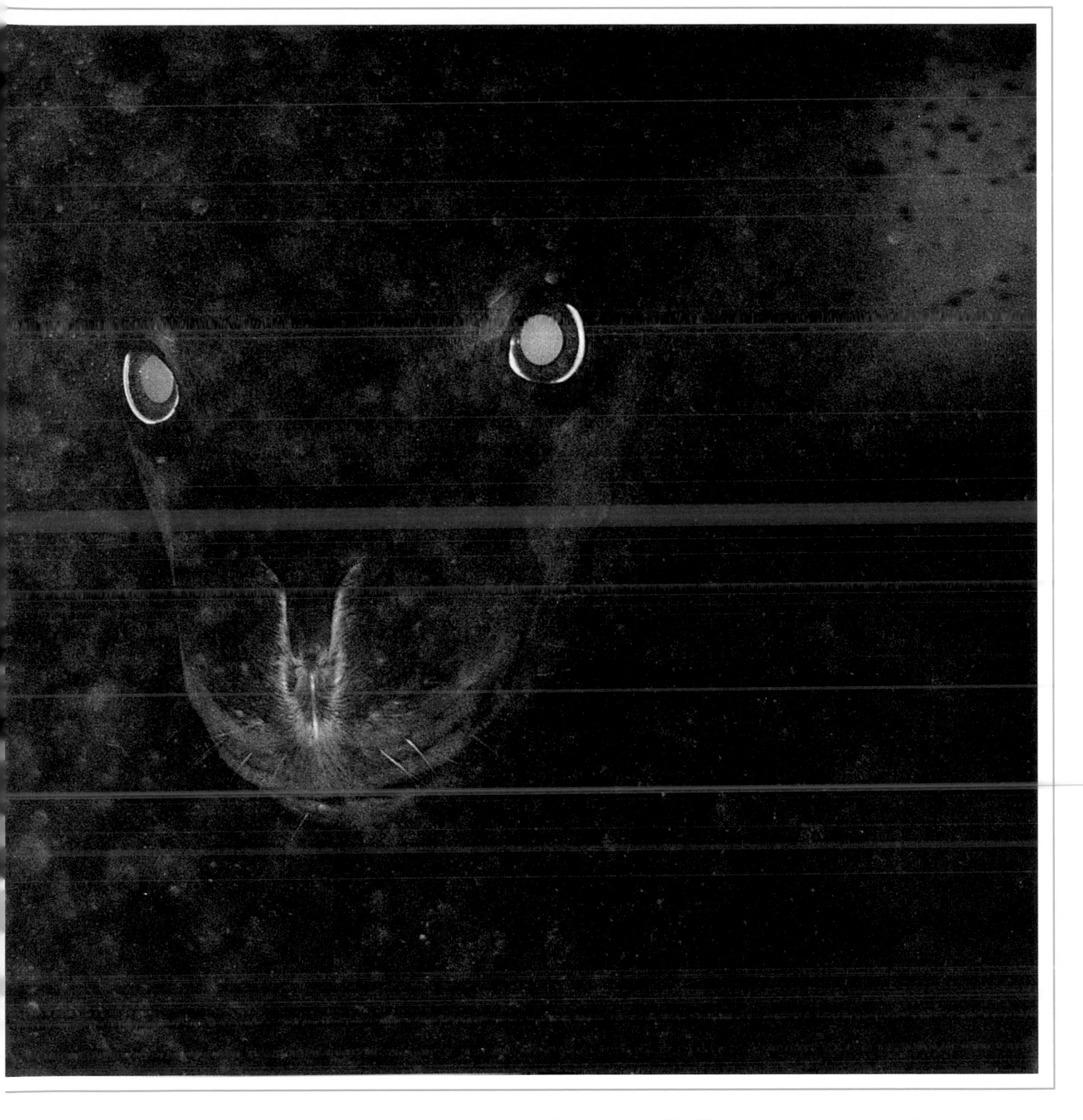

PORTRAIT OF A PREDATOR: A LEOPARD SEAL PEERS FROM COLD WATERS
WHERE IT PREYS ON FISH, KRILL, CRABEATER SEALS, AND PENGUINS.
SHACKLETON'S MEN FEARED THE SEALS, CALLING THEM "SEA-LEOPARDS."

PRESENT-DAY EXPLORERS ARE EXPERTS AT USING DOGS AND SKIS
TO CROSS ANTARCTICA'S HARSH TERRAIN. SHACKLETON'S MEN MASTERED
NEITHER TECHNIQUE AND SUFFERED GREATLY AS A RESULT.

THE *ENDURANCE* CRUSHED BY ICE, CREWMEN TRIED IN VAIN TO
HAUL THE *JAMES CAIRD* LIFEBOAT OVER WEDDELL SEA PACK ICE TO OPEN
WATER. SHACKLETON HALTED THE BACKBREAKING EFFORT.

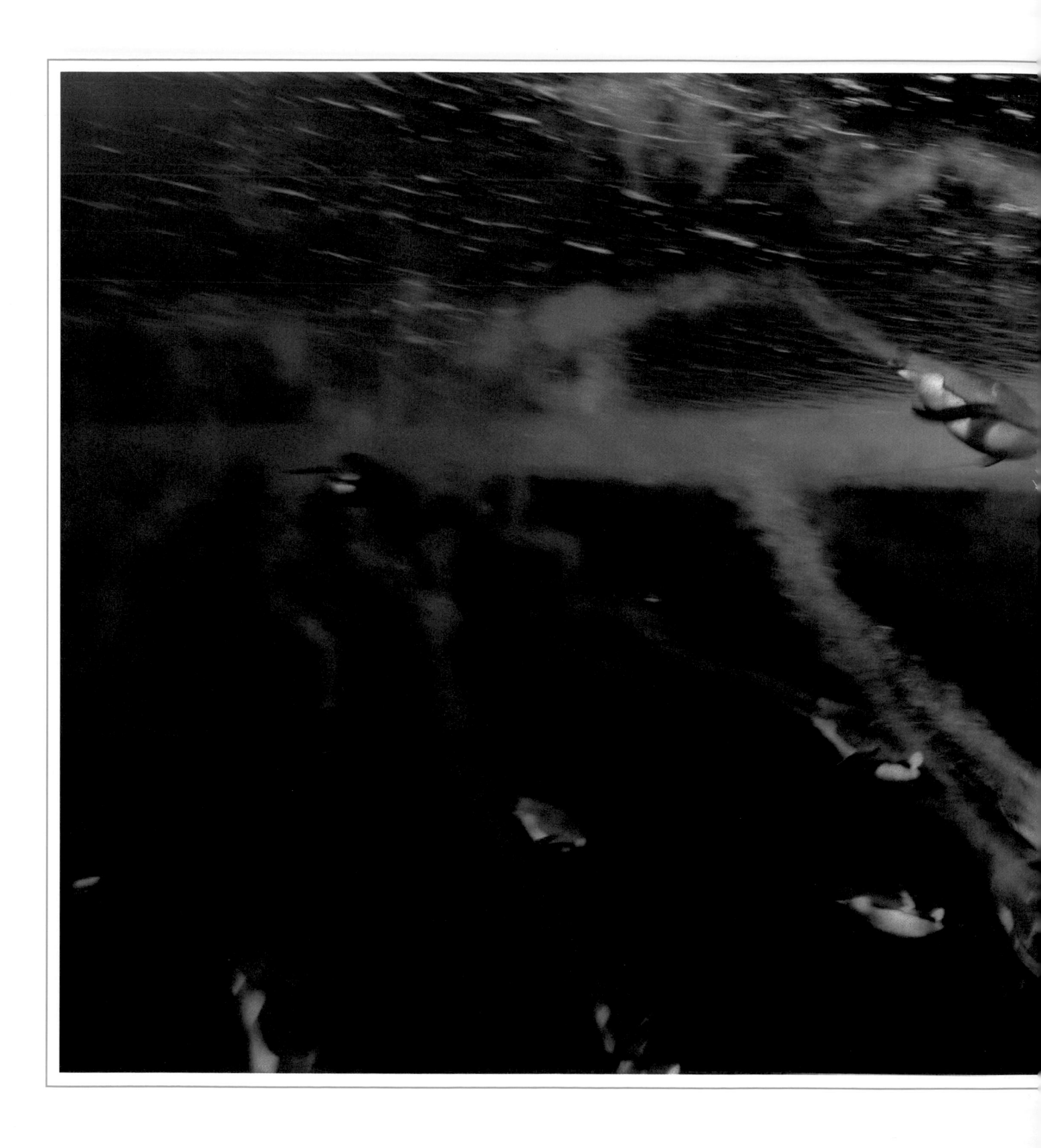

LARGEST OF 17 PENGUIN SPECIES, EMPERORS LEAVE AWKWARDNESS
BEHIND WHEN THEY SWIM, DIVING AS DEEP AS 800 FEET TO FIND FISH
AND SQUID. THEY CAN SPEND A LIFETIME NEVER SETTING FOOT ON LAND.

MODERN EXPLORERS WITNESS ANTARCTICA'S ICY TECTONICS WHEN
A GLACIER CALVES A LARGE ICEBERG THAT ROLLS OVER AND CRASHES
THROUGH SURROUNDING PACK ICE, SPEWING SNOW LIKE SMOKE.

The Old Dog for the Hard Road

On the final day of December 1908, four starving men huddled in their sleeping bags at the bottom of the world, on the great polar plateau of Antarctica, 10,477 feet above sea level. They spoke in calm voices that belied the seriousness of their situation. Every so often a berserk wind would shriek against their tent and the men would fall silent, each harboring private fears and thinning hopes. Their prize, the South Pole, now 126 nautical miles away, seemed less and less attainable at the end of each passing

Crewmen haul supplies onto Ross Island during Robert F. Scott's 1902 Discovery *expedition.*

day, after each brutal march and meager meal.

Nobody spoke of turning back, least of all their expedition leader, the indigo-eyed Anglo-Irishman with small hands but an iron grip, Ernest Shackleton. Yet the surgeon among them, Dr. Eric Marshall, believed that Shackleton showed the most worrisome signs of physical distress. His pulse was weak, his headaches severe. His behavior was sometimes giddy, sometimes listless.

This was not without precedent. Six years earlier, on Great Britain's National Antarctic Expedition under the command of Robert Falcon Scott of the Royal Navy, Shackleton had suffered from scurvy, spit up blood, and been forced to ride in a sled he was supposed to pull, relying on the strength and stamina of others. He had also crossed swords with Scott on the Ross Ice Shelf and challenged his command. For that as much as anything, Scott had invalided him back to England early, an embarrassment Shackleton would never forget.

Now he had returned to the birthplace of blizzards, but this time as a husband and a father, with his family waiting back home. And most important, he had returned as an expedition leader.

"Head too bad to write much," he wrote in his journal the next day, New Year's Day, 1909, after he and his men covered little more than 11 miles. He noted with subdued satisfaction, "so we have beaten North and South Records." Nobody had ever been this close to either geographic pole, north or south.

To stand at the axis of the Earth, around which all else spins, was the explorer's polar grail of the early 1900s. Such places lived in extremes of summer light and winter dark, veiled by distance, wind, and cold. Emerging, however, was an understanding of their contrasts: the Arctic as an ocean surrounded by land—Alaska, Canada, Greenland, Scandinavia, and Russia; the Antarctic as a continent surrounded by ocean, with its heart, the South Pole, as best Shackleton could now guess, somewhere on this hostile plateau high above sea level, a much colder, drier, windier—and altogether more unforgiving—place than the Arctic.

In every direction stretched a prebiotic world of ice and snow. Altocirrus clouds etched the sky and obscured a reluctant sun that offered only cold, interrogating light.

How different things had been one year earlier, on New Year's Day, 1908, when Shackleton's little expedition ship, *Nimrod*, left Port Lyttelton, New Zealand, amid a cheering crowd of 30,000 well-wishers. Those voices were mute now, lost in the wind. While Shackleton's polar party pushed south on foot, the *Nimrod* and most of the expeditioneers waited at base quarters at Cape Royds, on Ross Island, McMurdo Sound, 700 miles to the north. Earlier in the season a six-man party from the *Nimrod* had climbed 12,448-foot Mount Erebus, the southernmost active volcano in the world, a marvelous success considering that en route a fierce storm

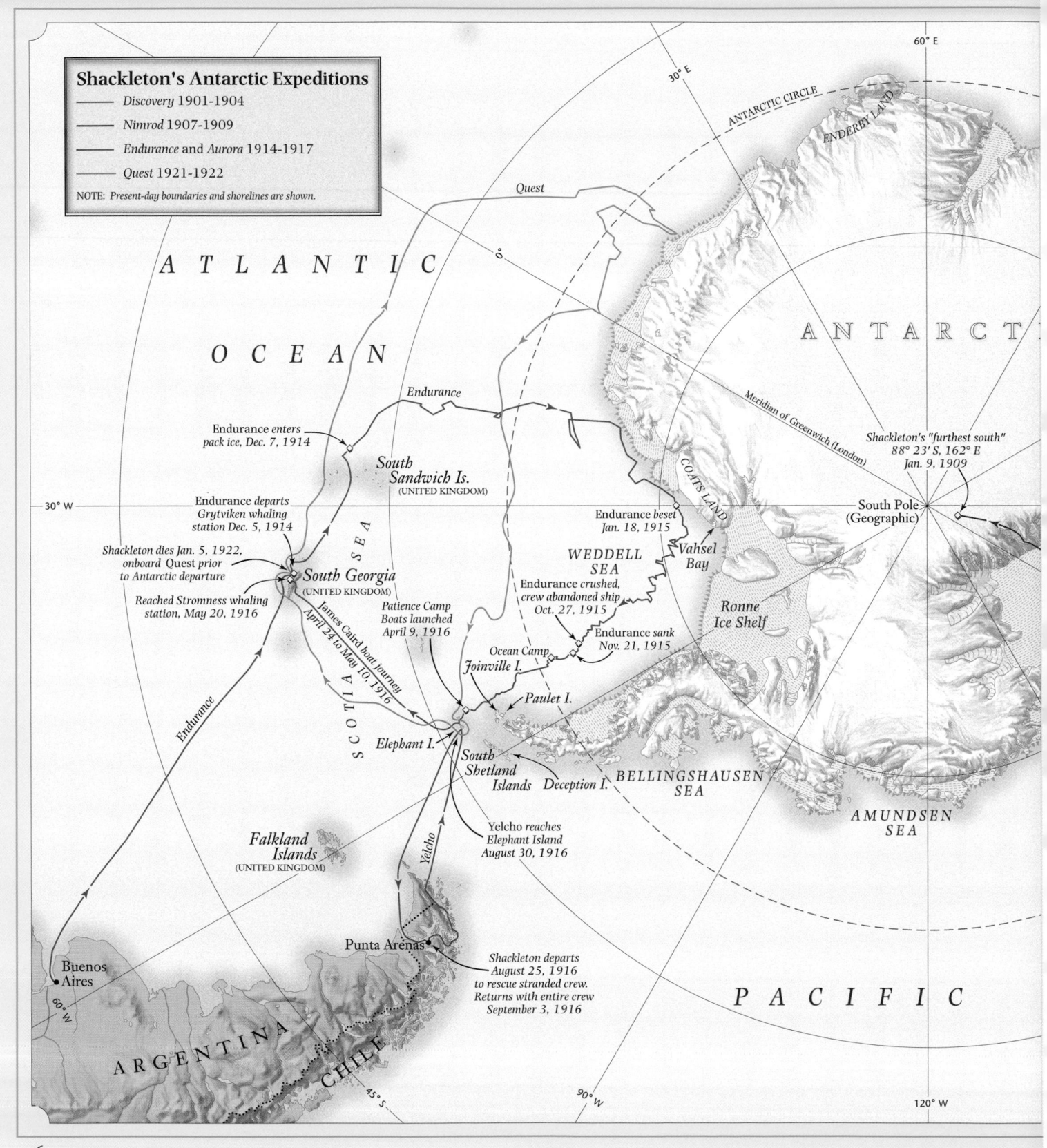

Shackleton's Antarctic Expeditions

- Discovery 1901-1904
- Nimrod 1907-1909
- Endurance and Aurora 1914-1917
- Quest 1921-1922

NOTE: Present-day boundaries and shorelines are shown.

ATLANTIC

OCEAN

Quest

60° E

30° E

ANTARCTIC CIRCLE

ENDERBY LAND

ANTARCTI

0°

Endurance

Endurance enters
pack ice, Dec. 7, 1914

South
Sandwich Is.
(UNITED KINGDOM)

Meridian of Greenwich (London)

Shackleton's "furthest south"
88° 23' S, 162° E
Jan. 9, 1909

30° W

Endurance departs
Grytviken whaling
station Dec. 5, 1914

Endurance beset
Jan. 18, 1915

COATS LAND

South Pole
(Geographic)

Shackleton dies Jan. 5, 1922,
onboard Quest prior
to Antarctic departure

South Georgia
(UNITED KINGDOM)

WEDDELL
SEA

Vahsel
Bay

Reached Stromness whaling
station, May 20, 1916

Endurance crushed,
crew abandoned ship
Oct. 27, 1915

Ronne
Ice Shelf

James Caird boat journey
April 24 to May 10, 1916

Patience Camp
Boats launched
April 9, 1916

Endurance sank
Nov. 21, 1915

SCOTIA

Ocean Camp

Joinville I.

Endurance

Paulet I.

Elephant I.

South
Shetland
Islands

Deception I.

BELLINGSHAUSEN
SEA

AMUNDSEN
SEA

Falkland
Islands
(UNITED KINGDOM)

Yelcho

Yelcho reaches
Elephant Island
August 30, 1916

Buenos
Aires

60° W

Punta Arenas

Shackleton departs
August 25, 1916
to rescue stranded crew.
Returns with entire crew
September 3, 1916

PACIFIC

ARGENTINA

CHILE

45° S

90° W

120° W

26

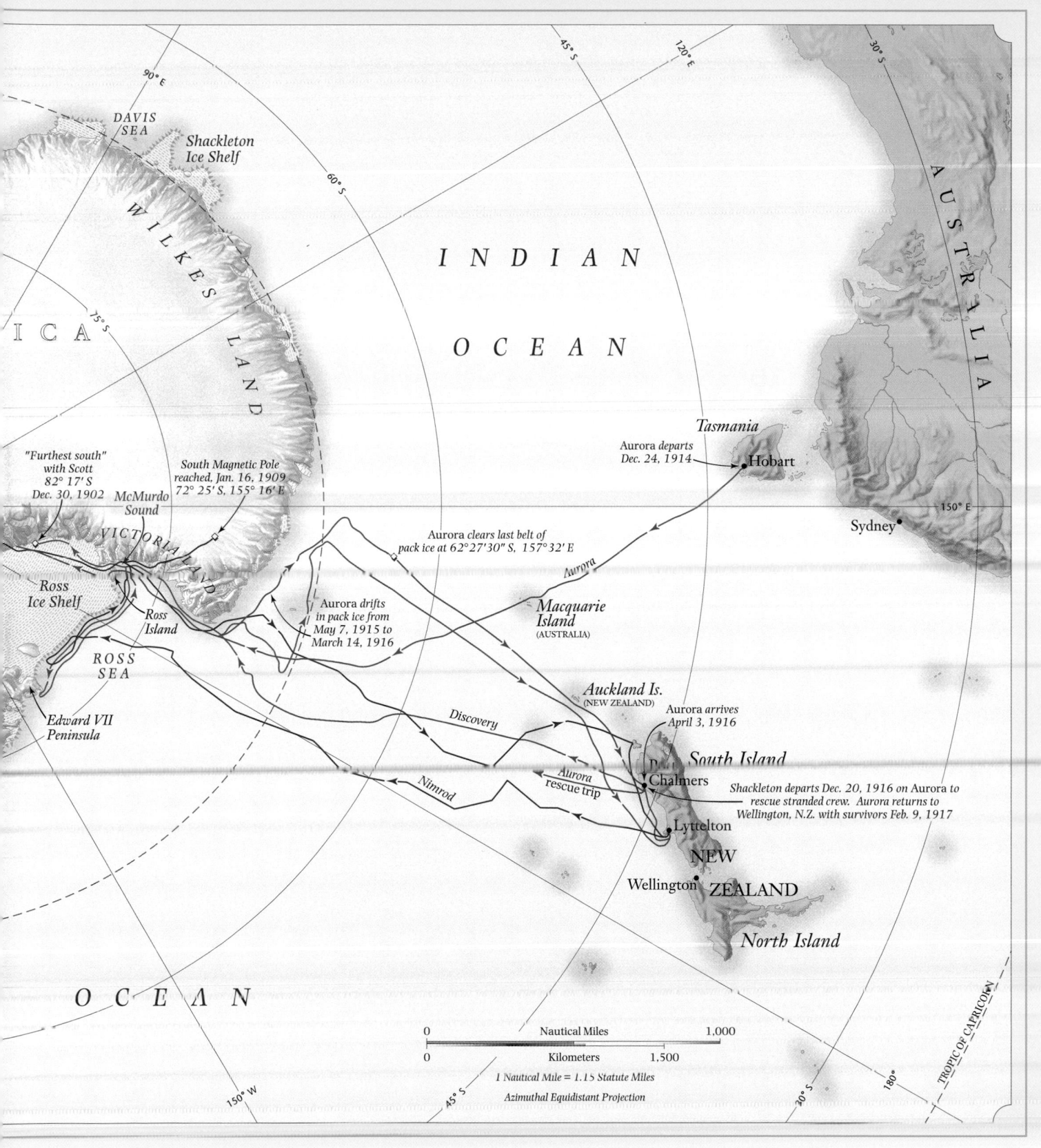

DAVIS
SEA

Shackleton
Ice Shelf

90° E

WILKES LAND

75° S

I C A

60° S

45° S

120° E

30° S

AUSTRALIA

150° E

INDIAN

OCEAN

Tasmania

Aurora departs
Dec. 24, 1914

Hobart

Sydney

"Furthest south"
with Scott
82° 17' S
Dec. 30, 1902

South Magnetic Pole
reached, Jan. 16, 1909
72° 25' S, 155° 16' E

McMurdo
Sound

VICTORIA LAND

*Aurora clears last belt of
pack ice at 62°27'30" S, 157°32' E*

Aurora

Ross
Ice Shelf

*Aurora drifts
in pack ice from
May 7, 1915 to
March 14, 1916*

Ross
Island

Macquarie
Island
(AUSTRALIA)

ROSS
SEA

Auckland Is.
(NEW ZEALAND)

Aurora arrives
April 3, 1916

Edward VII
Peninsula

Discovery

South Island

Chalmers

*Aurora
rescue trip*

*Shackleton departs Dec. 20, 1916 on Aurora to
rescue stranded crew. Aurora returns to
Wellington, N.Z. with survivors Feb. 9, 1917*

Nimrod

Lyttelton

NEW

Wellington

ZEALAND

O C E A N

North Island

150° W

45° S

20° S

180°

TROPIC OF CAPRICORN

0   Nautical Miles   1,000

0   Kilometers   1,500

1 Nautical Mile = 1.15 Statute Miles

Azimuthal Equidistant Projection

had pinned them down for 30 hours, yet no man was lost. And now, while Shackleton moved south, another party—including two of Australia's preeminent geologists, Edgeworth David and Douglas Mawson—marched across frozen McMurdo Sound to the coast of South Victoria Land, then inland onto the polar plateau. Per Shackleton's orders, they were to proceed with due swiftness and caution to the South Magnetic Pole, an arduous round-trip journey of 1,260 miles that would require 122 days. It would be another grand discovery, one explorers had wanted to attain ever since James Clark Ross and Francis Crozier sailed their three-masted navy war frigates, H.M.S *Erebus* and H.M.S *Terror,* into the area in 1841. Indeed the *Nimrod* expedition would make many important discoveries and scientific observations in volcanology, geomagnetism, meteorology, marine biology, and other disciplines.

But for Shackleton it was all secondary to the South Pole itself. After four years of preparation, little else mattered. Thus focused, he and his polar party—Dr. Marshall, Frank Wild, and Lt. Jameson Boyd Adams—had departed Cape Royds on October 29, 1908, with three months rations weighing 773 pounds. Ever the meticulous planner, Shackleton determined that each man should receive a daily allotment of 34 ounces of food: a diet of pemmican (dried beef with 60 percent extra fat added), biscuit, cheese or chocolate, cocoa, plasmon (hydrolyzed protein), sugar, and Quaker Oats, with a little tea, salt, and pepper thrown in. Support parties accompanied them some of the distance, complete with four tough little Manchurian ponies pulling supplies. A specially designed motorcar—the first in the Antarctic—was also used. Shackleton had hoped it would cover 150 miles in a single day. But after only eight miles on solid ice and easy going, it hit soft snow and proved useless.

∽

NOW ALONE AND DEEP in the Antarctic freezer, the four men had marched 400 miles across the Ross Ice Shelf, then climbed 10,000 feet up the 125-mile-long Beardmore Glacier onto the polar plateau. Continuing south in bitter cold and wind, on rough surfaces and soft, they man-hauled their sledges—work that Norwegians believed only sled dogs should do. They had cached several food depots for their return trip. Progress was slower than expected, and once again they cut rations, stretching their food while trying to stretch their stamina. With fuel running low for their primus stove, less and less snow could be melted into drinking water.

Compounding their problems, on December 7, 1908, they lost Socks, their last pony and strongest sledger. As Frank Wild would later describe it, they were "making for the centre of the glacier...and the sledges were running nicely; [Shackleton, Adams, and Marshall] were ten yards ahead, when I suddenly stepped into space, felt a violent blow on my shoulder and a fearful rush of something past me, a vicious snatch at my right hand, and found myself hanging by my left arm only, in a horrible chasm. Socks gone, and the sledge with a broken bow very near following; I got out somehow, and the other three running back, we quickly got the sledge into safety. Socks must have been killed instantly, as we could hear no sound from below, and see nothing but an intense black depth."

With Socks gone and the sledge damaged, each man had to pull 250 pounds under a strain, and there would be no immediate horse meat for the return trip to Cape Royds.

"I cannot think of failure yet," Shackleton wrote on the plateau on January 2, 1909. "I must look at the matter sensibly and consider the lives of those who are with me. I feel that if we go on too far it will be impossible to get back...and then all the results will be lost to the world.... Man can only do his best, and we have arrayed against us the strongest forces of nature...."

On January 4 he wrote, "The end is in sight...we are weakening rapidly. Short food and a blizzard wind from the south...." The temperature was minus 15° F. They had jettisoned food and gear to lighten their loads. Each man now had no extra clothes; what he sweated in by day he slept in by night. Their sleeping bags were rimed with ice. Each pulled 70 pounds across the plateau, not 250 pounds up the glacier as he had three weeks earlier. Yet each found it harder going, which to Shackleton was "a clear indication of our failing strength." Their elevation was now 11,200 feet. After a difficult stretch, with the ill-running sledge askew in soft snow behind them, each man would bend at the waist, hands on his knees, shoulders in harness, and inhale the thin air in ragged, rasping breaths.

They cached a final food depot and pushed on, hoping—"trusting" was Shackleton's word—that their previous footprints would guide them back to valuable provisions.

The next day they did 13 miles; the day after that, 12. These forced marches were "some of the most astonishing marches ever achieved," a biographer would later write. Shackleton's ambition required perfect conditions and a better tomorrow. Then came a blizzard, with winds up to 90 miles an hour. The men lay tent-bound for 60 straight hours. They were so cold they suffered from cramps, all of them with temperatures three to five degrees below normal human body temperature, which Wild noted, "spells death at home."

"All nearly paralyzed with cold," added Marshall in his diary.

Sheets of ice formed on their beards and their Burberry jackets, and made

"I do not know what 'moss' stands for in the proverb, but if it stood for useful knowledge... I gathered more moss by rolling than I ever did at school."

ERNEST SHACKLETON
APRIL 1914

movement painful. To keep spirits up, Shackleton read to them from *The Merchant of Venice.* Perhaps in a lucid moment they realized that never in 300 years had Shakespeare found such a preposterous stage as the Antarctic ice cap.

On January 8 Shackleton wrote, "we simply lie here shivering. Every now and then one of our party's feet go, and the unfortunate beggar has to take his leg out of the sleeping bag and have his frozen foot nursed into life again by placing it inside the shirt and against the skin of his equally unfortunate neighbour."

The storm broke on January 9, and the men made a dash. Leaving behind their sledge and theodolite (used to measure their location), they carried Queen Alexandra's flag and another Union Jack, plus a camera, glasses, a compass, and a brass cylinder containing some stamps and documents. Half walking, half running over a surface hardened by the blizzard, Shackleton observed, "It was strange for us to go along without the nightmare of a sledge dragging behind us." At latitude 88° 23' S they stopped, 97 nautical miles short of the South Pole. They hoisted the flags and Shackleton took possession of the area, naming it the King Edward VII Plateau.

"We have shot our bolt," Shackleton wrote. "While the Union Jack blew out stiffly in the icy gale that cut us to the bone, we looked south with our powerful glasses, but could see nothing but the dead white snow plain.... We stayed only a few minutes, and then, taking the Queen's flag and eating our scanty meal as we went, we hurried back...."

Time to march or die.

❧

WHAT CONCERNED SHACKLETON now, far beyond the scourges of fatigue or frost-bite or scurvy, was pessimism. He knew from his time at sea since the age of 16, sailing around Cape Horn, and from his first expedition to Antarctica in 1901-03, that stress was a beast more dangerous than any rogue wave or a maverick wind. When they were packed together under severe physical strain for long periods of time, men tended to magnify the faults and shrink the virtues of others around them. Frank Wild, who was small but tough and reliable as granite, didn't think Marshall and Adams were pulling their weight. He privately wished Shackleton had brought the indefatigable seaman Ernest Joyce and the big bear of an artist George Marston instead. The extra sledging burden must have been hard on him. Marshall in turn nursed a growing resentment for Shackleton for getting them into this bloody mess.

Added to their misery was the disappointment of defeat. They had not reached the Pole, and this bitter pill could slow them down like a strong wind. Yet as the other three slogged along, losing strength each day, Shackleton, who had been the weakest before, grew stronger, as if supreme danger were somehow his elixir. The Pole was lost and behind him. There would be no looking back, only looking forward. Only better tomorrows. He would invest every ounce of himself into this new challenge: the art of polar survival and saving his men and doing the impossible—a personal magic he played better than anybody in the heroic age of polar travel.

They followed their footprints, which the wind had sculpted into pedestals above the rest of the ice and snow. The clouds vanished and the sun circled them in its low orbit, burning their skin and eyes. They reached each food depot without a biscuit to spare. They looked like shadows of their former selves, eyes hollow, faces gaunt, four weather-beaten scarecrows made of grit and bone. Through labyrinthine icefalls they negotiated the headwaters of the Beardmore Glacier, sometimes making 25 and 30 miles in a day. Down, down, down they raced for the next food depot, more afraid of starving to death than of falling into a crevasse.

"I do not know how [Shackleton] stands it," wrote Wild, "both his heels are split in four or five places, his legs are bruised and chafed, and today he has had a violent headache...and yet he gets along as well as anyone."

By the end of January Shackleton was stumbling and falling in his harness. One night after supper, he collapsed. "For a good six weeks," Wild noted, Shackleton had been "doing far more than his share of work." Marshall worried that the others might have to haul him in the sled, not unlike the debacle with Scott in 1903.

They descended to below 6,000 feet, where they could breathe without effort. Then they got dysentery, probably from eating half-cooked horsemeat cached at lower elevations (where the horses had been butchered earlier, according to plan). Their pace slowed to a crawl. Frank Wild buckled with pain. Yet from some deep reserve Shackleton gathered the strength to spirit them on. He never complained to the others, nor did they to him.

One night in mid-February on the Ross Ice Shelf, still many miles from safety and by no means assured they would survive, Shackleton and Frank Wild shared a tent, and Shackleton asked Wild if he would return with him to Antarctica someday, have another go at the Pole. Starving, dehydrated, sunburned, frostbitten, shivering in their sleeping bags for the hundredth-odd time, it was an absurd yet noble moment. Wild had decided earlier that, "This trip has completely cured me of any desire for more polar exploration." But Shackleton's magnetism turned his compass needle. Upon hearing the invitation, Wild instantly said yes. The two men spent many hours discussing details, warming each other with their enthusiasm, forging a partnership that would someday enter the pantheon of polar greatness.

They struggled on. Minna Bluff and other familiar landmarks came into view. Then Mount Erebus, lording over Ross Island. It was late February. If they didn't reach the *Nimrod* by March 1, the crew would sail north, assuming Shackleton was dead. The ship could not delay, for each additional day meant greater likelihood of entrapment by winter's encroaching pack ice. Shackleton told his three companions that if they didn't reach the *Nimrod* in time, they could use a small open boat to sail and row to New Zealand, one thousand miles across tempestuous seas, an absurd proposition that he somehow made sound credible. He would get his open boat journey...someday.

They reached a cornucopia food depot recently stocked by crewmen from the *Nimrod,* and feasted like paupers at a banquet. Back on the march, Marshall, who had eaten too much, suffered severe cramps and couldn't continue. Shackleton left him in a tent under Adams's care and pushed on with Wild. Every hour counted as the last two days of February flickered away. At one point Shackleton grasped his friend's hand and said breathlessly, "Frank old man, it's the old dog for the hard road every time." He and Wild were 35; the two men left behind not yet 30.

The weather smiled with clear skies and a following wind. The last day of February broke with 15 miles to go. They had no more food; Adams had under-packed their lunch sack. The wind changed and a snowstorm swallowed the two men. Still, they pushed on. They had no choice. "To give way to despair," wrote Wild, "was not possible for Shackleton."

On the *Nimrod,* spirits were low. Shackleton was assumed dead. He had departed 120 days ago with 91 days of food. The crew considered a search party to "find the bodies." But would their little ship then get frozen in?

Shackleton and Wild reached Scott's old abandoned base at Hut Point, built in 1901-02. They tried to burn some wood as a signal, but it wouldn't ignite. They tried to tie a Union Jack onto a high cross, but their cold fingers couldn't manage the knots. They stayed that night in the hut, shivering.

On the morning of March 1, the *Nimrod* approached from Cape Royds and saw the two men waving a flag. Cheers of joy erupted on deck. "We had almost overlooked the fact that we were in the Land of Surprises," wrote Second Officer Arthur Harbord.

"No happier sight ever met the eyes of man," said Frank Wild when he and Shackleton saw the masts of the *Nimrod* appear over the horizon.

To those on board, Shackleton and Wild looked like the walking dead. "Did you get to the Pole?" they asked eagerly.

"No," Shackleton said, "we got within 97 miles." His own words seemed to ridicule him. He was the man who almost got to the Pole.

He could not think of that now. Marshall and Adams were still tentbound on the Ross Ice Shelf. Though weak, Shackleton insisted that he lead the rescue party. He was the one who got them into this mess. He would get them out. Wild stayed on the *Nimrod*, too exhausted to travel. Shackleton departed and returned with Marshall and Adams in two days.

Back home in England, Shackleton received a hero's welcome. No longer an obscure lieutenant in the Mercantile Marine, he was knighted and made a Commander of the Victorian Order. His name appeared everywhere. He played to the crowd as the beau-ideal polar explorer, cutting his rugged image, salting his lectures with high-stakes drama, pluck, humor, and wit. His rival, Captain Scott, a reserved man who lacked Shackleton's magnetism, listened carefully and planned his own return to Antarctica. The great Norwegian explorers, Fridtjof Nansen and Roald Amundsen, praised Shackleton's efforts. Amundsen said his name "will forevermore be engraved with letters of fire in the history of Antarctic exploration." Shackleton's polar shortfall was an irresistible invitation for these men to go south, and Amundsen, like Scott, had plans.

For all his success, Shackleton was restless, a moth to the cold white flame of Antarctica. He burned to return. But it would take years to finance another expedition. Leaving the South Pole unattained haunted him. To Emily, his wife, he asked, "A live donkey is better than a dead lion, isn't it?"

"Yes, darling," she responded.

THE NEWSPAPERS CALLED him many things, among them a "splendid failure." The dark implication being that if he could get so close, why not go all the way? Sacrifice himself and his men for the pride of the Empire, reach the Pole with no food for the return. Die there, wrapped in the Union Jack. The perfect Edwardian English hero. It was perhaps prophecy. England did not have to wait long for her polar martyr.

In early 1912, Robert Falcon Scott and four companions froze to death en route back from the South Pole. They had reached the great prize only to find a Norwegian flag flapping in the bitter wind, mocking them, and a letter from Amundsen who had arrived five weeks before by pioneering a new route through the Transantarctic Mountains:

"Dear Captain Scott, As you are probably the first to reach this area after us, I will ask you kindly to forward this letter to King Haakon VII [of Norway]. If you can use any of the articles left in the tent please do not hesitate to do so. With kind regards I wish you a safe return. Yours truly, Roald Amundsen."

The intent was simple. If Amundsen disappeared on the return trip, so would his proof of priority at the Pole. If Scott reached the Pole and returned home, the letter would be Amundsen's insurance package, delivered by the man he beat. Yet it was Amundsen, not Scott, who made it back, and all cordiality was blinded by a perceived insult. Raymond Priestly, the geologist on the *Nimrod* and the *Terra Nova* noted that Scott, already dispirited, was degraded from explorer to postman.

Later, as he and his men lay in their tent freezing to death on the Ross Ice Shelf, not far from where Marshall and Adams had waited for Shackleton, Scott wrote in his diary, "We shall die like gentlemen.... These rough notes our dead bodies must tell the tale."

Amundsen had won the Pole, but Scott trumped him to become the larger hero. He paid the greatest price. He left a widow and a fatherless son. His "rough notes" electrified the world. England had its dead lion.

Shackleton faded but would not disappear.

An American had claimed the North Pole, a Norwegian the South. Yet in Shackleton's mind a suitably outrageous prize remained: a sledging journey across the icy continent from one end to the other via the South Pole. He believed it was "up to the British nation to accomplish...the most striking of all journeys—the crossing of the Continent." He called it the Imperial Trans-Antarctic Expedition. One apocryphal notice read: "Men Wanted for Hazardous Journey. Small wages, bitter cold, long months of complete darkness, constant danger, safe return doubtful. Honour and recognition in case of success. Ernest Shackleton." A formal letter from Shackleton to the *Times* of London announced the expedition.

The expedition ship would be called the *Endurance.* To captain her Shackleton wanted John King Davis, a fellow strong-willed Anglo-Irishman with tarnished red hair who had been the chief officer, and later skipper, aboard the *Nimrod.* But Davis declined.

Thus in the early summer of 1914, with war brewing in Europe, Shackleton was consumed as always by the Antarctic. He needed a captain. The man for the job came from the volcanic hills of Akaroa, New Zealand, guided by a dream.

Growing up in Akaroa, little Frank Worsley courted trouble far out of proportion to his size. At age six he drank carbolic acid and nearly died. At eight he and his brother built a raft made of flax stems and crossed three-mile-wide Akaroa Harbor—a flooded, seaside volcanic crater—using makeshift paddles and their jackets as sails. They had to fight for their lives when a wind kicked up, and they arrived home well after dark, hungry, wet, and cold.

Labeled a "wild bush boy," he was caned constantly at school by a headmaster who aimed to civilize him. In four years Worsley received an estimated 3,000 "cuts" of cane to the palms of his hands. Yet not once did he cry, whimper or try to evade punishment. He seemed to pride himself in testing his limits for pain. By 1887, at age 15, he finished top in every class and won 12 prizes and the Dux Medal by becoming the head boy of Fendalton School. The next year he went to sea, where the Earth's far latitudes became his classroom.

Years later in a London hotel, he had a dream that changed his life. As he later wrote, "One night I dreamed that Burlington Street was full of ice-blocks, and that I was navigating a ship along it—an absurd dream. Sailors are superstitious, and when I woke up next morning I hurried like mad into my togs, and down Burlington Street I went. I dare say that it was only a coincidence, but as I walked along, reflecting that certainly my dream had been meaningless and uncomfortable and that it had cost me time that I could have used to better purpose, a sign on a door-post caught my eye. It bore the words 'Imperial Trans-Antarctic Expedition,' and no sooner did I see it than I turned into the building with the conviction that it had some special significance for me."

Inside he met Shackleton. Worsley was the smaller man, yet he possessed a sturdy build and confidence, and a permanent mirthful expression as if on the edge of an unveiled jest. Of Shackleton he wrote, "the moment I set eyes on him, I knew that he was a man with whom I should be proud to work."

Shackleton's intuition told him that Worsley's demeanor would not render him an altogether effective leader; he couldn't look stern if he had to. But the New Zealander spoke in a breezy, nautical way, as if storm petrels were his kin. They agreed on terms and Shackleton told him, "You're engaged. Join your ship until I wire for you."

Then a second officer on a transatlantic freighter, Worsley wrote, "I was committed to my fate. Not a superfluous word had been spoken on either side, but we knew by instinct that we were to be friends from that hour." ■

The Boss

*S*hackleton was everything that men of the sea expected him to be. As John King Davis described him on a first encounter years earlier, he was "dressed in a blue suit. He had thick black hair carefully brushed down and parted in the middle, heavy eyebrows, a piercing glance and a clean shaven jaw of the variety known as 'bulldog.' There was about him the unmistakable look of a deep-water sailor."

A young, determined Shackleton faces the camera (above). The ice that beckoned him endures (opposite).

Born in Kilkea, County Kildare, Ireland in 1874, the same year as Winston Churchill and Herbert Hoover, Ernest Henry Shackleton was part of the Protestant Ascendancy—descendants of English settlers in Ireland—who recognized the green isle not as an independent country but as a colony of the crown. He shared his Anglo-Irish roots (yet not all his political views) with Jonathan Swift, Oscar Wilde, and George Bernard Shaw, and like those men of words he fancied himself a poet and a wit, or at least a student of poetry and wit. He reminded others that his birthday, February 15, was the same as Galileo's. Perhaps he felt his life, like that of the Italian radical, would somehow be unorthodox and remarkable.

The second oldest of ten children, he had one brother and eight sisters who intermittently adored and tolerated him. Biographer Roland Huntford wrote that his mother had a "total lack of pretension, and an unshakable, almost exasperating optimism...." and that "The tales clustering around Ernest Shackleton the child suggest an ordinarily troublesome boy, and very much the Irishman. They seem largely to illustrate persuasiveness, plausibility, and a capacity to hide shrewd calculation under the onion skins of charm. In one, he induces a housemaid to help him dig in the garden for buried treasure, having first salted the claim with a ruby ring belonging to his mother. In another, he convinces one of his sisters that the Monument in London had been erected in his honour."

When Ernest was six, the family moved to Dublin, where his father earned a medical degree with distinction from Trinity College. Four years later they moved to England and settled amid the comfortable estates of Victorian Sydenham, in surburban London. The family flourished, and young Ernest continued his games and good humor. Sitting on the garden wall surrounded by friends and ginger-beer bottles, he would hoodwink his younger sisters into the oddball and the absurd. He developed a strong memory for quotations, and the ability to sprinkle them at perfect moments.

Teased by classmates about his brogue, he became quick with his fists and earned the nickname Mick. Despite having a fertile imagination, or perhaps because of it, he struggled in school. Provincial halls and walls didn't challenge him. Like many boys his age he no doubt read about Captain Nemo in Jules Verne's *Twenty Thousand Leagues Under the Sea.* He must have fancied himself on deck with Admiral Nelson at Trafalgar, or with Francis Drake in the Channel, fighting the Spanish Armada for Good Queen Bess—Elizabeth I.

In Dulwich College his report cards consistently read "could do better." In time Dr. Shackleton accepted the reality that his eldest son belonged to the sea, not the streets. The Royal Navy was beyond family means, so he contacted a cousin who secured for Ernest a probationary position with the Mercantile Marine working for the Northwestern Shipping Company. Ernest worked hard and his grades improved. For the first time in his life he had a goal, a purpose, a horizon beyond temperate, manicured England.

∼

AT 16 HE SAILED from Liverpool to Valparaiso in the square-rigged *Hoghton Tower,* a three-masted clipper ship with acres of canvas and more than 200 lines, each with its own name. "I can tell you Nic," he wrote to a school chum, "that it is pretty hard work, and dirty work too. It is a queer life and a risky one...you carry your life in your hand whenever you go aloft, in bad weather; how would you like to be 150 feet up in the air; hanging on with one hand to a rope while with the other you try to get the sail in...and there is the ship rocking, pitching, and rolling about like a live creature...."

He rounded Cape Horn in the middle of the southern winter. A gale snapped spars and injured several members of the crew. Yet young Ernest fared well. His captain was a kind man in sharp contrast to the martinet who commanded the next run. Ever the watchful apprentice, Shackleton absorbed these early lessons in good leadership versus bad. When asked years later how he became interested in Antarctica, he recalled his first journey around the Horn, fighting "one continuous blizzard all the way.... Yet many a time, even in the midst of this discomfort, my thoughts would go out to the southward."

Terra Australis Incognita, the "unknown southern land." That was how ancient maps depicted Antarctica. The Greeks loved symmetry and believed the earth round. Furthermore, they believed lands to the north under the constellation of the great bear, Arctos, must be balanced by lands to the south, Anti-arctos. More than two millennia would be required to confirm the existence of such a

THE SHACKLETON BROOD (opposite) comprised two sons and eight daughters of Dr. Henry Shackleton, a member of the Royal College of Surgeons, and Henrietta Letitia Sophia Shackleton, an energetic, good-humored woman. The girls left to right are Kathleen, Ethel, Clara, Amy, Eleanor, Alice, Gladys, and Helen. Frank is seated, and Ernest towers above.

place. Even Capt. James Cook, sailing in search of Antarctica in the 1770s and "surrounded on every side by danger," failed to sight land. He lamented that "The risque one runs in exploring a coast in these unknown and icy seas, is so very great, that I can be bold enough to say that no man will ever venture farther than I have done, and the lands which may lie to the South will never be explored...."

Bold indeed, and for Cook uncharacteristically incorrect. What greater challenge did an adventurer need? Antarctica was one of the few places in the world—perhaps the only place—that could prove Cook so wrong. Men did go farther, beginning with sealers in the early 1820s, and what they found intoxicated them: white ice and black rock, castle bergs and tuxedoed birds, a constant edge and seductive fear. For Shackleton, his spirit just beginning to soar, Antarctica would become irresistible.

By age 20 he had sailed around Cape Horn five times and earned the rank of second mate. Two years later he was first mate; two years after that, a certified master, qualified to command British ships on any sea. He sailed on tramp steamers to China, Japan, Cape Town, and the Mediterranean, ports of call exotic and strange. Returning home to his adoring sisters, whom he called his "harem," he would burst through the door and shout, "Come all my wives. Come Fatima, tickle my toes. Come, oh favoured one and scratch my back."

"Of course," said his sister Kathleen, "we all loved it."

He regaled them with stories. In one he said he met Lord Rothschild, a passenger on his ship who one night after dinner gave Ernest a magnificent cigar. Ernest carefully wrapped it in foil and boasted of his relationship with the famous baron,

FIVE-PANEL PANORAMA shows Scott's ship, Discovery, *beset in pack ice off Ross Island in the summer of 1903-04. Two rescue ships reached her in February 1904, and blasted away the ice with explosives. Subsequent to the expedition, Scott claimed "prior rights" to all Ross Island, and forbade Shackleton from landing there on the* Nimrod *in 1908. Shackleton obliged him for a while, but when ice conditions made alternatives impossible, he landed at the island's Cape Royds. Scott never forgave him.*

saying they were pals. When two crewmen stole the cigar from his cabin and flipped a coin to see who would smoke it, the winner discovered a foul taste. Ernest had anticipated their theft—he had in fact provoked it—and smoked the cigar and replaced it with a cheap fake.

He encouraged his sisters to follow their ambitions. Kathleen became a professional artist, Eleanor a nurse. In some respects they were his first crew; the women he would love most in his life. Yet, in 1897, when Kathleen introduced him to her friend, Emily Dorman, the daughter of a prosperous Sydenham solicitor, Ernest found a love he'd never experienced before. Emily admired the poems of Robert Browning, as did he. They took long walks together, her hand at his elbow, and when it came time to return to sea Ernest felt a reluctance that was new to him.

To impress Emily—and her father—he took a position on the elite Union Castle Line, with its coal-fired ships painted red and black, and Ernest, as an officer, dressed in navy blue with gold braid. In 1899-1900 he served on transport ships that carried bright-eyed boys to their tragic deaths in the Boer War in South Africa. The end of the century spelled deepening uncertainty for England. Queen Victoria died after a prosperous 64-year reign. Colonialism continued to collapse, and the British Empire spiraled down in a slow yet steady decline. People worked hard for little money in factories and on farms, laying brick upon brick, and young Ernest felt restless.

He wanted to make something of himself, be somebody, find a destiny—forge one if necessary—beyond the banal and routine. The work a day, grind-away life would never satisfy his implacable drive. Halfway around the world, Klondike

stampeders were rushing to riches and adventure in Alaska and the Yukon. Jack London was developing his best stories—*The Call of the Wild* and *White Fang*—about the primordial versus the civilized. Teddy Roosevelt and his Rough Riders had charged San Juan Hill. Sigmund Freud had just published *The Interpretation of Dreams* as a repudiation of secular Victorian codes.

Shackleton needed a broader brush, his own call of the wild. In the summer of 1900 he heard about the National Antarctic Expedition, the first British imperial venture to the far south in 60 years, a grand opportunity. He applied and was rejected. Undaunted, he befriended fellow members of the Royal Geographical Society, a major sponsor of the expedition, and they commended him as "more intelligent than the average officer. His brother officers considered him to be a very good fellow, always quoting poetry and full of erratic ideas."

The president of the Royal Geographical Society, Sir Clements Markham, might have seen in Shackleton something of his younger rambunctious self, a tough lad who compensated a mediocre formal education with voracious reading, nursing books through a thousand quiet nights at sea under the watchful stars of a single heaven. He might have even chosen Shackleton to lead the expedition, as Markham was a powerful man, "one of those imposing Victorian figures," said one source, "who commanded respect and dispensed patronage like an eastern potentate." But Shackleton was in the Mercantile Marine, not the Royal Navy, and although he was eventually enlisted for the expedition, the leadership post went to Markham's first protégé, Robert Falcon Scott.

∽

SHACKLETON AND SCOTT: From here forward, in life and in death, each man's name would cast a shadow across the other. Beyond ambition and Antarctica they had little in common. While Scott was reserved and regimented, Shackleton was intuitive and adaptive. In the years ahead he would display uncommon optimism, decisiveness, fellowship, and good humor. Leadership, not poetry, would be his true art; the chisel by which he would sculpt men's lives and make them believe in the greater whole of themselves and each other.

He was only 27 when he accompanied Scott in 1901, each going to Antarctica for the first time. His skills in leadership were just beginning to crystallize. Why Scott selected him for the three-man polar party one year later remains unknown; unaccountable decisions were his specialty. Shackleton no doubt distinguished himself with hard work, and positioned himself well. But he secretly disapproved of Scott's distant and mercurial manner. Scott had intended that the polar party be only two men, himself and his closest friend, Dr. Edward Wilson, a physician, naturalist, and artist. But Wilson felt that a third man should join the party; if one fell ill the other two would fare better getting him back. A deeply religious man, Wilson might have recommended Shackleton, with whom he shared a love of literature and a bent for horseplay and conviviality, traits foreign to Scott. Regardless, the three inexperienced men didn't make it far. They were poor skiers and poorer dog handlers, and it was Shackleton who fell ill. En route back Wilson expressed concern to Scott that Shackleton might not make it. Shackleton overheard them and vowed that he would outlive them both.

Upon return to base camp, Scott invalided Shackleton back to England, an extreme disgrace for the young explorer. As the British Broadcasting Company reported years later, Shackleton "came home in his late twenties, embarrassed and with bleak immediate prospects, and no job. Near despair. His one burning dream, to become an Antarctic explorer, now seemed horribly remote. He had failed. Some historians believe that Shackleton's breakdown in early 1903, and Scott's invaliding him home, were watershed moments that transformed his life—It required this trauma to rise to the level of 'rival' with Captain Scott. The realization slowly dawned on him that the only way for him to get back to the Antarctic was to lead his own expedition."

He needed an income and began at the bottom, as subeditor at *Royal Magazine*. Then the position of secretary/treasurer opened at the prestigious Royal Scottish Geographical Society, and with help from influential patrons Sir Clements Markham and Hugh Robert Mill, Shackleton got the post. His prospects brightened. He married Emily in London in April 1904, and settled into an amiable life in Edinburgh. That summer he took her on a belated honeymoon, and they played many games of golf, which Emily loved. She always won.

Biographers Margery and James Fisher wrote that in his early years of marriage Shackleton had a way of "becoming the centre of every gathering he went to, without making any effort to be so," and that he and Emily "without any ostentation, entertained delightfully those people whose company they liked."

Still, he was a cat in a cage. The secretaryship would have satisfied if not honored most men, but Shackleton wanted more and he wanted it yesterday. He managed to increase the society's membership and bank account and attendance at lectures, due in large part to his effervescence. But Edwardian protocol and armchair adventure didn't suit him. He puffed on cigarettes and wore light tweed suits that distressed his colleagues. One day he found an assistant who was practicing his golf swing by hitting balls into heavy curtains in a large and lavishly decorated room. Rather than scold the man, Shackleton borrowed a club, tried a few shots himself and hit a ball through a windowpane onto the street below.

During the Discovery expedition, Shackleton, Scott, and Dr. Edward Wilson return from their sledging push for the South Pole, having reached a farthest south latitude of only 82°17', not even beyond the Ross Ice Shelf, a disappointment for them all. Here Shackleton trails behind, far right. Louis Bernacchi, the expedition physicist, described the three men: "Long beards, hair, dirt, swollen lips & peeled complexions, & blood-shot eyes made them almost unrecognizable.... Shackleton appeared very ill indeed." Soon thereafter Scott invalided Shackleton home on the relief ship, Morning.

After only 18 months at the RSGS, he resigned his post to enter politics as the Liberal-Unionist candidate for Dundee. He canvased the shipyards as a working-man and a fighter, and gave some stirring speeches. But he lost. "It cannot be regretted now that Shackleton was not elected to a seat in Dundee," noted the Fishers 50 years later. "A Parliamentary career would have masked for him, for a time at least, the true nature of his gifts."

Again without work, and now with an infant son and domestic responsibilities, Shackleton faced a bleak year in 1906. Being allergic to any long road to financial success, he cooked up one grandiose scheme after another to make instant money and a name for himself, and reaped nothing but disappointment.

That same year, 1906, Roald Amundsen completed his three-year journey across the frozen inlets of Canada's high Arctic to claim the Northwest Passage, a geographical prize long sought by such luminaries as Martin Frobisher, Henry Hudson, William Parry, John Ross, James Cook, George Vancouver, and John Franklin. Known as "the man who ate his shoes," Franklin had nearly starved to death on his first expedition to the high Arctic. On his second expedition he mapped hundreds of miles of new coastline and for it was knighted. On his third and final expedition, in the 1840s, Franklin searched for the Northwest Passage with 129 men and two venerated ships under his command, H.M.S. *Erebus* and H.M.S. *Terror,* and disappeared into the icy oblivion with all hands lost, an epic tragedy that still haunted Britain.

The year 1906 also saw the American Dr. Frederick Cook claim the summit of Mount McKinley, the top of North America, a claim that would later be proved false. Another American, Robert Peary, was making noise about stalking the North Pole, as was Amundsen. And Robert Falcon Scott, back from Antarctica and now a captain, would no doubt try again for the South Pole.

Ernest Shackleton couldn't stand it. The world was passing him by. He had to do something.

Few people in the distinguished arena of polar exploration expected to hear from him again. But that changed on the night of February 11, 1907, at a Royal Geographical Society black-tie dinner at the Kosmos Club in London, when Shackleton—back from the misty Scottish moors—unveiled his intentions to return to Antarctica and reach both the South Geographic Pole and the South Magnetic Pole. He would lead the expedition himself and do it by private funds if necessary. He had already received generous donations. The urbane gentlemen in attendance nearly dropped their cigars and spilled their brandy. It was "more than some of them could stand," wrote Christopher Ralling for the British Broadcasting Company. "Words like 'blunder' and 'upstart' were heard in the smoking room. With its long and distinguished history in the field of exploration, the Royal

Return of the Southern Sledge party. Feb 9 1903. Capt. Scott. Skelton. Bernacchi. E.a.wilson. Cross. Shackleton. Armitage.

Geographical Society had acquired the role of major sponsor to British expeditions, wherever they might be heading. With the Society's official backing, funds became easier to acquire, assistance from the Armed Services more readily granted, and where necessary, the cooperation to keep its hand firmly on the tiller. Most expeditions of any size could expect to be under the control of a committee, usually dominated by senior officers of the Society itself. Suddenly here was Shackleton abjuring the very idea of a committee and prepared to proceed with or without the Society's backing. In the climate of those times, it must have seemed like a direct challenge to their authority and prestige." Which, of course, it was. Shackleton was not a clubbish man, and certainly not a committee puppet.

He called his private venture the British Antarctic Expedition, 1907. But like most expeditions of the day it came to be known simply by the name of its vessel.

Thus the *Nimrod* expedition sailed south, into what Shackleton called "the indescribable freshness that permeates one's being." For the first time gallant men reached the summit of Mount Erebus, and the South Magnetic Pole, and almost the South Pole itself.

Almost. Ninety-seven miles seemed such an unattainable distance back then, and such a short one now in mild England. Time and circumstance spawned cruel reexamination, and vows had a wicked way of coming true. Edward Wilson froze to death with Scott in 1912, writing his last letters and saying his final prayers. Shackleton had outlived them both. He no doubt suspected that a combination of poor decisions and bad luck killed Scott and his men, though Scott in his journal blamed everything but himself: horses, dogs, motor sledges, weather. A little more bad luck in 1909 would have killed Shackleton and Wild, too, leaving the *Nimrod* to sail home with sad news. But now was a time for redemption, another voyage, this one an unprecedented crossing of the continent.

"I have often been asked," Shackleton wrote in the *London Daily Mail* in December 1913, "what can one see in the cold, inhospitable regions of the Antarctic? And confronted with a bald question such as that, it is hard to give an answer. The mere fact that one cannot answer in a terse sentence, and that one feels what Keats calls 'The dearth of human words, the roughness of mortal speech,' shows that there must be an intangible something that draws one back to the wild wastes of Antarctica." He wrote of the immense silence and untrodden vistas and the wonder of the unknown. "Those are the memories that remain, and not the bitter cold, and the hard work, and the rough and often salty food, and the constant effort to do just a little more than one should expect...."

But how to find such men, those who will always do a little more?

First, enlist Frank Worsley, a sharp-eyed sailor with an uncanny sense of direction and dead reckoning, who could safeguard a chronometer and handle a sextant through any gust and gale. Second, enlist proven Antarctic argonauts: Frank Wild, Thomas Crean, Alfred Cheetham, George Marston, Frank Hurley, and Thomas McLeod.

For second-in-command of the expedition, Shackleton chose Frank Wild. A tough Yorkshireman who grew up with his sleeves rolled to the elbows, Wild was a small man, smaller than Worsley, but very strong. He possessed a never-say-die spirit and an incurable appetite for adventure that Shackleton admired. If the crew ever became mutinous—a leader's worst nightmare—Shackleton knew that Wild would stand beside him. The allegiance had cemented one morning during the

SIX YEARS older than Shackleton, Emily Mary Dorman (above) was described by one biographer as "a tall, dark-haired...woman with a...formidable hint of motherly firmness behind a soft manner." Married in April 1904, she and Ernest shared a love of poetry, especially the works of Robert Browning. Their first child, Raymond (with Ernest, opposite), was born in February 1905. On first seeing Raymond, the proud father boasted that the boy had "good fists for fighting."

Nimrod expedition, when Wild was starving and sick with dysentery on the Ross Ice Shelf, and Shackleton, who was also starving, gave him his only biscuit. "S. privately forced upon me his one breakfast biscuit," wrote Wild, "and would have given me another tonight had I allowed him. I do not suppose that anyone else in the world can thoroughly realise how much generosity and sympathy was shown by this; I DO, and BY GOD I shall never forget it. Thousands of pounds would not have bought that one biscuit." Wild's dedication to Shackleton was complete. Their alliance, said one observer, "could be broken only by death."

WHEN APPLICANTS CAME CALLING at Burlington Street, they often found Frank Wild in the office with Shackleton, a pipe clenched between his teeth, an untrimmed moustache over his mouth, a faintly bemused look on his face, his eyes alert and studious beneath thinning hair.

A raw-boned Irishman with big ears and an easy disposition, Tom Crean was one of the few men from the 1901-04 *Discovery* expedition chosen by Captain Scott for the 1910-12 *Terra Nova* expedition. Five men died on that later expedition—Scott, Wilson, Henry Bowers, Edgar Evans, and Titus Oates—and more would have without the heroism of Crean. Shackleton enlisted him for second officer on the *Endurance.*

Alfred "Alf" Cheetham signed on as third officer, or bo'sun, in charge of supervising the able seamen, tough trawlerhands from Hull, Grimsby, and Labrador. On first impression Cheetham might have seemed a poor choice for this. He was small and spoke in a squeaky voice. But he had deep experience in the ice—three expeditions to Antarctica—and Shackleton called him "the veteran of the Antarctic," which conveyed upon him instant status. He was also likable and fair-minded, a man who worked the decks and lines as hard as the seamen and won their respect.

In *Pearson's* magazine Shackleton wrote about the qualities that "are necessary to the explorer—and I put them in the order of their relative importance: First, optimism; second, patience; third, physical endurance; fourth, idealism; fifth and last, courage. No explorer can ever expect to overcome the difficulties that will daily present themselves unless he is endowed with a large share of optimism.

During the years that I have been exploring, especially in the Polar Regions, I have rarely seen a day begin bright and clear, and with the promise of good work, that did not end badly. And again, days that have begun badly have ended well."

To illustrate this he told a story from 1907, when he was looking for an artist for the *Nimrod* expedition. From 30 applicants he found 3 that showed promise. "Finally, one Friday afternoon I sent a telegram to each of the three, asking him to be present at my office on Saturday afternoon...."

One replied that he was going out of town for the weekend and would be there on Monday. Another asked if he made the four-hour trip into London could he be guaranteed the job? "I received no communication from the third," wrote Shackleton, "but on the Saturday afternoon, just as I was leaving my office, in he walked, somewhat disheveled and rain-soaked. He informed me that he had been on a walking tour in Cornwall; my telegram had been forwarded to him where he was putting up for the night; he had just caught a train, and after many changes had arrived in London."

Shackleton hired him immediately. He was George Marston, 25, a strong but sensitive man willing to brave the cold and learn any task. A shipmate later described him as having "the frame and face of a prizefighter and the disposition of a fallen angel." He loved to read late at night in his bunk with a candle balanced on his head. So valuable was he on the *Nimrod* that Shackleton asked him to join the *Endurance*. Despite being married and with children, Marston said yes.

Thomas McLeod, also a veteran from the *Nimrod,* signed on as an able seaman and completed the core of experienced Antarctic hands. Now came the task of finding new scientists and crew.

"In the manner of selecting newcomers," wrote American journalist Alfred Lansing, "Shackleton's methods would appear to have been almost capricious. If he liked the look of a man, he was accepted. If he didn't, the matter was closed. And these decisions were made with lightning speed."

A young doctor named Alexander Macklin presented himself at Shackleton's office early one morning after receiving no reply to his letter of application. In Macklin's words, Sir Ernest came tearing down the stairs like "a living avalanche," in a hurry to go out. He told Macklin to wait upstairs. Not until afternoon did Shackleton return, still in hurry, to find Macklin still waiting, a portrait of patience.

"Why do you want to go?" Shackleton asked him.

"I don't know. I just want to."

"You look fit enough. Are you perfectly healthy?"

"Perfectly fit."

Shackleton sized him up: neatly trimmed moustache, wire-rimmed glasses. He looked older than his 24 years. "What's wrong with your eyes?"

FIRST ASCENT of Mount Erebus, the world's southernmost active volcano, was made on March 10, 1908, by six crewmembers of Shackleton's Nimrod *expedition. From the 12,448-foot summit, overlooking Ross Island, Dr. Eric Marshall described in his diary McMurdo Sound below: "Very still. Never forget sunset...opal tints on open sea." Ten months later, three of the men, including Douglas Mawson, would be first to reach the South Magnetic Pole.*

NIMROD EXPEDITION members stand with a Scottish-built motor-car (below) donated to Shackleton. Capable of 16 miles an hour on a solid surface, in Antarctica's soft summer snow "The wheels would simply sink in...," Shackleton wrote. He relied on Manchurian ponies and the British custom of man-hauling. The polar plateau party (opposite), exhausted upon return to the Nimrod after a harrowing ordeal, are from left, Frank Wild, Shackleton, Eric Marshall, and Lt. Jameson Boyd

"Nothing," Macklin said. He was nearsighted. Then he added, "Many a wise face would look foolish without specs."

Shackleton laughed. After a brief moment when he seemed to weigh balances and measures only he could fathom, he said, "All right, I'll take you." Then he pushed Macklin out of his office saying they would talk later; he had a lot to do.

Reginald James was a physics student who remembered, "I was about to leave Cambridge and had gone to say goodbye to a friend who was ill in a nursing home, when I was hailed from a window in a street I had never passed through before in my whole five years at Cambridge, by a fellow student at the Cavendish Laboratory, with the words, 'Hi, James, do you want to go to the Antarctic?' I said, 'No, not particularly. Why?' He then told me that Shackleton had not so far got a physicist...." And James had been recommended by the Master of Christ's College. Was this a prank? That night at his relatives' home James found a telegram waiting from the famous Sir Ernest, asking him to report the following morning to London. "I did so," James said, "and was appointed after an interview of about ten minutes at the outside, probably more nearly five. So far as I remember he asked me if my teeth were good, if I suffered from varicose veins, if I had a good temper, and if I could sing. At this question I probably looked a bit taken aback, for I remember he said, 'I don't mean any Caruso stuff; but I suppose you can shout a bit with the boys?' He then asked me if my circulation was good. I said it was except for one finger, which frequently went dead in cold weather. He asked me if I would seriously mind losing it. I said I would risk that."

James developed an immediate high regard for Shackleton, saying "his energy & vitality in those days of preparation were wonderful and a thing to remember. You

always felt that however busy you were he was busier. He had a remarkable adaptability & a habit of suddenly changing plans to meet a changed situation...."

Leonard Hussey was a cheerful, banjo-strumming student on an archaeology dig in the Sudan when he saw an old newspaper notice about the expedition and wrote to Shackleton, expressing interest. He hurried to London and received the typical short interview followed by a brusque acceptance. Shackleton said he was amused to receive an application from the heart of Africa. Besides, he thought Hussey "looked funny," which was Shackleton's way of saying he regarded him to be of good cheer, a bit servile perhaps, but an eternal optimist whose banjo might buoy spirits when things got bad.

"You'll do, Hussey," he said.

"At that," Hussey later wrote, "I felt two inches taller and was the happiest man in England. He wrung my hand in his grasp and that was that. I was committed to my fate...." Shackleton quickly arranged for him to receive training in meteorology and magnetism.

Buried in the mound of inquiries and applications was a letter from three women:

> Dear Sir Ernest
>
> We "three sporty girls" have decided to write & beg of you, to take us
> with you on your expedition to the South Pole. We are three strong, healthy
> girls, & also gay and bright, & willing to undergo any hardships that you

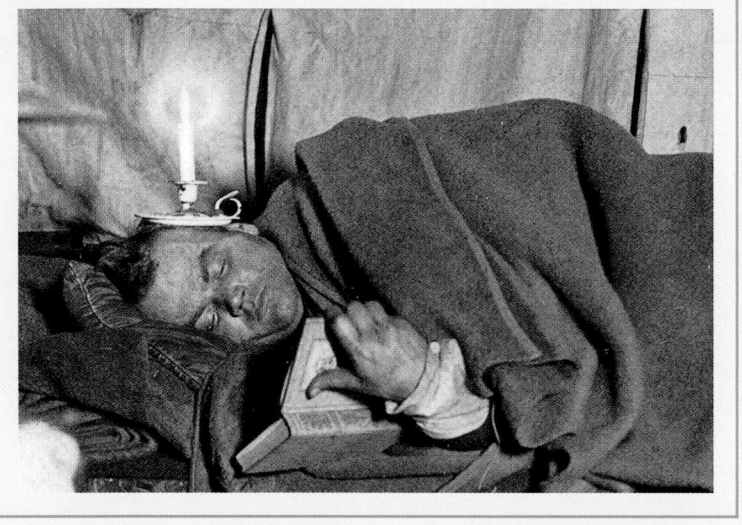

yourselves undergo. If our feminine garb is inconvenient, we should just love to don masculine attire. We have been reading all books & articles that have been written on dangerous expeditions by brave men to the Polar regions, & we do not see why men should have all the glory, & women none, especially when there are women just as brave & capable as there are men.

"This was perhaps the only time in his life when Shackleton refused a challenge," wrote an observer. "His reply was terse and diplomatic. He regretted that there were 'no vacancies' for the opposite sex on the Expedition."

Funding was a constant challenge. Promises fell through. Grants and aid, always forthcoming, never got there. Hundreds of people made small donations from around the world. An alderman in Birmingham, Neville Chamberlain (who would later become prime minister) gave five pounds. The Royal Geographical Society gave $5,000, hardly a grand endorsement, but enough to fly their flag over any significant claim Shackleton might make. The government gave a remarkable sum given the volatile political climate at the time, with war clouds over Europe. Substantial amounts came from Dudley Docker and Miss Janet Stancomb-Wills, the bejeweled adopted daughter of a tobacco millionaire. Now in her later years, Miss Wills wrote to Sir Ernest, "Into my life you flashed, like a meteor out of the dark...." The extent of her donation was never made public.

Shackleton had to mortgage whatever income he derived from his lectures and from books, motion pictures, and still photographs after the expedition. This, of course, assumed that he would return home alive. The possibility that he would not, or that he would fail to achieve his goal of crossing the continent, appeared to never enter his mind.

To lure additional investments he formed a film syndicate and baited it with commercial profit sharing, then went fishing for Frank Hurley, a talented and tireless Australian photographer who had just completed an expedition with Douglas Mawson. In the growing volume of Antarctic tragedies, Mawson's expedition had produced another chapter. One man had fallen into a crevasse and died. Another had eaten sled dogs and died, probably from Vitamin A poisoning from the livers. Mawson himself, alone and starving, had staggered and crawled back to his base on the edge of death, so gaunt and unrecognizable when he arrived that his mates asked, "Which one are you?" Hurley's cinematography showed raw and brutal Antarctica as it had never been seen before, due in part to the fact that Mawson had established his base at Commonwealth Bay, one of the windiest places in the world. Now in London working on a book, Mawson recommended to Hurley that he not join Shackleton; he would never see any money out of it. But the idea of crossing Antarctica was too much, and Hurley, stricken by the romance of rambling, agreed to go.

The single largest donation to the expedition, 24,000 pounds, came from Sir James Caird, a Scottish jute magnate and a friend of Winston Churchill who admired Shackleton's pluck and personality. "This magnificent gift," Shackleton told the *Morning Post*, "relieves me of all anxiety."

But it did not. Sir Ernest's younger brother, Frank, was a dubious financier and social climber suspected of stealing the Irish crown jewels, among other dark deeds. He had recently been convicted of defrauding an older woman of her money, and a judge had sentenced him to 15 months hard labor with the admonishment that he "violated all the rules of commercial morality." This blighted Sir Ernest badly. Furthermore, things with Emily were not sweet as before. She understood now that her husband was made of equal parts sugar and salt; that although he loved her and their children deeply, he loved adventure more. Every woman, even his wife, was a mistress after Antarctica.

❧

HE TRAVELED TO NORWAY in May to test equipment in the snow, including two motor sledges driven by large propellers. He practiced his skiing, as Nansen and Amundsen had convinced him he must if he were to have any chance of crossing Antarctica. Shackleton found it "rather hard after my sedentary life at the office.

Also in Norway, he retrieved his ship, the *Endurance*, which arrived in the Thames in early June 1914. She was a masterpiece. Constructed in the Framnaes shipyard in Sandefjord, her builders were proud men descended from Vikings who had sired a long lineage of rugged whaling and sealing vessels. They suspected she might be the last of her kind, so they built her with courage to fight the icy teeth of Antarctica, to go deep into the Weddell Sea where few ships had gone before.

Being northerners, they named her *Polaris*. But when Shackleton purchased her for $67,000 he rechristened her *Endurance*, in honor of his family motto, "*Fortitudine vincimus*—By endurance we conquer." Little did he realize how apt a name it would be, more for himself and his hardy men than for the ship.

She measured 144 feet long by 25 feet at the beam; bigger than the *Nimrod*, by a little. The greatest differences were in age, character, comfort, and speed. Whereas the *Nimrod* had been a 41-year-old shabby tramp that smelled of seal oil when Shackleton first saw her in 1907, the *Endurance* in 1914 was a beautiful maiden only 18 months out of the shipyard. A barkentine, she sported a square-rigged mast forward and two schooner-like masts center and aft, each with a Norwegian krone placed beneath it to bring good luck. The coal-fired *Nimrod* had had a top speed of 6 knots; to ration coal Shackleton towed her half way to Antarctica from New Zealand in 1908. The *Endurance,* with a 350-horsepower steam engine designed to burn both oil and coal, would achieve 10.2 knots and need no assistance.

Her oak keel was 7 feet thick; her flanks, made of oak and Norwegian fir, tapered from 30 inches to 18. "Outside this planking, to keep her from being chafed by the ice," reported Alfred Lansing, "there was a sheathing from stem to stern of greenheart, a wood so heavy it weighs more than iron and so tough it cannot be worked with ordinary tools. Her frames were not only double-thick...but they were double in number, compared with a conventional vessel. Her bow, where she would meet the ice head-on, had received special attention. Each of the timbers there had been fashioned from a single oak tree especially selected so that its natural growth followed the curve of her design."

SHACKLETON WORE a Burberry helmet (opposite) on the Nimrod expedition, to within 97 miles of the South Pole. On November 17, 1911, he inscribed it: "To Frank Thornton, I give this helmet, though it is not of any use in his combat in 'When Knights Were Bold,' it may be liked as it was worn 'When nights Were Cold,' when the most Southerly point in this world was reached by man. With kindest wishes from E. H. Shackleton."

IN MID-JULY the dowager Queen Alexandra, widow of King Edward VII, visited Sir Ernest and the *Endurance* on the Thames. She intended to stay for only 30 minutes, but the impeccable ship and courteous crew so charmed her, her sister the dowager Empress Marie Feodorovna of Russia—who snapped many pictures, and Princess Victoria, that the three royal women stayed well over an hour. Lady Emily made a rare public appearance with her children, including three-year-old Edward, who declined an invitation to walk with the queen. He said he wanted to walk with his nurse instead. Everybody took the rebuff in good humor.

The queen presented Shackleton with a Union Jack and two Bibles, one for him and one for the ship. In the flyleaf of each she had inscribed verses from the Book of Job, and had added her own good tidings: "For the Crew of the *Endurance* from Alexandra, May 31, 1914. May the Lord help you to do your duty & guide you through all dangers by land and sea. May you see the Works of the Lord & all His wonders in the Deep."

The royal visit landed the *Endurance* in the newspapers. It was the last time that summer that the expedition would receive its rightful place in the headlines.

Day and night Shackleton made final preparations, the culmination of four years of planning. It should have been a rewarding time for him. But dark days shadowed Europe and his imminent departure south. Archduke Franz Ferdinand, heir to the Austrian throne, had been assassinated in late June. National ranks closed. Austria-Hungry declared war on Serbia. Germany declared war on Russia. Dominoes fell as one country after another entered the fray, each adept at seeing the other as the unprovoked aggressor. It was a hot, unsettling summer as naïve young men who had lived in peace and prosperity and never tasted war suddenly hungered for it, crowed about it, convinced they could win in a few short months and remake the world. The people of England, until now certain that a continental war would not consume them, began to have their doubts as British Navy vessels chugged up and down the Channel, belching smoke, pacing.

The *Endurance* sailed down the Thames on August 1, 1914, the same day that Germany declared war on France. Two days later, as the ship lay off Margate, Shackleton went ashore to read the disquieting news. England had sent an ultimatum to Germany to respect the neutrality of Belgium, and had received no reply. Time was running out. Back onboard, Shackleton mustered all hands. "I proposed to send a telegram to the Admiralty," he wrote, "offering the ships, stores, and, if they agreed, our own services to the country in the event of war breaking out. All hands immediately agreed, and I sent off a telegram in which everything was placed at the disposal of the Admiralty. We only asked that, in the event of the declaration of war, the Expedition might be considered as a single unit, so as to preserve its homogeneity. There were enough trained and experienced men amongst us to man a destroyer. Within an hour I received a laconic wire from the Admiralty saying 'Proceed.' Within two hours a longer wire came from Mr. Winston Churchill, in which we were thanked for our offer, and saying that the authorities desired that the Expedition, which had the full sanction and support of the Scientific and Geographical Societies, should go on."

Still, Shackleton was uneasy. Opposing allegiances pulled at him. General mobilization had begun. Patriotism thickened the air. How could he go to Antarctica now? How could he not? The next day, August 4, he visited King George V and received his blessings: Go south. The *Endurance* sailed for Plymouth, and that night at midnight England declared war on Germany.

In Plymouth, the last port of call in England for the *Endurance*,

Chief Officer D. G. Jeffrey resigned his position to join the war. Worsley and Shackleton replaced him with Lionel Greenstreet, who arrived on board half an hour before the *Endurance* sailed for Buenos Aires on August 8.

While Worsley commanded the little ship across the big pond, Shackleton and Frank Wild remained behind to tie up financial arrangements. Convinced that the Russian juggernaut would smash Germany and bring the war to a quick end, the two explorers departed England in late September on a mail steamer that would overtake the *Endurance*.

Finally at sea, Shackleton could relax and reflect. "Life is a puzzle," he wrote to Emily. They had quarreled upon his departure and he wanted to make amends. "I expect I have a peculiar nature that the years have hardened." he said. "I don't want to go away into the South with any misunderstanding between us; I know that if you were married to a more domesticated man you would have been much happier.... It seems a hard thing to say but this I know is my Ishmaelite life and the one thing that I am suited for and in which I yield to no one...."

Always the explorer, Sir Ernest seemed to find intimacy in the distance. Only from afar could he say certain close things. Only when he was bound for the cold could he unveil elements of his warmth. While Emily raised their children with constant affection, her arms around them like a harbor, Sir Ernest, who loved them no less, was at times a rough sea who imparted his ambitions onto them and became openly critical when they fell short of his expectations.

"I am just good as an explorer and nothing else," he lamented to Emily, again from the comfort of afar. "I am hard also and damnably persistent when I want anything: altogether a generally unpleasing character...."

What he needed and would soon get was comradeship and the chance to lead his men through an impossible situation, a task only he could accomplish.

In Buenos Aires he reunited with the *Endurance* and found discipline sorely lacking. Frank Worsley, though an excellent sailor, understood one end of the whip but not the other. Shackleton shaped things up quickly; not that he was a brutal Bligh—he was not. He merely had an intuitive sense of how to motivate men beyond their desires; to create within them a sense of teamwork, synergy and purpose. To his credit Worsley had discharged four men in Buenos Aires for causing trouble during the crossing. Two were replaced. Charles Green was hired as baker and pastry chef, a duty that would magnify in importance with each passing day. And William Bakewell, who had been wandering the docks when he spied the *Endurance* and fell in love with her, was enlisted as an able seaman. He said he was Canadian, a lie, as he figured a Commonwealth man would have a better chance than a Yank of joining the expedition. Illinois born, Bakewell had run away from home at the age of 12. He worked as a lumberjack and a sailor, and found himself shipwrecked in South America. The only American on board the *Endurance*, he later would be described as "one of the staunchest and hardest working members of the expedition."

On the third day out from Buenos Aires, southbound toward what Shackleton called "our white warfare," a hungry and seasick stowaway was discovered and hauled before him. Sir Ernest put his chin into the young man's face and bellowed, "Do you know that on these expeditions we often get very hungry, and if there is a stowaway available he is the first to be eaten?"

The young man, a wobbly 19-year-old bantamweight named Pierce Blackboro, assessed the deep-chested Shackleton and replied, "They'd get a lot more meat off you, sir."

Shackleton turned away to hide a grin, then told Frank Wild to take the boy to Bo'sun Cheetham, adding, "Introduce him to the cook first." Not lost on Shackleton were the telltale expressions of William Bakewell and another able seaman, sail maker Walter How, who had squirreled Blackboro aboard. They explained that the expedition was two men short, would not a diligent hand like Blackboro be of valuable service? Shackleton reminded them that these were his decisions to make, not theirs. Walter How had left his wife with a six-month-old baby, so Shackleton went easy on him. He also reserved judgment on Blackboro, who had asked to join the expedition in Buenos Aires and been told he was too young. But the kid showed boldness and enthusiasm; he just might work.

In early November the *Endurance* arrived at South Georgia, the southernmost outpost of the British Empire, an elongated island of splintered mountains, shimmering glaciers, storm-cut headlands, and deep fjords. One hundred miles long by 20 miles wide at its widest, it remained largely unexplored, with an interior blank on every map. Only its shores had been charted, a coastline rich with wildlife. Though little was recorded of their enchantment, many crewmen must have felt as if they had sailed into the heart of the Swiss Alps, a magical place of snowy peaks, king penguins, elephant seals, and great gliding albatrosses. Only Lewis Carroll and Rudyard Kipling could imagine such a place.

Captain Cook had sighted South Georgia and sailed around it in 1775, think-

WITH ENDURANCE soon to launch, The Daily Mirror commented on December 13, 1913: "Quite a lot of people stopped to look into the shops in Oxford-street yesterday, but few, if any, gave a glance of recognition to the great explorer, Sir Ernest Shackleton, who was standing near the curb—not far from the motor-omnibus danger zone. It was noticeable that Sir Ernest, perhaps in preparation for his Antarctic experience, was not wearing an overcoat...."

ing it was connected to Antarctica. It was not. So he named its southern tip Cape Disappointment. Shackleton found disappointment here, too, as Norwegian whalers told him it was an usually heavy ice year in the Weddell Sea, his destination to the south.

The Norwegians knew these waters well. Ten years earlier they had established a number of whaling stations along the island's north shore and begun a harvest that would continue for another half century. Using means such as exploding harpoons, catcher ships, and factory ships, they would eventually devastate populations of right, blue, fin, sei, and humpback whales, some to less than one percent of their original numbers. "Below 40 degrees is no law," the whalers would say, "beyond 50 degrees, no God."

The *Endurance* crew was fascinated by this rough-and-tumble life. Shackleton had cooked up many get-rich-quick schemes in his life; now, seeing this bounty of whales, he decided he would form a whaling company after the expedition was finished. Hurley was also enamored of the whole affair. At Grytviken Station, where the ship rested dockside and at anchor, he literally got into his subject when he fell into a whale carcass while photographing it. He yelled for help and finally was hoisted out by muttering Norwegians. Later, hiking upslope with Hurley and hauling 40 pounds of photographic gear, Lionel Greenstreet wrote that the determined Australian was "a warrior with his camera & would go anywhere or do anything to get a picture." His prophetic image of the *Endurance* taken from a peak high above Grytviken Harbor made the ship look small and vulnerable.

The stolid Norwegians were astounded by Shackleton's trans-Antarctic plan. His proposed route from Vahsel Bay to the Pole had never been traveled. And only three or four of his crew had ever been on skis. Was he another Scott, taking off on a heroic tragedy?

Shackleton had hoped to land his six-man trans-Antarctic team in November and make the 1,500-mile crossing of the continent in one austral summer, 1914-15, a hope now dashed by reports of heavy pack ice. His new plan was to wait, let the pack ice clear, get down there in December and make safe landfall. The trans-Antarctic party—himself, Wild, Crean, Macklin, Marston, and Hurley—would then overwinter in a prefabricated hut and push for the Pole the following spring. He stocked the *Endurance* with more sugar, flour, tinned butter, and foul weather gear. He waited for a mail boat to arrive from home with news about the war.

On December 5, 1914, he could wait no longer. The *Endurance* sailed that morning. The ship's storekeeper/mechanic, Thomas Hans Orde-Lees, wrote in his diary, "What thoughts are ours, setting out at such a time, with no chance of news from our dear ones at home who are passing through the greatest national crisis of modern times. God grant that England may stand where she is this day & that all those dear to us may be spared any privations or sufferings." Two hours after the *Endurance* sailed, the mail boat arrived at Grytviken. The news would have depressed them. Blood soaked the soil of France and Flanders. Millions of soldiers were huddled along the Western Front in trenches wet with rats and rain, waiting and dying behind barbed wire that stretched from the Channel to the Alps. Many of the young elite, already dead, were fodder for generals who used land tactics outdated by destructive technologies. The event that would be recorded in history books as World War I was horrific—and it was just beginning.

Shackleton's "white warfare" would involve no German submarines, tanks, or poisonous gases; no hostile natives with spears and clubs, the sort of thing that had killed Magellan, Cook, and La Perouse, great explorers all. His adversary would be Antarctica, home for no human yet savage in its own way with ice, cold, wind, and sea. He would also fight himself, his own war, a hunger for success weighed against a history of turning back, the will to survive. This expedition was his idea, his responsibility. The eyes of his men would pin their hopes on him and ask for something beyond words.

The whalers' ice warnings concerned him. He would proceed with caution. Only two and a half years earlier, in April 1912, a captain had failed to take ice warnings seriously and had gone to the bottom of the North Atlantic with 1,500 passengers and his ship, also on her maiden voyage—the *Titanic*. Shackleton had testified at an inquiry on the disaster, speaking as an authority on ice navigation.

Now he was about to enter a sinister sea of ice far more treacherous than the North Atlantic.

&

IN 1901, Swedish paleontologist Otto Nordenskjold, entering the Weddell Sea in search of fossils, wrote, "We were now sailing a sea across which none had hitherto voyaged. The weather had changed as if by magic; it seemed as though the Antarctic world repented of the inhospitable way in which it had received us on the previous day, or, maybe, it merely wished to entice us deeper into its interior in order the more surely to annihilate us." Indeed, Nordenskjold's relief ship, the *Antarctic*, was crushed by the Weddell Sea pack ice, stranding him and others during the brutal winter of 1903.

More recently, the German explorer Wilhelm Filchner had discovered Vahsel Bay, deep in the Weddell Sea, as a portal into the Antarctic interior. He erected a *stationhaus* on a flat iceberg that he assumed rested on the ocean floor. One February morning in 1912 he reported that, "A racket erupted as if one hundred pieces of heavy artillery were firing in rapid succession." Capt. Richard Vahsel observed that, "All the ice in the bay is moving and the stationhaus-berg has begun to rotate." A sudden spring tide had set the ice free, sending monstrous bergs moving in all directions at once, threatening to crush Filchner's ship, the *Deutschland*, and carry away men stranded on the stationhaus-berg. All hands were saved. But after a second attempt to land on the mainland, the late season trapped the ship in pack ice for nine long months, and Captain Vahsel died of illness. Such were the precedents for disaster in the Weddell Sea, now about to wrap its icy arms around Shackleton and his ship.

The *Endurance* sailed east-southeast past South Georgia and slowly turned toward the Weddell Sea. Sixty-nine sled dogs crowded the decks as the able seamen moved about and climbed aloft to carry out Alf Cheetham's commands. Shackleton noted that, "The wind freshened during the day, and all square sail was set, with the foresail reefed in order to give the look-out a clear view ahead.... The ship was very steady in a quarterly sea, but certainly did not look as neat and trim

as she had done when leaving the shores of England four months earlier. We had filled up with coal in Grytviken, and this extra fuel was stored on deck, where it impeded movement considerably. The carpenter had built a false deck, extending from the poop-deck to the chart-room. We had also taken aboard a ton of whale meat for the dogs. The big chunks of meat were hung up in the rigging, out of reach but not out of sight of the dogs, and as the *Endurance* rolled and pitched, they watched with wolfish eyes for a windfall."

The *Endurance* carried 28 men: 11 forecastle hands (mostly able seamen), 8 officers, and 9 scientists and specialists. The pay was $240 a year for an able seaman, $750 for a scientist, though Shackleton felt passage alone was pay enough. A scientist could build a career on a single trip such as this, something his peers could never equal.

Shackleton watched each man closely for his strengths and weaknesses, his response to authority, and contribution to morale. He had no tolerance for sloth, yet seemed to half expect his scientists to be absentminded. Those who adapted

beyond their specialties and made themselves proficient at ship's chores won his immediate approval. He cultivated a personal relationship with each man.

"When he came across you by yourself," noted Macklin, the young bespectacled doctor, "he would get into conversation and talk to you in an intimate sort of way, asking you little things about yourself—how you were getting on, how you liked it, what particular side of the work you were enjoying most—all that sort of thing. Sometimes when you felt he'd been perhaps a bit ruthless, pushing you round a bit hard, he seemed to have the knack of undoing any bad effect he'd had with these little intimate talks; he immediately put you back on a feeling of rightness with him.... He'd be mostly talking about books and poetry. One found it rather flattering at the time, to have him discussing Thackeray...or asking you if you'd ever read Browning. I never had, and he would tell me what I was missing."

In time all on board came to call him "the Boss," an endearment Shackleton accepted without comment or expression. Forty years old and beginning his third Antarctic expedition, he did everything with purpose. By learning to obey he had learned to command. Beyond that, he possessed a genius for leadership that would carry men's lives into a white hell and God willing carry them out again.

❧

THREE DAYS AFTER LEAVING South Georgia, still shy of latitude 57° S, the *Endurance* hit pack ice. The Norwegians had been right; it was indeed a bad year, with ice this far north. The little ship quickly circumvented the narrow white belt and rigged sail for open sea. Worsley watched the water for guidance, noting telltale tones of "sea green...Indigo, or Reeves French blue," colors that spoke to him of Neptune's temperament.

On December 11, the pack was back, a vast icescape that stretched to the horizon, punctuated here and there by seals and penguins, austral animals perfected by fin and feather. How comfortable they appeared in a protean world of ice that would kill most men. Whales were sighted spouting in leads (open water between ice floes) far ahead. Albatrosses and southern giant petrels glided by, their dark eyes watchful of this strange wooden beast coughing black smoke into the cold air, bringing men's ambitions to the last place on Earth.

Shackleton ordered the *Endurance* forward. Worsley obeyed with enthusiasm. The little ship nosed into the ice, her engine chugging. Crewmen gathered on deck to watch the floes crack and move aside, then slowly engulf the *Endurance* as they closed around her astern. Ice rasped against the hull. The air temperature dropped. What a thrill to finally bite into Antarctica. Unburdened by the responsibilities of

ICE CLEAR, FIFTEEN DEGREES to port: Frank Worsley (opposite) directs the Endurance *helmsman through loose pack ice in the Weddell Sea. Worsley hailed from New Zealand and claimed to be part Maori. His mother died when he was two, and he grew up rambunctious. Shackleton told a friend that Worsley "is not the type to hold men well together." He soon learned that what Worsley lacked in leadership he compensated for in navigation.*

ultimate command—a position better suited for Shackleton—Worsley was ebullient and full of jokes, always hungry for adventure.

"Worsley specialized in ramming," observed Macklin, "and I have a sneaking suspicion that he often went out of his way to find a nice piece of floe at which he could drive at full speed and cut in two; he loved to feel the shock, the riding up, and the sensation, as the ice gave way and we drove through."

Worsley's gift for navigation gained luster when he was freed from larger tasks, and Shackleton used him accordingly. He even forgave him a mischievous indiscretion now and then. But Frank Wild did not. According to Macklin, Wild was "always calm, cool, or collected, in open lanes or in tight corners he was just the same; but when he did tell a man to jump, that man jumped pretty quick. He possessed that rare knack of being one with all of us, and yet maintained his authority as second-in-command. We had no 'Worsley' thrills in Wild's watch."

On the recommendation of the Norwegians, Shackleton steered the *Endurance* toward the eastern shore of the Weddell Sea, where currents would make ice conditions more favorable. Yet progress was slow. For two weeks the ship slalomed and prodded her way through difficult conditions. On December 17, Shackleton recorded large floes that "presented a square mile of unbroken surface, and among them were patches of thin ice and several floes of heavy old ice. Many bergs were in sight and the course became devious." That same day a piece of ice torqued the ship's rudder with tremendous force. Helmsman Leonard Hussey, the smallest crewman, reported that "the wheel spun round and threw me over the top of it."

The next day Shackleton wrote, "Shortly before noon further progress was barred by heavy pack, and we put an ice anchor on the floe and banked the fires." Whereas earlier the *Endurance* had averaged 200 miles a day in open sea under steam and sail, now, in heavy pack, she managed only 30 miles a day. "I had been prepared for evil conditions in the Weddell Sea," Shackleton reflected, "but had hoped that in December and January, at any rate, the pack would be loose.... What we were encountering was fairly dense pack of a very obstinate character."

Such was the temptress Antarctica, the dangerous beauty. Diaphanous ice showers anointed the men with millions of tiny crystals floating down from above, glittering in fairyland light that filled day and night as they approached the Antarctic Circle. Great tabular bergs patrolled every vista, sculpted by wind and wave into arches, castles, temples, and towers. Ice floes patterned the sea like so many leaves on a lake. While charmed by the beauties of sea ice, the explorers were nevertheless aware of its dangers and kept an eye on its changing character. Shackleton had earlier noted that "The surface of the ice showed a rounded polygon structure something like the tops of a number of large weathered basaltic columns...close in shore the pancake ice was traversed by deep tidal cracks."

One afternoon, Shackleton recorded that "three Adélie penguins approached the ship across the floe while Hussey was discoursing sweet music on the banjo. The solemn-looking birds appeared to appreciate *It's a Long Way to Tipperary*, but fled in horror when Hussey treated them to a little of the music that comes from Scotland."

While passing another group of Adélies, Worsley teased Robert Clark, the expedition biologist, who was at the wheel. The penguins, Worsley wrote, "rushed along as fast as their legs could carry them yelling out 'Clark! Clark!' & apparently very indignant & perturbed that he never...even answered them, tho' we often called his attention to the fact that they all knew him."

Bright spirits and good humor buoyed the men, though some began to tire of the vagaries of the ice and the unknown, what Worsley called the "Up and Down."

The Weddell Sea was not so kind as its counterpart on the other side of Antarctica, the Ross Sea. Embraced by land on three sides, the Weddell was a maelstrom of ice twisted by a clockwise gyre, a sea current that rotated from southeast to northwest and jammed the floes into the Antarctic Peninsula.

In his private cell of responsibility, Shackleton worried. When he left South Georgia he had expected to land at Vahsel Bay by the end of December. But the *Endurance* had made little more than 300 miles in two weeks. On the day before Christmas, they were at the 64th Parallel, roughly 600 miles from Vahsel Bay, and just inching along. Shackleton recalled a poem by Oxford don St. John Lucas, "The Ship of Fools:"

The world where wise men sit at ease,
Fades from my unregretful eyes
And blind across uncharted seas
We stagger on our enterprise.

That night, Christmas Eve, the *Endurance* found open water and increased speed to seven knots. It seemed like a blessing, a gift. Beyond optimism, Shackleton would take whatever providence he could get. He was going to need it. ∎

"*Mountains tipped with gold and base of Erebus with glaciers a sea of gold and purple. Sun dipped, whole scene changed to cold purple.*"

DR. ERIC MARSHALL
NIMROD EXPEDITION
MARCH 1908

∿

SMOKE AND DISTANT RUMBLING of Mount Erebus, Earth's southernmost active volcano, appear not to faze the local denizen, a Weddell seal. First sighted by Capt. James Clark Ross in 1841, Erebus has been noted by subsequent explorers for its smoke columns tinged with flame. Shackleton used it as a landmark on his journeys south.

AFTER A 60-YEAR ABSENCE from Antarctica (since the 1840-43 voyage of James Ross and Francis Crozier), Great Britain returned to the far south with Discovery, *beset here in pack ice after a gale. Under the auspices of the Royal Navy and commanded by Robert Falcon Scott, the scientific expedition was the first to Antarctica for Scott and for his crewmember Ernest Shackleton.*

ANTARCTICA SHOWS her moods in ice, from the polar plateau where ice achieves a thickness of 15,000 vertical feet, to the many faces of sea ice—pan ice, pack ice, pancake ice (above), and others—around the continent. The type of ice that forms depends on water conditions, such as temperature and chemistry, at the time of freezing.

"[I noted] a fine crop of ice flowers
springing up on the lead & they,
illuminated by the morning sun,
resembled pink carnations."

FRANK HURLEY
ENDURANCE EXPEDITION

"They are...like children, these little people of the Antarctic world, either like children or old men, full of their own importance and late for dinner...."

APSLEY CHERRY-GARRARD
THE WORST JOURNEY IN THE WORLD
Published 1922

A CHINSTRAP PENGUIN punctuates an iceberg in Gerlache Strait off the Antarctic Peninsula. Unlike its relative the Adélie, which lives farther south, the chinstrap resides in northern Antarctic waters. Explorers of the early 1900s, including Shackleton, ate penguins when their rations dwindled.

THE EXPLORER'S DICTUM, *"find a way or make one,"* is evident in Frank Hurley's image (above), shot from the Endurance *foremast and showing the stern as she pushes her way through loose pack ice in the Weddell Sea, in December 1914. Today, vessels cut through pack ice with far greater power and when possible follow leads— open water between floes (opposite)—to reach mainland Antarctica.*

*"It was impossible to manoeuvre the
ship in the ice owing to the strong wind,
which kept the floes in movement
and caused lanes to open and close
with dangerous rapidity."*

ERNEST SHACKLETON
ENDURANCE EXPEDITION
DECEMBER 1914

STILL UNCONVINCED of the superiority of dogs, Shackleton used ten Manchurian ponies on his 1907-09 Nimrod expedition. Two had to be put down before making landfall. Four ponies died later from eating volcanic grit from Mount Erebus mixed with the snow around their stables. Others foundered in the cold and were shot for meat. The last pony, Socks, disappeared into a crevasse, nearly taking Frank Wild with it.

Life by the Fathom

Standing on deck, his face into the wind, Shackleton found

precious moments to enjoy the scenery and rediscover his youth.

How grand to be a sailor again, free of the hobnobbing and

hypocrisy required to raise money at home, of the false promises

and petty territorialities of the past, and yes, he had to admit,

free of his conventional-minded wife and her provincial problems.

How marvelous to be Odysseus again on a frozen Poseidon,

Amid ice-packed seas (opposite), Endurance's night watch enjoys company (above).

among real men, in real geography, under real circumstances, the future beckoning.

Christmas Day, 1914 began with midnight grog served to all hands on deck, and again at breakfast. T. H. Orde-Lees had decorated the wardroom with little flags, and prepared a small present, neatly wrapped, for each man. Dinner was a splendid affair of turtle soup, whitebait, jugged hare, pudding, mince pies, dates, figs, crystallized fruits, and rum and stout. More desserts than main courses, all washed down by liberal drinks that contributed to a memorable esprit de corps. Later that night everybody sang songs and Hussey, in the words of Worsley, "discoursed quite painlessly" on a one-string violin.

"Here endeth another Christmas Day," wrote Greenstreet. "I wonder how and under what circumstances our next one will be spent."

A southeast gale blew through the night and the next two days. The *Endurance* waited, anchored to a floe. Using a Lucas sounding machine, the scientists determined the Weddell Sea depth at 2,819 fathoms (nearly 7,000 feet). Blue glacial mud was hauled up from the bottom and found to contain marine protozoans of the order Radiolarian. It was hard work, all that pulling. The men worked in two-man teams on ten-minute shifts.

"Though I sympathize with the scientists," Hurley wrote, "I am afraid I have not the patience to enthuse over these microscopical 'bug hunts.' Evidently they stimulate in the scientific mind some highly specialized emotion which I lack. However, I admire the zeal and indefatigable patience of these learned men."

Perched on the foremast of the *Endurance*, his legs and tripod dangling, his big box camera balanced precariously like so much else, Hurley framed his images of the improbable ship against the vastness of ice, black on white, a positive negative. He seemed to belong to a different gravity up there, consumed by apertures and shutter speeds and the artist's elements of composition. Captain Worsley described him as "a marvel—with cheerful Australian profanity he preambulates alone and aloft & everywhere, in the most dangerous and slippery places he can find, content & happy at all times but cursing so if he can get a good or novel picture. Stands bare & hair waving in the wind, where we are gloved & helmeted, he snaps his snap or winds his handle turning out curses of delight & pictures of Life by the fathom."

Nobody questioned Hurley's devotion to his work, or his toughness and ability to perform multiple tasks. Confidence defined him. If he failed at anything, it was in hiding his vanity. Most of the crew found him easier to admire than to like, and called him "the Prince." Shackleton watched him closely.

During this time the ship's carpenter, a 40-year-old crusty Scot name Harry McNeish, rigged a platform over the stern where crewmen could watch for ice that might strike and damage the rudder or propeller.

Fine weather returned on December 30. The *Endurance* followed a long lead to the southeast and late that night crossed the Antarctic Circle, latitude 66° 33' S, roughly 1,400 nautical miles from the South Pole.

The next day, the last of 1914, the first sign of danger rattled the men when two ice floes grabbed the ship like a vise. One floe thrust over the other and tilted the *Endurance* six degrees. The men quickly fixed an ice anchor and hauled on a chain to free the ship, then watched in amazement as huge slabs of ice buckled upward ten feet, pushed from the onslaught of colliding floes below.

∾

NEW YEAR'S DAY, 1915 found the men in good cheer, shaking hands and sharing bright wishes. Yet an undertow of concern suffused them. Again, ice blocked their path south, so they dodged north and west looking for a route. Shackleton wrote that the "good run had given me hope of sighting the land on the following day, and the delay was annoying. I was growing anxious to reach land on account of the dogs, which had not been able to get exercise for four weeks, and were becoming run down."

For several days the *Endurance* steamed back and forth, picking her way through leads in the ice. While moored to a floe, the crew disembarked to exercise the dogs. "The weather was clear," wrote Shackleton, "and some enthusiastic football-players had a game on the floe until...midnight. Worsley dropped through a hole in rotten ice while retrieving the ball. He had to be retrieved himself."

They backtracked the next day and passed a berg they had seen 60 hours earlier. They were running in circles, locked in a vortex while looking for leads. Shackleton recorded that "The ship passed no fewer than five hundred bergs that day, some of them very large." The *Endurance* pushed through loose pack ice at half speed, then hit open water and found clear sailing for one hundred miles south. Shackleton wrote that "Two very large whales, probably blue whales, came up close to the ship, and we saw spouts in all directions. Open water inside the pack in that latitude might have the appeal of sanctuary to the whales, which are harried by man further north."

Seldom did Shackleton express such concern for wildlife. Like most self-actualized Western men of his day, he was a utilitarian who regarded the natural world as grist to the mill of human enterprise. That mankind could drive another species extinct by excessive killing or habitat destruction would have seemed nearly impossible to him. That's not to say such sentiments didn't exist. Douglas Mawson was alarmed by the killing of whales, seals, and penguins. As early as 1820, Adm. Thadeus Bellingshausen, the first Russian to circumnavigate

Antarctica, expressed concern for seals plundered by rapacious men in the South Shetland Islands, off the Antarctic Peninsula. But extinction? For Shackleton, the world was simply too big and resilient for mankind to inflict serious damage. More of an Elizabethan buccaneer than a dedicated ecologist, he had never heard the terms "ecosystem" or "biodiversity." In his era they didn't exist. He had no idea that the passenger pigeon, a bird so abundant it once clouded the skies of North America, had just gone extinct. Times were changing at an accelerating rate. Henry Ford had just introduced the assembly line to build more automobiles for more people to drive faster and faster, which improved commerce but pumped more pollutants into the air. Someday even the climate of remote Antarctica, Shackleton's white muse, would be altered by human meddlings. But in these halcyon days of polar adventure when the world was wild, such a notion would have seemed preposterous.

Physicist Reginald James recalled that Shackleton "had really very little sympathy with the scientific point of view, & had no idea about scientific methods or the time taken to produce results in research ...he had little patience with the academic mind & would openly ridicule it.... He would like scientific work to be good, yet felt that it was only because it would add to the prestige of the expedition & not because he had any real interest in it."

What James saw as ridicule, Shackleton saw as good-spirited teasing, one of many ways to test his men to find their strengths and weaknesses, answers he needed to know now instead of later when things could get suddenly dangerous. When the expedition began, the 28 men had composed three separate societies: officers, scientists, and the tough forecastle hands (able seamen), each with its own strata, vernacular, and decorum. By humor and easy talk, Shackleton worked to relax the barriers between them and build a single cohesive team. He downplayed rank and hierarchy. He insisted that each man receive the same portion at mealtime. And he announced that nobody would make fun of the cook.

"Shackleton afloat was I think a more likable character than Shackleton ashore," James observed. "Once at the head of his party his natural qualities of leadership became apparent.... I think he could persuade anyone to do almost anything if he could at once talk to him. There was a mixture of personal magnetism, bluff, and blarney that could be irresistible."

By now the dogs—mostly mongrels acquired from the Hudson's Bay Company in Canada—had colorful names that reflected the dispositions of the men as much as their own personalities. Among them were the more pedestrian Bob, Tim, Roy, Mack, Jerry, Sandy, Sally, and Sadie; the more descriptive Fluffy, Slippery, Rufus, Splitlip, and Slobber; the lyrical Caruso and Songster; the literary Shakespeare and Ulysses; the questionable Bummer, Snapper, and Stumps, the mysterious Chirgwin; the wise Saint and Judge; the mighty Hercules and Samson; and the most respectful name of all, Amundsen.

❧

REGARDED AS THE FINEST POLAR EXPLORER of his day, Norwegian Roald Amundsen possessed such intense single-mindedness and high-latitude grit that he made the difficult look easy. That was part of his failing. His quiet heroism didn't play well on the British stage, where polar suffering was regarded as an art. Better to fail flamboyantly than to succeed quietly. Unlike Shackleton, Amundsen possessed little humor or charm. A brooding oak post of a man with a narrow nose and Rasputin-like eyes, he seldom embellished, he didn't have to. But he did deceive. When he left Norway in 1910 aboard the famous little ship, the *Fram*, everybody, even his crew, thought he was going to the North Pole. He wasn't. Two Americans, Dr. Frederick Cook and Comdr. Robert E. Peary, had already claimed that prize, and each was busy debunking the claims of the other. Amundsen wanted no part of that mess, so he secretly planned to go south.

When he beat Scott to the South Pole, the response in Great Britain was one of anger and disbelief: the impudence of that "interloper" to outdo our man and steal our prize. Shackleton at first criticized Amundsen, but later annoyed his countrymen when he publicly praised the Norwegian's deeds. They shared the same rival, Captain Scott, and as circumstances would have it, they shared the same mentor as well, Fridtjof Nansen.

Ever since Nansen skied across the Greenland Ice Cap in 1888, the Norwegian approach to overland polar travel had been simple and successful: Men should ski, dogs should pull. Again and again Nansen told those who came seeking his advice: Don't treat your dogs like men, or your men like dogs. Forget horses and motor sledges and cumbersome science experiments. Forget man-hauling and Byzantine

FRANK WILD COMMISERATES (opposite) with one of nearly 70 Canadian sled dogs on the Endurance. Early in the expedition Shackleton wrote, "The dogs gave promise, after training, of being able to cover 15 to 20 miles a day with loaded sledges." It was an optimistic assessment, vintage Shackleton. The dogs, in fact, were unruly, and the men not adept at driving them. But both improved. In early 1915, as the situation worsened from one of exploration into mere survival, the dogs would have to be shot. "This duty fell upon me," Wild wrote, "and was the worst job I ever had in my life. I have known many men I would rather shoot than the worst of the dogs."

expeditions with too much of everything but common sense. Forget noble suffering; there's no such thing. Travel light and fast, kick and glide, Nordic style. If food runs low on the return, kill and eat the dogs one by one, but not the livers. They're toxic.

Not until Amundsen's South Pole triumph and Scott's tragic death did Shackleton look critically at his own methods and biases. Only then did he forsake horses for dogs. Yet before departing London, he received some biting criticism. Sir Clements Markham, by now a curmudgeonly octogenarian bitter over the death and defeat of his protégé, Scott, had huffed at the "absurdity of Shackleton's plan" that was "designed solely for self-advertisement." John King Davis had declined command of the *Endurance* not because of other commitments, but because the idea seemed reckless to him. Many people praised the expedition, however, and embraced its romantic ideals. Amundsen himself called it a "marvelous undertaking."

On January 10, the *Endurance* crew sighted the snowy shoulders of Coats Land —mainland Antarctica—and two days later had an opportunity to make landfall at a place Shackleton called Glacier Bay. Worsley suggested that the overland journey begin there, but Shackleton said no. His objective was Vahsel Bay, three degrees farther south. To begin at Glacier Bay would add extra burdensome miles to the overland journey. So the *Endurance* pushed on and left behind her first and last chance to land on the Antarctic continent. "Shackleton afterwards regretted that he had not landed here...." Worsley wrote. "He mentioned this to me the next day, but it is easy to be wise after the event."

The *Endurance* ran briskly through open water along the imposing tidewater face of an ice shelf that Shackleton called a "barrier-edge." He recorded "large schools of seals swimming from the barrier to the pack off shore." The next day a vast armada of grand and grounded icebergs came into view, some 200 feet high and showing tidemarks near the water. Too dangerous to slalom through, the bergs presented only one option: The *Endurance* would turn away from the coast to go around them. At one point the ship sidled up to a small berg to disembark geologist James Wordie. A quiet Cambridge man like his friend and colleague, physicist Reginald James, Wordie collected samples of granite embedded in the ice until a loud crack sent him scrambling back on board.

A gale blew up and the *Endurance* found shelter in the lee of a stranded berg. Tendrils of brash ice closed around her. The temperature dropped, the ice thickened. The weather eased and Captain Worsley took the *Endurance* forward under fore topsail alone, sparing the propeller damage from the ice. For a moment the ship hit open water and again made good speed. Eighty miles from her objective, Vahsel Bay, she slid into loose pack ice. But the pack was like wet cement that hardened quickly. Worsley shut down the engines. "We must possess ourselves in patience till a Southerly gale occurs," he noted in his log, "or the ice opens of its own sweet will."

But this was different. There was no sweet will. The northeast gale had kicked up an insurrection of Weddell Sea pack ice and pushed it against the nearby coast. Unlike before, when the ice would rasp and grind against the wooden ship, now it was strangely silent. Hurley wrote, "It is now seven weeks since we first entered the pack ice, & since then it has been almost an incessant battle."

Several days later a crack appeared in the ice at right angles to the ship, less than one hundred yards off her bow. By the next morning, January 25, the crack was a quarter mile across, taunting the imprisoned men. With full steam ahead and sails set, the *Endurance* pushed against the ice for three hours and hardly moved. The men hacked at the ice with pickaxes, chisels, crowbars, and saws, trying to no avail to cut a path to freedom. With maddening caprice the crack closed. The temperature plummeted to 9°F. "An ominous happening," Hurley wrote, as the ice hardened all around. Alfred Lansing would later say, "The *Endurance* was beset. As Orde-Lees, the storekeeper, expressed it, 'frozen, like an almond in the middle of a chocolate bar.'"

The Weddell Sea takes its name from the amiable Scottish seafarer, James Weddell, who was fond of his rum and who, in the benevolent antipodal summer of 1823, sailed to latitude 74°15' South, a feat that wouldn't be exceeded in the area for 88 years. He sighted many spectacular bergs and little pack ice, and returned home believing the South Pole was occupied by ocean, not continental land. He also claimed the geographic prize of *ne plus ultra*—"farthest south." Fifty years earlier, when Capt. James Cook was the first to cross the Antarctic Circle, he hit gales and thick ice, conditions opposite of those found by Weddell. As Cook prepared to turn his ship back north, a young apprentice named George Vancouver climbed onto the bowsprit so he too could claim ne plus ultra. That same southern fever infected Shackleton when he first rounded Cape Horn in his youth.

As seasons varied back home in Great Britain, with some summers wetter than others, and some winters colder, so too did they vary in the polar regions. But here the variations reached extremes, with the Weddell Sea largely free of pack ice some years (which was rare) or jammed with ice other years (which was common). For decades explorers failed to grasp the nature of polar weather and climate, how it related to sea temperatures and currents, and how the whole scheme affected local ice conditions.

James Weddell hit a good year and got lucky. James Cook did not. Amundsen and Nansen made their own luck. And Shackleton? His cards remained on the table, face down.

～

WITH HELP FROM REGINALD JAMES, navigator Hubert Hudson rigged the wireless in hopes of hearing a monthly message from the Falkland Islands, more than 1,600 miles to the north. A primitive radio, the wireless could receive but not send. Still, the men hungered for voices from home, news of the war, anything. They huddled over the apparatus, described as a "cumbersome array of condensers, spark gaps, and coils the size of half gallon jars," and listened for anything familiar. All they heard was static.

By the middle of February the sun, which had been up 24 hours a day, began to wink away, first at midnight, then with longer absences, presaging the polar winter to come.

Lanes of open water appeared ahead, and again efforts by the crew to cut a path to them proved vexing. Even Charlie Green, the cook with bad knees, finished baking his many loaves of bread and trundled onto the ice to lend a hand. During one strenuous episode the pack ice was cleared around the ship into a slushy brash, and the *Endurance* was able to ram forward and advance about 200 yards. But the lead was another 400 yards away, and the pack in between measured 12 to 18 feet thick. Temperatures dropped. The brash ice froze solid and gripped the ship. Shackleton ordered the fires turned down, as coal was running low. Every shovelful burned in ramming would be one less for staying warm through the winter.

By the end of February the *Endurance* had drifted to the 77th parallel, her farthest south, only 25 miles from Vahsel Bay. Her maiden voyage had brought her 15,000 miles through the tempestuous Atlantic, and 1,000 miles through the semifrozen Weddell Sea, only to end up icebound, as Sir Ernest put it, "in the inhospitable arms of the pack," a one-day voyage from her destination.

"It was more than tantalizing," observed Macklin, "it was maddening.

"FOR TWO DAYS IN FEBRUARY," Hurley wrote in his diary, *"the crew chopped a channel for the* Endurance *in hopes of reaching open water. But they gave up 400 yards short of a lead, thwarted by layered ice up to 18 feet thick."* One week later, on February 22, 1915, the Endurance *drifted to the 77th parallel, her farthest point south. "The summer had gone,"* Shackleton added. *"Indeed the summer had scarcely been with us at all. The temperatures were low day and night, and the pack was freezing solidly around the ship."*

Shackleton at this time showed one of his sparks for real greatness. He did not rage at all, or show outwardly the slightest sign of disappointment; he told us simply and calmly that we must winter in the pack; explained its dangers and possibilities; never lost his optimism and prepared for winter."

If Shackleton harbored regrets over having not landed at Glacier Bay, he didn't share them. It was his burden alone. Looking back would get him nowhere. He would invest his energy in looking ahead, anticipating problems, improvising. Seldom if ever did he second-guess himself. He had not given up on the trans-Antarctic idea. When liberated from the ice next spring or early next summer (October to December), he hoped to sail the *Endurance* back to South Georgia, resupply her, then return to the Weddell Sea to travel overland to the Pole and beyond. This icy incarceration was to him not an acute danger, just a delay. Men had overwintered in ships in pack ice before, some in the far north, others in the far south. He had studied their journals and the reasons behind their successes and failures. His primary goals: Keep his men active, alert, and well fed; create games and contests; exercise men and dogs; maintain scientific and literary inquiry. Avoid despair. Break free as soon as possible. Let no opportunity slip away.

His door was always open. No crewman was of so little importance that a decision was kept from him. According to authors James and Margery Fisher, every change of plan was "freely discussed and commented on, and although Shackleton had the final decision at all times, he was known to be approachable. All hands could go to him with suggestions, and all hands were made to feel that they were important in the general scheme. The fact that no changes or dangers were hidden from them, and that Shackleton never gave anyone false hope, was of incalculable importance. Not only this, but it meant that Shackleton was liked by his men, because he took the trouble to keep a living human relationship with each of them."

≈

THE ENDURANCE no longer served as a ship, but rather as a winter shore station. Sea watches were discontinued. All hands would work by day and sleep by night, with one man as a night watchman, accompanied if he wished by a friend at the chessboard, or walking topside and talking softly of things back home. Shackleton made it clear that he be apprised of any sudden changes in ice conditions, no matter what the hour.

As the engine room generated no more heat, the officers and scientists moved from their cold cabins into the forehold. Stores were stashed into the empty coal bunkers, and a mid-decks area was converted into a cozy sleeping and gathering place complete with a long table for meals and a bogie stove for warmth. The men called it "the Ritz." Harry McNeish, the sour yet skilled carpenter and shipwright, fashioned several two-man cubicles, each customized for its new occupants. The forecastle hands remained comfortable in the fo'c'sle below, and were pardoned from having to serve on night watch, a small but strategic compensation for their hard work above decks and below. Shackleton slept in his cabin aft. Worsley, who said his quarters were too warm, often slept in the passageway where temperatures dropped to zero. He also enjoyed a snow bath now and then, rubbing down shirtless on the pack ice.

The dogs were moved onto the pack where the men built ice-block kennels called "dogloos." Two pigs, acquired in Buenos Aires, were accordingly housed in "pigloos." The ship's pet tomcat, Mrs. Chippy, remained on board where she was a close companion to McNeish, whom the crew called "Chippy," a common nickname for ship's carpenters.

All of February and March, Worsley climbed to the crow's nest and glassed the Filchner Ice Shelf far to the south. Each day it slipped farther away as the ship, locked in the Weddell Sea gyre, drifted west and north. Distant leads of open water created phantasmagoric smokelike curtains of steam. When the sun broke through brooding clouds, which was rare, the light was spectacular. Shackleton described a "wonderful golden mist to the southward, where the rays of shining sun shone through vapour rising from the ice. All normal standards of perspective vanish under such conditions, and the low ridges of the pack, with mist lying between them, give the illusion of a wilderness of mountain peaks...."

Hurley added that "Immense clouds of dark vapour rolled skyward from the water, as if from a boiling lake. These mists solidified into crystals, which fell in shimmering showers from the clear blue sky—a rain of jewels. The sun shone through the glinting fall in great rainbow circles, which spanned the sky. The crystal showers carpeted the pack ice and ship until she looked like a tinselled beauty on a field of diamonds."

From the crow's nest hawk-eyed Worsley also sighted seals, some as many as three miles away, dark specks in a netherworld of white. He instructed the men where to find them. Over floes and pressure ridges they would walk until, true to Worsley's directions, they found a seal lying near a lead, often a Weddell seal or a crabeater seal. Though quick and agile in the sea where they lived as predator and prey, the seals were docile and slow on the ice. Little stealth was required in the men's approach; the seals' genetic repertoire possessed nothing to warn them. Endemic to the unpeopled Antarctic, they simply had no fear of men. One rifle shot by the capable Frank Wild killed them. The challenge was then to haul the carcass back to the ship before it became too cold to butcher without freezing one's fingers.

By late March the nights were longer than the days, and the leads of open water scarce. Shackleton wrote that "The seals were disappearing and the birds were leaving us." The ship contained 5,000 pounds of seal meat and blubber, the meat as food for men and dogs, the blubber as fuel in lieu of dwindling coal reserves. Shackleton estimated the supply would last 90 days, enough to augment the standard-issue tinned and dried foods through the bitter cold polar night.

Fifteen dogs had died, most of them from worms. "Worm-powders were to have been provided by the expert Canadian dog-driver I had engaged before sailing south," Shackleton wrote later, "and when this man did not join the expedition the matter was overlooked." Two litters of pups helped to compensate for the loss, with eight furballs surviving into bounding puppyhood, a source of great delight for the crew. Shackleton divided the adult dogs into training teams and assigned one team to each of six men: Wild, Crean, Hurley, Marston, Macklin, and the other expedition physician, James McIlroy, a dashing Ulster man with a biting wit.

"JUST BEFORE MIDNIGHT," wrote Shackleton in his diary on January 24, 1915, "a crack developed in the ice five yards wide and a mile long." By ten o'clock the next morning it had widened to a quarter of a mile, "and for three hours we tried to force the ship (above) into this opening with engines at full speed ahead and all sails set." It didn't budge. A crewman's diary depicts a tabular iceberg (opposite).

But these dogs had no sense of humor. Unlike the 35-pound, narrow-chested, even-tempered marathon huskies typical of long-distance racing in the far north, these were large freight dogs, more mongrel than husky, boisterous and fun at times, but also capable of tremendous aggression and mean-spiritedness. The largest dog, Hercules, weighed 86 pounds. Samson tipped the scales at 75 pounds.

To properly handle a harnessed team of such powerful animals required skill and authority. After a rough beginning, each driver soon learned the basic dynamics of his team, which dogs to mix and match, how to be stern, when to be rewarding. In due time each team made forays across the ice.

In early May the men were surprised to see emperor penguins appear from small leads that opened near the ship. The crew had captured penguins before, and butchered them for meat, but didn't expect to find any this late in the season. Imitating their comical manner—arms stiff at their sides, bodies waddling with each imperious step—the men enticed the birds into capture. The penguins showed little fear, and in fact were curious about these fellow creatures upright on the ice. At one point a frightened 80-pounder knocked Second Engineer A. J. Kerr off his feet and jumped onto his chest before fleeing. Undeterred, Kerr and Cheetham captured another, bound his bill, and in Shackleton's words, "lead him, muttering muffled protests, to the ship like an inebriated old man between two policemen." During another roundup, James Wordie had corralled a penguin when Frank Wild approached, driving a dog team. According to Shackleton, "The dogs, uncontrollable in a moment, made a frantic rush for the bird, and were almost upon him when their harness caught upon an ice-pylon, which they had tried to pass on both sides at once. The result was a seething tangle of dogs, traces,

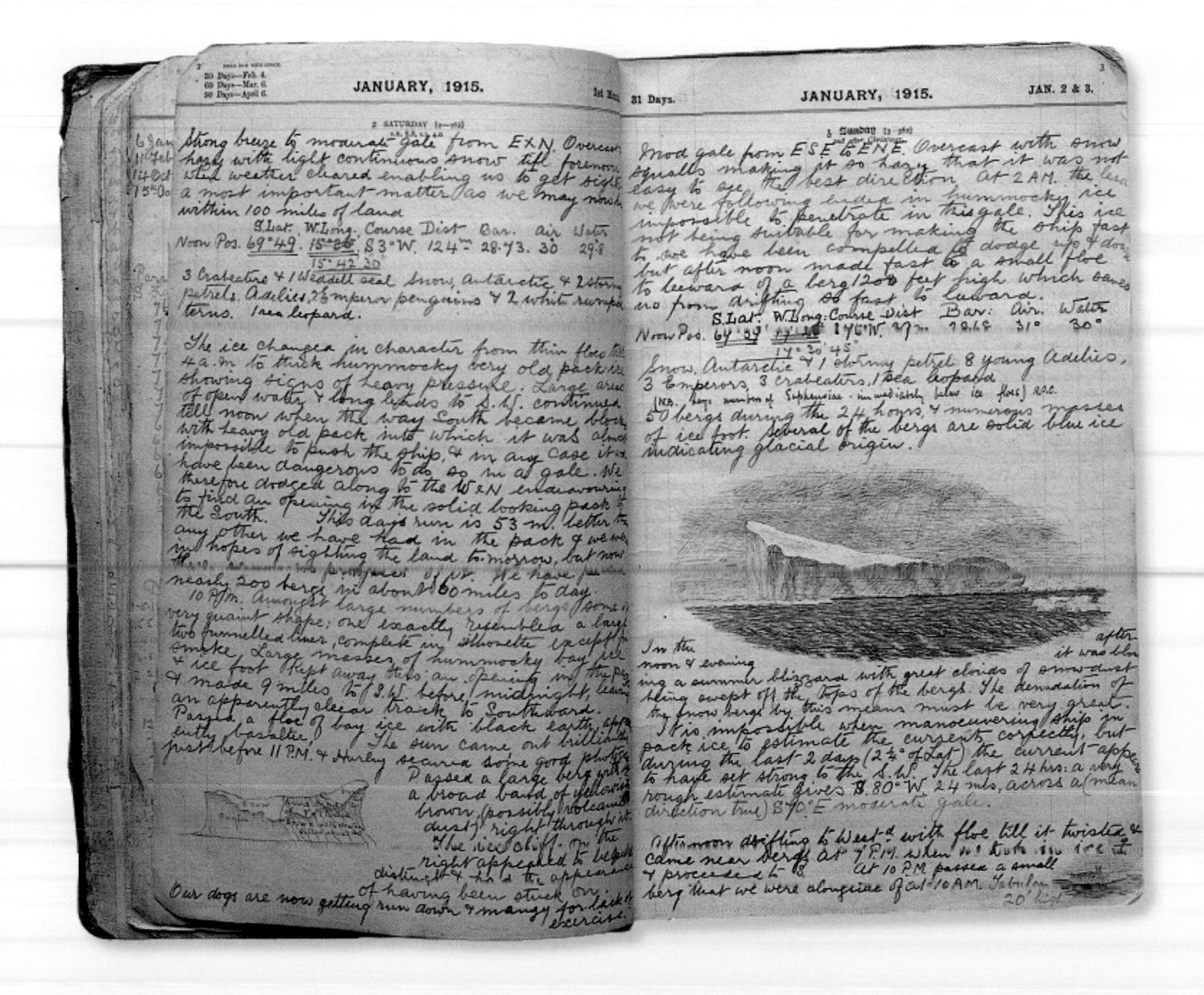

and men, and an overturned sledge, while the penguin, three yards away, nonchalantly surveyed the disturbance. He had never seen anything of the kind before and had no idea at all that the strange disturbance might concern him."

Green quickly skinned the birds, but not everybody was thrilled. Seaman Thomas McLeod, a superstitious Scot, believed the souls of dead fishermen inhabited penguins. He said he wouldn't eat a one.

Under normal circumstances a ship at sea is said to get a foot shorter each day, a reference to growing tensions among a confined crew. Add entrapment in pack ice and the polar night, and the recipe for tension thickens. On the *Belgica*, the first ship to overwinter in Antarctica in 1899, one man died, several became ill, and another got it into his head that his shipmates wanted to kill him. To pass the monotony the men walked the deck in a ritual called "madhouse promenade." When Nansen drifted in the Arctic pack ice for three years in the *Fram*, he chose men who showed supreme patience and tolerance. Regarding the virtues of patience, Nansen liked to tell a story about Greenland Eskimos who traveled afar one spring to get grass for hay. Finding the grass too short, they simply sat down and waited for it to grow. Such parables were not lost on Shackleton.

Aboard the *Endurance*, minor complaints were lodged with Frank Wild. A crewman might think Chippy McNeish too brusque, or Orde-Lees too lazy, or Marston too moody, or Bobby Clark, a dour Scot, more concerned with his biological specimens than the welfare of his shipmates. Wild would listen with paternal grace, offer a few judicious words to assuage the man, then send him out the door feeling redeemed. No further action taken. More serious matters were addressed by Shackleton. When a strong and stocky forecastle hand named John Vincent was reported for pirating food and bullying others, Shackleton called him into his cabin for a little chat. Vincent left with his face ashen and his manners improved. When another man grumbled about a spaghetti dinner, the noodles limp at the end of his fork, Shackleton reminded him that as a boy in Ireland he himself had been taught to eat what was placed in front of him, and to be grateful. The sailor finished his meal and complained no more.

∽

IN EARLY MAY the sun winked away, leaving a gauze of gray light that leaked along the northern horizon. Soon after, the ship slipped into winter's tunnel, the polar night, dark as a grave for 16 hours a day, now and then bejeweled by southern stars and a brittle moon. Faint twilight appeared only at the middle of each day. Shackleton had been through it before on previous expeditions on the Ross Sea side

WINTER 1915, trapped in the Weddell Sea ice, the Endurance *crew gather in the Ritz and give each other haircuts to break the monotony of the cold and dark. Worsley described "fits of laughter. All now look so irresistibly quaint, comical, or criminal that the camera is called in...to cure us...of conceit...." McNeish noted, "We do look a lot of convicts & we are not much short of that life at present." Winter diversions included dogsled races, mock trials, card games, and slide shows by Hurley.*

THE ANTARCTIC CHALLENGE

of Antarctica, as had a few others, but never on an ice-entombed ship.

The men took comfort in their growing camaraderie. With daily chores at a minimum, they had ample time to read, play cards, write in their diaries. Charlie Green filled the decks with the aromas of hot soups and baked bread. Blackboro, the young stowaway, made himself valuable as he collected ice for drinking water and helped Green in the galley. Everybody speculated about the war and wondered if the Germans had been booted from France. The cosmopolitan Dr. McIlroy told stories of his world travels, salted no doubt by wry comments from the crowd. A round of grog was served on Saturday nights, followed by the toast: "To our sweethearts and our wives, may they never meet."

Other ways to pass the time were more innovative. By now the men had given each other haircuts that bordered on scalpings, and many of the men had nicknames: "Chippy" McNeish, Frank "Wuzzles" Worsley, James "Jock" Wordie, Reginald "Gentle Jimmy" James. Amusements involved a mock trial that found Worsley accused of robbing a church of a trouser button. With Wild as the judge, Orde-Lees as defense attorney, and James as prosecutor, the trial descended into boisterous mayhem and vaudeville when Worsley, fearing for his life, offered to buy Judge Wild a drink after the trial, provided of course that he, the esteemed Mr. Worsley, be found innocent. Wild agreed. But the jury showed no sympathy and found Worsley guilty as charged.

In midwinter's darkness, Hurley rigged electric lights to port and starboard on the dogloos. Temperatures ballasted well below zero, and Tom Crean began to run the pups. Shackleton noted that "it was very amusing to see them with their rolling canter just managing to keep abreast by the sledge and occasionally cocking an eye with an appealing look in the hope of being taken aboard for a ride." He described the amiable Crean as the pups' "foster-father."

All in all, the month of May was a comfortable and largely uneventful time on the *Endurance.* But not so on the other side of Antarctica, on Ross Island, where in the early morning hours of May 7, 1915, disaster struck.

Since its birth, the Imperial Trans-Antarctic Expedition had involved not just one ship, but two, the second being the *Aurora,* a former Newfoundland sealer christened by the famous ballet dancer, Anna Pavlova, and used by Douglas Mawson to discover much of the western Antarctic coast. The mission of her crew now, as instructed by Shackleton, was to make safe landfall on Ross Island, and establish food and fuel depots across the Ross Ice Shelf to the Polar Plateau, depots that would sustain Shackleton's overland trans-Antarctic party on the second half of the journey. Under the command of one-eyed Aeneas Mackintosh, a veteran of the *Nimrod* expedition, the *Aurora* had started six weeks late, reached Ross Island under nerve-fraying conditions, and only laid a few depots before winter arrived. The night of May 6 found her crew hunkered down against the cold at Cape Evans, with some men in a hut on shore, and some on board the moored ship nearby. At three in the morning crewman Dick Richards was awakened in the hut by a violent wind pounding the roof and walls. Walking outside, he was shocked to see no ship in the moonlight; only the fixed anchors with their stocks bent seaward, and the iron hawsers twisted across the icy beach like strands of yarn. The wind had ripped the *Aurora* from her moorings, her hull encased in ice, and set her adrift in the Ross Sea.

TOM CREAN HUGS Alf Cheetham (above), who often rode as a passenger in Alex Macklin's sledge. Macklin described Cheetham as a "cheery little fellow who had a strange outlook on life...." While daylight lasts, a game of soccer (opposite), which the men called football, breaks the monotony of entrapment in the ice. "The idea of spending the winter in an ice bound ship," wrote Hurley, "is extremely unpleasant."

On board the crippled, ice-locked ship, her keel damaged and hull leaking, Chief Officer John Stenhouse wrote, "We are drifting God knows where! But what of the poor beggars at Cape Evans—and the returning southern party. It is a dismal prospect for them."

Two ships were now trapped in the ice. While the *Endurance* retained her entire crew and tight fittings, the *Aurora* did not. She had left ten men stranded on shore, their duties unfinished and vastly more daunting than before. Among this unlucky Ross Island crew was Ernie Wild, Frank's younger brother, a gentle clergyman named the Rev. A. Patrick Spencer-Smith, who served as expedition photographer, and their leader, Mackintosh.

Australian polar historian Lennard Bickel would later describe these men as "half-frozen wretches" who would make "the most horrendous sledge march in polar history in a cause of the highest nobility and the utmost futility. Committed to lay food depots every 60 miles...with no more than the clothes they wore, dependant on the discarded supplies from past expeditions, with faulty equipment and poor shelter, these heroes achieved a march of almost 2,000 miles and spent ten months in the field of ice laying down food and fuel weighing thousands of

pounds, and which they badly needed for their own survival, for the men of Shackleton's planned transcontinental party...six men who would never come.

In the past 16 years nearly two dozen wooden vessels had braved the icy seas of the far south. All but one had returned home. That ship, the *Antarctic*, was a 30-year-old tired whaler when the Weddell Sea pack crushed her like an apple crate and left her crew stranded on the ice in 1903. The *Aurora* was also old, and now in peril. The young *Endurance*, although the last of her kind in many respects, was also a first. Lloyd's of London and the Indemnity Marine Assurance Company had underwritten her hull, machinery, and equipment for 15,000 pounds. Just before she sailed, *The Times* of London had reported that "Hitherto the insurance of vessels taking part in Antarctic exploration has ceased at the last port touched, and the *Endurance* will be the first vessel to be insured in the ice zone."

Insurance gives little warmth to a freezing man. Nature underwrites the underwriters by behaving with certain predictability. But in Antarctica nature contains forces that Lloyd's of London and the *Endurance* crew could only partially understand and never control. *The Times* had praised the *Endurance* as "built specially for work in Polar seas," adding that "in an ice-coated sea there can be no turbulent waves which are the causes of so many disasters in warmer zones."

Turbulence of another kind defined the pack ice. Rafting atop the Weddell Sea gyre and pushed along by mad winds, the pack would twist and strain from differential pressure, then suddenly break, as it did on June 9, only 500 yards from the ship. Hearing deep and distant rumbles, a handful of men walked to the source, their feet crunching on hoarfrost at minus 20°F. Their shadows, cast by handheld lanterns, danced over hummocks like hobgoblins and ghosts. What they found was an ice wreck; massive blocks jammed together to a height of 15 feet, and still colliding. The rumblings continued for three days, then grew quiet.

∽

ON JUNE 15, the "Antarctic Derby" featured a 700-yard dog race from Khyber Pass, off the bow of the ship, to a point near the jibboom. Shackleton wrote that "Canvas handkerchiefs fluttered from an improvised grand stand and the pups, which had never seen such strange happenings before, sat round and howled with excitement." The teams dashed through the twilight amid great fanfare. Frank Wild won in little more than two minutes. Hurley called for a rematch.

One week later, on June 22, all hands gathered in the Ritz to celebrate Midwinter's Day with good food, bad theater, and terrible singing. The performances included McIlroy dressed as a Spanish temptress, Kerr as a tone-deaf tramp, Marston as a yokel, and Greenstreet as a ruddy-faced drunk. Orde-Lees delivered a sermon as Reverend Bubblinglove; Wild recited *The Wreck of the Hesperus*. Most memorable was Gentle Jimmy who, as Herr Professor von Schopenbaum, lectured on "The Calorie."

"Witty and unintelligible," summarized Worsley. "We laughed until tears ran down our cheeks," wrote Greenstreet. The evening ended with a rendition of *God Save the King*. Shackleton hoped for "success in the days of sunshine and effort...ahead."

A few days later Hurley got his dog derby rematch with Wild. The two teams dashed through the twilight neck and neck, pulling loads of equal weight. Wild's sledge went into a skid and spilled part of its load, giving him an advantage on the final dash. The spilled load was none other than Sir Ernest who'd rolled out onto the ice. Wild won by seven seconds but was disqualified for his lightened sledge.

Twilight lengthened in July, and new leads opened in all directions, some only

300 yards from the *Endurance.* The barometer fell and on July 13 a fierce gale struck. "I gave orders that no man should venture beyond the kennels," wrote Shackleton. "The ship was invisible at a distance of 50 yards, and it was impossible to preserve one's sense of direction in the raging wind and suffocating drift. To walk against the gale was out of the question. Face and eyes became snowed up within two minutes, and serious frost-bites would have been the penalty of perseverance." The temperature dropped to minus 35°F. Huddled in their kennels, the dogs pushed their paws through the drift for breathing holes. That night the wind screamed at 70 miles an hour. Ice quakes rolled through the pack. The wooden ship, according to Shackleton, "was trembling under the attack."

He called Wild and Worsley into his cabin. Pacing, he told them that the *Endurance* was in trouble. She couldn't take many beatings like this before breaking apart. It might be months or weeks, he said, "but what the ice gets, the ice keeps."

Wild accepted the news with patented aplomb. But Worsley couldn't believe it. An incurable romantic, he regarded the *Endurance* as a horse man would his horse, with deep fidelity and respect. His ship was his charter and his charge. Without her he would have no helm under his feet, no tangible mission. Shackleton's disclosure was calculated to give him time to accept the probability of loss, to prepare to make the most of it when it happened. Back with the crew, the three men divulged nothing.

Severe ice quakes hit the ship again in late July and rattled the men's nerves. Shackleton ordered hourly watches and the decks cleared in case breakup and open water required that the dogs be brought aboard quickly. The sun returned after a 79-day absence, but amid so much anxiety it was greeted with only half-hearted cheer. Six days later, on August 1, another gale hit, and the floe that had imprisoned the *Endurance* decided to torture her. Fracturing, thrusting, and sheering into massive plates and shards, the ice lifted the ship, shook her, and dropped her. The men hustled the dogs aboard in minutes, just in time as the ship jolted forward and sideways. Her beams and planks moaned in protest as the grinding ice seized and squeezed her again and again. After three days the violence ended, and the *Endurance* rested with a five-degree list, tossed like a toy in a fault zone. She was an estimated 37 miles north of her previous location, crunched in the middle of what Orde-Lees later called "a labyrinth of ice blocks and gullies."

Shackleton noted "the ruins of 'Dog Town' amid the debris of pressure ridges. Some of the little dwellings had been crushed flat beneath blocks of ice; others had been swallowed and pulverized when the ice opened beneath them and closed again. It was a sad sight, but my chief concern just then was the safety of the rud-

LEONARD HUSSEY, the banjo-playing meteorologist and smallest crewman, lifts 75-pound Samson, one of the expedition's largest dogs. Shackleton noted that when harnessed to pull, Samson "justified his name one day by starting off at a smart pace with a sledge carrying 200 pounds of blubber and a driver."

der, which was being attacked viciously by the ice. We managed to pole away a large lump that had been jammed between the rudder and the stern-post, but I could see that damage had been done...."

Worsley wrote that if such treatment continued, the *Endurance* "would crush up like an empty eggshell."

Shackleton ordered emergency rations stored with the sledges, and warm clothing packed for foot travel. The three lifeboats—*Dudley Docker, Stancomb-Wills* and *James Caird*—were made ready for quick deployment. The men gathered prized possessions, placed photographs of their families in their Bibles, and lay awake in their bunks, thinking too much, waiting for the next quake to shake their eggshell.

The sky cleared and the wind abated. Hockey games ensued on the ice, and every other day the dogs were disembarked to run. Spirits climbed with the returning sun. By sextant and chronometer Worsley determined that the ship had drifted 160 miles north since the gale in mid-July, all the closer to open water and freedom. Some men decided that the *Endurance,* though battered, was tough enough to take anything the Weddell Sea pack threw at her. Shackleton found them in the Ritz one night sharing bravado about their ship's resilience. Joining them at their table, he told a story about a mouse in a tavern that found a leaking barrel of beer: After drinking its fill, the mouse twirled its whiskers, puffed out its little rodent chest and said with smug satisfaction, "Now then, where is that damned cat?"

The parable fell on deaf ears. Shackleton allowed his men their fantasy. Besides, the young ship just might make it.

Hurley wrote in his diary that he "conceived the ambition of making some pictures of the *Endurance* that would last, and I spent weeks studying her from all angles. She was never twice the same...a lady of infinite variety."

His efforts culminated on August 27. Working late into the night at minus 36°F, his fingers already split around the nails from exposure to the extremes of outside cold and chemical baths in the ship's darkroom, he positioned 20 lights around the ship, "one behind each salient pressure hummock," he wrote. With the tripod firmly set and the working parts of the camera lubricated, he opened the shutter and tripped a brilliant succession of lights. "Half blinded...I lost my bearings amidst hummocks, bumping shins against projecting ice points & stumbling into deep snow drifts." The brittle film required delicate handling, a tedious process, but worth it. Hurley's images transformed the *Endurance* into a crystalline bird, feathered in ice, transcendent, as if she were flying above her fate.

August ended as it began, with the ship groaning and the men sleepless, under attack again. Sometimes the ice would explode with stupefying suddenness and the men would run up on deck bootless, and see nothing. Other times a tectonic wave would rumble through the pack like a runaway locomotive. All hands would hear

EYE ON THE SEA ICE in search of open lanes, Shackleton appears indifferent to Hurley's photographic acrobatics on the far end of the Endurance *topsail yard (opposite). A veteran of Australian Douglas Mawson's 1910-13* Aurora *expedition, Hurley was an innovative, self-confident Australian who found similarities between Mawson and Shackleton. "Both possessed the fearless, indomitable will of born leaders. Both were strong men, physically and mentally, able organisers, and accustomed to having their own way."*

THE ANTARCTIC CHALLENGE

it approach and brace themselves as the maddening sound roared into the ship, shook them, and moved on, never slowing. Worst of all, the men winced in their bunks as the ice rasped on the outside hull only three feet from their heads, clawing, chewing—that damned cat.

The quixotic ice fell silent again. In mid-September temperatures climbed above zero for the first time in seven months. Penguins and seals returned, here, there.

The last day of September delivered an hour of trauma when the pack shook the ship until the foremast appeared as if it might snap. Down in the Ritz, Chippy McNeish said the beams "bent like a piece of cane."

In the quiet that followed, Worsley wrote that the *Endurance* "shows almost unconceivable strength, when every moment it seems as though the floe must crush her like a nutshell. All hands are watching and standing by, but to our relief, just as she appears she can stand no more, the huge floe weighing possibly a million tons or more yields to our little ship by cracking and so relieves the pressure. The behavior of our little ship in the ice has been magnificent. Undoubtedly she is the finest little wooden vessel ever built."

Shackleton might have disagreed. The most famous of all polar vessels was the *Fram* (Norwegian meaning "forward"). Designed by Nansen for his famous three-year drift in the Arctic pack, 1893-96, she was built like a tub, small and flat-bottomed. When squeezed under pressure she would, in Nansen's words, "slip like an eel out of the embraces of the ice." Not so the *Endurance*. For all her strength, beauty, and craftsmanship, she did not have the *Fram*'s ingenuity, and now, caught in the jaws of the Antarctic pack, she was paying the price.

IN MID-OCTOBER water appeared around the hull, and a lead opened off the bow. Shackleton ordered boilers pumped for full steam ahead, but a leak in the fittings prevented start-up. The men set topsails and headsails to catch a favorable breeze, but the ship wouldn't move. The next day brought snow and cold; the jaws of the pack tightened. With sickening dread the men listened to the crunch of ice on wood. "All sorts of weird noises came from the engine room," wrote Wordie. Suddenly the ship heeled over 30 degrees to port, her bulwarks pressed to the ice. Men, supplies, and howling dogs careened across the decks.

Shackleton ordered the galley fires put out and battens nailed down. Worsley inspected the lifeboats. Hanging from their davits, they nearly touched the ice. Hurley disembarked to take photographs of the stricken ship. "Dinner in the wardroom that evening was a curious affair," wrote Shackleton. "Most of the diners had to sit on the deck, their feet against battens and their plates on their knees."

With equal suddenness the ship righted herself, ending another chapter of chaos in a continuing tale of uncertainty.

There followed a few days of quiet and anxious waiting. An orca—what the men called a killer whale—surfaced in an open lane next to the ship and cruised by like a dark omen, its tall dorsal fin slicing the sea.

On October 23, the pressure returned. The pack ripped the sternpost from its starboard planking. Seawater began to flood the forward hold and engine room. All hands jumped to action. When the bilge pumps proved ineffective, Worsley, Hudson, and Greenstreet hustled down to the bunkers along the keel—the basement of the ship—where amid floating coal and seal blubber they worked in knee-deep freezing water to thaw the intakes. Other men worked hand pumps along the mainmast. McNeish fashioned a cofferdam to hold the seawater abaft of the engines. Blankets were stuffed into the cracks as caulking. The stout oak timbers cried in agony, assaulted by incomprehensible forces. The ship was a twig in a juggernaut. Forecastle beams snapped and the decks buckled. Several hands hacked away at the pack ice to try to relieve the pressure.

Pieces of canvas were rigged into chutes from the port rail, and the 49 remaining dogs slid down to the ice below. Ordinarily filled with barking and excitement at a time like this, the dogs must have sensed the apocalypse around them. They went quietly. Not one tried to run away. There was nowhere to go. The dog-team drivers loaded sledges for quick deployment. Worsley lowered the lifeboats onto the starboard floe and provisioned them for travel.

Night and day the crew worked, fighting the inevitable. Every so often they would take an hour's rest and drink a bowl of porridge, their eyes closed, faces drawn. A man would just fall asleep, then be awakened for his next turn on the pumps. On the evening of the third day of struggle, a group of emperor penguins appeared. Commonly seen in singles and in pairs, this was an unusual procession of eight birds that walked solemnly up to the dying ship, lifted their ornate heads and uttered a strange, mournful wail. The men froze. No one had heard such a lamentation before. "Do you hear that?" the superstitious McLeod said to Macklin, "We'll none of us get back to our homes again."

Even Shackleton appeared unnerved. Macklin noticed him bite his lip.

That next afternoon, October 27, 1915, with the pressure unabated and seawater gaining on the pumps, rising a foot deep in the Ritz, Shackleton nodded gravely to Wild. The steady Yorkshireman walked the ruptured passageways and gave the order to abandon ship. "She's going boys. I think it's time to get off."

The men dutifully accepted what they knew had been coming for a long time. Nobody complained; most were too exhausted. Some men actually felt relieved to let the ship go, to bring to an end the seesawing psychosis of months of unknowing. Time to camp on the ice, to accept the cold, lonely impermanence of everything around them.

Shackleton was last to leave, and later recorded, "I looked down the engine-room skylight as I stood on the quivering deck, and saw the engines dropping sideways...the stays and bed-plates gave way. I cannot describe the impression of restless destruction...." He raised the signatory blue ensign and disembarked.

Greenstreet wrote of the ship, that he could hear "the ice being ground into her, and you almost felt your own ribs were being crushed." As if to bid farewell to the only crew she had ever known, the ship's short-circuited emergency light flickered on, then went dark. For Greenstreet, "It seemed like the end of everything."

Tired and forlorn, the men assembled on a floe about one hundred yards from the ship. They called the site "Dump Camp," as it was littered with supplies. Shackleton told them straight: Their situation was dangerous. With their cooperation he would do everything he could to get them back home. He offered no false promises or fancy heroics, only his clear eyes and brutal honesty, which in itself was a salve. They had drifted 570 miles northwest since the *Endurance* was beset ten months earlier. The nearest land with food and shelter was Paulet Island, 350 miles away. He explained that a rock hut had been built there a dozen years before by the crew of the *Antarctic* after their ship was crushed by ice. As fate would have it, Shackleton had purchased the stores for the relief expedition; he knew exactly what was in that hut. His plan: Do as the crew of the *Antarctic* had done, pull lifeboats over the pack until they hit open water, then take to the oars and row to Paulet.

Shackleton thanked the men for their "steadiness and good morale."

Green heated water on the blubber stove, and it warmed Shackleton to hear the men request their tea with the joking affectation of aristocrats. Said one, "Cook, I like my tea strong." Said another, "Cook, I like mine weak."

"It was pleasant to know that their minds were untroubled," Shackleton noted, "but I thought [it] opportune to mention that the tea would be the same for all hands and that we would be fortunate if two months later we had tea at all."

ABANDON SHIP, October 27, 1915: A painting by George Marston, the expedition artist and a Nimrod *veteran, shows the* Endurance *punished by ice as her crew off-loads supplies and prepares to camp. "It was a pitiful sight," Macklin wrote of the ship. "To all of us she seemed like a living creature...and it was awful to witness her torture."*

Homeless on the ice, the men received new winter clothing (Burberry jackets, underclothing, and socks) and drew lots for sleeping bags. While most of the able seamen got the warmer reindeer-fur bags, the officers settled for lighter wool bags. They snuggled into five tents and laid on groundsheets that did little to arrest heat loss or muffle the disquieting sounds of the ice. Three times that night they had to move camp over troublesome pressure ridges onto new floes as the ice cracked beneath them. The temperature dropped to minus 16°F. Moonlight leaked through the thin tent walls. "A terrible night," wrote Reginald James, "with the ship sullen dark against the sky & the noise of the pressure against her...like the cries of a living creature."

Shackleton paced much of the night. How ironic that the coming of spring, which they had hoped would free them, had stranded them. The objective was no longer exploration, but survival. They had no ship, and with spring upon them the ice could break up anywhere and everywhere. "The disaster had been looming ahead for many months," wrote Shackleton, "and I had studied my plans for all contingencies a hundred times. But the thoughts that came to me as I walked up and down in the darkness were not particularly cheerful. The task now was to secure the safety of the party, and to that I must bend my energies and mental power and apply every bit of knowledge that experience of the Antarctic had given me. The task was likely to be long and strenuous, and an ordered mind and a clear programme were essential if we were to come through without loss of life."

Early that next morning Wild and Hurley boarded the *Endurance* to fetch fuel. With Shackleton they built a fireplace from an old water tank and warmed a large pot of milk. "Then we three ministering angels went round the tents with the life-giving drink," Shackleton wrote, "and were surprised and a trifle chagrined at the matter-of-fact manner in which some of the men accepted this contribution to their comfort." Wild said, "If any of you gentlemen would like your boots cleaned, just put them outside."

That brought a tide of chuckles. Worsley recorded later that Wild's remark "made us laugh when we really didn't think we could smile."

∿

THE NEXT FEW DAYS the men made preparations for travel. They retrieved additional stores from the ship, and muscled the lifeboats onto the sledges. Tom Crean stoically shot three puppies and McNeish's tomcat, Mrs. Chippy, as they would burden the arduous pulling journey and reduce the rations of seal meat. It was Macklin's duty to put a shotgun to the neck of an older puppy, Sirius, and he made poor work of it, due in part to the dog's bounding exuberance and his own shaking hands.

Shackleton and Wild scouted a route through the pressure ridges. Shackleton then announced that personal gear would be limited to two pounds per man. By example, he set aside his gold sovereigns and a gold cigarette case. Holding aloft the Bible given to him and his men by Queen Alexandra, he tore out the flyleaf she had inscribed, a page containing the 23rd Psalm, and a page from the Book of Job, and then set the Bible on the ice to be consumed by the Weddell Sea.

He knew the cost of taking too much; how weakened men in extreme conditions became slaves to sentimentality. Franklin's men had frozen to death in their traces in the Arctic, pulling sledges loaded with books, silver sets, cutlery, and a backgammon game. En route back from the South Pole, Scott and his starving men had stopped on the Beardmore Glacier to gather 30 pounds of fossil rocks, which they added to their already heavy burden and hauled to within 11 miles of a large food depot, where, unable to go farther due to weather and fatigue, they died.

This was Shackleton's point with the Bible. He was not a godless man; any Scripture so important could be written down or memorized. And he did make exceptions. He instructed Hussey to keep his 12-pound banjo, as it would be "vital mental medicine" in the trials ahead.

Hurley was to keep his most precious photographic plates. "Sir Ernest and I went over the plates together," Hurley wrote, "and as a negative was rejected, I would smash it on the ice to obviate all temptation to change my mind." About 400 plates were thus destroyed; 120 retained. Those retained were placed in double tins and hermetically sealed. Later, according to Hurley, "All my photographic gear was compulsorily abandoned, except one small pocket-camera and three spools of unexposed film."

The going was slow and painful with the men pulling and pushing the heavy lifeboats on sledges. Loaded with gear, the boats weighed more than a ton. Shoving and jostling through notches cut in the pressure ridges, they made only one mile that first day, and about one mile the next. At this rate they would never reach Paulet Island. They made camp in the center of a thick floe that to Shackleton seemed safe from pressure. This new home would soon be called Ocean Camp. Over the ensuing days the men returned to the *Endurance,* about a mile and a half away, to retrieve supplies. When they ripped open a submerged deck, cases of walnuts, sugar, flour, rice, baking soda, barley, lentils, vegetables and jam floated to the surface. The following dinner was a feast.

One night in early November, Shackleton called Wild, Worsley, and Hurley into his tent to discuss food and options. Hurley's presence at this summit showed Shackleton at his diplomatic best. He feared nothing more than dissension among his men, and knew Hurley as a powerful personality who could break or buttress

cohesiveness. Now and then he would ask his opinion to flatter him and lessen the odds that the photographer might later question his authority and sow discord among others. Shackleton also assigned Hurley to his own tent, which the Australian considered an honor. Beyond that, Shackleton recognized Hurley as a resourceful, tireless, and intelligent man whose talents he could ill afford to lose.

The options discussed that night were not appealing. Hauling the lifeboats was slow and backbreaking. It seemed wisest to stay put, to balance the benefit of drifting north against the risk of sudden breakup. Margery and James Fisher wrote that, "Shackleton's policy showed an intelligent blend of optimism and caution. He saw no point in weakening the health of his men for the sake of the problematical future. Rather, he would feed them well now, while he could, so that they would be physically capable of standing up to greater hardships if such should come."

In one entry of his journal Shackleton wrote, "Put footstep of courage into stirrup of patience."

As Nansen would say: Time to sit and watch the grass grow.

Camping on ice was at first miserable compared with living in the ship, but

Shackleton dedicated himself to making his men as comfortable as possible, to giving them a sense of security. Several crewmen retrieved the ship's wheelhouse and fashioned it into a galley and storehouse, the focal point of camp. Others erected a watchtower. Wooden planks from the ship were made into tent flooring.

A daily routine evolved around Ocean Camp, as preparations were made for the days ahead. With help from the able seamen, Chippy McNeish used what few tools and supplies existed to improve the lifeboats for rough seas. He raised the gunwhales and used lamp wick and oil colors from Marston's artist box to caulk the planks. The men's hair and beards grew long, and their faces sooty from nights huddled around the blubber stove. Rings formed around their eyes where they wore glacier goggles against the glare of sun on ice. Shackleton wore a knife on his belt and a compass around his neck. By mid-November he had devised an evacuation plan should the floe suddenly break up around them, or worse, beneath them. He read the Emergency Stations Bill to the assembled crew, then posted a copy on each tent and issued a caveat: Daily routine was one thing, complacency another. Be ready. At anytime he might surprise them with a drill.

OCEAN CAMP was the crew's home, November to December 1915. While the men drifted north on the Weddell Sea ice, Frank Hurley composed this "Antarctic Gothic" of Shackleton, far left, with Wild beside him. On sunny summer days such as this, Shackleton called the weather "unbearably hot," when the men "were afraid of getting sunstroke." Yet conditions could turn nasty in hours, and the future was always uncertain. Hurley wrote, "I shall never forget those cold, hideous nights in our tents...with the floes hammering sinister warnings a few paces away."

On November 21, the 25th day after the crew abandoned the *Endurance*, Shackleton saw her stern in the distance, slipping away. "She's going boys," he yelled. The men scrambled from their tents to watch her disappear into the deep. "I cannot write about it," noted Shackleton. It was an expected death, but a death nonetheless, the end of the young ship Hurley had called a "bride of the sea."

WHAT HAS HAPPENED TO SHACKLETON? GRAVE NEWS.

As this page goes to press there is news of the Shackleton Antarctic Expedition, but it is conflicting. One message speaks of a return to safety. A more circumstantial story tells a tale of what may be tragedy. The Aurora was to have met Shackleton and the men with him on their emergence on the Ross Sea after travelling right across the Pole from the Weddell Sea. It is said that she broke adrift after the landing party had gone ashore to provision Shackleton and bring him away. If this is so, the men cannot be reached for a whole year. 1. Sir Ernest Shackleton. 2. The Aurora. 3. Petty Officer Crean and (4) Mr. F. Wild, who were probably members of the Pole party. 5. Captain Mackintosh, of the Aurora, said to have been left stranded after the mishap. 6. The Endurance, which conveyed the Polar party to the Weddell Sea. 7. Sir Ernest in his Antarctic attire.
[Photographed by Speaight.]
1109

Nobody talked much about it. Hurley later confided in his diary, "It is beyond comprehension, even to us, that we are dwelling on a colossal ice raft, with but five feet of ice separating us from 2,000 fathoms of ocean, & drifing along under the caprices of wind & tides, to heaven knows where."

To contravene depression after the ship sank, Shackleton called for increased rations for all hands, rations not always forthcoming from Orde-Lees, the miserly storekeeper who harbored an acute fear of running out of food and starving to death. While others approached meals like hungry wolves, Orde-Lees was a veritable squirrel, always hoarding a piece of his share of bannock or pemmican which he would later pull out and nibble in front of his fellow castaways. The nicknames given to him were less than complimentary, yet he didn't seem to mind. A former physical education trainer for His Majesty's Royal Marines, he possessed tremendous strength yet a noncombative, childlike personality. He loved to climb mountains and ski, but managed to disappear or openly avoid work whenever arduous tasks needed doing. On the pack, he would walk into severe storms and not return for hours, or recklessly jump wide leads from floe to floe. His practiced obsequiousness infuriated his shipmates but didn't fool Shackleton, who often assigned Worsley to reprimand him and restrict him.

Other crewmen posed challenges as well. Gentle Jimmy James, who was one hundred times more of a scholar than a sailor, showed signs of disenchantment with the very elements of adventure that motivated the likes of Wild, Worsley, and Crean. To keep James's spirits up, Shackleton assigned him to his own tent and engaged him in nightly banter with Hurley and Hudson. The irascible Chippy McNeish could be openly pessimistic and required careful handling. Shackleton assigned Wild to watch him at all times.

The human heart contains chambers weak and strong, and Shackleton, as the analog's cardiologist, sought to make the whole beat true. He assigned tent mates with a keen regard for compatibility. He let no indiscretion blind him. Orde-Lees was in fact a meticulous storekeeper, James a good scientist, and McNeish a magical craftsman who could seemingly make anything out of nothing. Each in his way was a chamber, and the group a single heart. The challenge was not just the physical aspects of Antarctica, but the subtle dynamics of the men who exerted themselves against it. How did they behave as individuals? How did they beat as a whole? Shackleton might have remembered Browning:

Welcome each rebuff
That turns earth's smoothness rough,
Each sting that bids nor sit nor stand but go!

With each passing week they had drifted north until early December when their drift turned slowly northeast, rafting them in an arc away from the Antarctic Peninsula and Paulet Island. By mid-December higher temperatures softened the ice. Shackleton wrote that "the moment of deliverance from the icy maw of the Antarctic was at hand." But what if that deliverance was into brash ice, for example, which was too thick to row through but too thin to stand upon?

Shackleton consulted with Wild, and on December 20 he announced that they would march to the west to "reduce the distance between us and Paulet Island."

NEWS FROM THE SOUTH reaches The Daily Graphic, *March 25, 1916 (opposite). Amid war in Europe, the world learns that the* Aurora (2), *Shackleton's Ross Sea ship under the command of Aeneas Mackintosh (5), was ripped from her moorings by high winds in May 1915 and held in pack ice out of radio range until March 1916. Ten men have been stranded on Ross Island. Meanwhile, where is Shackleton (1, 7), the* Endurance (6), *and her crew, including Tom Crean (3) and Frank Wild (4)?*

∽

AFTER SCOUTING A ROUTE and celebrating Christmas a few days early, the men broke Ocean Camp and headed out. They traveled at night when the sun was low and the ice not so mushy. Progress was slow as many times they found their route blocked by open leads or pressure ridges. The heavy loads had to be relayed, and the sledge runners often froze to the ice. A lunch of stale bannock and cocoa was consumed without a word as everybody sat about, backs bent with fatigue, faces lined with sweat. A dinner consisted of nothing more than one seal steak and a cup of tea. Men sometimes plunged knee-deep into water beneath a false surface of new snow. Christmas Day came and went with no celebration and little mention of it.

On the fifth day of the march Shackleton returned from a scouting trip to find McNeish, a self-described "sea lawyer," at odds with Worsley, refusing to push a

Monday

2 FRIDAY [92—273]
Good Friday.

Last night, a night of terror & anxiety—
On a par with the night of the ship's distress.
Shortly after 8 pm when all the gear was
hauled up onto an apparently safe floe, a
bang was heard. all made from tents—
False alarm—caused by subsidence of surface—
Heavy swell running causing floe to rock
dangerously & Floe cracks in halves, separating
Caird & our tent from rest of party & passing through
Sailors tent. Spreads rapidly, & before they have time
to struggle out of bags—Holness & How fall into
the gap but are speedily rescued, Party reassembled
with difficulty.—All tents struck in case of
further disaster & all Spend rest of the dismal
dark night shivering & waiting for morning.
We are thankful the floe remained intact till daylight—Hoosh at 6 am & Await opening of ice & Start
9 am. strong E Wind & heavy swell. Wind increases
to gale during day with Snow Squalls & Ice very
dissipated. Pass through old hummocky pack—the
survival ice of the pack margin, the thinner ice being
ground into slush, Enter what appeared an
Ice free sea at 11am. Take hourly spells at
rowing—Hoisted Sail on Caird & Dudley Docker
—both doing splendidly. Sea & wind increase
& have to draw up onto an old isolated
floe & pray to God it will remain

boat-loaded sledge as the skipper had ordered. Shackleton would not have tolerated such a countermand against himself. But Worsley didn't have the skills to deflect or defuse, and the situation had escalated. Sir Ernest was left no option but to read a copy of the ship's articles, reminding the men that although the *Endurance* was gone, they still answered to her officers. Typically laconic in his diary, he wrote the next day, "Everyone working well except the carpenter; I shall never forget him in this time of strain and stress."

Onward, the going proved difficult with soft ice, impassable pressure ridges, and weakening muscles and spirits. They settled on an old floe on December 30, and again resigned themselves to the vagaries of the pack, riding on it like a louse on a whale. They called their new home Mark Time Camp. They had traveled only seven and a half miles in five days. "Our rations are just sufficient to keep us alive," wrote Shackleton, "but we all feel that we could eat twice as much as we get."

On New Year's Day, 1916, Macklin wrote, "It is beginning to be an anxious time for us, for so far there is not much sign of any opening of the floe, and the broken mushy stuff is quite un-navigable for our boats. If we cannot get away very soon our position will be a very serious one...."

Five crabeater seals and an emperor penguin were killed and brought into camp that day, a veritable bounty after so little wildlife had been seen. Returning alone on skis, Orde-Lees was surprised by a leopard seal that lunged at him from a lead between floes. An efficient skier, Orde-Lees turned and glided away. The seal gave chase, rippling over the ice like an antediluvian dragon. Orde-Lees screamed for help as the seal gained on him. It had a huge head and a large mouth filled with sinister rows of teeth, all the better to shred and eat penguins, which it no doubt took Orde-Lees to be. Wild grabbed his rifle and ran to intervene, his short legs scurrying over the ice. At one point the seal dived into a lead and tracked Orde-Lees' shadow as it swam below him, then surfaced straight ahead. Orde-Lees turned. The seal saw Wild and charged, mouth agape, head low. Wild knelt and fired, chambered another round, fired again and again until the onrushing seal dropped 30 feet away, 1,100 pounds of predator plowing into the soft snow. It was 12 feet long and required two dog teams to haul it into camp.

The weather grew wet and warm into mid-January. Rain fell in what Worsley called "a regular Scottish mist." The men's spirits ebbed. Invoked Greenstreet, "God send us open water soon or we shall all go balmy."

With rations dwindling, Shackleton ordered all dogs shot except a couple teams, a sad duty, and not accepted as the right thing to do by every man, yet objections were kept private. The ice softened beneath their feet and they moved again, this time a short distance onto a more stable floe called Patience Camp. A gale blew up from the southwest in late January and pushed the party in precisely the direc-

"LAST NIGHT, A NIGHT of tension...," begins a crewman's journal for April 10, 1916, the men's first full day at sea in three crowded lifeboats, James Caird, Dudley Docker, *and* Stancomb-Wills. *Released from Patience Camp, the 28 men rowed and sailed toward landfall, only to find their early efforts canceled by mercurial currents and winds. With few belongings, Shackleton carried pages torn from the symbolic Book of Job: "Out of whose womb came the ice? The waters are hid as with stone and the face of the deep is frozen."*

tion they wanted to go: 84 miles north in six days. Everybody was elated.

A few men made sledging forays back to Ocean Camp and found it half flooded with meltwater. Of all the materials they ferried to Patience Camp, none was more valuable than the third lifeboat, the *Stancomb-Wills*. When faced with open water, 28 men would be much safer in three boats instead of two.

Through February and into March they waited. Shackleton and Hurley played six games of poker every afternoon. Hurley noted that "at the end of ten weeks our aggregate scores were within a few points of each other. I had become the possessor of an imaginary shaving glass, several top hats, enough walking canes to equip a regiment, several sets of sleeve-links, and library of books. Moreover, I had dined, at Sir Ernest's expense, at Claridges, and had occupied a box at the opera."

Their drift continued due north, even in the face of stiff winds from that direction. By mid-March all the dogs had been shot, and the enforced waiting was terribly wearisome, adrift on what Worsley called "this white interminable prison."

On March 23, Shackleton and his men sighted Joinville Island to the west, the end of the Antarctic Peninsula. Next to Joinville would be little Paulet, some 60 miles away. Yet all that was visible in that direction was rotting ice.

Shackleton climbed a hummock with Worsely and scanned the region with binoculars. "Will you try to make for it now?" Worsley asked him.

At length Shackleton said no. He told Worsley, "I can't risk the danger of crossing ice that will be opening and closing rapidly under the influence of the tides and currents.... The boats might get crushed. We might get separated. Many things could happen. But if we keep on as we are for another hundred miles or so, we are bound to drift to open water, and then we will make for the nearest whaling station."

Paulet was out. But where would they go? Clarence Island and Elephant Island, fangs of rock at the western end of the South Shetland archipelago, lay 100 miles north. South Georgia was 800 miles to the northeast, a long shot at best; "Our chances of reaching it would be very small," Shackleton wrote. All his seafaring life he had wanted a daring open boat journey. He would soon have it.

That very next day, on the other side of Antarctica, the crippled *Aurora*, ripped from her moorings off Ross Island more than ten months before, and released from the ice only ten days ago, had proceeded far enough north to make radio contact with Australia: "Hull severely strained...jury rudder, no anchors, short of fuel."

For the first time since 1914, the world heard news of the Imperial Trans-Antarctic Expedition, and of the *Aurora* crewmen stranded on Ross Island, left to lay food depots with only meager supplies for themselves. Winter was setting in there; no relief ship would be able to reach Ross Island for another nine months, December at the earliest. And what of Shackleton? Had he crossed the continent? A flurry of articles appeared in the British press, many flushed with patriotism.

"The whole situation is obscure," reported the *Daily Telegraph*. "They are men of our blood; they are men of instinct...." Amid a horrible war that was consuming Europe, it was comforting to assume that Sir Ernest was still alive. But where?

"What is Shackleton thinking about?" asked the *Weekly Dispatch*.

"I confess that I feel the burden of responsibility sit heavily on my shoulders," Sir Ernest confided in his diary. "Loneliness is the penalty of leadership, but the man who has to make decisions is assisted greatly if he feels that there is no uncertainty in the minds of those who follow him, and that his orders will be carried out confidently and in expectation of success."

On April 7, the peaks of Clarence and Elephant Islands came into view. For nearly a month the men had felt the swell of the ocean beneath the ice, subtle at first, now, in April, unmistakable as the floes rose and fell like chest armor on a breathing beast. Shackleton prepared for every contingency. Eagerness filled the camp.

The floe they camped upon was a triangle roughly a hundred yards long on each side. It drifted away from other floes, merged back, drifted, then began to break apart. "Strike the tents and clear the boats," shouted Shackleton. The men hustled into action. The boats were pushed to the edge of the floe for quick deployment. At one point the floe split in two with a thunderous crack. As the two halves separated, men jumped from one to the other to retrieve valuable stores.

The cook served a quick lunch of seal soup and powdered milk while the men remained standing, watching the ice, the sea, and Sir Ernest. If they took to the boats too early they might be crushed by colliding floes; too late and their floe—now only 50 yards across—might crumble beneath them and toss them into the frigid sea. Shackleton's strained eyes studied it all. Finally he said, "Launch the boats."

The men sprang to action and soon the entire party was in the boats, pulling on the oars and pushing away blocks of ice. Patience Camp disappeared into chaos off the stern. They had crossed their Rubicon, the point of no return. Not that anyone wished to go back. For five and a half months they had camped on the pack and had come to detest it. How good it was to be moving again, despite the slim odds of success. Hampered by their anxiety and atrophied arms, they rowed poorly, clunking the oars together, jamming the blades into uncompromising pieces of ice.

"Stroke, stroke," called the coxswains. Slowly the oars moved in unison and the little boats made progress. The sky filled with fulmars, petrels, and terns that cried on the wing, a celebration perhaps, or a warning from creatures born into circumpolar winds. Suddenly, killer whales surfaced in every direction and circled the boats. The men heard a roar and stared in mute fascination, not at the whales, but at a riptide, what Shackleton described as a wall of "foam-clad water and tossing ice" that advanced like an ominous assailant, threatening to sink them all. ■

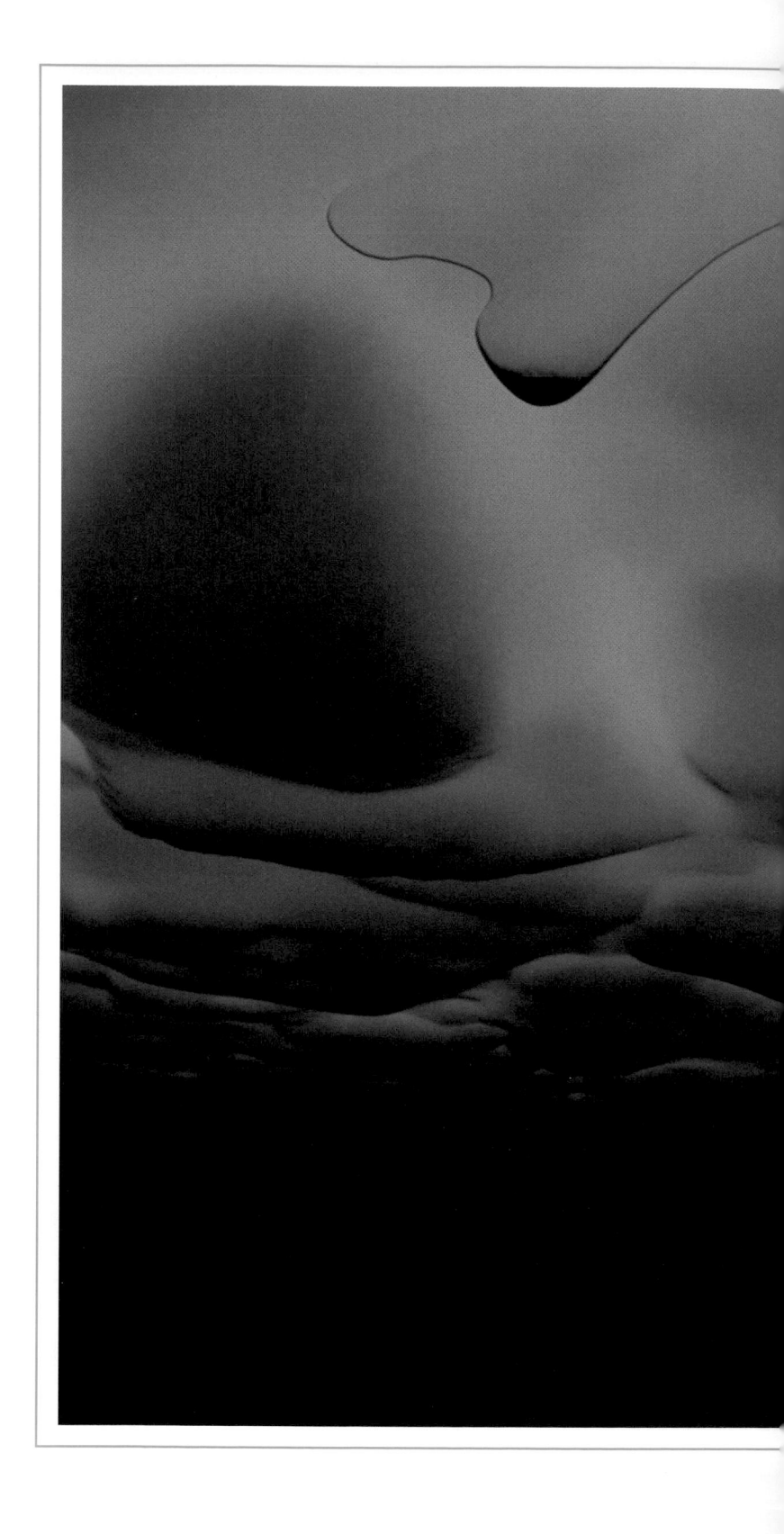

"And yet it [sea ice] makes a rare impact on our senses. In its details it has forms changing interminably, and colors playing on all shades of blue and green...."

FRIDTJOF NANSEN
GREENLAND EXPEDITION
1888

NANSEN, LIKE SHACKLETON, *witnessed sea ice in its many variations, but never from below (right) where the erosive effects of saltwater scallop ice walls into a feast of blue tones and shapes. Views like this greet seals and penguins as they search for a portal to surface for air.*

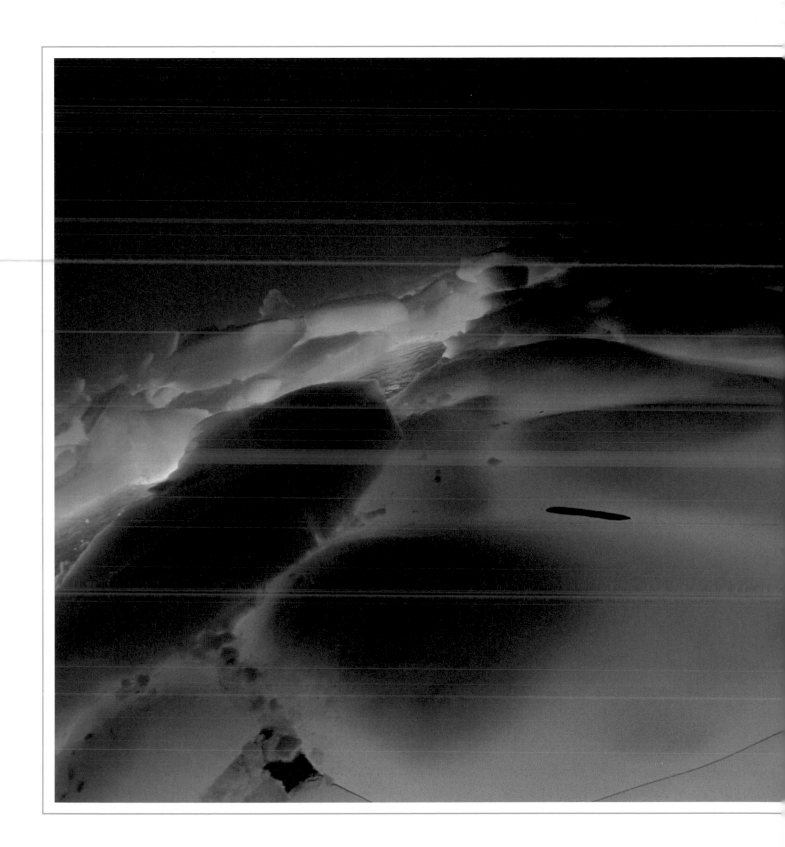

ENDURANCE *IN THE POLAR NIGHT*, *August 27, 1915, one of Hurley's most arresting photographs. He called her "the connecting link between the vast, lifeless solitude of the south and living humanity of the north.... She never looked so beautiful as when the moonlight etched her inky silhouette, transforming her into a fairyland vessel."*

A WEDDELL SEAL RESTS on a black volcanic beach on the Antarctic Peninsula. Like other species of Antarctic seals, Weddells were shot for meat by early explorers. Shackleton noted that once all their suet was gone, "we used seal blubber to fry the meat in." Southern light (opposite) creates an abstraction of a glacier.

"Seals and penguins now seemed to avoid us, and on taking stock of our provisions...I found that we had only sufficient meat to last ten days...so one biscuit had to be our midday meal."

ERNEST SHACKLETON
ENDURANCE EXPEDITION
MARCH 1916

ATOP AN ICY HUMMOCK, a crewman studies the Endurance *trapped in a white immensity, its fate, like his own, uncertain. Frank Hurley took this image with his large-format Graflex camera. "As a photographer," Orde-Lees observed of Hurley, "he excels...." To facilitate travel in the future, Hurley would abandon about 400 negatives, breaking each plate over his knee to "obviate all temptation to change my mind."*

WASH DAY COMES to Ocean Camp (above). December 1915 found variable winds pushing the pack ice toward land, away from land, and back again, seesawing the men's spirits with each change. Crewmen (opposite) pull a mate to safety after long hours working in vain to chop an open lane for the trapped Endurance.

OCTOBER 18, 1915, *Shackleton stands on the deck of the doomed* Endurance *tipped 30 degrees to port by overthrusting floes. He wrote, "Hurley...took photographs of the ship in her unusual position.... At 8 p.m. the floes opened and the* Endurance *was nearly upright again." This print was made from one of Hurley's hand-painted lantern slides.*

CHAPTER THREE

Never the Last Endeavour

"*S*troke, stroke, stroke."

The men pulled on the oars with all their might and

barely escaped the riptide, a vortex of ice and water that

nearly ended their journey before it began. "It was an unusual

and startling experience," wrote Shackleton.

He commanded the most seaworthy of the three boats, the *James*

Caird, a double-ended whaleboat, 22 feet 6 inches long,

Adélie penguins race across a floe; Endurance *crew (above) build an ice cave on Elephant Island.*

built in England to Worsley's specifications: American elm and English oak in the keel and hull, Baltic pine for planking. Worsley steered the Dudley Docker, Hudson the Stancomb-Wills, each a heavier, square-sterned cutter made in Norway of solid oak, 21 feet 9 inches long. The men rowed for another hour, until darkness began to fall, and they found an old floe rocking in the swell. They pitched camp in the twilight, ate a warm dinner from the blubber stove, and climbed into their tents, exhausted. A watchman was posted, but that night Shackleton couldn't sleep. He wrote, "Some intangible feeling of uneasiness made me leave my tent...and glance around the quiet camp. The stars between the snow flurries showed that the floe had swung round and was end on to the swell, a position exposing it to sudden strains."

As Shackleton walked across the floe, the ice cracked directly under his feet and continued on through the middle of camp. It split through a tent and dropped two men into the water. Hearing their muffled cries, Shackleton reached into the sea and with a mighty heave lifted one man to safety. It was Fireman Ernie Holness, still in his sleeping bag, wet to his waist. The other man climbed to safety seconds before the ice edges slammed together with a power that would have crushed both men.

The killer whales returned, spouting in the open lanes between floes, circling. Nobody slept the rest of that night. They gathered around the blubber stove and watched for new cracks, nursing cups of hot milk and pipes filled with wet tobacco. Holness had no dry set of clothes—nobody did—so Shackleton ordered him to walk off the chill and dry the clothes with his own body heat. Crewmates took turns walking with him to keep him cheered. It was a miserable situation, but still preferable to the doldrums of Patience Camp. "At any rate," wrote Shackleton, "we were on the move at last, and if dangers and difficulties loomed ahead we could meet and overcome them."

Daybreak came with snow squalls, poor visibility, and strong winds, while somewhere to the north, 30 or 40 miles away, Elephant and Clarence Islands seemed marginally attainable. The little boats struggled on through a nasty chop and a shifting witchery of floes pushed by the wind. Always the shepherd,

Shackleton watched the three boats and herded them together whenever they pulled too far apart. By midday they were in a large expanse of open water, and Sir Ernest ordered sails aloft.

This was the open ocean they had longed for since their internment in Ocean Camp, and now it bedeviled them. Breaking waves threw salt spray into their faces and down their necks. Everyone shivered from the cold and lack of sleep. Orde-Lees and Kerr curled onto the rolled sleeping bags below, green with seasickness. Shackleton ordered a strong ration for lunch and the boats forward into the weather until midafternoon, when the beating became too severe. They pulled into the lee of a deep blue berg and rested there, the boats tight abeam, the oars jammed into the ice to hold position.

The respite lasted only minutes. The winds freshened and soon the boats were rocking and chafing against the ice edge and each other. Swirls of stinging snow blew into the men's eyes. After the perils of the night before, Shackleton was reluctant to sleep on the ice. But given the current misery of his crew and the declining options, he had no choice.

They disembarked and handed up the stores. One boat was hauled onto the berg. A second was midway up when the ice edge collapsed and dumped Fireman Bill Stephenson into the water. His crewmates lifted him to safety, then hoisted up the third boat. After a warm meal, nearly every man fell into instant sleep, too tired to feel the pain of mild frostbite and blisters. Those who didn't sleep, prayed.

KILLER WHALES CIRCLED the three little boats en route to Elephant Island. "Shipwrecked mariners drifting in the Antarctic seas would be things not dreamed of in the killers' philosophy," Sir Ernest wrote, "and might appear on closer examination to be tasty substitutes for seal and penguin. We certainly regarded the killers with misgivings." Macklin knew them to be large dolphins, not whales, man-eaters, or an excuse for hyperbole; he found their presence both "companionable and rather comforting."

⁓

MORNING BROUGHT NO ABSOLUTION, but instead a tempest of ice. In every direction the pack was back. Where open ocean had surrounded the intrepid travelers the day before, all they could see now were horrifying floes driven by some invisible force, grinding away at their host berg, moving in a thousand directions at once. Shackleton climbed an icy promontory and scanned for open leads. For hours he stayed there, motionless, watching, his face creased with worry, while the floes chewed away at the host berg. Obviously they could not stay on the berg that night—it would never survive. Yet neither could they climb onto the hostile floes that shattered and buckled all around them.

Then suddenly, open water.

"Launch the boats," Shackleton yelled. In minutes they were at the oars, pulling madly. The pack disappeared as it had appeared, as if ordained by a mercurial god. The three boats drew alongside a single floe that night, and only Green disembarked to set up the blubber stove and make a hot dinner. The men slept fitfully in the boats and heard the percussive spouts of whales, great leviathans that sometimes surfaced under floes and lodged them aside. Would they surface under the boats as well, and upend them?

The next morning brought clear skies. Worsley pulled out his sextant and shot the disk of the sun at 10:30 and again at noon. He double-checked his damp navigational tables and ran his computations. All eyes were on him, red with bloodshot and strain; this was the first time since leaving Patience Camp he had taken their position. His figures didn't make sense, so he computed them again and came up with the same result. They were 61 miles southeast of Clarence Island, more than 20 miles farther away than when they began rowing three days earlier. So bitter was the news that some men refused to believe it.

While prevailing winds had pushed them in one direction, a strong current had pulled them in another.

Sir Ernest showed no sign of dismay. He had intended to make for Clarence Island, but when buffeted by winds, currents, and malevolent floes, had changed his destination to King George Island, toward the west end of the South Shetland archipelago, and then to Hope Bay, on the Antarctic Peninsula. Clarence Island was still the closest, yet safe landfall there might be impossible. The important thing was to get his men ashore and comfortable as soon as possible. Each single day in these boats was a greater hardship than an entire month at Patience Camp.

The *James Caird* moved briskly through the sea, and the *Dudley Docker* held her course well, but the *Stancomb-Wills* behaved more like a brick than a boat, and the other crews frequently waited upon her and escorted her.

Canvas sea anchors were deployed to hold steady into oncoming winds and swells. Shackleton would stand in the stern of the *James Caird* and guide the little fleet through one perilous ordeal after another: lanes in the floes, brash ice, rough open water, fog, wind, snow squalls beneath a diaphanous orb of moon. "It was Shackleton's style of leadership not only to be in command," wrote biographer Roland Huntford, "but to be seen in command." While the excitable Worsley always wanted to push on through the night, Shackleton said no. The boats might become separated.

Miserable night followed miserable day as they progressed northward. No more camping on the ice, no more hot meals. "We had emerged so suddenly from the pack into the open sea," wrote Shackleton, "that we had not the time to take aboard ice for melting...and without ice we could not have hot food." The men gnawed on cold seal meat, their lips cracked from salt spray and dehydration. Water everywhere yet none to drink. "Rest was not for us," wrote Shackleton.

That night, their sixth out, sea spray broke over the gunwales and froze topside on bow and stern, adding half a ton of ice to each boat. The fleet rafted together so the men could chip the ice away. "The temperature was below zero and wind

THE REELING BERG: *George Marston painted this scene that greeted them early on April 12, 1916, the third day out from Patience Camp. The night before they had hauled up the lifeboats, pitched camp, and fallen asleep, only to awaken to the sound of grinding ice. "Morning showed us we had been sleeping in a fool's paradise," James wrote. "Ice had surrounded the berg," Macklin added, "and the whole mass ...was rising and falling on enormous waves." Shackleton sat atop a hummock, straining his eyes for an opening to launch the boats. "You felt that if he led you," wrote Greenstreet, "everything was going to be all right."*

penetrated our clothes and chilled us most unbearably," observed Shackleton. He doubted if every man would make it through the night.

On the *Docker*, a tent cloth was spread topside for protection. "Never will I forget the writhing mass of humanity which tried to snatch a few moments sleep under it," wrote Macklin. "Men cursed each other, the sea, the boat, and everything cursable."

When Hurley lost his mittens, Shackleton offered him his own. Hurley declined, but Shackleton insisted. Orde-Lees wrote in his diary, "Sir Ernest was on the point of throwing them overboard rather than wear them when one of his subordinates had to go without."

Such an appraisal of altruism was interesting coming from Orde-Lees, who during this difficult time had refused to row, or when he did proved terrible at it, and whether seasick or not managed to requisition the only pair of oilskins and lie down in the bow, inert. When nobody else could sleep, he managed to snore.

In the *Stancomb-Wills*, Hudson collapsed after 72 hours straight at the tiller. The stoic Irishman, Tom Crean, spelled him.

Shackleton had to get to land. Every hour was critical. He shouted to Worsley that by nightfall they should make it to Clarence or Elephant Island. Worsley shouted back that it would be impossible, too far. Shackleton berated him, not for navigational blunders, of which Worsley was incapable, but for popping the bubble of hope Sir Ernest had floated above his blistered, chafed, and bleeding flock.

That afternoon came a southeast gale, and the horrible possibility that a following sea might push them right past land into the middle of the South Atlantic. With no chance of turning back, they would drift into oblivion.

The wind screamed in their ears.

In the *Docker*, a fatigued Worsley was 50 hours without sleep as he reefed the sails and shifted the weight of the crew to raise her seaward gunwales above the crashing waves. Still, she shipped water. Like a crazy man suddenly aware of his own mortality, Orde-Lees began to bail with incredible speed and stamina. Slowly the Docker gained buoyancy.

The *Stancomb-Wills* fared not so well, as her gunwales were the lowest of the three boats and she shipped water with alarm. Ernie Holness, one of the tough trawlerhands from the North Atlantic, buried his face and wept with fear. Young Blackboro, sitting knee deep in the freezing water, mentioned something about not being able to feel his feet.

In the *James Caird*, Shackleton distributed extra rations, yet many men were too sick with dysentery to eat.

The *Docker* cast out her sea anchor and the other two boats tied up behind, painter to stern, three in a row. Some men managed to lie down and steal precious moments of sleep, while most just sat with their backs to the weather, cursing. Marston managed to sing, his voice hoarse with fatigue. After a screaming pre-dawn blast of wind, the storm abated and a brilliant sunrise transfigured Clarence and Elephant Islands into citadels in the sea, crimson with promise, 30 miles away, precisely where Worsley's calculations said they would be.

Shackleton called out congratulations to the New Zealander who, according to Alfred Lansing, "looked away in proud embarrassment."

The radiant dawn unveiled horrors as well, boatloads of scarecrows staring at nothing if not death, the faces of forlorn men, their clothing frozen like icy body casts, their eyes red with fatigue, mouths swollen with thirst. Seawater had frozen to their beards and rendered boils on their arms and legs. Frank Wild noted that "At least half of the party were insane...not violent, simply helpless and hopeless."

Shackleton had not slept since leaving Patience Camp, yet, according to Wild, "he looked after those helpless men just as though they were babes in arms."

Back at the oars, they rowed with feeble focus, and by midafternoon were only ten miles off Elephant Island. The nearshore sea grew lumpy with tidal crosscur-rents, which Worsley described as "far more dangerous for small boats than the straight running waves of a heavy gale in open seas. The boats could never settle down, and to steer became a work of art." Every able hand rowed or bailed.

According to Shackleton, "A little later the *Dudley Docker* ran down to the *James Caird*, and Worsley shouted a suggestion that he should go ahead and search for a landing-place.... I told him he could try, but he must not lose sight of the *Caird*. Just as he left me, a heavy snow squall came down, and in the darkness the boats parted."

Shackleton hoisted a candlelit compass binnacle, but received no reply. He instructed Hussey to light matches against the white sail. Still no reply. The *Docker* was gone, swallowed in the somber night and a running cross-sea. To come so far and lose a boat distressed Sir Ernest deeply. He could only hope that Worsley's excellent seamanship and a divine hand would see the *Docker* to safety.

∾

IT WAS NOW APPARENT that they would spend another night in the rocking boats, a dismal prospect. Shackleton ordered the painter of the limping *Stancomb-Wills* to be tied to the stern of the *Caird*. All night he held the icy line as the *Wills* pitched on crests and troughs behind him, a ghost boat, its presence confirmed only rarely by white water breaking around her bow.

Half a mile away, the *Docker* broke free of a fierce riptide and tried to answer Shackleton's signal. A soundless black wave slammed into her, and she dropped

into an abyss. Macklin, Marston, Greenstreet, and Kerr pulled on the oars while Orde-Lees, refusing to row even after Worsley screamed at him, bailed with help from Alf Cheetham. It was blind madness, fighting rascal waves in the inky night.

Worsley ordered sails aloft, and with uncanny skill righted the boat into the teeth of the wind and held her there until conditions calmed. His chin dropped to his chest as he succumbed to exhaustion after five and a half days at the helm. Macklin offered to relieve him and Worsley agreed. But he had sat for so long in one position, he was unable to stand up straight. Marston and McLeod lifted him and set him into a soft spot like a bag of brittle bones, where he immediately fell asleep.

Lansing reported that "during that time almost everyone had come to look upon Worsley in a new light. In the past he had been thought of as excitable and wild—even irresponsible. But all that was changed now. In these past days he had exhibited almost phenomenal ability, both as a navigator and in the demanding skill of handling a small boat. There wasn't another man in the party even comparable with him, and he had assumed an entirely new stature because of it."

As Worsley slumbered, the others worried. Would they fetch up on a reef? Had they blown far out to sea, past Elephant Island into the dreaded Drake Passage, the roughest water in the world? Macklin and Greenstreet tried to read a compass by

matchlight in the darkness, but the wind snuffed their efforts. All hope seemed lost just as dawn leaked across the eastern sky and the men stared in awe at palisades of ice and rock only one mile away—Elephant Island. No sooner did they allow themselves a little elation than a fierce katabatic wind shrieked down the cliffs, seeming to shred the ocean and depress sea level. Suddenly a six-foot displacement wave was racing toward them. Greenstreet manned the helm, but in his debilitated state he had no idea what to do. McLeod tried to wake Worsley, shaking him again and again, but the New Zealander lay still as a corpse. McLeod kicked him until Worsley lifted his groggy head to see the imminent threat. "For God's sake," he yelled, "get her around. Get her away from it. Hoist the sail!"

The canvas began to fill as the first wave hit and washed over the stern. The second wave half filled the boat. All hands bailed madly, the waves subsided, and the *Docker* slowly rebounded. The men gasped for breath, their energy spent, as they moved along the treacherous coast a dozen miles, looking for safe landfall, convinced that the *Stancomb-Wills* and *James Caird* had foundered and they alone had survived. "Poor bighters," Greenstreet confided to Macklin, "They're gone."

Then the bobbing masts of the two other boats hove into view off Cape Valentine, the northeast tip of the island, and three rasping cheers were raised.

Seeing the *Docker*, said Shackleton, "took a great load off my mind."

Minutes later the boats passed through a gauntlet of shoals and onto a beach of shingle rocks. It was, to the best of Shackleton's knowledge, the first time anyone had landed on Elephant Island, so named for the large elephant seals that inhabited it. He decided that the honor of first ashore, "should belong to the youngest member of the expedition, so I told young Blackboro to jump over. He seemed to be in a state almost of coma and in order to avoid delay I helped him, perhaps a little too roughly, over the side of the boat. He promptly sat down in the surf and did not move. Then I suddenly realized what I had forgotten, that both his feet were frost-bitten badly." Shackleton felt terrible, and two crewmen carried Blackboro up the beach to a dry place. One by one, like shipwrecked apparitions, the men staggered ashore.

James noted that most were in a "semi-hysterical condition and hardly knew whether to laugh or to cry. We did not know, until it was released, what a strain the last few days had been. We took childish joy in looking at the black rocks and picking up stones...."

Some men filled their pockets, as if each pebble were a nugget of gold. Others fell face first into rivulets of fresh water and drank. Some just sat and mumbled, semidelirious. Never had such a godforsaken place seemed so much like paradise.

∾

UNIDENTIFIED CREWMEN, likely McNeish, Marston, and McLeod, outfit the James Caird *for its journey from Elephant Island to South Georgia. McNeish proposed that the decking be covered with sewn canvas that would shed rough seas like water off a duck's back.*

IT WAS APRIL 15, 1916, the first time they had stood on solid ground in 497 days, since leaving South Georgia on December 5, 1914. For one interminable week they had fought the sea to get here; for five and half months before that they had camped on the pack ice, and for ten months before that they had lived in their dying ship, at the mercy of the ice.

Within no time Green had the stove bubbling, and the men poured hot milk into the cold caves of their aching bodies. Shackleton stood with them and said little, his dirty hair framing a pallid face, his eyes red from salt and worry, his voice a whisper from all the shouting. If he had slept at all in the last six days, nobody could remember it. Spokes of sunlight spilled onto the beach, and like the hot milk, seemed to transfuse each man, pumping blood back into his long-numb limbs. How grand to be alive, even marginally, to stand on the lovely naked Earth and share an emerging sense of security. Blackboro received special attention from doctors Macklin and McIlroy, as did Louis Rickinson, first engineer, who appeared to have suffered a mild heart attack.

Hunters dispatched four seals, and soon the men were eating thick steaks, round after round in a languorous meal that lasted until midafternoon. They set up camp and slept, wrote James, "as we had never slept before, absolute dreamless sleep, oblivious of wet sleeping bags, lulled by the croaking of penguins."

The next morning Shackleton confirmed a disturbing rumor: They would have to move. He had inspected the beach and found "well-marked terraces" on the headwall cliffs immediately behind camp, clear evidence that a gale, "such as we might expect to experience at any time," would flood the camp and send the boats to sea in horrible conditions.

He sent Wild to reconnoiter for a better campsite, and late that morning the indefatigable Yorkshireman set out in the *Dudley Docker* with a crew of four.

On the *Discovery* expedition of 1901-04, Wild had belonged to the Guarantee Party, a team of sledgers so tough and determined they seemed capable of going anywhere under any conditions. Shackleton had unshakable faith in this small blue-eyed man whom he said was "unmoved by cold or fatigue...a tower of strength."

Night fell with no sign of the *Docker*. The men retired to their tents, and no sooner had they fallen asleep when the watchman heard a shout from the sea Frank Wild. He brought the *Docker* through the breakers and onto the beach. Indeed, he told Shackleton, Cape Valentine was a dangerous place, and the alternatives were slim. But there was a spot seven miles to the west along the island's north shore, a spit with abundant penguins and seals, and a glacier for fresh water.

The next morning everyone awoke early, broke camp, and launched the boats. They made good progress until a katabatic wind roared down the island's 2,000-foot cliffs and screamed into them. It lasted only minutes, but presaged a full gale that soon had every oarsman bending under terrible strain. So quixotic was the storm that one minute it threatened to sweep the *Docker* beyond the horizon, and the next to dash her onto a reef, carried there by large swells. "Lay back! Lay back!" Worsley yelled as the *Docker* teetered on the edge of destruction. "Pull harder than you can pull." By a narrow margin the *Docker* slipped past danger to safely join the other two boats, already pulled ashore.

Shackleton described the new site as "by no means an ideal camping-ground; it was rough, bleak, and inhospitable—just an acre or two of rock and shingle, with the sea foaming around it.... But some of the larger rocks provided a measure of shelter from the wind, and as we clustered around the blubber-stove, with the acrid smoke blowing into our faces, we were quite a cheerful company...another stage of our homeward journey had been accomplished and we could afford to forget for an hour the problems of the future." Ever the optimist, he added, "Life was not so bad. We ate our evening meal while the snow drifted down from the surface of the glacier, and our chilled bodies grew warm."

Others were less sanguine. "Elephant Island," said one, "had flattered only to deceive." The joy that had infused them at Cape Valentine was missing here. This new place, soon to be called Cape Wild, seemed a small improvement for such a risky move. But winter would soon be upon them, and Shackleton knew sea conditions would only worsen. Every improvement, no matter how slight, would factor into their survival.

All that night the wind roared down icy battlements of cliff and glacier with such intensity that the *Dudley Docker*, the heaviest boat, spun around on the rocky beach. A bag of old blankets was picked up and blown out to sea. The tents flapped as if they might rip apart. Unable to sleep, the men struck the tents and threw their bags on the ground where grit and snow covered them.

Morning offered no reprieve, yet Shackleton rousted everyone to kill penguins that would soon migrate north and be in short supply. The wind threatened to knock the men off their feet. Orde-Lees described "driving snow" that "rushed down one's throat." Butchering the penguins was brutal work; only by thrusting bare hands into the warm bodies while skinning them did the men prevent frostbite.

The next day, April 20, Shackleton announced that he and five others would take the *James Caird* and go for help as soon as possible, before winter's ice and storms imprisoned them. Their destination would not be the Falklands, 540 miles to the north, but South Georgia, 800 miles to the northeast, across angry seas but also in the direction of prevailing winds and currents, a blind bargain at best, yet many men volunteered to go.

Among them were Wild and Worsley. "I told Wild at once that he would have to stay behind," Shackleton recorded in his diary. "I relied upon him to hold the party together while I was away...." If Shackleton did not return by spring, Wild was to take the men and "make his way to Deception Island," 400 miles to the west-southwest, a remote port-of-call where whalers might find them. Shackleton decided that, "Worsley I would take with me, for I had a very high opinion of his accuracy and quickness as a navigator, and especially in the snapping and working out of positions in difficult circumstances."

Tom Crean begged to go and after long discussions with Wild, Shackleton accepted him. His pluck would be valuable in the face of daunting odds. Chippy McNeish and John Vincent were selected because they would fare poorly and erode morale on Elephant Island, yet would be resourceful and strong on the *Caird*. McNeish could improvise almost anything from nothing, and Vincent had been an ox at the oars in the journey from Patience Camp. The final choice, Seaman Tim

WHILE LAUNCHING the Caird on April 24, 1916 (opposite), a sudden swell nearly capsized her. Shackleton wrote, "Vincent and the carpenter, who were on deck, were thrown into the water. This was really bad luck, for the two men would have small chance of drying their clothes after we had got under way. Hurley...secured a picture of the upset, and I firmly believe that he would have liked the two unfortunate men to remain in the water until he could get a 'snap' at close quarters."

McCarthy, another ox, was unlike Vincent in that he had an ebullient spirit.

Having made his decision, Shackleton said he "walked through the blizzard with Worsley and Wild to examine the *James Caird*." Somehow the boat "appeared to have shrunk in some mysterious way when I viewed her in the light of our new undertaking. Standing beside her, we glanced at the fringe of storm-swept, tumultuous sea that formed our path. Clearly our voyage would be a big adventure."

Shackleton asked McNeish to make every improvement he could to the *Caird*, and for three days the carpenter worked his magic. He removed the mainmast from the *Docker* and bolted it into the keel, then fashioned a small mizzenmast to complement the jib and standing lug. With help from Marston and McLeod, he used old sledge runners and box lids to frame and deck the forecastle end, then covered the whole affair with watertight canvas. Meanwhile, Greenstreet and Bakewell sewed 1,500 pounds of shale rocks into canvas bags for ballast.

All this time the blizzard raged, with winds gusting up to 120 knots. On the evening of April 23, as the storm began to sigh, Shackleton ordered Orde-Lees and Vincent to melt ice from the glacier and fill water casks for the *Caird*. Late into the night Shackleton and Wild discussed every contingency, and when talk no longer sufficed, Sir Ernest wrote a letter into his log, addressed to Wild, asking the faithful man to watch after his interests. "I have every confidence in you and always have had," he ended the letter. "May God prosper your work and your life. You can convey my love to my people and say I tried my best. Yours sincerely, E. H. Shackleton."

The next morning, Easter Monday, April 24, the sun emerged for the first time in more than a week and Worsley was able to correct his one chronometer, the only one of 24 chronometers that remained from the beginning of the expedition.

The *Caird* was positioned offshore while the men ferried the ballast and supplies to her in the *Wills*. "As each boatload came alongside," wrote Worsley, "the contents were passed to us, with a running fire of jokes, chaff, and good wishes from dear pals whom we were leaving behind. Many were solicitous that I might not overeat myself, and that my behaviour on reaching civilization should be above reproach. As for Crean, they said things that ought to have made him blush; but what would make him blush would make a butcher's dog drop its bone."

Handshakes around, then the *James Caird* released its painter and hoisted sail.

"The men who were staying behind made a pathetic little group on the beach," observed Shackleton, "with the grim heights of the island behind them and the sea seething at their feet, but they waved to us and gave us their hearty cheers."

Ever mindful of the moment, Frank Hurley had his pocket Kodak and snapped his fellow castaways bidding farewell, their arms high in a final tribute to the one man who could accomplish a task so preposterous as that just beginning, crossing the south Atlantic in early winter in a boat not much bigger than a bathtub. "We watched them until they were out of sight," wrote Orde-Lees, "which was not long, for such a tiny boat was soon lost to sight on the great heaving ocean; as she dipped into the trough of each wave, she disappeared completely, sail and all."

Hussey remembered Shackleton's favorite quote from Browning: "Ah, that a man's reach should exceed his grasp, or what's heaven for?"

∽

THEY STEERED NORTH to catch the westerlies and to skirt the most immediate of many dangers: ice. Avoiding it in daylight would be one thing, at night another. One shard through the hull could sink them. They took to the oars to navigate a belt of loose pack and bergs, cleared it before nightfall, then hoisted the jib and lugsail on the mainmast, and the gaff sail on the mizzen, and made good progress in open sea. By daybreak the next morning all six men were cold and miserable, and Elephant Island was 45 miles off their starboard stern.

By noon a strong northerly was in their faces, the waves cresting at 20 feet, and all hands save Worsley and McCarthy were seasick.

Hunched in the cockpit, impervious to the odds against him, salt spray running off his neck and chin, Shackleton's entire being seemed coiled for this moment, all his years distilled into a single absurd challenge. His once boyish face, so full of promise, now looked ancient and drawn, his eyes burning with fatigue and resolve. He never questioned the appropriateness of it all; there was simply no alternative.

As Worsley wrote of the men marooned on Elephant Island, "We knew that a disaster to us would in all likelihood be a fatal one to them. One night, between the drunken lurches of the boat, Shackleton said to me, 'Skipper, if anything happens to me while those fellows are waiting for me, I shall feel like a murderer!'"

As the second day ended, everything in the *Caird* was wet. Waves drenched the canvas decking every three to four minutes. On the third day, as if to underscore their jeopardy, they sighted pieces of wooden wreckage on a passing swell, what Shackleton guessed to be the remains of a ship that had foundered off Cape Horn.

The clouds parted a fraction, and Worsley pulled out his sextant. Positioning himself spread eagle across the deck, elbows against the thwarts and legs held by Vincent and McCarthy—lest a wave wash him overboard—he snapped the sun as the boat pitched up to the open horizon. "Stop," he would yell at the critical moment. Crouched below, Shackleton would read the chronometer and check the almanac and logarithm charts, careful as he turned the wet and fragile pages. The result: 128 miles from Elephant Island, right where Worsley had guessed, feeling his dead reckoning a little "wide of the mark." They had traveled north more than 2° latitude. Free of the ice zone, they now turned northeast toward South Georgia, more than 600 hundred miles away.

Though the others had great faith in his navigational abilities, Worsley knew as Shackleton did, that the slightest error now would magnify over distance with disastrous results.

The seas climbed into mountainous swells, great rolling cordilleras pushed by winds that blew unimpeded around the world. "The sub-Antarctic Ocean lived up to its evil reputation," wrote Shackleton. "Deep seemed the valleys when we lay between the reeling seas. High were the hills when we perched momentarily on the tops of giant combers. Nearly always there were gales. So small was our boat and great were the seas that often our sail flapped idly in the calm between the crests of two waves. Then we would climb the next slope and catch the full fury of the gale. We had our moments of laughter—rare, it is true, but hearty enough. Even when cracked lips and swollen mouths checked the outward and visible signs of amusement we could see a joke of the primitive kind."

The three Irishmen—Shackleton, Crean, and McCarthy—engaged in running volleys of hardly decipherable badinage. "As they turned in," wrote Worsley when he spelled Shackleton at the helm, "a kind of wordless rumbling, muttering, growling noise could be heard issuing from the dark & gloomy lair in the bows, sometimes directed at one another, sometimes at things in general, & sometimes at nothing at all. At times they were so full of quaint conceits & Crean's remarks were so Irish that I ran the risk of explosion by suppressed laughter."

"Go to sleep Crean & don't be clucking like an old hen," Sir Ernest would say.

"Boss," Crean would respond as he climbed into his wet reindeer bag, the hairs shedding everywhere, even into his mouth, "I can't eat those reindeer hairs. I'll have an inside on me like a billygoat's neck. Let's give them to the Skipper and

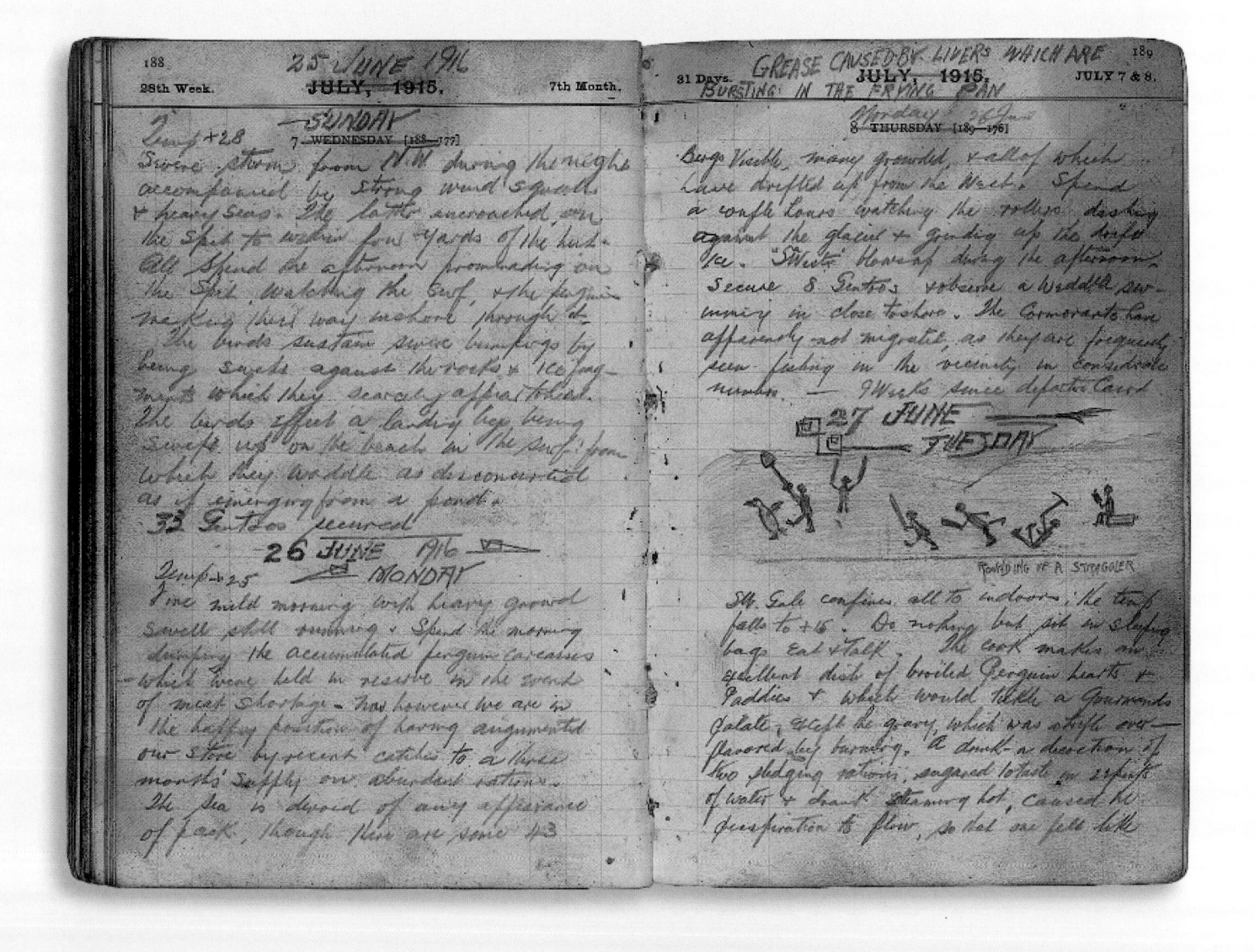

THE ANTARCTIC CHALLENGE

McCarthy. They never know what they're eatin'."

They cooked two hot meals per day on the primus stove, which they jammed between their feet so it wouldn't pitch overboard. To keep spirits and body temperatures up, Shackleton let any man eat as much as he could.

"There was no means of exercise," wrote Worsley, "unless one counts crawling like an infant. We crept at the end of our watch straight into our sleeping bags, or rather those just vacated by the other watch, for if we tried to get into our own they were sometimes frozen.... The routine was: three men in sleeping bags deluding themselves that they were sleeping, and three men 'on deck'; one man steering for an hour, while the other two, when not pumping, bailing, or handling sails, were sitting in our 'saloon' (the biggest part of the boat, where we had all the grub)."

A silver-gray fish-scale sky merged with the sea. The ceaseless roar of the wind deafened them to everything but the creak of timbers and the sloshing of water running up and down the bilges. In the endless cycles of day and night, trough and swell, wet and cold, April turned to May and the little boat pushed on, some days making good progress, and other days, battling into the wind with her sails trimmed and sea anchor deployed, making no progress at all.

Several times sea spume caked the *Caird's* topsides with ice, once up to a foot thick, and threatened to capsize the little boat, ponderous in the swells. Quickly the men went to work with ax and knife, cutting notches for their hands and knees, then chipping off heavy slabs of ice like exfoliating granite. The job required enormous strength and caution, as beneath the ice stretched the thin but vital layer of canvas protection. One careless slip and a man would be gone forever. Two sleeping bags became so rotten and heavy with ice that they were tossed overboard.

Shackleton watched the men carefully and ordered hot drinks whenever one seemed in danger of hypothermia or depression, symptoms of the arduous journey, what he called "supreme strife."

Navigating at night proved especially problematic, as Worsley would "feel" the strength and direction of the wind, and read the compass by match light or candle, and estimate by dead reckoning, what he whimsically called "a merry jest of guesswork." Once or twice a week he noted that "the sun smiled a sudden wintry flicker, through storm-torn clouds. If ready for it, and smart, I caught it."

By early May, John Vincent, the former ox, was so physically and mentally debilitated that according to Shackleton he "ceased to be an active member of the crew." McNeish, the oldest among them, also seemed listless at times, and though

FRANK WILD, SHACKLETON'S second-in-command, possessed the quiet strength and stamina to hold together the marooned party on Elephant Island. Macklin wrote that he "exercised a wonderful control without...outward sign of authority." Hurley's diary from June 1916 (opposite) depicts hunting penguins for food.

he never complained or joined in any banter, he sailed and bailed with unflagging heart. Crean seemed impervious to any discomfort, while Worsley, ever the boy from Akaroa, reveled in the adventure. He described young McCarthy as "the most irrepressible optimist I've ever met.... [Once when] I relieved him at the helm, seas pouring down our necks, [a wave] came right over us & I felt like swearing but just kept it back & he informed me with a cheerful grin, 'It's a foine day, sorr'."

On May 2, the eighth day out, the odds for success worsened when the painter, burdened by ice, snapped free and the sea anchor was lost. Sea spume froze to the men's clothes, creating an icy armor that abraded and seared their skin, already tender from saltwater exposure and mild frostbite. Every movement, no matter how slight, now became painful. Compounding his own discomfort, Shackleton suffered another bout of sciatica, a nerve disorder of the lower back and thighs that had plagued him in Ocean Camp.

That same day, at midnight, as Shackleton took the helm from Worsley during a gale, his tired eyes caught the white margin of a clearing horizon. He called to his mates that the weather was finally improving, then heard an ominous roar and realized his mistake. The white line was the crest of a monster wave, perhaps 60 feet high, bearing down on them. "For God's sake," he yelled, "hold on, it's got us."

The *Caird* slid into a broad valley, a disturbing split-second stillness that magnified their dread, then sky became sea and everything went dark. Gripping the tiller, Shackleton fought for control as, in his own words, "We felt our boat lifted and flung forward like a cork in a breaking surf...a seething chaos of tortured water; but somehow the boat lived through it, half full of water, sagging to the dead weight and shuddering under the blow."

They bailed for an hour afterward, and Sir Ernest noted that in 26 years at sea he had never encountered such a widow-maker wave. He looked at Worsley with shock, then his face filled with resoluteness, and an old New Zealand school song came to mind: "Never for me the lowered banner, never the last endeavour."

∽

THAT SAME DAY on Elephant Island, some 400 miles to the west-southwest, the sun came out for the first time since the *Caird* had left. Twenty-two bedraggled men stood in its light and drank its warmth like ambrosia. During the next two days everything was set out to dry: sleeping bags, clothes, boots, and tents.

On the suggestion of Marston and Greenstreet, the boats had been inverted, set side by side on a perimeter wall of rocks, and covered with canvas. In this new shelter—not exactly a hotel but better than a tent—the interiors of the boats became a loft wherein men could sleep above and below, packed together like sardines. Fierce winds blasted grit and snow through a thousand tiny holes, but after an equal number of improvements the shelter became tolerable.

Whatever the chore—capturing penguins, collecting ice for water, patching the shelter—each man would glance now and then toward the sea, to "scour the skyline daily," as Hurley wrote, "in the expectancy of a mast or plume of smoke."

Some estimated that Sir Ernest would return as early as mid-May; some said early June, others late June. Yet everyone banked on the same assumption: that the Boss would make it to South Georgia, reach a whaling station, and mount a rescue. To think otherwise was out of the question.

As a topic of discussion second after the return of Sir Ernest, sugar won hands down. Devonshire dumplings with cream, marmalade, blackberry and apple tarts, syrup pudding: The marooned men could have none of it so they discussed all of it, engaging in lengthy debates and voting with parliamentary seriousness as to which dessert would be most appropriate after which occasion. In the end all

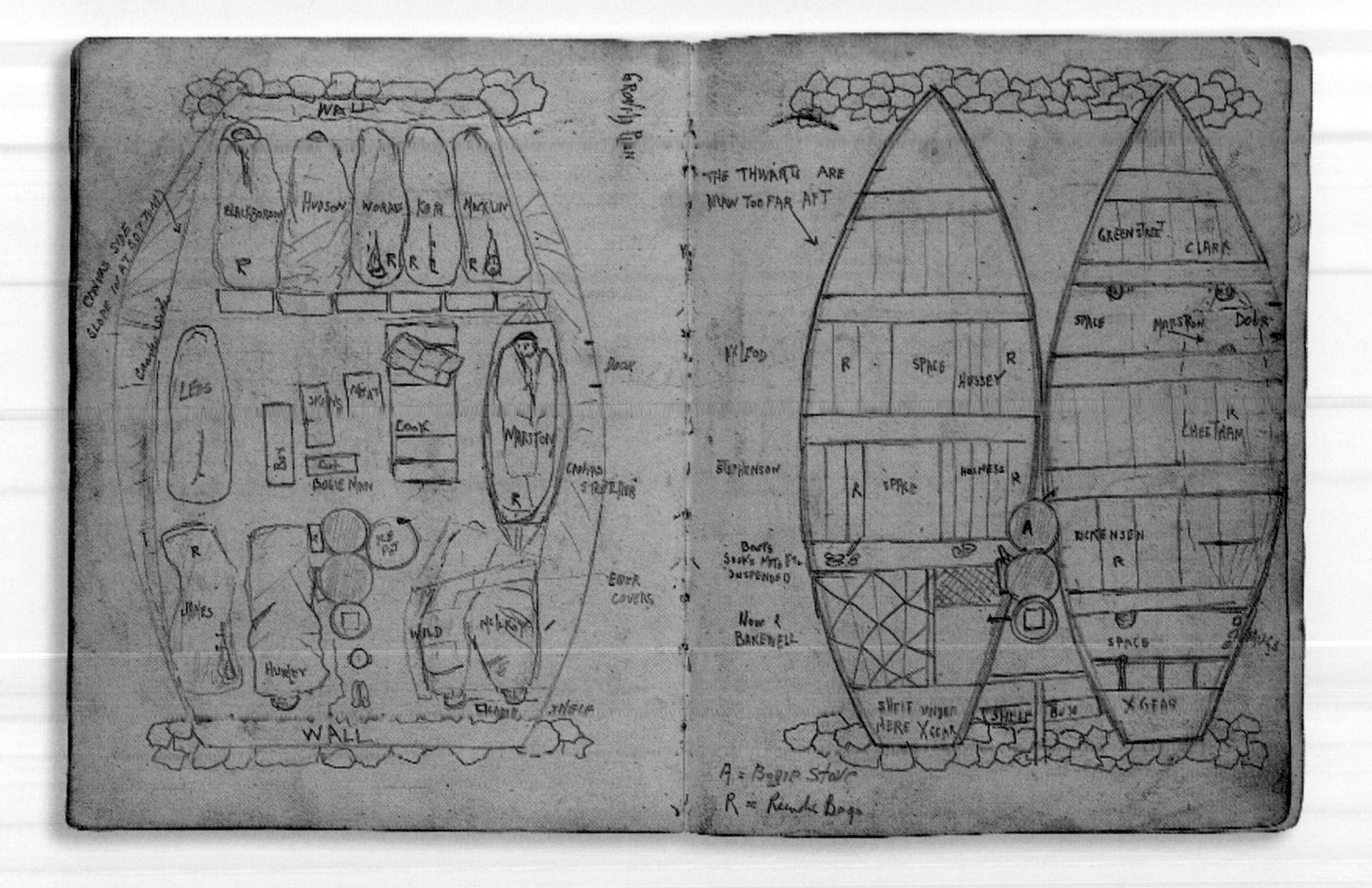

agreed that dessert should be eaten first. Orde-Lees wrote, "We want to be fed with a large wooden spoon and, like the Korean babies, be patted on the stomach with the back of the spoon so as to get a little more than would otherwise be the case. In short, we want to be overfed, grossly overfed, yes, very grossly overfed on nothing but porridge and sugar, black currant and apple pudding and cream, cake, milk, eggs, jam, honey and bread and butter till we burst, and we'll shoot the man who offers us meat. We don't want to see or hear of more meat as long as we live."

Hurley described an "epidemic of snoring. It was almost impossible to hear one's own snores above those of the others. Nevertheless there was one who easily outdid all and earned the title of 'the Snorer.' His consistent efforts outrivaled those of a wandering minstrel with a trombone. He survived all efforts—and there were many and varied—at suppression. Wild laid a cord through eyelets past each man's bunk, and attached one end to the Snorer's foot. When anyone was awakened, he hauled on the rope, with the result that up went the leg and down went the snores. But at the end of the week the Snorer grew accustomed to these interruptions and took no notice of the leg-pulling."

The levity, though clever, provided only punctuation to long weeks of boredom and misery, usually with the men packed together under the boats, waiting out wet and gloomy weather. "Everyone spent the day rotting in their bags with blubber and tobacco smoke," wrote Greenstreet, "so passes another goddam rotten day."

The invalids received the greatest attention from Macklin and McIlroy. Rickinson seemed to have recovered from his heart attack, but boils on his wrists left him disabled. Kerr had a tooth pulled without the aid of anesthesia. Wordie suffered from an infected hand. A large abscess confined Hudson to his sleeping bag, and bad feet confined Greenstreet to his. But poor young Blackboro concerned McIlroy the most. While the frostbitten toes on his right foot improved, those on his left turned gangrenous. McIlroy did his best to save them, but by the middle of June, with no relief in sight, the decision was made to amputate the toes.

To vaporize the chloroform, the only anesthetic they had, Hurley stoked the blubber stove with penguin skins until the shelter reached a sweltering 80°F. Macklin then uncorked the chloroform, soaked some surgical gauze, and placed it over Blackboro's face. The young Welshman slipped into unconsciousness on the makeshift operating table, and Wild handed McIlroy a scalpel and a pair of forceps sterilized in boiling water in a hoosh pot. One by one the toes, blackened and dead, clattered into a metal pot below, and in less than an hour the surgery was done. When Blackboro awoke he smiled and asked for a cigarette, and McIlroy rolled him one with a page torn from the *Encyclopedia Britannica*.

Macklin observed that during the surgery, while Hudson turned away, unable to watch, Wild observed every detail and never flinched.

As Shackleton knew he would, Wild treated the men with equality and humanity. He allowed them to debate and blow off steam now and then, but brooked no edge of pessimism. He kept them occupied with small chores and encouraged evening sing-alongs and storytelling. While seals were sometimes plentiful, he refused to stock large larders of meat that would imply a lack of faith in Shackleton's imminent return. "Lash up and stow boys," he would say each morning, "the Boss may come today."

But June turned to July, and July to August; ice, snow, and wind descended with the long nights of winter, and no mast appeared on the horizon.

ON THE *JAMES CAIRD*, six tired, anxious men peered through heavy fog, hungry for land. Cross swells tossed the boat on lumpy seas as the fog cleared and a squall cut across the port stern, bringing rain and gray skies burdened with clouds. Earlier that morning, May 8, the 14th day out, they had seen kelp, "a glad sight of the proximity of land," wrote Shackleton. An increasing number of albatrosses winged by, and most encouraging the men saw two shags, heavy-bodied diving birds that, said Worsley, guaranteed that the *Caird* was "within 15 miles of land."

In the two seeks since leaving Elephant Island, Worsley had shot the sun only four times, two of those he described as "mere snaps or guesses" in poor weather. The rest of the navigation had been dead reckoning and intuition. The monster wave of six days before had soaked everything, and two days ago the last cask of fresh water was found brackish and undrinkable. Shackleton rationed fresh water down to half a pint per man a day and noted, "our thirst grew to a burning pain."

Half an hour after noon, McCarthy gave an eager cry, "Land ho."

"There, right ahead," recorded Worsley, "through a rift in the flying scud, our glad but salt-blurred eyes saw a towering black crag, with a lacework of snow around its flanks. One glimpse and it was gone again. We looked at each other with cheerful, foolish grins. The thoughts uppermost were: 'We've done it. We'll get a drink tonight. In a week we'll get them off Elephant Island.'"

Worsley guessed they were off Cape Demidov, near King Haakon Bay. His navigation had been perfect. But a cross-sea was sweeping them to starboard along the island's uninhabited south side, not the north where the Norwegian whaling stations were, and the weather appeared to be deteriorating.

"We stood in towards the shore to look for a landing-place," wrote Shackleton, "and presently we could see the green tussock grass on the ledges above the surf-beaten rocks. Ahead of us and to the south, blind rollers showed the presence of uncharted reefs along the coast. Here and there the hungry rocks were close to the surface, and over them the great waves broke, swirling viciously and spouting 30 and 40 feet into the air. The rocky coast appeared to descend sheer to the sea. Our need for water and for rest was well-nigh desperate, but to have attempted a landing at that time would have been suicidal."

Against Worsley's wishes, Shackleton ordered that they stand off for the night. He knew that to come so far and be so close was a blessing and a curse. As a boy he had read books about shipwrecks and whaleback combers that splintered boats and turned triumph into tragedy in seconds. A grail can become a grave when desperate men fetch up too hard on the very shore they seek. In mountaineering, most climbers perish on the way down, not the way up, lulled by their accomplishment into carelessness. And those new contraptions, airplanes, flown by barons and barnstormers with great derring-do, the real trick wasn't aeronautics in blue skies, it was landing in nasty weather.

Yet this time Shackleton might have quietly cursed his patience, as that night the wind stiffened to a force 10 gale, a storm more severe than anything they'd yet encountered. They passed the hours with frayed nerves, and all the next day battled against wind and sea, finally gaining the lee of one shore only to be windward of another. Worsley did his best with tiller and sails, and saved their lives more than once, all while malevolent waves threatened to rip the little boat apart, and the men pumped and bailed. Worsley described the *Caird* hitting waves "like striking a stone wall with such force that the bow planks opened and lines of water spurted in from every seam, as she halted, trembling, and then leaped forward again."

One man steered, three pumped, one bailed with a hoosh pot, and the last stood ready to relieve any man who collapsed. "As we looked at the hellish rock-bound coast, with its roaring breakers," noted Worsley, "we wondered, impersonally, at which spot our end was to come." In the thick of the fight he lamented on their bad luck with this bloody gale, that they should lose now and be dashed against the rocks when "no one would ever know we had got so far."

As night fell, Shackleton noted that "The chance of surviving...seemed small. I think most of us had a feeling that the end was near." But in the darkness, "as the boat was in the yeasty backwash from the seas flung from this iron-bound coast...just when things looked their worst, they changed for the best. I have marveled often at the thin line that divides success from failure and the sudden turn that leads from apparently certain disaster to comparative safety. The wind suddenly shifted, and we were free once more to make an offing. Almost as soon as the

THE VENERATED SEXTANT used on the Endurance *and later on the* James Caird *by Frank Worsley (above) was not altogether familiar to him as it belonged to Hubert Hudson, the expedition navigator. After hiking over South Georgia, Worsley drew a memory map (opposite) of their route from King Haakon Bay, at far left and center, to Stromness, at far right and center, which he mistakenly marked Husvik.*

gale eased, the pin that locked the mast to the thwart fell out. It must have been on the point of doing this throughout the hurricane, and if it had gone nothing could have saved us; the mast would have snapped like a carrot."

After another night in the boat, their thirst now excruciating, the new day dawned windless but with a strong cross-sea. They steered the *Caird* toward King Haakon Bay, past reefs and through beds of kelp, as a new gale freshened. They had to tack for four hours to gain the entrance to the bay, then run before the wind toward a small cove. So narrow was the cove's entrance that they took to the oars to row through the rocky portal. One final stroke and a swell lifted the *Caird* onto a steep boulder beach and gentle landfall. It was late in the afternoon of May 10, 1916. Shackleton probably had little idea that he and the others had just accomplished one of the most outrageous boat journeys in the annals of nautical history.

Shackleton jumped out and held the bow as three others disembarked, stiff from the 16-day ordeal. They were too weak to haul the heavy boat up onto the beach.

While the others held the painter—what was left of it—Shackleton climbed a cliff to tie off a secure line. "A slip on the wet rocks twenty feet up nearly closed my part of the story just at the moment when we were achieving safety," he wrote. "A jagged piece of rock held me and at the same time bruised me sorely. However, I made fast the line, and in a few minutes we were all safe on the beach, with the boat floating in the surging water just off the shore."

LADY SHACKLETON LEARNS WITH JOY THAT HER HUSBAND IS SAFE.

Lady Shackleton and two of her children walking through the Park yesterday.

Then hearing the music of a creek at their feet, the men dropped to their knees and lapped up the water with steady gulps that, according to Shackleton, "put new life into us."

"At this time," wrote Worsley, "the boat's stern swung against the rocks, unshipping the rudder and carrying away the lanyard that held it, so that in the darkness it was lost."

Shackleton added that it was "a serious loss." A boat without a rudder was hardly a boat at all.

With a last measure of energy the men unloaded the *James Caird*, and carried their gear up the beach. In time, after rest and food and more fresh water, they managed to secure the boat safely up the beach. For the next four days they convalesced and slept in a cave and feasted on albatross chicks. "We did not enjoy attacking these birds," wrote Shackleton, "but our hunger knew no law. They tasted so very good and assisted our recuperation to such an extent that each time we killed one of them we felt a little less remorseful."

One night Shackleton shouted, "Look out, boys, look out," as he gripped Worsley's shoulder and awakened from a nightmare about the monster wave. Another night, while sleeping too close to the fire, Worsley burned the bottom of his bag and the heels of his socks, thinking in his dreams that the strange sensation was mild frostbite.

The next day, according to Shackleton, "a strange thing happened. The rudder, with all the broad Atlantic to sail in and the coasts of two continents to search for a resting place, came bobbing back into our cove...surely a remarkable salvage."

Fine weather allowed the men to dry their gear and make repairs. Shackleton, Worsley, and Crean reconnoitered from the hills above. With the mountains, glaciers, and coast of South Georgia in full view, they decided that to sail around the island more than 130 miles to Stromness, the nearest whaling station, would tax the boat and crew too much. From the head of King Haakon Bay, however, an overland hike to Stromness would be somewhat more than 20 miles, traveling east. Shackleton wrote that he "planned to climb to the pass and then be guided by the configuration of the country...," admitting that, "No man had ever penetrated a mile from the coast of South Georgia at any point, and the whalers regarded the country as inaccessible." Every map of South Georgia showed its interior as blank, terra incognita, the nothing that to Shackleton was everything.

On the morning of May 15, they sailed to the head of King Haakon Bay and came ashore on a low profile sandy beach near hundreds of elephant seals. They overturned the *Caird* for shelter, dined that night on seal steaks, and called their new home Peggotty Camp, the name of a boat hut in a Dickens story.

Shackleton was eager to begin the trek while the moon was full, and before winter worsened, but poor weather pinned them down for three days. McNeish managed to build a small sledge, and by removing boat screws from the *Caird* and driving them through the hikers' boots, he created crampons for glacier travel.

At 2 a.m. on the morning of May 19, with a clearing sky and the platinum light of a full moon glinting off glacier and peak, Shackleton knew no time would be better. After a breakfast of hoosh, he and Worsley and Crean shook hands with their mates and at 3:10 a.m. began their hike into the unknown, climbing onto snow and ice, taking with them the fragile hopes of McCarthy, McNeish, and Vincent left at Peggotty Camp, and 22 others on Elephant Island. Three men who had achieved one miracle at sea now intended to achieve another in the mountains. They carried no tent or sleeping bags, only a primus stove with fuel for six hot meals, plus three days of sledging rations and biscuits, a box of matches, a hoosh pot, two compasses, 90 feet of rope, and the carpenter's adze as an ice ax. Each man kept his food in a sock, and Worsley wore his chronometer around his neck. In the end Sir Ernest decided to leave the sledge in Peggotty Camp. They would travel light and fast, alpine style, and reach Stromness either quickly or not at all.

Shackleton set a brisk pace, and by 6 a.m. they had climbed 3,000 feet in ankle-deep snow to a broad saddle, the last couple hours roped together as diffuse moonlight shone through disorienting fog. Morning dawned and the fog lifted, and Shackleton could see their route ahead, long glacial undulations broken by a precipitous rampart of ice and rock. Downslope he sighted what appeared to be a large frozen lake along their route, its far shore still obscured by fog. They descended and soon found themselves in a sorcery of crevasses. "A little later the fog lifted completely," Shackleton wrote, "and then we saw that our lake stretched to the horizon, and realized suddenly that we were looking down upon the open sea on the east side of the island."

FROM BENEATH HER fashionable hat, Lady Shackleton (opposite), with daughter Cecily, 9, and son Edward, 4, surrendered a demure smile for The Daily Mirror *on June 2, 1916, after learning that her husband was safe in the Falkland Islands and attempting to rescue 22 crewmen stranded on Elephant Island. "The news was indeed a wonderful & glad surprise," she wrote to a friend, "& I can hardly realize it yet...."*

The shimmering light had deceived them, and their crude chart was inaccurate. They had crossed a narrow neck of the island from King Haakon Bay to Possession Bay. To regain their route they had to climb back to where they had been, losing precious time and energy.

The sun rolled skyward in rare good weather, but soon the three men were exhausted from its glare and their own exertion. Salt-encrusted clothing chafed their raw legs; deep fatigue seared their lungs. At midmorning they stopped and melted snow in the hoosh pot, stirred in a couple bricks of sledging rations, ate them scalding, and were on the march in half an hour.

By noon they reached a transverse series of five rocky spires, each spire separated from another by fins of ice, apparent passes to Stromness. Shackleton chose the nearest and southernmost pass and began the long ascent. Near the top, the slope became dangerously steep, and he cut steps in the ice with the adze.

"Anxiously but hopefully I cut the last few steps and stood upon the razorback," wrote Shackleton, "while the other men held the rope and waited for my news. The outlook was disappointing. I looked down a sheer precipice to a chaos of crumpled ice 1,500 feet below. There was no way down for us."

Except the way they had come.

They retraced their steps, ate another quick hot meal, and ascended the second pass, where again the other side proved breathtaking and daunting, with no possible descent, just suicide cliffs of ice and rock.

Down again, they stepped where they had before. With the afternoon dying and sea fog threatening to engulf them from behind, the threesome climbed the third pass, steeper and more arduous than the first two, and beheld again an icy panorama of terrible tranquility, and no safe route down.

THE SUN WINKED AWAY and long shadows coalesced into a deep blue chill. The temperature began to plummet and the men inched back downslope, careful with every footfall. En route to the fourth and final pass they encountered an ice chasm that Worsley described as a "gloomy gulf about 200 feet deep and 2,000 feet long...what impressed us most was the fearful force of the elements that had cut and chiselled it out, while we knew that, if a gale came on, we could live but an hour or so on these wind-threshed summits and uplands."

Gingerly inching by, they zigzagged upslope and arrived at the fourth and final pass as night fell and tendrils of fog licked at them from behind, threatening to spill over the rocky ramparts and engulf everything. They were nearly 5,000 feet above sea level, straddling the icy fin as they squinted into the Stygian vault below, a long steep slope of ice and snow that swept into mist and darkness.

"We'll try it," Shackleton said. He cut steps with the adze while the others followed. The going was slow, dangerous; they had to get down before they froze to death.

After half an hour of painfully slow progress, the icy slope turned to snow, indicating, wrote Shackleton, that the gradient was less severe." He stopped, lost in thought, as Worsley and Crean stood silently at his side.

"We'll slide," he said to them. "Are you game?"

The two men couldn't believe it, but in an instant they grasped its crazy genius. There could be no turning back, they had to get warm fast, and the fog was on their heels, spilling over the ramparts just a couple hundred feet above.

They coiled the rope and sat on it, three in a row, each with his legs wrapped around the man in front, Shackleton first, then Worsley and Crean. Then they let go. "The speed was terrific...," wrote Worsley, "quite suddenly I felt a glow, and knew that I was grinning! I was actually enjoying it." All three men yelled from the wild exhilaration and sheer velocity that squeezed the screams out of them. They might have pitched into a crevasse or hit a rock, but the slope leveled out and they landed in a snowbank. Picking themselves up, their trousers even more tattered than before, they laughed and shook hands and looked upslope with smug satisfaction. In roughly one minute they had descended more than one thousand feet.

Typically laconic in his diary, Shackleton wrote only that "we slid in the fashion of youthful days."

After a quick hot dinner they continued east up a gentle gradient. The moon rose at 8 p.m., its light dancing magically off rock, snow, and sea, making what Shackleton called "a silver pathway for our feet." Around midnight they reached a broad upland and the slope began to fall away, taking them down. They passed a great nunatak to their left, skirted a transverse range to their right, and sighted a bay ahead that looked like Stromness. "I suppose our desires were giving wings to our fancies," Shackleton observed, "for we pointed out joyfully various landmarks revealed by the now vagrant light of the moon. Our high hopes were soon shattered.

THEIR FACES FRESHLY washed and shaved, from left, Crean, Shackleton, and Worsley stand for a rare photograph likely taken on May 20, 1916, the day they arrived in Stromness whaling station after trekking for 36 hours over South Georgia. They wear clothes loaned to them by the Norwegians, but expressions distinctly their own. "When I look back on those days," wrote Shackleton, "I have no doubt that Providence guided us...."

Crevasses warned us that we were on another glacier, and soon we looked down almost to the seaward edge of the great riven ice mass." It was Fortuna Bay, not Stromness. Another ruse. Shackleton wrote that, "The disappointment was severe. Back we turned and tramped up the glacier again, not directly retracing our steps but working a tangent to the southeast. We were very tired."

At 5 a.m., a full 26 hours after leaving Peggotty Camp, they found shelter from a cold breeze behind a rock, sat down, and wrapped their arms around each other for warmth. Worsley and Crean immediately fell asleep, folded together like straw men. Of all the times they could have died in the last 16 months, on the pack ice or in the boats, in a gale or during a glissade, how ironic that they go like this, deceptively warm in the unconscious, intending to nap yet never awakening as they freeze to death. Shackleton knew this. He let them sleep for ten minutes, then awakened them and told them they'd been out for half an hour.

Climbing on, their knees bent with stiffness, they reached a wind-raked gap and beheld the unmistakable shores of Husvik Harbor and Stromness Bay 3,000 feet below. Their hearts pounded from excitement as much as exertion. "Boss," said Worsley, "it looks too good to be true."

A little farther on they stopped for breakfast, and while Worsley and Crean lit the primus stove, Shackleton climbed a slope and thought he heard the sound of a steam whistle. Hurrying back he told the others, and together they watched the chronometer. If indeed it had been a whistle, it would sound again at seven o'clock to call the whalers to work. "Right to the minute the steam whistle came to us," noted Shackleton, "borne clearly on the wind across the intervening miles of rock and snow. Never had any of us heard sweeter music."

They abandoned the primus stove, now empty of fuel, and trudged down through deep snow that fell away into a steep ice face above a cliff. Belayed by rope by the other two, Shackleton cut steps with the adze and his heels, one careful pitch at a time, slow going and dangerous as a belay is valuable only when the belayer is securely anchored, which Worsley and Crean were not. Had Shackleton slipped he would have pulled them all to injury if not death.

After several strenuous hours, they reached the far beach of Fortuna Bay and found gunshot carcasses of seals. Shackleton ruefully observed, "Here was the first evidence of the proximity of man whose work...is so often one of destruction."

While crossing the last headland, Crean fell to his waist through thin ice on a small lake, what they had assumed was a plateau. Moving delicately over the ice, they reached the opposite ridge and peered down at the commerce of Stromness Bay, ships at anchor, miniature men moving about, busy on the wharf and flensing plan. The three weary travelers shook hands for a final time and followed a stream down a deep-cut green ravine.

They had not crossed Antarctica; they had not even set foot on the continent. Their ship was lost, and Sir Ernest Shackleton would never achieve the South Pole. Yet something much greater had been accomplished, and each of them knew it. Despite their heavy feet sloshing through the ankle-deep stream, they moved with a lightness beyond their fatigue.

The stream ended in a 25-foot waterfall, flanked on both sides by cliffs. With no hesitation and little discussion, they secured the rope to a boulder and lowered themselves sputtering and coughing down through the frigid, surging water. They left the rope behind and continued on, their route now level and easy.

A few hundred yards from the whaling station, they suddenly took stock of their appearance, thinking women might be present. Worsley produced three safety pins that they used to hitch up their tattered trousers. Then into the station they walked at 3 p.m. on May 20, 1916, after hiking for 36 hours.

Two boys saw them first, and ran away. An old man saw them next, and hurried out of their path. The interior of South Georgia was a place nobody walked into, let alone out of, and these three beings looked frightful, their hair long and matted, faces bearded and black from blubber smoke, eyes red, clothes like rags. They walked with steady deliberation past several buildings and onto the wharf where the station foreman, Matthias Andersen, stared in disbelief.

In English Shackleton asked for the manager, Capt. Anton Andersen.

Captain Andersen was no longer there, replied the foreman. Thoralf Sørlle had taken his place.

Very well, Shackleton nodded. He knew Sørlle from when the *Endurance* had called in at Stromness 17 months before.

Andersen had never met Shackleton, but like every Norwegian on South Georgia he knew about him and the *Endurance*, and assumed all hands had been lost at sea. He led the three strangers to Sørlle's house, trailed by curious onlookers.

Andersen entered the house and told the manager, "There are three funny-looking men outside, who say they have come over the island and they know you. I have left them outside."

Sørlle, a stolid Norwegian, appeared at the door and said to the three, "Well?"

The man in the middle stepped forward and quietly asked, "Don't you know me?"

"I know your voice," Sørlle replied, a little uncertain.

"My name is Shackleton."

The disbelief was unanimous, and at least one old whaler who witnessed the exchange turned away and wept tears of joy. ■

> *"A* great cross-sea was running, and the wind simply shrieked as it tore the tops of the waves and converted the whole seascape into a haze of driving spray."

ERNEST SHACKLETON
SOUTH
Published 1919

AFTER SIGHTING South Georgia (right) on May 8, 1916, Shackleton, Worsley, Vincent, McNeish, McCarthy, and Crean, dehydrated and tired, maneuvered the James Caird *through a full gale. On May 10, they landed in a cove off King Haakon Bay, where they fell to their knees to drink from a stream.*

ON APRIL 15, 1916, after 497 days on ice and sea, the men land at Cape Valentine on Elephant Island. Frank Hurley snapped this image with his Kodak and later touched it up by brushing in a glacier in the background. "Our strength was...exhausted and it was heavy work....," Shackleton wrote. "We had to wade in the icy water to lift the gear from the boats."

HIGH WINDS ALOFT (above) portend bad weather. Shackleton called them "willy waws," fierce katabatic winds that would sweep down glaciers and batter the men on Elephant Island. Hurley composed an image of ice and rock (opposite) in an Elephant Island cave he found "adorned with a magnificence of icicles."

"In one heavy gale, sheets of ice
a quarter-inch thick and a foot square
were hurled about, making it
dangerous to venture out."

FRANK WORSLEY
ENDURANCE EXPEDITION
APRIL 1916

ON THEIR MAY 1916 moonlight hike over South Georgia, Shackleton, Crean, and Worsley used "a huge dome-shaped rock for a guide." This modern aerial photograph, taken in February, summer's end, shows the rock on the far left horizon. The snowy slope they glissaded lies at right, outside the picture.

FRANK WORSLEY
ENDURANCE EXPEDITION
MAY 1916

"We cleared the
threatening area of
crevasses and icefalls
and steadily
ascended
a long, sloping
upland....."

WHALES DOMINATE a flensing plan on South
Georgia (above). Having decimated whale populations in northern waters, whalers came south in
the early 1900s. Shackleton considered the enterprise a "gold mine." King penguins and southern
elephant seals (opposite) crowd the same South
Georgia beaches to breed and molt.

"To rest unperturbed...to hear
the music of the surf, the swirl of
the ice-blocks, the croak of the
penguins; to dream with hope
of the future...."

FRANK HURLEY
ENDURANCE EXPEDITION
APRIL 1916

ON APRIL 24, 1916, the James Caird departs Elephant Island for South Georgia 800 miles across the storm-torn South Scotia Sea as 22 men wave in hopeful farewell. Hurley captured this image using his vest pocket Kodak. He later manipulated it and called it "The Rescue." Of Shackleton Hurley wrote, "His unconquerable spirit inspired his team and made them invincible."

CHAPTER FOUR

The Best of the Brave

"Come in, come in," Sørlle said, extending hearty handshakes

to the three dirty men. Shackleton hesitated. "I'm afraid we smell."

Sørlle chuckled and reminded him that this was a whaling station.

"Tell me," Shackleton asked as he entered the house,

"when was the war over?"

"The war is not over," Sørlle replied. "Millions are being killed.

Europe is mad. The world is mad." He elaborated.

A storm rages over the Antarctic coast (opposite). The continent never ceased to beckon Shackleton (above).

How horrible and strangely futuristic it all sounded, the tear gas, submarines, aerial dogfights, and Zeppelin attacks. The carnage at Ypres and Gallipoli. For a blissful few hours, it was forgotten as the three men basked in Norwegian hospitality, eating sugars and starches, smoking dry tobacco, taking hot baths. Shackleton described how "we shed our rags and scrubbed ourselves luxuriously." Sitting in soft furniture in a warm home, each man felt a thousand muscles relax.

Shackleton told of his 25 castaways, and Sørlle arranged for a whaling vessel, the *Samson*, to retrieve the men in King Haakon Bay the following day. He and Shackleton then made plans to rescue the others on Elephant Island.

That night a storm kicked up and winds pelted the windows with driving snow. Tucked into soft beds in Sørlle's home, Shackleton described how he and Crean "were so comfortable that we were unable to sleep."

Worsley bunked on board the *Samson* for an early departure to King Haakon Bay. Listening to the gale and thinking of the rocky ramparts of South Georgia, he wrote, "had we been crossing that night, nothing could have saved us."

The next day the *Samson* arrived in King Haakon Bay, and Worsley went ashore in a small whaler. McNeish, Vincent, and McCarthy emerged from under the *James Caird*, relieved to be rescued yet disappointed that none of their own party had come for them.

"What do you mean?" asked Worsley.

"We thought the Boss or one of the others would have come...," said McCarthy.

"What's the matter with you?" Worsley said. "I'm here."

The three men gaped at him, dumbfounded. Bathed, shaved, and in a new change of clothes, Worsley was unrecognizable to them. They quickly gathered their meager possessions and boarded the *Samson*, while Worsley had the presence of mind to load the *James Caird*.

Back at Stromness, the Norwegians unloaded the *Caird* as if it were an icon. Worsley described how they "would not let us put a hand to her, and every man on the place claimed the honour of helping to haul her up to the wharf."

Word had spread around South Georgia, and that night Norwegian whalers gathered in Stromness to meet the men who had done the impossible. Worsley described it: "We went into a large, low room, full of captains, mates, and sailors, and hazy with tobacco smoke. Three or four white-haired veterans of the sea came forward; one spoke in Norse, and the manager translated. He said he had been at sea over 40 years, that he knew this stormy Southern Ocean intimately, from South Georgia to Cape Horn, from Elephant Island to the South Orkneys, and that never had he heard of such a wonderful feat of daring seamanship as bringing the 22-foot open boat from Elephant Island to South Georgia, and then to crown it, tramping across the ice and snow and rocky heights of the interior, and that he felt it an honour to meet and shake hands with Sir Ernest and his comrades." Then one by one the Norwegians "came forward and solemnly shook hands with us in turn."

It was the finest tribute Shackleton could have asked for, the ceremonial off-loading of the *James Caird,* and now this fraternity of the sea, bonded by stories that required no embellishment. For a brief moment he could enjoy it without outside complications, without the debts and details he knew would plague him at home. He learned that during the gale of May 9, which had held them off South Georgia in the *James Caird* and nearly killed them, a 500-ton steamer was lost not far away. Another tragedy also occurred then, one closer to Shackleton's heart: Two of his men disappeared in a storm on Ross Island. It would be months, however, before he knew of this.

He would have liked to cable Emily of his safe return, and hear about his children, but South Georgia had no wireless or cablehead. News would have to wait.

 ~

DIRECT PASSAGE BACK HOME from South Georgia was arranged for McNeish, McCarthy, and Vincent. On May 23, only three days after arriving in Stromness, Shackleton, Worsley, and Crean departed for Elephant Island on a large steam whaler called the *Southern Sky.*

Sixty miles from Cape Wild, thick ice and rough seas and a shortage of coal turned them back. Heartbroken, Shackleton retreated to the Falkland Islands to cable England of his safe return and the plight of the men on Elephant Island.

"Safe Arrival of Sir Ernest Shackleton at Falkland Islands," reported London's *Daily Chronicle* on June 1, 1916, a welcome diversion to the 102nd day of the Battle of Verdun. The news crackled through England and Western Europe; even Berlin reported the remarkable story. While Lady Emily said little in public, Kathleen Scott, the widow of Robert Falcon Scott, a flamboyant sculptress and constant critic of Sir Ernest, proclaimed,"Shackleton or no Shackleton, I think it one of the most wonderful adventures I ever read of, magnificent."

If Shackleton had felt among friends on South Georgia, he did not feel so in the Falklands, where the people of Port Stanley, according to one source, seemed to care not one scrap about him and his ongoing ordeal. Not a single flag was flown.... And why? An old kelper remarked, "'E ought ter 'ave been at the war long ago instead of messing about on icebergs."

Shackleton found no ship available for the Elephant Island rescue, and a stream of cables to the Admiralty brought only frustration. Finally a steam trawler was loaned to him from the Uruguayan fisheries research institute, and on June 17 she sailed south in nasty weather. At dawn on the third day, winter solstice in the

Antarctic, the peaks of Elephant Island hove into view only 20 miles distant. Pack ice blocked the way. They tried ramming through but pulled back quickly, aware that the pack could tighten around them and crush the ship. Shackleton wrote that "we approached close enough to fire a gun, in the hope that they would hear the sound...yet so accustomed were they to the noise made by the calving of the adjacent glacier, that either they did not hear or the sound passed unnoticed."

Again fuel ran low, the engine began to sputter and knock, and Shackleton retreated to the Falklands. Worsley wrote, "It was a dreadful experience to get so short a distance of our marooned shipmates and then fail to reach them."

As luck would have it, a Royal Navy light cruiser was in Port Stanley, idle between patrols for German war vessels. With her captain willing to go south, Shackleton cabled the Admiralty for permission to use her. "Your telegram not approved," came the terse reply.

Thus rebuffed, Shackleton, Worsley, and Crean sailed to Punta Arenas, in southern Chile on the Straits of Magellan, where they outfitted a 70-foot auxiliary-powered wooden schooner with a polyglot crew. Slammed by gales under sail most of the way, they met a belt of pack ice and entered it one hundred miles from Cape Wild. The auxiliary diesel engine quit, sea ice thrashed the hull, and once again they had to turn back. Worsley wrote that during all this time Sir Ernest "passed through hell...the lines on his face became furrows and his hair showed streaks of grey."

Finding no solace among adults, on August 1, Shackleton penned a letter to his nine-year-old daughter, Cecily, telling her of his anxiety, and how little his marooned men had to eat. "I will have many stories...when I return, but I cannot write them. I just hate writing letters but...I am thinking of you my little daughter."

On Elephant Island, August 2 marked the hundredth day since the departure of the James Caird. "Monotony of existence extreme," wrote James. Hurley bemoaned "sitting like an invalid in one's sleeping bag and rereading the same few books."

By mid-August the sugar and methylated spirits were gone, and the tobacco nearly so. Penguins and seals made infrequent visits. In their dark and dismal hut, dirt, penguin feathers, and reindeer hairs (from the sleeping bags) settled like cement into the stone floor and found their way into every pot of hoosh. One crewman noted, "It is at least comforting to feel that we can become no filthier."

Brash ice often filled the bays off Cape Wild, and a tight pack occasionally stretched to the horizon. Macklin confided that many times a day the men would climb the hill and look for a relief ship. "Some of the party," he recorded, "have quite given up all hope of her coming...." On August 19, Orde-Lees wrote, "There is no good in deceiving ourselves any longer."

"The last pipeful of genuine leaf was smoked by Wild on 23 August," Hurley wrote, "but long before this we had been stifled with fumes of penguin feathers,

rope-yarn, dried meat, and other pipe-fuel, with which the confined smokers had endeavoured to satisfy their cravings. One evening I was awakened from a doze by the familiar smell of an Australian bush-fire…. I beheld McLeod, one of the sailors, contentedly puffing out volumes of heavy smoke. He had borrowed all the pipes and boiled them down in a tin to extract nicotine juice. McLeod then discovered, that by steeping the grass lining of his padded footwear in the concoction, and drying it before the fire, an aromatic 'tobacco' of exceptional flavour resulted. The unusual 'perfume' awakened everyone and in a twinkling one and all were busy slitting open their boots to remove the padding. That we had worn those padded boots continuously for seven long months was an unconsidered trifle."

"Lash up and stow boys," Wild would say with unflagging determination, "the Boss may come today."

On August 30, 1916, the 137th day on Elephant Island, the men gathered in the hut for midday hoosh and boiled seal backbone. Marston lingered atop the bluff to complete some sketches and was soon heard running down the trail, in a hurry, the others assumed, so as not to miss lunch. He burst into the hut and said to Wild, "There's a boat. Shall we light a fire?"

For an instant they all looked at him as if he had cried wolf. Then they exploded in what Hussey described as a rugby scrum. "We were so excited...by the news that some of us tore down the canvas walls to...see the great sight."

Some neglected to put on boots; some grabbed whatever was available, big or small. Gentle Jimmy James the physicist got his boots on the wrong feet.

They ran to the beach.

Such an odd ship, only a mile away; it was not a wooden polar ice-breaker, as they expected, nor did it come from the northeast, the direction of South Georgia. It came from the west—a mysterious iron-plated tug flying a Chilean naval ensign. Wild quickly jammed an ice pick into a tin of petrol, soaked some coats and socks, and set them ablaze as a signal. Hurley helped with the fire, then pulled out his pocket Kodak, having saved a final few frames for this dreamed-of moment.

Macklin hoisted his tattered Burberry jacket up an extended oar, the flagpole, but the running gear jammed at half mast. Seeing this from the Chilean ship, the *Yelcho*, Shackleton's heart sank. The loss of even one man would be a terrible blow.

"As I manoeuveured the *Yelcho* between bergs and hidden reefs," Worsley recorded that "Shackleton peered through his binoculars with painful anxiety. I heard his strained tones as he counted the figures that were coming out from under the upturned boat. 'Two-five-seven'—and then an exultant shout, 'They're all there, Skipper. They're all safe!' His face lit up and years seemed to fall off his age."

The ship stopped. A boat was lowered. The men on shore recognized a stout, square-shouldered figure climb down into the boat. It could be only one man: the Boss. Crean was with him. They cheered and waved and laughed with giddy delight.

"I felt jolly near blubbering," Wild wrote, "& could not speak for several minutes."

Still unable to walk, Blackboro received assistance from Orde-Lees and Hudson to watch the memorable event.

Shackleton stood in the bow, and as the boat approached within hailing distance he asked if everyone was all right.

"All are well," came the reply.

Shackleton sidled ashore and offered firm handshakes around, then ordered an instant departure before winds and ice trapped them. In less than an hour they were aboard the *Yelcho* steaming north, the peaks of Elephant Island fading off the stern. Said one crewman, "We intend to keep August 30 as a festival for the rest of our lives."

FORGOTTEN HEROES: The seven survivors of the Ross Sea shore party (above), unaware of the sinking of the Endurance, worked long and hard—and suffered greatly—to lay food depots for Shackleton's polar party that never came. Seated in the center is Ernest Joyce, who assumed command after the breakdown (and later disappearance) of Aeneas Mackintosh. To Joyce's left, with his hat on his knee, is Ernest Wild, Frank Wild's younger brother.

Shackleton concluded that it was "largely due to Wild, and to his energy, initiative, and resource that the whole party kept cheerful all along...the demons of depression could find no foothold when he was around...."

Of his ordeal on the *James Caird* and hiking over South Georgia, Shackleton deferred the role of raconteur to Worsley and Crean. It was luxury just to listen.

"On Sunday September 3, the *Yelcho* chugged into Punta Arenas, bedecked with flags," wrote Hurley. "On nearing the jetty we were deafened by the tooting of whistles & cheering motor craft, which was taken up by the vast gathering on the piers & water-fronts." The reception was no accident; ever the impresario, Shackleton had disembarked at Rio Seco and telephoned authorities in Punta Arenas of his arrival. Still wearing their rancid Elephant Island clothes and scraggly beards, as Shackleton preferred, his men disembarked and walked through the crowd, smothered by well-wishers and the oompah-pah of a brass band.

Shackleton boarded a mail boat and fired off a letter to Emily. "My Darling, I have done it. Damn the Admiralty. I wonder who is to blame for their attitude to me. Not a life lost and we have been through Hell.... Give my love and kisses to the children. Your tired 'Mickey.'"

꙳

THE SOUTH AMERICAN RECEPTIONS would be his warmest, in Punta Arenas, Valparaiso, Buenos Aires, and Montevideo. Yes, the expedition had failed, yet Shackleton played to Latin sentiments and alchemized that failure into success. While his men sailed for home, he made arrangements to rescue the Ross Sea half of his Imperial Trans-Antarctic Expedition, the ten men stranded when the *Aurora* was ripped from shore in a storm 16 months ago.

Though Shackleton understood the tragedy of war, he did not yet grasp the scope and scale of this war. It consumed everyone. Three million killed already, and the tide was just beginning to turn against Germany. The casualty list was now called the Roll of Honour, with distinction won in dying, not in surviving. The safe return of the *Endurance* crew did indeed brighten the darkness, if only for a moment. Yet compared to the carnage of Europe, Shackleton's persistent efforts to save a few marooned men in Antarctica smacked of frivolousness.

Amid this global crisis, the governments of England, Australia, and New Zealand nevertheless had prepared the *Aurora* to rescue the men off Ross Island, and put John King Davis in command. Davis told Shackleton that when every man in uniform was a hero, people were a little impatient with polar explorers in general.

Shackleton got the point, and to his credit he agreed to join the *Aurora* as a supernumerary officer under Davis. He was bankrupt, after all, and joined the rescue of the Ross Sea party only through the generosity of others. He reached New Zealand in early December 1916.

On January 9, 1917, the eight-year anniversary of his farthest south on the polar plateau, Shackleton stood on deck and watched the profile of Mount Erebus hove into view. The *Aurora* approached Ross Island and the next day pulled up to Cape Royds. Shackleton went ashore to visit his old hut from the *Nimrod* days, and found a note saying the men were at Cape Evans. As the *Aurora* proceeded, figures were seen traveling across sea ice toward the ship. Davis tactfully remained aboard as Shackleton went to greet them. Roland Huntford noted that Shackleton was profoundly shocked by what he saw. The men were in a worse state than those who had been on Elephant Island. Scurvy, starvation, fatigue, depression, injuries, snow blindness, the Ross Sea party had suffered it all; and they had cut their own rations short to lay food depots for Shackleton's party that would never be used. They had sledged 199 days, a remarkable feat compared to 93 days for Scott and Wilson and Shackleton in 1902-03; to 120 days for Shackleton and his polar party in 1908-09; and to 150 days for Scott and his doomed men in 1911-12.

SIR ERNEST POSED for a final portrait with his family on the Quest *(above). After three hectic months of preparation, the* Quest *departed St. Katharine's Dock under London's Tower Bridge (opposite) on September 17, 1921. A 125-ton straight-stemmed wooden sealer with an awkward square-rigged mainmast and a cracked boiler, she would plod like a bucket and require repairs at every port.*

Aboard, Davis noted their behavior: "Their great physical suffering went deeper than their appearance. Their speech was jerky, at times semi-hysterical.... Their eyes had a strained harassed look—and no wonder! These events had rendered these hapless individuals as unlike ordinary human beings as any I have ever met. The Antarctic had given them the full treatment."

Shackleton wrote only that the men showed traces of the ordeal through which they had passed. Three of them had died: Aeneas Mackintosh, Victor Hayward, and the Rev. Arnold Patrick Spencer-Smith, whose heart failed within sight of Ross Island on March 9, 1916, the day when the icebound *Endurance* crew, on the other side of Antarctica, first felt the exciting swell of the sea in Patience Camp. Two months later, on May 8, the same day that Shackleton and his men first sighted South Georgia from the *James Caird,* Mackintosh and Hayward disappeared in a storm while trying to cross thin sea ice from Hut Point to Cape

Evans. As if angels could not work in two places at once, the greatest tragedies on the Ross Sea side of Antarctica coincided with the greatest elations on the Weddell Sea side.

Although the Ross Sea survivors had searched for Mackintosh and Hayward and found no trace, Shackleton mounted his own search. His compulsion for leadership would brook nothing less, yet he found only the same emptiness, inside and out. They erected a cross, beneath which Shackleton placed a copper tube containing the names of the three men, and lines from Browning's poem "Prospice:"

For sudden the worst turns the best of the brave,
The black minute's at end,
And the elements rage, the fiend voices that rave,
Shall dwindle, shall blend...

On January 17, 1917, the *Aurora* sailed north. Watching her bow cut through cold water, Shackleton considered the weights and balances of the last two and half years, the men he had saved and those he had lost; new friends made, and loved ones left behind. Little did he know that he would never see Antarctica again.

The heroic ideal had been stood on its head by cataclysmic events in Europe, yet he received a warm welcome in New Zealand and Australia. Patriotism became his new banner. In Sydney, where military service was voluntary, he delivered a rousing speech to 11,000 people that was later printed by the government as a recruiting rally: "We lived long dark days in the South...," he said. "We lived through slow dead days of toil, of struggle, dark striving and anxiety; days that called not for heroism in the bright light of day, but simply for dogged persistent endeavour to do what the soul said was right. It is in that same spirit that we...British...have to face this war...this call to fight means to men more than ease, more than money, more than love of woman, more even than duty; it means the chance to prove ourselves the captains of our own soul."

Shackleton founded a trust fund for Mrs. Aeneas Mackintosh, and refused lecture monies in New Zealand, as that nation had done so much for his bankrupt expedition.

He arrived in San Francisco in early April, three days after the United States had entered the war on the side of Great Britain and France. A tremendous vitality imbued America then, where barriers seemed made only to be broken. A man named Gil Anderson had driven a race car an incredible 102 miles an hour. A woman named Margaret Sanger, jailed for writing *Family Limitations,* a radical first book about birth control, had responded upon her release by founding a birth control clinic, another first, and Alexander Graham Bell in New York City had made the first transcontinental telephone call to Thomas A. Watson in San Francisco.

Shackleton's crackling Antarctica lectures filled halls in San Francisco, Portland, and Seattle. Only in sleepy Tacoma was turnout poor. He explained, "As it was a woman running this [lecture] I cut my guarantee down so that she would not lose on it. It was not her fault.... There has been a mistake in the name Tacoma —the 'T' and 'A' should come off and it should read 'Coma.'"

In Carnegie Hall, a packed audience arrived early and stirred with anticipation, as one source wrote, "to accept this as one of the greatest lectures in New York history." But a chairman who introduced the explorer "proceeded to give Shackleton's speech...for 40 minutes. It was agony. The audience tried to shout him down with cheers, which of course only encouraged him more.... Shackleton was going about like a lion, up and down, and the whole audience shouting for him. He was really worked up. Finally they got the chairman down and Shackleton repeated what had been said—but it was Shackleton. He did it magnificently, and the emotion between him and his audience was such as you seldom feel."

Not until late May 1917, nearly a full year since Emily had learned of his safety in the Falkland Islands, did he arrive home in London. His children delighted him, and together with Emily offered soothing domestication for a while. Husband

and wife settled into the role of intimate strangers they had crafted for themselves; she independent in her nest, living off a modest trust from her father of 700 pounds a year; he born to soar but tethered by debt, looking for work in the war effort, unable to pay a shilling.

Hurley's cinematography proved a sensation, and defrayed many of the expedition bills. But Hurley himself harbored ill feelings for Shackleton, whom he said owed him money. In a letter to Douglas Mawson, a fellow Australian, Hurley referred to Sir Ernest's financial dodgings as "contemptible." He had returned to South Georgia in the austral summer of 1916-17 to complete his portfolio and capture images forsaken on the ice after the *Endurance* was lost. He attempted to trek across the mountains as Shackleton had done, and found it impossible. Back in Europe, he shipped out to France as an official war photographer.

BY NOW, 30 FORMER CREWMEN from the *Endurance* and *Aurora* heard the guns of war. Wild was in Russia. Worsley, known as "Depth-Charge Bill," commanded an antisubmarine mystery ship. Wordie lived amid the thunder of the Royal Field Artillery on the Western Front. James joined the Royal Engineers, then served at the Sound Ranging School, teaching what Shackleton called "this latest and most scientific addition to the art of war." Macklin would win the Military Cross for aid to the wounded under fire on the Italian Front. McIlroy was seriously wounded in Ypres. Greenstreet worked barges on the Tigris. Most of the *Endurance* sailors served on minesweepers, yet sadly, young Timothy McCarthy, the affable Irish lad who had survived the *James Caird* journey, died at his gunpost in the English Channel.

All this time a frustrated Shackleton worked the warrens of the War Office in search of a commission. Britain had introduced military conscription for every able-bodied man aged 18 to 41. But he was 42, legally exempt, and spending more and more time with his American mistress, Rosalind Chetwynd, a vivacious stage actress many years his junior. He began to drink, and refused medical examinations, certain that the doctors would find something wrong.

England had paid little attention to his homecoming, and while his name and influence helped to advance others, he seemed powerless to advance himself. With his parents aging and ill, he, the eldest son, was forced to rely on the charity of friends to finance their needs. It was not easy. Sir Ernest Shackleton, polar hero, had become a relic, a Don Quixote jousting at windmills.

Finally he received an assignment to investigate and if possible forestall German propaganda in South America. He sailed through the dreaded German

U-boat offensive and arrived in Buenos Aires in November 1917. The Latin Americans welcomed him, and soon Shackleton was busy trying to convince both Argentina and Chile to drop their neutrality and join the war on the Allied side.

Back home in late April 1918, he once again found himself hustling for military service. The Bolsheviks had taken power in Russia and forged a separate peace with the Germans. One of the many places threatened by this new treaty was Spitsbergen, a cluster of islands north of Norway, where, as fate would have it, Shackleton had been asked to be a field leader for the Northern Exploration Company, a private mining firm that had received official approval from the War Office and offered profit sharing as part of the deal. Here was a chance to make money while simultaneously defending the interests of the Allies. A temporary major, he now had rank and a uniform. He asked for Frank Wild as his assistant, and got him. Dr. McIlroy, invalided out of the army, also joined. En route north, Shackleton fell ill, and McIlroy observed that "his colour changed very badly." The doctor suspected a heart attack, but noted that "the stubborn Shackleton wouldn't remove his shirt and let me listen to his heart."

SOLDIERS IN THE URUGUAYAN army guard Shackleton's coffin in a military hospital in Montevideo (above), before its return for burial on South Georgia, at the request of Lady Shackleton. In tribute to the explorer, the president of Uruguay, Baltasar Brum, said that "in an age of warlike heroism he was the hero, calm and strong, who left behind him neither death nor grief."

Meanwhile, a strong German offensive had marched to within 60 miles of Paris. To fracture their forces back to the Eastern Front, the Allies captured Murmansk, a vital ice-free submarine base in north Russia, where brutal winter would arrive soon. The War Office turned to Shackleton to organize transportation and supplies. Suddenly in great demand, he sailed for Murmansk in October, writing that "it was a job after my own heart...winter sledging with a fight at the end."

Two weeks after he landed in Murmansk, the Armistice was signed, in November 1918. Yet Shackleton stayed for winter operations, as the Allies faced a new foe: Russian revolutionaries called Bolsheviks. He was joined by three more *Endurance* veterans, Worsley, Macklin, and Hussey, plus the *Nimrod's* Eric Marshall.

Macklin described the British commanding general in Murmansk as rather a disgruntled, unsmiling, bad-tempered customer. The general commented, "I've heard about this man Shackleton. He's an impossible person. He likes to run everything in his own way.... I'm not going to have him." Yet Shackleton proved a nimble player who disarmed the general, leaving him in charge while he, Shackleton, commanded with magnetism. In time the general conceded that Sir Ernest was "a cheerful and amusing companion, and...did much to keep us free from...depression.

Still, ghosts appeared. The polar outpost attracted veterans from Scott's two Antarctic expeditions, men who did little to mask their contempt for Shackleton.

When Marshall and Macklin asked another doctor, Edward Atkinson, a Scott man, about scurvy among the troops in Russia, Atkinson said he recognized the symptoms from when he had served under Scott in Antarctica. Yet all official documents reported that Scott and his men had perished due to severe weather, not scurvy. Atkinson eventually confessed in private to a cover-up. "Marshall and Macklin," wrote Roland Huntford, "were scandalized at this intellectual dishonesty. The whole 'Scott camp' subscribed to it...to foster the burgeoning heroic legend. The denial was also aimed at Shackleton. Scurvy was concealed...because Shackleton had manifestly conquered the disease on the expeditions he had personally led."

Shackleton drank heavily that winter, and was heard by a naval officer talking softly about a mysterious fourth presence during his hike with Worsley and Crean over South Georgia.

To Emily he wrote, "I have not been too fit lately."

While out on ski patrol near Murmansk, an Army officer described how Shackleton stopped to "gaze over what seemed to me was the abomination of monotony...vast expanses of snow; in the distance the gun-metal of the Kola Inlet ...as though he wished to imprint it on his memory...and...began to declaim poetry." The officer recognized Browning and said so. Shackleton drew back, amazed, and said, "First man in...uniform I've met who'd even heard of Robert Browning."

He resigned his commission in February 1919, and returned home with plans to develop an economic relief agency for the Archangel-Murmansk region, complete with exclusive access to all mineral, timber, and fishing resources. In a letter to Emily he described the region as "hilly with birch forests and wonderful lakes nestling in valleys.... We could be very comfy up here." The grand idea merited him an interview in *The Times.* But soon thereafter the Allied forces withdrew, the region fell to the Bolshevik Red Army, and Shackleton's plans crumbled.

Two years earlier, in 1917, he had dictated his *Endurance* expedition notes to Edward Saunders, a self-effacing New Zealand journalist with whom he had collaborated on his first book, *The Heart of the Antarctic,* about the *Nimrod* expedition. Now, after months of hard work, Saunders had crafted Shackleton's *Endurance* material into a compelling manuscript, with volunteer help in the final draft from Leonard Hussey. The result was *South,* published in late 1919. It sold well and was critically acclaimed by none other than Apsley Cherry-Garrard, a member of Scott's *Terra Nova* expedition, who commented: "I get the feeling that [Shackleton] ...is a good man to get you out of a tight place. There is an impression, of the right thing being done without fuss or panic."

The book netted Shackleton no cash; it only lessened his debts. To pay Saunders, he sold all the chronometers from the Ross Sea party. That he used a ghost writer was not unusual or frowned upon. Scott's diaries, retrieved from his frozen body on the Ross Ice Shelf in 1912, had been edited by a master of purple prose, novelist and playwright Sir James Barrie, the author of *Peter Pan.*

Twice a day, six days a week, all that winter and into spring, Shackleton lectured on the *Endurance* expedition to receptive if not overflowing audiences in the Philharmonic Hall, while Hurley's film flickered on the screen above. No matter how clever his oratory or compelling Hurley's silent footage, to those who knew Shackleton well, he sounded tired.

By May of 1920, his lectures finished, and perhaps sensing that his time was short, Shackleton cooked up one final trip into the ice. "This will be the last," he wrote to a colleague. At first he aimed to go north to the Canadian high Arctic and the unexplored Beaufort Sea. But when those plans became mired in politics and business, he quickly changed his target to the unfettered Antarctic, his white muse, and sent out invitations to the "old guard" from the *Endurance.*

THE HOP RETURNED to his step as he trundled about London in search of money. Lady Emily did little to dissuade him. "One must not chain down an eagle in a barnyard," she had once confided to a friend, adding later in a moment of heartbreak, "I must have failed him somehow." He still called her endearing names, and adored his children, but most days he visited Rosalind Chetwynd's Mayfair flat.

An old Dulwich College schoolmate came to his rescue with funds, and Shackleton purchased a 125-ton Norwegian wooden sealer, the *Foca I.* Emily suggested he rename it the *Quest.*

She sailed on September 17, 1921, with a large crowd cheering and waving from St. Katharine's Dock under the Tower Bridge. On deck waving back was Shackleton, wearing suspenders and a slouchy hat. The old guard had indeed answered his call, for standing with him were Wild, Worsley, Macklin, McIlroy, Hussey, Kerr, Green, and the superstitious Scot, McLeod, ready again to face the odds. Some had not yet been paid for their service on the *Endurance,* and probably suspected they never would be paid, yet still they sailed. Cheetham might have joined them, singing his shanties, had he not drowned when his vessel was torpedoed just before the Armistice. And Ernie Wild, younger brother of Frank and a veteran of the Ross Sea party under Mackintosh, might have been there, too, had he not died while minesweeping in the Mediterranean.

Even as the *Quest* slipped from view down the Thames, her objective remained obscure. Shackleton had many ideas, including a circumnavigation of Antarctica in search of uncharted isles or Captain Kidd's treasure or a secret pearl lagoon. He talked about mapping the unknown Enderby Quadrant of Antarctica, and putting to rest, "the history and methods of the Pacific Natives in the navigation across the Pacific spaces hundreds of years before Columbus crossed the Atlantic." Basically, he wanted to be with the boys again in the high latitudes of adventure; perhaps get in a jam and get out again, accomplish the outlandish, discover the unknown, step where no man had stepped before.

The expedition geologist, Vibert Douglas, guessed that Shackleton wanted to find a bonanza of Antarctic minerals. Also on board was a 17-year-old boy scout, James Marr, selected from 1,700 entries. Shackleton sought to apprentice him in seamanship, comradeship, and polar exploration. To help with the cost of Marr's university education, Shackleton raised his wages by a pound a week.

In Rio de Janeiro, Shackleton suffered a heart attack but refused examination. By now Macklin and McIlroy could see he was not himself, as in fact could all the old *Endurance* hands. Still, they sailed south. Shackleton had outfitted the *Quest* with many mechanical devices: an electrically heated crow's nest, a new wireless, and an Odograph that would trace the ship's route. Yet how trite these gadgets seemed when the *Quest* crossed paths with the *France*, an old square-rigged, five-masted clipper ship. She sailed by as if in a dream, white and billowing on the wind, more of a cloud than a ship. She seemed to confirm to Shackleton and the others that the past, not the future, was what they hungered for; that each was a Phoenician born thousands of years too late, pining for a time when mariners used only their wits and courage to navigate and map the world, and thus mapped themselves.

The *Quest* weathered a storm, and in the calm that followed, Shackleton noted the first iceberg: "The old familiar sight aroused in me memories that the strenuous year had deadened." He reflected that "when things are going well I wonder what internal difficulty will be sprung on me...."

The next day, January 4, 1922, the peaks of South Georgia came into view. Shackleton and Worsley scurried about the deck "like a pair of excitable kids," said Worsley, to point out every feature familiar to them: Possession Bay, Fortuna Bay, the steep snow slope down which they glissaded with Tom Crean five and a half years ago, in May 1916. The Boss seemed to be himself again, full of vitality.

"When I look back at those days I have no doubt that Providence guided us," Shackleton had written in *South*, "not only across those snow fields, but across the storm-white sea that separated Elephant Island from our landing-place on South Georgia. I know that during that long and racking march of 36 hours over the

unnamed mountains and glaciers of South Georgia, it seemed to me often that we were four, not three. I said nothing to my companions on the point, but afterwards Worsley said to me, 'Boss, I had a curious feeling on the march that there was another person with us.' Crean confessed to the same idea."

After such an experience, everything that followed seemed like a codicil, and Shackleton sensed it. Macklin noted that he seemed desperate to get to South Georgia, after which his plans were utterly vague.

That evening the *Quest* dropped anchor in Grytviken, and a revived Shackleton went ashore to see old Norwegian friends. The navigating officer, Lt. D. G. Jeffrey, described him as "more like the Shacks I knew in 1914."

But late that night when he returned, he looked tired. Just before 3 a.m. the next morning Macklin was summoned to his cabin by a whistle; Shackleton was having another heart attack. By now a dear friend, Macklin tucked a blanket around him and lectured him on how he must change his habits, watch his diet, get more sleep.

"You're always wanting me to give up things," Shackleton replied. "What is it I ought to give up?" A few minutes later, seven weeks shy of 48, he gave up his life.

Frank Wild called all hands on deck after dawn and broke the sad news, and announced that the expedition "will carry on." Shackleton's death shocked them all, even those who knew he wasn't well; each had regarded him as indestructible.

A friend back home remembered that Shackleton had wanted to die on one of his expeditions, far from the tame and tidy fields of England. "I shall be going, old man," Shackleton had told him, "till one day I shall not come back."

The body was prepared for transport to England, accompanied by Hussey. But in Montevideo, where Shackleton received full military honors, word came from Emily that the far South had always been her husband's first love; he should be buried there. After a large memorial service at the Holy Trinity Church, attended by the president of the Republic of Uruguay and many officers in the diplomatic corps, Shackleton sailed south for the final time.

Only Hussey among the *Quest* crew was with him when his body arrived in South Georgia. The others had sailed into the ice, assuming the Boss was en route to England.

On March 5, 1922, he was laid to rest in a small cemetery in Grytviken, just upslope from king penguins and elephant seals. "No congregation of uniformed dignitaries and ministers of state here," wrote Margery and James Fisher, "but sailors and whaling captains; no military escort, but a company of hard-working, hard-handed men walking over the tussocks after a coffin carried by ex-service men from the Shetlands who were working at Leith harbour. On the grave was a wreath of flowers made by Mrs. Aarberg, the only woman on the island."

"Now that he is gone," wrote Hussey, "there is a gap in our lives that can never be filled." ■

SHACKLETON ON THE QUEST southbound for the final time (opposite). "I am mad to get away," he had written to Janet Stancomb-Wills. To where, exactly, didn't seem to matter, as his plans bounced between the Arctic and the Antarctic. Finally under way, he was overheard saying that he wished he were still young enough to cross Antarctica with intrepid men and dogs and nothing but trackless terrain ahead.

"*The friendly moon
seemed to pilot
our weary feet.
We could have had
no better guide.*"

ERNEST SHACKLETON
ENDURANCE EXPEDITION
MAY 1916

THE MOON RISES over tight pack ice and a tabular iceberg (right). Pressure ridges between the floes in the pack can reach ten feet high and become nearly impassable during travel, as Shackleton and the Endurance crew discovered when they attempted to man-haul sledges loaded with lifeboats that weighed a ton.

A RARE COLOR IMAGE by Frank Hurley shows hoarfrost bejeweling the Endurance *rigging, in some places up to three inches in diameter (above). The S.S.* City of New York *(opposite) moors along the Ross Ice Shelf at the Bay of Whales, in 1930, during Adm. Richard Byrd's pioneering flights in Antarctica.*

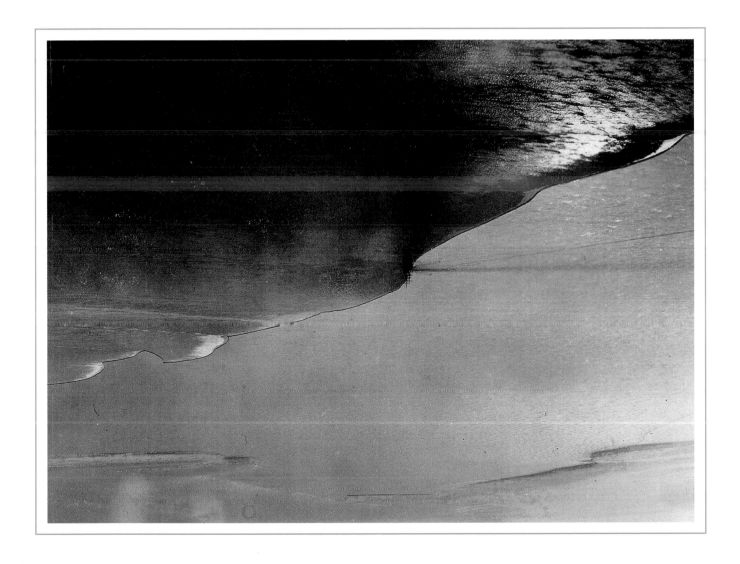

CIRCUMPOLAR WINDS whip up huge
seas in stormy southern latitudes sailors
call the roaring forties and the screaming
fifties. Such a full gale bedeviled
Shackleton en route to South Georgia on
the Quest on Christmas day, 1921, a
storm he said was among the most severe
in his career.

"Penguins always excite fresh interest in everyone who sees them.... They are the civilized nations of these regions, and their civilization...is in some respects higher [than ours]...."

JAMES MURRAY
NIMROD EXPEDITION
1907-1909

CHINSTRAP PENGUINS convene on an ice-berg off the Antarctic Peninsula. In the Straits of Magellan, 700 miles north, Francis Drake wrote in 1578 of seeing a "Great store of strange birds which could not flie...[yet] in the sea...nature may seeme to have granted them no small pre-rogative in swiftness."

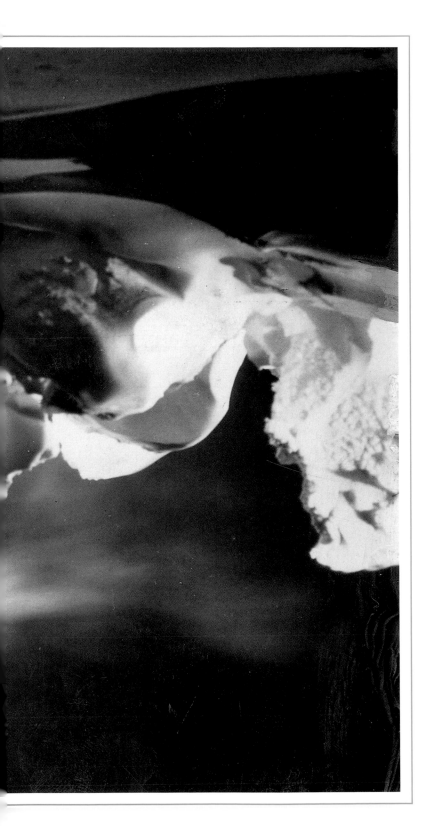

FRIDTJOF NANSEN said that when men cease to explore they cease to be men, even with the Endurance lost and his men marooned, Shackleton discussed a future expedition to Alaska with Worsley. "We are enthusiastic about our next trip," wrote Worsley, "before we settle on how the devil we are going to get out of this one." Such enthusiasm inspired later expeditions. A member of Admiral Byrd's party (right) casts light into the frigid polar night.

"Some bergs had been weathered into fantastic shapes…. Beautiful as this scene was, it gave rise to anxiety…for if we were caught in a breeze amidst this maze, it would go hard with us."

ERNEST SHACKLETON
NIMROD EXPEDITION
JANUARY 1908

❧

CALVED FROM the Larsen ice shelf and weathered into a cold castle, a tabular iceberg drifts in the Weddell Sea. Ice shelves command roughly one third of Antarctica's coastline, and were called "barriers" by Shackleton and other explorers. The largest, the Ross ice shelf, is the size of France.

Up the White Road

About the time Shackleton was buried, T. S. Eliot's poem "The Waste Land" appeared, wherein he wrote:

Who is the third who walks always beside you?

When I count, there are only you and I together

But when I look ahead up the white road

There is always another one walking beside you

Gliding wrapt in a brown mantle, hooded

I do not know whether a man or a woman

—But who is that on the other side of you?

In memory of the Boss, a cross was erected on South Georgia by the Quest crew.

A signature of the post-war era, the poem would become one of Eliot's most famous, which he admitted was inspired by an Antarctic expedition. "I forget which one," he wrote in his notes, "but I think one of Shackleton's...."

Sir Ernest was not a particularly religious man. As he did not turn to God during times of good fortune, he felt he had no right to turn to Him during bad fortune. In his book, *South,* he could only explain the mysterious Fourth Presence that had seemed to accompany him across South Georgia by turning to Keats, another poet, writing that "One feels 'the dearth of human words, the roughness of mortal speech' in trying to describe things intangible, but a record of our journeys would not be complete without a reference to a subject very near to our hearts."

On the snowy uplands of South Georgia, where moonlight guided them past crevasses and cliffs, Shackleton, Worsley, and Crean found a heaven on Earth, and their experience was later immortalized, of all places, in a poem, a literary device that to Shackleton was as magical as Antarctica itself.

The *Quest* remained in the pack ice until late March, then returned to South Georgia by way of Elephant Island, where Worsley held her off Cape Wild, unable to go ashore in rough seas. Overcome with emotion, Macklin described how they "stood gazing with binoculars picking out & recognizing old familiar spots, each reminiscent of some incident.... Few of us thought when we left it last that it would be our fate to see it again. Ah what memories—they rush to one like a great flood and bring tears to ones eyes.... Once more I see the little boat, Frankie Wild's hut, dark & dirty, but a snug little shelter.... Once more I see the old faces and hear the old voices—old friends scattered everywhere. But to express all I feel is impossible."

Upon their return to South Georgia in early April, the men found the Boss buried there, and they erected a cross and cairn in his honor, placing it high on a headland above the entrance to the harbor. "It is likely to be seen by few," wrote Macklin, "but the few who see it are men who themselves lead hard lives, & who are able to appreciate better than those at home, the work which he accomplished."

On the morning of May 6, 1922, the day they sailed north, Wild and the others climbed the headland to say their final farewells.

In England, Lady Shackleton received hundreds of letters and condolences. A service at St. Paul's Cathedral, attended by royalty, confirmed her husband's status as a national hero. He was compared to Sir Francis Drake, and one source gushed of "his likeness to Raleigh—courtier, poet, explorer, and lover of his country."

But in the minds of many he remained the man who almost got to the Pole; the other guy, second to Scott.

That year, 1922, Apsley Cherry-Garrard's book, *The Worst Journey in the World,* was published to wide acclaim. It described a near-fatal trek in 1911 across Ross Island in the dead of winter. Schooled in the arts and humanities, Cherry-Garrard wrote movingly about the esprit de corps of Scott and his men, further cementing Scott as the prime explorer of the South, dying with courage on the ice, a victim of anything but his own mistakes. "I have never known anybody," Cherry-Garrard observed, "man or woman, who could be so attractive when he chose.... Sledging he went harder than any man of whom I have ever heard."

Once Poles Apart—Now Shoulder to Shoulder.

AS IF SHACKLETON had been his compass, Frank Wild seemed to lose his bearing after the Boss died. He returned to southern Africa where he had been before the *Quest* expedition, and took up cotton farming. Years of drought and flood bankrupted him, and his drinking worsened. He bartended at a gold mine next to a Zulu village, and was living like a tramp when Teddy Evans, a shipmate from the *Terra Nova*, found him and secured for him a modest pension only months before he died in 1939.

Tom Crean settled in his old home of Anascaul, in County Kerry, Ireland. He married a local girl, raised a family, tended his garden, and opened a pub called the South Pole Inn. One observer said he "talked Irish as if he had never been away." A veteran of Scott's two Antarctic expeditions, he cried when Scott didn't select him for the 1912 polar party, turning him back atop the Beardmore Glacier, a decision that saved his life. Those whom Scott chose, all perished. Crean later wrote to Cherry-Garrard, "We had a hot time of it the last 12 months when we lost the *Endurance* and I must say the Boss is a splendid gentleman and I done my duty towards him to the last." Though he stood only five foot ten, Crean's strength and reliability made him seem much taller. Sir Clements Markham once compared him to the Duke of Wellington, adding that Crean was "universally liked." He died in 1938 at 63, according to a friend, "smoking his pipe to the last."

Frank Worsley never stopped adventuring or mismanaging his affairs. He won the Distinguished Service Order in World War I, but overspent his pay from the Admiralty, leaving him broke and lamenting that "bagging submarines was an expensive amusement." He transported troops to northern Russia, then invested in the schooner trade in the Baltic. One trip he estimated would take 32 hours took 32 days in heavy seas. Fearing mutiny, he slept with a revolver under his pillow.

THE ANTARCTIC CHALLENGE

One observer said, "Worsley seems to have been a hopeless businessman, displaying equal measures of unbridled optimism and complete disorganization."

After commanding the *Quest*, Worsley captained the *Lady of Avenel* for the 1925 British Arctic Expedition, taking the New Zealand flag farther north than ever before. He matured as a leader and learned to control powerful personalities around him, especially scientists, whom he chided when they misspoke nautical terms. He loved ridiculous moments, such as chasing jellyfish with a hundred-ton brigantine, and he seldom passed a chance to run under sail versus the abomination of modern steam power.

"The skipper...is really out of place in this century," observed the expedition leader, "he would be in his element in a frigate duel of the old days, or sailing some high-powered galleon with Morgan or Dampier."

In his later years, Worsley hunted for buried treasure with his wife, Theodora, and delivered private yachts to their owners around the world. He wrote three books about his time with Shackleton. In one, he tells of himself and the Boss in Ocean Camp just before the *Endurance* sank, when the odds didn't look good. "Shackleton remarked to me one day, in a rather melancholy tone, 'Perhaps it's a pity, Skipper, that you dreamed a dream, or a nightmare, or whatever it was, that sent you to Burlington Street that morning we met.' 'No,' I replied, 'I've never regretted it, and never shall, even if we don't get through.'"

With the outbreak of World War II, Worsley rejoined the Navy and served as an instructor at the Greenwich Royal Naval College. He died in 1943, eight days shy of his 71st birthday, and received full naval honors. His ashes were scattered to the winds and seas he had always loved.

Several of the *Endurance* scientists enjoyed notable careers. Reginald "Gentle Jimmy" James taught physics at the University of Cape Town, South Africa, where he advanced to department chairman and vice-chancellor. Bobby Clark worked as a director in fisheries research in Aberdeen. Wordie became master of St. John's College, Cambridge, and president of the Royal Geographical Society. He made nine expeditions to the Arctic, and was knighted Sir James Wordie for his many valuable contributions to science and exploration.

In his book, *South with Shackleton*, Leonard Hussey wrote of his talisman banjo: "I played some old tunes on it to Sir Ernest the night he died. He said, 'I love those tunes, Huss. They make me feel sad or cheerful, just as I wish. And they help me forget my troubles.'"

Hussey played Brahms's *Lullaby* as Sir Ernest was buried on South Georgia. He later earned a medical degree, served in World War II, and for the rest of his life, spoke wistfully of his time with Sir Ernest Shackleton.

Hurley served as an official photographer in both World Wars, and over the

ROBERT E. PEARY, first to reach the North Pole (opposite) stands with Shackleton in New York in 1910. In the dispute over who actually reached the North Pole first—if at all—Shackleton sided with Peary rather than his rival, Dr. Frederick Cook.

decades he compiled valuable portfolios of Palestine, Papua New Guinea, Tasmania, and Australia, none of which have the stark luminosity of his images from the *Endurance*. Innovative to the end, he altered and mislabeled several of his most notable compositions; hard-headed to the end, he defended his actions. He married an opera singer after a ten-day courtship, raised three children, and died in 1962.

ROALD AMUNDSEN took this photograph of a Norwegian crewmate (above) as they arrived first at the South Pole on December 14, 1911. "God be thanked," he wrote. Robert Falcon Scott (opposite, second from right), 360 miles behind, reached the Pole on January 17, 1912. "We built a cairn and put up our poor slighted Union Jack...," he wrote.

The dashing Dr. McIlroy recovered from the injuries he sustained in World War I, served with distinction in World War II—including time as a prisoner in Africa, and to the chagrin of many hopeful women, never married.

Macklin, who had quipped to Shackleton that "many a wise face would look foolish without spectacles," became chief of student health services at the University of Aberdeen. A dedicated chronicler of the *Endurance* expedition, he was disheartened to learn that Shackleton had denied the Polar Medal to McNeish, Vincent, Holness, and Stephenson. "Of all the men in the party," Macklin wrote, "no-one more deserved recognition than the old carpenter.... I think too that withholding the medal from the three trawlermen was a bit hard. They were perhaps not very endearing characters but they never let the expedition down."

Despite his skills and hard work, Chippy McNeish had committed a grave indiscretion on the Weddell Sea pack ice when he refused Worsley's order to man-haul a heavy sledge. Shackleton saw it as far more than a personal affront or harmless "backchat," for which McNeish was well known; it was a seed of insurrection that if left unchecked could doom the expedition. As for the three trawlermen, they lacked optimism, what Shackleton ranked as the most important ingredient in a polar expedition.

The other four trawlermen—Bakewell, How, McCarthy, and McLeod—were sterling chaps in Shackleton's estimation. Fearing bad luck, the superstitious McLeod had quietly picked up the Bible Sir Ernest abandoned on the ice after he ripped out pages from the Book of Job. McLeod bequeathed it to a family in Punta Arenas, who later sent it to the Royal Geographical Society in London.

A sailor to his core, Shackleton had harbored superstitions of his own, one in particular about the number nine. He was engaged and married on the ninth of a month, and turned back from his march to the Pole on January 9, 1909. As a personal insignia he chose a nine-point star, and affixed a silver 9 to his cabin door on the *Quest*.

Nothing suggests that Emily shared this preoccupation, yet after a long illness

THE ANTARCTIC CHALLENGE

she died on June 9, 1936. Her husband had done little to help raise their children or to help her financially, and this no doubt burdened her. "I have nothing to offer you," Shackleton had written during their courtship. "I am poor; I am not clever." Perhaps she had never expected from him a fraction of what he expected from himself.

Not until 1955, nearly 40 years after Shackleton, Worsley, and Crean crossed South Georgia, did another party do the same. The skilled British alpinists led by Duncan Carse followed a longer but easier route. Of his half-starved, intrepid predecessors of 1916, Carse wrote, "I do not know how they did it, except that they had to—three men of the heroic age of Antarctic exploration with 50 feet of rope between them, and a carpenter's adze."

Three years later, in 1958, Shackleton's dream of a great Trans-Antarctic Expedition was realized in distance if not in similar style when Sir Vivian Fuchs and Sir Edmund Hillary, of Everest fame, used Sno-cats and modified farm tractors to cross Antarctica via the South Pole. Fuchs barely made it. He reported that "the weather even at the height of summer was atrocious.... If these factors had affected Shackleton's party, his chances of success would have been small indeed. It may therefore be permissible to comment that the loss of *Endurance* may have saved a worse disaster." Many polar scholars agree. But then again, it was Shackleton, the man who made ordinary men do extraordinary things, who had what Cherry-Garrard called "great grip."

"Nothing is harder to a leader than to wait," Cherry-Garrard elaborated. "The unknown is always terrible, and it is so much easier to go right ahead and get it over one way or the other than to sit and think about it. But Shackleton waited... and waited...one seems to see [him] sticking out his jaw and saying to himself that he is not going to be beaten by any conditions which were ever created."

Nansen would have been proud.

Not until the 1980s, with the publication of Roland Huntford's landmark book *Scott and Amundsen*, did the public receive a thorough investigation of the famous 1911-12 race to the South Pole. Scott's achievement, Huntford concluded, "was to perpetuate the romantic myth of the explorer as martyr and, in a wider sense, to glorify suffering and self-sacrifice as ends in themselves."

A *Masterpiece Theater* presentation followed, and as Scott's star dimmed, Shackleton's brightened to where it is today, a supernova used by businesses, schools, and churches to model leadership and vision. Sledging "harder than any man," as Cherry-Garrard had said in praise of Scott, wasn't the point. It was sledging wisely, pacing oneself, putting the welfare of one's men before any geographical prize, even if it meant turning back only 97 miles from one's dream. That was Shackleton's uncommon courage; not an absence of fear, but a mastery of it, not walking into death, but to the edge and back.

"All bravery stands upon comparisons," Francis Bacon wrote nearly 300 years before Shackleton. And the comparisons never end.

Every great man has his detractors. Scott and Amundsen each had his, as did Shackleton, who blustered past his shortcomings and left others to deal with the detritus. But he was never ambiguous, even in his failings. He shone best in Antarctica, where the world was fresh and new. And while he made the same mistakes that others made, he learned from his. He listened, adapted, and had a genius for boldness. He never let hope die, and for this his men loved and admired him.

More than a participant in the heroic age, Shackleton became emblematic of it. From the *Discovery* expedition in 1901 to the *Quest* in 1922, he opened and closed an era. Next would come the mechanical age, when men conquered by contraption as much as by courage, running tractors and landing airplanes at the South Pole, circling the ice with nuclear-powered ships. Perhaps Shackleton had not been born too late; perhaps he had been born just in time.

In the little wooden boats with his tired men, pulling on the oars toward Elephant Island, he had remembered the poetry of Coleridge:

Alone, alone, all, all alone,
Alone on the wide, wide sea.

Many years after his death, when Dulwich College compiled a list of famous alumni by occupation—civic leader, banker, barrister, and such; men of high station and advanced degree—Sir Ernest, whose report cards had constantly read "could do better," defied categorization once more and indeed did better. He was simply listed by himself, as himself: Shackleton. ∎

Shackleton-Rowett Expedition.
May 3rd 1922.   Quest RYS

Frank Wild.
F. A. Worsley.
Alan J. Kerr
Douglas Jeffey.
J. McIlroy.
A. Helbach liu
C. E. Smith
J. Wedell
J. F. McLeod
S. S. Young.
G. H. Ross.
J. W. S. Marr.
H. A. Argles
C. Naisbitt.
C. J. Green
George Wilkins
W. Filmot Douglas.

Finder please report to the Royal Geographical Society London England.

"FINDER PLEASE REPORT to the Royal Geographical Society, London England," instructed the Quest crew on May 3, 1922, when they buried a signed photograph in a concrete compartment beneath a cross on South Georgia. "Shackleton-Rowett Expedition" refers to John Quiller Rowett, a school chum of Shackleton's who financed the expedition. Frank Wild commented that the cross and cairn, originally built in 1914, had been reconstructed in Shackleton's honor to "stand the ravages of frost and blizzards for many years to come." The photograph was removed by a Falkland Islands magistrate for safer keeping and in 1997 was delivered to the Royal Geographical Society.

GEORGE MARSTON

The big bear of an artist was adept at many chores, and a valuable explorer. He became director of the Rural Industries Bureau.

JAMES WORDIE

"Jock," a quiet man with a sense of humor, became president of RGS, master of Trinity College, made nine Antarctic expeditions, and was knighted.

FRANK HURLEY

Talented and innovative, he served as an official photographer in both World Wars, and later made wildflower portfolios in Australia and Tasmania.

LEONARD HUSSEY

The smallest crewmate played the banjo at Shackleton's funeral, later served in both World Wars, and became a doctor.

THE ANTARCTIC CHALLENGE

PIERCE BLACKBORO

The welsh stowaway who suffered frostbitten feet returned home to great fanfare, and later worked the docks as a longshoreman.

THOMAS HANS ORDE-LEES

The endurance storekeeper, the royal marine lived his later years in New Zealand.

TOM CREAN

This tough, reliable Irishman, liked and respected by all, retired to his hometown and opened the South Pole Inn.

FRANK WORSLEY

Endurance captain, he won the WWI distinguished service order, and taught at Greenwich Royal Naval College in WWII.

TWO MEN AT EASE AT SEA, *a final portrait. Barefooted and braced against the muscled waves, Frank Wild talks with Shackleton on the* Quest. *"I go exploring because I like it and it's my job," said Shackleton. "One goes once and then one gets the fever and can't stop going." Wild was more cryptic when asked why he returned, saying he couldn't escape the call of "the little voices" of the Antarctic.*

INDEX

Boldface indicates illustrations.

80, 84; surgical operation 146; trek across South Georgia 151–155, 163, 181, 183, 185, 199, 203–204; wireless 87; see also *Aurora* expedition; *Endurance* (ship)

Erebus, Mount, Antarctica 32, **66–67**, 77, 176; ascent of 25, 48, **49**

Evans, Cape, Ross Island, Antarctica 94, 176, 177

F

Falkland Islands, South Atlantic Ocean 138, 171, 172

Filchner Ice Shelf, Antarctica 89

Filchner, Wilhelm 60

Fisher, James and Margery 43, 44, 88, 106

Fortuna Bay, South Georgia 153–154, 183

Fram (ship) 83, 92, 100

Framnaes shipyard, Sandefjord, Norway 53–54

Franklin, Sir John 44, 104

Fuchs, Sir Vivian 204

G

Gerlache Strait, Antarctica **72–73**

Glacier Bay, Antarctica 84, 88

Glaciers 28, 31, 104, 137–138, 200, 202; calving **22–23**, 172

Goodenough, William 182

Green, Charles **57**, 87, 92–93, 102, 129, 136, 182

Greenland Ice Cap: crossing of (1888) 83

Greenstreet, Lionel 56, **61**, 96, 101, 111, 134–135, 139, 144, 146; journal entries 58, 80, 96, 102, 131, 146; military service 179

Grytviken whaling station, South Georgia 58–61; harbor **61;** Shackleton's grave 180, 185, 198

H

Harbord, Arthur 32

Hayward, Victor 176–177

Hillary, Sir Edmund 204

Holness, Ernie 132

Horn, Cape, South America 141, voyages around 30, 39, 86

How, Walter 57, **135**, 203

Hudson, Hubert 87, 101, 108, 132, 146, 149, 174

Huntford, Roland 38, 131, 176, 181, 204

Hurley, Frank 46, 52–53, 90, 92–93, 96, **99**, 102–103, 108, 132, **208;** death 202; ill-feelings toward Shackleton 179; journal entries 11, 71, 80, 86–89, 94, 98, 104, 107, 111–112, 117, **142,** 144–146, 165–166, 172–175; photography 58, 80, 84, 98, 100, 104, 140, 172, 179, 202, 208; photos by **10, 60–61, 74, 86, 106–107, 116–117, 120–121, 124–125, 158–159, 161, 166–167, 173;** sketch by **145;** war service 179, 202, 208

Hussey, Leonard 51, 80, **97,** 104, 111, 140, 181–182, 202, **208;** journal entries 172, 174, 185; military service 208

I

Ice: brash 87, 172; formation 70; ice flowers **71;** pan ice 70; pancake ice **70;** sea ice **12–13, 114–115,** 176; *see also* Pack ice

Ice floes **8–9,** 62, **75, 78,** 81, 89, 96, 100, 102, 109–113, **126, 128,** 128–133, 138, 176, 186

Ice shelves 25, 28, 31, 34, 44, 47, 84, 89, 94, 182, 188, **189,** 196

Icebergs **36,** 60, **78,** 81, 84, **85,** 86, 118, **119,** 129, 183, **192–193;** calving **23–24;** sketch of **91;** tabular **91, 186–187, 196–197**

Icequakes 96–98

Imperial Trans-Antarctic Expedition see *Endurance* expedition

J

James Caird (lifeboat) 97–98, 111, 127–128, 131–133, **134,** 135, 140, 143–144, 147–150, 156, **158–159,** 170–171, 175, 179; hauled over pack ice **18–19;** leaving Elephant Island 138, **139,** 166, **166–167;** outfitting of **136;** water rations 139, 147

James, Reginald 50–51, 84, 87, 93, 96, 108–109, 174, 201; journal entries 82–83, 102–103, 131, 136–137, 172; military service 179

Jeffrey, D.G. 56, 185

Joyce, Ernest 30, **174**

K

Katabatic winds 135, 137, 138, **160;** *see also* Storms

Kerr, A.J. 91, 96, 129, 134, **135,** 146, 182

Killer whales 100, 113, **128,** 128–129

King Edward VII Plateau, Antarctica 30

King George Island, South Shetland Islands 130

King Haakon Bay, South Georgia 147, 149, 151–152, 156, 170

Kodak cameras 140, 158, 166, 174

L

Lansing, Alfred 48, 54, 86, 133–134

Larsen, Anton 155

Larsen Ice Shelf, Antarctica: iceberg **196–197**

Leads (sea-ice channels) 62, 74, **75,** 80–81, 87, 89–90, 96, 100, 108–109, 129

M

Mackintosh, Aeneas 94, **108,** 109, 174, 177, 182; death 176, 178

Macklin, Dr. Alexander 48, 58, 90, 101, 134–135, 137, 146, 180–183, 185, 202; journal entries 62, 87–88, 111, 129, 131–132, 143, 172, 199, 202; military service 179

Markham, Sir Clements 42–43, 84, 201

Marr, James 183

Marshall, Dr. Eric 25, 28–31, 32–34, 50, **51,** 181; British North Russian expeditionary force 180–181; journal entries 29, 48, 66

Marston, George 30, 46, 48, **52,** 58, 90, 92, 96, 107, 133–134, **136,** 139, 144, 173, **209;** paintings **102, 130–131**

Mawson, Douglas 28, 48, 52–53, 81, 93–94, 98, 179

McCarthy, Tim 138–139, 141–142, 144, 147, 151, 156, 170–171, 203; military service 179

McIlroy, Dr. James 90, 93, 96, 137, 146, 182–183; military service 179, 202

McLeod, Thomas 46, 48, 92, 101, 134–135, **136,** 139, 173, 182, 203

McMurdo Sound, Antarctica 25, 28, 48

McNeish, Harry "Chippy" 80, 89, 92–93, 101, 103, 106–109, **136,** 138–139, 143–144, 151, 156, 170–171; journal entries 92, 100

Mill, Hugh Robert 151
Mrs. Chippy (cat) 89, **94**, 103
Murray, James 193

N

Nansen, Fridtjof 17, 33, 53, 83–84, 87, 92, 100, 114, 194, 204
National Antarctic Expedition see *Discovery* expedition
Nimrod expedition (1907-1909) 24–25, 28–34, 40, 46–50, **50–52**, 53–54, 66, 94, 102, 176, 181; announcement of 44–45; food rations 28–29, 31– 32; forced marches 29; illnesses and starvation 24–25, 29, 31–32, 46; Manchurian ponies **76–77**; map of route 26–27; motor car 28, 50, **50**; Mount Erebus ascent 25, 46, 48, **49**; rescue party 33; scientific discoveries 28; South Pole shortfall 30–33, 46, 54, 204
Nordenskjold, Otto 59
North Pole: expeditions to 34, 44, 62, 83, 100, 201
Northwest Passage 44

O

Ocean Camp, Antarctica 104, 106–107, **106–107**, 109, 111, **122**, 129, 144, 201
Orcas *see* Killer whales
Orde-Lees, Thomas Hans 80, 92–93, 96–97, 108–109, 111, 129, **135**, 139, 174, **209**; journal entries 59, 86, 120, 132, 138, 172

P

Pack ice 9, **22–23**, 32, **40–41, 68–69,** 70, 81, 84, 88–89, 93, 100–101, 104, **105**, 129, **130–131**, 172, **186–187**; Weddell Sea **10–11, 18–19,** 59–60, 62, **63, 74,** 85, 87, 92, 94–98, 202
Patience Camp, Antarctica 111, 113, 128, 130–131, 133, 138, 176
Paulet Island, Antarctica 19, 102, 104, 109, 112
Peary, Robert E. 44, 83, **200**, 201
Peggotty Camp, South Georgia 151, 154
Penguins 15, 40, 62, 98, 114, 119, **128**, 137, 172; Adélie 72, **126**; chinstrap 72, **73, 192–193**; emperor **20–21**, 21, 90–92, 101, 111; killed for food

72, 81, 90–92, 111, 129, 138, 145; king 58, **165**, 185; number of species 21; sketch of **142**
Polar Plateau, Antarctica 70, 94, 176
Polaris (ship): renamed *Endurance* 53
Ponies, Manchurian 28–29, 50, **76–77**
Ponting, Herbert G. 120

Q

Quest expedition (1921-1922) **176**, 182–183, **184**, 185, 191, 205, **210–211**; crew **207**; departure from London 176, **177**; map of route 26–27; signatures of crew **207**; storm **190–191**

R

Rickinson, Louis **135,** 137, 146
Ross Ice Shelf, Antarctica 25, 28, 31, 34, 44, 47, 94, 182, 188, **189**, 196
Ross Island, Antarctica 25, 32, **40–41**, 48, **49**, 93, 94, 109, 112; crewmen hauling supplies onto **24**; rescue of marooned crew 175–176; trek across 200
Ross Sea, Antarctica 92, 94, 109, 175
Ross, James Clark 28, 66, 68
Royal Geographical Society 42, 44–45, 52, 201, 203, 207; Shackleton statue 182, **183**
Royal Scottish Geographical Society 43, 44
Royds, Cape, Ross Island, Antarctica 25, 28–29, 32, 40, 176

S

Scott and Amundsen (Huntford) 204
Scott, Kathleen 34, 171
Scott, Robert Falcon 17, 24–25, 32, 34, 44, **45**, 58, 68, 171, 176, 180–181, 200, **203**, 204; character 42–43; death en route from South Pole 33–34, 46–47, 84, 104, 182; diaries 182; rivalry with Shackleton 25, 31, 40, 42, 43, 83; South Pole reached 42, 181, 202, **203**
Scurvy 25, 181
Sealing 40, 81, 82, 154
Seals 84, 98, 114, 119, 172; blubber 90, 97, 101, 118; crabeater 15, 89, 111; elephant 58, 136, 151, **165,** 185; killed for food 89, 109, 111, 118, 129, 131, 137, 147, 154, 173;

leopard **15,** 111; Weddell **66–67**, 89, **118**
Sextants 98, 130, 141, **148,** 149
Shackleton, Dr. Henry 38, 39
Shackleton, Lady Emily 33, 41, 43, **46,** 54, 56, 79, **150,** 151, **176,** 178–182, 185, 199–200; death 203
Shackleton, Sir Ernest H. 17, 19, **37, 51, 56, 106, 108, 124, 130, 135, 153, 169, 176, 184, 200, 210**; Antarctic expeditions see *Aurora; Discovery; Endurance; Nimrod; Quest;* birth 38; Burberry helmet 44, **55**; Cape Horn voyages 30, 39, 40, 86; character 31, 33, 42, 50–51, 88, 205; childhood **38,** 38–39; children 25, 44, 46, **47,** 54, 56, **150, 176,** 178, 182; coffin **180**; cross erected to **198,** 199, 207; death and burial place 180, 185, 198; family motto 53; financial problems 179, 181; health problems 179–181, 183; invalided home 25, 43, 44; journal entries 25, 29–30, 50, 61, 75, 81, 83, 87–91, 93, 96–97, 100–103, 107–109, 111–113, 119, 125–132, 136–141, 144, 147–154, 158, 172, 186, 196; knighthood 33; leadership qualities 42, 62, 82–83, 87–88, 92, 106, 108–109, 131; lecture tours 178, 182; letters home 56, 172, 175, 181; love of poetry 41, 46, 62, 181, 199, 205; marriage 43, 46; military service 179–181; parents 38–39; physical appearance 37; proposed Alaska expedition 194; rivalry with Scott 25, 31, 40, 42, 43, 83; siblings 38, **38,** 40–41, 53; statue 182, **183**; wife *see* Shackleton, Lady Emily
Skiing 43, 53, 58, 83–84, 108, 111
Sled dogs **16–17,** 28, 43, 60–61, 77, 81, **82,** 83–84, 90–91, 96–97, **97,** 104, **105, 202**; ice-block kennels 89, 93, 97; killed for food 52, 103, 111
Soccer game 94, **95**
Sørlle, Thoralf 155, 169–170
South (Shackleton) 156, 181, 183, 185, 199
South Georgia, South Atlantic Ocean 57–60, **60–61,** 88, 112, 136, 138, 149–152, **156–157,** 170, 191; aerial view **162–163**; cross erected to Shackleton **198,** 199, 207; grave of

SURVIVORS UNITE *in 1964 on the 50th anniversary of the* Endurance *expedition,
left to right: How, Green, Bakewell, McIlroy, Greenstreet, and Macklin. In 1970
the only three remaining—How, Green, and Greenstreet—would gather
for the ceremonial commissioning of H.M.S.* Endurance.

ACKNOWLEDGMENTS ~ ADDITIONAL READING ~ CREDITS

SHACKLETON: THE ANTARCTIC CHALLENGE
by Kim Heacox

Published by The National Geographic Society

John M. Fahey, Jr.   *President and Chief Executive Officer*
Gilbert M. Grosvenor   *Chairman of the Board*
Nina D. Hoffman   *Senior Vice President*

Prepared by The Book Division

William R. Gray   *Vice President and Director*
Charles Kogod   *Assistant Director*
Barbara A. Payne   *Editorial Director and Managing Editor*
David Griffin   *Design Director*

Staff for this book

Barbara Brownell   *Editor*
Annie Griffiths Belt   *Illustrations Editor*
Marianne Koszorus   *Art Director*
Elizabeth Booz   *Researcher*
Carl Mehler   *Director of Maps*
Joseph F. Ochlak   *Map Research*
Gregory Ugiansky   *Map Production*
Tibor Toth   *Map Relief*
R. Gary Colbert   *Production Director*
Lewis Bassford   *Production Project Manager*
Ric Wain   *Production*
Meredith Wilcox   *Illustrations Assistant*
Peggy Candore   *Assistant to the Director*
Alexander Cohn   *Staff Assistants*
Sandy Leonard
Elisabeth
MacRae-Bobynskyj   *Indexer*

Manufacturing and Quality Control

George V. White   *Director*
John T. Dunn   *Associate Director*
Vincent P. Ryan   *Manager*
James J. Sorensen   *Budget Analyst*

Acknowledgments

Many people contributed beyond their full measure to the making of this book—my heartfelt thanks to them all. Of special note I wish to acknowledge the staff at the Scott Polar Research Institute in Cambridge, England, especially archivist Robert Headland, for his expertise and good humor, and for inviting Melanie and me into the Friday 17:30 Club. On that note, a sincere thanks to Melanie Heacox for her tireless research, to Valerie Mattingley for her diplomacy, to Denise Landau for sending me to Antaractica, and to Peter Wordie for the long distance phone call. And to all those who face south toward the ice with dreams and desires, thanks for the shared vision of a wild Antarctica, the world of tuxedoed birds and castle bergs that inspired Shackleton.

In creating *Shackleton: The Antarctic Challenge*, The National Geographic Book Division gratefully acknowledges Valerie Mattingley, Shane Murphy, Chris Whitaker, Cary Wolinsky, and Heather Yule.

Additional Reading

The author included many of the following books in his research and recommends them for further reading:

Caroline Alexander, *The Endurance: Shackleton's Legendary Antarctic Expedition*; Pierre Berton, *The Arctic Grail*; Lennard Bickel, *In Search of Frank Hurley* and *Mawson's Will: The Greatest Survival Story Ever Written*; David G. Campbell, *The Crystal Desert*; Apsley Cherry-Garrard, *The Worst Journey in the World*; Harding Dunnett, *Shackleton's Boat: The Story of the James Caird*; Margery and James Fisher, *Shackleton and the Antarctic*; Alan Gurney, *Below the Convergence: Voyages Toward Antarctica*; Kim Heacox, *Antarctica: The Last Continent*; Kare Holt, *The Race*; Roland Huntford, *Shackleton*; Frank Hurley, *Shackleton's Argonauts*; L.D.A. Hussey, *South with Shackleton*; Alfred Lansing, *Endurance: Shackleton's Incredible Voyage*; Reinhold Messner, *Antarctica: Both Heaven and Hell*; Hugh Robert Mill, *The Life of Sir Ernest Shackleton*; Colin Monteath, *Wild Ice: Antarctic Journeys*; Michael Parfit, *South Light: A Journey to the Last Continent*; L.B. Quartermain, *Antarctica's Forgotten Men*; Christopher Ralling, *Shackleton: His Antarctic Writings Selected and Introduced by Christopher Ralling*; R.W. Richards, *The Ross Sea Shore Party, 1914-17*; Ernest Shackleton, *South*; John Thomson, *Shackleton's Captain*; Sara Wheeler, *Terra Incognita: Travels in Antarctica*; Frank A. Worsley, *Endurance: An Epic of Polar Adventure* and *Shackleton's Boat Journey*.

Illustrations Credits

All photos from Scott Polar Research Institute, Cambridge, U.K., unless noted below:

DUSTJACKET: Background, Maria Stenzel. Foreground, Scott Polar Research Institute, Cambridge, U.K.

ENDSHEETS: The photograph of "Nova Orbis Terrarum..." reproduced with permission of Universal Press Pty Ltd. DG 07/99

FRONTMATTER: 2-3, Maria Stenzel; 6, Cary Wolinsky, Courtesy Royal Geographical Society

PORTFOLIO ONE: 8-9, Rhonda Klevansky/Tony Stone Images; 10-11, Mitchell Library, State Library of New South Wales; 12-13, Norbert Wu/www.norbertwu.com; 14-15, Bill Curtsinger; 16-17, Damien Morrissot/Black Star; 20-21, Norbert Wu/www.norbertwu.com; 22-23, Mimi George

PROLOGUE: 24, Royal Geographical Society

CHAPTER ONE: 36, Frans Lanting/Minden Pictures; 37, Sean Sexton Collection/Corbis; 38, A.M.S. Shackleton Collection/Scott Polar Research Institute; 46, Taken from *South*, by Sir Ernest Shackleton, published by Trafalgar Square in the U.S.A. and by Ebury Press in all other territories; 55, Royal Geographical Society; 56, Mirror Syndication International

PORTFOLIO TWO: 66-67, Michael Castellini, University of Alaska; 70, Maria Stenzel; 71, Maria Stenzel; 72-73, Kim Heacox; 75, Bryn Campbell/Tony Stone Images; 76-77, Royal Geographical Society

CHAPTER TWO: 78, Tui De Roy/Minden Pictures; 82, Royal Geographical Society; 85, National Library of Australia; 91, Cary Wolinsky, Courtesy Scott Polar Research Institute; 99, Royal Geographical Society; 101, Royal Geographical Society; 104, "The *Endurance* Crushed in the Ice of the Weddell Sea," October, 1915, by George Edward Marston (1882-1940), Courtesy Christie's Images; 110, The British Library; 112, Mitchell Library, State Library of New South Wales

PORTFOLIO THREE: 116-117, Maria Stenzel; 120, Bill Curtsinger; 121, Maria Stenzel; 122-123, Royal Geographical Society; 124, Royal Geographical Society; 125, Royal Geographical Society

CHAPTER THREE: 128, Ben Osborne/Tony Stone Images; 129, Royal Geographical Society; 130, National Library of Australia; 132-133, 'The Reeling Berg,' April, 1916, by George Edward Marston (1882-1940), Courtesy Christie's Images; 136, Royal Geographical Society; 142, Mitchell Library, State Library of New South Wales; 145, Mitchell Library, State Library of New South Wales; 148, Cary Wolinsky; 149, Cary Wolinsky, Courtesy Scott Polar Research Institute; 150, The British Library

PORTFOLIO FOUR: 156-157, Frans Lanting/ Minden Pictures; 160, Gerry Ellis/ENP Images; 162-163, Maria Stenzel; 165, Art Wolfe/Tony Stone Images

CHAPTER FOUR: 168, Bill Curtsinger; 173, Royal Geographical Society; 183, Hulton Getty

PORTFOLIO FIVE: 186-187, Maria Stenzel; 188, Mitchell Library, State Library of New South Wales; 189, Ohio State University Archives, Papers of Admiral Richard E. Byrd, File Folder 7757; 190-191, Courtesy the Estate of Lincoln Ellsworth and the Estate of Mary Louise Ellsworth; 192-193, Kim Heacox; 194-195, St. Louis Post-Dispatch; 196-197, Kim Heacox

EPILOGUE: 198, Maria Stenzel; 200, The Illustrated London News Picture Library; 202, Anne-Christine Jacobsen, 1986, Photo by Roald Amundsen, 1912; 203, Lt. H.R. Bowers/ Popperfoto, London; 205, Royal Geographical Society

About the Author

Writer, photographer, musician, and conservationist, Kim Heacox has written feature articles for a dozen national magazines, opinion-editorials for the *Los Angeles Times/Washington Post* News Service, and a television script for WNET/Nature. The author/photographer of several books, including *In Denali* (winner of the Benjamin Franklin Nature Book Award) and *Alaska Light*, Kim is twice winner of the Lowell Thomas Award for excellence in travel journalism. He lives in a small town in Southeast Alaska, reachable only by boat or plane, where he and his wife, Melanie, are designing the Glacier Bay Institute. This is his third book for National Geographic.

Library of Congress Cataloging-in-Publication Data

Heacox, Kim.

    E.H. Shackleton : Ernest H. Shackleton, the Antarctic challenge / Kim Heacox.

    p. cm.

    Includes bibliographical references (p.).

    ISBN 0-7922-7536-5

    1. Shackleton, Ernest Henry, Sir, 1874-1922--Journeys. 2. Endurance (Ship) 3. Imperial Trans-Antarctic Expedition (1914-1917) 4. Antarctica--Discovery and exploration. I. Title.

    G850 1914 .S53H43 1999

    919.8'904--dc21

    99-35125   CIP

Composition for this book by National Geographic Book Division. Printed and bound by R.R. Donnelley & Sons, Willard, Ohio. Color separations by NEC, Nashville, Tennessee. Dust jacket by Miken Systems Inc., Cheektowaga, New York.

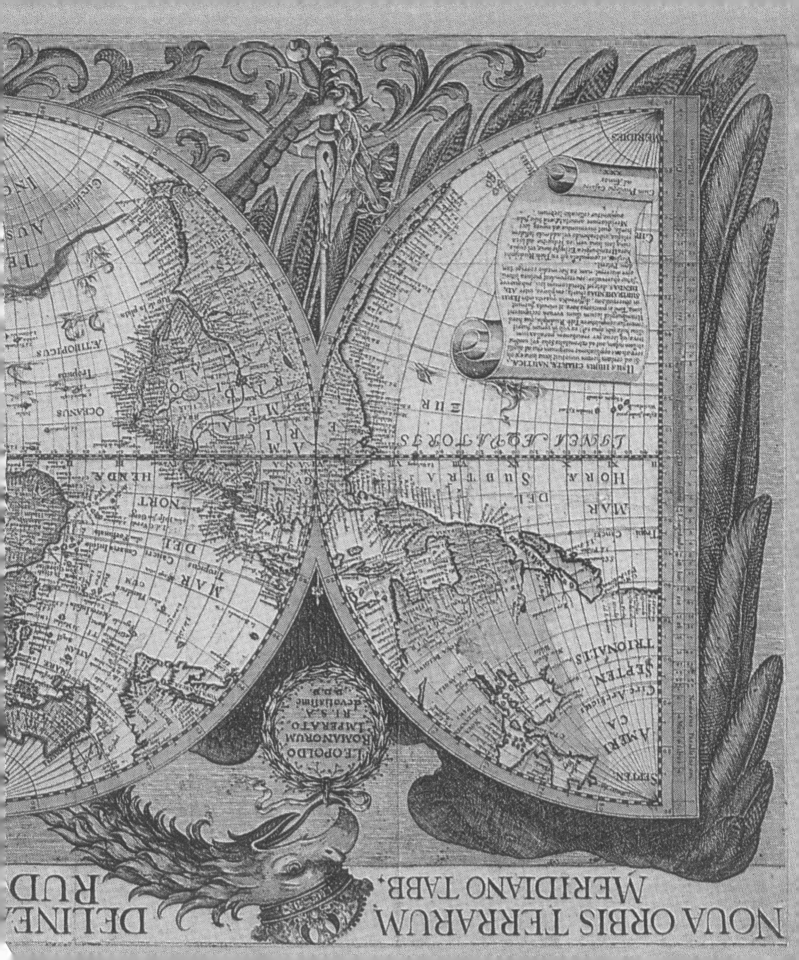

Abnormal Psychology

About the Authors

Richard P. Halgin and Susan Krauss Whitbourne are Professors of Psychology at the University of Massachusetts at Amherst. Both teach large undergraduate classes in addition to teaching and supervising doctoral students in clinical psychology. Their clinical experience has covered both inpatient and outpatient settings. Professors Halgin and Whitbourne are Fellows of the American Psychological Association and have served on the editorial boards of major professional journals. They recently published an edited book for Oxford University Press, *A Case Book in Abnormal Psychology: From the Files of Experts,* containing case studies written by leading international authorities in the field of psychopathology.

Professor Halgin received his PhD from Fordham University, and completed a 3-year fellowship in the Department of Psychiatry at New York Hospital-Cornell Medical Center, prior to joining the faculty of the University of Massachusetts in 1977. He is a Board Certified Clinical Psychologist and has over two decades of clinical, supervisory, and consulting experience. At the University of Massachusetts, his course in Abnormal Psychology is one of the most popular offerings on campus, attracting an enrollment of more than 500 students each semester. In recent years, he has also offered this course at Amherst College and Smith College. His teaching has been recognized at the university and national level. He was honored with the University of Massachusetts Distinguished Teaching Award and was recognized by The Society for the Teaching of Psychology of the American Psychological Association. Professor Halgin is the author of more than 50 journal articles and book chapters in the fields of psychotherapy, clinical supervision, and professional issues in psychology.

Professor Whitbourne received her PhD from Columbia University and has dual specializations in life-span developmental psychology and clinical psychology. She has taught at the State University of New York at Geneseo and the University of Rochester. At the University of Massachusetts, she received the College of Arts and Sciences Outstanding Teacher Award. She is the Honors Coordinator in the Psychology Department, the Faculty Advisor to Psi Chi, and a faculty advisor within the newly established Commonwealth Honors College. The author of 10 books and over 90 journal articles and book chapters, Professor Whitbourne is regarded as an expert in the field of personality development in adulthood and old age and has served as President of Division 20 of APA (Adult Development and Aging). She also serves as the Division 2 (Teaching of Psychology) Liaison to the APA Committee on Aging. Professor Whitbourne has developed nationally recognized approaches to technological innovations in teaching, and the web site she developed for her introductory psychology course was selected as a McGraw-Hill Web Cafe "Site of the Month."

Abnormal Psychology

Clinical Perspectives on Psychological Disorders, Third Edition

Richard P. Halgin
Susan Krauss Whitbourne
University of Massachusetts at Amherst

McGraw
Hill

Boston   Burr Ridge, IL   Dubuque, IA   Madison, WI   New York   San Francisco   St. Louis
Bangkok   Bogotá   Caracas   Lisbon   London   Madrid
Mexico City   Milan   New Delhi   Seoul   Singapore   Sydney   Taipei   Toronto

McGraw-Hill Higher Education
A Division of The McGraw-Hill Companies

ABNORMAL PSYCHOLOGY: CLINICAL PERSPECTIVES ON PSYCHOLOGICAL DISORDERS, THIRD EDITION

This book is printed on recycled, acid-free paper containing 10% postconsumer waste.

2 3 4 5 6 7 8 9 0 QPH/QPH 0 9 8 7 6 5 4 3 2 1 0

ISBN 0-07-228982-1

Editorial director: *Jane E. Vaicunas*
Senior sponsoring editor: *Joseph Terry*
Developmental editors: *Susan Kunchandy/Megan Rundel*
Senior marketing manager: *James Rosza*
Senior project manager: *Peggy J. Selle*
Senior production supervisor: *Mary E. Haas*
Coordinator of freelance design: *Michelle D. Whitaker*
Photo research coordinator: *John C. Leland*
Senior supplement coordinator: *Dave A. Welsh*
Compositor: *GTS Graphics, Inc.*
Typeface: *10/12 Times Roman*
Printer: *Quebecor Printing Book Group/Hawkins, TN*

Freelance cover/interior designer: *Jamie A. O'Neal*
Cover image: *© Diana Ong/SuperStock*
Photo research: *Rose Deluhery*

The credits section for this book begins on page 515 and is considered an extension of the copyright page.

Library of Congress Cataloging-in-Publication Data

Halgin, Richard P.
Abnormal psychology : clinical perspectives on psychological disorders/Richard P. Halgin, Susan Krauss Whitbourne.—3rd ed.
p. cm.
Includes bibliographical references and index.
ISBN 0-07-228982-1
1. Psychology, Pathological. 2. Social psychology.
I. Whitbourne, Susan Krauss. II. Title.
RC454.H334 2000
616.89—dc21 99–24532
CIP

www.mhhe.com

To our families,
with love and appreciation

Brief Contents

Contents

Assessment 62

Theoretical Perspectives 96

Contents

Anxiety Disorders 170

Personality Disorders 138

x   Contents

Somatoform Disorders, Psychological Factors Affecting Medical Conditions, and Dissociative Disorders 204

Sexual Disorders 240

Mood Disorders 276

Schizophrenia and Related Disorders 308

Contents

Eating Disorders and Impulse-Control Disorders 424

Ethical and Legal Issues 450

Preface

Illness is the night-side of life, a more onerous citizenship. Everyone who is born holds dual citizenship, in the kingdom of the well and in the kingdom of the sick." Susan Sontag, from *Illness as Metaphor.*

All human beings experience the duality of illness and wellness. Those who suffer from mental illnesses experience the "night-side" of life more intimately. Our hope is that the study of abnormal psychology will serve as the first step toward understanding, coping, and recovering from mental illness. Our goal in writing this text is to share our understanding with students who come to this course from a variety of socioeconomic and cultural backgrounds, as well as academic pursuits. In revising this edition of *Abnormal Psychology,* we have focused our efforts on transcending those boundaries to reach our readers on a purely human level. We begin by sharing with you the following stories.

Katya developed a deep interest in abnormal psychology after hearing about her friends' and family's immigrant experiences. An immigrant herself, Katya firmly believes that migration can adversely affect human behavior. For example, how does geographical displacement contribute to the onset of major depression? How crucial a factor is "culture shock" in the manifestation of psychological disorders? These are the issues Katya seeks to explore.

Chung, an English major and aspiring writer appreciates the fluctuations in human behavior. He is especially fascinated by and sensitive to its vast range, because he knows that characters cannot be written solely from the imagination. A credible character should reflect an individual one would meet on the street, at the local bar, or in the workplace. Thus, it is important to Chung to be as informed as possible about both ends of the spectrum of human behavior.

Jason's reason for taking a course in abnormal psychology is far more personal. A young man whose mother has long suffered from schizophrenia, Jason seeks to learn more about the disorder, so that he can better understand what his mother must endure daily and to assure that she is receiving treatment most suitable for her case. He also realizes that his genetic disposition makes him susceptible to developing the disorder, thus furthering his interest in the course.

Like Katya, Chung, and Jason, many students find themselves studying abnormal psychology either to deepen their own understanding or to satisfy a personal curiosity, or both. Whatever the specific reason, our goal as instructors and authors continues to be to engage students in the study of abnormal psychology from a clinical and human perspective.

Themes

Clinical Perspectives on Psychological Disorders

The study of abnormal psychology is strongly founded on clinical research. The subtitle of this third edition reflects our efforts to respond to the need for greater and clearer representation and articulation of disorders and their diagnostic features. We have expanded the wide presentation of case studies. Each disorder comes to life through a mini-case, accompanied by a listing of the *DSM-IV* diagnostic features associated with that disorder. Rather than merely list the features, we have paraphrased them into language that is easily understood.

The Human Experience of Psychological Disorders

Above all, the study of abnormal psychology is the study of profoundly human experiences. The varieties of disorders are as diverse as the students who take this course. We have written this text with that thought in mind and address the issue of diversity in such features as "How People Differ." This feature, woven throughout the text, highlights the range of human behavior and the experience of psychological disorders, spanning culture, gender, age, and ethnicity. In addition, the MIND M.A.P. CD-ROM that accompanies this text contains seven clips of real people living with a disorder. Students who view these clips will see firsthand how people live with and suffer from disorders. We hope that students will take from this course the understanding that abnormal behavior is a very real part of our society, our humanity, and our world and that it needs to be addressed with compassion and understanding.

The Scientist-Practitioner Framework

We have developed this text using a scientist-practitioner framework. While emphasizing empirically supported research, we share with the student stories of real people who are suffering from compelling personal problems and serious psychological disorders. As students take this course and long after they have moved on to their respective careers, our hope is that they will have learned to approach the study of abnormal psychology with the dispassionate eye of a scientist and the compassionate heart of a practitioner.

Organization

The Basics

The table of contents reflects a building block approach. The first four chapters provide the fundamentals of history and research methods (Chapter 1); diagnosis, classification, and treatment planning (Chapter 2); assessment (Chapter 3); and theories (Chapter 4). These chapters provide a foundation for subsequent discussions regarding the understanding and treatment of psychological disorders.

The Disorders

From the basics, we move on to a consideration of the disorders, beginning with those that we believe students will find most familiar, such as personality disorders (Chapter 5) and anxiety disorders (Chapter 6). Progressing through the major categories of psychological disorders, we end with eating disorders and impulse-control disorders. Using a biopsychosocial approach, theory and treatment are both discussed in each chapter. For example, we examine anxiety disorders in terms of biological, psychological, and sociocultural influences that cause and maintain these conditions. We also discuss intervention in terms of the relative contributions offered by each perspective.

Conclusion

In the final chapter of the text (Chapter 15), we cover legal, ethical, and professional issues. This new chapter provides expanded coverage of legal and forensic issues previously discussed in chapter 2.

Changes

This textbook fully incorporates diagnostic material from the *Diagnostics and Statistical Manual of Mental Disorders,* fourth edition *(DSM-IV).* For each disorder, *DSM-IV* diagnostic features are paraphrased rather than listed, in order to translate the features into language and concepts that are more easily understood by undergraduate students.

The burgeoning of research in psychopathology in the past several years has prompted us to draw from rich new empirical sources that document the scientific basis for the diagnosis and treatment of disorders. References that are no longer relevant have been deleted, while the classic sources in literature have been retained. Expanded epidemiological databases now accessible via the Internet have also helped improve this edition. Ultimately, our goal is to offer a contemporary and concise approach to the field.

A number of changes in the text reflect new research directions, feedback from reviewers and student readers, and experience from our teaching of abnormal psychology. Each chapter contains two feature boxes that focus on a particular research topic, a critical issue, or a discussion of diversity. Approximately 25 percent of the third edition consists of new material, including discussions that incorporate current, empirically supported approaches. Dated and discarded viewpoints and citations have been deleted. Following is a brief summary of the most significant changes that are specific to each chapter.

Chapter 1 History and Research Methods

- Clarified the biopsychosocial model and its applicability to understanding "abnormality." Increased the interest value of historical material. Enhanced the presentation of research methods in the second part of the chapter.

Chapter 2 Classification, Diagnosis, and Treatment Plans

- Removed the legal and forensic issues, which are now in Chapter 15. Presented a summary of all major disorders on Axis I of the *DSM-IV.*

Chapter 3 Assessment

- Added the WAIS-III and updated the information on biological assessment measures.

Chapter 4 Theories

- Combined the former Chapters 4 and 5 into one theories chapter, which emphasizes the biopsychosocial approach. Expanded the discussion of genetic theories of psychological disorders.

Chapter 5 Personality Disorders

- Condensed the sections on antisocial and borderline personality disorders. Added new biopsychosocial perspective sections. Added diagnostic features corresponding to mini-cases. Updated references.

Chapter 6 Anxiety Disorders

- Significantly tightened the sections dealing with post-traumatic stress disorder and obsessive-compulsive disorder and incorporated the biopsychosocial perspective. Added diagnostic features corresponding to mini-cases. Updated references on all disorders.

Chapter 7 Somatoform, Psychological Factors Affecting Medical Conditions, and Dissociative Disorders

- Condensed the section on dissociative disorders and presented the theories in terms of the biopsychosocial perspective. Added new material on the immune system to the "Psychological Factors Affecting Medical Conditions" section. Added diagnostic features corresponding to mini-cases. Updated references.

Chapter 8 Sexual Disorders

- Presented additional biological information on sexual dysfunctions. Added diagnostic features corresponding to mini-cases. Updated references, particularly with regard to treatment of male sexual dysfunction (included current material on Viagra).

Chapter 9 Mood Disorders

- Substantially revised section on major depressive disorder and clarified material relating to course and prevalence of the disorder, as well as genetic contributions. Added diagnostic features corresponding to mini-cases. Updated references.

Chapter 10 Schizophrenia

- Provided expanded coverage of Type I and Type II schizophrenia. Added diagnostic features corresponding to mini-cases. Updated references, particularly in the biological area.

Chapter 11 Development-Related Disorders

- Improved the coverage of ADHD and mental retardation with more complete explanations. Expanded the biopsychosocial approach to ADHD. Added diagnostic features corresponding to mini-cases.

Chapter 12   Cognitive Disorders

- Significantly updated the section on biological approaches to Alzheimer's disease and provided new material on diagnosis and treatment. Added diagnostic features corresponding to mini-cases.

Chapter 13   Substance-Related Disorders

- Revised the section on theoretical approaches to substance disorders and updated the information on substance abuse statistics. Added diagnostic features corresponding to mini-cases.

Chapter 14   Eating Disorders and Impulse-Control Disorders

- Reorganized chapter to give more emphasis to eating disorders. Added diagnostic features corresponding to mini-cases. Updated references and incorporated the biopsychosocial perspective.

Chapter 15   Legal, Ethical, and Professional Issues

- Moved material from Chapter 2 into this chapter and expanded the coverage of all topics. Included new examples of forensic issues in clinical psychology.

Ancillaries

Following is a list of available ancillaries to accompany Abnormal Psychology, 3e. Please contact your McGraw-Hill sales representative for details concerning policies, prices, and availability as some restrictions may apply.

Study Guide: 0-07-232387-6
Instructor's Manual: 0-07-229063-3
Test Bank: 0-07-229064-1
CTB, MAC: 0-07-229066-8
CTB, IBM: 0-07-229065-X
Overhead Transparencies: 0-07-229069-2
Faces of Abnormal Psychology Video: NEW! McGraw-Hill's new 85-minute video presents a compassionate portrait of real people suffering from disorders. This video is free to adopters.
0-07-232388-4
Halgin/Whitbourne web site: http:www.mhhe.com/halgin
NEW! MIND M.A.P. (Multimedia for Abnormal Psychology) CD-ROM: 0–07–236233–2 This new study aid contains a variety of interactive games, questions, and study material for *Abnormal Psychology*. Also included are seven video clips of people with seven different disorders from McGraw-Hill's new video *Faces of Abnormal Psychology*. A short narrative introduces each of the disorders, and is accompanied by a series of 10 essay questions that students can type responses to, then print out to hand in.

Pedagogy

Recognizing that many students find scientific research daunting, we have done our best to present this material in a way that is easily understood yet strongly founded in scholarship. The pedagogy in this text is carefully designed and set up to assist students in learning. Each element is tailored to provide an insight into the clinical and human aspects of abnormal psychology.

To the Instructor

Like us, most instructors have students like Katya, Chung, and Jason and are aware of the challenge that this heterogeneity of students presents. We want to excite aspiring researchers like Katya to pursue their goals and become immersed in this fascinating and rapidly changing field of abnormal psychology. However, even those of you who are extremely research-oriented realize the importance of including ample clinical material in order to make the scientific material understandable. For students like Chung, who come to the course with broader interests, we want to capture for them the fascinating and multifarious aspects of abnormal behavior. This includes highlighting interesting clinical phenomena and incorporating them with ideas derived from empirically supported research. Our goal is to infuse teaching with credible and validated scholarship. Students like Jason present the greatest teaching challenge, because their concerns are of such a personal nature. As instructors, we need to keep in mind the importance of not creating a therapy context in the classroom. We must recognize that emotionally provocative information can be discussed in a way that is informative and sensitively responsive to individual needs.

In this textbook, we speak to these various types of students in a manner that is informative, scholarly, and engaging. The scientist-practitioner framework is geared toward emphasizing current empirically supported research while conveying the compelling personal problems and serious psychological disorders of real people through case studies. The pedagogy is developed to communicate this framework as well. With this effective blending of science and clinical material, this textbook serves the needs of a diverse student body, while satisfying the preferences of a variety of instructors.

Acknowledgments

The following instructors were instrumental in the development of this text, offering their feedback and advice as reviewers: **Carol M. Baldwin,** University of Arizona Health Sciences Center; **Donald L. Bliwise,** Emory Sleep Disorders Center; **Barbara Brown,** Dekalb College, North Campus; **James F. Calhoun,** University of Georgia; **Ellen Cash,** Washington State; **Michele Catone-Maitino,** Hudson Valley Community College; **Kit Carman,** Golden Gate University; **Elaine Cassel,** Lord Fairfax Community College; **Sammie L. Cratch,** Mount Olive College; **Scott J. Dickman,** University of Massachusetts, Dartmouth; **Robert Emmons,** University of California; **Marc Henley,** Delaware County Community College; **Jacqueline Horn,** University of California, Davis; **Gayle Iwamasa,** Ball State University; **Jennifer Langhinrichsen-Rolling,** University of South Alabama; **Travis Langley,** Henderson State University; **Russell Lee,** Bemidji State University; **Mark Lenzenweger,** Harvard University; **Joseph Lowman,** University of North Carolina, Chapel Hill; **Jodi Mindell,** St. Joseph's University; **Leslie Morey,** Vanderbilt University; **Kim Mueser,** Dartmouth School of Medicine; **Jubemi O. Ogisi,** Brescia College; **Joseph J. Palladino,** University of Southern Indiana; **Judith Reade,** Central Wyoming College; **Lynn Hohm,** University of Houston; **Anita Rosenfeld,** Chaffey College; **Bruce M. Sliney,** North Central Technical College; **Michael D. Spiegler,** Providence College; **Timothy P. Tomczak,** Genesee Community College; **Tova Vitiello,** Kirkwood Community College; and **Fred Whitford,** Montana State University.

Our most heartfelt appreciation goes to our families, whose encouragement and patience gave both of us the energy to follow through on a task that consumed thousands more hours than either of us had ever imagined. The loving support of our spouses, Lucille Halgin and Richard O'Brien, made it possible for us to maintain a reasonable degree of emotional stability. The perspectives of our children, Daniel and Kerry Halgin, and Stacey Whitbourne and Jennifer O'Brien, helped keep before us the goal of writing in a way that would answer the questions of the inquisitive undergraduate.

A great book can't come together without a great publishing team. We'd like to thank our editorial team, all of whom worked with us through various stages of the publishing process. Our editor, Joe Terry, brought together the vision of this book while Megan Rundel, freelance development editor, worked with us to develop and refine this text. Susan Kunchandy, Lai Moy, Frederick Speers, and Barbara Santoro took care of all the odds and ends behind the scenes that polish a book to perfection. We'd also like to thank our project manager, Peggy Selle who has patiently worked with us through the production process.

We would especially like to acknowledge the contributions of the thousands of students who positively influence our teaching and keep us conscious of the need to communicate clearly in our writing. Many of our students have also given us specific ideas and feedback that are incorporated into this edition. It has also been our good fortune to have the creative input of three talented research assistants, Robert Murphy, Paige Fisher, and Alyssa Turkewitz, who worked with us on this project.

On a final note, we want to thank each other for a working relationship characterized by good humor, nondefensiveness, and mutual respect. We can honestly say that no part of this book is owned exclusively by either of us. In a most collaborative writing process, we created the wording of each phrase through discussion, debate, and occasional good-natured sarcasm. While working on this third edition, we managed to keep our sense of humor despite the pressures of many competing demands and a fast-paced revision schedule. We debated the order of authorship, each of us insisting that the other deserved to be first author, and ultimately we yielded to the tradition of alphabetical listing.

To the Student

Chapter Outline

Each chapter begins with an outline of the heading levels, setting the stage for and serving as an overview of the chapter.

Dr. Sarah Tobin Case Report

Each chapter begins with a case report, which sets the stage for the topics covered in the chapter. These cases, based on actual clinical material, are presented from the perspective of "Dr. Sarah Tobin," a clinical psychologist who relates a different client consultation story for each chapter. Through the voice of Dr. Tobin, we can illustrate the disorders more vividly, giving students an appreciation for the complexities of psychological disorders and a sense of what real-life clinical work involves. We return to the case at the end of each chapter.

Critical Issues

This feature is a thought-provoking discussion of controversial issues such as the debate over the role of DSM-IV in creating diagnoses as a reflection of the culture and politics of our time.

Mini-Case Study and *DSM-IV* Criteria

Each disorder is brought to life by a mini-case, which is presented alongside a listing of diagnostic features associated with that disorder. Rather than list *DSM-IV* criteria verbatim, we paraphrase features of each disorder in language more accessible to the student.

How People Differ

Variations according to age, gender, cultural background, and ethnicity are covered to highlight the range of human behavior and the experience of psychological disorder.

Research Focus

This feature highlights interesting and important research studies, giving the student an appreciation of the complexity of investigating important issues in abnormal psychology.

Tables

The tables highlight key concepts and distinctions in a straightforward and clear style.

Return to the Case

At the end of the chapter, students return to Dr. Sarah Tobin's case, introduced at the start of the chapter. At this point, the student is equipped with the knowledge to understand the diagnosis, formulation, and treatment of the case.

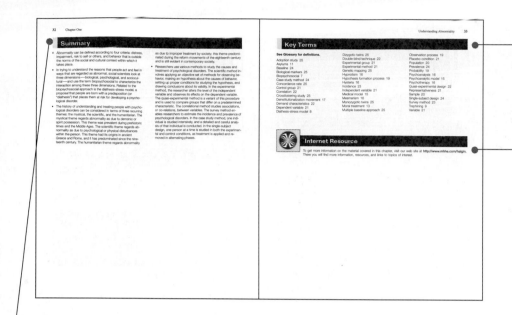

List of Key Terms

The key terms that are boldface in the chapter are listed alphabetically at the end of the chapter and defined in an alphabetical, page-referenced glossary at the end of the book.

Web Address

Access the Internet through this address for further reading on any topic in the chapter that contains this icon.

Chapter Summary

Each chapter ends with a comprehensive summary of the major points in the chapter, corresponding back to the chapter-opening outline.

Student Study Guide

Special Feature
All the key terms in the text are alphabetically organized by chapter and bound in the back of the text as glossary cards for the student.

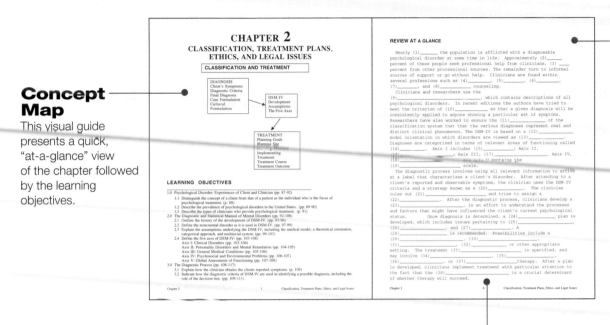

Concept Map
This visual guide presents a quick, "at-a-glance" view of the chapter followed by the learning objectives.

Review at a Glance
This is a fill-in-the-blank summarizing exercise that appears in each chapter.

Exercises
In addition to matching, identifications, and applicable games, each chapter contains critical thinking questions that relate back to the Dr. Sarah Tobin case reports, Research Focus, and How People Differ features in each chapter.

Practice Tests
Each chapter contains 20 multiple-choice questions, 10 true/false items and 8–10 fill-in-the-blanks per chapter.

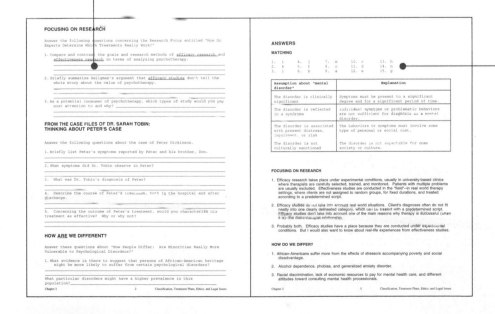

Answer Keys
At the end of each chapter are provided full explanations for each of the multiple-choice items, explanations for the false items in the true/false, and possible answers for the case-thought, essay, and short-answer items. The answers to the matching, identification, and games are also provided.

To the Instructor
Test Bank

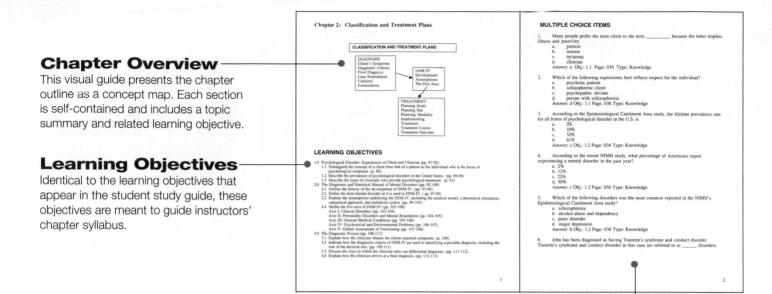

Chapter Overview

This visual guide presents the chapter outline as a concept map. Each section is self-contained and includes a topic summary and related learning objective.

Learning Objectives

Identical to the learning objectives that appear in the student study guide, these objectives are meant to guide instructors' chapter syllabus.

Multiple-Choice Questions

Each chapter contains an average of 140 questions, with more coverage of race, gender, and ethnicity. Select questions are included from the *Student Study Guide*.

True/False—No fewer than 15 per chapter
Matching—No fewer than 10 per chapter
Fill-in-the-Blanks—No fewer than 5 per chapter

Essay Items

No fewer than 5 per chapter, including questions based on Dr. Sarah Tobin Case Report, Research Focus, and How People Differ features.

For the Instructor
Instructor's Manual

Chapter Overview
This visual guide presents the chapter outline as a concept map. Each section is self-contained and includes a topic summary and related learning objective.

Learning Objectives
Identical to the learning objectives that appear in the student study guide, these objectives are meant to guide instructors' chapter syllabus.

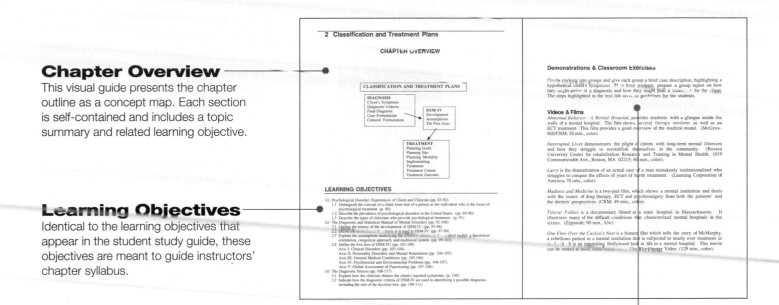

2 Classification and Treatment Plans

CHAPTER OVERVIEW

CLASSIFICATION AND TREATMENT PLANS

DIAGNOSIS
Client's Symptoms
Diagnostic Criteria
Final Diagnosis
Case Formulation
Cultural Formulation

DSM-IV
Development
Assumptions
The Five Axes

TREATMENT
Planning Goals
Planning Site
Planning Modality
Implementing
Treatment
Treatment Course
Treatment Outcome

LEARNING OBJECTIVES

1.0 Psychological Disorder: Experiences of Client and Clinician (pp. 87-92)
  1.1 Distinguish the concept of a client from that of a patient as the individual who is the focus of psychological treatment. (p. 88)
  1.2 Describe the prevalence of psychological disorders in the United States. (pp. 89-90)
  1.3 Describe the types of clinicians who provide psychological treatment. (p. 91)
2.0 The Diagnostic and Statistical Manual of Mental Disorders (pp. 92-108)
  2.1 Outline the history of the development of DSM-IV. (pp. 93-96)
  2.2 [illegible] ... for us it used in DSM-IV. (pp. 97-99)
  2.3 Explain the assumptions underlying the DSM-IV, including ... dinal model, a theoretical orientation, categorical approach, and multiaxial system. (pp. 99-103)
  2.4 Define the five axes of DSM-IV: (pp. 103-108)
      Axis I: Clinical Disorders (pp. 103-104)
      Axis II: Personality Disorders and Mental Retardation (pp. 104-105)
      Axis III: General Medical Conditions (pp. 105-106)
      Axis IV: Psychosocial and Environmental Problems (pp. 106-107)
      Axis V: Global Assessment of Functioning (pp. 107-108)
3.0 The Diagnostic Process (pp. 108-117)
  3.1 Explain how the clinician obtains the client's reported symptoms. (p. 109)
  3.2 Indicate how the diagnostic criteria of DSM-IV are used in identifying a possible diagnosis, including the role of the decision tree. (pp. 109-111)

Demonstrations & Classroom Exercises

Divide students into groups and give each group a brief case description, highlighting a hypothetical client's symptoms. Or ... have students prepare a group report on how they might arrive at a diagnosis and how they might plan a treatment for the client. The steps highlighted in the text can serve as guidelines for the students.

Videos & Films

Abnormal Behavior: A Mental Hospital, provides students with a glimpse inside the walls of a mental hospital. The film shows several therapy sessions as well as an ECT treatment. This film provides a good overview of the medical model. (McGraw-Hill/CRM; 28 min., color).

Interrupted Lives demonstrates the plight of clients with long-term mental illnesses and how they struggle to reestablish themselves in the community. (Boston University Center for rehabilitation Research and Training in Mental Health, 1019 Commonwealth Ave., Boston, MA 02215; 60 min., color).

Larry is the dramatization of an actual case of a man mistakenly institutionalized who struggles to conquer the effects of years of harsh treatment. (Learning Corporation of America; 78 min., color).

Madness and Medicine is a two-part film, which shows a mental institution and deals with the issues of drug therapy, ECT and psychosurgery from both the patients' and the doctors' perspectives. (CRM; 49 min., color).

Titicut Follies is a documentary filmed at a state hospital in Massachusetts. It illustrates many of the difficult conditions that characterized mental hospitals in the sixties. (Zipporah; 90 min., b/w).

One Flew Over the Cuckoo's Nest is a feature film which tells the story of McMurphy, a rebellious patient in a mental institution that is subjected to nearly ever treatment in ... . It is an interesting Hollywood look at life in a mental hospital. This movie can be rented at most video ... . The Blockbuster Video. (129 min., color).

Demonstrations and Classroom Exercises Videos and Films
Includes various demonstrations and exercises to be used in class as well as a list of videos related to chapter content.

Supplementary Lecture/Discussion Topics and Controversies
Includes additional lecture topics and discussion questions linked to learning objectives. These also reflect back to the main text case features.

Supplementary Lecture/Discussion Topics and Controversies

Linked to Objective 3.6
Since many forms of psychological disorders are intimately wed with the culture in which they occur, it should not be surprising that diagnostic systems developed in the west, like the DSM are culturally biased. There are several reports of a disorder characterized by confusion and dramatic excitement that is often brief in duration that has been observed in West Africa, the Caribbean and New Guinea and has been referred to by researchers as transient psychosis, acute confusional state or bouffée délirante aigie. Some researchers argue that this particular syndrome does not fit neatly into any of the standard psychiatric diagnoses established by the American Psychiatric Association (Draguns, 1980, p. 138). In some instances, other cultures do not have diagnostic labels for syndromes that we recognize in our culture. The Inuit of Alaska have no word or label to conveniently describe anxiety (Murphy, 1976, p. 1024). These facts lead many to criticize the reliability, validity and the basic utility of the DSM.

Draguns, J. G. (1980). Psychological disorders of clinical severity. In H.C. Triandis, & J. Draguns (Eds.), Handbook of cross-cultural psychology (Vol. 6). Boston: Allyn & Bacon.

Murphy, J.M. (1976). Psychiatric labeling in cross-cultural perspective. Science, 191, 1019-1028.

Linked to Objective 3.6
It is now well recognized that culture has an impact on the way in which certain psychological disorders are manifest in individuals. Yet culture itself is a very broad construct that encompasses a wide range of factors. Researchers have recently turned their interest to the specific cultural factors that may lead to differences in disorders that are observed between different ethnic and racial groups. Okazaki (1997) hypothesized that one potential factor that might lead to some well-documented differences in social anxiety and depression between Asian-Americans and White Americans is the ethnic difference in self-construals. Okazaki notes that Asian-Americans typically have more interdependent self-construals; that is, there self definition is based more on their relationships with significant others. White Americans typically have independent self-construals--their self-definition is based more on individual and personal factors. By using multivariate techniques, Okazaki correlated Asian-American and White American students' scores on measures of self-construal, depression and fear of negative evaluation. Although no differences were found on measures of depression, ethnic differences were found on measures of social anxiety. The author suggests that ethnic differences in self-construal might predispose Asian-Americans to certain types of disorders that have social anxiety (e.g., social phobia). Okazaki also points out that the current findings shed light on a culture-bound syndrome observed in Japan called Taijin Kyofusho characterized by avoidance of social situations due to a fear of offending or embarrassing others. More researchers will need to focus on the specific cultural factors that may lead to ethnic differences in psychopathology.

Okazaki, S. (1997). Sources of ethnic differences between Asian-American and white American college students on measures of depression and social anxiety. Journal of Abnormal Psychology, 106, 52-60.

Supplementary Topics/Lecture Launcher Discussion Questions

Case Report
In the case of Peter Dickinson, why do you think Peter was so resistant to the idea that he might need help? In Peter's own view, do you think he felt he needed help? What aspect of Peter's case most clearly indicates that Peter has a problem?

Research Focus
From a research standpoint, what advantages are there to conducting what Seligman calls efficacy studies as opposed to effectiveness studies? What are some of the disadvantages?

Literature Guide/Suggested Readings

Kirk, S. A. & Kutchins, H. (1992). The selling of the DSM: The rhetoric of science in psychiatry. Hawthorne, NY: Aldine De Gruyter.

Kirk, S. A. & Kutchins, H. (1997). Making us crazy: DSM: The psychiatric bible and the creation of mental disorders. New York: The Free Press Seligman, 1995

Ratey, J. & Johnson, C. (1997, May/June). Out of the shadows. Psychology Today, pp. 47-48, 50, 78, 80.

Seligman, M. E. P. (1995). The effectiveness of psychotherapy: The Consumer Reports study. American Psychologist, 50, 965-974.

Paper Topics

Using Seligman (1995; see above) as a starting point, students may want to look at several current studies on the effectiveness of therapy and analyze them in terms of Seligman's criteria.

Students may wish to read either of Kirk and Kutchins books (1992 or 1997) and report on their contents.

It may be interesting for students to look at the previous DSMs, compare and contrast them with the current DSM and report their findings.

Literature Guide/Suggested Readings Paper Topics
Includes a list of suggested readings and up to five paper topics based on suggested readings, Case Reports, and Research Focus features found in the main text.

Welcome to the
Halgin/Whitbourne
Abnormal Psychology 3e
Web site!

ABOUT THE BOOK

- **Overview**
Provides a quick synopsis of the edition and the material covered.

- **Table of Contents**
Lists the entire TOC.

- **What's New**
Introduces the new features of the textbook.

- **Supplements**
Includes title and ISBN information for all accompanying student and instructors' supplements.

- **NEW! Faces of Abnormal Psychology Video**
Links to a downloadable demo of McGraw-Hill's new 85 minute abnormal psychology video, containing 7 segments of real people with real disorders. FACES is free to adopters.

ABOUT THE AUTHOR

- **Meet the Authors**
Have questions or comments concerning the text? E-mail the authors!

Richard Halgin
rhalgin@psych.umass.edu

Susan Whitbourne
swhitbo@psych.umass.edu

STUDENT RESOURCES

- **Online Learning Center**
Links to every text chapter containing learning objectives, quizzes, crossword puzzles, and more!

- **Internet Primer**
Links to the McGraw-Hill Internet Guide providing students with valuable information on internet navigation.

- **Careers In Psychology**
Links to a list of resources for students interested in a career in psychology.

- **Statistics Primer**
Provides a quick overview of statistics.

- **Web Resources**
Links to interesting and useful psychology sites.

INSTRUCTOR'S RESOURCES

Online Learning Center
- CLICK HERE to see a web version of the Instructor's Manual. This area is password protected. Please contact your McGraw-Hill representative for the password.

PageOut
- FREE to adopters, PageOut is designed for the professor just beginning to explore web site options. In just a few minutes, even the novice computer user can have a course web site.

- **Movies & Mental Illness**
This text, by Danny Wedding and Mary Ann Boyd, utilizes the viewing and discussion of popular films to illuminate and enhance student understanding of abnormal behavior.

- **Psych In The News**
Links to issues of the Psychwatch: Newsletter

Abnormal Psychology

CASE REPORT: REBECCA HASBROUCK

Twenty years of clinical practice had not prepared me for my encounter with Rebecca Hasbrouck. Working in the outpatient department of a large psychiatric facility, I had encountered hundreds of people whose stories would move me, but, for some reason, Rebecca's seemed unusually troubling. Perhaps it was her similarity to me in so many ways that stirred me up. Like me, she was in her mid-forties and had mothered two sons when she was in her early thirties. She had been raised in a middle-class family and had attended excellent schools. In fact, when I first spoke with Rebecca, my attention was drawn to the faded Polaroid photo that she grasped tightly in her fist. It was the picture of a jubilant 22-year-old Rebecca on the day of her graduation from an Ivy League university. She stood beside her parents and her older sister, everyone gleaming with pride about all that she had accomplished and filled with the greatest of expectations about all that would lie ahead for her. I later learned that she was planning to attend one of the most prominent law schools in the country, where she would pursue a specialization in maritime law. Everyone, including Rebecca, assumed that a life of happiness and personal fulfillment would lie ahead.

Before telling you the rest of Rebecca's story, let me tell you more about my initial encounter with her. It was the Tuesday morning following Labor Day weekend. The summer was over, and I was returning from a restful vacation, burdened somewhat by the prospects of the correspondence, the messages, and the new responsibilities that awaited me. I had arrived early that morning, even before the receptionist, with the hope of getting a head start on my work. As I approached the clinic's entrance, I was shocked, however, to find a disheveled woman lying up against the locked door. Her hair was dirty and knotted, her clothes torn and stained. She looked up at me with piercing eyes and spoke my name. Who was this woman? How did she know my name? The sight of countless homeless people on the streets of the city every day had made me numb to the power of their despair, but I was suddenly startled to have one of them call me by name.

After unlocking the door, I asked her to come in and take a seat in the waiting room. As she emerged from a state of seeming incoherence, this woman told me that her name was "Rebecca Hasbrouck." She explained that an old college friend whom she had called after paging through a discarded phone book that she had found on the street had given her my name and address. Rebecca's friend apparently recognized the seriousness of her condition and urged her to get some professional help.

I asked Rebecca to tell me how I could be of assistance. With tears streaming down her face, she whispered that she needed to "return to the world" from which she had fled 3 years earlier. Not knowing what she meant, I asked her to tell me what that "world" was. The story that unfolded seemed unbelievable. She explained that just a few years earlier she was living a life of wealth and comfort in an upper middle-class suburb. Both she and her husband were very successful attorneys, and their two sons were bright, attractive, and athletically gifted. Oddly, Rebecca stopped there, as if that were the end of her story. Naturally, I asked her what happened then. Upon hearing my question, her eyes glazed over as she drifted into a detached state of apparent fantasy. I continued to speak to her, but she did not seem to hear my words. Several minutes went by, and she returned to our dialogue.

Rebecca proceeded to tell me the story of her journey into depression, despair, and poverty. Interestingly, the turning point in Rebecca's life was almost 3 years to the day of our encounter. As she and her family were returning from their vacation in the mountains, a large truck violently rammed their car, causing the car, which she was driving, to careen off the road and roll over several times. Rebecca was not sure how her body was propelled from the wreckage, but she does recall lying near the burning vehicle as fire consumed the three most important people in her life. For the weeks that she spent in the hospital, recovering from her own serious injuries, she wandered in and out of consciousness, convinced all the while that her experience was that of a bad dream from which she would soon awaken.

On her release from the hospital, she returned to her empty home but was tormented relentlessly by the voices and memories of her sons and husband. Realizing that she was in emotional turmoil, she turned to her mother for support and assistance. Sadly, Rebecca's mother was also struggling with one of her recurring episodes of severe depression and was unable to help Rebecca in her time of need. In fact, her mother sternly told Rebecca never to call again, because she did not want to be "burdened by" Rebecca's difficulties. Adding to Rebecca's dismay was the fact that she received a similar distancing response from the parents of her deceased husband, who told Rebecca that it was too painful for them to interact with the woman who had "killed" their son and grandchildren.

Feeling that she had no one to whom she could turn for help, Rebecca set out in search of her lost family members. In the middle of a cold October night, she walked out the front door of her home, dressed only in a nightgown and slippers. Walking the 4-mile distance into the center of town, she called out the names of these three "ghosts" and searched for them in familiar places. At one point, she went to the front door of the police chief's home and screamed at the top of her lungs that she wanted her sons and husband "released from prison." A police car was summoned, and she was taken to a psychiatric emergency room. However, during the process of her admission, she cleverly slipped away and set out on a path to reunite with her family members, who were "calling out" to her. During the 3 years that followed this tragic episode, Rebecca had fallen into a life of homelessness, losing all contact with her former world.

Sarah Tobin, PhD

1

Understanding Abnormality

A Look at History and Research Methods

In each chapter of this book, you will read a case study written in the words of Dr. Sarah Tobin, who is a composite of many of the qualities found in a good clinical psychologist. At the beginning of each chapter, Dr. Tobin tells us about her initial encounter with a client who has a problem pertinent to the content of that chapter. At the end of the chapter, after you have developed a better understanding about the client's disorder, we will return to Dr. Tobin's detailed discussion of the case. We believe that you will find each case to be an exciting opportunity to hear the thoughts of a clinician and you will develop an appreciation for the complexity and challenges involved in the diagnosis and treatment of psychological disorders.

The field of abnormal psychology is filled with countless fascinating stories of people who suffer from psychological disorders. In this chapter, we will try to give you some sense of the reality that psychological disturbance is certain to touch everyone, to some extent, at some point in life. As you progress through this course, you will almost certainly develop a sense of the pain and stigma associated with psychological problems. You will find yourself drawn into the many ways that mental health problems affect the lives of individuals, their families, and society. In addition to becoming more personally exposed to the emotional aspects of abnormal psychology, you will learn about the scientific and theoretical basis for understanding and treating the people who suffer from psychological disorders.

What Is Abnormal Behavior?

Think about how you would feel if you were to see someone like Rebecca walking around your neighborhood. You might be shocked, upset, or afraid, or you might even laugh. Why would you respond in this manner? Perhaps Rebecca would seem abnormal to you. But think further about this. On what basis would you judge Rebecca to be abnormal? Is it her dress, the fact that she is mumbling to herself, that she sounds paranoid, or that she is psychologically unstable? And what would account for your emotional responses to seeing this woman? Why should it bother you to see Rebecca behaving in this way? Do you imagine that she will hurt you? Are you upset because she seems so helpless and out of control? Do you laugh because she seems so ridiculous, or is there something about her that makes you nervous? Perhaps you speculate on the causes of Rebecca's bizarre behavior. Is she physically ill, intoxicated, or psychologically disturbed? And, if she is psychologically disturbed, how could her disturbance be explained? You might also feel concerned about Rebecca's welfare and wonder how she might be helped. Should you call the police to take her to a hospital? Or should you just leave her alone, because she presents no real danger to anyone? You may not have experienced a situation involving someone exactly like Rebecca, but you have certainly encountered some people in your life whom you regard as "abnormal," and your reactions to these people probably have included the range of feelings you would experience if you were to see Rebecca.

Conditions like Rebecca's are likely to touch you in a very

This woman is hesitant to use the phone, out of fear that her conversation might be recorded. How would you go about determining whether her concern is realistic or evidence of some kind of disturbed thinking?

personal way. Perhaps you have already been affected by the distressing effects of psychological disorders. Perhaps, you have been unusually depressed, fearful, or anxious, or maybe the emotional distress has been a step removed from you: your father struggles with alcoholism, or your mother has been hospitalized for severe depression; a sister has an eating disorder, or your brother has an irrational fear. If you have not encountered a psychological disorder within your immediate family, you have very likely encountered one in your extended family and circle of friends. You may not have known the formal psychiatric diagnosis for the problem, and you may not have understood its nature or cause. But you knew that something was wrong and that professional help was needed.

Until they are forced to face such problems, most people believe that "bad things" happen only to other people. Other people have car accidents, other people get cancer, and other people become severely depressed. We hope that reading this textbook will help you go beyond this "other people" syndrome. Psychological disorders are part of the human experience, touching the life—either directly or indirectly—of every person. As you read about these disorders and the people who suffer with them, you will find that most of these problems are treatable, and many are preventable.

What is "abnormal" behavior? You may have read this word in the title of the book without giving it much thought. Perhaps you told a friend that you were taking a course in "abnormal" psychology. Think about what you had in mind when you read or used the word *abnormal* as applied to human behavior. How would you define "abnormal" behavior? Read the following examples. Which of these behaviors do you regard as abnormal?

- Finding a "lucky" seat in an exam
- Being unable to sleep, eat, study, or talk to anyone else for days after a lover says, "It's over between us"
- Breaking into a cold sweat at the thought of being trapped in an elevator
- Swearing, throwing pillows, and pounding fists on the wall in the middle of an argument with a roommate
- Refusing to eat solid food for days at a time in order to stay thin
- Having to engage in a thorough hand-washing after coming home from a ride on a bus
- Believing that the government has agents who are listening in on telephone conversations
- Drinking a six-pack of beer a day in order to be "sociable" with friends after work

What is your basis for deciding between "normal" and "abnormal"? As you can see from this exercise, this distinction is often difficult to make. It may even seem arbitrary, yet it is essential that you arrive at a clear understanding of this term to guide you in your study of the many varieties of human behavior discussed in this book.

Defining *Abnormality*

Let's take a look at four important ways in which we will be discussing abnormality throughout the remainder of this book. As you read about these four criteria, you may notice some overlap, yet there are also some clear distinctions that should be apparent.

Distress

The story of Rebecca is that of a woman whose life was thrown into emotional chaos following a traumatic event in which she witnessed the death of her family members. The horror of this image propelled her into a state of profound psychological turmoil, as she looked for ways to cope with the loss of the most important people in her life. Distress, the experience of emotional or physical pain, is common in life. At times, the level of pain becomes so great that an individual finds it difficult to function. As you will see in many of the conditions discussed in this book, psychological pain, such as deep depression or intense anxiety, may be so great that some people cannot get through the tasks of daily life.

Impairment

In many instances, intense distress leads to a reduction in a person's ability to function, but there are also instances in which a person's functioning is deficient but he or she does not feel par-

The anxiety experienced by this business executive during a sales presentation may interfere with the quality of her performance.

ticularly upset. Impairment involves a reduction in a person's ability to function at an optimal or even an average level. For example, when a man consumes an excessive amount of alcohol, his perceptual and cognitive functioning is impaired, and he would be a danger behind the wheel of a car. He might not describe himself as feeling distressed, however; on the contrary, he may boast about how great he feels. For some of the conditions that you will read about, people feel fine and describe themselves with positive terms; however, others would regard them as functioning inadequately in primary spheres of life, such as at work or within their families. In the case of Rebecca, we see a woman who is both distressed and impaired.

Risk to Self or Other People

Sometimes people act in ways that cause risk to themselves or others. In this context, *risk* refers to danger or threat to the well-being of a person. For example, we would describe a severely depressed woman, such as Rebecca, as being at risk of committing suicide. In other situations, an individual's thoughts or behaviors are threatening to the physical or psychological welfare of other people. Thus, people who abuse children or exploit other people create a risk in society that is considered unacceptable and abnormal. Rebecca Hasbrouck certainly engaged in behavior that put her at risk, as she lived a life of a homeless person; out of contact with reality and loved ones, she roamed the streets, looking for the family members who had been killed.

Socially and Culturally Unacceptable Behavior

A final criterion for abnormality that will be relevant throughout this book is behavior that is outside the norms of the social and cultural context within which it takes place. For example, it wouldn't be odd to see people with painted faces and bizarre outfits cheering inside a college basketball arena, but such behavior would be abnormal in a college classroom. In this example, the social context calls for, and permits, very different kinds of behavior; people who deviate from the expected norms are regarded as abnormal.

Do you think that dressing as a Viking to run in the Boston marathon is normal or abnormal behavior?

In some instances, behavior that is regarded as odd within a given culture, society, or subgroup may be quite common elsewhere. For example, some people from Mediterranean cultures believe in a phenomenon called *mal de ojo,* or evil eye, in which they contend that the ill will of other people can affect them in profound ways. As a result, they may experience various bodily symptoms, such as fitful sleep, stomach distress, and fever. People expressing such beliefs in contemporary American culture might be regarded as odd, possibly a bit paranoid, or overly emotional. Returning to the case of Rebecca, we see behavior in which her attempts to contact deceased loved ones would be considered bizarre in the United States but not particularly unusual in an Asian culture. As you can see, the context within which a behavior takes place is a critical determinant of whether it is regarded as abnormal.

What Causes Abnormality?

Now that we have discussed criteria for defining *abnormality,* we can turn our attention to its causes. In trying to understand why people act and feel in ways that are regarded as abnormal, social scientists look at three dimensions: biological, psychological, and sociocultural. In other words, abnormal behavior arises from a complex set of determinants in the body, the mind, and the social context of the individual. Throughout this book, you will see that all three of these domains have relevance to the understanding and treatment of psychological disorders.

Biological Causes

In their efforts to understand the causes of abnormal behavior, mental health experts know that they must carefully evaluate what is going on in a person's body that can be attributed to ge-

netic inheritance or disturbances in physical functioning. As a routine component of every evaluation, Dr. Tobin knows that it is important for her to assess the extent to which a problem that seems to be emotionally caused can be explained in terms of biological determinants. Understanding the important causal role of biology also alerts Dr. Tobin to the fact that she may need to incorporate biological components, such as medication, into her intervention.

As is the case with many medical disorders, various psychological disorders run in families. For example, major depressive disorder is one of these disorders. The odds of a son or daughter of a depressed parent developing depression are statistically greater than they are for offspring of nondepressed parents. In the case of Rebecca Hasbrouck, Dr. Tobin would attend to the fact that Rebecca's mother suffers from recurring episodes of depression. Might Rebecca carry within her body a genetic vulnerability to developing a similar mood disorder?

In addition to considering the role of genetics, clinicians also consider the possibility that abnormal behavior may be the result of disturbances in physical functioning. Such disturbances can arise from various sources, such as medical conditions, brain damage, or exposure to certain kinds of environmental stimuli. Experts know that many medical conditions can cause a person to feel and act in ways that are abnormal. For example, a medical abnormality in the thyroid gland can cause wide variations in mood and emotionality. Brain damage resulting from a head trauma, even a slight one, can result in bizarre behavior and intense emotionality. Similarly, the ingestion of substances, either illicit drugs or prescribed medications, can result in emotional and behavioral changes that mimic a psychological disorder. Even exposure to environmental stimuli, such as toxic substances or allergens, can cause a person to experience disturbing emotional changes and behavior.

Psychological Causes

If biology could provide all the answers, then we would regard mental disorders as medical diseases. Obviously, there is more to the story. Disturbance commonly arises as a result of troubling life experiences. Perhaps an event an hour ago, last year, or in the early days of a person's life has left its mark in ways that cause dramatic changes in feelings or behavior. For example, a demeaning comment from a professor can leave a student feeling hurt and depressed for hours. A disappointment in an intimate relationship can evoke intense emotionality that lasts for months. A trauma that took place many years ago may continue to affect a person's thoughts, behavior, and even dreams during sleep. Life experiences may also contribute to psychological disorder by causing the individual to form negative associations to certain stimuli. For example, an irrational fear of small spaces may arise from being trapped in an elevator.

The trauma experienced by Rebecca Hasbrouck was so intense that her life was thrown into chaos and profound disturbance that would last for years. For Dr. Tobin to understand the nature of Rebecca's disorder, it would be important that she have a grasp of the extent of the trauma; such an understanding would also inform the treatment plan that she would develop to help Rebecca.

Thus, in evaluating psychological causes for abnormality, social scientists and clinicians consider a person's experiences. Most experiences are interpersonal—events that take place in interactions with other people. But people also have intrapsychic experiences, those that take place within thoughts and feelings. As you will see later in the text, emotional problems can arise from distorted perceptions and faulty ways of thinking. Take the case of a college student, Matt, who inferred that his girlfriend was angry with him because she failed to return his phone call. For more than a day, he was affected by feelings of anger, which led to feelings of depression. It was only after discussing the situation with his roommate that he realized that his response was irrational and probably related to a long history of disappointments with his parents, who had hurt him countless times because of their unreliability. Having internalized the notion that important people tend to disappoint, Matt goes through life expecting this to happen, even when the facts do not support his conclusion. Just as biology can lead to the development of abnormality, so can the psychologically significant events in a person's life.

Sociocultural Causes

So much of who we are is determined by interpersonal interactions that take place in the concentric circles of our lives. The term *sociocultural* refers to the various circles of social influence in the lives of people. The most immediate circle is comprised of those people with whom we interact on the most local level. For the typical college student, this would be a roommate, co-workers, and classmates who are seen regularly. Moving beyond the immediate circle are those people who inhabit the extended circle of relationships, such as family members back home or friends from high school. A third circle is comprised of the people in our environments with whom we interact minimally, and rarely by name, perhaps residents of our community or campus, whose standards, expectations, and behaviors influence our lives. A fourth social circle is the much wider culture in which we live, such as American society.

Abnormality can be caused by events in any or all of these social contexts. Troubled relationships with a roommate or family member can cause a person to feel deeply distressed. A failed relationship with a lover might lead to suicidal depression. Involvement in an abusive relationship may initiate an interpersonal style in which an abused person becomes repeatedly caught up with people who are hurtful and damaging. Being raised by a sadistic parent may cause a person to establish a pattern of close relationships characterized by control and emotional hurt. Political turmoil, even on a relatively local level, can evoke emotions ranging from disturbing anxiety to incapacitating fear. For some people, the cause of abnormality is much broader, perhaps cultural or societal. For example, the experience of discrimination has profound impact on a person who is part of a minority group, whether involving race, culture, sexual orientation, or disability.

Some social critics have taken an unorthodox stand in pointing out ways in which they believe that society can be at the roots of what is regarded and labeled as abnormal. Noted British psychiatrist R.D. Laing (1964) stirred up a debate that has lasted several decades by contending that modern society dehumanizes the individual, and that people who refuse to abide by the norms of this society are psychologically healthier than those who blindly accept and live by such restrictive social norms. Along similar lines, American psychiatrist Thomas Szasz (1961) argued that the concept of mental illness is a "myth" created by modern society and put into practice by the mental health profession. Szasz proposed that a better way to describe people who cannot fit into society's norms is that they have "problems in living." Such terminology avoids labeling people as "sick" and, instead, indicates that their difficulties stem from a mismatch between their personal needs and society's ability to meet those needs. Although most mental health professionals now regard the ideas of Laing and Szasz as simplistic, their ideas have caused mental health professionals to weigh the issues that these theorists have raised. The mental health community as a whole seems more sensitive today than in decades past to the need to avoid labeling people with psychological disorders as socially deviant. Such views also help promote social acceptance of people with emotional problems.

Criticisms of the mental health establishment, such as those raised by Laing and Szasz, became more credible when researcher David Rosenhan conducted a radical study, now regarded as a classic, that caused many people in the scientific community to take a second look at institutionalization. The Critical Issue box on page 8 describes the questions raised by Rosenhan's study, and it provides some insight into the ways in which sociocultural factors influence what people regard and label as abnormal.

Returning to the case of Rebecca, there are two ways in which sociocultural influences can be seen as playing a role in her depression. First, as the child of a depressed mother, Rebecca grew up in a family in which maternal impairment may have left its mark on her. Second, following the accident, Rebecca was profoundly affected by the decision of her mother and in-laws to distance themselves from her. Although these significant people in her life did not directly cause Rebecca's symptoms, they played a role in aggravating her impairment because of their emotional distancing.

Putting It All Together: A Biopsychosocial Perspective

The three categories of the causes of abnormality are summarized in Table 1.1. Disturbances in any of these areas of human functioning can contribute to the development of a psychological disorder. However, the causes of abnormality cannot be so neatly divided. There is often considerable interaction among the three sets of influences. Social scientists use the term **biopsychosocial** to refer to the interaction in which biological, psychological, and sociocultural factors play a role in the development of the individual. As you will see when reading about the conditions in this textbook, the degree of influence of each of these variables differs from disorder to disorder. For some disorders, such as schizophrenia, biology plays a dominant role. For some disorders, such as stress reactions, psychological factors predominate. And, for other

On Being Sane in Insane Places

On January 19, 1973, an article appeared in *Science* magazine that was to have an enormous impact on the entire mental health profession. This article, by David L. Rosenhan (1973), reported the findings of a study in which eight people successfully fooled the staffs of 12 psychiatric hospitals located across the United States. These people were all "sane" and were employed in a variety of mostly professional occupations. They each presented themselves at a hospital's admissions office, complaining that they had been hearing voices that said, "Empty," "Hollow," and "Thud." The kind of "existential psychosis" that these symptoms were supposed to represent has never been reported in the psychiatric literature, which is why those symptoms were chosen. No other details about the lives of the "pseudopatients" (except their names and employment) were changed when they described themselves; consequently, their histories and current behaviors outside of their symptoms could

not be considered abnormal in any way. All the hospitals accepted the pseudopatients for treatment. Once admitted to the hospitals, the pseudopatients stopped fabricating any symptoms at all. None of the staff in any of the hospitals detected the sanity of the pseudopatients and, instead, interpreted the ordinary activities of the pseudopatients on the hospital wards as further evidence of their abnormality. One of the most troubling experiences for the pseudopatients was a feeling of dehumanization, as they felt that no one on the staff cared about their personal issues and needs. Further, despite their efforts to convince the staff that they were normal, no one believed them, with the interesting exception of some of the patients, who guessed that they might be either reporters or researchers trying to get an inside look at mental hospitals.

It took from 7 to 52 days for the pseudopatients to be released from the hospitals. By the time they left, each had been given a diagnosis of schizophrenia "in remission"; in other words, their symptoms were no longer evident, at least for the time being. Rosenhan concluded that the misattribution of abnormality was due to a general bias among hospital staff to call a healthy person sick: "better to err on the side of caution, to suspect illness even among the healthy" (p. 251).

Rosenhan's study was criticized on both ethical and methodological grounds. Ethical concerns were raised about the

fact that the study involved the deception of the mental health professionals whose job it was to diagnose and treat the pseudopatients. Methodological questions were raised by the fact that no attempt was made to exercise the usual experimental controls on a study of this nature, such as having a comparison group (Spitzer, 1975). Other criticisms pertained to diagnostic issues. The pseudopatients were reporting serious symptoms (hallucinations) that would understandably cause alarm in others. At the point of discharge, the fact that the pseudopatients were labeled as being in remission implied that they were symptom-free. Technically, the staff probably felt reluctant to label these individuals as "normal" in light of the fact that the pseudopatients had previously complained of schizophrenia-like symptoms (Farber, 1975).

Despite these criticisms, Rosenhan's results and the debates that followed in the study's aftermath were part of the momentum in the late 1960s and early 1970s to change attitudes toward institutionalization of psychologically disturbed individuals. At the same time, mental health professionals were in the process of changing the system for diagnosing many disorders, including schizophrenia. The point of the study, however, is still pertinent today. When a patient in a psychiatric hospital claims to be "the sane one in an insane place," would anyone believe the patient?

conditions, such as post-traumatic stress disorder associated with experiences under a terrorist regime, the cause is primarily sociocultural.

Related to the biopsychosocial model is a very important concept that sheds light on the biopsychosocial approach. In many research articles and scholarly writings, you will come across the term **diathesis-stress model,** a proposal that people are born with a predisposition (or "diathesis") that places them at risk for developing a psychological disorder. Presumably, this vulnerability is genetic, although some theorists have proposed that the vulnerability may also be acquired due to certain early life events, such as traumas, diseases, birth complications, and even family experiences (Meehl, 1962; Zubin & Spring,

1977). When stress enters the picture, the person who carries such vulnerability is at considerable risk of developing the disorder to which he or she is prone. Rebecca Hasbrouck is a woman with a diathesis in the form of a genetic vulnerability to the development of a mood disorder. However, it was only following the experience of an intense life stress, the accident and family deaths, that the depression emerged. When we turn to the discussion of schizophrenia, you will read about the fascinating finding that this disorder, with a prominent genetic loading, cannot be fully explained by genetics. For example, in identical twin pairs, one twin may have the disorder while the other does not, even in instances involving a clear family history. As you will see, scientists believe that the affected twin

Table 1.1

Causes of Abnormality

Biological	Genetic inheritance
	Medical conditions
	Brain damage
	Exposure to environmental stimuli
Psychological	Traumatic life experiences
	Learned associations
	Distorted perceptions
	Faulty ways of thinking
Sociocultural	Disturbances in intimate relationships
	Problems in extended relationships
	Political or social unrest
	Discrimination toward one's social group

must have been exposed to a stressor not encountered by the unaffected twin.

The bottom line, of course, is that psychological disorders arise from complex interactions involving biological, psychological, and sociocultural factors. Special kinds of vulnerability, such as genetic, increase the likelihood of developing given disorders. You will also learn, however, that certain life experiences can protect people from developing conditions to which they are vulnerable. Protective factors, such as loving caregivers, adequate health care, and early life successes, reduce one's vulnerability considerably. By contrast, low vulnerability can be heightened when a person receives inadequate health care, engages in risky behaviors (such as using drugs), and gets involved in dysfunctional relationships. Some researchers provide quantitative estimates of the relative contributions of genes and environment to the development of a psychological disorder (McGue & Christensen, 1997). When we talk later in this book about specific disorders, such as schizophrenia, we will summarize the theories that scientists propose to explain the role of diathesis and stress in the development of each disorder.

■ Abnormal Psychology Throughout History

Now that you know about the complexities of defining and understanding abnormality, you can appreciate how very difficult it is to understand its causes. The greatest thinkers of the world, from Plato to the present day, have struggled to explain the oddities of human behavior. In this section, we will look at how the mental health field has arrived at current understandings of the causes and treatments of psychological disorders. You will see how ideas about psychological disorders have taken a variety of twists and turns throughout recorded history. There is every reason to expect that these concepts will continue to evolve.

Three prominent themes in explaining psychological disorders recur throughout history: the mystical, the scientific, and the humanitarian. Mystical explanations of psychological disorders regard abnormal behavior as the product of possession by evil or demonic spirits. The scientific approach looks for natural causes, such as biological imbalances, faulty learning processes, or emotional stressors. Humanitarian explanations view psychological disorders as the result of cruelty, nonacceptance, or poor living conditions. Tension among these three approaches has existed throughout history; at times, one or another has dominated, but all three have coexisted for centuries. Even in today's scientific world, the humanitarian and mystical approaches have their advocates. As you read about the historical trends in understanding and treating psychological disorders, see if you can identify which theme is most prevalent at each stage.

Prehistoric Times: Abnormal Behavior as Demonic Possession

There is no written record of ideas regarding psychological disorders in prehistoric times, but there is mysterious archeological evidence dating back to 8,000 B.C. during the Stone Age: skulls with holes drilled in them. Furthermore, there is evidence that the bone healed near these holes, evidence taken to indicate that the procedure was a surgical one and that people survived it. Why would prehistoric people perform such bizarre surgery?

Anthropologists have wondered whether this kind of surgery, called **trephining,** was performed as a way of treating psychological disorders. They theorize that prehistoric people thought that evil spirits that were trapped inside the head caused abnormal behavior and that releasing the evil spirits would

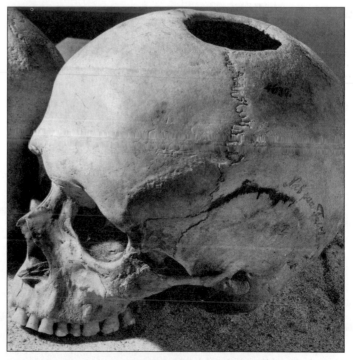

A trephined skull shows that prehistoric people tried to treat psychological disorders by releasing evil spirits from the head.

cause the person to return to normal. Another interpretation is that trephining was used to treat medical problems. For all we know, the procedure might have been an effective treatment for some psychological disturbances caused by physiological imbalances or abnormalities. In any case, the skulls are the only evidence we have from that period of history, and we can only speculate about their meaning (Maher & Maher, 1985).

Surprisingly enough, the practice of trephining did not end in the Stone Age. It was also practiced all over the world from ancient times through the eighteenth century, for various purposes from the magical to the medical. Evidence of trephining has been found from many countries and cultures, including the Far and Middle East, the Celtic tribes in Britain, ancient and recent China, India, and various peoples of North and South America, including the Mayans, Aztecs, Incas, and Brazilian Indians. The procedure is still in use among certain tribes in Africa for the relief of head wounds.

Another practice that was used in ancient times was the driving away of evil spirits through the ritual of exorcism. Although intended as a cure through the conjuring of spirits, the procedures involved in exorcism seem more like torture to our contemporary eyes. The possessed person might be starved, whipped, beaten, and treated in other extreme ways, with the intention of driving the evil spirits away. Some were forced to eat or drink foul-tasting and disgusting concoctions, which included blood, wine, and sheep dung. Some were executed, because they were considered a burden and a threat to their neighbors. These practices were carried out by a shaman, priest, or medicine man, a person thought by the community to possess magical powers. In some cases, the afflicted individual would simply be sent away from the community, forced to wander around the countryside, perhaps mocked by their neighbors but never helped by them. Although these practices are associated with early civilizations, variants of shamanism have appeared throughout history. The Greeks sought advice from oracles believed to be in contact with the gods. The Chinese practiced magic as a protection against demons. In India, shamanism flourished for centuries, and it still persists in Central Asia.

Had Rebecca lived at a time or in a culture in which exorcism was practiced, her symptoms might have been interpreted as signs of demonic possession. The voices she heard could have been devils speaking to her. Her bizarre behavior would have been perceived as evidence that she was under the control of a supernatural force. Frightened and disturbed by behaviors they could not understand, her neighbors might have sent her to a shaman, who would carry out the rites of exorcism. As you will see, such ideas played a prominent role in the understanding and treatment of psychological disorders for centuries to follow.

Ancient Greece and Rome: The Emergence of the Scientific Model

Even though their theories now may seem strange, early Greek philosophers established the foundation for a systematic approach to psychological disorders. Hippocrates (*ca.* 460–377

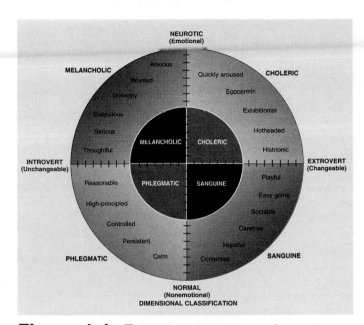

Figure 1.1   Four temperaments

An illustration of Eysenck's explanation of personality types. The two dimensions of neurotic-normal and introvert-extrovert interact to produce the four types described by Hippocrates.

B.C.), whom many people consider the founder of modern medicine, was concerned not only with physical diseases but with psychological problems as well. He believed that there were four important bodily fluids that influenced physical and mental health: black bile, yellow bile, phlegm, and blood. An excess of any of these fluids could account for changes in an individual's personality and behavior. For example, an excess of black bile would make a person depressed ("melancholic"), and an excess of yellow bile would cause a person to be anxious and irritable ("choleric"). Too much phlegm would result in a calm disposition bordering perhaps on indifference ("phlegmatic"). An overabundance of blood would cause a person to experience unstable mood shifts ("sanguine"). Treatment of a psychological disorder, then, involved ridding the body of the excess fluid through such methods as bleeding, purging (forced excretion), and administering emetics (nausea-producing substances) and establishing a healthier balance through proper nutrition.

As unlikely as it sounds, Hippocrates' classification of four types of fluid imbalances resurfaced in modern explanations of personality types. The classification proposed by Hans Eysenck (1967), shown in Figure 1.1, is based on a psychological test that provides scores on various personality dispositions. The two dimensions of neurotic–normal and introvert–extrovert interact to produce the four personality types shown in the figure. The resurfacing of ancient ideas in the form of a modern psychological theory suggests that, despite the very different philosophies that underlie these systems, there might be something to the notion that there are some enduring dimensions of personality.

The views of Hippocrates dominated medical thinking on the topic of psychological disorders for 500 years. However, these views were countered by the more popular belief in spiritual possession and the cruel treatment of psychologically disturbed people. The next significant advances in the medical approach were made by two Greek physicians living in Rome, separated by 200 years, who introduced new and more humane ideas about psychological disorders.

In the first century B.C., Aesclepiades rebelled against the Hippocratic belief that the imbalance of bodily substances caused psychological disorders. Instead, he recognized that emotional disturbances could result in psychological problems. This notion is comparable to many contemporary explanations of abnormal behavior. Aesclepiades also made diagnostic distinctions, such as the difference between acute and chronic psychological disorders and the difference between hallucinations and delusions. Today, these distinctions are taken for granted. As a therapist, Aesclepiades also developed some surprisingly modern ideas—for example, music therapy. In addition, he argued strenuously against the use of bleeding, imprisonment, and other cruel treatments.

Two hundred years later, Claudius Galen (A.D. 130–200) developed a system of medical knowledge that revolutionized previous thinking about psychological as well as physical disorders. Rather than rely on philosophical speculation, Galen studied anatomy to discover answers to questions about the workings of the human body and mind. He was the first "medical researcher" who conducted experiments on animals in order to study the workings of the internal organs. In fact, his books on anatomy were used until the nineteenth century. Unfortunately, although Galen made important advances in medicine, such as inventing the use of the pulse for diagnosis, he essentially maintained Hippocrates' beliefs that abnormality was the result of an imbalance of bodily substances. Nevertheless, the writings of Hippocrates and Galen formed the basis for the scientific model of abnormal behavior. These views were to be buried under the cloud of the Middle Ages and the return to superstition and spiritual explanations of abnormality.

The Middle Ages and Renaissance: The Re-emergence of Spiritual Explanations

The Middle Ages are sometimes referred to as the "Dark Ages." In terms of the approaches to psychological disorders, this was indeed a dark period. No scientific or medical advances occurred beyond those of Hippocrates and Galen. In the rare cases in which people with psychological disorders sought medical treatment, the physician could offer little beyond the barbaric methods of purging and bleeding, ineffectual attempts to manipulate diet, or the prescription of useless drugs.

During the Middle Ages, there was a resurgence of primitive beliefs regarding spiritual possession. People turned to superstition, astrology, and alchemy to explain many natural phenomena, including psychological and physical illnesses. So-called treatments corresponding to these beliefs, including magical rituals, exorcism, and folk medicines, were widely practiced. Beliefs in demonic possession were also used to account for abnormal behavior, and people who sought help from

Hieronymous Bosch's *Removal of the Stone of Folly* depicted the prevailing belief that spiritual possession was the cause of psychological disorder.

the clergy were treated as sinners, witches, or embodiments of the devil. The punishment and execution of people accused of being witches became more widespread toward the end of the Middle Ages, especially during the Renaissance.

The dominance of religious thinking in the Middle Ages had both positive and negative effects on the care of psychologically disturbed individuals. Beliefs in spiritual possession and the treatment of people as sinners had harmful effects. By contrast, ideas about Christian charity and the need to help poor and sick people formed the basis for more humanitarian approaches to treatment. Monasteries began to open their doors to give these people a place to stay and receive whatever primitive treatments the monks could offer. Poorhouses, or homes for people who could not pay their living expenses, were built all over Europe. Many of them sheltered people who were emotionally disturbed.

Later, the poorhouses became known as **asylums.** One of the most famous of these asylums was the Hospital of St. Mary of Bethlehem in London. Originally founded as a hospital for poor people in 1247, by 1403 it began to house people referred to at the time as "lunatics." In the centuries to follow, the term *bedlam,* a derivative of the hospital's name, became synonymous with the chaotic and inhumane housing of psychologically

The inhumane treatment at the Hospital of St. Mary of Bethlehem in London is shown in William Hogarth's *The Madhouse.*

disturbed people who languished unattended for years (Mac-Donald, 1981). As the hospital became more crowded and its occupants increasingly unruly, the hospital workers resorted to chains and other punishments to keep the inhabitants under control. Similar conditions prevailed in other asylums as they became more and more crowded. Unfortunately, the original intention of enlisting clergy to treat psychologically disturbed individuals with humanitarian methods had disastrous consequences. Not until several centuries later were the humanitarian ideals reinstated.

In contrast to what you might learn in a history class about the Renaissance as a period of enlightenment, you will see that this period was far from enlightened with regard to an understanding of psychological disorders. There were virtually no scientific or humanitarian advances during this entire period, and demonic possession remained the prevalent explanation for abnormal behavior of any kind. Some historical accounts have proposed that witch hunts, conducted on a wide scale throughout Europe and later in North America, were directed at people with psychological disturbances. These acts were seen as justified by the publication of the *Malleus Malificarum,* an indictment of witches written by two Dominican monks in Germany in 1486, in which witches were denounced as heretics and devils who must be destroyed in the interest of preserving Christianity. The "treatment" it recommended was deportation, torture, and burning at the stake. Women, particularly old women, as well as midwives, were the main targets of persecution. Once a woman was labeled a witch by the Church, there was no escape for her.

Were Rebecca to be treated during this era, she might have been regarded as a witch, especially if she were heard to refer to the devil or any other supernatural force. However, if she were lucky, someone might consult a medical practitioner. In the midst of the witch hunt frenzy, some voices of reason were starting to be heard, and, in the 1500s, the idea began to spread that people who showed signs of demonic possession might be psychologically disturbed. In 1563, a physician named Johann Weyer (1515–1588) wrote an important book called *The Decep-*

tion of Demons, in which he tried to debunk the myth that psychologically disturbed people were possessed by the devil. Although Weyer did not abandon the notion of demonic possession, his book represented the first major advance since the time of Galen in the description and classification of forms of abnormal behavior. Weyer's approach also formed the basis for what later became a renewal of the humanitarian approach to psychologically disturbed people. However, at the time of his writing, Weyer was severely criticized and ridiculed for challenging the views held by the powerful and influential religious and political leaders of the time. However, in another part of Europe, Weyer's "radical" ideas were being echoed by an Englishman, Reginald Scot (1538–1599), who deviated even further from the prevalent ideologies by denying the very existence of demons.

Europe and the United States in the 1700s: The Reform Movement

The eighteenth century was a time of massive political and social reform throughout Europe. By this point, public institutions housing individuals with psychological disorders had become like dungeons, where people were not even given the care that would be accorded an animal. The living conditions for poor people were miserable, but to be both psychologically disturbed and poor was a horrible fate. People with psychological disorders lived in dark, cold cells with dirt floors and were often

If Rebecca were living in New England during the height of the Salem witch trials, she might have suffered the fate of the woman in this picture who is shown here being arrested.

This painting shows Philippe Pinel having the irons removed from the inmates at La Salpêtrière Hospital. It was actually Pinel's employer, Jean-Baptiste Pussin, who performed this liberating gesture.

chained to straw beds and surrounded by their own excrement. It was widely believed that psychologically disturbed people were insensitive to extremes of heat and cold or to the cleanliness of their surroundings. The "treatment" given to these people involved bleeding, forced vomiting, and purging. It took a few courageous people, who recognized the inhumanity of the existing practices, to bring about sweeping reforms.

The leader of the reform movement was Vincenzo Chiarugi (1759–1820). Fresh from medical school, at the age of 26, he was given the responsibility of heading *Ospitdale di Bonifacio,* the newly built mental hospital in Florence. Within a year of taking charge of the hospital, he instituted a set of revolutionary standards for the care of mental patients. These standards were a landmark in creating general principles for care of the mentally ill, including a detailed history for each patient, high hygiene standards, recreational facilities, occupational therapies, minimal use of restraints, and respect for individual dignity. In 1793–1794, Chiarugi published a major work on the causes and classification of "insanity," which he regarded as due to impairment of the brain. Thus, Chiarugi made important contributions to both the humanitarian and scientific models of abnormality.

More attention was given, however, to the reforms of Philippe Pinel (1745–1826) in La Bicêtre, a hospital in Paris with conditions like those faced by Chiarugi. On his appointment as a hospital physician in 1792, a hospital worker, Jean-Baptiste Pussin, who had begun the process of reform, influenced Pinel. Together, they made changes to improve the living conditions of the patients. When Pinel left La Bicêtre 2 years later, Pussin stayed behind. It was then that Pussin made the bold gesture of freeing patients from their chains, an act for which Pinel is mistakenly given credit. After leaving La Bicêtre, Pinel became director of La Salpêtrière Hospital, where he and Pussin continued to spread these reforms.

England was the third country to see major reforms in its treatment of psychologically disturbed individuals. In 1792, an English Quaker named William Tuke established the York Retreat, an institution based on the religious humanitarian principles of the Quakers. Tuke's work was carried on by succeeding

generations of his family. Their methods became known as **moral treatment** and were based on the philosophy that the mentally ill deserved to be treated with humanity. Underlying this approach was the philosophy that, with the proper care, people can develop self-control over their own disturbed behaviors. Restraints were used only if absolutely necessary, and, even in those cases, the patient's comfort came first.

At the time of Europe's revolutionary reforms, similar changes in the care of psychologically disturbed people were being initiated in the United States. Benjamin Rush (1745–1813) became known as the founder of American psychiatry for his rekindling of interest in the scientific approach to psychological disorders. His text, *Observations and Inquiries upon the Diseases of the Mind,* written in 1812, was the first psychiatric textbook printed in the United States. Rush, who was one of the signers of the Declaration of Independence, achieved fame outside psychiatry as well. He was a politician, statesman, surgeon general, and writer in many diverse fields, ranging from philosophy to meteorology. Because of his prestigious role in American society, he was able to influence the institution of reforms in the mental health field. In 1783, he joined the medical staff of Pennsylvania Hospital. Rush was appalled by the poor conditions in the hospital and by the fact that psychologically disturbed patients were placed on wards with the physically ill. He spoke out for changes that were considered radical at the time, such as placing psychologically disturbed patients in separate wards, giving them occupational therapy, and prohibiting visits from curiosity seekers who frequented the hospital for entertainment.

In evaluating Rush's contributions, we must also mention that he advocated some of what we now regard as barbaric interventions that were accepted conventions at the time. For example, Rush supported the use of bloodletting and purging in the treatment of psychological disorders. Some of his methods were unusual and seem sadistic now—such as the "tranquilizer" chair, to which a patient was tied. The chair was intended to reduce stimulating blood flow to the brain by binding the patient's head and limbs. Rush also recommended that patients be submerged in cold shower baths and frightened with threats that

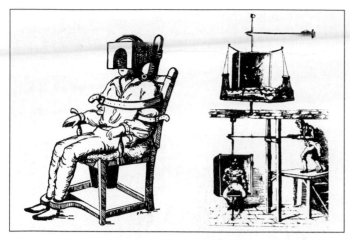

Benjamin Rush's methods of treatment, based on what he thought were scientific principles, would be considered barbaric by today's standards.

Source: National Library of Medicine.

they would be killed. Similar techniques were used by other physicians at the time, such as surprise immersions into tubs of cold water and the "well-cure," in which a patient was placed at the bottom of a well as water was slowly poured into it. Rush and his contemporaries thought that the fright induced by these methods would counteract the overexcitement responsible for their violent and bizarre behavior (Deutsch, 1949). It is ironic that, in the spirit of reform, methods just as primitive as those of the Middle Ages continued to be developed.

Despite the more humane changes Rush advocated, conditions in asylums worsened over the next 30 years with continued overcrowding. The psychologically disturbed patients were often forced to live in poorhouses and jails, where conditions were even less conducive to treatment than in the asylums. By 1841, when a Boston schoolteacher named Dorothea Dix (1802–1887) made her first venture into these institutions, conditions had become ripe for another round of major reforms. She was shocked and repulsed by scenes that were reminiscent of the horrifying conditions that European reformers had faced in the previous century. Her first encounter was with the prison system, in which many psychologically disturbed people were incarcerated. Inmates were chained to the walls, no heat was provided for them, and they were forced to live in filth. Viewing these conditions was enough to set Dix off onto an investigative path. She traveled throughout Massachusetts, visiting jails and poorhouses and chronicling the horrors she witnessed. Two years later, Dix presented her findings to the Massachusetts Legislature, with the demand that more state-funded public hospitals be built to care specifically for the psychologically disturbed. Dix believed, furthermore, that the proper care involved the application of moral treatment. From Massachusetts, Dix spread her message throughout North America, and even to Europe. She spent the next 40 years campaigning for the proper treatment of psychologically disturbed people. She was a very effective champion of this cause, and her efforts resulted in the growth of the state hospital movement.

In the century to follow, scores of state hospitals were built throughout the United States. Once again, as in the Middle Ages, the best intentions of the mental health reformers became lost and ultimately backfired. These new state hospitals became so overcrowded and understaffed that treatment conditions deteriorated. The wards in these hospitals were overflowing with people whose symptoms included violent and destructive behaviors. Under these circumstances, there was no way to fulfill Dix's goal of providing moral therapy. Instead, the staff resorted to the use of physical restraints and other measures that moral therapy was intended to replace. However, there were some reforms, such as allowing patients to work on the hospital grounds and to participate in various forms of recreation. At the same time, though, these institutions became custodial facilities where people spent their entire lives, an outcome that Dix had not anticipated. It simply was not possible to "cure" people of these serious disorders by providing them with the well-intentioned but ineffective interventions proposed by moral therapy. Furthermore, over the course of several decades, the emphasis of this form of treatment had shifted almost solely toward disciplinary enforcement of the institution's rules and away from the more humane spirit of the original idea.

Even though moral therapy was a failure, the humanitarian goals that Dix advocated had a lasting influence on the mental health system. Her work was carried forward into the 1900s by advocates of the "mental hygiene" movement—most notably, Clifford Beers. In 1908, Beers wrote the autobiographical *A Mind That Found Itself,* which recounted in alarming detail his own harsh treatment in psychiatric institutions. Beers had become so enraged by the inhumane treatments that he established the National Committee for Mental Hygiene, a group of people who worked to improve the treatment of those in psychiatric institutions.

Dorothea Dix worked throughout the late 1800s to move psychologically disturbed people from jails and poorhouses to state-funded hospitals, where they could receive more humane treatment.

The 1800s to the 1900s: Development of Alternative Models for Abnormal Behavior

While Dix was engaged in her reform campaign, the superintendents of existing state mental hospitals were also trying to develop better ways to manage patients. In 1844, a group of 13 mental hospital administrators formed the Association of Medical Superintendents of American Institutions for the Insane. The name of this organization was eventually changed to the American Psychiatric Association. The founding of this organization gave rise to the **medical model,** the view that abnormal behaviors result from physical problems and should be treated medically.

The goals of the American Psychiatric Association were furthered by the publication in 1845 of a book on the pathology and treatment of psychological disorders by William Greisinger, a German psychiatrist. Greisinger focused on the role of the brain, rather than spirit possession, in abnormal behavior. Another German psychiatrist, Emil Kraepelin, was also influential in the development of the American psychiatric movement. Kraepelin carried further Greisinger's ideas that brain malfunction caused psychological disorder. He is perhaps better known, however, for his efforts to improve the way that psychological disorders were classified. Kraepelin's ideas continue to be influential even today, and some of the distinctions he introduced are reflected in contemporary systems of psychiatric diagnosis. For example, Kraepelin's concept of manic-depression was a precursor to what is now called bipolar disorder; his concept of dementia praecox (premature degeneration) is now known as schizophrenia.

At the same time that the medical model was evolving, a very different approach to understanding psychological problems was also taking root. The **psychoanalytic model,** which

Anton Mesmer claimed that, by redistributing the magnetic fluids in the patient's body, he could cure psychological disorders. Mesmer, standing in the far right-hand corner of the room, is holding a wand while his patients hold metal rods.

seeks explanations of abnormal behavior in the workings of unconscious psychological processes, had its origins in the controversial techniques developed by Anton Mesmer (1734–1815), a Viennese physician. Mesmer gained notoriety for his dramatic interventions involving hypnotic techniques. Expelled from Vienna for what were regarded as false claims of cure, Mesmer traveled to Paris, where the same misfortune befell him. Wherever he went, the medical establishment regarded him as a fraud because of his unbelievable assertions and questionable practices. In 1766, Mesmer published a book called *The Influence of the Planets,* which promoted the idea that magnetic fluid filled the universe and, therefore, was in the bodies of all living creatures. He maintained that physical and psychological disturbances were the result of an imbalance in this magnetic fluid, called animal "magnetism." These disturbances could be corrected by a device Mesmer invented called a "magnetizer." So many people became interested in this cure that Mesmer began to treat them in groups. Mesmer's patients held hands around a "baquet," a large oak tub containing water, iron filings, and glass particles, while he walked around them, stroking them with a magnetic wand. This practice became exceptionally popular in Paris because of reports of beneficial effects. Hundreds of sick individuals, particularly women, went to Mesmer's clinic. The medical establishment decided to investigate Mesmer's practices, which aroused suspicion due to their questionable scientific basis. In 1784, the French government invited Benjamin Franklin to head a commission to investigate animal magnetism. The investigation lasted 7 years and concluded that the effects of magnetism were due to "excitement of the imagination" (Baker, 1990).

An English physician, James Braid (1795–1860), was intrigued by what he heard about magnetism's popularity in France and decided to investigate how such a questionable method could actually produce such dramatic benefits. Braid became convinced that whatever positive effects occurred were unrelated to animal magnetism. Instead, Braid proposed that

The work of Emil Kraepelin, a German psychiatrist, led to improved ways of classifying psychological disorders.

changes took place in people's minds, outside their conscious awareness, that could explain the "cures" attributed to mesmerism. In 1842, Braid introduced the term **hypnotism** to describe the process of being put into a trance, which he believed to be the cause of Mesmer's ability to effect changes in the minds of his subjects. He reasoned that some people treated by Mesmer's method improved because they were in a hypnotic state and were open to suggestions that could result in the removal of their symptoms. The term **mesmerized,** in fact, refers to this state of heightened suggestibility brought about by the words and actions of a charismatic individual. Braid's explanation of hypnosis played an important role in leading practitioners to realize how powerful the mind can be in causing and removing symptoms.

Two decades later, Ambrose-Auguste Liébault (1823–1904), a French doctor, began to experiment with mesmerism. Many of Liébault's patients were poor farmers, whom Liébault treated in his clinic in Nancy, France. Liébault discovered that he could use hypnotic sleep induction as a substitute for drugs. Liébault's clinic eventually became well known for innovative treatments. In 1882, another physician, Hippolyte-Marie Bernheim (1837–1919), who became one of the major proponents of hypnotism in Europe, visited Liébault. Bernheim was seeking Liébault's help in treating a patient with severe back pains for whom other forms of therapy were unsuccessful. Liébault's cure of this patient convinced Bernheim that hypnosis was the wave of the future.

From their work at the Nancy clinic, Bernheim and Liébault gained international attention for advances in the use of hypnosis as a treatment for nervous and psychological disorders. At the same time, an esteemed neurologist in Paris, Jean-Martin Charcot (1825–1893), was testing similar techniques in La Salpêtrière Hospital. However, Charcot's Salpêtrière "school" of hypnosis differed sharply in its explanation of how hypnosis worked. Charcot believed that hypnotizability was actually a symptom of a neurological disorder and that only people who suffered from this disorder could be treated by hypnosis. You can see how Charcot's notion that hypnosis involved physical changes in the nervous system was a radical departure from the Nancy school's position. The weight of evidence, however, was in favor of the Nancy school, and eventually Charcot adopted its position. Hypnosis was clearly understood as a psychological process that could be very instrumental in resolving certain kinds of disorders. In particular, hypnosis became the treatment of choice for **hysteria,** a disorder in which psychological problems become expressed in physical form. A girl whom Mesmer "cured" of her blindness was probably suffering from hysteria; in other words, a psychological conflict was converted into an apparent sensory deficit. Other forms of hysteria became widely known in the medical establishment, including various forms of paralysis, pain disorders, and a wide range of sensory deficits, such as blindness and hearing loss.

The development of hypnosis went on to play a central role in the evolution of psychological methods for treating psychological disorders. In fact, Sigmund Freud (1856–1939) was heavily influenced by both Charcot and Bernheim in his early work with hysterical patients. Freud originally studied medi-

French neurologist Jean-Martin Charcot is shown demonstrating a hypnotic technique during a medical lecture.

cine in Vienna, where he trained as a neurologist. After graduating from the University of Vienna, Freud traveled to France to learn about hypnosis, a method of treatment that fascinated him. In *Studies in Hysteria* (Breuer & Freud, 1892/1982), written with his colleague, Josef Breuer (1842–1925), Freud analyzed the famous case of "Anna O." and other women suffering from hysteria. Freud and Breuer described how Anna O. was cured of her many and varied hysterical symptoms by the use of hypnosis. In addition, however, Anna O. urged Breuer, who was actually the one treating her, to allow her to engage in "chimney sweeping," which she also called the "talking cure." When she was allowed simply to talk about her problems, she felt better, and her symptoms disappeared. Freud and Breuer called this the "cathartic method," a cleansing of the mind's emotional conflicts through talking about them. The cathartic method was the forerunner of **psychotherapy,** the treatment of abnormal behavior through psychological techniques. This discovery eventually led Freud to develop **psychoanalysis,** a theory and system of practice that relied heavily on the concepts of the unconscious mind, inhibited sexual impulses, and early development, as well as the use of the "free association" technique and dream analysis.

In the early 1900s, Freud attracted a variety of brilliant minds and courageous practitioners from across the Atlantic Ocean and all over Europe, who came to work with him at his home in Vienna. Although many of these people eventually broke rank and went on to develop their own theories and training schools, Freud's legacy continues to maintain an important position throughout the world.

The Late Twentieth Century: The Challenge of Providing Humane and Effective Treatment

When first encountering the various historical approaches to understanding and treating psychological disorders, you may wonder how it could be possible for people to have such extreme beliefs as demonic possession and to propose such

As recently as the 1970s, many patients in psychiatric hospitals were restrained physically, such as in cribs with bars.

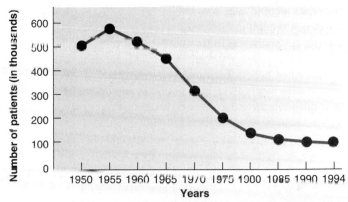

Figure 1.2   The Number of patients in psychiatric hospitals, 1950–1994

The number of patients in psychiatric hospitals in the United States has dropped steadily since 1960.

seemingly naive treatments as moral therapy and the use of mechanical devices as cures. However, if you look around at the popular media and perhaps even in your local bookstore, you can readily find examples of spiritual, mystical, or "new age" approaches to physical and psychological treatment. For the most part, mainstream contemporary society takes a more scientific approach to understanding and treating psychological disorders. The scientific approach, rooted in the ideas of ancient Greek philosophers and physicians, began to be applied systematically in the mid-1900s and is now the predominant view in Western culture.

In the 1950s, scientists introduced medications that controlled some of the debilitating symptoms of severe psychological disturbance. Because of the many reports of dramatic reduction in symptoms, these medicines were quickly incorporated into the treatment regimens of mental hospitals. They were seen as an easy solution to the centuries-old problem of how to control the harmful and bizarre behaviors of psychologically disturbed people and possibly even to cure them. The initial hopes for these "miracle drugs" were naive and simplistic. No one realized that these medications could have harmful physical side effects, some of which could cause irreversible neurological damage. Swept away by early enthusiasm, mental health professionals often became caught up in the indiscriminate and unselective use of large doses of powerful drugs. An extreme overemphasis on the medical model also had the unanticipated effect of inattention to the other mental health needs of these patients.

Until the 1970s, despite the growing body of knowledge about the causes of abnormal behavior, the actual practices used in the day-to-day care of psychologically disturbed people were sometimes as barbaric as those used in the Middle Ages. Even people suffering from the least severe psychological disorders were often housed in what were known as the "back wards" of large and impersonal state institutions, without adequate or appropriate care. Although patients were not chained to the walls of their cells, they were frequently severely restrained by the use of powerful tranquilizing drugs and strait-

jackets, coats with sleeves long enough to wrap around the patient's torso. Even more radical was the indiscriminate use of behavior-altering brain surgery or the application of electrical shocks—so-called treatments that were often used as punishments intended to control unruly patients (see more on these procedures in Chapter 2).

Public outrage over these abuses in mental hospitals finally led to a more widespread realization that dramatic changes were needed in the provision of mental health services. The federal government took emphatic action in 1963 with the passage of groundbreaking legislation. The Mental Retardation Facilities and Community Mental Health Center Construction Act of that year initiated a series of changes that would affect mental health services for decades to come. Legislators began to promote policies designed to move people out of institutions and into less restrictive programs in the community, such as vocational rehabilitation facilities, day hospitals, and psychiatric clinics. People were placed in halfway houses after their discharge from the hospital, which provided a supportive environment in which they could learn the social skills needed to reenter the community. By the mid-1970s, the state mental hospitals which had once been overflowing with patients, were practically deserted (see Figure 1.2). Hundreds of thousands of people who had been confined to dreary institutions were freed, to begin living with greater dignity and autonomy.

Unfortunately, like all other supposed breakthroughs in the treatment of psychologically disturbed people, the **deinstitutionalization movement** that promoted the release of psychiatric clients into community treatment sites did not completely fulfill the dreams of its originators. Rather than abolishing inhumane treatment, deinstitutionalization created another set of woes. Many of the promises and programs hailed as alternatives to institutionalization ultimately failed to come through because of inadequate planning and insufficient funds. Patients were often shuttled back and forth between hospitals, halfway houses, and shabby boarding homes, never having a sense of stability or respect. Some social critics have questioned whether the almost indiscriminate release of psychologically disturbed people was too radical a step that took place too rapidly. Although the intention of releasing patients from psychiatric hospitals was to free people who had been deprived of basic human rights, the result may not have been as liberating as many had hoped. In contemporary American society, many people who would have been found inside the walls of psychiatric hospitals three decades ago are being moved through a circuit of shelters, rehabilitation programs, jails, and prisons, with a disturbing number of these individuals spending long periods of time as homeless and marginalized members of society (Haugland, Siegel, Hopper, & Alexander, 1997).

While many of the reports regarding the effects of deinstitutionalization have been negative, some investigators have asserted that moving people out of institutions has been beneficial when the resources have been carefully reallocated. One researcher, Robert Okin (1995), compared patients who had been moved out of state hospitals in Massachusetts between the years 1978 and 1993. He compared communities in which there was greater reliance on returning disturbed individuals to the hospital with communities that made greater use of comprehensive community services. He found that the total expenditures per capita were roughly the same. Even though community care is very expensive, it is not cumulatively more expensive than the unnecessary use of inpatient care.

Emphasizing the importance of community follow-up, Okin and his colleagues (Okin, Borus & Baer, 1995) found some striking results in their longitudinal study of 53 chronically mentally ill people following their discharge from a state hospital into structured group home settings. Seven and a half years after discharge, 57 percent of these individuals continued to live in residential settings, and more than one fourth had moved on to independent living. Although more than half had to be readmitted to the hospital for some period of time, the amount of time spent in the hospital was relatively brief. Most important were the findings that almost all the individuals expressed a clear preference for life outside the hospital, with many showing impressive improvements in functioning.

Integral to the success of a community program are approaches that help individuals help themselves. The field is moving toward a recovery-oriented mental health system in which community support is viewed as crucial in helping seriously disturbed people cope with psychological disorders. Recovery from psychological disorder can be viewed as comparable to recovery from a physical condition. In both cases, there is a difference between cure and recovery. Even though people who have suffered an affliction may continue to have symptoms, they can develop coping strategies that help them adapt and move on with their lives. An important component of this approach is the notion that people can recover without professional intervention. Presumably, mental health professionals facilitate the recovery of a person with a psychological disorder, but it is really up to the client, who is called a consumer in this model, to take the steps toward recovery, usually by reaching out to others. Essential to recovery is the availability of people who are concerned about and supportive of the struggling individual, especially in times of active symptoms or intense stress. Self-help can be derived through contact with relatives, friends, groups, and churches. Although the recovery model rests on some lofty

ideals, influential changes have emerged from this framework, along with recommendations for new ways of responding to the needs of psychologically troubled people in the years to come.

In recent years, changes in the insurance industry have had a tremendous effect on the provision of mental health care. Managed health care has become the standard by which third-party payers, such as insurance companies, oversee reimbursement for health services. In a managed care system, all medical and mental health procedures are evaluated to ensure that they provide the best therapeutic value at the least financial cost. For example, if you are in need of a dental filling for a cavity, a dental managed care company will reimburse your dentist for a routine filling, but it would be unwilling to pay for monthly cleanings, because they would be viewed as unnecessary. In the field of mental health care, insurers also want to be certain that the care provided to clients is effective, inexpensive, and limited to what is absolutely necessary.

The rationale of managed care rests on the notion that everyone involved saves money when excessive costs are contained. Unfortunately, many practitioners feel that the ideals on which health maintenance organizations and related provider systems were developed three decades ago have been compromised by recent changes aimed at short-term cost savings with little foresight about the long-term effects on clients and society (Karon, 1995). For example, 15 years ago, a seriously depressed client might have remained in the hospital for several weeks of treatment, but today he or she might be released after a few days, because an insurance company would regard extended inpatient treatment as unnecessary and too expensive. What does this mean for the many individuals who suffer from chronic psychological disorders? In the worst-case scenario, they are released to the community, where they may be at risk of deterioration and neglect.

In a recent survey of nearly 16,000 licensed psychologists, four out of every five respondents reported that managed care was negatively affecting their clinical practice (Phelps, Eisman & Kohout, 1998). Of particular concern are the ethical dilemmas raised by working within a managed care system (Murphy, DeBernardo, & Shoemaker, 1998; Rothbaum et al., 1998). For

Group therapy provides a context for clients to share their stories with others, and in doing so obtain support and guidance from people dealing with similar problems.

example, clinicians are concerned about the compromise of confidentiality standards, as is the case when they must submit detailed personal information about their patients to seemingly anonymous utilization staff at the managed care company's central office. Many clinicians also complain that managed care decisions commonly lead to the provision of inadequate care or inappropriate treatment—decisions that are based on cost rather than clinical need.

In recent years, consumers have joined with providers in expressing their alarm about inadequacies in the health care system, and some promising changes have taken place. State legislatures have responded to public concern by enacting laws that regulate managed care practices and decisions, ranging from specifying the minimum number of hospital days following the birth of a baby to determining the minimum number of sessions provided for psychological disorders (Heldring, 1998).

As we enter the new century, we still face the prospect of many seriously disturbed people wandering homeless in the streets without adequate care and perhaps moving in and out of jails and shelters. Ironically, this situation is not unlike that which confronted Dorothea Dix 150 years ago. Like Dorothea Dix, some contemporary advocates have suggested new forms of compassionate treatment for people who suffer from psychological disorders. In particular, methods of collaboration between the mental health establishment and "consumers" of services are being developed in which the consumers are encouraged to take an active role in choosing their treatment. The community, in turn, can provide greater financial and emotional support, so that those with psychological disorders can survive more effectively outside the institution.

In the decades to come, experts and lay people will continue to struggle to find the proper balance between providing asylum for those in need and incarcerating people in institutions beyond the point at which they are helped. At the same time, scientific researchers will continue to search for the causes of abnormal behavior and the most effective forms of treatment. In the next section, we will examine research methods used by scientists to deal with these crucial issues.

Research Methods in Abnormal Psychology

Psychological disorders are such a fascinating and mysterious aspect of human behavior that people feel compelled to offer explanations, even without adequate support. Popular books claiming that psychological problems are due to everything from diet to radioactivity are regularly published. You can pick up almost any newspaper and read simplistic speculations about the profile of a murderer or a person who has committed suicide. Such easy explanations can be misleading, because they lack a grounding in psychological theory and scientific data.

The Scientific Method

Claims about the cause and treatment of abnormal behavior must be made on the basis of solid, scientific research rather than speculation. We will explain briefly the essentials of scientific methods as applied to abnormal psychology. In this process, we will discuss topics that you may have learned in introductory psychology or in a psychological methods course. Our review of this topic will explain the aspects of research methods that apply specifically to the study of abnormal psychology. This review will equip you to read reports in newspapers and magazines with an eye for scientific standards. An overview of research methods in abnormal psychology is contained in Table 1.2.

The essence of the scientific method is objectivity, the process of testing ideas about the nature of psychological phenomena without bias before accepting these ideas as adequate explanations. Taking a farfetched example, let's say you suspect that people who live on the East Coast are more stable psychologically than people who live on the West Coast (or vice versa, if you live on the West Coast). You should test this suspicion systematically before accepting it as "fact." As you set about this process, you would certainly want to hold open the possibility that your initial hunch was in error. The potential to discard an erroneous idea is an essential ingredient of the scientific method.

The underlying logic of the scientific method involves three concepts: observation, hypothesis formation, and the ruling out of competing explanations through proper controls. You have probably already used the scientific method yourself without referring to it in these terms. You may have found, for example, that it seems every time you have a caffeinated drink, such as coffee, after 6 P.M. you have trouble falling asleep. What would you need to do to test this possibility? You might go through the **observation process,** in which you mentally keep track of the differences between the nights you drink coffee and the nights you do not. The **hypothesis formation process** would be the step of predicting that drinking coffee causes you to stay awake at night. To test this hypothesis, you could try experimenting with drinking coffee on some nights but not on others. Next, you must rule out competing explanations. You must be careful not to drink coffee on a night that you have just watched a scary television program, for example. Otherwise, you would have no way of knowing whether your sleep problems were due to the coffee or to the anxiety created by the movie.

Although the coffee-drinking example may seem rather simple, it highlights the basic issues involved in most of the research we will encounter in this book. Researchers in abnormal psychology begin by observing a phenomenon of interest, form hypotheses to explain it, and then design ways to eliminate as many competing explanations as possible. This last step often is the most difficult, because abnormal behavior is such a multifaceted phenomenon.

To help make these important decisions, researchers rely on statistical procedures in which probability is a central concept. **Probability** refers to the odds, or likelihood, that an event will happen. The probability of a coin toss turning up heads is .5; that is, if a coin is tossed 100 times, it should show heads one half of the time because there are only two possibilities. All conclusions about the correctness of hypotheses are framed in terms of probability, because it is almost impossible to study every individual whose responses

Table 1.2

Research Methods in Abnormal Psychology

Type of Method	Application to Studying Depression
Experimental	The effectiveness of an antidepressant drug is evaluated by comparing the scores on a test of depression of people who receive the drug with those of people who do not. Purpose: To establish whether the drug works better than no drug. Advantages: If the group receiving the drug improves and the other group does not, the experimenter can conclude quite confidently that the drug had a therapeutic effect. Disadvantages: It can be difficult to withhold treatment from people who are depressed.
Quasi-experimental	People who differ in the number of friends they have are compared on a measure of depression. Purpose: To determine whether groups that differ in number of friends differ in level of depression. Advantages: It is useful when people are being compared on characteristics that cannot be manipulated. Disadvantages: Since people were not assigned randomly to groups, the experimenter cannot be sure that they actually were similar on all but the relevant variable.
Correlational	People who become depressed are tested on self-esteem to see if they have negative views about themselves. Purpose: To study the relationship of depression with other psychological states. Advantages: The experimenter can determine what other psychological qualities characterize depressed people. Disadvantages: The experimenter cannot determine whether depression causes people to have low self-esteem or whether low self-esteem is a cause of depression.
Survey	Anonymous questionnaires are sent to thousands of people, asking them to indicate whether they have symptoms of depression. Purpose: To obtain responses from a representative sample so that findings can be generalized to the population. Advantages: The responses of large samples of people can be obtained at relatively low cost. Disadvantages: Questions asked of respondents tend to be limited in depth.
Case study	A person with a history of depression is described in detail with particular emphasis on this person's development of the disorder. Purpose: To provide an in-depth analysis of one person to gain unique insight into the particular disorder. Advantages: Many circumstances in the person's life and psychological status can be explored in an attempt to gain a thorough understanding of that individual. Disadvantages: What characterizes one individual may not characterize others with depression.
Single-subject design	A depressed person is given a trial run of a treatment and is tested after this treatment to measure its effectiveness. Then the treatment is discontinued, and depression is measured again. This cycle is repeated one or more times. Purpose: To use one case for studying the effects of alterations in conditions on behavior. Advantages: By comparing the person receiving the treatment with himself or herself rather than with other individuals, differences between people in their life histories or current circumstances can be ruled out. Disadvantages: It can be emotionally draining for the individual to be run through a cycle of on-again, off-again treatments. Later treatments may be influenced by the outcome of earlier ones.

might be relevant to the question under study. For example, if you are studying people with serious depression, you cannot obtain data from every person in the world who is depressed. You can study only some people from this very large group. In other words, you would choose a **sample,** or selection, from the **population,** or entire group, of depressed people. After you have studied the sample, you would proceed to draw conclusions about the larger population. For example, you might find that, in your sample of 50 depressed people, most of them have a disturbance in their appetite. You could then infer that appetite disturbance is a common feature of serious depression. However, you would have to be careful to state this inference in terms of probabilities. After all, you did not sample every depressed person in the population. Assuming your results were statistically "significant," there would be at most a 5 percent probability that your results were due to chance factors.

All statistics rely on some very important assumptions about the samples on which the results are based—namely, that the sample is representative of the whole population and that it was randomly selected. **Representativeness** is the idea that your sample adequately reflects the characteristics of the population from which it is drawn. For example, if you interview only 50 men, you cannot draw conclusions about men and women. Random selection increases the likelihood that your sample will not be contaminated by a selective factor. Ideally, every person who is representative of the population of depressed people should have an equal likelihood of being selected for the sample. Let's say you have identified 1,000 potential participants for your study who are representative of the population of depressed people. Of those 1,000, you have resources to interview only 50. To ensure that your final sample is randomly selected you need to use a method, such as drawing names out of a hat. You can see how it would be a mistake to select your final sample by choosing the first 50 people who responded to your initial request for participants. These people might be unusually compulsive or desperate in pursuit of relief from their depression. Either of these attributes might bias your sample so that it no longer represents the full spectrum of people with depression.

The Experimental Method

The purpose of psychological research is to develop an understanding of how and why people differ in their behavior. The dimensions along which people, things, or events differ are called **variables.** For example, depression is a variable. Some people are more depressed than others; if given a test of depression, some people would receive high scores and others would receive low scores. The purpose of research on depression is to find out what accounts for these differences among people.

The experimental method is one approach to discovering the source of differences among people on psychological variables. The **experimental method** involves altering or changing the conditions to which participants are exposed and observing the effects of this manipulation on the behavior of the participants. In research involving this method, the experimenter attempts to determine whether there is a cause-effect relationship between two kinds of variables. The experimenter adjusts the level of one variable, called the **independent variable,** and observes the effect of this manipulation on the second variable, called the **dependent variable.** In our example about the effects of coffee on sleep patterns, the independent variable would be the caffeine in the coffee, and the dependent variable would be ease of falling asleep. In depression research, the independent variable would be a factor the researcher has hypothesized causes depression. For example, a current hypothe-

In an experimental study on light therapy and depression, participants in the treatment group might receive exposure to a light source, such as the one shown here.

sis is some people in northern climates become more depressed in the winter, when the daylight hours are shorter and the light is less intense. To test this hypothesis, you would need to create an artificial situation in which you could manipulate light exposure for at least several days and observe the effect on depression scores in your participants.

The experimental method usually involves making comparisons between groups exposed to varying levels of the independent variables. The simplest experimental design has two groups: an experimental and a control group. In this design, the **experimental group** receives the "treatment" thought to influence the behavior under study and the **control group** does not. Returning to the coffee example, you would test the hypothesis that caffeine causes sleeplessness by designing an experiment in which the experimental group is given caffeine and the control group is not given caffeine. By comparing sleep patterns in the two groups, you would be able to determine whether caffeine causes sleeplessness.

Many studies involve a special kind of control group—a "placebo" condition. In the **placebo condition,** people are given an inert substance or treatment that is similar in all other ways to the experimental treatment. Thus, to test the caffeine hypothesis, you might give one group of participants a sugar pill that has no caffeine in it but looks identical to the caffeine pill you give the experimental participants. What is the purpose of the placebo condition? Think about your own experience in taking pills or in exposing yourself to other treatments that supposedly affect your behavior or health. Sometimes you feel better (or, perhaps, worse) just knowing that you have taken a substance that you think might affect you. The purpose of a placebo is to eliminate the possibility that a participant will experience a change that could be attributed to his or her expectations about the outcome of a treatment. Again, in the case of the caffeine example, if you wanted to test the effects of coffee (as opposed to caffeine), you might give the experimental group a cup of caffeinated coffee and the placebo group a cup of decaffeinated coffee. That way, people in both groups would be drinking a hot, brown beverage. You might compare their sleeping patterns, then, with those of the "no treatment" control group, who drink nothing before going to sleep.

In abnormal psychology, studies on the effectiveness of various therapeutic treatments should, ideally, include a placebo condition. For example, researchers who are investigating whether a new medication will be effective in treating a certain psychological disorder must include a group receiving a placebo to ensure that any therapeutic benefit in the treatment group can be attributed to the active ingredients in the medication. If the medication was found to be an effective treatment or if the researcher was interested in establishing further control, the researcher might then make medication available to the people in the placebo and other control conditions and test the effect of the intervention at that point. Comparable procedures would be carried out in investigating the effects of certain kinds of psychotherapy. In these cases, however, the task of providing a placebo treatment is much more complicated than in the case of medication studies. What would a placebo treatment be for psychotherapy? Ideally, the researchers would want the placebo participants to receive treatments of the same frequency and duration as the experimental group participants who are receiving psychotherapy. As you might imagine, this would provide a real challenge for the researchers, who would be faced with trying to devise a method in which the people in the placebo condition would be meeting with a "therapist" but not participating in a therapeutic interaction. Perhaps they would talk about the weather or politics, but you might ask whether even such apparently neutral conversations might not have some therapeutic effect.

Researchers in the field of abnormal psychology must also make allowances for the **demand characteristics** of the experimental situation. People in an experiment have certain expectations about what is going to happen to them and about the proper way they should respond, particularly when these people suspect that the research may reveal something very personal about themselves. For example, if you know that you will be given caffeine, you might anticipate difficulty falling asleep that night. Similarly, if the experimenter knows that you have been given caffeine, he or she might make comments that could further influence how easily you fall asleep. The "demand" in this situation is the pull toward responding in ways based not on the actual effects of caffeine but on how you or the experimenters *think* the caffeine will affect you. Imagine how seriously the demand characteristics could bias an experiment on the effects of an antianxiety medication. An experimenter administers a drug and tells participants that they will feel relaxed in a little while. The chances are that they will feel more relaxed, but there is no way of knowing whether this is the result of the experimenter's leading comments or a true response to the medication. Or perhaps a participant notices labeling on the bottle, indicating that the pill is an antianxiety drug. This alone might have some influence on how the participant feels.

To control for demand characteristics on both sides, most researchers use a **double-blind technique,** in which neither the person giving the treatment nor the person receiving the treatment knows whether the participant is in the experimental or the control group. Even if this technique cannot be applied, as in the case of research on the effects of psychotherapy on depression, a minimal requirement for methodologically sound research is that neither the experimenter nor the participant knows the study's hypotheses. Otherwise, they will behave in ways that fulfill the expectations of the research.

In all of these cases, it is essential that the experimenter assign participants to conditions in a totally random manner. You would not want to put all the people with sleep problems in the coffee-drinking group, or vice versa. Instead, the researcher would place people in groups according to a predetermined method of random assignment.

The experimental method can be a powerful way to determine cause-effect relationships. However, it is not always possible to manipulate a variable in an experiment by assigning participants randomly to conditions. For instance, you cannot use "number of friends" as an independent variable, because there is no practical way you can control how many friends someone has. In this case, you would use a **quasi-experimental design,** one that looks a bit like an experimental design but lacks the key ingredient of random assignment. You would choose groups that appear to be as similar as possible, except on the characteristic of number of friends, and then compare them on the dependent variable of interest. The problem with this method is that, because people are not assigned randomly to groups, you cannot be sure that they actually are similar on all but the relevant variable. Any pre-existing differences between the groups may affect the outcome of the study. For instance, the group with few friends may have poor social skills, compared with the group with many friends. If the dependent variable is depression, it may be differences in social skills rather than number of friends that account for differences in their depression scores. Despite these problems, it is necessary to use a quasi-experimental design in research in which groups whose characteristics have been predetermined are compared. For example, comparisons of males vs. females, older vs. younger individuals, or people of different ethnicities would all involve this type of quasi-experimental design.

The Correlational Method

It is not always possible or desirable to frame a research problem in experimental or even quasi-experimental terms. In such cases, researchers use the correlational method. A **correlation** is an association, or co-relation, between two variables. The relationship described in the previous section between depression and number of friends is a perfect example of a correlation. The advantage of using a correlational procedure is that the researcher can study areas that are not easily tested by the experimental method. For example, it is theorized that people who have depressive disorders think very negatively about themselves and have very low levels of self-esteem. The most direct way to test this theory is to measure the levels of depression and self-esteem in people and see if the scores are correlated, or related to each other.

The correlation statistic is expressed in terms of a number between plus and minus one. Positive numbers represent positive correlations—meaning that, as scores on one variable increase, scores on the second variable increase. For example, because one aspect of depression is that it causes a disturbance in normal sleep patterns, you would expect, then, that scores on a measure of depression would be positively correlated with scores on a measure of sleep disturbances. Conversely, negative correlations indicate that, as scores on one variable increase, scores on the second variable decrease. An example of a negative correlation is the relationship between depression and self-esteem. The more depressed people are, the lower their scores are on a measure of self-esteem. In many cases, there is no correlation between two variables. In other words, two variables show no systematic relationship with each other. For example, depression is unrelated to height. Illustrations of different types of correlations are shown in Figure 1.3.

Just knowing that there is a correlation between two variables does not tell you whether one variable causes the other. The correlation simply tells you that the two variables are associated with each other in a particular way. Sleep disturbance might cause a person to score higher on a measure of depression, just as a high degree of depression can result in disturbed sleep patterns. Furthermore, a third variable that you have not measured could account for the correlation between the two variables that you have studied. Both depression and sleep disturbance could be due to an unmeasured physical problem, such as a biochemical imbalance. People who use correlational methods in their research are always on guard for the potential existence of unmeasured variables influencing the observed results.

The Survey Method

Almost every day you can pick up a newspaper or magazine and read the results of the most recent survey report on any aspect of human behavior. It might be nationwide surveys of people's attitudes toward the guilt or innocence of a major figure in the news, a campuswide survey about satisfaction with dormitory food, or a report in a newsmagazine comparing sexual practices in America with those in Europe. The **survey method** is a research tool used to gather information from a sample of people considered representative of a particular population. The reason there are so many surveys published in the news is that people are interested in what other people think and do. Sometimes the most interesting surveys are the ones that do not seem to "fit" with what you might expect, or the ones that pertain to a particular issue that is on people's minds. Surveys vary, of course, in their scope and relevance, with some pertaining more to political attitudes and others to the general health and well-being of a large segment of the population. Although they have the advantage that they can be administered to thousands of people, they tend to be limited in depth, especially when they rely on the self-reports of respondents.

In abnormal psychology, the surveys that have the most relevance are those that focus on the mental health of the popu-

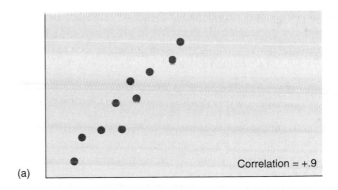
(a) Correlation = +.9

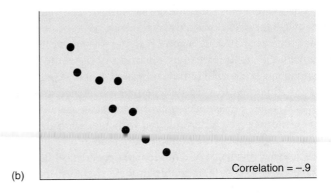
(b) Correlation = −.9

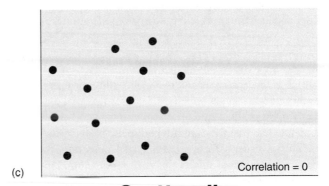
(c) Correlation = 0

Figure 1.3   Scatter diagrams
Hypothetical scatterplots illustrate different types of correlations: (a) a high positive correlation between sleep disturbance and depression, (b) a high negative correlation between self-esteem and depression, and (c) a zero-order correlation between height and depression. It is rare in psychology to find correlations as high as those in (a) and (b).

lation, reporting the frequency of various psychological disorders. Other aspects of human behavior are also of interest, such as the frequency of drug use, sexual experiences, and child abuse and the use of mental health services.

In the pages to follow, you will read many statistics about the frequency of psychological disorders. Researchers gather information about these disorders by conducting surveys. The statistics they obtain fall into two categories: incidence and prevalence. The **incidence** of a disorder is the frequency of new cases within a given time period. For example, the public health commissioner in a large city may be interested in the number of newly reported cases of AIDS during the month of January.

This number would represent the 1-month incidence of AIDS cases for the population of that city. In other cases, incidence may be based on a 1-year period, so that the number represents all new cases reported during that 12-month period. Sometimes researchers do not have access to the entire population in attempting to determine the number of people who develop the disorder in a given time period. In this case, incidence rates are based on a sample that is assumed to be representative of the entire population. For example, researchers interested in estimating the incidence of depression in a 1-month period may base their figures on interviews in which they ask people if they have begun to experience symptoms of depression within the past month.

The **prevalence** of a disorder is the number of people who have ever had the disorder at a given time or over a specified period. The time period could be the day of the survey (the "point" prevalence), the month preceding the study, or the entire life of the respondent. The period of time on which the prevalence rate is based is important to specify. Lifetime prevalence rates are higher than point prevalence rates, because the chances of a person developing a disorder increase with age. The age group of people in their fifties, for example, are more likely to have a higher lifetime prevalence rate of alcohol dependence, because they have lived longer than people in their twenties. Interestingly, the incidence rate for the disorder might actually be higher for the 20-year-olds than for the 50-year-olds, even though the lifetime prevalence might be lower. New cases of alcohol dependence are more likely to arise in the younger group.

The Case Study Method

Sometimes a researcher is interested in studying a condition that is very rare but has compelling features that make it worth investigating. For example, transsexualism is a disorder in which people feel that they are trapped in the body of the wrong gender. This disorder affects a fraction of 1 percent of the population, so researchers would not have access to sufficient numbers to conduct a statistically rigorous study. Instead, they would perform a case study. The **case study method** allows the researcher to describe a single case in detail. For example, a therapist treating a transsexual client would describe the client's developmental history, psychological functioning, and response to interventions. Other clinicians and researchers reading about this case would have the opportunity to learn about a rare phenomenon to which they might otherwise not have access. Furthermore, case studies can be particularly useful in helping others develop hypotheses about either psychological disorders or treatment.

Single-Subject Design

A **single-subject design** adds an experimental component to the study of the individual. In this type of research, one person at a time is studied in both the experimental and control conditions. Often, this method is used in research in which the focus is really on treatment. For example, a school psychologist wants to assess the effectiveness of a particular approach to

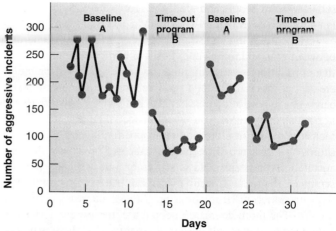

Figure 1.4   An example of an A-B-A-B design

This graph shows the frequency of aggressive incidents recorded during 20-minute morning observation periods of a child in a classroom.

Source: From J.S. Bailey, H.M. Hutchinson, & H.A. Murphy, *Journal of Applied Behavior Analysis*, 16:33. Copyright © 1983. Used by permission of the Journal of Applied Behavior Analysis.

treating a kindergartner named Bruce for aggressive outbursts. She could use a four-phase variant of the single-subject design called the "A-B-A-B" method. The "A" phase is the **baseline**, the period in which Bruce is observed but given no treatment for a fixed period of time. During phase "B," the treatment is administered. In Bruce's case, this might consist of sending Bruce to the "time-out" corner. The baseline and treatment conditions are repeated at least once to provide greater assurance that improvements in behavior during treatment were due to the intervention and not other, chance factors. To show this method in its simplest form, the schedule for the experiment might be conducted as follows:

Week 1: Condition A is followed. The frequency of Bruce's aggressive incidents is observed, but no attempt is made to regulate them.

Week 2: Bruce is put on a time-out program. This is Condition B. Bruce's aggressive incidents continue to be monitored, but, every time one occurs, he spends 10 minutes in the time-out corner of the classroom.

Week 3: The time-out program is discontinued (Condition A).

Week 4: The time-out program is reinstituted (Condition B).

Throughout this period, the frequency of Bruce's aggressive outbursts is monitored. If the treatment is effective, the number of aggressive incidents should be less frequent in the "B" periods than in the "A." You can see from the graph in Figure 1.4 how an A-B-A-B design would look.

Sometimes the withdrawal of treatment in the A-B-A-B design would be considered unethical. In Bruce's case, this would be true if Bruce were physically harming himself or other children. The psychologist would not want to suspend treatment that was regarded as effective. As an alternative, the psychologist could use a **multiple baseline approach.** This method involves observing different dependent variables in the same person over the course of treatment. The intervention would be introduced at different times and its impact evaluated on multiple dependent variables. In Bruce's case, a baseline would be established for verbal outbursts, the treatment introduced, then his number of verbal outbursts measured. Another baseline would be established at a different point for another type of aggressive behavior, such as punching his fists. The time-out procedure would be introduced and the frequency of punching measured. A similar process would be repeated for another type of aggressive behavior, such as kicking. If the time-out procedure is working, then it should result in reduced frequency of all three dependent variables.

Single-subject designs are most appropriate for studying behaviors that are easily observed and measured. A mood state, such as depression, would be difficult to study using this procedure, but specific behaviors, such as number of pessimistic statements (which are thought to reflect depressed mood), could be studied in this manner. One advantage of this method is that it allows the investigator to make precise manipulations whose effect can be carefully measured. The disadvantage is that the study is carried out on only one individual, thus limiting its generalizability. To avoid this problem, some researchers report the results of several single-subject designs in one study.

Studies of Genetic Influence

So far, we have been discussing psychological methods of research. Although psychological research provides valuable information about the causes and treatment of abnormal behavior, it cannot answer all the questions. In fact, there has been a tremendous amount of excitement over the past decade as researchers have plunged into new areas of inquiry that focus on the genetic transmission of behavioral characteristics. We all know that we inherit many physical characteristics from our parents, but, as researchers discover more about genetics, it is becoming apparent that behavioral characteristics have a strong genetic component as well (McGue & Christensen, 1997). In the chapters to follow, you will see that many psychological disorders are being examined from a genetic perspective. Depression, schizophrenia, alcoholism, and panic disorder are just a few that geneticists and psychologists are actively researching.

Most researchers begin the search for genetic causes of a disorder by establishing that the disorder shows a distinct pattern of family inheritance. This process requires obtaining complete family histories from people who are identified as having symptoms of the disorder. Their genealogy must be traced in order to calculate the prevalence of the disorder among blood relatives. Another way to trace inherited causes of psychological disorders is to compare the **concordance rate,** or agreement ratios, between people diagnosed as having the disorder and their relatives. For example, a researcher may observe that out of a sample of 10 twin pairs, the members of 6 pairs each has the same diagnosed psychological disorder. This would mean that, among this sample, there is a concordance ratio of .60 (6 out of

10). An inherited disorder would be expected to have the highest concordance between **monozygotic,** or identical, **twins** (whose genes are the same), with somewhat lower rates between siblings and **dizygotic,** or fraternal, **twins** (who are no more alike genetically than siblings of different ages), and even lower rates among more distant relatives.

A more powerful way to determine whether a disorder has a genetic basis is the study of families in which an adoption has taken place. The most extensive evidence gathered from these studies comes from the Scandinavian countries, where the governments maintain complete records for the population. Two types of adoptions are studied in this research. In the first, simply called an **adoption study,** researchers look at children whose biological parents have diagnosed psychological disorders but who are adopted by "normal" parents. In the second and rarer kind of adoption situation, called a **crossfostering study,** researchers look at children who are adopted by parents with psychological disorders but whose biological parents are psychologically healthy.

These kinds of studies enable researchers to draw strong inferences about the relative contributions of biology and family environment to the development of psychological disorders. Take the example of a boy who is born to two seriously depressed parents but who is adopted by two parents with no diagnosed psychological disorder. If this child also develops serious depression later in life, it makes sense to infer that he is genetically predisposed. When researchers study many dozens of people in similar situations and observe a heightened prevalence rate of psychological disorders among these children, they are able to draw these conclusions with a high degree of certainty. Conversely, consider the case of a girl born to parents with no diagnosed psychological disorder who is adopted and whose adoptive parents later become psychologically disturbed. If she develops the adoptive parents' psychological disorder, family environment would be one logical cause.

Researchers trying to understand the specific mechanisms involved in models of genetic transmission have found it helpful to study measurable characteristics whose family patterns parallel the pattern of a disorder's inheritance, called **biological markers.** For example, hair color would be a biological marker if a certain hair color always appeared in people within a family who have the same disorder. Other marker studies involve **genetic mapping,** a process researchers currently use in studying a variety of diseases thought to have a hereditary basis. In the chapters to follow, we will explore many of the important discoveries about a variety of psychological disorders that have been made using these methods.

■ The Human Experience of Psychological Disorders

As researchers continue to make progress in understanding the causes of psychological disorders, interest and attention have become increasingly focused on the impact of these disorders on every level—the family, community, and society. The widespread distribution of information, such as research findings, along with society's increased openness to confronting the concerns of people with psychological disorders, has led to a dramatic increase in public awareness of how psychological disorders affect many aspects of life. Psychological problems touch upon many facets of human experience. Not only is the individual with the problem deeply troubled; the family is disturbed, the community is moved, and society is affected.

Impact on the Individual: Stigma and Distress

One of your reactions to seeing people like Rebecca Hasbrouck might be to consider them as very different from you. You may even feel a certain degree of contempt or disgust for them. Many people in our society would react to her in such disdainful ways, not fully realizing the powerful impact of their discriminatory response. Such reactions are common, and they are the basis for the discrimination and stigma experienced by many people with severe psychological disturbance. A **stigma** is a label that causes certain people to be regarded as different, defective, and set apart from mainstream members of society. The phenomenon of stigma was brought to public attention in the writings of famous sociologist Erving Goffman in the 1960s, and, several decades later, stigma continues to be a major focus in publications and discussions pertaining to the rights and treatment of psychologically disturbed individuals.

It is common for people with serious psychological disorders, especially those who have been hospitalized, to experience profound and long-lasting emotional and social effects. These "survivors" commonly report feeling isolated and rejected by others. In time, they come to think less of themselves, take less advantage of opportunities for growth and development, and actually come to believe in society's myths and expectations for the mentally ill (Reidy, 1994) (See Table 1.3).

Although tremendous efforts have been undertaken to humanize the experiences of patients within psychiatric institutions, for most people the process of hospitalization is deeply upsetting, and possibly traumatizing. A number of institutional procedures are seen as dehumanizing and contributing to stigma. For example, patients who are out of control may be physically restrained. Others may be forced to give up personal possessions or to limit their contact with loved ones, even by telephone. They are expected to participate in group activities, such as occupational or recreational therapy, and to share their private concerns in group therapy. While such structures are designed to be therapeutic, some individuals find them too intrusive and controlling. Even clinic routines that require patients to wait for appointments can be dehumanizing, causing them to feel that they are less important than the staff. Loss of privacy, inadequate access to information about diagnosis and treatment, patronizing or infantilizing speech, offensive slang, and language with a medical orientation are additional objectionable practices that stigmatize individuals. Finally, being forced to accept a psychiatric label may be experienced as stigmatizing. The individual may be made to feel as though he or she cannot argue or dispute the diagnosis once it has been given. In the words of one patient, "The whole system is set up . . . to create and preserve stigma" (Reidy, 1994, p. 5).

Table 1.3

Myths of Mental Illness

Read the following statements and see how many you find yourself agreeing with. Each of these myths will be dispelled in the corresponding chapters of this book.

1. Creative people are usually a little "crazy."
2. Psychologically disturbed persons are dangerous.
3. Inkblot personality tests are bogus.
4. Freud's theory was all about sex.
5. Behaviorists have no interest in thoughts or feelings.
6. Criminals are born "bad."
7. People who make a big deal out of a traumatic experience are just looking for the "easy way out."
8. Asthma is caused by emotional problems.
9. Most of the people who sexually abuse children are gay men.
10. Suicidal individuals keep their intentions to themselves.
11. People with schizophrenia have multiple personalities.
12. Kids become hyperactive from eating too much sugar.
13. Most older people are "senile."
14. It's easy to spot a drug addict.
15. People with eating disorders are uninterested in food.

Most people would outwardly espouse an understanding and a tolerance for people with psychological disorders. Reflected more subtly in their language, humor, and stereotypes, however, are usually some fairly negative attributions. Watch television for an hour, or listen to the everyday conversation of those around you, and you will probably encounter some comments about emotional illness. Colloquialisms relating to emotional illness abound in our language. Statements about being "nuts," "crazy," "mental," "maniac," "flaky," "off-the-wall," "psycho," "schizo," or "retarded" are quite common. Popular humor is filled with jokes about "crazy people." Imagine the response of a group of teenagers walking past Rebecca; they might make derogatory comments and jokes about her appearance and behavior. What toll do you think this would take on Rebecca's already unstable sense of self?

Considering the tremendous impact of psychological disorder on the individual, why are some people so cruel as to joke about a person's distressed state? One reason might be that people often joke about issues that make them anxious. There is something very frightening about psychological disorder that makes people want to distance themselves from it as much as possible, perhaps feeling frightened about the prospect of losing control over their own behavior and thoughts. Consequently, they joke about oddities in other people's behavior.

What about your attitudes? Imagine the following scenario. An urgent message is waiting for you when you return to your room. It is from the mother of Jeremy, your best friend in high school. You call Jeremy's mother, who says she wants you to meet her at the psychiatric hospital in your hometown as soon as possible. Jeremy has just been admitted there and says that he has to see you, because only you can understand what he is going through. You are puzzled and distressed by this news. You had no idea that he had any psychological problems. What will you say to him? Can you ask him what's wrong? Can you ask him how he feels? Do you dare inquire about what his doctors have told him about his chances of getting better? What will it be like to see him in a hospital that cares for "crazy" people? Does that mean he is "crazy" too? Do you think you could be friends with someone who has spent time in a mental hospital?

Now imagine the same scenario, but instead you receive news that Jeremy has just been hospitalized for treatment of a kidney dysfunction. As you imagine yourself going to visit him, you will probably not think twice about how you will respond to him. Of course, you will ask him how he feels, what exactly is wrong with him, and when he will be well again. Even though you might not like hospitals very much, at least you have a pretty good idea about what hospital patients are like. It does not seem peculiar to imagine Jeremy as a patient in this kind of hospital. Your friend's physical illness would probably be much easier to understand and accept than his psychological disorder, and you would probably not even consider whether you could be friends with him again after he is discharged.

Apart from the distress created by stigma is the personal pain associated with the actual psychological disorder. Think about Rebecca and the dramatic turn that her life took as she was shaken from her successful and stable existence. Not only was she devastated by the trauma of losing her family, but she lost her own identity and sense of purpose as well. By the time she reached out for help, she no longer had even the remnants of her former self. Think about how you would feel if everything you had were suddenly gone in the course of a few weeks—your family, your home, your identity. For many people who develop a serious psychological disorder, whatever the cause, the symptoms themselves are painful and possibly terrifying. The sense of loss of control over one's thoughts and behaviors adds to one's torment.

Of course, not all cases of psychological disorder are as severe as Rebecca's, nor do they necessarily follow from an identifiable event. In the chapters to follow, you will read about a wide range of disorders involving mood, anxiety, substance abuse, sexuality, and thought disturbance. The case descriptions will give you a glimpse into the feelings and experiences of people who have these disorders, and you may find that some of these individuals seem similar to you or to people you know. As you read about the disorders, put yourself in the place of the people who have these conditions. Consider how they feel and how they would like to be treated. We hope that you will realize that our discussion is not about disorders but about the people with these disorders.

Impact on the Family

Typically, even before a person with a psychological disorder has been seen by a professional, the family has been affected by the person's behavior and distress. The degree of the impact depends in part on the nature of the problem and in part on the dynamics of the family.

Most commonly, family members are touched by the pain of a relative who is wounded emotionally. For example, a mother loses sleep for many months as she struggles to understand what role she might have played in the development of her teenage daughter's suicidal depression. A father worries that his son might once again drink insecticide as he responds to visions of giant insects crawling down his throat. A wife feels anxious every time the phone rings, wondering whether it might be the police or an acquaintance calling to tell her that her husband has passed out in a drunken stupor at the neighborhood bar.

The stigma of a psychological disorder also taints the family. Many families speak of the shame and embarrassment they feel when neighbors, schoolmates, and co-workers discover that someone in the family is schizophrenic, depressed, addicted to drugs, or abusive. You can imagine how Rebecca's relatives might have felt when news of her wandering and disruptive behavior with the police was broadcast on the local media.

For much of the twentieth century, the mental health profession in general was unsympathetic regarding the impact of psychological disorder on the family. Not only were families kept uninformed about treatment, but they were often blamed for the problem. Theories of many disorders, such as schizophrenia, depression, and sexual problems, typically blamed families—usually mothers. Families found themselves distressed by the turbulence caused by the problems of one of their relatives, hurt, and confused by what they heard as accusations from mental health professionals. Much of that has changed in recent years, as some prominent mental health professionals, such as psychiatrist E. Fuller Torrey, have recognized the distress of these families and have written books specifically directed to them (Torrey, 1995), letting them know that they are not alone; in fact, their worries, concerns, and problems are similar to those experienced by millions of other Americans.

Families also have banded together for support and mutual education. Across the country, families of people with serious psychological disorders have formed organizations, such as the National Alliance for the Mentally Ill (NAMI). These groups have helped many families better understand the nature of the problems they face, and the organizations have also served an important political function. Many such family advocacy groups have played a crucial role in ensuring that psychiatrically hospitalized people are properly treated, that their legal rights are respected, and that adequate posthospitalization care is planned.

Impact on the Community and Society

Anyone who has lived in a community where a state psychiatric hospital is located knows that there are many challenges involved in accommodating the mental health care needs of psychologically disturbed people following their discharge from the hospital. As we discussed earlier, beginning in the 1970s, there has been a national movement toward relocating psychiatric inpatients from hospitals to less restrictive environments.

RESEARCH FOCUS

How "Crazy" Are Creative People?

Most of us have encountered people who possess a remarkable sense of creativity, wit, or insight that enables them to see the world in unique ways. Perhaps they have a keen sense of humor or an unusual perspective on life that engenders a response of awe in other people with whom they interact. Maybe it is another student in one of your classes who comes up with some "far-out" ideas that captivate the imagination of others. Perhaps it is a person whom you know socially who is able to come up with great ideas for parties, and whose spark of creativity is able to ignite the fantasies and creative fires within others. Among the select group of very creative people you've encountered, it is quite possible that one or more of these individuals have been described as being just a little bit "crazy." You might have even wondered, as have some prominent researchers, about the possibility that there might actually be a relationship between some forms of creativity and some psychological disorders.

In an effort to assess the relationship between creativity and psychological disorders, Nancy Andreasen, a leading researcher in the area of schizophrenia, examined the rate of mental illness among 30 creative writers and 30 matched control participants. Andreasen was aware of the commonly held belief about a relationship between creativity and a serious form of psychological disturbance called schizophrenia. However, she was also aware that there existed no research evidence to support this belief. Consequently, she set out to investigate the nature and extent of such a connection. Andreasen did not find a relationship between schizophrenia and creativity, but her research uncovered some intriguing facts about creative people. Although creative writers are not more likely than others to suffer from schizophrenia, they, and their close relatives, are more likely to suffer from a mood disorder. (As you will see later in this book, a mood disorder is a condition in which a person has disturbances in mood in the forms of depression, elation, or both.) Let's take a closer look at the way in which Andreasen came to her conclusion. (Andreasen, 1987).

Andreasen began her investigation by systematically evaluating a sample of creative writers at the University of Iowa Writers' Workshop, an established and highly respected creative writing program that boasts of an enviable list of previous participants, including such internationally respected writers as Kurt Vonnegut, John Irving, Flannery O'Connor, Philip Roth, and John Cheever. During a 15-year period, Andreasen's research team used a structured interview to evaluate 30 workshop faculty members (27 men and 3 women, with an average age of 37 years) to determine their patterns of creativity, their personal histories of psychological disorder, and the extent of the mental health problems among their close relatives. (Of course, it was necessary for Andreasen to guarantee confidentiality regarding the identity of all participants who agreed to take part in her study.) The researchers recruited a control group of 30 people matched for age, sex, and educational status but different in occupation. For each group of participants, the

---

It was commonplace in the mid-1970s for a state hospital to contain several thousand people. By the 1990s, those numbers had dwindled. (Review Figure 1.2.) Many institutions had closed; others were left open but operated at a far smaller scale. Some of the discharged individuals moved back to the homes of their families, but most moved into community-based homes with several other deinstitutionalized people. In some programs and communities, these people are adequately cared for; however, in many areas, particularly large cities, there are dozens, even hundreds of formerly institutionalized people who go without homes, food, or health attention.

The impact of psychological disorder on society is not easily measured, but there is agreement among mental health professionals and public health experts that psychological problems exact a tremendous toll on society. Families are often torn apart and communities are divided. Once again, consider Rebecca's story. The loss of her productivity and

As a kick-off to National Mental Health Month, several thousand people joined in a Washington march to bring attention to the concerns of people with mental illness.

(continued)

searchers used specific criteria to determine the presence of a psychological disorder in the participant and in that participant's close relatives.

Andreasen wanted to know whether the participants had experienced a period of psychological disorder at any point in their lives, and the results were startling—80 percent of the writers had suffered from a mood disorder. Was mood disorder absent from the lives of the controls? Interestingly, no. In fact, 30 percent of the control participants had suffered from mood disorder at some point in life, but statistical analysis demonstrated that the higher proportion of mood disorder among the writers was much greater than chance. Andreasen realized that there was something curious about the rate of 30% among the control group; this figure was higher than one would expect to find in a group of individuals selected randomly from the population. However, keep in mind one important fact—these people were not randomly selected; rather, they were matched with the controls along several dimensions. Of specific relevance is the fact that studies have shown a relationship between mood disorder and occu-

pational achievement. This fact, and other issues pertaining to the diagnostic criteria used by Andreasen, led her to conclude that the differences in rates of psychological disorder between the two groups could be attributed to the very important variable of whether the participant was a writer, not the person's high level of occupational achievement.

When Andreasen inquired about the prevalence of mental illness among the participants' relatives, once again she found that the rate of psychological disturbance, particularly mood disorder in the form of depression, was higher among the group of writers than among the control group. It was not surprising, either, to find that the creative participants were much more likely than the controls to have relatives who were creative in such diverse areas as art, music, dance, and mathematics.

Every study has its limitations, and Andreasen recognized some in her own. One obvious one was that the investigator knew which of her participants were in the creative group and which were in the control group. Ideally, the investigator would be blind to the status of the participant, so as not to be biased in such a way that she might inadvertently look for evidence to support her hypothesis.

However, keep in mind that Andreasen had set out to study a very different connection—the connection between creativity and schizophrenia, not mood disorder.

How would you explain this puzzling relationship between creativity and mood disorder? On one level, we might consider what makes creative writing so appealing to read. Certainly, one facet of creativity that others find appealing is the creative writer's ability to see the world in different, moving, and provocative ways. Perhaps successful writers are able to do this because of the inner turmoil with which they struggle. Sometimes inner pain gives people a view and understanding of the world that are not otherwise accessible.

---

participation in the community can be considered costs to society. More directly measured are the actual financial costs of her rehabilitation. Her treatment will require intensive therapy, inpatient hospitalization, relocation within the community, and follow-up support. The expenses of her treatment must be weighed against the human cost of the continued suffering she would experience if she were not able to receive proper care. When you think of the fact that there are hundreds of thousands of people like Rebecca on the streets of America, you can appreciate the tragedy of the unfulfilled lives that takes its toll on society.

◼ Bringing It All Together

As you come to the close of this chapter, you now have an appreciation of the issues that are central to your understanding of abnormal psychology. We have tried to give you a sense of

how complex it is to define *abnormality,* and you will find yourself returning to this issue as you read about many of the disorders in the chapters to follow. The historical perspective we have provided will be elaborated on in subsequent chapters, as we look at theories of and treatments for specific disorders. Currently, developments are emerging in the field of abnormal psychology at an unbelievable pace, due to the efforts of researchers applying the techniques described here. You will learn more about some of these research methods in the context of discussions regarding specific disorders. Our discussion of the impact of psychological disorders forms a central theme for this book, as we return time and again to consideration of the "human experience" of psychological disorders.

RETURN TO THE CASE

Rebecca Hasbrouck

Course and Outcome

My professional relationship with Rebecca provided a powerful glimpse into the mind and experiences of a woman who had been emotionally devastated by a personal trauma. Little did I expect that my encounter with her on that Tuesday morning in September would be the start of a psychotherapy that would prove to be so instrumental in helping a troubled woman set on a new life course, nor did I anticipate the impact that this year-long therapy would have on my professional work with my other clients. Somehow, this relationship helped me increase my level of empathy and responsiveness to my clients.

I often think back to the first hour I spent with Rebecca and how I was called on to make some important decisions regarding her needs. Of immediate concern was Rebecca's physical health and comfort. I escorted her to the admissions office of the psychiatric unit, where a nurse welcomed her to the unit and assisted her in washing and dressing in clean clothes. I recall being startled, on returning to speak with Rebecca later in the day, to find a woman who looked so dramatically different from the helpless figure I had encountered only a few hours earlier. Although she continued to have a look of numbness, she seemed much more responsive in her interactions with me. She asked me what would happen to her. At one point, she became agitated for a few moments, telling me that she really should be on her way. I asked her to be patient and to listen to my recommendations. Although she could not be retained in the hospital against her will, it made sense for her to rest and recuperate, so that a plan could be developed to return her to a "normal life."

I explained to Rebecca that I would be her therapist during her stay in the hospital, which I expected to last approximately 2 weeks. During that time, I would collaborate with a social worker, Beverly Mullins, who would focus on helping Rebecca re-enter the world she had fled 3 years ago. Practical matters would be planned, such as where Rebecca would live and how she would gain access to the financial resources she had left behind. My task would be to help Rebecca understand what had happened to her emotionally—to return to the trauma of the car accident and to develop a basic understanding of how this trauma and the loss of her family precipitated a flight from reality. I would try to help her develop some of the psychological strength she would need to recover from the torment that had lasted for 3 years.

During the first few days of Rebecca's stay in the hospital, the medical staff conducted a comprehensive assessment of her physical health. The list of her physical maladies was lengthy and included gastrointestinal problems, skin infections, and head lice. By the end of the first week, her medical needs were being treated, and she was on a nutritional regimen designed to address various deficiencies. Concurrent with attention to her physical condition, the clinical staff and I formulated a treatment plan to address her psychological state. During her 14 days in the hospital, Rebecca met with me six times and attended group therapy each day. She also met several times with Beverly Mullins, who contacted Rebecca's sister and parents to involve them in developing a plan of action. I joined Bev Mullins for the initial meeting of Rebecca and her family members. The emotion that filled the room was overwhelming; Rebecca was greeted as a person "coming back from the grave."

In my own work with Rebecca in those six sessions during her inpatient stays, we reviewed in painful detail Rebecca's memories of what had happened to her during the past 3 years. Much of this period was blotted out, but Rebecca did remember the accident and her psychological devastation in the weeks that followed. She recalled her desperate pursuit of her lost loved ones, and she spoke in disbelief about how she thought she had heard their voices calling out to her. The depth of her depression was so great that Rebecca had become immobilized after the death of her family. She spent nights and days for many months

RETURN TO THE CASE

Rebecca Hasbrouck (continued)

crying constantly and wandering the streets of the city. As strange as it came to seem to Rebecca, she found comfort in the community of other homeless people who befriended her. These people became her "family" and taught her the ways of the streets.

Rebecca was never quite sure what prompted her to emerge from the dismal life she had come to live. Perhaps it was the anniversary of the car accident that caused her to think about what was happening to her life and to consider the possibility of returning to the world from which she had tried to escape.

The intensity of Rebecca's connection with me was evident from our very first sessions. As we planned her discharge from the hospital, she asked me if she could continue to see me until her functioning was more stable. I agreed.

Bev Mullins was able to arrange a posthospital placement for Rebecca in a halfway house for women who were capable of working and gradually assuming independent control of their lives. Although none of the other six clients in the halfway house had stories as dramatic as that of Rebecca's, each had suffered a serious break with reality and was trying to return to an independent life in the community.

Rebecca remained in the halfway house for a month. During that time, she worked out her financial situation with an attorney and found an apartment not far from her sister's house. She decided to take this apartment, feeling that she wanted to be in some proximity to a relative until she felt more comfortable returning to a normal life.

Both during her stay in the halfway house and for 11 months following her departure from the house, Rebecca came to see me twice a week for outpatient therapy. Although dealing with her grief always remained a component of our work, in time we refocused our attention on tapping her talents and abilities so that she could return to work and social involvement with other people.

Rebecca felt that she had fallen out of touch with the practice of law, and she had little desire to return to that kind of work. Because of a large insurance settlement, she did not feel pressured to find a high-paying position, but she realized that it was important for her psychological health to be active and to work. Always having had an affinity for writing, Rebecca decided to pursue a career as a freelance writer of feature articles for popular magazines. This route seemed ideal for her, because it permitted her to work in a more private space, in which she would feel less burdened by having to interact with people who would inquire about her personal life.

The success story that unfolded for Rebecca seemed to have a fairy tale quality to it. Her writing was very well received, and she returned to a healthy psychological state over the course of a year. In our work together, she slowly reacquired a sense of her identity and learned to compartmentalize her traumatic experience, so that it would be less intrusive in her day-to-day life.

After a year of regular therapy sessions, Rebecca made the decision that she was ready to separate from therapy. I suggested that she might wish to gradually reduce the frequency of sessions, a practice I have found useful with other long-term clients. Although Rebecca initially considered this possibility, she decided against it, because she felt it important to make a "clean break" in order to prove to herself that she could be truly independent. In the years that followed, I heard from Rebecca only once. About 4 years after we had terminated, I received an engraved announcement of her wedding on which she wrote, "Thanks for everything. I've now come back to the world." Because there was no return address, I concluded that Rebecca did not need, or wish, for me to respond. Her note did mean a great deal to me, however. I was now able to have a sense of completion about our work, and, in contrast to many other cases with less-than-happy outcomes, I was able to feel a sense of comfort that my efforts with Rebecca were instrumental in bringing her "back." ■

Sarah Tobin, PhD

Summary

- *Abnormality* can be defined according to four criteria: distress, impairment, risk to self or others, and behavior that is outside the norms of the social and cultural context within which it takes place.

- In trying to understand the reasons that people act and feel in ways that are regarded as abnormal, social scientists look at three dimensions—biological, psychological, and sociocultural—and use the term biopsychosocial to characterize the interaction among these three dimensions. Related to the biopsychosocial approach is the diathesis-stress model, a proposal that people are born with a predisposition (or "diathesis") that places them at risk for developing a psychological disorder.

- The history of understanding and treating people with psychological disorders can be considered in terms of three recurring themes: the mystical, the scientific, and the humanitarian. The mystical theme regards abnormality as due to demonic or spirit possession. This theme was prevalent during prehistoric times and the Middle Ages. The scientific theme regards abnormality as due to psychological or physical disturbances within the person. This theme had its origins in ancient Greece and Rome, and it has predominated since the nineteenth century. The humanitarian theme regards abnormality as due to improper treatment by society; this theme predominated during the reform movements of the eighteenth century and is still evident in contemporary society.

- Researchers use various methods to study the causes and treatment of psychological disorders. The scientific method involves applying an objective set of methods for observing behavior, making an hypothesis about the causes of behavior, setting up proper conditions for studying the hypothesis, and drawing conclusions about its validity. In the experimental method, the researcher alters the level of the independent variable and observes its effects on the dependent variable. The quasi-experimental method is a variant of this procedure and is used to compare groups that differ on a predetermined characteristic. The correlational method studies associations, or co-relations, between variables. The survey method enables researchers to estimate the incidence and prevalence of psychological disorders. In the case study method, one individual is studied intensively, and a detailed and careful analysis of that individual is conducted. In the single-subject design, one person at a time is studied in both the experimental and control conditions, as treatment is applied and removed in alternating phases.

Key Terms

See Glossary for definitions.

Adoption study 25
Asylums 11
Baseline 24
Biological markers 25
Biopsychosocial 7
Case study method 24
Concordance rate 25
Control group 21
Correlation 22
Crossfostering study 25
Deinstitutionalization movement 17
Demand characteristics 22
Dependent variable 21
Diathesis-stress model 8

Dizygotic twins 25
Double-blind technique 22
Experimental group 21
Experimental method 21
Genetic mapping 25
Hypnotism 16
Hypothesis formation process 19
Hysteria 16
Incidence 23
Independent variable 21
Medical model 15
Mesmerism 16
Monozygotic twins 25
Moral treatment 13
Multiple baseline approach 25

Observation process 10
Placebo condition 21
Population 20
Prevalence 24
Probability 19
Psychoanalysis 16
Psychoanalytic model 15
Psychotherapy 18
Quasi-experimental design 22
Representativeness 21
Sample 20
Single-subject design 24
Survey method 23
Trephining 9
Variable 21

Internet Resource

To get more information on the material covered in this chapter, visit our web site at **http://www.mhhe.com/halgin**. There you will find more information, resources, and links to topics of interest.

CASE REPORT: PETER DICKINSON

It was an unbearably hot and humid Friday afternoon in July. As I was wrapping up my work for the week, feeling relieved that I would be able to leave the office on time, I received the seemingly inevitable call from the admissions unit. The head nurse on the unit, Hank Mahar, emphasized that I should get right down to the unit because "this guy's out of control!"

I entered the admitting room and came face to face with Peter, who leaped out of his chair and tried to give me a hug. With ardent enthusiasm in his voice, Peter said, "Thank God you've arrived. Please tell my idiot brother that I don't need to be in this looney bin!" Peter's brother, Don, sat quietly nearby and softly spoke to Peter, "Please calm down so that we can tell the doctor what has been going on."

After settling down a bit, Peter agreed to answer my questions about his background and to tell me what had been going on in his life during the days and weeks prior to being brought to the hospital. He explained that he was 23 years old and divorced. Explaining that he worked as a janitor at a bank and lived in a rooming house, he quickly interjected that he would soon be "moving up in the world as soon as the contract arrived from the recording company." I decided to wait to ask him what he meant by this, feeling that it was more important at that moment to focus on specific symptoms.

In response to my questions about how he had been feeling, Peter did acknowledge that he had been recently having "bouts of anxiety," which caused him to feel "hyper" and restless. In fact, throughout our interview, Peter showed a great deal of edginess as he became intermittently irritable and annoyed with me. He also mentioned that 4 months previously he had experienced a serious depression in which he felt as if he wanted to kill himself. Peter became defensive when discussing the depression, as he explained that the depression was understandable in light of all that he had gone through. Peter's wife, Christine, had thrown him out of the house and had filed for divorce, because she felt he was a "loser with a lousy job and no future."

This deep depression had lasted about a month, and somehow Peter managed to pull himself out of it. He characterized the depression as "a living hell" and stated with stern emphasis that he "would never become depressed again." At this point, Peter insisted on leaving the room to go out into the hallway for a cigarette. He told me that, if I wanted information, I should talk to his brother.

Don agreed that Peter had been acting "hyper" for several weeks and had been causing quite a disturbance for the preceding several days. Peter's mother had called Don to tell him that Peter seemed to be heading toward a psychological crisis similar to the kind that she had struggled with earlier in her life. Mrs. Dickinson had received a call from the owner of Peter's rooming house, who had become increasingly concerned about Peter's odd behavior. He had been staying up all night, playing his electric guitar, writing what he described as his "first million-dollar recording hit." On several occasions, he ran from room to room in the middle of the night, waking everyone up, urging them to come and "witness a creative genius at work." From what Don could tell, Peter was operating on "nervous energy," as he hadn't slept or eaten anything for several days. There were no signs that Peter had been drinking or abusing drugs, and he had no history of substance abuse. Night after night, Peter had been working on his song. He devoted 4 or 5 daytime hours to making countless telephone calls to recording company executives in an effort to sell his song. He had called one company more than 40 times, insisting that someone listen to him play his song over the phone.

Peter's strange behaviors were also evident outside the rooming house. He had stopped going to work. When he wasn't calling the record companies, he was pursuing outlandish purchases. For example, he had gone to a luxury car dealership and had submitted a credit application to buy a $50,000 car. He also went to a realtor, who spent many hours showing him expensive homes in the belief that Peter was about to come into a large amount of money. In the evenings, Peter spent time at bars, reportedly looking for a talented singer who would be willing to record his songs. Peter had met a woman, Marnie, who was captivated by Peter's dramatic tales of past success and future potential. They spent 48 hours together and decided to get married, but Marnie never showed up for their planned meeting at city hall to apply for a marriage license. Peter was devastated and infuriated. He made threatening comments about Marnie, although Don felt that there was no real likelihood that Peter would harm her. For one thing, he had no way of finding her; furthermore, he was the kind of individual whose "bark was worse than his bite," Don commented.

Peter was certainly an interesting individual. I was struck by his air of bravado, while at the same time believing that he had many endearing qualities. Beneath his loud and demanding demeanor, there seemed to be a man who was terrified by what he had been experiencing since the day his wife, Christine, left him. I was confident that the hospital treatment staff could help Peter, but I wasn't sure whether he would let us. In as calming a manner as possible, I asked Peter for his cooperation, explaining that it was my sense that he had been through very difficult times since his wife had left him. I also explained that it would take only a couple of weeks to get him back to a normal level of function—somewhere between the deeply depressed and the highly energized extremes he had experienced in recent months.

Sarah Tobin, PhD

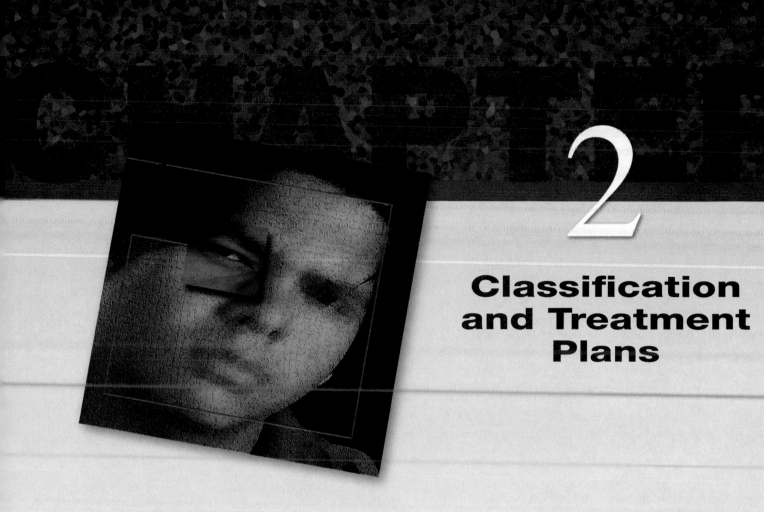

2

Classification and Treatment Plans

You have just read the case of a young man whose life was thrown into havoc by the experience of extreme psychological symptoms ranging from deep depression to frenzied hyperactivity. Imagine that you are a professional and are faced with the responsibility of treating an individual like Peter. How would you begin? One of the first things you might try to do is establish a working relationship, so that you can gain a better understanding of what is going on with Peter and how you might be of assistance to him. In addition, you would attempt to determine which diagnostic label might best apply to his symptoms, so that you could implement the most appropriate treatment. In this chapter, we will take you through the issues that clinicians face every time they encounter a new client.

In therapy, the client and clinician work jointly to help the client resolve psychological problems.

Psychological Disorder: Experiences of Client and Clinician

The field of abnormal psychology goes beyond the academic concern of studying behavior. It encompasses the large range of human issues involved when a client and a clinician work together to help the client resolve psychological difficulties. Throughout this text, we will continually return to these human issues and focus on the individual experiences of the client and the clinician, as well as the drama that unfolds when they interact. Here, we will orient you to these issues with a discussion of who these people are.

The Client

We use the term *client* in this text to refer to a person seeking psychological services. This term conveys certain meanings that are important to clarify at the outset of our discussion. After providing clarification on the meaning of the term, we will go on to another major point that underlies this book: the "client" can be anyone. Psychological disorders are highly prevalent among the population; therefore, we should not think of clients as distant from or removed from the rest of the world.

Definitions

What do you think when you hear that someone you know is in psychotherapy? Do you think of the person being treated as a "patient"? This is a common view, with roots in the medical model, and it is reinforced by popular characterizations of therapy on television and in films. **Patient** is a term used to refer to someone who is ill and, consistent with the medical model, someone who passively ("patiently") waits to be treated. Some people, including those who provide as well as those who receive treatment, object to the term *patient* because of its association with illness. They prefer to use an alternative term, *client*. In this sense, **client** refers to the person seeking psychological treatment, to reflect the fact that psychotherapy is a collaborative endeavor. Although these are the terms most commonly used, in recent years, other terms have been suggested, such as *resident, consumer,* and *member.* It may be helpful for you to

think about how you would want to be referred to if you were seeking professional psychological services. In this book, we will use the term *client,* except in instances in which other terms have been more commonly used, as in the phrases "outpatient treatment" and "patients' rights."

While we are on the topic of appropriate terms, it is important to understand that people are not disorders. By calling someone a "schizophrenic," one implies that the individual is synonymous with the disorder, and it hides the person's identity as an individual behind the label. A more sensitive phrase is "a person with schizophrenia." Even though this may sound unwieldy, it communicates respect for the individual by putting the person first.

Prevalence of Psychological Disorders

Although this book focuses on people with severe psychological problems, it is important to keep in mind that everyone faces crises, dilemmas, or a desire for greater self-understanding. The National Institute of Mental Health (NIMH) cites the statistic that 22 percent of all Americans have experienced a mental disorder during the preceding year, and nearly half of these people have obtained professional help (http://www.nimh.nih.gov/research/amer.htm) (National Institute of Mental Health, 1998). Two comprehensive investigations in recent years have provided ample documentation of the extent to which people of all ages and walks of life experience psychological disturbance at some point. We will refer to these studies throughout this book when we provide epidemiological data on each of the disorders.

Researchers at the National Institute of Mental Health designed the Epidemiological Catchment Area (ECA) study to determine the prevalence of psychological disorders in the United States (Robins & Regier, 1991). More than 20,000 people from five U.S. communities were given structured interview protocols to assess their psychological symptoms. In contrast to many earlier studies, which had relied on samples of individuals already being treated for psychological problems, the ECA study drew on a community sample and allows us to estimate how

Table 2.1

Lifetime prevalence of psychiatric disorders as reported in the National Comorbidity Survey

Disorder	Lifetime Prevalence	Proportion of These People Who Had at Least One Other Diagnosis in Their Lives
Mood disorders	19.6%	82.2%
Anxiety disorders	28.7%	74.1%
Substance use disorder	26.7%	73.3%
Other disorders (conduct disorder, adult antisocial behavior, and nonaffective psychosis)	18.9%	78.9–96.2%
Any disorders	52.5%	59.8%

frequently various disorders occur in the general public (Ade-bimpe, 1994; Narrow et al., 1993). The lifetime prevalence of any psychological disorder was 32 percent, and about 25 percent of the sample had experienced symptoms within the previous year. Alcohol abuse and dependency was among the most common of all disorders, with a lifetime prevalence rate of 13.8 percent.

The second study, the National Comorbidity Survey, provided even more impressive evidence of the extent to which psychological disorders appear in so-called normal samples (Kessler, 1997). This study was conducted on a representative sample of more than 8,000 adults from across the United States, with the intention of documenting the extent to which psychiatric disorders are **comorbid,** or co-existing. The results, in fact, confirmed the suspicions of the investigators, who were following up on some intriguing leads from the ECA study, in which it had been reported that 54 percent of the respondents with one psychiatric disorder had a second diagnosis as well at some point in life. Interestingly, a similar rate of comorbidity emerged from this more focused study. Of the respondents with a lifetime history of one psychiatric disorder, over half of the sample had at least one other diagnosis. The most common comorbidities involve drug and alcohol abuse with other psychiatric disorders. The lifetime prevalence and comorbidity rates from this study are summarized in Table 2.1.

As you read about the conditions described in this book, it will be important for you to keep in mind these facts about the frequency of psychological disorders. Furthermore, the NIMH statistics also provide strong indications that obtaining help from others is a normal and natural part of life. The data would be even more impressive if routes of informal helping were included. Some people receive this help from friends, family, or other helpers, such as teachers or clergy. Others turn to mental health professionals in pursuit of assistance, and still others are mandated to obtain help, possibly by a court or an employer. Each of these situations involves one person, a client, accepting assistance from another person in changing troubling or mal-adaptive behavior or emotional experiences.

The Clinician

Many people respond in an understandably defensive manner to the idea of consulting a mental health professional. They fear being scrutinized and labeled by a total stranger who is in a position to judge them as being "crazy." This negative view of the clinician accounts in part for the resistance some people express about seeing a "shrink."

Optimally, however, a clinician is an astute observer of human nature, an expert in human relations, a facilitator of growth, and a resource who aids others in making crucial life choices. A good clinician assesses others, not out of arrogance and insensitivity, but out of concern for understanding and responding to the problems of people seeking help. There are many types of clinicians, who approach clinical work in a variety of ways, based on their training and orientation. In the early 1900s, people in need of psychological help saw physicians or **psychiatrists**—medical doctors (MDs) with advanced training in treating people with psychological disorders. During World War II, the mental health needs of the nation increased, necessitating an expansion of the mental health provider network. University-based doctoral (PhD) psychology programs were created to increase the number of mental health professionals with training in the behavioral sciences who provided direct service to clients. Along with the growth of PhD programs has been the development of programs that are called "professional schools" of psychology, some of which offer a PhD and some of which offer a newer degree, the doctor of psychology (PsyD). Individuals trained in either type of doctoral program are known as **clinical psychologists.** Some psychologists are trained within the field of counseling psychology, where the emphasis is on normal adjustment and development, rather than on psychological disorder.

Psychiatrists and clinical psychologists currently predominate in the mental health field. An important distinction between them is that psychiatrists are licensed to administer medical treatment, and psychologists are not. In addition to providing psychotherapy, then, psychiatrists are responsible for prescribing medication for the treatment of psychological disorders when necessary. Psychologists and other mental health professionals often work closely with psychiatrists and consult with them when a client needs medication. Another difference is that clinical psychologists are trained in conducting **psychological testing,** a broad range of measurement techniques, all of which involve having people provide scorable information about their psychological functioning.

In addition to doctorally trained professionals, several other groups of professionals provide mental health services, including counseling and school psychologists, psychiatric social workers, nurse clinicians, and marriage and family counselors. The mental health field also includes a large group of individuals who do not have graduate-level training but serve a critical role in the functioning and administration of the mental health system. Included in this group are the thousands of nurses, occupational therapists, recreational therapists, and counselors who devote their careers to working with emotionally troubled people in institutions, agencies, schools, and homes.

We realize that abstract discussions may not enable you to appreciate fully who the clinician is and what the clinician does. Consequently, throughout this book, we will use examples involving one clinician and some of the cases she has treated. This clinician, whom we call Dr. Sarah Tobin, is a composite of many of the qualities found in a good clinical psychologist. Her cases are similar to those in psychological clinics and psychiatric institutions. As you read about Dr. Tobin's work, think of yourself as her apprentice or intern. Imagine yourself discussing the cases with her and consulting with her about the diagnosis and treatment of each client. At the beginning of each chapter, you will read a case report that relates to the content of that chapter. As you read the chapter, use an inquisitive and problem-solving approach to develop your own understanding of the case. Try to form your own hypotheses about the most appropriate diagnosis, the cause of the client's problems, and ways that the client might best be treated.

The *Diagnostic and Statistical Manual of Mental Disorders*

In making a diagnosis, mental health professionals use the standard terms and definitions contained in the *Diagnostic and Statistical Manual of Mental Disorders (DSM),* a publication that is periodically revised to reflect the most up-to-date knowledge concerning psychological disorders. The title of this book, and the diagnostic system it contains, is abbreviated as *DSM;* this is followed by an indication, in Roman numerals, of the edition currently in use (now the *DSM-IV*). This diagnostic system was originally developed in 1952, when the American Psychiatric

Association published the first *DSM.* In the years since then, the *DSM-II, DSM-III, DSM-III-Revised,* and *DSM-IV* have reflected advances and refinements in the system of diagnosis that is most commonly used in the United States. We will discuss the history of the development of this system later, but first it is important for you to have a grasp of what we mean by a diagnostic system, or "nomenclature," as it is sometimes called.

The *DSM-IV* contains descriptions of all psychological disorders, alternatively referred to as mental disorders. In developing recent editions of the *DSM,* various task forces have been appointed, each consisting of a group of expert clinicians and researchers knowledgeable about a particular subset of disorders. Based on their research, these experts have listed several hundred disorders, ranging from relatively minor adjustment problems to long-term chronic and incapacitating disorders. The *DSM-IV* provides both clinicians and researchers with a common language for delineating disorders, so that they can feel relatively confident that diagnostic labels have accepted meanings.

The authors of recent versions of the *DSM* have taken an atheoretical approach. In other words, they have attempted to describe psychological disorders in terms that refer to observable phenomena, rather than presenting the disorders in terms of their possible causes. In describing an anxiety disorder, for example, various psychological and physical symptoms associated with the experience of anxiety are listed, without consideration of whether the cause is physical or emotional.

By characterizing a client's symptoms in terms of a *DSM-IV* diagnosis, the clinician can use that system of knowledge as the basis for a treatment plan. For example, a clinician would plan a very different kind of treatment for a person with an anxiety disorder than for a person with schizophrenia. Furthermore, the clinician often is asked to provide a diagnosis, with the accompanying *DSM-IV* numerical code, to help a client obtain insurance payments to cover the cost of treatment.

The authors of the *DSM-IV* continued in the footsteps of their predecessors to arrive at a system that would be scientifically and clinically accurate (Millon, 1991). They had to ensure that the diagnoses would meet the criterion of **reliability,** meaning that a given diagnosis will be consistently applied to anyone showing a particular set of symptoms. Returning to the case of Peter, if he were to describe his symptoms to a clinical psychologist in Spokane, Washington, that psychologist should be able to use the *DSM-IV* to arrive at the same diagnosis as would a psychiatrist seeing Peter in Baton Rouge, Louisiana. Further, any knowledgeable mental health professional should be able to use the criteria specified in the *DSM-IV* to make a diagnosis, regardless of that professional's theoretical orientation or particular experience with clients. Working toward reliability of diagnoses, the authors of successive versions of the *DSM* have refined the criteria for disorders. At the same time, teams of researchers throughout the United States have continued to investigate the **validity** of the classification system, meaning that the diagnoses represent real and distinct clinical phenomena. In all of these efforts, experts have had to keep in mind the **base rate** of a disorder, the frequency with which it occurs in the general population. The lower the base rate of a disorder, the

Does *DSM-IV* Make You Crazy?

Without even realizing it, you may have had a mental disorder at some point in your life. Maybe you were so sad and depressed following an unhappy event that you found it difficult to eat, sleep, or concentrate for several weeks. With a few more symptoms, such as a loss of interest in important aspects of your life, feelings of worthlessness, and negative thoughts, you would have met the diagnostic criteria for a serious mood condition called major depressive disorder. How would you feel about being labeled in such a way? With a diagnosis such as depression, perhaps you might not feel stigmatized, but consider some other conditions that carry a label of a mental disorder.

Consider the case of a woman whose lack of sexual desire has caused relationship problems with her partner. Or consider a man whose persistent difficulty in falling asleep each night causes him to experience social and occupational problems. Or take the case of a boy who vocalizes sounds uncontrollably to such an extent that his classmates

ridicule him. Would it surprise you to learn that each of these conditions is a diagnosable "mental disorder"? Some social critics regard the work of the American Psychiatric Association, as expressed in the recent versions of the *Diagnostic and Statistical Manual of Mental Disorders,* as highly politicized, money-making publications that are laden with problems of reliability and validity. Herb Kutchins is a professor at California State University at Sacramento, and Stuart Kirk a professor at UCLA. In their 1992 book, *The Selling of DSM* (Kirk & Kutchins, 1992), they skewered the authors of *DSM-III,* who purportedly "used the language, paradigms, and technology of research to gain influence over clinical language and practice" (p. 14). Kutchins and Kirk continued the attack in a more recent book, *DSM: The Psychiatric Bible and the Creation of Mental Disorders* (Kutchins & Kirk, 1997), stating that *DSM-IV* is a strange mix of social values, political compromise, scientific evidence and material for insurance claim forms.

Kutchins and Kirk highlight some interesting points by noting the extent to which *DSM* diagnoses reflect the politics and culture of the time. For example, because of pressure from outside groups, homosexuality was dropped and post-traumatic stress disorder was added when *DSM-III* was published in 1980. The fact that homosexuality had previously been listed in *DSM-II* highlighted the complexity of defining a "mental disorder." It took nearly 10 years of debate for the American Psychiatric Association

to conclude that pathologizing people because of sexual orientation was absurd. As for post-traumatic stress disorder, pressure from Vietnam veterans forced *DSM-III* authors to recognize the constellation of symptoms experienced by thousands of survivors of traumatic events, such as combat.

Kutchins and Kirk raise many legitimate concerns about this publication, which has become an indispensable book on the shelf of every mental health practitioner. Even clinicians who detest the document know that their income depends on the inclusion of a *DSM-IV* diagnosis on every insurance form they submit. Consequently, they must be familiar with the workings of this complex diagnostic system and must learn to live with its limitations.

In response to the criticisms of the *DSM-IV,* many mental health professionals ask what the alternative is. Even with its limitations, the diagnostic manual provides a common language that clinicians and researchers can use to describe the phenomena of abnormal conditions. For example, clinicians treating clients with mood symptoms such as those mentioned at the beginning of this discussion know that the diagnosis is major depressive disorder, and they know that there are well-established treatments for it. Thus, even though you might feel odd about having your sadness labeled a mental disorder, you would certainly feel reassured by the knowledge that your symptoms could be understood and treated.

more difficult it is to establish the reliability of the diagnosis because there would be so few cases to compare.

How the *DSM* Developed

The first edition of the American Psychiatric Association's *DSM,* which appeared in 1952, was the first official psychiatric manual to describe psychological disorders and, as such, was a major step forward in the search for a standard set of diagnostic criteria. Although a step in the right direction, these criteria were very vague and had poor reliability. A second limitation of

the *DSM-I* was that it was based on the theoretical assumption that emotional problems or "reactions" caused the disorders it described. The second edition, or the *DSM-II,* was published in 1968. This was the first classification of mental disorders based on the system contained in the International Classification of Diseases (ICD). The *DSM-II* represented a movement away from the conceptualization of most psychological disorders as being emotional reactions. The authors of this edition tried to use diagnostic terms that would not imply a particular theoretical framework, but, in retrospect, it is clear that they based their criteria on psychoanalytic concepts. Furthermore, these criteria were sufficiently loose that a clinician with a particular theoretical preference could fit in a client's diagnosis with his or her theory, rather than with the client's actual condition.

To overcome these problems with low reliability, in 1974 the American Psychiatric Association appointed a task force of eminent scholars and practitioners to prepare a new and more extensive classification system that would reflect the most current information on mental disorders. The task force was directed to develop a manual that would have an empirical basis and be clinically useful, reliable, and acceptable to clinicians and researchers of different orientations.

When the *DSM-III* was published in 1980, it was widely heralded as a major improvement over its predecessors. It provided precise rating criteria and definitions for each disorder. These criteria enabled clinicians to be more quantitative and objective in assigning diagnoses. However, the *DSM-III* had some problems. For example, in some instances the manual did not go far enough in specifying criteria. Because of these limitations, the American Psychiatric Association tried once again to improve and refine the diagnostic system. The *DSM-III-R* by the American Psychiatric Association in 1987 was published with the intention that it would serve as an interim manual until a more complete overhaul, the *DSM-IV*, could be introduced in 1994.

Shortly after the publication of the *DSM-III-R*, the American Psychiatric Association established the Task Force on the *DSM-IV* with the intent of providing an empirical base for the diagnoses in the new manual. Work groups investigating specific disorders were appointed to conduct a three-stage process involving further reliability and validity testing of the diagnoses. In Stage 1 of this process, comprehensive reviews of the published research were conducted. Stage 2 involved thorough analyses of research data, some of which had not previously been published. Criteria from the *DSM-III-R* were rigorously applied to these analyses, with the intention of adding or changing criteria on the basis of the analytical findings. Stage 3 was the largest and most ambitious phase of the project, involving field trials in which interviewers evaluated thousands of people with diagnosed psychological disorders. These field trials were attempts by researchers to establish the reliability and validity of the new diagnostic criteria. In reliability testing, pairs of clinicians provided independent ratings of clients through videotaped interviews. Evaluating the validity of diagnostic categories was an even more challenging task. Clinicians conducted focused field trials in which individuals diagnosed as having specific disorders were studied. The purpose of these field trials was to determine the number and nature of the criteria needed for clients to be diagnosed with specific disorders. As you will see later in this book, diagnoses are made on the basis of the kind and number of relevant symptoms. The field trials were used to provide an empirical basis for deciding on which symptoms and how many of those symptoms would be necessary for the diagnosis to be applied. For example, for a diagnosis of major depressive disorder, the client must demonstrate at least five symptoms out of a possible list of nine, including such symptoms as disturbed sleep, recurrent thoughts of death, and feelings of worthlessness.

Dr. Robert Spitzer chaired the work group that developed *DSM-III* and *DSM-III-R*, and served as an advisor for the development of *DSM-IV*.

Definition of "Mental Disorder"

In Chapter 1, we discussed the alternate conceptions of abnormality and how difficult it is to define what constitutes abnormal behavior or, for that matter, how it should be labeled. The authors of the *DSM* had to confront the task of defining "mental disorder" and arrived at a definition that serves as the foundation for every diagnosable condition within the manual. According to this definition, a mental disorder is "a clinically significant behavioral or psychological syndrome or pattern that occurs in an individual and that is associated with present distress (e.g., a painful symptom) or disability (i.e., impairment in one or more important areas of functioning) or with a significantly increased risk of suffering death, pain, disability, or an important loss of freedom. In addition, this syndrome or pattern must not be merely an expectable and culturally sanctioned response to a particular event, for example, the death of a loved one" (American Psychiatric Association, 1994, p. xxi). The concept of mental disorders is central to the whole enterprise of diagnosis and treatment. Let's take a closer look at the definition given in the *DSM-IV* and its implications.

A mental disorder is "clinically significant." For each disorder, the *DSM-IV* specifies the length of time during which the symptoms must be present for the diagnosis of a disorder. Thus, a fleeting thought or mood, an occasional strange behavior, or a temporary feeling of instability or confusion does not constitute a mental disorder. You probably can think of a time when you felt emotionally distraught following an upsetting event in your life. Such experiences are common and would not be regarded as mental disorders, unless they are so severe that they result in serious consequences. To be considered "clinically significant," the disorder must be consistently present over time and have enough impact that the person's life is dramatically affected.

The disorder is reflected in a behavioral or psychological "syndrome." A **syndrome** is a collection of symptoms that forms a definable pattern. A behavioral or psychological syndrome is a collection of observable actions and the client's reported thoughts and feelings. Thus, an isolated behavior or a single thought or feeling would not constitute a disorder. Rather, a diagnosable condition is an organized unit that manifests itself in a wide range of thoughts, feelings, and behaviors. If you feel sad for a few days, and this feeling is your only symptom, a diagnosis of depression would be inappropriate.

The disorder is associated with present distress, impairment in life, or serious risk. In other words, a disorder involves personal or social cost. For example, a woman's fear of leaving the house may cause her to be very distressed. She wishes she could overcome her extreme fearfulness but feels incapable of changing her behavior. Her syndrome, then, in addition to being severe, is also causing her a great deal of personal distress. In addition, her functioning is impaired, because she is unable to hold a job or take care of household errands.

Not everyone with a psychological disorder is distressed. Consider a man who has developed an unusually cold, constricted, and impersonal style of relating to other people because of a disturbed view of interpersonal relationships. Although this man might not be bothered by this style, it will make it difficult, if not impossible, for him to develop intimate relationships. Moreover, unless he has a job that involves absolutely no social interaction (and there are not many such jobs), this style of relating to others will invariably hurt his chances of having a productive career.

Some disorders can lead a person to commit suicide or inflict severe physical pain through self-mutilation. Other disorders place the individual at risk, because they lead to acts involving physical peril. A man in a hyperexcited state of euphoria may go out and rent a hang glider, because he feels like flying, unconcerned that he lacks the proper training. Still other disorders threaten the individual with physical harm, because they lead to the adoption of an unhealthy lifestyle. A person who is driven to work excessively hard without taking time for relaxation is likely, over a period of years, to suffer from heart problems due to stress. Finally, a psychological disorder can lead a person to give up personal freedom if it leads to criminal acts, resulting in punishment or incarceration.

The disorder is not an expectable and culturally sanctioned response. Some behaviors and emotional reactions are understandable, given the circumstances. For example, in an oppressive political system, one might expect people to be on the alert for danger, perhaps to the point of seeming paranoid. Such individuals would not be regarded as having a mental disorder because their reaction is expectable. Another example would be a woman who becomes depressed following the death of her partner. She may lose sleep, cry frequently, and have difficulty eating or concentrating. Her symptoms would not constitute a mental disorder. In some cultures, reactions to the death of a loved one may involve rituals and behaviors that might seem bizarre to outsiders but are acceptable within the culture.

Assumptions of the *DSM-IV*

Throughout the history of the *DSM* system, its authors have debated a number of complex issues, including the theoretical basis of the classification system. Each edition of the manual has represented thousands of hours of discussion among experts in several related fields from very different theoretical backgrounds. The *DSM-IV* today contains the result of these discussions, and underlying its structure and organization are several important assumptions.

Medical Model

One of the most prominent assumptions of the *DSM-IV* is that this classification system is based on a medical model orientation, in which disorders, whether physical or psychological, are viewed as diseases. In fact, as we mentioned earlier, the *DSM-IV* corresponds to the International Classification of Diseases, a diagnostic system developed by the World Health Organization to provide consistency throughout the world for the terms that are used to describe medical conditions. For example, proponents of the medical model view major depressive disorder as a "disease" that requires treatment. The use of the term *patient* is consistent with this medical model.

Also consistent with the medical model is the use of the term *mental disorder*. If you think about this term, you will notice that it implies a condition that is inside one's "mind." This term has been used historically to apply to the types of conditions studied within psychiatry, as in the terms *mental hospital* and *mental health*. For many professionals, though, the term *mental disorder* has negative connotations, because it has

Severe depression can be so devastating that some people consider suicide the only option.

historically implied something negative. In this book, we use the term *psychological disorder* in an attempt to move away from some of the negative stereotypes associated with the term *mental disorder;* we also wish to emphasize that these conditions have an emotional aspect. For example, a person who has unusually low sexual desire would have a diagnosable condition within the *DSM-IV* called "hypoactive [low] sexual desire disorder." Does it make sense to refer to such a condition as a mental disorder?

Atheoretical Orientation

The authors of the *DSM-IV* wanted to develop a classification system that was descriptive rather than explanatory. In the example of hypoactive sexual desire disorder, the *DSM-IV* simply classifies and describes a set of symptoms without regard to their cause. There might be any number of explanations for why a person has this disorder, including relationship difficulties, inner conflict, or a traumatic sexual experience.

Previous editions of the *DSM* were based on psychoanalytic concepts and used such terms as *neurosis,* which implied that many disorders were caused by unconscious conflict. Besides carrying psychodynamic connotations, these terms were vague and involved subjective judgment on the part of the clinician. **Neurosis** is not part of the official nomenclature, but you will still find it in many books and articles on abnormal psychology. When you come across the term, it will usually be in reference to behavior that involves some symptoms that are distressing to an individual and that the person recognizes as unacceptable. These symptoms usually are enduring and lack any kind of physical basis. For example, you might describe your friend as neurotic because she seems to worry all the time over nothing. Assuming that she recognizes how inappropriate her worrying is, your labeling of her behavior as neurotic might be justified. However, a mental health practitioner might diagnose her as having an anxiety disorder, a more precise description of her constant worrying behavior. Mental health professionals still use the term *neurotic* informally to refer to a person who experiences excessive subjective psychological pain and to distinguish such conditions from those referred to as psychotic.

The term **psychosis** is used to refer to various forms of behavior involving loss of contact with reality. In other words, a person showing psychotic behavior might have bizarre thoughts and perceptions of what is happening. This might involve delusions (false beliefs) or hallucinations (false perceptions). The term *psychotic* may also be used to refer to behavior that is so grossly disturbed that the person seems to be out of control. Although not a formal diagnostic category, *psychotic* is retained in the *DSM-IV* as a descriptive term.

Categorical Approach

Implicit in the medical model is the assumption that diseases fit into distinct categories. For example, pneumonia is a condition that fits into the category of diseases involving the respiratory system. The *DSM-IV,* being based on a medical model, has borrowed this strategy. Thus, conditions involving mood fit into the category of mood disorders, those involving anxiety fit into the category of anxiety disorders, and so on. However, the authors of the *DSM-IV* are the first to acknowledge that there are

limitations to the categorical approach. For one thing, psychological disorders are not neatly separable from each other or from normal functioning. For example, where is the dividing line between a sad mood and diagnosable depression? Furthermore, many disorders seem linked to each other in fundamental ways. In a state of agitated depression, for example, an individual is suffering from both anxiety and saddened mood.

The difficulty of establishing clear boundaries between psychological conditions prompted the *DSM-IV* Task Force to consider adopting a dimensional rather than a categorical model. In a dimensional model, people would be rated according to the degree to which they experience a set of fundamental attributes. Rather than being classified as "depressed" or "nondepressed," individuals would be rated along a continuum. At one end would be no depression, and at the opposite extreme would be severe incapacitation, with varying degrees in between. In the current system, the many separate categories for depressive disorders lead to a proliferation of diagnoses. A dimensional system with numerical ratings would provide a cleaner and perhaps more accurate representation of psychological (Livesley, Schroeder, Jackson, & Jang, 1994). The categorical system has been retained, however, because the *DSM-IV* authors believe that it is less confusing for clinicians and researchers to think in terms of disorders as clustering into discrete groups.

Multiaxial System

In the *DSM,* diagnoses are categorized in terms of relevant areas of functioning within what are called axes. There are five axes, along which each client is evaluated. An **axis** is a class of information regarding an aspect of an individual's functioning. The **multiaxial system** in the *DSM-IV* allows clients to be characterized in a multidimensional way, accommodating all relevant information about their functioning in an organized and systematic fashion.

As you might imagine, when a clinician is developing a diagnostic hypothesis about a client, there may be several features of the individual's functioning that are important to capture. For example, consider the case of Greg, a young man who is suffering from periods of intense depression that have troubled him for the past few months. Greg says that since high school he has had personality problems as well as a problem with ulcers. Six months ago, Greg's girlfriend was killed in an automobile accident. Before then, he was managing reasonably well, although his personality problems and ulcer sometimes made it difficult for him to function well on his job. Each fact the client presents is important for the clinician to take into account when making a diagnosis, not just the client's immediate symptoms. In Greg's case, the symptom of depression is merely one part of a complex diagnostic picture. As we saw earlier, most clients, such as Greg, have multiple concerns that are relevant to diagnosis and treatment. Sometimes there is a causal relationship between comorbid disorders. For example, a man with an anxiety disorder may develop substance abuse as he attempts to quell the terror of his anxiety by using drugs or alcohol. In other situations, the comorbid conditions are not causally related, as would be the case of a woman who has both an eating disorder and a learning disability.

The Five Axes of the *DSM-IV*

Each disorder in the *DSM-IV* is listed on either Axis I or Axis II. The remaining axes are used to characterize a client's physical health (Axis III), extent of stressful life circumstances (Axis IV), and overall degree of functioning (Axis V).

Axis I: Clinical Disorders

The major clinical disorders are on Axis I. In the *DSM-IV* system, these are called "clinical syndromes," meaning that each is a collection of symptoms that constitutes a particular form of abnormality. These are the disorders, such as schizophrenia and depression, that constitute what most people think of as psychological disorders. As you can see from Table 2.2, however, there are a wide variety of disorders encompassing many variants of human behavior.

Another set of disorders in Axis I are **adjustment disorders.** These are reactions to life events that are more extreme than would normally be expected, given the circumstances. To be considered an adjustment disorder, this reaction must persist for at least 6 months and must result in significant impairment or distress for the individual. Adjustment disorders manifest themselves in several forms: emotional reactions, such as anxiety and depression; disturbances of conduct; physical complaints; social withdrawal; or disruptions in work or academic performance. For example, a woman may react to the loss of her job by developing a variety of somatic symptoms, including headaches, backaches, and fatigue. A man may respond to a diagnosis of a serious illness by becoming reckless, self-destructive, and financially irresponsible. In these cases, the individual's reaction can be temporally linked to the occurrence of the life event. Moreover, the reactions are considered out of proportion to the nature of the stressful experience.

Some conditions are the focus of clinical attention but are not psychological disorders. In *DSM-IV,* these conditions are referred to as V (vee) codes and include a variety of difficulties, such as relational problems, bereavement reactions, and the experience of being abused or neglected. When these problems are the primary focus of clinical attention, they are listed on Axis I. When these problems are evident but are not the primary focus of concern, they are noted on Axis IV, which you will read about later in this section.

Axis II: Personality Disorders and Mental Retardation

Axis II includes a set of disorders that represents enduring characteristics of an individual's personality or abilities. One set of disorders is the personality disorders. These are personality traits that are inflexible and maladaptive and that cause either subjective distress or considerable impairment in a person's ability to carry out the tasks of daily living. The second component of Axis II is mental retardation. Although not a "disorder" in the sense of many of the other conditions found in the *DSM-IV,* mental retardation nevertheless has a major influence on behavior, personality, and cognitive functioning.

To help you understand the differences between Axis I and Axis II, consider the following two clinical examples. One case involves Juanita, a 29-year-old woman who, following the birth of her first child, becomes very suspicious of other people's intentions, to the point of not trusting even close relatives. After a month of treatment, she returns to normal functioning and her symptoms disappear. Juanita would receive a diagnosis of an Axis I disorder, because she has a condition that could be considered an overlay on an otherwise healthy personality. In contrast, the hypersensitivity to criticism and fear of closeness shown by Jean, another 29-year-old woman, is a feature of her way of viewing the world that has characterized her from adolescence. She has chosen not to become involved in intimate relationships and steers clear of people who seem overly interested in her. Were she to seek treatment, these longstanding dispositions would warrant an Axis II diagnosis.

An individual can have diagnoses on Axes I and II. For example, Leon is struggling with substance abuse and is characteristically very dependent on others. Leon would probably be diagnosed on both Axis I and Axis II. On Axis I, he would be assigned a diagnosis pertaining to his substance abuse; on Axis II, he would receive a diagnosis of dependent personality disorder. In other words, his substance abuse is considered to be a condition, and his personality disorder is considered to be part of the fabric of his character.

Axis III: General Medical Conditions

Axis III is for documenting a client's medical conditions. Although these medical conditions are not the primary focus of the clinician, there is a solid logic for including Axis III as part of the total diagnostic picture. At times, physical problems can be the basis of psychological problems. For example, a person may become depressed following the diagnosis of a serious physical illness. Conversely, such conditions as chronic anxiety can intensify physical conditions, such as a stomach ulcer. In other cases there is no obvious connection between an individual's physical and psychological problems. Nevertheless, the clinician considers the existence of a physical disorder to be critical, because it means that something outside the psychological realm is affecting a major facet of the client's life.

The clinician must keep Axis III diagnoses in mind when developing a treatment plan for the client. Take the example of a young man with diabetes who seeks treatment for his incapacitating irrational fear of cars. Although his physical and psychological problems are not apparently connected, it would be important for the clinician to be aware of the diabetes, because the condition would certainly have a major impact on the client's life. Furthermore, if the clinician considers recommending a prescription of antianxiety medication, the young man's physical condition and other medications must be taken into account.

Axis IV: Psychosocial and Environmental Problems

On Axis IV, the clinician documents events or pressures that may affect the diagnosis, treatment, or outcome of a client's psychological disorder. Examples of Axis IV stressors are shown in Table 2.3. As you can see, Axis IV conditions include the negative life events of losing a job, having an automobile accident, and breaking up with a lover. All of these conditions are stressors that can cause, aggravate, or even result from a

Table 2.2

Axis I Disorders of the *DSM-IV*

Category	Description	Examples of Diagnoses
Disorders usually first diagnosed in infancy, childhood, or adolescence	Disorders that usually develop during the earlier years of life, primarily involving abnormal development and maturation	• Mental retardation • Learning disorders • Motor skills disorders, communication disorders, pervasive developmental disorders (e.g., autistic disorder) • Attention-deficit disorders and disruptive behavior disorders • Feeding and eating disorders of infancy and early childhood • Tic disorders • Elimination disorders
Delirium, dementia, amnestic, and other cognitive disorders	Disorders involving impairments in cognition that are caused by substances or general medical conditions	• Delirium • Dementia (e.g., Alzheimer's type) • Amnestic disorder
Mental disorders due to a general medical condition	Conditions characterized by mental symptoms judged to be the physiological consequence of a general medical condition	• Personality change due to a general medical condition • Mood disorder due to a general medical condition • Sexual dysfunction due to a general medical condition
Substance-related disorders	Disorders related to the use or abuse of substances	• Substance use disorders (e.g., substance dependence and substance abuse) • Substance-induced disorders (e.g., substance intoxication and substance withdrawal)
Schizophrenia and other psychotic disorders	Disorders involving psychotic symptoms (e.g., distortion in perception of reality; impairment in thinking, behavior, affect, and motivation)	• Schizophrenia • Schizophreniform disorder • Schizoaffective disorder • Delusional disorder • Brief psychotic disorder
Mood disorders	Disorders involving a disturbance in mood	• Major depressive disorder • Dysthymic disorder • Bipolar disorder • Cyclothymic disorder
Anxiety disorders	Disorders involving the experience of intense anxiety, worry, or apprehension that leads to behavior designed to protect the sufferer from experiencing anxiety	• Panic disorder • Agoraphobia • Specific phobia • Social phobia • Obsessive-compulsive disorder • Post-traumatic stress disorder • Generalized anxiety disorder

Table 2.2 (continued)

Axis I Disorders of the *DSM-IV*

Category	Description	Examples of Diagnoses
Somatoform disorders	Disorders involving recurring complaints of physical symptoms or medical concerns not supported by medical findings	• Somatization disorder • Conversion disorder • Pain disorder • Hypochondriasis • Body dysmorphic disorder
Factitious disorders	Conditions in which physical or psychological symptoms are intentionally produced in order to assume a sick role	• Factitious disorder • Factitious disorder by proxy
Dissociative disorders	Disorders in which the normal integration of consciousness, memory, identity, or perception is disrupted	• Dissociative amnesia • Dissociative fugue • Dissociative identity disorder • Depersonalization disorder
Sexual and gender identity disorders	Disorders involving disturbance in the expression or experience of normal sexuality	• Sexual dysfunctions (e.g., sexual arousal disorder, orgasmic disorder, sexual pain disorder) • Paraphilias (e.g., fetishism, pedophilia, voyeurism) • Gender identity disorder
Eating disorders	Disorders characterized by severe disturbances in eating behavior	• Anorexia nervosa • Bulimia nervosa
Sleep disorders	Disorders involving recurring disturbance in normal sleep patterns	• Dyssomnias (e.g., insomnia, hypersomnia) • Parasomnias (e.g., nightmare disorder, sleepwalking disorder)
Impulse-control disorders	Disorders characterized by repeated expression of impulsive behaviors that cause harm to oneself or others	• Intermittent explosive disorder • Kleptomania • Pyromania • Pathological gambling • Trichotillomania
Adjustment disorders	Conditions characterized by the development of clinically significant emotional and behavioral symptoms within 3 months following the onset of an identifiable stressor	• Adjustment disorder with anxiety • Adjustment disorder with depressed mood • Adjustment disorder with disturbance of conduct
Other conditions that may be a focus of clinical attention	Conditions or problems for which a person may seek or be referred for professional help	• Relational problems • Problems related to abuse or neglect • Psychological factors affecting medical condition • Other conditions (e.g., bereavement, academic or occupational problem, religious problem, phase of life problem)

On *Axis III* a clinician would document a medical condition such as diabetes, realizing that a physical disorder can cause or aggravate psychological symptoms.

The Diagnostic Process

The diagnostic process involves using all relevant information to arrive at a label that characterizes the client's disorder. This information includes the results of any tests given to the client, material gathered from interviews, and knowledge about the client's personal history. The end result of the diagnostic process is a diagnosis that can be used as the basis for the client's treatment.

Although this definition makes the diagnostic process sound straightforward, it usually is not so simple. In fact, the diagnostic process can be compared to the job of a detective trying to solve a complicated case. A good detective is able to piece together a coherent picture from many bits and pieces of information, some of which may seem insignificant or even random to the untrained observer. Similarly, a good clinician uses every available piece of information to put together a coherent picture of the client's condition. Fortunately, some of this information is readily available, such as the client's age, gender, and ethnicity. This background data can help the clinician gauge the likelihood of the client's having particular disorders. For example, if a 20-year-old were to seek treatment for symptoms that appeared to be those of schizophrenia, the clinician's ideas about diagnosis would be different than if the individual were 60 years old. Schizophrenia often makes its first appearance in the twenties, and, with a client of this age who shows possible symptoms of schizophrenia, the diagnosis is plausible. On the other hand, if the client were 60 years old and showing these symptoms for the first time, other disorders would seem more likely. Similarly, the client's gender can provide some clues for diagnosis. Some conditions are more prevalent in women, so the clinician is more likely to consider those when diagnosing a woman. Finally, the individual's social and cultural background may provide some clues in the diagnostic process. The clinician may find it helpful to know about the religious and ethnic background of clients if these are relevant to the kind of symptoms they are exhibiting. For example, a client from a country in which the voodoo religion is practiced might complain that she has been "cursed." Without knowing that such a belief is perfectly acceptable within the voodoo religion, the clinician may mistakenly regard this statement as evidence of a serious psychological disorder. We will talk more about the role of culture when we examine the issue of cultural formulations later in the chapter.

We will return now to Peter's symptoms and will discuss the diagnostic process Dr. Tobin would use to evaluate him. You will see how she uses the tools of the detective to arrive at the diagnosis.

The Client's Reported and Observable Symptoms

Remember that Peter first describes his symptoms as involving "bouts of anxiety." When Dr. Tobin hears the word *anxiety,* she immediately begins thinking about the *DSM-IV* criteria for what is called an anxiety disorder. This is the first step in the diagnostic process. Dr. Tobin listens for a key word or phrase in the client's self-report of symptoms and observes how the client

psychological disorder. A depressed man may get into a serious accident, because he is so preoccupied with his emotions that he does not concentrate on his driving. Alternatively, a person may become clinically depressed in the aftermath of a serious car accident. As you can see, the same life event can be either the result or the cause of a psychological problem.

For the most part, the life events on Axis IV are negative. However, "positive" life events, such as a job promotion, might also be considered stressors. A person who receives a major job promotion may encounter psychological difficulties, due to the increased responsibilities and demands associated with the new position.

Axis V: Global Assessment of Functioning

Axis V is used to document the clinician's overall judgment of a client's psychological, social, and occupational functioning. Ratings are made for the client's current functioning at the point of admission or discharge, or the highest level of functioning during the previous year. The rating of the client's functioning during the preceding year provides the clinician with important information about the client's **prognosis,** or likelihood of recovering from the disorder. If a client has functioned effectively in the recent past, the clinician has more reason to hope for improvement. The prognosis may not be so bright if a client has a lengthy history of poor adjustment.

The **Global Assessment of Functioning (GAF) scale,** which is the basis for Axis V, allows for a rating of the individual's overall level of psychological health. The range of scores on the GAF is from 100, indicating good functioning in all areas, to 1, indicating that the individual is violent, suicidal, or unable to perform the basic functions of life. The full scale is shown in Table 2.4.

Table 2.3

Axis IV of the *DSM-IV*

Problem Category	Examples
Problems with primary support group: childhood	Death of parent Health problems of parent Removal from the home Remarriage of parent
Problems with primary support group: adult	Tensions with partner Separation, divorce, or estrangement Physical or sexual abuse by partner
Problems with primary support group: parent-child	Neglect of child Sexual or physical abuse of child Parental overprotection
Problems related to the social environment	Death or loss of friend Social isolation Living alone Difficulty with acculturation Adjustment to life cycle transition (such as retirement)
Educational problems	Academic problems Discord with teachers or classmates Illiteracy Inadequate school environment
Occupational problems	Unemployment Threat of job loss Difficult work situation Job dissatisfaction Job change Discord with boss or co-workers
Housing problems	Homelessness Inadequate housing Unsafe neighborhood Discord with neighbors or landlord
Economic problems	Extreme poverty Inadequate finances Serious credit problems
Problems with access to health care services	Inadequate health insurance Inadequate health care services
Problems related to interaction with the legal system/crime	Arrest Incarceration Victim of crime
Other psychosocial problems	Exposure to disasters Loss of important social support services

From American Psychiatric Association: *Diagnostic and Statistical Manual of Mental Disorders*, Fourth Edition. Washington DC, American Psychiatric Association, 1994.

acts. That gives her a clue about what to look for next. In the process of following up on this clue, Dr. Tobin will gain more information about the symptoms that Peter reports.

In addition to listening to the client's description of symptoms, the clinician also attends to the client's behavior, emotional expression, and style of thinking. For example, a client with very severe depression may be immobilized and unable to verbalize, leaving the clinician to infer that the client is depressed.

Diagnostic Criteria and Differential Diagnosis

The next step is to obtain as clear an idea as possible of the client's symptoms and to determine the extent to which these symptoms coincide with the diagnostic criteria of a given disorder. What does Peter mean when he says that he has "bouts of anxiety"? After Dr. Tobin asks him this question, she listens to determine whether any of his symptoms match the *DSM-IV*

Table 2.4

Axis V: Global Assessment of Functioning Scale

Rating	Level of Symptoms	Examples
91–100	Superior functioning; no symptoms	
81–90	No symptoms or minimal symptoms; generally good functioning in all areas; no more than everyday problems	Occasional worries such as feeling understandably anxious before taking examinations or feeling or concerns disappointment following an athletic loss
71–80	Transient, slight symptoms that are reasonable responses to stressful situations; no more than slight impairment in social, occupational, or school functioning	Concentration difficulty following an exciting day; trouble sleeping after an argument with partner
61–70	Mild symptoms, or some difficulty in social, occupational, or school functioning	Mild insomnia; mild depression
51–60	Moderate symptoms or moderate difficulties in social, occupational, or school functioning	Occasional panic attacks; conflicts with roommates
41–50	Serious symptoms or any serious impairment in social, occupational, or school functioning	Suicidal thoughts; inability to keep job
31–40	Serious difficulties in thought or communication or major impairment in several areas of functioning	Illogical speech; inability to work; neglect of responsibilities
21–30	Behavior influenced by psychotic symptoms or serious impairment in communication or judgment or inability to function in almost all areas	Delusional and hallucinating; incoherent; preoccupied with suicide; stays in bed all day every day
11–20	Dangerous symptoms or gross impairment in communication	Suicide attempts without clear expectation of death; muteness
1–10	Persistent danger to self or others or persistent inability to maintain hygiene	Recurrent violence; serious suicidal act with clear expectation of death
0	Inadequate information	

From American Psychiatric Association: *Diagnostic and Statistical Manual of Mental Disorders,* Fourth Edition. Washington DC, American Psychiatric Association, 1994.

criteria for "anxiety." Do his hands tremble? Does he get butterflies in his stomach? Does he feel jittery and irritable or have trouble sleeping? Dr. Tobin keeps a mental tally of Peter's symptoms to see if enough of the appropriate ones are present before she decides that his state is, in fact, anxiety and that he might therefore have an anxiety disorder.

As she listens to Peter's symptoms, Dr. Tobin discovers that he has also experienced severe depression within the past few months. This discovery leads her to suspect that perhaps Peter does not have an anxiety disorder after all. Now, as she sorts through the facts of his story, she starts to see his highly energized behavior as the classic symptoms of a mood disturbance. Based on this decision, Dr. Tobin then turns to a guide that she will follow to sort through the information she has gathered. This guide takes the form of a **decision tree,** a series of simple yes/no questions in the *DSM-IV* about the client's symptoms that lead to a possible diagnosis. Like the branches of a tree, the assessment questions proposed by the clinician can take different directions. There are different decision trees for many of the major disorders. Dr. Tobin can use the decision tree for mood disorders to narrow down the possible diagnoses and make sure that she has considered all the options in Peter's case.

The decision tree with the specifics of Peter's case is shown in Figure 2.1. Although there are many more steps in this tree than represented here, you can see the basic logic of the

process in this simplified version. Dr. Tobin begins with the mood disturbance decision tree, because she has already decided that Peter's symptoms might fit the diagnostic criteria for a mood disorder. Going through the steps of the decision tree, Dr. Tobin begins with the recognition that Peter has been depressed and that his mood is now both expansive and irritable. Although she will request a complete medical workup, there is no evidence at the moment that his symptoms are physiological effects of a medical condition or drugs. She then focuses on the nature of the present mood episode and concludes that Peter may be experiencing a manic episode. It also appears that Peter has suffered a major depressive episode as well. Now, the question is whether Peter has psychotic symptoms at times other than during these episodes. Assuming he does not, it means that Peter should be diagnosed as having bipolar disorder (formerly referred to as manic depression), a mood disorder that involves the experience of a manic episode and very commonly a depressive episode. If he did have psychotic symptoms at times other than during his mood episodes, Peter would be diagnosed as suffering from another disorder related to schizophrenia.

The final step in the diagnostic process is for Dr. Tobin to be sure that she has ruled out all possible alternative diagnoses, either by questioning Peter or by reviewing the information she has already collected. This step, called **differential diagnosis,** will probably have been completed already, because Dr. Tobin

Diagnostic questions

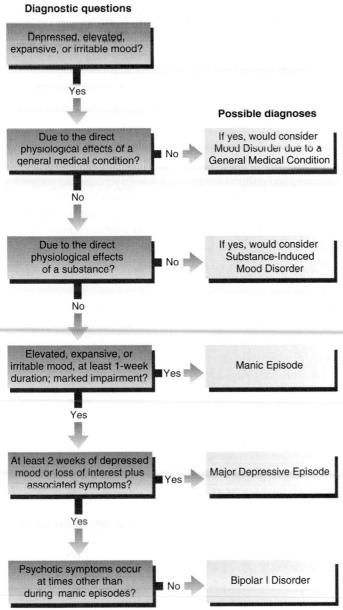

Figure 2.1 Dr. Tobin's decision tree for Peter

Decision trees provide choices for the clinician based on the client's history and symptoms. Follow the choices made by Dr. Tobin throughout the tree for mood disturbances, the area that seems most appropriate for Peter.

has been through the decision tree process. However, Dr. Tobin must be confident that Peter fits the diagnostic criteria for bipolar disorder.

One of the questions that Dr. Tobin might have is whether Peter's symptoms might be due to drug use or to an undiagnosed medical condition. If Peter had been abusing amphetamines, he might have had symptoms like those of a manic episode. Alternatively, a person with a brain tumor might show mood disturbances similar to those of a person with mania. In the process of differential diagnosis, the clinician must ensure that there is not a physiological basis for the symptoms. Virtually all the diagnoses on Axis I of the *DSM-IV* specify that the

clinician should rule out this possibility. There is an entire category of disorders on Axis I termed "mental disorders due to a general medical condition." Another category applies to disorders due to the abuse of psychoactive substances.

The diagnostic process often requires more than one session with the client, which is why some clinicians prefer to regard the first few psychotherapy sessions as a period of evaluation or assessment. While some therapeutic work may be accomplished during this time, the major goal is for the client and clinician together to arrive at as thorough an understanding as possible of the nature of the client's disorder. This paves the way for the clinician to work with the client on an agreed-upon treatment plan.

Peter's diagnosis was fairly straightforward; however, there are many people whose problems do not fit neatly into a diagnostic category. The problems of some individuals meet the criteria for two or more disorders. The most common instance is when a person has a long-standing personality disorder as well as another more circumscribed problem, such as depression or a sexual disorder. It is also possible for an individual to have two concurrent Axis I diagnoses, such as alcoholism and depression. When clinicians use multiple diagnoses, they typically consider one of the diagnoses to be the **principal diagnosis**—namely, the disorder that is considered to be the primary reason the individual is seeking professional help.

Final Diagnosis

The final diagnosis that Dr. Tobin assigned to Peter incorporates all the information gained during the diagnostic phase of his treatment. Clinicians realize the importance of accuracy in designating a final diagnosis, as this label will set the stage for the entire treatment plan. Dr. Tobin's diagnosis of Peter appears in her records as follows:

Axis I: 296.43 Bipolar I Disorder, most recent episode manic, severe without psychotic features

Axis II: Diagnosis deferred (no information yet available on Peter's long-standing personality traits)

Axis III: No physical conditions reported

Axis IV: Problems with primary support group (divorce)

Axis V: Current Global Assessment of Functioning: 43
Highest Global Assessment of Functioning (past year): 80

Case Formulation

Once the formal diagnosis is made, the clinician is still left with a formidable challenge—to piece together a picture of how the disorder evolved. A diagnosis is a categorical judgment, and, although it is very informative, it does not say much about the client as an individual. To gain a full appreciation of the client's disorder, the clinician develops a **case formulation:** an analysis of the client's development and the factors that might have influenced his or her current psychological status. The formulation provides an analysis that transforms the diagnosis from a set of code numbers to a rich piece of descriptive information about the client's personal history. This descriptive information helps the clinician design a treatment plan that is attentive to the client's symptoms, unique past experiences, and future potential for growth.

Let's return to Peter's case. Having diagnosed Peter as having bipolar disorder, Dr. Tobin uses the next two therapy sessions with him to obtain a comprehensive review of his presenting problem, as well as his life history. Based on this review, Dr. Tobin makes the following case formulation:

> Peter is a 23-year-old divorced White male with a diagnosis of bipolar disorder. He is currently in the middle of his first manic episode, which follows his first major depressive episode by about 4 months. The precipitant for the onset of this disorder several months ago seems to have been the turbulence in his marriage and the resulting divorce. Relevant to Peter's condition is an important fact about his family—his mother has been treated for a period of 20 years for bipolar disorder. Peter's diagnosis appears to be a function of both an inherited predisposition to a mood disorder and a set of experiences within his family. The younger child of two boys, Peter was somehow singled out by his mother to be her confidant. She told Peter in detail about her symptoms and the therapy she was receiving. Whenever Peter himself was in a slightly depressed mood, his mother told him that it was probably the first sign of a disorder he was bound to inherit from her. Her involvement in his emotional problems creates another difficulty for Peter in that it has made him ambivalent about seeking therapy. On the one hand, he wants to get help for his problems. Counteracting this desire is Peter's reluctance to let his mother find out that he is in therapy, for fear that this information will confirm her dire predictions for him.

This case formulation gives a more complete picture of Peter's diagnosis than does the simple diagnosis of bipolar disorder. Having read this case formulation, you now know some

A clinician works on developing a case formulation for her new client.

important potential contributions to Peter's current disorder. In effect, in developing a case formulation, a clinician proposes an hypothesis about the causes of the client's disorder. This hypothesis gives the clinician a logical starting point for designing a treatment and serves as a guide through the many decisions yet to be made.

Cultural Formulation

In a diverse society, such as American culture, experienced clinicians know that they must be broad in their understanding of ethnic and cultural contributions to psychological problems. To middle-class White clinicians, some conditions might seem strange and incomprehensible without an awareness of the existence of these conditions within certain other cultures. Consequently, with clients from culturally diverse backgrounds, it is important for clinicians to go beyond the multiaxial diagnostic process of the *DSM-IV* and to evaluate conditions that might be culturally determined. In these cases, a cultural formulation is developed. This is a formulation that takes into account the client's degree of identification with the culture, the culture's beliefs about psychological disorder, the ways in which certain events are interpreted within the culture, and the cultural supports available to the client.

The individual's degree of involvement with the culture is important for the clinician to know, because it indicates whether the clinician should take into account cultural influences on the client's symptoms. Clients who do not identify with their culture of origin would not be expected to be as affected by cultural norms and beliefs as would those who are heavily involved in their culture's traditions. The client's familiarity with and preference for using a certain language is one obvious indicator of cultural identification. Second, assuming that the client does identify with the culture, it is necessary to know about cultural explanations of the individual's symptoms. In certain cultures, psychological disorders may be expressed as particular patterns of behavior, perhaps reflecting predominant cultural themes that date back for centuries, known as **culture-bound syndromes.** For example, "ghost sickness" is a preoccupation with death and the deceased that is reported by members of American Indian tribes. This phenomenon includes a constellation of extreme bodily and psychological reactions (see Table 2.5). Such symptoms would have a different meaning if reported by a middle-class White person, rather than an American Indian. Third, the clinician takes into account how events are interpreted within the individual's cultural framework. An event may be extremely stressful to members of a given culture who attribute significant meaning to that event. By contrast, members of another cultural group may have a more neutral interpretation of that event. For example, within certain Asian cultures, an insult may provoke the condition known as "amok," in which a person (usually male) enters an altered state of consciousness in which he becomes violent, aggressive, and even homicidal. Cultural supports available to the client form the fourth component of the cultural formulation. Within certain cultures, extended family networks and religion provide emotional resources to help individuals cope with stressful life events.

In the process of developing a case formulation, clinicians know that it is important to be aware of the ways in which the client's age, gender, and ethnicity may be salient.

Apart from the role of cultural factors in the formulation, clinicians must also take cultural factors into account when conceptualizing the treatment relationship they will have with clients. The clinician should take care not to make assumptions about how the client would like to be treated, based on the clinician's own cultural background. Seemingly minor aspects of the relationship, such as how familiar the clinician acts toward the client, may have tremendous bearing on the rapport that is established in their relationship. In some cultures, for example, it would be regarded as rude for the clinician to use an individual's first name. Another aspect of the relationship that may be affected by cultural factors is the role of eye contact. The clinician should be aware of whether people within the client's culture make eye contact during conversation. It would be erroneous for the clinician to assume that a client's lack of eye contact implies disrespect.

Attention to all of these factors helps the clinician formulate a diagnosis and treatment that are sensitive to cultural differences. Going a step further, clinicians can benefit from becoming familiar with the culture-bound syndromes such as those in Table 2.5. If some of these seem bizarre to you, think about how someone from another culture might regard conditions that are prevalent in Western culture, such as eating disorders. You might also think about the meaning of these culture-bound syndromes for our understanding of abnormal behavior. The fact that psychological disorders vary from one society to another supports the claim of the sociocultural perspective that cultural factors play a role in influencing the expression of abnormal behavior.

Treatment Planning

We have discussed the steps through which a clinician develops an understanding of a client's problem. This understanding provides the basis for the clinician's next phase, which is to plan the most appropriate treatment for the client. In an optimal situation, the clinician has the client's cooperation in addressing several questions regarding treatment choices: What are the goals of the treatment? What would be the best treatment setting? Who should treat the client? What kind of treatment

should be used? What kind of treatment is financially feasible and available? Finally, what theoretical orientation would be best suited to the client's particular needs? All of these considerations would form Dr. Tobin's treatment plan for Peter as she moves from the diagnostic phase toward the treatment phase.

Goals of Treatment

The first phase of treatment planning is to establish treatment goals, which are the objectives the clinician hopes to accomplish in working with the client. These goals range from the immediate to the long term. To understand this critical phase of the process, put yourself into the shoes of a clinician for the moment and think of an analogous situation in which you are trying to help a friend through a crisis. Although you are not "treating" your friend in a professional sense, the steps you take would be very much like the approach a clinician takes with a client in developing a treatment plan. Let's say this friend knocks on your door late one night, in tears because she has had another of her many arguments on the phone with her father. Because of her problems with her father, she has had academic difficulties all semester. Tomorrow, she has an important exam, and she is panic-stricken.

Now, consider what you would do in helping your friend. Your first reaction would be to help her calm down. You might talk to her and try to get her in a better frame of mind, so that she will be able to take the exam. However, you would also realize that she has other problems, which she will need to attend to after she gets through the next day. In the short term, she needs to catch up on the rest of her course work. Over the long term, she will need to deal with the difficulties that recur between her and her father. A clinician treating a client would also think in terms of three stages—immediate management, short-term goals, and long-term goals.

In dealing with immediate management, the clinician addresses the most pressing needs at the moment. Short-term goals involve change in the client's behavior, thinking, or emotions but do not involve a major personality restructuring. Long-term goals include more fundamental and deeply rooted alterations in the client's personality and relationships.

These three stages imply a sequential order, and in many cases this is the way a treatment plan is conceived. First the clinician deals with the crisis, then handles problems in the near future, and finally addresses issues that require extensive work well into the future. However, in other cases, there may be a cyclical unfolding of stages. New sets of immediate crises or short-term goals may arise in the course of treatment. Or there may be a redefinition of long-term goals as the course of treatment progresses. It is perhaps more helpful to think of the three stages not as consecutive stages per se, but as implying different levels of treatment focus.

Immediate management, then, is called for in situations involving intense distress or risk to the client or others. A person experiencing an acute anxiety attack would most likely be treated on the spot with antianxiety medication. A client who is severely depressed and suicidal may need to be hospitalized. In the case of Peter, Dr. Tobin decides that Peter's possible

Table 2.5

Culture-Bound Syndromes in the *DSM-IV*

Certain psychological disorders, such as depression and anxiety, are universally encountered. Within particular cultures, however, idiosyncratic patterns of symptoms are found, many of which have no direct counterpart to a specific *DSM-IV* diagnosis. These conditions, called culture-bound syndromes, are recurrent patterns of abnormal behavior or experience that are limited to specific societies or cultural areas.

Culture-bound syndromes may fit into one or more of the *DSM-IV* categories, just as one *DSM-IV* category may be thought to be several different conditions by another culture. Some disorders recognized by the *DSM-IV* are seen as culture-bound syndromes, because they are specific to industrialized societies (e.g., anorexia nervosa).

This table describes some of the best-studied culture-bound syndromes and forms of distress that may be encountered in clinical practice in North America, as well as the *DSM-IV* categories they most closely resemble.

Term	Location	Description	*DSM-IV* Disorders
Amok	Malaysia	Dissociative episode consisting of brooding followed by violent, aggressive, and possibly homicidal outburst. Precipitated by insult; usually seen more in males. Return to premorbid state following the outburst.	
Ataque de nervios	Latin America	Distress associated with uncontrollable shouting, crying, trembling, and verbal or physical aggression. Dissociation, seizure, and suicidal gestures possible. Often occurs as a result of a stressful family event. Rapid return to premorbid state.	Anxiety Mood Dissociative Somatoform
Bilis and colera	Latin America	Condition caused by strong anger or rage. Marked by disturbed core body imbalances, including tension, headache, trembling, screaming, and stomach disturbance. Chronic fatigue and loss of consciousness possible.	
Boufée delirante	West Africa and Haiti	Sudden outburst of agitated and aggressive behavior, confusion, and psychomotor excitement. Paranoia and visual and auditory hallucinations possible.	Brief psychotic
Brain fag	West Africa	Difficulties in concentration, memory, and thought, usually experienced by students in response to stress. Other symptoms include neck and head pain, pressure, and blurred vision.	Anxiety Depressive Somatoform
Dhat	India	Severe anxiety and hypochondriacal concern regarding semen discharge, whitish discoloration of urine, weakness, and extreme fatigue.	
Falling-out or blacking out	Southern United States and the Caribbean	A sudden collapse, usually preceded by dizziness. Temporary loss of vision and the ability to move.	Conversion Dissociative
Ghost sickness	American Indian tribes	A preoccupation with death and the deceased. Thought to be symbolized by bad dreams, weakness, fear, appetite loss, anxiety, hallucinations, loss of consciousness, and a feeling of suffocation.	
Hwa-byung (wool-hwa-byung)	Korea	Acute feelings of anger resulting in symptoms including insomnia, fatigue, panic, fear of death, dysphoria, indigestion, loss of appetite, dyspnea, palpitations, aching, and the feeling of a mass in the abdomen.	
Koro	Malaysia	An episode of sudden and intense anxiety that one's penis or vulva and nipples will recede into the body and cause death.	
Latah	Malaysia	Hypersensitivity to sudden fright, usually accompanied by symptoms including echopraxia (imitating the movements and gestures of another person), echolalia (irreverent parroting of what another person has said), command obedience, and dissociation, all of which are characteristic of schizophrenia.	

Table 2.5 (continued)

Term	Location	Description	DSM-IV Disorders
Mal de ojo	Mediterranean cultures	Means "the evil eye" when translated from Spanish. Children are at much greater risk; adult females are at a higher risk than adult males. Manifested by fitful sleep, crying with no apparent cause, diarrhea, vomiting, and fever.	
Pibloktog	Arctic and sub-Arctic Eskimo communities	Abrupt dissociative episode associated with extreme excitement, often followed by seizures and coma. During the attack, the person may break things, shout obscenities, eat feces, and behave dangerously. The victim may be temporarily withdrawn from the community and report amnesia regarding the attack.	
Qi-gong psychotic reaction	China	Acute episode marked by dissociation and paranoia that may occur following participation in qi-gong, a Chinese folk health-enhancing practice.	
Rootwork	Southern United States, African American and European populations, and Caribbean societies	Cultural interpretation that ascribes illness to hexing, witchcraft, or sorcery. Associated with anxiety, gastrointestinal problems, weakness, dizziness, and the fear of being poisoned or killed.	
Shen-k'uei or Shenkui	Taiwan and China	Symptoms attributed to excessive semen loss due to frequent intercourse, masturbation, and nocturnal emission. Dizziness, backache, fatigue, weakness, insomnia, frequent dreams, and sexual dysfunction. Excessive loss of semen is feared, because it represents the loss of vital essence and therefore threatens one's life.	
Shin-byung	Korea	Anxiety and somatic problems followed by dissociation and possession by ancestral spirits.	
Spell	African American and European American communities in the southern United States	Trance state in which communication with deceased relatives or spirits takes place. Sometimes connected with a temporary personality change.	
Susto	Latinos in the United States and Mexico, Central America, and South America	Illness caused by a frightening event that causes the soul to leave the body. Causes unhappiness, sickness (muscle aches, stress headache, and diarrhea), strain in social roles, appetite and sleep disturbances, lack of motivation, low self-esteem, and possibly death. Healing methods include calling the soul back into the body and cleansing to restore bodily and spiritual balance.	Major depressive, Post-traumatic-stress Somatoform
Taijin kyofusho	Japan	Intense fear that one's body parts or functions displease, embarrass, or are offensive to others regarding appearance, odor, facial expressions, or movements.	
Zar	Ethiopia, Somalia, Egypt, Sudan, Iran, and other North African and Middle Eastern societies	Possession by a spirit. May cause dissociative experiences characterized by shouting, laughing, hitting of one's head against a hard surface, singing, crying, apathy, withdrawal, and change in daily habits.	

From American Psychiatric Association: *Diagnostic and Statistical Manual of Mental Disorders,* Fourth Edition. Washington DC, American Psychiatric Association, 1994.

Razors pain you;
Rivers are damp;
Acids stain you;
And drugs cause cramps.
Guns aren't lawful;
Nooses give;
Gas smell[?]
You might [?]

SUICIDE HOT LINE

At this suicide hot line, telephone counseling is available 24 hours a day.

dangerousness to others warrants hospitalization. Furthermore, his manic symptoms of irrational behavior and agitation suggest that he needs intensive professional care. Not all clinical situations require that action be taken in the immediate management stage, but it is important for the clinician to think about various options to help the client deal with pressing concerns of the moment.

When a client's most troubling symptoms are under control, it is possible for the clinician to work with the client in developing more effective ways of resolving current difficulties. The plan at this point might include establishing a working relationship between the clinician and client, as well as setting up specific objectives for therapeutic change. If Dr. Tobin is to treat Peter's mood disorder, she must establish rapport with him, and he, in turn, must feel committed to working with her. Another short-term goal might be to stabilize Peter on medication, so that his symptoms will be alleviated.

Long-term goals are the ultimate aims of therapeutic change. Ideally, the long-term goals for any client are to overcome the problem and to develop a strategy to prevent recurrence. In reality, these goals are difficult to achieve. The restructuring of a personality can be a lifelong endeavor. With the help of Dr. Tobin, Peter will need to plan his life, taking his disorder into account. For example, Dr. Tobin may advise Peter to take medication aimed at preventing a recurrence of his symptoms. He may also need to prepare himself for some of the ways this disorder may affect his life. In addition, Peter will have to work with Dr. Tobin to deal with the emotional scars he has suffered as a result of his own disorder and the troubled childhood caused by his mother's disorder.

A treatment plan, then, includes a set of goals for short- and long-range interventions. Having established these goals, the clinician's next task is to specify how to implement the plan. This requires decisions regarding the optimal treatment site, the treatment modality, and the theoretical perspective on which the treatment is based.

Treatment Site

The severity of the client's problem is one of the first issues a clinician considers in deciding what kind of treatment site to recommend. Treatment sites vary in the degree to which they

provide a controlled environment and in the nature of the services they offer to clients. Treatment sites include psychiatric hospitals, outpatient treatment settings, halfway houses and day treatment centers, and other treatment sites, such as the school or workplace, that provide mental health services. The more serious the client's disturbance, the more controlled the environment that is needed and the more intense the services.

The severity of the client's symptoms is assessed on several dimensions. Is the client suicidal, at risk of harming others, delusional, or otherwise incapable of maintaining control? Does the client have physical problems, such as those that might result from a brain dysfunction, an eating disorder, or illness? What is the client's support system at home? Are people there who can help the client deal with the problems caused by the disorder and its symptoms? Further, the clinician must be sensitive to the financial resources available to the client. In an age in which cost-effectiveness is of major concern to insurance companies, treatment decisions are commonly dictated by decisions to pursue the least expensive care. The clinician's recommendation of a treatment site is also based on the match between the client's needs and the services provided in a particular treatment setting. Depending on how clinical and financial issues are addressed, the clinician will recommend a psychiatric hospital, outpatient treatment, or a halfway house or group home that provides a combination of services.

Psychiatric Hospitals

The decision to hospitalize a client depends largely on the risk the client presents. A clinician usually recommends that the client be admitted to a psychiatric hospital when the client is at risk of harming self or others or seems incapable of self-care. Although some clients choose inpatient psychiatric care quite willingly, there must be demonstrable clinical need and evidence that the client presents a risk in order for this very expensive form of treatment to be covered by insurance or public programs. Often, clients who are at high risk of harm to self or others are involuntarily hospitalized by a court order until their symptoms can be brought under control (this is discussed in more detail in Chapter 15).

Hospitalization is also recommended for clients who have disorders that require medical interventions and intensive forms of psychotherapeutic interventions. Some medical interventions, such as a trial on a new drug regimen, are best done in a hospital setting, where the risks of potential side effects and treatment efficacy can be monitored continuously. Some psychotherapeutic interventions are also best done in a setting where the contingencies of the client's behavior can be monitored and reinforced by trained personnel. For example, a young man prone to violent outbursts may require an environment in which he is rewarded when he is quiet and is responded to aversively when he loses control.

In some cases, the clinician might recommend a specialized inpatient treatment center. Such a treatment site would be appropriate for adults with substance abuse problems or for children and adolescents who need professional treatment in a residential setting.

Returning to the case of Peter, a hospital would be the treatment site of choice, because he is a threat to others, he needs medication monitoring, and the hospital could offer him various forms of therapy. As he improves, Dr. Tobin will develop a discharge plan that will undoubtedly include outpatient care.

Outpatient Treatment

Because hospitalization is such a radical and expensive intervention, most clients receive outpatient treatment, in which they are treated in a private professional office or clinic. Professionals in private practice offer individual or group sessions, usually on a weekly basis. Some prepaid health insurance plans cover the cost of such visits, either to a private practitioner or to a clinician working in a health maintenance organization (HMO). Outpatient treatment may also be offered in agencies supported partially or completely by public funds. **Community mental health centers (CMHCs)** are outpatient clinics that provide psychological services on a sliding fee scale for individuals who live within a certain geographic area.

Outpatient services are, by necessity, more limited than those in a hospital, in terms of both the time involved and the nature of the contact between client and clinician. However, additional services may be made available to clients who need vocational counseling, help with domestic management, group therapy, or the support of a self-help organization, such as Alcoholics Anonymous.

Halfway Houses and Day Treatment Programs

Clients with serious psychological disorders who are able to live in the community need more services than can be provided through conventional outpatient treatment. For such individuals, halfway houses and day treatment programs are the most

One of the nation's premier psychiatric hospitals, McLean Hospital in Belmont, Massachusetts, is a nationally recognized leader in mental health and outcomes assessment, and maintains the largest research program of any private U.S. psychiatric hospital.

appropriate treatment sites. These facilities may be connected with a hospital, a public agency, or a private corporation. **Halfway houses** are designed for clients who have been discharged from psychiatric facilities but who are not yet ready for independent living. A halfway house provides a living context with other deinstitutionalized people, and it is staffed by professionals who work with clients in developing the skills they need to become employed and to set up their own living situations. **Day treatment programs** are designed for formerly hospitalized clients as well as for clients who do not need hospitalization but do need a structured program during the day, similar to that provided by a hospital. Many day treatment programs are based on a social club model. Some of the clients who participate in day treatment programs reside in halfway houses and some live independently, with relatives or in apartments supervised by paraprofessional mental health workers.

Other Treatment Sites

Psychological treatment is also provided in settings not traditionally associated with the provision of mental health services, such as the schools and the workplace. Guidance counselors and school psychologists are often called on to intervene in cases in which a student is emotionally disturbed or is upset by a pathological living situation. These professionals handle much of the intervention in the school, but they often find it necessary to refer the student or family for outside professional help. In the workplace, many employers have recognized the importance of intervening in the lives of employees whose emotional problems are interfering with their job performance and could possibly result in termination from employment. A common program is the Employee Assistance Program (EAP) provided by most large companies. The EAP provides the employee with a confidential setting in which to seek help for emotional problems, substance abuse difficulties, or relationship problems. Often the EAP professional can work with the employee toward a resolution of the problem; at times, the EAP professional can help the employee locate appropriate treatment resources for the problem at hand.

Modality of Treatment

The **modality,** or form in which psychotherapy is offered, is another crucial component of the treatment plan. In **individual psychotherapy,** the therapist works with the client on a one-to-one basis. Typically, the therapist and client meet on a regular schedule—most commonly, once a week for about an hour. In couple therapy, partners in a relationship both participate, and, in **family therapy,** several or all of the family members are involved in the treatment. In family therapy, one person may be identified by family members as being the "patient." The therapist, however, views the whole family system as the target of the treatment. **Group therapy** provides a modality in which troubled people can openly share their problems with others, receive feedback, develop trust, and improve interpersonal skills.

Milieu therapy, which has been found to be helpful for hospitalized clients, is based on the premise that the milieu, or environment, is a major component of the treatment; a new setting, in which a team of professionals works with the client to

Psychological treatment is also provided in settings other than hospitals and clinics. This high-school counselor is talking with a student about drug abuse.

In family therapy, all available members of a family are involved in treatment.

improve his or her mental health, is considered to be better than the client's home and work environments, with their stresses and pressures. Ideally, the milieu is constructed in such a way that clients will perceive all interactions and contexts as therapeutic and constructive. In addition to traditional psychotherapy, other therapeutic endeavors are made through group or peer counseling, occupational therapy, and recreational therapy.

The clinician's decision to recommend a particular modality of treatment is based, again, on a match between the client's specific needs and the treatment's potential to meet these needs. For example, a teenage girl with an eating disorder may be seen in both individual therapy and family therapy if the clinician believes that the eating disorder is rooted in disturbed parent-child interactions. As this example illustrates, the clinician has the option of recommending multiple modalities, rather than being restricted to one form of therapy. We will discuss the modalities in more detail in Chapter 4, along with their conceptual underpinnings.

In Peter's case, three treatment modalities would be recommended, at least in the initial phase of his treatment. Along with his individual therapy needs, Peter would benefit from both family therapy and group therapy. Family therapy would be useful in helping Peter develop his support system with his mother and brother, and group therapy would provide Peter with the opportunity to interact with and derive support from other clients who have similar disorders.

Theoretical Perspective on Which Treatment Is Based

Whatever modality of treatment a clinician recommends, it must be based on the choice of the most appropriate theoretical perspective or the most appropriate aspects of several different perspectives. Many clinicians are trained according to a particular set of assumptions about the origins of psychological disorders and the best methods of treating these disorders. Often, this theoretical orientation forms the basis for the clinician's treatment decisions. However, just as frequently, clinicians adapt their theoretical orientation to fit the client's needs. Further, the growing movement toward integrating diverse theoretical models in treatment planning is addressing the concerns of clinicians who feel that a single theoretical model is too narrow. Increasingly, clinicians are combining the best elements of various theoretical orientations in tailoring the treatment plan to have the greatest likelihood of success for a given client (Norcross, 1992).

Treatment Implementation

When the diagnostic process and treatment planning have taken place, the clinician then implements the treatment. Despite all the thinking and preparation that have gone into this plan, though, the exact way in which treatment unfolds varies according to the characteristics of the clinician, the client, and the interaction between the two. There are many individual variations among both clients and clinicians. Consequently, the potential for variation is virtually unlimited in the interactions between any one client and any one clinician. Some common issues, though, characterize all therapeutic interactions.

Above and beyond whatever techniques a clinician uses to treat a client's problems, the quality of the relationship between the client and clinician is a crucial determinant of whether therapy will succeed or not. A good clinician does more than coldly and objectively "administer" treatment to a client. A good clinician infuses a deep personal interest, concern, and respect for the client into the therapeutic relationship. In this regard, psychotherapy is as much an art as a skill.

The Course of Treatment

The way that treatment proceeds is a function of the contributions made by the clinician and the client. Each has a part to play in determining the outcome of the case, as does the unique interaction of their personalities, abilities, and expectations.

How Do Experts Determine Which Treatments Really Work?

For many medical problems, physicians know that there is a standard treatment that would be applied to most patients presenting with a given set of symptoms. For example, antibiotics would be prescribed for an infection. You might assume that most psychotherapists treating a given disorder would use a standard intervention, but, in fact, this has not been the case in the twentieth century. Consider a client with major depressive disorder. Some clinicians would recommend a brief intervention that focuses on the client's distorted thoughts. Other clinicians would suggest that the client engage in lengthy psychotherapy to explore early life experiences that caused or contributed to adult depression. Still others would dispense with "talk therapy" and recommend antidepressant medication. And others would integrate components of each of these approaches.

Which treatment method is the most effective, and how can effectiveness be measured? In an effort to answer these questions, psychotherapy researchers have devoted considerable effort in recent years to reviewing all pub-lished outcome studies on specific disorders. From these efforts to identify empirically supported treatments have emerged treatment recommendations called "practice guidelines" (Nathan, 1998). Although the process of developing practice guidelines might seem straightforward and relatively uncontroversial, these efforts have unleashed a storm of controversy. Nathan (1998) noted that many clinical scientists were concerned about the adequacy of the research that served as the basis for these recommendations. Complicating the picture is the fact that many of the empirically supported treatments and practice guidelines are based on behavioral principles, thus leaving some practitioners who work within different theoretical models to feel left out in the cold. The debate has intensified as insurance companies have looked to clinical recommendations to support briefer, and less expensive, interventions that focus on observable behavioral change. Adding to the debate is the belief of some insurance company executives that, with treatment manuals, relatively untrained clinicians can now conduct therapy. The obvious benefit would be a reduction in the cost of therapy provided by professionals with a doctoral or master's degree.

Even though efforts to designate the most effective treatments have been admirable, these efforts have not yielded the simple solutions that experts had hoped would be found. To shed some light on the complexity of the issues, Martin Seligman, a leading psychotherapy researcher, has attempted to highlight some of the differences between research that is conducted in laboratory settings (called efficacy research) and outcome studies involving people who have sought professional help in a traditional helping context (effectiveness research) (Seligman, 1995). Efficacy studies are commonly conducted in university-based clinics, where therapists are carefully selected, trained, and monitored; furthermore, patients are also carefully screened in order to exclude those with multiple problems (DeRubeis & Crits-Cristoph, 1998).

Seligman contends that what is measured in efficacy studies has only a slight resemblance to what takes place in a real-world therapy setting. In the real world, clients are not assigned to random groups for fixed durations and treated according to a predetermined script. Furthermore, rarely does a client's diagnosis fit neatly into one clearly delineated category. For example, a client with major depressive disorder may also have a personality disorder, an eating disorder, and a sexual dysfunction. In such a case, which practice guidelines would be followed? Seligman points out that, in effectiveness research, investigators study therapy as it is practiced in the field. Therapy is conducted without a manual; patients may have several presenting problems, and they are choosing therapists in whom they believe.

As you are reading about various disorders in this book, and the treatments that have been demonstrated as most effective, it will be important to keep in mind the empirical basis for the treatment conclusions. Findings from efficacy studies shed light on appropriate interventions, but they are insufficient for making conclusive determinations about what is most effective with real people with complex problems.

The Clinician's Role in Treatment

One of the skills the clinician develops is an ability to scan the client-clinician interaction for meaningful cues that will provide insight into the nature of the client's problems. An important piece of information the clinician gathers is the way the client seems to respond to the clinician. Let's use Dr. Tobin as an example to illustrate this point. Dr. Tobin is a woman in her early forties. Each of her clients forms a unique impression of the kind of person she is. One client thinks of Dr. Tobin as an authority figure, because Dr. Tobin's mannerisms and appearance remind him of his seventh-grade teacher. Another client perceives Dr. Tobin as a peer, because they are about the same age and professional status. A third client is in his sixties, and Dr. Tobin reminds him of his daughter. Thus, the same clinician is perceived in three different ways by three different clients. With each client, Dr. Tobin has a markedly different basis for a therapeutic relationship.

Not only do clients have unique responses to Dr. Tobin, but she also has individualized responses to each client. As a professional, Dr. Tobin is trained to examine her reactions to each client and to try not to let her reactions interfere with her ability to help. Moreover, she has learned how to use her perception of each client and the way she thinks she is perceived as aids in diagnosing the client's disorder and in embarking on a therapeutic procedure.

The Client's Role in Treatment

In optimal situations, psychotherapy is a joint enterprise in which the client plays an active role. It is largely up to the client to describe and identify the nature of his or her disorder, to describe personal reactions as treatment progresses, and to initiate and follow through on whatever changes are going to be made.

The client's attitudes toward therapy and the therapist are an important part of the contribution the client makes to the therapeutic relationship. There is a special quality to the help that the client is requesting; it involves potentially painful, embarrassing, and personally revealing material that the client is not accustomed to disclosing to someone else. Most people are much more comfortable discussing their medical, legal, financial, and other problems outside the realm of the emotions. Social attitudes toward psychological disorders also play a role. People may feel that they should be able to handle their emotional problems without seeking help. They may believe that, if they can't solve their own emotional problems, it means they are immature or incompetent. Moreover, having to see a clinician may make a person believe that he or she is "crazy." You would not hesitate to tell your friends that you have an appointment with a physician because of a sore knee. Most people would, though, feel less inclined to mention to acquaintances that they are in psychotherapy for personal problems. The pressure to keep therapy secret usually adds to a client's anxiety about seeking professional help. To someone who is already troubled by severe problems in living, this added anxiety can be further inhibiting. With so many potential forces driving the troubled individual away from seeking therapy, the initial step is sometimes the hardest to take. Thus, the therapeutic relationship requires the client to be willing to work with the clinician in a partnership and to be prepared to endure the pain and embarrassment involved in making personal revelations. Moreover, it also requires a willingness to break old patterns and to try new ways of viewing the self and relating to others.

The Outcome of Treatment

In the best of all possible worlds, the treatment works. The client stays through the treatment, shows improvement, and maintain this improved level of functioning. Many times, though, the road is not so smooth, and either the goals of the treatment plan are never attained or unanticipated problems arise. Some of the obstacles that clinicians face in their efforts to help clients include some curious and frustrating realities. The most frustrating involve the client who is unwilling to change. It may sound paradoxical, but, even though a client may seem terribly distressed by a problem, that client may fail to follow through on a very promising treatment. Mental health professionals know that change is very difficult, and many clients have become so accustomed to living with a problem that the effort needed to solve the problem seems overwhelming. At times, clinicians also face frustration over financial constraints. They may recommend a treatment that they are quite confident can succeed but that is financially infeasible. In other cases there may be an involved party, such as a lover or parent, who refuses to participate in the treatment, even though he or she plays a central role. Other pragmatic issues can disrupt therapy: clients may move, lose jobs, or lack consistent transportation to the clinic. Over time, those in the mental health field learn that they are limited in how effective they can be in changing the lives of people who go to them for help.

RETURN TO THE CASE

Peter Dickinson

Treatment Plan

After only a brief interaction with Peter during our first encounter, I knew that he needed to be hospitalized. As is common when dealing with individuals in a manic state, there was a tremendous amount of resistance to such a suggestion, however. I realized that Peter would balk at my recommendation, so I was prepared to make my viewpoint as unambiguous as possible. In my thoughts, I realized that there was no way that I would feel comfortable sending Peter back out onto the streets. Of particular concern was the intensity of his anger toward Marnie. Might he threaten to harm her in some way? It seemed unlikely, but possible. What did seem likely, however, was that Peter would not be able to take adequate care of himself in this disordered state of mind.

I explained to Peter that I was deeply concerned about his psychological state and that I was prepared to commit him. Not only did I consider him to be a possible danger to others, but I feared for his physical and psychological well-being. As I had anticipated, Peter began ranting and raving in response to this. At one point, he jumped up and began yelling that I had no authority to push him around. I knew that it was important for me to let him know that I was not intimidated. In a gentle but determined voice, I explained to Peter that I was prepared to take this action, which I was quite clear was in his best interest. Even I was surprised, however, by Peter's sudden turnaround. Apparently, on some level, he recognized that he was out of control. He was then able to accept help in regaining his stability. Peter admitted to me that the disturbed reaction of his brother, Don, to his outlandish behavior had helped him realize that "something was seriously wrong."

Peter admitted himself voluntarily to the hospital, asking me to "promise" that he would be discharged within 2 weeks. I explained that a 2-week time frame seemed reasonable, but providing a guarantee was too difficult, because I was not sure how quickly he would respond to treatment.

My treatment recommendations for Peter were relatively straightforward. First, he needed medication to help control his manic symptoms. Beginning Peter on lithium made sense, because this medication has proven to be effective in the treatment of mania. Second, Peter needed to begin a course of psychotherapy that would have several components. In individual therapy, Peter could work with me in developing an understanding of the nature and causes of his psychological disturbance. We would also discuss choices he could make to reduce the amount of stress in his life and to manage his symptoms over the longer course. In addition to individual therapy, I suggested that Peter's mother and brother join Peter for a few family therapy sessions to be conducted by Bev Mullins, the treatment unit's social worker. Family therapy would focus on establishing a more stable source of emotional connection between Peter and his immediate family. The benefits of such an improved alliance would be multiple. Those most concerned about Peter could be available for support in the event that his disturbance reappeared. Furthermore, his mother's personal experience with the same disorder could serve as an invaluable source of insight into the nature and treatment of this condition. Group therapy was the third form of therapy I recommended to Peter. During his stay on the treatment unit, he would participate in three groups per week, during which he would share his own experiences with others who were also struggling with the powerful experiences associated with a psychological disorder. With expressions of reluctance, Peter agreed to go along with my plan.

Outcome of the Case

As it turned out, Peter's stay in the hospital lasted precisely 14 days. He had shown dramatic improvement after only 4 days on lithium, at which point he expressed relief that he was now calmer and "getting back to normal." For the first time in several weeks, he was able to get some sound sleep and return to normal eating habits.

In his sessions with me, Peter told the story of a troubled childhood, having been raised by a mother with extreme and unpredictable mood variations. Making matters worse, his mother saw Peter, the younger of the two boys, as the son in whom she could confide. By doing so, she set up an uncomfortable alliance with him, and he felt unduly responsible for her well-being.

After graduating from high school, Peter didn't choose the college route taken by most of his classmates; instead, he eloped with his girlfriend and took a job at a local convenience store. Peter and his wife fought almost constantly—mostly about money issues—for the 4 years of their marriage, but they had developed an emotional dependence on each other that made separation seem too difficult. When his wife finally threw him out

RETURN TO THE CASE

Peter Dickinson (continued)

of the house, he was devastated and found himself burdened by feelings of depression and rage. In the weeks that followed the breakup, he "bottomed out." He couldn't work, eat, sleep, or think clearly. At one point, he came close to making a suicide attempt one night while driving alone in his car. Instead of acting on his impulse, he pulled over to the side of the road and cried until dawn. Eventually, over subsequent weeks, the depression subsided. Following a period of relative serenity, however, he found himself unbelievably energized and traveling down the path to mania.

During Peter's stay in the hospital, we met six times. In these sessions, he was able to see how stressors in his life brought on a mood disorder to which he was biologically predisposed. His ongoing interpersonal and financial difficulties placed him at increased risk, and, when his marriage broke up, the psychological turmoil reached a level too intense for him to tolerate.

In the three family sessions Bev Mullins conducted, Peter's mother and brother were remarkably responsive in communicating their concern and support. For the first time that Peter could remember, Mrs. Dickinson acknowledged the turmoil that her mood disorder must have created for Peter, as well as the pressures she placed on her young son to help her solve her problems. In an emotionally charged session, all three family members were brought to tears as they spoke of the hurt and confusion of years past. They also became closer to each other, as they spoke of ways they would try to make their relationships different in the months and years to come.

As successful as individual and family therapy proved to be for Peter, the same was not true for group therapy. Although the group was scheduled to meet three times each week, Peter refused to attend the meetings during the second week of his stay in the hospital. He asserted that, since his symptoms had gone away, he had nothing in common with the "psychos in the therapy group." This issue had the potential of becoming the basis of a power struggle between Peter and the treatment staff. Peter realized that he would be forfeiting some unit privileges, but he was firm in his insistence. Although I would have preferred that he participate, I realized that on some level he was trying to make a statement about his need to be autonomous. Because he was so cooperative in every other way, and he did not balk about the ad-

ministrative consequences of his choice, I decided to let the issue rest.

As we approached the point of discharge, I asked Peter what his preference would be regarding aftercare. He asked me if I would be willing to continue seeing him for "a couple more weeks." I believe that Peter realized that his condition warranted a longer term of follow-up therapy. I pointed out to Peter that he had been through a bout with a major psychological disorder. Even though he was feeling fine, he was still vulnerable, and ongoing treatment made sense. I remember the tone of his sarcasm as he asked me, "So how many weeks of therapy do I need, Dr. Tobin?" I responded that 6 months of regular follow-up sessions, perhaps one every other week, would be most helpful. At that point, we would re-evaluate and make a decision about subsequent treatment. He went along with my plan and responded quite positively in our work, every other week, for the following 6 months. He continued to take lithium, and there was no evidence of mood symptoms throughout that period.

At the end of 6 months, Peter had made some important life changes. He had applied for a job as a bank teller, and he had enrolled in an educational support program in which the bank subsidized part-time college courses. Once he had made this move, Peter communicated that he was "feeling OK" and that he wanted to reduce the frequency of sessions to once a month. I concurred with this plan. What I was less comfortable with, however, was Peter's decision to stop taking lithium. He felt that he was over his "sickness" and that he didn't want to take medication he no longer needed. I reviewed the risks with him, but I respected his right to make his own decision. Five months went by, and Peter was doing very well, when suddenly he found himself feeling energized and "high." He called me with a tone of euphoria in his voice to cancel our session, and I sensed that he might once again become manic. He responded to my urgent request that he come in for a session that day. With great ambivalence, he followed my recommendation to resume his medication.

We met monthly for another year, and now Peter contacts me, usually with a brief phone call once every year, on the day after his birthday, to let me know that "all's well." ■

Sarah Tobin, PhD

Summary

- Nearly half the population is afflicted with a diagnosable psychological disorder at some point in their lives. Approximately 25 percent of these people seek professional help from clinicians, 15 percent from other professional sources; the remainder from informal sources of support or go without help. Clinicians are found within several professions, such as psychiatry, psychology, social work, nursing, and family counseling. They are professionals who are trained to be objective observers of behavior, facilitators of growth, and resources for people facing difficult situations.

- Clinicians and researchers use the *Diagnostic and Statistical Manual of Mental Disorders, Fourth Edition (DSM-IV)*, which contains descriptions of all psychological disorders. In recent editions, the authors of the *DSM* have strived to meet the criterion of reliability, so that a given diagnosis will be consistently applied to anyone showing a particular set of symptoms. At the same time, researchers have worked to ensure the validity of the classification system, so that the various diagnoses represent real and distinct clinical phenomena. The development of the most recent edition, *DSM-IV*, involved a three-stage process, including a comprehensive review of published research, thorough analyses of the research data, and field trials. The authors of *DSM* consider a phenomenon a mental disorder if it is clinically significant; if it is reflected in a behavioral or psychological syndrome; if it is associated with distress, impairment, or risk; and if it is not expectable or culturally sanctioned. The *DSM-IV* is based on a medical model orientation, in which disorders, whether physical or psychological, are viewed as diseases. The classification system is descriptive rather than explanatory, and it is categorical rather than dimensional. Diagnoses are categorized in terms of relevant areas of functioning, called axes: Axis I (Clinical Disorders), Axis II (Personality Disorders and Mental Retardation), Axis III (General Medical Conditions), Axis IV (Psychosocial and Environmental Problems), and Axis V (Global Assessment of Functioning).

- The diagnostic process involves using all relevant information to arrive at a label that characterizes a client's disorder. Clinicians first attend to a client's reported and observable symptoms. The diagnostic criteria in *DSM-IV* are then considered, and alternative diagnoses are ruled out by means of a differential diagnostic process. Going beyond the diagnostic label, clinicians develop a case formulation, an analysis of the client's development and the factors that might have influenced his or her current psychological status. Clinicians also attend to ethnic and cultural contributions to a psychological problem.

- Once a diagnosis is determined, a treatment plan is developed. The treatment plan includes issues pertaining to immediate management, short-term goals, and long-term goals. A treatment site is recommended, such as a psychiatric hospital, an outpatient service, a halfway house, a day treatment program, or another appropriate setting. The modality of treatment is specified and may involve individual psychotherapy, couple or family therapy, group therapy, or milieu therapy. The clinician will also approach the treatment within the context of a given theoretical perspective or a combination of several perspectives. After a plan is developed, clinicians implement treatment, with particular attention to the fact that the quality of the relationship between the client and the clinician is a crucial determinant of whether therapy will succeed. Although many interventions are effective, some are not. Mental health professionals know that change is difficult and that many obstacles may stand in the way of attaining a positive outcome.

Key Terms

See Glossary for definitions.

Adjustment disorder 43
Axis 42
Base rate 38
Case formulation 49
Client 36
Clinical psychologists 37
Community mental health centers
    (CMHC) 55
Comorbid 37
Culture-bound syndromes 50

Day treatment programs 55
Decision tree 48
*Diagnostic and Statistical Manual of
    Mental Disorders (DSM)* 38
Differential diagnosis 48
Family therapy 55
Global Assessment of Functioning
    (GAF) scale 46
Group therapy 55
Halfway houses 55
Individual psychotherapy 55
Milieu therapy 55

Modality 55
Multiaxial system 42
Neurosis 42
Patient 36
Principal diagnosis 49
Prognosis 46
Psychiatrists 37
Psychological testing 38
Psychosis 42
Reliability 38
Syndrome 41
Validity 38

 # Internet Resource

To get more information on the material covered in this chapter, visit our web site at **http://www.mhhe.com/halgin**. There you will find more information, resources, and links to topics of interest.

CASE REPORT: BEN ROBSHAM

Wednesday afternoons provided me with interesting opportunities outside of the psychiatric institution where I worked most of my week. My half-day of consultation at the nearby university's counseling center afforded a different perspective on clinical work. Not only did I supervise some of the graduate student trainees, but I also taught a seminar in psychological testing. For the seminar, I relied on the assessment material that I collected from testing clients in the counseling center.

It was a Wednesday afternoon early in October when Ben Robsham, a 21-year-old college junior, stopped by the clinic during walk-in hours. My schedule was completely full for the afternoon, but my 2:00 supervision student was running late. Marie Furcolo, the clinic's receptionist, came down to my office and asked me if I could possibly spend a few minutes with a young man, Ben Robsham, who was in the waiting room. Marie explained that she felt bad for Ben, because this was the third time he had stopped by the clinic during walk-in hours. Each time he had been turned away, because the clinician on duty was busy with clinical crises and was unable to meet with him to answer a few questions he had about psychological testing. Despite my hectic schedule, I felt it important to be responsive to Ben, thinking in the back of my mind that his simple request might be a cover for a serious problem.

The testing case of Ben was different from the customary assessments I had conducted and presented to my class. Most of the assessment clients were individuals about whom there were diagnostic or treatment planning questions. I couldn't think of an instance of a person coming to the clinic requesting testing because he was "interested in finding out what psychological tests were like."

When I approached Ben in the waiting room to introduce myself, I was struck by my initial impression of him. He was sitting in a distant corner of the room, staring intently at the floor. It seemed that he was muttering something, but I wasn't sure if he was talking to himself or humming a song. His clothing was the typical casual clothing commonly worn by college students—jeans and a plaid shirt—but there were a few aspects of his appearance that seemed odd. Although it was a relatively warm afternoon, Ben wore a wool knit hat over his hair and ears. On his hands he wore sleek black leather gloves, the kind that athletes use in sports, such as golf and handball. In introducing myself, I reached out my hand, which Ben firmly grasped without removing his glove. He stared intensely into my eyes and said with a tone of fear in his voice, "Can we please go to your office, and get out of this public place?" Although his request seemed emphatic and intense, it is not uncommon for clients who come to the counseling center to feel self-conscious and concerned that they might be embarrassed if someone they know were to see them seeking professional help.

As we walked down the hallway, it was evident that Ben was not interested in small talk but, rather, was eager to get right to the business at hand. Even in the few moments since we had met, I had been able to develop a fairly clear impression that Ben had more on his mind than just curiosity about the nature of psychological testing. I quickly came to the conclusion that I was interacting with a young man who was experiencing emotional instability and was feeling needy and frightened.

As soon as Ben took a seat in my office, he got right to the point. He had heard from one of his friends that psychological testing was done in the counseling center, and he had become curious about what it would be like to be tested. He stated that he might even learn some "neat stuff" about himself. Although many people are intrigued by psychological testing, there was a strange quality about the way in which Ben discussed the testing issue. He asked me whether "the police would have access to the testing results." When I asked why he would have such a concern, he claimed that police officers had been following him for several months, since the day he had collided with a police car while riding his bike. Apparently, a police officer had been quite stern with him that day, yelling at Ben as he lay in the street with a minor concussion. No citation was written, nor did Ben suffer any lasting injury, but he grew increasingly concerned that there would be legal repercussions. After hearing this story and Ben's concerns, I reassured him that the test results would be kept confidential. At the same time, I felt a certain level of alarm about the fact that he was troubled by such worries. My concern intensified after asking him why he was wearing a hat and sports gloves. At first, Ben hesitated, apparently reluctant to share the reason for this strange attire, but he then cautiously proceeded to explain. Almost as if he was joking, he said, "It's a good idea to cover up some of your identifying characteristics, just in case . . ." When I asked him, "In case of what?" he responded, "I know it sounds far out to you, but in case someone is trying to identify you for something they think you've done—like a crime or something." I continued to probe about why Ben thought it possible that he could be perceived as a criminal, but he laughed it off and said that he was "just kidding."

By this point in my dealings with Ben, it was evident that this young man had more on his mind than just some questions about psychological testing. Rather, it was quite likely that he was suffering from a psychological disorder and was using the pretext of psychological testing as a route by which to gain access to professional help. I gently raised this possibility with Ben, to which he responded with annoyance by saying, "Can't you shrinks just take something at face value, without reading all sorts of weird meanings into it?" Rather than be offended by what Ben said, I decided to put it aside and accommodated his request for psychological testing. For whatever reason, this was the route Ben was choosing to reach out for help, and I felt I might be able to make a difference in his life.

Sarah Tobin, PhD

3

Assessment

Chapter Outline

As you read the opening case report about Ben's request for psychological testing, certain questions probably came to mind. Perhaps you wondered whether the police might actually be following Ben. Maybe you thought that Ben seemed paranoid. Perhaps it crossed your mind that Ben was actually looking for professional help. If you were Dr. Tobin, how would you go about finding the answers to these questions? First, you would want to talk with Ben and find out more about his concerns. You would possibly find, however, that talking with him did not really answer your questions. He could sound very convincing and present you with "facts" to document his concerns about the police. At the end of your interview, you still would not know whether his concerns were legitimate. You would want to gather more data that would include a careful study of how Ben thinks, behaves, and organizes his world. You would also want to know about his personality and emotional stability. The most efficient way to gather this information is to conduct what is called a psychological assessment.

What Is a Psychological Assessment?

When you meet people for the first time, you usually "size them up." You may try to figure out how smart they are, how nice they are, or how mature they are. In certain circumstances, you may be trying to solve other puzzles, such as whether a car salesperson really has your best interests in mind or is trying to take advantage of your naiveté. Perhaps you are trying to decide whether to accept a classmate's invitation to go on a date. You will probably base your decision on your appraisal of that person's motives and personality. Or consider what you would do if a professor suggests that members of the class pair up to study. You are faced with the task of judging the intelligence of the other students to find the best study partner. All of these scenarios involve **assessment**, a procedure in which a clinician evaluates a person in terms of the psychological, physical, and social factors that have the most influence on the individual's functioning.

Clinicians approach the tasks of assessment with particular goals in mind. These goals can include establishing a diagnosis for someone with a psychological disorder, determining a person's intellectual capacity, predicting a person's appropriateness for a particular job, and evaluating whether someone is mentally competent to stand trial. Depending on the questions to be answered by the assessment, the clinician selects the most appropriate tools. For example, a psychologist asked by a teacher to evaluate a third-grader's mathematical ability would use a very different kind of assessment technique than if asked to evaluate the child's emotional adjustment.

The kinds of techniques used in assessment vary in their focus and degree of structure. There are assessment tools that focus on brain structure and functioning, others that assess personality, and still others that are oriented toward intellectual functioning. These tools range from those that are very structured and follow carefully defined instructions and procedures to those that allow for flexibility on the part of the examiner.

A clinician uses the clinical interview to gather information and establish rapport with a client.

Interview

The clinical interview is the most commonly used assessment tool for developing an understanding of a client and the nature of the client's current problems, history, and future aspirations. An assessment interview consists of a series of questions administered in face-to-face interaction. The clinician may construct the questions as the interview unfolds or may follow a standard set of questions designed prior to the interview. Methods of recording the interview also vary. The interview may be audio- or videotape-recorded, written down during the interview, or reconstructed from the clinician's memory following the interview. In clinical settings, two kinds of interviews are used: the unstructured interview and the structured interview.

Unstructured Interview

The **unstructured interview** is a series of open-ended questions aimed at determining the client's reasons for being in treatment, symptoms, health status, family background, and life history. The interview is called "unstructured," because the interviewer adjusts the exact content and order of the questions rather than following a preset script. The interviewer formulates questions during the interview on the basis of the client's verbal responses to previous questions. Other information the clinician uses to construct questions includes nonverbal behaviors, such as eye contact, body position, tone of voice, hesitations, and other emotional cues.

The way the clinician approaches the interview depends, in part, on what kind of information the clinician is seeking. If the clinician seeks to make a diagnosis, for example, the interview questions would concern the precise nature of the client's symptoms and behaviors, such as mood disturbances, changes in eating or sleeping patterns, or levels of anxiety. However, as you saw in Chapter 2, some people seek professional psychological help for problems that are not diagnosable psychological disorders. For example, when interviewing a woman who is dissatisfied with her job and her deteriorating marriage, the clinician may feel that it is inappropriate to focus entirely on diagnosis. Instead, the clinician works toward developing insight into what factors are causing this woman's current distress.

An important part of the unstructured interview is history taking, in which the clinician asks the client to provide family information and a chronology of past life events. The main objective of history taking is to gain a clear understanding of the client's life and family. History taking should provide the clinician with enough information to write a summary of the major turning points in the client's life and the ways in which the client's current symptoms or concerns fit into this sequence of events. In some cases, clear links can be drawn between the current problem and an earlier event, such as childhood trauma. Most of the time, however, the determinants of current problems cannot be identified this precisely, and the clinician attempts to draw inferences about the possible contributors to current problems. For example, a man told a college counselor that he was looking for help in overcoming his intense anxiety in situations involving public speaking. The counselor first looked for connections between the student's problem and specific events related to this problem, such as a disastrous experience in high school. Finding no clear connection, the counselor inquired about possible relationships between the student's current problem and a more general pattern of insecurity throughout childhood and adolescence.

In most cases, history taking covers the client's personal history and family history. **Personal history** includes important events and relationships in the client's life. The clinician asks about experiences in such realms as school performance, peer relationships, employment, and health. **Family history** covers major events in the lives of the client's relatives, including those who are closest to the client as well as more distantly related family members. The questions asked about family history may be particularly important when attempting to determine whether a client may have inherited a diathesis for a disorder with strong genetic components. For example, the fact that a client has relatives going back several generations who suffered from serious depression would be an important piece of information for a clinician to use in evaluating a client who is showing symptoms of depression.

Let's return to the case of Ben, so that you can get an idea of what might take place in an unstructured interview. Read the excerpt from Dr. Tobin's interview focusing on Ben's history (Table 3.1). Take note of how her questions follow naturally from Ben's answers and how there appears to be a natural flow in the dialogue. Imagine yourself interviewing someone like Ben, and try to think of some of the questions you might want to ask in your effort to understand his needs and concerns. What features of this interview stand out? You probably notice that Ben seems quite fearful and evasive as he talks about some matters, particularly his current experiences. He is particularly concerned about the issue of privacy, more so than might be warranted, given the confidential nature of the professional context. At the same time, he is unduly worried about the possibility that he may sound so disturbed that hospitalization might be considered, yet he has very unusual beliefs and perceptions that might lead you to wonder whether he is, in fact, out of touch with reality. As he describes some of his relationships, even the one with his father, you may notice some seemingly paranoid thinking. All of these issues are of considerable concern to Dr. Tobin in her effort to understand the nature of Ben's problems.

Structured Interview

The **structured interview** consists of a standardized series of questions, with predetermined wording and order. The items are formally written, and the sequence of questioning is prescribed, thus involving less reliance on the clinical experience and judgment of the interviewer. The evaluation of structured interviews is based on objective, predetermined criteria and, consequently, differs from unstructured interviews, which differ substantially from one interviewer to the next.

Structured interviews are designed to help researchers and clinicians attain precise accuracy in diagnosing clients. While some structured interviews cover a range of possible disorders, others have a narrow focus, with the goal of determining whether the interviewee has a given disorder, such as schizophrenia, a mood disorder, or an anxiety disorder.

Examples of commonly used structured interviews are the Anxiety Disorders Interview Schedule for *DSM-IV* (ADIS-IV) (Dinardo, Brown, & Barlow, 1994) and the Structured Clinical Interview for *DSM-IV* (SCID) (First, Spitzer, Gibbon Miriam, & Williams, 1997). The developers of the SCID have formulated the SCID-I for the diagnosis of *DSM-IV* Axis I disorders. The SCID-II is used in the diagnosis of *DSM-IV* Axis II disorders.

More recently, researchers and clinicians working within the U.S. Alcohol Drug and Mental Health Administration (ADAMHA) and the World Health Organization (World Health Organization, 1997) have developed assessment instruments that can be used cross-culturally. The Composite International Diagnostic Interview (CIDI), which has been translated into 18 languages, is a comprehensive standardized instrument for the assessment of mental disorders that facilitates psychiatric epidemiological research throughout the world. Table 3.2 contains some sample items from this instrument.

The International Personality Disorder Examination (IPDE), another cross-cultural instrument, was developed by Armand Loranger and his colleagues (Loranger et al., 1994) to assess the personality disorders that are listed in the *DSM-IV* and the International Classification of Diseases. The authors have demonstrated that this instrument is remarkably accurate in assessing personality disorders (Lenzenweger, Loranger, Korfine, & Neff, 1997), which is especially impressive in light of the fact that it relies on self-report. The researchers developed this scale by using the structure of an earlier instrument that had been designed for use in North America. The international version provided a valuable opportunity for the standardized assessment of personality disorders in different cultures and countries, and it has been published in many languages, including German, Hindi, Japanese, Norwegian, Swahili, Italian, Spanish, Russian, and Estonian. The test developers were concerned about consistency in the administration of this instrument, but they found it was important to acknowledge that departures would have to be made from the literal text to maintain communication with illiterate subjects and those speaking a regional or tribal dialect.

Because the intent of the IPDE is to assess personality disorders, the focus of the instrument is on the subjects' behaviors and characteristics that have been enduring, defined by the authors as having been present for at least a 5-year period. The

Table 3.1

Excerpts from Ben's History Taking

Dr. Tobin: Can you tell me what brings you here today?

Ren: I'd like to take some of the psychological tests I've heard about.

Dr. Tobin: Explain to me what you mean.

Ben: Well, my psychology teacher said that these tests can help you tell whether you're crazy or not.

Dr. Tobin: Is that a concern for you?

Ben: I've had some pretty strange experiences lately, and, when I tell other people about them, they tell me I'm nuts.

Dr. Tobin: Tell me about these experiences.

Ben: Well, sometimes . . . [pause] . . . I don't know if I should tell you this, but . . . [pause] . . . I know that as soon as you hear this you'll want to lock me up . . . but, anyway, here goes. For the past few months, the police have been following me. It all started one day when I was walking by a student demonstration on campus where people were being arrested. I stayed away from the action, because I didn't want to get involved, you know, but I know that the police were watching me. A few days after the demonstration, I saw Nazi soldiers out in my backyard taking pictures of my house and looking in through the windows. You know, this sounds so crazy, I'm not sure I believe it myself. All I know is, it scares the hell out of me, so can I please have the testing to see if I'm losing my mind or not?

Dr. Tobin: We can talk about that a little bit later, but right now I'd like to hear more about the experiences you're having.

Ben: I'd really rather not talk about them anymore. They're too scary.

Dr. Tobin: I can understand that you feel scared, but it would be helpful for me to get a better sense of what you're going through.

Ben: [pause] . . . Well, OK, but you're sure no one else will hear about this? . . .

[Later in the interview, Dr. Tobin inquired about Ben's history.]

Dr. Tobin: I'd like to hear something about your early life experiences, such as your family relationships and your school experiences. First, tell me something about your family when you were growing up.

Ben: Well . . . there's me and my sister, Doreen. She's 2 years older than me. And we haven't ever really gotten along. My mother . . . well . . . Doreen claims that my mother treated

me better than Doreen. Maybe that's true, but not because I wanted it that way.

Dr. Tobin: Tell me more about your relationship with your mother.

Ben: I hated the way she . . . my mother . . . hovered over me. She wouldn't let me make a move without her knowing about it. She always worried that I would get sick or that I would hurt myself. If I was outside playing in the backyard, she would keep coming outside and telling me to be careful. I would get so mad. Even my father would get angry about the way she babied me all the time.

Dr. Tobin: What about your relationship with your father?

Ben: I can't say that I had much of one. No one in the family did. He always came home late, after we had gone to bed. Maybe he was trying to avoid the rest of us or something. I don't know, maybe he was working against the family in some way.

Dr. Tobin: What do you mean, "working against the family"?

Ben: I don't want to get into it.

[Later in the interview]

Dr. Tobin: I'd like to hear about the things that interested you as a child.

Ben: You mean like hobbies, friends, things like that?

Dr. Tobin: Yes.

Ben: I was a loner. That's what Doreen always called me. She would call me a "loser and a loner." I hated those names, but she was right. I spent most of the time in my room, with earphones on, listening to rock music. It was sort of neat. I would imagine that I was a rock star, and I would get lost in these wild thoughts about being important and famous and all. Staying home was OK. But going to school stunk.

Dr. Tobin: Let's talk about your experiences in school.

Ben: Teachers hated me. They liked to embarrass me . . . always complaining that I wouldn't look them in the eye. Why should I? If I made the smallest mistake, they made a federal case out of it. One time . . . we were studying state capitals and the teacher, Mrs. Edison, asked me to name the capital of Tennessee. I didn't know what a capital was. I said, "I don't know anything about capitalism." She got pissed off and called me a "wise guy."

---

interviewer begins by giving the subject the following instructions: "The questions I am going to ask concern what you are like most of the time. I'm interested in what has been typical of you throughout your life, and not just recently." The interviewer then moves into six realms of inquiry: work, self, interpersonal relationships, affects, reality testing, and impulse control.

Such instruments as the IPDE present challenges because of their reliance on the respondent's self-report. Sometimes people are unaware of personal characteristics that are regarded as objectionable, or they may be reluctant to admit to negative

personal aspects. To offset this problem, clinicians can use additional sources of data, such as information from relatives, other mental health professionals, and clinical records.

■ Mental Status Examination

Clinicians use the term **mental status** (or present status) to refer to what the client thinks about and how the client thinks, talks, and acts. Later, when we discuss particular psychological disorders, we will frequently refer to symptoms reflecting

Table 3.2

Sample items from the CIDI

These questions are from the section of the CIDI concerning symptoms related to animal phobias. They illustrate both the scope and the depth of the items on this structured diagnostic interview. Similar questions on this interview concern other DSM-IV Axis I disorders, including substance abuse, mood disorders, schizophrenia, other anxiety disorders, and sleep disorders.

Modified Sample CIDI Anxiety Disorder Questions

A. There are things that make some people so afraid that they avoid them, even when there is no real danger. Have you ever had an unusually strong fear or needed to avoid things like animals, heights, storms, being in closed spaces, and seeing blood?

If Yes:

1. Have you ever had an unusually strong fear of any of these living things, such as insects, snakes, birds, or other animals?

2. Have you ever avoided being near insects, snakes, birds, or other animals, even though there was no real danger?

3. Did the (fear/avoidance) of insects, snakes, birds, or other animals ever interfere with your life or activities a lot?

4. Was your (fear/avoidance) of insects, snakes, birds, or other animals ever excessive, that is, much stronger than in other people?

5. Was your (fear/avoidance) of insects, snakes, birds, or other animals ever unreasonable, that is, much stronger than it should have been?

6. Were you ever very upset with yourself for (having the fear of/avoiding) insects, snakes, birds, or other animals?

7. When you had to be near insects, snakes, birds, or other animals, or thought you would have to be, did you usually become very upset?

B. When you were near insects, snakes, birds, or other animals, or thought you would have to be . . . (the following questions are asked until two are answered "no").

1. Did your heart pound or race?

2. Did you sweat?

3. Did you tremble or shake?

4. Did you have a dry mouth?

5. Were you short of breath?

6. Did you feel like you were choking?

7. Did you have pain or discomfort in your chest?

8. Did you have nausea or discomfort in your stomach?

9. Were you dizzy or feeling faint?

10. Did you feel that you or things around you were unreal?

11. Were you afraid that you might lose control of yourself, act in a crazy way, or pass out?

12. Were you afraid that you might die?

13. Did you have hot flushes or chills?

14. Did you have numbness or tingling sensations?

C. When was the (first/last) time you (were afraid of/avoided) insects, snakes, birds, or other animals?

D. Between the first time and the last time, was this (strong fear/avoidance) of insects, snakes, birds, or other animals usually present whenever you were near them or thought you would have to be near them?

---

disturbances in mental status. A clinician uses the **mental status examination** to assess a client's behavior and functioning, with particular attention to the symptoms associated with psychological disturbance (Trzepacz & Baker, 1993).

Although for the most part mental status examinations are not in standardized form, a few specialized mental status examinations focus on the diagnosis of specific disorders. The Mini-Mental State Examination (Folstein, Folstein, & McHugh, 1975) is one example of a structured mental status instrument shown to have success in the psychological assessment of individuals with Alzheimer's disease and other brain syndromes that are difficult to identify through other assessment methods.

In conducting a mental status examination, the clinician takes note of the client's behavior, orientation, content of thought, thinking style and language, affect and mood, perceptual experiences, sense of self, motivation, intelligence, and insight. The report of a mental status examination incorporates both the client's responses to specific questions and the clinician's objective observations of how the client looks, behaves, and speaks.

A clinician conducts a mental status examination.

Appearance and Behavior

What do you notice when you meet someone for the first time? In all likelihood, you attend to the way the person responds to you, whether there are any oddities of behavior, and even how the individual is dressed. Similarly, in gathering data about the total picture of the individual, the clinician takes note of the client's appearance, level of consciousness, mannerisms, attire, grooming, activity level, and style of interaction. Consider one of Dr. Tobin's cases, a 20-year-old man whom she assessed in the emergency room. Dr. Tobin was struck by the fact that Pierre looked at least 10 years older, that he was dressed in torn and tattered clothing, and that he had a crusty wound on his forehead. In her report, she also made note of the fact that Pierre maintained a stiff posture, refused to remove his hands from his jacket pockets, and never made eye contact with her. In response to Dr. Tobin's questions, Pierre mumbled some unintelligible comments under his breath. These are odd behaviors in our culture that might be important pieces of information as Dr. Tobin develops a more comprehensive understanding of Pierre. Some of these behaviors are found in people with certain forms of psychosis.

Although every bit of information can have diagnostic significance, the movements of a person's body and level of activity are especially noteworthy. The term **motor behavior** refers to the ways in which a client moves. Even clients who are unwilling or unable to speak can communicate a great deal of important information through their bodily movements. For example, one man may be so restless that he cannot stop pacing, whereas another man is so slowed down that he moves in a lethargic and listless manner. **Hyperactivity** involves abnormally energized physical activity, characterized by quick movements and fast talking. Sometimes hyperactivity is evidenced by **psychomotor agitation**, in which the individual appears to be restless and stirred up. In contrast, **psychomotor retardation** involves abnormally slow movements and lethargy.

Perhaps the individual shows some oddities of behavior that are not particularly bizarre but are nevertheless notable, and possibly diagnostically important. These include unusual mannerisms, such as dramatic gesturing or a facial tic in which the individual blinks rapidly when speaking.

Abnormalities of bodily movements can take extreme forms, such as rigid posturing or immobilization. **Catatonia** refers to extreme motor disturbances in a psychotic disorder not attributable to physiological causes. In some instances of catatonia the individual appears to be in a coma, with rigid and unmovable limbs. In other cases, the catatonic person may be extremely flexible and responsive to being "molded" into position by someone else. Consider the case of Alice, who sits motionless all day long in a catatonic state. Even if someone were to stand in front of her and shout or try to startle her, she would not respond. There are other forms of catatonia, in which the individual engages in excited, usually repetitive behavior, such as repeated flailing of the arms. Later in this book, you will read about certain disorders that are characterized by various forms of catatonia.

Another disturbance of behavior is a **compulsion**, a repetitive and seemingly purposeful behavior performed in response to uncontrollable urges or according to a ritualistic or stereotyped set of rules. Compulsions, which involve unwanted behaviors, can take over the individual's life, causing considerable distress. A compulsion can be a simple repetitive action, such as a clap of the hand before speaking, or it can be a complex series of ritualized behaviors. For example, before opening any door, a woman feels that she must scratch her forehead and then clean the doorknob with her handkerchief five times prior to turning the knob. There are many types of compulsive behavior, and you will learn more about them in the chapters in which we discuss certain anxiety and personality disorders.

Orientation

People with some kinds of disorders are disoriented and out of touch with basic facts about themselves and their surroundings. **Orientation** is a person's awareness of time, place, and identity. Disturbances in orientation are used in diagnosing disorders associated with some forms of brain damage and disease, such as amnesia and dementia. They may also be signs of psychotic disorders, such as schizophrenia.

Content of Thought

The **content of thought**, or ideas that fill a client's mind, is tremendously significant in the assessment process. The clinician must carefully seek out information about the various types of disturbing thought content that can be associated with many psychological disorders. Some of this inquiry takes place in the flow of clinical conversation with the client, but, in some parts of the mental status examination, the clinician may ask pointed questions, especially when there is some suggestion of serious thought disturbance. The clinician may ask a question, such as "Do you have thoughts that you can't get out of your head?" Or the clinician may follow up on something that seems odd or idiosyncratic about what the client has reported, as when a client reports having had previous occupations that cannot possibly have a basis in reality. A man who has spent his adult life in a state hospital but believes he is a famous movie actor may answer questions about his occupation that are consistent with his belief, and in the process he may reveal his particular disturbance of thought content. Clinicians listen for these kinds of clues to develop a better understanding of the nature of the client's disorder.

Of particular interest to the clinician are disturbances of thought content known as obsessions. An **obsession** is an unwanted thought, word, phrase, or image that persistently and repeatedly comes into a person's mind and causes distress. No amount of effort can erase this obsession from the individual's thinking.

Most people have experienced transient obsessional thinking, such as following a breakup with a lover or even a heated argument in which the dialogue of the argument recurrently intrudes into consciousness. One common form of obsession involves torturous doubt about an act or a decision, usually of a trivial nature, such as whether one paid too much for a 20 dollar item. Unlike these ordinary occurrences, clinically significant obsessions are enduring and can torment a person for years.

Another common obsession is an individual's irrational concern that he or she has done or is about to do something evil or dangerous, such as inadvertently poisoning others. Obsessions and compulsions often go hand in hand, as in the case of a man who was obsessively worried that a car accident might take place outside his apartment. Consequently, he walked to the window every 10 minutes to make sure that the streetlight had not burned out. He was afraid that a burned-out streetlight would increase the likelihood of cars colliding in the darkness.

Obsessions are certainly irrational, but even further removed from reality are **delusions**, which are deeply entrenched false beliefs that are not consistent with the client's intelligence or cultural background (Table 3.3 gives some examples of delusions). Despite the best efforts of others to convince an individual that these beliefs are irrational, people who have delusions are highly resistant to more realistic views. In determining the presence of delusional thinking, the clinician needs to be aware of the person's intelligence and cultural background. For example, a very religious woman may believe in miracles, which people who are not familiar with her religion might regard as delusional.

Sometimes a person has very unusual ideas that are not so extreme as to be regarded as delusional. **Overvalued ideas** are thoughts that have an odd and absurd quality but are not usually bizarre or deeply entrenched. For example, a man believes that a credit card that ends in an odd number will cause him to have bad luck. Each time he submits an application for a new credit card, he explains to the issuer that he will refuse to accept the card unless the last digit is an even number. In **magical thinking**, there is also a peculiar and illogical content to the individual's thought, but in this case there is a connection in the individual's mind between two objects or events that other people would see as unrelated. For example, a woman believes that, every time she takes her clothes to the dry cleaners, a natural disaster occurs somewhere in the world within the following day. Although the presence of overvalued ideas or magical thinking does not provide evidence that a person has a psychotic disorder, clinicians make note of these symptoms, because they can be signals that a client is psychologically deteriorating.

Violent ideation is another important area to assess. Clinicians assess the possibility of violent thoughts, either in the form of suicidal thinking or thoughts about harming, and possibly killing, someone else. As you will see later in this book, when we discuss the assessment of suicide in Chapter 9, clinicians are usually quite direct when inquiring about self-injurious intentions, particularly with depressed clients.

Thinking Style and Language

In addition to listening to what a person thinks, the clinician also listens for evidence of **thinking style and language** to indicate how a person thinks. This includes information on the client's vocabulary use and sentence structure. For example, when conversing with a man who is psychotic, you may have a difficult time grasping his words or meaning. His language may be illogical and unconnected. In listening to him during a mental status examination, a clinician would suspect that he has a thought disorder, a disturbance in thinking or in using language. Examples of thought disorders are shown in Table 3.4 .

Affect and Mood

Affect is an individual's outward expression of emotion. A feeling state becomes an affect when others can observe it. Clinicians attend to several components of affect, including appropriateness, intensity, mobility, and range.

In assessing affect, the clinician takes note of **inappropriate affect**, the extent to which a person's emotional expressiveness fails to correspond to the content of what is being discussed. For example, affect would be considered inappropriate if a woman were to giggle when asked how she feels about a recent death in her family.

The **intensity of affect**, or strength of emotional expression, provides important clinical clues that the clinician uses in forming a diagnosis. To describe abnormally low affective intensity, the clinician uses such terms as *blunted affect* (minimal expressiveness) and *flat affect* (complete lack of reactivity). By contrast, when the individual's affect seems abnormally strong, the clinician uses such terms as *exaggerated*, *heightened*, and *overdramatic affect*.

If you observe the emotional expressiveness of people who are close to you, it will become apparent that people have very different styles of emotional reactivity. **Mobility of affect** is the ease and speed with which people move from one kind of feeling or level of emotional intensity to another. You can probably think of acquaintances who are very slow to show emotional responsiveness, even in compelling situations. Their affect might be described as being decreased or constricted. Alternatively, there are people who are overreactive, with a suddenness or unpredictability that may be jarring; their affect might be characterized as labile.

This woman's affect seems to be an inappropriate response to her friend telling her a humorous story.

Table 3.3

Examples of Delusions

All of these delusions involve a form of *false belief;* that is, they are inconsistent with external reality, and have no validity to anyone except the person who believes in them.

Type of Delusion	Description
Grandeur	A grossly exaggerated conception of the individual's own importance. Such delusions range from beliefs that the person has an important role in society to the belief that the person is actually Christ, Napoleon, or Hitler. Milton Rokeach's 1964 book entitled *The Three Christs of Ypsilanti* describes the interesting situation involving three state hospital patients who each thought he was Jesus Christ; when they met, each one believed that the others were frauds.
Control	The feeling that one is being controlled by others, or even by machines or appliances. For example, a man may believe that his actions are being controlled by the radio, which is "forcing" him to perform certain actions against his will.
Nihilism	The feeling that one's self, others, or the world is nonexistent. Commonly, this delusion is associated with feelings of unreality, and the individual becomes absorbed with the thought that he or she is only "part of a dream."
Reference	The belief that the behavior of others or certain objects or events are personally referring to oneself. For example, a woman believes that a soap opera is really telling the story of her life. Or a man believes that the sale items at a local food market are targeted at his own particular dietary deficiencies.
Persecution	The belief that another person or persons are trying to inflict harm on the individual or on that individual's family or social group. For example, a woman feels that an organized group of politically liberal individuals is attempting to destroy the right-wing, political organization to which she belongs.
Self-blame	Feelings of remorse without justification. A man holds himself responsible for a famine in Africa because of certain unkind or sinful actions that he believes he has committed.
Somatic	Inappropriate concerns about one's own body, typically relating to a disease. For example, without any justification, a woman believes she has brain cancer. Adding an even more bizarre note, she believes that ants have invaded her head and are eating away at her brain.
Poverty	The belief that the individual has no material possessions worth any value. Even when confronted with facts about her sound financial condition, a woman may assert that the possessions or the money do not belong to her.
Infidelity	A false belief usually associated with pathological jealousy involving the notion that one's lover is being unfaithful. A man lashes out in violent rage at his wife, insisting that she is having an affair with the mailman because of her eagerness for the mail to arrive each day.
Thought broadcasting	The idea that one's thoughts are being broadcast to others. A man believes that everyone else in the room can hear what he is thinking, or possibly that his thoughts are actually being carried over the airways on television or radio.
Thought insertion	The belief that thoughts are being inserted into one's mind by outside forces. For example, a woman concludes that her thoughts are not her own but that they are being placed there to control her or upset her.
Thought withdrawal	The belief that thoughts are being removed from one's mind. A man believes that he forgot an appointment because someone intentionally removed the thought from his mind.

Affect is also described in terms of **range of affect**, or the extent and variety of emotional expression. Most people have a broad range of affect and are able to communicate sadness, happiness, anger, agitation, or calmness as the situation or discussion warrants. People with restricted affect show very few variations in their emotional responsiveness. This would be the case of a woman who remains tearful and sad in her emotional expressiveness, regardless of what is taking place or being discussed.

In contrast to affect, which is behavior that is outwardly expressed, **mood** refers to a person's experience of emotion, the way the person feels "inside." Some examples of emotions are

Table 3.4

Examples of Thought Disorder

Types of Thought Disorder	Description
Incoherence	Speech that is incomprehensible. Incoherent speech is impossible for others to understand because of a lack of meaningful connections between words or sentences. For example, a client who is asked how he is feeling responds, "The gutter tree ain't here go far."
Loosening of associations	A flow of thoughts that is vague, unfocused, and illogical. In response to the question about how he is feeling, a man responds, "I'm feeling pretty good today, though I don't think that there is enough good in the world. I think that I should subscribe to *National Geographic*."
Illogical thinking	Thinking characterized by contradictions and erroneous conclusions, which characterizes the individual's entire cognitive system. People who think illogically are typically unable to see how others might perceive them as being illogical. For example, a client who likes milk thinks that she must be part cat, because she knows that cats like milk.
Neologisms	Words invented by a person, or distortions of existing words to which a person has given new personalized meanings. For example, a woman expresses concerns about her homicidal fantasies, saying, "I can't stand these *gunly* thoughts of *murdeviousness*."
Poverty of content of speech	Speech that conveys very little information, because the speaker is vague, overabstract, overconcrete, or repetitive. A client, when asked how he is feeling, responds, "I could say that I'm OK, and I could say that I'm not OK, but I think that it's best to say that I'm like the squirrel on a rusty piece of metal."
Blocking	The experience in which a person seemingly "loses" a thought in the midst of speaking, leading to a period of silence, ranging from seconds to minutes. This differs from the common experience of losing one's train of thought occasionally; by contrast, blocking involves a frequent intrusion into the thought and communication processes of some seriously disturbed people.
Circumstantiality	Speech that is indirect and delayed in reaching the point because of irrelevant and tedious details. In response to a simple question about the kind of work he does, a man responds with a long-winded description of his 20-year work history, with overdetailed comments about the nature of his relationship with each of the seven supervisors he has worked under during that period. Though his talk remains remotely connected to the topic, it is filled with unnecessary and inconsequential details.

depression, elation, anger, and anxiety. A clinician is particularly interested in assessing a client's mood, because the way the client characteristically feels has great diagnostic and treatment significance. A **normal,** or **euthymic, mood** is one that is neither unduly happy nor sad but shows day-to-day variations within a relatively limited and appropriate range. **Dysphoric mood** refers to unpleasant feelings, such as sadness and irritability. **Euphoric mood** is more cheerful and elated than average, possibly even ecstatic. Although your mood might be elevated after succeeding at an important task, euphoric mood is a state in which you feel an exaggerated sense of happiness, elation, and excitement.

In addition to the characterizations of mood as normal, low, or high, there are other clusters of mood, including anger, apprehension, and apathy. As you might infer, angry mood is experienced as feelings of hostility, rage, sullenness, and impatience. Apprehension connotes feeling anxious, fearful, overwhelmed, panicky, and tense. Those who are apathetic have feelings of dullness and blandness and are lacking motivation and concern about anything.

Perceptual Experiences

Individuals with psychological disorders often have disturbances in perception. A clinician would find out whether a client has these disturbances by asking questions such as whether he or she hears voices or sees things of which other people are not aware. **Hallucinations** are false perceptions not corresponding to the objective stimuli present in the environment. Unlike illusions, which involve the misperception of a real object, such as misperceiving a tree at night to be a man, hallucinations involve the perception of an object or a stimulus

Table 3.4 (continued)

Types of Thought Disorder	Description
Tangentiality	Going completely off the track and never returning to the point in a conversation. For example, when asked how long she has been depressed, a woman begins speaking about her unhappy mood and ends up talking about the inadequacy of care in the United States for people who are depressed.
Clanging	Speech in which the sound, rather than the meaning of the words, determines the content of the individual's speech. When asked why he woke up so early, a man responds, "The bell on my clock, the smell from the sock, and the well was out of stock."
Confabulation	Fabricating facts or events to fill in voids in one's memory. These are not conscious lies but are attempts by the individual to respond to questions with answers that seem to approximate the truth. For example, although a client is not fully sure of whether or not he had eaten breakfast that morning, when queried about what he had for breakfast, he replies, "Oatmeal with honey." He gives a description of a typical breakfast in his household rather than a confident reporting of precisely what he had eaten that morning.
Echolalia	Persistent repetition or echoing of words or phrases, as if the person is intending to be mocking or sarcastic. When a woman is asked by her roommate, "What's the time?" she responds, "The time, the time, the time."
Flight of ideas	Fast-paced speech that, while usually intelligible, is marked by acceleration, abrupt changes of topic, and plays on words. A man rapidly speaks: "I have to go to work. I have to get there right away. I have to earn some money. I'll go broke. My kids need food. Food is expensive. The prices are way too high. I need the money. I need it now!"
Pressure of speech	Speech that is so rapid and driven that it seems as though the individual is being inwardly compelled to utter a stream of nonstop monologue. Flight of ideas usually involves pressure of speech.
Perseveration	Repetition of the same idea, word, or sound. A woman says, "I have to get dressed. I have to get dressed. My clothes, my clothes, I have to get dressed." Another example is giving the same response regardless of the question.

that is not there. As you can imagine, the experience of a hallucination can be distressing, even terrifying. Clinicians carefully scrutinize a client's experience of hallucinations, knowing that this symptom may be caused by a range of conditions, including reaction to trauma, the effect of substance intoxication or withdrawal, or a neurological condition, such as Alzheimer's disease or temporal lobe epilepsy.

Hallucinations are defined by the sense with which they are associated. **Auditory hallucinations**, which are the most common, involve hearing sounds, often voices or even entire conversations. With **command hallucinations**, an individual hears an instruction to take an action. For example, one man reported that, while eating at a lunch counter, he heard a voice that directed him to punch the person sitting next to him. Other common auditory hallucinations involve hearing voices making derogatory comments, such as "You're stupid."

Visual hallucinations involve the false visual perception of objects or persons. For some people, the visual hallucination

may be chronic, as is reported in some individuals with Alzheimer's disease. For example, a woman claimed that she saw her deceased husband sitting at the table whenever she entered the kitchen.

Olfactory hallucinations, which are relatively uncommon, pertain to the sense of smell, possibly of an unpleasant odor, such as feces, garbage, or noxious gases. **Somatic hallucinations** involve false perceptions of bodily sensations, the most common of which involve tactile experiences. For example, a man reported the feeling that insects were crawling all over his body. **Gustatory hallucinations** are the least commonly reported and involve the false sensation of taste, usually unpleasant.

It is common for hallucinations to be associated with delusions. For example, a man who had a delusion of persecution also had olfactory hallucinations in which he believed that he constantly smelled toxic fumes that he believed were being piped into his room by his enemies.

Sense of Self

A number of psychological disorders alter the individual's personal identity or sense of "who I am." Clinicians assess this altered sense of self by asking clients to describe any strange bodily sensations or feelings of disconnectedness from their body. **Depersonalization** refers to an altered experience of the self, such as a feeling that one's body is not connected to one's mind. At times, the person may not feel "real." Other disturbances in sense of self become apparent when the clinician discovers that a client is experiencing **identity confusion**, which is a lack of a clear sense of who one is. This experience can range from confusion about one's role in the world to actual delusional thinking in which one believes oneself to be under the control of an external person or force.

Motivation

The clinician assesses motivation across a wide range of areas by asking the client to discuss how strongly he or she desires a lasting personality change or relief of emotional distress. With some psychological disorders, the client's motivation is so severely impaired that even ordinary life tasks seem insurmountable, much less the process of embarking on the time-consuming and effortful course of therapy. As surprising as it may seem, some individuals seem to prefer to remain in their present familiar state of unhappiness, rather than risk the uncertainty of facing a new and unknown set of challenges.

Cognitive Functioning

In a mental status examination, a clinician attempts to gauge a client's general level of intelligence as evidenced by level of general information, attention and concentration, memory, physical coordination, and capacity for abstraction and conceptualization. For example, a woman with an IQ significantly above average might use unusual or abstract words that give the impression that she has a thought disorder. Or a man's memory may be so impaired that the clinician hypothesizes that he is suffering from a neurological condition, such as Alzheimer's disease. In the mental status examination, the clinician's task is not to conduct a formal IQ test but, rather, to develop a general idea about the client's cognitive strengths and deficits.

Insight and Judgment

In a mental status examination, the clinician also attempts to assess a client's ability to understand the nature of his or her disorder. Along these lines, the clinician needs to determine a client's receptivity to treatment. A woman who has no understanding of the debilitating nature of her paranoid delusions is certainly not going to be very receptive to intervention by a mental health professional. She may even resist any such attempts because she regards them as proof that others are trying to control or hurt her.

Insight is a sense of understanding and awareness about oneself and one's world. For example, a college student notices that she becomes depressed on most Friday afternoons as she prepares to return home for weekend visits. On discussing her reaction with her roommate, she develops insight into the fact that she resents her father treating her like a child. In more serious clinical contexts, the client's level of understanding about the nature of problems and symptoms will set the stage for treatment. A man who is paranoid, but unable to see how his defensive style with others creates interpersonal distance, is not likely to be open to changing his behavior in order to become more emotionally accessible to others.

Judgment is the intellectual process in which an individual considers and weighs options in order to make a decision. Every day, each of us makes many judgments, some of which are inconsequential and others of which may have long-lasting effects. You have probably encountered people who have very poor judgment and make choices that are obviously unwise. Perhaps you know someone who repeatedly gets intimately involved with abusive partners and seems to lack the ability to make an objective assessment of these people before becoming involved. Or you may know someone who, when intoxicated, says or does things that are dramatically different from his or her behavior in a sober state. Similarly, people who are seriously disturbed lack the ability to make choices in their lives that are constructive or wise. They may put their physical health and safety at risk, and in some cases it is necessary for others to step in and help them make decisions that are self-protective.

Psychological Testing

Psychological testing covers a broad range of measurement techniques, all of which involve having people provide scorable information about their psychological functioning. The information that test-takers provide may concern their intellectual abilities, personalities, emotional states, attitudes, and behaviors that reflect lifestyle or interests.

It is very likely that you have had some form of psychological testing in your life and that your scores on these tests had a bearing on decisions made by you or about you, since psychological tests have become increasingly important in contemporary society. Because of this importance, psychologists have devoted intensive efforts to developing tests that accurately measure what they are designed to measure.

What Makes a Good Psychological Test?

Many popular magazines and newspapers publish so-called psychological tests. Items on these tests claim to measure such features of your personality as your potential for loving, how lonely you are, how devoted your romantic partner is, whether you have "too much anger," or whether you worry too much. These tests contain a number of scorable items, accompanied by a scale to tell you what your responses indicate about your personality. Although interesting and provocative, most tests published in the popular press fail to meet accepted standards for a good psychological test.

Many magazines contain "personality" tests. This woman is completing a quiz to measure her self-esteem.

To show you the many issues involved in developing a good psychological test, we will take an in-depth look at each criterion that plays a role in the process. These criteria are covered by the general term **psychometrics**, whose literal meaning, "measurement of the mind," reflects the goal of finding the most suitable tests for the psychological variables of interest to the researcher and clinician.

Reliability and validity are generally considered to be the two features most essential to determining a test's psychometric qualities. **Reliability** indicates the consistency of test scores, and **validity** the extent to which a test measures what it is designed to measure. Table 3.5 describes the types of reliability and validity.

A good psychological test is also one that follows **standardized**, or uniform, procedures for both test administration and scoring. For example, a national college entrance examination is supposed to be given under strict standardized conditions. The room should be quiet and well lit, the seats should be comfortable for test-taking, proctors should monitor the students so that no one has any unfair advantages, and the same instructions should be given to everyone. A standardized psychological test is intended to follow the same guidelines. Particularly important is the requirement that each person taking the test receives the same instructions. At times, because people with certain psychological disorders have problems focusing on test items or following instructions, the examiner may need to provide extra assistance or encouragement to complete the test. However, the examiner must not suggest how the test-taker should answer the questions or bias the test-taker's performance in any way. It is also important that the examiner not stretch the time limits beyond those allowed for the test.

Standardization also applies to the way tests are scored. The most straightforward scoring method involves adding up responses on a multiple-choice test or a test with items that are rated on numerical scales. Less straightforward are tests that involve judgments on the part of raters who must decide how to score the test-taker's responses. For the scoring to be standardized, the examiner must follow a prescribed set of rules that equates a given response with a particular score. The examiner must be sure not to let any biases interfere with the

scoring procedure. This is particularly important when only one person does the scoring, as is the case with many established tests whose reliability has already been documented. When scoring an intelligence test, for example, it may be tempting for the examiner to try to give the test-taker the benefit of the doubt if the test-taker is someone who seems to have been trying hard and wants to do well. Conversely, examiners must be sensitive to their negative biases regarding certain types of clients and not inadvertently penalize them by scoring them lower than they deserve. As guarantees against the misuse of tests, people who administer and score standardized psychological tests receive extensive training and supervision in all of these procedures.

The term *standardization* is also used to refer to the basis for evaluating scores on a particular test. The college entrance examination, for example, has been given to vast numbers of high-school seniors over the years, and there is a known distribution of scores on the parts of this test. When evaluating a student's potential for college, the student's scores are compared with the national scores for the student's gender, and a percentile score is given. This **percentile score** indicates what percentage of students scored below a certain number. Such a score is considered to be an objective indication of the student's college potential and is preferable to basing such an evaluation on the personal judgment of one individual. As you will see in our discussion of intelligence tests, however, there are many questions about the appropriateness of percentile scores when the person taking the test differs in important ways from the people on whom the test was standardized.

Once the psychometric qualities of a measurement instrument have been established, the measure becomes one of many types and forms of tests that the clinician can incorporate into an assessment. Psychologists then choose measurement instruments on the basis of the assessment goals and theoretical preferences. We will examine each of the various types of assessment devices from the standpoint of its most appropriate use in assessment, its theoretical assumptions, and its psychometric qualities.

Standardized tests are sometimes administered in group settings for personnel selection. These people have applied for jobs at a large manufacturing company.

Table 3.5

Criteria for a Good Psychological Test

Reliability: the consistency of test scores

Type of Reliability	Definition	Example
Test-retest	The degree to which test scores obtained from people on one day (the "test") agree with the test scores obtained from those people on another day (the "retest")	A test of intelligence should yield similar scores for the same person on Tuesday and on Thursday, because intelligence is a quality that is assumed not to change over short time periods
Interjudge	The extent to which two or more people agree on how to score a particular test response	On a 5-point scale of thought disorder, two raters should give similar scores to a psychiatric patient's response
Internal consistency	How well items on a test correlate with each other	On a test of anxiety, people answer similarly to the items designed to assess how nervous a person feels

Validity: how well the test measures what it is designed to measure

Type of Validity	Definition	Example
Content	How well the test reflects the body of information it is designed to tap	The professor's abnormal psychology exam concerns knowledge of abnormal psychology, rather than familiarity with music from the 1960s.
Criterion	The extent to which the test scores relate in expected ways to another benchmark	(See more specific examples below.)
Concurrent	How well scores on a test relate to other measures taken at the same time	A test of depression should produce high scores in people with known diagnoses of depression.
Predictive	The extent to which test scores relate to future performance	People who receive high scores on college entrance examinations are expected to achieve high grade-point averages in college.
Construct	The extent to which a test measures a theoretically derived psychological quality or attribute	A test of depression should correlate with recognized characteristics of depression, such as low self-esteem, guilt, and feelings of sadness.

Intelligence Testing

Psychologists have long been interested in studying intelligence because of its wide-ranging influence on many aspects of an individual's functioning. Psychologists and others have made many attempts to define the elusive quality of intelligence. Although debate continues, for all practical purposes, current intelligence tests are based on the concept of "g," the proposal by psychologist Charles Spearman (Spearman, 1904) that there is a broad quality ("general" intelligence) that underlies the individual's ability to "see relations." The quality of "g" is theorized to reflect in part the individual's inherited capability and in part the influence of education and other experiences. Tests that assess intelligence reflect, to varying degrees, the individual's level of "g."

Intelligence tests serve various purposes. One important purpose is to help educators determine whether certain students might benefit from remedial or accelerated learning op-

portunities. Intelligence tests can also be useful for employers who wish to know whether a prospective employee has the intellectual capacity to carry out the duties of a given job. For the mental health professional, intelligence tests provide crucial information about a client's cognitive capacities and the relationship between these capacities and the expression of emotional problems. For example, an exceptionally bright young woman might make very esoteric but bizarre associations on a test of personality. Knowing that this young woman's intellect is at a higher level than the norm can provide the clinician with an understanding that such associations are probably not due to a psychological disorder. Alternatively, a man whose intelligence is significantly below average might say or do things that give the appearance of a psychotic disorder.

Intelligence tests can yield fairly specific information about a person's cognitive deficits or strengths, which can be helpful to a therapist working on a treatment plan. Clients who have little capacity for abstract thinking are likely to have difficulty in insight-oriented psychotherapy. Instead, a clinician treating a client with such cognitive deficits would focus on practical, day-to-day problems.

Some intelligence tests are designed to be administered to relatively large groups of people at a time. These tests are more commonly used in nonclinical settings, such as psychological research, schools, personnel screening, and the military. Most of these tests use a multiple-choice question format, and scores are reported in terms of separate subscales assessing different facets of intellectual functioning. Group tests are used, because they allow mass administration and are easily scored, with no special training required of the examiner. However, clinicians fault these tests for their impersonality and their insensitivity to nuances in the test-taker's answers. A test-taker may give a creative but wrong answer to a question that the computer simply scores as incorrect, without taking into account the originality of the response.

Individual testing methods have the advantage of providing rich, qualitative information about the client. Open-ended answers to questions regarding vocabulary, which cannot conveniently be obtained in group testing, may reveal that the client's thoughts follow a rather bizarre chain of associations. This sort of information would be lost in a group intelligence test, which does not provide any opportunities to scrutinize the client's thought processes and judgment.

Stanford-Binet Intelligence Test

The first intelligence test was developed in 1905 by Alfred Binet (1857–1911) and Theophile Simon (1873–1961), whose work for the French government involved screening mentally retarded children and adults. In 1916, Stanford University psychologists Lewis Terman and Maude Merrill revised the original Binet-Simon test, and scales were added in an effort to increase the test's reliability and validity. The version published in 1986 is known as the Stanford-Binet Fourth Edition (Thorndike, Hagen, & Sattler, 1986a, 1986b).

Scores on the Stanford-Binet tests have traditionally been expressed in terms of **intelligence quotient (IQ)**. When Lewis Terman originally proposed this term in 1916, it literally referred to a ratio measure or quotient—namely the individual's "mental age" (calculated on the basis of test performance) compared with the individual's chronological age. An IQ of 80, in this system, meant that a child had a mental age of 8 and a chronological age of 10, or was moderately retarded. An IQ of 100 indicated average intelligence; in other words, a child's mental age was equal to his or her chronological age. This scoring system worked reasonably well for children, but it created problems with adults, because 16 is the highest achievable mental age on the Stanford-Binet.

Wechsler Intelligence Scales

More widely used than the Stanford-Binet test are the three Wechsler scales of intelligence published by Psychological Corporation. In 1939, psychologist David Wechsler developed

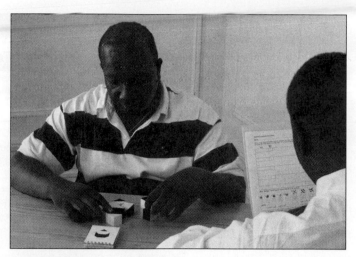

The Block Design is one of the subtests of the Wechsler Adult Intelligence Scale III (WAIS-III).

the Wechsler-Bellevue Intelligence Scale to measure intelligence in adults. The format of the Wechsler-Bellevue has persisted until the present day, serving as the basis for revisions of the original adult test and the addition of tests for younger age groups: the Wechsler Adult Intelligence Scale-Third Edition (WAIS-III) (Wechsler, 1997), the Wechsler Intelligence Scale for Children-Third Edition (WISC-III) (Wechsler, 1991), and the Wechsler Preschool and Primary Scale of Intelligence-Revised (WPPSI-R) (Wechsler, 1989).

Because Wechsler's tests were initially designed for adults, they required a different method of scoring than the traditional IQ formula, which relies on the ratio of mental to chronological age. The concept of mental age is not really appropriate for adults. Wechsler developed a new method of scoring, called the **deviation IQ,** a concept that is completely different from the ratio concept. Eventually, the deviation IQ was adopted on a more widespread basis for children and adults and was incorporated into the 1960 revision of the Stanford-Binet. The deviation IQ score is calculated by converting a person's actual test

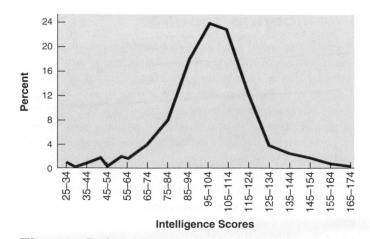

Figure 3.1

An approximate distribution of intelligence scores in the population. The distribution follows a bell-shaped curve, with the highest percentage of people in the "normal" range between 85 and 114.

score to a score that reflects how high or low the score is, compared with the scores of others of similar age and gender. An average IQ, in Wechsler's system, is 100 (see Figure 3.1). An IQ of 80, using this calculation method, reflects the fact that, relative to others in the same age group, the individual's score is significantly below the mean.

All Wechsler tests share a common organization in that they are divided into two scales: Verbal and Performance. The Verbal scale includes measures of vocabulary, factual knowledge, short-term memory, and verbal reasoning. The Performance subtests measure psychomotor abilities, nonverbal reasoning, and the ability to learn new relationships. On the basis of the Verbal IQ and the Performance IQ, a Full Scale IQ is computed as a more comprehensive intelligence quotient. In addition to the three IQ scores, the WAIS-III provides four characterizations of intelligence based on more refined domains of cognitive functioning: Verbal Comprehension, Perceptual Organization, Working Memory, and Processing Speed.

Intelligence tests, such as the Wechsler scales, are used for various purposes, including psychoeducational assessment, the diagnosis of learning disabilities, the determination of giftedness or mental retardation, and the prediction of future academic achievement. IQ tests are also sometimes used in the diagnosis of neurological and psychiatric disorders, in which cases they are a component of a more comprehensive assessment procedure. Finally, IQ tests may be used in personnel selection when certain kinds of cognitive strengths are especially important.

Although IQ numbers provide valuable information, they do not tell the whole story; consequently, clinicians know that they must evaluate many factors that may contribute to a subject's test performance and scores. A low IQ may reflect a low level of intellectual functioning, but it may also be the result of the subject's intense anxiety, debilitating depression, poor motivation, oppositional behavior, sensory impairment, or even poor rapport with the examiner. The case of Ben, whom you read about earlier in this chapter, provides an interesting example of how a clinician would use subtle findings from IQ testing to formulate some hypotheses that go beyond intellectual functioning. Dr. Tobin noted that Ben has average intelligence, with no striking strengths or deficits. She also took note of the fact that, even though Ben was distressed at the time of testing, he was able to function adequately on the various subtests of the WAIS-III. From this, Dr. Tobin concluded that, when tasks are clear and structure is provided, Ben is able to respond appropriately. At the same time, Dr. Tobin wondered why Ben's IQ was not as high as might be expected in an academically successful college junior; perhaps emotional problems, such as anxiety or depression, were interfering with Ben's test performance. She would keep these concerns in mind as she continued to collect assessment data from Ben.

Cultural Considerations in Intelligence Testing

Psychologists know that when they assess intelligence they must take into account the person's cultural, ethnic, and racial background. In recent years, the publishers of psychological tests, especially those measuring intelligence, have worked to remove culture-specific items, such as definitions that would be familiar primarily to middle- or upper-middle-class White Americans. Going a step further, as discussed in the How People Differ box, test publishers have developed specialized tests to provide culture-fair assessments of individuals from diverse backgrounds. The Research Focus box raises other issues relevant to cultural and ethnic biases in standardized intelligence tests. Attempts to disentangle genetic from environmental contributions have stimulated a voluminous amount of discussion about the validity of IQ scores and tests.

Personality and Diagnostic Testing

Personality and diagnostic tests provide additional means of developing an understanding of a person's thoughts, behaviors, and emotions. Sometimes these tests are used independently, and at other times they supplement clinical or research interviews. For example, Dr. Tobin completed an interview with a new client, Vanessa, and hypothesized two possible diagnoses that both seemed plausible. Vanessa explained that she was "penniless and had no hope of ever earning a cent." Dr. Tobin, realizing that Vanessa was delusional, wondered whether this delusion of poverty reflected severe depression or whether it was a symptom of serious personality disorganization. Vanessa's responses on personality tests that Dr. Tobin selected to help make this differential diagnosis led her to conclude that Vanessa was suffering from pervasive personality disorganization.

There are two main forms of personality tests: self-report and projective. These tests differ in the nature of their items and in the way they are scored.

Self-Report Clinical Inventories

A **self-report clinical inventory** contains standardized questions with fixed response categories that the test-taker completes independently, "self"-reporting the extent to which the responses are accurate characterizations. The scores are computed and usually combined into a number of scales, which serve as the basis for constructing a psychological profile of the client. This type of test is considered "objective" in the sense that scoring is standardized and usually does not involve any judgment on the part of the clinician. However, the clinician's judgment is needed to interpret and integrate the test scores with the client's history, interview data, behavioral observations, and other relevant diagnostic information. The clinician's judgment is also required in determining whether the diagnostic conclusions from computer-scored tests are accurate, keeping in mind that computerized tests have both strengths and limitations.

A major advantage of self-report inventories is that they are easy to administer and score. Consequently, they can be given to large numbers of people in an efficient manner. Extensive data are available on the validity and reliability of the more well-known self-report inventories because of their widespread use in a variety of settings.

Psychological Testing of Minorities

A psychologist has been asked to respond to two referrals for psychological testing. The first involves an 8-year-old Hispanic girl, with only limited fluency in English, who has been doing poorly in school; the second is an African American teenager who has been hospitalized for the first time on a psychiatric unit. In the first instance, school officials want to know if special education services are needed. In the second, the adolescent's therapist wants more information about the client's personality functioning and psychological problems. How should the psychologist go about testing these individuals?

Researchers and clinicians have debated for years about using common psychological tests for assessing individuals from diverse cultural and ethnic backgrounds. Questions have been raised about how valid such tests are with people other than middle-class White Americans. Some experts contend that many personality and cognitive tests are biased against minorities, who are more likely to receive lower IQ scores and higher psychological disturbance scores than Whites. Is the issue one of intelligence, or is the issue one of flawed assessment? Are members of minority groups more psychologically disturbed, or is the measurement of such variables problematic?

Consider the challenge of evaluating children in need of special education interventions. An IQ test, such as the WISC-III, is typically a component of a special education evaluation. Some have pointed out that the use of this instrument results in an overrepresentation of minority children in special education programs (Cronbach, 1990). In response to concerns about the validity of this test with minority children, alternative tests have been developed.

The SOMPA, or System of Multicultural Pluralistic Assessment (Mercer, 1979), provides a method for the cognitive assessment of children that takes cultural and linguistic differences into account. The SOMPA includes three categories of assessment: medical, social, and pluralistic. For the medical section, the examiner assesses the child's physical dexterity, perceptual ability, physical maturity, vision, hearing, and health history. The social section includes measures of general knowledge and an assessment of the ways in which the child conforms to or deviates from the norms of his or her culture. The pluralistic section is still more specific to ethnic and cultural background. Children complete "sociocultural scales" to determine the extent to which their culture differs from the dominant, Anglo-American culture. Scores on the sociocultural scales are translated into "estimated learning potential" scores, predictions of IQ relative to a child's cultural and ethnic background. Researchers have reported modest success in using the SOMPA to predict academic placement and achievement (Figueroa & Sassenrath, 1989), but controversy also exists about the validity of this test for assessing cognitive abilities.

Another commonly used test is the Test of Nonverbal Intelligence-3 (TONI-3) (Brown, Sherbenou, & Johnsen, 1997), a language-free measure of intelligence, aptitude, abstract reasoning, and problem solving. The respondent is required to provide only a gesture, such as a point or nod to indicate response choices. The instructions are also presented nonverbally. There are no words, numbers, pictures, or symbols, so that the test can be given to anyone regardless of cultural background or reading ability.

Although personality tests for the assessment of ethnic minorities are somewhat less controversial than IQ testing, researchers have also disagreed about their validity. Some investigators have translated objective personality measures, such as the MMPI, into other languages, but their efforts have not resolved basic concerns about the items' applicability to different ethnic groups. Similar criticisms have been leveled at projective tests, such as the TAT, which contain no depictions of minority members.

One alternative to traditional personality instruments is the Tell-Me-A-Story (TEMAS) test, a projective test designed specifically for Hispanic and African American children and adolescents (Constantino, Malgady, & Rogler, 1988; Malgady, Constantino, & Rogler, 1984). The TEMAS consists of 23 chromatic pictures depicting African American and Hispanic characters engaged in interpersonal situations in an urban setting. Children tell stories in response to each portrayal of an ambiguous interpersonal conflict. For example, one picture could be interpreted as an episode either of stealing or of helpful interpersonal behavior. How the subject thinks about these situations and the resolution of conflicts provides data about adaptive and maladaptive aspects of personality.

The TEMAS pictures are designed to evoke nine aspects of personality: interpersonal relations, aggression, anxiety/depression, achievement motivation, delay of gratification, self-concept, sexual identity, moral judgment, and reality testing. Researchers have successfully used the TEMAS to differentiate disturbed from nondisturbed urban children in clinical and school samples (Constantino et al., 1988), and the test appears particularly useful with bilingual and inner-city minority children.

Tests such as the SOMPA and TEMAS can provide valuable information about the intelligence and personality of people outside of mainstream American society. Clinicians and educators know that such tests have their limitations and must be used with caution. These tests can be particularly useful in combination with traditional instruments in developing a comprehensive understanding of the client that is especially sensitive to different backgrounds and experiences.

RESEARCH FOCUS

Is Intelligence Destiny?

You take it for granted that the color of your eyes, hair, and skin is determined by genetics. But what about your intelligence? Is your IQ the result of your experiences, your genetic makeup, or a combination of nurture and nature? Taking the questions a step further, to what extent are your successes and failures in life due to the cognitive structure you have inherited? These questions are among the most controversial in psychology, as scientists labor to understand the relative contributions of genetics and environment in determining a person's intelligence and innate predisposition to succeed in life's endeavors. These questions are so important, because many life opportunities and decisions are made on the basis of how "smart" people are, such as the schools they attend, the occupations they choose, and how they are perceived by teachers, bosses, and even their own family members.

The nature/nurture debate has a significant general bearing on social policy. If political leaders believe that IQ can be affected by environmental stimulation, they are more likely to support programs that enhance environments for lower socioeconomic groups. On the other hand, if IQ is believed to be determined exclusively by genetics, they might question why millions of tax dollars should be spent on environmental enhancement.

The debate about the heritability of intelligence leaped from academia to the public forum with the publication of *The Bell Curve* (Herrnstein & Murray, 1994). In essence, Herrnstein and Murray conclude that intelligence is largely, although not completely, a heritable trait that predicts and possibly causes a variety of beneficial and problematic social outcomes. They believe that the capacity for social attainment or failure is attributable to the intelligence that people inherit.

Taking their argument to the next level, Herrnstein and Murray suggest that the genetic endowment of intelligence may be the root cause of many societal problems. Individuals fortunate enough to possess considerable intelligence are channeled upward into a "cognitive elite," distinguished by educational, occupational, and personal success. Individuals with limited intelligence do not fare as well and experience a social decline, marked by poverty, educational failure, unemployment, family breakdown, and crime. Herrnstein and Murray apply their assertions to Whites and nonwhites alike, but their most controversial claim is for the existence of an innate difference in intelligence between people of different races.

Other writers (Jensen, 1987; Rushton, 1995; Rushton, 1997) have claimed that there are consistent differences in IQ among three races of people: the Mongoloid (or Asian), the Caucasoid (or White), and the Negroid (or Black). They have cited differences in head size, brain mass, and IQ scores as evidence for cognitive disparity in intelligence, with the IQs of Asians exceeding those of Whites and Blacks, and the IQs of Whites exceeding those of Blacks. In their book, Herrnstein and Murray report small differences of several points in IQ score, favoring Asians over Whites. In discussing the IQ of Whites and Blacks, they report an average difference of approximately one standard deviation, or 15 points on the Wechsler scales. They acknowledge that other factors, such as socioeconomic status and learning opportunities, contribute to differences in IQ. At the same time, they maintain that such factors cannot erase the basic difference in genetically endowed intellectual heritage and subsequent social maladjustment.

To the casual reader, Herrnstein and Murray's arguments may seem convincing and reasoned, as they attempt to explain the ways in which environmental factors interact within the genetic parameters of intelligence, yet a flurry of controversy followed the publication of this book as their assertions led to an outcry from the public and scientists alike. Indeed, intelligence may be largely inherited, but the picture is more complicated. Intellectual abilities can be enhanced by nurturance or inhibited by a deficient environment. It is understandable that the intelligence of people from low socioeconomic groups can be affected by poverty, diminished educational and social opportunities, and greater exposure to psychological disturbance (Gould, 1981). Researchers point to a long history of support for the idea that intellectually and economically rich environments can increase intelligence (Frumkin, 1997; Neisser, 1997). However, some researchers looking at the same data have drawn a different conclusion—that enriching the environments of low-income children does not significantly affect IQ (Spitz, 1997). At this point in time, it seems that environment is only one piece of the puzzle.

Similar confusion exists in the effort to assess the role of genetics (Melnick, 1997; Neisser, 1997; Reed, 1997). Some investigators believe that it is useless to try to measure the heritability of intelligence due to the range and diversity of environments of different groups of people (Velden, 1997). There is disagreement about which aspects of human thinking should be assessed, about the meaning of intelligence, and about which tests are best for measuring intelligence (Naglieri, 1997).

Adding racial questions to the debate about intelligence complicates an already confusing picture. Some theorists attack the ideas of Herrnstein and Murray, contending that there is no agreement about what "race" actually is (Neisser, 1997; Yee, 1997) and that this concept is commonly defined in arbitrary and superficial terms. Consider the complexity of the case of a young man born of one White parent and one Black parent who chooses to define himself as White. Herrnstein and Murray (1994) have for the most part defined *race* through physiological differences stemming from different biological and

(continued)

gies and biased views of investigators. He suggests that apparent racial differences are of relatively recent evolutionary origin, too recent in the evolution of the human species for there to be different developmental pathways of psychological abilities. Gould asserts that the notion that there are distinct races is contradicted by generations of interbreeding among people from varying ancestries.

Clearly, current questions about what determines intelligence are far from answered. Arbitrary definitions, contradictory research findings and interpretations, and other methodological problems make it impossible to draw firm conclusions. The relationship be-

tween IQ and race will become a fuzzier and less important focus of attention, as racial distinctions become less relevant in a society comprised of people from a spectrum of ethnic ancestries. As the race issue diminishes in importance, concerns will grow about the relative contributions of genetics and environment. These concerns will intensify as genetic scientists develop more refined techniques of predetermining various human characteristics, ranging from eye color to musical ability, and social scientists clarify the aspects of environment that most powerfully affect the unfolding of cognitive ability.

evolutionary bases. Other researchers have attempted to debunk the notion of distinct races of people. In his book *The Mismeasure of Man* (Gould, 1981), paleobiologist Stephen Gould describes the ways in which racial differences in intelligence have been misrepresented as a result of studies with weak methodolo-

MMPI and MMPI-2 The most popular self-report inventory for clinical use is the Minnesota Multiphasic Personality Inventory (MMPI), published in 1943, and a revised form, the MMPI-2, published in 1989. The original MMPI, which was cited in thousands of research studies, had flaws, such as psychometric limitations and a narrow standardization sample that did not reflect the contemporary population diversity of the United States. In response to these criticisms, in 1982 the University of Minnesota Press embarked on a restandardization project and commissioned a team of researchers to develop the MMPI-2 (Hathaway & McKinley, 1989). Data were collected from a sample of 2,600 persons all across the United States who were chosen to be representative of the general population in terms of regional, racial, occupational, and educational dimensions. Additional data from various clinical groups were also obtained, including people in psychiatric hospitals and other treatment settings.

The MMPI-2 consists of 567 items containing self-descriptions to which the test-taker responds "true" or "false." These self-descriptions refer to particular behaviors (for example, alcohol use), as well as thoughts and feelings (such as feelings of sadness or self-doubt). The MMPI-2 yields a profile of the test-taker's personality and psychological difficulties, as well as three scales that provide the clinician with information about the validity of each individual's profile.

The MMPI and MMPI-2 provide scores on 10 "clinical" scales and 3 "validity" scales. The clinical scales provide the clinician with a profile of an individual's personality and possible psychological disorder. The validity scales provide the clinician with important information about how defensive the test-taker was and whether the individual might have been careless, confused, or intentionally lying during the test. Scales 1–10 (or 1–0) are the clinical scales, and the remaining 3 are the validity

scales (see Table 3.6). An additional scale—the "?," or "Can't say," scale—is the number of unanswered questions, with a high score indicating carelessness, confusion, or unwillingness to self-disclose.

Although the authors of the MMPI had initially hoped that scores on specific MMPI scales could be used for diagnosis, over time it became apparent that this hope was unrealistic. Elevated scores on individual scales can form the basis for only limited clinical interpretations, leading most clinicians to look at patterns of high scale scores, such as elevated scores on 2 or 3 of the 10 scales. Current interpretive guides to the MMPI-2 provide detailed psychological descriptions that correspond to these two-point or three-point codes, as they are called. The validity scales supplement these descriptions and, in some cases, can provide information about the individual's test-taking attitude.

The development of a variety of scales based on item content, including anxiety, alcoholism, and college maladjustment, has also enhanced the original interpretive procedure. "Critical items" are responses of the test-taker that are regarded as particularly indicative of psychological problems, such as depression and worry, deviant thinking and experiences, problematic anger, and family conflict. The vast amount of research on the MMPI and MMPI-2 has led, then, to a rich store of descriptive information to be used for clinical interpretation, going well beyond the original aim of providing a simple and straightforward psychiatric diagnosis.

Let's return once again to the case of Ben. As you study his MMPI-2 profile (see Figure 3.2), you will notice that there are several extremely high scores. First, look at the validity scale scores, which give some important clues to understanding the clinical scales. Ben's high F tells us that he reports having many unusual experiences, thoughts, and feelings. This could be due

Table 3.6

Clinical and Validity Scales of the MMPI-2, with Adapted Items

Scale	Scale Name	Content	Adapted Item
1	Hypochondriasis	Bodily preoccupations, fear of illness and disease, and concerns.	I have a hard time with nausea and vomiting.
2	Depression	Denial of happiness and personal worth, psychomotor retardation and withdrawal, lack of interest in surroundings, somatic complaints, worry or tension, denial of hostility, difficulty controlling thought processes.	I wish I were as happy as others appear to be.
3	Hysteria	Hysterical reactions to stress situations. Various somatic complaints and denial of psychological problems, as well as discomfort in social situations.	Frequently my head seems to hurt everywhere.
4	Psychopathic deviate	Asocial or amoral tendencies, lack of life satisfaction, family problems, delinquency, sexual problems, difficulties with authorities.	I was occasionally sent to the principal's office for bad behavior.
5	Masculinity-femininity	Extent to which individual ascribes to stereotypic sex-role behaviors and attitudes.	I like reading romantic tales (male item).
6	Paranoia	Paranoid symptoms, such as ideas of reference, feelings of persecution, grandiosity, suspiciousness, excessive sensitivity, rigid opinions and attitudes.	I would have been a lot more successful had others not been vindictive toward me.
7	Psychasthenia	Excessive doubts, compulsions, obsessions, and unreasonable fears.	Sometimes I think thoughts too awful to discuss.
8	Schizophrenia	Disturbances of thinking, mood, and behavior.	I have had some rather bizarre experiences.
9	Hypomania	Elevated mood, accelerated speech and motor activity, irritability, flight of ideas, brief periods of depression.	I become excited at least once a week.
O	Social introversion	Tendency to withdraw from social contacts and responsibilities.	I usually do not speak first. I wait for others to speak to me.
L	"Lie" scale	Unrealistically positive self-presentation.	
K	"Faking good"	Compared with the L scale, a more sophisticated indication of a person's tendency to deny psychological problems and present oneself positively.	
F	"Faking bad"	Presenting oneself in an unrealistically negative light by responding to a variety of deviant or atypical items.	

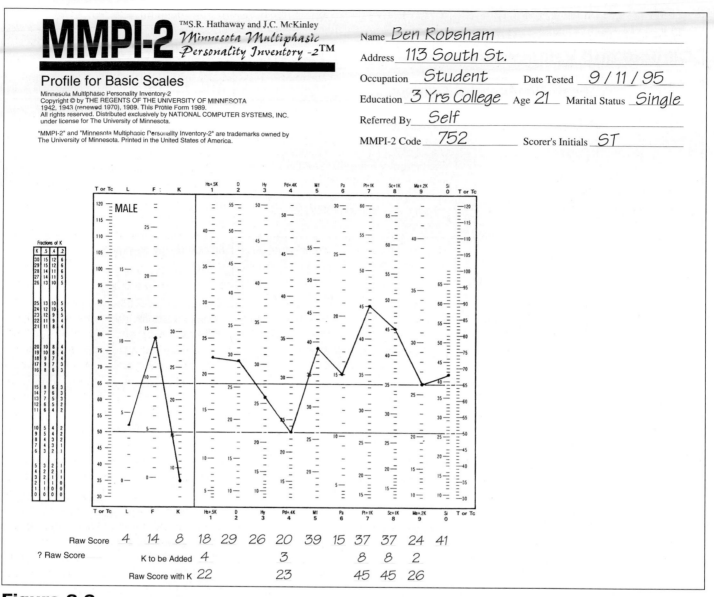

Figure 3.2
Ben Robsham's MMPI-2 profile

Source: Minnesota Multiphasic Personality Inventory-2. Copyright © by the Regents of the University of Minnesota 1942, 1943 (renewed 1970), 1989. This profile form 1989.
All rights reserved. "MMPI-2" and "Minnesota Multiphasic Personality Inventory-2" are trademarks owned by the University of Minnesota.

to a deliberate attempt on Ben's part to make himself appear "sick" for some ulterior motive. On the other hand, an exaggeration of symptoms sometimes reflects a person's desperation, a "call for help." Looking next at Ben's K scale, you can see that he is not particularly defensive; however, recall that Ben appeared to be quite guarded in the opening phase of his interview with Dr. Tobin. How would you reconcile these seemingly conflicting impressions? Perhaps the more anonymous nature of the MMPI-2 allowed Ben to be self-disclosing. The validity scales yield important information, then, about Ben's personality, as well as the fact that Ben's clinical profile is a valid one. The clinical scales show a picture of severe disturbance. The highest elevations are on scales 7 and 8, which measure obsessional anxiety, social withdrawal, and delusional thinking. He also has physical concerns and depression, and very possibly sexual conflicts.

In summary, Ben's MMPI-2 profile is that of a young man on the verge of panic. He is extremely alarmed by very unusual thoughts, feelings, and conflicts. He is calling out for help, while at the same time he feels conflicted about asking for it. Keep these observations about Ben in mind when you read about his responses on the other tests.

Other Self-Report Inventories   There are literally hundreds of self-report clinical inventories, many of which have been developed for specific research or clinical purposes. Several are used as adjuncts to the MMPI-2, providing information on personality functioning apart from or in addition to data that might be diagnostically useful. The NEO Personality Inventory (Revised), known as the NEO-PI-R (Costa & McCrae, 1992), is a 240-item questionnaire that measures personality along five personality dimensions, or sets of traits. These traits, the authors theorize, can be seen as underlying all individual differences in personality. Some authors have proposed that the traits measured by the NEO-PI-R provide a better way to classify personality disorders than the current system. Measures such as the NEO-PI-R would be instrumental in providing such a classification. Whether or not such changes in classification come to pass, the NEO-PI-R provides useful data on personality functioning. The five dimensions include three labeled N, E, and O (hence the title of the measure), plus two additional scales added as the result of empirical testing of the original measure. These scales, then, consist of Neuroticism (N), Extraversion (E), Openness to Experience (O), Agreeableness (A), and Conscientiousness (C). The scales can be completed by individuals rating themselves (Form S) as well as by others who know the individual, such as spouses, partners, or relatives (Form R). Within each of the five dimensions or trait domains, six underlying facets are also rated. For example, the O scale includes the six facets of openness to fantasy, aesthetics, feelings, actions, ideas, and values. Profiles based on the NEO-PI-R allow the clinician to evaluate relative scores on the five domains of personality, as well as the six facets within each domain.

Another instrument focusing on personality is the Millon Clinical Multiaxial Inventory, which is now referred to as the MCMI-III (Millon, 1994). In contrast to the NEO-PI-R, which is specifically intended to assess personality dimensions rather than specific disorders, the MCMI-III is primarily designed to assist clinicians in the diagnosis of *DSM-IV* personality disorders (Millon & Davis, 1997). The theoretical base of the MCMI-III is a theory of personality and psychopathology developed by Millon (Millon & Davis, 1996), which we will describe in more detail in Chapter 5. Briefly, the classification system is based on two dimensions considered fundamental to personality. The first dimension focuses on whether individuals tend to seek positive reinforcement or whether they are more likely to avoid emotional pain (negative reinforcement). There are five types, or points, along this dimension: detached (receives few rewards in life), discordant (those who substitute pain for pleasure), dependent (needs others to provide pleasure), independent (relies on the self for pleasure), and ambivalent (experiences conflict over dependence on others). The second theoretical dimension refers to the individual's characteristic pattern of seeking rewards (positive reinforcement) and minimizing pain (negative reinforcement). The two points along this dimension are active (seeking gratification through personal efforts) and passive (taking an apathetic, fatalistic, or resigned approach to life).

The two dimensions provide the basis for the 175 true/false items composing the MCMI-III. Scale scores derived from these items provide a profile along 11 personality disorders, 3 "severe" personality disorder scales, 7 Axis I clinical syndromes, and 3 Axis I "severe" syndromes. A version of the MCMI-III for adolescents, called the Millon Adolescent Clinical Inventory (MACI), has also been developed (Millon, 1993). This 160-item scale provides a profile with scores on 12 personality "patterns," such as introversive, dramatizing, and egotistic; 8 content areas of "expressed concerns," including identity diffusion, body disapproval, and family discord;

and 7 clinical syndromes, including substance abuse proneness, anxious feelings, and suicidal tendency. Both the MCMI-III and the MACI include scales that assess social desirability, willingness to disclose, and the tendency to complain or be self-pitying. These instruments were developed on a sample of psychotherapy clients (with corroborating evidence from their clinicians), rather than a representative sample of adults in the general population, on the assumption that the Millon scales would be used for clinical purposes rather than general personality testing. This is another important difference between the Millon and the NEO-PI-R scales. The Millon scales are intended to identify clinical "prototypes," or factors that capture the core distinguishing features of the individual's personality.

Researchers and clinicians interested in a quantitative measure of an individual's symptoms might use the SCL-90-R (Derogatis, 1994), a self-report measure in which the respondent indicates the extent to which he or she experiences 90 physical and psychological symptoms. The scales derived from these symptoms include somatization, obsessive-compulsiveness, interpersonal sensitivity, depression, anxiety, hostility, phobic anxiety, paranoid thinking, and psychoticism. There are also general symptom index scales that can be used to assess overall functioning. The SCL-90-R is used to measure current symptoms and can therefore be given on multiple occasions. For example, the SCL-90-R might be used to evaluate whether a certain kind of therapy is effective in reducing symptoms by administering it before and after therapy.

For every clinical issue and syndrome, there are inventories that can be used for the purposes of assessment. Sometimes researchers and clinicians want to assess a clinical phenomenon or theory for which there is no published scale, and they may be faced with the challenge of developing one that fits their needs. Examples of scales developed in this way measure such varied phenomena as eating disorders, fears, impulsivity, attitudes about sexuality, hypochondriasis, homophobia, assertiveness, depressive thinking, personality style, and loneliness.

Projective Testing

We have discussed several tests that are based on the premise that an effective method of understanding psychological functioning involves a highly structured task in which the test-taker provides self-report information. In many instances, such information is sufficient to understand the individual. However, many clinicians take the theoretical position that unconscious issues exist below the surface of conscious awareness. Projective tests were developed with the intention of gaining access to these unconscious issues. A **projective test** is a technique in which the test-taker is presented with an ambiguous item or task and is asked to respond by providing his or her own meaning. Presumably, the test-taker bases this meaning on unconscious issues or conflicts; in other words, he or she "projects" unconscious meanings onto the item. It is assumed that the respondent will disclose features of his or her personality or concerns that could not easily be reported accurately through more overt or obvious techniques. For example, take the case of a client named Barry, who, in response to items on a self-report inventory about interpersonal relationships, says that he gets along very well with other people. In contrast, his responses on a projective technique reveal hidden hostility and resentment toward others.

The most famous of the projective techniques is the Rorschach Inkblot Test. This technique is named after Swiss psychiatrist Hermann Rorschach, who created the test in 1911 and in 1921 published his results of 10 years of using this technique in the book *Psychodiagnostik*. Rorschach constructed the inkblots by dropping ink on paper and folding the paper, resulting in a symmetrical design. Before arriving at the final set of 10 inkblots, Rorschach experimented with many hundreds, presumably until he found ones that produced the most useful responses. Although Rorschach did not invent the inkblot technique (it had been proposed by Binet in 1896), he was the first to use standardized inkblots as the basis for assessing psychological disorder. Unfortunately, Rorschach did not live long after the publication of his book; he died a year later, in his late thirties.

The initial response to the idea of the Rorschach test was unenthusiastic, and Rorschach's book was not even reviewed by the psychiatric journals in his own country. When the test made its way to the United States, it created little interest, but eventually its use caught on in the mental health community, and it continues to be a widely used and researched technique (Watkins, Campbell, Nieberding, & Hallmark, 1995).

The Rorschach test consists of a series of 10 cards showing inkblots. Half of these inkblots are colored, and half are black-and-white. The test-taker is instructed to look at each inkblot and respond by saying what the inkblot looks like. After explaining the procedure, the examiner shows the inkblots one at a time, without giving any guidance as to what is expected, except that the test-taker should indicate what each inkblot looks like. The examiner is trained to provide no clues as to how the inkblot will be scored. The test-taker is then asked to describe what about the inkblot makes it look that way. While the test-taker is talking, the examiner makes a verbatim record of his or her response and how long it takes to respond.

Throughout the history of the Rorschach, clinicians and researchers have debated the best way to evaluate Rorschach responses. Soon after the test was introduced in the United States, clinicians and researchers began to explore ways of scoring it, developing a number of different systems until, by the 1950s, there were five approaches for administering, scoring, and interpreting the Rorschach. Some of these methods were based on the subjective judgment of the clinician, and others attempted to rely more on empirical methods (Groth-Marnat, 1997), which understandably led to questions and concerns about this instrument.

In response to criticisms, the Rorschach Foundation began a concerted effort in the late 1960s to improve the psychometric qualities of the Rorschach. This effort was organized and led by psychologist John Exner, who undertook the massive job of bringing together the best features of all the available scoring systems. Exner's efforts resulted in a method that is becoming the standard in the field, and as data based on this system accumulate, the value of the Rorschach as a diagnostic tool should become clearer. An objective evaluation of the Rorschach leads

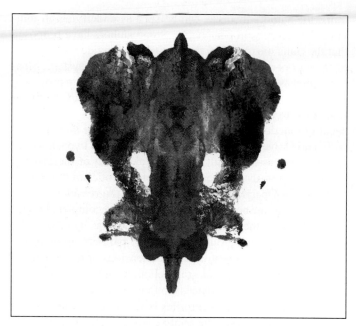

Ben's perception of this Rorschach-like inkblot was "An evil mask that's jumping out to get you. Also a seed, some kind of seed which is dividing itself into two equal halves. It could be a sign of conception and yet it's dying. It's losing part of itself, falling apart, raging."

©Rorschach: Psychodiagnostic

to the conclusion that this instrument has both limitations and assets. As Groth-Marnat (1997) points out, there are concerns about the Rorschach, because its reliability and validity have been shown to be variable, scoring and interpretation are complicated, and the potential for error is considerable. On the other hand, the Rorschach provides a wealth of information that can be acquired through simple test administration; furthermore, the instrument can bypass faking and conscious resistance.

You may be wondering how responses to a set of inkblots can be used to help understand an individual's personality. The Rorschach test is one of several types of projective techniques that can be integrated with the more objective information gained from a self-report clinical inventory. Let's return to the case of Barry mentioned earlier, who responded in different ways on self-report and projective techniques regarding his attitudes toward other people. The clinician working with his test data would look for ways to integrate these divergent views and might conclude that Barry deludes himself into believing that he feels more positively about other people than might be the case. This hypothesis about Barry's personality could be tested with other projective methods, a clinical interview, or more specific self-report inventories focusing on interpersonal styles.

It is important to remember that the theoretical stand of the clinician usually influences the choice of what test to incorporate in a battery. Projective techniques are most commonly associated with approaches that focus on unconscious determinants of behavior. In contrast, a clinician who is more interested in conscious and overt behaviors might select a very different battery of tests to assess a client with serious disturbance. We have chosen to emphasize projective tests in describing Ben's case to show the richness of the information that can be derived from these techniques.

Ben's response to Rorschach Card I shows that the ambiguity of the projective test stimulated a variety of unusual and idiosyncratic perceptions. He sees in this card an "evil mask." Many people look at this card and see a mask; however, Ben sees this mask as "evil," a more ominous image than simply a mask. Furthermore, Ben sees the mask as "jumping out to get you." Not only does the mask have ominous elements, but it is seen as an attacker. In his next response to the same card, Ben sees the inkblot as "a seed . . . which is . . . losing part of itself, falling apart, raging." Is Ben talking about himself in this description?

Ben's response to another card, which contains color, reflects an even more extreme trip into fantasy. By the time Ben saw this card, which came near the end of the test, he had become preoccupied with fantasies of people and objects coming together and splitting apart. His responses had become increasingly bizarre and unconnected with the stimuli. When unusual responses such as these are paired with Ben's MMPI-2 profile, the clinician would hypothesize that Ben is losing control and feels panicked by the experience of losing control.

The Thematic Apperception Test (TAT), another widely used projective test, works on the same premise as the Rorschach; when presented with ambiguous stimuli, test-takers reveal hidden aspects of their personalities. Instead of inkblots, the stimuli are black-and-white ink drawings and photographs that portray people in a variety of ambiguous contexts. Parts of these pictures are vague and sketchy. The TAT is far more structured than the Rorschach in that it presents the test-taker with more clearly defined pictures, many of which contain people. These pictures are ambiguous in that their meaning is not totally obvious, but they nevertheless provide the test-taker with a context within which to respond. The instructions for the TAT request the respondent to tell a story about what is happening in each picture, including what the main characters are thinking and feeling, what events preceded the depicted situation, and what will happen to the people in the picture. Some test-takers become very involved in telling these stories, as the pictures lend themselves to some fascinating interpersonal dramas.

TAT stories are interpreted either on the basis of such quantitative ratings as the number and type of different words or ideas or on the basis of qualitative interpretations based on the themes and issues present in the characters and stories. The premise of the TAT is that themes or issues can be accessed that are not conscious or that are too painful to discuss. For example, one man's stories were filled with caricatures of people acting in harsh and abusive ways, which led the clinician to hypothesize that he might have been the victim of abuse at some point in his life or, alternatively, might be fearful of being exploited in the future.

The TAT was originally conceived by Christina Morgan and Henry Murray (Morgan & Murray, 1935), working at the Harvard Psychological Clinic, and was published as a method of assessing personality several years later (Murray, 1938; Murray, 1943). The test was intended to uncover personality "needs"—forms of motivation proposed by Murray's theory of personality—in ways that could not be assessed through self-report methods. Examples of some of these needs include the needs for achievement, power, and nurturance. However,

within 10 years the test became used more as a general projective assessment device, both in clinical work and research, to assess a wide variety of motivation and personality themes assumed to operate below the level of conscious awareness. In the process of changing the focus of the TAT from Murray's theory to a wider range of issues, researchers and clinicians began to experiment with different ways of administering the TAT and different ways of interpreting the responses. Over subsequent decades, variations on the TAT were developed for use with populations other than the White, college age individuals for whom it was designed, including children, adolescents, older adults, and minority groups. In recent decades, the TAT has become a widely used research instrument for measuring forms of motivation, such as achievement, power, and affiliation.

As much as the TAT has become a fixture among psychological assessment devices, there is still considerable debate over its psychometric qualities. In large part, this debate is a function of the way the TAT has evolved over the years, in that there is no standard way of administering or scoring it. Many who use the TAT adapt it to their own theoretical interests, and their interpretations are often based on subjective impressions and familiarity gained through experience in deriving possible meaning from test-takers' responses. As with other projective techniques, though, the TAT is best used as part of a set of assessment measures, rather than as a single index of personality functioning (Anastasi & Urbina, 1996).

One of the advantages of the TAT is its flexibility. The pictures lend themselves to a variety of interpretations that can be used for both research and clinical purposes. In one clever adaptation of the TAT, Harvard Medical School psychologist Drew Westen has developed a comprehensive theoretical framework for understanding TAT responses. This framework is based on object relations theory, a perspective you will read about in Chapter 4, which is based on contemporary psychodynamic theory. Westen's system, called the Social Cognition and Object Relations Scale (SCORS) (Westen, 1991a, 1991b), involves scoring the TAT along dimensions that incorporate the quality of descriptions of people and their relationships. For example, affect-tone is assessed by analyzing how people in the TAT stories are portrayed; at one extreme people may be described as malevolent or violent, and at the opposite extreme they may be portrayed as positive and enriching. The scoring manual for this system involves specific procedures for assigning scores along these dimensions, ensuring that the measure has high reliability (Westen, Lohr, Silk, & Kerber, 1994).

The themes that emerge from Ben's TAT responses are consistent with the issues identified in the other personality tests, in that they reflect such concerns as family problems, depression, and fears about what is going on around him. Ben describes a character who is frightened by the chaos in her environment. In Ben's story, the character observes someone being rescued from a suicide attempt. One might wonder whether Ben's description of the relationship between the character and her mother is a parallel of his own relationship with his mother. Interestingly, the character describes leaving home as "breaking out," as if home were a prison from which to escape. He pessimistically concludes that the character will not be able to

Ben told the following story about this TAT card: "This is a story of a woman who has lived too long with her mother. She wants to break away but knows she can't. Her whole life is wrapped up in her mother and the house. She's a successful businesswoman and yet she feel like a failure because she can't break out because of what she sees going on outside the house. She is looking out at the sky and sees a plane about to make a crash landing on the street. Across the street she sees a man about to jump off the top of a six-story building, but he stops when someone comes to rescue him. Because of all the crazy things going on outside, the woman thinks that maybe it is better to stay with her mother."

fulfill the wish to separate. In the report at the end of this chapter, Dr. Tobin will integrate the data from this test with the other test results, as she puts together the pieces of Ben's puzzle.

Behavioral Assessment

So far, we have discussed forms of assessment that involve psychological testing. These forms of assessment are the ones that most people think about when they imagine how a psychologist approaches the task of diagnosing psychological disorder. Another form of psychological assessment has emerged since the late 1960s, and it relies on a very different set of assumptions than those of projective testing. **Behavioral assessment** includes a number of measurement techniques based on a recording of the individual's behavior. Clinicians use these techniques to identify problem behaviors, to understand what maintains

these behaviors, and to develop and refine appropriate interventions to change these behaviors.

As originally conceived, behavioral assessment relied almost exclusively on recording observable behaviors—namely, actions carried out by the individual that other people could watch. This was in large part a reaction against traditional models that rely on inferences about hidden causes, such as unconscious determinants or unobservable personality traits. Since the late 1970s, though, behavioral assessments have increasingly come to include the recording of thoughts and feelings as reported by the individual, in addition to outward actions. Commonly used approaches include the behavioral self-report of the client and the clinician's observation of the client.

Behavioral Self-Report

Behavioral self-report is an assessment method in which the client provides information about the frequency of particular behaviors. The rationale underlying behavioral self-report techniques is that information about troublesome behavior should be derived from the client, who has the closest access to information critical for understanding and treating the problem behavior. This information can be acquired in a number of ways, including interviews conducted by the clinician, the client's self-monitoring of the behavior, and the completion of any one of a number of checklists or inventories specifically designed for this purpose.

It is commonly accepted within clinical contexts that the best way to find out what troubles clients is to ask them; the interview is the context within which to undertake such inquiry. **Behavioral interviewing** is a specialized form of interviewing in which the clinician focuses on the behavior under consideration, as well as what preceded and followed the behavior. Events that precede the behavior are referred to as **antecedents**, and events following the behavior are called **consequences**.

Behavioral interviewing has long been regarded as an integral part of behavioral assessment and therapy, for it is within this context that the clinician works to understand the problem under consideration. When interviewing the client about the problem behavior, the clinician gathers detailed information about what happens before, during, and after the enactment of the behavior. For example, take the case of Ernesto, a young man who develops incapacitating levels of anxiety whenever it begins to rain while he is driving his car. In interviewing Ernesto, the clinician tries to develop as precise an understanding as possible of the nature of these attacks of anxiety and asks very specific questions pertaining to the time, place, frequency, and nature of these attacks. Although the clinician wants to obtain some background information, in most cases this is limited to information that seems relevant to the problem behavior. In this example, the clinician would be more likely to focus on particular experiences in Ernesto's history that relate to fears of driving under risky conditions than to ask about early life relationships.

Within the behavioral interview, the clinician not only tries to understand the precise nature of the problem but also seeks to collaborate with the client in setting goals for intervention.

Psychologists use behavior records to monitor the frequency of target behaviors, as in the case of this person trying to quit smoking.

What is it that the client wants to change? In the example of the anxiety attacks, presumably the client wants to be able to continue driving after the rain starts, without being impaired by the anxiety that had previously afflicted him. The clinician tries to ascertain whether the client's goal is realistic or not. If the young man asserts that he wants to work toward a goal of never feeling any anxiety while in a car, the clinician would consider such a goal unrealistic and would help the client set a more attainable objective.

Self-monitoring is another behavioral self-report technique in which the client keeps a record of the frequency of specified behaviors, such as the number of cigarettes smoked or calories consumed, or the number of times in a day that a particular unwanted thought comes to the client's mind. Perhaps a woman is instructed to keep a diary of each time she bites her fingernails, documenting the time, place, and context of the **target behavior,** the behavior that is of interest or concern in the assessment. With such careful attention to the troubling behavior, she may come to realize that she is prone to biting her nails primarily in certain situations. For example, she may notice that her nail-biting is twice as likely to occur when she is speaking on the telephone.

Self-monitoring procedures have some limitations. Such habits as nail-biting are so deeply ingrained that people are almost unaware of engaging in the behavior. Another problem with self-monitoring procedures is that the individual must have the discipline to keep records of the behavior. As you might imagine, it could be quite disruptive for the nail-biter to take out a note pad each time she raises her fingernails to her mouth. In response to such concerns, some clinicians acknowledge that the measurement of the behavior in and of itself may be therapeutic.

Behavioral checklists and inventories have been developed to aid in the assessment or recording of troubling behaviors. In completing a behavioral checklist or inventory, the client checks off or rates whether certain events or experiences have transpired. For example, in the Beck Depression Inventory-II (BDI-II) (Beck, Steer, & Brown, 1996), the client indi-

cates the occurrence of depression-related thoughts. Another commonly used behavioral inventory is the Fear Survey Schedule (Wolpe & Lang, 1977), in which an individual is asked to indicate the extent to which various experiences evoke feelings of fear. Checklists and inventories such as these often appeal to both clinicians and clients, because they are relatively economical and easy to use.

However, in many instances it is important to observe and measure the behavior that is the focus of concern. A client can tell a clinician about the nature and frequency of a troubling behavior, but a person may have trouble reporting a behavior that is embarrassing or otherwise upsetting.

Behavioral Observation

Observation of the client's behavior is an important component of behavioral assessment (Foster, Bell-Dolan, & Burge, 1988). In **behavioral observation**, the clinician observes the individual and records the frequency of specific behaviors, along with any relevant situational factors. For example, the nursing staff on a psychiatric unit might be instructed to observe and record the target behavior of an individual who bangs his head against a wall every time something out of the ordinary occurs. Or a classroom observer of a hyperactive boy might count the number of times each minute the boy gets out of his seat. The consequences of each behavior would also be recorded, such as the number of times the teacher tells the child to sit down.

The first step in behavioral observation is to select the target behaviors that are of interest or concern. In the example of the hyperactive child, the target behavior would be the boy's getting up from his desk at inappropriate times. The second step is to define the target behavior clearly. Vague terms are not acceptable in a behavioral observation context. For example, a target behavior of "restlessness" in the hyperactive boy is too vague to measure. However, a measurement can be made of the number of times he jumps out of his seat.

Ideally, behavioral observation takes place in the natural context in which the target behavior occurs. This is called *in vivo* **observation**. For the hyperactive boy, the classroom setting is particularly problematic, so it is best that his behavior be observed and measured there, rather than in a laboratory. However, many challenges are involved in conducting such assessments, including overcoming the possible effects of the observer's presence. It is possible that the boy's behavior will be affected by the fact that he knows he is being observed, a phenomenon behaviorists refer to as **reactivity**.

To deal with some of the limitations of *in vivo* observation, the clinician or researcher may conduct an **analog observation**, which takes place in a setting or context specifically designed for observing the target behavior. For example, the hyperactive boy may be taken to the clinician's office, where his behavior can be observed through a one-way mirror. Perhaps other children will be included, so that the boy's interactions can be observed and certain target behaviors measured. Analog observation has its limits, however, primarily because the situation is somewhat artificial.

Environmental Assessment

In evaluating an individual, it is often helpful to obtain a perspective on his or her social or living environment. As you read about various approaches to understanding psychological disorders, you will see that some emphasize the role of the individual's family or social context in the development and continuation of symptoms. **Environmental assessment scales** ask the individual to rate certain key dimensions hypothesized to influence behavior. Psychologist Rudolf Moos has been influential in developing such instruments, which include ratings of the family environment, the school, the community setting, or a long-term care institution. For example, the Family Environment Scale (Moos & Moos, 1986) involves having individuals rate their families along dimensions including the quality of relationships, the degree of personal growth the family promotes, and the activities in which the family engages to maintain the system. Within the relationship domain, separate scales assess how much cohesion or commitment exists among family members, how expressive family members are to each other, and how much conflict they express. Specific items on these scales ask about what might seem to be mundane family experiences, such as when the dishes are washed and what family members do together for recreation. Other questions tap into more sensitive issues, such as whether family members hit each other when they are angry and whether family members share religious beliefs. The Family Environment Scale can be used to assess the quality of, for example, a delinquent adolescent's home life or the degree of supportiveness family members show during a crisis. Such a scale can provide important information to mental health professionals about the influence of the social environment on the individual's adaptation.

Physiological Assessment

Many psychological disorders occur in the presence of physiological disturbances that must either contribute to or at least may have a bearing on the individual's condition. Sometimes the disturbance is localized in the brain, perhaps in the form of a structural abnormality. Or perhaps a person has a physical disorder, such as diabetes, AIDS, or hyperthyroidism (an overactive thyroid), that causes the individual to experience altered psychological functioning. Increasingly, as psychological disorders are being found to have accompanying physiological abnormalities, the evaluation of the individual's physiological status has become a central aspect of a complete psychological assessment. In some cases, abnormalities of physiological functioning become a central feature of diagnosis.

Psychophysiological Assessment

Since the early days of behavior therapy, many clinicians and researchers have been interested in assessing changes in the body that are associated with psychological or emotional experiences, especially changes in a person's cardiovascular system, muscles, skin, and brain. To measure these changes, they use psychophysiological assessment procedures, which provide a wealth of information about the bodily responses of an individual to a given situation.

The cardiovascular system is composed of the heart and blood vessels. As you know from thinking about any situation in which you have felt frightened, your heart rate can change drastically in a short period of time. Even thinking about something that frightens you can cause changes in your cardiovascular system. Various measurement devices are used to monitor cardiovascular functioning, the most common of which is the **electrocardiogram (ECG),** which measures electrical impulses that pass through the heart and provides an indication of whether the heart is pumping blood normally. **Blood pressure** is a measure of the resistance offered by the arteries to the flow of blood as it is pumped from the heart. Assessments of cardiovascular functioning may be used to provide information about a person's psychological functioning, as well as his or her level of risk for developing various stress-related conditions that affect the heart and arteries.

Muscular tension, another physiological indicator of stress, is assessed by means of **electromyography (EMG),** a measure of the electrical activity of the muscles. This technique is used in the assessment and treatment of tension-related disorders, such as headaches, that involve severe and continuous muscle contractions.

An individual's skin also provides important information about what the person is experiencing emotionally. Many people sweat when they feel nervous, which causes electrical changes in the skin called the **electrodermal response**. This response, also called the **galvanic skin response (GSR),** is a sensitive indicator of emotional responses, such as fear and anxiety.

Brain Imaging Techniques

The growth of increasingly powerful computer technology in the 1980s led to the development of a new generation of physiological measures of brain structure and activity. These techniques have made it possible for psychologists, psychiatrists, and neurologists to gain greater understanding of the normal brain and the brain's changes as a function of various physical and psychological disorders.

One of the earliest techniques to assess the living brain was the **electroencephalogram (EEG),** which measures electrical activity in the brain, an indication of the individual's level of arousal. An EEG recording is taken by pasting electrodes (small metallic discs) with an electricity-conducting gel to the surface of the scalp. A device called a galvanometer, which has an inkpen attached to its pointer, writes on the surface of a continuously moving paper strip, producing a "wave" drawing on the paper.

EEG activity reflects the extent to which an individual is alert, resting, sleeping, or dreaming. The EEG pattern also shows particular patterns of brain waves when an individual engages in particular mental tasks. For diagnostic purposes, EEGs provide valuable information for determining diseases of the brain, such as epilepsy (convulsions caused by a chaotic

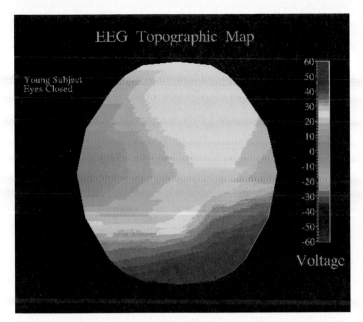

In an EEG topographical map, computer software converts EEG amplitude waves into tones of color depicting electrical activity.

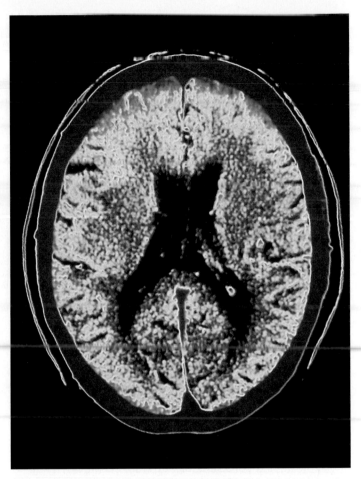

CT scans are increasingly important in helping professionals pinpoint abnormalities associated with psychological disorders.

activity of neurons), sleep disorders, and brain tumors. When clinicians detect abnormal EEG patterns, they may use this information as preliminary evidence of brain abnormalities that can be investigated further with more in-depth physical and psychological assessments.

In recent years, computerized interpretations of EEG patterns have replaced the subjective interpretations of technicians and clinicians. A computer can translate wave patterns into color-coded plots of activity, such as black and blue to indicate areas of low EEG amplitude and yellow and red to indicate higher amplitude. This approach yields an easily comprehensible view of the patterns of electrical rhythm and amplitude across the surface of the brain. Animations of these images make it even easier to appreciate variations in brain activity patterns, particularly when computer graphing techniques are used to generate three-dimensional video images.

The EEG, particularly the computerized version, provides a "picture" of the living brain that can be extremely useful for diagnosis. Other imaging techniques of the brain provide X-raylike images that can be used to diagnose abnormalities in brain structure caused by disease, tumors, or injury.

A **computed axial tomography (CAT or CT scan)** (*tomo* means "slice" in Greek) is a series of X-rays taken from various angles around the body that is integrated by a computer to produce a composite picture. During a CT exam, the individual lies with his or her head in a large X-ray tube. A beam of X-rays is shot through the brain; as it exits on the other side, the beam is blunted slightly, because it has passed through dense areas of living tissue. Very dense tissue, such as bone, causes the greatest bending of the beam, and fluid causes the least. X-ray detectors collect readings from multiple angles around the circumference of the scanner, and a computerized formula reconstructs an image of each slice. This method can be used to provide a cross-sectional slice of the brain from any angle or level. CT scans provide an image of the fluid-filled areas of the brain

(ventricles). As you will see later in this book, such as in the discussion of schizophrenia, this kind of information is very valuable in determining the structural brain differences between people with this disorder and nonschizophrenic individuals.

Another imaging technique used to assess brain structure is **magnetic resonance imaging (MRI),** which uses radiowaves rather than X-rays to construct a picture of the living brain based on the water content of various tissues. The person being tested is placed inside a device that contains a powerful electromagnet. This causes the nuclei in hydrogen atoms to transmit electromagnetic energy (hence the term "magnetic resonance"), and activity from thousands of angles is sent to a computer, which produces a high-resolution picture of the scanned area. The picture obtained from the MRI delineates areas of white matter (nerve fibers) from gray matter (nerve cells) and is useful for diagnosing diseases that affect the nerve fibers that make up the white matter. Tumors that cannot be seen on a CT scan can sometimes be seen in an MRI. In a variant of the traditional MRI, which produces static images, **functional magnetic resonance imaging** makes it possible to construct a picture of actual activity in the brain.

Another neuroimaging technique used to assess abnormalities of brain function is the **positron emission tomography (PET)** or a variant of this technique known as **single photon emission computed tomography (SPECT).** In this method,

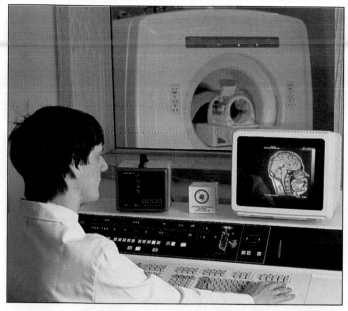

The MRI is a scanning procedure that uses magnetic fields and radio-frequency pulses to construct an image of the brain.

radioactively labeled compounds are injected into a person's veins in very small amounts. The compounds travel through the blood into the brain and emit positively charged electrons called positrons, which can then be detected much like X-rays in a CT. The images, which represent the accumulation of the labeled compound, can show blood flow, oxygen or glucose metabolism, and concentrations of brain chemicals. These vibrant colors at the red end of the spectrum represent higher levels of activity, and colors at the blue-green-violet end of the spectrum represent lower levels of brain activity. What is so intriguing about this process is that the PET scan can show where in the brain specific mental activities are taking place; this is accomplished by assessing the increase in blood flow to a given region. Thus, a thought or specific mental task causes a region of the brain to light up. In addition to the utility of the PET scan in measuring mental activity, this procedure is valuable in studying what happens in the brain following the ingestion of substances, such as drugs.

Sophisticated physiological assessment techniques are not routinely included in a battery because of the tremendous expense involved. At the same time, however, astute clinicians recognize the importance of evaluating the possibility that a medical abnormality may be causing or contributing to an individual's psychological disorder. Let's return to the case of Ben. Recall how he told Dr. Tobin that his concern about the possibility of the police following him dated back to the time that he suffered a minor injury following a bike collision with a police car. As Dr. Tobin attempted to understand the nature of Ben's symptoms, she considered the possibility that he might have sustained a previously undiagnosed brain injury in this accident. Consequently, she recommended that Ben consult with a neurologist for an evaluation. In this procedure, an MRI was done; although the results showed no diagnosable brain damage, the neurologist did note some slight brain abnormalities in the form of enlarged ventricles. Although a clinician would not make a psychiatric diagnosis on the basis of this information, Dr. Tobin did make a mental note of the fact that enlarged ventricles are sometimes associated with schizophrenia.

Neuropsychological Assessment

As valuable as physical assessment techniques are in pinpointing certain kinds of abnormalities in the brain or other parts of the body, they have limitations. Often the clinician needs information about the kind of cognitive impairment that has resulted from a brain abnormality, such as a tumor or brain disease. Perhaps information is needed about the extent of the deterioration that the individual has experienced to that point. **Neuropsychological assessment** is the process of gathering information about a client's brain functioning on the basis of performance on psychological tests.

The most well-known neuropsychological assessment tool is the Halstead-Reitan Neuropsychological Test Battery, a series of tests designed to measure sensorimotor, perceptual, and speech functions. This battery was developed by psychologist Ralph Reitan, based on the earlier work of an experimental psychologist, Ward Halstead (Halstead, 1947). Each test in the battery involves a specific task that measures a particular hypothesized brain-behavior relationship. Clinicians can choose from an array of tests, including the Halstead Category Test, Tactual Performance Test, Rhythm Test, Speech-Sounds Perception Test, and Finger Oscillation Task. These tests were developed by comparing the performance of people with different forms of brain damage as determined through independent measures, such as skull X-rays, autopsies, and physical examinations. In addition to these tests, the battery may include the MMPI-2 as a measure of personality variables that may affect the individual's performance. Also, the WAIS-III may be administered in order to gather information on overall cognitive functioning.

Although the Halstead-Reitan is regarded as an extremely valuable approach to neuropsychological assessment, some clinicians prefer the more recently developed Luria-Nebraska Neuropsychological Battery. A.R. Luria was a well-known Russian neuropsychologist who developed a variety of individualized tests intended to detect specific forms of brain damage. These tests were put into standardized form by a group of psychologists at the University of Nebraska (Golden, Purisch, & Hammeke, 1985). This battery comprises 269 separate tasks, organized into 11 subtests, including motor function, tactile function, and receptive speech. It takes less time to administer than the Halstead-Reitan; furthermore, its content, administration, and scoring procedures are more standardized.

Though the Halstead-Reitan and the Luria-Nebraska are regarded as impressively precise, their administration involves very sophisticated skills and training. Rather than begin with these tests, most psychologists administer simpler global screening indicators, such as the Bender Visual Motor Gestalt Test (Bender, 1938) and the Benton Revised Visual Retention Test (Benton, 1974). These tests are diagnostic tools used to

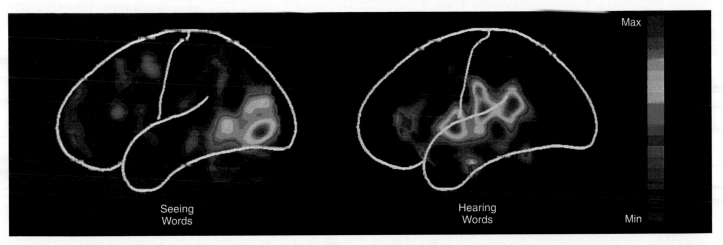

Seeing Words

Hearing Words

Max

Min

The PET scan on the left shows the two areas of the brain (red and yellow) that became particularly active when volunteers read words on a video screen: the primary visual <u>cortex</u> and an additional part of the visual system, both in the back of the left hemisphere. Other brain regions became especially active when the subjects heard words through earphones, as seen in the PET scan on the right. Since brain activity involves an increase in blood flow, more blood—and radioactive water—streamed into the areas of the volunteers' brains that were most active while they saw or heard words. The radiation counts on the PET scanner went up accordingly. This enabled the scientists to build electronic images of brain activity along any desired "slice" of the subjects' brains. These images were produced by averaging the results of tests on nine volunteers (www.hhmi.org/senses).

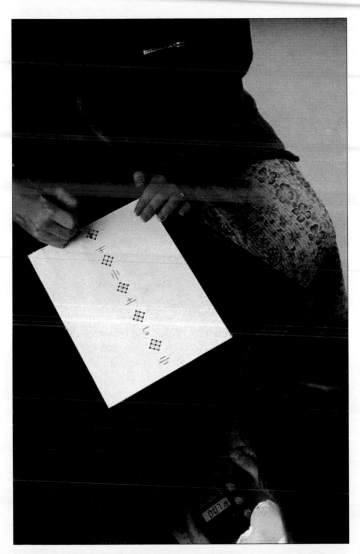

In neuropsychological tests such as the one this woman is taking, the ability to copy simple objects is used to assess brain functioning.

assess general visual perception, motor coordination, memory, concepts of time and space, and ability to organize. If the clinician detects an abnormality, the next step is to refer the client for more comprehensive neuropsychological testing.

Putting It All Together

At the end of the assessment period, the clinician should have a broad-based understanding of the client as a total individual, as well as an understanding of the client's specific areas of concern. The clinician puts together a "case" that describes the client's current situation and background in a comprehensive, detailed fashion. Using the biopsychosocial model, the clinician would evaluate the extent to which biological, psychological, and sociocultural factors have contributed to and maintained a person's problem. Thus, the clinician is faced with the formidable task of discerning a multitude of possible factors. When we return to the case of Ben, you will see the ways in which Dr. Tobin considers the three major sets of factors. In the biological realm, Dr. Tobin wonders about the extent to which Ben's problem has been genetically influenced. She also questions the possibility that his minor biking injury might have contributed to his problems. Did he suffer a closed head injury that might have been the cause of his current abnormal thinking and behavior? Or might this accident have been a stressor that ignited the already brittle structure of his vulnerable personality? In the psychological realm, Dr. Tobin questions the extent to which past and current emotional difficulties may be contributing to Ben's problems. Finally, she evaluates sociocultural factors, such as family problems, difficulties with peers, and other social forces, that might be causing or adding to Ben's disturbance. As you will see in reading the assessment report about Ben, Dr. Tobin attends to the complex of biopsychosocial issues that may be affecting his thoughts, emotions, and behavior.

RETURN TO THE CASE

Ben Robsham

Reason for Testing

Although Ben Robsham had stated that his reason for requesting psychological testing was his curiosity about the nature of these tests, it was apparent that he had concerns about his psychological state. Unable to express these concerns in a clear way, it seemed that Ben saw psychological testing as a context within which his disturbance would become apparent, thus opening the door to his obtaining professional help.

Two facts justified the administration of a battery of psychological tests, as well as a neurological evaluation. First, Ben had expressed ideas that sounded delusional, including his belief that the police might be following him. Second, he described an accident in which he sustained minor injuries, possibly including an undiagnosed head injury.

Identifying Information

At the time of the assessment, Ben was 21 years old, living with his family, and working part-time in a supermarket. He was completing his junior year in college, majoring in political science with career aspirations of eventually running for public office.

Behavioral Observations

Ben was casually dressed in typical college student clothing, except for the fact that he wore a wool hat covering his hair and ears, as well as black leather gloves similar to those worn by athletes playing golf or handball. He was initially tense and ostensibly concerned about the possibility of being seen in the counseling center by people who knew him. In subsequent meetings, this concern diminished. For the most part, Ben was well-mannered and cooperative. During testing, Ben made frequent comments, such as "this really makes you take a good look at yourself." At times, he seemed defensive about his responses. For example, when questioned about the meaning of two unclear sentences on the Incomplete Sentences Blank, he curtly responded, "That's what I meant." In several instances, he responded tangentially to test and conversational questions, relating personal incidents that had little to do with the task or topic.

Relevant History

Ben Robsham grew up in a middle-class family.

He described his early childhood years as being troubled, both at home and at school. Most of Ben's time was spent in solitary hobbies such as listening to rock music. He had no close friends and preferred to stay at home rather than to socialize. He described an antagonistic relationship with his sister, Doreen, who is 2 years older. Ben spoke of how he fought almost constantly with Doreen and how Mrs. Robsham invariably sided with Ben in any dispute. This reflected what Ben believed to be his mother's overprotective parenting style. In describing his mother, Ben spoke of her as a "nut case, who would go ranting and raving about crazy stuff all the time." He also noted that she had been psychiatrically hospitalized at least twice during his childhood for what was described as a "nervous breakdown." Ben described his father as having been minimally involved with the rest of the family, especially in the years following his wife's first hospitalization.

Ben recalls how, from the earliest grades, his teachers repeatedly commented about his failure to look people in the eyes. They were also bewildered when he responded to classroom questions with answers that they found difficult to understand. Ben clearly remembers one incident in which he was asked to name the capital of Tennessee and he replied, "I don't know anything about capitalism." His teacher became angry with him for sounding like a "wise guy," although Ben did not intend to make a joke. Despite his idiosyncrasies, Ben managed to get through high school and get accepted into college.

Several months before the assessment, Ben was involved in a minor traffic collision with a police car while riding his bike. In the accident, he fell off his bike and injured himself slightly. Greater than the physical hurt, however, was the intense fear he felt when confronted by the officer driving the car. The officer spoke sternly to Ben about his careless biking, causing Ben to feel frightened. In the months that followed, Ben's worries about the police intensified. For example, he described one incident in which he was walking by a student demonstration protesting a campus research project that was being funded by the Central Intelligence Agency. On seeing a police officer, Ben became alarmed and feared that he might be arrested. In the following days and weeks, he grew more fearful. He began to worry that his phone might be tapped, his mail read, and his food treated with truth serum. Since that

RETURN TO THE CASE

Ben Robsham (continued)

time, Ben reported, he has continued to worry that he was being followed by the police and that they were trying to put together trumped-up charges against him. According to Ben, on several occasions he saw "Nazi agents who were sent by the police" to trail him.

Evaluation Procedures

Diagnostic interview, WAIS-III, MMPI-2, Rorschach, and TAT

Neurological evaluation conducted by Mariel Machmer, MD, including an MRI

Impressions and Interpretations

Ben Robsham is a very troubled young man who is desperately seeking help. He is beginning to show signs of thought disorder, emotional instability, and loss of contact with reality.

Ben is of average intelligence, with no exceptional strengths or deficits. However, the quality of many of his responses reflects unusual thought processes. For example, when asked to define the word *winter*, he responded, "It means death." It is possible that conflicts and unusual thought processes, as reflected by this response, interfere with his intellectual test performance, which is lower than the norm for college students.

Ben suffers from intense anxiety, and he is frightened by his gradual loss of touch with reality. In this state of near panic, he is calling out for help. Ben sees the world as an ominous place, filled with people who are either evil or on the verge of a horrible calamity. To cope with his fright, Ben escapes into fantasy, in which he imagines that he will be cared for, that people will live in happiness, and that conflict will disappear.

Ben keeps his distance from other people. His feelings about women are characterized by ambivalence. On the one hand, he wishes for women to be nurturant caretakers yet, on the other hand, sees them as controlling and seductive. This ambivalence about women is further aggravated by his confusion about his own sexuality. He speaks of a secret problem that he is finally admitting to himself. Although he is not explicit about this problem, there are many allusions in his responses to concerns about his sexual orientation.

Several sets of factors seem to be contributing to Ben's disturbance. Ben's mother has a history of psychiatric disturbance. Although no diagnosis is available for this woman, the history and behavior that Ben describes in his mother is that commonly found in people with schizophrenia. Compounding Ben's vulnerability is the fact that he has experienced a lifelong history of feeling socially isolated and unhappy. These feelings are rooted in a family system characterized by disharmony, tension, and psychological disorder. The stresses of adolescence and college achievement may have seemed tremendous for him, intensifying his feelings of vulnerability. Ben's slight accident several months ago may have caused physical and emotional injury, which pushed him to the brink of losing control over his thoughts, behavior, and emotions. Although neurological assessment (MRI) data have yielded no diagnosable brain injury, Dr. Machmer did make note of slight brain abnormalities in the form of enlarged brain ventricles.

In summary, this young man is on the verge of a break with reality and is in immediate need of professional help. Ben needs regular psychotherapy at this time and should be immediately evaluated regarding the possibility of prescribing medication that can address his deteriorating mental health and his heightened level of anxiety.

Recommendations

I will refer Ben for a psychiatric consultation. I recommend that he be evaluated for antipsychotic medication to treat his emerging signs of severe psychological disturbance: delusional thinking, hallucinations, and extreme anxiety. I will also refer Ben for long-term psychotherapy that focuses on helping him develop more appropriate adaptive behaviors, such as social skills and coping strategies.

Sarah Tobin, PhD

Summary

• Assessment is a procedure in which a clinician evaluates a person in terms of the psychological, physical, and social factors that influence the individual's functioning. Clinicians approach the tasks of assessment with various goals, such as determining a person's intellectual capacity, predicting a person's appropriateness for a job, and evaluating whether someone is mentally competent to stand trial. Some assessment tools focus on brain structure and functioning, others assess personality, and still others are oriented toward intellectual functioning.

• The clinical interview is the most commonly used assessment tool for developing an understanding of a client and the nature of the client's current problems, history, and future aspirations. An unstructured interview is a series of open-ended questions aimed at determining the client's reasons for being in treatment, symptoms, health status, family background, and life history. The structured interview consists of a standardized series of questions, with predetermined wording and order. The evaluation of structured interviews is based on objective criteria and differs from that of unstructured interviews, which differs substantially from one interviewer to the next.

• Clinicians use the mental status examination to assess a client's behavior and functioning, with particular attention to the symptoms associated with psychological disturbance. In the mental status examination, several areas of functioning are assessed, including the client's appearance and behavior, orientation, thought content, thinking style and language, affect and mood, perceptual experiences, sense of self, motivation, cognitive functioning, and insight and judgment.

• Psychological testing covers a broad range of techniques in which scorable information about psychological functioning is collected. Those who develop and administer psychological tests attend to psychometric principles, such as validity, reliability, and standardization. Intelligence tests, particularly the Wechsler scales, provide valuable information about an individual's cognitive functioning. Personality tests, such as self-report clinical inventories (e.g., MMPI-2) and projective techniques (e.g., Rorschach), yield useful data about a person's thoughts, behaviors, and emotions.

• Other forms of assessment include behavioral assessment, environmental assessment, physiological assessment, and neuropsychological assessment. Behavioral assessment includes measurement techniques based on the recording of a person's behavior, such as behavioral self-report, behavioral interviewing, self-monitoring, and behavioral observation. In environmental assessment, ratings are provided about key dimensions, such as family environment, that influence behavior. Psychophysiological and physiological techniques assess bodily functioning and structure. Psychophysiological techniques include such measures as ECG, blood pressure, EMG, and other measures of emotional responses. Physiological measures include brain imaging techniques, such as EEG, CT scan, MRI, PET, and other techniques for assessing abnormalities in the body, particularly the brain. Neuropsychological assessment techniques provide additional information about brain dysfunction based on data derived from an individual's performance on specialized psychological tests such as the Halstead-Reitan Neuropsychological Test Battery. Based on information from various sources, clinicians formulate an understanding of a client's specific areas of concern with attention to the biological, psychological, and sociocultural factors that may play a role.

Key Terms

See Glossary for definitions.

Key Terms

Mood 70
Motor behavior 68
Neuropsychological assessment 90
Normal (or euthymic) mood 71
Obsession 68
Olfactory hallucinations 72
Orientation 68
Overvalued ideas 69
Percentile score 74
Personal history 65

Positron emission tomography (PET) 89
Projective test 83
Psychometrics 74
Psychomotor agitation 68
Psychomotor retardation 68
Range of affect 70
Reactivity 87
Reliability 74
Self-monitoring 87
Self-report clinical inventory 77

Single photon emission computed
tomography (SPECT) 89
Somatic hallucinations 72
Standardized 74
Structured interview 65
Target behavior 87
Thinking style and language 69
Unstructured interview 64
Validity 74
Visual hallucinations 72

Internet Resource

To get more information on the material covered in this chapter, visit our web site at **http://www.mhhe.com/halgin**. There you will find more information, resources, and links to topics of interest.

CASE REPORT: KRISTIN PIERPONT

A year prior to contacting me for therapy, Kristin Pierpont had been a student in a large undergraduate abnormal psychology course that I had taught at the state university. More than 300 students were enrolled in this course, and I often regretted the fact that I had so little opportunity to get to know them. However, I did recall Kristin, due to the tragedy that she experienced midway through the semester.

I first learned of the terrible events in Kristin's life when I received a phone call from Joanne MacKimmie, the Dean of Students, who told me that she had just received news that Kristin's father had committed suicide. As is customary in such exceptional circumstances, the Dean urged me to give Kristin every possible consideration regarding the fulfillment of course requirements. As told to Dean MacKimmie by a family member, Kristin's father was 47 years old, reportedly a "healthy and happy man," to whom she was especially close. He had hung himself in the family home without any warning. One of Kristin's sisters had reportedly discovered Mr. Pierpont's body, as well as the very disturbing suicide note that he had written. In the note, he mentioned the name of his wife and each of his four daughters, stating that he felt so "unloved" by them that he felt that there was no option but to end his life.

The day after Kristin received news of this terrible event, she approached me after class, explained what had happened, and in a matter-of-fact manner asked if she could reschedule the examination that was to be given later that week, because she would have to attend her father's funeral. I immediately reacted with sympathy and solicitous concern, stating that we could, of course, work something out. With a notable lack of emotion in her voice, Kristin thanked me and began to walk away. I was stunned by the numbness of her emotional state, yet at the same time I realized that Kristin was responding to her personal crisis with emotional distancing, a response that is common in people who have experienced a trauma.

I suggested that she come to my office and talk for a while, an invitation she accepted. As soon as I closed my office door, she broke down in tears and blurted out that she didn't want to go on living. After meeting for more than an hour, she agreed to follow my suggestion that she meet with a clinician at the mental health service, so we phoned for an appointment that afternoon.

The following week, I approached Kristin after class and asked how she was doing. All she said was "Fine, thanks." From that point on, she made it clear—mostly through nonverbal cues, such as avoiding eye contact—that she did not wish to talk to me about personal matters, and I respected her wish for privacy. For the subsequent 7 weeks of the semester, she dressed completely in black and sat in a place far removed from her classmates.

In light of the manner in which she had chosen to keep her distance from me for the duration of that semester, I was surprised and perplexed that a year later she chose to pursue therapy under my care. When she phoned me, she began the discussion by stating, "I'm sure that you have no recollection of me, but I was in your class last year." She seemed genuinely surprised when I told her that indeed I did recall her and that I remembered what a difficult time it had been for her.

Kristin was now 23 years old, and she was seeking therapy to deal with her feelings of "isolation and loneliness." She didn't use the word *depression*, but there was a profound sadness in the tone of her voice. While speaking to me on the phone, Kristin asked me whether she might be "untreatable." When I stated that I wasn't sure what she meant, Kristin explained her worry that these feelings of sadness may have become a "part of" her personality. I suggested that we hold off discussion of this concern until we could talk face to face. We set an appointment for later that week.

On meeting Kristin in the reception room on the day of our first appointment, I immediately noticed the black clothing she was wearing. The image took me back to the sight of her, a year earlier, as she sat in a remote corner of the auditorium during the weeks following her father's death. It had been apparent to me a year ago that she was in a state of mourning, and even after all these months she continued to suffer from unrelenting feelings of sadness. With a faint smile, she meekly responded to my invitation to proceed into my office. Despite my effort to walk beside her, she paced her steps in such a way that she became a follower.

Kristin began our first session by telling me she had lived through the "worst year" of her life. On graduating from college, she had found a job as a housewares buyer for a large department store, but she felt this job was not particularly gratifying. She explained that she viewed herself as a "failure" because of her "low salary" and the lack of a boyfriend, or "any friends, for that matter." In fact, she had spent social time with no one since the day she graduated, other than a few "compulsory" visits with her mother. When her former college friends invited her to go to concerts with them, she turned them down, explaining that she felt too busy and exhausted.

In our interview, I returned to the issue of her father's death and inquired about the ways in which that traumatic event continued to affect her. At first, she stated that it was something she had "gotten over," but then admitted she thought of him several times every day, sometimes feeling very sad and at other times feeling "furious about what he did."

Sarah Tobin, PhD

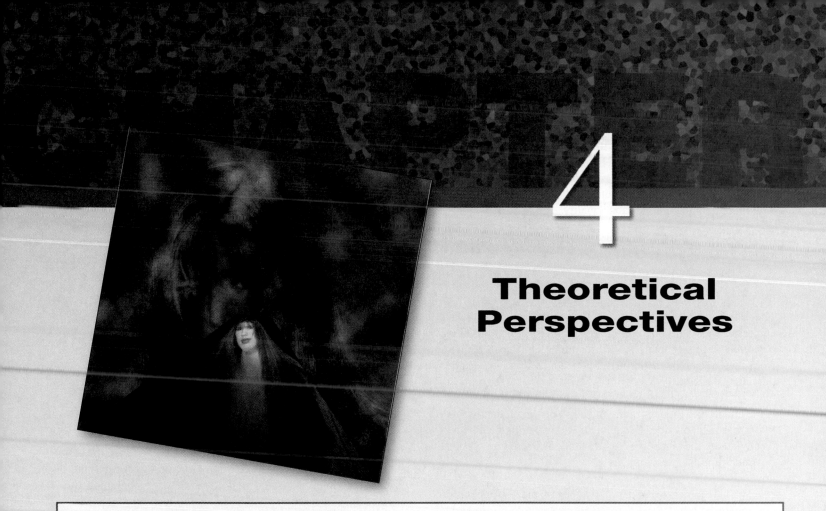

4

Theoretical Perspectives

As you read Kristin's case, you probably formed your own hunches about the causes of her behavior. Dr. Tobin would have done the same from the first moments that she observed Kristin acting in unusual ways. Her thinking would have been influenced by the beliefs and assumptions she has developed about human behavior and abnormality. These beliefs and assumptions are based on a **theoretical perspective,** an orientation to understanding the causes of human behavior and the treatment of abnormality.

The Purpose of Theoretical Perspectives in Abnormal Psychology

Theoretical perspectives influence the ways in which clinicians and researchers interpret and organize their observations about behavior. In this chapter, we will examine abnormal behavior from the five major theoretical perspectives that have shaped the field as it is today. We will see what answers each perspective provides to questions regarding abnormal behavior. What is the underlying model of human nature on which the perspective is based? How does the perspective explain human behavior? What are the perspective's implications for research? What treatment approaches would follow from the perspective, and how well do these treatments work?

When it comes to actual practice, experienced clinicians do not adhere strictly to one theoretical perspective but integrate techniques and perspectives from multiple approaches. As you read this chapter, you will find it helpful to recall our discussion in Chapter 1 of the biopsychosocial model, keeping in mind that most disorders have a complex set of causes, warranting a multidimensional treatment.

Psychodynamic Perspective

The **psychodynamic perspective** is the theoretical orientation that emphasizes unconscious determinants of behavior. You will recall from Chapter 1 that Sigmund Freud's (1856–1939) view of psychological disorder focused on unconscious motives and conflicts. His ideas about the cause and treatment of psychological disorder form the foundation for the psychodynamic perspective. As you will see, this theory has come a long way from Freud's original formulations.

Freudian Psychoanalytic Theory

Freud theorized that disorders of the mind produce bizarre and exotic behaviors and symptoms and that these behaviors and symptoms can be scientifically studied and explained. The term *psychoanalytic* is identified with Freud's original theory and approach to therapy. The term *psychodynamic* refers more broadly to the perspective that focuses on unconscious processes and incorporates a wider variety of theoretical perspectives on personality and treatment.

Freud's Background

According to Freud, the "child is father to the man," meaning that early life experiences play a formative role in personality. This observation stemmed from analyzing his own childhood (Gay, 1988; Jones, 1953). When in his thirties and forties, Freud came to the dramatic realization that the events of his early childhood had taken root in the deepest level of awareness, the region of the mind he called the "unconscious." He came to this conclusion through extensive analysis of his dreams and of the thoughts and memories they triggered (Freud, 1900). In the process of this self-analysis, he found that he was able to obtain relief from a variety of disturbing symptoms, such as a fear of trains he developed during a traumatic ride from his hometown to Vienna at the age of 4.

Freud's medical training led him to the convictions that an understanding of disorders of the mind could be achieved by using scientific methods, and that all psychological phenomena could be traced to physiological processes. The scientific approach was also evident in his work, as he sought to confirm his theory through observation and analysis of his patients.

Freud's Structural Model of Personality

According to Freud (1923) the mind has three structures: the id, the ego, and the superego. The three structures constitute the psyche (the Greek word for "soul"), and they are continuously interacting with one another in a "dynamic" fashion. Freud coined the term **psychodynamics** to describe the process of interaction among the personality structures that lie beneath the surface of observable behavior. The **id** is the structure of personality that contains sexual and aggressive instincts, what Freud called a "seething cauldron." Inaccessible to conscious awareness, the id lies entirely in the "unconscious" layer of the mind. The id follows the **pleasure principle,** a motivating force oriented toward the immediate and total gratification of sensual needs and desires. According to Freud, pleasure can be obtained only when the tension of an unmet drive is reduced. The way

Psychoanalyst Sigmund Freud with his daughter, psychoanalyst Anna Freud, in 1928.

the id attempts to achieve pleasure is not necessarily through the actual gratification of a need with tangible rewards. Instead, the id uses "wish fulfillment" to achieve its goals. Through wish fulfillment, the id conjures up an image of whatever will satisfy the needs of the moment.

Freud (1911) used the phrase **primary process thinking** to describe the id's loosely associated, idiosyncratic, and distorted cognitive representation of the world. In primary process thinking, the thoughts, feelings, and desires related to sexual and aggressive instincts are represented symbolically with visual images that do not necessarily fit together in a rational, logical way. Time, space, and causality do not correspond to what happens in real life. Primary process thinking is best illustrated in dreams.

The center of conscious awareness in personality is the **ego.** The ego's function is to give the individual the mental powers of judgment, memory, perception, and decision making, which enable the individual to adapt to the realities of the external world. Recall that the id is incapable of distinguishing between fantasy and reality. The ego is needed to transform a wish into real gratification. Freud (1911) described the ego as being governed by the **reality principle,** a motivational force that leads the individual to confront the constraints of the external world.

In contrast to the id's illogical primary process thinking, the ego functions are characterized by **secondary process thinking,** which is involved in logical and rational problem solving. Imagine a hungry student, working late in the library, who goes to a coin-operated vending machine, inserts her last quarter, and finds that the machine fails to respond. Primary process thinking leads her to bang angrily on the machine, achieving nothing but an injured hand. The secondary process thinking of her ego eventually comes into play, and she searches for a more practical solution, such as borrowing some change from a friend.

In Freud's theory, the ego has no motivating force of its own. All of the ego's energy is derived from the energy of the id, a pressure for gratification that Freud called the **libido.** The ego performs the functions that allow the id's desires to be gratified in reality, not just in fantasy. The id, then, is the ego's taskmaster.

Although the ego is the center of consciousness, not all of the ego's contents are accessible to conscious awareness. The unconscious part of the ego contains memories of experiences that reflect unfavorably on the individual's conscious self. These experiences include events in which the individual acted selfishly, behaved in sexually inappropriate ways, or was unnecessarily cruel and violent.

The **superego** is, as the name implies, "over" the ego, controlling the ego's pursuit of the id's desires. Freud believed that, without a superego, people would pursue for pleasure the satisfaction of the "taboo," or socially unacceptable, desires of the id, such as rape, murder, and incest. In addition to serving as one's conscience, the superego also serves an inspirational function. It includes the **ego ideal,** which is the individual's model of how the perfect person should be.

Psychodynamics

In the personality of a healthy individual, according to Freud (1923), the id achieves instinctual desires through the ego's ability to navigate in the external world within the confines placed on it by the superego. Psychodynamics, or the interplay among the structures of the mind, is the basis for both normal and abnormal psychological functioning.

Defense Mechanisms

To protect against anxiety, people use various tactics to keep unacceptable thoughts, instincts, and feelings out of conscious awareness, tactics that Freud called **defense mechanisms**. According to Freud, everyone uses defense mechanisms on an ongoing basis to screen out potentially disturbing experiences. It is when defense mechanisms become used in a rigid or extreme fashion that they are the source of psychological disorder.

Current views on defense mechanisms place them into categories or groups based on theoretical considerations and empirically demonstrated relationships to overall mental health (Vaillant, 1994). Based on this approach, the authors of the *DSM-IV* developed a categorical scheme called the Defensive Functioning Scale. These categories provide a helpful way to think about the defense mechanisms and the way they are manifested in various psychological disorders. Examples of some of these defense mechanisms are presented in Table 4.1.

Psychosexual Development

Freud (1905) proposed that there is a normal sequence of development through a series of what he called **psychosexual stages.** Each stage focuses on a different sexually excitable zone of the body (erogenous zone); the way the child learns to fulfill the sexual desires associated with each stage becomes an important component of the child's personality. According to Freud, failure to pass through these stages in the normal manner causes various psychosexual disturbances and character disorders.

Freud based his description of the psychosexual stages almost entirely on his observations of adults he treated in

This college student's thumb-sucking might be considered regression to infantile behavior associated with an earlier psychosexual stage.

Table 4.1

Categories and Examples of Defense Mechanisms

Defense Mechanism	Definition	Example
High Adaptive Defenses	*Healthy responses to stressful situations*	
Humor	Emphasizing the amusing aspects of a conflict or stressful situation	Maria jovially reenacted the humiliating experience in which she slipped on the ice while a group of guys watched.
Self-assertion	Dealing with difficult situations by directly expressing feelings and thoughts to others	Pedro told his father that he was disappointed and angry when his father stated that he was too busy to attend Pedro's graduation.
Suppression	Avoiding thoughts about disturbing issues	Maureen made a conscious decision to avoid thinking about financial problems while studying for her final exams.
Mental Inhibitions	*Unconscious tactics that help people keep out of conscious awareness disturbing thoughts, feelings, memories, wishes, and fears*	
Displacement	Shifting unacceptable feelings or impulses from the target of those feelings to someone less threatening or to an object	After his boss criticized him, Fred remained quiet but later barked at one of his subordinates for no good reason.
Dissociation	Fragmenting of the usually integrated cognitive, perceptual, and motor processes in a person's functioning	While being publicly humiliated by his coach in front of the entire hockey team for getting a penalty, Tim "spaced out" by thinking about a party later that night.
Intellectualization	Resorting to excessive abstract thinking in response to issues that cause conflict or stress	Rather than focus on the upsetting aspects of placing her mother in a nursing home, Gabrielle spoke at length about the limitations of the social security system.
Reaction formation	Transforming an unacceptable feeling or desire into its opposite in order to make it more acceptable	Jared, who was secretly addicted to pornography, publicly criticized his daughter's high-school teacher for assigning a classic novel with a sexual theme.
Repression	Unconsciously expelling disturbing wishes, thoughts, or experiences from awareness	Janine was unable to recall any of the details associated with her traumatic automobile accident.
Minor Image-Distorting Defenses	*Distortions in the image of the self, the body, or others in order to regulate self-esteem*	
Devaluation	Dealing with emotional conflict or stress by attributing negative qualities to oneself or others	Patrick claimed that the communication difficulties with his girlfriend were due to her immaturity, low IQ, and lack of sophistication.
Idealization	Dealing with emotional conflict or stress by attributing exaggerated positive qualities to others	Kathleen disregarded her husband's inattentiveness by convincing herself and others that he was absorbed in thoughts of genius and creativity.
Omnipotence	Responding to stress by acting superior to others	The greater the tension in his job as a stock broker, the more likely it was that Norman would speak in demeaning ways to his co-workers.

Table 4.1 *(continued)*

Categories and Examples of Defense Mechanisms

Defense Mechanism	Definition	Example
Disavowal Defenses	*Keeping unpleasant or unacceptable stressors, thoughts, feelings, impulses, or responsibility out of awareness*	
Denial	Dealing with emotional conflict or stress by refusing to acknowledge a painful aspect of reality or experience that would be apparent to others	Rather than contend with the painful emotions about her cancer diagnosis, Candace acted matter-of-factly as though she were unaffected.
Projection	Attributing undesirable personal traits or feelings to someone else to protect one's ego from acknowledging distasteful personal attributes	Unaware of her reputation for being selfish and miserly, Isabel often complained about the cheapness of others.
Rationalization	Concealing true motivations for thoughts, actions, or feelings by offering reassuring or self-serving but incorrect explanations	To deal with his disappointment about not making the baseball team, Pete convinced himself that he really didn't want to be on "such a weak team" anyway.
Major Image Distorting Defenses	*Gross distortion of oneself or others*	
Splitting	Compartmentalizing opposite affect states and failing to integrate positive and negative qualities of self or others into cohesive images	Although she had idealized a professor for the entire semester, immediately following a test on which she received an *A-* Marianne began to view him as an "evil and hostile person."
Defenses Involving Action	*Responses to conflict or stress that involve an action or withdrawal*	
Acting out	Dealing with emotional conflict or stress by actions rather than thoughts or feelings	Rather than telling his wife that he was hurt by her resistance to sexual intimacy, Rafael decided that he would get even by having an affair with a co-worker.
Passive aggression	Presenting a facade of overcompliance to mask hidden resistance, anger, or resentment	Kevin's resentment about his job as a janitor was reflected in his "overdoing" the office cleaning chores in such a way that the executives were repeatedly distracted by the noise and commotion when he cleaned.
Regression	Dealing with emotional conflict or stress by reverting to childish behaviors	Following even the most minor of disagreements with her co-workers, Adrianne rushed off to the bathroom in tears and waited until someone came to soothe her hurt feelings.
Defenses Involving Breaks with Reality	*Responses to stress or conflict that involve bizarre thought or behavior*	
Delusional projection	Delusionally attributing undesirable personal traits or feelings to someone else to protect one's ego from acknowledging distasteful personal attributes	Although it was Harry who disdained everyone he encountered, he convinced himself that his neighbors hated him so much that they intended to murder him.
Psychotic distortion	Dealing with emotional conflict or stress by resorting to delusional misinterpretation of reality	As his college grades continued to fall, Yev developed the belief that all his professors were intentionally grading him harshly because of their wish to rid the university of Russian immigrants.

CRITICAL ISSUE

Repressed Memories—Fact or Fiction?

When 35-year-old Elizabeth Carlson began seeing psychiatrist Dr. Diane Humenansky, she was a severely depressed woman with memories of having been sexually molested by two male relatives. Four years after beginning therapy, Elizabeth's life was in utter turmoil, as she came to believe that she had more than 25 personalities and that she had "recovered memories" of having been molested by more than 50 relatives. Adding to these shocking assertions was Carlson's report that she "remembered" being forced to participate in satanic rituals and cannibalism. The story of Elizabeth Carlson, which appeared in an article in *The New Yorker* (Acocella, 1998) is but one example of the attention being given in the media to dramatic cases involving clients who have been led to believe that they have multiple personalities.

When Carlson entered therapy, it was her hope and expectation that, within a brief period of time, her depression would subside and she would return to normal functioning. However, that is not what happened. In fact, Elizabeth's condition worsened dramatically to a point that she became so depressed that she dropped out of school, often slept more than 18 hours a day, and suffered from terrible nightmares that left her vomiting and screaming. She cut off all contact with her relatives, believing that they had forced her into horrendous acts earlier in life.

Carlson gradually came to her senses and, along with another patient, sued Dr. Humenansky for malpractice, claiming that this psychiatrist was responsible for creating false memories of abuse and torture and had erroneously led these patients to believe that they had multiple personalities. The court agreed and awarded over $2.5 million to each plaintiff. Dr. Humenansky lost her license to practice medicine in Minnesota.

How could a person possibly come to believe such far-fetched notions about close family members? And how could images of events that never took place develop into "memories" that seemed so real? Can memories of traumatic events, such as abuse, lie dormant in our minds, ready to be "recovered" many years later? Such questions have been the focus of intense debate in recent years, especially as some individuals have come forth with realizations that "memories" of early life abuse that emerged in therapy were actually false images evoked by the therapist.

Most psychotherapists have recognized that they must proceed with tremendous caution when treating clients who report having been abused earlier in life. They realize that it is very difficult to differentiate actual occurrences of trauma from "false" memories of events. On the one hand, a therapist would not want to respond to a client's report of a trauma with an attitude of disbelief; on the other hand, the therapist must avoid colluding with a client in whom false memories are brewing. Researchers have brought considerable attention to the fact that some therapists have used questionable techniques to

---

psychotherapy, whose recollections convinced him that their difficulties stemmed from repressed sexual instincts left over from their early years (Freud, 1925). According to Freudian theory, the notions of regression and fixation are central to the development of psychological disturbance. An individual may regress to behavior appropriate to an earlier stage or may become stuck, or fixated, at that stage. In **fixation,** then, the individual remains at a stage of psychosexual development characteristic of childhood.

During the **oral stage** (0–18 months) the main source of pleasure for the infant is stimulation of the mouth and lips. This stage is divided into two phases. The first is the oral-passive, or receptive phase, in which pleasurable feelings come from nursing or eating. In the second phase, called oral-aggressive, pleasure is derived from gumming and biting anything the infant can get into the mouth. Regression to or fixation at the oral-passive phase results in excessive reliance on oral sources of gratification (thumb-sucking, cigarette smoking, overeating). People who regress to or fixate at the

oral-aggressive phase are hostile and have a critical (biting) attitude toward others.

During the **anal stage** (18 months–3 years) the toddler's sexual energy focuses on stimulation in the anal area from holding onto and expelling feces. The person who becomes fixated at this stage may have an overcontrolled, hoarding type of character structure, called anal retentive, relating to the world by holding back. Conversely, fixation at the anal stage may result in a sloppy, impulsive, and uncontrolled character, called anal expulsive. In regression to the anal stage, the individual may become excessively sloppy or, conversely, excessively neat. For example, a woman who cleans out her dresser drawers in a frenzied manner every time she has an argument with her husband is regressing to anal-like behaviors.

In the **phallic stage** (3–5 years) the genital area of the body is the focus of the child's sexual feelings. Freud believed that the fate of the child's future psychological health was sealed during this phase, when the child must deal with the most important issue of early life. During the phallic stage, the child

influence the experience and reporting of memories by their clients (Hyman & Loftus, 1997, Loftus, 1997).

Arguments have been forceful on both sides of the debate. Some professionals insist that repressed memories of childhood abuse are common and that those who refuse to recognize the phenomenon of recovered memories are hindering an important healing process. Those on the other side of the issue believe that working with clients to recover memories may actually involve ethical violations. In response to the realization that many lives have been thrown into chaos by a few misguided therapists, the False Memory Foundation was started by a parent who had been falsely accused by his daughter. This group is comprised of concerned relatives, clients, and researchers who are trying to shed light on this controversial phenomenon. What is still lacking is sufficient rigorous scientific study of false memory (Pope, 1997).

Of particular interest to this discussion is the work of Elizabeth Loftus (1997), who asserts that memory is fallible and that people can become convinced that an event that never occurred actually did take place. In one study, Loftus showed that some adults could be convinced that they had been lost in a shopping mall at age 5, even when no such event had happened (Loftus, 1993a, 1990b). Based on extensive memory research, Loftus and other scientists have concluded that attempts to uncover repressed memories are dangerous and improper (Hyman & Loftus, 1997).

Those disagreeing with Loftus assert that she does not adequately address the true issues of repressed memory; instead, she compares relatively trivial experiences, such as getting lost in a mall, with extreme cases of traumatic abuse, which people may understandably be motivated to forget (Christianson & Engelberg, 1997). Scheflin and Brown (1996) reviewed 25 studies of the relationship between amnesia and child sexual abuse; in every study, there was evidence of amnesia of child sexual abuse. They concluded that recovered memories are no more or less accurate than continuous memories. Leavitt (1997) found that patients with recovered memories of child sexual assault are actually less susceptible to suggested misinformation than are normal or psychiatric control subjects. In an effort to find a middle ground, some experts now believe that, although it is possible to form false memories, it is also possible to forget traumatic experiences and to remember them much later in life (Alpert et al., 1996; Schacter, Norman & Koutstaal, 1997).

As the issue of repressed memories has entered the mainstream media, many clients have wondered if they, too, might have repressed memories of abuse. Prudent therapists are faced with a daunting challenge. Some clinicians advocate the use of active techniques to recover repressed memories that may not yet have emerged into consciousness. Others argue that memories of abuse should only become relevant when they spontaneously emerge into consciousness. The reactions of therapists are tremendously influential in determining how these concerns will be addressed and the extent to which they might escalate into disruptive concerns for the client. Of primary importance is the therapist's responsibility to respond to clients who report repressed memories with concern and understanding for the clients' feelings of vulnerability and victimization.

becomes sexually attracted to the opposite-sex parent. Freud (1913) called this scenario in boys the Oedipal complex, after Oedipus, the tragic character in ancient Greek literature who unknowingly killed his father and married his mother. Freud described a parallel process in girls, the Electra complex, based on Electra, the ancient Greek character who conspired to kill her mother. Freud believed there were important sex differences in how the crisis is resolved but that, for both sexes, it is resolved favorably when the child identifies with the same-sex parent. The child acquires a superego, which enforces society's taboo against incest and sets the stage for all later struggles in dealing with unacceptable sexual and aggressive desires. Freud believed that failure to resolve the Oedipal complex, as it is now referred to for both sexes, becomes the major source of neurosis.

Following the turmoil of the Oedipal complex, the child's sexual energies recede entirely, according to Freud. During **latency** (5–12 years) the child interacts with peers and imitates the behavior of parents and other adults of the same sex as the

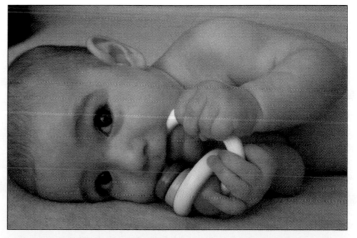

During the oral stage of development, infants put anything they can find into their mouths.

child. With sex presumably out of the picture, little that is of psychological interest happens during this stage.

In the **genital stage** (12 years through adulthood), coinciding with the resurfacing of sexual energy just prior to puberty, sexual feelings associated with the Oedipal complex begin to reappear. The adolescent must learn to transfer feelings of sexual attraction from the parent figure to opposite-sex peers. Adult **genitality,** the ability to express sexual feelings in a mature way and in appropriate contexts, is reached when an individual is able to "work and love" (in Freud's words) with another person. Any prior fixations and regressions, however, restrict the individual's ability to complete this stage satisfactorily.

Freud's Place in History

You can probably imagine that Freud's theories created a great deal of controversy, especially since he wrote in the early 1900s, when sex was not as openly discussed as it is today. Freud himself often compared his role to that of a conqueror and explorer, paving the way for revolutionary approaches to understanding the mind. During his lifetime, Freud experienced rejection and derision from his colleagues in the medical establishment. By the time he died, however, he had achieved international renown, and his work was beginning to have a major impact on many fields besides psychology.

Even though Freud's ideas have been influential, his theory is far from perfect. As you read further, you will see that important refinements came from both his followers and his critics. However, we must not lose sight of the major role that Freud played in redefining ways of understanding human behavior.

Post-Freudian Psychodynamic Views

Post-Freudian theorists departed from Freudian theory, contending that Freud overemphasized sexual and aggressive instincts as the root of personality. Instead, they focused on interpersonal and social needs and the role of sociocultural factors. Carl Jung (1875–1961) developed a theory that differed radically from Freud's emphasis on sexuality (Jung, 1961) and in the conceptualization of the unconscious. According to Jung, the deepest layer of the unconscious includes images common to all human experience, which he called archetypes. Some of these archetypes include images of "good" versus "evil," the "hero," rebirth, and the self. Jung believed that people respond to events in their daily lives on the basis of these archetypes, because they are part of our genetic makeup. For example, Jung asserted that such characters as *Batman* and *Superman* are popular because they activate the hero archetype. Jung (1916) believed that the goal of healthy personality development involves the integration of the unconscious life with conscious thoughts and that psychological disorders result from an imbalance between these parts of the personality.

Alfred Adler (1870–1937) and Karen Horney (1885–1952) made important contributions to psychodynamic theory in their emphasis on the ego and the self-concept. People are motivated to maintain a consistent and favorable view of the self, according to these theorists, and they develop psychological defenses to protect this positive self-view. Both Adler and Horney also emphasized social concerns and interpersonal relations in the development of personality. Close relationships with friends and family and an interest in the life of the community are seen as gratifying in their own right, not because a sexual or an aggressive desire is indirectly satisfied in the process. According to these theories, the "neurotic" adult is someone who feels very inferior or unworthy, feelings that originated in childhood.

Erik Erikson (1902–1994) proposed that personality development proceeds throughout the life span in a series of eight "crises" (Erikson, 1963) (see Figure 4.1). Each "crisis" is a critical period during which the individual is maximally vulnerable to two opposing forces: one that pulls the person to healthy, age-specific ego-functioning and one that pulls the person to unhealthy functioning. Depending on how the crisis is resolved, the individual's ego will acquire a new "strength" unique to that crisis stage. When the forces of a particular crisis pull the individual toward the unhealthy resolution of that issue, the individual becomes more vulnerable to the development of subsequent problems. Crisis resolutions have a cumulative effect—if one stage is unfavorably resolved, it becomes more likely that succeeding stages will also be unfavorably resolved. Failure to resolve the early psychosocial issues has particularly serious consequences for later development.

Psychosocial issue

Age period / Stage	1	2	3	4	5	6	7	8
Infancy	Basic trust vs. mistrust							
Toddler-hood		Autonomy vs. shame and doubt						
Pre-school			Initiative vs. guilt					
School age				Industry vs. inferiority				
Puberty & adolescence					Identity achievement vs. diffusion			
Young adulthood						Intimacy vs. isolation		
Middle adulthood							Generativity vs. stagnation	
Later adulthood								Ego integrity vs. despair

Figure 4.1   The eight stages of development in Erikson's theory

According to this theory, in each stage of the life span there is a theme or an issue that the individual must resolve. However, these stages do not turn "on" and "off" at clearly distinct times. Earlier stages can reappear in later life, and later stages may appear before their "scheduled" time. When a young child must confront the death of a close relative, this experience may trigger the issue of ego integrity versus despair.

Object Relations Theories

Rejecting Freud's belief that the instinctual desire for sexual and aggressive release of tension is the sole basis for the formation of personality, object relations theorists proposed instead that interpersonal relationships lie at the core of personality (Greenberg & Mitchell, 1983). These theorists, including Melanie Klein (1882–1960), D. W. Winnicott (1896–1971), and Heinz Kohut believed that the unconscious mind contains images of the child's parents and of the child's relationships to the parents. These internalized images remain at the foundation of personality throughout life. This perspective is called **object relations** in keeping with Freud's use of the term *object* to refer to anyone or anything that is the target (object) of an individual's instinctual desires.

Integrating the work of these theorists with systematic observations of infants and young children, Margaret Mahler (1897–1985) and her co-workers sketched out a timetable for the emergence of phases in the development of object relations (Mahler, Bergman & Pine, 1975). Psychological disturbance,

The writings of Sigmund Freud and his daughter, Anna Freud, had tremendous impact on the development of theories and psychotherapeutic techniques in the 20th century.

according to Mahler's theory, can result from problems arising during development.

Treatment

The main goal of traditional psychoanalytic treatment as developed by Freud (Freud, 1913–14/1963) is to bring repressed, unconscious material into conscious awareness. This is accomplished largely through two therapeutic methods. In **free association,** the client speaks freely in therapy, saying whatever comes to mind. **Dream analysis** involves the client relating the events of a dream to the clinician and free associating to these events. The psychoanalyst attempts to interpret the meaning of the dream both from its content and from the associations the client makes to the dream. These methods of accessing the unconscious mind were best accomplished, according to Freud, by having the client recline on a couch, in as relaxed a state as possible.

According to Freud, the psychoanalytic process is stimulated by **transference** in which the client presumably relives conflictual relationships with his or her parents by transferring feelings about them onto the clinician. The clinician best promotes the transference by maintaining an attitude of **neutrality,** not providing any information that would reveal the clinician's preferences, personal background, or reactions to the client's revelations in therapy.

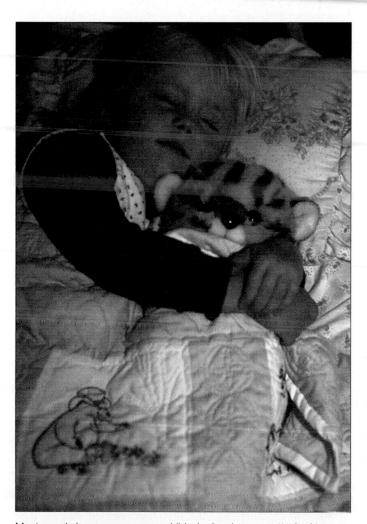

Most people have seen a young child who has become attached to a soft, cuddly toy or "security blanket." According to Winnicott, these are useful "transitional objects." The child transfers attachment from the mother to the object and eventually from the object to people outside the family.

Once conflictual feelings about parents are aroused by evoking transference feelings, the clinician can help the client begin the difficult process of **working through.** In this process, the client is helped to achieve a healthier resolution of these issues than had actually occurred in the early childhood environment. For example, the client might transfer onto the clinician the feelings of having been neglected as a child. With these feelings brought out into the open within the therapeutic relationship, the clinician can explore with the client the reasons for feeling neglected. Over time, the client may learn that it is possible to trust a parent figure (the clinician, in this case), and this realization will help the client feel more secure in relationships outside therapy.

The client's **resistance,** or holding back within the therapy, often impedes the progress of therapy. Confronting unconscious fears and desires is a painful and difficult process, and clients may forget important material, refuse to free associate, or stop therapy altogether to protect themselves from the anxiety associated with this process. An important part of the clinician's job is to help the client overcome resistance through the process of interpretation. For example, if a client consistently arrives late for therapy appointments, the clinician would try to help the client realize that this behavior may reflect an unconscious desire to avoid anxiety.

Although psychoanalysts who broke with the Freudian tradition developed their own theories of personality, their methods of therapy nevertheless relied heavily on Freud's principles of encouraging the client to explore unconscious personality dynamics. Contemporary clinicians who are psychodynamically oriented are likely to base much of their work on object relations views, in which therapy is viewed as an effort to reverse the destructive processes that occurred in the client's early life by providing a new kind of relationship. The clinician attempts to restore, through good "parenting," the client's sense of self and control over the boundaries that define the self.

Evaluation of Psychodynamic Theories

The psychodynamic perspective, just over 100 years old, is still evolving today. Clinicians, researchers, and theorists continue to debate basic issues, such as the role of instincts in shaping the unconscious mind and personality dynamics, the influence of early childhood on later adult functioning, and the role of the clinician in promoting psychological change. The debate centers on several fundamental issues; although these issues are not likely to be resolved in the near future, the writings and research stimulated by this debate have helped refine and clarify some of Freud's most important teachings.

Freud is often given credit for having developed the first comprehensive psychological theory and the first systematic approach to psychotherapy. Although trained in neurology, Freud discovered early in his career that physical symptoms could have psychological causes, and these discoveries formed the cornerstone of a revolutionary approach to understanding the nature and treatment of psychological disorders. Freud can also be credited with introducing into popular culture some

> ## Box 4.1
>
> ### Psychodynamic Approaches to Treating Kristin
>
> A clinician working from a psychodynamic perspective would assume that her difficulties stem from conflicts in early life. Examining the various elements of Kristin's case shows which themes would be important to each of the theorists we have covered. Freud would focus on Kristin's unconscious guilt about feeling angry toward her father for abandoning her through death (Freud, 1917). Interpreting Kristin's resistance to confronting her feelings of grief would also be important. Jung would attempt to help Kristin overcome her conscious unwillingness to speak about her father's death by exploring the symbolic meaning of archetypal images in Kristin's dreams. Adler would suggest that perhaps it is time for Kristin to move on to use her talents and education in a more productive way and to try to establish new friendships. He might see Kristin's lengthy period of unrelenting grief over her father's death as an excuse for not getting involved in a more challenging career or in an intimate relationship.
>
> Horney would help Kristin realize that part of her unhappiness comes from following various "shoulds": she "should" have a higher salary, she "should" be involved in a steady relationship, she "should" have recovered from her father's death. By accepting the reality of her situation, Kristin can become more comfortable with who she really is. Erikson would approach Kristin's depression as being due to unresolved identity and intimacy issues.
>
> The object relations theorists would focus on Kristin's early relationships to her parents, both as she perceived these relationships then and as she perceives them now. A clinician working within this perspective would be alert to problems in early attachment relationships that might be affecting her current difficulty in developing a sense of identity and direction in life.

important psychological concepts that have given people insights into their behavior and have changed the way that Western society views itself.

Just as Freud's theory led to radical alterations in the way psychological disorder was conceptualized, it also led to intense debates in academic circles regarding its scientific validity. Perhaps the most serious charge levied against psychoanalysis is that its major premises are difficult to test through empirical research. Although researchers have made efforts to translate some of Freud's ideas about the unconscious mind into experimental studies (Erdelyi, 1985; Fisher & Greenberg, 1977; Masling, 1983), these attempts have been relatively few in number, and most of the concepts have little hard data to back them up. Furthermore, on logical grounds, Freud's theory contains many assumptions that are difficult to disprove. For instance, if you challenge the Freudian position that anxiety over sexual impulses lies at the root of defense mechanisms, a Freudian might tell you that it is your own anxiety over sexuality that keeps you from acknowledging the role of sexuality in personality.

Other criticisms of psychodynamic theory concern the way Freud characterized women. Feminists have argued strongly against Freud's teachings about women, a position articulated by Horney during Freud's lifetime and carried further by contemporary feminist critics (Chodorow, 1978; Dinnerstein, 1976; Mitchell, 1974; Sayers, 1991).

In broadening the scope of psychodynamic theory to include the relationship between the individual and society, the post-Freudians set the stage for many later theorists and researchers to explore the role or cognitive processes, interpersonal relationships, and social context in the development of personality and psychological disorder. Many studies involving object relations theory have been conducted during the past few decades, particularly on the social behavior of infants and young children. Especially interesting and important has been the work of the late psychologist Mary Salter Ainsworth and her associates (Ainsworth, Blehar, Waters & Wall, 1978), who developed characterizations of infants according **attachment style,** or the way of relating to a caregiver figure. Ainsworth and her colleagues found dramatic evidence pointing to the relationship between the attachment style of infants and subsequent development of competence in social relationships. For example, in one follow-up study of adolescents, by the age of 18 those who had insecure attachment styles as infants were more likely to develop anxiety disorders than those who had shown secure attachment style in early childhood (Warren, Huston, Egeland, & Stroufe, 1997).

Researchers have also adapted the concept of infant attachment style to the ways that individuals relate as adults to significant figures in their lives, such as a romantic partner (Bartholomew, 1997; Hatfield & Rapson, 1994). In one adaptation (Hazan & Shaver, 1994), individuals are classified on the basis of how they say they feel about romantic love relationships. People are classified into one of three attachment styles: secure, ambivalent (or preoccupied), and avoidant (which

Mary Ainsworth, shown on the right, in the laboratory, conducting research on infant attachment.

includes fearful and dismissive). People with a secure attachment style find it easy to relate to others in close relationships and are comfortable with emotional interdependencies. Ambivalent, or preoccupied, individuals seek closeness with others but worry that others will not value them in relationships. For people with a fearful attachment style, relationships create conflict because of the potential for being hurt by rejection, betrayal, or disloyalty within the relationship. Finally, dismissive individuals have little interest in emotional relationships and prefer to remain self-sufficient. Measuring attachment style involves having respondents rate each of these four approaches to relationships as they apply to themselves (see Table 4.2).

The impact of psychodynamic viewpoints continues to be evident in emerging treatment methods. One approach involves the development of forms of treatment that, while relying on interpretation of transference relationships, focus the therapy more intensely on specific issues of current concern to the client (Barber, 1994; Grenyer & Luborsky, 1996; Luborsky, 1984; Malan, 1979; Sifneos, 1979; Sifneos, 1981). Instead of trying to reconstruct the client's personality, the clinician helps the client overcome disappointment in a romantic relationship, or the stress of adjusting to a major life change, such as parenthood. A client may participate in weekly therapy for a prearranged period up to 3 to 4 months. At the end of this period, the client uses the strengths developed in treatment to attempt to cope independently with the life stress or issue. The client may seek therapy again later, when new circumstances arise or the gains from therapy have eroded. Brief psychotherapy is gaining acceptance because of its demonstrated effectiveness (Shadish et al., 1997). Not surprisingly, briefer approaches have been endorsed within managed care health programs (Budman, 1996).

■ Humanistic Perspective

At the core of the **humanistic** perspective is the belief that human motivation is based on an inherent tendency to strive for self-fulfillment and meaning in life. According to humanistic theories of personality, people are motivated by the need to

Freud's theory pointed out the many neurotic aspects of contemporary society that cause us to experience inner conflict.

Table 4.2

Attachment Style Questionnaire

Each of the items below is first rated on a 7-point scale. Then the respondent chooses the one item from the four that best applies to how he or she feels in romantic love relationships.

ATTACHMENT STYLE: Fearful

1. I am uncomfortable getting close to others. I want emotionally close relationships, but I find it difficult to trust others completely, or to depend on them. I worry that I will be hurt if I allow myself to become too close to others.

ATTACHMENT STYLE: Preoccupied

2. I want to be completely emotionally intimate with others, but I often find that others are reluctant to get as close as I would like. I am uncomfortable being without close relationships, but I sometimes worry that others don't value me as much as I value them.

ATTACHMENT STYLE: Dismissive

3. I am comfortable without close emotional relationships. It is very important to me to feel independent and self-sufficient, and I prefer not to depend on others or have others depend on me.

ATTACHMENT STYLE: Secure

4. It is easy for me to become emotionally close to others. I am comfortable depending on others and having others depend on me. I don't worry about being alone or having others not accept me.

understand themselves and the world and to derive greater enrichment from their experiences by fulfilling their unique potential.

The work of humanistic theorists was heavily influenced by **existential** psychology, a theoretical position that emphasizes the importance of fully appreciating each moment as it occurs (May, 1983). According to existential psychology, people who are tuned in to the world around them and experience life as fully as possible in each moment are psychologically healthy. Psychological disorder arises when people are unable to experience this kind of living "in the moment." It is not a fundamental flaw in human nature that causes psychological disorder; rather, people become disturbed because they must live within the restrictions on human freedom that modern society imposes (Frankl, 1963; Laing, 1959).

By the mid-twentieth century, psychologists who were disenchanted with the major theoretical approaches to understanding human behavior and psychological disorder had come to believe that psychology had lost its contact with the "human" side of human behavior. These humanists joined together to form the "third force" in psychology, with the intention of challenging psychoanalysis and behaviorism. Two of the most prominent theorists within this tradition were Carl Rogers and Abraham Maslow.

Person-Centered Theory

The **person-centered theory** of Carl Rogers (1902–1987) focuses on the uniqueness of each individual, the importance of allowing each individual to achieve maximum fulfillment of potential, and the individual's need to confront honestly the reality of his or her experiences in the world. In applying the person-centered theory to the therapy context, Rogers (1951) used the term **client-centered** to reflect his belief that people are innately good and that the potential for self-improvement lies

within the individual, rather than in the therapist or therapeutic techniques.

A central feature of Rogers' theory is the idea that a well-adjusted person's self-image should match, or have **congruence** with, the person's experiences. When this happens, a person is said to be **fully functioning,** with an accurate view of the self and experiences. The term *fully* implies that the individual is putting psychological resources to their maximal use. Conversely, psychological disorder is the result of a blocking of one's potential for living to full capacity, resulting in a state of **incongruence**—a mismatch between a person's self-perception and reality.

As an example of incongruence, consider Noah, a high-school boy who believes he is unpopular but fails to recognize that most of his classmates like him. According to Rogers, Noah's view of himself is "incongruent" with the reality of his situation. By telling himself that he is unpopular, Noah keeps from his awareness the fact that other people try to approach him in an effort to be friendly. You can see how such a situation would lead to problems over time because of his distorted perceptions of reality. These distortions cause Noah to interact with others in ways that lead to frustration rather than happiness.

Rogers regarded the fully functioning person as being in a process of continual evolution and movement, rather than in a static, or fixed, place. The development of these qualities has been an important focus of Rogers' theory (1959) and is the basis for the application of this theory in schools, parent education, and counseling. According to Rogers, psychological disorder develops in an individual who, as a child, is subjected to parents who are too critical and demanding. The child feels overanxious about doing things that will be disapproved of. In this case, the parents are setting up what Rogers referred to as **conditions of worth** or conditions in which the child receives love only when he or she fulfills certain demands. The parents,

According to Rogers, when a parent constantly communicates the message that the child must be "good" to be loved, the child becomes insecure and anxious.

Abraham Lincoln

Harriet Tubman

Martin Luther King, Jr.

Mother Teresa

in effect, tell the child, "If you want us to love you, you have to meet our conditions. That is the only way we will treat you as a worthy person." Children then become so fearful of being punished that they cannot admit to having done something "wrong," and the stage is set for a lifetime of low self-esteem.

Self-Actualization Theory

Related to Rogers' views of the fully functioning person is the theory Abraham Maslow (1962) developed, which centers on the notion of **self-actualization,** the maximum realization of the individual's potential for psychological growth. It is perhaps because of this focus on healthy human functioning that Maslow's theory has gained popularity as a guide to optimal living in such contexts as personnel management and human resources. Maslow's theory also focuses on motivation, in that he wanted to draw attention to the experiences that propel people toward realizing their fullest potential. According to Maslow, self-actualized people are accurate in their self-perceptions and are able to find rich sources of enjoyment and stimulation in their everyday activities. They are capable of **peak experiences** in which they feel a tremendous surge of inner happiness, as if they were totally in harmony with themselves and their world. But these individuals are not simply searching for sensual or spiritual pleasure. They also have a philosophy of life that is based on humanitarian and egalitarian values.

Maslow's theory is best known, perhaps, for its pyramid-like structure, which he called the **hierarchy of needs,** which describes the order in which human needs must be fulfilled (see Figure 4.2).

The basic premise of the hierarchy is that, for people to achieve a state of self-actualization, they must have satisfied a variety of more basic physical and psychological needs. Needs that are lower on the hierarchy are called **deficit needs,** because they describe a state in which the individual seeks to obtain something that is lacking. An individual who is still struggling to meet those needs cannot progress to the top of the pyramid.

Maslow's theory is as much a philosophy of life as it is a psychological theory. In part, this is because Maslow based his concept not on psychotherapy patients but on observations of the lives of extraordinary people who were extremely productive and who seemed to have reached their maximum potential. The individuals shown here are examples of such self-actualized people.

Maslow would contend that a philosopher who is hungry is unable to philosophize. Of course, there are exceptions, in which people sacrifice their lower-order needs, even their lives, to achieve self-actualization. People who climb Mt. Everest, take off on a space mission, go on a hunger strike, or risk their lives to protest unjust military leaders are risking a variety of deficit needs. The underlying assumption is still that at some point in their lives these individuals satisfied their deficit needs, and for the purpose of achieving self-actualization, were able to set them aside.

Like Rogers, Maslow (1971) defined *psychological disorder* in terms of the degree of deviation from an ideal state and had similar views about the conditions that hamper self-actualization. To progress beyond the "deficit" needs, children must feel a stable sense of being physically cared for, safe from harm, loved, and esteemed. They must also be allowed to express the higher-level needs required to achieve actualization. For example, a person who is raised in an environment of dishonesty is deprived in satisfaction of the need for truth and becomes cynical and mistrusting as a result.

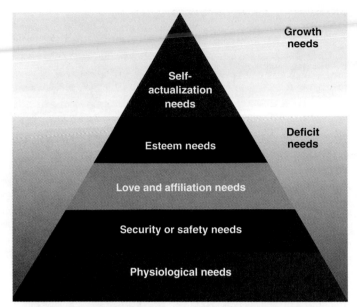

Figure 4.2   The hierarchy of needs according to Maslow's theory

In Maslow's hierarchy of needs, it is assumed that lower-order (deficit) needs must be met before self-actualization can be achieved.

Treatment

According to Rogers' client-centered approach, therapy should focus on the needs of the client, rather than on the predetermined views of the clinician. A clinician's job is to help clients discover their inherent goodness and in the process to help each client achieve greater self-understanding. To counteract the problems caused by conditions of worth in childhood, Rogers recommended that therapists treat clients with **unconditional positive regard.** This method involves total acceptance of what the client says, does, and feels. As clients feel better about themselves, they become better able to tolerate the anxiety associated with acknowledging weaknesses. The clinician tries to be as empathic as possible and attempts to see the client's situation as it appears to the client.

Therapists working within the client-centered model often use such techniques as reflection and clarification. In reflection, the therapist mirrors back what the client has just said, perhaps rephrasing it slightly. For example, the client might say, "I'm really down today, because last week my girlfriend told me to get lost." The therapist's reflection of this statement might be, "So, when your girlfriend threatens to leave you, it makes you feel sad." In clarification, the therapist clarifies a vague or poorly formulated statement the client makes about how he feels. If the client says, "I'm really mad at my girlfriend for the lousy way she treated me," the therapist might say, "And perhaps you're very sad about that too."

Rogers also maintained that clinicians should provide a model of genuineness and willingness to disclose their personal weaknesses and limitations. Presumably, clients can learn a great deal from observing these behaviors in the therapist. Ideally, the client will see that it is acceptable and healthy to be honest in confronting one's experiences, even if those experiences have less than favorable implications. For example, the Rogerian clinician might admit to having experiences similar to those the client describes, such as feeling anxious about speaking before a group.

In contrast to the detailed therapy methods Rogers described, Maslow did not specify a particular model of therapy, because he developed his ideas in an academic context, rather than through clinical observation and treatment. His theory presents more of a map for optimal human development than a concrete basis for treatment of psychological disorders.

Evaluation of Humanistic Theories

The humanistic approach has generated a considerable body of research based on the ideas of both Rogers and Maslow. Much of this research was conducted by the originators of these theories, both of whom were interested in translating their ideas into measurable concepts. Maslow developed his theory on the basis of case studies, gathered from 60 individuals, which involved combining biographical information about each individual's life with extensive interviews. His sample was purposefully limited to individuals showing signs of optimal psychological functioning, because Maslow maintained that psychology had ignored the study of healthy individuals in favor of those who suffered from various forms of psychopathology (Maslow, 1954–1970). Maslow's ideas have been widely applied in industry and business, as in the notion that worker productivity can be enhanced by satisfying self-actualization needs; if workers feel personally involved in what they do, they will presumably be happier and more productive.

Rogers was interested in researching two central facets of the client-centered approach: self-concept and the therapy process. In his research on self-concept, Rogers focused on the extent to which a person experiences incongruence between the

---

Box 4.2

Humanistic Approaches to Treating Kristin

As an approach to treating a client like Kristin, humanistic therapists would focus on providing her with a secure sense of positive self-regard. Consistent with Carl Rogers' emphasis on becoming more aware of one's feelings, Kristin would be encouraged to experience more fully her feelings regarding her father's death and to link her sadness about his passing with her overall dissatisfaction with her life. In this process, the clinician would help Kristin identify her feelings and accept them without undue self-criticism. In keeping with the concept of therapist self-disclosure, the clinician might share with Kristin personal reactions to losses or feelings of sadness in hearing Kristin talk about the hurt she has experienced.

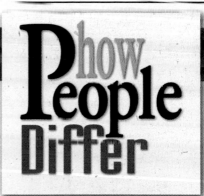

Feminist-Relational Approaches to Therapy

Imagine a young woman who consults a therapist for the first time. Since marrying, she has become depressed, as she finds it difficult to balance the demands of marriage and her desire for a career. How might a therapist develop a formulation of this young woman's presenting problem? The answer to this question, as you know by now, depends on the therapist's theoretical orientation. When offering hypotheses about psychological problems, psychodynamic therapists have traditionally focused on deficits and problems in early development with a parent, usually the mother; however, over the past several decades, prominent female authors have criticized this approach for neglecting crucial aspects of women's psychological development (Brodsky & Steinberg, 1995).

Influenced by the advances in women's rights and by dissatisfaction with an emphasis on male development in psychological theory and research, feminist authors have proposed an alternative view of psychodynamic therapy, emphasizing the importance of relationships in the lives of women. These writers (Brodsky & Steinberg, 1995; Miller, 1001) assert that traditional dynamic theories have been dominated by a masculine point of view that blames mothers for inadequate parenting. Earlier theorists neglected the social disadvantages women encountered and tended to define psychological health in terms of masculine ideals of independence and self-reliance. In place of such approaches, these contemporary authors offer a conceptualization of women's development based on the ability to form mature and nurturing relationships, a theme that is carried over in innovative approaches to psychodynamic psychotherapy with female clients.

Dynamic theorists have traditionally viewed development in terms of separation from parental or maternal authority, as the individual goes on to acquire an autonomous sense of self. Feminist authors, such as Nancy Chodorow (1978) and Jean Baker Miller (1976), suggest an alternative. Both boys and girls usually form their first and closest emotional bond with their mother. During development, boys must recognize differences between themselves and their mothers, which may mark the onset of the process of separation. Girls, on the other hand, might proceed along a different track. They do not have to incorporate this recognition of gender differences, so they are able to maintain a consistent relationship with their mothers based on their innate physical and psychological similarities. While boys are encouraged to separate and individuate (Mahler et al., 1975), the development of girls continues uninterrupted in the context of the maternal relationship and caring for others (Brodsky & Steinberg, 1995; Otivor, 1991)

Miller (1991) suggests that therapists who encourage traditional notions of separation and autonomy actually fail their female clients. They may neglect the importance of relationships to the psychological health of women. When female clients emphasize the importance of relationships in their lives, some therapists mistakenly see these clients as being excessively dependent on others for happiness and satisfaction. Contemporary theorists contend that, from a relational perspective, a therapist who urges a female client toward independence is doing her a serious disservice and may contribute to a deepening of her psychological symptoms. Instead, women should be encouraged to develop a sense of self based on their ability to care for themselves in the context of caring for others. The goals of therapy should involve growth in the capacity for connectedness with others, rather than independence from others (Jordan, 1991).

Returning to the example of the woman struggling to choose between her career and her marriage, a relationally oriented therapist might help a client consider the implications of each alternative in terms of the client's feelings and important relationships. Her therapist would help her understand and appreciate her own need to determine the course of her life and develop intimate and mutually supportive relationships.

"actual self" and the "ideal self." The aim of therapy would be to reduce incongruence between a client's self-concept and the person he or she would like to be. Rogerian concepts about therapy emphasized the factors that contribute to successful psychotherapy, such as the therapist's empathy. Many contemporary clinicians, irrespective of theoretical orientation, acknowledge the importance of empathy (Kahn, 1991). The teaching of empathic communication styles has become integrated into current models of self-help, counseling, and advising programs.

Research on the effectiveness of client-centered therapy has not gone without criticism. Lacking in this research are some of the fundamental requirements for a scientific approach, such as using appropriate control groups or adopting acceptable levels of statistical significance in evaluating outcome. Although some advocates of the client-centered model are open to the importance of research, they have not been particularly successful at ensuring that their work is scientifically rigorous. There are several reasons for this, some have to do with the fact that the humanistic perspective relies heavily on the individual's

Table 4.3

Items from a Self-Actualization Scale

1. I do not feel ashamed of any of my emotions.
2. I feel I must do what others expect of me.
3. I believe that people are essentially good and can be trusted.
4. I feel free to be angry at those I love.
5. It is always necessary that others approve of what I do.
6. I don't accept my own weaknesses.
7. I can like people without having to approve of them.
8. I fear failure.
9. I avoid attempts to analyze and simplify complex domains.
10. It is better to be yourself than be popular.
11. I have no mission in life to which I can feel especially dedicated.
12. I can express my feelings even when they may result in undesirable consequences.
13. I do not feel responsible to help anybody.
14. I am bothered by fears of being inadequate.
15. I am loved because I give love.

High self-actualization scores result from agreeing with items 1, 3, 4, 7, 10, 12, and 15, and disagreeing with the rest.

self-report of psychological functioning, rather than objective assessment.

Humanistic theorists and clinicians saw their ideas as a radical departure from the traditional focus of psychology, which minimized the role of free will in human experience. These theorists also saw human behavior in much more positive terms and viewed psychological disorder as the result of restricted growth potential. It is clear today that, although humanistic theories have limitations and do not play a central role in the understanding of psychological disorder, their influence has been widespread and is felt in many indirect ways.

Sociocultural Perspective

Theorists within the **sociocultural perspective** emphasize the ways that individuals are influenced by people, social institutions, and social forces in the world around them. As we discussed in Chapter 1, these influences can be organized into those that have an immediate impact on the person, such as the family, and more far-reaching circles, such as society. Unlike the other theoretical perspectives covered in this chapter, the sociocultural perspective is a more loosely connected set of orientations. Theorists within this perspective tend to focus on one or more realms of influence, but all share an emphasis on factors external to the individual as the cause of psychological disorder.

Family Perspective

Proponents of the **family perspective** see abnormality as caused by disturbances in the patterns of interactions and re-

lationships that exist within the family. Although there are distinct theories within the family perspective, all share a focus on **family dynamics**, the interactions among family members. There are four major approaches within the family perspective: intergenerational, structural, strategic, and experiential (Sharf, 1996). Murray Bowen's intergenerational approach emphasizes the ways in which the parents' experiences in their own families of origin affect their interactions with their children; parents who experienced family dysfunction in their own childhoods are likely to repeat these disturbed patterns when raising their children. In the structural approach, Salvador Minuchin assumes that, in normal families, parents and children have distinct roles, and there are boundaries between the generations; problems can arise when family members are too close or too distant. Jay Haley proposed the strategic approach, in which the focus is placed on the resolution of family problems, with particular attention to power relationships within the family. Within the experiential approach, such theorists as Carl Whitaker emphasize the unconscious and emotional processes of families; dysfunctional behavior results from interference with personal growth.

Family theorists have made important contributions to the understanding and treatment of people with various disorders. Consider the examples of eating disorders and schizophrenia. As you will read in Chapter 14, some experts on eating disorders have suggested that the girls and young women who starve themselves are acting out a wish to assert their independence from their parents. Eating disorders may also arise from other family disturbances, such as conflictual relationships, parental withholding of affection, or familial chaos. In Chapter 10, you will read how some researchers

According to family systems theories, the cause of psychological disorder lies in family relationships.

believe that a person with schizophrenia can be profoundly affected by a disturbed pattern of interactions within the family. Thus, in a family in which members are critical, hostile, and emotionally overinvolved with each other, a person with schizophrenia is more likely to experience symptoms of the disorder.

Neglect and abuse are also important factors that increase vulnerability to psychological disorder. For example, some theorists contend that dissociative identity disorder, formerly known as "multiple personality disorder," is a response to early abuse; in this condition alternate identities emerge from a fantasy world markedly different from the horrors of the real home life. Researchers attempting to understand personality disorders also focus on the early life experiences of these individuals, especially circumstances involving trauma and abuse within the family. For example, many people with borderline personality disorder (a condition involving a pervasive pattern of instability in relationships) are thought to have difficulty with intimate adult relationships, because they fear they will be subjected to the same harsh treatment they experienced as children.

Social Discrimination

It is an unfortunate but well-recognized fact that many people experience discrimination because of gender, race, or age and that stresses associated with such discrimination can cause psychological problems. For example, as long ago as the 1950s, social scientists assessing the personal effects of discrimination showed that psychological disturbance is more commonly diagnosed among people of lower social class (Hollingshead & Redlich, 1959). In trying to explain this relationship, researchers have focused on the fact that people of lower social class experience many economic hardships and have limited access to quality education, health care, and employment. Many people within the lower classes are also members of ethnic or racial minorities, for whom the power of socioeconomic discrimination is compounded. Furthermore, the stressful environ-

ments in which they live—with high rates of poverty, crime, substance abuse, and unemployment—make matters even worse. The intense stress with which they contend on a daily basis adversely affects their physical and mental health, and for many it leads to premature death (Lantz et al., 1998). Although discriminatory processes associated with social class differ from those pertaining to gender and age, the impact can be similar. When people are given few opportunities or when they encounter oppression because of unalterable human characteristics, they are likely to experience inner turmoil, frustration, and stress, which lead to the development of psychological symptoms.

Social Influences and Historical Events

In addition to personal attributes, such as gender or social class, we can all be adversely affected by general societal forces. For example, Theodore Millon (1998), a major researcher in the area of personality disorders, contends that fluid and inconsistent societal values have contributed to the increase in these disorders in Western society. He believes that social instability and a lack of clear cultural norms make their way into the home, causing children to feel that life is unpredictable and causing them to become more prone to developing psychological disorders later in life.

Psychological disorders can also emerge as a result of destructive historical events, such as the violence of a political revolution, the turmoil of a natural disaster, or the poverty of a nationwide depression. Since World War I, American psychologists have conducted large-scale studies of the ways in which war negatively affects psychological functioning. As you will read in Chapter 6, people who are traumatized as the result of exposure to battle, persecution, or imprisonment are at risk for developing serious anxiety disorders. Similarly, fires and natural disasters, such as earthquakes, tornadoes, and hurricanes, leave more than physical destruction in their wake.

Treatment

How do clinicians intervene with people suffering from conditions caused or exacerbated by sociocultural factors? Clearly, it is not possible to "change the world." However, clinicians can play a crucial role in helping people come to grips with problems that have developed within a family system, the immediate environment, or extended society.

Family Therapy

In family therapy, the family is encouraged to try new ways of relating to each other or thinking about their problems. The family therapist, sometimes working with a co-therapist, meets with as many family members as possible. To facilitate communication, family therapists commonly use techniques that would be considered unusual in individual psychotherapy. For example, it is not unusual for the therapist to move around the room, sitting next to one family member for a period of time and then getting up to sit near another. The purpose of doing so may be to draw attention to individual family members or to establish an emotional alliance with a family member who appears to be resistant to the therapy process. At other times, the therapist may initiate a conversation between two family members and "coach" them as they talk to one another, so that the family begins to see their relationship from the therapist's perspective. Some family therapists conduct sessions in rooms with one-way mirrors, so that colleagues can observe and provide ideas and suggestions for improvements.

The particular techniques used in the therapy depend greatly on the training and theoretical approach of the family therapist. An intergenerational family therapist might suggest drawing a genogram, a diagram of all relatives in the recent past, in an effort to understand the history of family relationships and to use this understanding to bring about change. A structural family therapist might suggest that one of the family members enact a disagreement as if they were characters in a play about the family. Strategic family therapists would work with family members to develop solutions to the issues that are causing difficulty. An experiential family therapist might work with the family members to develop insight into their relationships with each other.

Group Therapy

For many troubled people, the experience of sharing their stories and experiences with other, similar people can be life changing. Irvin Yalom (1995), a prominent group therapy theorist, speaks of several factors in the group experience that are therapeutic. Clients in therapy groups commonly find relief and hope in the realization that their problems are not unique. In the group, they can acquire valuable information and advice from people who share their concerns. Furthermore, in the process of giving to others, people generally find that they themselves derive benefit. For some individuals, the group can compensate for painful and unsatisfactory experiences in their families of origin, as clients have the opportunity to develop more appropriate social skills and to imitate the successful behavior of peers in a context that facilitates corrective and cathartic emotional experiences.

Often the best advice can be provided by other people experiencing the same condition. This principle has been well documented with peer groups—such as Alcoholics Anonymous, in which recovering alcoholics share their histories of substance abuse and the methods they use to abstain from drugs and alcohol. Group therapy in a more formal structure also has been a component of the treatment protocol for many other conditions. For example, clinicians treating pedophiles, people who have sexually abused children, have demonstrated that group therapy is especially effective in confronting denial and rationalizations, while providing pedophiles with a supportive context conducive to frank discussions of their urges and methods of self-control (Berlin, 1998).

Some clinicians find it particularly valuable to include a group therapy component in the treatment of people with eating disorders. As with substance abusers and pedophiles, eating-disordered clients can benefit from hearing the stories of people like themselves whose capacity for understanding the nature of the condition is especially insightful.

Milieu Therapy

Another form of therapy that is based on intervention in the environment, rather than with the individual alone, is **milieu therapy,** in which staff and clients in a treatment setting work as a therapeutic community to promote positive functioning in clients. Members of the community participate in group activities, ranging from occupational therapy to training classes. Staff members encourage clients to work with and spend time with other residents, even when leaving on passes. The entire community is involved in decision making, sometimes including an executive council, with elected members from units of the treatment setting. Every staff person, whether a therapist, nurse, or paraprofessional, takes part in the overall mission of providing an environment that supports positive change and appropriate social behaviors.

Box 4.3

Sociocultural Approaches to Treating Kristin

Family therapists treating Kristin would focus on various aspects of her family, both before and after her father's suicide. Most family therapists would prefer that Kristin be treated not as an individual client but as a member of a family; as such, they would suggest that Kristin's mother and three sisters participate in the therapy. Regardless of the specific approach, her father's powerful suicide message, that he "felt unloved" would play a central role in understanding and treating this dysfunctional system.

An intergenerational theorist, such as Murray Bowen would focus on the childhood experiences of Kristin's patterns in an attempt to understand how the stage was set for the tragedy that unfolded in Kristin's immediate family. The therapist might suggest drawing a genogram in an effort to understand the history of family relationships to use this understanding to bring about change.

Salvador Minuchin would focus on the structure of the family before and after the suicide. A structural therapist might ask one or more of the family members to enact a conflict in the family therapy session, such as an argument that might have taken place just prior to the suicide.

A strategic therapist would return to Jay Haley's problem solving approach and help Kristin's family members look for ways to move beyond their current state of grief and dysfunction.

Carl Whitaker would take a more humanistic and experiential approach to treating Kristin and her family by trying to help the family grow beyond the tragedy, learn how to express their feelings, and to appreciate the unique aspects of each family member.

In addition to recommending family therapy for Kristin, a clinician, such as Irvin Yalom, might also suggest that she participate in group therapy, particularly with a focus on bereavement. By hearing the stories and experiences of others who have lost loved ones, Kristin might come to the realization that her reactions are not unique. The insights shared by others might help her move out of her grief. Furthermore, the help she provides others might prove to be therapeutically beneficial to Kristin.

The underlying idea behind milieu therapy is that the pressure to conform to conventional social norms of behavior discourages a severely disturbed client, such as a person with schizophrenia, from expressing problematic symptoms. The "normalizing" effects of such an environment are intended to help the individual make a smoother and more effective transition to life outside the therapeutic community.

Evaluation of the Sociocultural Perspective

For the past several decades, clinicians have recognized the role of contextual factors in causing and maintaining abnormality, while also realizing that changing systems can be extremely difficult. For example, the detrimental effects of discrimination are widely recognized, but the solutions to this divisive social problem are not apparent. On a more local level, a client's family may play a central role in causing or aggravating a psychological problem, but these other people may be resistant to or unavailable for participation in treatment. In such cases, family therapy would not be possible, even if it were the treatment of choice. Although group therapy may be quite beneficial, many individuals are unwilling to disclose their problems to people they perceive to be strangers, because they feel ashamed or too shy.

As important as the sociocultural model is to understanding the causes and treatment of psychological disorders, this perspective does have significant limitations. In recent years, the importance of biological determinants has resulted in a devaluing of the role of family systems factors for certain disorders. For example, no credible contemporary theorist would support theories, considered tenable earlier in the century, that schizophrenia could be caused by disturbed family relationships. Science has certainly gone beyond such naive assumptions. At the same time, however, as previously noted, some experts believe that disturbed family communication can aggravate schizophrenic symptomatology. For most psychological disorders, the sociocultural perspective provides a valuable lens for looking at psychological disorders, but most conditions are best viewed from a viewpoint that also includes attention to psychological and biological forces.

Behavioral and Cognitively Based Perspectives

In this section, we will discuss two perspectives that focus on behaviors and thought processes. According to the **behavioral perspective** abnormality is caused by faulty learning experiences, and, according to the **cognitive-behavioral perspective** abnormality is caused by maladaptive thought processes, which result in dysfunctional behavior. The cognitive-behavioral perspective is sometimes referred to simply as "cognitive," although most people who work in this field prefer "cognitive-behavioral" (Craighead, Craighead, Kazdin & Mahoney, 1994).

As you read the sections that follow, you will see how early behaviorists focused exclusively on observable behaviors, but over time they expanded their views to include a broader consideration of the relationship between thoughts and behaviors. The early behavioral psychologists resisted elaborate speculations about the "whys" of behavior, preferring to look at the "whats." In looking for "what" behaviors occur, they attempted to determine the functional relationships between events in the environment and the individual's behaviors. We will begin with a review of the principles of classical and operant conditioning, which lie at the heart of the behavioral perspective on psychological disorder.

Classical Conditioning

According to behaviorists, many of our automatic, emotional reactions are acquired through the process of **classical conditioning,** in which we associate a reflexive response with an unrelated stimulus. For instance, the smell of a certain brand of cologne may make you feel unaccountably sad, until you realize that this was the cologne you wore when you saw the movie *Titanic*. In this example, you formed an association between an originally neutral stimulus (the cologne) and a naturally evoking stimulus (seeing the romantic hero die), which produces an emotional reaction (becoming teary-eyed). This connection is formed through repeated pairings of the two kinds of stimuli. The neutral stimulus is called the **conditioned stimulus,** because only after conditioning does it cause the response. The naturally evoking stimulus is called the **unconditioned stimulus,** because it produces the response before any conditioning

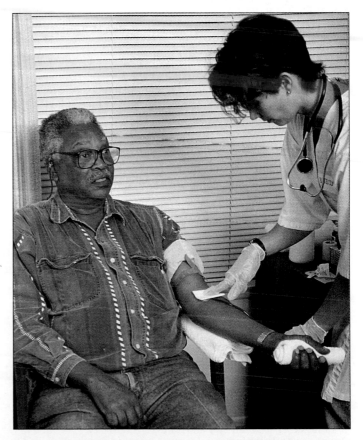

A frightening experience with a medical procedure during childhood can provoke intense fears that last throughtout life.

takes place. The emotional reaction, once it has become associated with the conditioned stimulus (cologne), is called the **conditioned response.** Prior to conditioning, this reflex is called the **unconditioned response;** in other words, no learning is necessary for you to begin to cry when you witness the death of the heroine's lover.

As an explanation of psychological disorder, the classical conditioning paradigm accounts for acquiring or learning, through conditioning, the emotional reactions that interfere with a person's ability to carry out everyday tasks. For example, 6-year-old Jerry has been accidentally locked in a dark closet. The next time he needs something from that closet, he might feel nervous, almost panicky. His problem will become exacerbated through **generalization,** the expansion of learning from the original situation to one that is similar. For example, he may feel uncomfortable when he has to ride in an elevator, another enclosed space. This kind of reaction, called **stimulus generalization,** takes place when a person responds in the same way to stimuli that have some common properties. By contrast, **discrimination** is the process in which learning becomes increasingly specific to a given situation. Perhaps Jerry comes to realize that he will not be harmed if he rides the elevator, because it is not the same as a dark, locked closet. Differentiating between two stimuli that possess similar but essentially different characteristics is called **stimulus discrimination.**

One of the best known examples of conditioned fear is "Little Albert," an 11-month-old infant who was studied by John B. Watson (1878–1958), one of the most prominent early behaviorists. Watson and his associate, Rosalie Rayner, conducted an infamous set of experiments in which Albert was exposed to a loud noise while he petted a white rat; Albert subsequently acquired a fear of white rats. Their experiment represented a form of **aversive conditioning,** in which an aversive or a painful stimulus (the noise) was paired with an initially neutral stimulus (the rat). Albert's conditioned fear of rats generalized to other white, furry objects. Fortunately, this kind of experiment is now forbidden by ethical guidelines for research on human subjects; furthermore, its scientific merits have been questioned.

Even though Watson's analysis may have been misguided, we can draw inferences from it regarding how people acquire irrational fears. You can probably think of instances when you were exposed to a similar kind of aversive conditioning. Perhaps you ate too much pizza and became ill shortly afterward. The following week, when going by a pizzeria, you started to feel queasy. The pizza, previously a neutral or positive stimulus, acquired an aversive meaning for you. This particular principle is very useful in certain forms of behavior therapy, as in the treatment of alcoholism. As you will see in Chapter 13, one form of treatment involves giving a person a medication that causes nausea when alcohol is consumed. The individual then learns to associate alcohol with nausea; theoretically, this should reduce the frequency of alcohol consumption.

Operant Conditioning

Operant conditioning is a learning process in which an individual acquires a set of behaviors through reinforcement. In contrast to classical conditioning, operant conditioning involves the learning of behaviors that are not automatic. The learner tries to become proficient at performing behaviors that will lead to a positive outcome, such as attention, praise, or the satisfaction of a biological need. The "positive" outcome could also consist of the removal of an unpleasant or aversive circumstance. If your next-door neighbor's stereo is blasting, you may "operate" on the environment by making a phone call requesting that it be turned down. Your behavior results in the removal of an aversive stimulus.

The principles of operant conditioning were developed by B.F. Skinner, who, along with Freud, is probably one of the most well-known names in psychology. Of course, Skinner's theory is diametrically opposed to Freud's, inasmuch as it emphasizes that observable behavior is the only appropriate subject matter for psychology. Like Freud, however, Skinner's ideas about behavior became the basis for a broad-ranging philosophy about human nature.

In your introductory psychology class you probably learned that Skinner was the originator of operant conditioning. He developed the "Skinner box," a device containing a mechanism that delivers food pellets when the occupant pushes a lever. Using this mechanism, Skinner taught pigeons a number of "tricks," including pecking out a tune on a xylophone and playing Ping-Pong. These antics proved instructive, however, for studying the fundamental processes involved in learning

Burrhus Frederick Skinner (1904–1990) grew up in a small town in Pennsylvania. An English major in college, Skinner tried a career as a writer but soon gave it up for the study of psychology. He received his doctorate from Harvard and later returned there as a professor.

complex behaviors. Skinner moved considerably beyond the laboratory in his theories, with ideas that helped shape later advances in the field of childhood education and the treatment of psychologically disturbed individuals. Particularly noteworthy was Skinner's preference for the use of positive rewards in bringing about desirable changes in people, rather than using punishment or other aversive techniques. *Walden Two,* his view of utopia, was one in which positive reinforcement was the main basis for promoting socialization and human development (Skinner, 1953).

Reinforcement is the principle that underlies Skinner's model of operant conditioning. *Reinforce* means "to strengthen"; think of **reinforcement** as the "strengthening" of a behavior, increasing the likelihood that the behavior will be performed again. You can probably recall many examples in which your own behavior was reinforced. Perhaps a friend responded positively to an expression you used in conversation. Soon you realize you are using that expression quite often. Your friend's laughter served as a positive reinforcer that increased the frequency of your remark-making behavior. Extending this principle to psychological disorder, you can see how a disturbed behavior that is reinforced may become ingrained in a person. For example, an overprotective parent may inadvertently reinforce a child's pathological dependency by consoling the child with hugs, kisses, and cookies every time the child expresses a minor fear.

As these examples imply, there can be many kinds of reinforcers. The ones that satisfy a biological need (hunger, thirst, relief from pain, sex) are called **primary reinforcers,** because they are intrinsically rewarding. Behavior is also driven by **secondary reinforcers,** which derive their value from association with primary reinforcers. Money is a good example of a secondary reinforcer, because its value comes from the fact that it can be used to obtain primary reinforcers. As you will see later, some forms of behavior therapy use "tokens" as reinforcers, which are like money in that they can be used to purchase special treats or privileges.

Other kinds of secondary reinforcers do not have material value but are reinforcing for other reasons. Praise, attention, and recognition are rewarding to us as adults because earlier in our lives they were associated with the pleasurable feelings of being fed and held by a parent. The value of secondary reinforcers extends beyond the family, in such areas as school, work, hobbies, and athletics. Secondary reinforcers can also be involved in the acquisition of various forms of abnormal behavior. For example, a hypochondriacal person who exaggerates the severity of normal physical signs may derive secondary reinforcement in the form of attention from family, friends, or health care professionals.

In operant, as in classical, conditioning, reinforcement can have a pleasurable or unpleasurable effect. So far, our discussion has focused on **positive reinforcement,** in which a person repeats a behavior that leads to a reward. Sometimes, individuals operate on the environment to remove an unpleasant stimulus, as in the case of your request that the neighbor turn the stereo down. The removal of the unpleasant stimulus is called **negative reinforcement.**

It is easy to confuse negative reinforcement with the idea that a person is being penalized for engaging in a certain behavior. However, **punishment** involves applying an aversive stimulus, such as scolding, which is intended to reduce the frequency of the behavior that preceded the punishment. When a parent scolds a misbehaving boy, the presumption is that the scolding will cause the child to stop misbehaving. If you receive a speeding ticket, this punishment is intended to stop you from speeding in the future.

The purpose of negative reinforcement is to increase, not decrease, the frequency of the behavior that preceded it. For example, the parent of the misbehaving boy may tell him that, as soon as he does what he is told, the scolding will stop. Your call to the neighbor stops the aggravating noise of the stereo. Negative reinforcement makes it more likely that you will repeat the behavior that succeeded in removing the unpleasant stimulus. Behaviorists prefer negative reinforcement to punishment, because research has shown that punishment has unpredictable effects on behavior. For example, a child who is spanked may rebel, learn to fear the parent, or even imitate the parent by being physically aggressive with peers and siblings.

In the absence of reinforcement, most learned behaviors tend to diminish and finally cease. If you go to your favorite music store and find that it is unexpectedly closed for the afternoon, you might return one or two more times, but, if this keeps happening, eventually you will stop going there. **Extinction** is the term used to describe the cessation of behavior in the absence of reinforcement. In treating a behavior problem, such as that of a girl who yells out answers in the classroom, the teacher might attempt to extinguish the behavior by ignoring the child, thereby withholding the reinforcement provided by attention. At the same time, the teacher would strengthen appropriate behaviors by attending to the child only when she raises her hand to answer a question.

We have discussed the learning of relatively simple behaviors. However, operant conditioning is also intended to apply to the acquisition of skilled new behavior, such as learning language or becoming a proficient musician. **Shaping** is the process of reinforcing increasingly complex behaviors that come to resemble a desired outcome. It is the method an animal trainer uses, for example, to teach a dolphin to jump through a hoop. The dolphin does not naturally perform this behavior but is capable of doing so with the right incentives. The trainer establishes this "operant" behavior in stages until the desired response sequence is completely established. Shaping is an important component in certain behavioral treatments when combined with other methods of reinforcement, as you will see shortly.

Social Learning and Social Cognition

Many parents object to their children watching television programs with violent or adult content, particularly in recent years, in which murders committed by high-school students have raised national attention. The concern is that children will see that violent behavior produces outcomes desirable to the perpetrator and, therefore, will be inclined to act in a similar fashion. The process of acquiring new responses by imitating the behavior of another person, called **modeling,** has been studied by behaviorists who focus on **social learning.** Theorists who work within social learning theory are interested in understanding how people develop psychological disorders through their relationships with others and through observation of other people. Some theorists within this perspective also focus on **social cognition,** the factors that influence the way people perceive themselves and others and form judgments about the causes of behavior. According to these perspectives, not only do direct reinforcements influence behavior, but so do indirect reinforcements, which people acquire by watching others engaging in particular behaviors and seeing them being rewarded or punished.

According to social learning theorist Albert Bandura (b. 1925), when you watch someone else being reinforced for a behavior, you receive **vicarious reinforcement** because you identify with that person (called the "model") and put yourself in that person's place. When the model is reinforced, it is as if you are being reinforced as well. This kind of reinforcement is the underlying process through which advertisements have their effect. People in beer commercials seem to be having a good time with their attractive friends, so, if you want to have a good time and be popular, you should drink that beer!

Social learning theory was considered revolutionary when it was first proposed, because it expanded the realm of influence of learning from direct consequences of behavior to the many indirect reinforcements that exist in life. Furthermore, social learning theory added the idea that people acquire "expectancies" for reinforcement as part of the learning process. This was a step toward a more cognitively oriented form of behavioral theory, which focuses on the role of thoughts and ideas in influences on behavior. Gradually, social learning theory has come to be known as **social cognitive theory** because of its increased focus on thought processes and how they influence overt behavior.

One important contribution of the social learning and social cognitive theories was to show how maladaptive behaviors are learned through observing other people engaging in these behaviors and seeing them receive rewards. The process of vicarious reinforcement can explain why parents who were abused as children are more likely to be physically violent with their own children. A boy who observes his father beating his mother may batter his own wife years later.

Bandura has also become known for his work on **self-efficacy,** the individual's perception of competence in various life situations. According to Bandura, people will try harder to succeed in difficult tasks if they are confident that they can complete these tasks. The concept of self-efficacy can be applied to a variety of psychological phenomena (Bandura, 1997), including motivation, self-esteem, addictions, and interpersonal relations. People who lack self-efficacy in a given situation can be trained to increase their confidence in their abilities to succeed, thus, enhancing their feelings of self-worth.

Cognitively Based Theory

Although many have contributed to cognitive approaches, two individuals are particularly prominent in this field: Aaron Beck (b. 1921), and Albert Ellis (b. 1913). Both emphasize the role of disturbed thinking processes in causing maladaptive behavior.

According to Beck, a pervasive feature of many psychological disorders is the existence of **automatic thoughts**—ideas so deeply entrenched that the individual is not even aware that they lead to feelings of unhappiness and discouragement. (Beck drops the word *behavioral,* referring to his approach simply as cognitive theory.) Automatic thoughts appear to arise spontaneously and are difficult to ignore. For example, in conversation with a friend, a person might start to think "What a boring person I am," "That was a dumb thing to say," or "Why can't I be more clever and interesting?" Beck compared automatic thoughts to the "shoulds" described by Horney, which lead the person to try to achieve unrealistic goals of perfection. In the case of depression, automatic thoughts are inevitably followed by sadness, because these thoughts are so discouraging (Beck, Rush, Shaw & Emery, 1979).

Automatic thoughts are the product of **dysfunctional attitudes,** personal rules or values people hold that interfere with adequate adjustment. The sample items in Table 4.4 from the Dysfunctional Attitudes Scale give an idea of the range of beliefs in this domain. These attitudes prime the individual who is prone to depression to interpret experiences in negative ways through faulty logical processes, as shown in Figure 4.3. Automatic thoughts emerge from this process, leading to the negative emotion of depression. In other psychological disorders, automatic thoughts of a different nature prevail. However, whatever form of disorder is involved, the process through which negative emotions follow from these thoughts remains the central focus of cognitive theory.

Ellis describes a linkage of cognitive and emotional processes in his "A-B-C" model, in which he proposes that people can make themselves either happy or miserable by the way they think about experiences. In this model, the "A" refers to "activating experience" or "adversities," the "B" to beliefs, and the "C" to consequences (Ellis, 1998) (see Figure 4.4). It is the "Bs" that are often faulty or irrational in people with psychological disorders. Ellis called these **irrational beliefs**—views

The process of vicarious reinforcement, according to social learning theorists, accounts for children acquiring the behaviors of adults.

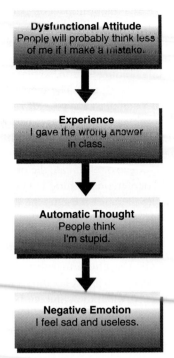

Figure 4.3

The relationship among dysfunctional attitude, experience, automatic thought, and negative emotion

Table 4.4

Examples of Items from the Dysfunctional Attitudes Scale

1. It is difficult to be happy unless one is good-looking, intelligent, rich, and creative.
2. People will probably think less of me if I make a mistake.
3. If a person asks for help, it is a sign of weakness.
4. If I fail partly, it is as bad as being a complete failure.
5. I am nothing if a person I love doesn't love me.
6. I should be upset if I make a mistake.
7. If I ask a question, it makes me look inferior.
8. Being isolated from others is bound to lead to unhappiness.
9. If someone disagrees with me, it probably indicates he does not like me.
10. If I do not do well all the time, people will not respect me.

Agreeing with these items indicates that the person holds dysfunctional attitudes.

From Arlene Weissman, "Dysfunctional Attitudes Scale." Copyright © 1978. Reprinted by permission.

---

about the self and world that are unrealistic, extreme, and illogical. Some examples of irrational beliefs are shown in Table 4.5. These irrational beliefs cause people to create unnecessary emotional disturbance by sticking rigidly to the "musts" (what Ellis has called "musturbation") and then punishing themselves needlessly ("awfulizing"). They then engage in unnecessary self-pity ("I-can't-stand-it-itis") and refuse to admit that they need help. Rather than trying to change themselves, many people find ways to change their situations, such as seeking a divorce rather than learning what facets of their personalities contribute to marital distress. If we are to believe Ellis, it would seem that few people are ever really happy. On a more positive note, as we will see later, Ellis also offers some practical suggestions for how people can get out of the mess they create for themselves.

Treatment

According to behavioral and cognitively based perspectives, abnormality arises from faulty learning and thinking and can be changed by methods that address these processes. In interventions based on behavioral theory, clinicians use behavioral analysis in which they attempt to provide a precise understanding of the factors that maintain the behavior before proposing methods that are likely to be effective (Mueser & Liberman, 1995). In interventions based on cognitive theory, the clinician works with the client to change maladaptive thought patterns.

Conditioning Techniques

Behavior therapists use both classical conditioning and operant conditioning, relying on such mechanisms as positive reinforcement, negative reinforcement, punishment, and extinction.

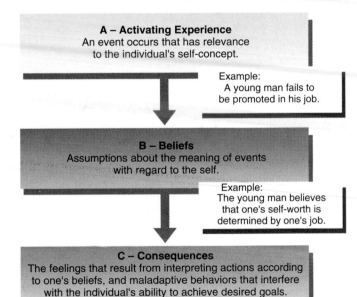

Figure 4.4   The A-B-C process in rational-emotive therapy

A narrow focus on his job led this young man to overreact when he did not get the promotion he desired. A more rational belief is that a job is a part, but by no means all, of what determines one's self-worth. If the man's beliefs had been more rational, he would have reacted less extremely, and probably would be in a good position to receive a promotion at a later time.

Table 4.5

Examples of Irrational Beliefs as Described by Ellis

Ellis (1987) distinguishes between two types of irrational beliefs: those that are "obvious or blatant" and those that are "subtle or tricky." They are equally maladaptive, but the subtle beliefs are more difficult to change because detecting their irrationality is more difficult. See if you can recognize the difference as you read the following list.

1. Because I strongly desire to perform important tasks competently and successfully, *I absolutely must* perform them PERFECTLY WELL!

2. Because I strongly desire to perform important tasks competently and successfully, and because I REALLY TRY HARD to succeed at these tasks, I DESERVE to perform well and *absolutely must* perform that way!

3. Because I strongly desire to be approved by people I find significant, *I absolutely must* have their TOTAL AND PERFECT approval!

4. Because I strongly desire to be approved by people I find significant, and BECAUSE I AM A *SPECIAL KIND* OF PERSON, *I absolutely must* have their approval!

5. Because I strongly desire people to treat me considerately and fairly, and BECAUSE I AM UNUSUALLY WEAK AND UNABLE TO TAKE CARE OF MYSELF, people *absolutely must* treat me well!

6. Because I strongly desire people to treat me considerately and fairly, they *absolutely must* AT ALL TIMES *PERFECTLY* DO SO!

The obvious irrational thoughts are numbers 1, 3, and 6, and the rest are of the subtle variety. Could you tell the difference? How many of them apply to you?

From Albert Ellis. "The Impossibility of Achieving Consistently Good Mental Health." In *American Psychologist*, 264–375, 1987. Copyright © 1987 American Psychological Association. Reprinted by permission.

These methods are combined in various procedures that involve helping the client "unlearn" the maladaptive behaviors and replace them with ones that will allow them to move on with their lives.

One method that is particularly useful in treating irrational fears is based on **counterconditioning,** the process of replacing an undesired response to a stimulus with an acceptable response. Counterconditioning is particularly effective when the new response is incompatible with the existing one. The assumption underlying counterconditioning is that, if the undesired response was learned, it can be unlearned, and the acceptable response can be acquired through the same process.

Physician Joseph Wolpe (b. 1915) is the primary figure in the development of counterconditioning approaches. After classically conditioning cats to experience "anxiety" in a room in which they had been shocked, Wolpe developed methods to inhibit the anxiety by training them to associate the room with eating rather than shocks. From this experiment, Wolpe speculated that the counterconditioning of anxiety could serve as a basis for a radically new therapy model. His insights (Wolpe, 1958, 1973) have had a major impact on behavioral therapy as it is practiced today.

Counterconditioning might be used to help a client overcome a fear of handling knives. The client would be reinforced to feel relaxed while holding a knife, so that relaxation replaces the undesirable response of fear. The therapist would train the client in relaxation techniques and provide rewards for showing a relaxation response instead of fear when presented with a knife. Over time, the pairing of rewards with relaxation in the presence of the previously feared stimulus should establish the new response and reduce or eliminate the old one.

A variant of counterconditioning is **systematic desensitization,** in which the therapist presents the client with progressively more anxiety-provoking images of stimuli while the client is in a relaxed state. This is considered to be a form of counterconditioning in that, in each successive presentation, the therapist encourages the client to substitute the desired response for the undesired one—relaxation rather than anxiety. This technique is used when the clinician believes that having to confront the actual stimulus that has provoked the undesirable behavior would overwhelm the client. For example, if this client has a full-blown anxiety reaction at the sight of a knife, it might be unwise to use counterconditioning, because relaxation would be impossible under these circumstances. Instead, the therapist exposes the client to the knife gradually, in steps, developing a list, or "hierarchy," of images associated with the fear. At each step, the therapist helps the client enter a relaxed state while looking at or handling the feared object. Eventually, the client reaches the point of being able to handle a knife without panicking. However, at any point, if the client suffers a setback, the therapist must move back down the hierarchy until the client is ready to move on.

Another counterconditioning technique developed by Wolpe (1973) is assertiveness training, in which the client is taught to express justified anger, rather than to be anxious and intimidated when other people are exploitive, unduly demanding, or disrespectful. As in counterconditioning, the underlying rationale is that a person cannot experience opposing emotions (anger and anxiety, in this case). By strengthening the desired emotion (anger), the opposite emotion (anxiety) is unlearned in that situation. At the same time, the client learns effective communication methods to manage difficult situations more effectively.

Contingency Management Techniques

Another category of behavioral therapy techniques uses a simple principle that many people follow in their daily lives; that is, desired behavior can be established through rewards, and undesirable behavior can be eliminated by removing its rewards. **Contingency management** is a form of behavioral therapy that involves this principle of rewarding a client for desired behaviors and not providing rewards for undesired behaviors. This treatment teaches the client to connect the outcome of the behavior with the behavior itself, so that a contingency, or connection, is established.

In everyday life, people use contingency management to stop smoking, control their weight, discipline their children, or develop better study habits. Some people turn to therapy if their own contingency management efforts have failed to change undesirable behaviors. A therapist can help monitor the client's behavior and suggest alternative ways to try to control it. A common form of contingency contracting used in psychiatric hospitals is the **token economy,** in which residents who perform desired activities earn plastic chips that can later be exchanged for a tangible benefit (Ayllon & Azrin, 1965).

Modeling and Self-Efficacy Training

In the behavioral therapy methods we have discussed so far, clients directly experience reinforcement for actions they carry out in the context of therapy. However, we have seen from Bandura's research that people can learn new behaviors vicariously. Bandura, in fact, successfully applied the principle of vicarious reinforcement to behavioral therapy by exposing clients to videotapes or real-life models who were being rewarded for demonstrating the desired behaviors (Bandura, 1971). In this approach, a girl who is afraid of dogs might be shown a videotape of a girl happily petting a dog and playing ball with it. By seeing the videotape, the client presumably develops the idea that playing with dogs can be fun and, more important, need not be dangerous. Going one step further, the therapist might use **participant modeling,** a form of therapy in which the therapist first shows the client a desired behavior and then guides the client through the behavior change. The therapist might first play with the dog and then have the girl do the same while the therapist offers encouragement.

Another form of behavioral therapy relies on Bandura's concept of self-efficacy. According to Bandura, maladaptive responses, such as irrational fears, arise from the perception that one lacks the resources for handling a potentially threatening situation. If the client's feelings of self-efficacy are strengthened, then the client should be able to overcome the irrational fear (Bandura, 1991). Self-efficacy training can also help clients gain control over undesired habits, such as smoking (Prochaska & DiClemente, 1983). In this approach, em-

phasis is placed on helping clients feel that they have the emotional strength to follow through on their wish to stop smoking.

Cognitive Therapies

The principles of cognitive and cognitive-behavioral therapies are straightforward and follow logically from the premise that dysfunctional emotions are the product of dysfunctional thoughts. One of the fundamental techniques is **cognitive restructuring,** in which the clinician helps the client alter the way he or she views the self, the world, and the future. In this method, the therapist reframes negative ideas into more positive ones to encourage the development of more adaptive ways of coping with emotional difficulties. The therapist questions and challenges the client's dysfunctional attitudes and irrational beliefs, and makes suggestions that the client can test in behavior outside the therapy session.

In Ellis' rational-emotive behavior therapy (REBT), the clinician makes a systematic attempt to dissuade clients from their irrational beliefs by showing them how mistaken they are and helping them arrive at more rational ways of thinking about themselves. Consider the case of a young man, Patrick, who is distraught over his failure to be promoted. Ellis would attempt to uncover Patrick's irrational beliefs that are causing him to feel upset and are interfering with his chances for future success. Ellis would try to show Patrick that focusing on a job as a source of self-worth is irrational. He might suggest that a more rational belief would be "It was disappointing not to get that promotion, but I have other rewards in life outside my work." Ellis might also try to show Patrick that there will

---

Box 4.4

Behavioral and Cognitively Based Approaches to Treating Kristin

Although Kristin's psychological condition is a type not generally treated with strict behavioral methods, she might benefit from interventions that focus on interpersonal skills and communication. For example, Wolpe might suggest that Kristin could benefit from assertiveness training, in which she would be taught to express her feelings and needs to others, such as her supervisors at work and her family.

Cognitive therapists would focus on the aspects of Kristin's thought processes that contribute to her unrelenting depression. Beck would help Kristin see the ways in which her automatic thoughts lead to feelings of unhappiness, and he would work toward the goal of helping her change her views of self, the world, and her future through cognitive restructuring.

Ellis might zero in on Kristin's irrational beliefs through rational-emotive behavior therapy. He would try to help Kristin see the ways in which her father's suicide was an activating event (A) that led to the beliefs (B) that she was responsible for this tragedy and for disappointments in her own life; the consequence (C) is that she feels depressed and incompetent. He would look for ways to help Kristin realize that she can control her life and her destiny in much more satisfying ways.

In a token economy, clients are given tangible rewards, or "tokens," which they exchange for desired activities or privileges.

be other opportunities and that all is not lost, unless he sabotages himself in his current job.

As with Beck's version of cognitive therapy, Ellis' rational emotive behavior therapy focuses on the client's thoughts and puts far less emphasis on the relationship between the client and the therapist. In fact, Ellis tends to be quite confrontational with clients yet, at the same time, maintains that the rational-emotive perspective is based on principles of philosophy and humanistic psychology that suggest that people can control their own destinies.

Evaluation of the Behavioral and Cognitively Based Perspectives

Perhaps the main appeal of the behavioral perspective is its relative simplicity and reliance on concepts that can be translated into objective measures. This perspective uses a limited set of empirically based principles and circumvents sticky philosophical questions by not proposing complex structures that underlie behavior. The very simplicity of the behavioral perspective is also its undoing, in the minds of many psychologists. Humanists contend that, by restricting the definition of *psychology* to the study of observable behavior, behaviorists have failed to capture the complexity of human nature and have portrayed free will as a negligible influence on humans, compared with outside forces in the environment. Psychoanalysts argue that the de-emphasis on unconscious influences, which is characteristic of behavioral approaches, leaves out most of what is interesting and unique about human beings.

Cognitively oriented theorists have come closest to satisfying both sets of criticism, in that they regard thought processes as worthy of studying (satisfying the humanist concerns) and propose that behavior can be influenced by unstated assumptions about the self (satisfying the psychoanalytic contentions). However, even the cognitively oriented theorists fail to provide an overall explanation of personality structure, restricting their observations to particular problem areas.

Although not comprehensive, the behavioral and cognitive theories have a strong empirical base. Each of the major theoretical approaches has been grounded in research from its inception. The methods of therapy proposed by these theories were tested from and developed through controlled studies. When studies have failed to provide supportive evidence, the theory or proposed method of therapy has been revised accordingly. As a result, contemporary researchers continue to broaden the applications of these theories to a variety of clients and settings. Behavioral treatment is used for disorders ranging from alcoholism to sexual dysfunction, as well as a variety of anxiety disorders, and for social skills training in schizophrenia. You will see many instances throughout this book in which the contributions of behavioral and cognitive theorists play prominent roles in understanding and treating various psychological disorders. Even though clinicians may not adhere entirely to behavioral or cognitive approaches, most would recognize that certain strategies within these models have special advantages.

Biological Perspective

Within the **biological perspective,** disturbances in emotions, behavior, and cognitive processes are viewed as being caused by abnormalities in the functioning of the body. As you will read in the following sections, the nervous system and endocrine systems play important roles in determining abnormality, as does the genetic makeup of an individual.

The Nervous System and Behavior

Complex behaviors, thoughts, and emotions are the result of activities of the central nervous system (see Figure 4.5). The central nervous system consists of the brain and the nerve pathways going to and from the brain through the spinal cord. You can think of the central nervous system as a core information processing unit within the body, transmitting information regarding the body's current state to various decision-making centers, and then carrying these decisions back to the body as the basis of action. These activities occur at a rate of speed that exceeds even the most sophisticated computer and involve millions of decisions every second in which trillions of cells participate.

The central nervous system communicates with two other networks in the **peripheral nervous system,** called peripheral because its pathways lie outside the brain and spinal cord. The two subdivisions are the somatic nervous system and the autonomic nervous system. In the **somatic nervous system,** information from outside and inside the body is brought to the central nervous system through sensory pathways, which communicate information from the eyes, ears, and other sensory organs. Instructions for action from the central nervous system are communicated through motor pathways in the somatic system, which give instructions to the muscles and certain glands. The autonomic nervous system controls various involuntary functions, such as the digestion of food and beating of the heart, which rarely enter the sphere of the conscious thoughts and actions regulated by the central nervous system.

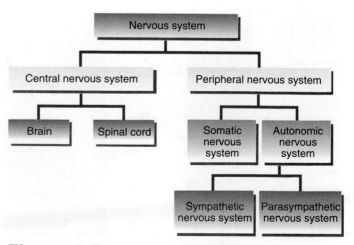

Figure 4.5
A schematic representation of the nervous system.

Neurons and Synapses

A **neuron,** or nerve cell, is the basic unit of structure and function within the nervous system. The neuron is a communicator, whose job it is to transmit information. There are different types of neurons, but all possess the same parts, including the cell body, the axon, and dendrites (see Figure 4.6). The **cell body** houses the structures, found in all cells of the body, that are responsible for keeping the neuron alive. The axon is the section of the neuron that transmits information to other neurons. This information passes from fibers at the end of the axon to the fibers on the dendrites of the neurons that receive the information. Spines along the length of the **dendrites** increase their effective surface area many thousands of times.

The transmission of information throughout the nervous system takes place at **synapses,** or points of communication between neurons. Electrical signals containing information are transmitted chemically across the synapse from one neuron to the next. Through this transmission, neurons form interconnected pathways, along which information travels from one part of the nervous system to another. Most synapses involve information transmission from the axon of one neuron to the dendrites of another, since the dendrites comprise such a large surface area, but there are also axon-axon synapses and axon-cell body synapses. Each neuron is surrounded by many others that synapse on it.

Synapses can have one of two effects—either "turning on" or "turning off" the neuron that receives information. An **excitatory synapse** is one in which the message communicated to the receiving neuron makes it more likely to trigger a response. By contrast, an **inhibitory synapse** decreases the activity of the receiving neuron. At any given moment, the activity of a neuron, and whether it sends off a signal to other neurons in its pathway, depends on the balance between excitatory and inhibitory synapses. In this way, each neuron integrates information from all the signals feeding into it, and it responds according to which of these signals is stronger.

Right now, as you read the words on this page, millions of electrochemical transmissions are taking place in your brain. What are these transmissions like? You might imagine something like the set of electrical wires that connects the components of your stereo system. As the signal passes from one wire to another, the sound is transmitted until it finally reaches the speaker. The nervous system is like this, but with one important difference: there are no "hard-wire" connections between the neurons. The neurons do not touch; instead, there is a gap at the juncture between neurons, called the **synaptic cleft.** The

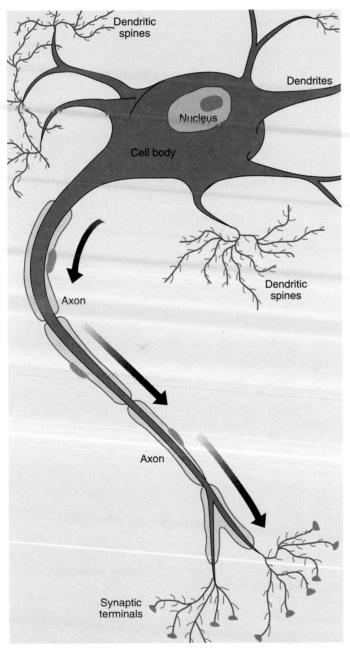

Figure 4.6   The neuron

A typical neuron has a cell body, containing the cell's nucleus; dendrites, which receive impulses from other neurons; dendritic spines, which enlarge the receptive surface of the neuron; an axon, which transmits impulses through the neuron; and synaptic terminals, which communicate the impulses to other neurons.

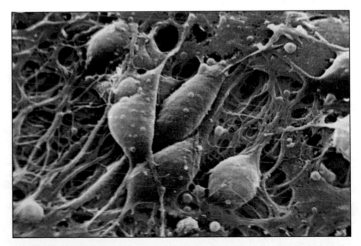

This colorized magnification, known as a scanning electron micrograph, affords a close-up view of neurons from the cerebral cortex.

transmission of information from the axon of one neuron to the dendrites of other neurons involves chemical and electrical activities occurring across the synaptic cleft. (The fact that synapses do not involve direct connections will prove to be particularly important later, when we discuss how psychoactive medications affect the brain.) A chemical substance is released from the transmitting neuron into the synaptic cleft, where it drifts across the synapse and is absorbed by the receiving neuron. This substance is called a **neurotransmitter** (see Figure 4.7).

There are several kinds of neurotransmitters, which differ in their chemical composition. Some of the more important ones are acetylcholine (ACh), gamma-aminobutyric acid (GABA), serotonin, dopamine, norepinephrine, and enkephalins. Other chemicals involved in the regulation of neural activity are hormones, growth factors, and various proteins, such as amino acids and neuropeptides. Some neurotransmitters are excitatory, in that they increase the likelihood that the receiving neuron will trigger a response. Norepinephrine is generally considered an excitatory neurotransmitter, and a deficit in this substance is thought to be a causal factor in depression. Other neurotransmitters, such as GABA, have an inhibitory effect when they pass through the synapse. Some tranquilizers work by facilitating GABA activity—which, in effect, "slows down" the nervous system. The enkephalins have received particular attention

since the early 1980s, because they have been recognized as the body's naturally produced painkillers. Abnormalities in other neurotransmitters are considered likely sources of some forms of abnormal behavior. For example, researchers hypothesize that serotonin is involved in a variety of disorders, including obsessive-compulsive disorder, depression, and eating disorders. An excess of dopamine activity has been hypothesized to cause symptoms of schizophrenia. Conversely, a dopamine deficit causes trembling and difficulty walking, which are symptoms of Parkinson's disease.

You can see by these examples that neurotransmitters play a central role in affecting a variety of behaviors. Other disorders, particularly those that respond to medication, may someday be found to have their source in neurotransmitter imbalances. The potential that this approach offers to the understanding and treatment of psychological disorders cannot be overemphasized, because it suggests relatively direct, simple interventions that can reduce the toll these disorders take on the quality of human life. However, it is unlikely that a "magic" cure will be found that, like penicillin for bacterial diseases, can eliminate a broad spectrum of serious mental disorders.

Role of the Brain in Behavior

Now that you have seen how neurons communicate information, let's move on to the big picture—that is, how the brain's functioning determines whether a person behaves abnormally. We will approach this by taking a brief "tour" of the brain from the "bottom" to the "top," focusing on these areas that are most relevant to abnormal behavior.

The simplified representation of the central nervous system shown in Figure 4.8 shows the location of the major structures of the brain. In speaking of brain-behavior relationships, it is helpful to think of behavior along a continuum of "lower" to "higher," or lower-order to higher-order functions. Lower-order functions require little analysis or planning, and the individual cannot easily control them. Examples of lower-order functions are the perception of an object as round and the transmission of signals to the lungs to control breathing. Higher-order functions involve judgment and planning and can be voluntarily controlled. Determining the best route to take to your destination is a higher-order behavior, as are reading and singing.

The higher-order functions are made possible by the activities of the structures within the **cerebral cortex,** the thin covering of neural tissue surrounding the outer surface of the brain. The lower-order, or more automatic, functions are served by the structures underneath and within the cerebral cortex. These **subcortical structures** operate much of the time as relay stations, to prepare information for processing in the cerebral cortex and to carry out the instructions for action that the cerebral cortex gives to the muscles and glands.

The brain stem is the site of transition between the brain structures and the spinal cord. There are three structures within the brain stem: the medulla oblongata, pons, and midbrain. Running vertically to and through these structures is a diffuse collection of ascending and descending pathways called the **reticular formation.** This structure controls the level and direction of arousal of brain activity through the excitation of

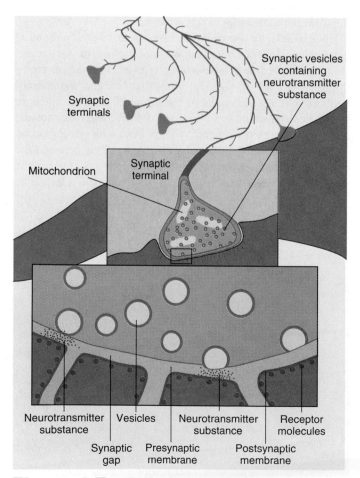

Figure 4.7

Neurotransmitters released across the synapse.

Synaptic terminals

Synaptic vesicles containing neurotransmitter substance

Mitochondrion

Synaptic terminal

Neurotransmitter substance | Vesicles | Neurotransmitter substance | Receptor molecules

Synaptic gap | Presynaptic membrane | Postsynaptic membrane

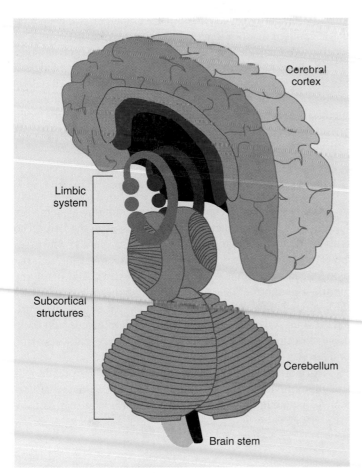

Figure 4.8   A diagram of the human brain

This illustration shows the cerebral cortex and the internal structures that lie under it, including the limbic system, the cerebellum, and the brain stem.

(Figure labels: Cerebral cortex; Limbic system; Subcortical structures; Cerebellum; Brain stem)

these centers. There also are centers in the hypothalamus that, when stimulated, arouse pain. These motivational functions of the hypothalamus clearly influence human behavior. The hypothalamus is also involved in several other bodily control systems, integrating a wide range of thoughts, feelings, and bodily reactions. It is involved, for example, in responding to stress by controlling the individual's emotional state and the physiological arousal that accompanies stress.

The **limbic system** is a set of loosely connected structures that forms a ring within the center portion of the brain. This system, which contains the hypothalamus, provides the neurological basis for the interaction between "rational" and "irrational" human behaviors. The limbic system also contains the **hippocampus,** which is responsible for the consolidation of short-term memory into long-term memory. Other limbic system structures, called the amygdala and septal area, are involved in the control of emotional reactivity. In summary, through its structures and pathways, the limbic system serves as the basis for the integration of memory, learning, and motor behavior and the emotional states of pleasure, pain, and arousal.

The cerebral cortex covers the upper portion of the two halves of the brain. The two parts of the cerebral cortex, the **cerebral hemispheres,** are connected by a band of tissue called the **corpus callosum.** There is a degree of specialization between the hemispheres, so that some functions are carried out by structures on the right side of the brain and others on the left. For example, language is typically carried out by left hemisphere structures in people who are right-handed.

The cerebral cortex has four major subdivisions: parietal, temporal, occipital, and frontal lobes (see Figure 4.9). Simply put, the parietal lobe is involved in the perception of bodily sensations, such as touch; the temporal lobe is involved in speech and language; the occipital lobe is involved in vision; and the frontal lobe is involved in movement. The **prefrontal**

certain pathways and the inhibition of others. It is responsible for "consciousness," and most brain researchers believe that it plays a role in dreaming. Some of the other functions carried out by the structures in this part of the brain include the regulation and control of eye movements, facial muscles, sleep patterns, and bodily position.

The cerebellum controls finely tuned voluntary movements. The ice skater or tightrope walker who performs elaborate balancing tricks is relying on the functioning of the cerebellum. Also involved in balance and motor control is the basal ganglia, a set of nuclei located deep within the brain. It is in the basal ganglia, specifically, that a dopamine deficiency can cause Parkinson's disease.

Because of its central role in many aspects of human behavior, the **hypothalamus** is the focus of extensive research attention. A tiny but crucial structure, it coordinates the activities of the central nervous system with systems involved in the control of emotion, motivation, and bodily regulation. Parts of the hypothalamus control hunger, thirst, and sexual needs. When stimulated, reward centers in the hypothalamus produce such pleasurable feelings that rats will spend long periods of time pushing electrode-connected levers that deliver excitation to

Neurosurgical procedures are sometimes used to alleviate extreme symptoms of some disorders such as Parkinson's disease, a condition that causes uncontrollable bodily shaking.

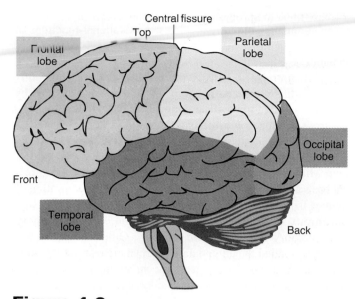

Figure 4.9
The four lobes of the cerebral cortex.

area at the very front of the brain is responsible for abstract planning and judgment. The largest area of the cerebral cortex is made up of the association cortex, which synthesizes and integrates information from all over the brain.

The Autonomic Nervous System

Right now your body is attending to many functions that you are probably not even thinking about. Stop for a moment and feel your pulse. You are not consciously instructing your heart to beat, yet your pulse indicates that your heart is beating at a rate of approximately 60 times per minute. At the same time, your stomach is digesting your last meal. You are not controlling this process in the way that you would use your right hand to turn the page. The automatic, involuntary processes that keep your body alive are controlled by the autonomic nervous system.

The two complementary functions of the autonomic nervous system are carried out by its two subdivisions: the parasympathetic nervous system and the sympathetic nervous system. The **parasympathetic nervous system** takes care of the maintenance functions of the body when it is at rest, directing most of the body's activities to producing and storing energy to be used when the body is in action. After you eat, the parasympathetic nervous system takes over and "instructs" the digestive system to begin to process what you have eaten.

The **sympathetic nervous system** is primarily responsible for mobilizing the body's stored resources when these resources are needed for activities that require energy. When you are in danger or when you are exercising, your sympathetic nervous system directs blood flow to the muscles and prepares you for action. Your heart pumps faster and your blood vessels constrict; as a result, your blood pressure increases. The actions of the sympathetic nervous system are commonly referred to as the "fight or flight" reaction.

The operation of both the parasympathetic and sympathetic systems is coordinated by structures in the brain that receive and translate sensory information from inside and outside the body and transmit instructions through the spinal cord for the appropriate autonomic response. The hypothalamus plays a major role in this process, regulating many autonomic functions and communicating with other regions of the brain regarding the body's temperature, energy needs, and level of comfort or satisfaction.

The Endocrine System

In addition to the nervous system, the endocrine system (see Figure 4.10) also maintains control processes in the body. The **endocrine system** consists of a number of glands, which secrete **hormones,** chemical messengers that travel through the bloodstream and influence the internal organs. The **pituitary gland,** sometimes called the "master" gland, is controlled by the hypothalamus and is located directly underneath it. Thus, the nervous system and endocrine system are linked, and these connections play an important role in psychological well-being or distress.

Hormones that the pituitary gland releases into the bloodstream stimulate other glands to release a broad range of hormones, including growth hormone, sex hormones, and cortisol,

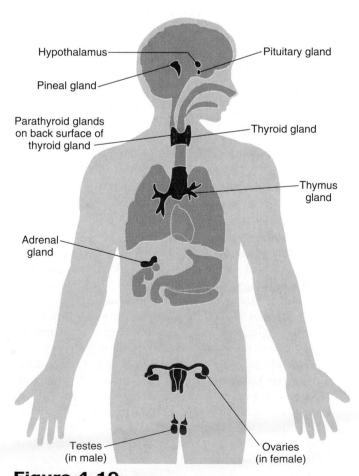

Figure 4.10
The organs in the endocrine system.

which is released by the adrenal gland and is involved in the body's response to stress. The endocrine system operates mainly on the principle of negative feedback. When the level of a hormone in the blood becomes too low, the hypothalamus sends a signal to the pituitary gland to stimulate the production of more of that hormone. One important exception to this negative feedback cycle is the onset of puberty, when sex hormones are released in large amounts, an experience appropriately labeled "raging hormones."

Disturbances in the endocrine system can have widespread effects on behavior and health. For example, an excess of thyroid hormone can cause a person to become overexcitable, restless, and irritable. In contrast, a deficiency of thyroid hormone can cause a person to feel sluggish and depressed. Abnormal levels of cortisol are particularly significant in the body's response to stress.

Genetic Influences on Behavior

Many people have an intuitive understanding of the genetic influences on behavior. It is common for parents to scrutinize their children to see which of their own characteristics have emerged, from the father's long fingers to the mother's small nose. Relatives often engage in ample speculation about the origins of this or that characteristic in the younger generation. Perhaps an aunt or uncle has told you that you have your grandmother's smile or that you are as mischievous as your father was when he was young. Apart from these informal assessments, most people would find it difficult to trace precisely the genetic routes through which offspring come to acquire the behaviors, appearance, mannerisms, and personality traits that have made their way through the family tree. There is good reason for this. The mechanisms of genetic inheritance often stump even the most sophisticated researcher.

Basic Concepts in Genetics

When we speak of inherited characteristics, we are talking about the components of the **genome,** the complete set of instructions for "building" all the cells that make up an organism. The human genome is found in each nucleus of a person's many trillions of cells. As is true for any building plan, things can change as a result of environmental factors. This interaction of the gene with the environment is reflected in the **phenotype,** which is the external expression of the genes. We will return to this crucial point later.

The genome for each living creature consists of tightly coiled threads of the molecule **deoxyribonucleic acid (DNA).** The DNA resides in the nucleus of the body's cells as 23 sets of paired strands each spiraled into a double helix, a shape that resembles a twisted ladder. There are four nitrogen-containing chemicals, called bases, that appear like beads of a necklace on each strand of DNA and form a particular sequence. This sequence of bases contains the information the cells need to manufacture protein, the primary component of all living things. Another function of DNA is to replicate itself before the cell divides. This makes it possible for each new cell to have a complete copy of the DNA's vital message, so that it can continue the process of protein manufacturing carried out by the original cell.

A **gene** is a functional unit of a DNA molecule carrying a particular set of instructions for producing a specific protein. There are between 60,000 and 100,000 genes, and every gene is made up of two million pairs of bases. Human genes vary widely in length, often extending over thousands of bases, but only about 10 percent of the genome actually contains sequences of genes used to code proteins. The rest of the genome contains sequences of bases that code for nothing of known value.

The genome is organized into **chromosomes**—distinct, physically separate units of coiled threads of DNA and associated protein molecules. In humans, there are two sets of chromosomes, one set contributed by each parent. Each set has 23 single chromosomes: 22 are called "autosomes" and contain nonsex-linked information, and the twenty-third is the X or Y sex chromosome. A normal female has a pair of X chromosomes, and a male has an X and Y pair. Although each chromosome always has the same genes on it, there is often no rhyme or reason to the distribution of genes on chromosomes. A gene that produces a protein that influences eye color may be next to a gene that is involved in cellular energy production.

Chromosomes can be seen under a light microscope and, when stained with certain dyes, reveal a pattern of light and dark bands. These bands reflect variations in the amounts of the four bases. Each chromosome has a characteristic size and banding pattern that can be seen through the microscope. This sort of inspection can reveal a few types of major chromosomal abnormalities—such as a missing or an extra copy of a chromosome, as in Down syndrome, a cause of mental retardation in which the individual has a third copy of chromosome 21. Most chromosomal abnormalities, however, are too subtle to be detected by this fairly crude method and require more sophisticated forms of analysis.

Genes undergo alterations, called **mutations,** some from faulty copying when a cell reproduces itself, some from chemical alterations by sunlight or carcinogens. Genetic mutations can be either inherited from a parent or acquired over the course of one's life. Inherited mutations originate from the DNA of the cells involved in reproduction (sperm and egg). When reproductive cells containing mutations are combined in one's offspring, the mutation will be in all the bodily cells of that offspring. Inherited mutations are responsible for such diseases as cystic fibrosis and sickle cell anemia and may predispose an individual to cancer, major psychiatric illnesses, or other complex diseases.

Acquired mutations are changes in DNA that develop throughout a person's lifetime. Remarkably, cells possess the ability to repair many of these mutations. If these repair mechanisms fail, however, the mutation can be passed along to future copies of the altered cell.

Models of Genetic Transmission

Recall that the cells of the body contain two sets of chromosomes, one inherited from the mother and one from the father. Each set of chromosomes has the same genes, but many of these genes come in different variants, called alleles. Many genetically based traits (such as hair color and eye color) are determined by the combination of the gene's two alleles that the individual inherits. Many alleles are described as either dominant or recessive, depending on whether one or both must be present in the individual's genome for the trait to be expressed. A **dominant** allele always expresses the trait that it codes, no matter what the other allele is. Brown hair is a dominant allele. If one parent is brown-haired and the other is blond, the offspring will have brown hair. A **recessive** allele is expressed only if it is paired with another recessive allele. Blond hair fits this pattern of inheritance, because blondness is a recessive trait.

Certain genetic disorders are based on a dominant pattern of inheritance. In this case, a person has inherited a "normal" allele and a "disease" allele. Since the disease allele is dominant, it is expressed in the individual, who is likely to become afflicted with the disorder. The affected individual, therefore, carries one normal and one disease allele. Let's say the affected individual is a male. When he has children, each of his children has a 50 percent chance of inheriting the disease allele and, therefore, has a 50 percent chance of developing the disorder. This situation is summarized in Figure 4.11(a). Another pattern of disease inheritance involves altered recessive genes. In this case, both parents carry one normal allele and one disease allele. Although neither parent has the disease, each is a "carrier." Think of the alleles as "ND" and "ND," with "N" for normal and "D" for disease. Two NDs can produce four possible combinations: NN, ND, DN, and DD. Therefore, as shown in Figure 4.11, each child has a 1/4 chance of being diseased, a 1/4 chance of being normal, and a 2/4 (1/2) chance of being a carrier, like the parents.

When scientists attempt to determine the genetic origins of particular psychological and physical characteristics, they often begin with the assumption that a characteristic was acquired through this type of dominant-recessive pattern of transmission. Although this model is complex, only a limited number of factors can influence the inheritance of a characteristic from generation to generation; with the right tools, it is possible to trace the route of genetic transmission by knowing which genes are dominant and which are recessive. Infinitely more challenging is the process of determining patterns of inheritance when the pattern does not follow one of dominant-recessive transmission. **Complex traits** are characteristics that reflect an inheritance pattern that does not follow the simple rules of dominant and recessive combination. This inheritance pattern follows a **polygenic** model of genetic inheritance, in which two or more genes participate to determine a characteristic. In a polygenic model, multiple genes are assumed to play a role in combining, perhaps at different levels, to determine the overall expression of a characteristic. Unlike the case of one brown-hair gene combining with one blond-hair gene, it may be the combined pattern of as many as 10 or 100 genes that determines whether the individual acquires a certain characteristic, such as body size.

Researchers have come to accept the notion that an interaction of "nature" and "nurture" causes most forms of psychological disorder. As we saw in Chapter 1, current models propose interactions between genetic and environmental contributors to behavior in which nature and nurture have reciprocal influences on each other. Let's take a look at these interactions in more depth.

Consider the example of extraversion (outgoing behavior), which researchers have claimed to be a partially inherited characteristic that influences the choices people make over controllable events in their lives (Saudino et al., 1997). A girl born with "extraversion" genes may trigger friendly responses from people in her environment that encourage her to be even more extraverted, leading to the growth of this trait within her personality. A variation on this model is that people select environments that are consistent with their genetically determined interests and abilities and that these environments, in

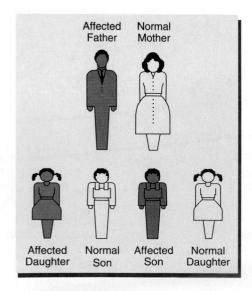

(a) Dominant pattern

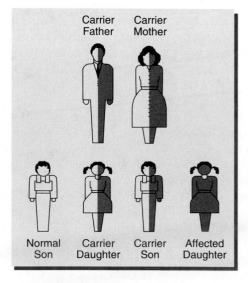

(b) Recessive pattern

Figure 4.11   Patterns of inheritance

turn, further influence the expression of these qualities (Scarr, 1992). According to this model, genetically based characteristics are enhanced by experiences that people have chosen because they possess these interests. Estimates of **heritability,** the proportion of the offspring's phenotype that is due to genetic causes, have been applied to traits as diverse as religiosity, political orientation, job satisfaction, leisure interests, proneness to divorce, and even perceptions of one's talents or abilities. Theorists claim that these characteristics have a strong genetic component as indicated by high heritability indices (Bouchard et al., 1990; McGue, Hirsch & Lykken, 1993).

Another interactive view of the relationship between genes and the environment is the **diathesis-stress model,** a proposal that people are born with a genetic predisposition ("diathesis") or acquire a vulnerability very early in life due to such formative events as traumas, diseases, birth complications, and even family experiences (Zubin & Spring, 1977). Such vulnerability places individuals at risk for the development of a psychological disorder. Previously researchers believed that people possessed this vulnerability as an enduring trait; therefore, they always would be at risk for developing a disorder, such as schizophrenia or depression, if exposed to certain extremely stressful life experiences. In more recent formulations, however, researchers are attempting to quantify the diathesis-stress model by providing quantitative estimates of the relative contributions of genes and the environment to the development of psychological disorder (Cadoret et al., 1996; Zinbarg & Barlow, 1996). Some theorists have taken the diathesis-stress model a step further by suggesting that the "diathesis" can actually be a cognitive factor that is established early in life (Spangler, Simons, Monroe & Thase, 1996). For example, a woman's tendency to attribute negative events to her personal flaws may have been established in early childhood; when she encounters difficulties in adulthood, she assumes that she is the cause.

Complicating the gene-environment equation even further is the fact that, as pointed out earlier, the genome is not always expressed in the phenotype, or observed characteristics of the individual. Some people with a genotype that would predispose them to developing a certain disease may not manifest the disease, a phenomenon referred to as incomplete **penetrance.** Such factors as age, gender, environment, and other genes influence the degree of penetrance of a genetically inherited characteristic. In other cases, a person may develop a disease due to environmental or random causes, without having inherited a predisposition for that disease.

Just when you thought the situation could hardly become more confusing, consider the **multifactorial polygenic threshold** model (Gottesman, 1991; Moldin & Gottesman, 1997). Researchers who hold to this model maintain that several genes with varying influence are involved in the transmission of a disorder or characteristic. The vulnerability for a disease is seen as ranging from low to high, depending on the combination of genes that the individual inherits. The disorder's symptoms are produced when the accumulation of genetic and environmental factors exceeds a certain threshold value. Most contemporary researchers agree that this model provides a better explanation for the actual patterns of family incidence than does the single

gene model or others based on simpler mechanisms of genetic inheritance.

Which model is correct? It is possible that all hold partial answers, depending on the modifiability of the characteristic being considered. A person with a tallness genotype does not become taller by playing basketball, but a person with artistic talent may become more proficient with training. Physical characteristics may also vary in the degree to which they can be modified; a person with "heavy" genes may maintain an average weight through careful dieting and exercise. Similarly, a person who is genetically predisposed to inherit heart disease may lower the risk of acquiring the disease through careful monitoring of dietary intake. However, blue eyes cannot be changed to brown, no matter what the person looks at or does. Apart from such obviously restricted physical characteristics, the idea of modifying the expression of genetically acquired traits or health problems through the control of lifestyle factors represents an exciting possibility.

Treatment

Therapies that follow from the biological perspective are primarily oriented to reducing or alleviating the symptoms of a disorder. **Somatic** (bodily) **therapies** involve treatments that act on known or presumed causes of the disorder.

Psychosurgery

The first form of somatic therapy is in some ways the most extreme: surgical intervention on the brain, also known as **psychosurgery.** The most typical form of psychosurgery involves disconnecting the frontal lobes from the rest of the brain. The basic procedure of this type of surgery was developed by the Portugese neurosurgeon Egas Moniz in 1935 as a way to relieve the symptoms of people with severe psychosis. The technique was considered a major breakthrough at the time, and Moniz received a Nobel Prize in 1949 for his work. After the development of antipsychotic medications in the 1950s, psychosurgery as a widespread practice was discontinued. Even though psychosurgery is rarely performed today, some mental health professionals still recommend this procedure to treat people with otherwise intractable forms of obsessive-compulsive disorder and major depressive disorder who do not respond to medications (Marino-Junior & Cosgrove, 1997).

Electroconvulsive Therapy

Less extreme than psychosurgery, but also controversial, is **electroconvulsive therapy (ECT)** for the treatment of severe depression. In ECT, an electric shock is applied through electrodes attached across the head, producing bodily convulsions. This method was developed in 1937 by Ugo Cerletti, an Italian neurologist who developed the procedure through his work in the field of treatment for epilepsy, a brain seizure disorder. Cerletti noticed in his experiments that dogs who were induced to undergo convulsions from electroshocks were much calmer afterwards. At about the same time, other physicians in Europe were using chemicals to produce convulsions, but Cerletti felt these methods were too risky and uncontrollable. The attempt to treat severe psychological disorder by causing radical alterations in the brain's environment was based on the notion that these chemical changes would stimulate beneficial changes in the neurons, thus reducing the patient's symptoms. As ECT began to spread throughout Europe, refinements were added that reduced the risk of muscle injury during the convulsions.

As ECT's popularity grew in the 1940s and 1950s, so did the criticisms against it, in part because it was often abused as a means of controlling disruptive patients in hospitals. This was the image depicted in Ken Kesey's *One Flew over the Cuckoo's Nest*. As a result of the controversy surrounding ECT, the method had largely fallen into disuse by the mid-1970s. However, it was still used for treating a narrow range of disorders, and in 1985, the National Institutes of Health issued a statement in support of its limited application to these disorders. (Health, 1985). In recent years, there has been a resurgence of interest in ECT as a method of treatment for severe depression (Sobin et al., 1996; Thase & Kupfer, 1996). It has also been used successfully with severely depressed older adults (Tomac, Rummans, Pileggi & Li, 1997), people in the manic phase of bipolar disorder (Kusumakar et al., 1997), and individuals suffering from psychotic symptoms and depression (Coryell, 1998). However, the procedure is more common in certain areas of the United States, where there is a greater proportion of psychiatrists and more private hospital beds. Practitioners are not in total agreement about its value as a clinical tool (Hermann, Dorwart, Hoover & Brody, 1995).

Medication

The most common somatic intervention is medication. As we discuss many disorders later in this book, we will also describe the medications demonstrated to be effective in alleviating the symptoms of these disorders. These medications typically alter body chemistry in ways that affect the levels and actions of brain neurotransmitters. During the past decade, major advances in psychopharmacology have resulted in the introduction of medications that are dramatically more effective than those previously in use. As you will read later in this book, medications called **selective serotonin reuptake inhibitors (SSRI)** (e.g., fluoxetine/Prozac) have been remarkably effective in treating the symptoms associated with depression and obsessive-compulsive disorder. As you will read in the chapter on mood disorders, selective serotonin reuptake inhibitors block the reuptake of serotonin at the synapse, enabling more of this neurotransmitter to be available at the receptor sites. For clients suffering from schizophrenia, the recently introduced atypical antipsychotic medications (e.g., clozapine/Clozaril) have changed the lives of people whose debilitating cognitive, emotional, and behavioral symptoms had previously caused havoc. Clozapine blocks serotonin, as well as dopamine to a lesser degree.

Biofeedback

In **biofeedback,** a somatic intervention is combined with behavioral principles with the goal of providing clients with the means of controlling their own physiological responses. These responses can be ones that are under voluntary control, such as the actions of the skeletal muscles that are controlled by the central nervous system. More important, clients can also learn to control the so-called visceral functions of the autonomic nervous system and the hormonal responses of the endocrine system, including heart rate, blood pressure, contractions of the intestinal muscles, and galvanic skin response. In cases where physical symptoms are the result of disturbances in autonomic functions, the ability to control such functions can help the individual achieve tremendous relief. For example, biofeedback can be used to treat migraine headaches, insomnia, pain from injured muscles, asthma, high blood pressure, intestinal disorders, and heart rhythm abnormalities.

The basis for biofeedback was largely in the pioneering work of in the 1960s and 1970s conducted by Rockefeller University psychologist Neal E. Miller. Based on extensive experimental work on the instrumental (operant) conditioning of laboratory animals (Miller & Banuazizi, 1968), Miller concluded that it was possible to use reinforcement to alter physiological responses. He further theorized that some physiological symptoms in humans resulted from misinterpretations of the cues from their bodies (Miller & Dworkin, 1977). Biofeedback allows clients to learn to "read" their bodily signals more clearly and then go on to the next step, which is to alter them through instrumental conditioning. For example, clients could be taught to recognize the presence of tense muscles and then learn to relax them.

The training methods used in biofeedback are relatively simple, as they are based on principles of learning and reinforcement, and the client can easily carry them outside of the clinician's office. However, the initial training requires very sophisticated instruments to provide precise measurements of bodily responses. After determining what treatment method is best suited to the client's symptoms (such as muscle relaxation for tension headaches), the clinician hooks up the client to an instrument whose output can be easily read. When a desirable outcome is achieved (such as a reduction of muscle tension), reinforcement is provided (such as a light or music going off).

In biofeedback, a person learns to regulate autonomic functions by attending to bodily changes registered on recording instruments.

Shaping is used, so that initially the thresholds are easily within the client's reach, and gradually, they become more challenging. The goal is for the client to be able to accurately read bodily signals without the machine and then be able to control the response at will.

Evaluation of the Biological Perspective

Biology is the foundation on which all behavior is based. Ultimately, any psychological approach to abnormal behavior must consider the role of biology. Researchers have increasingly realized that, for decades, many disorders that had been explained in psychological terms may have had biological components. In some cases, it is being recognized that the connection between biology and psychology is reciprocal. For example, such emotions as anxiety can cause changes in the body, such as increased heart rate and sweating. These changes can interfere with a number of psychological processes, such as concentration. The realization that one is not concentrating well can lead to even greater anxiety. Chronic anxiety, in turn, can cause physical changes that create long-standing health problems. Cases such as that of Kristin raise some fascinating questions about the role of biology in psychological disorders. Many people reading Kristin's story would regard the traumatic loss of her father as the direct cause of her depression. However, as you will discover in the chapter on mood disorders, depression often has a prominent biological component. Many people who develop depression have a family history in which one or more relatives have also suffered from mood disturbance. Having this information available, clinicians can develop hypotheses about the kind of mood disorder that is most likely.

The search for genetic contributions to psychological characteristics and disorders is progressing rapidly with the development of new technologies for unlocking biological secrets. Complicating this search, however, is the fact that most psychological characteristics follow a polygenic rather than Mendelian pattern of inheritance. As genetic technologies and understanding increase regarding the complexities of the gene-environment equation, improved understanding of and treatments for genetically based disorders will not be far behind.

Developing a Perspective: An Integrative Approach

Now that you have read about the major perspectives on abnormal behavior, you probably can see value in each of them. Certain facets of various theories may seem particularly useful and interesting. In fact, you may have a hard time deciding which approach is the "best." However, as we have said repeatedly, most clinicians select aspects of the various models, rather than adhering narrowly to a single one. In fact, in recent decades, there has been a dramatic shift away from narrow clinical approaches that are rooted in a single theoretical model. Most clinicians now identify themselves as integrative, or eclectic. The therapist views the needs of the client from multiple perspectives and develops a treatment plan that responds to these particular concerns. Some cases might involve focusing on the client's family; others may call for a more detailed analysis of the client's early development. One client may need a great deal of direction and education from the therapist, whereas another client may benefit from support and nurturance. Similarly, in the course of therapy, components of several different models may be integrated.

Let's take a look at three ways in which clinicians integrate different therapeutic models (Goldfried & Norcross, 1995): (1) technical eclecticism, (2) theoretical integration, and (3) the common factors approach. Those adhering to technical eclecticism seek to match a specific intervention to each client and presenting problem (Beutler, Consoli, & Williams, 1995). These therapists do not affiliate with the particular theoretical models but are willing to acknowledge that a particular technique is effective for a certain kind of problem. For example, a therapist who does not often use behavioral techniques may recognize the value of systematic desensitization in treating a phobic client, while using exploratory techniques to understand the developmental roots of the client's fears and dependent style.

Theoretical integration involves formulating a psychotherapeutic approach that brings divergent models together on a consistent basis in one's clinical work (Wachtel, 1977, 1997). For example, a clinician may consistently choose two theoretical bases, such as family systems and cognitive behaviorism, from which to develop an intervention model. In a way, the clinician is developing his or her own model by means of a conceptual synthesis of the contributions of previously established models. Somewhat independent of the presenting problem, this therapist would consistently look for ways in which both the family system and maladaptive cognitions have contributed to the client's distress. The intervention would be based on an approach that brings these two models together.

Box 4.5

Biological Approaches to Treating Kristin

An extreme procedure, such as psychosurgery, would not even be considered for a client such as Kristin. Neither would electroconvulsive treatment, unless Kristin's depression became so incapacitating that the usual therapeutic efficacy period of antidepressant medication was deemed to be too long and too risky.

Because most clinicians would view Kristin's depression as stemming from the trauma caused by her father's suicide, treating Kristin just with antidepressant medication would be unlikely. Some clinicians might consider the possibility of including medication, such as a selective serotonin reuptake inhibitor, into a more comprehensive treatment plan if Kristin complained about severe symptoms, such as appetite disturbance, sleep disturbance, and incapacitating sadness. In such a treatment regimen, the medication would be a single facet of a broader psychotherapeutic intervention.

When using the common factors approach to integration, the clinician develops a strategy by studying the core ingredients that various therapies share and choosing the components that have been demonstrated over time to be the most effective contributors to positive outcomes in psychotherapy. In their review of 50 publications, Grencavage and Norcross concluded that "the single most frequent commonality was the development of a collaborative therapeutic relationship/alliance" (Grencavage & Norcross, 1990, p. 377). Psychotherapy outcome literature frequently emphasizes that the quality of the rapport between the therapist and the client is crucial to the improvement of the client's condition.

When reading Dr. Tobin's cases throughout this text, you will see how she approaches her work from an integrative framework. In addition to incorporating techniques from various models into her treatment approach, Dr. Tobin is attuned to the importance of attending to certain common factors in her clinical work. For example, you will read about the emphasis Dr. Tobin places on her working relationship with her clients. She realizes that the most effective of techniques will be worthless unless she and her clients are allied in a collaborative working relationship.

As you read about the various psychological disorders in the chapters to follow, imagine the approach you might take if you were treating people with these disorders. Think of the extent to which you might rely on psychodynamic, humanistic, family systems, behavioral, cognitive, and biological models in understanding and treating these conditions. We will discuss the current state of the science regarding which explanations and interventions are regarded as most appropriate and effective. At the same time, it is important for you to keep in mind that knowledge about many of these conditions and the efficacy of certain interventions is still limited. The science of psychopathology and the art of psychotherapy are still evolving.

Box 4.6

Integrative Approach to Treating Kristin

An integrative therapist, such as Dr. Tobin, would face several choices in treating a client such as Kristin. Perhaps Kristin's depression is rooted in lifelong conflicts that would warrant some exploratory work. At the same time, Kristin might benefit from cognitive strategies aimed at helping her change her views of herself, her world, and her future. Although Kristin's depression is not so severe as to warrant extreme biologically based interventions, some clinicians might consider suggesting antidepressant medication if her symptoms worsened. Furthermore, the therapist might suggest that Kristin's family participate in the therapy, because Kristin's depression developed in response to a family trauma. The family therapy decision would rest primarily on Kristin's preference; some clients feel strongly about limiting their psychotherapy to a private endeavor, uncomplicated by involving family members. Regardless of the therapeutic techniques tapped, a skilled clinician would base Kristin's therapy on a foundation of empathy, acceptance, and support. When we return to the case at the end of this chapter, you will see just what Dr. Tobin chose to include in her work and how her integrative approach played out.

RETURN TO THE CASE

Kristin Pierpont

Kristin's History

Until the day of her father's death, Kristin had thought of her family as "typical, American, and middle class." She was the youngest of four girls, each of whom had reportedly gone on to successful careers and marriages. Kristin's parents owned their own real estate business, which they had started prior to the birth of any of the children.

Kristin remembered that, from a very early age, she perceived her three older sisters as being "great" at everything they did. Succeeding at academics, sports, and social pursuits, life seemed to be so easy for them. Her mother had similar expectations for Kristin, and she made her displeasure evident whenever Kristin failed to attain her mother's predefined goals. Even in the early grades of school, Kristin recalls feeling an inner pressure to do well and an accompanying feeling of fright that she would not succeed. In time, she developed perfectionistic tendencies about which her sisters and mother frequently chided her. Everything had to be just right—every homework assignment, every piece of clothing, even the placement of the things in her room. Her father responded differently to Kristin's perfectionistic style, however. He took a softer approach, in which he tried to talk to her about the ways in which she was getting herself "too upset" by trying to make everything perfect. He tried to communicate his appreciation of what she did and who she was and that "perfect wasn't necessarily the best."

RETURN TO THE CASE

Kristin Pierpont (continued)

As the years went by, Kristin found herself taking comfort in her father's words, and she learned how to accept healthy compromises. She didn't feel compelled to attend an Ivy League college or to have a large circle of friends. She participated in activities, such as the marching band and intramural sports, because she found them to be fun, and she liked the other people who were attracted to these activities. Even Kristin was able to acknowledge that, for most of her college years, she felt happy and healthy, both physically and psychologically. Although she had not been involved in an intimate relationship, she felt confident that the "right guy" would come along sooner or later.

Kristin's sense of psychological stability and serenity was dramatically shaken on that day in March of her senior year, when she received the "still unbelievable" phone call from her sister with the news of her father's death. In the months that followed, Kristin became consumed by feelings of sadness and loss, and she pulled away from her friends and family. She managed to finish her academic courses, although her grade point average for that semester was the lowest of her college career. Despite her mother's urging that Kristin participate in commencement, Kristin chose to stay away from the festivities, stating that it would be too emotional for her to be at the event without her father being present.

During the summer months following Kristin's completion of college, she remained in her apartment and made half-hearted attempts to find a job. When fall approached, her depression began to lift, and she realized that she would have to find a means of support. The job as a buyer was one of the first for which she applied, and she was surprised to land the position.

In her year in the job, she performed her duties quite adequately. She received high performance evaluations and corresponding salary raises. As with anything positive that happened in her life, Kristin did not take much satisfaction in these successes. She went about her work, mostly in a solitary manner, interacting with others only when the circumstance necessitated doing so. As the months passed, however, this solitary style of living became increasingly unbearable, so she decided to contact me to initiate psychotherapy.

Assessment

Kristin's case provided an interesting assessment challenge. In some ways, her issues seemed very evident; she was suffering from unresolved grief associated with the tragic death of her father. However, I felt that Kristin's clinical issues were far more complicated, as is so often the case. I wanted to get a better grasp of subtle interpersonal issues, especially those pertaining to early development and family relationships. At the same time, I wanted to understand the extent to which Kristin's low self-esteem was impeding her satisfaction in life. In addition to an extensive clinical interview, I decided to administer two assessment procedures that are markedly different but complementary: the Thematic Apperception Test and the Beck Depression Inventory-II.

As I might have expected, Kristin's TAT stories were filled with themes of loss and interpersonal pain. However, somewhat surprising was the depth of rage that characterized the interactions between the people in her TAT stories. One of the TAT cards is a drawing of an older woman who dressed in black, standing behind a younger woman [see Chapter 3]. Kristin described this scenario as follows: "The two women are attending the funeral of a friend, Adam. They are standing outside the church as the coffin is being carried out. The younger woman is feeling annoyed, actually furious, that the older woman even came to the funeral. In her mind she is thinking, 'Who the hell is she to be here! She didn't even like Adam.' She is also irked that the woman is standing so close to her, breathing down her neck. After a couple of moments, she turns around and gives her a nasty look, then walks away."

The relevance of Kristin's TAT story to events in her life was evident. Touching upon the most obvious themes, it was reasonable to interpret that Kristin was identifying with the younger figure in the picture, attending the funeral of a close one (her father), accompanied by someone else (possibly her mother) in the background. Perhaps she felt resentful of her mother's emotionally distant relationship with her father and angered by a woman whom she perceived to be "breathing down her neck" in life. Similar conflictual themes characterized Kristin's other stories, but in most instances there was little resolution to the conflict. Instead, the person in the story evaded the conflict while internalizing some intense feelings about other people.

The information from Kristin's Beck Depression Inventory-II confirmed my impression that she was seriously depressed. On this measure, Kristin's responses reflected sadness, pessimism, loss of pleasure, and self-criticalness. Although she expressed no suicidal thoughts or wishes, I was concerned about the extent and depth of Kristin's depression.

RETURN TO THE CASE

Kristin Pierpont (continued)

Diagnosis

Kristin was certainly depressed, but her depression was not severe enough to warrant a diagnosis of major depressive disorder or the duration long enough for the diagnosis of dysthymic disorder. The *DSM-IV* does provide the option of assigning the diagnosis of "bereavement" for the period following the death of a loved one, but the length and nature of Kristin's condition made this diagnosis inappropriate. In light of the profound nature of Kristin's depression, I viewed her as suffering from an unspecified mood disorder.

In addition to her depression following the loss of her father, Kristin was struggling with questions about her long-term goals in life, specifically pertaining to the role of intimate relationships and career development. Kristin needed to develop a sense of herself in the present and a vision of herself for the future. She was trying to delineate an identity that was a good fit.

Axis I: Mood Disorder Not Otherwise
Specified (296.90)
Identity Problem (313.82)
Axis II: None
Axis III: No medical diagnosis
Axis IV: Bereavement issues pertaining to unresolved feelings about the death of her father
Axis V: Global Assessment of Functioning (current): 68

Highest Global Assessment of Functioning (past year): 68; some difficulties in social functioning but satisfactory work involvement and performance

Case Formulation

I was impressed by Kristin's recognition of the central issues that had been upsetting her. She knew, as did I, that the suicide of her father would be a focal point of our work but that her issues were deeper and more long-lasting. Feelings of personal inadequacy had been a part of Kristin's emotional life for as long as she could remember. Fears of not being accepted, particularly by her mother and sisters, led Kristin to feel particularly vulnerable in any close relationship.

Kristin's lack of closeness with her mother early in life initiated a pattern of insecurity in other important relationships. For much of her life, she was able to compensate by turning to her father for support and affection. His suicide traumatized Kristin, leading her to panic about whether anyone would be there to help her through the next phase of her life. Insecurities that had always haunted her became explosive. Not knowing how to deal with others, even close friends and relatives, she retreated into a world of emotional isolation. Without consciously realizing what she was doing, she dismissed the important people from her life and felt unable to develop new relationships. In her heart was the fear that if she were to become close to another person, she might once again be abandoned.

Treatment Plan

I felt that the nature of Kristin's issues warranted a psychotherapy that integrated exploratory, supportive, and cognitive techniques. It was important for Kristin to understand the developmental antecedents of her current emotional problems. An approach rooted in an object relations framework would enable me to help Kristin understand how her unsatisfying relationship with her mother and sisters throughout life might be interfering with the establishment of intimacy in adult life. I wanted our work together to focus on the sequence of life events, particularly in her family, that brought her to such a stage of unhappiness.

In addition to exploratory work, Kristin needed someone to help her feel good about herself once again. Having become so reliant on her father for positive feedback, she was emotionally starved for someone to respect her and take joy in her accomplishments. Ideally, this role would eventually be filled by an intimate partner. For the time being, however, Kristin would benefit from a humanistic component to the therapy characterized by a strong positive regard and acceptance.

Complementing the exploratory and supportive work, I would also incorporate cognitive techniques focusing on the ways in which Kristin's dysfunctional emotions were the product of dysfunctional thoughts. Through the process of cognitive restructuring, Kristin could alter the ways she viewed herself, her family, and other significant people in her world. She could learn how to reframe negative ideas into positive ones that would facilitate the development of more adaptive coping strategies.

I also considered the possibility of medication as well as a family therapy component in my work with Kristin, but I ruled out both of these interventions. As for family therapy, Kristin explained that it was important to her to have an opportunity to have a therapeutic relationship that was a private and safe place in which she could openly explore family issues, without the pressure to contend with her sisters and mother in the therapy context. As for medication, it was my sense that her depression was not so incapacitating as to

RETURN TO THE CASE

Kristin Pierpont (continued)

warrant antidepressant medication; furthermore, Kristin explained that she preferred to tackle her depression psychotherapeutically. I agreed with her, explaining that we could come back to the medication issue if her depression deepened.

Outcome of the Case

My work with Kristin, which lasted 3 months, stands out in my mind as having been very special. I saw myself as a "provocative guide" in her evolving sense of herself. At first our work focused on dealing with her feelings about the death of her father. In particular, Kristin wanted and needed an opportunity to be openly expressive of her sadness about the loss of this relationship and her anger toward her father for having taken his life. Following the assessment sessions, during which I conducted a clinical interview and administered the TAT and Beck Depression Inventory-II, we moved into a discussion of her depression and unresolved rage.

For several sessions, Kristin told me stories of the warm and nurturing relationship she had with her father. With tears streaming down her face, she put forth unanswerable questions, such as "Why did he do this?" There was no clear answer to this query, particularly in light of the fact that her father's cryptic suicide note provided no clues about his life-ending decision, other than the accusatory comment directed to his family members.

By the end of our first month of working together, I felt that Kristin had experienced a certain "cleansing" of her emotions relating to pent-up feelings about her father's death. She and I both realized that she would never be able to fully put her father's suicide behind her; nevertheless, she did respond to my notion that she "file it away" for the time being. As I explained to her at the time, there are many past events in each of our lives that we can't change; however, we do have some control over the extent to which they intrude into our lives. With a supportive and affirming style, we incorporated cognitive techniques to help Kristin perceive herself as strong and competent and to find ways for her to take power over this past hurt, rather than being controlled by painful memories.

During the second and third months of our work together, the integrative therapy that I was conducting tapped more developmental aspects. With an approach rooted in object relations theory, we explored Kristin's early life relationships and the impact of these family relationships on her current life. At the same time, Kristin learned the techniques of cognitive restructuring, in which she was able to alter her thoughts about those relationships and thereby change the feelings about important people in her past and in her present. I helped Kristin realize how her interactions with others were being defined by her trauma. Since her father's suicide, Kristin had come to expect that any important person in her life would eventually abandon her, so she retreated from any possible intimacy. By capturing this understanding of what she was doing, Kristin felt free to venture into new relationships.

In time, not only did Kristin's self-perception improve, but so also did her interactions with others. She was able to let go of some of her perfectionistic traits, while coming to view her relationships with others in more positive terms. Kristin came to understand how she had desperately pursued acceptance in her family, all the while feeling like an outsider. The distance between her and her mother, whatever the basis, had caused her to approach intimate relationships with caution and distrust. By using Kristin's transference to me, I was able to point out the ways in which she seemed to approach me with fear and apprehension. I broadened this interpretation to other important relationships in Kristin's life, including her interactions with co-workers and friends. In a remarkably short period of time, Kristin came to see how the template of her interpersonal style had been established early in life and how she had adhered to that style for the past two decades.

By the end of 3 months of work together, Kristin was clearly happier. Her approach to other people had changed dramatically. She had begun to accept the invitations from her friends and had begun to date a man who worked with her.

It was rewarding to see Kristin grow and change. I realized that I would have liked to continue working with her, because I found the work so rewarding; however, I recognized that my own countertransference was the basis for this kind of thinking. I guess I was gratified by the success that she was achieving, and I wanted to continue to witness Kristin's growth, but my own curiosity would not be justification for recommending that she continue in treatment. I realized that it was important for Kristin to separate from me—in a way that felt good to her, that helped her feel she had the emotional strength to leave her work with me when the time seemed right. We mutually agreed after 3 months of progress that the time was, indeed, right.

RETURN TO THE CASE

Kristin Pierpont (continued)

Several years have passed since Kristin's therapy with me. Each December, she sends me a holiday greeting and provides a brief sketch of what has happened in her life—usually happy and upbeat accomplishments but also a few comments about difficult events, experiences, and choices. Kristin has found herself. ■

Sarah Tobin, PhD

Summary

- Theoretical perspectives influence the ways in which clinicians and researchers interpret and organize their observations about behavior. In this chapter, we discussed five major theoretical perspectives: psychodynamic, humanistic, sociocultural, behavioral and cognitively based, and biological; we concluded the discussion with a consideration of an integrative approach in which theorists and clinicians bring together aspects and techniques of more than one perspective.

- The psychodynamic perspective is a theoretical orientation that emphasizes unconscious determinants of behavior and is derived from Freud's psychoanalytic approach. The term *psychodynamics* is used to describe interaction among the id, the ego, and the superego. According to psychodynamic theorists, people use defense mechanisms to keep unacceptable thoughts, instincts, and feelings out of conscious awareness. Freud proposed that there is a normal sequence of development through a series of what he called psychosexual stages, with each stage focusing on a different sexually excitable zone of the body: oral, anal, phallic, and genital. Post-Freudian theorists, such as Jung, Adler, Horney, and Erikson departed from Freudian theory, contending that Freud overemphasized sexual and aggressive instincts. Object relations theorists, such as Klein, Winnicott, Kohut, and Mahler, proposed that interpersonal relationships lie at the core of personality, believing that the unconscious mind contains images of the child's parents and of the child's relationships to the parents. Treatment within the psychodynamic perspective may incorporate such techniques as free association, dream analysis, analysis of transference, and analysis of resistance. Considerable debate about the tenets and techniques of the psychodynamic perspective continues to take place; much of this debate focuses on the fact that psychodynamic concepts are difficult to study and measure and that some Freudian notions are now regarded as irrelevant in contemporary society. Newer approaches, based on object relations theory, have adapted the concept of infant attachment style to understanding the ways that adults relate to significant people in their lives.

- At the core of the humanistic perspective is the belief that human motivation is based on an inherent tendency to strive for self-fulfillment and meaning in life, notions that were rooted in existential psychology. Carl Rogers' person-centered theory focuses on the uniqueness of each individual, the importance of allowing each individual to achieve maximum fulfillment of potential, and the need for the individual to confront honestly the reality of his or her experiences in the world. Maslow's self-actualization theory focuses on the maximum realization of the individual's potential for psychological growth. In client-centered therapy, Rogers recommended that therapists treat clients with unconditional positive regard and empathy, while providing a model of genuineness and a willingness to self-disclose.

- Theorists within the sociocultural perspective emphasize the ways that individuals are influenced by people, social institutions, and social forces. Proponents of the family perspective see the individual as an integral component of the pattern of interactions and relationships that exists within the family. The four major approaches are intergenerational, structural, strategic, and experiential. Psychological disturbance can also arise as a result of discrimination associated with such attributes as gender, race, or age or of pressures associated with economic hardships. People can also be adversely affected by general social forces, such as fluid and inconsistent values in a society and destructive historical events, such a political revolution, natural disaster, or nationwide depression. Treatments within the sociocultural perspective are determined by the nature of the group involved. In family therapy, family members are encouraged to try new ways of relating to each other and thinking about their problems. In group therapy, people share their stories and experiences with other, similar people. Milieu therapy provides a context in which the intervention is the environment, rather than the individual, usually consisting of staff and clients in a therapeutic community.

- According to the behavioral perspective, abnormality is caused by faulty learning experiences; according to the cognitive-behavioral (sometimes called cognitive) perspective, abnormality is caused by maladaptive thought processes. Behaviorists contend that many emotional reactions are acquired through classical conditioning. Operant conditioning, with Skinner's emphasis on reinforcement, involves the learning of behaviors that are not automatic. The process of acquiring new responses by observing and imitating the behavior of others, called modeling, has been studied by social learning theorists. The cognitive theories of Beck and Ellis emphasize disturbed ways of thinking. In interventions based on behavioral theory, clinicians focus on observable behaviors, while those adhering to a cognitive perspective work with clients to change maladaptive thought patterns.

- Within the biological perspective, disturbances in emotions, behavior, and cognitive processes are viewed as being caused by abnormalities in the functioning of the body, such as the brain and nervous system or the endocrine system. A person's genetic makeup can play an important role in determining certain disorders. In trying to assess the relative roles of nature and nurture, researchers have come to accept the notion of an interaction between genetic and environmental contributors to abnormality. Treatments based on the

biological model involve a range of somatic therapies, the most common of which is medication. More extreme somatic interventions include psychosurgery and electroconvulsive treatment. Biofeedback is a somatic intervention in which clients learn to control various bodily reactions associated with stress.

- In contemporary practice, most clinicians take an integrative approach, in which they select aspects of various models rather than adhering narrowly to a single one. Three ways in which clinicians integrate various models include technical eclecticism, theoretical integration, and the common factors approach.

Key Terms

See Glossary for definitions.

Anal stage 102
Attachment style 107
Automatic thoughts 118
Aversive conditioning 116
Behavioral perspective 115
Biofeedback 130
Biological perspective 122
Cell body 123
Cerebral cortex 124
Cerebral hemispheres 125
Chromosomes 127
Classical conditioning 115
Client-centered 108
Cognitive-behavioral
perspective 115
Cognitive restructuring 121
Complex traits 128
Conditioned response 116
Conditioned stimulus 115
Conditions of worth 108
Congruence 108
Contingency management 120
Corpus callosum 125
Counterconditioning 120
Defense mechanisms 99
Deficit needs 109
Dendrites 123
Deoxyribonucleic acid
(DNA) 127
Diathesis-stress model 129
Discrimination 116
Dominant 128
Dream analysis 105
Dysfunctional attitudes 118

Ego 99
Ego ideal 99
Electroconvulsive therapy
(ECT) 129
Endocrine system 126
Excitatory synapse 123
Existential 108
Extinction 117
Family dynamics 112
Family perspective 112
Fixation 102
Free association 105
Fully functioning 108
Gene 127
Generalization 116
Genitality 104
Genital stage 104
Genome 127
Heritability 129
Hierarchy of needs 109
Hippocampus 125
Hormones 126
Humanistic 107
Hypothalamus 125
Id 98
Incongruence 108
Inhibitory synapse 123
Irrational beliefs 118
Latency 103
Libido 99
Limbic system 125
Milieu therapy 114
Modeling 117
Multifactorial polygenic
threshold 129

Mutations 127
Negative reinforcement 117
Neuron 123
Neurotransmitter 124
Neutrality 105
Object relations 105
Operant conditioning 116
Oral-stage 102
Parasympathetic nervous
system 126
Participant modeling 121
Peak experiences 109
Penetrance 129
Peripheral nervous system 122
Person-centered theory 108
Phallic stage 102
Phenotype 127
Pituitary gland 126
Pleasure principle 98
Polygenic 128
Positive reinforcement 117
Prefrontal area 125
Primary process thinking 99
Primary reinforcers 117
Psychodynamic perspective
98
Psychodynamics 98
Psychosexual stages 99
Psychosurgery 129
Punishment 117
Reality principle 99
Recessive 128
Reinforcement 117
Resistance 106
Reticular formation 124

Secondary process thinking 99
Secondary reinforcers 117
Selective serotonin reuptake
inhibitors (SSRI) 130
Self-actualization 109
Self-efficacy 118
Shaping 117
Social cognition 118
Social cognitive theory 118
Social learning 118
Sociocultural perspective 112
Somatic nervous system 122
Somatic therapies 129
Stimulus discrimination 116
Stimulus generalization 116
Subcortical structures 124
Superego 99
Sympathetic nervous system
126
Synapses 123
Synaptic cleft 123
Systematic desensitization 120
Theoretical perspective 98
Token economy 121
Transference 105
Unconditional positive regard
110
Unconditioned response 116
Unconditioned stimulus 115
Vicarious reinforcement 118
Working through 106

 # Internet Resource

To get more information on the material covered in this chapter, visit our web site at **http://www.mhhe.com/halgin.** There you will find more information, resources, and links to topics of interest.

CASE REPORT: HAROLD MORRILL

My first interaction with Harold Morrill involved his phone call to schedule an intake session. Prior to initial sessions, it is common for prospective clients to ask about my clinical approach and to inquire about such issues as billing and scheduling. Although I was expecting such questions, I was not prepared for the kind of encounter we had in that 20-minute telephone exchange. Harold began the call by stating, "Dr. Tobin, I want to begin therapy with you as soon as possible. I've heard about your reputation from several people, so I know that you are probably the most skilled and sensitive therapist in the area." After speaking on the phone for only 10 or 15 minutes, Harold enthusiastically exclaimed, "Yes, you are exactly the kind of therapist I've been looking for. You seem like a person who is genuinely caring and would be able to understand all that I've been through in this miserable life. Please, please take me as your patient!"

As I listened to Harold's lush praise, I had to resist the temptation to be flattered, realizing that this kind of idealization is often a signal that there will be trouble in the relationship later on. The overly positive response to me, after only a few minutes on the phone, seemed unwarranted. I could think of a dozen clients whom I had treated over the years who began therapy with similar idealizing words but whose emotional responsiveness to me was at the other end of the continuum after only a session or two. I couldn't be sure, of course, if Harold would show such extremes in his dealings with me, but I knew that it would be important for me to watch out for this possibility. As a matter of fact, I caught a glimpse of this style of splitting when we turned our attention to setting the intake appointment. When I explained to Harold that I had no openings until the following week, he responded with a tone of annoyance: "Busy little bee, aren't you?" Rather than take offense at Harold's comment, I tried to assure him that I was committed to working with him.

When I approached Harold Morrill in the waiting room, I immediately noticed the two small gold earrings in his left ear. His appearance caught my attention in other ways as well. Perhaps it was his shaggy, unkempt look or the fact that he appeared to be so much younger than 29, which was the age listed on his intake form.

Harold's initial description of his distress gave me a first glimpse into his confused state: "I feel lost and empty. I can't stand being alone, and yet I'm furious that people can't accept me for what I am. Sometimes I just want to kill myself to make other people feel some of the pain I feel all the time!" He then shared his long history of emotional problems—a life he characterized as filled with depression, anxiety, irritability, and uncontrollable anger. He spoke of the "emotional roller coaster" of his life, which had left others, as well as himself, feeling bewildered.

As Harold spoke of his dealings with other people, I found myself affected by the intensity of his interactions with others, both at work and in his personal life. When I asked about his numerous job changes, he described a series of bitter disputes with co-workers, most of which culminated in his abrupt departures from jobs, either because Harold was fired or because he stormed out in anger. In each situation, Harold rationalized his sudden departure by placing blame on an "airhead" supervisor or a "screwed up" company. To compensate for what he perceived to be his unjust treatment at each terminated job, Harold typically stole items from the workplace. Some items were relatively inexpensive office supplies, but Harold boasted that on one occasion he walked off with a laptop computer. He laughed as he explained, "Not only did they lose the computer, but I managed to walk away with some important inventory information that existed only on this computer. Guess they should've made a back-up, and I guess they'll learn that it's a good idea to treat their employees better than they treated me."

His intimate relationships were similarly unstable. Moving from partner to partner every few months, Harold had a long string of relationships, most of which ended when he became enraged over seemingly small matters. Often, these episodes of rage were followed by violent outbursts. In discussing his most recent lover, for instance, Harold told me gleefully about the time he punctured the tires on her car in a fit of rage when she told him that she planned to take a vacation without him. Harold also described an experience during this incident that left him feeling a bit frightened that things were really getting out of control—he believed that a voice in his thoughts was telling him that his partner was a "she-demon who should be punished."

Although recognizing that desperate behaviors such as those he described had chased away previous lovers, Harold dreaded the pain of not being in an intimate relationship. Driven to panic and despair by these feelings of emptiness, Harold found himself rushing into new relationships with people whom he instantaneously idealized in his mind. Each time, the infatuation quickly deteriorated into vicious animosity.

When I asked Harold about his sexual orientation, he acknowledged that he was not sure whether he preferred intimate relationships with men or with women. He explained his ambivalence by stating that the gender of his partner was less important than was the person's ability to make a commitment to him.

After listening to Harold describe his chaotic and unsatisfying relationships, I became increasingly concerned about his ability to commit himself to a psychotherapy relationship. I also felt concerned about his capacity to act in abusive ways toward his therapist. My concerns intensified as Harold told me about his three prior experiences with psychotherapy, each of which he ended abruptly because of the "incompetence" of the professionals who were treating him. When I asked whether he could make a commitment to long-term therapy, Harold tried to assure me that he was now "ready" to get the help he needed to become happier in life.

Sarah Tobin, PhD

5

Personality Disorders

Think about a few people you know, and then think of four or five adjectives that describe each of their personalities. You might describe a well-adjusted friend as enthusiastic, talkative, pleasant, warm, and cooperative. Another acquaintance annoys everyone, because all she seems to care about is herself. You might describe her as egocentric, manipulative, selfish, and attention-seeking. These adjectives may not convey the subtle distinctions between these two people, but they give you a sense of the fundamental characteristics of each person—what psychologists call personality traits. A **personality trait** is an enduring pattern of perceiving, relating to, and thinking about the environment and others, a pattern that is ingrained in the matrix of the individual's psychological makeup. In this chapter, you will read about people whose patterns of behavior are so rigid and maladaptive that they experience significant psychological problems and interpersonal difficulties.

The Nature of Personality Disorders

A **personality disorder** involves a longlasting maladaptive pattern of inner experience and behavior, dating back to adolescence or young adulthood, that is manifested in at least two of the following areas: (1) cognition, (2) affectivity, (3) interpersonal functioning, and (4) impulse control. This inflexible pattern is evident in various personal and social situations, and it causes distress or impairment. The personality disorders represent a collection of diverse and complex patterns of behavior. The expression of psychological disturbance is quite different for each, yet the problems that people with personality disorders experience are present every day and in most of their interactions with others. Whether their problems involve excessive dependency, overwhelming fear of intimacy, intense worry, exploitative behavior, or uncontrollable rage, these individuals are usually unhappy and maladjusted. They become caught in a vicious cycle in which their disturbed personal style alienates others, thus intensifying their problematic styles of relating. Because personality disorders involve the whole fabric of an individual's being, clinicians typically perceive them as being the most challenging of the psychological disorders to treat.

In evaluating whether an individual has a personality disorder, a clinician considers the person's life history. Have the person's problems been long-term and pervasive throughout life? Or are they related to a particular event or relationship? If the problems appear to be deeply entrenched and longstanding, characteristic ways of feeling and acting, this person may have a personality disorder.

Consider a sensitive young woman who worries about whether the co-workers at her new job like her or not; she fears that they may be making critical comments about her work when she is out of the office. Assuming this is a one-time occurrence, she would not be considered to have a personality disorder. By contrast, if the woman has lifelong concerns that others might talk about her, ridicule her, harm her, or try to stand in the way of her succeeding, this would be considered a rigid and maladaptive pattern indicative of a personality disorder.

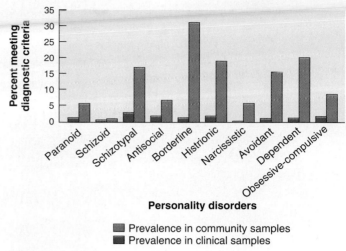

Figure 5.1

The prevalence of personality disorders in the general population and those in clinical samples. Source: *Textbook in Psychiatric Epidemiology* by M.T. Tsaung, M. Tohen, & G.E.P. Zuhner, Copyright ©1995 by John Wiley & Sons, Inc. Reprinted by permission of John Wiley & Sons, Inc.

The diagnosis of a personality disorder is particularly difficult, because many personality disorders share similar features (Morgenstern, Langenbucher, Labouvie, & Miller 1997). Although the authors of *DSM-IV* used large-scale empirical studies to provide clearly delineated diagnostic criteria (Widiger & Shea, 1991), concerns about reliability and validity of personality disorder diagnoses remain. There are wide ranges of estimates for the prevalence of many personality disorders, due to variations in the ways that specific criteria are defined and

---

Box 5.1

Diagnostic Features of Personality Disorder

An enduring pattern of inner experience and behavior that differs markedly from what is expected in the person's culture. This pattern is manifested in at least two of the following areas:

● Cognition—ways of perceiving self, other people, and events

● Affectivity—range, intensity, and appropriateness of emotional expression

● Interpersonal functioning

● Impulse control

The pattern is inflexible and pervasive across a range of personal and social situations.

The pattern causes distress or impairment.

The pattern is stable and of long duration, with an onset that can be traced back to adolescence or early adulthood.

measured. For example, *DSM-IV* specifies "inappropriate, intense anger or difficulty controlling anger" as a criterion for diagnosing borderline personality disorder, Harold Morrill's condition. As you might imagine, one clinician might see outrageous acts of revenge (puncturing tires and stealing a computer) as expressions of inappropriate anger, while another clinician might see these behaviors as criminal behaviors that would relate more to a diagnosis of antisocial personality disorder. Further complicating issues of diagnosis is the fact that an individual may have an Axis I disorder that interacts with the symptoms of the personality disorder. What if Harold Morrill also suffers from a severe depression? It might be difficult to determine whether certain symptoms are due to Harold's depression or to longlasting characteristics of his personality. Yet another problem is the fact that individuals tend to change over the adult years, as they adapt their personality traits to various life demands. As the symptoms change, the individuals may no longer meet the diagnostic criteria for the disorder (Zimmerman, 1994). For example, people who are exploitative and impulsive during youth and the middle years of life may change as they develop a more mature understanding of the negative consequences of their behavior.

The present system in the *DSM-IV* includes a set of separate diagnoses grouped into three clusters based on shared characteristics. Cluster A comprises paranoid, schizoid, and schizotypal personality disorders, which share the features of odd and eccentric behavior. Cluster B includes antisocial, borderline, histrionic, and narcissistic personality disorders. People with these disorders are overdramatic, emotional, and erratic or unpredictable. In Cluster C are avoidant, dependent, and obsessive-compulsive personality disorders. These are linked because they involve anxious and fearful behaviors. We will begin our discussion with Cluster B disorders—specifically, antisocial and borderline personality disorders. For each of these disorders, there is a relatively specific set of theoretical perspectives and treatment approaches. They are also the most extensively researched. Therefore, we will devote full sections to these two personality disorders before going on to describe the disorders that fall into Clusters A and C.

Antisocial Personality Disorder

When you hear a news story about a shocking crime in which the perpetrator has a long history of criminal behavior, you may wonder whether that individual has any sense of morality. Chances are that many such criminals have personality traits consistent with a diagnosis of **antisocial personality disorder,** which is characterized by a lack of regard for society's moral or legal standards.

Characteristics of Antisocial Personality Disorder

Although you may never have heard the label "antisocial personality disorder," you may have heard of people called psychopaths or sociopaths, terms commonly used to refer to people

with a pattern of traits that would currently be labeled antisocial personality disorder. In 1801, Philippe Pinel first recognized this disorder as a defect of "moral character." Widespread publicity still is given to this disorder, particularly when it is reflected in violent crime. Consider the case of Ted Bundy, a serial killer who sexually assaulted and ruthlessly murdered several dozen women yet was able to deceive people with his charming style. Bundy committed these brutal acts without concern for right or wrong, and without remorse for his deeds.

Most cases of antisocial personality disorder are far less extreme than that of serial killers, such as Ted Bundy, yet all share a lack of concern for what is right or wrong. People with this disorder wreak havoc in our society, and for this reason they have been the focus of a great deal of research. Antisocial personality disorder is disturbingly common, with an estimated lifetime prevalence of 4.5 percent of the adult males and .8 percent of the adult females in the United States (Robins & Regier, 1991).

The diagnosis of antisocial behavior used today in the *DSM-IV* has its origins in the work of Hervey Cleckley, whose 1941 book, *The Mask of Sanity,* represented the first scientific attempt to list and categorize the behaviors of the "psychopathic" personality, a work that appeared in its most recent edition more than 30 years later (Cleckley, 1976). Cleckley developed a set of criteria for **psychopathy,** a personality type characterized by a cluster of traits that constitutes the core of what is now called antisocial personality disorder. He outlined more than a dozen characteristics of psychopathy, which have provided the foundation for current diagnostic criteria. Cleckley's characteristics of psychopathy include lack of remorse or shame for harmful acts committed to others; poor judgment and failure to learn from experience; extreme egocentricity and incapacity for love; lack of emotional responsiveness to others;

Ted Bundy, one of the most notorious serial killers in the United States, was an example of an extreme antisocial personality disorder. Some clinicians still use the term psychopath or sociopath to describe a person with this behavior.

impulsivity ("fantastic and uninviting behavior"); absence of "nervousness"; and unreliability, untruthfulness, and insincerity. Cleckley used the term _semantic dementia_ to capture the psychopath's inability to react appropriately to expressions of emotionality. Cloaking these socially offensive behaviors is a veneer of superficial charm and seeming intelligence.

Cleckley's notion of psychopathy remains a key concept in descriptions of antisocial personality disorder. Building on Cleckley's work, Canadian psychologist Robert D. Hare developed an assessment instrument known as the Psychopathy Check List (PCL-R) (Hare, 1997), which has two factors: (1) affective interpersonal traits and (2) unstable and antisocial traits and behaviors. These factors were based on large-scale studies of forensic populations (Hare, 1991, 1993). The first factor includes such traits as glibness and superficial charm, a grandiose sense of self-worth, a tendency toward pathological lying, a lack of empathy for others, a lack of remorse, and an unwillingness to accept responsibility for one's own actions. The second key set of traits revolves around impulsivity, a characteristic that can lead to behaviors expressed in an unstable lifestyle, juvenile delinquency, early behavioral problems, lack of realistic long-term goals, and a need for constant stimulation.

The diagnostic criteria in the _DSM-IV_ go beyond the central traits of psychopathy and include the behavioral aspects of the disorder as reflected in a long list of chronic disreputable or manipulative behaviors. Consequently, not all individuals with psychopathic personalities meet the diagnostic criteria for antisocial personality disorder. These criteria involve a pervasive disregard for the rights of others as shown by such behaviors as unlawfulness, deceitfulness, and impulsivity. Individuals with this disorder may behave impulsively, aggressively, and recklessly without showing signs of remorse. At times, they may feign remorse with the intention of extricating themselves from a difficult situation. Rather than being outwardly aggressive, some are "smooth talkers," who are able to get what they want by presenting themselves in a favorable light. For example, a man with this disorder may persuade others to give him money by using manipulative sales tactics, or he may play on their sympathy by convincing them that he is a victim of circumstances and, in the process, get them to do something special for him.

It is important to distinguish between antisocial personality disorder and **adult antisocial behavior,** which refers to illegal or immoral behavior, such as stealing, lying, and cheating. A further distinction should be made between the terms _antisocial_ and _criminal_. The term _criminal_ has meaning in the legal system but is not a psychological concept. Nevertheless, many individuals who are sent to prison meet the psychological criteria for antisocial personality disorder. Estimates within prison populations of individuals with this disorder range from 40 to 75 percent (Hare, 1993; Widiger & Corbitt, 1995). Although some people tend to think only of men when discussing antisocial personality disorder, it is important to recognize that a significant number of women also have this condition, and many of them spend lengthy prison terms as convicted felons (Jordan, Schlenger, Fairbank, & Caddell, 1996). However, not all individuals with antisocial personality disorder are criminals. For many, the qualities of an antisocial personality disorder are reflected in acts that would not be considered violations of the law, such as job problems, promiscuity, and aggressiveness.

As is the case with all personality disorders, the problematic characteristics of people with antisocial personality disorder are enduring. That is, their problems begin in childhood and continue throughout most of their adulthood. In one fascinating study, researchers who assessed individuals at the age of 3 and again at the age of 21 found that undercontrolled young children (i.e., children who are impulsive, restless, and distractible) are more likely to meet the diagnostic criteria for antisocial personality disorder and to be involved in crime as adults (Caspi, Moffitt, Newman, & Silva 1996). As you will read in Chapter 11, problems with impulse control are common among children with conduct disorder, a condition that predisposes young people to develop antisocial personality disorder. Children and adolescents with conduct disorder get in trouble at home, in school, and in their neighborhoods. The more frequent and diverse the childhood antisocial acts are, the more likely the individual is to have a lifelong pattern of antisocial behavior (Lynam, 1997).

Although we have a good understanding of predisposing factors, we know less about the long-term prospects of individuals with antisocial personality disorder. Statistics show that the criminal activities of people with antisocial personality disorder seem to decrease when they reach the age of 40 (Hare, McPherson, & Forth, 1988) and that 94 percent of all serious crimes are committed by men under the age of 45 (U.S. Department of Commerce, 1989). The components of psychopathy involving impulsivity, social deviance, and antisocial behavior are less prominent in prison inmates who are older than the mid-40s (Harpur & Hare, 1994). Perhaps antisocial individuals experience "burnout" or have just become more adept at avoiding detection. Or perhaps some of the more extreme cases are eliminated from the population, because these people are killed or arrested in the course of their criminal activities.

Much research has focused on the relationship between juvenile delinquency and antisocial personality disorder.

Antisocial Personality Disorder

MINI-CASE

Tommy was the leader of a teenage street gang that was reputed to be the most vicious in the neighborhood. He grew up in a chaotic home atmosphere, his mother having lived with a series of violent men who were heavily involved in drug dealing and prostitution. At the age of 18, Tommy was jailed for the brutal mugging and stabbing of an elderly woman. This was the first in a long series of arrests for offenses ranging from drug trafficking to car thefts to counterfeiting. At one point, between jail terms, he met a woman at a bar and married her the next day. Two weeks later, he beat her when she complained about his incessant drinking and involvement with shady characters. He left her when she became pregnant, and he refused to pay child support. From his vantage point now as a drug trafficker and leader of a child prostitution ring, Tommy shows no regret for what he has done, claiming that life has "sure given me a bum steer."

■ Which of Tommy's behaviors would lead you to regard him as having antisocial personality disorder?

■ What does Tommy's lack of remorse suggest about his prospects for treatment?

DIAGNOSTIC FEATURES

This diagnosis is assigned to adults, who as children showed evidence of conduct disorder and who, from the age of 15, have shown a pervasive pattern of disregard for and violation of the rights of others, as indicated by three or more of the following:

● Repeated engagement in behaviors that are grounds for arrest

● Deceitfulness, such as lying, using false identities, or conning others for personal profit or pleasure

● Impulsivity, or failure to plan ahead

● Irritability and aggressiveness, such as repeated fights or assaults

● Reckless disregard for the safety of self or others

● Consistent irresponsibility, such as repeated failure to keep a job or honor financial obligations

● Lack of remorse, such as being indifferent to or rationalizing one's hurtful or dishonest behavior

Theories and Treatment of Antisocial Personality Disorder

As you have seen, antisocial personality disorder represents a deeply entrenched pattern of behavior, with wide-ranging effects on both the individual and the people with whom the individual comes into contact. In this section, we will consider the most compelling explanations for the development of this personality disorder. It is important to remember that some of these investigations pertain to criminals, who may or may not have been diagnosed specifically with antisocial personality disorder.

Biological Perspectives

When you hear about a terrible crime, such as a vicious mugging or ruthless murder, you probably don't presume that a biologically based disorder caused the perpetrator to commit this act. You may be surprised, then, to learn that there are a number of biological hypotheses about criminal behavior. Various brain abnormalities are cited as possible causes of antisocial personality disorder, including defects in the prefrontal lobes of the cerebral cortex (Deckel, Hesselbrock, & Bauer, 1996), areas of the brain involved in planning future activities and in considering the moral implications of one's actions. Abnormalities in the processing of emotionally charged words have also been demonstrated with SPECT studies comparing psychopaths with nonpsychopaths.

These abnormalities in the brain may have genetic causes. It has been observed for decades that criminal behavior runs in families. As with other behaviors found to show such a pattern, scientists have questioned whether antisocial behavior is learned or is genetically acquired. We will turn next to adoption studies and the studies of family inheritance patterns used in research on criminal behavior as clues to understanding the roots of antisocial personality disorder.

Studies of family inheritance patterns show that there is a modest heritability of criminality and psychopathy (Kendler, Davis, & Kessler, 1997). Strong evidence in favor of the inheritance of antisocial personality disorder comes from a study of more than 3,200 male twin pairs (Lyons et al., 1995). The researchers assessed the relative contributions of sharing an environment and sharing the same genotype. Although the environment seemed to play a role in determining the antisocial behavior of these people as juveniles (under the age of 15), the expression of antisocial behaviors in the adults reflected the influence of inheritance. In other words, adults who engage in antisocial behavior are expressing a genetic predisposition. Antisocial behavior in juveniles, on the other hand, reflects the influence of external factors, such as peers and home life.

Although the study of twins provides an important perspective, adoption studies are able to control more effectively for the influence of shared environments on estimates of heritability. In a study of almost 200 male and female adoptees who had been separated shortly after birth from their biological parents, researchers found that the children of parents with documented antisocial personality disorder were more likely to develop this disorder, particularly if they were then raised in an adverse adoptive home environment. However, the children without a biological predisposition for the disorder did not develop symptoms, even if they were raised in similarly harsh settings (Cadoret et al., 1995).

On the basis of these and other studies, experts have concluded that genetics can explain over one half of the gene-environment equation, with one heritability estimate reaching as high as 56 percent (O'Connor et al., 1998). Now let's take a look at other contributors to the equation.

Psychological Perspectives

Closely related to the biological perspective is the hypothesis that antisocial personality disorder is due to neuropsychological deficits reflected in abnormal patterns of learning and attention. Following along the lines of Cleckley's characterization of the psychopath as lacking emotional reactivity was a pivotal study conducted by David Lykken (1957), in which psychopathic individuals failed to show the normal response of anxiety when they were subjected to aversive stimuli. Lykken's hypothesis that the psychopath is unable to "feel" fear or anxiety (Lykken, 1995) has continued to gather support (Day & Wong, 1996; Patrick, Bradley, & Lang, 1993; Patrick, Cuthbert, & Lang, 1994). This fearlessness hypothesis has evolved into a more general proposition called the response modulation hypothesis, which proposes that psychopaths are unable to process any information that is not relevant to their primary goals (Newman, Schimitt, & Voss, 1997). According to the response modulation hypothesis, psychopaths are able to learn to avoid punishment when this is their main goal. However, if their attention is focused elsewhere, they do not pay attention to information that would allow them to avoid aversive consequences. This hypothesis would explain many aspects of the core psychopathic traits Cleckley identified, such as the inability to think about someone else's needs when one is focused on one's own personal interests. It might also explain the lack of remorse when causing pain to victims (Goldstein et al., 1996).

Another psychological perspective based on social-cognitive theory regards low self-esteem as a causal factor in antisocial personality disorder. As children, people who develop this disorder feel the need to prove their competence by engaging in aggressive acts (Lochman & Dodge, 1994).

Sociocultural Perspectives

Sociocultural perspectives on antisocial personality disorder focus on factors in the family, early environment, and socialization experiences that can lead individuals to develop a psychopathic lifestyle. One of the landmark studies investigating the role of early life influences was a 30-year follow-up study of juvenile delinquents carried out by Washington University psychologist Lee Robins (1966). Although it is commonly assumed that children of divorce later develop problems because of a lack of adequate discipline, Robins found that it is not the divorce itself but disharmony between parents that precede the child's development of antisocial behavior. According to Robins, this may be because the type of parents who are likely to argue excessively, especially fathers, may have psychological difficulties, including antisocial tendencies.

In the research by Robins and others on the effect on a child of different kinds of childrearing, inconsistent discipline appears to be especially problematic. When parents vacillate between unreasonable harshness and extreme laxity, they send confusing messages to the child about what is right and what is wrong, or what is acceptable and what is unacceptable. Children with such parents fail to make a connection between their actions, bad or good, and the consequences.

The relationship between childhood abuse and the development of antisocial personality disorder has become the focus of some very important research. Luntz and Widom (1994) tracked more than 400 individuals with substantiated histories of having been abused or neglected during childhood. When they interviewed and assessed these people in early adulthood, they found that the experiences of childhood victimization played a major role in influencing the likelihood that they would become antisocial adults. In a related study, Widom (as cited in Goleman, 1995) found that adults who had been neglected during childhood went on to have 50 percent more arrests for violent crimes than did matched subjects. Even more startling was the finding that physical abuse during childhood led to a rate that was double that of those in the comparison group.

In summing up the research on the impact of life experiences on the development of sociopathic behavior, Lykken (1997) views many of the parents of sociopathic individuals to have been overburdened, incompetent, and sociopathic themselves. To compensate for parental inadequacy, greater attention could be given to placement in foster care, group homes,

Popular movies such as "Natural Born Killers" glamorize violence in ways that some researchers regard as having disturbing influence on young people.

and boarding schools. The suggestion has been raised that parents should be "licensed," or at least given greater training in childrearing, especially when dealing with high-risk children.

Treatment of Antisocial Personality Disorder

From our discussion of antisocial personality disorder, you could conclude that people with this disorder do not change easily. For that matter, they are unlikely to seek professional help voluntarily, because they see no reason to change (Hare, 1993; Widiger, 1998). If they do see a clinician, it is often because treatment is mandated by a court order. Furthermore, by attending therapy sessions, the client may simply be attempting to impress a judge or a probation officer of a serious intent to reform. In such a situation, the clinician may have difficulty knowing whether or not to believe the client. Without giving up on the client or operating on the basis of preconceived biases, the clinician must be careful not to become unduly optimistic.

Given the difficulty of working with people with antisocial personality disorder, how can a clinician achieve a satisfactory treatment goal? Experts maintain that these people change their behavior only when they realize that what they have done is wrong. Therefore, the goal of therapy, ironically, is not to help these individuals feel better but, rather, to get them to feel worse about themselves and their situation. To do so, the clinician must initially adopt a confrontational approach, showing ostensible disbelief regarding the client's presumed fabrications, while continually reflecting back to the client the selfish and self-defeating nature of such behavior. Group therapy can be helpful in this process, because feedback from peers, who cannot be easily deceived, can have a forceful impact.

Inmates participating in group therapy such as the Lifeline Recovery Program confront each other while openly admitting their own problems and maladaptive behaviors.

When the therapeutic process is "successful," the client begins to feel remorse and guilt about his or her behavior, followed by feelings of hopelessness and despondency, which, it is hoped, will lead to behavior change. Keep in mind, though, that such a "positive" outcome is extremely difficult to achieve.

■ Borderline Personality Disorder

The names of most of the personality disorders include words that convey the essence of the disorder, such as "antisocial" and "paranoid." What does it mean to be "borderline"? In the current *DSM-IV* terminology, **borderline personality disorder** is characterized by a pervasive pattern of poor impulse control, fluctuating self-image, and unstable mood and interpersonal relationships. Because this is a somewhat elusive diagnosis, the authors of the *DSM-IV* have specified observable behaviors and symptoms that characterize the disorder.

Characteristics of Borderline Personality Disorder

When the term *borderline* first became popular in psychiatry, it was used as a catchall for the most difficult and treatment-resistant clients (Stern, 1938). These individuals were felt to be functioning somewhere at the "border" between neurosis and psychosis, on the fringes of schizophrenia (Knight, 1953). Despite the vagueness of the concept of borderline, the term remained in use because it described a subgroup of clients that did not seem to fit into the existing diagnostic categories. Efforts to clarify and define the nature of the disorder continued through the 1980s. Some researchers have maintained that borderline personality disorder is a variant of schizophrenia or mood disorder, or possibly a hybrid. However, by the time the *DSM-IV* was in its final stages of preparation, most experts had come to regard it as a singular personality disorder (Berelowitz & Tarnopolsky, 1993).

The female character Alex in the movie *Fatal Attraction* is a good example of what a person with borderline personality is like. In a very dramatic scene in the movie, Alex becomes overwhelmingly distraught following a one-night sexual encounter, and she slashes her wrists at the moment her sexual partner is preparing to leave. In the weeks that follow, Alex obsessively pursues this man. Her intense emotionality and rage terrify him, as she acts out many outrageous and disturbing behaviors, such as boiling the pet rabbit that belongs to the man's family. The intensity of this relationship, even one so brief, gives you a glimpse into a central characteristic of people with this disorder—unstable interpersonal relationships.

People with borderline personality disorder often experience a distinct kind of depression that is characterized by feelings of emptiness and variable negative emotionality (Southwick, Yehuda, & Giller, 1995; Westen & Cohen, 1993). Although they rarely go as far as to harass other people, they tend to be deeply affected by interpersonal incidents that most other people would let pass. It is common for people with this

Explaining the Prevalence of Borderline Personality Disorder Among Women

As you read about borderline personality disorder, perhaps a relative or an acquaintance comes to mind. Is this person a man or woman? You may be surprised to learn that most individuals with this diagnosis are women (Grilo et al., 1996), while far more men are diagnosed with narcissistic, antisocial, and obsessive-compulsive personality disorder (Akhtar, 1996). What could account for these gender differences?

For years, there has been controversy about the fact that women are much more likely than men to be diagnosed with personality disorders in general. Some experts have questioned whether there is a gender bias that results in feminine personality characteristics being perceived as pathological. In their efforts to understand gender differences, these investigators have looked at overlapping features of antisocial and borderline personality disorder (Paris, 1997a). For example, impulsivity is a characteristic associated with both conditions, yet this criterion is interpreted quite differently for each disorder. For antisocial personality disorder, *DSM-IV* specifies "impulsivity or failure to plan ahead" but for borderline personality disorder states "impulsivity in at least two areas that are potentially self-damaging (e.g., spending, sex, substance abuse, reckless driving, binge eating)." Which gender comes to mind as you read these criteria? Taking the issue a step further, we see that several behaviors associated with antisocial personality disor-

der, such as violence and aggression, are stereotypically male, while characteristics associated with borderline personality disorder, such as intense relationships and affective instability, are stereotypically female (Grilo et al., 1996). Additionally, some scientists believe the diagnosis of mental disorders in general is plagued by biases and methodological problems that result in over-diagnosis of personality disorders in women (Hartung & Widiger, 1998).

Moving beyond the question of possible gender bias in diagnosis, researchers have explored the possibility that differing biology and differing life experiences might account for the gender imbalance between these disorders in adulthood. Hormonal differences may explain the disparity; perhaps females are predisposed to developing borderline characteristics because of a gender-specific reaction to endorphins (Holden, Pakula, & Mooney, 1997).

Other researchers and clinicians highlight environmental factors as the most important contributors to the development of borderline personality disorder (Sabo, 1997; Zanarini et al., 1997). Experts have focused on the childhood years as a time during which many of these individuals experienced disturbed and chaotic parental relationships which interfered with emotional and interpersonal development. Such experiences as sexual abuse, physical abuse, neglect, and parental substance abuse or criminal behavior are commonly reported in the childhood histories of individuals who grow into borderline personality disorder (Guzder, Paris, Zelkowitz, & Marchessault, 1996). But, since such experiences affect both boys and girls, researchers realize that there must be more to the story.

In scrutinizing the differences between the troubling childhood experiences of boys and girls, investigators have focused on the powerful and lasting effects of sexual abuse in the development of borderline personality disorder (Figueroa & Silk, 1997; Wagner & Linehan, 1997; Zanarini et al., 1997). Females are more likely than males to have been sexually abused during childhood, and an alarming number of women with borderline personality disorder report having been the victims of re-

peated or prolonged sexual molestation during childhood (Paris, 1997b).

Some experts have proposed conceptualizing borderline personality disorder as a complex reaction to the trauma of childhood sexual abuse (Herman, Perry, & van der Kolk, 1989). In contrast to clients with post-traumatic stress disorder, individuals with borderline personality disorder are less likely to experience flashbacks and other intrusive recollections of their trauma. Instead, their symptoms are usually consistent with their overall character. Wagner and Linehan (1994; 1997) have suggested that parasuicidal symptoms, such as cutting or burning oneself, may be related to a history of sexual abuse. In their study, women with borderline personality disorder who had also been sexually abused committed more self-destructive acts than those who had not been sexually abused. In addition, their attempts to hurt themselves were more lethal and reflected a stronger wish to commit suicide. For people with borderline personality disorder, parasuicide may be an attempt to cope with intolerable thoughts and feelings through their transformation into palpable, physical pain. Dissociation, another symptom of the disorder, may represent a similar effort to cope with the intolerable by preventing conscious awareness of painful thoughts, feelings, and experiences.

The likely result of chronic childhood sexual abuse is that the experiences become integrated into a child's developing personality, interfering with most spheres of psychological development. It is important to remember, however, that childhood sexual abuse is neither the sole cause, nor the sole route, to borderline personality disorder. Not all individuals who are sexually abused develop the disorder. Not all people with the disorder have been sexually abused. Nonetheless, knowledge of the abuse histories of clients with borderline symptoms can be tremendously important in understanding a possible reason for the higher prevalence of borderline personality disorder among women. By recognizing the importance of early history, as well as biological contributors, clinicians can develop more effective interventions for these individuals.

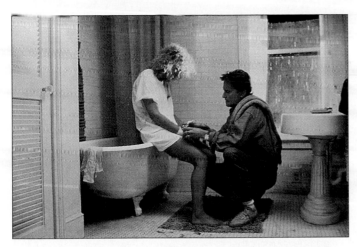

The movie, "Fatal Attraction," captured many of the symptoms and behaviors associated with borderline personality disorder, such as this scene following a suicidal gesture of Alex in response to her rage about being abandoned.

disorder to form suddenly intense, demanding relationships with others and to perceive other people as being all good or all bad—a phenomenon referred to as **splitting.** The inappropriate intensity of their relationships results in recurrent experiences of distress and rage. In fact, anger and hostility are enduring characteristics found in many people with this disorder.

In addition to having disturbed relationships, people with borderline personality disorder are often confused about their own **identity,** or concept of who they are. Even after they have passed through the customary time of identity questioning in adolescence, they are unsure of what they want out of life and, at a deeper level, lack a firm grasp of their sense of self. Their uncertainty about who they are may be expressed in sudden shifts in life choices, such as career plans, values, goals, and types of friends. This identity confusion may reach a point at which they become unclear about the boundaries between themselves and others. For example, in close relationships, they may have difficulty distinguishing between their own feelings and the feelings of the other person. Other identity problems appear in the area of sexual orientation; these individuals may shift between identifying as homosexual or heterosexual, perhaps going through phases in which they abruptly redefine their own sexuality (Munich, 1993).

Chronic feelings of boredom lead people with borderline personality disorder to seek stimulation. In part, the drama of their relationships reflects this search for intense emotional experiences. In their attempt to fend off boredom, they may engage in impulsive behaviors, such as promiscuity, careless spending, reckless driving, binge eating, substance abuse, or shoplifting. The excitement from these activities makes them feel alive. Furthermore, their moods are as unstable as their behavior. They may vacillate between extreme emotional states, one day feeling on top of the world and the next feeling depressed, anxious, and irritable.

The extremes of feelings that people with borderline personality disorder experience may drive them precipitously into a state of suicidal thinking and self-injurious behavior. As was illustrated in the discussion on page 146, sometimes they

are not intent on killing themselves, and their behavior—called **parasuicide**—is considered a gesture to get attention from family, a lover, or professionals. In other cases, they may actually hurt themselves with a knife or razor in an act of self-directed aggression. For people with borderline personality disorder, such behavior sometimes serves as a test of whether they are actually alive, a concept that most people take for granted but one that becomes a source of uncertainty for these individuals. The sight of blood and the physical pain reassure them that their bodies have substance. Interestingly, some of these individuals do not experience pain while cutting themselves. These individuals seem to comprise a subtype of borderline personality disorder who experience especially severe symptoms of depression, anxiety, impulsiveness, and dissociation; furthermore, many in this high risk group have histories of early abuse. It is not surprising that the intensity of emotional pain leads to serious suicide attempts (Kemperman, Russ, & Shearin, 1997; Russ, Shearin, Clakin, & Harrison, 1993). The risk of suicide is especially high in individuals with deficient problem-solving ability who may see suicide as the only way out of a difficult situation (Kehrer & Linehan, 1996).

Many individuals with borderline personality disorder seem intensely angry much of the time. Even without provocation, they fly into a fury. A friend's seemingly innocent comment may cause them to lash out sarcastically or to become bitter for an unreasonable length of time. A common trigger for their rage is the feeling that they have been neglected or abandoned by a lover or another important person. At times, their intense anger may lead them to express physical violence against others. After their angry outbursts, they may feel ashamed and guilty and become convinced of their inherent evil nature.

Stress is particularly problematic for people with borderline personality disorder. During stressful experiences, their vulnerability intensifies, causing them to feel highly suspicious and untrusting of others to the point of being paranoid. They may also develop dissociative symptoms, such as feeling disconnected from others and even their own conscious self.

Although many aspects of their functioning are disturbed, most people with this disorder can manage the responsibilities of everyday life. Some are actually successful in various contexts (for instance, the character Alex, in *Fatal Attraction*, had a well-paid, important job). However, for many, there is a constant undercurrent of interpersonal conflict and the risk that their unpredictability, dependency, and moodiness may drive away people to whom they are close. At times, the demands of their lives may become overwhelming. They may experience a transient, psychotic-like state, possibly characterized by delusional thinking or dissociative symptoms, which can necessitate hospitalization.

Theories and Treatment of Borderline Personality Disorder

Tremendous effort has been devoted to the development of theories and treatment for people with this condition, perhaps because these individuals create so much chaos in the lives of everyone with whom they interact. It is also an inherently

Borderline Personality Disorder

MINI-CASE

Lisa is a 28-year-old account executive with a long history of interpersonal problems. At the office, her co-workers see her as being intensely moody and unpredictable. On some days, she is pleasant and high-spirited, but on others she exhibits uncontrollable anger. People are often struck by her inconsistent attitudes toward her supervisors. She vacillates between idealizing them and devaluing them. For example, she may boast about the "brilliance" of her supervisor one day, only to deliver a burning criticism the next day. Her co-workers keep their distance from her, because they have become annoyed with her constant demands for attention. She has also gained a reputation in the office for her promiscuous involvements with a variety of people, male and female. On several occasions, she has been reprimanded for becoming inappropriately involved in the personal lives of her clients. One day, after losing one of her accounts, she became so distraught that she slashed her wrists. This incident prompted her supervisor to insist that Lisa obtain professional help.

■ What would lead you to diagnose Lisa as having borderline personality disorder, rather than a mood disorder, such as depression?

■ How does Lisa's disorder interfere with her ability to succeed at her profession?

DIAGNOSTIC FEATURES

This diagnosis is assigned to people who show recurrent impulsivity and a pervasive pattern of instability of interpersonal relationships, self-image, and affects, as indicated by five or more of the following:

● Frantic efforts to avoid real or imagined abandonment

● A pattern of unstable and intense interpersonal relationships characterized by changes between idealizing and devaluing others

● Identity disturbance—unstable self-image or sense of self

● Impulsivity in at least two areas, such as spending, sex, substance abuse, and reckless driving

● Recurrent suicidal behavior, gestures, or threats or self-mutilating behavior

● Emotional instability, such as intense episodes of sadness, irritability, or anxiety, usually lasting a few hours and sometimes several days

● Chronic feelings of emptiness

● Inappropriate, intense anger or difficulty controlling anger, such as frequent displays of temper, constant anger, or recurrent physical fights

● Occasional stress-related paranoid thinking or dissociative symptoms

---

fascinating disorder, because it revolves around a disturbance in the very essence of self-definition.

The biopsychosocial model is particularly well-suited to understanding this disorder. Researchers are increasingly recognizing that the disorder evolves from a combination of a vulnerable temperament, traumatic early experiences in childhood, and a triggering event or set of events in adulthood (Zanarini & Frankenburg, 1997). Together, these influences interact to create the volatile behaviors and difficulties in identity and relationships that plague the life of the individual with the disorder.

Biological Perspectives

Researchers studying possible biological contributors to this disorder are trying to identify physiological markers that distinguish borderline personality disorder from mood disorders and schizophrenia. Although most theories regarding this disorder are psychological, some investigators have examined the possibility that some of the psychological factors thought to be involved in the development of this disorder have biological correlates. Specifically, as you will see, early childhood trauma in

the form of sexual abuse is regarded as a prime suspect in the search for psychological factors. The possibility that such abuse leaves an imprint on the individual's brain led researchers to suggest that sexual abuse in childhood may make the noradrenergic (sympathetic nervous system) pathways hypersensitive, so that the individual is constantly primed to overreact to experiences of any kind later in adulthood. This altered sympathetic functioning may interact with a predisposition toward impulsivity, due to abnormalities in serotonergic receptors in the brain. The self-destructive and impulsive behaviors of people with this disorder, combined with the distress they experience due to their tendency to overreact to life events, may produce the characteristics of borderline personality disorder (Figueroa & Silk, 1997).

Psychological Perspectives

The notion of early childhood trauma forms the cornerstone of the psychological approaches to understanding borderline personality disorder (Sabo, 1997). This emphasis on trauma emerged from a wealth of clinical observations that all pointed to a common theme in the stories clients told of their early histories. Researchers have provided evidence to support these clinical hunches, and several theories have emerged that attempt to connect trauma to the development of the traits associated with the disorder. In fact, there seems to be a direct relationship between the extent to which a person was abused or neglected as a child and the likelihood of developing borderline personality disorder. In one investigation of more than 750 women between the ages of 16 and 45, over 93 percent of the respondents had experienced at least some abuse or trauma during childhood. Even worse, many of the abused women had suffered combined abuse from several perpetrators (Laporte & Guttman, 1996). Theories regarding the basis for the relationship between early abuse and neglect and the development of borderline personality disorder propose that these experiences cause children to expect that others will harm them (Silk, Lee, Hill, & Lohr 1995). As adults, people with borderline personality disorder report that their caretakers withdrew from them emotionally, treated them inconsistently, denied the validity of their thoughts and feelings, and did not carry out their roles as parents in terms of providing them with protection, often from sexual abuse by a male noncaretaker (Zanarini et al., 1997). Abnormal bonding with a parent and an anxious attachment style, particularly with the mother, are additional risk factors (Salzman, Salzman, & Wolfson, 1997).

Clinical observations led the psychodynamic theorists who

first described the characteristics of borderline personality disorder to propose a different model of parent-child relationships to explain the development of borderline pathology (Gunderson, 1984; Kernberg, 1967; Masterson, 1981). These theorists believed that deficits in the formation of the self were the underlying pathology of this disorder. One disturbed pattern of parenting they identified is that of a mother who is overinvolved with her child but also inconsistent in her emotional responsiveness. By failing to bolster the child's independent sense of self, she sets the stage for her child's later lack of an identity and a sense of commitment to life goals. The individual fails to develop a healthy "real" self that can form the basis for intimate, sharing, and committed relationships with others or that can be creative, spontaneous, and assertive. The individual perceives other people in a distorted way and builds a false self that is fused with these distorted perceptions of others (Masterson & Klein, 1989).

In contrast to theories that emphasize abnormalities in parenting, cognitive-behavioral approaches to understanding people with borderline personality disorder focus on their maladaptive thoughts. According to Beck's cognitive approach (Beck, Freeman, & Associates, 1990), people with this disorder have a tendency to dichotomize their thinking about themselves and other people; in other words, they think in terms of "all or nothing." Such thinking could account for the individual's tendency to shift moods so readily and to use splitting in relationships with others. For example, if an individual with borderline personality disorder originally perceives someone as all good, and that person then fails to follow through on a promise, the person immediately appears to become all bad. People with borderline personality disorder also apply this limited set of standards when evaluating themselves; when they perceive themselves as falling short, even on minor grounds, their entire self-evaluation becomes negative. Finally, a low sense of self-efficacy related to their weak identity causes a lack of confidence in their decisions, low motivation, and an inability to seek long-term goals.

Sociocultural Perspectives

Millon contends that the pressures of contemporary society that have placed a strain on families and individuals may exacerbate the deficient parenting that can give rise to this disorder (Millon & Davis, 1996). People with borderline personality disorder are particularly vulnerable to the diminished cohesion in society that is associated with urbanization and modernization in contemporary culture. Their lack of psychic cohesion reflects the instability within society and a lack of clearly defined cultural norms and expectations. Further contributing to their development of this disorder is a pattern of instability within their family. A child who is subjected to parental conflict comes to feel internally divided and, furthermore, starts to question basic assumptions about life's predictability and stability. From another perspective, family difficulties, including depression, substance abuse, and antisocial behavior, can lead to the development of this disorder through the perpetuation of childrearing patterns that are

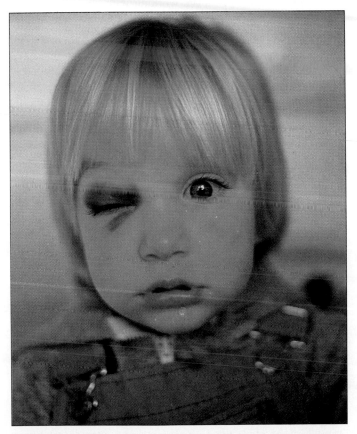

A childhood history of abuse is thought to be one cause of borderline personality disorder. The tragic face of this badly abused child provides compelling evidence of emotional scars that will last throughout life.

carried from generation to generation (Goldman, D'Angelo, & DeMaso, 1993). An adult with borderline personality disorder who was abused as a child passes on this pattern of parenting to the next generation, who then become vulnerable to developing the disorder (Stone, 1990).

Treatment of Borderline Personality Disorder

Due to their volatility, inconsistency, and intensity, people with borderline personality disorder have difficulty remaining in therapy long enough to make progress. Also, these individuals commonly become pathologically dependent on their therapist; as a result, they may feel uncontrollably enraged when the therapist fails to live up to their idealizations. Consequently, therapists are watchful of their own emotional reactions, recognizing that these clients may evoke intense feelings of anger or helplessness. Furthermore, since these clients are prone to distort their relationship with the therapist, it is necessary to try to keep the client grounded in reality (Kernberg et al., 1989).

Although clinicians agree on certain key facets of therapy for people with borderline personality disorder, controversy remains about whether to focus more on confrontive or supportive approaches (Gunderson, 1989). Some clinicians believe that the client's manipulative behavior can be held in check only by confrontation (Gunderson, 1984; Kernberg, 1984; Masterson & Klein, 1989). In contrast, other clinicians recommend a more supportive, nurturant technique. For example, Millon (1998a) suggests that, once clear limits have been established early in the therapy relationship, the therapist should be as responsive and supportive as possible within those limits; he contends that a failure to be responsive causes the client to feel abandoned. Consider the situation in the case study at the beginning of the chapter, when Harold Morrill made a sarcastic comment to Dr.

Tobin about her inability to schedule an immediate appointment. When Harold stated, "Busy little bee, aren't you?" Dr. Tobin felt that it would be therapeutically wiser for her to assure Harold of her commitment to helping him than to confront his sarcasm. In the course of therapy, a client may make derogatory remarks about the therapist, which the therapist can then use as opportunities to show the client the inappropriateness and destructiveness of misdirected anger. The therapist, then, would respond to the client's anger with concern and understanding. This approach is based on the assumptions that the client's disorder is the result of poor parenting and that the therapist can provide a positive parental role. As Millon notes, much can be gained as the client comes to realize that others need not be perceived as people who are dangerous or likely to abandon the client out of an unwillingness to put up with the client's problems and difficult interpersonal style.

Some clinicians integrate supportive and cognitive-behavioral techniques to reduce the frequency of self-destructive acts and to improve the client's ability to handle disturbing emotions, such as anger and dependency. Psychologist Marsha Linehan has developed a treatment method that she calls "Dialectical Behavioral Therapy (DBT)," in which the term *dialectical* refers to systematically combining opposed ideas with the goal of reconciling them (Heard & Linehan, 1994; Linehan, 1993a). Thus, the therapist's strategy is to alternate between accepting clients as they are and confronting their disturbing behavior to help them change. In a detailed manual, Linehan provides guidelines for therapists working with clients who have borderline personality disorder (Linehan, 1993b). These guidelines are based on the underlying principle that therapists should move between acceptance and change within the context of a supportive therapeutic relationship. Much of Linehan's work is based on therapy with suicidal individuals, in which the relationship becomes a crucial factor, not only for keeping the client in therapy but also for keeping the client alive. In her work with suicidal clients, Linehan applies the dialectical approach by "reframing" suicidal behaviors as dysfunctional, maladaptive efforts to solve problems. This reframing constitutes acceptance or an attempt to understand the origins of the behavior. At the same time, she focuses therapy on new ways to analyze the problem and to develop healthier solutions, a process that stimulates change. Specific methods used within this framework are regulating emotions, developing interpersonal effectiveness, learning to tolerate emotional distress, and developing self-management skills. One process, called "core mindfulness," teaches clients to balance emotions, reason, and intuition in their approach to life's problems.

Linehan points out that the results from several of her studies support the effectiveness of this intervention. Compared with clients who received standard weekly psychotherapy, DBT clients showed a decreased frequency of suicidal or self-destructive behavior and became more able to control anger and anxiety. The DBT clients described themselves as more emotionally adjusted, described their interpersonal relationships in more positive terms, and experienced fewer problems in social and vocational settings. Furthermore, the DBT clients remained in therapy for longer periods of time

People with borderline personality disorder often have a difficult time with good-byes. Reluctant to end the session, such a client may bring up an "important" new issue, ignoring the therapist's cues that it is time to get up and leave.

and were hospitalized less frequently. On the other hand, DBT was not more effective in reducing hopelessness, depression, and suicidal ideation. Researchers studying the long-term effects of this intervention have found that clients maintain improved functioning for 1 year after treatment (Shearin & Linehan, 1994).

As an adjunct to the psychological treatment of people with borderline personality disorder, some clinicians recommend medication. Although no medication can effectively treat borderline personality disorder, several pharmacological interventions have been shown to be effective in treating specific symptoms (Maxmen & Ward, 1995). The group of medications used to target borderline symptoms includes antidepressants, antipsychotics, anticonvulsants, lithium, and minor tranquilizers (Markovitz, Calabrese, Schultz, & Meltzer 1991; Soloff et al., 1993). Physicians realize that these medications must be prescribed with careful assessment of the specific symptoms that are most problematic for the client. For example, serotonergic medications, such as fluoxetine (Prozac), have been shown to be especially effective in controlling depression and impulsive aggression while helping the client manage anxiety, sensitivity about possible rejection, psychotic-like thinking, and obsessive-compulsive symptoms (Coccaro & Kavoussi, 1997).

Clearly, both the symptoms and the treatment of people with borderline personality disorder are challenging and complex. In severe cases, successful treatment can be undertaken only in an inpatient setting. This is particularly true when clients are suicidal, experience psychotic-like episodes, or threaten harm to other people. The hospital provides a safe and secure setting, in which limits are established and maintained (Stone, 1990). Alternatively, day treatment partial hospitalization can offer these clients intensified treatment that is less likely to cultivate too much dependency (Miller, 1995).

■ Histrionic Personality Disorder

Some people tend to express themselves in very dramatic ways. When carried to an extreme, these tendencies form the basis for **histrionic personality disorder.** The term *histrionic* is derived from a Latin word meaning "actor." People with this disorder display theatrical qualities in their everyday behavior. For example, someone with this disorder may put on a "show" of being overwhelmed with tears and sentimentality at the wedding of a distant relative or may greet an acquaintance at a party with ostentatious and attention-getting hugs and exclamations of affection. What differentiates people with this disorder from those who show appropriate emotionality is the fleeting nature of their emotional states and the fact that they use excessive emotions to manipulate others rather than to express their genuine feelings. This disorder is more commonly diagnosed in women, though it is not clear whether this is because the disorder is more common in women or because those who are assigning the label regard histrionic behaviors as stereotypically feminine.

People with histrionic personality disorder enjoy being the center of attention and behave in whatever way necessary to ensure that this happens. They are excessively concerned with their own physical appearance, often trying to draw attention to themselves in such extreme ways that their behavior seems ludicrous. Furthermore, they are likely to be seen as flirtatious and seductive, demanding the reassurance, praise, and approval of others and becoming furious if they don't get it. They want immediate gratification of their wishes and overreact to even minor provocations, usually in an exaggerated way, such as by weeping or fainting. Although their relationships are superficial, they assume them to be intimate and refer to acquaintances as "dear" friends. They are easily influenced by others, lack analytic ability, and see the world in broad, impressionistic terms. You can imagine how such histrionic behaviors would cause others to keep their distance; being in a relationship with a person with a histrionic personality disorder can be exasperating and unsatisfying. The result, of course, is that people with this disorder have few, if any, close and reciprocal relationships.

Cognitive-behavioral theorists propose that people with this personality disorder have several mistaken assumptions underlying their approach to life (Freeman, Pretzer, Fleming, & Simon, 1990). One basic belief of the person with this disorder is that "I am inadequate and unable to handle life on my own," which leads to the next step of assuming that it is necessary to find someone else to make up this deficit (Millon, 1991; Millon & Davis, 1996). These individuals seek attention and approval by acting in ways that are stereotypes of hyperfemininity or hypermasculinity, believing that this will elicit admiration and support from others. Given the

Trying to catch other people's attention is a common characteristic of people with histrionic personality disorder.

Histrionic Personality Disorder

MINI-CASE

Lynnette is a 44-year-old high-school teacher who is notorious for her outlandish behavior and inappropriate flirtatiousness. Several of her students have complained to the principal about her seductive behavior during individual meetings. She often greets students with overwhelming warmth and apparent concern over their welfare, which leads some to find her appealing and engaging at first; however, they invariably become disenchanted, once they realize how shallow she is. To her colleagues, she brags about her minor accomplishments, as if they were major victories, yet, if she fails to achieve a desired objective, she sulks and breaks down into tears. She is so desperate for the approval of others that she will change her story to suit whomever she is talking to at the time. Because she is always creating "crises," and never reciprocates the concern of others, people have become immune and unresponsive to her frequent pleas for help and attention.

- How does Lynnette's behavior differ from that of Lisa, who was described as having borderline personality disorder?

- If you were a friend of Lynnette's, how would you react to the dramatic style and behaviors characteristic of her histrionic personality disorder?

DIAGNOSTIC FEATURES

This diagnosis is given to people who show a pervasive pattern of excessive emotionality and attention seeking, as indicated by five or more of the following:

- Discomfort when not the center of attention

- Interactions characterized by inappropriate sexually seductive or provocative behavior

- Rapid shifts and shallow expression of emotions

- Use of physical appearance to draw attention

- Speech that is excessively impressionistic and lacking in detail

- Self-dramatization, theatricality, and exaggerated expression of emotion

- High suggestibility

- Misinterpretation of relationships as being more intimate than they are

---

cognitive-behavioral position that emotions are a product of one's thoughts, it follows that the global nature of the histrionic individual's thinking style leads also to diffuse, exaggerated, and rapidly changing emotional states. The way these individuals evaluate people and situations is equally imprecise and subject to distortion; therefore, their opinions can change on a daily basis from one extreme to another.

A therapist using cognitive-behavioral techniques would help the client develop more effective ways of approaching problems and situations, would work with the client to focus on goals, and would teach the client how to think more precisely and objectively. By taking this approach, the therapist models good problem-solving behavior and gives the client practical help in dealing with various life issues. Clients also learn self-monitoring strategies to keep their impulsive tendencies in check, as well as assertiveness skills to improve interpersonal relationships.

■ Narcissistic Personality Disorder

People with **narcissistic personality disorder** have an unrealistic, inflated sense of their own importance, a trait known as **grandiosity.** The name of this disorder comes from the Greek legend of Narcissus, the youth who fell in love with his own reflection in a pond. Although people with this disorder expect

others to compliment them and gratify all their wishes and demands, they lack sensitivity to the needs of others. Because they perceive themselves as being so special, they feel that only high-status people can appreciate their special needs and problems. They possess excessive aspirations for their own

A person with narcissistic personality disorder is preoccupied with appearance and extremely concerned about impressing others with an attractive and suave presentation.

Narcissistic Personality Disorder

MINI-CASE

Chad is a 26-year-old man who has been desperately trying to succeed as an actor. However, he has had only minor acting jobs and has been forced to support himself by working as a waiter. Despite his lack of success, he brags to others about all the roles he rejects because they aren't good enough for him. Trying to make inroads into acting, he has been selfishly exploitive of any person whom he sees as a possible connection. He has intense resentment for acquaintances who have obtained acting roles and devalues their achievements by commenting that they are just "lucky," yet, if anyone tries to give him constructive criticism, Chad reacts with outrage, refusing to talk to the person for weeks. Because of what he regards as his "terrific" looks, he thinks he deserves special treatment from everyone. At the restaurant, Chad has recurrent arguments with his supervisor, because he insists that he is a "professional" and that he should not have to demean himself by clearing dirty dishes from the tables. He annoys others, because he always seeks compliments on his clothes, hair, intelligence, and wit. He is so caught up with himself, that he barely notices other people and is grossly insensitive to their needs and problems.

- How has Chad's self-absorption and grandiose sense of himself, characteristic of narcissistic personality disorder, caused problems in his life?

- Compare Chad's sense of self-importance with Lynnette's, who has histrionic personality disorder. In what ways are they similar? In what ways do they express their grandiosity differently?

DIAGNOSTIC FEATURES

This diagnosis applies to people who show a pervasive pattern of grandiosity, need for admiration, and lack of empathy, as evidenced by five or more of the following:

- Grandiose sense of self importance

- Preoccupation with fantasies of success, power, brilliance, beauty, or ideal love

- Belief that they are so "special" that they should associate only with other special people, who can understand them

- Need for excessive admiration

- Sense of entitlement

- Exploitive interpersonal style

- Lack of empathy

- Envy of others or belief that others are envious

- Arrogant behaviors and attitudes

---

lives and intense resentment for others whom they perceive as more successful, beautiful, or brilliant. They are preoccupied with and driven to achieve their own goals and think nothing of exploiting others in order to do so. Despite their show of grand self-importance, they are often troubled by self-doubt. Relationships with others, whether social, occupational, or romantic, are distorted by the perception of other people as tools for self-gratification. Furthermore, they can be haughty and arrogant, characteristics that interfere with their interpersonal relationships.

Noting the many types of behaviors incorporated into the definition of the narcissistic personality disorder, Millon (1998b) proposed subtypes: the normal, the unprincipled, the amorous, the compensatory, the elitist, and the fanatic narcissistic personalities. According to Millon, differentiation among these subtypes would add greater refinement to the *DSM* diagnostic criteria and would reflect the distinctions made by the various theories regarding the disorder. More generally, questions about the validity of the diagnostic category were raised in a follow-up study. Three years after an

initial diagnosis of narcissistic personality disorder, 60 per cent of the group no longer met the criteria for this diagnosis (Ronningstam, Gunderson, & Lyons, 1995). Another difficulty in conceptualizing narcissism is that it is a common feature of other personality disorders, especially histrionic and borderline personality disorders. As many as one fifth of those with another personality disorder also meet the diagnostic criteria for narcissistic personality disorder (Gunderson, Ronningstam, & Smith, 1991).

Apart from these empirical considerations, the construct of narcissism is an interesting one and has stimulated some important theoretical analyses regarding its origins and development. The traditional Freudian psychoanalytic approach regards narcissism as the failure to progress beyond the early stages of psychosexual development. More current object relations conceptualizations focus on the effect of disturbances in the parent-child relationship on the developing child's sense of self. Every child needs parents to provide reassurance and positive responses to accomplishments. Without these, the child becomes insecure. This insecurity is expressed, paradoxically, in an inflated sense of self-importance that can be understood as the individual's attempt to make up for what was missing earlier in life (Kohut, 1966, 1971). Lacking a firm foundation of a healthy self, these individuals develop a false self that is precariously based on grandiose and unrealistic notions about their competence and desirability (Masterson & Klein, 1989). Narcissistic personality disorder can be understood, then, as the adult's expression of this childhood insecurity and need for attention.

Cognitive-behavioral theorists (Beck et al., 1990) contend that people with narcissistic personality disorder hold maladaptive ideas about themselves, including the view that they are exceptional people who deserve to be treated far better than ordinary humans. They lack insight into or concern for the feelings of other people, because they consider themselves to be superior to others. These beliefs hamper their ability to perceive their experiences realistically, and they encounter problems when their grandiose ideas about themselves clash with their experiences of failure in the real world.

The psychodynamic approach to treating individuals with narcissistic personality disorder is based on the notion that they lack early experiences of admiration for their positive qualities. Therapy is intended to provide a corrective developmental experience, in which the therapist uses empathy to support the client's search for recognition and admiration but, at the same time, attempts to guide the client toward a more realistic appreciation that no one is flawless. Somewhat paradoxically, the more recognition and support the therapist gives the client, the less grandiose and self-centered the client becomes (Kohut, 1971).

Cognitive-behavioral therapy for narcissistic personality disorder also is oriented toward reducing the client's grandiosity and enhancing the client's ability to relate to others. In working toward this goal, the therapist structures interventions that work with, rather than against, the client's self-aggrandizing and egocentric tendencies. For example, rather than try to convince the client to be less selfish, the therapist might try to show that there are better ways to reach important personal goals. At the same time, the therapist avoids giving in to the client's demands for special favors and attention. When the therapist establishes and follows an agenda with clear treatment goals, the client may learn how to set limits in other areas of life (Freeman et al., 1990).

Paranoid Personality Disorder

The term *paranoia,* as you have already learned, means suspiciousness, guardedness, and vigilance toward other people, based on the belief that others intend harm. As you will see later in this book, paranoid thinking is present in various psychological disorders. In this section, we will look at the personality disorder that is characterized by paranoia.

People with **paranoid personality disorder** are extremely suspicious of others and are always on guard against potential danger or harm. Their view of the world is very narrowly focused, in that they seek to confirm their expectations that others will take advantage of them, making it virtually impossible for them to trust even their friends and associates. They may accuse a spouse or partner of being unfaithful, even if no substantiating evidence exists. For example, they may believe that an unexplained toll call that appears on a telephone bill is proof of an extramarital affair. They are unable to take responsibility for their mistakes and, instead, project blame onto others. If others criticize them, they become hostile. They are also prone to misconstrue innocent comments and minor events as having a hidden or threatening meaning. They may hold grudges for years, based on a real or an imagined slight by another person. Although individuals with this disorder might be relatively successful in certain kinds of jobs requiring heightened vigilance, their emotional life tends to be isolated and constrained.

As you can imagine, people with paranoid personality disorder have problematic relationships. They keep other people at a distance because of irrational fears that others will harm them, and they are particularly sensitive to people in positions of power. For example, they may create a "paper trail" of their work, keeping records of everything, in case they are ever accused of a mistake or an impropriety. A certain amount of paranoid thinking and behavior might be appropriate in some situations, such as in dangerous political climates in which people must be on guard just to stay alive; however, people with paranoid personality disorder think and behave in ways that are unrelated to their environment.

Particularly frustrating to the relatives and acquaintances of these people is the fact that they refuse to seek professional help, because they don't acknowledge the nature of their problem. In the unlikely event they do seek therapy, their rigidity and defensiveness make it very difficult for the clinician to make inroads and work toward any kind of lasting change.

Psychodynamic theorists have explained paranoid personality disorder as a style of viewing the world in which the individual relies heavily on the defense mechanism of projection, meaning that other people, rather than the self, are perceived as having negative or damaging motives (Shapiro, 1965). In contrast, cognitive-behavioral theorists (Beck et al., 1990) regard the person with paranoid personality disorder as someone who suffers from mistaken assumptions about the world and who attributes personal problems and mistakes to others.

The cognitive-behavioral perspective (Freeman et al., 1990) incorporates these ideas but presents an alternate view, emphasizing the three basic mistaken assumptions that people with paranoid personality disorder hold: "People are malevolent and deceptive," "They'll attack you if they get the chance," and "You can be OK only if you stay on your toes." The difficulty these assumptions create is that the behavior of others inevitably causes them to conclude that their impressions are correct. If a woman is primed to suspect other people's motives, she is likely to interpret what they do as proof. For instance, Caroline believes that retail merchants deliberately take advantage of consumers. The next time a salesperson gives her the wrong change, she will interpret this not as a casual error but as confirmation of her fears. According to the cognitive-behavioral view, the third mistaken assumption, that people have to be vigilant to avoid being harmed, is related to

Paranoid Personality Disorder

MINI-CASE

Anita is a computer programmer who constantly worries that other people will exploit her knowledge. She regards as "top secret" the new database management program she is writing. She even fears that, when she leaves the office at night, someone will sneak into her desk and steal her notes. Her distrust of others pervades all her interpersonal dealings. Her suspicions that she is being cheated even taint routine transactions in banks and stores. Anita likes to think of herself as rational and able to make objective decisions; she regards her inability to trust other people as a natural reaction to a world filled with opportunistic and insincere corporate ladder climbers.

■ How does Anita's sense of mistrust impair her relationships with others?

■ What would lead you to think that Anita has a paranoid personality disorder, rather than a form of psychosis involving paranoid symptoms?

DIAGNOSTIC FEATURES

People with this personality disorder show pervasive distrust and suspiciousness of others whose motives they interpret as malevolent, as indicated by four or more of the following:

● Unjustified suspicion that others are exploiting, harming, or deceiving them

● Preoccupation with unjustified doubts about others' loyalty or trustworthiness

● Reluctance to confide in others, for fear that the information will be used against them

● Tendency to read hidden demeaning or threatening meanings into harmless remarks or events

● Tendency to bear grudges

● Perception of personal attacks that are not apparent to others and tendency to respond with angry counterattacks

● Recurrent unjustified suspicions about the faithfulness of spouse or sexual partner

feelings of low self-efficacy, leading paranoid people to believe that they cannot detect the harmful intentions of others and, therefore, must perpetually stay on guard.

The treatment of paranoid personality disorder that follows from the cognitive-behavioral perspective (Freeman et al., 1990) involves countering the client's mistaken assumptions in an atmosphere aimed at establishing a sense of trust. The therapist attempts to increase the client's feelings of self-efficacy, so that the client feels able to handle situations without resorting to a defensive and vigilant stance. Because the client with paranoid personality disorder is likely to enter therapy feeling distrustful of the therapist, the therapist must make a special effort to help the client feel that therapy is a collaborative process. Other beneficial interventions involve helping the client become more aware of other points of view and develop a more assertive approach to conflict with others. These increased interpersonal skills improve the quality of the client's interactions outside therapy and eventually contribute to disproving the client's mistaken assumptions.

■ Schizoid Personality Disorder

The term *schizophrenia,* as discussed in Chapter 2, refers to a psychological disorder in which the individual experiences severe disturbances in thought, affect, and behavior. Two personality disorders, schizoid and schizotypal, involve disturbances in personality that have schizophrenia-like qualities but do not take on the psychotic form seen in schizophrenia. As you will see in Chapter

10, researchers are studying the relationship between these personality disorders and schizophrenia. In fact, some researchers refer to these three disorders as **schizophrenia spectrum disorders,** implying that all three are on a continuum of psychological disturbance and may be related. For the present, we will describe the characteristics of the two personality disorders that share some aspects of the symptoms found in schizophrenia.

Schizoid personality disorder is characterized by an indifference to social and sexual relationships, as well as a very limited range of emotional experience and expression. Individuals with this disorder prefer to be by themselves rather than with others, and they appear to lack any desire to be accepted or loved, even by their families. Sexual involvement with others holds little appeal. As you might expect, others perceive them as cold, reserved, withdrawn, and seclusive, yet the schizoid individual is unaware of, and typically insensitive to, the feelings and thoughts of others.

Throughout their lives, many people with schizoid personality disorder seek out situations that involve minimal interaction with others. It is no surprise, then, that employment is problematic for these individuals, and they are unlikely to retain jobs for more than a few months (Fulton & Winokur, 1993). Those who are able to tolerate work are usually drawn to jobs in which they spend all of their work hours alone. They rarely marry but, rather, choose solitary living, possibly in a single room, where they guard their privacy and avoid any dealings with neighbors. Although they are not particularly distressed or a risk to others, their self-imposed isolation and emotional constriction can be considered

Schizoid Personality Disorder

MINI-CASE

Pedro, who works as a night security guard at a bank, likes his job, because he can enter the private world of his thoughts without interruptions from other people. Even though his numerous years of service make him eligible for a daytime security position, Pedro has repeatedly turned down these opportunities, because daytime work would require him to deal with bank employees and customers. Pedro has resided for more than 20 years in a small room at a rooming house. He has no television or radio, and he has resisted any attempts by other house residents to involve him in social activities. He has made it clear that he is not interested in "small talk" and that he prefers to be left alone. Neighbors, co-workers, and even his own family members (whom he also avoids) perceive Pedro as a very peculiar person who seems strikingly cold and detached. When his brother died, Pedro decided not to attend the funeral, because he did not want to be bothered by all the "carrying on" and sympathetic wishes of relatives and others.

■ To what extent might Pedro's eccentricity be due to his social isolation?

■ If Pedro is not unhappy because of his self-imposed isolation, what would justify a diagnosis of schizoid personality disorder?

DIAGNOSTIC FEATURES

This diagnosis applies to people who show a pervasive pattern of detachment from relationships and a restricted emotional range, as indicated by four or more of the following:

● Lack of desire for or enjoyment of close relationships

● Strong preference for solitary activities

● Little or no interest in sexual experiences with another person

● Lack of pleasure in few, if any, activities

● Lack of close friends or confidants, other than immediate relatives

● Indifference to praise or criticism

● Emotional coldness, detachment, or flat emotionality

---

maladaptive. They take pleasure in few, if any, activities. As maladaptive as their behavior may seem, people with schizoid personality disorder are not likely to seek psychotherapy. If they do enter therapy, perhaps for another psychological disorder, such as a mood disorder or substance abuse, these people are difficult to treat because of their lack of interest in interpersonal relationships.

The construct of schizoid personality disorder is closely tied to the schizophrenia spectrum concept in terms of causal factors. However, in an interesting examination of possible risk factors for the development of this particular personality disorder, a team of researchers investigating the effect of early life experiences found that nutritional deficiency during the prenatal period was a risk factor for the development of schizoid personality disorder by the age of 18 years. This study was conducted in the Netherlands, on men born during the famine of 1944–1946. Schizophrenia was also more prevalent in men whose mothers suffered through the famine (Hoek et al., 1996).

Treating people with schizoid personality disorder is extremely difficult, because they lack the normal patterns of emotional responsiveness that play a role in human communication. The therapist must be careful to avoid setting unrealistically high goals for therapy, because progress with these individuals is likely to be slow and limited in scope. Most promising is an approach geared toward helping them work on their styles of communication (Freeman et al., 1990).

Schizotypal Personality Disorder

People tend to regard individuals with **schizotypal personality disorder** as peculiar, eccentric, and oddly bizarre in the way they think, behave, and relate to others, even in how they dress. Their peculiar ideas may include magical thinking and beliefs in psychic phenomena, such as clairvoyance and telepathy. They may have unusual perceptual experiences in the form of illusions. Though their speech is not incoherent, the content sounds strange to others. Their affect is constricted and inappropriate. They are often suspicious of other people and may have ideas of reference, beliefs that the behavior of others or a random object or event refers to them. Unable to experience pleasure, their lives are characterized by a sense of blandness, which robs them of the capacity for enthusiasm. Like people with schizoid personality disorder, these individuals find it difficult to establish close relationships, because they experience discomfort around others—in part, due to their suspiciousness.

The symptoms of social isolation, eccentricity, peculiar communication, and poor social adaptation associated with schizotypal personality disorder are regarded by some researchers as cause to place it within the schizophrenic spectrum (Torgersen, 1985). According to this view, the symptoms of schizotypal personality disorder represent a **latent** form of schizophrenia, meaning that people with schizotypal symptoms are vulnerable to developing a full-blown psychosis if exposed to difficult life circumstances that challenge their ability to maintain contact with reality. This position received support from a 15-year follow-up study of people who met the criteria for schizotypal personality disorder, schizophrenia, and borderline personality disorder. At the end of the follow-up period, the schizotypal individuals were functioning more like people diagnosed with schizophrenia than like those with borderline personality disorder (McGlashan, 1983). There is also evidence that people with schizotypal personality disorder have some of the same biological anomalies as people with schizophrenia, such as attentional deficits (Roitman et al., 1997) and abnormalities of eye movement (Keefe et al., 1997; Thaker et al., 1996). Another view is that schizotypal personality disorder and schizophrenia are genetically linked but constitute distinct disorders. Rather than schizotypal personality disorder representing a latent version of schizophrenia, it may be a different disorder found in people with a family history of schizophrenia (Kendler, Neale, & Walsh, 1995). In other words, the offspring of schizophrenic parents have a heightened genetic vulnerability to developing either schizophrenia or schizotypal personality disorder, depending on a complex of other biological and environmental factors.

Odd behavior and appearance are characteristics of people with schizotypal personality disorder.

Schizotypal Personality Disorder

MINI-CASE

Joe is a college junior who has devised an elaborate system for deciding which courses to take, depending on the course number. He will not take a course with the number 5 in it, because he believes that, if he does so, he might have to "plead the Fifth Amendment." Rarely does he talk to people in his dormitory, believing that others are intent on stealing his term paper ideas. He has acquired a reputation for being "kind of flaky" because of his odd manner of dress, his reclusive tendencies, and his ominous drawings of sinister animals displayed on the door of his room. The sound of the nearby elevator, he claims, is actually a set of voices singing a monastic chant.

■ How does Joe's lack of interest in social relations compare with the case of Pedro, who has a schizoid personality disorder?

■ Why would Joe's odd behaviors constitute schizotypal personality disorder, rather than a psychotic disorder?

DIAGNOSTIC FEATURES

This diagnosis is given to people who show a pervasive pattern of social and interpersonal deficits marked by acute discomfort with, and reduced capacity for, close relationships and who experience cognitive or perceptual distortions and behavioral eccentricities, as indicated by five or more of the following:

● Ideas of reference

● Odd beliefs or magical thinking, which influences their behavior (e.g., belief in mind reading)

● Unusual perceptual experiences, including bodily illusions

● Odd thinking and speech

● Suspiciousness or paranoid ideation

● Inappropriate or constricted affect

● Behavior or appearance that is odd or eccentric

● Lack of close friends or confidants other than immediate relatives

● Excessive social anxiety that tends to be associated with paranoid fears

Avoidant Personality Disorder

Most people feel some degree of shyness on occasion—for example, in an unfamiliar situation in which they do not know other people. They may be concerned about committing a social blunder and appearing foolish; however, if a person is always intimidated by social situations, fearful of any kind of involvement with others, and terrified by the prospect of being publicly embarrassed, he or she may have **avoidant personality disorder.**

People with avoidant personality disorder refrain almost entirely from social encounters, especially avoiding any situation with the potential for personal harm or embarrassment, and they steer clear of an activity that is not part of their usual, everyday routine. Sometimes they imagine terrible calamities resulting from novel activities and use this concern as a reason to avoid new situations where they can be seen by other people. Convinced that they are socially inferior to others, they become extremely sensitive to rejection and ridicule, interpreting the most innocent remark as criticism. As a result of their desire to avoid the imagined disapproval of others, they tend to be loners. Their job preferences reflect this desire to keep away from others; they avoid occupations that would involve interacting with people. If they can be assured of unconditional acceptance, they can enter into close and even intimate relationships. However, they remain restrained in their relationships, guarding against possible criticism, embarrassment, or rejection.

You might think that this disorder is very similar to schizoid personality disorder. In both disorders, the person tends to stay away from intimate relationships. However, the person with the avoidant disorder truly desires closeness and

Although wanting to do so, a person with avoidant personality disorder cannot join in a lively conversation, due to the fear of saying something embarrassing.

feels a great deal of emotional pain about the seeming inability to make connections with others. By contrast, the schizoid individual prefers to be alone and lacks a sense of distress about being uninvolved with others.

Contemporary psychodynamic explanations of this disorder emphasize the individual's fear of attachment in relationships (Sheldon & West, 1990), while cognitive-behavioral approaches regard the individual as hypersensitive to rejection, due to childhood experiences of extreme parental criticism (Beck et al., 1990; Freeman et al., 1990). According to this approach, the dysfunctional attitudes these individuals hold center around the core belief that they are flawed and unworthy of other people's regard. Because of their perceived unworthiness, they expect that people will not like them; therefore, they avoid getting close to others to protect themselves from what they believe to be inevitable rejection. Contributing to their dilemma are their distorted perceptions of experiences with others. Their sensitivity to rejection causes them to misinterpret seemingly neutral and even positive remarks. Hurt by this presumed rejection, they retreat inward, placing further distance between themselves and others.

The main goal of cognitive-behavioral therapy is to break the negative cycle of avoidance. The client learns to articulate the automatic thoughts and dysfunctional attitudes that are interfering with interpersonal relations and to see the irrationality of these beliefs, but in a supportive atmosphere. These interventions are most successfully accomplished after the client has come to trust the therapist. Other therapeutic measures based on a cognitive-behavioral model include graduated exposure to increasingly threatening social situations and the training of specific skills to improve intimate relationships. Interestingly, individuals who are more distrustful and angry toward others seem to benefit from graduated exposure. By contrast, people with this disorder who allow themselves to be coerced and controlled by others respond particularly well to skills training (Alden & Capreol, 1993).

Dependent Personality Disorder

Unlike people with avoidant personality disorder, individuals with **dependent personality disorder** are strongly drawn to others. However, they are so clinging and passive that they may achieve the opposite of their desires as others become impatient with their lack of autonomy. Convinced of their own inadequacy, they cannot make even the most trivial decisions on their own. For example, a man may feel incapable of selecting his clothes each day without consulting his live-in partner. In more important spheres, he may rely on his partner to tell him what kind of job to seek, whom he should be friends with, and how he should plan his life.

Others may characterize individuals with this disorder as "clingy." Without others near them, people with dependent personality disorder feel despondent and abandoned. They become preoccupied with the fear that close ones will leave them. They cannot initiate new activities on their own, because they feel that they will make mistakes unless others guide their actions. They go to extremes to avoid being disliked—for example, by

Avoidant Personality Disorder

MINI-CASE

Max is a delivery person for a large equipment corporation. His co-workers describe Max as a loner, because he does not spend time in casual conversation and avoids going out to lunch with others. Little do they know that every day he struggles with the desire to interact with them but is too intimidated to follow through. Recently, he turned down a promotion to become manager, because he realized that the position would require a considerable amount of day-to-day contact with others. What bothered him most about this position was not just that it would require interaction with people but also that he might make mistakes that would be noticed by others. Although he is 42 years old, Max has hardly ever dated. Every time he feels interested in a woman, he becomes paralyzed with anxiety over the prospect of talking to her, much less asking her for a date. When female co-workers talk to him, he blushes and nervously tries to end the conversation as soon as possible.

- How do the symptoms of Max's avoidant personality disorder compare with the isolation shown by Pedro, who has a schizoid personality disorder?

- What potential do you think Max has to benefit from treatment?

DIAGNOSTIC FEATURES

This diagnosis applies to people with a pattern of social inhibition, feelings of inadequacy, and hypersensitivity to negative evaluation, as indicated by four or more of the following:

- Avoidance of activities that involve significant interpersonal contact because of fears of criticism, disapproval, or rejection

- Unwillingness to get involved with others unless certain of being liked

- Restraint within intimate relationships due to fear of being shamed or ridiculed

- Preoccupation with being criticized or rejected in social situations

- Inhibition in new interpersonal situations because of feelings of inadequacy

- Self-view as socially inept, personally unappealing, or inferior to others

- Reluctance to take personal risks or new activities due to fear of being embarrassed

---

agreeing with other people's opinions, even when they believe these opinions to be misguided. Sometimes they take on responsibilities that no one else wants, so that others will approve of and like them. If anyone criticizes them, they feel shattered. They are likely to throw themselves wholeheartedly into relationships and, therefore, become devastated when relationships end. This extreme dependence causes them to seek another relationship urgently to fill the void.

Psychodynamic theory has traditionally regarded individuals with dependent personality disorder as having regressed to or become fixated at the oral stage of development because of parental overindulgence or parental neglect of dependency needs. Object relations theorists regard such individuals as being insecurely attached, constantly fearing abandonment (West & Sheldon, 1988). Because of their low self-esteem, they rely on others for guidance and support (Lively, Schroeder, & Jackson, 1990). Consistent with these theories, researchers using the Family Environment Scale have found that the families of people with dependent personality disorder tend to have high ratings on the factor of control but low ratings on the factor of independence (Baker, Capron, & Azorlosa, 1996).

A cognitive-behavioral approach to dependent personality disorder maintains that resting at the heart of the disorder are unassertiveness and anxiety over making independent decisions. Dependent individuals believe that they are

When waiting to meet a late-arriving friend, a person with dependent personality disorder may feel helpless, not knowing what to do.

Dependent Personality Disorder

MINI-CASE

Betty has never lived on her own; even while a college student, 30 years ago, she commuted from home. She was known by her classmates as someone who was dependent on others. Relying on others to make choices for her, she did whatever her friends advised, whether it involved the choice of courses or the clothes she should wear each day. The week after graduation, she married Ken, whom she had dated all senior year. She was particularly attracted to Ken, because his domineering style relieved her of the responsibility to make decisions. As she has customarily done with all the close people in her life, Betty goes along with whatever Ken suggests, even if she does not fully agree. She fears that he will become angry with her and leave her if she rocks the boat. Although she wants to get a job outside the home, Ken has insisted that she remain a full-time homemaker, and she has complied with his wishes. However, when she is home alone, she calls friends and desperately pleads with them to come over for coffee. The slightest criticism from Ken, her friends, or anyone else can leave her feeling depressed and upset for the whole day.

■ Why would Betty be regarded as having a dependent personality disorder, instead of being a product of a society that once fostered dependency in women?

■ How does Ken's behavior reinforce Betty's lack of assertiveness?

DIAGNOSTIC FEATURES

People with this disorder have a pervasive and excessive need to be taken care of, which leads to their submissive, clinging behavior and fears of separation, as indicated by five or more of the following:

● Difficulty making everyday decisions without advice and reassurance

● Need for others to assume responsibility for most major areas of life

● Difficulty expressing disagreement with others due to fear of loss of support or approval

● Difficulty initiating projects or tasks because of low self-confidence in judgment or abilities

● Tendency to go to excessive lengths to obtain nurturance and support to the point of volunteering to do things that are unpleasant

● Feelings of discomfort or helplessness when alone due to fear of being unable to care for themselves

● Pursuit of another relationship as a source of care and support immediately following the end of a close relationship

● Preoccupation with fears of being left to take care of themselves

---

inadequate and helpless and, therefore, are unable to deal with problems on their own. For them, the natural solution is to find someone else who will "take care" of them and relieve them of the obligation to make independent decisions. Having arrived at this solution, they dare not act in assertive ways that might challenge the relationship's security.

In psychotherapy based on cognitive-behavioral principles, the therapist provides structured ways for the client to practice increasing levels of independence in carrying out daily activities. The client also learns to identify actual areas of skill deficits and then to acquire the abilities necessary to perform these skills. However, while helping the client, the therapist avoids becoming an authority figure to the client. Clearly, it would be counterproductive for the client to become as dependent on the therapist as on others in his or her life (Beck et al., 1990; Freeman et al., 1990).

Obsessive-Compulsive Personality Disorder

People with obsessive-compulsive personality disorder struggle continuously with an overwhelming concern about neatness and the minor details of everyday life. You can probably think of instances in your own life when you have found it very diffi-

cult to make a decision. Perhaps you worried about the matter for days, going back and forth between two choices, somewhat tormented by the process of evaluating the pros and cons of each choice. Imagine what it would be like to go through life this way. People with **obsessive-compulsive personality disorder** feel immobilized by their inability to make a decision. (The words *obsessive* and *compulsive* in this context have a different meaning from the way you will see them used in the next chapter, when we discuss the anxiety disorder known as obsessive-compulsive disorder, a condition in which the individual suffers with the kind of diagnosable obsessions or compulsions we discussed in Chapter 3). In addition, people with obsessive-compulsive personality disorder are intensely perfectionistic and inflexible and express these attributes in a number of maladaptive ways. In striving for unattainable perfection, they become caught up in a worried style of thinking, and their behavior is inflexible to the point of being rigid.

The disturbance of people with obsessive-compulsive personality disorder is also evident in how they act. They have an inordinate concern with neatness and detail, often to the point of losing perspective on what is important and what is not. This style is both irksome to others and inefficient for the individual with the disorder, because it makes it impossible to complete a project. Every single detail must come out

Obsessive-Compulsive Personality Disorder

MINI-CASE

For as long as he can remember, Trevor has been preoccupied with neatness and order. As a child, his room was meticulously clean. Friends and relatives chided him for excessive organization; for example, he insisted on arranging the toys in his toy closet according to color and category. In college, his rigid housekeeping regimens both amazed and annoyed his roommates. He was tyrannical in his insistence on keeping the room orderly and free from clutter. Trevor has continued this pattern into his adult life. He is unhappy that he has not found a woman who shares his personal habits but consoles himself by becoming immersed in his collection of rare record albums featuring music of the 1940s. Trevor, a file clerk, prides himself on never having missed a day of work, regardless of health problems and family crises. However, his boss will not offer him a promotion, because she feels he is overattentive to details, thus slowing up the work of the office as he checks and rechecks everything he does. He enhances his sense of self-importance by looking for opportunities in the office to take control. For example, when his co-workers are planning a party, Trevor tends to slow down matters because of his annoying concerns about every detail about the event. More often than not, his co-workers try to avoid letting him get involved, because they object to his rigidity even in such trivial matters.

- In assessing Trevor's behavior, where would you draw the line between careful attention to detail and obsessive-compulsive personality disorder?

- How does Trevor's behavior create problems in his personal and social life?

DIAGNOSTIC FEATURES

This diagnosis applies to people with a pervasive pattern of preoccupation with orderliness, perfectionism, and mental and interpersonal control, at the expense of flexibility, openness, and efficiency, as indicated by four or more of the following:

- Preoccupation with details, rules, order, organization, or schedules to such an extent that the major point of the activity is lost

- Perfectionism that interferes with task completion

- Excessive devotion to work and productivity to the exclusion of leisure activities and friendships (not due to economic necessity)

- Tendency to be overconscientious, scrupulous, and inflexible about matters of morality, ethics, or values (not due to culture or religion)

- Inability to discard worn-out or worthless objects

- Reluctance to delegate tasks to others unless they agree to an exact way of doing things

- Miserly spending style toward self and others

- Rigidity and stubbornness

Just right, and, by the time these details are handled, the person has run out of time or resources. Similarly, these individuals' daily lives are ruled by a fanatical concern with schedules. For example, they might refuse to start a meeting until precisely the second it is scheduled to begin, or they might insist on seating each person in a room in alphabetical order. They are stingy with time and money and tend to hoard even worn-out and worthless objects. People with this disorder have a poor ability to express emotion, and they have few intimate relationships. Their intense involvement in their work contributes to this pattern, because they have little time for leisure or socializing. When they do interact with other people, they tend to be so rigid that they will not concede or compromise when there is disagreement. Others may regard them as excessively moralistic or prudish because of their narrow views on social, religious, and political issues.

It is important to keep in mind that there is a difference between the hard-working, well-organized person with high standards and a concern about getting a job done right and the per-

son with an obsessive-compulsive personality disorder. People with this disorder are unproductive, and their pursuit of perfectionism becomes self-defeating rather than constructive. Obsessive-compulsive personality disorder is one of the more common personality disorders (Weissman, 1993), and it is more common in men than women (Golomb, Fava, Abraham, & Rosenbaum, 1995).

Freud believed that the obsessive-compulsive style represented fixation at or regression to the anal stage of psychosexual development. Psychodynamic thinking about this disorder has advanced somewhat from the time of Freud, however, with more attention given to cognitive factors and prior learning experiences as central in its development (Shapiro, 1965).

From the standpoint of cognitive-behavioral theory, people with this disorder have unrealistic expectations about being perfect and avoiding mistakes (Beck et al., 1990; Freeman et al., 1990). Their feelings of self-worth depend on their behaving in ways that conform to an abstract ideal of perfectionism;

if they fail to achieve that ideal (which, inevitably, they must), they regard themselves as worthless. In this framework, obsessive-compulsive personality disorder is based on a problematic way of viewing the self.

Cognitive-behavioral treatment can be made more difficult by particular problems in this personality disorder. The person with obsessive-compulsive personality disorder tends to go over past actions constantly and to consider further actions in light of whether or not there is a danger of making a mistake. Cognitive-behavioral therapy, with its focus on examining the client's thought processes, may reinforce this ruminative tendency.

Personality Disorders: The Perspectives Revisited

Now that you have read about the wide variety of ingrained patterns represented in the personality disorders, you can appreciate that it is difficult to make general statements about the causes and treatment of this diverse group. As we have seen throughout this chapter, researchers working in the field of personality disorders have struggled with the issue of overlap among these disorders (Bornstein, 1998). The jury is still out on whether *DSM-IV* has brought about greater refinement.

While researchers continue to investigate the best system for diagnosing personality disorders, clinicians continue to look for the most effective methods for treating people whose symptoms have endured over many years and whose problems have been resistant to change. Given the uncertainties regarding the causes and nature of these personality disorders, clinicians focus their therapeutic efforts on the primary causes of the client's current distress, a more realistic goal than bringing about total change. Although some clinicians follow a set of specific ideas about treatment, most individualize their treatment to respond to the particular problems of each client. For example, when treating a person with a dependent personality disorder, the clinician can help the client understand the roots of this dependency and then intervene in ways to reinforce autonomy. In contrast, when treating a client with avoidant personality disorder, the therapist focuses on helping the client develop more satisfying interpersonal relations.

At times, the clinician may rely more heavily on particular theoretical perspectives if they seem pertinent to the client's history and current symptoms. For example, when treating clients with borderline personality disorder, more and more clinicians are finding that cognitive-behavioral approaches, such as Dialectical Behavior Therapy, are quite helpful. Even clinicians who identify with other approaches may incorporate some of these techniques in treating clients with this personality disorder.

Because of the chronic and persistent nature of personality disorders, as well as the difficulty in precisely identifying their qualities, these disorders are likely to remain a challenging area for researchers and clinicians. It is also quite likely that the diagnostic criteria for these disorders, and even their names, will undergo continued revision in future editions of the *DSM*, as theorists and researchers continue to refine and elaborate on their scientific base. In this process, mental health professionals will develop not only a better understanding of this form of disturbance but also perhaps a richer appreciation for the factors that contribute to normal personality growth and change through life.

Brief Psychodynamic Treatment of Personality Disorders

Because personality disorders are so deeply ingrained in the fabric of personality, therapies for individuals diagnosed with personality disorders have traditionally been lengthy endeavors, often resulting in only limited change in the individuals, enduring patterns of relating with others (Reich & Green, 1991). With increasing pressures to provide effective therapy in briefer periods of time, researchers and clinicians have begun to question the traditional assumption that personality change requires years of intensive psychotherapy. Of course, many therapists have relied on cognitive and behavioral approaches, in which brief therapy is viable. But how are therapists who adhere to a psychodynamic model to respond to the pressures of the marketplace to conduct briefer therapies, even for deeply disturbed clients? Many are being inspired by research that supports the appropriateness of a brief psychodynamic approach to the treatment of various psychological disorders, including personality disorders. In a statistically based reanalysis of studies of short-term dynamic therapy, Crits-Cristoph (1992) concluded that these therapies are effective forms of treatment for a variety of disorders, with effects comparable in scope to those of other forms of psychotherapy.

Therapists using short-term psychodynamic therapies approach their work with a frame of reference comparable to what they would use in lengthier treatments; however, they modify their work in important ways. Specifically, they intentionally try to heighten a client's emotional arousal during sessions, possibly steering the client toward a central, maladaptive theme that might explain certain emotional and interpersonal problems. In their efforts to help clients change longstanding emotional patterns and psychological defenses, some therapists have relied on frequent, active confrontation, but research suggests that confrontation in the absence of empathic support can actually increase a client's defensiveness (McCullough-Vaillant, 1994).

In Time-Limited Dynamic Therapy (TLDP), which was developed by Hans Strupp and his colleagues at Vanderbilt University (Binder, Strupp, & Henry, 1995; Strupp & Bonder, 1984), the therapist organizes treatment around a central interpersonal theme and watches carefully for the emergence of this theme during therapy sessions. For example, the therapist may confront a client about her ineffective styles of relating, by calling her attention to such behaviors when they arise during the therapeutic hour. This heightens the client's emotional involvement and ability to evaluate alternative courses of action. Brief dynamic therapies, such as Strupp's TLDP, usually last from several months to a year.

Arnold Winston and his associates (Winston et al., 1991, 1994) have conducted several studies evaluating brief psychodynamic therapies for clients with personality disorders. Although the particular type of dynamic treatment did not influence outcome, the clients who participated in an average of 37 sessions of dynamic therapy became less depressed and anxious and experienced significant improvements in their interpersonal functioning. Winston and his colleagues continued to follow their individuals beyond the termination of therapy and found that those who participated in 30 or more sessions of therapy maintained their therapeutic gains for several years (Hoglend, 1993; Winston et al., 1994).

In considering the appropriateness of a brief dynamic therapy for a client with a personality disorder, a therapist must attend to some essential variables. First, a prominent interpersonal theme should be present. Second, the therapist should be able to establish a working relationship with the client. As you consider the usefulness of brief treatments for personality disorders, keep in mind that, by some standards, treatments lasting 6–12 months are still relatively lengthy. Furthermore, the dynamic approaches described here require a more focused and intensive treatment than is typical of most psychotherapies. At the same time, short-term dynamic treatments can be a cost-effective alternative for some individuals who might not need or have access to the lengthier treatments associated with traditional dynamic models.

RETURN TO THE CASE

Harold Morrill

Harold's History

The story Harold told about his life helped me make sense of the turmoil of the past few years. The only child of middle-class parents, Harold spent much of his childhood seeking a compromise between his mother's demands that he stay "out of trouble" and his own desires to play and explore in his backyard and neighborhood. When explaining even relatively minor incidents that occurred, the words he used to describe his mother reflected the intensity of his feelings about her, as well as his pained ambivalence toward her. She was a "bitch . . . always yelling at me for anything I did. She controlled my every move, yelled at me for playing too long with my friends, going too far from the house, leaving her home all alone. If I stayed in the backyard and near her, I was the good boy, and she praised me and rewarded me with candy and cookies. But, if I strayed for an hour, even when I was a teenager, she yelled down the street and humiliated me. Maybe it was her way of showing she loved me and worried about me, but it was a tough thing to deal with."

Harold's description of his father was certainly no more positive than that of his mother. He spoke of his resentment about the fact that his father was hardly ever home and that, when he was there, he virtually ignored Harold. The message his mother repeated so often to Harold haunts him to the present day. She told him that she needed him to be the "man of the house." According to Harold, this was how she rationalized her need for him to stay so close to her—he had "important responsibilities, after all."

Harold told me that during adolescence he desperately tried to flee his mother's clutches. He became caught up in substance abuse, which seemed like his only chance "to escape."

RETURN TO THE CASE

Harold Morrill (continued)

Introduced to the world of street drugs, Harold became involved in a promiscuous and dangerous lifestyle, as he became caught up in drug trafficking and petty thievery. He finally moved out of his mother's apartment to a squalid room in a boarding house, and he hasn't spoken to his mother in more than 5 years. Occasionally, he sees his father but is not interested in maintaining a relationship with him.

Throughout most of his twenties, Harold drifted from job to job, without any sense of purpose. He tried college several times but dropped out, because the "teachers were such losers." Harold contended that his employment instability was due mostly to a series of health problems. He told me about three hospitalizations, each of which resulted from a serious motorcycle accident. He enumerated a long list of broken bones, concussions, and internal injuries he had sustained and, with a laugh in his voice, commented, "You'd think I was trying to kill myself, wouldn't you?"

Relationships have been terribly unhappy for Harold. Throughout adolescence and adulthood, he has moved from one relationship to another, abruptly walking out on people who have been unable to satisfy his insatiable demands for love and affection. As Harold described the many stormy relationships of his life, he found it difficult to acknowledge the possibility that he might have played a role in their failure.

Assessment

I told Harold that a psychological assessment battery would help me derive a clearer understanding of the nature of his problem. Initially, he responded with irritation, but he finally agreed. This ambivalence was evident throughout the testing sessions. At times, he was cooperative and pleasant, but he became irascible and impatient a short while later.

Harold's IQ is above average, but his IQ score alone did not tell the whole story about Harold's intelligence. The variability among the WAIS-III subtest scores reflected the unevenness in his cognitive functioning, with impressive strengths on certain tasks (such as vocabulary) but notable deficits on others (such as comprehension). Harold's problem with comprehension tasks revealed his inadequate understanding of appropriate behavior in common situations. For instance, he responded to a question about why stoplights are needed by saying, "So that people won't murder each other." Although the essence of Harold's response to this question suggested that he understood the issue, I noted the angry content of what he said and how he said it.

Harold's profile on the MMPI-2 revealed serious personality disorganization, with some psychotic-like features. This impression was supported by his performance on the Rorschach test, in which he gave many unusual responses, describing images that are rarely reported by others who take the test. In the color cards, Harold saw fire, explosions, and bursts of ammunition, coupled with sadistic human destruction: "a grenade blowing up in the middle of a Sunday picnic." Themes of rage in the face of abandonment were particularly pronounced in Harold's TAT stories. He described people's moods as changing suddenly and chaotically, and the plots of his stories were similarly disorganized.

Diagnosis

Most striking about Harold's story is the chaos that has permeated most facets of his life. His relationships have been turbulent and unfulfilling, his emotions volatile, his behavior self-destructive and impulsive, and his sense of self seriously confused.

My initial interaction with Harold left me with a fairly certain diagnostic impression of borderline personality disorder. In part, my inference was based on his presenting problems and history, but I was also deeply affected by my personal reactions to Harold. I found myself feeling sympathetic toward him at times and at times feeling disturbed by his abusive responses to my efforts to understand and help him. I was tuning in to the process by which Harold was "splitting" in his dealings with me, at times complimenting me about my clinical skillfulness but soon thereafter questioning my competence and ability to establish rapport with him.

As I considered the diagnostic criteria for borderline personality disorder, I confirmed my initial diagnostic hunch. Harold has a history of unstable and intense interpersonal relationships in which he responded to people in dramatically different ways, vacillating between idealization and devaluation of anyone close to him. This was commonly intertwined with affective instability, in which he felt tossed from one emotional state to another, feeling extremes of depression, anxiety, and irritability. At times, his mood escalated into inappropriate and intense expressions of anger in the form of temper tantrums and victimizing behavior. At other times, the anger was self-directed and took the form of impulsive and self-destructive pursuits—such as reckless motorcycle driving, promiscuity, and drug abuse. Never really sure about his own identity, he wandered from

RETURN TO THE CASE

Harold Morrill (continued)

lifestyle to lifestyle, from lover to lover, and from job to job, in a desperate attempt to fill the void that he painfully carried with him everywhere.

Axis I:	Rule out cocaine dependence
Axis II:	Borderline personality disorder
Axis III:	History of motorcycle injury that may include head trauma
Axis IV:	Problems with primary support group (lack of contact with parents) Occupational problems (discord and job instability)
Axis V:	Current Global Assessment of Functioning: 32
	Highest Global Assessment of Functioning (past year): 32

Case Formulation

My diagnosis of Harold seemed clear and accurate, in that he met the criteria for borderline personality disorder. But how did Harold develop this personality structure? By putting together the information from my interview, the psychological assessment, and Harold's history and current presenting problems, I was able to formulate hypotheses based on what clinicians and researchers know about this personality disorder.

When trying to understand the etiology of an individual's personality disorder, it is common to consider the family's contributions, both genetic and environmental. According to Harold, both his parents were "troubled people." We can see this disturbance in his mother's overprotective and anxious interactions with Harold and in his father's aloofness and emotional unavailability. Could these personality disturbances have been transmitted genetically? Scientific understanding of this possibility remains limited, but it is reasonable to conclude that, as a result of his parents' disturbance, Harold grew up in an emotionally unhealthy home environment.

Looking at these issues more closely, we see a family system ripe for the development of a personality disorder. Harold's father was distant, rejecting, and ineffective in moderating his wife's overcontrol of their son. Moreover, at a time when children need to be able to exercise some autonomy, Harold's mother was overcontrolling. She punished him by withdrawing her love if he ventured away from her. The only way he could gain her love was by not leaving her in the first place. Harold's mother exerted similar pressure on him during his adolescence. Under these circumstances, Harold's

ability to differentiate himself psychologically from his mother would have been extremely impeded, contributing to his current identity confusion.

Behavioral and systems perspectives help augment this understanding of Harold's problems. For example, it is reasonable to imagine that Harold modeled his interpersonal relationships after the disturbed relationships he observed in his home life. Perhaps Harold "learned" negative attitudes about himself and inadequate strategies for coping with stresses, particularly those his mother imposed on him.

Harold's difficulties may also be seen as resulting from a disturbed family system in which an overinvolved mother formed a unit with Harold that excluded his father. Her overinvolvement continued into adolescence, a time when he should have been allowed to break away from the family. His involvement in the world of street drugs could be seen as the result of his mother having placed him in an impossible situation of not being able to satisfy her and his own needs simultaneously. Perhaps he saw drugs as the only escape from this dilemma. In addition, Harold's inability to develop an adult identity reflects his mother's reluctance to let Harold grow up. He went on to substitute dependence on lovers for the pathological relationship with his mother.

Treatment Plan

After my initial evaluation of Harold, I felt that intervention should involve an attempt at restructuring his personality, while attending to his current stresses and self-defeating behaviors. Had Harold been suicidal or more seriously self-destructive, I might have recommended that he admit himself to an inpatient treatment program, which is sometimes beneficial for people with borderline personality disorder. This is especially true for those who seem to need the security and stability of the milieu. Although I considered this for Harold, his limited financial resources made hospitalization impossible. Therefore, I recommended outpatient psychotherapy.

Harold asked me if I would be his psychotherapist, stating that I was the "only person to seem to understand" his problems. Having treated a number of people with borderline personality disorder, I was alert to the probability that Harold's positive response involved idealization, commonly noted in people with this personality disorder. At the same time, I found myself feeling interested in treating Harold. Something about him affected me deeply. Perhaps I was moved by the belief that I could help him undertake major life changes. Some might call this a "rescue fantasy"—the

RETURN TO THE CASE

Harold Morrill (continued)

notion that psychotherapists can rescue clients from the unhappiness that has become so much a part of their lives. With a bit of apprehension, and following a consultation with my colleagues about the wisdom of my treating Harold, I agreed to accept him into treatment and recommended that we schedule two sessions weekly for the first 3 months. I believed that the increased frequency of sessions would facilitate the development of rapport.

The treatment approach I have found to be most effective in treating people like Harold involves an integration of psychodynamic and cognitive-behavioral approaches. Within the psychodynamic perspective, I planned an intense psychotherapy, in which the pattern of Harold's early life relationships could be brought to the surface and re-examined. I was not so naive as to consider such an approach with Harold to be simple. I expected that his initial laudatory comments about my clinical expertise would very likely be replaced by devaluing critiques of my "incompetence." I was prepared for the likelihood that he would act and speak in provocative ways, perhaps testing me to see if I would angrily reject him, thereby proving that I wasn't really concerned about him. I knew that there was a strong possibility that he would end treatment precipitously and go to another therapist, to whom he might describe me in very unflattering ways. In addition to the psychodynamic framework, I planned to incorporate some cognitive-behavioral techniques with which Harold could learn appropriate styles of interacting with others, more constructive ways of perceiving himself, and more effective strategies for dealing with ordinary life stresses.

Outcome of the Case

To no one's surprise, including mine, Harold's treatment did not go very well. The first few months were difficult and, frankly, fairly stressful for me. Harold became increasingly demanding of my attention and time, making emergency telephone calls on weekends, asking for extra sessions, and ruminating in therapy sessions about how frustrating it was not to be able to find out more about my personal life. One incident troubled me greatly. It took place on a Friday afternoon as I was leaving my office, several hours after a session with Harold. As I got into my car, I noticed in the rearview mirror that Harold was sitting in his car across the parking lot, ostensibly ready to follow me home. Feeling both alarmed and angry, I walked over and spoke to Harold; he acknowledged that my hunch was correct but became very angry with me when I pointed out the inappropriateness of this plan. When he didn't show up for either of our sessions the following week, I felt greatly relieved. At the same time, I recognized my responsibility to reach out to Harold in a therapeutic manner, so I decided to drop him a note, urging him to come to our regularly scheduled sessions.

Harold returned to therapy, but his response to me remained troubling from that point on. His expressions of anger were more aptly characterized as rage, as he derided many of my efforts to help. By contrast, there were numerous times when he seemed responsive, and he made temporary changes in his life that reflected a more healthy way of thinking and acting. We continued our therapy sessions for another year, during which our work could best be described as rocky.

Another crisis unfolded when I informed Harold that I would be taking a 3-week vacation several weeks hence. Once again, he failed to show up for our sessions, and I tried to reach out to him by urging him to resume therapy sessions. A week after I mailed my letter to him, I received a disturbing phone call from the emergency room physician in the hospital where I worked. Harold had taken an overdose of heroin and wanted to see me. I did see Harold and made arrangements for him to be admitted to the inpatient psychiatric unit. He told me how grateful he felt about my expression of concern and how relieved he felt that our sessions would resume, this time on the inpatient unit. I wondered whether he had manipulated me, but I felt that the seriousness of his self-destructive behavior warranted inpatient treatment.

Harold remained on the unit for 2 weeks and seemed to stabilize, both physically and emotionally. However, in our session just prior to his discharge from the hospital, Harold angrily told me of his plans never to return to therapy with me. He stated that he wanted to find a therapist who would be "more giving" than I was. My efforts to work through this issue with Harold failed, and I never did see him again. Several months after our termination, I read in the newspaper that Harold had been arrested and charged with reckless driving while intoxicated. The photograph accompanying the newspaper story showed Harold staring into the camera with knife-like intensity. I could see the rage in his eyes, yet at the same time I knew that underlying his rage were feelings of confusion, loneliness, and desperation.

Sarah Tobin, PhD

Summary

- A personality disorder involves a long-lasting, maladaptive pattern of inner experience and behavior, dating back to adolescence or young adulthood, that is manifested in at least two of the following areas: (1) cognition, (2) affectivity, (3) interpersonal functioning, and (4) impulse control. This inflexible pattern is evident in various personal and social situations, and it causes distress or impairment. Because personality disorders involve the whole fabric of an individual's being, clinicians typically perceive these as being the most challenging of the psychological disorders to treat. Personality disorders cause major intrapsychic and interpersonal difficulty, leading to long-lasting impairment. The diagnosis of personality disorders is difficult, because many personality disorders share similar features, causing some concerns about the reliability and validity of these diagnoses. The *DSM-IV* uses separate diagnoses that are grouped into three clusters based on shared characteristics. Cluster A comprises paranoid, schizoid, and schizotypal personality disorders, which share the features of odd and eccentric behavior. Cluster B includes antisocial, borderline, histrionic, and narcissistic personality disorders. People with these disorders are overdramatic, emotional, erratic, or unpredictable. In Cluster C are avoidant, dependent, and obsessive-compulsive personality disorders. These are linked because they involve anxious and fearful behaviors.

- People with antisocial personality disorder lack regard for society's moral or legal standards. This diagnosis has its origins in Cleckley's notion of psychopathy, a personality type characterized by several features, such as lack of remorse, extreme egocentricity, lack of emotional expressiveness, impulsivity, and untruthfulness. *DSM-IV* diagnostic criteria add behavioral aspects involving disreputable and manipulative behaviors. Biological theories have focused on brain abnormalities, such as defects in the prefrontal lobes of the cerebral cortex. There is considerable support for the notion that genetic makeup plays an important, though not exclusive, role. Psychological theories have focused on the notion that these individuals are unable to feel fear or anxiety or to process any information that is not relevant to their immediate goals. Sociocultural perspectives focus on family, early environment, and socialization experiences. As for treatment, experts recommend confrontation, especially in group therapy.

- Borderline personality disorder is characterized by a pervasive pattern of poor impulse control, fluctuating self-image, and unstable mood and interpersonal relationships. Many people with this condition engage in splitting and parasuicidal behavior. An interesting biological theory focuses on brain differences, particularly hypersensitive noradrenergic pathways, that may have

evolved as a result of earlier trauma. Psychological theories have dwelled on trauma and abuse as predisposing factors. Sociocultural views focus on the possibility that many people develop this disorder as a result of diminished cohesion in contemporary society. As for treatment, clinicians try to balance levels of support and confrontation, while giving special attention to issues of stability and boundaries. Linehan's Dialectical Behavior Therapy involves components of acceptance and confrontation. As an adjunct to psychological treatment, some clinicians recommend medication.

- In addition to antisocial and borderline personality disorders, which have received extensive attention in the research and clinical literature, there are eight other personality disorders. The diagnosis of histrionic personality disorder is given to people who show a pattern of excessive emotionality and attention seeking, while narcissistic personality disorder applies to people who show a pervasive pattern of grandiosity, need for admiration, and lack of empathy. Paranoid personality disorder is characterized by extreme suspiciousness of others. People with schizoid personality disorder show a pattern of detachment from relationships and a restricted range of emotional expression in their dealings with others. Those with schizotypal personality disorder show a pattern of social and interpersonal deficits marked by acute discomfort with, and reduced capacity for, close relationships; they also experience cognitive or perceptual distortions and behavioral eccentricities. Avoidant personality disorder is characterized by a pattern of social inhibition, feelings of inadequacy, and hypersensitivity to negative evaluation. People with dependent personality disorder have an excessive need to be taken care of, which leads to their submissive and clinging behavior and fears of separation. The diagnosis of obsessive-compulsive personality disorder is characterized by a preoccupation with orderliness, perfectionism, and mental and interpersonal control, at the expense of flexibility, openness, and efficiency. Given the lack of certainty about the causes of personality disorders, clinicians tend to focus efforts on improving the client's current life experiences, rather than attempts to bring about total change; consequently, most therapists individualize treatments to respond to the particular present needs and difficulties of each client.

Key Terms

See Glossary for definitions.

Adult antisocial behavior 142
Antisocial personality disorder 141
Avoidant personality disorder 158
Borderline personality disorder 145
Dependent personality disorder 158
Grandiosity 152
Histrionic personality disorder 151

Identity 147
Latent 156
Narcissistic personality disorder 152
Obsessive-compulsive personality
    disorder 160
Paranoid personality disorder 154
Parasuicide 147
Personality disorder 140

Personality trait 140
Psychopathy 141
Schizoid personality disorder 155
Schizophrenia spectrum disorders 155
Schizotypal personality disorder 156
Splitting 147

Internet Resource

To get more information on the material covered in this chapter, visit our web site at **http://www.mhhe.com/halgin.** There you will find more information, resources, and links to topics of interest.

CASE REPORT: BARBARA WILDER

Before I left my office to meet Barbara Wilder for the first time, the clinic receptionist, Marie, pulled me aside in the hallway to warn me about the situation in the waiting room. Marie explained that Barbara's friend, who had come along for support, offered the reassuring words that Barbara was fine and that she commonly had these kinds of "attacks." Even with her warning, the scene would leave a lasting mark in my memory—in a distant corner of the otherwise empty waiting room, Barbara was writhing on the floor in what appeared to be a convulsion. Her friend knelt next to her, offering soothing words that had a powerful impact on helping Barbara regain control of herself.

As I walked across the waiting room, I sorted through a number of options about how I would enter this very dramatic situation. I momentarily wondered if I should return to my office and wait until Barbara had calmed down, but I felt it might appear as though I was intimidated by Barbara's behavior. Instead, I reached out my hands to Barbara and, in a reassuring voice, introduced myself and helped her rise from the floor and take a seat in a nearby chair. For a moment, Barbara continued to gasp for breath but gradually recovered as she sat between her friend and me. She seemed like a frightened child whose fears were contained by the presence of caregivers sitting beside her. I sat there for 5 minutes and offered calming words in an effort to offer her further comfort. Barbara then looked into my eyes and said, "I'm really sorry for all this drama. I hope you'll understand that this condition is beyond my control." I told Barbara that I realized this and that I also recognized how disturbing and frightening such reactions could be. I asked her to come with me to my office. At first, she asked if her friend could join us but quickly reconsidered and stated, "Actually, I think I should try to do this on my own."

As Barbara walked alongside me, my occasional glances caused me to wonder about whether I had correctly recalled her age. How could this woman be only 22 years old? The way she carried her body and shuffled her feet, along with the look of worry on her face, caused me to think that she must be at least in her mid-thirties. I wondered whether she was suffering from a medical problem, such as arthritis, that caused her to walk and move her body with such rigidity. The more we talked, the more I realized that her bodily tension was telling the story of inner turmoil rather than physical impairment. Barbara began her story by telling me how the preceding 6 months had been "pure hell." It all began one evening when she was waiting in a crowded airport lounge to fly home to visit her parents, her first visit since starting her new job. She suddenly felt incredibly dizzy, and the words on the page of her paperback novel began to dance in front of her eyes. She felt a roaring sound in her ears and a sudden stabbing pain in her chest. Her heart pounded wildly, and she broke out into a cold sweat. Her hands trembled uncontrollably. Just that day, Barbara had heard about the sudden death of a young woman due to a rare heart condition. Struggling to overcome the choking sensation in her throat, she was convinced that she was about to die.

In what seemed to Barbara to be an absolute miracle, the woman next to her saw what was happening and summoned paramedics. Neither they nor the physicians who examined Barbara could find anything physically wrong. The doctor told Barbara that she was probably exhausted and that the airport lounge must have been too stuffy. She spent the night at the hospital and was released the next morning.

Barbara had to cancel her visit to her parents, but her alarm about the incident gradually subsided. Two weeks later, though, the same thing happened again. She was shopping at the mall for a present for her roommate, who was to be married in a few days. Once again, a medical exam showed no physical abnormalities. Barbara began to suspect that the physicians were hiding something from her about the seriousness of her condition. Over the next several months, Barbara went from physician to physician, searching in vain for someone who could diagnose her illness and put her on a proper course of therapy. All they did, though, was advise her to get some rest. One physician prescribed a mild tranquilizer, but it offered no relief from her attacks, which became even more intense, occurring once every 2 weeks.

Little by little, Barbara found herself staying away from situations in which she would be trapped if she were to have an attack. She quit her job, because she was terrified that she would have an attack in the elevator while riding up to her office on the 26th floor. Eventually, Barbara became virtually a total recluse. She could not even walk out of her front door without feeling an overwhelming sense of dread. The only time she left the house was when her former roommate, who was now married, took her to the grocery store or for a walk. At this friend's suggestion, Barbara sought help at the mental health clinic. This young woman appeared to others, for much of her early years, to be an individual who functioned quite well. They did not realize, however, that within Barbara's hidden emotional life she was tremendously insecure and felt intensely dependent on others. When confronted with the challenging life transitions of her first job, she became caught up in overwhelming anxiety.

Sarah Tobin, PhD

6

Anxiety Disorders

Chapter Outline

Everyone becomes anxious from time to time—an examination, a sporting match, a meeting with an important person, and concern over a new relationship can all create feelings of apprehension. Often a person's anxieties are about the future, whether long-term concerns about a career or more immediate worries about a Saturday night date. Think about your own experiences involving anxiety. Perhaps you were so nervous while taking an examination that your mind went blank, or you were so "wound up" while playing in a close basketball game that you missed an easy shot. The anxiety of giving an oral presentation in class may have left you tongue-tied and embarrassed. As upsetting as any of these experiences may be, none would be considered abnormal functioning. It is even possible that such experiences had beneficial aspects. You may have developed ways to calm yourself, which you then found useful in other circumstances, or your anxiety may have energized you to overcome obstacles and perform more effectively. Thus, in moderation, anxiety may serve some positive functions.

Although the terms fear and anxiety are commonly used interchangeably, psychologists make a distinction between them in a clinical context. **Fear** refers to an innate, almost biologically based alarm response to a dangerous or life-threatening situation. People who suffer from the disorders covered in this chapter experience "false alarms," in which harmless stimuli or situations are regarded as dangerous (Street & Barlow, 1994). **Anxiety,** by contrast, is more future-oriented and global, referring to the state in which an individual is inordinately apprehensive, tense, and uneasy about the prospect of something terrible happening. Anxiety has both cognitive and affective components. When you are anxious, you have a feeling that something terrible will happen and that you are powerless to change it. You start to focus on your inner concerns, while becoming hypervigilant, or overly watchful, regarding the possibility of danger or threat.

Sometimes anxiety can be so overwhelming that people feel unable to cope with the ordinary demands of life.

Anxiety becomes a source of clinical concern when it reaches such an intense level that it interferes with the ability to function in daily life, as a person enters a maladaptive state characterized by extreme physical and psychological reactions. These intense, irrational, and incapacitating experiences are the basis of the anxiety disorders, which affect as many as 12 percent of Americans every year (Robins & Regier, 1991).

The Nature of Anxiety Disorders

People with **anxiety disorders** are incapacitated by chronic and intense feelings of anxiety, feelings so strong that they are unable to function on a day-to-day basis. Their anxiety is unpleasant and makes it difficult for them to enjoy many ordinary situations, but, in addition, they try to avoid situations that cause them to feel anxious. As a result, they may miss opportunities to enjoy themselves or to act in their own best interest. For example, people who are afraid to fly in airplanes face job problems if their work requires air travel. You may have heard of John Madden, the sportscaster who travels around the country by bus because he experiences severe panic attacks in airplanes. The lives of people whose anxiety prevents them from even the more ordinary task of leaving the house are even more disrupted. It is perhaps because of the disabling nature of anxiety and related disorders that prescription drugs for anxiety are among the most widely used in the United States.

Panic Disorder

People with **panic disorder** experience **panic attacks,** periods of intense fear and physical discomfort, in which they feel overwhelmed and terrified by a range of bodily sensations that causes them to feel they are losing control. These attacks have a sudden onset and usually reach a peak within a 10-minute period. The sensations the person experiencing a panic attack feels include shortness of breath or the feeling of being smothered, hyperventilation, dizziness or unsteadiness, choking, heart palpitations, trembling, sweating, stomach distress, feelings of unreality, sensations of numbness or tingling, hot flashes or chills, chest discomfort, and fear of dying, "going crazy," or losing control. While this is happening, the individual has a sense of impending doom and feels an overwhelming urge to escape. If you have ever had any of the symptoms of a panic attack, even to a small degree, you can imagine how upsetting it must be to someone who experiences a full-blown episode.

For panic disorder to be diagnosed in an individual, at least some of the person's panic attacks must arise "out of the blue," meaning that there is no situational cue or trigger. Such an attack is called an **unexpected (uncued) panic attack.** An individual may also experience a panic attack immediately following exposure to a specific stimulus or cue in the environment. For example, every time Jonathan hears an ambulance siren, he begins to experience the symptoms of a panic attack. This is an example of a **situationally bound (or cued) panic attack.** In cases in which the person has a tendency to have a panic attack

DIAGNOSTIC FEATURES OF PANIC ATTACK A panic attack is a period of intense fear or discomfort, during which a person experiences four or more of the following symptoms, which develop abruptly and reach a peak within 10 minutes:

- Palpitations, pounding heart, or accelerated heart rate
- Sweating
- Trembling or shaking
- Sensations of shortness of breath or smothering
- Feeling of choking
- Chest pain or discomfort
- Nausea or abdominal distress
- Feelings of dizziness, unsteadiness, lightheadedness, or faintness
- Feelings of unreality (derealization) or a sensation of being detached from oneself (depersonalization)
- Fear of losing control or going crazy
- Fear of dying
- Sensation of tingling or numbness
- Chills or hot flashes

in the situation but does not have one every time, the episode is referred to as a **situationally predisposed panic attack.** For example, Samantha may occasionally have a panic attack when she is riding in a subway car, but she does not have a panic attack on every occasion that she rides the subway.

When evaluating the situation of a client who experiences panic attacks, the clinician must consider the possibility that the client has a medical condition that causes the symptoms. Physical disorders, such as hypoglycemia, hyperthyroidism, insulin-secreting tumors, and cardiovascular or respiratory diseases, can cause panic-like symptoms. Some drugs can also cause reactions that mimic panic attacks. People who are intoxicated with cocaine, amphetamines, or even caffeine may appear to be experiencing a panic attack, when, in fact, they are having a toxic reaction to the substances in their bodies.

Characteristics of Panic Disorder

The diagnosis of panic disorder is made when panic attacks occur on a recurrent basis or when a month has elapsed since the first panic attack but the individual has continued to feel apprehensive and worried about the possibility of recurring attacks. A fairly high percentage of Americans, as many as 15 percent, have experienced one or more panic attacks. However, the diagnosis of panic disorder is fairly uncommon, with estimates of lifetime prevalence rates ranging from 1.4 percent to 2.9 percent both in the United States and in other countries around the world (Weiss-

man et al., 1997). Most cases of panic disorder develop in people who are around the age of 20, with a second, smaller group of cases arising among people in their mid-thirties. Although some children and adolescents experience symptoms of panic attacks (Spence, 1997), the disorder is relatively rare among this age group (Ollendick, Mattis, & King, 1994). Like other anxiety disorders, panic disorder is less likely to arise in later adulthood (Flint et al., 1998). Women are approximately twice as likely to be diagnosed with this disorder (Dick, Bland, & Newman, 1994; Eaton, Kessler, Wittchen, & Magee, 1994).

The course of panic disorder, if left untreated, is quite variable. For some individuals, panic attacks occur only periodically, sometimes with months or years between episodes. Then, suddenly and without warning, an attack strikes. More typically, however, the disorder creates continuous problems for many years (Katschnig & Amering, 1994), particularly among women (Yonkers et al., 1998). People who suffer from these symptoms are faced with the daily uncertainty that they may experience a panic attack when they are not in a position to find someone who can help them. It is the unpredictability of the symptoms that is particularly distressing to these individuals. Researchers have found that people who are able to predict that a panic attack will occur, based on specific cues in the environment, experience less distress (Craske, Glover, & DeCola, 1995).

Over time, people with panic disorder learn to avoid places where they fear they may be trapped, such as elevators, crowded stores, or movie theaters. However, such avoidance can lead to the development of a related condition, **agoraphobia,** which is intense anxiety about being trapped, stranded, or embarrassed in a situation without help if a panic attack were to occur. Although panic disorder is usually linked with agoraphobia, it is possible for people to experience agoraphobia without panic disorder, or panic disorder without agoraphobia. These conditions vary in their severity and impact. People with agoraphobia commonly find the condition severely disruptive,

A person with agoraphobia becomes panicky at the prospect of being in a crowd.

DIAGNOSTIC FEATURES OF AGORAPHOBIA

- People with this condition experience anxiety about being in places or situations from which escape might be difficult or embarrassing, or in which they may not be able to get help should they have panic symptoms or a panic attack. Common agoraphobic fears involve such situations as being outside the home alone, being in a crowd or standing in line, being on a bridge, and traveling in a bus, train, or car.

- People with this condition avoid the feared situations, or they endure them with marked distress or anxiety about having a panic attack or panic symptoms, or they insist that a companion be present in the event that they panic.

cited location of a first panic attack (Shulman et al., 1994). Because people with agoraphobia become so fearful of panic attacks, they develop idiosyncratic personal styles and behaviors in order to avoid these situations. If forced to be in the dreaded situation, they experience intense distress about the possibility that they will experience a panic attack or panic-like symptoms. For example, they may refuse to leave the house unless they are accompanied by someone who knows about their disorder and will be ready to help if needed. They go to extremes to avoid being in a crowd or going to an unfamiliar place. Even when they are not experiencing feelings of immediate danger, people with agoraphobia constantly worry about unexpectedly being put into what they perceive as risky situations. It is common for people with agoraphobia to seek out "safety cues," such as a "safe person," who, the individual believes, can be of help in case of a panic attack. Other safety cues might be medication, a pet, or the home itself (Street & Barlow, 1994).

Theories and Treatment of Panic Disorder and Agoraphobia

In trying to understand the causes of panic disorder and agoraphobia, researchers have tended to discuss both phenomena together, although some give more emphasis to one than to the other. The available theories suggest that both disorders have psychological and physiological components, but it is unclear whether psychological factors cause physiological changes, or vice versa. In the following paragraphs, we will focus on both biological and psychological perspectives, because these are regarded as most relevant to the understanding and treatment of the conditions of panic disorder and agoraphobia.

Researchers have long suspected that changes in the body trigger the sensation of panic. Conditions such as asthma (Carr, 1998), chronic dizziness or vertigo (Asmundson, Larsen, &

while many whose diagnosis is panic disorder without agoraphobia are able to function adequately in their daily lives (Goisman et al., 1994). By contrast, the lifetime prevalence of agoraphobia without panic disorder is surprisingly high, with estimates of 5 percent of the adult population and twice as many women as men suffering from the condition at some point in life (Kessler et al., 1994). Women are also more likely to have symptoms of panic disorder with agoraphobia, while men are more likely to have uncomplicated panic disorder. Furthermore, compared with men, women are more likely to suffer recurring symptoms of panic disorder over time (Yonkers et al., 1998).

Common fears of people with agoraphobia involve such situations as being home alone, in a crowd, on a bridge, or in a moving vehicle. Public transportation is the most frequently

Panic Disorder With Agoraphobia

MINI-CASE

Frieda is a 28-year-old former postal worker who sought treatment because of recurrent panic attacks, which have led her to become fearful of driving. She has become so frightened of the prospect of having an attack on the job that she has asked for a medical leave. Although initially she would leave the house when accompanied by her mother, she now is unable to go out under any circumstances, and her family is concerned that she will become a total recluse.

- How does Frieda's case illustrate the symptoms of panic disorder with agoraphobia, compared to panic disorder without agoraphobia?

- What role do you think Frieda's panic attacks played in her development of agoraphobia?

DIAGNOSTIC FEATURES

This diagnosis is assigned to people who experience panic attacks not due to the physiological effects of substances or to a medical condition, and who do not have the symptoms of agoraphobia. They experience both of the following:

- Recurrent, unexpected panic attacks

- At least one of the attacks has been followed by at least one month during which they experience one of the following: persistent concern about having more attacks, worry about the implications of the attack or its consequences (e.g., fear that they will lose control, have a heart attack, or "go crazy"), significant change in behavior related to the attacks.

Stein, 1998), heart disease (Morris, Baker, Devins, & Shapiro, 1997), a tendency toward heavy sweating (Janszky, Szedmak, Istok, & Kopp, 1997), and breathing disturbances (Papp et al., 1997) have been linked to experiences of panic. One of the first theories to consider physiological factors focused on the role of lactate in panic attacks. **Lactate** is a chemical in the blood that normally produces no psychological problems; in fact, its production is stimulated by aerobic exercise, such as running or swimming. According to the **lactate theory** of panic disorder, the intense anxiety experienced during a panic attack results from an increase of lactate in the blood. In studies testing the lactate theory, people diagnosed with panic disorder are injected with sodium lactate, causing them to experience symptoms reportedly similar to their routine panic attacks (Liebowitz et al., 1984; Pitts & McClure, 1967). The infusion of sodium lactate in people who do not have panic disorder does not produce this experience, and the test seems to be highly reliable in identifying people with this disorder (Cowley & Arana, 1990; Papp, Coplan, & Gorman, 1994). Since the emergence of the lactate theory, researchers have continued to investigate the causes of heightened lactate sensitivity in people with panic disorder (Bourin, Baker, & Bradwejn, 1998). One possibility is that heightened cortisol levels increase the susceptibility of people with panic disorder to lactate infusion (Coplan et al., 1998). Research is also underway to investigate the interaction of lactate infusion with other chemicals thought to provoke panic attacks, such as medications that lower the activity of benzodiazepine receptors (Strohle et al., 1998). To date, however, the cause of the increased sensitivity of people with panic disorder to lactate infusion remains a mystery.

Other biological theories focus on abnormalities in the levels of particular neurotransmitters. According to one view, people with panic disorder have an excess of norepinephrine in the brain (Hoehn, Braune, Scheibe, & Albus, 1997). Norepinephrine, a neurotransmitter, is activated when the individual is placed under stress or in a dangerous situation. Tests of this theory are similar to tests of the lactate theory. For example, when a drug that increases norepinephrine activity is administered to people with a history of panic disorder, they are more likely than people without the disorder to experience a panic attack. Another theory involving neurotransmitters proposes that people with this disorder suffer from a defect in gamma-aminobutyric acid (GABA), a neurotransmitter with inhibitory effects on neurons (Insel et al., 1984). Supporting this theory is evidence of diminished numbers of GABA receptors in the brains of individuals with panic disorder (Marazziti et al., 1994). According to this theory, the anxiety that people with panic disorder experience is due to underactivity of the GABA neurotransmitter system. Neurons in the subcortical parts of the brain involved in panic attacks become more active with less GABA to inhibit them.

Researchers have also focused on a system in the brain that signals when there is insufficient air available to breathe. People with panic disorder are thought to have a hypersensitive "suffocation" mechanism, so that they feel as though they cannot breathe, even though others would feel nothing unusual in that situation. As the level of carbon dioxide in their blood ac-

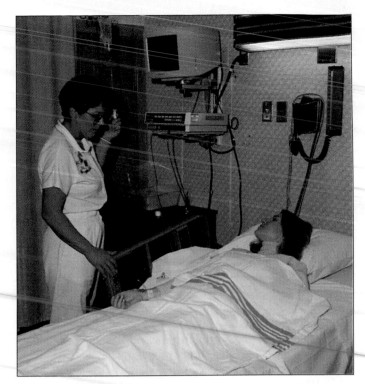

In an experiment to test the lactate theory of panic disorder, this woman is given an injection of sodium lactate to see if she will respond by having a panic attack.

cumulates, this false alarm mechanism is triggered, causing the individual to hyperventilate. If this increase in the rate of breathing fails to lower blood levels of carbon dioxide, the individual is thrown into a panic state (Klein, 1993). Evidence supporting this suffocation hypothesis comes from a study in which people with panic disorder were found more likely to have suffered from traumatic suffocation at an earlier point in their lives (Bouwer & Stein, 1997).

According to another, related hypothesis, people with panic disorder are hypersensitive to their body's internal functioning, particularly anxiety cues that arise within their bodies, such as a slight pounding of the heart or difficulty breathing (Schmidt, Lerew, & Trakowski, 1997). Adding to their plight is a tendency to misunderstand and exaggerate the meaning of these cues (Clark et al., 1997). They may even be awakened from sleep by minor heart palpitations, feeling that their heart is "pounding" or "racing" (Barsky, Cleary, Sarnie, & Ruskin, 1994). Some people with this disorder may be predisposed to a histrionic exaggeration of their body's normal indicators (Hoffart, Thornes, Hedley, & Strand, 1994).

As is suggested by the previous discussion of the misinterpretation of bodily cues among people with panic disorder, any physiological disturbances that account for this disorder interact with psychological processes. One approach that focuses on psychological factors regards **conditioned fear reactions** as contributing to the development of panic attacks. This means the individual associates certain bodily sensations with memories of the last panic attack, causing a full-blown panic attack to develop even before measurable biological changes have occurred (Gorman & Liebowitz, 1986). Over time, the individual begins to anticipate the panic attack before it happens, leading to the avoidance behavior seen in agoraphobia (Klein, 1981).

In a cognitive-behavioral model of anxiety disorders, psychologist David Barlow and his co-workers (Barlow, 1988; Barlow & Brown, 1998) proposed that anxiety becomes an unmanageable problem for an individual through the development of a vicious cycle. The cycle begins with the individual's experiencing the sensation of highly negative feelings (such as unpleasant bodily sensations in a panic attack), which in turn causes the person to feel that what is happening is unpredictable and uncontrollable. As these feelings increase in intensity, they draw the individual's attention like a magnet. The individual is now left awash in these unpleasant sensations and cannot do anything else except think about them. Faulty cognitions and the misperception of cues, both within the person's body and in the environment, further contribute to the sensation of anxiety, as in the case of phobias. Cognitive factors also play a role, as the individual develops distorted beliefs, which add to the anxious apprehension of a panic attack occurring in an uncontrollable manner in the future (Barlow, Brown, & Craske, 1994).

Given that biological factors play at least some role in causing panic disorder, many clinicians recommend treatment with medications. The most effective antianxiety medications are **benzodiazepines.** These medications bind to receptor sites of GABA neurons, which then become activated by this stimulation, leading to the inhibition of the brain sites involved in panic attacks. Some commonly prescribed benzodiazepines are chlordiazepoxide (Librium), diazepam (Valium), chlorazepate (Tranxene), and alprazolam (Xanax). To be effective in treating panic disorders, these medications must be taken for at least 6 months, and possibly as long as a year. Because these medications often lose their therapeutic efficacy and lead to physiological or psychological dependence, clinicians have sought alternatives, including antidepressants and serotonin reuptake inhibitors, such as fluoxetine (Prozac) and fluvoxamine (Luvox).

As useful as medications are in alleviating the symptoms of panic, they are regarded as insufficient in the treatment of panic disorder. Experts are now most inclined to recommend that, when medication is prescribed, a psychotherapeutic intervention should also be incorporated into the treatment.

Relaxation training is one behavioral technique used in the treatment of panic disorder and agoraphobia. In this approach, the client learns to systematically alternate tensing and relaxing muscles all over the body, usually starting at the forehead and working downward to the feet. After training, the client should be able to relax the entire body when confronting a feared situation.

Hyperventilation, a common symptom in panic attacks, is sometimes treated with a form of counterconditioning. In this approach, the client hyperventilates intentionally and then begins slow breathing, a response that is incompatible with hyperventilation. Following this training, the client can begin the slow breathing at the first signs of hyperventilation. Thus, the client learns that it is possible to exert voluntary control over hyperventilation.

Although relaxation training and counterconditioning have some appeal, experts now recognize that more comprehensive interventions involving cognitive techniques are necessary. The focus in recent years has been on treatments geared to giving the individual a sense of being able to control the attacks. Experts generally recommend *in vivo* exposure when treating individuals with panic disorder, especially for those suffering with agoraphobia. The assumption is that treatment is most effective when clients can confront the dreaded situation. When this intervention was initially developed in the 1970s, intensive exposure was recommended. However, more recently, experts have suggested the use of graduated exposure, a procedure in which clients gradually expose themselves to increasingly greater anxiety-provoking situations. For example, Martha finds visits to large shopping malls to be emotionally overwhelming. Martha's therapist would recommend that her exposure to stressful environments begin with a small shop in which she feels safe and relatively anxiety free. Step by step, Martha would progress to environments that are higher on her list of anxiety-provoking settings.

Barlow and his colleagues developed the most comprehensive model for treating clients with panic disorder with agoraphobia. **Panic control therapy (PCT)** consists of cognitive restructuring, the development of an awareness of bodily cues associated with panic attacks, and breathing retraining (Barlow, Craske, Cerny, & Klosko, 1989). Studies of this model have demonstrated that clients treated with PCT show marked improvement, at levels comparable to the improvement shown by clients treated with antianxiety medication. Interestingly, however, later assessments of these clients showed that a greater percentage of those treated with PCT remained symptom free (Klosko, Barlow, Tassinari, & Cerny, 1990). In another comparison of cognitive therapy with other forms of treatment (relaxation and antidepressant medication) and control conditions, cognitive therapy was reported to be particularly beneficial for clients suffering from panic, anxiety, and associated avoidance, both at the end of the treatment and at follow-up (Street & Barlow, 1994). The model proposed by Barlow has stimulated a growing body of research, both in his clinic and elsewhere throughout the world, with dramatic data supporting the efficacy of cognitive-behavioral treatments for panic disorder (Barlow, Esler, & Vitali, 1998) (see Figure 6.1).

Although panic disorder and agoraphobia are not viewed as socioculturally caused, clinicians treating clients with these conditions recognize the importance of including in the treatment partners and others intimately involved in the person's life. For example, a professional might recommend the addition of marital communications and problem-solving training to standard exposure-based couples treatment (Street & Barlow, 1994).

■ Specific Phobias

Everyone has fears about or unpleasant responses to certain objects, situations, or creatures. Perhaps you shrink away from the sight of a spider, rodent, or snake. Or maybe looking

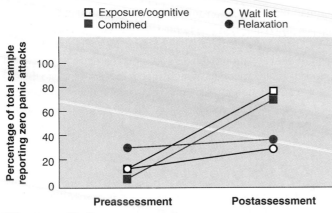

Figure 6.1

The percentage of total sample from Barlow (1990) reporting zero panic attacks before and after treatment

down from a high place causes you to tremble and feel nauseated. Standing in a crowded hallway may lead you to feel uncomfortable, even a bit edgy, and you seek an open space. Such responses of discomfort or dislike, called **aversions,** are common and are not much cause for concern. However, if a person's response to one of these experiences is far out of proportion to the danger or threat posed by the stimulus, the person is considered to have a phobia. A **specific phobia** is an irrational and unabating fear of a particular object, activity, or situation that provokes an immediate anxiety response, causes significant disruption in functioning, and results in avoidance behavior.

Characteristics of Specific Phobias

You have probably heard the word *phobia* many times, perhaps in a humorous context, such as when someone jokes about having a phobic reaction to computers. For people with genuine phobias, however, their condition is not a humorous matter. Rather, they live with an intense level of anxiety about the prospect of encountering the object of their dread, and they often go to great lengths to avoid contact with it. In circumstances in which they must come face-to-face with the phobic stimulus, anxiety level intensifies as they come closer to the stimulus, or as the possibility of escaping the feared situation decreases. For example, in the case of a man with a fear of airplanes, his anxiety increases as he drives to the airport and boards the plane, and it peaks after take-off, when he realizes that he cannot exit the plane. When phobic individuals confront the object of their fear, or anticipate that they will, they become intensely anxious, occasionally to such an extent that they experience a full-blown panic attack. They are overwhelmed by the prospect of such encounters and often imagine the dire consequences that would result. For example, the prospect of seeing someone else bleeding terrifies Maria. There is no real danger that anything would happen to her if she saw someone else's blood, but her fear of this situation (hematophobia) causes her to avoid any circumstance in which she fears she might see blood, such as watching certain movies. Her anxiety is so intense that, if she inadver-

tently faces this situation, as when her child cuts his hand, she feels faint, panicky, and breathless. Phobias fall into several categories, with the most commonly reported phobias being those pertaining to animals, the natural environment, and blood or injury.

You may be wondering whether it is appropriate to refer to a feared situation as a phobia if it is avoidable and causes no significant anxiety for an individual. In fact, such a circumstance would not meet the criteria for this condition. For example, an urban woman who is terrified by the prospect of encountering a snake (ephidiophobia) can be fairly confident that she will be able to avoid such encounters if she stays away from the countryside. Therefore, she would rarely have cause for concern about this matter, and her condition would not be clinically significant (See Table 6.1 for a list of terms used to label various rare phobias. Although they are not part of any current diagnostic classification system, these labels illustrate the variety of phobias documented throughout history.)

Some phobias—such as animal phobias (McNally & Steketee, 1985), blood-injury phobias (Marks, 1988), claustrophobia, and dental phobias (Ost, 1987)—can be traced back to childhood. Most children do experience certain fears, such as fear of the dark, of strangers, of death, and of imaginary creatures; however, most of these dissipate on their own (Emmelkamp, 1982). Other phobias, such as choking phobia, may arise in response to a traumatic episode of choking on food (McNally, 1994). Females are about twice as likely as males to have specific phobias and to develop phobic symptoms earlier (age 10 for females and age 14 for males) (Dick et al., 1994).

Specific phobias sometimes arise in conjunction with another psychological disorder. For example, almost two thirds of people who have panic disorder with agoraphobia also suffer from a specific phobia, such as situational phobia, dental

Climbing an outside staircase causes this man with acrophobia (fear of heights) to feel panicky.

Table 6.1

Some Rare Phobias

Word	Fear
Ailurophobia	Cats
Antlophobia	Floods
Chionophobia	Snow
Dromophobia	Crossing streets, wandering about
Erythrophobia	The color red
Gymnophobia	Naked bodies, the left side of naked bodies
Harpaxophobia	Robbers
Metallophobia	Metals
Osphreisiophobia	Body odors
Phasmophobia	Ghosts
Ponophobia	Work
Scopophobia	Being stared at
Theophobia	God
Triskaidekaphobia	The number 13

phobia, blood-injection-injury phobia, natural environment phobia, and death-related phobia (fear of funerals, dead bodies, and cemetaries). Many of these phobias preceded the development of panic disorder with agoraphobia by many years, except for death-related phobias, which appear closer in time to the onset of panic disorder. There may be some connection between the fear of death in certain people and their developing panic disorder (Starcevic & Bogojevic, 1997).

Theories and Treatment of Specific Phobias

As you have just seen, there are many types of specific phobias, ranging from the common to the relatively obscure. However, the fact that they are grouped together suggests that there is a common theme or element that underlies their cause and potentially their treatment. As is true for panic disorder, the primary explanations of specific phobias rely on biological and psychological perspectives. Nevertheless, as is also true for panic disorder, the existence of a specific phobia in an individual can have a significant impact on those who are close to that person. Consequently, treatment sometimes involves partners and family members.

The primary biological perspective on specific phobias involves the notion that humans are essentially preprogrammed to fear certain situations or stimuli that could threaten our survival. According to this view, there is an evolutionary advantage to the fear of death, disaster, or injury. This "biological preparedness" theory is based on the assumption that there might be a biological "wiring" that causes people to react with fear to threatening situations (Seligman, 1971). This biological propensity might explain how people can so rapidly acquire

Specific Phobia

MINI-CASE

Herbert is a 32-year-old lawyer seeking treatment for his irrational fear of thunderstorms. He has had this phobia since the age of 4, and throughout life he has developed various strategies for coping with his fear. Whenever possible, he avoids going outside when a storm is forecast. Not only will he stay within a building, but he will ensure that he is in a room with no windows and no electrical appliances. As his job has grown in responsibility, Herbert has found that he can no longer afford to take time off because of his fear, which he knows is irrational.

- Which of Herbert's symptoms would lead you to conclude that he has a specific phobia?

- Given that Herbert is afraid to leave the house if a storm is imminent, why would he not be regarded as having agoraphobia?

DIAGNOSTIC FEATURES

- This diagnosis is assigned to people who experience marked and persistent fear that is excessive or unreasonable, and that is brought on by the presence or anticipation of a specific object or situation (e.g., flying, heights, animals, injections, the sight of blood).

- When they encounter the phobic stimulus, they experience immediate anxiety, possibly in the form of a panic attack.

- They recognize that the fear is excessive or unreasonable.

- They avoid the situation or endure it with intense anxiety or distress.

- The condition causes distress or disruption in normal routines and functioning, activities, or relationships.

irrational fears that are so resistant to extinction. Although this theory has been questioned by behaviorists who favor a learned association theory of phobias (Forsyth & Chorpita, 1997), there has been some supporting evidence for the notion of biological preparedness (McNally, 1987), and it seems to account for such phobias as the fear of snakes and spiders.

Speculation about the psychological causes of phobias goes back at least as far as the time of Freud. Although Freud did not initially consider phobias to be psychologically based, his later writings reflect his notion of phobias as psychological symptoms that defend the ego against anxiety. Around the time that Freud was writing on the topic, behavioral psychologists, such as Watson, were demonstrating in the laboratory that animals and humans alike could acquire phobic behavior through conditioning, which led to the conclusion that phobias resulted from maladaptive learning. Current conceptualizations add to this behavioral model the notion that the individual's thoughts also play a role in acquiring and maintaining specific phobias. Many people with phobias report that they had an aversive experience during childhood that has remained with them, or whose parents, and even grandparents, displayed phobic behavior when confronted with the feared object (Fredrikson, Annas, & Wik, 1997; Merkelbach & Muris, 1997).

Cognitive-behavioral theorists (Beck, Emery, & Greenberg, 1985) view anxiety disorders, such as specific phobias, as rooted in and maintained by the client's cognitive styles. According to this view, phobic individuals have overactive "alarm systems" to danger, and they perceive things as dangerous because they misinterpret stimuli. Their perceptions are based on faulty inferences and overgeneralizations. Consider the case of Roberto, a 30-year-old man who experiences a fear of dying that is triggered by unexpected physical sensations. He inter-

prets the physical sensations as a sign of a physical disease and becomes anxious; in this way, a chain reaction is set up. Roberto then generalizes in such a way that everything looks dangerous. His attention becomes "stuck" on potentially dangerous stimuli, leaving him with less ability to think rationally. Roberto begins to think that he is losing his mind, and this makes matters worse.

Some people have feelings or beliefs about a stimulus that set the stage for developing a phobia. For example, the perception of an object or a situation as uncontrollable, unpredictable, dangerous, or disgusting is correlated with feelings of vulnerability. These attributions might explain the common phobia of spiders, an insect about which people have many misconceptions and apprehensions (Armfield & Mattiske, 1996). In another common phobia, that of blood-injury-injection, disgust for these phenomena plays a prominent role in the development of phobic reactions (Tolin, Lohr, Sawchuk, & Lee, 1997). As you can see, in addition to being associated with prior aversive experiences, specific phobias can also arise from a person's thoughts and perceptions, which heighten the individual's feelings of vulnerability.

People with specific phobias respond well to behavioral therapy, because their symptoms are relatively easy to identify and the stimuli are limited to specific situations or objects. Systematic desensitization, described in Chapter 4, rests on the premise that an individual can best overcome maladaptive anxiety by approaching feared stimuli gradually, while in a relaxed state. A therapist might decide, though, that systematic desensitization is either too time consuming, impractical, or unnecessary. Consider the case of Florence, a medical student who sees a therapist in desperation one week before she starts an anatomy course. She has fainted on past occasions when watching videotapes of surgical procedures and is sure that she will make a fool

Behavioral treatment of a person with a spider phobia sometimes involves live exposure to the feared object.

of herself in anatomy class. One week is not enough time to go through the systematic desensitization procedure. Furthermore, Florence's anxiety is not so severe as to be terrifying. Her therapist, therefore, decides to use a behavioral technique called **flooding,** in which the client is totally immersed in the sensation of anxiety, rather than being more gradually acclimated to the feared situation. Florence's therapist chooses a variant of flooding called **imaginal flooding,** in which Florence listens to someone read several vivid descriptions of the dissection of human cadavers. Florence is told to imagine exactly what these scenes look like. Exposure to the threatening stimulus while in a safe context will condition her to confront the target of her phobia without feeling unduly anxious.

Both of the behavioral techniques described so far use imagery in conditioning the client to feel less anxious toward the phobic stimulus. The alternative to imagery, and one that is generally more effective (Emmelkamp, 1994), is actually exposing the client to the feared object or situation until the client no longer feels anxious. Obviously, this *in vivo* method requires that the therapist have ready access to the phobic stimulus. Florence's therapist could just as easily show her a surgical videotape as encourage her to imagine the sight of blood. However, if the client fears flying in an airplane, it would be impractical for the therapist to embark on *in vivo* treatment by accompanying the client on an airplane ride (although cases of such treatment are occasionally reported).

In vivo flooding is probably the most stressful of any of the treatments described. An alternative is a graded *in vivo* method, involving a graduated exposure to increasingly anxiety-provoking stimuli. In the **graduated exposure** method, clients initially confront situations that cause only minor anxiety and then gradually progress toward those that cause greater anxiety (Street & Barlow, 1994). Often the therapist tries to be encouraging and to model the desired nonanxious response. In treating a client named Tan, who has a fear of enclosed spaces, the therapist could go with him into smaller and smaller rooms. Seeing his therapist showing no signs of fear could lead Tan to model the therapist's response. The therapist could also offer praise, to further reinforce the new response that Tan is learning. As illustrated in Table 6.2, behavioral treatments vary according to the nature of the client's exposure to the phobic stimulus (live or imagined) and the degree of intensity with which the stimulus is confronted (immediate full exposure or exposure in graduated steps).

Positive reinforcement is implicit in all behavioral techniques. The therapist becomes both a guide and a source of support and praise for the client's successes. The therapist may also find it useful to incorporate some techniques from the cognitive perspective into the behavioral treatment, because maladaptive thoughts are often part of the client's difficulties. Cognitive-behavioral treatment focuses on helping the client learn more adaptive ways of thinking about previously threatening situations and objects.

Cognitive restructuring, described in Chapter 4, can help the client view the feared situation more rationally by challenging his or her irrational beliefs about the feared stimulus. For example, a therapist may show Victor, who has an elevator phobia, that the "disastrous" consequences he believes will re-

Table 6.2

Methods of Exposure Used in Behavioral Therapy of Phobias

	Graduated Exposure	Immediate Full Exposure
Imagery	Systematic	Imaginal flooding, desensitization
Live	Graded *in vivo*	*In vivo* flooding

sult from riding in an elevator are unrealistic and exaggerated. Victor can also learn the technique of "talking to himself" while in this situation, telling himself that his fears are ridiculous, that nothing bad will really happen, and that he will soon reach his destination.

In **thought stopping,** the individual learns to stop anxiety-provoking thoughts. In therapy, the client is supposed to alert the therapist when the anxiety-provoking thought is present; at that point, the therapist yells, "Stop!" Outside therapy, the client mentally verbalizes a similar shout each time the anxiety-provoking thought comes to mind.

Through stress inoculation, the client can learn coping self-statements (Meichenbaum, 1985), another cognitive-behavioral method. The client prepares a list of statements to use when confronting the feared situation, which provides reassurance that he or she can adequately manage the situation. Examples of such statements are "I can cope with this," "It is irrational for me to feel so scared," "I've gotten through difficult situations before, so I can get through this one," and "Don't think about my fear." These statements increase the individual's sense that he or she can conquer the situation.

Bolstering the client's sense of self-efficacy is a related therapy component (Bandura, 1986) that helps the client feel more confident about being able to manage the phobic stimulus. For example, Florence, whose blood-injury phobia was described earlier, could learn through self-efficacy training to see herself as successfully handling her fears. She may observe or imagine observing someone else treating patients who are bleeding, using vicarious reinforcement to change her beliefs about her own ability to come close to a bleeding person. As Florence herself is put into actual situations with increased exposure to blood or injury, she can practice telling herself that she has the capability to cope with the situation, until she no longer experiences anxiety.

■ Social Phobia

Many people become nervous or jittery before speaking in front of a group, appearing in a musical performance, or participating in an athletic contest or a game. People with **social phobia,** however, feel tremendous anxiety not only in these situations but also in virtually all situations in which others might be observing them.

Characteristics of Social Phobia

The primary characteristic of social phobia is an irrational and intense fear that one's behavior in a public situation will be mocked or criticized by others. People with this disorder recognize that their fears are unreasonable, yet they cannot stop themselves from worrying that others are scrutinizing them. Although people with social phobia go to extremes to avoid such public situations, there are situations in which they have no choice; when this happens, they become crippled with anxiety.

People who have social phobia have many fears about such situations as speaking in public. They are afraid they will do or say something embarrassing, have their minds go "blank," be unable to continue speaking, say foolish things or not make any sense, or show signs of anxiety, such as trembling or shaking (Stein, Walker, & Forde, 1996). Even if their fears are not confirmed and their performance goes smoothly, people with social phobia doubt their ability to do well in these situations and fear that others will expect more of them in the future as a result (Wallace & Alden, 1997).

It may be understandable to think of becoming overwhelmed with fear regarding a public performance, but people with social phobia can have these experiences in seemingly innocuous situations, such as while eating in a restaurant. The simple act of picking up a fork or swallowing food can be seen as an insurmountable task for people with this disorder, who fear that others will laugh at how they hold their fork or swallow their food. They dread the possibility that they will blush, sweat, drop something, choke on their food, or vomit. These fears evaporate when the individual is alone or unobserved, because it is the public aspect of the situation that causes the individual to experience anxiety. In addition to their fears about appearing foolish or clumsy, people with social phobia have low self-esteem and underestimate their actual talents and areas of competence (Uhde, Tancer, Black, & Brown, 1991). They also tend to be perfectionistic and believe that others expect perfect performance of them (Bieling & Alden, 1997).

Social phobia can have effects similar to agoraphobia in that fears about public embarrassment may prevent the individual from leaving the house. However, the two disorders differ in that the anxiety that people with social phobia experience is specific to certain situations, whereas agoraphobia tends to be more generalized.

Although social phobia occurs in both children and adults, there are differences in the experience of the disorder. Namely, children are not necessarily aware that their fear is unreasonable. Secondly, children do not have the freedom that adults do to avoid anxiety-provoking situations, such as having to speak publicly in school. Because they have no escape, they may express their anxiety in indirect ways, such as poor school performance or refusal to interact with other children. Unfortunately, many who suffer with social phobia during childhood and adolescence will experience the symptoms of this disorder in adulthood (Pine et al., 1998). In one 29-year follow-up study, children who showed symptoms similar to social phobia (school phobia, separation anxiety, and school refusal) were more likely as adults to live with their parents, less likely to have children of their own, and more likely to have psychiatric symptoms (Flakierska-Praquin, Lindstrom, & Gillberg, 1997). For some people, the disorder arises gradually during childhood and adolescence within personalities that are shy and inhibited. For other people, social phobia arises suddenly, perhaps as the

---

Social Phobia

MINI CASE

Ted is a 19-year-old college student who reports that he is terrified at the prospect of speaking in class. His anxiety about this matter is so intense that he has enrolled in very large lecture classes, where he sits in the back of the room, slouching in his chair to make himself as invisible as possible. On occasion, one of his professors randomly calls on students to answer certain questions. When this occurs, Ted begins to sweat and tremble. Sometimes he rushes from the classroom and frantically runs back to the dormitory for a few hours and tries to calm himself down.

- What symptoms lead you to regard Ted as having social phobia?

- To what extent has Ted become caught up in a vicious cycle in which he avoids opportunities to confront anxiety-provoking situations?

DIAGNOSTIC FEATURES

- People with this diagnosis experience marked or persistent fear of social or performance situations in which they will encounter unfamiliar people or the scrutiny of others. They fear that they will appear anxious or act in embarrassing or humiliating ways.

- When they encounter the feared situation, they experience anxiety, possibly in the form of a panic attack.

- They recognize that the fear is excessive or unreasonable.

- The condition causes distress or disruption in normal routines and functioning, activities, or relationships.

result of a humiliating public experience, such as a disastrous piano recital or embarrassing incident of public speaking. The stage is then set for the person to experience subsequent feelings of vulnerability in similar situations. For many people with this disorder, the anxiety persists throughout life. Among the phobias, social phobia is second only to panic disorder in frequency, with a lifetime prevalence estimated at 3 percent of the general population for severe symptoms and a range of 8.5 percent to 13.3 percent for nonsevere symptoms. The lifetime prevalence of the disorder is somewhat higher in females than in males (Kessler et al., 1994; Robins & Regier, 1991; Weissman et al., 1996).

Social phobia may appear in a generalized or a specific form, depending on whether the phobia occurs in *any* public situation or whether it is associated with one specific type of situation. Individuals with generalized social phobia dread all interactions with others, not just situations in which they must perform or be observed. Individuals with the more specific type of social phobia have fears only in certain situations, such as public speaking (Kessler, Stein, & Berglund, 1998). In both forms of social phobia, the individual's occupational and social functioning are impaired by the disorder. For example, people with musical talent might steer away from careers as musicians because of the anxiety their social phobia engenders (Clark, 1989). However, the more generalized form of social phobia imposes many limitations, as individuals with this condition avoid careers with the potential for public exposure. They also are limited in their ability to enjoy many kinds of social relationships and social roles (Bech & Angst, 1996; Wittchen & Beloch, 1996). Individuals with this severe form of social phobia are also more likely to have coexisting conditions—notably, depression, agoraphobia, alcohol abuse, and suicidal thinking and attempts (Lecrubier & Weiller, 1997).

Theories and Treatment of Social Phobia

Although social fears and anxieties have always existed, social phobia was not understood as a separate category of the anxiety disorders until relatively recently. More and more attention is being paid to this disorder, as increasing numbers of clients seek professional help for the symptoms of this condition that interferes with the quality of life (Weissman et al., 1996).

Theories regarding the causes of social phobia are still preliminary, and some are quite speculative. For example, in one interesting realm of investigation, researchers have studied the relationship between a deficiency of growth hormone in childhood and adolescence and the development of social phobia. Working with the hypothesis that young people who are significantly shorter than their peers at a time when height is important to social status, some researchers have found that many such young people develop symptoms of social phobia—in fact, 38 percent of their sample, (Stabler, Tancer, Ranc, & Underwood, 1996). Other researchers, however, did not find support for the notion that social phobia develops as the result of low levels of growth hormone during youth (Nicholas et al., 1997). A more traditional biological approach examines alter-

ations in neurotransmitter levels that may characterize people with social phobia, and there is some evidence of disturbed serotonergic functioning in these individuals (Chatterjee, Sunitha, Velayudhan, & Khanna, 1997).

Psychological perspectives on social phobia revolve around understanding the thought processes of people with the disorder. As already noted, individuals with this disorder have a variety of maladaptive thoughts about their abilities to perform, and these thoughts can cause them to become distracted from the task at hand. Think about a time when you were called on to perform in public, such as hitting a baseball, delivering a speech, or giving a solo musical performance. Perhaps your hands shook and your heart pounded as you prepared to go into the spotlight. You may have imagined hearing the laughter or criticism of others if you made a mistake. Once you started performing the action, though, chances are that you forgot about these distractions and concentrated on doing the best job you possibly could. According to cognitively oriented explanations of social phobia, people with this disorder are unable to take the step of shifting their attention away from anticipated criticism and onto their performance. They fear making a mistake while performing or speaking, and, because their concentration is impaired, they are likely to make that dreaded mistake. Their fears acquire a solid basis in experience each time this happens, and these people soon avoid similar situations. Even if the individual manages to keep from making a mistake, the unpleasantness of the situation is so intense that it creates a desire to avoid repetition.

Information on sociocultural variations in social phobia is slowly beginning to emerge as this phenomenon gains more attention. For example, Taijin Kyofusho (TKS) is a form of social anxiety found in Japan, in which individuals are concerned about offending others through their appearance or behavior. In a study comparing Japanese and American college students on scores on scales derived from both the *DSM-IV* definition of social phobia and the definition of TKS, there was a high degree of overlap, with half the people in the sample receiving high scores on one scale also receiving high scores on the other (Kleinknecht et al., 1997). Such findings suggest that there are similarities in the expression of this disorder across cultures. Epidemiological studies also suggest that the disorder has similar patterns of prevalence and comorbidity in other countries (Lecrubier & Weiller, 1997; Weissman et al., 1996).

Treating people with social phobia involves helping them learn more appropriate responses to the situations they fear. Behavioral and cognitive-behavioral techniques, such as those used to treat people with specific phobias, are particularly helpful in reaching this goal. Social phobics need to develop new ways of thinking about their interactions with others. Combining such techniques as cognitive restructuring and *in vivo* exposure can have impressive results (Clark & Agras, 1991; Heimberg & Barlow, 1988). Another treatment approach involves social skills training to help social phobics learn methods for coping with interpersonal stress, so that they can feel more confident and comfortable in their interactions (Ost, Jerremalm, & Johansson, 1984). Some severe cases warrant pharmacological treatment, either in the form of antidepressants (Katzelnick et al., 1995) or antianxiety medication (Davidson, Ford, Smith, & Potts, 1991). However, even in cases in which medications are prescribed, cognitive behavioral techniques have also been recommended (Gelerneter et al., 1991).

For next test 10/30

Generalized Anxiety Disorder

Sometimes anxiety is not associated with a particular object, situation, or event but seems to be a constant feature of a person's day-to-day existence. The diagnosis of **generalized anxiety disorder** applies to this category of anxiety-related experiences.

Characteristics of Generalized Anxiety Disorder

Generalized anxiety disorder is one of the more common anxiety disorders, affecting an estimated 5 percent of adults (Wittchen, Zhao, Kessler, & Eaton, 1994), and a much smaller percentage of children. People with this disorder struggle with uncontrollable anxiety much of the time. Efforts to control their worry are usually unsuccessful, and they are afflicted with a number of symptoms, both physical and psychological, which interfere with social, occupational, and general life functioning. They are prone to feeling restless and keyed up much of the time and find it difficult to concentrate, sometimes feeling so tense that their mind goes blank. At night, they find it difficult to fall or stay asleep; during the day, they are likely to feel fatigued, irritable, and tense. As you will learn later in this text, many of the symptoms of this disorder are also associated with other Axis I disorders. For example, the physiological effects of some substances and the psychological components of mood disorder or a psychotic disorder may cause symptoms similar to those of generalized anxiety disorder.

The bodily reactions, feelings, and thoughts associated with generalized anxiety disorder often have no direct connection with a discernible issue in the person's life. If the individual does verbalize specific fears or concerns, these are usually unrealistic and extend to several domains. For example, Ben

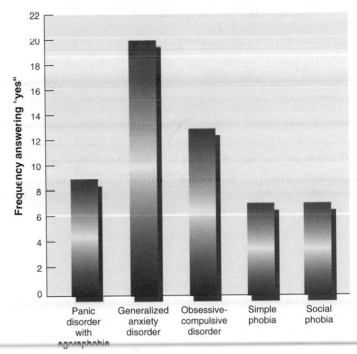

Figure 6.2

This graph shows the number of patients from five anxiety disorder categories who worry excessively about minor things.

may worry that his college-age son, who is in good health, will develop a life-threatening disease, and he may worry about going bankrupt, even though his business is thriving. Both sets of worries are without grounds, yet Ben finds himself consumed with anxiety and distracted from his daily responsibilities.

The worries that people with generalized anxiety disorder experience can linger for years. In fact, these individuals often state that at no time in their lives have they *not* felt tense and anxious. Other people tend to see them as "worrywarts." Figure 6.2 provides statistics on people with various anxiety disorders who report that they worry excessively about minor concerns (Sanderson & Barlow, 1990).

Generalized anxiety disorder is more common in women and, among women, more common in those over the age of 24. In addition to gender and age, there are other interesting factors that are associated with higher rates of this disorder, such as having a history of previous marriage, being a homemaker without outside employment, and living in the Northeast section of the United States. As with all studies of the relationship between variables, it is important to keep in mind that these are correlations but do not explain the causes of the disorder. Most people with generalized anxiety disorder also have at least one other disorder, particularly dysthymic disorder (Pini et al., 1997).

When the disorder appears in children, the anxieties and fears they express often relate to their performance in school or athletic activities. They worry incessantly that they will not do well in schoolwork or sports, even in situations in which their performance is not evaluated. Some children may worry more about potentially tragic matters, such as the possibility that there will be a nuclear war or an unlikely natural disaster that will affect them or their parents.

People with generalized anxiety disorder have many worries and physical symptoms that prevent them from enjoying life.

There is some debate in the literature about whether generalized anxiety disorder should stand on its own as a diagnostic category. Some researchers (Margraf, Ehlers, & Roth, 1986) have suggested that generalized anxiety disorder should be categorized with panic disorder, because some individuals who have generalized anxiety disorder develop panic disorder. However, there is evidence that the two disorders, although occasionally linked, are separate diagnostic entities and that generalized anxiety disorder can be reliably assessed (Wittchen, Kessler, Zhao, & Abelson, 1995). People with generalized anxiety experience heightened autonomic arousal reactivity, thoughts about threat, and heightened feelings of subjective anxiety and tension (Clark, Beck, & Beck, 1994). Evidence from epidemiological, family, and twin studies further supports the contention that they are separate disorders (Weissman, 1990). Evaluating the weight of such clinical and empirical evidence, specialists in the field of anxiety disorders support the view of generalized anxiety disorder as a distinct diagnostic entity. The fact that the somatic symptoms associated with this disorder are not so evident in other anxiety disorders provides a particularly compelling argument for this distinction (Brown, Barlow, & Liebowitz, 1994).

Theories and Treatment of Generalized Anxiety Disorder

Despite the fact that so many people suffer from this disorder, generalized anxiety disorder has not been extensively researched, and there are relatively few explanations for how it develops. From a biological perspective, it is suggested that people with this disorder have a biological abnormality similar to that proposed to account for other anxiety disorders involving abnormalities of benzodiazepine receptors (Insel et al., 1984).

From a cognitive-behavioral perspective, generalized anxiety is seen as resulting from cognitive distortions that arise in the process of worrying. People with generalized anxiety disorder also appear to become easily distressed and worried by the minor nuisances and small disruptions of life. If something goes wrong in their day-to-day existence, such as car trouble, an argument with a co-worker, or a home repair problem, they magnify the extent of the problem and become unduly apprehensive about the outcome. Their attention shifts from the problem itself to their own worries; as a result, their concern becomes magnified. As a result of their constant worrying, they are less efficient in their daily tasks and, consequently, develop more to worry about as more goes wrong for them. For whatever reason, once the anxiety is initiated, it begins to spiral out of control, with worry piling on worry (Barlow, 1988). Particularly damaging is the individual's lack of confidence in his or her ability to control or manage anxious feelings and reactions, as well as a lack of confidence in the ability to manage daily tasks effectively.

Finally, it is important to recognize the role of sociocultural factors in generalized anxiety disorder. Life stresses can significantly increase the basis for a person's tendency to experience chronic anxiety. In one study, men who had experienced four or more unexpected negative life events (such as loss of a job) over a 1-year period had nearly nine times the risk of developing generalized anxiety disorder than men reporting fewer

---

Generalized Anxiety Disorder

MINI-CASE

Gina is a 32-year-old single mother of two children seeking professional help for her long-standing feelings of anxiety. Despite the fact that her life is relatively stable in terms of financial and interpersonal matters, she worries most of the time that she will develop financial problems, that her children will become ill, and that the political situation in the country will make life for her and her children more difficult. Although she tries to dismiss these concerns as excessive, she finds it virtually impossible to control her worrying. Most of the time, she feels uncomfortable and tense, and sometimes her tension becomes so extreme that she begins to tremble and sweat. She finds it difficult to sleep at night. During the day she is restless, keyed up, and tense. She has consulted a variety of medical specialists, each of whom has been unable to diagnose a physical problem.

- Which of Gina's symptoms would lead you to believe she has generalized anxiety disorder?

- How would you distinguish Gina's disorder from panic disorder?

DIAGNOSTIC FEATURES

- This diagnosis is assigned to people who experience excessive anxiety and worry occurring more days than not for at least 6 months, pertaining to a number of events or activities, such as work or school.

- Their anxiety, worry, or related physical symptoms cause significant distress or impairment.

- They find it difficult to control their worry.

- Their anxiety and worry are associated with at least three of the following:

  - Restlessness
  - Being easily fatigued
  - Concentration difficulty
  - Irritability
  - Muscle tension
  - Sleep Disturbance

stressful life events (Blazer, Hughes, & George, 1987). When people with generalized anxiety disorder turn for professional help, many are likely to seek out medical care, especially from a gastroenterologist, to whom they turn for help for the alleviation of stomach and intestinal distress (Kennedy & Schwab, 1997). Astute physicians recognize the importance of differentiating this condition from a medical problem and usually suggest psychotropic medications or refer the patient to a mental health professional. The medications most likely to be prescribed are benzodiazepines and newer antianxiety drugs that are less habit-forming (such as buspirone, or BuSpar) (Gitlin, 1990; Saletu et al., 1994). However, clinicians are reluctant to prescribe such medications on a long-term basis. Some antidepressant medications have been used successfully with these individuals, even those who are not especially depressed (Maxmen & Ward, 1995).

An alternative to medication is cognitive-behavioral therapy (Butler, Fennell, Robson, & Gelder, 1991), in which clients learn how to recognize anxious thoughts, to seek more rational alternatives to worrying, and to take action to test out these alternatives (Beck et al., 1985). The emphasis is on breaking the cycle of negative thoughts and worries. Once this cycle is broken, the individual can develop a sense of control over the worrying behavior and become more proficient at managing and reducing anxious thoughts. In reviewing the treatment outcome literature for generalized anxiety disorder, Barlow and his colleagues (Barlow et al., 1998) concluded that active treatments are better than nondirective approaches. In particular, cognitive-behavioral therapy that combines relaxation exercises and cognitive therapy seems to help clients bring their worry under control.

■ Obsessive-Compulsive Disorder

If you have ever had a thought that you could not seem to force out of your consciousness, you have some insight into the experience of an **obsession**—a persistent and intrusive idea, thought, impulse, or image. People with obsessions recognize the fact that these cognitions arise within their own disturbed thought processes. They desperately try to ignore or suppress these intrusive thoughts, and in some cases they try to neutralize them by taking an action or thinking about something else. To get a sense of obsessive thought, think of a time when you had an argument with someone important in your life, which you relived in your thoughts for hours, even days, afterward. Even as you tried to attend to other matters, you found your mind returning time and again to the argument. Perhaps you tried desperately to erase these thoughts by engaging in an activity that might distract you. Multiply this experience dozens of times in intensity, such that most of every day is filled with similar experiences, and you will have a sense of the experience of clinical obsession.

Many people with obsessions also struggle with compulsions. A **compulsion** is a repetitive and seemingly purposeful behavior performed in response to uncontrollable urges or according to a ritualistic or stereotyped set of rules. Unlike obsessions, which cause anxiety, compulsions are carried out in an effort to reduce anxiety or distress. The disorder known as **obsessive-compulsive disorder** (OCD) involves both components of recurrent obsessions and compulsions that interfere significantly with an individual's daily life.

Characteristics of Obsessive-Compulsive Disorder

The obsessions and compulsions that characterize OCD greatly interfere with life and trap the individual in a cycle of distressing, anxiety-provoking thought and behavior. The symptoms of OCD are time-consuming, irrational, and distracting, and the individual may desperately wish to stop them. You can imagine how distressing it is for people whose thoughts are filled with concerns about contamination (e.g., germs), doubts (e.g., leaving the gas on), or aggression (e.g., fear of harming another person).

The most common compulsions involve the repetition of a specific behavior, such as washing and cleaning, counting, putting items in order, checking, or requesting assurance. Another compulsion that has recently caught the attention of experts in this area involves hoarding (Frost, Krause, & Steketee, 1996), in which an individual stores useless items such as outdated newspapers, mail, shopping bags, and empty food containers. When other people urge them to discard any of the items, they respond with concern that the item may be needed later for some reason.

As you have probably figured out, a compulsion often goes hand-in-hand with an associated obsession. The man obsessed with a concern that he has left a pot on the stove is compelled to return repeatedly to the kitchen to make sure the stove is turned off. Compulsions may also take the form of mental rituals, such as counting up to the number 15 every time an unwanted thought intrudes. Or perhaps a person conjures up a particular image in response to obsessive fears (Steketee, 1994).

In general, there appear to be four major dimensions to the symptoms of OCD: obsessions associated with checking compulsions, the need to have symmetry and to put things in order, obsessions about cleanliness associated with compulsions to wash, and hoarding-related behaviors (Leckman et al., 1997). Table 6.3 lists examples of common obsessions and compulsions experienced by people with this disorder.

Many students reading about obsessive-compulsive disorder are unclear about how this condition differs from obsessive-compulsive personality disorder, which we discussed in Chapter 5. The person with obsessive-compulsive personality disorder is a rigid and inflexible worrier who does not engage in the extremely disturbed kinds of thinking and behaving that characterize people with obsessive-compulsive disorder. For example, a man with an obsessive-compulsive personality disorder may have a very rigid classification system for all of his books and become very upset if anyone puts a book back in the wrong place. By contrast, the person with obsessive-compulsive disorder may have a compulsion to check the order of the books on the shelf many times a day to ensure that they have not somehow been moved. If anything interferes with his checking of the books, he feels a great deal of distress. As you

In the movie "As Good As It Gets," Jack Nicholson plays the role of a man with obsessive-compulsive disorder. Even expressing affection to a pet is complicated by his need to wear protective gloves.

can see, there is some relationship between these two disorders, but there are also some important differences. Only about one third of all people with OCD also have obsessive-compulsive personality disorder (Diaferia et al., 1997).

Epidemiologists have documented that obsessive-compulsive disorder has a lifetime prevalence rate of 2 percent, a figure derived from various places around the world (Sasson et al., 1997). Some researchers argue for caution in accepting this figure, however, because when conservative screening instruments are used the prevalence estimate drops to less than 1 percent (Stein, Forde, Anderson, & Walker, 1997a). Compounding the problem of estimating prevalence is the fact that, in the Epidemiological Catchment Area study, most of the people who met the diagnostic criteria for OCD when first tested no longer fit the diagnosis when they were retested 1 year later (Nelson & Rice, 1997).

OCD usually first appears in childhood and adolescence. However, it is interesting to note that not all children who develop compulsive rituals retain them; many lose them by adolescence (Zohar & Bruno, 1997). Many of the children who do develop OCD show a unique pattern of characteristics—they are more likely to be male, to have a family history of OCD, to lack insight into their symptoms, and to suffer from other conditions, such as attention-deficit/hyperactivity disorder (Geller et al., 1998).

Theories and Treatment of Obsessive-Compulsive Disorder

The symptoms of OCD are increasingly being understood as a reflection of abnormalities in the brain regions that are involved in the control of motor movements (Greenberg et al., 1997; Purcell, Maruff, Kyrios, & Pantelis, 1998), as well as dysfunctions in serotonergic pathways in the brain, perhaps reflecting a deficit in a gene controlling the production of this serotonin (Hanna et al., 1998). Thus, people with OCD are seen as having thoughts and actions that they literally cannot inhibit, as though the brain structures involved in this process are, in essence, "working overtime" to try to control them (Rosenberg, Dick, O'Hearn, & Sweeney, 1997). As you can see from the PET scans shown on this page, people with OCD have heightened levels of activity in the brain motor control centers of the basal ganglia and frontal lobes (Rauch et al., 1997).

Other disorders involving abnormal serotonin levels are also thought to be related to obsessive-compulsive disorder along a continuum or spectrum (Hollander, 1993). This spectrum includes a wide range of disorders involving dissociation, somatization, hypochondriasis, eating disorders, pathological gambling, borderline personality disorder, and disorders that involve uncontrollable impulses, such as hair pulling, face pick-

Table 6.3

Examples of Obsessions and Compulsions

Obsessions	Compulsions
A student has the urge to shout obscenities in a quiet classroom while listening to a lecture.	She feels driven to screw and unscrew the cap of a ballpoint pen exactly five times each time she thinks of an obscene word.
A woman cannot get the thought out of her mind that she might accidentally leave her gas stove turned on, causing her house to explode.	Each day before leaving for work, she feels the irresistible urge to check the stove exactly 10 times.
A 9-year-old boy worries incessantly that something terrible might happen to his mother while his family is sleeping.	On his way to bed each night, he insists that he must climb the stairs according to a fixed sequence of three steps up, followed by two steps down, in order to ward off danger.
A young woman is constantly terrified by the image that cars might careen onto the sidewalk and run her down.	She feels that she must walk as far from the street pavement as possible, and she always wears red clothes when in town, so that she will be immediately visible.
A man is tormented by the concern that he might inadvertently contaminate food as he cooks dinner for his family each night.	On a daily basis, he sterilizes all cooking utensils in boiling water, scours every pot and pan before placing food in it, and wears rubber gloves while handling food.

ing, compulsive shopping, and gambling (Christensen, Mackenzie, & Mitchell, 1991). There may also be a relationship between OCD and Tourette's syndrome (discussed in detail in Chapter 11), in which an individual exhibits a pattern of abnormal motor symptoms, such as uncontrollable twitches, vocalizations, and facial grimaces. When these disorders overlap, the symptom picture tends to be much more severe than is found when just one of the conditions is diagnosed (Coffey et al., 1998). In fact, when tics are evident in adolescents with OCD, these individuals are more likely to have aggressive and sexual images than are adolescents without tics (Zohar et al., 1997).

As important as biological notions are to the understanding and treatment of OCD, they do not tell the entire story, and the behavioral perspective adds an important dimension. Behaviorally oriented theorists have long focused on the possibility that the symptoms of OCD become established through a process of conditioning, in which they become associated with the momentary relief of anxiety (Foa, Steketee, & Ozarow, 1985).

The cognitive-behavioral perspective focuses on maladaptive thought patterns as contributing to the development and maintenance of OCD symptoms (Steketee, 1994). Individuals with OCD may be primed to be overreactive to anxiety-producing events in their environment (Hoehn-Saric, McLeod, & Hipsley, 1995). It is assumed that these clients are disturbed by thoughts related to the need to be perfect, the belief that they are responsible for harm to others, and concerns over the possibility of danger (Jones & Menzies, 1997; Shafran, 1997). They struggle with disturbing images related to these thoughts and try to suppress or counteract them through engaging in compulsive rituals. The more they try to suppress these thoughts, the greater their discomfort and inability to stop them (Salkovskis et al., 1997).

Another possibility emerging from a cognitive perspective is that people with OCD have memory deficits, causing them to have difficulty remembering behaviors, such as turning off the stove or locking the door. Their constant doubting and need to check is related to a true inability to remember whether they have completed these acts (Tallis, 1997). Even their memory for past events in their lives may be impaired by the presence of their intrusive thoughts, particularly if they also suffer from depression (Wilhelm, McNally, Baer, & Florin, 1997).

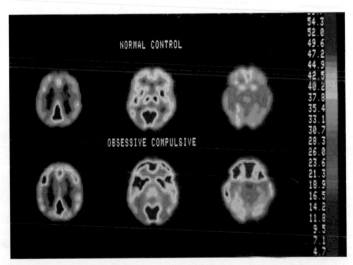

PET scans of the brains of people with obsessive-compulsive disorder show increased metabolic activity, as indicated by larger red areas in the caudate nucleus of the basal ganglia (bottom center figure) and frontal lobes (bottom right figure).

Table 6.4

Sample Items from the Yale-Brown Obsessive-Compulsive Symptom Checklist

Scale	Sample Items (Check Yes or No)
Aggressive obsessions	Fear might harm self
	Fear of blurting out obscenities
	Fear will be responsible for something else terrible happening (e.g., fire, burglary)
Contamination obsessions	Concerns or disgust with bodily waste or secretions (e.g., urine, feces, saliva)
	Bothered by sticky substances or residues
Sexual obsessions	Forbidden or perverse sexual thoughts, images, or impulses
	Sexual behavior toward others (aggressive)
Hoarding/saving obsessions	Distinguish from hobbies and concern with objects of monetary or sentimental value
Religious obsessions	Concerned with sacrilege and blasphemy
	Excess concern with right/wrong, morality
Obsession with need for symmetry or exactness	Accompanied by magical thinking (e.g., concerned that another will have an accident unless things are in the right place)
Miscellaneous obsessions	Fear of saying certain things
	Lucky/unlucky numbers
	Colors with special significance
	Superstitious fears
Somatic obsessions	Concern with illness or disease
	Excessive concern with body part or aspect of appearance (e.g., dysmorphophobia)
Cleaning/washing compulsions	Excessive or ritualized hand-washing
	Excessive or ritualized showering, bathing, toothbrushing, grooming, or toilet routine
Checking compulsions	Checking locks, stove, appliances, etc.
	Checking that nothing terrible did not/will not harm self
	Checking that did not make mistake completing a task
Repeating rituals	Rereading or rewriting
	Need to repeat routine activities (e.g., in/out door, up/down from chair)
Counting compulsions	(Check for presence)
Ordering/arranging compulsions	(Check for presence)
Hoarding/collecting compulsions	Distinguish from hobbies and concern with objects of monetary or sentimental value (e.g. carefully reads junk mail, sorts through garbage)
Miscellaneous compulsions	Excessive list making
	Need to tell, ask, or confess
	Need to touch, tap, or rub
	Rituals involving blinking or staring

The Yale-Brown Obsessive Compulsive Scale is completed following this checklist. The individual completes ratings on scales involving time spent, interference, distress, resistance, and control over compulsions and obsessions (Goodman et al., 1989a, 1989b).

Obsessive-Compulsive Disorder

MINI-CASE TITLE

Mark is a 16-year-old high-school student referred for treatment by his teacher, who became disturbed by Mark's irrational concern about the danger posed by an electrical outlet at the front of the classroom. Mark pleaded daily with the teacher to have the outlet disconnected to prevent someone from accidentally getting electrocuted while walking by it. The teacher told Mark that his concerns were unfounded, but he remained so distressed that he felt driven, when entering and leaving the classroom, to shine a flashlight into the outlet to make sure that a loose wire was not exposed. During classtime, he could think of nothing else but the outlet.

■ What is Mark's obsession and what is his compulsion?

■ How does Mark's behavior differ from that of a person with obsessive-compulsive personality disorder?

DIAGNOSTIC FEATURES

● People with this disorder suffer from either obsessions or compulsions, which the person recognizes at some point as excessive or unreasonable. These obsessions or compulsions cause marked distress, consume more than an hour a day, or significantly interfere with normal routine, functioning, or social activities or relationships.

● Obsessions are defined by the following four features:

  ● Recurrent and persistent thoughts, impulses, or images that sufferers recognize as intrusive and inappropriate and that cause marked anxiety or distress

  ● Not simply excessive worries about real-life problems

  ● Attempts to ignore or suppress these thoughts, impulses, or images or to replace them with another thought or action

  ● Recognition that these are products of his or her own mind (rather than the delusional belief that they are thoughts being inserted into the mind)

● Compulsions are defined by the following two features:

  ● Repetitive behaviors (e.g., hand-washing, checking, putting items in order) or mental acts (e.g., counting, silent repetition of words) that the person feels driven to perform in response to an obsession or according to rigid rules

  ● The behaviors or mental acts are intended to prevent or reduce distress or to prevent a dreaded event or situation, but they are clearly excessive or not connected in a realistic way with what they are intended to neutralize or prevent

Treatment

The most promising interventions for people with obsessive-compulsive disorder are rooted in biological and psychological approaches, which are commonly combined in an integrative treatment. Advances in psychopharmacology during the past three decades have been especially important. In the mid-1970s, it was discovered that an antidepressant medication, clomipramine (Anafranil), had the unanticipated effect of reducing obsessions in depressed people. This led investigators to wonder whether clomipramine would be an effective treatment for nondepressed people suffering from obsessive-compulsive disorder. Extensive experimental tests of this medication yielded very encouraging results, and researchers began to hypothesize that at least for some people, obsessive-compulsive disorder might have biological rather than psychological origins. Researchers noted that serotonin activity was reduced in people who responded favorably to clomipramine. From this they inferred that serotonin probably played a central role in causing the symptoms of this debilitating disorder (Rapaport, 1990). Individuals with these disorders are responsive to a category of medications that make larger amounts of serotonin available within the brain.

So far, treatment with clomipramine or other serotonin reuptake inhibiting medications, such as fluoxetine (Prozac) or sertraline (Zoloft), has proven to be the most effective biological treatment available for obsessive-compulsive disorder (Abramowitz, 1997; Greist et al., 1995; Rauch & Jenike, 1998). The excitement generated by success stories with these medications has led to the development of newer medications, which have shown promising results for people who do not respond to clomipramine or fluoxetine. In particular, fluvoxamine (Luvox), which has milder side effects than other medications, works in similar fashion to allow more serotonin to be available at receptor sites in the brain (Laird, 1995).

Many clinicians recommend psychological interventions instead of, or in addition to, medication. For example, thought stopping is recommended to help some clients reduce obsessional thinking, as is exposure to situations that provoke compulsive rituals or obsessions (Greist, 1990; Jenike, Baer, & Minichiello, 1986). Response prevention may also be used, in which the clinician instructs the client to stop performing compulsive behaviors, either totally or in graded steps (Salkovskis & Westbrook, 1989). Several experts advocate treatment that contains both exposure to the feared obsessions and prevention of the rituals that accompany the obsessions (Abramowitz, 1997; Franklin & Foa, 1998; Rauch & Jenike, 1998). Steketee (1998) explains that exposure helps reduce the obsessive anxiety, while the prevention of responses controls a person's rituals. For example, Steketee describes her treatment of a woman who compulsively checked faucets and the buttons on her child's clothing, as she was obsessed with the notion that certain numbers and activities were connected with the devil. Steketee helped the client identify her obsessive ideas and accompanying rituals; that information was used to construct a hierarchy of increasingly obsessive situations and associated rituals. Specific situations—such as fastening children's clothing snaps or having angry thoughts about the children or even reading about devils and demons—were selected for exposure. Each step of the way, the client agreed not to use any ritual, such as checking or repeating, that would have previously relieved her anxiety. In an effort to confront her tremendous difficulty with words associated with the devil, she engaged in some interesting forms of exposure; namely, she began to serve devil's food cake and deviled eggs, as well as to write the words devil and satan in her appointment book. Although there was not a rapid or miraculous cure, over time this woman reported that she felt 80 percent to 90 percent improved, compared with when she had first come for treatment. Unfortunately, for some people, neither pharmacological nor psychotherapeutic interventions offer any relief. In extreme cases involving people with debilitating symptoms, the radical intervention of psychosurgery, as discussed in the Critical Issue box, may be used. Although this intervention is understandably a disturbing option, some individuals for whom daily life is torturous consider this a viable option. Although reports of efficacy offer some hope, ethical factors and technical limitations have made it impossible to conduct control studies to establish with certainty the effectiveness of these neurosurgical interventions (Rauch & Jenike, 1998).

Acute Stress Disorder and Post-Traumatic Stress Disorder

A **traumatic experience** is a disastrous or an extremely painful event that has severe psychological and physiological effects. Traumatizing events include such personal tragedies as being involved in a serious accident, being the victim of violence, or experiencing a life-threatening calamity. At the other end of the spectrum are life-threatening events that affect large numbers of people, such as fires, earthquakes, riots, and war.

Each traumatic event takes its toll in human suffering, as the survivors cope with the loss of close ones who were victims of the disaster, with the loss of property when homes are destroyed, or with the sense of personal violation after being assaulted or raped. Survivors must cope with the painful memories of the traumatic event, which often involve vivid images of seeing other people killed or seeing their own lives nearly ended.

Some people develop an **acute stress disorder** soon after a traumatic event. In this condition, the individual develops intense fear, helplessness, or horror. Dissociative symptoms may appear, such as feeling numb, unreal, or detached, and amnesia about the event may develop. These individuals continue to reexperience the event in images, thoughts, dreams, and flashback episodes. They go to extremes to avoid anything that reminds them of the horrific event, whether it is a place, a person, an activity, or even a thought, feeling, or conversation, because these may evoke intense distress or a sense of reliving the trauma. Intensely anxious much of the time, they are likely to find it difficult to sleep or concentrate. They often become irritable and hypervigilant, perhaps easily startled by a minor noise or disruption.

Despite the extreme nature of the symptoms of acute stress disorder, most people are able to return to relatively normal functioning within days or weeks. Others, however, do not. They go on to develop **post-traumatic stress disorder (PTSD),** a diagnosis that is appropriate when the symptoms persist for more than a month.

Characteristics of Post-Traumatic Stress Disorder

In the aftermath of an acute stress disorder, the symptoms of PTSD may start to take hold and take on a chronic and unremitting course. Reminders of the trauma, either in the person's own thoughts or in the environment, evoke intense levels of psychological or physiological distress. Even the anniversary of the event may stir up intense psychological and physical disturbance. These symptoms are so painful that people who suffer from PTSD intentionally go to great lengths to avoid anything that may remind them of the trauma. For example, a woman avoids driving by the site where her house burned to the ground several years ago, because she knows that even a fleeting reminder of the trauma will result in great psychological distress, nightmares, and physical symptoms of anxiety and dread.

Many people with this disorder seem to "shut down" in a sort of numbness, which causes them to be generally unresponsive in most situations. For example, a woman finds that she is unable to feel or express the love for her husband that was so evident prior to the trauma. A traumatized man loses interest in the activities that had been pleasurable for so much of his life. For an extended period of time, these individuals feel an increased level of arousal that is evident in sleep difficulty, anger outbursts, concentration problems, an exaggerated startle response, or general hypervigilance.

The symptoms of PTSD seem to fall into two related clusters. The first, called "intrusions and avoidance" includes intrusive thoughts, recurrent dreams, flashbacks, hyperactivity to cues of the trauma, and the avoidance of thoughts or reminders. The second cluster, "hyperarousal and numbing," includes symptoms that in-

Psychosurgery for Obsessive-Compulsive Disorder

Prior to the advent of neuroleptic medications in the 1950s, psychosurgery was the treatment of choice for several serious psychological disorders. As described in Chapter 1, psychosurgery techniques, pioneered in 1937, involved severing the connections between the areas of the brain that were thought to be responsible for the symptoms of such disorders as schizophrenia. These relatively primitive surgical techniques resulted in a reduction of problematic symptoms but also sometimes caused unwanted personality changes. Although psychosurgery is only rarely performed these days, some professionals continue to advocate this intervention for individuals who do not benefit from more benign forms of treatment, such as psychotherapy and medication. However, some scientists still believe that psychosurgery can be effective for a small group of psychiatric disorders, such as obsessive-compulsive disorder (Rapoport & Inoff-Germain, 1997; Rauch, Baer, & Jenike, 1996a; Sachdev & Hay, 1996; Sachdev & Sachdev, 1997).

Most people diagnosed with obsessive-compulsive disorder benefit from medication, behavior therapy, or a combination of the two. Treatments generally include the prescription of a selective serotonin reuptake inhibitor (SSRI), such as fluoxetine or fluvoxamine, accompanied by a course of behavioral therapy. Through behavioral therapy, clients learn to confront feared thoughts and situations and to decrease their reliance on compulsions to control their anxiety. Nonetheless, medication does not help all individuals with obsessive-compulsive disorder, and many others are not helped by psychotherapy.

Severe cases of obsessive-compulsive disorder have been treated with psychosurgery, the most common and safe form of which is a cingulotomy. In contrast to the procedures of decades past, cingulotomy involves the precise lesioning of the cingulate bundle, an area of the brain that researchers have implicated in the development of anxiety and compulsive behavior (Jenike et al., 1991). Small holes, less than 2 centimeters in diameter, are drilled into the skull, and electrodes are carefully positioned in each cingulate bundle. Correct positioning is sometimes verified with magnetic resonance imaging. Electric current is then passed through the electrodes to create lesions between 1 and 2 centimeters in diameter, which ideally results in a reduction in obsessions and compulsions. Other forms of psychosurgery have also been refined in recent years. For example, surgeons conducting anterior capsulotomies, in which the anterior capsule is lesioned, have found this procedure to be even more effective than cingulotomies (Sachdev & Hay, 1996) but, unfortunately, not as safe (Rauch et al., 1996a).

As encouraging as this intervention may seem, psychosurgery is reserved for only the most seriously afflicted individuals with obsessive-compulsive disorder, and it is performed only rarely. One of the most serious concerns about promoting psychosurgery as an intervention pertains to the limited amount of research that has been conducted on the efficacy of these procedures; the research that has been conducted has demonstrated that psychosurgery is effective for some, but not for most of those who undergo the procedure. For example, Baer and his colleagues (Baer et al., 1995) at Massachusetts General Hospital studied 18 patients with obsessive-compulsive disorder who underwent cingulotomies. Their findings were consistent with other research data, in which 25 to 30 percent of people whose suffering was not aided by medication or psychotherapy were helped by psychosurgery.

In the past, psychosurgery has produced serious side effects, including unwanted personality changes and the blunting of emotional responses. Modern psychosurgical techniques are certainly safer than those of decades ago, and serious side effects are less common, yet there remain some worrisome unintended surgical aftereffects, such as the possibility of postoperative seizures, which must be controlled with medication.

Cingulotomy and other focused surgical techniques alleviate some of the suffering of individuals with severe cases of OCD; however, this highly invasive procedure should be a treatment of last resort. Some scientists believe that a combination of medication and behavioral therapy is still the best treatment method, even for the more severe cases of OCD (Park, Jefferson, & Greist, 1997). Clinicians and researchers must strive to understand why these more benign treatments might fail. Factors that could influence treatment failure include biological responses to medication, as well as personality and environmental factors that interfere with treatment gains. Only when a careful scrutiny of all interfering variables has been completed can professionals recommend that an individual consider an intervention as extreme as psychosurgery.

volve detachment, a loss of interest in everyday activities, sleep disturbance, irritability, and a sense of a foreshortened future. Thus, intrusive thoughts give rise to the avoidance of disturbing reminders, and hyperarousal leads to a numbing response (Taylor et al., 1998).

Following a traumatic life event, people go through a series of characteristic responses, identified as occurring in two phases (Horowitz, 1986). The initial reaction is the **outcry phase,** during which the person reacts with alarm and a strong

Acute Stress Disorder

MINI-CASE

Brendan is a 19-year-old college freshman who was well-liked, psychologically healthy, and quite successful in life until two weeks ago when he experienced a traumatic event that seemed to change every aspect of his functioning. The life changing event involved a devastating dormitory fire from which Brendan barely escaped. In fact, his roommate perished from smoke inhalation. Since the fire Brendan has been tormented by graphic images of waking to see his room filled with smoke, as flames encompassed the overstuffed chair in which his roommate had fallen asleep while smoking a cigarette. Tears come to his eyes as he recalls the experience of grabbing his roommate's leg and dragging the unconscious body out of the room only to realize that he was pulling a corpse. Feeling helpless and terrified, he screamed cries of horror, while suddenly becoming drenched by a sprinkler system that became activated several minutes too late. Brendan spent the days following the tragedy in the university health center where he was treated for inhalation and several psychological symptoms. He described himself as feeling in a daze, as if in a dream state that was more like a nightmare. Despite the efforts of family and friends to connect emotionally with him, Brendan was emotionally unresponsive and seemingly numb. In fact, he found it difficult to talk with people because his thoughts were filled with intrusive images of the fire. After being discharged from the health service, he was unable to go anywhere near the dorm building for fear that he would "really lose it," and ultimately decided to withdraw from school because he felt too anxious and distressed.

- In what way is Brendan's acute stress disorder different from post-traumatic stress disorder?

- How would the fact that Brendan was a psychologically healthy young man prior to the trauma affect his prognosis for recovery?

DIAGNOSTIC FEATURES

- This disorder, which occurs within a month of a traumatic event, causes clinically significant distress or impairment that lasts between 2 days and 4 weeks. The diagnosis is assigned to people who experience significant distress or impairment associated with exposure to a traumatic event in which

  - They experienced, witnessed, or confronted event(s) involving actual or threatened death or serious injury, or a physical threat to themselves or others.

  - They responded with intense fear, helplessness, or horror.

- Either during or after the event, the individual has three or more of the following dissociative symptoms:

  - Sense of detachment, numbing, or lack of emotional responsiveness

  - Reduced feeling of awareness of surroundings, as if in a daze

  - Feelings of unreality (derealization)

  - Sensation of being detached from oneself (depersonalization)

  - Inability to recall an important aspect of the trauma (dissociative amnesia)

- The traumatic event is reexperienced through recurrent images, thoughts, dreams, illusions, flashback episodes, or a sense of reliving the experience, or the person feels intense distress when exposed to reminders of the event.

- The individual avoids stimuli that evoke recollections of the trauma.

- The individual experiences symptoms of anxiety or increased arousal, such as difficulty sleeping, irritability, poor concentration, hypervigilance, exaggerated startle response, and restlessness.

---

emotion, such as fear or sadness. The person may shriek or hit something during this phase. When the event involves the immediate threat of personal danger, such as in an earthquake, the outcry phase may not occur immediately, because people need to cope with the situation at hand. The outcry takes place later, perhaps in a safer place, when the imminent threat has passed.

The second phase of response to a traumatic life event is the **denial/intrusion phase,** during which the person alternates between denial, the experience of forgetting the event or pretending it did not occur, and intrusion, the experience of disruptive thoughts and feelings about the event. Sometimes it is not until days or months following the trauma that intruding thoughts first emerge. Some people find that the traumatic event repeatedly intrudes into consciousness in the form of a flashback, a recurrence

of a powerful feeling or perceptual experience from the past, sometimes involving graphic and terrifying illusions and hallucinations. Nightmares and unwanted thoughts about the event may plague the individual during this phase, along with physical symptoms, such as a racing heartbeat or heavy sweating. Consider a young man, Gary, who was in a car accident that killed his friend. Gary had recurrent images of the scene of the fatal crash. When riding in cars, he overreacted to every approaching car, repeatedly bracing himself for another imagined crash. He thought he could hear the voice of his deceased friend crying, "Watch out!" For weeks following the accident, he repeatedly "saw" his friend's face when he tried to sleep. He could not get out of his mind the thought that he should have done something to prevent his friend's death.

Following a disaster such as the 1995 Oklahoma City bombing, many victims struggle with immediate losses, anxiety, and long-lasting psychological problems such as post-traumatic stress disorder.

In the 1980s, when the diagnosis of PTSD was added to the *DSM,* the media drew attention to the psychological aftereffects of combat experienced by Vietnam War veterans. The Vietnam War was the most publicized, but certainly not the only, war to produce psychological casualties. Reports of psychological dysfunction following exposure to combat emerged after the Civil War (Hyams, Wignall, & Roswell, 1996). Following World War I and World War II, there were numerous reports of psychological impairment described with such terms as "shell shock," "traumatic neurosis," "combat stress," and "combat fatigue." Concentration camp survivors were also reported to suffer long-term psychological effects, including the "survivor syndrome" of chronic depression, anxiety, and difficulties in interpersonal relationships (Chodoff, 1963; Eaton, Sigal, & Weinfeld, 1982).

Television reports brought the Vietnam War, and the horrors of combat, into American living rooms each night, perhaps leading to greater concern on the part of the public and professionals about the lasting effects of war on those involved. Many studies about the post-traumatic effects of the war were initiated, several of which continue decades after the end of the conflict. The statistics emerging from these studies are not always consistent, however, with estimates of the incidence of PTSD among Vietnam veterans ranging from 19 to 30 percent of those exposed to low levels of combat, and 25 to 70 percent of those exposed to high levels. Although the customary image of the Vietnam veteran is a male, there were also many women involved in the conflict, many of whom have also suffered from PTSD (Zatzick et al., 1997).

Many children also develop PTSD each year, with symptoms arising from their exposure to various kinds of trauma, many taking place in or near the home. There have been reports of children developing PTSD after witnessing violent family arguments and beatings (Kilpatrick & Williams, 1997a) and of others becoming symptomatic following the loss of a sibling to violence and murder (Freeman, Shaffer, & Smith, 1996). As we will see later, exposure in childhood to physical and sexual abuse at the hands of a family member accounts for many cases of PTSD.

Biological Perspectives

Although by definition PTSD has its origins in life experiences, researchers have increasingly been turning up evidence linking its symptoms to biological abnormalities. In recent years, some researchers have formulated the theory that, once a traumatic experience has occurred, parts of the individual's nervous system become primed or hypersensitive to possible danger in the future. Subcortical pathways in the central nervous system, as well as structures in the sympathetic nervous system, are permanently on "alert" for signs of impending harm (Heim, Owens, Plotsky, & Nemeroff, 1997; Rauch et al., 1996b). Altered neurotransmitter functioning would also play a role in this scenario. For some individuals with PTSD, alterations seem to occur in the norepinephrine pathways, while in others abnormalities in the serotonin pathways are more likely (Southwick et al., 1997). Dopamine, particularly in neurons in the prefrontal area that are sensitive to stress, may also be involved in the symptoms of PTSD (Horger & Roth, 1996). It seems that even the structure of the brain can change as a result of trauma; for example, researchers have noted that women with PTSD who had been victimized in childhood show brain changes similar to those of combat veterans—namely, a reduction in the size of the hippocampus (Stein et al., 1997b). This surprising observation suggests that some of the symptoms of PTSD may be associated with changes in the temporal lobe of the brain, resulting from the experience of trauma. Finally, genetic predisposition may also play a role in the development of PTSD. In one study of more than 4,000 twin pairs who fought in Vietnam, genetic factors seemed to play an important role in their susceptibility to the development of reexperiencing, avoidance, and arousal symptoms (True et al., 1993).

Years after the Vietnam War ended and their physical wounds healed, many veterans were left tormented by the emotional scars of combat.

Post-Traumatic Stress Disorder

MINI-CASE

For the past 25 years, Steve has suffered from flashbacks, in which he relives the horrors of his 9 months of active duty in Vietnam. These flashbacks occur unexpectedly in the middle of the day, and Steve is thrown back into the emotional reality of his war experiences. These flashbacks, and the nightmares he often suffers from, have become a constant source of torment. Steve has found that alcohol provides the only escape from these visions and from the distress he feels. Often, Steve ruminates about how he should have done more to prevent the deaths of his fellow soldiers, and he feels that his friends, rather than he, should have survived.

- If Steve could be convinced that he did all he could to help his friends, how might this affect him?

- To what extent do you think Steve's flashbacks and nightmares are due to the emotional effects of stress, rather than to his alcohol use?

DIAGNOSTIC FEATURES

- This disorder, which causes clinically significant distress or impairment, is assigned to people who have been exposed to a traumatic event in which
  - They experienced, witnessed, or confronted an event involving actual or threatened death or serious injury, or a physical threat to themselves or others.
  - They responded with intense fear, helplessness, or horror.
- For at least 1 month, there is a persistent reexperiencing of the traumatic event in one or more of the following ways:
  - Recurrent and intrusive distressing recollections of the event
  - Recurrent distressing dreams of the event

- Acting or feeling as if the event were recurring (e.g., a reliving of the experience, illusions, hallucinations, dissociative flashbacks)
- Intense distress at exposure to internal or external cues that symbolize or resemble an aspect of the event
- Physiological reactivity on exposure to internal or external cues that symbolize or resemble an aspect of the event
- For at least 1 month, there is avoidance of stimuli associated with the trauma and a numbing of general responsiveness, as indicated by at least three of the following:
  - Efforts to avoid thoughts, feelings, or conversations associated with the trauma
  - Efforts to avoid activities, places, or people that evoke recollections of the trauma
  - Inability to recall an important aspect of the trauma
  - Markedly diminished interest or participation in significant activities
  - Feelings of detachment or estrangement from others
  - Restricted range of affect (e.g., inability to experience loving feelings)
  - Sense of foreshortened future (e.g., pessimism about career, family, and life)
- For at least 1 month, there are persistent symptoms of increased arousal, as indicated by at least two of the following:
  - Difficulty falling or staying asleep
  - Irritability or outbursts of anger
  - Concentration difficulty
  - Hypervigilance
  - Exaggerated startle response

Psychological Perspectives

It is clear that psychological factors play a central role in the development of PTSD. Theorists have discussed and studied human responses to trauma for many decades. Freud described symptoms such as those in the disorder currently labeled PTSD as representing a flooding of the ego's defenses, with uncontrollable anxiety originating from the intense and threatening experiences. The experiences themselves may be traumatic enough to cause this reaction, or they may trigger painful memories of earlier unresolved unconscious conflicts and may cause anxiety to overflow as a result of an inability to keep these memories repressed (Lidz, 1946). For example, the experience of killing another person in battle may stimulate the emergence of previously repressed aggressive impulses. Anxiety over the expression of these impulses could trigger the stress reaction.

According to classical behavioral approaches, it is assumed that the person with PTSD has acquired a conditioned fear to the stimuli that were present at the time of the trauma. Because of a learned association, the individual experiences anxiety when these or similar stimuli are present, even in the absence of the traumatizing experience. Presumably, such reactions lead to avoidance. To escape, at least in fantasy, from the traumatic event becomes reinforcing for the individual, and this reinforcement then strengthens the withdrawal reaction seen in PTSD victims.

Cognitive-behavioral theorists (Foa, Steketee, & Rothbaum, 1989) have incorporated the concept of how people's beliefs about a traumatic event influence how they cope with it. Thoughts that are likely to have a detrimental effect, and can ultimately lead to PTSD, include excessive self-blame for events that are beyond personal control, as well as guilt over the outcome of these events (Kubany, 1994; Ramsay, Gorst-Unsworth, & Turner, 1993). The individual's unsuccessful attempts to reduce the stress experienced in the aftermath of the event can also increase the risk for PTSD. Some of these problematic coping methods include avoiding of problems for long periods of time, blaming and lashing out at other people, adopting a cynical and pessimistic view of life, catastrophising or exaggerating the extent of current difficulties, isolating oneself socially, and abusing drugs and alcohol (Hobfall et al., 1991).

Clearly, not everyone exposed to traumatic experiences, combat-related or otherwise, suffers from PTSD. What are the factors that increase the likelihood that a particular individual will become one of the victims of trauma-related symptoms? One has to do with the nature of the traumatic experience itself. A general principle that emerges from a variety of studies on trauma victims is that there is a direct relationship between the severity of the trauma and the individual's risk of developing PTSD later (Davidson & Foa, 1991). This principle applies to war-related combat experiences (Spiro, Schnurr, & Aldwin, 1994; Sutker, Uddo, Brailey, & Allain, 1993), natural disasters (Goenjian et al., 1994; Lonigan et al., 1994), the torture of political prisoners (Lavik, Hauff, Skrondal, & Solberg, 1996; Ramsay et al., 1993), crime (Resnick et al., 1993), physical abuse (Silva et al., 1997), sexual abuse in childhood (Briggs & Joyce, 1997), and the experience of living in a country ravaged by war and political or religious violence (Macksoud & Aber, 1996; Weine et al., 1995). Underlying these experiences is the individual's perceived threat to life.

In their studies of the kinds of experiences associated with PTSD symptoms, experts have come upon a number of fascinating correlates. For example, in a study of soldiers involved in Operation Desert Storm in 1991, individuals who had the job of handling human remains were more likely to develop intrusive and avoidant symptoms of PTSD. Experienced workers were less likely to suffer these symptoms, but even among experienced workers there was a positive relationship between the number of body remains that they handled and the degree of their symptoms (McCarroll, Ursano, & Fullerton, 1993). Even 1 year later, those who handled human remains still suffered psychological disturbance (McCarroll, Ursano, & Fullerton, 1995).

Individuals vary in their propensity to suffer from PTSD. One factor that mediates the relationship between the extent of trauma and PTSD symptoms is the individual's state of mind while the trauma is occurring. People who experience a period of dissociation during the traumatic episode are more likely to be the ones who will develop PTSD after the trauma has ended (Koopman, Classen, & Spiegel, 1994; Marmar et al., 1994; Shalev, Peri, Canetti, & Schreiber, 1996). In some cases, the individual's reaction to trauma may take precedence over the severity of the trauma as a risk factor. For example, there has

Movies such as "Saving Private Ryan" can stir up disturbing memories and symptoms in combat survivors with histories of PTSD.

not been a general relationship observed between the extent of exposure to trauma in motor vehicle accidents and the severity of PTSD symptoms. Instead, the individual's tendency to worry about the flashbacks and intrusions that occur in the weeks and months after the accident seems to be most predictive of the emergence of later symptoms (Ehlers, Mayou, & Bryant, 1998).

Investigators have long wondered whether some people might be predisposed to develop PTSD as a result of prior trauma, or even some characterological traits that put them at greater risk of a more intense reaction to adversity. As is true for other anxiety disorders, women are more likely than men to suffer from PTSD symptoms, even when exposed to the same trauma (Kessler et al., 1995). The co-existence of another psychological disorders—(Blanchard et al., 1996; North, Smith, & Spitznagel, 1994), such as depression (Bleich, Koslowsky, Dolev, & Lerer, 1997) or substance abuse (Najavits, Weiss, & Shaw, 1997)—is also a predisposing risk factor. However, the relationship between PTSD and other disorders also cuts the other way, because people who develop PTSD are also at higher risk for the subsequent development of both depression and substance abuse (Breslau et al., 1997).

Sociocultural Perspectives

As mentioned, the devastating wars in the second half of the twentieth century—most notably, the conflict in Vietnam—brought many cases of PTSD to the attention of clinicians and researchers, and they provided important opportunities to understand some sociocultural contributions to the development of this disorder. Investigators were particularly attuned to the fact that, for many Vietnam soldiers, symptoms did not emerge until they returned home. In explaining this phenomenon, researchers point out that the Vietnam War was not politically popular. Instead of receiving a hero's welcome on their return home, many soldiers felt that their efforts were neither valued nor respected. This lack of social support, rather than the combat experience itself, may have contributed to the development of the disorder (Sparr & Pankratz, 1983).

With information available on the Vietnam War experience, mental health professionals were better prepared to develop strategies for helping the veterans of the 1991 Operation Desert Storm action cope following their return from active duty (Hobfall et al., 1991). Outreach workers were available to help soldiers in the early days of the conflict, and it is thought that this early recognition played an important role in helping alleviate PTSD symptoms among those exposed to combat (West, Mercer, & Altheimer, 1993). Even with this proactive approach, however, approximately 8 percent of those returning from Operation Desert Storm developed PTSD symptoms (Stretch et al., 1996). As with the veterans of the Vietnam War, lack of support on their return from action seemed to play a role in the Gulf War veterans' development of PTSD symptoms (Viola, Hicks, & Porter, 1993).

Other sociocultural factors, such as education, income level, and social status, provide additional pieces to the puzzle of PTSD. Consider one study of Vietnam veterans, in which such factors as precombat personality, intensity of combat experiences, and postcombat experiences and social support were compared as predictors of PTSD symptoms (Green et al., 1990). What emerged from this study was the notion that people with certain backgrounds are more likely to get involved in exactly the high-exposure combat situations that would place them at most risk for later psychological problems. Soldiers with histories of mood disorder or substance abuse were more likely to become involved in situations in which they were exposed to grotesque combat experiences, such as witnessing or participating in the mutilation of Vietnamese citizens. On their return home, these veterans were also the least likely to engage in behaviors that might help reduce their anxiety symptoms, such as talking to friends or seeking outside help.

Interestingly, among World War II veterans, the picture seemed to be somewhat different. The unusual circumstances of one particular study (Lee, Vaillant, Torrey, & Elder, 1995) has shed some important light on the relationship between prewar personality and subsequent development of PTSD symptoms. This study, the Harvard Grant Study, was conducted between 1939 and 1944 on a group of 268 men, consisting of the top half of the undergraduate class (all men), considered medically and psychologically healthy and having a high potential for success. A number of notable individuals were included in this sample, many of whom went on to achieve national and international renown for their life's accomplishments. George Vaillant, working in the 1970s at Harvard Medical School, undertook a follow-up of these individuals at midlife, and he and his colleagues have continued their studies up to the present time. Having extensive data available on the college years of these men, the Harvard researchers had the unusual opportunity to examine the relationship between predisposing factors to trauma and PTSD in the war-related experiences that 90 percent of the sample had shortly after their college graduation. Interestingly, among this group, the relatively economically advan-

taged were more likely to enter combat roles in World War II. The men who experienced heavy combat were also more athletically active and more enthusiastic about their involvement in the armed forces. High combat exposure, in turn, was associated with more symptoms of PTSD; however, these symptoms did not interfere with the veterans' subsequent psychological adjustment. Those who engaged in heavy combat were more likely to appear in the prestigious *Who's Who in America* and to have more satisfying work and family lives. The subjective distress of PTSD did not interfere with their ability to function in the world. Furthermore, PTSD symptoms were not related to general levels of stress in these men's lives, either before or after their war experiences. It is noteworthy, though, that the heavy combat veterans also suffered more chronic illness and were more likely to die by the age of 65 than those who did not experience heavy combat. This study provides a model for analyzing the impact of pre-existing psychosocial characteristics on reactions to combat, but it is limited to a particular generation of advantaged White men.

In assessing the role of sociocultural factors in the determination of PTSD, investigators have been particularly interested in the ways that disadvantaged economic settings may set the stage for increased vulnerability. It has been established that people who live in certain sociocultural contexts are more likely to be victimized (Ensink, Robertson, Zissis, & Leger, 1997). Living in high-crime urban neighborhoods increases the likelihood of exposure to traumatizing events. So does living in impoverished locales in developing countries where the inadequacy of support and mental health services in the event of a disaster can aggravate the psychological responses of large numbers of people (Lima, Pai, Santacruz, & Lozano, 1991).

Cultural factors are also evident in the ways that people from various ethnic groups respond to traumatic events, such as disasters or devastation (de Silva, 1993). In some groups, tremendous stigma is associated with the idea of seeking professional psychological help, regardless of the severity of the distress. Lacking sufficient emotional support, in the family and in one's social group, can aggravate the experience of PTSD symptoms for some.

Treatment

Within the biological perspective, clinical investigators have reported the successful treatment of PTSD symptoms with a variety of medications, with the choice relying primarily on the client's particular symptoms (Maxmen & Ward, 1995). For example, clients with symptoms involving hyperexcitability and startle reactions may benefit from antianxiety medications, such as benzodiazepines. Those contending with irritability, aggression, impulsiveness, or flashbacks may find anticonvulsants, such as carbamazepine or valproic acid, helpful. Antidepressants, such as selective serotonin reuptake inhibitors and monoamine-oxidase inhibitors, are often therapeutic in treating the symptoms of numbing, intrusion, and social withdrawal. In one study, fluoxetine (Prozac) was especially helpful in reducing depression, anxiety, and panic attacks, and it's use resulted in overall improvement in veterans with combat-related PTSD (Nagy, Morgan, Southwick, & Charney, 1993).

The Enduring Effects of Psychological Trauma

Post-traumatic stress disorder was first identified among military combat veterans, yet in recent years we have learned that the symptoms of PTSD are relatively common responses to various psychologically damaging events. Severe traumas, such as those involving serious physical injury or a life-threatening event, are especially damaging (Nash et al., 1993; Robinson, Rapaport, & Rapaport, 1994). Clinicians and researchers have long been aware of the immediate effects of trauma and, in recent years, have expanded their focus to a consideration of the ways in which the symptoms of PTSD are manifested long after the traumatic event has passed.

Researchers studying different types of trauma have concluded that there is no single constellation of delayed post-traumatic symptoms. Rather, the symptoms depend on a combination of factors having to do with the nature of the event and with the psychological health of the trauma victims. Consider, for example, research on women who were victims of sexual and physical abuse during either childhood or adulthood. Relative to women who had not been abused, the abused women experienced higher levels of depression, anxiety, substance abuse, sexual dysfunc-

tion, dissociation, and interpersonal problems (Astin, Ogland-Hand, Coleman, & Foy, 1995; Daniel, Park, Jefferson, & Greist, 1997; Dutton & Painter, 1993; Halgin & Vivona, 1995). They often described themselves as "fundamentally damaged" by their trauma, highlighting the potential serious and lasting consequences of their experience (Nash et al., 1993).

Childhood is a particularly impressionable period for exposure to trauma; several researchers have found evidence suggesting that violent traumas during childhood can have long-lasting emotional effects (Famularo, Fenton, Augustyn, & Zuckerman, 1996; Klein & Janoff-Bulman, 1996; Timmons, Chandler-Holtz, & Semple, 1996; Van der Kolk, 1997). In one project, researchers studied 156 children who had been severely maltreated by their parents and found that many of the children continued to show signs of PTSD years after being separated from their abusive parents (Famularo et al., 1996). Equally disturbing is the fact that even witnessing a traumatic event is sufficient for the development of PTSD symptoms (Kilpatrick & Williams, 1997b).

Although the effects of trauma can endure for decades after the actual event, not all people who experience traumatic events will suffer long-term psychological consequences. Several factors can contribute to the resilience or vulnerability of these individuals. Psychologically healthy individuals who have close, supportive relationships seem better able to cope with the damaging effects of trauma. Further, those who have experienced trauma of relatively limited duration and severity tend to be less damaged over the longer term. On the other hand, many traumatic events occur in the context of serious social and family disturbance, which may in them-

selves be psychologically damaging. Such events are likely to touch the core of an individual's psyche and have residual effects in many spheres of life. For example, combat veterans and concentration camp survivors who were forced to endure unimaginably dangerous and threatening circumstances go on to suffer from disturbing effects that are both immediate and enduring. Months and years after the trauma, these people may be struggling to contend with the normal stresses of life that others find manageable. Their family environment is often a place of chaos, meeting few of their psychological needs and desires.

How can we explain the psychological aftereffects of traumatic events, which can irrevocably alter the lives of formerly well-adjusted individuals? One compelling explanation comes from the work of trauma researcher Ronnie Janoff-Bulman (1992). She has suggested that a trauma affects the deepest levels of personality. Children who are raised in relatively healthy and responsive environments develop "fundamental assumptions" (p. 3) about the world as a benevolent and meaningful place and about themselves as worthy individuals. Because a traumatic event cannot be easily integrated with a positive view of oneself and the environment, or with a belief in the predictability and meaning of life events, a traumatic experience can lead to a "shattering" of these basic beliefs about the self and the world (p. 52). For trauma victims, the world is no longer safe, predictable, and understandable; their sense of self may be jeopardized as they attempt to understand how they came to be victims of horrible events or others' malevolent actions. It is no surprise, therefore, that the experience of trauma can touch the deepest level of personality functioning and result in effects that last a lifetime.

Even though medications can provide some symptom relief, it would be naive to think that medication alone is sufficient for ameliorating the distressing psychological and interpersonal problems that burden those with PTSD. Consequently, clinicians recommend ongoing psychotherapy, not only to deal with emotional issues but also to monitor the individual's reactions to medical treatments (Southwick & Yehuda, 1993). The most effective psychological treatments for PTSD involve a combination of "covering" and "uncovering" techniques. "Covering" techniques, such as supportive therapy and stress management, help the client seal over the pain of the trauma. They may also help the client reduce stress more effectively and, in the process, eliminate some of the secondary problems that the symptoms cause. For example, PTSD victims who isolate themselves from friends and family are cutting themselves off from social support, which is an important therapeutic agent. By learning alternate coping methods, clients can become better able to seek out this kind of support.

"Uncovering" techniques, which involve a reliving of the trauma, include the behavioral treatments of imaginal flooding and systematic desensitization. Exposing the person with PTSD to cues that bring back memories of the event in a graded fashion, or in a situation in which the individual is taught simultaneously to relax, can eventually break the conditioned anxiety reaction. Other treatments, such as psychodrama, can also be useful in bringing to conscious awareness, under a controlled setting, repressed memories of the traumatic event.

PTSD victims can also learn to reduce stress by approaching their situations more rationally and by breaking down their problems into manageable units. They can work toward achieving a better balance between self-blame and avoidance. Individuals who feel excessively guilty for their role in the traumatic incident can learn to see that their responsibility was not as great as imagined. Conversely, those who feel they have no control over what happens to them and, therefore, avoid confronting problems can learn to feel a greater sense of mastery over the course of their lives (Hobfall et al., 1991).

Donald Meichenbaum (1998) describes a six-step cognitive-behavioral therapy plan that incorporates strategies he has found beneficial for clients suffering from PTSD:

1. Establish a good working relationship with clients, characterized by nurturance and compassion.

2. Encourage clients to view their symptoms in a more positive light; for example, numbing can be viewed as a way of slowing the pace in order to deal with intense levels of distress.
3. Help clients translate global problem descriptions into specific, problem-solving terms.
4. Take behavioral steps, such as confronting the feared situation, in thoughts and in real settings.
5. Confront barriers in the form of feelings (e.g., fears, guilt, depression) and distorted beliefs (e.g., negative self-views) that get in the way of implementing change and mustering hope.
6. Help clients anticipate possible lapses (e.g., a recurrence of flashbacks, bouts of anxiety or depression).

■ Anxiety Disorders: The Perspectives Revisited

As you can see, anxiety disorders cover a broad spectrum of problems, ranging from very specific, seemingly idiosyncratic responses to diffuse and undifferentiated feelings of dread. These disorders involve an intriguing intertwining of biological, psychological, and sociocultural phenomena. Fortunately, relatively straightforward behaviorally based treatments are available that can successfully alleviate the symptoms of anxiety for many people who suffer from these disorders. Furthermore, a number of other strategies involving cognitive, insight-oriented, and psychopharmacological interventions can enhance the effectiveness of behavioral techniques. Knowledge gained from research on the causes and treatment of anxiety disorders can also have some practical benefits for managing lesser difficulties.

RETURN TO THE CASE

Barbara Wilder

Barbara's History
As Barbara shared her life history with me, the flow of her speech frequently was interrupted by sobs and pleas that I be patient with her. As Barbara's story unfolded, I came to understand how the emotional scars left by growing up in a dysfunctional family plagued her throughout childhood and adolescence.

Barbara was raised almost exclusively by her mother. Her father spent very little time at home, because he worked as a sales representative for a company that had branch offices spread across a three-state area. When he was home, he was almost always inebriated. Barbara's mother was very protective of her, restricting almost all social and after-school activities. Barbara remembers feeling somewhat resentful of her mother's strong control over her, but she justified her mother's behavior, because "after all, she couldn't count on my father to help her, and, besides, I was a pretty difficult kid and she didn't want me getting into trouble."

Barbara's father was known to have out-of-town affairs with women, and everyone regarded him as a failure in his job. However, no one

RETURN TO THE CASE

Barbara Wilder (continued)

discussed these problems openly. Barbara remembers being frightened of her father because, when he was drinking, he became furious over even her slightest failure to respond instantly to his instructions. Usually, he gave unclear or contradictory instructions, so she could not predict when he would yell at her and when he would be satisfied with her response. When she tried to apologize, he criticized her even more. Barbara learned that the best way to deal with him was to stay out of his way.

Barbara explained to me that it was not only her father who struggled with psychological impairment. Her mother had, for most of her adult years, an intense fear of leaving the house alone, and she experienced deep depression related to her unhappy marriage. Going back a generation, Barbara's grandmother was considered by most people to be peculiar. She insisted on living the life of a recluse and acted toward her husband in ways that others considered domineering, bordering on sadistic. Barbara's maternal grandfather put up with the abuse, never complaining, always appearing to others as a quiet, accommodating "gentleman." It was quite a shock to the whole community when, at the age of 62, he asphyxiated himself and left a note filled with rage about his "miserable marriage."

In her senior year of high school, Barbara began to write away to a number of colleges for applications. It never occurred to her that her parents would object to her going to college, as long as she realized that she would have to support herself. Since Barbara's grades were excellent, she felt quite certain that she would earn some kind of financial aid. One day, her mother stopped Barbara as she was leaving the house to mail a stack of envelopes and asked Barbara what she was doing. When Barbara explained, her mother burst into tears. She told Barbara that it was time for them to have a talk. They sat down in the kitchen, and Barbara's mother poured forth an amazing "confession." Ever since Barbara was a child, it had been very important for her mother to have Barbara with her at home. That was why she found it so hard to let Barbara go out with her friends and do things after school. She said that Barbara's father had been so impossible that she was unhappy almost all the time. She couldn't even leave the house to run a simple errand unless she had Barbara with her. She begged Barbara not to go away to school, saying that she could not bear the thought of her leaving. Barbara was stunned. She did not realize how much she meant to her mother.

There was no way she could even consider going away to school under these circumstances. Barbara threw away all her letters and applied to the community college located 10 miles away from home.

After college, Barbara took a job in an insurance company, where she became a top-notch typist and receptionist. When her boss was transferred to another city, he told Barbara that he wanted her to move also. She could enroll in the university and take courses there to complete her bachelor's degree, all at company expense. According to her boss, Barbara had a lot of potential to advance in a career if she had the proper training. Concerned about leaving her mother, Barbara asked her what she should do. Barbara's mother assured her that she would "manage somehow." Barbara made the move, and all seemed to be going well. She felt particularly lucky to have found a roommate with whom she shared many common interests, ideas, and feelings. They soon became inseparable. Unfortunately, however, things did not remain so serene for Barbara; the ghosts of unresolved conflicts and pain reappeared and took the form of her current emotional crisis.

Assessment

Although I had some reasonable hypotheses about the nature of Barbara's disorder, important gaps needed to be filled in. Of particular concern was the possibility that Barbara might be suffering from a medical problem. It is not uncommon for people with certain medical problems, such as hypoglycemia, hyperthyroidism, or insulin-secreting tumors, to have symptoms that are strikingly similar to those found in anxiety disorders. However, the physician who conducted the physical examination found no physiological basis for Barbara's problems. Drugs and alcohol were ruled out as well. Barbara had never abused drugs, and she only occasionally drank alcohol in desperate attempts to calm herself down.

Because of the prominent features of anxiety in Barbara's presentation, I recommended that she meet with one of my colleagues, Dr. Michelle Herter, for a comprehensive behavioral assessment. Dr. Herter's assessment protocol consisted of three segments: (1) a symptom-focused interview, (2) the administration of a questionnaire, and (3) Barbara's collection of self-monitoring data.

In her interview, Dr. Herter collected extensive information about the frequency, intensity, and duration of Barbara's bodily and cognitive reactions to her periods of panic. She also discussed

RETURN TO THE CASE

Barbara Wilder (continued)

with Barbara the quality of her relationships, particularly those with her immediate family members. In her report, Dr. Herter described Barbara as a "well-dressed and attractive young woman who looked self-conscious and nervous throughout the interview." She felt that nothing about Barbara suggested intellectual impairment or a personality disorder, but she did discuss Barbara's prominent style of dependency, passive acquiescence to other people's demands, and discomfort in situations involving interpersonal conflict.

Barbara completed the Body Sensations Questionnaire and Agoraphobia Cognitions Questionnaire (Chambless & Goldstein, 1982), which provided compelling data about the nature of her overpowering fear of having disturbing bodily sensations, such as rapid heartbeat and feelings of dizziness. Furthermore, Barbara's responses suggested that she genuinely feared that she was losing her mind.

For the self-monitoring portion of the assessment, Barbara kept a Panic Attack Record (Barlow et al., 1994), on which she documented the time, duration, and intensity of each panic attack. She indicated who was with her at the time, as well as the specific symptoms she experienced. The assessment picture that emerged from these sources of data was that of a woman who was overcome by intense and incapacitating episodes of panic that occurred primarily in situations involving conflict or minor stress, especially when she was alone.

Diagnosis

The most striking feature of Barbara's presenting problems was the occurrence of panic attacks. After experiencing several of these on a frequent basis, Barbara could not leave her apartment because of her fears of having an attack in public. After ruling out the possibility of a physically based disorder on the basis of the medical work-up, I felt confident in the diagnosis of an anxiety disorder involving panic attacks and agoraphobia. I focused my attention on Barbara's symptoms during the episodes she described to me and to Dr. Herter, which included experiences of dizziness, speeded-up heart rate, uncontrollable trembling, sweating, choking sensations, chest discomfort, and fear of dying. I was secure in the belief that these episodes constituted panic attacks, because they involved sudden, unexpected periods of intense fear. Compounding the distress for Barbara was the fact that symptoms of agoraphobia accompanied these panic attacks.

Axis I:	Panic Disorder with Agoraphobia
Axis II:	Rule out Personality Disorder. Not otherwise specified
Axis III:	No physical disorders or conditions
Axis IV:	Problems with primary support group (family tensions) Occupational problems (job transitions)
Axis V:	Current Global Assessment of Functioning: 37 Highest Global Assessment of Functioning (past year): 83

Case Formulation

As I pondered what factors might have contributed to Barbara's developing such a troubling and incapacitating disorder, I considered her genetic history as well as her family system. In evaluating genetic contributions, my thoughts were drawn to the problems that both her mother and her grandmother experienced. Their problems seemed similar to Barbara's, leading me to hypothesize that Barbara had inherited a biological propensity to develop panic attacks.

In reviewing information about Barbara's family, I noted her stories of being so distraught about her father's frequent absences, and her resentment toward her overcontrolling mother, who could not protect her from the tyrannical ways of her unreliable and unpredictable father. The family did not air conflicts, and Barbara learned that the best way to get along with people was to do what they wanted or to stay out of their way. At a time when Barbara should have been allowed to begin her independent life, her mother made it virtually impossible for her to do so. When Barbara finally did leave her mother, she experienced considerable guilt when she realized how much her mother depended on her.

As her life went on, Barbara came to realize more and more that she could not please everyone. Perhaps her first panic attack grew out of this unresolvable conflict. Indeed, all of Barbara's early panic attacks were connected with some kind of emotional conflict in her life. The second attack occurred when Barbara was about to experience separation from the roommate to whom she had become so attached. Other panic attacks occurred when Barbara was going to her office, as thoughts of leaving her mother filled her mind. Although the panic attacks started in situations that had a link to an emotional conflict, they

RETURN TO THE CASE

Barbara Wilder (continued)

eventually generalized to all places outside Barbara's apartment. Barbara came to fear not the situations themselves but the attacks, which caused her to experience an excruciating degree of pain, embarrassment, and terror.

Treatment Plan

As I wrote up my treatment recommendations for Barbara, I realized that she would benefit most from an intervention that tapped behavioral and cognitive-behavioral techniques. Although I was familiar with these techniques, I felt that Barbara's needs would best be served by a clinician who specialized in interventions for people with anxiety disorders. Michelle Herter had offered her services, should such a recommendation seem appropriate, and I chose to accept her offer. I explained to Barbara that Dr. Herter was a leading expert in the kind of treatment she needed. Barbara made it clear that she was committed to obtaining the very best treatment available, even though she expressed disappointment that I would not be her therapist.

I called Dr. Herter and we reviewed the impressions of Barbara that each of us had derived. As we spoke about this case, Dr. Herter put forth a treatment approach not commonly used by most other clinicians. She thought it would be a good idea to begin the therapy in Barbara's home, a nonthreatening context in which she could begin establishing a trusting alliance with Barbara. In time, Dr. Herter would introduce *in vivo* techniques and graded exposure training, in which she would guide Barbara step-by-step through situations that more closely approximated those that had terrified her in the past. At the same time, Dr. Herter planned to work with her in restructuring her beliefs about her inability to control her panic attacks. Dr. Herter told me that, as time went on, she might also incorporate assertiveness training.

Outcome of the Case

I concurred with Dr. Herter's initial optimism about the likelihood that Barbara would show fairly quick improvement once treatment was begun. Barbara responded very positively to Dr. Herter's willingness to provide home-based therapy. During the first 3 weeks, which included six sessions, Dr. Herter took a comprehensive history of the problem and developed a relationship with Barbara that facilitated the initiation of behavioral techniques during the second phase. In the beginning of the second

phase, Dr. Herter taught Barbara techniques she could use to change the way she thought about panic-arousing situations. For example, Barbara was to imagine herself conquering her fear and feeling a sense of increased self-esteem following her success. She became able to envision herself as competent in situations that previously had seemed so threatening. In the third phase, Dr. Herter accompanied Barbara outside her apartment to a nearby convenience store. Step by step, in the weeks that followed, Dr. Herter introduced situations that were increasingly more threatening, culminating in Barbara's successful trip to a crowded shopping mall unaccompanied by her therapist.

Along with conquering her fears of leaving home, Barbara also began to gain some insight into the connection between interpersonal conflicts and her panic attacks. Several weeks into treatment, Barbara reported that her mother was telephoning her more and more frequently. Barbara's mother had developed terrible headaches that made her incapable of doing anything for hours at a time. Although she did not ask directly, Barbara felt very strongly that her mother was hinting for Barbara to move back home. Barbara missed a session, something that was very unusual for her. Dr. Herter became concerned that Barbara was experiencing a relapse. A call to Barbara confirmed this. Barbara had experienced another panic attack during the week and was unable to leave her apartment. The cognitive techniques she had practiced so faithfully had failed to work. Barbara had wanted to call Dr. Herter but felt too ashamed. After discussing this situation, Barbara was able to understand how this particular panic attack had been provoked by interpersonal conflict; this insight proved useful in motivating Barbara to resume and follow through with her treatment program.

In time, Barbara's mother began making fewer demands on her, and Barbara was able to recover the gains she had made in individual therapy prior to the most recent panic attack. Barbara and Dr. Herter continued to meet for another 6 months, during which time Barbara's progress was cemented. Soon after Barbara terminated with Dr. Herter, she sent me a note to thank me for the referral. In the note, she boasted about her success in overcoming the problem that had been so threatening and devastating for her. She explained how she had developed new ways of solving her problems, whether they pertained to possible panic attacks or to the difficulties she was likely to encounter in her relationship with her mother. ■

Sarah Tobin, PhD

Summary

- Anxiety disorders are characterized by the experience of physiological arousal, apprehension or feelings of dread, hypervigilance, avoidance, and sometimes a specific fear or phobia. Panic disorder is characterized by frequent and recurrent panic attacks—intense sensations of fear and physical discomfort. This disorder is often found in association with agoraphobia, the fear of being trapped or unable to escape if a panic attack occurs. Biological and cognitive-behavioral perspectives have been particularly useful for understanding and treating this disorder. Some experts explain panic disorder as an acquired "fear of fear," in which the individual becomes hypersensitive to early signs of a panic attack, and the fear of a full-blown attack leads the individual to become unduly apprehensive and avoidant of another attack. Treatment based on the cognitive-behavioral perspective involves such methods as relaxation training and *in vivo* or imaginal flooding as a way of breaking the negative cycle initiated by the individual's fear of having a panic attack. Medications can also help alleviate symptoms, with the most commonly prescribed being antianxiety and antidepressant medications.

- Specific phobias are irrational fears of particular objects or situations. Cognitive behaviorists assert that previous learning experiences and a cycle of negative, maladaptive thoughts cause specific phobias. Treatments recommended by the behavioral and cognitive-behavioral approaches include flooding, systematic desensitization, imagery, *in vivo* exposure, and participant modeling, as well as procedures aimed at changing the individual's maladaptive thoughts, such as cognitive restructuring, coping self-statements, thought stopping, and increases in self-efficacy. Treatment based on the biological perspective involves medication.

- A social phobia is a fear of being observed by others acting in a way that will be humiliating or embarrassing. Cognitive-behavioral approaches to social phobia regard the disorder as due to an unrealistic fear of criticism, which causes people with the disorder to lose the ability to concentrate on their performance, instead shifting their attention to how anxious they feel, which then causes them to make mistakes and, therefore, to become more fearful. Behavioral methods that provide *in vivo* exposure, along with cognitive restructuring and social skills training, seem to be the most effective in helping people with social phobia. Medication is the treatment recommended within the biological perspective for severe cases of this disorder.

- People who are diagnosed as having generalized anxiety disorder have a number of unrealistic worries that spread to various spheres of life. The cognitive-behavioral approach to generalized anxiety disorder emphasizes the unrealistic nature of these worries and regards the disorder as a vicious cycle that feeds on itself. Cognitive-behavioral treatment approaches recommend breaking the negative cycle of worry by teaching individuals techniques that allow them to feel they control the worrying. Biological treatment emphasizes the use of medication.

- In obsessive-compulsive disorder, individuals develop obsessions, or thoughts they cannot rid themselves of, and compulsions, which are irresistible, repetitive behaviors. A cognitive-behavioral understanding of obsessive-compulsive disorder regards the symptoms as the product of a learned association between anxiety and the thoughts or acts, which temporarily can produce relief from anxiety. A growing body of evidence supports a biological explanation of the disorder, with the most current research suggesting that it is associated with an excess of serotonin. Treatment with medications, such as clomipramine, seems to be effective, although cognitive-behavioral methods involving exposure and thought stopping are quite effective as well.

- In post-traumatic stress disorder, the individual is unable to recover from the anxiety associated with a traumatic life event, such as tragedy or disaster, an accident, or participation in combat. The aftereffects of the traumatic event include flashbacks, nightmares, and intrusive thoughts that alternate with the individual's attempts to deny that the event ever took place. Some people experience a briefer but very troubling response to a traumatic event; this condition, called acute stress disorder, lasts from 2 days to 4 weeks and involves the kinds of symptoms that people with PTSD experience over a much longer period of time. Cognitive-behavioral approaches regard the disorder as the result of negative and maladaptive thoughts about one's role in causing the traumatic events to happen, feelings of ineffectiveness and isolation from others, and a pessimistic outlook on life as a result of the experience. Treatment may involve teaching people with PTSD new coping skills, so that they can more effectively manage stress and reestablish social ties with others who can provide ongoing support. A combination of "covering" techniques, such as supportive therapy and stress management, and "uncovering" techniques such as imaginal flooding and desensitization, is usually helpful.

Key Terms

See Glossary for definitions.

Acute stress disorder 190
Agoraphobia 173
Anxiety 172
Anxiety disorders 172
Aversions 177
Benzodiazepines 170
Compulsion 185
Conditioned fear reactions 175
Denial/intrusion phase 192
Fear 172

Flooding 180
Generalized anxiety disorder 183
Graduated exposure 180
Imaginal flooding 180
Lactate 175
Lactate theory 175
Obsession 185
Obsessive-compulsive disorder 185
Outcry phase 191
Panic attack 172
Panic control therapy (PCT) 176

Panic disorder 172
Post-traumatic stress disorder (PTSD) 190
Relaxation training 176
Situationally bound (or cued) panic attack 172
Situationally predisposed panic attack 173
Social phobia 180
Specific phobia 177
Thought stopping 180
Traumatic experience 190
Unexpected (uncued) panic attack 172

Internet Resource

To get more information on the material covered in this chapter, visit our Web site at **http://www.mhhe.com/halgin.**
There you will find more information, resources, and links to topics of interest.

CASE REPORT: ROSE MARSTON

Late on a Friday afternoon, I received a call from Dr. Thompson, one of the hospital's emergency room physicians, asking me to conduct an evaluation of Rose Marston, a 37-year-old woman who had become a frequent visitor to the emergency room with an array of physical problems. The story Dr. Thompson told me about Rose was similar to previous histories he had told me about other problematic patients. I found myself completing some of his sentences as he described the frustrations the emergency room staff felt in their dealings with Rose. Dr. Thompson was convinced that Rose's recurrent "physical problems" were attributable to psychological rather than physical factors.

During the preceding year, Rose had come to the emergency room on 15 occasions and each time complained about what seemed like serious medical problems. Doctors conducted extensive medical testing and consulted specialists, but no diagnosable medical conditions had ever been confirmed. Her medical chart included complaints about gastrointestinal problems, such as vomiting, nausea, and bloating; complaints of pain in her chest, back, joints, and hands; neurological symptoms, including double vision and dizziness; and problems of irregular menstruation. On occasion, she had fainted, and several times she could not move her legs.

Dr. Thompson shared with me his own distress about his most recent emergency room contact with Rose. Following one of Rose's customary listings of physical complaints, Dr. Thompson told Rose he had come to believe that her problems were emotionally based, rather than medical in origin. Moments later, Rose collapsed on the floor in what appeared to be an epileptic seizure. When she became conscious, Rose stated that she remembered nothing of what had just happened and, indeed, could not even recall how she had gotten to the emergency room. When Dr. Thompson reviewed the situation with Rose, she became enraged and yelled out with a voice that echoed through the corridors, "I know you wish I would go away. Maybe you'd be relieved if I'd just kill myself." After calming down, Rose reluctantly agreed to take Dr. Thompson's recommendation to consult with me about her problems.

When Rose first contacted me to arrange the intake appointment, she insisted that our first meeting take place at my office in the hospital, rather than in the more customary outpatient setting in which I see my clients. When I asked Rose her reasons for this request, she stated rather emphatically that it "made sense" to be near medical personnel in the event of a physical crisis she might have. I was initially uncomfortable with the idea of agreeing to this request, feeling that I might reinforce her maladaptive behavior. After some thought, however, I agreed; perhaps it would help Rose establish an alliance with me if she viewed me as responsive to her concerns and worries.

Even with the concession I had made about the place of our first meeting, I could sense in our initial encounter that Rose was approaching me with considerable skepticism. Her first words were "I guess they've tried to convince you that I'm some kind of hypochondriac crackpot." I assured Rose that I wanted to hear what she had to tell me about her problems. Although I would ask for her permission to speak to the medical staff, I wanted her to know that I was committed to helping her find a way to feel better, both psychologically and physically. I tried tactfully to point out that people often develop physical problems when they are upset about something and that real physical problems become aggravated during times of stress. I could tell that she was cautious about speaking with me, but nevertheless she seemed willing to give it a try.

Though I was eager to proceed with the interview, I found myself wondering about what might be inside the large picnic basket Rose kept on her lap. Rose seemed a bit irked when I inquired about the contents but went on to say, "I guess you should learn about my conditions right away, so you'll be able to understand how serious my medical problems are." She lifted the top of the basket to expose what seemed to be a mini-pharmacy—a thermometer, a box of bandages and gauze pads, several tubes and jars of ointment, and a dozen medication bottles. With her face reddening, either from embarrassment or annoyance, Rose emphasized her need to be prepared for the aches and pains that commonly afflict her without warning. I wasn't quite sure how to respond to this display but chose to move right into our discussion of the history of her medical problems.

Rose explained that many of her physical problems dated back to childhood. In fact, she had come to believe that she suffered some bodily problems that "ran in the family." When I asked for clarification, Rose explained that her younger sister, Emily, had been born with serious medical problems and actually died from them during her teenage years. Although Rose was relatively healthy as a young child, she began to develop physical problems of her own, which caused her to wonder whether she was "catching some of Emily's medical problems." By the time she reached adolescence, Rose's problems had worsened; even a common cold or flu would cause her mother to comment that Rose seemed to get "much sicker than other people." In fact, Rose's mother frequently had to stay home from work to nurse Rose back to health. Over time, Rose's problems worsened, as she went from doctor to doctor, seeking answers to the disturbing mysteries of her bodily afflictions. Rose's frustration with the medical profession increased over the years because of the inability of physicians, even leading specialists, to determine what was wrong with her. Rose ultimately came to believe that she had unusual medical problems for which science and medicine did not yet have the answers.

Sarah Tobin, PhD

7

Somatoform Disorders, Psychological Factors Affecting Medical Conditions, and Dissociative Disorders

Chapter Outline

In this chapter, we will focus on three sets of disorders: somatoform disorders, conditions in which psychological factors affect medical conditions, and dissociative disorders. In
each of these sets of disorders, the body expresses psychological conflict and stress in unusual, and sometimes bizarre, fashion. These conditions have an important role in the history of
abnormal psychology because they alerted the medical community of the 1800s to the role that psychological processes can
play in causing otherwise unexplained symptoms. Recall our
discussion in Chapter 1 about hysteria and how medical experts
with training in neurology were confused and astounded by
case after case of patients with mysterious "physical" symptoms that seemed to have no physical basis. Freud's insight that
these physical symptoms could have a psychological basis led
to a revolution in the understanding and treatment of many unusual disorders. Although somatoform and dissociative disorders are relatively uncommon today, these disorders have not
disappeared, and they remain one of the more fascinating areas
of abnormal behavior. Situations in which psychological factors
affect medical conditions, on the other hand, seem to be receiving increased attention in contemporary medical circles, as
health professionals develop their understanding of the interactions between stress and a variety of medical problems.

Somatoform Disorders

Imagine the following scenario. A classmate of yours, a star
hockey player, wakes up one morning complaining that he is unable to move his hand. He then says in an oddly indifferent manner that the situation is very unfortunate, because he has an important game that night. He casually dismisses the problem as
"bad luck" and goes back to bed. You may be perplexed at his lack
of alarm but would nevertheless presume that there was something physically wrong with his hand. But might there be more to
the story? Perhaps you are wondering whether your classmate's
problem is "all in his head." Maybe he is very concerned about his
performance in the game and is "faking" his injury. Or, on a
deeper level, perhaps his anxiety is so great that he does not consciously make the connection between his inability to move his
hand and his concern about playing in the game.

Somatoform disorders include a variety of conditions in
which psychological conflicts become translated into physical
problems or complaints that cause distress or impairment in a
person's life. The term *somatoform* comes from the Greek word
soma, meaning "body." However, somatoform disorders are
considered psychological rather than physical disorders, because there is no physical abnormality that can explain the bodily complaint. If your classmate's condition is due to a somatoform disorder, his dysfunctional hand will not produce
abnormal responses on neurophysiological testing. In fact, the
pain or stiffness he feels would probably not correspond to the
symptoms of any known physical disorder.

Conversion Disorder

As the example of the hockey player illustrates, psychological
conflict can be converted into physical problems in some very

Some people suffering with apprehension and anxiety about performance, as in an athletic contest, unconsciously develop physical symptoms that pull them out of the upsetting situation.

dramatic ways. **Conversion disorder** involves this translation of
unacceptable drives or troubling conflicts into bodily motor or
sensory symptoms that suggest a neurological or other kind of
medical condition. The essential feature of this disorder is an involuntary loss or alteration of a bodily function due to psychological conflict or need, causing the individual to feel seriously
distressed or to be impaired in social, occupational, or other important areas of life. The person is not intentionally producing the
symptoms; however, clinicians cannot establish a medical basis
for the symptoms, and it appears that the person is "converting"
the psychological conflict or need into a physical problem.

In the mid-1800s, a French physician named Paul Briquet
systematically described and categorized the symptoms of hysteria based on his review of more than 400 patients. In the latter
part of the nineteenth century, French neurologist Jean Martin
Charcot used hypnosis to show that psychological factors played
a role in the physical symptoms of hysteria. In a person who was
under hypnosis, hysterical symptoms could be produced or removed at the hypnotist's suggestion. A student of Charcot's,
Pierre Janet, theorized that this difference between normal and
hysterical people was due to the presence, in hysterics, of dissociated contents of the mind. According to Janet, these parts of the

mind had become dissociated because of hereditary degeneration of the brain. The ideas and functions within the dissociated part of the mind took autonomous hold over the individual and created symptoms that appeared to be beyond the person's voluntary control. Hippolyte Marie Bernheim, another French neurologist, maintained that hypnotizability could be demonstrated in both normal and hysterical people.

The work of Janet and Bernheim attracted attention all over Europe, and Freud became fascinated with their ideas. Through contact with Janet and Bernheim, Freud eventually developed a radically different theory of hysteria in his work with Breuer in the 1890s. Freud called conversion disorder **hysterical neurosis,** implying that it was a physical reaction to anxiety (neurosis).

The mechanism through which the symptoms of conversion disorder arise is still as much in dispute as it was in Freud's day. What is fascinating about conversion symptoms is the way in which they shed light on the relationship between psychological processes and the workings of the body. It is known that many physical disorders can be produced or aggravated by emotional problems that place undue demands on a part of the body or on a particular organ system. Similarly, conversion symptoms are also the physical expression of a psychological disturbance, but the translation from "mind" to "body" occurs in a way that defies medical logic.

An intriguing feature of a conversion symptom for many people with this disorder is that, once the symptom is moved from the realm of the psychological to the realm of the physical, it no longer poses a threat to the individual's peace of mind. The individual may pay little attention to the symptom and dismiss it as minor, even though it may be incapacitating. This phenomenon is called **la belle indifférence,** or the "beautiful" lack of concern, to indicate that the individual is not distressed by what might otherwise be construed as very inconveniencing physical problems. Once thought to be a criterion for diagnosing conversion disorder, la belle indifférence is now regarded as an interesting but not defining aspect, seen in about one third to one half of clients with this disorder (Ford & Folks, 1985).

Conversion symptoms fall into four categories, each involving mystifying and very different kinds of disturbances: (1) motor symptoms or deficits, (2) sensory symptoms or deficits, (3) seizures or convulsions, and (4) mixed presentations. In motor functioning, the individual may experience such problems as impaired coordination or balance, paralysis or specific weakness, swallowing difficulties, speaking difficulty, and urinary retention. Sensory problems include feelings that one has lost a sense of touch or the ability to experience physical pain, as well as double vision, blindness, or deafness. Some individuals experience dramatic seizures or convulsions that lack a physiological basis, and others have a combination of symptoms or deficits from the other symptom subtypes.

Conversion disorder is a rare phenomenon, affecting 1 to 3 percent of those referred for mental health care. The disorder, which often runs in families, can appear at any age in adulthood and is more frequently observed in women (Tomasson, Kent, & Coryell, 1991) and people with less education (Binzer, Andersen, & Kullgren, 1997). The condition usually appears suddenly and dissipates in less than 2 weeks. The symptoms may recur, however, within a year of their initial development. Symptoms involving paralysis, speaking problems, and blindness have a better prognosis than others. Clinicians are less optimistic about clients who complain of seizures or bodily tremors (American Psychiatric Association, 1994).

As you can imagine, it is very difficult for a health professional to diagnose conversion disorder. One concern about helping a person who shows conversion-like symptoms is that a real physical or cognitive problem may be wrongly attributed to psychological causes, and the client may not receive prompt medical attention. Indeed, as many as one half of those who are diagnosed as having conversion disorder are sometimes years later found to have had a physical illness not apparent when they were first seen for treatment (Couprie et al., 1995; Ford & Folks, 1985).

Somatization Disorder and Related Conditions

Like conversion disorder, **somatization disorder** involves the expression of psychological issues through bodily problems that have no basis in a physiological dysfunction. The difference between somatization disorder and conversion disorder is that somatization disorder involves multiple and recurrent bodily symptoms, rather than a single physical complaint. This condition, which usually first appears before the age of 30, results in serious social, occupational, and interpersonal functioning problems. The individual seeks help from

Anna O. (Bertha Pappenheim). In what was one of psychotherapy's first "success stories," Anna became one of the founders of the modern social-work movement. Ironically, in her own work she never placed much stock in psychoanalysis as a means of treatment.

Conversion Disorder

MINI-CASE

Tiffany, a 32-year-old banker, thought she had already suffered more stress than one person could handle. She had always thought of herself as a person to whom weird things usually happened, and she commonly made more out of situations than was warranted. Driving down a snowy road one night, she accidentally hit an elderly man who was walking on the side of the road, causing a near fatal injury. In the months that followed, she became caught up in lengthy legal proceedings, which distracted her from her work and caused tremendous emotional stress in her life. On awakening one Monday morning, she found herself staggering around the bedroom, unable to see anything other than the shadows of objects in the room. At first, she thought she was just having a hard time waking up. As the morning went on, however, she realized that she was losing her vision. She waited 2 days before consulting a physician. When she did go for her medical appointment, she had an odd lack of concern about what seemed like such a serious physical condition.

■ What factors in Tiffany's personality and immediate past might have contributed to her developing a conversion disorder?

■ What might be the symbolic connection between her physical symptom and the event that apparently precipitated her loss of vision?

DIAGNOSTIC FEATURES

● This diagnosis is assigned to people with one or more symptoms or deficits that affect voluntary motor or sensory function that suggest a neurological or general medical condition.

● Psychological factors are judged to be associated with the condition, which began or was aggravated following a conflict or stressor.

● The condition is not intentionally produced or faked.

● After appropriate investigation, the condition cannot be attributed to a general medical condition, substance use, or culturally sanctioned behavior or experience.

● The condition causes significant distress or impairment, or it warrants medical evaluation.

● The condition is neither limited to pain or sexual dysfunction nor better explained by another mental disorder.

● Types are (1) with motor symptom or deficit, (2) with sensory symptom or deficit, (3) with seizures or convulsions, and (4) with mixed presentation.

---

physicians, often several different ones simultaneously over the course of years, with seemingly exaggerated physical complaints. In a small number of cases, the individual suffers from a diagnosable medical condition, but his or her complaints are far in excess of what is customarily associated with the condition, and the level of the person's impairment is also much more extreme. Although it may appear that people with this diagnosis are intentionally "faking" a complex medical problem, they actually are not consciously attuned to the ways in which their psychological problems are being expressed physically.

In most cases, somatization disorder first appears during adolescence and progresses to a fluctuating, lifelong course, during which stressful events can cause episodic intensification of the symptoms. Individuals with somatization disorder rarely go through a year without seeking medical treatment for an undiagnosable physical problem. These people go to extreme lengths, compulsively seeking medical and surgical treatment for their vague and unsubstantiated physical problems. Not surprisingly, the disorder can cause significant work and social impairment.

Somatization disorder is relatively rare. Estimates of its prevalence in the general U.S. population are .23 percent in women and .02 percent in men (Swartz et al., 1991). People with somatization disorder tend to be from lower socioeco-

nomic classes, with relatively little education or psychological sophistication. They may have come from a culture that gives less emphasis to the expression of emotions than to the expression of bodily symptoms. Many grew up in a home where they witnessed frequent sickness in a parent and suffered from physical illnesses themselves. In many cases, their home life was lacking in emotional support and was disturbed by alcoholic or antisocial problems on the part of one or both parents. These people generally experienced school problems during their youth, and in many cases they have records of delinquency. As they grew into adolescence, many were sexually promiscuous and married at a young age into unstable relationships with spouses who were substance abusers. Often, they themselves have a history of substance abuse problems (Ford, 1995).

Because they do not consider their difficulties to have an emotional cause, people with somatization disorder do not voluntarily seek psychotherapy. Only on the insistence of a physician are they likely to do so; even then, they make it clear to the psychotherapist that they feel misunderstood and that their physical problems have not been adequately assessed. The therapist tries to help the client draw the connections between physical problems and psychological conflicts; however, even in the best of these therapies the chances for success are slim.

Somatization Disorder

MINI-CASE

Helen, a 29-year-old woman, is seeking treatment, because her physician said there was nothing more he could do for her. When asked about her physical problems, Helen recited a litany of complaints, including frequent episodes when she could not remember what has happened to her and other times when her vision is so blurred that she could not read the words on a printed page. Helen enjoys cooking and doing things around the house, but she becomes easily fatigued and short of breath for no apparent reason. She often is unable to eat the elaborate meals she prepares, because she becomes nauseated and is prone to vomit any food with even a touch of spice. According to Helen's husband, she has lost all interest in sexual intimacy, and they have intercourse only about once every few months, usually at his insistence. Helen complains of painful cramps during her menstrual periods, and at other times says she feels that her "insides are on fire." Because of additional pain in her back, legs, and chest, Helen wants to stay in bed for much of the day. Helen lives in a large, old Victorian house, from which she ventures only infrequently "because I need to be able to lie down when my legs ache."

- How do Helen's symptoms correspond to the symptoms of somatization disorder?

- What circumstances in Helen's life might have contributed to her disorder?

DIAGNOSTIC FEATURES

- This diagnosis is assigned to people who, even before they reach the age of 30, have many physical complaints for years, for which they seek treatment or experience impairment in social, occupational, or other important areas of functioning.

- These individuals experience symptoms in each of the following four categories:

  - Pain: history of at least four pain symptoms (e.g., in head, abdomen, back, joints, chest, rectum)

  - Gastrointestinal: history of at least two gastrointestinal symptoms (e.g., nausea, bloating, vomiting, diarrhea)

  - Sexual: history of at least one sexual or reproductive symptom other than pain (e.g., erectile or ejaculatory dysfunction, irregular menstruation, menstrual bleeding)

  - Pseudoneurological: history of at least one symptom or deficit suggesting a neurological condition not limited to pain (e.g., conversion symptoms, such as impaired coordination or balance, paralysis or localized weakness, difficulty swallowing, hallucinations, loss of touch or pain sensation, dissociative symptoms)

- Either: (1) the symptoms cannot be fully attributed to a known medical condition or substance use or (2) when there is a medical condition, the physical complaints or impairment is in excess of what would be expected.

- The symptoms are not intentionally produced.

Pain disorder is yet another related condition. In contrast to the multisymptomatic picture of somatization disorder, in **pain disorder,** a form of pain (which causes intense personal distress or impairment) is the predominant focus of the client's medical complaint. As with all the conditions in this group, the client is not faking the experience of pain. People with pain disorder find that their life becomes consumed by the experience of their pain and the pursuit of relief. In many cases, a diagnosable medical condition exists, but the nature of the pain complaint is regarded as being intricately associated with psychological issues. In other cases, no diagnosable medical condition exists. Although psychological factors are not usually the cause of the pain, emotional problems can trigger and intensify an episode of pain and maintain the pain disorder (Turk, 1994).

The diagnosis of pain disorder is particularly complicated in cases in which a medical condition is evident, such as hernias, arthritis, and tumors—which certainly cause a good deal of pain. However, for people with this disorder, much more than the medical condition seems to be associated with the onset, severity, intensification, and maintenance of their pain. In many instances, these individuals have other psychological disorders, such as a mood disorder or an anxiety disorder, conditions that can become intricately intertwined with the experience and complaint of pain.

Body Dysmorphic Disorder

Perhaps, like most people, you are self-conscious about one aspect of your body, such as your height, your weight, your shape, the size of your nose, or something about your hair. If you confide in friends, they may tell you that they are also self-conscious about a feature of their bodies. In fact, many people have distorted negative concerns about their body (Phillips, 1996); for example, in one study of college students, as many as 70 percent of the group complained of some dissatisfaction with an aspect of their appearance (Fitts, Gibson, Redding, & Deiter, 1989).

People with **body dysmorphic disorder** are not just dissatisfied but preoccupied, almost to the point of being delusional, with the idea that a part of their body is ugly or defective. They are so consumed with distress about their bodily problem that their work, social life, and relationships are impaired. They may believe that there is something wrong with the texture of their skin, that they have too much or too little

Pain Disorder

MINI-CASE

Brian, a 48-year-old store manager, has complained for more than 3 years of constant pain in two distant parts of his body: his teeth and his feet. At times, the pain is so severe that he spends the entire day flat on his back at home. He has visited numerous dentists and podiatrists, who are unable to find any medically diagnosable cause of these complaints. Although several of the doctors pointed out that these symptoms first appeared soon after Brian's painful divorce, he is unable and unwilling to acknowledge that there might be a connection. Brian has missed an extensive amount of work and is at risk of losing his job. The thought of this terrifies him for both financial and emotional reasons. He has worked since the age of 19, beginning his career in merchandising as a shipping clerk for a large retail discount chain. He advanced to his current managerial position and fears that he would never be able to find another job or return to successful employment again.

- What symptoms does Brian have that fit the definition of pain disorder?

- Is there anything about Brian's symptoms that might lead you to suspect that he is faking them?

DIAGNOSTIC FEATURES

- People with this condition complain of pain in one or more places that is of sufficient severity to warrant clinical attention.

- The pain causes significant distress or impairment.

- Psychological factors are judged to have an important role in the onset, severity, aggravation, or maintenance of the pain.

- The pain is not intentionally produced or faked.

- The condition is not better accounted for by another mental disorder.

- Types are (1) acute if of less than 6 months' duration or (2) chronic if 6 months or longer.

---

facial hair, or that there is a deformity in the shape of their nose, mouth, jaw, or eyebrows. In one study of 54 women in treatment for this disorder, bodily concerns in order of frequency included concerns about thighs, abdomen, breast size or shape,

Some people with body dysmorphic disorder are preoccupied with the texture of their hair, and resort to wearing a wig to cover the imagined defect.

skin blemishes, buttocks, facial features, overall weight, scars, aging, hair, height, hips, teeth, and arms (Rosen, Reiter, & Orosan, 1995). There appear to be gender differences in the nature of bodily dissatisfaction, in that men are more likely to be preoccupied with their body build, their genitals, and the thinning of their hair (Phillips & Diaz, 1997).

For the most part, the defects these people are concerned about are imaginary. In other instances, there really is something abnormal about the body part, but the person's concern is grossly exaggerated. Mirrors and other reflecting surfaces are commonly problematic. The urge to stare at their "deformity" may be irresistible; they may have a special mirror with focused lighting that enables them to scrutinize the flaw, and they spend long periods of time trying to mask the body part that causes them such great distress. In one study of 13 individuals with this disorder, each person engaged in compulsive behaviors associated with their preoccupation for long durations, usually 3 hours or more each day (Neziroglu & Yaryura-Tobias, 1993). Others go to great lengths to avoid any reflection of their "grotesque" problem, possibly covering mirrors in a hotel room or crossing the street to avoid a reflecting store window. At times, their thinking borders on paranoia, as they imagine that others are talking about them or staring. Perhaps they take some measures to conceal the object of their concerns. For example, a woman who is distressed by her brittle hair texture wears a baseball hat all the time. A man who is distressed by a pock mark on his face grows a beard, which he dyes a deep color to mask the flaw that others hardly notice.

Medical Illness or Somatoform Disorder?

Imagine you are a health professional evaluating a woman who recently began having seizures the day after a traumatic disappointment in her life. One of your most difficult challenges is determining whether there is a medical basis to this woman's problems, or whether her seizures are actually psychologically based responses to her upsetting experience.

Somatoform disorders and somatic symptoms that cannot be traced to physical causes are quite common in medical settings where they evoke considerable frustration among medical practitioners (Dreher, 1996; Katon et al., 1995; Kirmayer, Robbins, & Paris, 1994). Because individuals with somatoform disorders view themselves as medically ill, they rarely seek psychological help and, instead, turn to primary care physicians for help. Their pursuit of medical help is both time-consuming and costly. In fact, the yearly health care cost of the typical individual with a somatoform disorder is estimated to be nine times the average cost of care for a typical American (Smith, 1990). In a vain attempt to confirm a medical diagnosis, physicians may resort to costly tests or medical procedures, and even surgery. When a physician does raise the possibility that

the cause of a problem might be psychological, the response is usually anger.

In some cases, the health professional is fairly convinced that the presenting problem is psychological rather than medical. Nevertheless, it is imperative to conduct a careful medical evaluation to make sure. This may be more difficult than you think, because some conditions are not easy to diagnose. For example, the early signs of multiple sclerosis involve episodic vision problems, muscle tremors, and bladder control difficulties, all of which can be mistaken for the neurologic-like symptoms of somatization disorder (Smith, 1990). Rare and obscure illnesses might also be incorrectly diagnosed as somatoform disorders. It is alarming for health professionals to realize that many people diagnosed as having a somatoform disorder are subsequently determined to have a very serious medical condition (Martin, 1992; Martin & Yutzy, 1996).

To rule out a medical condition, mental health professionals and physicians usually look for certain patterns that have been documented as common in people with somatoform disorders. For example, the symptoms of most somatoform disorders wax and wane over a period of years, even when untreated, so individuals with a history of these disorders are likely to continue to report similar symptoms to medical personnel over the course of years. Another interesting facet is the style with which these individuals discuss their symptoms. Oddly, there seems to be no middle point. Either they are intensely worried and hysterical, or they seem strangely unconcerned about the seriousness of their "medical" condition. People with hypochondriasis are often very upset about the cause of their concern, while those with conversion disorder are not necessarily so panic stricken.

Individuals diagnosed with somatoform disorders frequently have comorbid personality disorders, and some researchers have suggested that somatoform disorders might be caused in part by a trait known as alexithymia, a difficulty integrating emotions with daily thoughts and activities. Individuals with alexithymia tend to have problems distinguishing physical and emotional sensations; they avoid emotional expression and tend to seek external rather than internal explanations for their problems (Kirmayer et al., 1994). This condition, which is surprisingly common among men (Levant, 1998), is considered by some as a predisposing factor for developing a somatoform disorder. The assumption is that people who do not know how to express their emotions effectively will deal with their stress in pathological ways.

Returning to the case of the woman with unexplained seizures, the health professional must make a differential diagnosis between conversion disorder and epilepsy. Seizures are, in fact, a common conversion symptom, and dangers are inherent in misdiagnosis in either direction. Someone with psychogenic seizures, incorrectly diagnosed with epilepsy, could be prescribed powerful medications or surgery, while untreated epilepsy could be life-threatening. Assuming that physically caused seizures are ruled out, the health professional conducts a careful and thorough psychosocial history, with particular attention to the client's style of coping with symptoms, history of similar types of distress, and experience of psychologically painful events that may not have been resolved at an emotional level.

Researchers have begun to provide data that document the incidence and characteristics of this puzzling disorder. In one in-depth investigation, Katherine Phillips and colleagues described the nature of the disorder among a group of 30 individuals (Phillips, McElroy, Keck, & Pope, 1993). Ranging in age from 17 to 80, more than a third of these clients had a preoccu-

pation with their bodily concern that was of delusional proportion. The average age of onset for the condition was 15. The impact on their lives was dramatic, with 97 percent reporting that they avoided normal social and work involvements; a third remained housebound. Serious associated psychological disorders occurred in most of these individuals at some point in life,

Body Dysmorphic Disorder

MINI-CASE

Lydia is a 43-year-old woman who was referred to the mental health clinic by a local surgeon. For the past 8 years, Lydia has visited plastic surgeons across the country to find one who will perform surgery to reduce the size of her hands, which she perceives as being "too fat." Until she has this surgery, she will not leave her house without wearing gloves. The plastic surgeon concurs with Lydia's family members and friends that Lydia's perception of her hands is distorted and that plastic surgery would be inappropriate and irresponsible.

■ What symptoms of Lydia's would lead you to regard her as having body dysmorphic disorder?

■ In your opinion, would plastic surgery alleviate Lydia's suffering?

DIAGNOSTIC FEATURES

● People with this condition are preoccupied with an imagined defect in their appearance. Even if a slight abnormality is present, their concern is excessive.

● Their preoccupation causes significant distress or impairment.

● Their preoccupation is not better accounted for by another mental disorder, such as anorexia nervosa.

---

with 93 percent experiencing a major mood disorder, 73 percent an anxiety disorder, and 33 percent a psychotic disorder. Almost a fifth of the clients had made suicide attempts. Their efforts to obtain relief through medical procedures were generally unsuccessful and included surgical, dermatological, and dental treatments. Many people with this disorder also suffer with major depressive disorder (Phillips, Nierenberg, Brendel, & Fava, 1996), and some go so far as to attempt suicide (Veale, Boocock, Gournay, & Dryden, 1996).

Medications that are effective in treating obsessive-compulsive disorder and serious depression—particularly SSRIs, such as fluoxetine (El-khatib & Dickey, 1995; Heimann, 1997; Phillips & Taub, 1995)—also alleviate the emotional distress of some people with this disorder. Cognitive-behavioral group therapy, in which participants with the disorder give each other feedback about their actual appearance, can also be successful, as can training in behavioral methods, such as thought stopping, relaxation, and exposure therapy with response prevention (McKay, Todaro, Neziroglu, & Campisi, 1997; Rosen et al., 1995).

Hypochondriasis

People with the somatoform disorder known as **hypochondriasis** believe or fear that they have a serious illness, when in fact they are merely experiencing normal bodily reactions. For example, a stomachache that lasts for more than a day might lead a hypochondriacal woman to worry that she has an advanced case of stomach cancer. Or a recurrent headache might lead a hypochondriacal man to infer that he has a brain tumor. Even the most minor of bodily changes, such as itching skin, can cause the person with hypochondriasis to urgently seek medical attention. To the dismay of people with hypochondriasis, medical tests fail to confirm their assumptions that they have a serious medical illness.

Unlike conversion disorder or somatization disorder, hypochondriasis does not involve extreme bodily dysfunction or unexplainable medical symptoms. Instead, the person with hypochondriasis misinterprets or exaggerates normal bodily occurrences. Hypochondriacs sometimes become so alarmed about their symptoms that they appear to be on the verge of panic. Further, unlike some of the disorders we have seen so far, a characteristic of hypochondriasis is the person's intense preoccupation with the perceived abnormality of functioning, despite medical

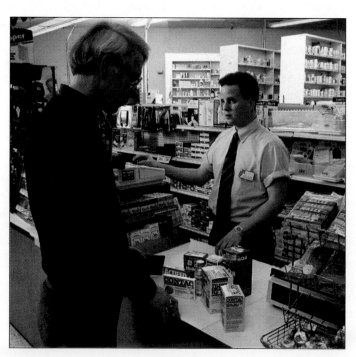

A hypochondriac may spend a small fortune on unnecessary medications to treat imagined bodily disorders.

Hypochondriasis

MINI-CASE

Beth is a 48-year-old mother of two children, both of whom have recently moved away from home. Within the past year, her menstrual periods have become much heavier and more irregular. Seeking an explanation, Beth began to spend days reading everything she could find on uterine cancer. Although medical books specified menstrual disturbance as a common feature of menopause, one newspaper article mentioned the possibility of uterine cancer. She immediately made an appointment with her gynecologist, who tested her and concluded that her symptoms were almost certainly due to menopause. Convinced that her physician was trying to protect her from knowing the awful "truth," Beth visited one gynecologist after another, in search of someone who will properly diagnose what she was certain was a fatal illness. She decided to give up her job as a department store clerk for two reasons. First, she was concerned that long hours of standing at the cash register would aggravate her medical condition. Second, she felt she could not be tied down by a job that was interfering with her medical appointments.

■ How would you determine whether or not Beth's hypochondriasis is a transient response to her concerns about her aging body?

■ What symptoms differentiate Beth from a person who has somatization or conversion disorder?

DIAGNOSTIC FEATURES

● People with this disorder are preoccupied with fears of having, or the idea that they have, a serious disease, due to their misinterpretation of bodily symptoms.

● Their preoccupation persists, despite appropriate medical evaluation or reassurance.

● Their concern is neither of delusional intensity nor related exclusively to a concern about appearance.

● Their preoccupation causes significant distress or impairment.

● The disturbance lasts at least 6 months.

● Their preoccupation is not better accounted for by another mental disorder.

---

evaluations and reassurances that nothing is wrong. No amount of reassurance from medical authorities can relieve their fears, yet these fears are not delusional, because the individual is aware of the possibility that the fears are unfounded or exaggerated. Thus, people with hypochondriasis do not show la belle indifference, experienced by some people with conversion disorders. In fact, rather than being unaffected by their medical concerns, many individuals suffer from intense symptoms of anxiety or depression (Gureje, Ustun, & Simon, 1997).

There are a number of explanations for the exaggeration of bodily symptoms seen in people with hypochondriasis. One possibility is that these individuals are more sensitive to what is happening inside their bodies, such as their heart rate and other somatic processes (Barsky, Brener, Coeytaux, & Cleary, 1995; Haenen, Schmidt, Kroeze, & van den Hout, 1996). Furthermore, some people with this condition are so concerned with efforts geared toward being in a state of good health that they become almost fanatical about their bodies (Lecci, Karoly, Ruehlman, & Lanyon, 1996). Another possible explanation is that traumatic life events in childhood, such as physical and sexual abuse, may set the stage for the later development of hypochondriasis in adulthood (Loewenstein, 1990; Salmon & Calderbank, 1996).

Physicians as well as mental health professionals regard the treatment of hypochondriasis as difficult. Because clients with this condition often react with anger and impatience when they feel their concerns are not taken seriously, they often provoke intense frustration and exasperation in those trying to help them recognize the psychological origins of their concerns. Some experts recommend that, when treating people with hypochondriasis, especially elderly individuals, it is best to conceptualize the intervention as care rather than cure; in this approach, the health professional helps the client cope with, rather than eliminate, the symptoms (Barsky, 1996). In some cases, such medications as fluoxetine are of value, particularly in reducing obsessional worrying about health concerns (Demopulos et al., 1996).

Conditions Related to Somatoform Disorders

Malingering involves deliberately feigning the symptoms of physical illness or psychological disorder for an ulterior motive. Returning to the example of the hockey player with the seemingly paralyzed hand, we might consider the possibility that he has fabricated the complaint to avoid playing in a game

Malingering

MINI-CASE

Linda is a 33-year-old janitor who had an accident at work 1 year ago. She slipped on a freshly mopped floor and badly bruised her right knee; since the accident, she has been unable to bend her knee or to support her weight on that leg. Consequently, she has found it necessary to rely on crutches and even a wheelchair. Linda has undergone numerous medical assessments, but no physical bases for her problems have been found. She has been unable to work and has filed a worker's compensation claim that would provide disability benefits. Linda states that this accident occurred at the worst possible time in her life, because her husband recently left her, and she is concerned about her ability to support herself and her 2-year-old daughter. She is comforted by the thought that, if she is awarded disability benefits, she would have permanent financial security and would be able to remain at home to take care of her daughter. She is annoyed by her physician's doubt that she has a real physical disability, and she has vowed to find the "best orthopedic surgeon in the country" to support her claim. If necessary, she will sue her employer and the worker's compensation insurance company to get her benefits.

■ What conditions in Linda's life might lead you to suspect that she is malingering?

■ Contrast Linda with Helen, who was described as having somatization disorder. How do their life circumstances differ, and what features of their symptoms differentiate them?

DIAGNOSTIC FEATURES

● People who malinger intentionally produce false or grossly exaggerated physical or psychological symptoms.

● They are motivated by such incentives as avoiding military duty, avoiding work, obtaining financial compensation, evading criminal prosecution, and obtaining unneeded medications.

---

his team is certain to lose. Another example of malingering is a case in which a physical problem enables a person to obtain financial gain, such as disability benefits. Sometimes a person wants to appear psychologically disturbed for a hidden motive, such as financial benefit. For example, Alex, who was involved in a minor car accident, may claim that he has sustained serious memory dysfunction or that he has developed the symptoms of post-traumatic stress disorder.

The question of possible malingering presents a challenge for clinicians. On the one hand, clinicians want to believe their clients' stories and problems. On the other hand, clinicians need to maintain an objectivity that permits them to assess the possibility that a client may have an ulterior motive. In recent years, psychologists have developed various assessment methods that help clinicians determine whether someone is malingering (Rogers, 1997). Many clinicians rely on the validity scales of the MMPI-2 to help them determine whether clients are malingering, or "faking bad" (Dannenbaum & Lanyon, 1993). Another instrument is the *Validity Indicator Profile* (Frederick, 1998), which consists of verbal and nonverbal tasks designed to determine whether a subject is responding legitimately or is trying to look impaired. Subjects are presented with verbal items, such as one in which they are asked to match a word (e.g., *house*) with one of two presented words that comes closest to it in definition (e.g., *home, shoe*). As you might guess, a person trying to appear impaired would choose the wrong word. Researchers have come across some interesting stylistic aspects of malingerers; for example, in one study of people presenting with symptoms of amnesia, researchers asked 40 amnestic subjects and 40 individuals faking amnesia to count backward under differing levels of distraction. The fakers tended to exaggerate their memory deficit relative to those with genuine amnesia (Baker et al., 1993).

In **factitious disorder,** people fake symptoms or disorders, not for the purpose of any particular gain but because of an inner need to maintain a sick role. The symptoms may be either physical or psychological, or they may be a combination of both. In some instances, the person fabricates a problem, such as excruciating headaches. In other instances, the individual inflicts physical harm, perhaps creating body bruises with a hammer. In other situations, the person makes an actual medical condition worse, as in the case of a person intentionally aggravating a skin infection by rubbing it with dirt.

Factitious Disorder

MINI-CASE

Jon is a 27-year-old man who has not completed his undergraduate degree, even though he had been continuously enrolled in college for 9 years. Only three credits short of his bachelor's degree, Jon tearfully presented himself each semester to the professor of his final college course with stories about physical illnesses that prevented him from finishing his last assignment, a three-page paper. One time, he appeared with cuts and bruises on his face and arms, explaining that he had fallen down a flight of stairs. Another time, he sat in his professor's office, gasping for breath and asserting that he had been suffering repeated bouts of pneumonia. In response to Jon's apparently serious health problems, Jon's professor told him that the final paper could be waived; to the professor's surprise, Jon declined the offer, stating that he preferred to do the work. Although Jon's professor agreed, he became suspicious about Jon's health issues when Jon presented a letter on a physician's stationery, stating that Jon had just been diagnosed with colon cancer. Suspecting that Jon was not telling the truth, his professor sent a copy of the letter to the physician, who called immediately, exclaiming that he had never met Jon and that Jon had somehow gotten his letterhead and typed a fraudulent letter. When Jon's professor confronted him, Jon ran out of the office, never to return to discuss the issue or to complete his college degree.

■ What do you think motivates Jon to fabricate stories about health problems?

■ What distinguishes Jon's factitious disorder from malingering?

DIAGNOSTIC FEATURES

● This label applies to people who intentionally produce or fake physical or psychological symptoms.

● The motivation of these individuals is to assume a sick role.

● There are no external incentives, such as economic gain or the avoidance of legal responsibility.

● Symptoms may be predominantly psychological, physical, or a combination of both.

What makes factitious disorder so intriguing is that the individual has no ulterior motive, such as economic gain or the avoidance of responsibilities. Rather, these individuals relish the notion of being ill and may go to great lengths either to appear ill or to make themselves sick. For some, the thought of undergoing surgery is appealing, and they gladly submit themselves to multiple invasive procedures. A man may inject saliva into his skin to produce abscesses, or a woman who is allergic to penicillin may willingly accept an injection to induce a reaction. The medical and mental health literature contains numerous accounts each year of almost unbelievable instances of factitious disorder. For example, in one case, a 29-year-old nurse was treated for septic arthritis in the knee, a condition brought on when she injected contaminated material into her knee joint to cause an infection (Guziec, Lazarus, & Harding, 1994).

These individuals present themselves as dramatically as possible, trying to create scenarios in which their illness plays a starring role. They may simulate a heart attack, appendicitis, kidney stone pain, or fevers of unknown origin. If no one believes them, however, they may become incensed and immediately seek medical help elsewhere, possibly flying all over the country to different medical centers, where their baffling diseases can become the center of concern. Many develop an impressive level of medical knowledge to ensure that their story corresponds to the technical aspects of the disorder about which they are complaining. Some go to great lengths to create a medical profile, possibly even stealing a physician's stationery and writing a "medical report" for others to read. People with factitious disorder seem to be energized by the opportunity to present their symptoms with a sense of drama and alarm.

Munchausen's syndrome is a type of factitious disorder. This syndrome is named after Baron von Munchausen, a retired German cavalry officer in the 1700s known for his "tall tales" (Asher, 1951). **Munchausen's syndrome** is used to describe chronic cases in which the individual's whole life becomes consumed with the pursuit of medical care. These individuals usually spend an inordinate amount of time inflicting injury on themselves in order to look "sick."

In factitious disorder with psychological symptoms, the individual feigns psychological problems, such as psychosis or depression. In such cases, the individual's symptoms tend to be vague and fail to correspond to any particular psychological disorder. However, such individuals tend to be suggestible and to take on new symptoms, which a clinician inadvertently implies are commonly associated with the hypothesized psychological disorder. Those trying to present themselves as psychologically disturbed may take drugs that produce such symptoms as restlessness, insomnia, or hallucinations, in an attempt to mimic psychological disorders.

At times, clinicians encounter an especially intriguing form of factitious disorder. In **factitious disorder by proxy** (or **Munchausen's syndrome by proxy**), a person induces physical symptoms in another person who is under that individual's care. For example, Loretta caused her young daughter to become sick by feeding her toxic substances; she then went from physician to physician with this sick and helpless child and used her daughter to gain access to medical attention and concern. For the most part, this disorder is reported in women, although increased familiarity with factitious disorder by proxy has alerted professionals to the possibility that men may have this condition. In one reported case, a father repeatedly produced symptoms of illness in his infant daughter during the first 6 months of her life, and he sought medical help for her while denying he knew the cause of her problems. The father finally admitted that he had been holding his daughter so tightly that

she would become breathless, at which point he would revive her (Jones, Badgett, Minella, & Schuschke, 1993).

Some cases of factitious disorder by proxy are so extreme that murder takes place. One case that captured the attention of the nation was that of Waneta Hoyt, an upstate New York woman who was convicted of murdering five of her children (Firstman & Talan, 1997). Health professionals thought that Hoyt's children were dying from sudden infant death syndrome (SIDS) and looked at this family as providing evidence that SIDS deaths can run in families. Only years later did the fact come to light that Hoyt had murdered her own offspring, seemingly for no other reason than to get attention from health professionals. Such cases have led researchers to scrutinize unexplained infant deaths and to come to some very disturbing conclusions. Using covert videotaping of suspicious medical cases in two British hospitals, David Southall and his colleagues taped 39 children to investigate suspicions of induced illness (Southall et al., 1997). They reported shocking instances of abuse in 33 of the 39 suspected cases, and they observed the efforts of 33 parents to suffocate their young children, who ranged in age from 2 to 44 months. They also observed attempts to poison, fracture, or otherwise abuse these children. The 39 children being secretly observed had 41 siblings, 12 of whom had previously died suddenly and unexpectedly, presumably from sudden infant death syndrome.

Following the jury verdict of guilt for the murder of her five children, Waneta Hoyt looks perplexed while her son Jay reacts with despair.

Why would people exert such extreme effort to present themselves or their children as being ill or having died for unexplainable reasons? In addition to wanting to be the center of attention, they seem to be motivated by a desire to be nurtured in a medical setting; some are also driven by a bizarre wish to inflict pain on others or to experience it themselves. Looking into the childhood backgrounds of these individuals, it appears that many were physically abused. Disease or an experience with the medical profession may also have figured into their childhood experiences, possibly creating a diathesis that set the stage for them to perceive professional attention and the hospital environment as positively reinforcing (Trask & Sigmon, 1997).

Although professionals may find it difficult to be sympathetic with these clients, clinicians realize that this strange behavior is often beyond their volition. Many of these individuals have an impaired sense of reality and a poorly consolidated sense of self. When they feel inner distress, they reach out for help in the only way they know, by seeking care in a relatively safe, structured context. Professionals may question whether they should take a confrontative approach in which the client is "accused" of faking; in cases in which the physical health of the client or the client's child is at stake, dramatic responses will be needed. However, a nonconfrontational approach seems preferable, in which the clinician attempts to help the client integrate reality and fantasy, while supporting the client's strengths and avoiding rewards for the client's acting-out behavior (Parker, 1993).

Theories and Treatment of Somatoform Disorders

To understand what motivates people to be "sick," it is helpful to look at what psychologists call the primary gain and secondary gain associated with sickness. **Primary gain** is the avoidance of burdensome responsibilities because one is "disabled." Going back to the case of the hockey player, his primary gain is the avoidance of playing in a game that entails high risk, in terms of both physical injury and loss of self-esteem. **Secondary gain** is the sympathy and attention the sick person receives from other people. For example, the hockey player might be secretly gratified by the solicitous concern of his friends and teammates.

Many potential costs are involved in adopting the sick role, however. Disability can result in lost or reduced wages, and the incapacitation it causes may engender others' annoyance or anger, not sympathy. However, people who take on the sick role find that more rewards than costs become available to them. Society also tends to make it more acceptable for people to receive care for a physical illness than for stress-related problems that seem to be more under voluntary control.

Somatoform disorders can best be explained as an interplay of biological factors, learning experiences, emotional factors, and faulty cognitions (Keller et al., 1992; Lipowski, 1988). According to this integrative approach, childhood events set the stage for the later development of symptoms. As children, people with this disorder may have had parents who dealt with stress by complaining about various unfounded physical ailments. As adults, they are primed to react to emotional stress with physical complaints. Some of these complaints may have a basis in reality, in that stress

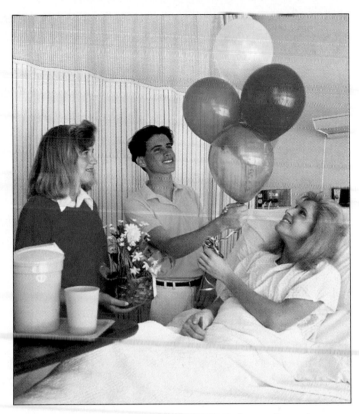

Illness usually elicits secondary gain in the form of sympathy and concern from others. Might this kind of attention contribute to the maintenance of symptoms in a person with a conversion disorder?

can cause muscle tension in parts of the body, such as the head, back, or gastrointestinal system. Although too subtle to show up on diagnostic tests, these symptoms of muscle tension create discomfort, on which the individual focuses attention and concern. A cycle is established, in which concern over these physical sensations becomes magnified, creating more tension and leading to more distress. Reinforcing this process are the rewards the individual stands to gain from being sick, such as disability benefits or attention from friends and family members.

Most contemporary approaches to treating somatoform disorders involve exploring a person's need to play the sick role, evaluating the contribution of stress in the person's life, and providing clients with behavioral techniques to control symptoms (McLeod, Budd, & McClelland, 1997). Irrespective of the specific techniques the therapist uses, developing a supportive and trusting relationship with a client who has a somatoform disorder is very important. As was true for Rose Marston, whose case was presented at the outset of this chapter, a client may become upset if a disbelieving therapist challenges physical symptoms that seem very real and troubling.

■ Psychological Factors Affecting Medical Conditions

Most people are aware that bodily conditions can be adversely affected by psychological factors. For example, intense emotional stress can increase one's vulnerability to getting sick and can seem

Table 7.1

Sleep Disorders

The *DSM-IV* category of sleep disorders includes a number of conditions highlighting the relationship between psychological and bodily disturbance. For some people, conflict and stress are expressed through disturbed sleep. For others, sleep disturbance caused by a neurological problem creates considerable emotional disturbance. Sleep disorders are chronic conditions that cause a great amount of emotional distress and interfere with normal life functioning. At times, these conditions might cause so much fatigue that an individual is in danger while performing the normal tasks of life, such as driving (Roth, Roehrs, & Rosenthal, 1994). Although sleep disorders do not technically fall into the category of psychological factors affecting medical conditions, they are relevant to our discussion of these topics.

Disorder	Symptoms
Dyssomnias	Disturbances in the amount, quality, or timing of sleep
Primary insomnia	Chronic difficulty with sleeping, taking various forms: trouble falling asleep, frequent awakening, or getting a full night's sleep but not feeling rested
Primary hypersomnia	An excessive need for sleep, expressed in having difficulty getting out of bed, yearning for sleep during the day, sneaking naps, and unintentional dozing off
Circadian rhythm sleep disorder	Disturbance in both sleep and daytime functioning caused by disruptions in the normal sleep-wake cycle, usually due to rotating work shifts or jet lag
Breathing-related sleep disorder	Excessive sleepiness during the day caused by frequent awakening during the night because of breathing problems (e.g., loud snoring, gasping for breath, or breathing interruptions)
Parasomnias	Conditions involving abnormal behavior or bodily events occurring during sleep or sleep-wake transitions
Nightmare disorder	The experience of recurrent vivid dreams from which a person awakes and has detailed recollection of extended frightening images
Sleep terror disorder	Condition in which an individual repeatedly wakes up suddenly and in a panic from a sound sleep, causing feelings of intense anxiety, confusion, and disorientation, for which there will be no recall in the morning
Sleepwalking disorder	Condition involving recurrent episodes of arising from sleep, usually walking about with a blank stare and lack of responsivity to other people, with amnesia for the episodes the following morning
Narcolepsy	The experience of irresistible attacks of sleep that can take place at any time and any place, usually lasting between 10 and 20 minutes

to slow down recovery from an ailment. Various bodily problems can be brought on or aggravated by the experience of anxiety, depression, and even anger. In some circumstances, the condition is quite serious and warrants clinical attention. There is a special *DSM-IV* diagnostic category, called psychological factors affecting medical conditions, that addresses conditions in which there is a marked relationship between psychological and bodily disturbance.

Characteristics of the *DSM-IV* Category of Psychological Factors Affecting Medical Conditions

The *DSM-IV* diagnostic category **psychological factors affecting medical conditions** includes situations in which psycho-logical or behavioral factors have an adverse effect on a medical condition. The psychological factors include the following: Axis I disorders (e.g., major depressive disorder), psychological symptoms (e.g., anxiety that aggravates asthma), personality traits (e.g., hostility), maladaptive health behaviors (e.g., unhealthy diet), stress-related physiological responses (e.g., stress-related aggravation of an ulcer), and less specific psychological factors (e.g., interpersonal problems).

This diagnosis is given to clients who suffer from a recognized medical condition that is adversely affected by emotional factors that influence the course of the medical condition, interfere with treatment, create additional health risks, or aggravate its symptoms. Consider the case of Joachim, a man with a history of panic disorder whose recovery from heart surgery is impeded because of his intense bouts with anxiety. Sometimes

Psychological Factors Affecting Medical Conditions

MINI-CASE

Brenda is a 41-year-old manager of a large discount chain store. Despite her success, she struggles with an agitated depression, which causes her to feel impatient and irritable most of the time. She recognizes that her emotional problems relate to issues with her parents, and she resents the fact that she chronically suffers from an inner tension that has always been part of her personality. The youngest in a family of four children, she perceived that throughout her childhood she had to do "twice as much" as her siblings to gain her parents' attention and affection. Now, as an adult, she is caught up in a drive toward success that literally makes her physically sick. She has intense headaches and stomachaches on most days, yet she is reluctant to seek medical help, because she doesn't want to take time away from her work.

■ How would you explain the relationship between Brenda's physical problems and her emotional problems?

■ How does Brenda's condition differ from the condition of a person with a somatoform disorder?

DIAGNOSTIC FEATURES

● This diagnosis is applied to people who have a medical condition and for whom psychological factors adversely affect the medical condition in one of the following ways:

  ● There is a close relationship in time between psychological factors and the beginning of a medical condition, the worsening of the condition, or the delay in recovering from the condition.

● The psychological factors interfere with the treatment of the condition.

● The psychological factors create additional health risks for the individual.

● Stress-related bodily responses bring on or worsen the symptoms of the medical condition.

● Psychological factors can be represented in various ways, such as psychological symptoms (e.g., depression that delays recovery from surgery, anxiety that aggravates asthma), personality traits (e.g., hostility that contributes to heart disease), maladaptive health behaviors (e.g., overeating), and stress-related physiological response (e.g., tension headache).

---

personality traits or coping style adversely affects an individual's health. For example, Marissa, who is characteristically hostile and impatient, experiences recurrent bodily problems, such as high blood pressure and gastrointestinal discomfort. Some medical conditions are quite sensitive to stress. For example, Alec knows that his asthma is likely to flare up during periods of intense stress.

Emotional and psychological factors can aggravate just about any physical problem. Researchers have conducted extensive investigations of such relationships in trying to better understand cancer, cardiovascular disease, skin conditions, endocrine problems, and difficulties affecting the stomach, breathing, kidney, and neurological functioning. Health professionals now are aware that psychological factors can initiate, aggravate, and prolong medical diseases and problems, and they continue to develop interventions that help enhance both physical and psychological well-being.

Theories and Treatment of the *DSM-IV* Category of Psychological Factors Affecting Medical Conditions

When you have an upset stomach or bad headache during exam time or when an important assignment is due, you probably recognize that there is a connection between what is happening in your emotions and what is happening in your body. Although the connection seems simple on the surface, it is more complex than you might think. Researchers who study the "mind-body" relationship attempt to determine why some people develop physiological or medical problems when their lives become busy, complicated, or filled with unpleasant events.

Stress

Most researchers use the term **stress** to refer to the unpleasant emotional reaction a person has when he or she perceives an event to be threatening. This emotional reaction may include heightened physiological arousal due to increased reactivity of the sympathetic nervous system. The **stressor** is the event itself, which may also be called a **stressful life event.** When a person experiences stress, he or she is likely to try to reduce this unpleasant feeling. Making an effort to reduce stress is called **coping.** It is when coping is unsuccessful, and the stress does not subside, that the individual may seek clinical attention for medical or psychological problems that have developed as a consequence of the constant physiological arousal caused by chronic stress.

Let's take a closer look at all of these components, beginning with the nature of stressful life events. Researchers in this area have developed measures that quantify the degree to which an individual has been exposed to difficult life situations. One of the most well known of these is the Social Readjustment Rating Scale (SRRS) (Holmes & Rahe, 1967), which assesses life stress in terms of "life change units" (LCU). Events are given LCU scores, based on how strongly they are associated with

When stress is high, many people develop physical ailments for which they seek medical care without giving much thought to the role that emotions play in the development of health problems.

physical illness. The rationale behind this measure is that, when people experience a large number of LCUs in a relatively brief period of time, they are at greater risk for developing a major illness within a 2-year period. You can assess your own stressful life events score by taking a scale developed for college students (see Table 7.2), the College Undergraduate Stress Scale (CUSS) (Renner & Mackin, 1998), which was developed to assess the kinds of stressors most familiar to traditional-age college students (90 percent of the people in the sample were under the age of 22 years).

Although the assessment of stress by the use of life events scales has merits, there is one problem in this kind of measurement instrument. Scales, such as the SRRS and the CUSS, are based on the assumption that the same event is equally stressful to all individuals who experience it. Although there may be compelling reasons for making this assumption, it does not fit with commonsense notions about stressful events or the views of researchers. According to cognitive models of stress, it is not just the event itself but also the way it is interpreted that determine its impact. One person may view the death of a spouse as a horrible calamity; another person may see it as distressing but not devastating. Further, the context of the event plays a role in determining its impact. For example, if the death of a spouse follows a long, debilitating illness, the survivor may feel a sense of relief.

Coping   Another factor in the mind-body equation is how people attempt to reduce the sensation of stress through coping. There are many ways to think about coping, but one of the most useful is that which distinguishes between **problem-focused coping** and **emotion-focused coping** (Lazarus & Folkman, 1984). In problem-focused coping, the individual reduces stress by acting to change whatever it is that makes the situation stressful. The person might make alternative plans or find a new and better way to correct the situation. In either case, the individual makes the attempt to "fix things." By contrast, in emotion-focused coping, a person does not change anything about the situation itself but, instead, tries to improve his or her feelings about the situation. "Thinking positively" is one

emotion-focused coping method people use to make themselves feel better under stressful conditions. Avoidance is another emotion-focused strategy. This coping method is similar to the defense mechanism of denial, in which the individual refuses to acknowledge that a problem or difficulty exists. In extreme form, avoidance as a coping strategy can involve escape into drugs or alcohol and can lead to additional problems in the person's life. Examples of these coping strategies are shown in Table 7.3.

Which coping style more effectively reduces stress depends on the nature of the stressor itself. In some cases, particularly when there is nothing one can do about a problem, feeling as good about it as possible is probably best. Consider the case of Elena, who broke her ankle while ice skating. Dealing with the stress may become more tolerable if she reframes the temporary disability as an opportunity to slow down her hectic life. When the situation is more controllable, problem-focused coping is more adaptive (Folkman, Lazarus, Gruen, & DeLongis, 1986). For example, if Leonard is refinancing his mortgage, he may become very upset because the interest rates suddenly rise. Rather than save money, he stands to lose thousands of dollars. Problem-focused coping would involve Leonard's developing alternative financial plans to resolve his monetary problems.

Coping strategies can play an important role in whether or not an individual will suffer health problems. A person who is able to manage stress effectively experiences fewer adverse consequences of stress. Furthermore, as you may know from personal

People who use emotion-focused coping strategies often resort to escape through drugs or alcohol to handle the stress in their lives.

Table 7.2

Items from the College Undergraduate Stress Scale

The number next to each item represents the "stress rating" that each was given by large samples of undergraduates. See how many have applied to you in the past year and then add up your score. The average score reported by the scale's authors is 1247, with scores ranging from 182 to 2571. A "normal" range would be between 800 and 1700.

Event	Stress Ratings	Your Items	Event	Stress Ratings	Your Items
Being raped	100		Talking in front of class	72	
Finding out that you are HIV-positive	100		Lack of sleep	69	
Being accused of rape	98		Change in housing situation (hassles, moves)	69	
Death of a close friend	97		Competing or performing in public	69	
Death of a close family member	96		Getting in a physical fight	66	
Contracting a sexually transmitted disease (other than AIDS)	94		Difficulties with a roommate	66	
Concerns about being pregnant	91		Job changes (applying, new job, work hassles)	65	
Finals week	90		Declaring a major or concerns about future plans	65	
Concerns about your partner being pregnant	90		A class you hate	62	
Overstudying for an exam	89		Drinking or use of drugs	61	
Flunking a class	89		Confrontations with professors	60	
Having a boyfriend or girlfriend cheat on you	85		Starting a new semester	58	
Ending a steady dating relationship	85		Going on a first date	57	
Serious illness in a close friend or family member	85		Registration	55	
Financial difficulties	84		Maintaining a steady dating relationship	55	
Writing a major term paper	83		Commuting to campus, or work, or both	54	
Being caught cheating on a test	83		Peer pressures	53	
Drunk driving	82		Being away from home for the first time	53	
Sense of overload in school or work	82		Getting sick	52	
Two exams in one day	80		Concerns about your appearance	52	
Cheating on your boyfriend or girlfriend	77		Getting straight A's	51	
Getting married	76		A difficult class that you love	48	
Negative consequences of drinking or drug use	75		Making new friends; getting along with friends	47	
Depression or crisis in your best friend	73		Fraternity or sorority rush	47	
Difficulties with parents	73		Falling asleep in class	40	
			Attending an athletic event (e.g., football game)	20	
			Total		

Source: Renner & Mackin, 1996.

Table 7.3

Sample Items from the Ways of Coping Questionnaire

The Ways of Coping Questionnaire assesses the strategies that people use to manage internal and external demands in a stressful encounter. In research using this questionnaire, Susan Folkman and Richard Lazarus and their associates found that people use a variety of these coping methods in any one stressful encounter. As you read about the eight types of coping listed below, think of a recent stressful situation you experienced and consider which styles characterized your way of managing the stress. Then use this rating scale to indicate whether this is a method you use to handle stress.

1—Does not apply or not used
2—Used somewhat
3—Used quite a bit
4—Used a great deal

Confrontive coping	I tried to get the person responsible to change his or her mind.
Planful problem solving	I knew what had to be done, so I doubled my efforts to make things work.
Distancing	I went along with fate; sometimes I just have bad luck.
Self-control	I tried not to burn bridges but leave things open somewhat.
Seeking social support	I talked to someone to find out more about the situation.
Accepting responsibility	I apologized or did something to make up.
Escape-avoidance	I slept more than usual.
Positive reappraisal	I was inspired to do something creative.

Two of these scales (confrontive coping and planful problem solving) reflect problem-focused coping strategies that are directed primarily at changing something about the situation to make it less stressful. Four of the scales (distancing, self-control, accepting responsibility, and positive reappraisal) reflect emotion-focused coping. Seeking social support serves both emotion- and problem-focused functions.

experience, situations that create high levels of activation in a person do not always have negative consequences. Some people thrive on a lifestyle filled with challenges and new experiences, feeling energized by being under constant pressure (DeLongis, Folkman, & Lazarus, 1988). Perhaps you perform (or think you perform) at your best when you are facing an urgent deadline.

Stress and the Immune System   We still have not addressed the questions of why and how the experience of stress can lead to physiological abnormalities. To look into this issue, we can draw from the field of **psychoneuroimmunology,** the study of the connections among stress ("psycho"), nervous system functioning ("neuro"), and the immune system ("immuno"). To an increasing degree, researchers in medicine and psychology are beginning to understand such disorders as heart and respiratory disease, some forms of diabetes, and gastrointestinal disorders as being influenced by stress-related responses initiated in the central nervous system. It is becoming clearer that experiences of stress, negative affect, depression, lack of social support, and repression and denial can influence immune status and function (Cohen & Herbert, 1996).

As illustrated in Figure 7.1, a stressful event can initiate a set of reactions within the body that lower its resistance to disease. These reactions can also aggravate the symptoms of a chronic, stress-related physical disorder. One explanation of these relationships is that stress stimulates hormones regulated by the hypothalamus, and these hormones lower the activity of the immune system. With less protection, the body is less resistant to infection, allergens, and the more serious intruders, such as carcinogens. Nervous system reactions also alter immune system functioning through nerve endings in the parts of the body involved in the immune system, such as the lymph nodes, thymus, and spleen. These processes appear to account for a wide range of physical disorders, including cancer, hypertension, and rheumatoid arthritis (Costa & VandenBos, 1996). Severe life stress and depression can accelerate the symptoms in people who have HIV disease (Evans et al., 1997; Leserman et al., 1997).

Researchers have used some innovative methods to assess the relationship between illness and stress. For example, Sheldon Cohen, a researcher at Carnegie Mellon University, conducted an intensive study of the relationship between stress and the common cold (Cohen et al., 1998). In this study, 276 volunteers completed a life stressor interview and psychological questionnaires,

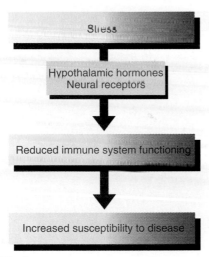

Figure 7.1

The relationship among stress, immune functioning, and disease.

and they provided blood and urine samples. After the subjects were injected with common cold viruses, the researchers monitored them and found that severe chronic stressors that lasted at least a month were associated with a greater likelihood of their becoming ill; however, stressful events lasting less than a month did not seem to have this negative effect on health. The most salient stressors were employment problems and enduring interpersonal problems with family or friends.

The relationship between stress and health goes both ways. People under stress also tend to neglect good health habits, possibly smoking more, drinking more alcohol, eating less nutritious meals, and getting less sleep. When in a state of stress, most people are more susceptible to becoming sick, possibly due to an increased vulnerability to infectious diseases. They turn to other people for support, and, ironically, their increased social interaction with others increases their exposure to viruses and infectious agents. Some people in states of stress seek out sexual intimacy, possibly indiscriminately and with inadequate attention to safe sex practices. If stressed individuals become sick, regardless of the cause, they are less likely to comply with recommended treatment, putting themselves at even greater physical risk (Cohen & Williamson, 1991).

Emotional Expression

The inhibition of emotional expression seems to be another key ingredient in the relationship between psychological functioning and health. For example, cancer researchers have focused on the role of emotional suppression, which characterizes a certain personality style (Eysenck, 1991, 1994). An individual with a cancer-prone personality, called "Type C personality," suppresses emotional expression, especially anger, and tends to be highly compliant and conforming. According to this proposal, when a person becomes emotionally aroused, the sympathetic nervous system reacts with heightened activity, and expressing emotion is an important outlet for this activation. Failure to express emotion causes the body to remain in a state of heightened activation. As was shown in Figure 7.1, this state is unhealthy, because high levels of arousal of the sympathetic nervous system reduce the efficiency of the immune system, leading to the greater risk of developing cancer. Although biological factors play the major role in cancer susceptibility (Tross et al., 1996), psychosocial factors can affect the progress of the disease. Specifically, people who become deeply depressed after being diagnosed with cancer or who lack social support to help them cope with their disease seem to be at higher risk for progression of the disease (Levenson & Bemis, 1991). However, when cancer patients obtain treatment for depression, their immune functioning can improve (McDaniel et al., 1995).

If emotional suppression is unhealthy, it seems reasonable to conclude that expressing emotion is beneficial to one's physical and mental well-being. Research connecting emotional expression with immune system functioning is bearing out the common belief that you should "get it off your chest" when you feel unhappy or upset. In a series of innovative experiments, psychologist James Pennebaker and his colleagues have shown that actively confronting emotions that arise from an upsetting or a traumatic event can have long-term health benefits (Pennebaker, 1997a, 1997b). For example, writing about a distressing experience facilitates coping and contributes to physical health. In one study, researchers asked college freshmen to write about the experience of coming to college and asked a control group of students to write about superficial topics. Although those who wrote about their college adjustment experiences reported higher levels of homesickness than the control subjects, they made fewer visits to physicians. By the end of the year, the experimental subjects were doing as well as or better than the control subjects in terms of grade point average and the experience of positive moods. From this study, the researchers concluded that confronting feelings and thoughts regarding a stressful experience can have long-lasting positive effects, even though the initial impact of such confrontation may be disruptive (Pennebaker, Colder, & Sharp, 1990).

Personality Style

People who frequently feel a sense of impatience, irritability, or pressure to get something done in a hurry may be at risk for developing heart problems. This pattern of being hard-driving, competitive, impatient, cynical, suspicious of and hostile toward others, and easily irritated, is described as Type A (see Table 7.4). Oddly, although individuals with a Type A personality are highly competitive, they seem driven by an internal set of standards; compared with more relaxed individuals (Type B), Type A individuals are less likely to cheat in academic situations (Davis et al., 1995). They want to do well based on their own abilities, rather than take the easy way out.

Converging evidence from several large studies points to the higher risk that people with Type A behavior patterns have for developing hypertension and associated heart problems (Barefoot et al., 1987; Eaker, 1998), problems that increase their mortality rate (Carmelli & Swan, 1996; Miller et al., 1996). Type A individuals tend to react explosively to stressful situations (Walsh, Eysenck, Wilding, & Valentine, 1994); in doing so, they set off "alarms" throughout their bodies. The sympathetic nervous systems of Type A people are in a state of alert, which puts physiological stress on sensitive bodily organs, which can result in coronary heart disease, cerebral atherosclerosis ("hardening" of the blood vessels in the brain), and atherosclerosis in other parts of the body. Associated psychological attributes, including hostility (Miller, Dolgoy, Friese, & Sita, 1996; Siegman, 1994) and the need to dominate others (Houston et al., 1997) appear to heighten the risk of heart disease for people with the Type A behavior pattern. These individuals may also have a high genetic vulnerability to cardiovascular disease—which, in conjunction with the Type A behavioral characteristics, becomes lethal (McClearn, Vogler, & Plomin, 1996).

People with Type A behavior patterns, particularly those with high levels of hostility, commonly engage in unhealthy behaviors, such as smoking and consuming large amounts of alcohol, behaviors that are well-established as detrimental (Whiteman, Fowkes, Deary, & Lee, 1997). They also are more likely to engage in high-risk behaviors, such as reckless driving, so it is no surprise that many of these individuals die in accidents and violent situations (Magnavita et al., 1997; Suls & Sanders, 1988). Even those who are not especially wild are prone to contend with intense levels of anger, vexed by even the slightest annoyance, an emotional style that has been shown to play a role in provoking a heart attack (Verrier & Mittleman, 1996).

Sociocultural factors also play a role in causing and aggravating stress-related disorders. For example, living in a harsh social environment that threatens a person's safety, interferes with the establishment of social relationships, and involves high levels of conflict, abuse, and violence can compound the health risks associated with certain personality

For a person with a Type A behavior pattern, minor frustrations, such as a traffic jam, can evoke a storm of outrage with accompanying physical and psychological disturbance.

characteristics (Taylor, Repetti, & Seeman, 1997). Furthermore, environmental stressors related to racial conflict and discrimination may interact with genetic factors to increase the risk of hypertension. African-Americans living in the U.S. have higher rates of hypertension than Blacks living in other parts of the world where there is less racial discrimination (Cooper, Rotimi, & Ward, 1999).

Treatment
Because the conditions in the category of psychological factors affecting medical conditions include such a vast array of physical problems, no single treatment model exists. During the past 2 decades, clinicians have increasingly realized that medical treatments alone are insufficient and that they must also introduce and reinforce new health behaviors. Psychologists have collaborated with physicians to develop an interdisciplinary approach to these conditions known as **behavioral medicine** (Compas et al., 1998; Gentry, 1984). Behavioral medicine techniques are rooted in behavioral theory and use learning principles to help the client gain psychological control over unhealthy bodily reactions. Clients learn to take responsibility for their health, to initiate and maintain health-producing behaviors, and to terminate unhealthy ones. They learn to be alert to unhealthy bodily processes and to take action to avoid or modify circumstances in which they are likely to become sick. Individuals learn to monitor early signs of mounting tension and to initiate steps to avert the further development of pain, including learning various emotion- and problem-focused coping strategies, such as leaving a stressful situation or reframing one's perspective on a situation that is inescapable.

Behavioral medicine techniques are being incorporated into standard medical treatments, as in the case of insomnia, chronic pain (Jacobs, Benson, & Friedman, 1996), and chronic migraine headaches (Kropp et al., 1997). Patients with chronic disorders that require constant medical management can also benefit from behavioral techniques to increase compliance, as in the case of diabetes (Jenkins, 1995).

Table 7.4

Are You Type A?

The Jenkins Activity Survey assesses the degree to which a person has a coronary-prone personality and behavior pattern. People with high scores, referred to as Type A, tend to be competitive, impatient, restless, aggressive, and pressured by time and responsibilities. In the items below, you can see which responses would reflect these characteristics.

Do you have trouble finding time to get your hair cut or styled?

Has your spouse or friend ever told you that you eat too fast?

How often do you actually "put words in the person's mouth" in order to speed things up?

Would people you know well agree that you tend to get irritated easily?

How often do you find yourself hurrying to get to places even when there is plenty of time?

At work, do you ever keep two jobs moving forward at the same time by shifting back and forth rapidly from one to the other?

Drawing on the research linking the Type C personality style to cancer proneness, clinicians have developed treatments for cancer that involve behavioral methods (Compas et al., 1998). Some clinicians recommend teaching cancer patients to vent their emotions when they would otherwise have suppressed their feelings of anger, as well as to practice meditation techniques to facilitate relaxation. In addition, cancer patients are taught to use imagery as a means of activating their immune system to "fight" the cancer cells (Lerner & Remen, 1987). Of course, few people would suggest that these methods should replace the conventional medical treatment of cancer, but the psychological techniques are thought to be an important adjunct.

The successful treatment of people whose physical problems are associated with the Type A behavior pattern integrates education, training in coping strategies, and behavioral interventions (Friedman et al., 1996; Roskies et al., 1989). The educational component includes helping clients understand coronary problems and the relationship between these problems and Type A behavior. The coping strategies include relaxation training and cognitive restructuring techniques. For example, instead of responding with anger to standing in line at the bank, a person could learn to be more relaxed about it. Imaging is a behavioral intervention in which the client learns to imagine a troublesome situation and to practice adaptive coping strategies for managing stress in that situation. Behavior modification gives individuals opportunities to rehearse

Exercise can help relieve potentially harmful effects of stress on the body.

more adaptive behaviors to use when provoked (Nunes, Frank, & Kornfeld, 1987). Such interventions can be reasonably effective, particularly if the client is given sufficient opportunity to incorporate relaxation exercises into his or her everyday life (Carlson & Hoyle, 1993).

Other treatment approaches involve preventive strategies. People can learn that exercising and taking advantage of available social supports help offset the harmful effects of stress on the body. Psychologists are also studying methods of intervention that can promote the resilience individuals can develop to living in a harsh urban environment (Wandersman & Nation, 1998). In addition to improving neighborhood conditions, these interventions can reduce the distress that people feel in these environments.

A particularly effective method of treatment for stress and stress-related disorders was developed by psychologist Donald Meichenbaum (Meichenbaum, 1985, 1993), who developed a technique known as **stress inoculation training.** Like its medical counterpart of inoculation against physical illness, this psychological inoculation helps people prepare for difficult situations that have occurred in the past and are likely to occur again in the future. People are taught to anticipate these situations and are given help in practicing ways to control stress when they next encounter the situations. Meichenbaum emphasizes the role of cognitive factors in stress inoculation, including the way that individuals explain to themselves the situations that create stress in their lives. The technique has gained wide acceptance in many circles, ranging from its use as a method of reducing stress among athletes (Kerr & Goss, 1996) to its use as a method of pain control for chronic pain sufferers (Weisenberg, 1998).

Particularly important in Meichenbaum's approach is the method of self-instruction, or guided self-dialogue, in which the individual practices "coping self-statements" that are unique to the client and that can help control the client's reaction when silently repeated in the actual stressful situation. Read the list of coping self-statements in Table 7.5 and see which might be beneficial for you to rehearse.

Other stress management techniques involved in the stress inoculation procedure are also readily applied to one's own life, particularly the notion that people can make changes in their behavior that help them resist the harmful effects of everyday stress. For example, if you wait until the last minute to begin important projects, you are probably setting yourself up to experience pressures that you could avoid. If you put yourself in situations in which you are likely to feel resentful, powerless, and frustrated, perhaps you can do something to heighten your sense of control. If you consistently keep your emotions bottled up and internalize anger and tension, you are putting yourself at a health risk. Identifying unhealthy behavioral patterns can prompt people to look for ways to change.

■ Dissociative Disorders

The conditions you have read about so far in this chapter involve a range of disorders involving emotions, such as anxiety and stress, that have varying degrees of disturbance and impact

Table 7.5

Examples of Coping Self-Statements

I can work out a plan to handle this.

Stop worrying. Worrying won't help anything.

What are some of the helpful things I can do instead?

I'm feeling uptight—that's natural.

I can convince myself to do it.

One step at a time.

Look for positives; don't jump to conclusions.

As long as I keep my cool, I'm in control of the situation.

Things are not as serious as I make them out to be.

Time to take a slow, deep breath.

I can be pleased with the progress I'm making.

Don't try to eliminate stress entirely; just keep it manageable.

Source: Meichenbaum (1985).

on a person's life. Dissociative disorders are far more extreme, involving anxiety or conflict so severe that part of the individual's personality actually separates from the rest of his or her conscious functioning. The individual with a dissociative disorder experiences a temporary alteration in consciousness involving a loss of personal identity, decreased awareness of immediate surroundings, and odd bodily movements. Once the dissociation has occurred, the contents of the dissociated part become inaccessible to the rest of the client's conscious mind.

Psychologists have learned some fascinating clues to understanding normal personality functioning from studying individuals with dissociative disorders. We generally take for granted the idea that within one person's body, only one personality can exist. However, dissociative disorders show that this assumption about human nature does not apply to everyone.

Dissociative Identity Disorder

In **dissociative identity disorder,** a person develops more than one self or personality. These personalities are referred to as **alters,** in contrast to the core personality, called the **host.** This condition was formerly called multiple personality disorder, a term that continues to be used by some lay authors and even a few health professionals. The disorder was made famous in novels and movies, such as *Sybil* (Schreiber, 1973) and *The Three Faces of Eve* (Thigpen & Cleckley, 1957), each of which tells the fantastic but true story of a woman who had several distinct "personalities." In dissociative identity disorder, each alter is a consistent and enduring pattern of perceiving, relating to, and thinking about the environment and the self.

Characteristics of Dissociative Identity Disorder

The individual with dissociative identity disorder has at least two distinct identities or personality states, each with its own pattern of perceiving, thinking, and relating, as well as its own style of behavior, personal history, and self-image. Most cases involve fewer than 10 identities, but reports range well into the hundreds. At different times, one of these identities or personality states takes control of the person's behavior. People with dissociative personality disorder have a primary identity associated with their given name. This primary identity, or host, is customarily passive and dependent, possibly also depressed and guilty. The alters are usually strikingly different, possibly acting in ways that are hostile, demanding, or self-destructive. They may have different ages, races, levels of intelligence, and affective styles, and they may even be of the opposite gender. The transition from one alter to another is usually sudden, triggered by psychosocial stress or a personally salient stimulus. At any given moment, only one alter interacts with the external environment, although the others may actively perceive what is happening or influence what is going on. Most of the personalities have a sense of lost or distorted experiences of time. An alter may piece together memories to make up for unaccounted gaps, or an alter may have access to memories of the other alters.

Psychiatrist Richard Kluft has played a major role in disseminating information about dissociative identity disorder in the scientific community. Kluft has described several key features of this disorder, including the nature of the personalities that reside within the same individual and their relationships to each other. The classic host personality, who seeks professional help, tends to be depressed, anxious, compulsively "good," masochistic, and moralistic. The most frequently seen alters include children, "protectors," "helpers," expressers of forbidden impulses, personalities based on lost loved ones, carriers of lost memories or family secrets, avengers who express anger over abusive experiences, and defenders of the abusers (Kluft, 1984a).

People with dissociative identity disorder also experience a form of amnesia, in which they have gaps in their memory about some aspects of their personal history. Some individuals have gaps that span years, or even a decade or more. This inability to recall important personal information cannot be explained by ordinary forgetfulness. Sometimes only when other people tell them about events do they become aware of something they have done or said. For example, the husband of a woman with dissociative identity disorder witnessed his wife going to the hardware store and buying a set of tools, yet she insisted that someone else must have purchased them and couldn't fathom what he was talking about.

In 1980, the condition that was then called multiple personality disorder began to gain a great deal of recognition, with the publication of four major papers on the topic (Bliss, 1980; Coons, 1980; Greaves, 1980; Rosenbaum, 1980). That year, the disorder was first included in the *DSM* and was defined in such a way that it was no longer reserved for cases as extreme as those of Eve and Sybil. The diagnosis could then be applied in situations in which a person experienced a disorganization of the self and attributed discrepant experiences to separate

Mark Peterson, a 31-year-old grocery worker from Oshkosh, Wisconsin, defends himself in court against a rape charge brought against him by Sarah, a woman with multiple personality disorder. He met 26-year-old "Franny" at a bar and asked her for a date. Franny told Peterson about fun-loving, 20-year-old "Jennifer" and, reportedly, he summoned Jennifer and invited her to have sex with him. During intercourse, 6-year-old "Emily" emerged; he reportedly told Jennifer to keep their activites secret from Sarah. But Franny and Emily told Sarah, who pressed charges against him. Although the jury voted to convict Peterson, the judge overturned the verdict on the grounds that the defense was not allowed to have Sarah examined by a psychiatrist before the trial.

individuals residing within the self. Along with this broadening of the definition came a proliferation of cases of multiple personality disorder, to the point that it became referred to as an "epidemic" (Boor, 1982). In the 50 years prior to 1970, only a handful of cases had been reported, but since 1970, the number of reports increased astronomically, into the thousands. In fact, more cases of this disorder were reported during one 5-year period in the 1980s than had been documented in the preceding two centuries (Putnam et al., 1986). Clinicians and researchers began to wonder if this increase was actually due to the increased prevalence of the disorder or whether it was an artificial phenomenon due to the broadening of the definition of the disorder. Some maintained that popular first-person characterizations of the disorder, media attention, and efforts by dedicated clinicians and people claiming to have had this disorder contributed to an inappropriate degree of emphasis on this rare but fascinating condition (Frankel, 1996).

A leading skeptic on the topic of multiple personality disorder (MPD) was the late Canadian psychologist Nicholas Spanos, who believed that social factors shape the display of MPD. Following exhaustive reviews of twentieth-century reports and studies of multiple personality disorder, Spanos asserted that this condition became a legitimate way for people to rationalize their failures and manipulate the sympathy of others (Spanos, 1996). Even more alarming is the question raised by Spanos and others (Orne, Dinges, & Orne, 1984; Simpson, 1989) about whether psychotherapists play a central role in

generating and maintaining the symptoms of multiple personalities. Are some clients responding to their therapists' suggestions that their problems are attributable to dissociative identity disorder, rather than more common disorders, such as depression or personality disorder? According to this view, some clients are highly suggestible and may pick up on cues from their therapist to construe their problems as resulting from dissociation. Sometimes, without even realizing it, therapists engage in leading and suggestive procedures that persuade some clients to develop the notion of multiplicity (Merskey, 1992). Hypnotic interviews are the most common procedure for eliciting multiple personalities, and it is not uncommon during such exercises for the therapist to suggest explicitly that the alter come forth. Over time, the clients tell stories about alternate personalities and may actually develop behaviors that fit these different personalities.

Following on the heels of professional attention to the possibility of overdiagnosis were reports in the media of individuals fabricating the diagnosis to seek external gain, such as being excused from responsibility for a crime. These reports further questioned the validity of a diagnosis that apparently could be so easily faked. These sensationalistic reports aside, some experts maintained that the increase in reported prevalence of a multiple personality condition was a valid phenomenon due to the fact that diagnostic standards for the disorder had improved in the 1980s. To help refine and standardize the diagnosis of this disorder, Canadian psychiatrist Colin Ross and his colleagues (Ross, 1989) developed the Dissociative Disorders Interview Schedule. Some of the key questions, reproduced in Table 7.6, give further insight into the nature of the symptoms associated with this disorder.

The availability of more sensitive diagnostic instruments has led clinicians and researchers to the discovery of previously undiagnosed cases of the disorder. In one study, it was found that 300 people who ultimately were diagnosed as having this disorder had experienced symptoms for an average of almost 7 years until they received the correct diagnosis. During that time, these individuals were given many other erroneous diagnoses, including depression, "neurotic disorder," personality disorder, schizophrenia, "hysterical schizophrenia," substance abuse, bipolar disorder, and epilepsy (Putnam et al., 1986; Ross et al., 1990). In one extreme case, it took 23 years for an individual to be correctly diagnosed.

Although it may seem shocking that misdiagnosis can occur, the problems in diagnosis are understandable. Several lines of investigation link the disorder to epilepsy, major depressive disorder, schizophrenia, somatoform disorder, and borderline personality disorder (Brodsky, Cloitre, & Dulit, 1995; Devinsky et al., 1989; Kluft, 1987a; Lauer, Black, & Keen, 1993; Shalev et al., 1998). The problem of diagnosis may further be exacerbated because the symptoms are not consistent over time; the individual may attempt to cover up the symptoms, and the dissociative symptoms may be mixed with a mood disturbance or personality disorder. In some cases, the individual may have a high level of functioning in various areas of life, and the symptoms of dissociative identity disorder may never even be suspected (Kluft, 1986). All of these factors could contribute to the underdiagnosis of this disorder.

Dissociative Identity Disorder as a Legal Defense

Dissociative identity disorder (formerly called multiple personality disorder) has become a vexing problem for forensic psychologists and other participants in the legal system, who are confronted with criminal defendants using the disorder as an explanation for their offenses. One dramatic legal case brought to light some of the complexities involved in the multiple personality disorder defense. Kenneth Bianchi, a serial murderer also known as the Hillside Strangler, faked multiple personality disorder in an attempt to avoid criminal prosecution for his offenses (Orne et al., 1984; Watkins, 1984). Forensic psychologists and other members of the judicial system are faced with the difficult task of differentiating a true dissociative disorder from instances of malingering.

Individuals who seek to explain their crimes as products of alter personalities typically invoke an insanity defense or claim that they are not competent to stand trial (Slovenko, 1993; Steinberg, Bancroft, & Buchanan, 1993). Defendants who claim insanity assert that symptoms of the disorder precluded their appreciation and understanding of criminal actions. Those who make the case that they are not competent to stand trial argue that their symptoms would interfere with their participation in court proceedings. In the more dramatic case of the insanity defense, the accused may admit to having committed the crimes, but under the control of an alter personality. They may claim that the offense was committed in a state of dissociation and that they have no recall of what happened. The more credible these reports of dissociation and amnesia are, the more likely it is that the court will accept the insanity defense (Serban, 1992).

The accurate diagnosis of a psychologically disturbed defendant can lead to appropriate treatment; by contrast, an improper diagnosis can have dire effects for the individual and for the legal system. A missed diagnosis may deprive a person of potentially effective psychological treatment. An incorrect diagnosis of dissociative identity disorder could allow a dangerous individual to escape the consequences of his or her criminal behavior. Psychologists must typically rely on their clinical skills to detect malingering among defendants who claim they have dissociative identity disorder, and some have argued that the differential treatment of these defendants is contrary to sound legal and therapeutic practice. According to Ross (1989), the legal system favors malingering as a means for avoiding responsibility and consequences for criminal actions. Similarly, defendants who successfully use the insanity defense jeopardize their ability to make progress in therapy, which typically emphasizes the acceptance of responsibility for all of one's actions, even those carried out by alter personalities.

Although there is no foolproof way to detect malingering in a claim of multiple personalities, there are some strategies that can be used (Brick & Chu, 1991). Legal experts have found it helpful to work with psychologists using sophisticated assessment techniques, such as the *Structured Clinical Interview for DSM-IV Dissociative Disorders (SCID-D)* (Steinberg, 1993). This instrument has been particularly useful in evaluating the severity of dissociative symptoms and in diagnosing dissociative disorders in both psychiatric and legal contexts (Steinberg & Hall, 1997). In genuine cases of this disorder, new personalities may be discovered during the course of therapy. When this happens, clinicians should regard these with skepticism. The client may be motivated by the belief that additional personalities could create a stronger legal defense. More reliable evidence can come from diaries or journals that the client kept, as well as testimony from relatives and friends. These sources may reveal information about periods of amnesia, personality change, and other aspects of fragmented experience that either support or contradict the diagnosis. Another distinction pertains to the nature of the symptoms involved in dissociative identity disorder. True cases of this disorder are often a product of extreme abuse in childhood. Furthermore, the symptoms create troublesome interference in the client's everyday life. The malingerer, however, shows none of the emotional scars of early abuse and appears to be suspiciously at ease when discussing actions of alter personalities and past instances of trauma. In other words, malingerers do not experience the acute psychological reactions typical of genuine dissociative identity disorder.

Although dissociative identity disorder is relatively easy to fake, malingerers generally find it difficult to maintain a consistent facade of dissociated feelings, thoughts, and memories that they can then associate with different personality states. Unlike clients who truly have the disorder, malingerers rarely have histories marked by confused and fragmented experiences and failed treatment attempts. Malingerers may describe stereotypical personalities that carry out bad or criminal actions, but their alter and host personalities are less likely to be explainable in terms of their traumatic experiences. Clients who truly have dissociative identity disorder may feel strange and ashamed of their disorder, whereas malingerers play up their symptoms for greater attention, especially from legal authorities (Kluft, 1987b).

Table 7.6

Items from the Dissociative Disorders Interview Schedule

"Yes" responses to all questions would be rated in the direction of a high dissociative disorder score:

Did you have imaginary playmates as a child?

Were you physically abused as a child or adolescent?

Were you sexually abused as a child or adolescent? (Sexual abuse includes rape or any type of unwanted sexual touching or fondling that you may have experienced.)

Have you ever noticed that things are missing from your personal possessions or where you live?

Have you ever noticed that there are things present where you live, and you don't know where they came from or how they got there (e.g., clothes, jewelry, books, furniture)?

Do people ever come up and talk to you as if they know you but you don't know them, or only know them slightly?

Do you ever speak about yourself as "we" or "us"?

Do you ever feel that there is another person or other persons inside you?

If there is another person inside you, does he or she ever come out and take control of your body?

Source: *Multiple personality disorder: Diagnosis, clinical features, and treatment* by C. Ross. Copyright © 1989 by John Wiley & Sons, Inc. Reprinted by permission of John Wiley & Sons, Inc.

As a way to put to rest some of the arguments, pro and con, about the existence of the disorder, the authors of the *DSM-IV* chose to apply the label "dissociative identity disorder," rather than the more popular term "multiple personality disorder." The new term captures the essence of an individual's detachment and disorganization, without getting caught up in the issue of multiplicity. Adding the criterion of amnesia to the list of symptoms further refined the diagnostic label (Cardena & Spiegel, 1996).

Theories and Treatment of Dissociative Identity Disorder

The primary explanation of dissociative identity disorder focuses on disturbances in childhood in the development of the sense of self. As children, most of us develop a sense of self through interactions with parents and peers; in this process, we maintain a sense of continuity over time. People with dissociative identity disorder fail to develop an integrated and continuous sense of self, because they were severely traumatized at some point in their childhood. Many if not most clients with dissociative identity disorder report having been victims of childhood sexual or physical abuse. (Ellason, Ross, & Fuchs, 1996; Kluft, 1997; Lewis et al., 1997; Lussier, Steiner, Grey, & Hansen, 1997; Ross et al., 1991; Scroppo, Drob, Weinberger, & Eagle, 1998). Intensive studies of hundreds of individuals who meet the diagnostic criteria for the disorder reveal a common history of extreme abuse in childhood (Coons, Bowman, Pellow, & Schneider, 1989; Ross et al., 1990; Terr, 1991; van der Hart, Boon, & Heijtmajer Jansen, 1997; Wilbur & Kluft, 1989).

What is the connection between a traumatic childhood and the development of a dissociated identity? Most theorists believe that children develop alters as an escape, through fantasy, from the horrors of their daily reality. They learn to enter a dissociative, self-hypnotic state filled with fantasy and thoughts of being someone else. According to one theorist, the "I" disappears into the background in the child's perceptual experience (Beere, 1995). Repeated victimization leads the child to enter this state more and more frequently. As this happens, the split-off, dissociated parts of experience and memory develop independently, and the child's personality and sense of self fail to become integrated (Ross, 1997b). Biological factors may also play a role, as the extreme stress to which the child was exposed during incidents of abuse may have triggered alterations in brain functioning (Bremner, Krystal, Charney, & Southwick, 1996).

As compelling as this explanation may be, only a small percentage of traumatized children develop such dissociative disorders. Although many people with dissociative identity disorder have a history of abuse, the converse does not necessarily hold true. Researchers do not yet understand what makes certain children vulnerable to developing this disorder. An unknown factor, which could be either biological or psychological, seems to predispose a subset of traumatized children to develop different personalities in response to their experiences of abuse, whereas

The terror of abuse drives some children into a dissociative state in which their fantasies provide them with an escape from the harsh realities of their lives.

Dissociative Identity Disorder

MINI-CASE

Myra is a young single woman who works as a clerk in a large bookstore. She lives by herself, never goes out socially except to see her relatives, and dresses in a conservative manner, which her associates ridicule as "prudish." In her early teens, she was involved in an intimate relationship with a middle-aged man who was quite abusive toward her. Although others remind her of this troubled relationship, Myra claims that she has no recollection of that person, and she has even wondered at times whether others have made up the story to annoy her. At the age of 25, Myra says that she is "saving" herself sexually for marriage, yet she seems totally uninterested in pursuing any close relationships with men. So far, this describes Myra as her work acquaintances and family know her. However, alters reside within Myra's body, and they go by other names and behave in ways that are totally incongruous with "Myra's" personality. "Rita" is flamboyant, outgoing, and uninhibited in her sexual passions. She has engaged in numerous love affairs with a variety of unsavory characters she picked up in nightclubs and discotheques. "Rita" is aware of "Myra" and regards her with extreme disdain. A third personality, "Joe," occasionally emerges from "Myra's" apartment. Dressed in a man's three-piece business suit, "Joe" goes downtown to do some shopping. According to "Joe," "Rita," is nothing but a "slut," who is heading for "big trouble someday." Myra's alters are oblivious to the details of her life.

- What factors in Myra's personal history might her therapist look for when trying to understand the basis of Myra's dissociative identity disorder?

- Can you see any relationship among the alters; if so, how do they relate to the host?

DIAGNOSTIC FEATURES

- This diagnosis is given to people who experience two or more distinct identities or personality states, each with an enduring pattern of perceiving, relating to, and thinking about the environment and the self.

- At least two of the identities or personality states recurrently take control of the person's behavior.

- The person is unable to recall important personal information, well beyond what could be explained by ordinary forgetfulness.

- The disturbance is not due to substance use or a medical condition.

others are able to cope successfully and develop normal personalities (Binder, McNiel, & Goldstone, 1996). One group of researchers has noted that people who develop pathological dissociative symptoms are especially hypnotizable, leading them to hypothesize that hypnotizability may increase vulnerability to this disorder, particularly in instances when such individuals experience acute stress (Butler et al, 1996).

Working on the assumption that dissociative identity disorder is a response to trauma, Kluft contends that treatment is a form of post-traumatic therapy, in which the clinician works with the client to recover. Therapy involves helping the client integrate the alters into a unified whole and develop adequate coping strategies to deal with the painful memories of the past and the stresses of current life without resorting to fragmentation. The most common treatment approach involves techniques derived from psychoanalytic psychotherapy, often including **hypnotherapy,** in which the client is hypnotized and encouraged to recall painful past experiences while in a trance state. The various alters with their associated memories are brought out one-by-one and are unified into a consistent whole. Each alter may require a separate treatment, and the therapist may need to establish a positive working relationship with each. Because some alters may be abrasive and antagonistic, while others may be dependent and seductive, each may respond differently to alternate interventions (Kluft, 1984b).

Some clinicians prefer to use cognitive-behavioral techniques instead of or in addition to hypnotherapy in an effort to change the client's dysfunctional attitudes (Fine, 1996; Ross, 1997a). These attitudes, arising from the client's history of abuse, include the beliefs that different parts of the self are separate selves, that the victim is responsible for abuse, that it is wrong to show anger or defiance, that the host cannot handle painful memories, that one of the alters hates the parents (but the primary personality loves them), that the host must be punished, and that neither the self nor others can be trusted. According to

Hypnotherapy is often used in treating clients with dissociative disorders, such as multiple personality disorder, to help the client achieve an integrated personality.

Ross (1997b), each of these core beliefs carries with it a set of assumptions that further guides the individual's behavior. Although countering these beliefs is not considered sufficient for treating dissociative identity disorder, it would seem to be an important component of an overall treatment plan.

Another aspect of cognitive-behavioral therapy that might be helpful is to bolster the individual's sense of self-efficacy through a process called temporizing (Kluft, 1989), in which the client controls the way that the alters make their appearance. This may be accomplished through hypnosis in an effort to help the client develop coping skills that can be used when dealing with stress, which otherwise might precipitate a personality shift.

As more reliable information becomes available on dissociative identity disorder, improved methods of treatment are certain to be developed. Nevertheless, several factors contribute to difficulty in treating this disorder. First, this is a very broadly defined disorder that ranges from cases such as those of Sybil and Eve to people who show far less dramatic symptoms. Second, clinicians and researchers have ascertained that most people with this disorder also suffer from other psychological problems, such as mood disorders or personality disorders. Third, repairing the damage done by abuse and trauma that took place decades earlier in the client's life can be very difficult. Finally, consider what it must be like for the clinician to work with a client whose problems and style of presentation are so diverse and contradictory. Given all these obstacles, you can see why it can take many years to reach the desired goal of personality integration. Even so, experts in this area have been inspired by the fact that some recent research points to positive outcome in the treatment of people with dissociative identity disorder. In one study of 135 individuals with this disorder, 54 were located and reassessed after a 2-year period and continued to show significant improvement, compared with their status at admission (Ellason & Ross, 1997). Kluft asserts that his work with dissociative clients has been quite successful; in fact, he notes that he has brought over 160 individuals to integration (Kluft, 1998).

Other Dissociative Disorders

Although dissociative identity disorder is the most dramatic form of dissociative disorder, there are several other related conditions that are equally compelling in terms of impact on the individual's life.

Dissociative Amnesia

In **dissociative amnesia,** formerly called psychogenic amnesia, the individual is unable to remember important personal details and experiences, usually associated with traumatic or very stressful events. This memory loss is not attributable to brain dysfunction associated with brain damage or drugs, nor is it a matter of common forgetfulness. People who develop dissociative amnesia most commonly describe a gap or series of gaps in their memory about past troubling events or parts of their lives. Dissociative amnesia is rare, yet it is the most common of the dissociative disorders. It received a great deal of attention following the two world wars, in which many individuals with combat-related trauma experienced amnesia (Kardiner & Spiegel, 1947).

There are four forms of dissociative amnesia, each associated with the nature of a person's memory loss. In **localized amnesia,** the most common form, the individual forgets all events that occurred during a specified time interval. Usually, this interval immediately follows a very disturbing event, such as a car accident, fire, or natural disaster. In **selective amnesia,** the individual fails to recall some, but not all, details of events that have occurred during a given period of time. The survivor of a fire may remember the ambulance ride to the hospital, but not having been rescued from the burning house. **Generalized amnesia** is a syndrome in which a person cannot remember anything at all from his or her life. **Continuous amnesia** involves a failure to recall events from a particular date, up to and

An automobile accident can be so traumatizing that a person may forget events that happened only moments earlier.

Dissociative Amnesia

MINI-CASE

In a daze, Norma entered the mental health crisis center, tears streaming down her face, "I have no idea where I live or who I am! Will somebody please help me?" The crisis team helped her search her purse but could find nothing other than a photograph of a blond-haired little girl. Norma appeared to be exhausted and was taken to a bed, where she promptly fell asleep. The crisis team called the local police to find out if there was a report of a missing person. As it turned out, the little girl in the photograph was Norma's daughter. She had been hit by a car in the parking lot of a shopping center. Although badly injured with a broken leg, the child was resting comfortably in the pediatrics ward of the hospital. Her mother, however, had disappeared. Norma had apparently been wandering around for several hours, leaving her wallet and other identifying papers with the hospital social worker in the emergency room. When Norma awoke, she was able to recall who she was and the circumstances of the accident, but she remembered nothing of what had happened since.

■ How would a clinician determine that Norma is suffering from dissociative amnesia rather than amnesia caused by physical injury?

■ What is the possible relationship between Norma's disorder and the circumstances surrounding her daughter's accident?

DIAGNOSTIC FEATURES

● People with this disorder experience one or more episodes during which they are unable to recall important personal information, usually of a traumatic or stressful nature, that is well beyond ordinary forgetfulness.

● The disturbance does not occur as a result of another mental disorder, the use of substances, or a medical or neurological condition.

● The symptoms cause significant distress or impairment.

including the present time. For example, a war veteran may remember his childhood and youth until the time he entered the armed services, but he may have forgotten everything that took place after his first tour of combat duty.

Dissociative amnesia is very difficult for clinicians to diagnose, because there are so many possible causes of memory loss. For example, as you will see in later chapters, amnesia can be caused by a physical dysfunction due to brain injury, psychoactive substance abuse, or epilepsy. Alternatively, other psychological disorders have symptoms that may cause the individual to appear amnestic. For example, a catatonic person who does not communicate may be construed to be amnestic. When the individual is questioned, though, it may be possible to elicit some information about the person's past.

As is sometimes the case with other dissociative disorders, a person might fake symptoms to gain certain benefits or advantages. For example, a man who has committed a serious crime may claim that he remembers nothing of the incident or even who he is. Understandably, someone interviewing this man would be skeptical of his memory loss and would try to ascertain whether the amnesia is genuine or not. Clinicians usually try to rule out the possibility of malingering when evaluating symptoms of amnesia by being alert to hidden motivations for "forgetting."

Dissociative Fugue

You may have read newspaper accounts or heard news stories of the fascinating story of a person who has found his way to a community far away from home, with no idea of how he got there or who he is. Although such cases are rare, they capture our attention because they seem so unbelievable. Many of the people in such stories are experiencing a **dissociative fugue,** formerly called psychogenic fugue, a condition in which a person who is confused about personal identity suddenly and unexpectedly travels to another place. The venture may be brief, lasting only hours or days, or it may last for weeks or months. People in a fugue state are unable to recall their own history or identity, and a few may even assume a new identity. If a person assumes a new identity, he or she is likely to appear to be much more outgoing than the core personality of the individual and may even go so far as to create a new name, find a place to live, get a job, and interact with others in ways that do not suggest anything out of the ordinary. In fact, in many cases, others do not suspect anything unusual, because the person in the fugue state appears very normal. After the fugue state has passed, the individual often has no recall of what took place during the fugue.

A fugue is rare and usually passes quickly. The disorder is more likely to occur at certain times, such as during a war or following a natural disaster. Personal crises or extreme stress, such

Dissociative Fugue

MINI-CASE

George was an administrator at a small college in a rural town. He was a reliable worker, keeping mostly to himself and rarely discussing his personal life with his colleagues. All they knew about him was that he lived with his wife, Judy, and their two teenage children. Family life was quiet until one afternoon, when Judy received a telephone call from George's secretary, asking if she knew George's whereabouts. He had not shown up at work in the morning, nor had he called in sick. The secretary was concerned that George might be very upset, because the college president had announced on the previous day that the college would be closing permanently at the end of the academic year. Judy was startled by the news, because George had not mentioned it at dinner the evening before. No one heard from George for 3 weeks following the date of his mysterious disappearance. During that time, he traveled to Stanford University, with the intention of applying for a position as a philosophy professor. One day, he woke up in a California hotel room and was mystified about how he had gotten there.

■ What symptoms of a dissociative fugue were evident in George's behavior?

■ What factors in George's life might have contributed to his symptoms?

DIAGNOSTIC FEATURES

● People with this disorder travel suddenly and unexpectedly away from home or job and are unable to recall their past.

● They are confused about personal identity, or they assume a partial or complete new identity.

● The disturbance does not occur as a result of another mental disorder, the use of substances, or a medical or neurological condition.

● The symptoms cause significant distress or impairment.

---

as financial problems, the desire to escape punishment (Spiegel & Cardena, 1991), or the experience of a trauma (Classen, Koopman, & Spiegel, 1993) can also precipitate fugue states.

Depersonalization Disorder

You may be able to think of a time when you had a feeling of being "unreal." Perhaps you had not slept or eaten for a long period of time and had the sensation that you were an outsider observing the movements of your body, as if in a dream. The phenomenon of depersonalization includes alterations of mind-body perception, ranging from detachment from one's experiences to the feeling that one has stepped out of one's body. Depersonalization experiences occur in normal people when they are placed under great stress or when they use mind-altering drugs, such as marijuana or LSD. In **depersonalization disorder,** however, distortions of mind-body perceptions happen repeatedly and without provocation by drugs. Periods of extreme stress, such as the time immediately following an accident, can also precipitate an episode of depersonalization in a vulnerable individual. Some experts have noted that the experience of depersonalization commonly follows a stressful event and emerges in the "calm following the storm" (Shader & Scharfman, 1989).

People with depersonalization disorder feel as though they are not "real," that their body is changing in shape or size, or that they are being controlled by forces outside of themselves, as if they were an automaton or a robot. At the same time, however, they realize

that they are not really robotic but that something odd is happening in their body and mind. At times, the individual may experience "conversations" between an observing self and a participating self (Steinberg, 1991). People with this disorder are aware that something is wrong with them, and this awareness is a further source of distress, however, they may be reluctant to tell other people about their experiences, because they fear they will sound "crazy." Therefore, they can feel quite alone and isolated from others, as well as frightened about their loss of contact with reality.

The onset of depersonalization disorder typically occurs in adolescence or early adulthood. The disorder tends to be chronic, with remissions and exacerbations that are triggered by anxiety, depression, or stress.

Theories and Treatment of Dissociative Amnesia, Dissociative Fugue, and Depersonalization Disorder

Most experts agree that dissociative disorders may be the end product of intensely traumatic experiences during childhood, especially those involving abuse (Maldonado, Butler, & Spiegel, 1998). However, in addition to childhood abuse experiences, other kinds of traumatic events can also result in dissociative experiences, some of which are transient and some of which are longer-lasting. In the discussion of reactions to

Depersonalization Disorder

MINI-CASE

Robert entered the psychiatrist's office in a state of extreme agitation, almost panic. He described the terrifying nature of his "nervous attacks," which began several years ago but had now reached catastrophic proportions. During these "attacks," Robert feels as though he is floating in the air, above his body, watching everything he does but feeling totally disconnected from his actions. He reports that he feels as if his body is a machine controlled by outside forces: "I look at my hands and feet and wonder what makes them move." Robert's thoughts are not delusions, though; he is aware that his altered perceptions are not normal. The only relief he experiences from his symptoms comes when he strikes himself with a heavy object until the pain finally penetrates his consciousness. His fear of seriously harming himself adds to his main worry that he is losing his mind.

- If you were Robert's therapist, how would you differentiate whether he is hallucinating or experiencing symptoms of depersonalization disorder?

- What differentiates Robert's symptoms from those of a panic attack?

DIAGNOSTIC FEATURES

- This diagnosis is given to people with persistent or recurrent experiences of feeling detached from their mental processes or body, as if in a dream or as if they were external observers.

- During the depersonalization experience, they are in touch with reality.

- The symptoms cause significant distress or impairment.

- The disturbance does not occur as a result of another mental disorder, the use of substances, or a medical or neurological condition.

Sometimes people with depersonalization disorder look as though they are on psychotropic drugs. They may feel that they are in a dream-like state, observing their own actions.

traumatic events in Chapter 6, we pointed out that people who dissociate during a traumatic event are at higher risk for the later development of PTSD.

Treatments for dissociative disorders are varied, in great part because the conditions themselves are so variable. As you can tell from reading the preceding sections, dissociative identity disorder is a markedly different phenomenon from depersonalization disorder. Nevertheless, a central goal in the treatment of clients with dissociative symptoms is to bring stability and integration into their lives. Essential to their treatment is the establishment of a safe environment, away from the threatening stressors that presumably evoked dissociation. In this security of the treatment context, the clinician will introduce soothing techniques, some psychotherapeutic and others psychopharmacological. Psychotherapeutic techniques include hypnosis to help the client recover repressed or dissociated memories at a pace that the client can tolerate. Some clinicians would also add medications to the intervention, also aimed at enhancing a state of calm. The most commonly used medications are sodium pentobarbital and sodium amobarbital, which facilitate the interview process, particularly in clients with dissociative amnesia or dissociative fugue. Once amnesia has been reversed, the clinician helps the client figure out what events and factors evoked the amnesia. While these medications can help with some forms of dissociation, they are not particularly helpful with clients who have dissociative identity disorder, for which there is no easy cure for core symptoms of fragmentation (Maldonado et al., 1998).

The dissociative disorders provide a unique opportunity to appreciate the complexity of the human mind and the very unusual ways in which people respond to stressful life experiences. As fascinating as they are, it is important to keep in mind that these disorders are very rare and very difficult to treat. Although current explanations rely heavily on psychological perspectives, in the future perhaps more will be learned about a biological substrate for the development of these conditions.

Somatoform Disorders, Psychological Factors Affecting Medical Conditions, and Dissociative Disorders: The Perspectives Revisited

At this point, it should be clear why, historically, disorders involving somatization and dissociation were regarded as neuroses rather than psychoses. People with these disorders have experienced conflict or trauma during their lives, and these circumstances have created strong emotional reactions that they could not integrate into their memory, personality, and self-concept. The symptoms of somaticizing and dissociating represent not a loss of contact with reality but a translation of these emotions into terms that are less painful to acknowledge than is the original conflict or trauma.

Stressful events can trigger maladaptive responses in physical functioning, ranging from a variety of physical conditions to sleep dysfunctions to the more elusive disorders involving somatization. Stress related factors, not repressed sexuality, are currently regarded as central in understanding somatoform disorders. In addition, learning seems to play a strong role, particularly as individuals with these disorders develop secondary gain from their symptoms. With regard to dissociative disorders, experts now believe that actual, rather than imagined, trauma is the source of such symptoms as amnesia, fugue, and multiple identities. Cognitive-behavioral explanations of stress-related disorders add to these understandings. Low feelings of self-efficacy, lack of assertiveness, and faulty ideas about the self can all be contributing factors to somatoform and dissociative disorders. For example, believing that one must be sick to be worthy of attention is a dysfunctional attitude that could underlie a somatoform disorder. Similarly, faulty beliefs about the self and the role of the self in past experiences of trauma seem to be important cognitive factors in dissociative disorders. Adding to these psychological components are the biological factors that may contribute to an individual's vulnerability to developing these maladaptive thoughts or susceptibility to trauma.

A variety of treatment modalities for the disorders covered in this chapter are being explored. To varying degrees, these focus on the management of intense and intrusive stress. Supportive therapy aimed at gradual exploration of the role of stress or trauma in the individual's life is important. Cognitive-behavioral methods of enhancing the individual's feelings of self-efficacy, assertiveness, and awareness of dysfunctional thinking patterns are also being incorporated into an integrative treatment approach.

RETURN TO THE CASE

Rose Marston

Rose's History

I remember feeling surprised when Rose returned to see me for the second session we had scheduled. People with stories involving numerous undiagnosable medical problems rarely come back after the intake meeting with a mental health clinician. In our second session, Rose told me a life story that gave me the basis for some reasonable hunches about the nature of her problems.

The older of two daughters, Rose grew up in the center of a city, close to the factory where her father worked. Rose vividly remembers the day her younger sister, Emily, was born, 2 days after Rose's seventh birthday. All the excitement surrounding Rose's birthday celebration and the birth of a baby in the family abruptly deteriorated to emotional chaos when Rose's parents were informed, hours after the birth, that Emily had serious abnormalities. This bad news about Emily caused Rose to become extremely worried, particularly about her father, whose drinking problem was apparent to her even at her young age and had already threatened the stability of the family. Rose began to fear that, with the added stress of Emily's health problems, her father might drift further into his alcoholic ways.

In the years that followed, Rose's parents were forced to devote most of their attention to her disabled sister. Feeling obliged to help her parents, Rose spent all her available time tutoring her sister, playing with her, and protecting her from the jeers of neighborhood children. When I inquired about Rose's remarkable level of devotion to her sister, she confided that it was largely the result of her intense feeling of guilt about being so much "luckier" than Emily. Tragically, Rose's sister died from heart trouble in her teenage years. Prior to this, Rose had planned to go to college and become a special education teacher, but her attempts to carry out this ambition were hampered after her sister's death by a series of unexplainable illnesses and ailments, none of which

RETURN TO THE CASE

Rose Marston (continued)

were very serious but which caused her to drop out of college.

After leaving college, Rose took a job as a cosmetics consultant in a department store, but she had to quit after a short time, due to her nagging and incapacitating physical symptoms. Because of her inability to work, Rose had recently applied for disability benefits from the government, and she told me that she lived from day to day in dread that she may be denied these benefits.

When I inquired about intimate relationships in her life, Rose became uncomfortable as she told me about her "lousy batting average" with men. Citing a long list of brief relationships, Rose explained that these relationships generally fell apart because her physical problems constantly got in the way. Recurrently frustrated by the lack of sympathy on the part of the men whom she had met, Rose concluded that she is "probably better off without them."

Assessment

Although the information provided by both Dr. Thompson and Rose gave me the basis for a diagnostic hypothesis, I was intrigued by the unconscious factors within Rose that might relate to her problems. Rose, who had submitted to countless medical tests in the past, was open to the psychological assessment I recommended. She did express some reservations about the validity of tests, pointing out that dozens of medical tests had been unable to pinpoint any of her problems.

Psychological testing showed Rose to be a bright woman, with an IQ in the above-average range. Her cognitive functioning was consistent across the subscales of the WAIS-III, although she did show some evidence of difficulty in breaking down a problem into component parts and in understanding social situations. Rose's MMPI-2 profile was predictable, with elevations on Scales 1 (Hypochondriasis), 2 (Depression), and 3 (Hysteria), suggesting the likelihood that Rose defends against depression by using denial and by dwelling on possible physical problems. Rose's TAT responses revealed a highly romanticized, superficial view of intimate relationships, with many unrealistic "happy endings" to her stories. There was also a strong element of jealousy in the relationships between female figures. On the Rorschach test, Rose's first few responses were quite creative and potentially very rich in content, but she seemed unable to sustain this high level of production and quickly reverted to simple images. Throughout testing, Rose complained frequently of various physical complaints, which made it necessary to interrupt testing. What struck me as odd about this was that Rose seemed to develop a physical symptom just at the point of becoming immersed in the assessment tasks.

Diagnosis

As I worked toward confirming a diagnosis, my thoughts focused on Rose's lengthy history of unsubstantiated medical complaints. Although I am reluctant to conclude that any person's medical complaints are without physical basis, the evidence supporting the assumption of a psychological, rather than medical, basis was substantial. For a brief moment, I considered the possibility that Rose might be malingering. But for what benefit? I did not believe she wanted to be "sick" just to collect disability benefits. Rose's problems and complaints predated any concern about financial support. Might Rose be a hypochondriac? Certainly, some facets of her story might lead to such a diagnosis, but a major difference was that Rose truly believed she was suffering from physical diseases. My sense was that, even though her problem was psychologically rooted, the discomfort and incapacitation Rose suffered were very real to her. Her lengthy list of recurrent bodily complaints and chronic pursuit of medical help for conditions that lacked any medical basis led me to diagnose Rose as having somatization disorder.

Axis I:	Somatization Disorder
Axis II:	Deferred. Rule out Histrionic Personality Disorder
Axis III:	No diagnosable physical disorders or conditions
Axis IV:	Problems related to the social environment (isolation) Occupational problems (disability)
Axis V:	Current Global Assessment of Functioning: 70 Highest Global Assessment of Functioning (past year): 70

Case Formulation

Rose's history was similar to that of the few other people with somatization disorder I had seen in my clinical practice. She was an individual with a long history of medical complaints, which had brought her much attention from others. As I thought about the possible origins of this psychological disorder, I noted that her physical complaints first developed after the death of her younger sister, an event that Rose described as devastating. It is my

RETURN TO THE CASE

Rose Marston (continued)

sense that Rose struggled with guilt about being more intelligent, more capable, and healthier than her sister. By taking over a parental role in relation to her sister, perhaps Rose was able to relieve some of this guilt. Also, as a result of her physical problems, Emily's parents naturally devoted more time, energy, and attention to her. Rose, with her feelings of guilt, found it difficult to acknowledge any of the jealous feelings she harbored. Thus, early in life, Rose had to cope with powerful feelings of guilt and jealousy; given her youth, she turned to the immature defense of denial. Had Rose's sister survived her illness, Rose might very well have learned to express her feelings in a more mature fashion. However, her sister's death cut this process off prematurely. Indeed, when her sister died, Rose's physical symptoms began. One hypothesis about the cause of the symptoms at this time was that Rose identified with her sister and took on symptoms that bore a superficial resemblance to those that characterized Emily's fatal medical problems. The symptoms also incapacitated Rose so that she could have a legitimate reason not to live up to her own potential. By punishing herself, she could unconsciously resolve her guilt over having been more capable and healthier than her sister and, at the same time, having been ineffective in saving her.

Rose's symptoms also served a function in the family. For years, Rose's parents had turned all their energies as a couple toward caring for their disabled child. This allowed them to deflect their attention away from their own marital problems, which centered around Mr. Marston's alcoholism. With the death of their ill child, they needed a substitute to serve a similar function in the marriage. Perhaps Rose's symptoms served, in this sense, as unconscious compliance with the needs of her parents. Additionally, Rose's symptoms gave her secondary gain in the form of attention and concern from her parents, reactions she had not gotten from them for many, many years.

Treatment Plan

I made my decision to accept Rose into psychotherapy with some ambivalence. I was well aware of the low odds for success, yet at the same time I was touched by Rose's willingness to give therapy a chance. From the outset, she acknowledged her skepticism about the usefulness of psychotherapy, particularly in light of her belief that her medical problems were genuine. At the same time, she acknowledged that she might derive some benefit if we directed our attention to stress management. I agreed that this should be a component of the treatment, but I also felt that a broad, integrative therapy was necessary. I believed that, for Rose's life to change for the better, psychotherapy would have to focus on some of the unconscious conflicts underlying her symptoms, the secondary gain she has received as reinforcement, and the problems in Rose's current family life that have maintained her disorder.

I recommended individual outpatient psychotherapy on a weekly basis; however, I also realized that individual psychotherapy for people with such problems is usually insufficient. Ideally, they should be seen in multiple contexts, including group therapy, family therapy, and vocational counseling. Rose agreed to participate in a therapy group with another therapist and a group of seven clients dealing with life stresses in general and with problems with close relationships more specifically. As for family therapy, she told me emphatically that her father would not agree to any kind of professional "intrusion."

Outcome of the Case

In the initial weeks of therapy, Rose tried to redirect my attention away from psychological concerns to her somatic complaints. Gently but firmly I tried to make it clear that our work must focus on emotional rather than medical matters, but Rose was not receptive to my efforts. After a few sessions, she began to question openly the value of therapy, and 2 weeks later she announced she had found a "cure" for her symptoms and was going to discontinue therapy. A friend had told Rose about a new technique of pain management through hypnosis, and Rose was sure it would be right for her.

Several months later, I received a note from the emergency room staff informing me that Rose had been admitted to the psychiatric unit following a suicide attempt involving an overdose of pain medication. She told the physician she was looking for a way to escape her physical problems and pains. After a brief hospital stay, Rose was released from inpatient care and agreed to resume psychotherapy under my care.

In her second round of therapy, Rose made some progress in terms of coming to understand the psychological causes of her symptoms. However, Rose's denial of conflict was firmly entrenched, and she never seemed very convinced of the connection between her physical problems and the difficulties in her emotional life. Whatever gains Rose started to make were wiped out when she had a car accident and required a series of

RETURN TO THE CASE

Rose Marston (continued)

minor operations. Rose phoned me several months later to say that she would not be returning for psychotherapy. She explained that she would not have time, because the physical problems she had sustained in the accident would require many months of intensive medical care and rehabilitation. I wondered to myself whether Rose had finally achieved what she had come to desire for so long—clearly diagnosable medical problems and the attention that would accompany these problems. ■

Sarah Tobin, PhD

Summary

- This chapter covered three sets of conditions: somatoform disorders, medical conditions affected by psychological factors, and dissociative disorders. In each of these sets of disorders, the body expresses psychological conflict and stress in an unusual fashion.

- Somatoform disorders include a variety of conditions in which psychological conflicts become translated into physical problems or complaints, which cause distress or impairment in a person's life. Conversion disorder is the translation of unacceptable drives or troubling conflicts into bodily motor or sensory symptoms that suggest a neurological or medical condition. Somatization disorder involves the expression of psychological issues through bodily problems that have no basis in physiological dysfunction. In pain disorder, some kind of pain, which causes intense personal distress or impairment, is the predominant focus of the client's medical complaint. People with body dysmorphic disorder are preoccupied, almost to the point of being delusional, with the idea that a part of their body is ugly or defective. Individuals with hypochondriasis believe or fear that they have a serious illness, when in fact they are merely experiencing normal bodily reactions. Phenomena sometimes associated with somatoform disorders are malingering and factitious disorders. Malingering involves deliberately faking the symptoms of physical illness or psychological disorder for an ulterior motive. In factitious disorder, people fake symptoms or disorders not for the purpose of any particular gain but because of an inner need to maintain a sick role. In factitious disorder by proxy, a person induces physical symptoms in another person under the individual's care.

- In trying to understand the basis for the development of somatoform disorders, theorists consider issues of primary and secondary gain. Somatoform disorders can also be viewed as developing as a result of an interplay of biological factors, learning experiences, emotional factors, and faulty cognitions. A combination of treatment techniques may be used, in which a clinician strives to develop a supportive and trusting relationship with the client with a somatoform disorder.

- The *DSM-IV* diagnostic category of psychological factors affecting medical conditions includes situations in which psychological or behavioral factors have an adverse effect on a medical condition. The psychological factors include Axis I disorders, psychological symptoms, personality traits, maladaptive health behaviors, stress-related physiological responses, and less specific psychological factors. Researchers and clinicians have focused on the processes by which people learn to deal with disruptive emotional experiences, and they have developed sophisticated theories and techniques pertaining to coping. In the field of psychoneuroimmunology, experts are finding answers to complex questions regarding the nature of the mind-body relationship.

- Dissociative disorders involve expressions of conflict that are so severe that part of the individual's personality actually separates from the rest of conscious functioning. In dissociative identity disorder, a person develops more than one self or personality. Although considerable controversy exists regarding the nature and prevalence of a condition involving multiple personalities, the *DSM-IV* includes the diagnosis of dissociative identity disorder to capture the essence of intense detachment, disorganization, and amnesia reported by many clients. In dissociative amnesia, the individual is unable to remember important personal details and experiences, usually associated with traumatic or very stressful events. Dissociative fugue is a condition in which a person who is confused about personal identity suddenly and unexpectedly travels to another place. In depersonalization disorder, distortions of mind-body perceptions happen repeatedly and without provocation.

- Experts agree that dissociative disorders commonly arise as the result of intense trauma usually associated with experiences of abuse during childhood. Treatment depends on the nature of the dissociative disorder, with the goal being integration of the fragmented components of the individual's personality and cognition. Hypnotherapy and other psychotherapeutic techniques are commonly used to attain this goal.

Key Terms

See Glossary for definitions.

Alters 226
Behavioral medicine 224
Body dysmorphic disorder 209
Continuous amnesia 231
Conversion disorder 206
Coping 219
Depersonalization disorder 233
Dissociative amnesia 231
Dissociative fugue 232
Dissociative identity disorder 226
Emotion-focused coping 220
Factitious disorder 214
Factitious disorder by proxy (Munchausen's
    syndrome by proxy) 216

Generalized amnesia 231
Host 226
Hypnotherapy 230
Hypochondriasis 212
Hysterical neurosis 207
La belle indifference 207
Localized amnesia 231
Malingering 213
Munchausen's syndrome 215
Pain disorder 209
Primary gain 217
Problem-focused coping 220

Psychological factors affecting medical
    conditions 218
Psychoneuroimmunology 222
Secondary gain 217
Selective amnesia 231
Somatization disorder 207
Somatoform disorders 206
Stress 210
Stressful life event 219
Stress inoculation training 225
Stressor 219

Internet Resource

To get more information on the material covered in this chapter, visit our web site at **http://www.mhhe.com/halgin**. There you will find more information, resources, and links to topics of interest.

CASE REPORT: SHAUN BOYDEN

When I first read the note on the intake form for Shaun Boyden, I felt a sense of uneasiness as I prepared to meet him in the intake interview. The words on the form were blunt and startling: "Pedophile . . . 46 years old . . . raped a 10-year-old boy. Court-ordered treatment." Perhaps I was struck and troubled by the fact that a tragedy of such proportions could be reduced to a few terse phrases. At the same time, I was aware of the difficult issues involved in treating pedophiles, many of whom are resistant to change and tend to regress to their molesting behavior. I knew that I would not be Shaun's therapist, because it was clinic procedure to assign such cases to Dr. Stephanie Draper, a staff psychologist with expertise in treating sex offenders. Frankly, I was relieved that I would not have responsibility for treating this client, feeling that it would be personally very difficult to sustain a relationship with a person who had exploited a child. As a mother, I found the notion of child abuse so despicable that I feared being unable to approach the client with empathy. In addition to my personal sensitivity to the issue, I felt pressures arising from my sense of social conscience; I have little patience with people who take advantage of those less powerful than themselves. I realized that these were issues that I should discuss in my ongoing consultation with my peer supervisor. Even though my interaction with Shaun Boyden would be limited to one or two sessions, I knew that it was important for me to approach these meetings with a mindset of objectivity, neutrality, and understanding. With a commitment to this kind of stance, I felt I would be able to conduct a professional evaluation of Shaun Boyden to determine if he was an appropriate candidate for the clinic's treatment program. My task was to conduct an intake evaluation and psychological assessment to assist Dr. Draper in formulating an appropriate treatment plan for Shaun.

In my initial encounter with Shaun, I found it difficult to view him as a 46-year-old man. His style of dress seemed more like the clothing of a teenager, while the harsh characteristics of his face made him seem at least a decade older than his age. He wore a flashy bicyclist's outfit consisting of brightly colored shorts and jersey, with matching Reeboks. At first, I thought it odd that he would come to a professional appointment so casually dressed, but I quickly came to recognize that he desperately wanted to be perceived as youthful and athletic. By contrast, however, his face was engraved with deep wrinkles, which reflected premature aging and exposure to the sun. I had the sense that Shaun fought an ongoing battle with the process of aging on one side and his fantasy of himself as a teenager on the other side.

In my meeting with Shaun, he was ostensibly humiliated and uncomfortable. Using such words as *humiliated* and *mortified*, Shaun tried to describe his deep feelings of distress about his uncontrollable urges to seduce young boys. A married man, Shaun described himself as the devoted father of two young daughters. He spoke of his relationship with the girls in the most endearing of terms, weeping as he uttered his fears that they might be taken away from him. When I asked him about his marriage, he said that he was at a loss for words and had been unable to face his wife to try to explain his behavior. Adding to his intense anxiety was his realization that with an arrest record for this kind of offense, he would lose his job as a bank teller and would probably never be able to land another job.

When I asked Shaun to tell me the details of these sexual urges and inappropriate behavior, he began to cry, and only after a long delay could he speak about what had happened. Shaun had often volunteered his time to take disadvantaged youths on overnight camping trips to a state park. While sleeping in the tent one night, he became overwhelmed with sexual desire and began to fondle the genitals of one of the boys. Shaun covered the boy's mouth to prevent him from screaming, and he mounted the child in an attempt at anal intercourse. Terrified, the young boy finally managed to scream, causing an adult in a nearby tent to rush over and witness what was taking place.

When I asked Shaun if anything like this had ever happened before, he immediately said no, but I sensed that he was not telling me the truth. Gazing at the floor, Shaun once again began to weep, and in his weeping I could hear the hint of stories involving other seductions. As he struggled to regain his composure, he proceeded to tell me that on many previous camping trips he had fondled boys who were sleeping in his tent, but they had always remained asleep, and Shaun had never attempted intercourse before.

Shaun's wife knew nothing of his problem, although he had struggled with these urges since adolescence. Until a few years ago, he had limited himself to sexual fantasies about young boys while masturbating. However, when being so close to sleeping youngsters, the urges became irresistible.

By the end of the intake hour with Shaun, I felt drained, and I realized that we needed to meet at least once more to gather information about his history before proceeding to the psychological testing. In my mind, the images of the boys who had been exploited were intertwined with the tormented face of this middle-aged man. His problem had been longstanding and had become so enmeshed with his psychological and sexual functioning that only an extreme form of intervention could provide any hope of altering this tragic life course. I sensed that Shaun's honesty about the nature and duration of his problem was rooted in his desperate wish to escape from this nightmarish struggle.

Sarah Tobin, PhD

8

Sexual Disorders

Sexual functioning is an essential aspect of human existence that can be a very rewarding or upsetting part of a person's life. Sexuality involves such a driving force in human nature, and is such an emotionally charged phenomenon, that it is not surprising that there are problems associated with this facet of human behavior.

What Is Abnormal Sexual Behavior?

How would you define abnormal sexual behavior? Look at the following list of sexual activities. On a scale of 1 to 10, with 1 being normal and 10 being abnormal, how would you rate each of these activities?

- Stimulating one's own genitals
- Making love in a place other than a bedroom
- Slapping, biting, pinching, or scratching one's partner
- Tying up or holding down one's partner
- Having anal intercourse
- Reading or looking at pornography
- Putting honey, whipped cream, wine, or other edibles on one's partner
- Having sex in a kneeling position
- Having one partner undress the other
- Wearing sexy bedroom clothing
- Kissing, licking, or sucking each other's genitals
- Having intercourse with an anonymous stranger

What criteria did you use in labeling any of these behaviors "abnormal"? For some people, all of these behaviors would be considered abnormal; for others, none would be. In and of themselves, these behaviors are not considered to represent psycho-

logical disturbance. For the sake of our discussion, we will assume that a sexual behavior is a psychological disorder if (1) it causes harm to other people or (2) it causes an individual to experience persistent or recurrent distress or impairment in important areas of functioning. According to the first criterion, sexual molestation of a child is clearly a psychological disorder. According to the second criterion, a distressing, ongoing aversion to sexuality is a psychological disorder. But what about cases in which the individual finds a behavior pleasurable that society regards as unacceptable or deviant? As you will see in this chapter, the distinction between normal and abnormal in the sexual domain of behavior is complicated and far from clear.

When evaluating the normality of a given sexual behavior, the context is extremely important, as are customs and mores, which change over time. Many attitudes and behaviors related to sex have changed since the 1970s and 1980s. For example, the kinds of magazines and videos featuring explicit sexual behavior that are commonplace in the 1990s would have been grounds for arrest in most American communities just 20 years ago.

For most of the twentieth century, surprisingly little factual evidence was available about sexual disorders because of such restrictive social attitudes. Much changed in the 1960s and 1970s, partly as a result of the dramatic and candid accounts of human sexual behavior published by world-renowned experts on human sexuality William Masters and Virginia Johnson (Masters & Johnson, 1966, 1970), whom you will read about later in the chapter. Following their pioneering efforts, researchers and clinicians made drastic changes in the way they explained sexual disorders and treated people with these conditions.

Some sophisticated survey and interview studies have been conducted that shed light on the complex behaviors associated with human sexuality. In a major study conducted at the National Opinion Research Center (NORC) at the University of

Sexually provocative web sites are among the most commonly visited sites on the internet, and have made sexually explicit images universally accessible.

Table 8.1

Examples of Paraphilias

Telephone scatologia	Making obscene phone calls, such as describing one's masturbatory activity in great detail, threatening to rape the victim, or trying to find out about the victim's sexual activities
Necrophilia	Deriving sexual gratification from viewing or having sexual contact with a corpse
Zoophilia	Having sex with animals or having recurrent fantasies of sex with animals
Coprophilia	Deriving sexual pleasure from contact with feces
Klismaphilia	Deriving sexual pleasure from the use of enemas
Urophilia	Deriving sexual pleasure from contact with urine
Autagonistophilia	Having sex in front of others
Somnophilia	Having sex with a sleeping person
Stigmatophilia	Deriving sexual pleasure from skin piercing or a tattoo
Autonepiophilia	Wearing diapers for sexual pleasure

Chicago, researchers conducted 90-minute interviews with more than 3,000 randomly chosen individuals between the ages of 18 and 59 (Laumann, Gagnon, Michael, & Michaels, 1994; Smith, 1996). Using sophisticated statistical analyses, these investigators provided some of the most comprehensive data about human sexuality since Alfred Kinsey's groundbreaking research more than four decades earlier (Kinsey, Pomeroy, & Martin, 1948; Kinsey, Pomeroy, Martin, & Gebhard, 1953). In the NORC study, behaviors that would have been considered abnormal or deviant a few decades ago had become part of mainstream sexuality. Least surprising was their finding that, among young people, only 5 percent of the women and 2 percent of the men waited until marriage to have their first sexual intercourse experience, in contrast to 45 percent of the women and 17 percent of the men in the older group. The researchers found similar generational differences regarding the frequency of oral sex, with the younger people engaging more commonly in this form of sexual intimacy. As we begin our discussion of sexual disorders, it is important to realize that what is regarded as "deviant" changes over time. In the next section of this chapter, we will discuss behaviors that are regarded as deviant in our society.

Paraphilias

The term *paraphilia* (*para* meaning "faulty" or "abnormal," and *philia* meaning "attraction") literally means a deviation involving the object of a person's sexual attraction. **Paraphilias** are disorders in which an individual has recurrent, intense sexually arousing fantasies, sexual urges, or behaviors involving (1) nonhuman objects, (2) children or other nonconsenting persons, or (3) the suffering or humiliation of oneself or a partner.

Characteristics of Paraphilias

There are several paraphilias (see Table 8.1) but all share the common feature that people who have these disorders are so psychologically dependent on the target of desire that they are unable to feel sexual gratification unless this target is present in some form. For some, the unusual sexual preferences occur in occasional episodes, such as during periods in which the individual feels especially stressed. Keep in mind that paraphilias are not fleeting whims or daydreams about unusual sexual practices but are conditions that last for at least 6 months. People with paraphilias find themselves recurrently compelled to think about or carry out their unusual behavior. Even if they do not actually fulfill their urges or fantasies, they are obsessed with them to the point of experiencing considerable personal distress. A paraphilia can become so strong and compelling that the individual loses sight of any goals other than the achievement of sexual fulfillment. By definition, paraphilias cause intense personal distress or impairment in social, work, and other areas of life functioning. Except for sexual masochism, almost all cases of paraphilia involve males.

To illustrate these points, let us compare the cases of Brian, who has a paraphilia, and Charles, who does not. Brian is extremely upset by his preoccupation with the sight and smell of women's leather gloves, is tormented by his intense arousal when he sees women wearing gloves, and can achieve sexual fulfillment only if he masturbates while fondling a leather glove. Brian has a paraphilia (namely, fetishism). Conversely, Charles finds it sexually stimulating when his girlfriend wears high heels to bed, but it is not necessary for her to wear these in order for him to be stimulated to orgasm. His attraction seems a little "kinky" to him, but not particularly unusual. Charles does not have a paraphilic disorder. Such distinctions are important to keep in mind as you read about the paraphilias.

Information about the incidence of paraphilias is limited, primarily because people with these disorders are so ashamed or embarrassed that they rarely seek psychological help. The extent to which paraphilias exist may be inferred indirectly by considering the large commercial market in pornographic magazines, movies, and objects sold in adult bookstores and over the internet.

As you begin to read about the paraphilias, you may question the extent to which they cause distress for an individual, or even for others. In fact, some people with paraphilias insist that neither they nor others are bothered by their unusual sexual practices; they insist that the negative reaction of an unaccepting society is what causes their behavior to be viewed as dysfunctional. Others, however, are tormented by guilt and shame, as they find their lives being consumed by the pursuit of sexual gratification in ways that they view as unacceptable.

Pedophilia

We begin our discussion of paraphilias with the most disturbing disorder you will study in this book—**pedophilia,** a paraphilia in which an adult (16 years or over) has uncontrollable sexual urges toward sexually immature children. Sometimes these stories take on gruesome proportions, as when children are submitted to horrifying forms of victimization, such as kidnapping and sexual abuse, that persist for months or even years. Although these extreme cases are rare, the prevalence of child sexual abuse is disturbingly high in the United States. Estimates are that as many as 10 to 15 percent of all children and adolescents are sexually victimized at least once during their early developmental years, with twice as many girls as boys being victims (Mrazek, 1984). The vast majority of pedophiles are male, and approximately 75 percent of them choose girls as their victims. People with this disorder are notoriously difficult to treat. It is well known that the disturbance is usually so deeply ingrained in the character of pedophiles that they are likely to return to their victimizing behavior, even following periods of incarceration or treatment (Prentky, Lee, Knight, & Cerce, 1997b)

Types of Pedophilia

Although pedophiles are by definition attracted to children, their sexual preferences and behavior vary a great deal. Some do not act out their impulses but have disturbing fantasies and inclinations to molest children. Those who do act on their pedophilic impulses commit such acts as undressing the child, touching the child's genitals, coercing the child to participate in oral-genital activity, and attempting vaginal or anal intercourse.

Researchers have used various systems to classify pedophiles. A particularly useful one (Lanyon, 1986) involves the distinction among situational molesters, preference molesters, and child rapists. Situational molesters have a history of normal sexual development and interests; as adults, they are primarily interested in relationships with other adults. However, in certain contexts, such as during a stressful time, they are overcome by a strong impulse to become sexual with a child. Rather than feeling relieved after the incident, though, situational molesters feel distress. For the preference molester, pedophilic behavior is ingrained into his personality and lifestyle, and he has a clear preference for children, especially boys. He will marry only out

A playground can be the setting for a pedophile to target a potential victim.

of convenience, to be near children or as a cover for his disorder. The preference molester sees nothing wrong with his behavior; if anything, he feels that society is too critical of what he regards as simply a variant of sexual expression. The child rapist is a violent child abuser whose behavior is an expression of hostile sexual drives.

Another model applies to the behavior of sexual aggressors in general, but it seems particularly well suited for understanding pedophilia. According to this model (Hall, Shondrick, & Hirschman, 1993), there are four subtypes of sexual aggressors: physiological, cognitive, affective, and developmentally related. The physiological aggressor, who experiences deviant sexual arousal patterns, is more likely to choose male children and to have multiple victims, while refraining from physical violence and nonsexual aggression. The cognitive aggressor plans his sexual aggression, which is more likely to be acquaintance rape or incest that is less impulsive and violent than found in the other subtypes. The affective aggressor, who lacks affective control, engages in sexual aggression that is opportunistic, unplanned, and often violent. Affective aggressors who violate children are more prone to suffer from depression, while those who victimize adults tend to be more angry. Sexual aggressors with developmentally related personality problems tend to have a long history of personality and adjustment difficulties, family and interpersonal conflicts, and childhood victimization, and they tend to engage in violent forms of sexual aggression. This last group has the poorest treatment prognosis.

Theories and Treatment of Pedophilia

Because of the extreme harm caused innocent victims that results from pedophilic behavior, it is one of the most widely investigated of the paraphilias. We will devote greater attention to the understanding and treatment of this disorder in this section and then return to more general theories and treatments of the other paraphilias later in the chapter. As you will see, the

A Relationship Between Pedophilia and a History of Being Sexually Victimized?

Researchers trying to understand the development of pedophilia have described a "victim-to-abuser cycle" (Bagley, Wood, & Young, 1994), in which some childhood victims of sexual abuse go on to perpetrate similar acts of sexual abuse as adults. Establishing such a connection would provide some greater insight into the minds of those who commit these disturbing crimes, and it might lead to the development of effective treatment programs for pedophiles. Unfortunately, the relationship between being victimized and becoming a victimizer is not quite so clear.

In retrospective studies, some researchers have found that many pedophiles were sexually abused as children (Bagley et al., 1994). Other researchers, however, have observed that the rate of childhood sexual abuse among pedophiles is only marginally higher than that found among individuals who commit sexual offenses against adults or violent offenses against a variety of victims (Freund, Watson, & Dickey, 1990). These researchers suggest that pedophiles might be motivated to mini-

mize responsibility for their offenses and offer the quasi-excuse that their own experience of having been victimized led to their exploitive behavior. Further complicating the issue is the tendency of pedophiles to deny that they are sexually interested in children and to minimize the appearance of their being psychologically disturbed (Haywood & Grossman, 1994).

Based on reports that approximately 3 percent of all college men admit that they have had fantasies about sex involving a child, or actual sexual contacts, Bagley and his colleagues (1994) set out to explore the relationship of sexual abuse histories to erotic interest in children among essentially normal men. Those who had been victims of more than one instance of sexual abuse and had also suffered emotional abuse were much more likely to express sexual interest in children and young adolescents and, to a lesser extent, to have engaged in sexual activities with minors. These men experienced more symptoms of emotional distress, including prominent feelings of depression and anxiety, than their counterparts without histories of sexual and emotional abuse. The authors suggested that painful histories of abuse may have led some to identify with their abusers in an attempt to make sense out of the disorganizing effects of their victimization.

In response to the inconsistent findings relating sexual abuse to subsequent pedophilia, other researchers have broadened their scope to investigate familial and developmental antecedents of pedophilia and sexual aggression. They note that the sexual abuse of children is rarely an isolated event; instead, it often occurs in the context of families struggling with considerable emotional and physical conflict. Parental figures may themselves

commit the abuse, or may simply be unavailable to provide adequate parenting and support for children who are victimized by others (Alexander, 1992).

Serious family disturbance may lay the groundwork for both sexual victimization and for offending later in life. Alexander (1992) suggested that parents' insecure patterns of attachment, their disturbed style of relating, and their sexually abusive behavior become models for the individual who later goes on to be sexually abusive himself. Sexually abusive parents are impaired in their ability to meet their relationship needs in mature and appropriate ways, and they are less able to seek assistance to stop abusive behavior. Thus, pedophiles come to view others, adults and children alike, as acting on their own desires and needs, while denying the effects of sexual transgressions on their victims. Similarly, Prentky and his colleagues (1989) determined that early relationship disturbances with caregivers, accompanied by sexual deviation within the family, are characteristics of the most violent sexual offenders. Lacking adequate models for relationships and for controlling aggressive and sexual impulses, sexual offenses become "acceptable" outlets for the feelings of isolation, anger, and sexual arousal these individuals experience.

No single model or theory can adequately explain all cases of pedophilia, yet careful study of the childhood experiences of pedophiles can shed light on the reasons these individuals commit such acts. With such improved understanding, more effective treatments can be formulated. Perhaps even more important, prevention programs can be developed in which those at greatest risk of perpetuating the cycle of abuse can be helped before they act on their fantasies and inclinations.

biopsychosocial model of pedophilia is particularly appropriate because of the complex interactions of physiological, psychological, and sociocultural influences on its development.

Clinicians and researchers working within a biological perspective take less interest in understanding the causes of pedophilia than in finding a somatic treatment that will reduce

the individual's sexual urges. Consequently, a number of approaches are aimed at the endocrine system, such as administering the female hormone progesterone to reduce the pedophile's sex drive by lowering his level of testosterone. Another approach is the administration of antiandrogens, which are intended to have the same effect. Most recently, researchers

Pedophilia

MINI-CASE

Shortly following his marriage, Kirk began developing an inappropriately close relationship with Amy, his 8-year-old stepdaughter. It seemed to start out innocently, when he took extra time to give her bubble baths and backrubs. But, after only 2 months of living in the same house, Kirk's behavior went outside the boundry of common parental physical affection. After his wife left for work early each morning, Kirk invited Amy into his bed on the pretext that she could watch cartoons on the television in his bedroom. Kirk would begin stroking Amy's hair and gradually proceed to more sexually explicit behavior, encouraging her to touch his genitals, saying that it would be "good" for her to learn about what "daddies" are like. Confused and frightened, Amy did as she was told. Kirk reinforced compliance to his demands by threatening Amy that, if she told anyone about their secret, he would deny everything and she would be severely beaten. This behavior continued for more than 2 years, until one day Kirk's wife returned home unexpectedly and caught him engaging in this behavior.

■ Would Kirk be regarded as a situational or a preference molester?

■ How is Kirk's pedophilic behavior likely to affect Amy when she becomes an adult?

DIAGNOSTIC FEATURES

● For a period lasting at least 6 months, people with this disorder have recurrent, intense sexually arousing fantasies, sexual urges, or behaviors involving sexual activity with a prepubescent child or children (generally 13 years old or younger).

● The fantasies, sexual urges, or behaviors cause significant distress or impairment.

● The individual with this disorder is at least 16 years old and at least 5 years older than the victimized child or children.

● The individual's pedophilic behavior may be characterized by sexual attraction to males, females, or both sexes.

● The pedophilic behavior is characterized by whether or not it is limited to incest.

● The pedophilic behavior is characterized by whether or not sexual attraction is exclusive to children.

have developed a treatment that involves administering a substance that reduces testosterone secretion by inhibiting the action of the pituitary gland. Although such an intervention appears to have positive effects, it is nevertheless considered necessary to combine medical treatments with psychotherapy (Rosler & Witztum, 1998).

The most radical medical interventions involve surgery. Castration, or removal of the testes, is intended to eliminate the production of testosterone. Another surgical intervention is hypothalamotomy, or destruction of the ventromedial nucleus of the hypothalamus. This procedure is intended to change the individual's sexual arousal patterns by targeting the source of these patterns in the central nervous system. Hypothalamotomies have been used most frequently in Germany, but with limited effectiveness. The problem with all of these procedures, in addition to their side effects, is that they do not eliminate the man's ability to be sexually aroused and to have intercourse or masturbate. They may reduce the level of testosterone and, thus, help curb the pedophile's sex drive, but the issue of the inappropriateness of his choice of a partner must also be addressed. Therefore, any of these somatic treatments must be combined with psychotherapy (Prentky, 1997).

Keep in mind that surgical treatments for sex offenders are performed very rarely and represent extreme forms of intervention. But it is also important to consider why these al-

ternatives are even regarded as viable methods of treatment. The men for whom these treatments are recommended are incorrigible individuals who have repeatedly exploited and seriously harmed vulnerable individuals. Even though it may be difficult for some people to understand or support the use of such radical interventions, it is also disturbing to consider the alternatives, which may include life imprisonment as the only means of preventing these men from repeating their offenses against children.

Psychological theorists focus on the early life experiences of people with this disorder. As discussed in the Research focus box, researchers have described a "victim-to-abuser cycle" (Bagley et al., 1994; Haywood et al., 1996), which leads childhood victims of sexual abuse to perpetrate similar acts of sexual abuse when they reach adulthood.

Other researchers have broadened their scope beyond looking specifically at abuse to investigate more general familial and developmental antecedents of pedophilia and sexual aggression. They note that sexual abuse of children is rarely an isolated event; instead, it often occurs in the context of families struggling with considerable emotional and physical conflict.

Another approach focuses on the psychological factors that lead to pedophilia by zeroing in on the personality traits of sex offenders. In one study (Serin, Malcolm, Khanna, & Barbaree, 1994), researchers found a strong relationship between psychopathy, or antisocial personality disorder, and deviant sexual arousal in a group of 65 offenders, some of whom were rapists and others child molesters. The pedophiles who preyed on unrelated children showed the strongest relationship between psychopathy and deviant sexual arousal. Next in degree of psychopathy were the rapists, followed by the incest offenders (those whose victims were relatives). Thus, there appears to be a strong antisocial element in the personalities of child molesters.

Both the diagnosis and treatment of pedophilia may be assisted by the use of a measure called a penile plethysmograph, an instrument that measures the blood flow in the penis and, hence, objectively registers the degree of a man's sexual arousal. This procedure, called phallometry, is an accurate technique for determining pedophilic responses in males that is far more reliable than self-report. Child molesters, for example, experience changes in penile circumference when shown stimuli depicting sexual scenes involving children (Maletzky, 1998).

In addition to looking at factors that predict pedophilic behavior, researchers have attempted to determine which offenders are more likely to repeat their acts. There appears to be a pattern or constellation of factors that leads to high rates of repeating pedophilic behavior among convicted offenders. In examinations of the records of 269 convicted child molesters, researchers found that, compared to non-repeaters, those who were likely to offend repeatedly had higher scores on measures of pedophilia, a history of previous sexual charges, were younger, tended to prey on male victims (frequently from outside the family), and were more likely to be living alone (Proulx et al., 1997). In a similar study of conviction records, another team of researchers also found that individuals who had a paraphilia besides pedophilia were more likely to engage repeatedly in pedophilic acts (Prentky, Knight, & Lee, 1997a). Overall, the reconviction rate for pedophilia was 13 percent.

The psychological treatments of pedophilia involve behavioral methods, cognitive-behavioral techniques, and biological interventions. Within the behavioral realm, clinicians use a variety of techniques. Electroshock is a form of aversive therapy rooted in classical conditioning; it involves the administration of shock in response to sexual arousal in response to a deviant stimulus, such as a depiction of a sexual situation involving a child. In another technique, the clinician attempts to replace the pedophile's attraction to a child as a sexual target with an appropriate adult object. For example, while masturbating using his customary fantasies of sexual activity with a child, the pedophile may be instructed to replace the child image with an adult image as he approaches the point of orgasm. Other behavioral techniques involve principles of aversive conditioning, with the stimulus being a child's picture or image. Alternatively, the pedophile might be instructed to talk about his sexual practices to an "audience" of other clients or clinicians who criticize and deride him. The behavioral techniques are intended not only to extinguish the inappropriate behavior and replace it with appropriate sexual behavior but also to reinforce socially acceptable ways of relating to other adults.

Cognitive interventions are another psychological treatment used for pedophilia. In relapse prevention, the therapist helps the client strengthen self-control by providing methods for identifying and analyzing problem situations and by developing strategies that help the client avoid and cope more effectively in these circumstances. Cognitive therapy for depression or anger may also be used in cases in which the pedophile has associated disorders.

There is no one best approach to treating people with pedophilia. The fact that people with this disorder are likely to repeat their behavior even after long term intensive treatment has led clinicians and researchers to conclude that a multifaceted approach is needed (Barbaree & Seto, 1997). Especially promising have been treatment approaches involving a combination of techniques, with particular attention to the inclusion of a group therapy component. Berlin (1998) describes an approach that has been successful in reducing repeated offenses to less than 8 percent of those participating. In this program, Berlin and his colleagues incorporate group therapy, which is combined in some cases with medications aimed at lowering sex drive. In the group therapy, efforts are made to confront denial and rationalizations, while providing a supportive context that is conducive to a frank discussion of desires and conflicts. Yet another component of this approach is the development of a family- and community-based support system to help the pedophile stick to his determination to remain healthy (Berlin, 1998).

Exhibitionism

In **exhibitionism**, a person has intense sexual urges and arousing fantasies involving the exposure of genitals to a stranger. The exhibitionist actually does not expect a sexual reaction from the other person but finds the sight of shock or fear in the onlooker to be arousing. Some exhibitionists have the fantasy, however, that the onlooker will become sexually aroused. When discussing exhibitionistic behavior, it is important to differentiate this psychological disorder from exhibiting behaviors that are associated with a neurological condition in which an individual lacks normal inhibitory capacity. The paraphilia of exhibitionism is also different from socially sanctioned display (Hollender, 1997), as would be found at a nudist beach or strip club. People with this paraphilia feel they cannot control their behavior or feel driven to this behavior in a desperate attempt to get attention; the result is emotional torment and significant disruption in life.

In trying to understand how people, most of whom are men, become so compulsively driven to display their genitals, it is useful to consider early developmental experiences having to do with comparable situations. According to one view, the exhibitionist is motivated to overcome chronic feelings of shame and humiliation. His exhibitionistic behavior provides a temporary reprieve from his feelings of incompetence by bolstering feelings of personal adequacy (Silverstein, 1996). A more behavioral explanation regards the exhibitionistic behavior as a product of learning experiences in childhood, when the individual was sexually aroused while displaying himself and was excited by the distress that his inappropriate behavior caused in other people. Over time,

Exhibitionism

MINI-CASE

Ernie is in jail for the fourth time in the past 2 years for public exposure. As Ernie explained to the court psychologist who interviewed him, he has "flashed" much more often than he has been apprehended. In each case, he has chosen as his victim an unsuspecting teenage girl, and he jumps out at her from behind a doorway, a tree, or a car parked at the sidewalk. He has never touched any of these girls, instead fleeing the scene after having exposed himself. On some occasions, he masturbates immediately after the exposure, fantasizing that his victim was swept off her feet by his sexual prowess and pleaded for him to make love to her. This time, seeing that his latest victim responded by calling the police to track him down, Ernie felt crushed and humiliated by an overwhelming sense of his own sexual inadequacy.

- Why do you think Ernie chooses teenage girls as his victims?

- Might there be a connection between Ernie's feelings of sexual inadequacy and the fact that he engages in exhibitionistic behaviors?

DIAGNOSTIC FEATURES

- This diagnosis is assigned to people who, for a period lasting at least 6 months, have intense sexually arousing fantasies, sexual urges, or behaviors involving genital exposure to unsuspecting strangers.

- The fantasies, sexual urges, or behaviors cause significant distress or impairment.

repetition of this behavior is reinforced to such an extent that it becomes addictive. In fact, exhibitionists often prefer this form of behavior to sexual intercourse, because they have come to associate intense feelings of sexual gratification with the display of their genitals to alarmed strangers (Money,

Exhibitionists take pleasure in the shock value of their behavior.

1984). Their behavior enhances their feelings of masculinity and power, especially as the shock value of their behavior is so strong and easily observed in the victim.

The treatment of exhibitionists takes a multifaceted approach (Maletzky, 1997), often involving a reliance on learning principles, such as counterconditioning or aversive conditioning. The person must unlearn the connection between sexual pleasure and the exhibitionistic behavior, either through creating new associations between sexuality and appropriate stimuli or through associating pain and embarrassment, instead of pleasure, with exhibitionistic behavior. For example, the therapist might use **covert conditioning,** a behavioral method in which the client imagines a great deal of shame when his acquaintances observe him engaging in his exhibitionistic behaviors.

Fetishism

A **fetish** is a strong, recurrent sexual attraction to a nonliving object. People with the paraphilia of **fetishism** are preoccupied with an object, and they become dependent on this object for achieving sexual gratification, actually preferring it over sexual intimacy with a partner. It is difficult to estimate how common fetishism is, because fetishists, virtually all of whom are men, are unlikely to seek treatment for their disorder.

The most common fetishistic objects are ordinary items of clothing, such as underwear, stockings, shoes, and boots; however, there are also reports in the psychiatric literature of a wide range of fetishes, including rubber items, leather objects, dia-

Fetishism

MINI-CASE

For several years, Tom has been breaking into cars and stealing boots or shoes, and he has come close to being caught on several occasions. Tom takes great pleasure in the excitement he experiences each time he engages in the ritualistic behavior of procuring a shoe or boot and going to a secret place to fondle it and masturbate. In his home, he has a closet filled with dozens of women's shoes, and he chooses from this selection the particular shoe with which he will masturbate. Sometimes he sits in a shoe store and keeps watch for women trying on shoes. After a woman tries on and rejects a particular pair, Tom scoops the pair of shoes from the floor and takes them to the register, explaining to the clerk that the shoes are a gift for his wife. With great eagerness and anticipation, he rushes home to engage once again in his masturbatory ritual.

- If Tom's fetishistic behavior did not involve the act of stealing, should it be considered a psychological disorder?

- If Tom is arrested, should he be sent to jail for committing a crime, or should he be ordered to participate in therapy for a psychological disorder?

DIAGNOSTIC FEATURES

- For a period lasting at least 6 months, people with this condition have recurrent, intense sexually arousing fantasies, sexual urges, or behaviors involving nonliving objects.

- The fantasies, sexual urges, or behaviors cause significant distress or impairment.

- The fetish objects are not limited to female clothing used in cross-dressing or devices used for tactile genital stimulation, such as a vibrator.

---

pers, safety pins, and even amputated limbs. Some fetishes involve very specific attractions—for example, brown boots lined with fur. **Partialism** is another paraphilia, which some experts regard as a variant of fetishism; people with partialism are interested solely in sexual gratification from a specific body part, such as feet. Cases in which a man's sexual excitement is dependent on female clothing used for cross-dressing fall into another category, transvestic fetishism, which we will discuss later. Also, behavior is not regarded as fetishistic when it involves the use of an object specifically designed for increasing sexual excitation, such as a vibrator.

A fetishist becomes sexually excited by the object. Some fondle or wear the fetishistic object. Some are aroused by smelling the object, rubbing against it, or observing other persons wearing it during sexual encounters. In some cases, the fetishist may not even desire to have intercourse with the partner, preferring instead to masturbate with the fetishistic object. Some men find that they are unable to attain an erection unless the fetishistic object is present. Some fetishists engage in bizarre behavior, such as sucking it, rolling in it, burning it, or cutting it into pieces.

When discussing fetishes, it is important to keep in mind the difference between what is considered "normal" sexual behavior and what would be considered deviant. Fantasies and behaviors that occasionally enhance a person's sexual excitement are different from the ritualistic preoccupations seen in true fetishism. Fetishism involves a compulsive kind of behavior that seems beyond the control of the individual, and it can be the source of considerable distress and interpersonal problems.

Although some people with fetishes incorporate their fetishistic behavior into their sexual relationship with a partner who accepts this divergent behavior, more often the fetishistic behavior interferes with normal sexual functioning, and it is more likely when relationship problems exist (de Silva, 1993).

Fetishism appears to develop in a way similar to exhibitionism, in that early life experiences result in a connection between sexual excitation and a fetishistic object. As the person grows older, he becomes conditioned to associate sexual gratification with the object, rather than with another person. For example, fetishists who prefer baby-related objects, such as diapers, crib sheets, or rubber diaper pants, may have developed an intense association in early childhood between pleasurable genital feelings and the touching of these objects. To test this learning hypothesis (in experiments that would be regarded as unethical by today's standards), one group of researchers reported that they could condition male subjects to acquire a fetish (Rachman, 1966; Rachman & Hodgson, 1968). In one of these studies, the researchers showed men pictures of nude or scantily dressed women (unconditioned stimulus) paired with pictures of fur-lined boots (conditioned stimulus) and used an apparatus to measure the men's erectile response. After repeated pairings of the pictures of women and boots (and other footwear), the men became aroused by the pictures of footwear alone (conditioned stimulus). Extinction of this behavior was then achieved by repeatedly showing the shoes and boots without the pictures of women. Over time, the men lost interest in these objects, which no longer had sexual associations.

Frotteurism

MINI-CASE

Bruce, who works as a delivery messenger in a large city, rides the subway throughout the day. He thrives on the opportunity to ride crowded subways, where he becomes sexually stimulated by rubbing up against unsuspecting women. Having developed some cagey techniques, Bruce is often able to take advantage of women without their comprehending what he is doing. As the day proceeds, his level of sexual excitation grows, so that by the evening rush hour he targets a particularly attractive woman and only at that point in the day allows himself to reach orgasm.

■ If the women who are the targets of Bruce's behavior are unaware of what he is doing, why does his behavior qualify as a paraphilia?

■ What therapeutic techniques might help Bruce replace his paraphilia with more normal sexual behavior?

DIAGNOSTIC FEATURES

● For a period lasting at least 6 months, people with this condition have recurrent, intense sexually arousing fantasies, sexual urges, or behaviors involving touching and rubbing against nonconsenting people.

● The fantasies, sexual urges, or behaviors cause significant distress or impairment.

As controversial as this study was, it provided a model for the treatment of fetishes, and researchers have established that extinction and other behavioral methods are effective treatment strategies. One technique is aversion therapy, in which the individual is subjected to punishment, such as taking a vomit-inducing drug or being hypnotized to feel nauseated, while masturbating with the fetishistic object.

Orgasmic reconditioning is another behavioral method geared toward a relearning process. In this procedure, developed by Davison (1968) for treating paraphilias, an individual is instructed to arouse himself with a fantasy of the unacceptable object, then masturbate while looking at an appropriate sexual stimulus, such as a picture of an adult partner. If his arousal decreases, he may return to the fantasy of the unacceptable object, but he is to attain orgasm only while focusing on the acceptable stimulus. In time, the individual presumably relies less and less on the unacceptable object for sexual excitement and increasingly on the desired sexual stimulus.

Frotteurism

The term **frotteurism** is derived from the French word *frotter* (meaning "to rub"), and it refers to masturbation that involves rubbing against another person. A **frotteur** has recurrent, intense sexual urges and sexually arousing fantasies of rubbing against or fondling another person. The target of the frotteur is not a consenting partner but a stranger. The frotteur seeks out crowded places, such as buses or subways, where he can select an unsuspecting victim and then usually rubs up against the person until he ejaculates. While rubbing against or touching the person, the frotteur may fantasize that they are involved in a close, intimate relationship. To avoid detection, he acts quickly and is prepared to run before his victim realizes what is happening. Customarily,

it is a very brief encounter and the victim may be unaware of what has just taken place.

As with other paraphilias, learning theory provides a useful model for understanding the development of frotteurism. According to this view, at a point in the frotteur's life, this behavior was acquired through a pleasurable, perhaps inadvertent experience, and each repetition of the behavior provides additional reinforcement. Treatment involves an unlearning of these associations through such methods as extinction and covert conditioning.

Sexual Masochism and Sexual Sadism

The term **masochism** comes from the name of nineteenth-century Austrian writer Leopold Baron von Sacher-Masoch (1836–1895), known for his novels about men who were sexu-

A crowded subway provides an opportunity for the frotteur to become sexually excited by rubbing against other people.

ally humiliated by women. A masochist is someone who seeks pleasure from being subjected to pain. The term *sadism* comes from the name of eighteenth-century French author Marquis de Sade (1740–1814), who wrote extensively about obtaining sexual enjoyment from inflicting cruelty. The psychiatric terms *sadism* and *masochism* were coined by Krafft Ebing (1840–1903), a German physician who pioneered the scholarly approach to understanding the broad range of human sexual behavior in his book *Psychopathia Sexualis* (Krafft-Ebing, 1886/1950).

Sexual masochism is a disorder marked by an attraction to achieving sexual gratification by having painful stimulation applied to one's own body, either alone or with a partner. Men and women with this disorder achieve sexual satisfaction by such means as binding with cloth or ropes, injuring the skin with pins or knives, or administering electric shocks. Some sexual masochists do not act on their fantasies, but they feel recurrent urges and may feel distressed by the power of these urges.

Sexual sadism is the converse of sexual masochism in that it involves deriving sexual gratification from activities that harm, or from urges to harm, another person. Seeing or imagining another's pain excites the sadist. In contrast to sexual masochism, which does not require a partner, sexual sadism clearly does require a partner to enact sadistic fantasies.

People with these disorders may alternate playing sadistic and masochistic roles. In some sexual activities, one of the partners acts in a very submissive role and begs to be hurt and hu-

Some people flaunt their sadomasochistic tendencies, asserting that it is just a personal expression of identity and preference.

miliated. In other activities, the partners reverse the roles such that the previously submissive person now inflicts the pain and dominates the interaction. The term **sadomasochist** refers to people who derive sexual pleasure from both inflicting and receiving pain.

The specialized nature of their sexual activities and their desire to meet other people with similar preferences lead some sadomasochistic individuals to join organizations designed to cater to their needs, such as the Till Eulenspiegel Society in New York City or the Janus Society in San Francisco. In a survey of sadomasochists who were members of

---

Sexual Sadism and Sexual Masochism

MINI-CASE

For a number of years, Ray has insisted that his wife, Jeanne, submit him to demeaning and abusive sexual behavior. In the early years of their relationship, Ray's requests involved relatively innocent pleas that Jeanne pinch him and bite his chest while they were sexually intimate. Over time, however, his requests for pain increased and the nature of the pain changed. At present, they engage in what they call "special sessions," during which Jeanne handcuffs Ray to the bed and inflicts various forms of torture. Jeanne goes along with Ray's requests that she surprise him with new ways of inflicting pain, so she has developed a repertoire of behaviors, ranging from burning Ray's skin with matches to cutting him with razor blades. Jeanne and Ray have no interest in sexual intimacy other than that involving pain.

- If Ray and Jeanne both consent to this form of sexual activity, why would it be considered a paraphilia?

- What kind of childhood experiences may have predisposed Ray to develop his preference for sexuality that involves the experience of pain?

DIAGNOSTIC FEATURES OF SEXUAL SADISM

- For a period lasting at least 6 months, people with this condition have recurrent, intense sexually arousing fantasies, sexual urges, or behaviors involving real or simulated acts in which they are sexually excited by the psychological or physical suffering or humiliation of another person.

- The fantasies, sexual urges, or behaviors cause significant distress or impairment.

DIAGNOSTIC FEATURES OF SEXUAL MASOCHISM

- For a period lasting at least 6 months, people with this condition have recurrent, intense sexually arousing fantasies, sexual urges, or behaviors involving real or simulated acts of being humiliated, beaten, bound, or made to suffer in other ways.

- The fantasies, sexual urges, or behaviors cause significant distress or impairment.

such a society, researchers found the most prevalent sadistic sexual interests to be spanking, master-slave relationships, bondage, humiliation, and restraint. Less common were infliction of pain, whipping, verbal abuse, bondage, and enemas and other toilet-related activities. Some people act out dramatic scenarios, such as being led around on a collar and leash and ordered to act like a submissive puppy who may be spanked for slight misbehaviors. Interestingly, women and men reported similar levels of interest in most of these behaviors, with somewhat higher percentages of women indicating interest in bondage and verbal abuse (Breslow, Evans, & Langley, 1985).

Activities such as cutting, bondage, pricking, and shocking can be dangerous, and this danger adds to the excitement sadomasochists feel. Even more extreme, however, is strangling to the point of oxygen deprivation, wearing a mask or plastic bag over the head, placing a noose around one's neck, or ingesting a nitrate gas, which causes asphyxiation. This type of activity, which some individuals practice while alone, is usually accompanied by fantasies of near escapes from death; however, such fantasies sometimes become reality when the limits are pushed too far (O'Halloran & Dietz, 1993).

One avenue to understanding sexual sadism and sexual masochism is to consider the role that punishment and discipline played in the early lives of people with these disorders. Presumably, these individuals formed a connection between sexual excitation and the experience of pain or chastisement. The attention they received in the process of being disciplined may have been the only caretaking they received from otherwise negligent parents. Perhaps even a beating was preferable to being ignored, leading to a later sexual preference for masochism. Another scenario involves the pairing of physical punishment with subsequent parental cuddling and reassurance, leading the individual to associate pain with love. Sadists, conversely, may be driven by a wish to conquer others in the way that harsh parental figures controlled them early in life. The fact that sadists and masochists may switch roles complicates this analysis, but it is possible that the need for cooperating partners drives their reversal of sexual roles.

Most sadists and masochists do not seek professional help. In fact, the vast majority have no interest in changing their behaviors. They usually come to the attention of professionals only when their behavior results in physical injury or when they become distressed over ending a relationship with a partner. For the small number of people who spontaneously seek help and wish to change their sadistic or masochistic behaviors, group and individual therapy focusing on the behavioral principles of conditioning and reinforcement have been found most effective.

Transvestic Fetishism

A syndrome found only in males is **transvestic fetishism,** in which a man has an uncontrollable urge to wear a woman's clothes (called cross-dressing) as his primary means of achieving sexual gratification. This sexual gratification has a compulsive quality, and it consumes a tremendous amount of the individual's emotional energy. Cross-dressing is often accompanied by masturbation or fantasies in which the man imagines that other men are attracted to him as a woman. When he is not cross-dressed, he looks like a typical man, and he may be sexually involved with a woman. In fact, the definition of this disorder implies that the man sees himself as a man and is heterosexual in orientation.

Transvestic behaviors vary widely. Some men wear only a single item of women's clothing, such as underwear, often under their masculine outer clothing. Others have complete feminine wardrobes and, while alone, put on an entire outfit, possibly including "breasts" made with water-filled balloons or padding, as well as makeup, wigs, shoes, and other accessories. Their experience while wearing these clothes is one of having assumed a different personality. They may also find that cross-dressing while alone relaxes them or, when having sex with a partner, increases their level of excitement. A phenomenon related to transvestic fetishism is autogynephilia, in which a man derives sexual excitement from the thought or image of himself as having female anatomy or experiencing such biological functions as menstruation, childbirth, and breast-feeding (Blanchard, 1989, 1992).

Unlike transsexuals, people with transvestic fetishism do not seek to change their assigned sex; rather, they are driven to cross-dress for sexual gratification.

Transvestic Fetishism

MINI-CASE

In the evenings, when his wife leaves the house for her part-time job, Phil often goes to a secret hiding place in his workshop. In a locked cabinet, Phil keeps a small wardrobe of women's underwear, stockings, high heels, makeup, a wig, and dresses. Closing all the blinds in the house and taking the phone off the hook, Phil dresses in these clothes and fantasizes that he is being pursued by several men. After about 2 hours, he usually masturbates to the point of orgasm, as he imagines that he is being seduced by a sexual partner. Following this ritual, he secretly packs up the women's clothes and puts them away. Though primarily limiting his cross-dressing activities to the evenings, he thinks about it frequently during the day, which causes him to become sexually excited and to wish that he could get away from work, go home, and put on his special clothes. Knowing that he cannot, he wears women's underwear under his workclothes, and he sneaks off to the men's room to masturbate in response to the sexual stimulation he derives from feeling the silky sensation against his body.

- Does Phil's transvestic behavior hurt anyone; if not, why would it be considered a sexual disorder?
- If Phil were to seek treatment, what might be the goals of therapy?

DIAGNOSTIC FEATURES

- For a period lasting at least 6 months, heterosexual men with this condition have recurrent, intense sexually arousing fantasies, sexual urges, or behaviors involving cross-dressing.
- The fantasies, sexual urges, or behaviors cause significant distress or impairment.

Homosexual men who make themselves up as women are not transvestic fetishists because they are generally not dressing this way to gain sexual satisfaction. They do not have the same sense of compulsion that transvestic fetishists have. Rather, cross-dressing for some homosexual men has more to do with their participation in a subculture that they find inviting.

Individuals who develop transvestic fetishism often begin cross-dressing in childhood or adolescence. Some may have been forced to wear girls' clothes as a form of humiliation or to fulfill a parental fantasy that they were actually girls. Others ventured into cross-dressing out of curiosity and found the behavior to be enjoyable. Over time, the cross-dressing behavior seems to take on a life of its own, perhaps pleasurable at first but ultimately compulsive in nature. This behavior is not without conflict; in fact, transvestic fetishists go through phases in which they destroy or give away all feminine clothing, swearing that they will give up this activity.

Relatively few transvestic fetishists seek professional help, because they are reluctant to give up their cross-dressing behavior. When these men do become distressed enough to seek help, it is usually attributable to another problem, such as depression or distress stemming from feeling that their behavior is out of control. Consequently, some therapists focus on helping the individual develop a sense of control rather than on extinguishing the behavior altogether. When a person is motivated to change, therapists use behavioral methods already described in the treatment of other paraphilias, such as aversive conditioning, covert sensitization, and orgasmic reconditioning. Keep in mind that cross-dressing usually serves the purpose of reducing anxiety for the individual; therefore, the therapist may encourage the client to try to gain insight into the stresses that precipitate the behavior through more traditional psychotherapy.

Voyeurism

The word *voyeur* comes from the French word *voir* ("to see"). **Voyeurism** is a sexual disorder in which the individual has a compulsion to derive sexual gratification from observing the nudity or sexual activity of others who are unaware of being watched. The disorder is more common in men. The colloquial term "Peeping Tom" is often used to refer to a **voyeur.** This is a reference to the character Tom the Tailor, who was the only one in town to violate Lady Godiva's request for privacy when she rode nude on horseback through her town.

Unlike people who become sexually aroused when watching a sexual partner undress or a performer in a sexually explicit movie, the voyeur has the recurrent and intense desire to observe unsuspecting people. The voyeur is sexually frustrated and feels incapable of establishing a regular sexual relationship with the person he observes. He prefers to masturbate either during or soon after the voyeuristic activity. "Peeping" provides him with a substitute form of sexual gratification.

As is the case with the other paraphilias we have discussed, very few voyeurs seek treatment voluntarily. Only when apprehended and coerced into treatment do they reluctantly obtain professional help. Once in therapy, many voyeurs are still unwilling to change. The preferred method of treatment for voyeurism includes behavioral techniques similar to those used for treating exhibitionists (Schwartz, 1994). For example, the voyeur may be told to imagine that he is apprehended and publicly humiliated as he is engaging in his voyeuristic behaviors. Therapy might also focus on self-esteem issues, because a poor self-image is thought to contribute to a predilection for voyeuristic activity (Rhoads, 1989).

Theories and Treatment of Paraphilias

In the preceding sections, you have read about the specific theories and treatment that relate to each of the paraphilias. Although each condition warrants an individualized approach, there are some general principles that apply across the board. Most paraphilias have their roots in childhood experiences, and they emerge during adolescent years, as sexual forces within the body intensify. Once established, the paraphilia tends to be chronic.

One of the most widely respected researchers in the area of human sexuality, John Money (Money & Ehrhardt, 1973/1996) believes that paraphilias are due to distorted "lovemaps." According to Money, a **lovemap** is the representation of an individual's sexual fantasies and preferred practices. Lovemaps are formed early in life, during what Money considers to be a critical period of development: the late childhood years, when an individual first begins to discover and test ideas regarding sexuality. "Misprints" in this process can result in the establishment of sexual habits and practices that deviate from the norm. A paraphilia, according to this view, is due to a lovemap gone awry. The individual is, in a sense, programmed to act out fantasies that are socially unacceptable and potentially harmful. Similarly, other experts describe paraphilias as courtship disorders, particularly those involving voyeurism and frotteurism (Freund, Seto, & Kuban, 1997), in which individuals have disturbed views of appropriate sexual behavior in relationships.

Although some theorists have suggested that individuals who become paraphilic are biologically predisposed to these behaviors through genetic, hormonal, or neurological abnormalities, as we saw in connection with pedophilia, a biological explanation alone is considered insufficient. According to a behavioral approach, one or more learning events have taken place in a person's childhood involving a conditioned response of sexual pleasure with an inappropriate stimulus object. Over time, the individual has become compulsively driven to pursue the gratification (reinforcement) associated with the object or experience. Often a sense of power accompanies this gratification. In other words, the voyeur experiences both sexual excitation and power when he is "peeping." Similarly, the exhibitionist, the frotteur, and the pedophile can satisfy both sexual and self-esteem needs through "successful" experiences with the object of desire.

As we have seen, the treatment of people with paraphilias is particularly difficult, because these individuals are often reluctant to give up the pleasurable behavior or are too ashamed to seek help. Biological, psychological, and sociocultural

Voyeurism

MINI-CASE

Edward is a university senior who lives in a crowded dormitory complex. On most evenings, he sneaks around in the bushes, looking for a good vantage point from which to gaze into the windows of women students. Using binoculars, he is able to find at least one room in which a woman is undressing. The thrill of watching this unsuspecting victim brings Edward to the peak of excitement as he masturbates. Edward has been engaging in this behavior for the past 3 years, dating back to an incident when he walked past a window and inadvertently saw a naked woman. This event aroused him to such a degree that he became increasingly compelled to seek out the same excitement again and again.

- As with the case of Bruce (the frotteur), Edward's disorder involves a target who is unaware of his behavior. Why is voyeurism, like frotteurism, considered a paraphilia?

- How does Edward's behavior compare with that of a person who derives gratification from watching adult movies with explicit sex?

DIAGNOSTIC FEATURES

- For a period lasting at least 6 months, people with this condition have recurrent, intense sexually arousing fantasies, sexual urges, or behaviors involving the act of observing unsuspecting people who are naked, in the process of undressing, or engaging in sexual activity.

- The fantasies, sexual urges, or behaviors cause significant distress or impairment.

interventions have been used in various combinations for these treatments. In the biological sphere, as we mentioned in our discussion of pedophilia, there are several forms of intervention, some much more extreme than others. The more commonly used medical interventions involve the prescription of pharmacological agents, such as antidepressant medications and hormones. Rarely would a clinician limit treatment to a medical intervention, however. Rather, psychological and sociocultural components would play very important roles. In the psychological realm, the most commonly used techniques are behavioral and cognitive-behavioral. In the sociocultural sphere, clinicians often look for ways to involve the client in group therapy, in which other people with similar problems share their experiences and their efforts to achieve self-control. Furthermore, couple and family therapy may be recommended, with the goal of obtaining support and assistance from the individuals who are closest to the client.

Gender Identity Disorders

The term **gender identity** refers to the individual's self-perception as a male or female. However, an individual's gender identity may or may not match the **assigned** (or **biological**) **sex** that is recorded on the birth certificate. Do not confuse these notions with the concept of **gender role,** which refers to a person's behaviors and attitudes that are indicative of maleness or femaleness in one's society.

Sexual orientation is the degree to which a person is erotically attracted to members of the same or opposite sex. Most people have a clear orientation to have sexual activity with members of the other sex, but some are attracted to members of the same sex, and yet others are attracted to members of both sexes. Constancy of sexual orientation is typical but not universal; some people change over time and due to circumstances.

Characteristics of Gender Identity Disorders

A **gender identity disorder** is a condition involving a discrepancy between an individual's assigned sex and the person's gender identity. People with gender identity disorders experience a strong and persistent cross-gender identification, which causes feelings of discomfort and a sense of inappropriateness about their assigned gender. Individuals with this condition have intense feelings of distress and usually have adjustment problems in social, occupational, and other areas of personal functioning. You may have heard the more commonly used term **transsexualism,** which also refers to this phenomenon in which a person has an inner feeling of belonging to the other sex. Some people with gender identity disorders wish to live as members of the other sex, and they act and dress accordingly. Unlike individuals with transvestic fetishism, these people do not derive sexual gratification from cross-dressing.

A girl with gender identity disorder may refuse to acknowledge that she possesses a girl's body and, instead, insists that she will grow a penis. She may express this rejection of her female sex in various behaviors, such as standing

Sister Mary Elizabeth Clark, formerly Joanna Michelle Clark, and before that Michael Clark, is an Episcopalian nun. Clark, also a former Navy flier and Army WAC, who took the veil and vows of poverty, celibacy, and obedience, stated that she has felt close to God since she was 8 years old, but through the wrong body. Clark became a woman in 1975.

while she urinates and refusing to have anything to do with normative feminine behavior or dress. When asked to wear a new dress, she may become angry and resentful and may choose to avoid social situations in which customs would dictate wearing feminine clothing. Similarly, a boy with gender identity disorder may disdain the fact that he is a male with a penis, and he may push it between his legs to make believe it is not part of his body. He may have an aversion to wearing pants and, instead, be attracted to more traditionally feminine clothing. Rather than play stereotypically male games, he may prefer, for example, to play house with other children and insist that he play the role of a female. Keep in mind that this is a profoundly experienced psychological disorder. It does not refer to what some would call transient "tomboy" or "sissy" behaviors.

Distress over their assigned sex is usually evident before children with gender identity disorder reach their fourth birthday. When the child begins school, parents may become increasingly concerned about the ways in which their child acts differently from peers. For many of these children, the overt cross-gender behaviors become less evident as they grow into adolescence, but the disorder persists as the individual struggles with an ongoing feeling of inappropriateness about being male or female along with recurrent fantasies or cross-dressing behavior. In time, many individuals with gender identity disorder find themselves feeling deeply depressed because of the "prison" in which they must live. They may become increasingly isolated and may involve themselves only in activities in which gender has no bearing.

Researchers on the topic of gender identity disorder have devoted tremendous effort to gauging the developmental age during which this condition is first evident. The determination of dissatisfaction about gender is complicated by the fact that many young children act and speak in ways suggesting that they would prefer to be the other sex. In fact, there is not a great gender difference in such expressions; if anything, in normal children girls show a greater likelihood than boys of wishing to be the opposite sex. It is very interesting to note, however, that gender-conflicted boys are seven times more likely than gender-conflicted girls to be referred for professional help. This difference is attributed to the lower tolerance in society for boys dressing like girls (Bradley & Zucker, 1997) . Even as gender-dysphoric individuals grow older, females report fewer emotional problems, perhaps because it is more acceptable for women to act and dress in stereotypically masculine ways than it is for men to act and dress in stereotypically feminine ways. Consequently, it is not surprising that men are more likely than women to seek professional psychological help (American Psychiatric Association, 1994).

Complicating efforts to understand gender identity disorder is the variable of sexual orientation. There is a strong relationship between childhood cross-gender behavior and later homosexual orientation in men and women (Bailey & Kucker, 1995). It is important to realize, however, that not all homosexual men and women have a history of cross-gender behavior in their childhood. The relationship between gender identity disorder and adult sexual orientation becomes even fuzzier when the issue is raised as to whether a person with gender identity disorder has a homosexual or heterosexual orientation. A transsexual individual whose body is female and whose gender identity is male would reject the label of homosexual just because of an attraction to females. Rather, this person would want to be considered heterosexual, because the object of sexual desire is the "other sex." To deal with this issue, clinicians specify the gender of those to whom people with gender identity disorder are attracted: males, females, both, or neither.

Theories and Treatment of Gender Identity Disorders

The causes of gender identity disorder are not well understood, but, as in many of our discussions so far, biological, psychological, and sociocultural factors seem to play important roles. Biological research has focused on the effects of hormones that affect the development of the fetus during the prenatal period of life. Thus, females exposed to increased levels of androgens in the uterus are more likely to display stereotypically male gender role behaviors during childhood (Collaer & Hines, 1995). Based on the assumption that children's play patterns are af-

fected by hormonal factors, there is additional evidence that supports the biological approach to gender identity disorder. In one study, the males in treatment for gender identity disorder were described by their mothers as having been less likely to engage in so-called rough and tumble play than their peers. The girls in treatment for gender identity disorder were described as more likely to prefer rough play (Bradley & Zucker, 1997).

Carrying biological inquiry in another direction, researchers have been trying to understand some fascinating findings about the relationship between birth order and the gender of siblings in individuals with gender identity disorder. For some reason, boys with this condition have a later birth order in the family than do boys in matched control groups (Blanchard & Bogaert, 1996), and they are more likely to have more brothers than sisters (Blanchard et al., 1996). The precise ways in which these variables interact with gender identity remain unclear.

In contrast to the big-picture characteristics of birth order and sibling structure, researchers have also studied more subtle characteristics that differentiate individuals with gender identity disorder. Boys with gender identity disorder are acutely sensitive to various sensory stimuli and to the emotional expressiveness of their parents. Once again, it is difficult to understand how these characteristics influence gender identity, but somehow a vulnerability to high arousal and a sensitivity to parental affect are important factors in the development of gender identity disorder (Bradley & Zucker, 1997).

In the psychological realm, the picture is even murkier, as researchers have sorted through many hypotheses. In one avenue of study, investigators wondered about the importance of a parent's preference for a child of the other gender. There are no data to confirm that a parent's wish to have a girl can cause a boy to develop gender identity disorder (or vice versa), but there are some interesting findings that suggest that, for some mothers of boys with gender identity disorder, disappointment with the birth of yet another son, rather than a daughter, may negatively influenced her relationship with the boy (Bradley & Zucker, 1997). This is an interesting finding, but certainly not sufficient to explain the development of gender identity disorder. Researchers will continue to study other factors, such as early attachment experiences, parents' unintentional reinforcement of cross-gender behavior, and the powerful inner image that can result in which an individual develops a cross-gender identity.

Although sociocultural theories would not be sufficient for explaining the development of gender identity disorder, it is important to consider various ways in which American society idealizes men and women according to certain stereotypical variables. An impressionable child who is struggling with confusion that is biologically and psychologically rooted may be drawn to a resolution of the confusion by idealizing the attributes of attractive and successful members of the opposite sex.

Clinical work with individuals with gender identity disorder depends greatly on the age of the individual. Psychotherapy involving a child distressed about gender might involve the discouragement of cross-gender behavior and encouragement of the development of same-sex skills and friendships. The intervention would be primarily with the parents, if the identified

Gender Identity Disorder

MINI-CASE

Dale describes himself as a woman living in a man's body. His memories back to the age of 4 are of feeling discomfort with his assigned sex. When he was a young child, people often mistook him for a girl, because his mannerisms, style of play, and clothes were stereotypically feminine. He was glad he had an ambiguous name, and throughout adolescence he led others to believe he really was a girl. Schoolmates teased him at times, but this did not bother him, because he took pride in his feminine attributes. Dale's parents became increasingly alarmed, and they sent him to a psychologist when he was 15 years old. The psychologist recognized that Dale had a gender identity disorder, and she explained to Dale that he could not pursue sex reassignment surgery until adulthood, because a surgeon would insist that Dale have the maturity and life experience necessary for making such a dramatic decision. Now, at the age of 25, Dale is about to follow through on his wish to have the body of a woman and is consulting sex reassignment specialists at a major medical school to prepare for the surgery. After an initial evaluation, Dale was told that he needed to begin a presurgery evaluation process that would last for at least a year and a half. During this time, he would live publicly as a woman. This would involve dressing as a woman and changing all documentation that referred to him as a male (such as voting records, credit card applications, and driver's license). He would have to enter psychotherapy to evaluate his psychological health and readiness for surgery. Dale also had to begin taking hormones that would cause him to develop female secondary sex characteristics. After successfully completing the evaluation process, Dale would be able to enter the next phase of the sex reassignment process in which his physical characteristics would start to be transformed.

■ How does Dale's gender identity disorder differ from transvestic fetishism?

■ What aspects of Dale's case would make him an acceptable candidate for sex reassignment surgery?

DIAGNOSTIC FEATURES

● People with this condition have a strong and persistent cross-gender identification that is far greater than a desire for perceived cultural advantages associated with the opposite sex.

● In children, the disorder is evident by four of the following: (1) they repeatedly state their desire to be the other sex, or insist that they already are; (2) boys prefer cross-dressing, while girls insist on wearing only stereotypical masculine clothing; (3) they have a strong and persistent preference for cross-sex roles in make-believe play, or persistent fantasies of being the other sex; (4) they have an intense desire to participate in the games and activities stereotypically associated with the other sex; and (5) they have a strong preference for playmates of the other sex.

● In adolescents and adults, this disturbance is manifested by such symptoms as a stated desire to be the other sex, frequent passing as the other sex, and the conviction that he or she has the typical feelings and reactions of a person of the other sex.

● An individual with this condition has persistent discomfort with his or her sex or feels a sense of inappropriateness in the gender role of his or her biological sex.

● The disturbance is not concurrent with a physical condition involving ambiguous genitals.

● The disturbance causes significant distress or impairment.

● Sexual attraction may be to males, females, both, or neither.

---

client is a very young child, with an emphasis on helping the child develop greater self-value as either a boy or a girl. For older children, the clinician would deal more directly with the client's cross-gender behavior and fantasy, as well as other distressing psychological experiences, such as low self-esteem and fear of familial and peer rejection (Bradley & Zucker, 1997). Clinicians working with gender-disordered adults approach the therapy in much the same way they approach therapy with clients who are very dissatisfied with their lives. They help clients understand the causes of their distress, focusing on possible biological, psychological, and sociocultural origins. Most important, they provide support and help clients with gender identity disorder learn how to live with these feelings and experiences.

A small minority of individuals with gender identity disorder seek sex reassignment surgery; for these people, the term *transsexual* is appropriate in that they are "crossing over" to the other sex. In this process, individuals confront several complex issues. First, the procedure is available at only a few medical facilities and can cost hundreds of thousands of dollars. Second, the few surgeons who carry out these procedures insist that the individual complete a lengthy course of psychotherapy and a comprehensive psychological assessment prior to being accepted for surgery. Along with this, the individual must have lived as a member of the other sex during the evaluation period; this includes changes in legal name, clothing, and self-presentation. Third, and perhaps most significant, the surgery is very complicated, and the physical results are never perfect. Female-to-male transsexuals cannot expect to have a penis that looks or functions normally. For example, a constructed penis may require artificial inflation to become erect. Although the male-to-female surgery is less complicated, there are still some risks, such as the possibility of the constructed vagina closing up following surgery. In addition, individuals also need hormonal supplements to facilitate the change and to maintain the secondary sex characteristics of the new gender (Asscheman & Gooren, 1992; Cohen-Kettenis & Gooren, 1992). Finally, although surgery changes a person's genitals, it cannot give a person the childbearing capability of the newly acquired gender.

Most studies evaluating the effectiveness of reassignment surgery provide evidence of psychological improvement following the surgery (Cohen-Kettenis & van Goozen, 1997). The people who are dissatisfied after treatment appear to be the male-to-female individuals who were disappointed with unalterable bodily characteristics, such as large hands and feet, the persistence of the Adam's apple, and the quality of their voice (Rakic, Starcevic, Maric, & Kelin, 1996).

The level of improvement in the lives of these people depends on a number of factors. First, satisfaction is usually greater when the transition is from female-to-male rather than male-to-female. Researchers are not sure why there is a difference, but they consider the possibility that men who become women may be surprised and troubled when they encounter some of the disadvantages that women experience in society as a result of sexist attitudes. Second, people who are better adjusted prior to the surgery are more likely to experience a favorable outcome. This is especially true if they encounter little difficulty in being accepted as a person of their newly assumed gender (Kuiper & Cohen-Kettenis, 1988). Third, the strength of the individual's commitment and identification as a member of the other sex prior to surgery is important, because this provides the motivation and determination to carry through with the procedures. Fourth, the quality of the surgery itself is related to successful adjustment. Individuals who receive high-quality surgical care with anatomically convincing results are likely to have an easier time adapting to their lives as members of the opposite gender (Green et al., 1990; Rakic et al., 1996).

Despite the controversy surrounding this complicated and costly surgery, sex reassignment appears to be a valid alternative for individuals with severe gender identity disorder (Snaith, Tarsh, & Reid, 1993). Selection criteria have been developed to ensure that individuals seeking sex reassignment are appropriate candidates for the surgery (Cote & Wilchesky, 1996), and psychotherapy can assist the person to resolve other psychological problems and to adjust to the new gender role prior to surgery. A possible complication following surgery is that the person may have expected the operation to resolve many other life problems; psychotherapy can be useful at this point to help the person develop a more balanced outlook about his or her postoperative future. Finally, the growth and acceptance of the gender identity movement may help individuals adjust and live more happily in the context of a supportive and understanding community.

■ Sexual Dysfunctions

The disorders we will discuss in this section are very different from the paraphilias and gender identity disorder in that they are not considered deviant behaviors, and they involve no victimization of others. The term **sexual dysfunction** refers to an abnormality in an individual's sexual responsiveness and reactions.

The prevalence of problems with sexual performance has been documented by recent research in which investigators surveying adults aged 18 to 59 years found that 43 percent of women and 31 percent of men reported symptons of sexual dysfunction (Laumann, Paik, & Rosen, 1999).

Characteristics of Sexual Dysfunctions

Sexual dysfunctions are defined by the individual, often in terms of an intimate relationship and almost invariably in the context of cultural expectations and values about what constitutes normal sexual functioning. There is no one "correct" pattern of sexual activity; what one individual considers dysfunctional, another may regard as healthy and normal. Unfortunately, people may regard themselves as having a sexual dysfunction without being aware of the extent to which their behavior falls within the range of normal behavior. For example, in one study that queried people about reaching orgasm, three quarters of the men interviewed reported that they always reach orgasm during sexual intercourse, whereas the proportion of women was nearer to one fourth (Laumann et al., 1994). Looking at these figures in another way, does this mean that the remaining one fourth of men and three fourths of women are "abnormal"? Do they have a sexual dysfunction? An important factor to keep in mind as you read about each of the disorders in this section is whether or not a person feels distressed about the behavior.

Another feature of sexual dysfunctions that will become evident as you read the clinical descriptions and case histories is that sometimes sexual dysfunctions are signs or symptoms of problems in a person's life that do not directly pertain to sexuality. For example, a person who is very upset about job-related stresses or family problems may develop sexual performance problems. At times, people are not even aware of the connection between the sexual problem and other life stresses. On the other hand, some sexual problems are more clearly connected to problems within a particular relationship or to experiences in the person's past in which the foundation of a sexual problem was established. Clinicians refer to several distinctions in characterizing the nature of a sexual dysfunction. First, they question whether a dysfunction is attributable to a psychological factor, such as depression or relationship problems, or is due to a combination of psychological factors and physical factors, such as illness or substance use. They also distinguish between lifelong and acquired types, as well as between situational and generalized sexual dysfunctions. A lifelong dysfunction has been present since the beginning of active sexual functioning, whereas an acquired problem has developed following a period of normal functioning. Situational dysfunctions occur with only certain types of sexual stimulation, situations, or partners, whereas generalized dysfunctions are not limited.

Although our discussion refers to disturbances in heterosexual functioning, it is important to realize that lesbians and gay men can also be affected by these disorders. Clinicians and researchers are increasing their attention to understanding and treating lesbians and gay men with sexual dysfunctions, but most of the publications to date have focused on heterosexuals.

To understand sexual dysfunctions, it is helpful to gain a perspective on the factors that contribute to healthy sexual functioning. Masters and Johnson (Masters & Johnson, 1966, 1970), in their pioneering research on human sexuality, systematically observed the sexual responses of men and women under controlled laboratory conditions. Their research was widely publicized and helped dispel many myths regarding sexuality. For example, their observational studies of women provided more or less definitive proof that there is no physiological difference between vaginal and clitoral orgasms. This finding vindicated those who had disagreed with Freud's vigorous assertions that they differ. Not only did Masters and Johnson provide a more scientific basis for understanding sexual dysfunctions, but they also took a more humanistic approach to these disorders, treating them, insofar as possible, in the context of the interpersonal relationships in which they often develop.

The work of Masters and Johnson is not without its flaws, however. One criticism is that the laboratory setting they used was too artificial to provide a valid indicator of sexual functioning in naturalistic settings. Other criticisms are based on the selectivity of the sample. Think about whether you would want to participate in this kind of research. Every aspect of a subject's sexual responses was monitored via electrophysiological recording devices, devices that obviously would be intrusive and uncomfortable. Even more to the point, the participants in this research had to be willing to allow a team of male and female researchers to observe them engaging in sexual acts. In addition, they had to be motivated enough to undergo the effort and expense of the therapy process. They also had to be willing to disclose highly personal details about their lives and sexual idiosyncrasies. Masters and Johnson have also been criticized for what some regard as a sex bias in some of their diagnostic criteria that tends to pathologize women who have few or no orgasms. Despite these limitations, the work of Masters and Johnson has received widespread recognition and continues to be used as the foundation for understanding the sexual dysfunctions.

Masters and Johnson identified four phases of the sexual response cycle: arousal, plateau, orgasm, and resolution. During the arousal stage, the individual's sexual interest heightens, and the body prepares for sexual intercourse (vaginal lubrication in the female, penile erection in the male). Sexual excitement continues to build during the plateau phase, and during the orgasm phase the individual experiences muscular contractions in the genital area that are associated with intense sensations of pleasure. The resolution phase is a period of return to a physiologically normal state. People differ in their typical patterns of sexual activity, in that some people progress more readily through the phases and others progress at a slower pace. Not every sexual encounter necessarily involves all phases, either; an individual may, for example, become sexually aroused but not have an orgasm.

Sexual dysfunctions are associated with the arousal and orgasm phases, as well as with a person's overall level of sexual

Virginia Johnson and William Masters brought into the open the discussion of human sexual functioning and dysfunctions.

desire (see Table 8.2). Some people with sexual dysfunctions have little or no interest in sex; others experience a delay in a particular phase of sexual arousal or do not become aroused at all. Others may become highly aroused but are unable to experience the sexual release of orgasm. Still other people proceed too rapidly through the phases from arousal to orgasm and, therefore, feel that sexual relations lack the emotional meaning associated with a more relaxed approach. In some cases, an individual's partner may feel distressed over what seems like unacceptable deviations from a desired pattern of activity. Yet other sexual dysfunctions are the result of the experience of pain rather than pleasure during a sexual encounter.

You may wonder where to draw the line between ordinary variations in human sexual responsiveness and the pattern of psychological disorder represented by a sexual dysfunction. Sexual dysfunctions involve persistent and recurrent symptoms. To illustrate this point, consider two examples. Six weeks after the birth of her third child, Heather finds that she cannot regain her former interest in having sexual relations with her husband. At her sister's advice, Heather and her husband take a 5-day vacation during which Heather's sister will care for the baby. Although she still experiences occasional fatigue that dulls her sexual appetite, Heather regains her previous interest in sexual activity. She does not have a disorder because her symptoms are temporary and nonrecurrent. Treatment would not necessarily be indicated, other than her sister's common-sense advice.

Contrast Heather's situation with that of Christine, whose desire for sexual relations with her husband has dwindled for the past 5 years, until it is now very infrequent. Christine eventually seeks treatment when she realizes that, unless things change, her husband will give up on her and find sexual gratifi-

cation elsewhere. Christine's loss of sexual desire has been persistent and is considered dysfunctional.

It is important to realize that, at times, other psychological problems are the basis of sexual difficulties. For example, abnormally low sexual desire in someone who is depressed would not be considered grounds for diagnosing a sexual dysfunction but, instead, would be regarded as part of the depression.

It is also important to keep in mind that sexual dysfunctions can be physically as well as psychologically based and that often there is an interaction between physical and psychological factors. Many people with sexual dysfunctions, and even some professionals treating them, are quick to conclude that all sexual problems must be emotionally caused; they fail to consider that a sexual problem may be associated with physical illness, medication, or general level of health. For example, diabetes mellitus is a medical condition that affects millions of people in the world and is known to cause sexual dysfunction, particularly erectile problems in men (Thomas & LoPiccolo, 1994). Without an understanding of this connection and a comprehensive medical assessment, a clinician could draw an erroneous conclusion that a man's sexual problem is due to emotional or interpersonal causes.

One final point about sexual dysfunctions is that sexual problems can begin fairly innocuously but then develop into something more serious because of anxiety about the problem. For example, Roger, who is preoccupied with work problems, experiences difficulty one night in getting an erection with his partner, and he becomes worried that he is becoming impotent. This concern may impair Roger's performance the next time he is sexually intimate, making it even more difficult the time after that. This process may soon escalate into a dysfunction. Masters and Johnson use the term

Table 8.2

Phases of Human Sexual Response Cycle and Associated Disorders

Phase	Male	Female
Sexual desire		
Normal response	Interest in sexual activity	Interest in sexual activity
Sexual dysfunctions	Hyperactive sexual desire disorder, sexual aversion disorder	Hyperactive sexual desire disorder, sexual aversion disorder
Sexual arousal		
Normal response	Penile erection	Lubrication and swelling of vagina
Sexual dysfunctions	Male erectile disorder	Female sexual arousal disorder
Orgasm		
Normal response	Feeling of inevitability of orgasm, followed by rhythmic contractions of prostate and urethra and expulsion of semen	Rhythmic contractions of vagina and uterus
Sexual dysfunctions	Male orgasmic disorder, premature ejaculation	Female orgasmic disorder

Hypoactive Sexual Desire Disorder

MINI-CASE

With the pressures of managing a full-time advertising job and raising 3-year-old twins, Carol says that she has "no time or energy" for sexual relations with her husband, Bob. In fact, they have not been sexually intimate since the birth of their children. Initially, Bob tried to be understanding and to respect the fact that Carol was recovering from a very difficult pregnancy and delivery. As the months went by, however, he became increasingly impatient and critical. The more he pressured Carol for sexual closeness, the more angry and depressed she became. Carol feels that she loves Bob, but she has no interest in sexuality. She does not think about sex and can't imagine ever being sexual again. She is saddened by the effect that this change has had on her marriage but feels little motivation to try to change.

■ In light of the fact that Carol does not feel especially distressed, why would she be regarded as having a sexual dysfunction?

■ If you were a clinician to whom Carol came for help, what kind of assessment would you conduct?

DIAGNOSTIC FEATURES

● People with this condition have persistent or recurrently deficient sexual fantasies and desire for sexual activity, with consideration given to factors that affect sexual functioning, such as age and the context of the person's life.

● The disturbance causes significant distress or interpersonal difficulty.

● The disturbance is not accounted for by another disorder, medical condition, or substance.

● The disturbance may be lifelong or acquired; generalized or situational; and due to psychological factors or a combination of psychological and physical factors.

spectatoring to refer to the experience in which the individual feels unduly self-conscious during sexual activity, as if evaluating and monitoring his or her performance during the sexual encounter.

Hypoactive Sexual Desire Disorder

The individual with **hypoactive sexual desire disorder** has an abnormally low level of interest in sexual activity. The individual neither seeks out actual sexual relationships, imagines having them, nor has the wish for a more active sex life. The distress associated with this disorder is usually in the realm of intimate relationships, which may be difficult to sustain. For some individuals, the condition applies to all potential sexual expression, while for others it is situational, perhaps occurring only in the context of a particular relationship. It is quite likely that people develop this disorder as the result of other psychological difficulties, such as depression, prior sexual trauma, poor body image or self-esteem, interpersonal hostility, or relationship power struggles. In some cases, the disorder may develop in association with a preexisting sexual dysfunction. For example, a man who lacks ejaculatory control may lose interest in sex because of embarrassment and anxiety about his problem.

Individuals with lifelong forms of hypoactive sexual desire disorder lack any interest in sexuality from the onset of puberty. Such cases are less common, however, than those cases of individuals who develop this condition in adulthood following a period of stress or interpersonal difficulties.

Sexual Aversion Disorder

Sexual aversion disorder is characterized by an active dislike and avoidance of genital contact with a sexual partner, which causes personal distress or interpersonal problems. The individual may be interested in sex and may enjoy sexual fantasies but is repulsed by the notion of sexual activity with another person. For some, the reaction is generalized and involves a disdain for all sexually intimate behavior, including kissing and hugging. For others, the aversion is to specific facets of interpersonal sexuality, such as vaginal penetration or genital odors. Reactions range from moderate anxiety reactions to panic attacks. People with sexual aversion disorder are distressed by the disdain they feel about sexual behavior, and they find themselves feeling lonely and resistant to entering into intimate relationships. If already in a close relationship, they usually encounter discord with their partner because of their disturbed reaction to the prospect of sexual intercourse.

Masters and Johnson (Masters, Johnson, & Kolodny, 1982) specify four primary causes of this disorder: (1) severely negative parental sex attitudes, (2) a history of sexual trauma, such as rape or incest, (3) a pattern of constant sexual pressuring by a partner in a long-term relationship, and (4) gender identity confusion in men. In the typical case, the individual has sexual activity only once or twice a year, if that often, and this is a source of strain in a long-term, monogamous relationship.

Sexual Aversion Disorder

MINI-CASE

Howard is a 25 year-old law school student who had done very well academically, but worries often about a sexual problem that has plagued him since adolescence. Although he yearns to be in an intimate relationship with a woman, he has steered away from dating because he dreads the prospect of being sexually intimate. Although he jokingly tells others, and himself, that he is asexual, he secretly acknowledges that he is disgusted by the idea of anyone touching his genitals. He feels sexual desire, and has no difficulty masturbating to orgasm. Although he feels attracted to women, the thoughts of sexual closeness cause him to feel anxious, distressed, and at times even nauseous. Howard dates the origin of his problem to an incident that took place when he was 14 years old when he was alone in a movie theater. Next to him sat a middle-aged woman who seductively pulled Howard's hand under her dress and rubbed her genitals with it. Shocked and repulsed, Howard ran out of the theater, carrying with him a powerful image and experience that would prove to be a lasting obstacle to sexual closeness.

■ How does Howard's sexual aversion disorder differ from a sexual arousal disorder?

■ What kind of behavioral techniques might a clinician recommend as part of the treatment plan for Howard's sexual aversion disorder?

DIAGNOSTIC FEATURES

● People with this disorder experience recurrent extreme aversion to, and avoidance of genital contact with a sexual partner.

● The disturbance causes significant distress or interpersonal difficulty.

● The disturbance is not accounted for by another disorder.

● The disturbance may be lifelong or acquired; generalized or situational; and due to psychological factors or a combination of psychological and physical factors.

Female Sexual Arousal Disorder

A woman with **female sexual arousal disorder** experiences the persistent or recurrent inability to attain or maintain the normal lubrication-swelling response of sexual excitement during sexual activity. The result is personal distress or interpersonal difficulty with her partner. The desire for sexual activity remains present, though, and some women with female sexual arousal disorder are able to have orgasms, especially when their clitoris is stimulated intensely, as with a vibrator. It is during normal intercourse that their bodies become unresponsive, and they do not experience the normal physiological reaction of vaginal swelling and lubrication. Consequently, penile penetration may cause considerable discomfort, and possibly pain.

Male Erectile Disorder

Male erectile disorder involves the recurrent partial or complete failure to attain or maintain an erection during sexual activity, causing the man to feel distressed or to encounter interpersonal problems in his intimate relationship. (The term *impotence* was formerly used to refer to this disorder, but it is now considered inappropriate because it implies a defect in an individual's personality.)

Like women who experience female sexual arousal disorder, men with erectile disorder retain their interest in sex. Some men can ejaculate with a flaccid penis, although their level of pleasure is less intense than they would experience with an erection. Because their erectile difficulty causes emotional distress and embarrassment, men with this disorder may avoid sex with a partner altogether. Some men experience this difficulty from the outset of every sexual encounter; other men are able to attain an erection but lose it when they attempt penetration, or soon afterwards. What is interesting, and medically important, is the fact that men with this disorder usually have no erectile difficulty while masturbating.

As with other sexual dysfunctions, this condition can be lifelong or acquired, generalized or specific to one partner. For those men with acquired erectile disorder, approximately 15 to 30 percent will find that the problem goes away in time, often as the result of a change in the intensity or quality of a relationship.

Female Orgasmic Disorder

Inability to achieve orgasm, or a distressing delay in the achievement of orgasm, constitutes **female orgasmic disorder**. This condition causes considerable personal distress or interpersonal

Female Sexual Arousal Disorder

MINI-CASE

Permella is a 40-year-old married woman who has been frustrated for the past 5 years because of sexual non-responsiveness. She describes her relationship with her husband in positive terms, and says that they love to caress and spend intimate time together. However, their positive feelings typically turn negative when they attempt intercourse. Permella states, "My mind is turned on, but my body doesn't respond." She elaborates by explaining that her vagina remains dry and uncomfortable throughout the sexual act. Although her husband manages penetration when using a genital lubricant, Permella does not find the experience to be pleasurable. She wants more from these sexual encounters, and has consulted her gynecologist about the problem.

- What kinds of questions might Permella's gynecologist ask in order to determine the extent of physical factors that may be playing a role in Permella's sexual arousal disorder?

- How does Permella's condition differ from hypoactive sexual desire disorder?

DIAGNOSTIC FEATURES

- Women with this condition experience persistent or recurrent inability to attain, or to maintain adequate genital lubrication and swelling through or during sexual activity.

- The disturbance causes significant distress or interpersonal difficulty.

- The disturbance is not better accounted for by another disorder, medical condition, or substance.

- The disturbance may be lifelong or acquired; generalized or situational; and due to psychological factors or a combination of psychological and physical factors.

Male Erectile Disorder

MINI-CASE

Brian is 34 years old and has been dating the same woman for more than a year. This is his first serious relationship and the first person with whom he has been sexually intimate. During the past 6 months, they have frequently tried to have intercourse, but each time they have become frustrated by Brian's inability to maintain an erection for more than a few minutes. Every time this happens, Brian becomes very upset, despite his girlfriend's reassurance that things will work out better next time. His anxiety level heightens every time he thinks about the fact that he is in his mid-thirties, sexually active for the first time in his life, and encountering such frustrating difficulties. He fears he is "impotent" and will never be able to have a normal sex life.

- To what extent do you think that Brian's anxiety over his sexual performance causes his erectile dysfunction?

- How do you think Brian might try to resolve this problem?

DIAGNOSTIC FEATURES

- Men with this condition experience persistent or recurrent inability to attain or to maintain an adequate erection until completion of sexual activity.

- The disturbance causes significant distress or interpersonal difficulty.

- The disturbance is not better accounted for by another disorder, medical condition, or substance.

- The disturbance may be lifelong or acquired; generalized or situational; and due to psychological factors or a combination of psychological and physical factors.

difficulty. Some women are unable to achieve orgasm in all situations; for others, the problem is situational. They may be able to reach orgasm by means of self-stimulation or with a partner engaging in sexual behaviors other than intercourse.

For many years, women with inhibited female orgasm and female sexual arousal disorder were labeled with the offensive and inappropriate term *frigid,* which implied a flawed personality style. To understand this disorder, it is important to realize that the female orgasm spans a range of experiences. Kaplan (1986) describes how at one extreme are a small number of women who can achieve orgasm merely by engaging in erotic fantasies, stimulation of the breasts, or kissing. Then there are the approximately 20 to 30 percent who are able to reach orgasm through intercourse alone, without direct stimulation of the clitoris. Some women can reach orgasm during intercourse, but only if assisted by manual stimulation of the clitoris. Next are those women who are unable to reach orgasm with a partner but who are able to stimulate themselves to the point of orgasm. At the far end of the continuum are the approximately 8 percent of women who have never had an orgasm at all. Kaplan points out that the demarcation between "normal" and "pathological" on this continuum is debatable, although most clinicians would regard individuals in the last two groups as having sexual dysfunctions.

Male Orgasmic Disorder

Male orgasmic disorder, also known as inhibited male orgasm, involves a specific difficulty in the orgasm stage. As with its female counterpart, this disorder may be generalized or situational. Men with generalized orgasmic disorder find it impossible to reach orgasm in any situation, whereas men with situational orgasmic disorder have difficulty in certain situations, such as intercourse, but not during masturbation.

The most common complaint of men with this disorder is that, though fully aroused during intercourse, they find it impossible to reach orgasm with a partner at the point of desired release.

This disorder ranges from mild situational delays in ejaculating to total inability to reach orgasm. At the mild end of the spectrum are men who take an exceptionally long time before they are able to ejaculate. Then there is a group of men who require added stimulation, either from a partner or themselves, in order to reach orgasm. Perhaps they can reach orgasm only when orally and manually stimulated. Next on the continuum are men who find it possible to reach orgasm only during masturbation. At the far extreme are men who find it impossible to reach orgasm regardless of the situation. In each of these cases, the man's concern over the problem or interpersonal difficulties that emerge in his close relationship result in psychological distress.

Premature Ejaculation

The man with **premature ejaculation** reaches orgasm in a sexual encounter long before he wishes to, perhaps even prior to penetration, and therefore feels little or no sexual satisfaction. The man may enjoy sexual intimacy and attraction to his partner, but as soon as he reaches a certain point of excitement he loses control. Usually, premature ejaculation occurs with all his partners, because the problem is that he has not learned volun-

---

Female Orgasmic Disorder

MINI-CASE

Like many of her friends, when Margaret was a teenager, she often wondered what intercourse and orgasm would feel like. When she later became sexually active in college, Margaret realized that she was probably still missing something, since she did not feel "rockets going off" as she had imagined. In fact, she never could experience orgasm when she was with a man in any kind of sexual activity. When Margaret fell in love with Howard, she fervently hoped that things would improve. However, even though he made her feel more sensual pleasure than anyone else she had known, her response to him always stopped just short of climax. She approached every sexual encounter with anxiety, and, afterwards, tended to feel depressed and inadequate. To avoid making Howard worry, however, Margaret decided it would be better to "fake" orgasm than to be honest with him. After 5 years together, she still has not told him that she is not experiencing orgasms, and she feels too embarrassed to seek professional help, despite her ongoing distress.

■ What factors do you think prevent Margaret from telling Howard about her problem?

■ How might Margaret go about resolving her orgasmic disorder?

DIAGNOSTIC FEATURES

● Women with this condition experience persistent or recurrent delay in, or absence of, orgasm following a normal phase of sexual excitement. Taking into consideration the wide variability in the type and intensity of stimulation that triggers female orgasm, the diagnosis is only appropriate in cases in which a woman's orgasmic capacity is less than would be reasonable for her age, sexual experience, and adequacy of sexual stimulation.

● The disturbance causes significant distress or interpersonal difficulty.

● The disturbance is not better accounted for by another disorder, medical condition, or substance.

● The disturbance may be lifelong or acquired; generalized or situational; and due to psychological factors or a combination of psychological and physical factors.

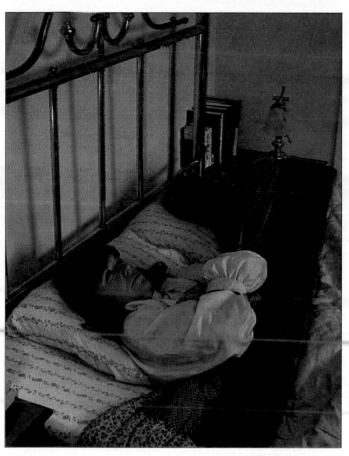

Frustrated by unsatisfying attempts at sexual intercourse, partners can feel hurt and rejected.

tary control over his ejaculatory reflexes (Kaplan 1986, 1998) Responses to this problem vary, from the men who are mildly distressed by it to the men and their partners who are severely distressed and are unable to develop other mutually satisfying lovemaking patterns. Premature ejaculation is more commonly reported in young men, perhaps associated with their lack of maturation and experience.

Sexual Pain Disorders

Sexual pain disorders, which involve the experience of pain associated with intercourse, are diagnosed as either **dyspareunia** or **vaginismus.** Dyspareunia, which affects both males and females, involves recurrent or persistent genital pain before, during, or after sexual intercourse. Vaginismus, which affects only females, involves recurrent or persistent involuntary spasms of the outer muscles of the vagina. Ordinarily, a sexually aroused woman experiences a relaxing of the vaginal muscles, but the woman with vaginismus experiences a closing of the muscles such that penetration is impossible or painful. Many women with vaginismus experience similar muscle spasms in response to any attempt at vaginal penetration, including attempts to insert tampons and pelvic examinations by medical professionals.

Theories and Treatment of Sexual Dysfunctions

Sexual dysfunction occurs for many different reasons. One man may experience inhibited male orgasm because of conflicts he has about physical intimacy; another man may experience the same problem because of a physical disorder, such as a prostate

Male Orgasmic Disorder

MINI-CASE

Chen is now 42 years old and has not been able to have an orgasm during sexual intercourse with a woman for more than a decade. He has been involved in four intimate relationships during this period and has encountered the same problem with each of his partners. He is able to become intensely aroused during foreplay, but he is unable to reach orgasm during intercourse, even after prolonged, and usually very frustrating, attempts to climax. Particularly perplexing for Chen and his partner is the fact that he is able to reach orgasm by masturbating or having his partner stimulate him manually. He has consulted physicians about this problem, but they have been unable to find any medical basis for his sexual dysfunction.

■ What psychological factors might explain Chen's orgasmic disorder?

■ What significance is there to the fact that Chen has experienced this same problem with four different partners?

DIAGNOSTIC FEATURES

● With consideration given to age, this diagnosis is assigned to men who experience persistent or recurrent delay in, or absence of, orgasm following a phase of normal excitement during sexual activity that is considered to be adequate in terms of focus, intensity, and duration.

● The disturbance causes significant distress or interpersonal difficulty.

● The disturbance is not better accounted for by another disorder, medical condition, or substance.

● The disturbance may be lifelong or acquired; generalized or situational; and due to psychological factors or a combination of psychological and physical factors.

Premature Ejaculation

MINI-CASE

Jeremy is a 45-year-old investment broker who has struggled with the problem of premature ejaculation for as long as he can remember. Since his first experience with sexual intercourse as a college student, he has been unable to control his orgasms. He customarily ejaculates seconds after penetration. Because of this problem, his relationships over the years have been strained and difficult. In each instance, the person he was dating at the time became frustrated, and Jeremy felt too embarrassed to continue the relationship. For a period lasting several years, he avoided sexual relations completely, knowing that each experience of failure would leave him feeling depressed and furious.

- Do you think that Jeremy's problem with premature ejaculation is due to learning experiences, or might it represent a deep-seated conflict?

- How is Jeremy's problem similar to those of Brian and Chen?

DIAGNOSTIC FEATURES

- A man with this condition experiences persistent or recurrent ejaculation with minimal sexual stimulation before, on, or shortly after penetration, and before he wishes to ejaculate. Consideration is given to factors that affect the duration of the excitement phase, such as the man's age, novelty of his sexual partner or the situation, and the recent frequency of sexual activity.

- The disturbance causes significant distress or interpersonal difficulty.

- The condition is not due exclusively to the effects of a substance.

- The disturbance may be lifelong or acquired; generalized or situational; and due to psychological factors or a combination of psychological and physical factors.

---

condition. Researchers now recognize that some sexual disorders result from physical problems, some from psychological problems, and others from an interaction between the two. Thus, once the disorder that is physiologically based has become established, psychological factors may come into play. In the example of the man with a prostate condition, you can imagine the emotional turmoil that might result from his sexual difficulty. Even knowing that his symptoms are physically based may not be particularly reassuring and might, in fact, cause other psychological problems, such as depression. Keeping in mind that most sexual dysfunctions arise from a complicated set of factors and interactions, let's now turn to the major theoretical approaches for understanding these disorders.

Biological Perspective

In recent years, increasing attention has been given to the fact that bodily processes, such as illness, reactions to medication, dietary factors, and even sleep, can cause or aggravate sexual difficulties. On the other hand, some physical experiences can enhance sexuality. For example, drinking a glass of wine makes some people feel more relaxed and open to sexual intimacy. In trying to understand the causes of a person's sexual dysfunction, the clinician must first conduct a comprehensive assessment of physical factors.

Various illnesses and diseases have direct connections to sexual problems. Some are quite obvious, such as a urinary infection, but others are not as evident and can involve a wide range of bodily systems, including neurological and cardiovascular disorders, liver or kidney disease, hormonal abnormalities, brain tumors, and hypothalamic-pituitary problems. As we mentioned earlier, diabetes mellitus is known to cause sexual

dysfunction, particularly in men. Specific problems associated with the male and female reproductive systems can also cause sexual dysfunctions. For example, dyspareunia in women can be the result of inadequate vaginal lubrication, which might in turn result from a glandular disorder. Menstrual abnormalities can contribute to changes in the uterus that make it very sensitive to the contractions that occur during orgasm. A man's dyspareunia might result from an anatomical abnormality, such as foreskin tightness. Painful orgasms in men might be attributable to a variety of conditions that can affect the genital region. The *DSM-IV* provides a separate category for sexual dysfunctions that are due to medical conditions. When treating people with such conditions, mental health professionals acknowledge the role of these physical factors, and they usually try to help the individual or couple expand the repertory of sexually intimate behaviors that take medical limitations into consideration.

These examples are just some of the many physical factors that can contribute to sexual functioning problems. But sexual problems can result from factors other than illnesses and physical abnormalities. For example, many chemical substances, both medications and illicit drugs, affect sexual functioning. For this reason, there is a *DSM-IV* category called substance-induced sexual dysfunction. Earlier, we mentioned that a small amount of alcohol can enhance sexual interest; however, alcohol in excess depresses sexual responsivity. Amphetamines and cocaine produce similar phenomena but as the result of different drug actions. Both of these drugs stimulate dopamine and norepinephrine activity. A man taking large amounts of cocaine may feel sexually aroused due to the stimulating effects of dopamine activity, but he may experience erectile and orgasmic problems as the result of the stimulation of norepinephrine activity.

Vaginismus

MINI-CASE

Shirley is a 31-year-old single woman who has attempted to have sex with many different men over the past 10 years. Despite her ability to achieve orgasm through masturbation, she has found herself unable to tolerate penetration during intercourse. In her own mind, she feels a sense of readiness, but her vaginal muscles inevitably tighten up and her partner is unable to penetrate. It is clear to Shirley that this problem has its roots in a traumatic childhood experience; she was sexually abused by an older cousin. Although she recognizes that she should seek professional help, Shirley is too embarrassed and has convinced herself that the problem will go away if she can find the right man who will understand her problems.

- Do you agree that Shirley's problems could be cured by finding a sensitive and caring partner?

- What do you think the connection is between Shirley's childhood experiences and her current vaginismus?

DIAGNOSTIC FEATURES

- Women with this condition experience recurrent or persistent involuntary spasm of the musculature of the outer third of the vagina, which interferes with sexual intercourse.

- The disturbance causes significant distress or interpersonal difficulty.

- The disturbance is not better accounted for by another disorder, or medical condition.

- The disturbance may be lifelong or acquired; generalized or situational; and due to psychological factors or a combination of psychological and physical factors.

Medications for both physical and psychological disorders can also interfere with sexual functioning. For example, medications that have vasoconstrictive effects, which are used for treating hypertension, reduce the amount of blood supply to the genitals, causing a man taking these medications to experience erectile difficulties. With some medications, the connection between the drug's effects and sexual dysfunction is not as obvious. For example, tricyclic antidepressants, which can interfere with sexual functioning, depress the activity of the parasympathetic nervous system, which is involved in sexual arousal. Unfortunately, many physicians fail to consider such side effects or to warn their patients about them. They face the dilemma of wanting to prescribe a medication that is effective for the patient's medical problem, while risking the difficulties that this medication may create for the patient's sex life. In some cases, the side effect of a psychotropic medication can have beneficial therapeutic effects. For example, some antidepressants (serotonin reuptake inhibitors, such as fluoxetine and sertraline) cause ejaculatory delay for many men (Montejo-Gonzalez et al., 1997). Although this may be a distressing side effect for most men, a man with premature ejaculation would perceive this as beneficial, and it is one effective treatment option (Lee, Song, Kim, & Choi, 1996).

An important change has taken place in the scientific understanding of male erectile dysfunction in the past 20 years. In 1970, Masters and Johnson claimed that virtually all men (95 percent) with erectile dysfunction had psychological problems, such as anxiety and job stress, boredom with long-term sexual partners, and other relationship difficulties. During the 1970s and 1980s, researchers arrived at very different conclusions as a result of new and more sophisticated assessment devices sensitive to the presence of physiological abnormalities.

More than half the cases of erectile dysfunction are now viewed by health care professionals as attributable to physical problems of a vascular, neurological, or hormonal nature, or to impaired functioning caused by drugs, alcohol, and smoking.

The distinction between physical and psychological causes of erectile dysfunction is more than just of academic interest; it helps determine the appropriate treatment. For example, if a man's erectile problems are due to psychological factors, individual or couple therapy is recommended. When the cause of erectile dysfunction is found to be physical, one of several somatic interventions may be used. The most invasive treatment is the surgical implantation of a penile prosthesis, such as a rod or an inflatable device. The inflatable device has the advantage of being adjustable, and it has a higher postsurgical success rate than the rod (Mohr & Beutler, 1990). Another somatic treatment is an arterial bypass operation, which is intended to correct problems due to vascular disease, or blockage of the arteries leading to the penis. Alternatively, an injection of medication into the penis may be used to induce an erection (Segraves & Althof, 1998; Szasz, Stevenson, Lee, & Sanders, 1987). Specially designed vacuum devices are also occasionally recommended, especially for men whose problems are the result of vascular insufficiency (Althof & Seftel, 1995). Finally, the latest entry into the treatment of erectile dysfunction, Viagra (sildanefil), which was introduced in 1998, has revolutionized the approach to this disorder, as it has a high effectiveness rate and is relatively noninvasive (see the Critical Issue box).

The other sexual dysfunctions do not have such clear-cut means of resolution. The clinician looks for possible physical causes and treatment routes and, in some cases, is able to recommend an effective medical intervention. For example, in cases involving side effects from medications, the physician may attempt to find substitutes that do not complicate sexual functioning. If a person has a physical disorder, treating this disorder would optimally resolve the sexual dysfunction. However, some medical problems are not easily treated. For example, a neurological impairment that results in sexual dysfunction may be incurable; consequently, the sexual problems will remain. In these instances, therapists may recommend other psychological interventions that help the individual develop alternative forms of sexual expression.

Psychological Perspective

For many people, the whole topic of sexuality is steeped in mystery and misinformation. In evaluating complaints of sexual dysfunction, clinicians first determine whether the individual has a reasonable understanding of the normal range of sexual behavior. For example, a man may complain of premature ejaculation because of his inability to sustain arousal for more than an hour. Or a woman may be frustrated by her inability to have multiple orgasms in a single sexual encounter. For these people, an educative approach that provides them with accurate information may be all that is needed.

Presently, the methods for treating sexual dysfunctions rely on conceptual models that incorporate physical, educative, attitudinal, intrapsychic, and interpersonal factors (Segraves & Althof, 1998). Most therapists treating clients with sexual dysfunctions rely at least in part on the methods originally developed by Masters and Johnson (Masters & Johnson, 1970), which have been refined over the past few decades. These methods typically focus on the couple's sexual behavior patterns and less on personality and relationship issues. Masters and Johnson conceptualized that much of the difficulty involved in sexual dysfunctions is due to spectatoring; hence, their treatment methods are attempts to reduce anxiety over sexual performance. For example, a man who is worried about losing his erection during intercourse may become so obsessed with his performance that he loses touch with the sexual experience itself. This objectification of the experience begins to interfere with his sexual arousal; consequently, he actually does lose his erection. His worst fears are then confirmed, and he approaches his next sexual encounter with increased anxiety (Barlow, 1986, 1988; Heimberg & Barlow, 1988; Segraves & Althof, 1998).

The treatment approach recommended by Masters and Johnson has several components. A primary objective is to refocus the individual's attention from anxiety over performance to the sensual pleasures of close physical contact with his or her partner. Also important is the need for the couple to clearly communicate their sexual wishes to each other. To achieve these two goals, Masters and Johnson recommend that couples use **sensate focus.** This method of treatment involves the partners taking turns stimulating each other in nonsexual but affectionate ways at first, then gradually progressing over a period of time toward genital stimulation. During the sensate focus exercise, individuals are instructed to focus on their own sensations, rather than on the partner's needs. During the early stage of treatment, intercourse is specifically forbidden, a fact that might seem surprising, given that this is a method of "sex" therapy. But the premise is that, when the option of having intercourse is eliminated, neither partner feels pressured to perform,

Sex therapy often helps couples resolve their sexual problems and focus on the more pleasurable aspects of the relationship.

thereby reducing the potential for failure. Further, the couple can learn to stimulate each other in a variety of new ways that they may never have tried before and, in the process, improve their communication about sex. The approaches developed by Masters and Johnson continue to be widely used in the treatment of sexual dysfunctions. For example, in one treatment program for men with hypoactive sexual desire disorder, the intervention focused on developing the individual's emotional aspects, increasing his sexual repertoire, and improving his attitude and response to these sexual experiences within the context of his relationship with his partner (McCabe, 1992).

Originally, Masters and Johnson insisted that couples come to their St. Louis clinic for a 2-week treatment program in which they would be free from distractions and able to concentrate on the development of more satisfying sexual behaviors. Since the 1970s, numerous clinicians have modified these techniques so that the couple can practice between sessions in the privacy of their own home and over a longer period of time. Some sex therapists take a more moderate stand on the issue of whether intercourse prohibition is absolutely necessary; instead they recommend that a decision regarding this matter be made on the basis of an individualized assessment of each couple. An important aspect of sex therapy is the assumption that it take place with a sexual partner; however, a client with a sexual dysfunction may not have a partner or may have a partner who is unwilling to participate in the treatment program.

Numerous other behavioral methods have evolved from the work of Masters and Johnson. For example, for treating premature ejaculation, the **squeeze technique** and the **stop-start procedure** have been recommended. In the squeeze technique, the partner stimulates the man's penis during foreplay and squeezes it when he indicates that he is approaching orgasm. This delays the ejaculatory response and, in turn, shows the man that he may have more control over ejaculation than he had previously thought possible. In the stop-start procedure, which was introduced several decades ago (Semans, 1956), either the man or his partner stimulates him

Viagra—Miracle Cure for Male Sexual Dysfunction?

A colorful ad in a popular recent newsmagazine contains a photo of a couple in their late sixties, smartly dressed, smiling, and enjoying a graceful dance together. The ad copy, "A pill that helps men with erectile dysfunction respond again . . . naturally the response has been positive . . . Viagra. Let the dance begin." What some social observers have termed the start of the next "sexual revolution" officially began on March 27, 1998, when the Federal Drug Administration approved the first medication in pill form for the treatment of male erectile disorder.

Even before Viagra (sildenafil) was introduced, pharmaceutical company Pfizer Inc. was preparing for a financial windfall that would result from the international marketing of this new wonder drug. Even with the unusually high cost ($10 per pill), and minimal or no insurance reimbursement, physicians were writing more than 200,000 prescriptions a week to approximately 30 million American men who were seeking relief from a notoriously embarrassing and depressing medical problem.

What makes Viagra especially appealing is the fact that it is so much less invasive than previous treatments for erectile dysfunction, such as surgery and implants, and so much less awkward than vacuum pumps or penile injections. Viagra works when it is accompanied by the experience of sexual excitement, unlike other treatments in which an erection is achieved artificially and independent of what is going on sexually with the man or his partner.

In addition to being easy to use, Viagra seems to be relatively safe, although initial cautions have been issued to men taking cardiac medications, such as nitroglycerine, since the combination of these two medications can be fatal. Some minor side effects have been reported, such as impaired vision and headaches, but these are not troubling enough to scare most men away from the use of Viagra. Effectiveness rates have been remarkable, with approximately 80 percent of men with erectile disorder reporting success with Viagra (Carlson, 1997; Goldstein & Feldman, 1997; Goldstein, Lue, & Padma-Nathan, 1998). Even men whose erectile disorder is due to medical problems, such as diabetes, spinal cord injury, or surgery, have found that Viagra has helped them achieve an erection. Men who have concluded that their erectile difficulty is psychologically caused have also reported that, despite the feeling of emotional conflict, erectile difficulty subsides with the ingestion of this small pill.

With all this good news about the effectiveness of this medication, is there a down side? Some clinicians wonder whether this miracle pill is making it too easy for men to gloss over more deeply rooted emotional issues that are reflected in erectile difficulty. For example, a man's difficulty in achieving an erection may be a way in which his body is signaling hostility, resentment, or even fear that he feels toward his partner. Might it not be more beneficial for him to understand the reasons for his problem, rather than to ignore the alarm system being activated within his body? As you will see in the next chapter (when we discuss other "wonder drugs," such as Prozac) , it is important to evaluate the extent to which people are using chemistry to change personality and emotions. For some problems, change might just as easily be achieved through self-understanding, cognitive change, or emotional exploration. In other words, a quick medical fix in the form of a pill might not be the best intervention for a problem that is emotionally complex and that reflects conflicts in an individual's emotional life. Yet another issue to consider with Viagra is its effect on an intimate relationship. For some couples, the sudden reintroduction of sexual intercourse may change their interpersonal system in ways that neither partner expects. Help columns in newspapers have contained many letters from exasperated women, complaining about the insensitivity of their newly aroused male partners since the introduction of Viagra. Rather than having a positive impact on the relationship, some women have found that their marital relationship has suddenly and dramatically been disturbed. In the months and years to come, researchers will investigate the impact of such medications on the quality of relationships, and possibly will introduce therapeutic components to the intervention that are aimed at enhancing commitment and affection. For the time being, men taking Viagra would be wise to consider the cause of their sexual difficulty; in cases involving psychological conflict, they should work toward understanding the nature of the problem, rather than naively concluding that a successful erection is an indicator that all is well.

---

to sexual excitement, and, as he approaches the point of orgasmic inevitability, stimulation is stopped. He regains his composure, and stimulation is resumed and stopped repeatedly. With recurrent exercising of this procedure, the man develops greater control over his ejaculatory response.

For women, in addition to sensate focus, behavioral techniques have been developed to help treat such dysfunctions as orgasmic disorder and vaginismus. A woman who feels frustrated because of her inability to reach orgasm may be instructed to begin a masturbation program (Heiman &

LoPiccolo, 1988), in which she moves through a series of steps beginning with bodily exploration, progressing through masturbatory orgasm, and culminating in sexual intercourse while her partner stimulates her genitals manually or with a vibrator. A woman with vaginismus would be instructed to penetrate her vagina with small, prelubricated cylindrical objects (called dilators) while in a relaxed state. Gradually, she would use dilators that are larger in circumference and that ultimately approximate the size of a penis. This approach is based on the theory that, as she grows more comfortable with this experience, her muscles will become reconditioned to relax rather than to constrict during intercourse.

As you read about these behavioral methods, you may wonder whether more is involved than just learning new sexual responses. Although some sexual dysfunctions can be successfully treated by a specific behavioral intervention, most sexual problems are multifaceted and require an approach that incorporates attention to relational and intrapsychic factors. The late Helen Singer Kaplan, a specialist in the treatment of sexual problems, advocated this integrative approach (Kaplan, 1979, 1983, 1986, 1998). She recognized that, because many sexual problems are the result of intrapsychic conflicts, successful treatment of the problem necessitates exploring the conflict and its roots. For example, inhibited orgasm could be associated with such intrapsychic problems as a strict religious upbringing, strongly suppressed hostility, mixed feelings about one's partner, or unconscious conflicts about sex.

Cultural expectations can be translated into sexual difficulties for both men and women, as men feel they must be "masculine" to perform adequately in the sexual relationship and women feel they must accept the "feminine" role of passivity and dependence. Disparities between the individual's personal preferences and these cultural norms can create conflict and, thus, inhibit the individual's sexual functioning. The challenge for the therapist working with such individuals is to focus treatment both on the source of their conflict and on the unsatisfactory sexual behaviors. Therapists using Kaplan's approach usually limit the exploration of the conflict to the extent needed to resolve the sexual problem, while recommending certain sexual exercises and changes in sexual patterns that are geared toward more sexual intimacy.

When treating people with sexual dysfunctions, it is important to determine whether the sexual problem reflects a relationship gone sour (LoPiccolo & Stock, 1986). If the therapist determines that the relationship is really the source of the trouble, then trying to treat the sexual problem while ignoring the other difficulties between the partners is fruit-less. The therapist would instead focus initially on improving communication between the partners and then move on to a sexual focus only when improved communication has been established.

As sensible and legitimate as the process of sex therapy appears, it does have some problems. For example, imagine yourself sharing very intimate details about your sexuality with a stranger. Most people would find this embarrassing enough to prevent them from seeking professional help. Thus, when considering the effectiveness of sex therapy methods, you must take into account that the people who have been studied are not representative of the population at large. The literature is filled with astounding claims of success in treating people with sexual dysfunctions, but these claims should be evaluated with considerable caution. Not only are the samples select, but the outcome measures are often poorly defined and the follow-up intervals too short to determine if the treatment has lasting effect.

Even if the success rates are not as high as some claim, sex therapy techniques have created new treatment opportunities for many people whose difficulties would never have received attention otherwise. Furthermore, the widespread publicity associated with these techniques has made it much easier for people seeking self-help treatments to find resources and suggestions for dealing with their problems on their own.

Sexual Disorders: The Perspectives Revisited

The sexual disorders constitute three discrete sets of difficulties involving varying aspects of sexual functioning and behavior. Although there are many unanswered questions concerning their causes, the behavioral perspective appears to hold the most promise as an explanation of how most of these diverse problems are acquired. Similarly, behavioral treatments of sexual disorders can be applied to the paraphilias and sexual dysfunctions. However, the biological perspective plays an important role as well, particularly with the gender identity disorders and the treatment of erectile dysfunction. Further, exploring personal history and relationship difficulties through insight-oriented and couple therapy seems to be an important adjunct to both the behavioral and biological approaches to treatment.

Interest in understanding and treating sexual disorders has a relatively recent history in the field of abnormal psychology. Even in this short time, though, significant advances have been made. We can expect these advances to continue as researchers and clinicians gain greater insight into the roles of biology and learning in these fascinating and often troubling conditions.

RETURN TO THE CASE

Shaun Boyden

Shaun's History

In our second intake session, Shaun told me some of the details of his life history, which enabled me to gain a perspective on how an otherwise normal man would have acquired such a serious disorder.

As is so common in the story of adults who abuse children, Shaun himself had been abused as a child. Primarily, Shaun's father beat him frequently because he was so "slow to catch on to anything." It was true that Shaun was not an *A* or even a *B* student in school, mainly because he had difficulty concentrating on his work. Shaun's mother was a quiet woman who told Shaun there was nothing she could do to intervene because his father was so unreasonable. Rather than try to help Shaun, his father only came down harder on him when his report card failed to live up to expectations. With a smirk on his face, Shaun pointed out the irony that his father was a dedicated volunteer in many social organizations yet was so cruel to Shaun.

His father's cruelty toward Shaun was compounded by the very different approach he took with Shaun's two brothers. It seemed to Shaun that the other two were spared their father's abuse by virtue of Shaun's "taking the rap" for them. If anything, they were inordinately treated to favorable attention. Later in life, the other two sons were to become partners in the father's furniture store, while Shaun was left to his own resources to make his way in the world.

Starting from the time Shaun was in high school, his main ambition in life, apart from finding a good job after graduation, was to help young boys in trouble and set them on the "right path." Unfortunately, before he knew what was happening, Shaun found himself drawn to sexual intimacy with young boys. Struggling with these impulses and fantasies during late adolescence, Shaun had naively hoped that, if he got married, his sexual preoccupation with young boys would disappear.

Assessment

Dr. Draper preferred to have the results of a comprehensive psychological assessment before planning a treatment, because pedophilia takes various forms and emerges for many different reasons. An understanding of the role of pedophilia in the conscious and unconscious realms of an individual's personality can facilitate a more effective treatment. A standard battery of psychological tests was supplemented by several specialized assessment techniques. Shaun was administered the WAIS-III, the MMPI-2, the Rorschach, and the TAT. In addition, Shaun was given specialized sexual assessment inventories pertaining to functioning and preferences.

Shaun's IQ fell in the average range, with his performance IQ much higher than his verbal IQ. His pattern of subscale scores suggested an inability to temper impulses with more cautious reflection. Shaun seemed to be oblivious to socially acceptable behaviors and prone to acting on his own desires rather than taking the needs of others into consideration. On the MMPI-2, Shaun responded in the direction of appearing guarded and suspicious, possibly because of concern over how the scores would be used in court proceedings. The responses he produced to the Rorschach indicated impulsivity and a restricted ability to fantasize. Both of these tendencies could lead to his acting on his immediate needs without considering the consequences of his actions. His TAT stories contained themes of victimization, but there was also denial of interpersonal problems. Most of the TAT stories had unrealistic, "happily ever after" endings, suggesting a naive and unfounded optimism.

The sexual assessment inventories confirmed Shaun's preference for sex with young boys, almost to the exclusion of any other sexual acts. Shaun tolerated sexual intercourse with his wife to maintain harmony, but he lacked any real interest or desire for intimacy with her. Shaun was not interested in sexual intimacy with adult males and, in fact, found the notion of such activities to be repulsive.

Diagnosis

It was clear to me that Shaun met the diagnostic criteria for pedophilia in that he has had recurrent, intense sexual urges and fantasies involving sexual activity with children which he has acted on.

Axis I: Pedophilia, same sex, exclusive type, severe
Axis II: Deferred
Axis III: No medical diagnosis
Axis IV: Problems related to interactions with the legal system (charged with child molestation)
Axis V: Global Assessment of Functioning in the past year: 48 Serious symptoms as well as serious impairment in social functioning due to the disorder

RETURN TO THE CASE

Shaun Boyden (continued)

Case Formulation

What would prompt a man who holds his own daughters so close to his heart to exploit children in order to satisfy his own cravings? Questions such as this are deeply perplexing. There are no clear answers, but, as I reviewed some of the facts about Shaun's life experiences, I began to develop a rudimentary understanding of why he might have developed along this path of deviance.

As a youngster, Shaun was subjected to very harsh treatment by his father and a not-so-benign neglect by his mother. Shaun could not live up to his father's unrealistic expectations of him and, consequently, was labeled a "failure." This label remained with him and eventually resulted in Shaun being left out of the favorable situation his younger brothers were to enjoy in the father's business. Although he managed to achieve a degree of material success and respect in the community, Shaun still longed for his father's approval and felt outraged at having been made to feel so worthless. He suppressed these powerful feelings through the very immature and fragile defense of denial. Shaun's poor ability to hold his impulses in check led him to act on the sexual desires he felt toward the boys he was ostensibly aiming to help. At the same time, Shaun's childlike view of himself caused him to identify with these boys, so that he did not see them as any different from himself. One remaining piece in the puzzle of Shaun's disorder concerned the possibility that he was sexually abused as a child. People with Shaun's disorder often have a background of sexual abuse.

Treatment Plan

In evaluating the context in which Shaun's treatment should take place, Dr. Draper and I concluded that outpatient care made sense. In some cases of pedophilia, inpatient care is warranted if there is concern that the individual may continue victimizing children. Shaun's mode of exploitation was limited to specific situations, which he would obviously have to avoid from that point forward. Dr. Draper agreed to accept Shaun into her treatment program, which consisted of intensive individual and group psychotherapy. Augmenting Shaun's psychotherapy would be his participation in an aversion therapy program aimed toward reducing and eventually eliminating his sexual responsiveness to children.

Outcome of the Case

Shaun responded to the aversion therapy offered by the sex offenders program, with minimal sexual arousal to stimuli involving young boys by the end of the 10-week treatment program. In his individual and group psychotherapy sessions, the story was much more complicated. Initially, Shaun was eager to impress Dr. Draper and the other members of the therapy group by showing what a "good patient" he was. However, Shaun revealed very little about himself, talking mostly in vague, superficial, and clichéd terms. This defensive style did not last very long, however, as the other men in the pedophile treatment group were harsh and direct in confronting Shaun. Once Shaun came to accept the reality of his behavior, he opened up remarkably in both group therapy and individual therapy. The real turning point came when Shaun publicly shared the fact that, at the age of 12, he had been sexually abused by a neighbor, a "good friend" of his father. Shaun felt afraid and guilty and had never told anyone. By talking about this incident with Dr. Draper and the other group members, Shaun was able to gain some insight into the fact that his own behavior with young boys was a repetition of the pattern that had been enacted with him in his childhood.

Shaun's legal difficulties were not as great as they might have been. In judicial proceedings on the matter, a compromise was reached in which Shaun was given a 6-month prison sentence and was placed on 5 years probation and required to participate in a sex offenders treatment program. Of course, he was ordered to refrain from participating in any situations with young children in which private interactions might take place.

Shaun continued in therapy for that 2-year period, but, immediately after terminating with Dr. Draper, Shaun moved his family to another state to "start a new life." He felt that the rumors about his child molestation would always haunt him and his family, and relocation was the only hope Shaun had of putting those rumors behind him.

Sarah Tobin, PhD

Summary

- Sexual behavior is considered a psychological disorder if (1) it causes harm to others or (2) it causes an individual to experience persistent or recurrent distress, or impairment in important areas of functioning. Paraphilias are disorders, lasting at least 6 months, in which an individual has recurrent, intense sexually arousing fantasies, sexual urges, or behaviors involving (1) nonhuman objects, (2) children or other nonconsenting persons, or (3) the suffering or humiliation of self or partner. Pedophilia is a disorder in which an adult (16 years or over) has uncontrollable sexual urges toward sexually immature children. In exhibitionism, a person has intense sexual urges and arousing fantasies involving genital exposure to strangers. People with the paraphilia of fetishism are preoccupied with an object, and they become dependent on this object for achieving sexual gratification, actually preferring it over sexual intimacy with a partner. A frotteur has recurrent, intense sexual urges and sexually arousing fantasies of rubbing against or fondling another person. Sexual masochism is a disorder marked by an attraction to achieving sexual gratification by having painful stimulation applied to one's own body, either alone or with a partner. Sexual sadism is the converse of sexual masochism, in that it involves deriving sexual gratification from activities that harm, or from urges to harm, another person. Transvestic fetishism is a disorder in which a man has an uncontrollable urge to wear a woman's clothes (called cross-dressing) as his primary means of achieving sexual gratification. Voyeurism is a sexual disorder in which the individual has a compulsion to derive sexual gratification from observing the nudity or sexual activity of others who are unaware of being watched. Most paraphilias emerge during adolescence, although there is usually a connection with events or relationships in early childhood. Once established, they tend to be chronic. Although biological factors play a role in some paraphilias, psychological factors seem to be central; in most cases, one or more learning events have taken place in childhood involving a conditioned response that results in a paraphilia. Treatment depends on the nature of the paraphilia and may include a biological component (such as medication), a psychological component (such as psychotherapy), and a sociocultural component (such as group or family therapy).

- A gender identity disorder is a condition involving a discrepancy between an individual's assigned sex and his or her gender identity, in which the person experiences a strong and persistent cross-gender identification that causes feelings of discomfort and a sense of inappropriateness about his or her assigned sex. Various theories have been proposed to explain the development of gender identity disorder. One biological explanation focuses on the effects of hormones that affect fetal development. Psychological theories focus on factors such as the role of a parent's preference for a child of the other gender, the impact of early attachment experiences, and parents' unintentional reinforcement of cross-gender behavior. Sociocultural theories consider various ways in which American society idealizes men and women according to certain stereotypical variables. Various factors influence the choice of intervention, with the most extreme method involving sex reassignment surgery.

- Sexual dysfunctions involve conditions in which there is abnormality in an individual's sexual responsiveness and reactions. The individual with hypoactive sexual desire disorder has an abnormally low level of interest in sexual activity. Sexual aversion disorder is characterized by an active dislike and avoidance of genital contact with a sexual partner, which causes personal distress or interpersonal problems. A woman with female sexual arousal disorder experiences a persistent or recurrent inability to attain or maintain the normal lubrication-swelling response of sexual excitement during sexual activity. Male erectile disorder involves the recurrent partial or complete failure to attain or maintain an erection during sexual activity, causing the man to feel distressed or to encounter interpersonal problems in his intimate relationship. An inability to achieve orgasm, or a distressing delay in achievement of orgasm, constitutes female orgasmic disorder. Male orgasmic disorder, also known as inhibited male orgasm, involves a specific difficulty in the orgasm stage. The man with premature ejaculation reaches orgasm in a sexual encounter long before he wishes to, perhaps even prior to penetration; therefore, he feels little or no sexual satisfaction. Sexual pain disorders, which involve the experience of pain associated with intercourse, are diagnosed as either dyspareunia or vaginismus. Dyspareunia, which affects both males and females, involves recurrent or persistent genital pain before, during, or after sexual intercourse. Vaginismus, which affects only females, involves recurrent or persistent involuntary spasms of the outer muscles of the vagina. Sexual dysfunctions can be caused by physical or psychological problems, or an interaction of both. The treatment of sexual dysfunctions includes a range of physiological interventions, such as medication, as well as psychological interventions that include behavioral, cognitive-behavioral, and couple therapy techniques.

Key Terms

See Glossary for definitions.

Assigned (biological) sex 255
Covert conditioning 248
Dyspareunia 265
Exhibitionism 247
Female orgasmic disorder 262
Female sexual arousal disorder 262
Fetish 248
Fetishism 248
Frotteur 250
Frotteurism 250
Gender identity 255
Gender identity disorder 255

Gender role 255
Hypoactive sexual desire disorder 261
Lovemap 254
Male erectile disorder 262
Male orgasmic disorder 264
Masochism 250
Orgasmic reconditioning 250
Paraphilias 243
Partialism 249
Pedophilia 244
Premature ejaculation 264
Sadomasochist 251
Sensate focus 268
Sexual aversion disorder 261

Sexual dysfunction 258
Sexual masochism 251
Sexual orientation 255
Sexual sadism 251
Spectatoring 261
Squeeze technique 268
Stop-start procedure 268
Transsexualism 255
Transvestic fetishism 252
Vaginismus 265
Voyeur 253
Voyeurism 253

Internet Resource

To get more information on the material covered in this chapter, visit our web site at **http://www.mhhe.com/halgin.**
There you will find more information, resources, and links to topics of interest.

CASE REPORT: JANICE BUTTERFIELD

I clearly recall the afternoon I received the phone call from a physician colleague, Eric Hampden. Frankly, I was surprised that Dr. Hampden was referring one of his patients to me in light of the fact that he had frequently reminded me of his lack of confidence in psychotherapy.

Eric Hampden explained to me that Janice had come to see him 2 months earlier with various bodily complaints, including ongoing exhaustion, sleep disturbance, and lack of appetite. She had described her feelings of sadness and gloom, as well as the difficulties that had emerged between her and her husband during the preceding 6 months. He was quite optimistic that a prescription of Prozac was all that Janice needed, but soon came to realize that he was wrong. Following 2 months of taking Prozac, Janice felt no better; in fact, she felt much worse and that very morning had made a suicide attempt. Apparently, wearing only her pajamas, Janice had gone into the garage after her husband had left for work and had turned on the car's ignition with the intention of asphyxiating herself. Having forgotten his briefcase, Janice's husband had returned to discover the disturbing scene of his wife trying to end her life. He called Dr. Hampden immediately, who in turn called me, admitting that this was a case beyond his competence to "cure." I instructed him to ask Janice's husband, Kurt, to call me, so that I could explain the process of admitting Janice to a psychiatric hospital.

When I answered the phone a few moments later, it was not the voice of Kurt Butterfield I heard but, rather, the faint whisper of a woman at the other end of the line. With a tremulous tone, Janice slowly spoke the words "Can you help me? Can you save me from myself?" With calmness and empathy, I assured Janice that I would do everything possible to help her, as long as she was willing to let me do so. I told her my emphatic opinion that it would be necessary for her to admit herself to a psychiatric hospital. At first, Janice said that she was unwilling to go to the "nut house" but didn't stop listening as I explained my reasoning. I told her, in no uncertain terms, that she had come dangerously close to death, a situation that warranted placing her in an environment in which she would be safe and cared for. Almost magically, Janice said, "I see what you mean. Yes, I am ready to go." In that momentary transition, the tone of her voice seemed to lighten a bit, as if a weighty burden had been lifted. I asked her to put Kurt on the phone, to whom I could give instructions about hospital admission. I explained to both of them that I would meet with her later that afternoon to complete the intake interview.

As the day progressed, I felt harried and a bit weary myself. Suicidally depressed clients are never easy, so I knew that I had to summon the stamina prior to my initial meeting with Janice, which would be my last appointment of the day. There were five women among the dozen people sitting in the waiting room, but there was no question in my mind which one was Janice Butterfield. With a blank stare on her face and her eyes glazed over and cast down to the floor, Janice sat motionless as if in an altered state. Her style of dress seemed odd. Underneath a stylish cardigan sweater she was wearing what appeared to be the top of a set of flannel pajamas. As I glanced down to her feet, I could see that the same flannel material extended beneath the hem of her jeans. Apparently, Janice had never taken off the pajamas from the early morning hour, when she had attempted to take her life. Noting my attention to Janice's attire, her husband explained that Janice had felt too weak to take off her pajamas prior to coming to the hospital.

I escorted Janice and Kurt to my office for the intake interview, where they shared with me the "nightmare" of the previous 6 months. Although it seemed difficult for Janice to participate actively in the interview, gradually she seemed to come to life. Janice explained that she felt like a "hopeless loser" who had no reason to live. She told me that, for at least 6 months, she had frequently been overcome by uncontrollable feelings of sadness. She repeated the bodily problems that Dr. Hampden had described and added that she had felt so weak that she could hardly find the energy to walk. When I inquired about the Prozac, she said that she had been taking the medication regularly but hated the edgy feelings it caused.

Both Janice and Kurt told me how the depression had taken its toll on their relationship and home life. Kurt said that he was finding himself complaining more and more about Janice's neglect of basic household responsibilities, her insensitivity to their 8-year-old daughter, and her total lack of interest in being affectionate or sexually intimate with him. The picture was painted of a woman, who for nearly a half year, had been spending the greater part of every day clothed in a bathrobe and slippers and staring at the walls. Even though Kurt had begged Janice to see a mental health professional, her only concession was agreeing to see their family doctor for her "fatigue."

When I asked Janice how she felt about entering the hospital in order to treat her depression, she admitted, even to her own surprise, that it felt "good." She then smiled faintly and asked if she might go to her room to get some rest. After the day she had been through, the choice seemed a wise one, but, as I explained to Janice, it was hospital policy that she be observed for the first 24 hours to ensure her safety. As Janice left my office, escorted by an aide from the unit, I felt confident she would begin to feel better in the days ahead but, at the same time, knew that my work with her would be difficult. Interactions with depressed people are usually stressful for therapists, and the stress intensifies when the client has been suicidal. Even though my work with Janice would be challenging, I was hopeful I might play a role in relieving her feelings of despair.

Sarah Tobin, PhD

9

Mood Disorders

It is common for people to feel happy and energized at times and sad and apathetic at other times; almost everyone experiences periodic mood fluctuations. Thinking about your own variations in how you feel can give you insight into the nature of mood disorders.

The disorders presented in this chapter are far more painful and disruptive than the relatively normal day-to-day variations in mood. As you will read later in this chapter, people with mood disorders that involve elation act in ways that are out of character for them, possibly acting wild and uncontrolled. In mood disorders that involve serious depression, as in the case of Janice, individuals experience pain that is so intense that they feel immobilized and possibly suicidal.

General Characteristics of Mood Disorders

A mood disorder involves a disturbance in a person's emotional state, or mood. People can experience this disturbance in the form of extreme depression, excessive elation, or a combination of these emotional states. The primary characteristic of depressive disorders is that the individual feels overwhelming **dysphoria,** or sadness. In another kind of mood disorder, called bipolar disorder, an individual has emotional experiences at the opposite "pole" from depression, feelings of elation called **euphoria.** As you will see later in this chapter, there are various subtypes of mood disorder involving dysphoria and euphoria.

To understand the nature of mood disorders, it is important to understand the concept of an **episode,** a time-limited period during which specific, intense symptoms of a disorder are evident. In some instances, an episode is quite lengthy, perhaps 2 years or more. People with mood disorders experience episodes of dysphoric or euphoric symptoms, or a

In the throes of a depressive episode, this woman probably feels that life is not worth living.

mixture of both. Episodes differ in a number of important ways that clinicians document in their diagnosis (Keller et al., 1995). Following are some of the ways that a mood episode can be characterized.

First, the clinician documents the severity of the episode with a specifier, such as *mild, moderate,* or *severe.* Second, the clinician documents whether it is the first episode or a recurrence of symptoms. For recurrent episodes, the clinician notes whether or not the client has fully recovered between episodes. Third, specifiers can also reflect the nature of a prominent set of symptoms. For example, some people in the midst of a mood episode have bodily movements that are strikingly unusual, possibly even bizarre. The adjective *catatonic,* which we discussed in Chapter 3, describes odd body postures and movements, such as immobility, rigidity, or excessive purposeless motor activity. Another specifier pertains to whether the episode is postpartum, which indicates that a woman's mood disturbance is presumed to be related to the delivery of a baby within the preceding month. We will discuss other specifiers used to characterize mood episodes in the relevant sections that follow.

Depressive Disorders

Mental health professionals differentiate between two serious forms of depression. **Major depressive disorder** involves acute, but time-limited, episodes of depressive symptoms. People with **dysthymic disorder,** on the other hand, struggle with more chronic but less severe depression. The clinician diagnoses dysthymic disorder when these moderately depressive symptoms have lasted at least 2 years in adults and a year or more in children.

Major Depressive Disorder

Think of a time in your life when something very sad or tragic happened to you and you felt overwhelmed with feelings of unhappiness, loss, or grief. Try to recall what those feelings were like and how despondent you were. As painful as this experience was, you probably could see the connection between the tragic event and your feelings, and you probably recovered after a period of time. Now imagine that these feelings just hit you without any obvious cause, or that you were unable to overcome your sense of loss. Then imagine feeling unremitting hopelessness, fatigue, worthlessness, and suicidality. This is comparable to what it's like for a person experiencing a major depressive episode.

Characteristics of a Major Depressive Episode

The emotional symptoms of a **major depressive episode** involve a dysphoric mood of an intensity that far outweighs the ordinary disappointments and occasional sad emotions of everyday life. Such dysphoria may appear as extreme dejection or a dramatic loss of interest in previously pleasurable aspects of life. In some cases, the depression has its roots in an experience of bereavement following the loss of a loved one. Although intense depression following the death of a loved one is normal, it would be considered

DIAGNOSTIC FEATURES OF A MAJOR DEPRESSIVE EPISODE

- For most of the time during a 2-week period, a person experiences at least five of the following symptoms, which involve a change from previous functioning (at least one of the first two symptoms must be present).

  - Depressed mood

  - Diminished interest or pleasure in all or most daily activities

  - Significant unintentional weight loss or appetite decrease or increase

  - Insomnia or hypersomnia

  - Psychomotor agitation or retardation

  - Fatigue or energy loss

  - Feelings of worthlessness or inappropriate guilt

  - Concentration difficulty or indecisiveness

  - Recurrent thoughts of death or suicidality

- The symptoms are not part of a mixed (manic/depressive) episode and are not attributable to a medical condition, use of a substance, or bereavement.

- The symptoms cause significant distress or impairment.

a mood disorder if the disabling sadness lasts inordinately long (more than 2 months). Most major depressive episodes are not precipitated by a painful loss, however. The fact that this intense sadness arises without cause often causes people who experience one of these episodes to feel overwhelmed and perplexed. Usually the life of an individual in a major depressive episode is thrown into chaos because of the impairment experienced at work and home.

Physical signs of a major depressive episode are called somatic, or bodily symptoms. Lethargic and listless, the person may experience a slowing down of bodily movement, called psychomotor retardation. Alternatively, some depressed people show the opposite symptom, psychomotor agitation; as a result, their behavior has a frenetic quality. As previously mentioned, when these behaviors are bizarre and extreme, they may be characterized as catatonic. Eating disturbances are also common, as the individual deviates from usual appetite patterns, either avoiding food or overindulging, usually with sweets or carbohydrates. People in a depressive episode also show a significant change in their sleeping patterns, either sleeping much more than usual or experiencing insomnia.

In addition, people in a major depressive episode have cognitive symptoms that include an intensely negative self-view reflected by low self-esteem and feelings that they deserve to be punished. They may become tyrannized by guilt as they dwell

unrelentingly on past mistakes. Unable to think clearly or to concentrate, they may find themselves indecisive about even the most insignificant matters. Activities that may have sparked their interest only weeks ago now lack any appeal. Feelings of hopelessness and negativity lead many people to become consumed by thoughts of death and to possibly look for escape, by thinking about or actually committing suicide. We will look specifically at suicide later in this chapter.

The symptoms of a major depressive episode usually arise gradually over the course of several days or weeks. Some people report that, prior to the full-blown symptoms of depression, they were noticeably anxious and mildly depressed, sometimes for months. Once the active episode of major depression begins, they may experience symptoms for 2 weeks to a period of months. If untreated, most major depressive episodes seem to run their course some time after 6 months, and most people return to normal functioning. However, for approximately one fourth of these severely depressed people, some symptoms continue for months or even years.

Types of Depression

In addition to the specifiers used to characterize depressive and manic episodes, there are terms used only to describe the nature of depressive episodes. People whose depressive episodes have **melancholic features** lose interest in most activities or find it difficult to react to events in their lives that would customarily bring pleasure. Morning is a particularly difficult time of the day for people with this type of depression. They may wake up much earlier than usual, possibly feeling more gloomy throughout the morning and struggling with a number of other symptoms throughout the day, such as psychomotor agitation or retardation, significant appetite disturbance, and excessive or inappropriate guilt.

People whose episodes show a **seasonal pattern** develop a depressive episode at about the same time each year, usually for about 2 months during the fall or winter, but then they return to normal functioning. During these episodes, they lack energy, and they tend to sleep excessively, overeat, and crave carbohydrates. As you will see later, studies of people with seasonal depression have led some researchers to propose that an alteration in biological rhythms linked to seasonal variations in the amount of daylight causes depression in these individuals. In fact, this variant of major depressive disorder is more frequently diagnosed in people who live at higher latitudes, such as the more northerly states, where there is less sunlight.

Prevalence and Course of the Disorder

Major depressive disorder is a relatively common psychological disorder. Out of every 100 people, approximately 13 men and 21 women develop this disorder at some point in life (Kessler et al., 1994). Reflected in these statistics is the fact that women are much more likely than men to experience this disorder (Spaner, Bland, & Newman, 1994).

In trying to define the course of major depressive disorder, researchers have come to realize that depression is a heterogeneous disorder with many possible courses. Approximately half of the people who have one episode never have another major

Men and women in U.S. society are socialized to express emotions in different ways. After the death of a child, a mother may feel more freedom to express her grief openly, while the father suppresses his grief.

depressive episode (Coryell et al., 1994). Among those who do have repeated episodes, the course of the disorder may take one of several forms. About 20 percent of those with a chronic condition experience recurrent and severe depressive episodes. The tendency of people with a chronic condition to ruminate over their symptoms can prolong the disorder (Nolen-Hoeksema,

Parker, & Larson, 1994), yet some people are able to carry on normal lives between their depressive periods, although they remain fearful that at any unexpected moment the depression will resurface.

Dysthymic Disorder

Not all forms of depression involve the severe symptoms we have discussed so far. For some people, depression involves sadness that is not as deep or intense as that of a major depressive episode but is nevertheless quite distressing and long-lasting. Keep in mind that we are not talking about normal blue moods that everyone experiences from time to time but a more serious, unrelenting depression. People with dysthymic disorder have, for at least 2 years, some of the same kinds of symptoms as those experienced by people with major depressive disorder, such as appetite disturbance, sleep disturbance, low energy or fatigue, low self-esteem, poor concentration, decision-making difficulty, and feelings of hopelessness. However, they do not experience as many symptoms, nor are these symptoms as severe. They feel inadequate in most of their endeavors and unable to feel pleasure or interest in the events of life. As you can see, dysthymic disorder differs from major depressive disorder on the basis of its course, which is chronic (Klein et al., 1998). People with dysthymic disorder are likely to withdraw from others, to spend much of their time brooding or feeling guilty, and to act with anger and irritability toward others. During this extended depression,

Major Depressive Disorder

MINI-CASE

Jonathan is a 37-year-old construction worker whose wife took him to a psychiatric facility. Although Jonathan has been functioning normally for the past several years, he suddenly became severely disturbed and depressed. At the time of admission, Jonathan was agitated, dysphoric, and suicidal, even going as far as to purchase a gun to kill himself. He had lost his appetite and had developed insomnia during the preceding 3 weeks. As each day went by, he found himself feeling more and more exhausted, less able to think clearly or to concentrate, and uninterested in anything or anyone. He had become hypersensitive in his dealings with neighbors, co-workers, and family, insisting that others were being too critical of him. This was the second such episode in Jonathan's history, the first having occurred 5 years earlier, following the loss of his job due to a massive layoff in his business.

■ What symptoms of major depressive disorder does Jonathan have?

■ What information would you need in order to determine whether Jonathan's depression is melancholic or seasonal?

DIAGNOSTIC FEATURES

● This diagnosis is assigned to people who have either a single major depressive episode (see features on page 279) or recurrent episodes with 2 or more months intervening between episodes.

● The major depressive episode is not better explained by another disorder.

● The individual has never had a manic, mixed, or hypomanic episode.

Dysthymic Disorder

MINI-CASE

Miriam is a 34-year-old community college instructor who, for the past 3 years, has had persistent feelings of depressed mood, inferiority, and pessimism. She realizes that, since her graduation from college, she has never felt really happy and that, in recent years, her thoughts and feelings have been characterized as especially depressed. Her appetite is low, and she struggles with insomnia. During waking hours, she lacks energy and finds it very difficult to do her work. She often finds herself staring out the window of her office, consumed by thoughts of how inadequate she is. She fails to fulfill many of her responsibilities and, for the past 3 years, has received consistently poor teacher evaluations. Getting along with her colleagues has become increasingly difficult; consequently, she spends most of her free time alone in her office.

■ How do Miriam's symptoms of dysthymic disorder differ from those of a person with major depressive disorder?

■ To what extent do Miriam's symptoms lead her to create situations that worsen her depression?

DIAGNOSTIC FEATURES

● For a period lasting at least 2 years, people with this disorder experience depressed mood for most of the day, for more days than not, as indicated either by their own report or by the observation of others.

● While depressed, these individuals experience at least two of the following: poor appetite or overeating; insomnia or hypersomnia; low energy or fatigue; low self-esteem; poor concentration or difficulty making decisions; and feelings of hopelessness.

● During the 2-year period (1 year for children and adolescents), the individual has never been without these symptoms for 2 continuous months.

● The individual has not (1) had a major depressive episode during the first 2 years of the disturbance, (2) ever had a manic, mixed, or hypomanic episode, (3) met the criteria for cyclothymic disorder, (4) experienced the symptoms during the course of a chronic psychotic disorder, and (5) has not developed the symptoms as the direct result of a medical condition or use of a substance.

● The symptoms cause significant distress or impairment.

these individuals are never symptom-free for an interval longer than 2 months. They commonly have other serious psychological disorders as well. Approximately one tenth will go on to develop major depressive disorder. A sizeable number also have a personality disorder, which makes accurate diagnosis difficult. Others are likely to develop a substance abuse disorder, because they use drugs or alcohol excessively in misguided attempts to reduce their chronic feelings of depression and hopelessness.

This woman's chronic depression interferes with her ability to concentrate and study for an exam.

Hospitalization is uncommon for people with this disorder, except in cases in which the depression leads to suicidal behavior. The disorder is also diagnosed in children and adolescents. In these cases, however, the duration need only be 1 year, and the depression may be more evident in an intense, chronic irritability than in depressed mood.

Approximately 8 percent of women and nearly 5 percent of men will develop this disorder in the course of their lives (Kessler et al., 1994). This condition begins quietly—often in childhood, adolescence, or early adulthood—as the symptoms subtly begin to affect functioning.

Disorders Involving Alternations in Mood

There are two forms of mood disorder in which alternations in mood are the primary characteristic: bipolar disorder and cyclothymic disorder. **Bipolar disorder** involves an intense and very disruptive experience of extreme elation, or euphoria, possibly alternating with major depressive episodes. A full-blown expression of extreme symptoms involving abnormally heightened levels of thinking, behavior, and emotionality that cause impairment in social or occupational functioning is called a **manic episode.** In some instances, the individual experiences psychotic symptoms, such as delusions and hallucinations. An individual may also experience a **mixed episode,** characterized by a period lasting at least a week, in which the symptoms of both a manic episode and a major depressive episode occur in rapidly alternating fashion. **Cyclothymic disorder** involves alternations between dysphoria and briefer, less intense, and less disruptive states of euphoria, called **hypomanic episodes.**

Bipolar Disorder

Think of a time when you felt unusually energetic and happy. You may have felt "on top of the world," with excitement filling your emotions and intense energy rushing through your body. During such a time, you may have slept and eaten less than usual, and you may have felt "hyped" to accomplish a remarkable task. You may have maintained this heightened energy level for several days but then suddenly "crashed," perhaps becoming exhausted or even a bit depressed. Experiences such as these, but in a much more extreme form, constitute the basis for manic episodes, the crucial component of bipolar disorder.

Characteristics of a Manic Episode

People who have manic episodes, even if they have never had a depressive episode, are diagnosed as having *bipolar disorder,* a term that has replaced *manic depression* in the diagnostic system. From what you may know about the more commonly used term, *manic depression,* you might expect that a bipolar disturbance would involve mood swings. The term *bipolar* does imply two

Composer Robert Schumann's bipolar disorder was reflected in the dramatic alternating styles of his music—some pieces filled with wild energy, others subdued and melancholic. Despite his success as a composer, he and his musician wife, Clara, suffered greatly because of the torment created by his disorder.

poles, mania and depression; however, not all people with bipolar disorder show signs of depression. The assumption underlying the diagnostic term is that, at some point, people with this disorder will become depressed.

A person in the midst of a manic episode may seem outgoing, alert, talkative, creative, witty, and self-confident. However, the experience of people in a manic episode is far more complicated. Their feelings of expansiveness and energy can cause serious dysfunction. Their self-esteem may be grossly inflated, and their thinking may be grandiose and even have a psychotic quality. For example, a manic man told his friends that he had just realized he possessed divine attributes and that soon he would be able to perform healing miracles. A manic woman asserted that the newspapers contained clues that suggested she would soon be called on by the White House to assume the vice presidency.

Most people in a manic episode do not have such bizarre thoughts, but they may have unusual ideas and bouts of uncharacteristic creativity. Their thoughts may race, and they may jump from idea to idea or activity to activity, easily distracted and craving stimulation. They may be more talkative and louder than usual, speaking with such rapidity that others find it difficult to keep up with them or to interrupt. They may make jokes, puns, and sexual comments, perhaps becoming theatrical and melodramatic, or hostile and aggressive. Strangers may view these individuals as being extraordinarily outgoing, friendly, and imaginative. Those who know them, however, recognize that something is seriously wrong and that their behavior and thinking are out of control.

DIAGNOSTIC FEATURES OF A MANIC EPISODE

- A period of abnormally and persistently elevated, expansive, or irritable mood lasting at least 1 week

- During this period, three or more of the following symptoms have persisted (four if the mood is only irritable):

  - Inflated self-esteem or grandiosity

  - Decreased need for sleep

  - Increased talkativeness

  - Flight of ideas or racing thoughts

  - Distractibility

  - Increase in goal-directed activity or psychomotor agitation

  - Excessive involvement in pleasurable activities with potentially painful consequences

- The symptoms are not part of a mixed (manic/depressive) episode and are not attributable to a medical condition or use of a substance.

- The symptoms cause significant distress or impairment or necessitate hospitalization to prevent harm to self or others.

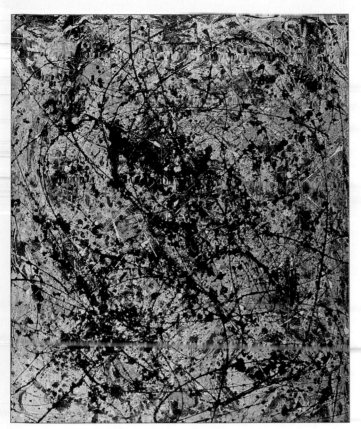

The work of abstract expressionist painters, such as Jackson Pollack, may reflect their experience of depression. Analysis of the biographies and archives of a group of these artists has linked their work with depressive symptoms that may have prompted them to turn inward and reexamine painful existential questions regarding the meaning of life (Schildkraut, Hirshfeld, & Murphy, 1994).

People in a manic episode are unusually energetic, possibly getting by with only a few hours of rest each night. During this time, they feel driven in tireless pursuit of outlandish goals. When others ask them how they feel, they report feeling "on top of the world." However, there is also a down side to a manic episode: the euphoria may suddenly turn into extreme irritability, even aggressiveness and hostility, especially if other people thwart their unrealistic and grandiose plans. For example, Harry, a relatively unsuccessful dealer in rare coins, suddenly concocted a grand scheme to overhaul the U.S. monetary system. When he told his family that he was flying to Washington to present the plan to the president, his family and friends thought he was kidding, and he responded with rage. Manic individuals also tend to seek out pleasurable activities, disregarding the possibility of any negative consequences that may result from their sexual indiscretions, unrestrained buying sprees, and foolish investments. Manic individuals whose family and friends suggest that they obtain professional help often respond with annoyance and anger.

In contrast to a major depressive episode, which tends to emerge and diminish rather gradually, a manic episode typically appears and ends suddenly. Often the individual develops a range of symptoms in a period of only a few days. Manic episodes typically last from a few weeks to a few months, depending, in part, on whether or not professional treatment is obtained.

Types of Bipolar Disorder

There are several variations in the expression of bipolar disorder, with a primary distinction in the *DSM-IV* between bipolar I disorder and bipolar II disorder. A diagnosis of **bipolar I disorder** describes a clinical course in which the individual experiences one or more manic episodes with the possibility, though not the necessity, of having experienced one or more major depressive episodes. In contrast, a diagnosis of **bipolar II disorder** means the individual has had one or more major depressive episodes and at least one hypomanic episode. In other words, those with bipolar II disorder have never experienced a full-blown manic episode but have become sufficiently energized to meet the criteria for a hypomanic episode.

Prevalence and Course of the Disorder

Bipolar disorder is much less common than major depressive disorder. Of the U.S. population, 1.6 percent have bipolar disorder at some point in life. Bipolar disorder is almost equally

People with bipolar disorder can become hyperagitated and irritable. They may develop exaggerated views of their own importance and may behave in ways that reflect those views, such as directing traffic, unaware of the inappropriateness of their behavior.

prevalent in males and females (Kessler et al., 1994), yet there is an interesting gender difference in the way that the disorder first appears. The first episode for men is more likely to be manic, but for women it is more likely to be a major depressive episode. As in the case with major depressive disorder, women with bipolar disorder are at greater risk of developing a manic episode during the postpartum period than at other times in their lives (American Psychiatric Association, 1994). Bipolar disorder most commonly appears in people in their twenties (Carlson, Fennig, & Bromet, 1994).

Following a single manic episode, there is a 90 percent probability that the individual will experience subsequent episodes. Experts speak about the phenomenon of "kindling." Once individuals have experienced a manic episode, they are at greater risk for experiencing another episode, even if they are taking medications to control the disorder (Goldberg & Harrow, 1994). Most subsequent manic episodes occur just prior to or soon after a major depressive episode. People who do not receive medication for the treatment of their bipolar disorder average about four episodes within the span of a decade, with the interval between these episodes decreasing as the individual grows older. In fact, in one longitudinal study, only 4 percent continued to experience manic episodes 10 years following their first episode (Winokur et al., 1994). A small percentage (less than 15 percent) of individuals with bipolar disorder have between four and eight mood episodes within the course of a single year; these individuals are referred to as **rapid cyclers** (Bauer et al., 1994; Coryell, Endicott, & Keller, 1992), and the specifier "rapid cycling" is part of the diagnosis. Most people with bipolar disorder act and feel normal between episodes, although approximately one fourth continue to show unstable mood and to have problems in their dealings with other people, both at home and at work (American Psychiatric Association, 1994). They are likely to have continuing difficulties at work following an initial episode, and less than half are fully adjusted within the 5 years after hospitalization (Goldberg, Harrow, & Grossman, 1995).

Cyclothymic Disorder

Everyone experiences mood changes, but the mood shifts that people with cyclothymic disorder exhibit are unusually dramatic and recurrent, though not as intense as those experienced by people with bipolar disorder. The hypomania is never severe enough to be diagnosed as a manic episode, and the dysphoria is never severe enough to be diagnosed as a depressive episode. Still, the destabilizing effects of this disorder disrupt their lives.

Cyclothymic disorder is a chronic condition that lasts a minimum of 2 years (1 year in children and adolescents). On the surface, some people with cyclothymic disorder seem to get along satisfactorily, and they may claim that their periods of heightened energy are welcomed periods of creativity. Un-

---

Bipolar I Disorder

MINI-CASE

Isabel is a 38-year-old realtor who, for the past week, has shown signs of uncharacteristically outlandish behavior. This behavior began with Isabel's development of an unrealistic plan to create her own real estate "empire." She went without sleep or food for 3 days, spending most of her time at her computer developing far-fetched financial plans. Within 3 days she put deposits on 7 houses, together valued at more than $3 million, although she had no financial resources to finance even one of them. She made several visits to local banks, where she was known and respected, and "made a scene" with each loan officer who expressed skepticism about her plan. In one instance she angrily pushed over the banker's desk, yanked his phone from the wall, and screamed at the top of her lungs that the bank was keeping her from earning a multimillion dollar profit. The police were summoned, and they brought her to the psychiatric emergency room, from which she was transferred for intensive evaluation and treatment.

- Which of Isabel's behaviors are symptoms of a manic episode?

- How would you distinguish Isabel's manic outburst from a realistic response to frustration over having her plan thwarted?

DIAGNOSTIC FEATURES

- People with this disorder have experienced at least 1 manic episode, but no current or past major depressive episode. (This contrasts with Bipolar II Disorder in which an individual experiences recurrent major depressive episodes, and a history of at least 1 hypomanic episode but no manic episodes.)

- The condition is not attributable to another disorder.

- The symptoms cause significant distress or impairment.

DIAGNOSTIC FEATURES OF A HYPOMANIC EPISODE

- A period of persistently elevated, expansive, or irritable mood lasting at least 4 days, which clearly differs from normal mood and is observable by others

- During this period, three or more of the following symptoms have persisted (four if the mood is only irritable):

  - Inflated self-esteem or grandiosity

  - Decreased need for sleep

  - Increased talkativeness

  - Flight of ideas or racing thoughts

  - Distractibility

  - Increase in goal-directed activity or psychomotor agitation

  - Excessive involvement in pleasurable activities with potentially painful consequences

- There are no psychotic features, and the episode is not severe enough to cause marked impairment or to necessitate hospitalization.

- The symptoms are not attributable to a medical condition or the effects of a substance.

fortunately, the individual with this disorder is actually more likely to feel some distress or impairment in work or interpersonal dealings due to the mood disorder. Problems are especially likely for individuals who struggle with unpredictable mood changes that recur in rapid cycles, because other people regard them as moody and unreliable. The onset of this disorder generally occurs when a person is in his or her twenties. The symptoms may not be apparent at first, but, over time, individuals with this disorder notice that their moods fluctuate dramatically, and people who know them find it increasingly difficult to deal with the individuals. People with cyclothymic disorder are at considerable risk of developing full-blown bipolar disorder. This disorder affects less than 1 percent of the population.

Theories and Treatments of Mood Disorders

For centuries, people have tried to gain an understanding of the causes of mood disorders and the ways in which people with these conditions should be treated. Due to the intense focus on these disorders, researchers and theorists have made considerable progress in recent years. Although no single perspective is sufficient, together they provide important insights into mood disorders, which may lead to more effective treatments.

Biological Perspectives

From our discussion so far, you are already aware that biology is connected in an important way to mood disorders. On the very simplest level, mood disorders cause physical changes, such as disturbances of appetite and sleep patterns. More complex is the effect of biological processes on feelings of depression and elation.

Genetics

The most compelling evidence supporting a biological model of mood disorders involves the role of genetics. The observation that these disorders run in families is well established. In families in which one parent has a mood disorder, approximately 30 percent of the children are at risk of developing a disorder. When both parents have a mood disorder, between 50 and 75 percent of the children will also develop a mood disorder (Gershon, 1983).

Studies of twins provide further evidence of the role of genetics in determining mood disorder. The concordance rates in dizygotic twins (nonidentical, or fraternal), who have the same level of genetic relationship as other siblings, vary between 15 and 20 percent. This means that, in a fraternal twin pair, if one twin has a mood disorder, the odds are approximately one in five that the other twin will also have a mood disorder. However, in monozygotic (identical) twins, who share the same genetic inheritance, the concordance rate more than triples, reaching as high as 67 percent (Torgerson, 1986; Wender et al., 1986).

Because of the purity of their genetic lineage and the care with which they keep marriage and birth records, the Amish have been interesting subjects for genetic researchers.

Cyclothymic Disorder

MINI-CASE

Larry is a 32-year-old bank cashier who has sought treatment for his mood variations, which date back to the age of 26. For several years, co-workers, family, and friends have repeatedly told him that he is very "moody." He acknowledges that his mood never feels quite stable, although at times others tell him he seems more calm and pleasant than usual. Unfortunately, these intervals are quite brief, lasting for a few weeks and usually ending abruptly. Without warning, he may experience either a depressed mood or a period of elation. During his depressive periods, his confidence, energy, and motivation are very low. During his hypomanic periods, he willingly volunteers to extend his work day and to undertake unrealistic challenges at work. On weekends, he acts in promiscuous and provocative ways, often sitting outside his apartment building, making seductive comments and gestures to women walking by. Larry disregards the urging of his family members to get professional help, insisting that it is his nature to be a bit unpredictable. He also states that he doesn't want some "shrink" to steal away the periods during which he feels "fantastic."

■ How do Larry's symptoms of cyclothymic disorder differ from those of Isabel, who has bipolar disorder, and Miriam, who has dysthymic disorder?

■ What aspects of Larry's symptoms might contribute to his experiencing distress in his daily life?

DIAGNOSTIC FEATURES

● For at least 2 years, people with this disorder experience numerous periods with hypomanic symptoms and numerous periods with depressive symptoms that do not meet the criteria for a major depressive episode.

● During the 2-year period (1 year for children and adolescents), the individual has never been without these symptoms for 2 continuous months.

● No major depressive episode, manic episode, or mixed episode has been present during the first 2 years of the disturbance.

● The symptoms are not attributable to another disorder, medical condition, or substance.

● The symptoms cause significant distress or impairment.

Additional evidence for genetic contributions to mood disorders comes from a large longitudinal study of people with mood disorders sponsored by the National Institute of Mental Health (Rice et al., 1987). This study, which was carried out in five prestigious psychiatric facilities in the United States, provides some of the most thoroughly documented family prevalence data on mood disorders. In the sample, of the 955 **probands** (people with symptoms of the disorder—in this case, mood disorder), 612 had relatives who were willing to be interviewed as part of the study. This group consisted of 2,225 people, including parents, siblings, children, and spouses. On the basis of family interviews, the researchers were able to estimate the prevalence of mood disorders among these relatives. Of the relatives of probands with major depressive disorder, 1 percent showed symptoms of the same disorder.

A large, long-term follow-up of individuals with various mood disorders showed that bipolar disorder clustered in the families of people with bipolar disorder but not in the families of people with major depression or nonmood-disordered controls (Winokur et al., 1995).

Although researchers have struggled to pinpoint the precise genetic abnormality in families with especially high rates of bipolar disorder, their attention has been drawn in recent years to chromosome 18 (Berrettini et al., 1994, 1997; McMahon et al., 1997). One of the genes on this chromosome may control a neurotransmitter receptor involved in the action of lithium and antidepressants, and a second gene may relate to disturbances in cortisol activity. These suggested genetic-biochemical links could ultimately prove crucial in understanding the biological basis for bipolar disorder.

Researchers also use adoption studies to study the relative effects of genetics and environment on mood disorders. For example, Mendlewicz and Rainer (1977) found that 31 percent of individuals who were adopted and later developed mood disorders had biological parents with this type of disorder, whereas only 2 percent of the adoptees who did not have mood disorders had a biological parent with a mood disorder. Researchers in a later study (Wender et al., 1986) looked at the biological and adoptive relatives of adoptees, including not only parents but also siblings and half-siblings. They found that the adoptees with major depressive disorder were 8 times more likely than were the matched controls (adoptees who had no psychiatric diagnosis) to have relatives with a history of depression. Another impressive statistic from this study was the finding that the suicide rate was 15 times higher among the biological relatives of the adoptees with a mood disorder.

Genetics cannot tell the whole story, however. For example, one group of researchers studying major depressive disorder in twins arrived at a heritability estimate of 40 to 45 percent, meaning that almost half the variation in depression within the population can be explained by genetic factors (Kendler et al., 1993). This statistic also means, however, that half of the variation in depression cannot be explained by heredity. This tells us that life experiences must also play a role in determining whether a person develops a mood disorder. As we will see later, stressful life experiences are also thought to predispose individuals to depressive disorders, and there is intriguing evidence that life stress may interact with genetic factors. Among a sample of more than 2,000 female twin pairs classified according to genetic liability for depression, those who had not experienced stressful life events were equally likely (about 1 percent) to develop actual symptoms. However, among women who had experienced a significant stressful event such as assault, serious relationship problems, or death of a close relative, the women with the highest genetic liability had a rate of major depression of 15 percent, compared with a rate of 6 percent among the women with the lowest genetic liability (Kendler et al., 1995) (see Figure 9.1). Therefore, genetic liability played virtually no role in predisposing an individual to developing a mood disorder unless compounded with stressful life experiences.

Biochemical Factors

The mechanisms that genetically predispose high-risk people to become depressed or have manic episodes are still unknown. At present, the most widely held biological theories focus on altered neurotransmitter functioning as the cause of mood disorders. Because scientists cannot directly observe the actions of

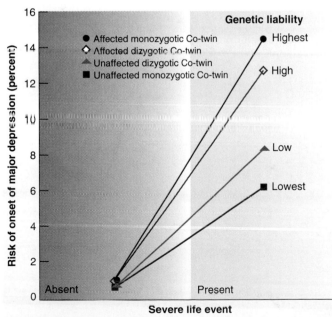

Figure 9.1

Risk of onset of major depression (per person-month) as a function of genetic liability and the presence or absence of a severe, stressful life event (in that month) among, 2,060 female twins.

The experience of a manic episode can be as exhilarating as a ride on a roller coaster. Sometimes people in this state don't want the manic ride to end.

neurotransmitters in the human brain, research in this area must involve studies of animals and observations of people who take certain types of drugs.

The earliest theory along these lines was the **catecholamine hypothesis** (Schildkraut, 1965), which asserts that a relative shortage of norepinephrine (a catecholamine) causes depression, and an overabundance of norepinephrine causes mania. The catecholamine hypothesis emerged from observing people's reactions to medications that affect the functioning of this type of neurotransmitter. For example, clinical evidence suggested that people who take certain antihypertensive medications become depressed, presumably because the drug depletes the levels of norepinephrine and other catecholamines. An alternative to the catecholamine hypothesis is the **indolamine hypothesis** (Glassman, 1969), which states that a deficiency of serotonin contributes to the behavioral symptoms of depression. The processes that cause a deficiency of serotonin are thought to be similar to those that cause norepinephrine deficits.

These neurotransmitter deficit hypotheses provided an important breakthrough in the understanding of the biological factors of mood disorders; however, they are now considered far too simplistic. One problem with such theories is the fact that antidepressant medications do not have immediate effects, as would be the case if a rise in the catecholamine level were enough to alleviate depression. These medications typically take at least 2 weeks to become therapeutically effective, yet they change neurochemical transmission in less than a day. Second, the observation that antihypertensive medications cause depression by altering catecholamine activity has been called into question by a study of medical claims among a sample of more than 4,000 adults, in which no relationship was found between the use of these medications and the clinical diagnosis of depression (Bright & Everitt, 1992).

Neuroendocrine research has also pointed out an important relationship between hormonal activity and depression. Researchers have proposed that certain "stress" hormones become activated in cases of melancholic depression, leading to the behavioral expression of anxiety and fearfulness (Schulkin, 1994). Furthermore, the known fact that adults and adolescents with mood disorders have abnormal levels of thyroid hormones suggests a link between the rate of metabolism in the body and the occurrence of manic or depressive symptoms (Sokolov, Kutcher, & Joffe, 1994). Researchers have also focused on the body's production of **cortisol,** a hormone involved in mobilizing the body's resources in times of stress. For example, a steroid called dexamethasone ordinarily suppresses the production of cortisol for at least one day after people take it. The **dexamethasone suppression test,** or **DST,** measures their cortisol levels during this period. When people with certain forms of depression take the DST, they do not show the suppression response (Nelson & Davis, 1997). These results further support the role of biological factors in many forms of mood disorders.

Although our understanding of the role of biology in mood disorders is still incomplete, multiple lines of research seem to point to a biological contribution to the causes and symptoms of mood disorders. Particularly compelling are the research findings in the area of genetics. As we discuss other theories of mood disorders, keep in mind the interaction among biological, psychological, and social factors. Regardless of what precipitates depression, depressed people experience biological changes. Any intervention must address the individual's physical as well as psychological state.

Psychological Perspectives

As important as biological factors appear to be in the understanding of mood disorders, it is clear that psychology plays a crucial role as well. Each of the major theoretical perspectives in the field has something to offer in understanding the causes of depression.

Psychodynamic Theories

Early psychoanalytic theories of mood disorders reflected themes of loss and feelings of rejection (Abraham, 1911/1968). Later psychodynamic theories retain a focus on inner psychic processes as the basis for mood disturbances, although they involve less of an emphasis on loss. For example, well-known British psychoanalyst John Bowlby proposed that people can become depressed as adults if they were raised by parents who failed to provide them with a stable and secure relationship (Bowlby, 1980). Another variant on the theme of deficient parenting comes from Jules Bemporad (1985), who proposed that children in these families become preoccupied with the need to be loved by others. As adults, they form relationships in which they overvalue the support of their partners. When such relationships end, the depressed person becomes overwhelmed with feelings of inadequacy and loss. Psychoanalytic explanations of mania are similar to those of depression, in that mania is seen as a defensive response by which an individual staves off feelings of inadequacy, loss, and helplessness. Presumably, people develop feelings of grandiosity and elation or become hyperenergetic as an unconscious defense against sinking into a state of gloom and despair.

Behavioral Theories

One of the earliest behavioral formulations of theories of depression was that the symptoms of depression are the result of a reduction in positive reinforcements (Lazarus, 1968; Skinner, 1953). According to this view, depressed people withdraw from

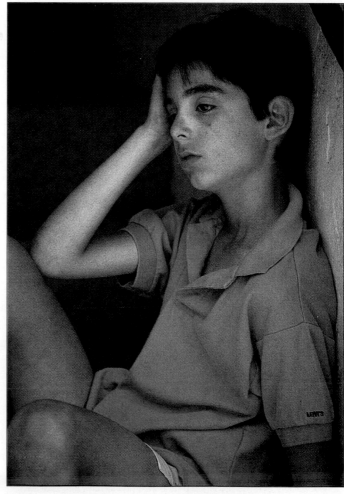

Neglectful parents can leave a child feeling unlovable.

CRITICAL ISSUE

Prozac— a Cure for Many Maladies?

During each of the recent decades, one medication was hailed as a revolutionary medication that would change psychiatric treatment forever, leading to widespread use. For example, in the 1960s, Thorazine was heralded as the medication that would end the institutionalization of people with psychotic disorders. In the 1970s, lithium was regarded as the ultimate treatment for mania. Valium also became widely used at this time for symptoms of anxiety.

Although all of these medications have been used with some success, they all have drawbacks as well. The fact that Thorazine was not a cure for schizophrenia, but just a treatment for some of the symptoms of the disorder, soon became evident. Lithium is effective when used in its recommended dose, but manic individuals are typically reluctant to take a medication that lowers their elevated moods. The abuse of Valium, as you may know, became a national scandal; its indiscriminate use led to millions of people becoming dependent on this drug to resolve everyday life stresses. Furthermore, even when used properly, each of these medications has side ef-

fects, some of them very serious, which were not understood completely when the medications were first introduced.

Prozac (fluoxetine), which was introduced in the late 1980s, is the latest psychotropic medication to make a big splash. This antidepressant has become one of the most widely prescribed medications in the world; for example, in 1994, Americans spent approximately $712 million on this most popular of all psychotropic medications (Standard & Poor's Industry Survey, 1995). Part of the reason for the large sales figure is its higher price relative to the other antidepressants; because of its effectiveness and relatively minor side effects, more than 10 million people have been willing to pay this price and have been prescribed Prozac. In addition to being therapeutically effective for people who have depression, Prozac also alleviates symptoms of obsessive-compulsive disorder and panic disorder (Barondes, 1994).

As the popularity of Prozac has grown, so have its applications. In his national bestseller, *Listening to Prozac,* psychiatrist and psychotherapist Peter Kramer (1993) suggests that Prozac need not be reserved for people diagnosed with a psychological disorder, such as depression. According to Kramer, Prozac can quickly and easily help people who have problems with low self-esteem or sensitivity to interpersonal rejection. People who take Prozac often claim that they feel more themselves than they did before taking it, and they believe that, if the medication helps them feel better, they should continue to take it, whether or not they are diagnosed with a psychological disorder (Konner, 1994). If Kramer's thesis is borne out by scientific research, the aspects of our

personalities that we view as most unique and particular to our own experiences might have to be reconsidered in terms of our biological development. Because little research supports using Prozac to alter personality characteristics, it is still too early to know if these claims represent a genuine advance in psychopharmacology or the latest trend in prescription (Barondes, 1994).

Prozac actually is not that different in its actions from the tricyclic antidepressants; however, it is unique in that it targets its effects on only one of the catecholamines—serotonin—rather than the broader range of neurotransmitters on which the tricyclics act. Like other medications, Prozac usually takes some weeks for its effects to be felt.

Similar to the miracle drugs of previous decades, a risk is associated with Prozac's precipitous rise in use. There have been some anecdotal reports of troubling side effects, including suicidality and dangerous impulsivity (Steiner, 1991; Teicher, Glod, & Cole, 1990). However, in a large-scale, controlled study of more than 1,000 people with major depressive disorder, researchers concluded that there was no basis for alarm regarding the prescription of Prozac (Fava & Rosenbaum, 1991). In fact, one of the primary advantages of Prozac is its side effect profile (Stokes, 1993). Because it has far fewer troubling side effects than the tricyclics, people are more willing to stay on Prozac until it achieves its desired effect. Prozac is also far less lethal than the older tricyclic antidepressants when taken in an overdose. For depressed individuals, some of whom might feel suicidal, this can be particularly important.

---

life because they no longer have incentives to be active. Consider the example of a formerly successful athlete who suffers an injury. Lacking the positive reinforcement of the athletic successes to which he has become accustomed, he might retreat into a depressive state.

Another classic behavioral position maintains that deficient social skills contribute to depression. A person with poor

interpersonal relationships loses the reinforcements provided by the attention and interest of other people (Lewinsohn & Shaw, 1969). Consequently, the individual is likely to become depressed and stay depressed. In time, the depressed person may derive a certain amount of secondary gain. Escape from responsibility, such as work and family commitments, may be reinforcement for remaining depressed.

Stressful life events are a third contributor to depression, according to behavioral models, because they disrupt the individual's ability to carry out important and relatively automatic behavior patterns (Hoberman & Lewinsohn, 1985). These patterns, called "scripts," include the many daily routines in which people engage every day, such as getting dressed in the morning and going to work. The changes in scripts that result from many different types of life events result in the mood changes that contribute to depression. The important factor determining whether a person will become depressed is the extent to which the circumstances or events interfere with the individual's scripts. The greater the disruption, the greater the distress. It is not only the inconvenience of such disruptions that contribute to depression, however. People feel more self-conscious when they lose the cues provided by their familiar routines and surroundings. This heightened self-consciousness can lead the person to become more self-critical, to take responsibility for negative outcomes, and to withdraw from others.

As an example of how disruptions in scripts can lead to depression, consider the case of Martina, who was recently widowed. She has not only lost a close relationship but also must make vast changes in her day-to-day life. Martina's life becomes less predictable, and her responsibilities are doubled. In this behavioral formulation of depression, such an interruption in Martina's daily life patterns results in a loss of positive reinforcements (the loss of a close relationship) and makes her feel more self-conscious in carrying out activities that are unfamiliar to her. For example, when she goes to a restaurant, she feels awkward and embarrassed about sitting alone; when she goes to the bank for the first time to discuss her financial situation, she feels uncomfortable and afraid of making a mistake in front of the bank personnel.

One important variant of the behavioral approach to depression is the **learned helplessness model,** which proposes that depressed people have come to view themselves as incapable of having an effect on their environment. Perhaps in your introductory psychology course you studied the phenomenon of *learned helplessness,* a term coined by psychologist Martin Seligman (Maier & Seligman, 1976). In their controversial and disturbing experiments, Seligman and his co-workers studied the conditioning of fear and escape learning in dogs. They placed a group of dogs in a cage from which they could not escape, and an electrical apparatus subjected them to electric shock. A warning light preceded each administration of shock. Next, experimenters placed the dogs in a chamber from which they could escape shock by jumping over a partition, if they did so at the signal of a warning light. Seligman had originally hypothesized that the dogs would immediately jump over the partition to escape the painful consequences. To his surprise, rather than escape, the dogs lay down "helplessly" until the experimenter finally turned off the shock. In contrast, dogs that were never subjected to inescapable shock took the normal action of jumping across the partition, once they learned that this escape route was available.

Naturally, Seligman and his co-workers were interested in the applicability of the learned helplessness phenomenon to humans. Of course, they could not present humans with the same kind of stimuli they applied to the animals. Instead, they

A parent who suddenly loses a spouse may have trouble adjusting to the doubling of household and family responsibilities, leading to depression and despondency.

conditioned helplessness in humans (college students) by presenting them with uncontrollable noise delivered through earphones. When given the opportunity to turn off the noise, the conditioned helplessness group failed to do so and, instead, listened passively to the noise (Hiroto, 1974). In addition to responding this way to a physiological stimulus, humans showed the same response to a cognitive task. When confronted with unsolvable cognitive problems, such as anagrams, college students gave up attempting to find solutions when given new problems that could be solved (Hiroto & Seligman, 1975). Perhaps you have felt this way when taking a particularly difficult exam, and you know the feeling of "giving up" because it does no good to keep trying.

What does this have to do with depression? According to Seligman's initial explanation, the apathy and passivity that depressed people show are behavioral symptoms of learned helplessness. People show these symptoms in response to prior experiences in which others made them feel powerless to control their destiny. Almost as soon as Seligman proposed this connection, his position was criticized as an oversimplistic translation from animal data to clinical problems in humans. One important limitation of the original explanation of depression was that it did not account for the fact that depressed people blame themselves for their failures. If they feel powerless to control the outcome of what happens to them, how could they blame themselves?

Seligman and his group modified their theory to take this factor into account, developing the "revised formulation" of the learned helplessness theory (Abramson, Seligman, & Teasdale, 1978; Peterson & Seligman, 1984). The revised version of the learned helplessness theory takes into account the role of **attributions,** explanations that people make of the things that happen to them. For example, if your stereo is stolen, you might attribute this to the fact that you forgot to lock your door before you left for the evening. In the revised learned helplessness model, exposure to situations inducing helplessness (traumatic or negative life events) leads depressed people to attribute their powerlessness to a lack of personal resources. They see this situation as unremitting and their powerlessness as extending to every aspect of their lives. Such attributions are "internal, stable, and global." By contrast, nondepressed people attribute their problems to situations outside their control (external attributions), they see their problems as temporary (not stable), and they regard them as fairly specific to the situation (not global).

Returning to the example of the stolen stereo, a depressed woman would see the theft as being typical of her stupidity in failing to lock the door. She would regard the theft as part of an overall life pattern and would see her carelessness as something that causes her grief in many situations. A nondepressed woman would attribute blame to the general rise of crime in her city, instead of seeing the theft as her own fault. She also would view the theft as an isolated incident in her life and would regard it as atypical of the other things that happen to her. The kinds of attributions depressed people make, according to later work on learned helplessness theory, render these individuals particularly vulnerable to feelings of hopelessness when confronted with negative life events (Metalsky, Halberstadt, & Abramson, 1987).

Although the learned helplessness theory has attracted considerable attention among depression researchers, the theory is limited in its power to explain individual differences in vulnerability to depression. Much of the research in this area would lead one to think that all depressed people are alike. As you know from reading about dysthymic disorder and major depressive disorder, these are different disorders, which vary in their symptoms and causes. Specifically, depression is a broad-spectrum disorder that ranges from mild yet chronic dysphoria to intense but episodic despair. Another problem with the revised learned helplessness theory of depression is that the research evidence used to support it relies on samples of people who would not be considered clinically depressed but, rather, mildly dysphoric (Alloy & Abramson, 1979). Among depressed individuals, there is no evidence of a "learned helplessness" subtype whose self-attributions match those proposed by the theory (Haslam & Beck, 1994). Nevertheless, the revised learned helplessness model has added a cognitive element to the behavioral models that has proved to have theoretical and practical value. We will now turn to the approaches that are more prominently cognitive.

Cognitively Based Theories

Think of a time when you were depressed, and try to recall the reasons for your depression. Perhaps you lost a close friend or felt pessimistic about your future. Maybe you misinterpreted something that someone said to you, which caused you to feel bad about yourself. Cognitively based approaches propose that serious mood changes can result from events in our lives or from our perceptions of events.

According to the cognitive perspective, people develop depressive disorders if they have been sensitized by early experiences to react in a particular way to a particular kind of loss or stressful event. Depressed people react to stressful experiences by activating a set of thoughts that Beck (Beck, 1967) called the **cognitive triad:** a negative view of the self, the world, and the future. Beck proposed that, once activated, this depressive way of viewing the self, the world, and the future (called a depressive schema) perpetuates itself through a cyclical process. For example, consider a young man, Anthony, who constantly looks at the negative side of life. Even when something good happens to him, he manages to see the downside of the situation. What is happening, according to theorists such as Beck, is that Anthony interprets every situation in terms of his schema, which prevents him from seeing anything but problems, hopelessness, and his own inadequacy. Because Anthony is so pessimistic, he can never take anything positive from his experiences, and his negative outlook proves to be a handicap. People become bored and irritated with Anthony and eventually give up trying to involve him in social activities. Thus, the cycle of depression is perpetuated.

Adding to the cycle of depressive thinking are **cognitive distortions,** errors that depressed people make in the way they draw conclusions from their experiences (Beck, Rush, Shaw, & Emery, 1979; Beck & Weishaar, 1989). These cognitive distortions involve applying illogical rules, such as making arbitrary inferences, jumping to conclusions, overgeneralizing, and taking a detail out of context (see Table 9.1). Using these rules makes the depressed person ascribe negative meanings to past and present events and make gloomy predictions about the future. The person is probably not even specifically aware of having these thoughts, because they have become such a constant feature of the individual's existence. The situation is comparable to what you might experience if you were sitting for a long time in a room with a noisy air conditioner. You do not actually notice how noisy the room is until someone else walks in and comments on it. Similarly, it takes a specific effort to isolate and identify automatic thoughts when they have become such permanent fixtures in the person's consciousness.

Contributing further to the unhappiness of depressed people, according to Beck, is the content of their thought. Depressed people feel sad because they believe they are deprived of something important that threatens their self-esteem. Further, depressed people are convinced that they are responsible for the loss. Their dysfunctional attitudes cause them to assume that they are worthless and helpless and that their efforts are doomed to fail. They distort any experience, including a positive one, so that it fits in with this generalized belief (Safran, 1990). As a consequence of these cognitive distortions, depressed individuals experience low feelings of well-being, energy, desire to be with others, and interest in the environment. These phenomena contribute to their depressed affect (Clark, Steer, & Beck, 1994).

Sociocultural and Interpersonal Perspectives

Some depressed people have had lifelong difficulties in their interactions with other people. Consider the case of Willy, a 40-year-old man who for most of his life has acted in abrasive ways that alienate others. As the years go by, Willy becomes increasingly saddened by the fact that he has no friends and realizes that it is unlikely that he will ever have a close relationship. For depressed people like Willy, whose social skills are so deficient, a cycle is created as their constant pessimism and self-deprecation make other people feel guilty and depressed. As a result, other people respond in unhelpful ways with criticism and rejection, and this further reinforces the depressed person's negative view of the world.

Table 9.1

Examples of Cognitive Distortions

Overgeneralizing

| If it's true in one case, it applies to any case that is even slightly similar. | "I failed my first English exam so I'm probably going to fail all of them." |

Selective Abstraction

| The only events that the person takes seriously are those that represent failures, deprivation, loss, or frustration. | "Even though I won the election for school committee, I'm not really popular because not everyone voted for me." |

Excessive Responsibility

| I am responsible for all bad things that happen to me or others to whom I am close. | "It's my fault that my friend didn't get the job—I should've warned her about how hard the interview would be." |

Assuming Temporal Causality

| If it has been true in the past, then it's always going to be true. | "My last date was a wipe-out; my next date will probably hate me too." |

Making Excessive Self-References

| I am the center of everyone else's attention, and they can all see when I mess up. | "When I spilled the coffee, everyone could see what a klutz I am!" |

Catastrophizing

| Always thinking the worst and being certain that it will happen. | "Because my sales figures were lower last quarter, I will never make it in the business world." |

Dichotomous Thinking

| Seeing everything as either one extreme or another rather than as mixed or in between. | "Everything about this school is rotten—the students, the professors, the dorms, and the food." |

From Aaron T. Beck, et al., *Cognitive Therapy of Depression: A Treatment Manual.* Copyright © 1979 Guilford Publications, Inc., New York, NY. Reprinted by permission of Dr. Aaron T. Beck.

Expanding on these ideas, Columbia University researcher Myrna Weissman, with her late husband Gerald Klerman and their associates, developed a model of understanding mood disorders that emphasizes disturbed social functioning (Klerman, Weissman, Rounsaville, & Chevron, 1984; Weissman & Markowitz, 1994). This theory incorporates the ideas of behavioral psychologists who focus on the poor social skills of the depressed individual, but it goes one step further in looking at the origins of the depressed person's fundamental problems (see feature box p. 298-299). The interpersonal theory of depression is rooted in the interpersonal approaches of Adolph Meyer (1957) and Harry Stack Sullivan (1953a; 1953b) and the attachment theory of John Bowlby. Meyer was known for his psychobiological approach to abnormal behavior, emphasizing how psychological problems might represent an individual's misguided attempts to adapt to the psychosocial environment. He believed that physical symptoms can also develop in association with psychological distress. Sullivan characterized abnormal behavior as a function of impaired interpersonal relationships, including deficiencies in communication. Each of these theories could apply to a variety of psychological disorders, but Bowlby's theory, with its specific focus on disturbed attachment bonds in early childhood as the cause of unhappiness later in life, is particularly relevant to depression.

Interpersonal theory connects the ideas of these theorists with the behavioral and cognitively oriented theories by postulating a set of steps that leads to depression. The first step is the person's failure in childhood to acquire the skills needed to develop satisfying intimate relationships. This failure leads to a sense of despair, isolation, and resulting depression. Once a person's depression is established, it is maintained by poor social skills and impaired communication, which lead to further rejection by others. Reactive depressions in adulthood may arise when the individual experiences a stressful life event, such as the end of a relationship or death of a significant other. After the depressive symptoms begin, the individual's maladaptive social skills perpetuate them. For example, a man whose wife dies may become so distraught over an extended period of time that he alienates his friends and family members. In time, a vicious cycle establishes itself, in which his behavior causes people to stay away; because he is so lonely, he becomes even more difficult in his interactions with others. Although the individual circumstances differ in each case, it is this cycle of depression, lack of social interaction, and deterioration of social skills that interpersonal theory regards as the core problem of depression.

In another line of discussion and research about social and interpersonal influences on mood disorders, some theorists and clinicians have attended to the ways in which conflict with close ones, particularly family members, is sometimes associated with the onset and course of depression (Moos, Cronkite, & Moos, 1998). It makes sense that unhappiness in a person's most intimate relationships has a profound impact on emotional functioning.

Some investigators interested in sociocultural issues have focused attention on the ways in which the prevalence of mood disorders differs between men and women in various countries of the world. In developed countries, the rate of depression among women is twice that of men, but, in developing countries, the ratios vary, with most reporting no gender difference. Drawing conclusions from these data is complicated by a number of factors, such as international differences in the definition of *depression* and other methodological problems. Of particular interest are views that the experience of depression may be conceptualized in markedly different ways when cross-cultural studies are conducted. For example, in some countries, men who act aggressively are referred for professional help, which may be explained in terms of depression; by contrast, women who are upset may seek support from alternative systems, such as spiritual healers (Culbertson, 1997). Although such theories and findings have limited applicability in the United States, clinicians know that they must be especially alert to the ways in which gender and culture influence the experience and definition of mood disorders.

Treatment

Biological Treatment

Because of the strong support for biological influences on mood disorders, people with these disorders often receive somatic treatments. Antidepressant medication is the most common form of somatic treatment for people who are depressed, and lithium carbonate (lithium) is the most widely used medication for people who have bipolar disorder. The most common medications used to treat depression are tricyclic antidepressants, monoamine oxidase inhibitors (MAOIs), and selective serotonin reuptake inhibitors (SSRIs).

Tricyclic antidepressants derive their name from the fact that they have a three-ring chemical structure. These medications, such as amitriptyline (Elavil, Endep), desipramine (Norpramin), imipramine (Tofranil), and nortriptyline (Aventyl, Pamelor), are particularly effective in alleviating depression in people who have some of the more common biological symptoms, such as disturbed appetite and sleep. Although the exact process by which tricyclic antidepressants work still remains unclear, it is known that they block the premature reuptake of biogenic amines back into the presynaptic neurons, thus increasing their excitatory effects on the postsynaptic neuron.

The antidepressant effects of MAOIs, such as phenelzine (Nardil) and tranylcypromine (Parnate), are believed to occur because the medications inhibit the enzyme monoamine oxidase, which converts the biogenic amines, such as norepinephrine and serotonin, into inert substances, so that they cannot excite the postsynaptic neurons. MAOIs prolong the life of neurotransmitters, thus increasing neuronal flow. These medications are particularly effective in treating depression in people with chronic depression that dates back many years and

who have not responded to the tricyclics. However, MAOIs are not as commonly prescribed as the other two types of medications, because their interactions with certain other substances can cause serious complications. Specifically, people taking MAOIs are not able to take certain allergy medications or to ingest foods or beverages containing a substance called tyramine (for example, beer, cheese, and chocolate), because the combination can bring on a hypertensive crisis, in which blood pressure rises dramatically and dangerously.

Selective serotonin reuptake inhibitors (SSRIs) have become very popular alternatives to the tricyclics and MAOIs. These medications block the uptake of serotonin, enabling more of this neurotransmitter to be available for action at the receptor sites. The SSRIs are distinguished from the tricyclics because of their selectivity. Unlike the other antidepressants, they do not block multiple receptors, which would cause unpleasant side effects, including sedation, weight gain, constipation, blood pressure changes, and dry mouth. The newer SSRI medications are not without side effects, however; the most commonly reported complaints are nausea, agitation, and sexual dysfunction. Despite some of these problems, these medications have received a tremendous amount of positive publicity, leading some to tout them as the miracle drugs of the decade, if not the past century (see feature box). SSRIs such as fluoxetine (Prozac), sertraline (Zoloft), fluvoxamine (Luvox), paroxetine (Paxil), trazadone (Desyrel), and bupropion (Wellbutrin) have had a dramatic impact on the lives of millions of depressed people. Interestingly, investigators have not found these medications to be substantially more effective than the tricyclics in alleviating the symptoms of depression (Greenberg et al., 1994). Another difference between SSRIs and tricyclics is the fact that an SSRI often has positive effects on symptoms other than depression; for example, some individuals taking Prozac report that they are less sensitive to criticism and fear of rejection, while also feeling higher levels of self-esteem and ability to experience pleasure (Barondes, 1994).

Antidepressant medications take time to work—from 2 to 6 weeks before a client's symptoms begin to lift. Once the depression has subsided, the client is usually urged to remain on the medication for 4 or 5 additional months, and much longer for clients with a history of recurrent, severe depressive episodes. Because of medication side effects and client concerns, clinicians have found it helpful to develop therapeutic programs that involve regular visits early in treatment, expanded efforts to educate clients about the medications, and continued monitoring of treatment compliance (Katon et al., 1995).

The traditional treatment for the manic symptoms of bipolar disorder is lithium carbonate, referred to as lithium (Klein & Hurowitz, 1998). Lithium is a naturally occurring salt (found in small amounts in drinking water) that, when used medically, replaces sodium in the body. The psychopharmacological effect of this medication is to calm the manic individual by decreasing the catecholamine levels in the nervous system. Researchers have studied the efficacy of lithium in numerous studies over the past three decades, and the conclusion seems clear—lithium is effective in treating the symptoms of acute mania and in preventing the recurrence of manic episodes (Keck & McElroy, 1998).

People who have frequent manic episodes, such as two or more a year, are advised to remain on lithium continuously as a preventive measure. The drawback is that, even though lithium is a natural substance in the body, it can have side effects, such as mild central nervous system disturbances, gastrointestinal upsets, and more serious cardiac effects. Because of these side effects, some people who experience manic episodes are reluctant or even unwilling to take lithium continuously. Furthermore, lithium interferes with the "highs" associated with bipolar disorder, and manic individuals may be reluctant to take the medication because they enjoy the pleasurable feelings that accompany escalation into the manic episode. By the time a full-blown episode develops, these individuals may have become so grandiose that they deny they even have a problem. Those taking lithium face a difficult choice regarding whether or not to remain on maintenance doses of the medication. On the one hand, side effects must be considered. On the other hand, not taking the medication puts them at risk of having another episode. Some therapists encourage their clients to participate in lithium groups, in which members who use the medication on a regular basis provide support to each other regarding the importance of staying on the medication.

Because of the variable nature of bipolar disorder, additional medication is often beneficial in treating some symptoms. For example, people in a depressive episode may need to take an antidepressant medication in addition to the lithium for the duration of the episode. However, this can be problematic for a person who is prone to developing mania, because an antidepressant might provoke hypomania or mania (Dantzler & Salzman, 1995). Those who have psychotic symptoms may benefit from taking antipsychotic medication until these disturbing symptoms subside (Dubovsky, 1994). People who experience rapid cycling present a challenge for clinicians because of the sudden changes that take place in emotions and behavior. Psychopharmacologists have reported that rapid cyclers, especially those for whom lithium has not been sufficient, seem to respond positively to prescriptions of anticonvulsant medication, such as carbamazepine (Tegretol) or valproate (Depakote) (Brown, 1995).

For some clients with mood disorders, medication is either ineffective or slow in alleviating symptoms that are severe and possibly life-threatening. In cases involving incapacitating depression, the clinician may recommend electroconvulsive therapy (ECT). Although ECT is the most powerful somatic treatment for major depressive disorder, it is the least commonly used because of the negative connotations associated with it, as well as concern about short-term and long-term side effects. If you saw the movie *One Flew over the Cuckoo's Nest,* you will probably never forget the dramatic presentation of the misuse of ECT. Indeed, negative attitudes toward ECT are due mainly to historical misuse of this procedure as punishment rather than treatment. Today ECT continues to be administered, because it has been shown to be a lifesaving treatment for severely depressed people for whom medications alone are ineffective. This is especially true for people over the age of 60. In fact, this is the age group most likely to receive ECT for depression, probably because so many other treatments have been tried and discarded as ineffec-

tive (Niederehe & Schneider, 1998). In addition to being used for the treatment of depression, ECT is recommended for individuals in an acute state of mania who are not responding to medication (Mukherjee, Sackeim, & Schnur, 1994).

For depressed individuals, ECT is usually administered six to eight times, once every other day until the person's mood returns to normal. The person undergoing this treatment receives anesthesia to reduce discomfort, a muscle relaxant, oxygen, and medication to help control heart rhythm. The lowest voltage needed to induce a convulsion is delivered to the client's head for less than a second. This is followed 2 to 3 seconds later by a tonic phase, lasting for 10 to 12 seconds, during which all muscles in the body under voluntary control undergo involuntary contractions. Last, there is a clonic phase, consisting of 30 to 50 seconds of convulsions, which appear more like a slight bodily tremor because of the muscle relaxant. A few minutes later, the individual emerges from the anesthesia, alert, without pain, and without recollection of what has transpired. Some seriously depressed individuals benefit from what is called "maintenance" ECT, in which the treatment is administered over a period of several months to prevent a recurrence of depressive symptoms (Stiebel, 1995).

One aspect of ECT that troubles some clinicians and clients is the fact that no one understands why ECT works. Most current hypotheses center on ECT-induced changes in neurotransmitter receptors and in the body's natural opiates. As for side effects, the primary complaints of clients following an ECT trial are short-term memory loss and confusion, which disappear within 2 weeks of the final treatment. No permanent brain damage or memory loss is known to result from ECT (Calev et al., 1991).

Light therapy is yet another intervention for people with depression that follows a seasonal pattern. Exposing some depressed individuals to special lights during the winter can alleviate depressive symptoms (Eastman et al., 1998; Lewy et al., 1998). In one version of light therapy, individuals with seasonal depression use a "dawn simulation" procedure, in which they

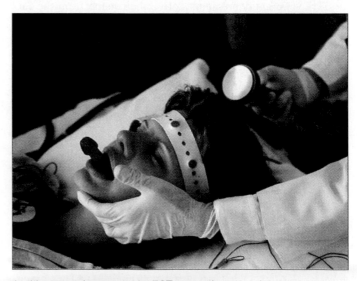

As this woman is prepared for ECT, precautions are taken to prevent injury. She is administered muscle relaxants, and a device is inserted into her mouth to prevent her from biting her tongue.

are exposed for a 2-hour period of gradual, dawn-like light each morning during the winter months. Another, less well-known but promising somatic treatment is sleep deprivation. Some people who do not respond well to medications improve when deprived of sleep for a period of 36 hours; they report that the sleep deprivation has the surprising effect of increasing the efficacy of antidepressant medications (Leibenluft et al., 1993).

Although somatic interventions, such as medication, ECT, and light therapy, provide effective and sometimes lifesaving help for many people, most therapists regard these treatments as insufficient by themselves. Consequently, clinicians typically recommend individual, family, or group psychotherapy as an adjunct to help the individual understand both the etiology of the disorder and the strategies for preventing recurrences. Let's turn now to the contributions of the various perspectives that address these psychological issues.

Psychological Treatment

In recent decades, clinicians and researchers have demonstrated the effectiveness of behavioral and cognitively based techniques for treating people with mood disorders (Craighead, Craighead, & Ilardi, 1998). Sometimes these techniques are part of a more comprehensive intervention, which also includes a somatic treatment (e.g., medication) or a sociocultural modality (e.g., couple therapy). In other instances, psychological interventions are sufficient.

Behavioral therapy for depression begins with a careful assessment of the frequency, quality, and range of activities and social interactions in the client's life. The clinician then implements a treatment involving a combination of helping the client change his or her environment, teaching the client certain social skills, and encouraging the client to seek out activities that help restore a proper mood balance. Specific reinforcements might be found from among activities that the client enjoyed in a nondepressed state.

In behavioral interventions, clients are given homework assignments that encourage them to engage in more pleasurable activities.

Education is an essential component of behavioral intervention. Depressed clients often set unrealistic goals and then are unable to implement behaviors to reach these goals. The therapist gives regular homework assignments that help the client make gradual behavioral changes and that increase the probability of successful performance. Behavioral therapy also incorporates contracting and self-reinforcement procedures. For example, every time the client follows through on initiating a social activity, reward should follow. Such rewards may consist of self-congratulatory statements or may involve more concrete behaviors, such as having a favorite snack. If these procedures do not succeed, the behavioral therapist moves toward more extensive instruction, modeling, coaching, role-playing and rehearsal, and "real-world" trials.

Cognitively based therapy usually involves a short-term, structured approach that focuses on the client's negative thoughts and includes suggestions for activities that will improve the client's daily life. This technique involves an active collaboration between the client and the therapist and is oriented toward current problems and their resolution. The cognitive approach incorporates didactic work, cognitive restructuring, and behavioral techniques.

Didactic work involves explaining the theory to the client—teaching the client how depression results from faulty thinking. Cognitive restructuring (Sacco & Beck, 1985) involves a multistep approach. First, the client needs to identify and monitor dysfunctional automatic thoughts. Second, the client needs to recognize the connection between thoughts, emotions, and behavior. Third, the client must evaluate the reasonableness of the automatic thoughts. Fourth, the client must learn how to substitute more reasonable thoughts for the dysfunctional automatic thoughts. Finally, the client must identify and alter dysfunctional assumptions. In other words, the therapist attempts to break down the maladaptive thinking patterns that underlie the depressed individual's negative emotions.

The dim days of winter cause people with seasonal affective disorder to be particularly prone to dysphoric moods.

Behavior change is needed in order to identify and alter dysfunctional cognitions. Behavioral methods include pleasure prediction experiments, weekly activity schedules, and graded task assignments. Pleasure prediction experiments involve planning an activity, predicting how much pleasure it will produce, and then observing how much it actually does produce. Such an exercise can help a depressed client see that he or she is mistaken about gloomy predictions. The weekly activity schedule helps the client monitor activities on an hour-by-hour basis, with the goal of showing the client that it is not true that he or she "never accomplishes anything." The client rates the mastery and pleasure of each activity. If the client really is inactive, then activities are planned hour-by-hour for each day of the week. Graded task assignments involve identifying a goal that the client wishes to attain but thinks is impossible, breaking the goal into simple component tasks, and helping the client experience the success of accomplishing a task, however simple.

The cognitively based method reduces the symptoms of depression by helping clients learn to restructure their thoughts. However, the method appears to have greater effectiveness for treating individuals whose depressive disorder has an acute course (Thase et al., 1994). Researchers working within this perspective are also attempting to integrate their treatment approach with biological methods and factors related to life stress (Simons, Gordon, Monroe, & Thase, 1995). Emerging from this approach is the finding that people who have experienced severe life events are more responsive to cognitive therapy than are individuals with, presumably, more deeply entrenched dysfunctional attitudes.

Although clinicians treating people with bipolar disorder customarily turn first to pharmacological interventions, they are also likely to incorporate psychological interventions designed to help clients develop better coping strategies in an effort to minimize the likelihood of relapse (Craighead, Miklowitz, Vajk, & Frank, 1998). Psychoeducation is an especially important aspect of treating people with bipolar disorder, in order to help clients with this condition understand its nature, as well as the ways in which medication is so important in controlling symptoms. Many people who have experienced a manic episode are tempted to forego taking their medication in the hope that they might once again experience the exciting highs of a manic episode. If they can develop insight into the risks involved in noncompliance, as well as an improved understanding of such medications as lithium, they are more likely to adhere to the treatment program.

Sociocultural and Interpersonal Intervention

Often in the treatment of people with mood disorders, clinicians find it extremely valuable to involve people who are close to the client. Couple or family therapy may provide a therapeutic context in which partners and family members can come to understand the experiences of the mood-disordered loved one and develop strategies for dealing with this individual's symptoms and disorder within the interpersonal system.

Interpersonal therapy (see Research Focus Box) was originally developed as a brief intervention, lasting between 12 and 16 weeks, which emerged from interpersonal theory. This approach adheres to a set of guidelines derived from research data. Although interpersonal therapy involves many of the techniques that most therapists use spontaneously, it frames these techniques in a systematic approach, including manuals to guide therapists in applying the method (Rounsaville, O'Malley, Foley, & Weisman, 1988).

Interpersonal therapy is divided into three broad phases. The first phase involves assessing the magnitude and nature of the individual's depression, using quantitative assessment measures. Interview methods are also used to determine the factors that precipitated the current episode. At that point, depending on the type of depressive symptoms the individual shows, the therapist considers treatment with antidepressant medications.

In the second phase, the therapist and the client collaborate in formulating a treatment plan that focuses on the primary problem. Typically, these problems are related to grief, interpersonal disputes, role transitions, and problems in interpersonal relationships stemming from inadequate social skills. The treatment plan is then carried out, with the methods varying according to the precise nature of the client's primary problem. In general, the therapist uses a combination of methods, such as encouraging self-exploration, providing support, educating the client in the nature of depression, and providing feedback on the client's ineffective social skills. Therapy focuses on the "here and now," rather than on past childhood or developmental issues.

Behavioral marital therapy is an approach that has been used successfully in treating depressed people who are having relational difficulties (Jacobson et al., 1991; O'Leary & Beach, 1990). Therapists providing this form of therapy use behavioral principles and techniques to help couples communicate more clearly with each other and solve problems more effectively. The clinician works with the couple to plan changes in their behaviors in ways that increase positive interactions while

According to the interpersonal theory of depression, poor social skills can contribute to a cycle of disturbed relationships, which intensifies the individual's experience of depression.

While the pain and depression of many people who commit suicide are usually evident to others, sometimes this is not the case. Scott Croteau, a 17 year old from Lewiston, Maine, was a star football player, honor student, and popular classmate. He was found hanging from a tree with a bullet wound in his head, leading authorities to wonder why such a seemingly successful and happy person would take his own life. Portrait photographer Emmett Stuart, Jr., set up a window display in memory of Scott at his studio in Lewiston. Croteau had posed in his football jersey for a yearbook photo on the last day he was seen alive.

minimizing negative ones. For example, the couple may work out a plan to engage regularly in pleasant activities, such as going for a walk or attending a movie. Reviews of research on behavioral marital therapy have shown that this approach is impressively effective in treating maritally distressed couples; in fact, it may be preferable to individual psychotherapy among maritally discordant couples, for whom both depression can be alleviated and marital discord can be reduced (Baucom et al., 1998).

For clients with bipolar disorder, marital and family interventions can serve an important therapeutic function in helping all participants in the system understand the nature and treatment of the disorder. Such interventions can also work in developing strategies to use when the mood-disordered individual is in the middle of a manic episode.

■ Suicide

For some people, depression is so painful that their thoughts turn recurrently to ideas about escaping from the torment that characterizes every day. People who reach this point feel that they lack the resources to cope with their problems. Not all suicides are in-

tended to be an end to life, however. Some suicide attempts are a "call for help" by people who believe the only way they can get help from others is by taking desperate actions. Rather than follow through on the act, they communicate their suicidal intent early enough so that they can be rescued.

Who Commits Suicide?

Each year, more than 31,000 Americans kill themselves (Anderson, Kochanek, & Murphy, 1997). In general, men are more likely to commit suicide than women, with the rate for adult men amounting to about four times the suicide rate for women. Women are more likely to *attempt* suicide, but they do not carry these attempts through to completion as often as men do. In turn, men are far more likely than women to take their own lives with firearms. When race is considered, White men are much more likely than are non-White men to commit suicide. Married people commit suicide less frequently than unmarried people, leading some researchers to conclude that marriage acts as a protective factor against suicide. (Klerman, 1987).

No formal diagnostic category in the *DSM* specifically applies to people who attempt suicide. Although most suicidal people have a mood disorder, suicidal behavior can also be associated with other disorders, such as schizophrenia, somatoform disorders, and anxiety disorders (Winokur, Black, & Nasrallah, 1988) especially panic disorder (Woodruff-Borden, Stanley, Lister, & Tabacchi, 1997). Some panic-stricken individuals become so terrified that they perceive this drastic measure as the only route of escape (Anthony & Petronis, 1991; Johnson, Weissman, & Klerman, 1990; Weissman et al., 1989). Suicidality is also a prominent feature in some personality disorders. Recall our discussion in Chapter 5 of people with borderline personality disorder who commonly make suicidal gestures and attempts. Finally, the combination of major depressive disorder and alcohol dependence is particularly lethal as a risk factor for suicide (Cornelius et al., 1995).

Why Do People Commit Suicide?

Theories about the causes of suicide focus both on the experience of depression that often precedes a suicide attempt and on related conditions that may serve as predisposing factors.

Biological Perspective

Statistics about family history of suicide support the notion that biological factors may predispose many individuals to the kinds of clinical states that lead to suicidality. There are higher rates of concordance between indentical (13.2 percent) compared with fraternal (.7 percent) twins (Roy, Segal, & Sarchiapone, 1995)—a link that adoption studies have shown cannot be attributed to environmental factors. Clinicians and researchers routinely ask about instances of suicide among relatives, knowing that a family history of suicide statistically increases the risk of suicide.

More direct support for biological contributions to suicide comes from findings of anatomical and physiological differences between suicide completers and controls. Autopsies of suicide completers reveal evidence of abnormalities in brain

Interpersonal Therapy for Depression

A groundbreaking study funded by the National Institute of Mental Health explored the controversy over the relative effectiveness of medications compared with psychotherapy in the treatment of depression (Elkin et al., 1989; Klein & Ross, 1993). In this study, researchers randomly assigned 250 people at six different sites to one of four treatment groups: (1) interpersonal psychotherapy, (2) cognitive-behavioral psychotherapy, (3) tricyclic antidepressant medication, and (4) placebo. In both the placebo and antidepressant conditions, which were conducted in a double-blind fashion, participants met weekly for 20 to 30 minutes with a therapist who monitored their progress and provided them with support. To assure consistency across sites and therapists in the way that the treatments were administered, the researchers developed a standardized manual describing the underlying theory of the approach the therapists were to use, the general strategies to be adopted, and suggested ways to deal with specific problems. The study continued for 16 weeks.

The researchers compared the outcomes of the four treatments using a variety of clinical indices, including clinician and self-report ratings of depression and other psychological symptoms. The outcomes of treatment differed, depending on the severity of the client's initial level of depression. As you can see from Figure 9.2, on the depression rating scale, the people with less severe depression benefited nearly equally from medication and the two psychotherapy conditions. For the more severely depressed, though, in-

terpersonal therapy was equivalent in effectiveness to medications, but cognitive-behavioral therapy was not. However, this finding did not hold true on all measures and all analyses. Figure 9.3 indicates the results in terms of the Global Assessment

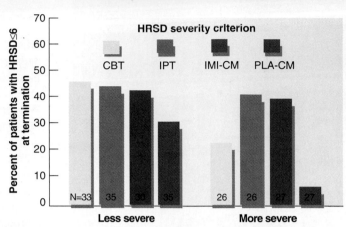

Figure 9.2

A comparison of Hamilton Rating Scale Depression (HRSD) scores of cognitive-behavioral therapy (CBT), interpersonal psychotherapy (IPT), imipramine hydrochloride plus clinical management (IMI-CM), and placebo plus clinical management (PLA-CM).
Percentages are for all subjects, including those who dropped out before receiving treatment.

Source: I. Elkin et al., in *Archives of General Psychiatry,* 46:971–982, 1989.

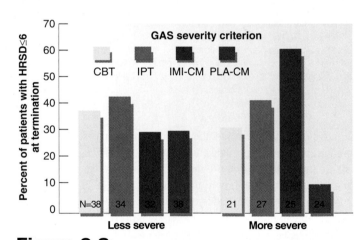

Figure 9.3

A comparison of Global Assessment Scale (GAS) scores of cognitive-behavioral therapy, interpersonal psychotherapy, imipramine plus clinical management, and placebo plus clinical management.
Percentages are for all subjects, including those who dropped out before receiving treatment.

Source: I. Elkin et al., in *Archives of General Psychiatry,* 46:971–982, 1989.

Scale (Axis V of the *DSM*) and shows that the less severely depressed people showed equivalent results with all forms of treatment, including the condition involving a placebo drug plus clinical management. Surprisingly, clinical contact alone (the placebo condition) seemed to have therapeutic value for those people. For these individuals who were severely depressed, the nature of the intervention did make a difference, and medications plus support proved to be more effective than the psychotherapies.

Recent investigations using these and other data show support for the long-term effectiveness of interpersonal therapy (Weissman & Markowitz, 1994). In another investigation (Ogles, Lambert, & Sawyer, 1995), researchers re-examined the clinical significance of the changes in depressive symptoms due to the different treatments in the NIMH study. Overall, these results were similar to those of earlier reports, yet, when the researchers limited the analysis to the individuals who had completed at least 12 therapy sessions, they found interpersonal therapy and medication to be superior to cognitive-behavioral therapy or placebo. Of the medication group, 81 percent experienced clinically significant changes in depression, as did 85 percent of those receiving interpersonal therapy. Cognitive-behavioral therapy and placebo plus clinical management benefited relatively fewer people—65 percent and 62 percent, respectively.

One of the most compelling studies to compare medication and psychother-apy found that depressed people whose therapy included a consistent interpersonal focus were symptom-free for up to 3 years after the end of treatment (Frank et al., 1990, 1991). Interpersonal therapy delivered on a fairly infrequent basis (for example, monthly sessions) outperformed relatively high doses of medication (for example, mean dosage of 200 mg of imipramine per day) in alleviating depression. The combination of medication and interpersonal therapy appeared most effective in preventing a relapse of depressive symptoms, suggesting that the combination of medication and psychotherapy using the interpersonal approach can be very effective in helping people with severe and recurrent depression.

Other researchers have more closely scrutinized the NIMH data to determine if certain treatments might be effective for certain types of people. For example, the quality of the relationship between client and therapist appears particularly salient in interpersonal therapy, and patients who both receive interpersonal therapy and form productive alliances with their therapists benefit the most from their treatment (Krupnick et al., 1994). Along the same lines, depressed people with higher levels of social functioning tend to benefit from interpersonal therapy, whereas those with higher levels of cognitive functioning fare better with cognitive-behavioral treatment (Blatt & Felson, 1993). Although conclusions about who benefits from which type of therapy are tentative, the efforts of these researchers highlight the growing interest in tailoring proven treatments to particular populations.

The success of interpersonal therapy for treating acute and chronic depression has led to a proliferation of outcome studies applying interpersonal therapy to the treatment of various populations and disorders (Weissman & Markowitz, 1994). Interpersonal therapy for depression has been adapted for the treatment of depressed geriatric, adolescent, and HIV-infected individuals, as well as other medically ill people. Researchers have also supported its use in treating dysthymic disorder, bipolar disorder, and bulimia nervosa, as well as its application in couple and group formats. However, researchers have not reached firm conclusions about the specific interaction of interpersonal therapy and medication and about the frequency of sessions needed to achieve optimal therapeutic results. They will continue to evaluate interpersonal therapy for a myriad of psychological disorders and problems and to clarify the particular circumstances that call for this promising treatment approach.

neurotransmitter systems, including GABA (Korpi, Kleinman, & Wyatt, 1988), serotonin (Arango, Underwood, & Mann, 1992; Hrdina et al., 1993; Pandey et al., 1995) and adrenaline (Meana, Barturen, Martin, & Garcia-Sevilla, 1993). Immune system dysfunction may also play a role in suicide risk. One study of suicide attempters found an imbalance in an essential measure of immune system functioning (Nassberger & Traskman-Bendz, 1993). It is not possible to determine whether the stress associated with the suicide attempt provoked an abnormal immune response or whether the immune dysfunction precipitated the suicidal behavior. However, this kind of research suggests an intriguing link between physiological indicators of stress and the risk of suicide.

Psychological Perspective

One of the more compelling explanations of the psychological factors that predispose individuals to committing suicide is provided by Edwin Shneidman, who views the act of taking one's own life as an attempt at interpersonal communication. According to Shneidman, people who attempt suicide are trying to communicate frustrated psychological needs to important people in their lives (Shneidman, 1984). Approaching the problem from a cognitively oriented view, Beck proposes that suicide is the expression of feelings of hopelessness triggered by perceiving one's stress to be insurmountable (Beck, Steer, Kovacs, & Garrison, 1985; Dixon, Heppner, & Rudd, 1994; Rudd, Rajab, & Dahm, 1994).

The role of stress as a cause of suicide has emerged from research on adolescent suicide. The death of a relative, family financial problems, and substance abuse problems are some of the situational factors that appear to predispose young people to seek an end to their lives. In addition, young people who commit suicide are more likely to have a close relative who was psychologically disturbed, to have experienced recent legal or disciplinary problems, and to have firearms present in their homes (Brent et al, 1993; Bukstein et al., 1993). Interpersonal separations and conflicts are particularly common events in the 24-hour period prior to suicide (Marttunen, Aro, & Lonnqvist, 1993).

Following the suicide of an adolescent, counselors often bring together high-school students to talk about their feelings. Such discussions are important to help teenagers cope with their sense of loss and to reduce the likelihood that they will see suicide as a way out of their problems.

Sociocultural Perspective

The earliest and most well-known sociocultural theory is that of French sociologist Emile Durkheim (1897/1952). A principal reason for suicide, according to Durkheim, is *anomie,* or a feeling of alienation from society. In the twentieth century, sociocultural theories have shifted to an emphasis on the role of the media in publicizing suicides, particularly among teenagers. In particular, concern about the role of "copycat" suicides has increased in the past decade. There is no question that adolescent friends and acquaintances of suicide victims experience intense psychological reactions, grief that might be characterized as pathological (Brent et al., 1992). However, although grieving peers may have suicidal thoughts, they are not necessarily more likely to follow through with an attempt (Brent et al., 1993).

Assessment and Treatment of Suicidality

Although suicide statistics are alarming, they nevertheless reflect a low incidence in the population. When a clinician is attempting to evaluate whether a particular client is at high risk for committing suicide, this low probability must be factored into the assessment, because it means that few people are likely to carry through with a suicidal wish. Nevertheless, clinicians tend to err on the conservative side, and, if there is any chance that a client is suicidal, all precautions are taken to ensure the client's safety.

Various methods are available to improve the odds of predicting whether a client presents a serious suicide risk. First, the clinician assesses the individual's suicidal intent and lethality. **Suicidal intent** refers to how committed a person is to dying. A person who is committed to dying would be regarded as having a high degree of suicidal intent. In contrast, a person who is ambivalent about the wish to die would be regarded as having lower suicidal intent. **Suicidal lethality** refers to the dangerousness of the person's intended method of dying. Some examples of highly lethal methods include combining high doses of barbiturates with alcohol, hanging, shooting oneself, and jumping from high places. Methods that are low in lethality include taking over-the-counter medications and making superficial cuts on one's wrist.

Suicidal intent and lethality are usually linked, but not always, and the clinician must consider both factors when evaluating a person who is suicidal. One aid to assessing suicidality is asking the individual if he or she has a "plan"; a carefully worked out plan is usually a very worrisome indicator. Consider the example of Shari, who is convinced that she wants to die and chooses a method that would clearly be lethal, such as heavy overdosing on barbiturates. Shari figures out a way to obtain the drugs and sets a time and place where she can carry out her act without being interrupted. This is a carefully worked out plan, indicating a high risk of attempting suicide. Both the intent and the lethality of Shari's plan are high.

Many suicidal people are willing to tell others about their intentions, but they may find that other people become uncomfortable and are reluctant to discuss their concerns. There is a common misconception that asking a person if he or she is suicidal might suggest the idea to the individual. Many people conclude that it might be better to avoid the topic and even go as far as to ignore warning signs. Even trained health practitioners may not pick up on the signs that an individual is suicidal. In a 1-year "psychological autopsy" study conducted in Finland, in which researchers analyzed the apparent causes of suicidal deaths, close to half of the victims saw a health care professional prior to committing suicide (41 percent), most seeing a psychiatrist. Of those, only 22 percent of the victims discussed suicidal intent on their last office visit. In most of the cases, the office visit took place within a week of the suicide, and most of the victims had a diagnosed depressive disorder (Isometsä et al., 1995). Thus, even trained professionals may not take the opportunity to ask about suicidal intent when treating depressed clients.

A sense of hopelessness is one of the strongest predictors of suicide.

Even if a person denies suicidal intent, behavioral clues can indicate a person's level of suicidality. For example, a depressed young man who gives away his stereo and mementos and puts his financial affairs in order might be preparing to end his life. However, it is easy to mistake the normal emotional and behavioral instability associated with puberty for signs of suicidality (Curran, 1987). Changes in mood, declining grades, recklessness, substance abuse, the giving up of former interests, and stormy relationships are frequently cited as suicide risk signs but are common experiences of adolescence, particularly during the early teen years.

As you have probably realized by this point, each potential suicide involves a unique set of factors. For example, a teenage girl who is upset about her poor academic performance is quite different from an individual with a long history of bipolar disorder and multiple suicide attempts. Clinicians must evaluate a range of factors, such as the individual's age, gender, race, marital status, health, and family history; however, experienced clinicians know that these risk factors can be used only as guides, rather than as conclusive evidence of suicidality.

Suicidality is assessed in many contexts, including suicide hot lines, hospital emergency rooms, mental health clinics, and in-patient psychiatric facilities. The interventions offered in these settings vary considerably in their scope and depth. Cutting across the varying intervention contexts are two basic strategies for treating suicidal individuals: providing social support and helping these individuals regain a sense of control over their lives.

The need to provide social support is based on the idea that, when an individual is suicidal, he or she feels very alone; having other people around reduces that sense of isolation. Professionals follow through on this idea by establishing a formal connection to the suicidal individual by way of a "contract." This contract is a two-way agreement in which the client promises to contact the clinician on experiencing suicidal impulses. The clinician, in turn, agrees to be available in the event of such a crisis. If a client will not agree to these conditions, the clinician is likely to consider having the client hospitalized.

The therapist can use cognitive-behavioral techniques to help the individual gain control over suicidal feelings by thinking of alternative ways to deal with stress. The therapist might also encourage the client to consider reasons for living and to shift the focus away from death to life. In any case, having an opportunity to talk about suicidal feelings is important for the client, in order to develop some perspective on the situation and a sense of control (Boyer & Guthrie, 1985).

During the past several decades, suicide prevention centers have been established in most parts of the United States, with moderately positive impact (Lester, 1993). Some of the most significant reasons that the effect has not been more dramatic are that many suicidal people do not call these services when they are at highest risk, and callers who are under the influence of psychoactive substances or who have serious emotional difficulties do not respond as well to the assistance provided by such services. However, telephone hot lines tailored to the needs of specific populations may be effective. For example, in one innovative program in Italy, more than 12,000 elderly individuals were connected to a combination of services involving a kind of suicide "911" with a "tele-check," or outreach, pro-

Providing comfort and support to a depressed person can help that person see alternatives to suicide.

gram. Only one suicide was reported in the 3-year study period, compared with an expected number of approximately seven (De Leo, Carollo, & Buono, 1995). This study also illustrates one of the problems with demonstrating the effectiveness of suicide prevention programs: that of the relatively low base rate of suicide attempts in the population. It is difficult to provide statistical evidence of the reduction in suicide rates when the rate is so low to begin with.

Nevertheless, people who do seek help from crisis intervention centers are likely to receive lifesaving services. The effectiveness of crisis intervention also depends, of course, on the quality of services provided. Table 9.2 summarizes some of the more effective strategies for suicide intervention.

Mood Disorders: The Perspectives Revisited

As you learned about each of the perspectives on mood disorders, you probably saw features that you felt were convincing, only to read on and find another approach that seemed equally compelling. This is because each approach has something valuable to offer in the way of understanding and treating mood disorders. You may be wondering how a clinician decides which techniques to use when treating clients with mood disorders. Many clinicians have preferences for one form of treatment over another, but, in addition to these preferences, they turn to the latest research findings to guide them in developing treatment plans responsive to each client's needs. For the most part, clinical decisions are based on the nature of the individual's problems. For example, a client having a manic episode would probably be prescribed medication, such as lithium, and this treatment would be supplemented by psychotherapy. A depressed client who has suffered a recent loss would be treated with psychotherapy; medication would be unlikely.

Much of what you have read should lead you to conclude that biology is an important contributor to mood disorders. Consequently, you may expect that somatic treatment approaches would be the most effective. Many experts in the field of depression would agree. However, as we have pointed out, medication alone has its limitations and in some instances may not be as effective as psychotherapy, or a combination of both.

It is encouraging to see the substantial progress being made in the understanding and treatment of mood disorders. Given the relatively high prevalence of these disorders, such progress will have a broad impact on many individuals and on society as a whole, and it is likely to enrich science's knowledge about the functioning of the brain and the role of genetics in human behavior as well. In the coming years, you will read and hear about many more advances in this heavily researched area.

Table 9.2

Telephone Strategies for Suicide Intervention

Assess Lethality

The first step in telephone intervention is to evaluate the caller's potential for self-harm. The following areas should be addressed:

Ask about a plan:	"Do you have a plan?" "How are you going to kill yourself?" The answers to these questions should be evaluated in terms of the individual's lethality.
Find out about history of suicide attempts:	"Have you ever tried to commit suicide before?" "What methods did you use?" "How often have you attempted to kill yourself?" People who have made previous attempts are at higher risk.
Evaluate the person's resources:	"Do you have any friends?" "Is help available from clergy or acquaintances?" "How do you usually cope with stress?" The availability of external and internal resources reduces the individual's suicide risk.
Determine degree of isolation:	"Do you live alone?" "Is there anyone at home now?" "Do you feel lonely?" The more isolated the person feels, the higher the risk.
Rate the degree of current life stresses:	"What kind of stresses have you experienced lately?" "Have you lost anyone close to you?" Suicide often follows stressful life experiences.

Evaluate other relevant factors such as ambivalence, level of distress, attempts to mask suicidal intent, the possibility that the individual has already acted, temporal factors (suicides are more frequent on weekends and Monday mornings), the presence of delusional thinking, hopelessness, and possible risk to other people.

Interventions

After assessing lethality, the next step is to intervene. Contact with the caller must be maintained at all costs through the development of a helping relationship. This is especially important because unlike face-to-face contact, the client can easily terminate the intervention.

Allow for ventilation of feelings	Let the caller talk about painful emotions and distress. This might include anger directed at the helper, which the helper must tolerate.
Reassure the caller of your availability	Restate your willingness to listen when the caller complains that no one cares.

Table 9.2 (continued)

Telephone Strategies for Suicide Intervention

Reinforce positive responses	Support any statements made by the caller that reflect attempts to obtain help, see things in a more positive light, or take constructive action.
Avoid superficial restating of negative statements	If a caller says "I'm upset about losing my job," it is not particularly useful for the helper to say "You sound upset about losing your job." Instead, it is better to offer problem-solving statements that provide the caller with a sense of direction and hope. In this example, it would be better for the helper to say "What steps could you take to find a new job?"
Provide alternative avenues of expression	Give the caller suggestions for other methods of coping with distress such as continuing to talk with the helper, relying on previously used coping strategies, and seeking social support.
Acknowledge the person's distress	Take the caller's concerns seriously while avoiding simplistic reflective statements. The helper can recognize the caller's obvious feelings of despair with statements such as "The fact that you are calling here shows how unhappy you are but that you are also willing to allow yourself to be helped."
Negotiate a "no-suicide" contract	Urge the caller to agree not to engage in self-destructive behavior. The contract should specify a time period and spell out contingencies in case the caller feels a mounting urge to act self-destructively.
Explore lethality	Talk about the caller's lethality at the moment whenever it seems appropriate in the conversation.
Avoid nontherapeutic interactions	Do not express hostility, sarcasm, impatience, or indifference. Do not let yourself be drawn into power struggles in the form of arguing with the caller.

From D. Neville and S. Barnes, "The Suicidal Phone Call" in *Journal of Psychosocial Nursing and Mental Health Services*, 23:14–18, 1985. Copyright ©1985 Slack, Inc. Reprinted by permission.

RETURN TO THE CASE

Janice Butterfield

Janice's History

Janice's voice quavered and tears streamed down her face as she recounted the story of her life, reminding me of her inner pain. The oldest daughter in a family of three girls, Janice described a harmonious family life during her early years that took a very sad turn when her father passed away when she was 14 years old. Prior to that unhappy date, Janice's mother had been a charming and energetic woman who devoted herself to the family. Everything changed dramatically following the death of Janice's father, when her mother became extremely withdrawn and uninvolved with her children. A few months later, Janice's mother was hospitalized for the first of several episodes of serious depression.

During each of her mother's hospitalizations, Janice was required to take over much of the family responsibilities, a pattern that continued throughout her remaining years in high school.

On graduation, Janice realized that she couldn't leave home because of her mother's reliance on her, so she enrolled in a local community college and earned a degree in business administration. She continued to play an important role in caring for her two younger sisters until they left home.

Janice stayed with her mother and worked as a buyer for a local clothing store. She fell in love with a man named Jed, whom she had met at a church-sponsored function. Jed asked her to marry him, but she insisted that her mother needed her at home and that she could not possibly leave her. Several years later, Janice's mother became terminally ill, and Janice nursed her until her death. Janice was so distraught over her mother's death that she could not return to work for many months. The death was particularly traumatic for Janice, because it left her without a living parent. At this time, Janice was 30 years old. Jed had not yet gotten married, and he again proposed to her. Janice accepted and they were married.

RETURN TO THE CASE

Janice Butterfield (continued)

Janice explained that, during the early years of her marriage, she felt relatively happy, despite occasional periods of sadness over the loss of her parents. She had used some of the insurance money she acquired after her mother's death to begin her own consulting firm, where she worked for more than a year, until the birth of her daughter. Although she had intended to keep working after her baby was born, she acquiesced to her husband's request that she sell the business so she could be a full-time homemaker. She agreed to go along with this plan but harbored resentment about it.

Assessment

Although it was evident to me that Janice was depressed, I felt that psychological testing would provide me with some insight into her mood disorder. On each of the tests that Janice took, she showed evidence of deep sadness and discontent. Janice's MMPI-2 profile was that of a person experiencing serious depression and obsessional thinking. Her Rorschach and TAT responses reflected themes of emotional constriction, guilt, depression, and anxiety. On the WAIS-III, Janice received a performance IQ in the below average range as a result of her lethargy, in contrast to her verbal IQ, which was well above average. Her score on the Beck Depression Inventory-II confirmed my clinical impression that the depth of Janice's depression was extreme, warranting immediate and intensive treatment.

Diagnosis

The prominence of Janice's mood disturbance led me to feel certain that she had a serious form of depression. She showed no psychotic symptoms or any history of a manic episode. I was able to rule out dysthymic disorder as a diagnosis because of the relative brevity of her disturbance. All signs pointed to a diagnosis of major depressive disorder—depressed mood, diminished interest in ordinary activities, appetite disturbance, sleep disturbance, psychomotor retardation, fatigue, feelings of worthlessness and guilt, poor concentration, and suicidality.

Axis I:	Major Depressive Disorder
Axis II:	No evidence of personality disorder
Axis III:	No physical disorders or conditions
Axis IV:	Problems with primary support group (marital tensions)
Axis V:	Current Global Assessment of Functioning: 45 Highest Global Assessment of Functioning (past year): 90

Case Formulation

In reviewing Janice's story in my attempt to understand why she became so severely depressed, my attention was first drawn to the fact that her mother had also experienced serious depression. Genetic factors, of course, have been shown to play an important role in the etiology of mood disorders, but I also felt that there was more to Janice's story that warranted consideration. Specifically, she had experienced several major shifts in her life within the past decade. She felt a great deal of conflict about her mixed feelings regarding her mother's death. Janice felt her mother's death as a painful loss, yet she had contrasting feelings of elation, because she was freed from her mother's excessive demands. Any sense of relief that she felt in this regard caused her to feel guilty, and her guilt led Janice to berate herself for not having been more attentive to her mother.

Over the course of several years, events within Janice's current family added further stress to her already fragile level of emotional functioning. As Janice's daughter reached toddlerhood, Janice's conflict around the issue of mother-daughter relationships was reactivated. Furthermore, her husband's demands that she become a full-time homemaker affected her self-esteem, because she was thwarted from fulfilling her career aspirations. I wondered whether her feelings of inadequacy, listlessness, and unhappiness were a turning-inward of the resentment she felt toward her husband. She saw suicide as her only escape from the unsatisfying trap of her life.

Treatment Plan

As with all cases involving a serious suicide attempt, Janice needed to be hospitalized, even if only for a brief period of time, for continued evaluation and mood stabilization. She remained in the hospital for 3 weeks. Following her discharge, I continued to see her weekly in individual psychotherapy for a year.

My work with Janice combined several approaches. Several factors about her current functioning and family history led me to the conclusion

RETURN TO THE CASE

Janice Butterfield (continued)

that antidepressant medication was warranted. Specifically, she was in a deep state of depression, involving both psychological and biological processes. In addition, the fact that her mother had had a mood disorder suggested to me that Janice was biologically predisposed to depression; therefore, biological intervention should be considered as a component of the treatment plan.

Regarding psychological intervention, I chose a combination of cognitive-behavioral and psychodynamically based techniques in my individual therapy, augmented by couple therapy provided by one of my colleagues.

I felt that cognitive-behavioral techniques would be effective in helping Janice reduce the frequency of her depressive thoughts and develop appropriately assertive interpersonal styles. In addition, I felt that Janice needed to explore her feelings about her mother to gain some insight into the ways in which unresolved mother-daughter issues had interfered with her own happiness. Also, couple therapy would allow Janice and Jed to begin working on some of the problems in their relationship—in particular, how he had stood in the way of Janice's feeling a greater sense of fulfillment in her professional life.

Outcome of the Case

During her stay in the hospital, Janice's mood improved as the antidepressant medication began to take effect. By the time she was ready to return home, she felt much more capable of handling her responsibilities.

In therapy, Janice learned to identify the ways in which her thinking was distorted and self-blaming, as well as to replace those thoughts with healthier ones. Focusing on becoming more assertive helped Janice become better able to express her needs to her husband. In time, Janice came to see how the conflicts she had harbored all these years about her relationships with her mother and her husband had seriously interfered with her achievement of happiness. Early in our work together, Janice came to the conclusion that she would seek a part-time job, an idea with which I concurred. It seemed to me that Janice needed a context other than her family from which to derive improved feelings of self-worth.

In couple therapy, Janice and Jed worked on developing clearer styles of communication. Jed came to recognize that his wife's depression was related to her loss of power in their relationship. Reluctantly, he began to accede to her requests for greater independence outside the home and more influence in their relationship. When he saw that these changes correlated with Janice's improved psychological functioning, he began to understand the impact of his behavior not only on Janice but also on the whole family system.

As I think back on my work with Janice, I feel a sense of satisfaction. When I first met Janice, she had just been rescued from a serious suicide attempt. Her self-esteem had been severely damaged, and her ability to live life as a happy and fulfilled person seemed only a remote possibility. That picture changed dramatically. Our work together, combined with the couple therapy, helped bring this woman from a period of despair to a state of fulfillment. ■

Sarah Tobin, PhD

Summary

- A mood disorder involves a disturbance in a person's emotional state, or mood. People can experience this disturbance in the form of extreme depression, excessive elation, or a combination of these emotional states. An episode is a time-limited period during which specific intense symptoms of a disorder are evident. Major depressive disorder involves acute, but time-limited, episodes of depressive symptoms, such as feelings of extreme dejection, a loss of interest in previously pleasurable aspects of life, bodily symptoms, and disturbances in eating and sleeping behavior. Individuals with major depressive disorder also have cognitive symptoms, such as a negative self-view, feelings of guilt, an inability to concentrate, and indecisiveness. Depressive episodes can be characterized as melancholic or seasonal. Dysthymic disorder is characterized by depression that is not as deep or intense as experienced in major depressive disorder but that has a longer-lasting course. People with dysthymic disorder have, for at least 2 years, depressive symptoms, such as low energy, low self-esteem, poor concentration, decision-making difficulty, feelings of hopelessness, and disturbances of appetite and sleep.

- Bipolar disorder and cyclothymic disorder involve alternations in mood. Bipolar disorder involves an intense and very disruptive experience of extreme elation, or euphoria, called a manic episode, which is characterized by abnormally heightened levels of thinking, behavior, and emotionality that cause significant impairment. A mixed episode consists of symptoms of both a manic episode and a major depressive episode, which alternate rapidly. Cyclothymic disorder involves a vacillation between dysphoria and briefer, less intense, and less disruptive states called hypomanic episodes. In bipolar I disorder, an individual experiences one or more manic episodes, with the possibility, though not the necessity, of having experienced one or more major depressive episodes. In bipolar II disorder, the individual has had one or more major depressive episodes and at least one hypomanic episode.

- Mood disorders have been explained in terms of biological, psychological, and sociocultural approaches. The most compelling evidence supporting a biological model of mood disorders involves the role of genetics, with the well-established fact that these disorders run in families. Biological theories focus on neurotransmitter and hormonal functioning. Psychological theories have moved from early psychoanalytic approaches to more contemporary viewpoints that emphasize the behavioral, cognitive, and interpersonal aspects of mood disturbance. In the behavioral viewpoint, it is assumed that depression is the result of a reduction in positive reinforcements, deficient social skills, or the disruption caused by stressful life experiences. According to the cognitive perspective, depressed people react to stressful experiences by activating a set of thoughts called the cognitive triad: a negative view of the self, the world, and the future. Cognitive distortions are errors people make in the way they draw conclusions from their experiences, applying illogical rules, such as arbitrary inferences or overgeneralizing. Interpersonal theory involves a model of understanding mood disorders that emphasizes disturbed social functioning.

- Treatments for mood disorders are also based on biological, psychological, and sociocultural perspectives. Antidepressant medication is the most common form of somatic treatment for people who are depressed, and lithium carbonate is the most widely used medication for people who have bipolar disorder. In cases involving incapacitating depression and some extreme cases of acute mania, the clinician may recommend electroconvulsive therapy. The psychological interventions that are most effective for treating people with mood disorders are those rooted in the behavioral and cognitive approaches. Sociocultural and interpersonal interventions focus on the treatment of mood symptoms within the context of an interpersonal system, such as an intimate relationship.

- Although no formal diagnostic category specifically applies to people who commit suicide, many suicidal people have a mood disorder, and some suffer from other serious psychological disorders. The dramatic act of suicide is explained from biological, psychological, and sociocultural perspectives. The treatment of suicidal clients varies considerably, depending on the context, as well as intent and lethality. Most intervention approaches incorporate support and directive therapeutic involvement

Key Terms

See Glossary for definitions.

Attributions 290
Bipolar disorder 281
Bipolar I disorder 283
Bipolar II disorder 283
Catecholamine hypothesis 287
Cognitive distortions 291
Cognitive triad 291
Cortisol 288
Cyclothymic disorder 282

Dexamethasone suppression test (DST) 288
Dysphoria 278
Dysthymic disorder 278
Episode 278
Euphoria 278
Hypomanic episodes 282
Indolamine hypothesis 287
Learned helplessness model 290
Major depressive disorder 278

Major depressive episode 278
Manic episode 281
Melancholic features 279
Mixed episode 281
Probands 286
Rapid cyclers 284
Seasonal pattern 279
Suicidal intent 300
Suicidal lethality 300

Internet Resource

To get more information on the material covered in this chapter, visit our web site at **http://www.mhhe.com/halgin.** There you will find more information, resources, and links to topics of interest.

CASE REPORT: DAVID MARSHALL

I was on call in the Emergency Room on that afternoon when 22-year-old David Marshall was brought in by his parents who were deeply troubled by his odd thinking and behavior. As I approached the consulting room in which David was sitting with his parents, I could hear a booming but argumentative voice from within the room yell out, "I want to see Zoroaster. That's the only reason I've allowed you to bring me to this dump!" I opened the door and came on the curious sight of a large young man, sitting wedged between two adults, much smaller in stature. Dora and Alfred Marshall were apparently trying to restrain their son David, who seemed ready to bolt from the room any minute. Even though David was tightly cushioned by his parents, his left arm was extended outward from his body, as he made sweeping circular movements that seemed beyond his control. Before I was able to introduce myself, David said, with great annoyance in his voice, "You are not he! Where is he whom I have come to see?" I responded by explaining to David that I wasn't sure what he meant, but I would like to spend some time talking to him and to his parents.

As I sat in the chair across from David, my attention was drawn immediately to the look of torment on David's face, and the ways in which this look was mirrored in the eyes of both his father and his mother. At first, David said nothing, but permitted his parents to tell me about the events of the preceding several days. They explained that David had been uttering a string of bizarre statements, such as "You can't stop me from my mission! Zoroaster is coming to save us all!" As David's parents struggled to tell me the story, David continued to interrupt with loud, dramatic assertions that he had a mission to "protect humankind from the evil force of 'thools,' creatures from the planet Dortanus." Hearing just a few such comments led me to guess that he was in a psychotic state.

In a threatening tone of voice, David told his parents and me that anyone who stood in the way of his destiny might be at great risk. Mr. and Mrs. Marshall sat by quietly, allowing me to assess the severity of David's problem as he told me the story of how he had been chosen as a special envoy for Zoroaster, an alien god with an "intergalactic message of salvation." In response to my questioning, David told me that he had been informed of this special assignment by way of television commercials targeted especially at him, and by "the voice of Zoroaster," which spoke to him at two o'clock each afternoon. At that point, his parents interjected that, "in preparation for his mission," David had hoarded a roomful of spray cans to be used to break through the ozone layer in order to save the world from destruction.

I soon realized that, because of David's disordered state of mind and disruptive behavior, he would be unable to give me accurate information about his current emotional state or a clear sense of important experiences in his life. Consequently, I asked to meet privately with his parents to collect some of this very important information—a request that provoked a moment of rage from David. Warning me that they were "part of a plot" to suppress his message, he stormed out of the room and then bolted from the hospital. I was somewhat startled at David's departure. Mr. Marshall explained that scenes like this took place every day. Sometimes David disappeared for a few days, but he always returned home, primarily because he wished to return to the private enclave of his room.

The Marshalls described David's deterioration during the course of his late adolescent years. David failed every course during the first semester of his first year in college, because he spent most of his time alone in his dormitory room, listening to rock music. After flunking out of college, David returned home, where he spent his time reading science fiction and esoteric religious writings. Mrs. Marshall noted that other oddities in his behavior became apparent around that time; she told of how David often attracted attention on the street because of his peculiar bodily movements and postures. For example, he would gaze heavenward, begin to wave his hand in a kind of spraying motion, and laugh with a sinister tone. Mrs. Marshall wept as she commented, "If only we had asked for help then, maybe David wouldn't have gotten so bad."

Three days after my initial meeting with the Marshalls, during which David had darted from the hospital moments before being admitted, Mr. and Mrs. Marshall brought David back to the hospital. This time we took security precautions to prevent David from leaving again and made arrangements to have him involuntarily admitted. The events of the preceding few days had left the Marshalls feeling exhausted and deeply upset about David's poor judgment and bizarre behavior. They explained to me that David had not returned home the night following our last meeting. The Marshalls had become alarmed, because the weather had turned very cold and snowy. They knew that it was unlikely for David to seek shelter anywhere other than his own room. Consequently, they decided to notify the police, who organized a search of the area around David's home.

Two nights passed without David being found, but, finally, in the early morning hours, the police located him. With the help of police dogs, David was tracked down deep in the woods a mile from the Marshall home. Perched on a rock, sitting in a lotus position, David was staring at the tops of the trees and speaking in a loud voice, apparently conversing with his "friends in the planets." He seemed unaffected by the dire weather conditions, despite his lightweight clothing, and appeared oblivious to the small group of searchers who tried to speak to him. He acquiesced to their request that he follow them to their nearby vehicle. As David spoke to his rescuers, it was clear that he believed they had been sent by Zoroaster and that it was his duty to adhere to their wishes. Moments after David was returned to his home, Mr. Marshall called for an ambulance to take David back to the psychiatric hospital.

Sarah Tobin, PhD

10
Schizophrenia and Related Disorders

Chapter Outline

he disorders we will discuss in this chapter include ones that afflict people like David and are commonly referred to as falling in the category of psychosis. As you will discover in this chapter, the forms of psychotic disorders differ in a number of important ways, but they share the central feature of a severe disturbance in the individual's experience of reality about the world and the self. People with psychotic disorders may have difficulty thinking or speaking in a coherent manner and may be distracted, and possibly tormented, by vivid images or voices.

Psychotic episodes are among the most frightening and tormenting of human experiences, but perhaps even more frightening is their apparent uncontrollability. The distress of people going through psychotic episodes is made worse by the fear and aversion such behaviors create in other people. It is difficult for the ordinary person not to be disturbed by the eccentricities and strange ramblings of people in a psychotic state. Because people who have psychotic disorders are so often rejected by others, they frequently are isolated and have little opportunity for social interaction.

Characteristics of Schizophrenia

Have you ever seen a man on the street muttering to himself, gesturing oddly, and acting as though he is hearing voices that no one else can hear? You may have wondered what was wrong with him. Although such behaviors can be associated with a number of conditions, including drug reactions, in many cases they are symptoms of a form of psychosis called schizophrenia, which affects slightly more than 1 percent of the adult population (Keith, Regier, & Rae, 1991). This means that approximately 1.8 million have the disorder—the same number of people residing in the entire state of West Virginia (Torrey, 1995).

Schizophrenia is a disorder with a range of symptoms involving disturbances in content of thought, form of thought, perception, affect, sense of self, motivation, behavior, and interpersonal functioning. Although statistically a small percentage of the population has this disorder, the 1 percent figure translates into a tremendous need for resources to care for these people. As the deinstitutionalization movement has taken hold, the burden of care has moved increasingly to families, and the costs, both in emotional and financial terms, are staggering. In one study, it was estimated that the direct cost of schizophrenia in the United States in 1 year was $33 billion, with the costs of treating people with this disorder accounting for 2.5 percent of all expenditures on health care (Rupp & Keith, 1993). However, this figure does not include indirect costs, such as family caregiving and lost income. As you read about this disorder, you will see that its symptoms are frightening and distressing, not only to the individuals who experience them but also to their families and friends, who carry a tremendous burden in so many tangible and intangible ways.

The disorder that we currently call schizophrenia was first identified as a disease by a French physician, Benedict Morel (1809–1873), and was systematically defined by German psychiatrist Emil Kraepelin (1856–1926). **Dementia praecox,** as it was called, was thought to be a degeneration of the brain (dementia) that began at a relatively young age (praecox) and ultimately led to disintegration of the entire

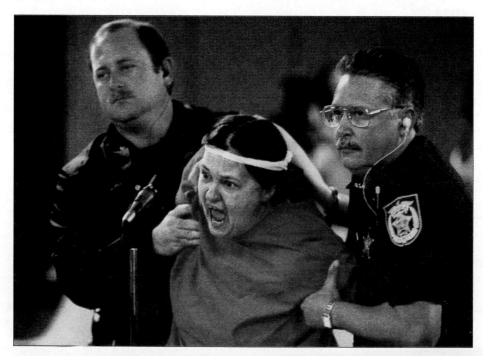

The disturbing disorder schizophrenia has been brought to public attention by such people as Margaret Mary Ray, who stalked David Letterman. Following years of delusional pursuit of celebrities and multiple arrests and hospitalizations, Ray committed suicide in October 1998, when she stepped in front of a moving train.

personality. Kraepelin believed that the hallucinations, delusions, and bizarre behavioral disturbances seen in people with schizophrenia could ultimately be traced to a physical abnormality or disease.

Swiss psychologist Eugen Bleuler (1857–1939) challenged Kraepelin's views that dementia praecox was a disease of the brain. Bleuler (1911) proposed a dramatic change in both the name and the understanding of the disorder. According to Bleuler, a more appropriate name for the disorder was schizophrenia, a term that incorporated ideas central to his understanding of the disorder: a splitting of (schiz) or lack of integration among the individual's psychological functions. Unlike Kraepelin, Bleuler thought it was possible for people with schizophrenia to recover from the disorder. Furthermore, Bleuler considered schizophrenia to represent a group of disorders, rather than a single entity. Even though he wrote about this disorder nearly a century ago, Bleuler's ideas about schizophrenia are still influential. The four fundamental features of the disorder that he identified are still commonly referred to as Bleuler's Four *A*s:

1. Association: thought disorder, as might be evident through rambling and incoherent speech
2. Affect: disorder of the experience and expression of emotion—for example, inappropriate laughter in a sad situation
3. Ambivalence: the inability to make or follow through on decisions
4. Autism: the tendency to maintain an idiosyncratic style of egocentric thought and behavior

Disagreeing with Bleuler's broad characterization of schizophrenia was a German psychiatrist, Kurt Schneider (1887–1967), who introduced the idea that, for the diagnosis of schizophrenia, certain "first-rank" symptoms must be present (Schneider, 1959). These include hearing voices that comment on one's actions and believing that an outside agent is inserting thoughts into one's mind. We now know that first-rank symptoms are also associated with disorders other than schizophrenia, such as certain forms of mood disorder, so Schneider's idea about using these symptoms as the sole diagnostic indicators of schizophrenia is no longer considered valid. As you will see later in our discussion, debate about the nature of schizophrenia continues among contemporary researchers and clinicians.

Phases of Schizophrenia

Schizophrenia is a complex and multifaceted disorder that can take one of many forms. Essential to the diagnosis of schizophrenia is a marked disturbance lasting at least 6 months. During this 6-month period is an **active phase** of symptoms, such as delusions, hallucinations, disorganized speech, disturbed behavior, and negative symptoms (e.g., speechlessness or lack of initiative).

The active phase does not usually appear without warning signs. Most, but not all, cases have a **prodromal phase,** a period prior to the active phase during which the individual shows progressive deterioration in social and interpersonal functioning. This phase is characterized by several maladaptive behaviors, such as social withdrawal, inability to work productively, eccentricity, poor grooming, inappropriate emotionality, pecu-

DIAGNOSTIC FEATURES OF SCHIZOPHRENIA

- People with this disorder experience a disturbance that lasts at least 6 months and includes at least 1 month of active symptoms, including at least two of the following:
  - delusions,
  - hallucinations,
  - disorganized speech,
  - disturbed or catatonic behavior, or
  - negative symptoms, such as flat affect or severe lack of motivation.
- For a significant portion of the time since symptom onset, they have experienced dysfunction in work, relationships, or self-care.
- The symptoms are not due to another disorder, a medical condition, or substances.

liar thought and speech, unusual beliefs, odd perceptual experiences, and decreased energy and initiative. For many people, the active phase is followed by a **residual phase,** in which there are continuing indications of disturbance similar to the behaviors of the prodromal phase. Throughout the duration of the disturbance, people with schizophrenia experience serious problems in work, relationships, and self-care.

Symptoms of Schizophrenia

The mysterious and dramatic symptoms of schizophrenia cover a range of categories from extreme disturbances in thought content to bizarre behaviors. Let's take a look at some of the defining characteristics of this disorder.

Disturbance of Thought Content: Delusions

Recall Dr. Tobin's interaction with David Marshall in the case study at the beginning of the chapter, and imagine yourself interacting with someone like David. What would you think if a friend were to tell you he had just received a message from someone named Zoroaster, telling him that he had been given the assignment to "protect humankind from the evil force of 'thools,' creatures from the planet Dortanus"? At first, you might think he was kidding around. Concluding that he was serious would cause you to become alarmed, because you would realize that your friend was delusional.

Delusions, or deeply entrenched false beliefs, are the most common disturbance of thought content associated with schizophrenia. David's false belief is an example of a delusion of grandeur. His delusion may also be persecutory, if he imagines that others are trying to harm him or prevent him from fulfilling his mission. David's thinking also seems to involve a delusion of reference, in that he believes that television commercials are targeted at him. As you recall from our discussion in Chapter 3, a delusion can take many forms, all of which are dramatic indicators of severe disturbance in a person's thinking.

Disturbance in Perception: Hallucinations

Have you ever had the experience as you were falling asleep of "hearing a voice" and thinking it was real? The mind often plays such tricks immediately before we fall asleep. But what if these voices, which no one else hears, were part of your everyday existence? What if you constantly heard the voice of an angry man telling you to hit someone sitting across from you or of someone telling you how stupid or unattractive you are? Certainly, you would be upset and frightened, and it might be a struggle for you to resist the commands. David Marshall reported that he had heard the "voice of Zoroaster," which had prompted him to take action to prepare for his "mission." David was experiencing an auditory hallucination. Recall that hallucinations are false perceptions involving one of the five senses. Although hallucinations do not correspond to actual stimuli, they are real to the person with schizophrenia. They are not under voluntary control but occur spontaneously, despite the individual's attempts to ward them off. As you can imagine, these experiences can be frightening and disruptive.

Disturbance of Thinking, Language, and Communication: Disorganized Speech

People with schizophrenia have such disorganized and dysfunctional cognitive processes that their thinking may lack cohesiveness and logic. Their language can be grossly distorted to the point of incomprehensibility. Attempting to communicate with a person who has a thought disorder is extremely perplexing. Dr. Tobin must have felt frustrated in her attempt to engage David Marshall in conversation. Because he was so consumed by his concerns about "Zoroaster" and the "evil forces," he was unable to interact in a normal conversation.

Some instances of disturbed communication in schizophrenia are not as dramatic; instead, some people with schizophrenia speak in a peculiar way and use awkward or pompous-sounding speech. For example, when casually asked about the weather, one man said, "It is an auspicious day for a feast on the grass, but the cumulus meanderings above us seem oh so ominous." Some individuals speak with odd intonations and lack the usual expressiveness and gestures common in everyday talk. Even when they write, they may use language so stilted and formal that it sounds artificial. In some extreme cases, the individual may be mute, saying nothing for hours or days.

Disturbed Behavior

People with schizophrenia may move in odd and disturbing ways. For example, David Marshall's odd circular movement of his arm as he waited with his parents in the consultation room was a visible behavioral symptom that would strike anyone as odd. At times, a person with schizophrenia may show signs of a catatonic disturbance, in the form of either stupor, rigidity, or excitement. Catatonic stupor is a state of being unresponsive to external stimuli, possibly to the point of being unaware of one's surroundings. Catatonic rigidity involves stiffened posturing of the body and resistance to pressure to move. Just as extreme is catatonic excitement, which involves apparently purposeless and repetitive bodily movements.

Sometimes auditory hallucinations involve negative and upsetting comments about a person or a command to engage in bizarre or threatening behavior.

Negative Symptoms

The four kinds of symptoms previously listed (delusions, hallucinations, disorganized speech, and disturbed behavior) are called **positive symptoms,** which are exaggerations or distortions of normal thoughts, emotions, and behavior. Many people with schizophrenia also have **negative symptoms,** those that involve functioning below the level of behavior regarded as normal. The most common negative symptoms are affective flattening, alogia, and avolition. In **affective flattening,** an individual seems unresponsive, with relatively motionless body language and facial reactions and minimal eye contact. **Alogia** is a loss of words or notable lack of spontaneity or responsiveness in conversation. The symptom of **avolition** involves a lack of initiative and unwillingness to act. Staring out the window may be preferable to doing anything else, even something that might be pleasant.

Clinicians often find it difficult to diagnose negative symptoms, because, in fact, most people at one time or another act in these ways, as when they are fatigued or depressed. Although less commonly noted, some people with schizophrenia also experience **anhedonia,** a loss of interest in or ability to experience pleasure from activities that most people find appealing.

Social and Occupational Dysfunction

The disturbing thoughts, feelings, and behaviors characteristic of schizophrenia affect every facet of functioning in people who have the disorder. They have troubled and tumultuous interactions with relatives, acquaintances, and even strangers, particularly during the active phase of symptoms. In the case of David Marshall, his argumentative and threatening interactions with Dr. Tobin and with his parents would be disconcerting for anyone with whom he is interacting, and they would certainly cause problems in most realms of his life.

People with schizophrenia often express their emotions in ways that seem abnormal to others, possibly expressing outward affect that is inconsistent with how they are feeling or how they would be expected to feel in a given situation. This inconsistency may cause confusion in other people, who are bewildered by a person who is giggling in a setting that others regard as serious, or crying in a context that most people view as humorous. Because of such oddities, other people may shun individuals with schizophrenia, because being around them is confusing and uncomfortable. The social isolation that ensues can trigger a vicious cycle of impairment in relational style. Over time, the socially disturbed and isolated person is likely to be rejected and to retreat further into a world of fantasy and delusion.

What would you think if you were participating in a serious conversation in which one person unexpectedly broke out laughing? Such inappropriate affect is found in some people with schizophrenia.

A stiff and bizarre posture characterizes catatonic rigidity.

Types of Schizophrenia

Although we speak of schizophrenia as a single disorder, it is actually diverse, taking on dramatically different forms from individual to individual, referred to in the *DSM-IV* as types. When the prominent symptom in a person with schizophrenia is bizarre motor behaviors, the person is diagnosed as having **schizophrenia, catatonic type.**

Schizophrenia, disorganized type is characterized by a combination of symptoms, including disorganized speech, disturbed behavior, and flat or inappropriate affect. Even the person's delusions and hallucinations, when present, lack any coherent theme. Individuals with this disorder are noticeably odd in their behavior and appearance and usually have serious impairment in work and other social contexts.

People with **schizophrenia, paranoid type,** are preoccupied with one or more bizarre delusions or have auditory hallucinations related to a theme of being persecuted or harassed, but without disorganized speech or disturbed behavior. The hallucinations are usually related to the content of the delusions. Interestingly, however, cognitive functioning and affect are reasonably normal. People with the paranoid type of schizophrenia have tremendous interpersonal problems, because of their suspicious and argumentative style.

In some people with schizophrenia, the symptoms are mixed, and the clinician cannot classify the disorder into one of the types just discussed; a diagnosis of **schizophrenia, undifferentiated type** is used when a person shows a complex of schizophrenic symptoms, such as delusions, hallucinations, incoherence, and disturbed behavior, but does not meet the criteria for the paranoid (systematic bizarre delusions), catatonic (abnormalities of movement), or disorganized (disturbed or flat affect) types of schizophrenia.

Schizophrenia, Catatonic Type

MINI-CASE

Maria is a 21-year-old college junior who has been psychiatrically hospitalized for a month. The resident assistant in Maria's dormitory brought her to the hospital in December, because she had grown increasingly concerned about Maria's deteriorating behavior over the course of the semester. When Maria returned to college in September, her roommate told others, including the resident assistant, that Maria was acting oddly. For example, she had an annoying habit of repeating other people's words, she stared listlessly out the window, and she ignored her personal hygiene. As the semester neared an end, Maria retreated more and more into her own world, until her behavior reached a point such that she was completely unresponsive to others. In the hospital, she maintains rigid posturing of her body, while staring at the ceiling and spending most of the day in a trance-like state that seems impenetrable. The treating staff are in a quandary about what intervention to use for Maria because of her hypersensitivity to most medications.

■ What specific catatonic symptoms does Maria show?

■ What were the early signs that Maria was becoming increasingly disturbed?

DIAGNOSTIC FEATURES

● In addition to meeting the general diagnostic criteria for schizophrenia (see page 311), people with this type of schizophrenia have a condition that is characterized by psychomotor disturbance that involves at least two of the following:
● Motor immobility or stupor;
● Excessive purposeless motor activity;
● Mutism or extreme negativism (e.g., rigid posturing or resistance to instructions);
● Peculiarities of movement (e.g., bizarre postures) or odd mannerisms or grimacing;
● Echolalia (senseless repetition of words or phrases) or echopraxia (repetition by imitation of another's movements).

Schizophrenia, Disorganized Type

MINI-CASE

Joshua is a 43-year-old man who can be found daily standing near the steps of a local bank on a busy street corner. Every day, he wears a Red Sox baseball cap, a yellow T-shirt, worn-out hiking shorts, and orange sneakers. Rain or shine, day in and day out, Joshua maintains his "post" at the bank. Sometimes he can be seen "conversing" with imaginary people. Without provocation, he sobs miserably; sometimes he explodes in shrieks of laughter. Police and social workers keep taking him to shelters for the homeless, but Joshua manages to get back on the street before he can be treated. He has repeatedly insisted that these people have no right to keep bothering him.

■ Which of Joshua's behaviors suggest that he has schizophrenia, disorganized type?

■ What are your thoughts about Joshua's insistence that he has the right to be left alone?

DIAGNOSTIC FEATURES

● In addition to meeting the general diagnostic criteria for schizophrenia (see page 311), people with this type of schizophrenia have (1) disorganized speech, (2) disturbed behavior, and (3) flat or inappropriate affect.

● The diagnosis is not given to people whose condition meets the criteria for the catatonic type of schizophrenia.

Some people who have been diagnosed as having schizophrenia may no longer have prominent psychotic symptoms but may still show some lingering signs of the disorder. Although they are not delusional, hallucinating, incoherent, or disorganized, they may retain some symptoms, such as emotional dullness, social withdrawal, eccentric behavior, or illogical thinking. These individuals would be diagnosed as having **schizophrenia, residual type.**

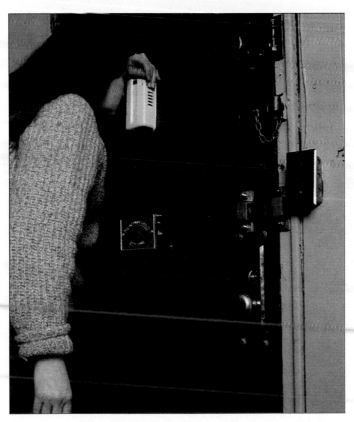

Convinced that assassins are in close pursuit, a person with paranoid schizophrenia might stay barricaded behind a heavily locked door.

Dimensions of Schizophrenia

In addition to the types of schizophrenia, researchers have been exploring other ways of categorizing the varieties of schizophrenia. Many clinicians and researchers feel that the current categories fail to capture the essential dimensions underlying individual differences in symptoms. Instead, they prefer ways of thinking about schizophrenia that focus on the presence or absence of dramatic symptoms (such as bizarre hallucinations, delusions, and prominent thought disorder), or they emphasize the progression, or course, of the disorder over time.

Positive-Negative Dimension

Building on the distinction between positive and negative symptoms, some experts have suggested that there are two fundamentally different categories of schizophrenia (Andreasen, 1998). This distinction can be traced to the original views of Kraepelin, who spoke of one kind of symptom picture as being more dramatic and observable and the other as being marked by deficit, such as loss of the ability to experience pleasure. This distinction was made more explicit by Bleuler, and it continued to be used by clinicians for the next half-century until it was replaced by a broader definition of *schizophrenia*.

New evidence for the validity of Kraepelin's formulation began to emerge in the early 1980s, with the publication of works by Thomas Crow (1985, 1990) on the distinction between what he calls Type I (positive) and Type II (negative) schizophrenia. Crow bases these categories on the nature of the symptoms, as well as a number of other characteristics related to the course of the disorder and responses to treatment. Scales are now available to assess the positive-negative distinction (Lin et al., 1998), and this dimension is considered important in predicting the long-term outcome of schizophrenia (Arndt et al., 1995; Eaton et al., 1995); people with negative symptoms have a worse prognosis than those with positive symptoms. The distinction between positive and negative symptoms is also important in helping clinicians choose the most appropriate medication, in light of the fact that some medications are more helpful in reducing positive symptoms, while others seem to be effective with negative symptoms (Buchanan et al., 1998).

Schizophrenia, Paranoid Type

MINI-CASE

Esther is a 31-year-old unmarried woman who lives with her elderly mother. A belief that the outside air is filled with radio waves that will insert evil thoughts into her head keeps Esther from leaving the house. The windows in her bedroom are "protected" with aluminum foil that "deflects the radio waves." She often hears voices that comment on these radio signals. For example, one comment is the slow, deep voice of an elderly man, who angrily states, "We're going to get these thoughts into your head. Give up your fight!"

■ What behaviors of Esther's would lead you to consider her as having schizophrenia, paranoid type?

■ How do Esther's symptoms differ from those of a person with paranoid personality disorder?

DIAGNOSTIC FEATURES

● In addition to meeting the general diagnostic criteria for schizophrenia (see page 311), people with this type of schizophrenia are preoccupied with frequent auditory hallucinations or with one or more delusions.

● The diagnosis is not given to individuals with any of the following prominent symptoms: disorganized speech, disturbed or catatonic behavior, or flat or inappropriate affect.

Schizophrenia, Undifferentiated Type

MINI-CASE

Bruce, a 24 year-old maintenance worker, is considered "peculiar" by almost everyone he meets. He has a "strange" look in his eyes, and he often mumbles to himself, as if he were holding a conversation with someone. The words he uses sometimes sound like those of a foreign language, but no one else can understand them. At times, he stares out the window for hours, and he barks angrily at anyone who disturbs him. It seems as though he is lost in a world of fantasy, but he nevertheless manages to keep up with his custodial duties.

■ What symptoms of various types of schizophrenia are evident in Bruce, who has a diagnosis of schizophrenia, undifferentiated type?

■ In light of the fact that Bruce is able to function in a job, do you feel that he should be urged to get professional help or simply be left alone?

DIAGNOSTIC FEATURES

● This diagnosis is assigned to individuals who have the general symptoms of schizophrenia but do not meet the diagnostic criteria for paranoid, disorganized, or catatonic type.

Schizophrenia, Residual Type

MINI-CASE

Three years after her third hospitalization for schizophrenia, Joyce's condition seems to have stabilized. She has a set routine for taking her antipsychotic medications, for checking in regularly at the Center for Independent Living (which supervises her work placement in a glove factory), and for visiting with her sister and family. At 45, Joyce shows only occasional signs of the illness that, at one time, had totally incapacitated her. She still sometimes becomes preoccupied with the idea that her former mother-in-law is sending her poisoned envelopes in the mail. At other times, she cannot stop herself from pacing the floor. These symptoms never last very long, though, and she is soon able to resume her daily schedule without being unduly distressed.

■ What warrants referring to Joyce as a person with schizophrenia, residual type?

■ Do you think that Joyce should be receiving psychotherapeutic treatment?

DIAGNOSTIC FEATURES

● This diagnosis is given to people who have had at least one episode of schizophrenia but currently lack prominent positive symptoms (i.e., delusions, hallucinations, disorganized speech, or grossly disorganized or catatonic behavior).

The authors of the *DSM-IV* had considered the proposal of defining a subtype of schizophrenia, called simple schizophrenia, to be used in diagnosing people with only negative symptoms (McGlashan & Fenton, 1991). However, the ultimate decision was to apply the diagnosis of schizophrenia only when an individual shows positive symptoms. In part, this debate over diagnostic categories and dimensions reflects increasing scientific understanding of the disorder. At the same time, there is a human side to the issue; clinicians are reluctant to assign the diagnosis to an individual who shows no positive symptoms.

Process-Reactive Dimension

A second dimension of schizophrenia is called process versus reactive (Garmezy, 1970). As the terms imply, **process** refers to

The difference between the experiences of this woman and those of this man captures the distinction between the positive and negative symptoms of schizophrenia. The woman's hallucinations and bizarre delusions are positive symptoms. The man's flat affect and apathy are negative symptoms.

the gradual appearance of the disorder over time, and **reactive** indicates that a precipitant provoked the onset of symptoms. Differences also exist between these two types with respect to **premorbid functioning,** which is the individual's functioning during the period prior to the onset of symptoms. People with process schizophrenia are more likely to show signs of maladjustment before diagnosable symptoms become apparent, in contrast to people with reactive schizophrenia, who appear normal until their symptoms develop.

Although the process-reactive distinction was popular from the 1950s to the 1980s, it is currently less accepted. Originally, the distinction was intended to help clinicians and researchers understand variations in the etiology and prognosis of schizophrenia. However, as we pointed out earlier, the diagnosis of schizophrenia that had evolved by the 1980s was much narrower than that of the 1950s. Thus, many people who were diagnosed with schizophrenia and fit the reactive definition would no longer be regarded as even having schizophrenia if

Table 10.1

Characteristics of Positive and Negative Subtypes of Schizophrenia

Distinguishing Feature	Positive Subtype "Type I"	Negative Subtype "Type II"
Types of symptoms	Hallucinations Delusions Thought disorder Bizarre or disorganized behavior	Poverty of speech Poverty of content of speech Affective flattening Anhedonia Asociality Avolition Apathy Attentional impairment
Onset	Sudden	Slow
Course	Exacerbations and remissions	Chronic
Response to treatment	Favorable response to traditional antipsychotic medications	Poor response to traditional antipsychotic medications
Intellectual impairment	Minimal	Significant
Brain abnormalities	Increased dopamine receptors Abnormalities in parts of the limbic system	Enlarged ventricles Frontal lobe abnormalities Normal CT scans
Social functions	Normal social functioning between episodes	Poor social functioning in general

diagnosed today. For example, a previously normal young man who is admitted to the hospital with disturbing delusions, hallucinations, and bizarre thoughts and behavior following a traumatic event would not currently be diagnosed with schizophrenia, although such a diagnosis may have been applied to him 20 years ago. The process-reactive distinction has, therefore, lost some of its relevance, because a person with "reactive" onset would probably now be regarded as having another disorder—for example, a personality disorder, a mood disorder, or brief psychotic disorder, which we will discuss later in this chapter.

Courses of Schizophrenia

Schizophrenia may take one of several courses, or patterns. In the most serious of cases, the individual experiences continuous positive symptoms with no remission. Other people have episodes of positive symptoms, but, between these episodes, only negative symptoms are evident. In some cases, individuals who have had only a single episode of schizophrenia can live the rest of their lives without a recurrence of the disorder. These people are considered to be "in remission."

Can Delusions Be Changed?

You have read about the rigidity with which individuals hold on to delusional beliefs, despite their obvious contradiction by common sense and reality. For many years, clinicians and researchers held little hope for altering the delusions of people diagnosed with schizophrenia and other, related conditions; neither medication nor psychotherapy seemed to alter their most firmly held beliefs. Recently, some cognitive-behavioral researchers have questioned the assumption that delusions are qualitatively different from other forms of human beliefs, and they have proposed using cognitive-behavioral techniques, similar to those used in the treatment of mood and anxiety disorders, to modify the delusions of people with schizophrenia (Alford & Beck, 1994; Kingdon, Turkington, & John, 1994).

Efforts to modify delusions through psychotherapy are still in their infancy, but the preliminary work of Chadwick and Lowe (1994), two researchers from the United Kingdom, may provide a useful adjunct to traditional medication and psychosocial treatments for schizophrenia. Their work is rooted in the view that delusions are attributions or judgments that people make in an effort to make sense of particular experiences or perceptions. Individuals with schizophrenia may develop delusions to bring order and understanding to unusual, frightening, or hallucinatory experiences.

Cognitive therapists have primarily used two therapeutic techniques in their efforts to modify delusions: verbal challenge and reality testing. In verbal challenge, therapists help clients understand how delusions and other beliefs exert profound effects on behavior and views of the world. They begin a collaborative examination of the evidence supporting or contradicting the delusional beliefs and develop alternate explanations that are more accurate and realistic. For example, Chadwick and Lowe helped a person with schizophrenia examine his belief that communicating with people from the past could prevent accidents. They examined instances of accidents in the person's life and in the lives of others and were able to gradually weaken this particular belief. In the second technique, reality testing, the person carries out activities or "behavioral experiments" (Chadwick & Lowe, 1994, p. 358) aimed at invalidating the delusion.

The researchers used a multiple-baseline design to evaluate the effects of verbal challenge and reality testing on four aspects of delusions: (1) the conviction with which the person held the delusion, (2) the amount of preoccupation with the delusion, (3) the amount of anxiety and depression associated with the delusion, and (4) the person's bias toward evidence that would confirm the delusion. After four to six weekly sessions of cognitive therapy, 10 of the 12 people were less convinced of the accuracy of their delusions, and 5 had rejected their delusions outright. Verbal challenge seemed particularly helpful, perhaps because it involved more support and collaboration with the therapist than did the reality testing exercises. The interventions were somewhat less successful in changing the people's preoccupation with their delusions; in other words, even some of the individuals who were less convinced of the accuracy of their delusions continued to think about them on a relatively frequent basis. Following therapy, the individuals were less depressed and somewhat less anxious. Finally, the individuals who had delusions frequently sought out and modified experiences in order to confirm them, while ignoring a multitude of disconfirming experiences. As a result of therapy, many of these individuals were able to spontaneously consider evidence contrary to their delusions.

Clearly, cognitive-behavioral therapy for delusions is at a very early stage in its development. These techniques cannot cure schizophrenia by any means, nor should they be considered replacements for established pharmacological and psychosocial treatments. Preliminary evidence supports their use in modifying and weakening delusions. This approach appears most effective when it extends beyond the several sessions involved in a research study and incorporates a strong, supportive therapeutic relationship.

Estimates of recovery from schizophrenia range from a low of about 20 percent of people to a high of 67 percent, with the estimates varying according to how narrowly recovery is defined. As you can imagine, people who do not recover at all are profoundly affected by their disorder in every facet of life. They experience troubled relationships, have difficulty maintaining stable employment, and often struggle with depression and loneliness. For many, their painful existence culminates in premature death due to suicide, violence, or impaired health. In one project, researchers studying the psychiatric histories of people who died suddenly found that sudden death was five times higher than normal in people with histories of psychiatric care. Although suicide accounted for part of the excess mortality, rates of death from natural causes and accidents were also elevated, especially among those who had misused substances. Findings such as these point to the importance of attending to the increased risk of death from inadequate care or suicide among people with schizophrenia (Ruschena et al., 1998).

Other Psychotic Disorders

At one time, the diagnosis of schizophrenia was applied so broadly to people with a wide range of maladaptive behaviors that most people living in institutions were labeled with this diagnosis. One of the most troubling facets of the overuse of this diagnosis was the corresponding notion that, once a person was diagnosed as having schizophrenia, that person was doomed to carry that label for life. Even for people with only brief psychotic symptoms, clinicians mistakenly assumed that schizophrenia would subsequently lie dormant beneath the surface, waiting to burst out again in the form of new symptoms at any time. Many clinicians advised clients who had shown psychotic symptoms to take antipsychotic medication for life to prevent their symptoms from occurring again. This situation began to change during the 1970s, in part because researchers defined a group of disorders that shared some but not all symptoms with schizophrenia.

The schizophrenia-like disorders share three features: (1) each is a form of psychosis representing a serious break with reality, (2) the condition is not caused by a disorder of cognitive impairment (e.g., Alzheimer's disease), and (3) mood disturbance is not a primary symptom. Each disorder has aspects similar to certain features of schizophrenia, but other facets of the disorder, such as presumed cause and course, distinguish it from schizophrenia. Further, each of the schizophrenic-like disorders has a different set of proposed causes, symptom picture, and recommended course of treatment.

Brief Psychotic Disorder

Most people have heard the phrase "nervous breakdown" used to describe people who suddenly lose control, behave in bizarre ways, and have strange experiences, such as delusions or hallucinations. The term is actually a misnomer, because these symptoms are not due to a breakdown in nerves. The correct term is **brief psychotic disorder,** a disorder characterized by a sudden onset of psychotic symptoms that lasts less than a

For some people, personal stresses reach such intensity that they develop brief psychotic disorder, with transient symptoms that resemble those of schizophrenia.

month. These symptoms are often reactive, appearing after a stressful event or set of events, and eventually the person returns to normal functioning. The stress may be something that others would clearly recognize as serious, such as the death of a spouse or a house fire; however, in some instances, the stressor is personally quite disturbing, though others might not construe it to be so serious (e.g., an academic or a financial problem). Some individuals become briefly psychotic without any apparent stressor, leaving clinicians and family members mystified about the cause of the dramatic change in the individual. Yet another variant of brief psychotic disorder involves women with postpartum onset, who develop transient psychotic symptoms within a month following childbirth.

Although experts believe that most cases of brief psychotic disorder are the result of psychological rather than biological factors, it is possible that certain people are biologically predisposed to develop this disorder when faced with considerable psychological stress. Most people have adequate resources for dealing with difficulties and anxiety. Some people, however, are more vulnerable, and, when their customary defenses fail or when a crisis is unusually stressful, they "fall apart."

This disorder can be terrifying for the individual who is experiencing intense and overwhelming changes in thoughts, feelings, and behavior. Individuals in such a state may act in ways that are completely uncharacteristic of their premorbid personality, failing to take care of themselves or interacting

Brief Psychotic Disorder

MINI-CASE

Anthony is a 22-year-old senior at a prestigious small college. His family has traditionally held high standards for Anthony, and his father had every expectation that his son would go on to enroll at Harvard Law School. Anthony felt intensely pressured as he worked day and night to maintain a high grade point average, while diligently preparing for the national examination for admission to law schools. His social life became devoid of any meaningful contact. He even began skipping meals, because he did not want to take time away from studying. When Anthony received his scores for the law school admission exam, he was devastated, because he knew that they were too low to allow him to get into any of the better law schools. He began crying uncontrollably, wandering around the dormitory hallways, screaming obscenities and telling people that there was a "plot" on the part of the college dean to keep him from getting into law school. After 2 days of this behavior, Anthony's resident advisor convinced him to go to the infirmary, where his condition was diagnosed and treated. After a week of rest and some medication, Anthony returned to normal functioning and was able to assess his academic situation more rationally.

- What factors in Anthony's life appear related to his development of brief psychotic disorder?

- Which of Anthony's symptoms are also found in schizophrenia?

DIAGNOSTIC FEATURES

- For at least 1 day, but less than a month, individuals with this disorder experience at least one of the following symptoms before returning to normal functioning:
  - delusions,
  - hallucinations,
  - disorganized speech, or
  - grossly disturbed or catatonic behavior.
- The condition is not attributable to another disorder, a medical condition, or substances.
- The condition can be specified as (1) with marked stressor(s); (2) without marked stressor(s); or (3) with postpartum onset.

with others in ways that are incomprehensible to those who care about them. Particularly worrisome is the possibility that the individual will attempt suicide in an effort to escape psychological torment.

Treatment of brief psychotic disorder usually consists of a combination of medication and psychotherapy. Individuals often require short-term use of antianxiety or antipsychotic medication to help them return to normal functioning. The nature of the psychological intervention depends on the nature of the stressor, when one is evident. Sometimes removing the person from the stressful situation can reduce the disturbance. At other times, this may not be possible. In either case, effective psychotherapy integrates support, education, and the development of insight regarding the determinants of the person's disturbed reaction.

Schizophreniform Disorder

The term *schizophreniform* means that a disorder takes the form of schizophrenia but is somehow different. People with **schizophreniform disorder** have psychotic symptoms that are essentially the same as those found in schizophrenia, except for duration. The symptoms of schizophreniform disorder last longer than those of brief psychotic disorder but not so long that the

clinician would diagnose the person as having schizophrenia. Specifically, active symptoms last from 1 to 6 months. If the symptoms last longer than 6 months, the clinician is more likely to make a diagnosis of schizophrenia.

Biology appears to play a prominent role in determining whether a person will develop schizophreniform disorder. For example, researchers have found that people with this disorder have unusually large brain ventricles (DeLisi et al., 1991), a phenomenon also observed in people with schizophrenia. Also suggesting a link to schizophrenia is the finding of similar patterns of brain activity during a cognitive task as measured by a PET scan (Rubin et al., 1991). The fact that relatives of people with this disorder have a higher likelihood of having the disorder also suggests a biological explanation for schizophreniform disorder. Researchers are working to sort out the significance of these strands of evidence supporting a biological explanation.

Most people with the diagnosis of schizophreniform disorder need medication to help bring their symptoms under control. For some, the symptoms will go away spontaneously, but the behavior of people with schizophreniform disorder is usually so disturbed that family and friends insist on an intervention. Most commonly, the clinician prescribes antipsychotic medication, particularly for the acute phase of the disorder.

Schizophreniform Disorder

MINI-CASE

At the time that Edward developed a psychological disorder, he was 26 years old and worked for a convenience store chain. Although family and friends always regarded Edward as unusual, he had not experienced psychotic symptoms. This all changed as he grew more and more disturbed over the course of several months. His mother thought that he was just "stressed out" because of his financial problems, but Edward did not seem concerned about such matters. He gradually developed paranoid delusions and became preoccupied with reading the Bible. What brought his disturbance to the attention of his supervisors was the fact that he had submitted an order to the district office for 6,000 loaves of bread. He had scribbled at the bottom of the order form "Jesus will multiply the loaves." When his supervisors questioned this inappropriate order, Edward became enraged and insisted that they were plotting to prevent him from fighting world hunger. Paranoid themes and bizarre behaviors also surfaced in Edward's dealings with his wife and children. Following 2 months of increasingly disturbed behavior, Edward's boss urged him to see a psychiatrist. With rest and relatively low doses of antipsychotic medication, Edward returned to normal functioning after a few weeks of hospitalization.

■ How do Edward's schizophreniform symptoms differ from those of schizophrenia?

■ What differentiates Edward's disorder from brief psychotic disorder?

DIAGNOSTIC FEATURES

● People with this disorder experience an episode (at least 1 month but less than 6 months in duration) of at least two of the following schizophrenic symptoms:

● delusions,

● hallucinations,

● disorganized speech,

● disturbed or catatonic behavior, or

● negative symptoms, such as flat affect or severe lack of motivation.

● The symptoms are not due to another disorder, a medical condition, or substances.

Because people with this disorder function normally when not experiencing a psychotic episode, most clinicians prefer to reduce and discontinue medication after a period of time. In cases in which the symptoms are dangerously out of control, electroconvulsive therapy can offer quick improvement. People with this disorder can also benefit from psychotherapy. Initially, the therapist helps the individual regain control, but eventually the focus shifts to possible causes of the disorder.

Schizoaffective Disorder

A major controversy pertains to the issue of whether schizophrenia and mood disorders are mutually exclusive or whether some people have symptoms of both disorders. Bleuler believed that the diagnosis of schizophrenia should take precedence, regardless of how severe a client's mood disturbance might be. Many clinicians and researchers have moved away from this position, insisting that some individuals have both schizophrenic and mood symptoms. The diagnosis of **schizoaffective disorder** applies to people who experience either a major depressive episode, a manic episode, or a mixed episode at the same time that they meet the diagnostic criteria

for schizophrenia. You may be wondering why this condition is not labeled a mood disorder if mood disturbance is so central to the diagnosis. This is because, during the period of active symptoms, there is a period of at least 2 weeks during which the person does not have prominent mood symptoms but continues to have psychotic symptoms, such as hallucinations or delusions.

Debate has focused on whether schizoaffective disorder is a variant of schizophrenia, with similar etiology, or whether it is a mood disorder. After reviewing the evidence on both sides of the issue, Nancy Andreasen, a prominent expert in the field, concluded that the term *schizoaffective disorder* most probably refers to a combination of schizophrenic and mood disorder symptoms that cannot clearly be separated (Andreasen, 1987). Researchers studied individuals during a 5-year period following hospitalization for schizoaffective disorder and found that these individuals attained somewhat better overall posthospital functioning than people with schizophrenia, somewhat poorer functioning than bipolar patients, and much poorer functioning than people who had been diagnosed with unipolar depression. Because poor outcome is apparently associated with the presence of schizophrenia-like psychotic symptoms during the active

Schizoaffective Disorder

MINI-CASE

At the time of her admission to a psychiatric hospital, Hazel was a 42-year-old mother of three children. She had a 20-year history of schizophrenia-like symptoms, and she experienced periodic episodes of mania. Her schizophrenia-like symptoms included delusions, hallucinations, and thought disorder. These symptoms were fairly well controlled by antipsychotic medications, which she received by injection every two weeks. She was also treated with lithium to control her manic episodes; however, she often skipped her daily dose because she liked "feeling high." On several occasions following extended periods of abstinence from the lithium, Hazel became manic. Accelerated speech and bodily activity, sleepless nights, and erratic behavior characterized these episodes. At the insistence of her husband and her therapist, Hazel would resume taking her lithium, and shortly thereafter her manic symptoms would subside, although her schizophrenia-like symptoms were still somewhat evident.

- Which symptoms of Hazel's schizoaffective disorder are indicative of schizophrenia, and which are indicative of a mood disorder?

- Why do you think Hazel repeatedly places her mental health in jeopardy by stopping her lithium?

DIAGNOSTIC FEATURES

- This diagnosis is appropriate for people who have experienced an uninterrupted period of disturbance, during which they have had either a major depressive episode, a manic episode, or a mixed episode concurrent with at least two of the following schizophrenic symptoms: (1) delusions, (2) hallucinations, (3) disorganized speech, (4) disturbed or catatonic behavior, or (5) negative symptoms, such as flat affect or severe lack of motivation.

- During the period of disturbance, the person has experienced delusions or hallucinations for at least 2 weeks in the absence of mood symptoms.

- The mood episode symptoms are present for a significant portion of the duration of the active and residual periods of the disturbance.

- The symptoms are not due to another disorder, a medical condition, or substances.

phase of the disorder, these researchers concluded that schizoaffective disorder is not just a variant of mood disorder (Grossman, Harrow, Goldberg, & Fichtner, 1991). In a related vein, retrospective studies of people discharged from a psychiatric hospital over a 25-year period also indicated that, the more schizophrenic the symptom picture, the worse the outcome was among people with schizoaffective disorder (McGlashan & Williams, 1990). Further evidence from a large epidemiological study in Ireland continues to support the validity of the diagnosis (Kendler, Neale, & Walsh, 1995). In this study, researchers observed different outcomes for people with schizoaffective disorder, compared with the outcomes for those with schizophrenia or mood disorder. Even more impressive, perhaps, were data from family members. The relatives of the people with schizoaffective disorder had higher rates of mood disorder than did the relatives of individuals with schizophrenia, as well as higher rates of schizophrenia than did the relatives of the people with mood disorder.

Clinicians are sometimes reluctant to use the diagnosis of schizoaffective disorder, because it has no systematic treatment protocol. Pharmacological intervention for people with this diagnosis usually involves a trial-and-error approach, which may include lithium, antidepressants, and antipsychotic medication, either alone or in various combinations. For the most part, antipsychotic medication is combined with lithium for clients with manic symptoms and with antidepressants for clients who are depressed. Psychotherapy needs to be individualized for

each client with this diagnosis. The psychotherapist must be prepared to deal with abrupt symptom changes and with the client's unpredictable feelings and behaviors.

Delusional Disorders

People with **delusional disorders** have a single striking psychotic symptom— an organized system of nonbizarre false beliefs. Although they may have hallucinations, such symptoms are not prominent. They do not show the other symptoms that would make a diagnosis of schizophrenia or mood disorder an appropriate one. Their delusions are systematized and prominent but lack the bizarre quality commonly found in schizophrenia. In fact, it is sometimes initially difficult for others to determine whether these people are delusional, because they can be quite convincing and coherent in the expression of their beliefs. However, with continued contact, most people are able to discern that the beliefs of a person with a delusional disorder are very strange. Interestingly, these individuals are usually able to function satisfactorily, and they do not seem odd to others, except when discussing the particular content of their delusion.

There are five types of delusional disorder. People with erotomanic type have a delusion that another person, usually of great prominence, is deeply in love with them. For example, an otherwise healthy woman may be firmly convinced that a famous talk show host is in love with her and that he communicates secret

Delusional Disorder

MINI-CASE

Paul is a 28-year-old man who has recently experienced tremendous stress at his job. Although he has avoided dwelling on his job problems, he has begun to develop irrational beliefs about his lover, Elizabeth. Despite Elizabeth's repeated vows that she is consistently faithful in the relationship, Paul has become obsessed with the belief that Elizabeth is sexually involved with another person. Paul is suspicious of everyone with whom Elizabeth interacts, questioning her about every insignificant encounter. He searches her closet and drawers for mysterious items, looks for unexplained charges on the charge card bills, listens in on Elizabeth's phone calls, and has contacted a private investigator to follow Elizabeth. Paul is now insisting that they move to another state.

■ What symptoms point to the diagnosis of jealous type of delusional behavior?

■ How do Paul's symptoms differ from those of a person with schizophrenia, paranoid type?

DIAGNOSTIC FEATURES

● People with this disorder have nonbizarre delusions lasting at least 1 month.

● They have never had schizophrenic symptoms, other than possible tactile or olfactory hallucinations related to the delusional theme.

● For the most part, their functioning is not impaired; nor is their behavior bizarre.

● If mood disturbances have occurred concurrent with the delusions, the duration has been brief.

● The symptoms are not due to a medical condition or substance use.

● Types include erotomanic, grandiose, jealous, persecutory, somatic, mixed, and unspecified.

love messages to her in his monologue each night. Grandiose type is characterized by the delusion that one is an extremely important person. For example, a man may believe that he is the Messiah, waiting for a sign from heaven to begin his active ministry. Jealous type is characterized by the delusion that one's sexual partner is being unfaithful. For example, a man may be mistakenly convinced that his wife is having an affair, and he may construct a set of "evidence" of routine domestic events (such as an unexplained charge on the phone bill) to "prove" her infidelity. People with persecutory type believe that they are being harassed or oppressed. For example, a woman may believe that she is the object of a government plot, and she may misconstrue insignificant events as evidence that she is a target for assassination. People with somatic type believe that they have a dreaded disease or that they are dying. Their adherence to such a belief is extreme and incorrigible. For example, a woman may believe that her teeth are turning to chalk and that this deterioration process will then lead to the deterioration of her skull.

Shared Psychotic Disorder

In **shared psychotic disorder,** one or more people develop a delusional system as a result of a close relationship with a psychotic person who is delusional. Typically, two people are involved in this disorder, and the term *folie a deux* (folly of two) is applied to the pair. Occasionally, three or more people or the members of an entire family are involved (Glassman, Magulac, & Darko, 1987).

A person with delusional disorder, erotomanic type may develop an imagined love affair with a movie star and conceive a far-fetched explanation for why the celebrity is not responding to love letters and phone calls.

Unlike schizophrenia, which develops with no apparent external provocation, shared psychotic disorder develops in the context of a close relationship in which there is a history of pathological dependence. The nonpsychotic person gets caught up in the delusional system of the psychotic person and becomes equally consumed by the irrational belief. If the two separate, the previously nonpsychotic person will very likely return to normal functioning and thinking.

This disorder is very rare. In the few instances that it is diagnosed, it is usually found among members of the same family, with the most common cases involving two sisters. This is followed in frequency by mother/child, father/child, and husband/wife combinations. Occasionally, it is found between two friends or lovers.

Shared psychotic disorder is explained primarily from a psychological perspective. The dominant person in these pairs feels desperately isolated from others due to numerous psychological problems. This person seeks out another person who can serve as an ally. The dependent person usually needs the dominant person for some reason, such as safety, financial security, or emotional support, and is therefore willing to surrender to the delusions of the dominant member.

People with shared psychotic disorder rarely seek treatment, because they do not perceive themselves as being disturbed. Occasionally, relatives or friends of the submissive partner urge this person to get professional help. Effective intervention involves separating the two people, at which point the submissive person sometimes becomes more open to rational discussion of the disturbed relationship. At that point, therapy can focus on personal issues that seem related to this person's vulnerability to being dominated. The therapist would explore ways to bolster the client's self-esteem in order to prevent such a situation from occurring again.

Theories and Treatment of Schizophrenia

In the previous sections, you read about the nature of schizophrenia. We now turn our attention to explanations of how schizophrenia develops and how people with this disorder are treated. As you prepare to read about views that may sound technical and theoretical, it is important to keep in mind that schizophrenia involves a disruptive and heartbreaking set of symptoms. Many people, when they hear about schizophrenia, think about a problem that happens only to other people, not to anyone they know. But, as you will discover as you proceed through life, schizophrenia touches the lives of millions of people—possibly someone in your own life. The experience of people with schizophrenia was stated well by William Carpenter, a prominent researcher (Carpenter, 1987): "This illness strikes at the very heart of what we consider the essence of the person. Yet, because its manifestations are so personal and social, it elicits fear, misunderstanding, and condemnation in society instead of sympathy and concern."

A review of the past century of research on schizophrenia shows that, despite major advances in our understanding of this disorder, we remain ignorant about its essence and causes. Experts still lack a reliable, valid set of diagnostic criteria for

In shared psychotic disorder, a nonpsychotic person becomes drawn into the delusional system of a psychotic person. This phenomenon usually occurs in a longstanding, close relationship.

schizophrenia. When researchers attempt to identify the causes of this disorder, this lack of specificity makes their job far more difficult. Compounding the problem is the fact that the research on the causes of schizophrenia goes back over several decades, during which the definition of *schizophrenia* evolved from a very vague, broad concept to a specific, narrow set of criteria. Many people who were diagnosed as having schizophrenia in 1960 would not meet the current criteria for the disorder. Furthermore, evaluating the results of studies from the 1960s is difficult, because the people with "schizophrenia" who were studied constituted such a diverse group.

Some researchers have addressed these definitional problems by reanalyzing data from early studies using present-day criteria. Unfortunately, even this approach does not provide a solution, because the definition of *schizophrenia* still varies from researcher to researcher. As a way of dealing with these differences in definitions, many researchers decided to look at a broad cluster of associated conditions related to schizophrenia, called the schizophrenic spectrum disorders. This term refers to schizophrenia-like conditions ranging from some of the personality disorders (for example, schizoid and schizotypal) to certain psychotic disorders (for example, delusional disorder, schizophreniform disorder, and schizoaffective disorder). At the extreme ends of the spectrum are schizophrenia and mood disorders with psychotic features; between these two poles are schizotypal/personality disorder, other psychoses without prominent mood features, and schizoaffective disorder (Kendler & Diehl, 1993).

Theories accounting for the origin of schizophrenia have traditionally fallen into two categories: biological and psychological. In the first part of this century, a debate raged between proponents of both sides. More recently, researchers have begun to accept that both biology and experience interact in the determination of schizophrenia and have begun to build complex theoretical models that incorporate multiple factors (Malmberg, Lewis, David, & Allebeck, 1998). These models are based on the concept of vulnerability, proposing that

Shared Psychotic Disorder

MINI-CASE

Julio and Carmen, both in their thirties, had been dating for 6 months. Having met at the accounting office where they both worked, they kept their intimate relationship a secret from co-workers at the insistence of Julio, the dominant partner in the relationship. Carmen submitted, and the couple kept exclusive company with each other. Most of their conversation centered around Julio's unwavering belief, which Carmen had come to share, that other people at their office did not like them and that several people wanted them fired. The two of them often stayed after work to search the desks and files of co-workers for evidence that would support Julio's notion. The slightest comment directed toward either of them was construed as evidence of this plot. On the rare occasions when they talked to co-workers, they immediately recorded the conversation in a secret log book. They refused to use the office computer, because they were convinced that it was programmed to keep tabs on them. Eventually, both lost their jobs, but not for the reasons they had constructed. Their odd behaviors aroused so much suspicion that the office routine was disrupted, and they had to be let go.

- What symptoms of shared psychotic disorder are evident in the case of Carmen and Julio?

- If Carmen were not in a relationship with Julio, do you think that she would have other serious psychological problems?

DIAGNOSTIC FEATURES

- This diagnosis is appropriate in cases in which a person develops a delusion similar to an already established delusion held by a person with whom he or she shares a close relationship.

- The disturbance is not due to another disorder, a medical condition, or substance use.

---

individuals have a biologically determined predisposition to developing schizophrenia but that the disorder develops only when certain environmental conditions are in place. As we look at each of the contributions to a vulnerability model, keep in mind that no single theory contains the entire explanation.

Biological Perspective

Biological explanations of schizophrenia have their origins in the writings of Kraepelin, who thought of schizophrenia as a disease caused by a degeneration of brain tissue. Kraepelin's ideas paved the way for the later investigation of such factors as brain structure and genetics, which are now recognized as contributing to an individual's biological vulnerability to schizophrenia.

Brain Structure and Function

Interest in possible brain abnormalities in people with schizophrenia dates back to the nineteenth century, to the first scientific attempts to understand schizophrenia. Some of the early efforts to examine the brains of these individuals were crude and imprecise, because they could be examined only after the person died. Not until the latter half of the twentieth century were sophisticated techniques developed to enable researchers to study the living brain. The technologies of computerized tomography (CT, or CAT, scan) and magnetic resonance imaging (MRI) have enabled researchers in schizophrenia to take a picture of the brain and to analyze that picture quantitatively.

One of the most consistent discoveries using brain imaging methods has been that the brains of people with schizophrenia have enlarged ventricles (the cavities within the brain that hold cerebrospinal fluid). Ventricular enlargement is often accompanied by cortical atrophy, a wasting away of brain tissue (Wolkin et al., 1998). These changes are more likely to occur in people who show a deteriorating course of behavioral symptoms over time (Davis et al., 1998) and in people who had experienced an onset of the disorder at a relatively late age of over 45 years (Corey-Bloom et al., 1995). These findings seem to support Kraepelin's belief that schizophrenia is a process of brain degeneration. However, it is important to keep in mind that studies of total brain size or volume are inherently limited in the information they can provide about the organic basis for schizophrenia. The particular psychological symptoms that people with this disorder show must surely be accounted for by changes more specific than a reduction in the amount of brain tissue. Using such methods as PET scans and neurobehavioral measures, investigators have determined that schizophrenia is associated with abnormalities in the frontal and prefrontal cortex, the left temporal lobe, the basal ganglia, and parts of the limbic system, including the hippocampus and amygdala (Buchsbaum, 1990; Gur et al., 1998; Kirkpatrick & Buchanan, 1990; Kremen et al., 1994; Liddle et al., 1992; Spence, Hirsch, Brooks, & Grasby, 1998; Stanley & Turner, 1995; Wible et al., 1995). Abnormalities in these areas are thought to be associated with dopamine functioning (Csernansky & Bardgett, 1998) and may underlie behavioral disturbances associated with schizophrenia in thoughts and perceptions, attention, the planning and execution of organized behavior, and the regulation of motivation. Another hypothesis regarding brain abnormalities in schizophrenia is that they reflect a failure in the genetic program through which one hemisphere of the brain becomes dominant (Tiihonen et al., 1998). Brain dominance affects many facets of behavior, including speech and communication, functions that are seriously impaired in schizophrenia.

Yet another path in the search for brain-behavior connections has been followed by researchers investigating the role of neurotransmitters, particularly dopamine. According to what is called the **dopamine hypothesis,** the delusions, hallucinations, and attentional deficits found in schizophrenia can be attributed to an overactivity of neurons that communicate with each other via the transmission of dopamine (Carlsson, 1988). This hypothesis emerged from two related lines of evidence. The first was the observation that antipsychotic medications reduce the frequency of hallucinations and delusions by blocking dopamine receptors. The second line of evidence was that certain drugs that are biochemically related to dopamine, such as amphetamines, increase the frequency of psychotic symptoms.

When first introduced, the dopamine hypothesis was heralded as a breakthrough in accounting for the more bizarre and puzzling symptoms of schizophrenia. Gradually, though, as with most explanations of schizophrenia, later findings caused researchers to temper their original enthusiasm and to refine the hypothesis. Not all people with schizophrenia have an overabundance of dopamine. Instead, it is more likely that dopamine activity varies according to the nature of the symptoms. According to this revised version of the dopamine hypothesis, people with Type I schizophrenia have higher levels of dopamine, and those with Type II have lower dopamine activity (Pickar et al., 1990). Evidence is also emerging that abnormalities in the serotonin neurotransmitter system may play a more important role in schizophrenia than previously thought, based both on blood tests of serotonin levels (Csernansky & Newcomer, 1994) and the responsiveness of people with schizophrenia to the medication clozapine (Masellis et al., 1998), which we will discuss in more detail later in the chapter. There is also emerging evidence that abnormalities in GABA neurons in prefrontal brain circuits may play a role in the development of the cognitive impairments associated with schizophrenia (Woo, Whitehead, Melchitzky, & Lewis, 1998).

Genetic Explanations

As you will recall from Chapter 4, researchers study genetic contributions to psychological disorders in several ways. Schizophrenia researchers have used four kinds of studies in their attempt to assess the contributions of genetics: family and twin studies, adoption studies, high-risk studies, and studies of biological markers.

Family and Twin Studies   The family patterns of individuals who have schizophrenia provide convincing evidence in favor of a biological explanation. The closer a relative is to an individual with schizophrenia, the greater the likelihood of concordance. Identical twins have the highest concordance, close to 90 percent (Franzek & Beckmann, 1998), and increasingly more distant relatives have correspondingly lower concordance rates (See Figure 10.1).

Studies that report a higher rate of the disorder among genetically linked family members have the obvious limitation that the researchers have not been able to rule out the effects of a shared family environment. In other words, the high concordance rate may be attributable either to genetics or to the fact that family members live in the same home. Studies on the concordance rate of schizophrenia between identical twins fail to separate these two influences. Besides studying the data from identical twins reared together, researchers also need to examine evidence from identical twins reared apart, but such cases are infrequent. Based on the few cases that have been reported, there is an impressive concordance rate of 64 percent (Gottesman, 1991; Gottesman & Shields, 1982). Keep in mind, though, that even this design has possible confounds. Why were the twins separated and reared apart? Was there a problem in the family that led to the drastic action of separating identical twins? Another approach, which uses statistical methods to control for the shared environments of twins reared together, produces a higher heritability ratio of 83 percent (Cannon et al., 1998). Such research demonstrates the powerful role of genetics, irrespective of environmental influences.

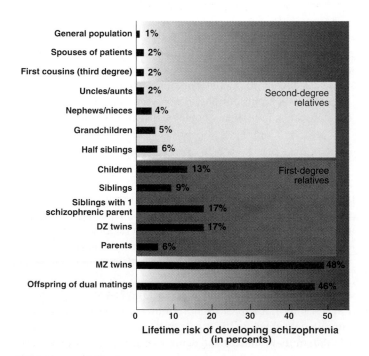

Figure 10.1

Grand average risks for developing schizophrenia, compiled from the family and twin studies conducted in European populations between 1920 and 1987. The degree of risk correlates highly with the degree of genetic relatedness.

In another research paradigm, investigators have studied discordant identical twin pairs, in which one twin has schizophrenia and the other does not. If genetics is a major determinant, then the child of a nonschizophrenic twin should still be at risk for developing the disorder. In fact, this is precisely what researchers have found. The rates of schizophrenia or a schizophrenia-like psychosis are roughly equal in the offspring of nonaffected twins and in children of twins with schizophrenia (McGue & Gottesman, 1989). This finding suggests that the twins who did not develop schizophrenia transmitted the risk of this disorder to their offspring as part of their genetic endowment. Researchers do not know why, though, the original nonschizophrenic member of the twin pair did not develop schizophrenia. If these people were carrying the genetic endowment for schizophrenia, what factors protected them from developing the disorder, and how were these factors different from the influences on their identical siblings?

One very persuasive explanation for the discordant findings for identical twins is that each member of the twin pairs was exposed to different sources of environmental harm, perhaps during the prenatal period (Prescott & Gottesman, 1993; Turnquist, 1993). In one investigation, researchers used magnetic resonance imaging to compare the brains of discordant identical twins. They identified structural differences indicating larger ventricular spaces and smaller hippocampal areas in the schizophrenic compared with the nonschizophrenic twins. Given the identical genetic makeup of the twins, the fact that their brains developed differently indicates that some type of exposure during the formative stages of brain development triggered a process resulting in adult brain abnormalities (Stabenau & Pollin, 1993). These brain abnormalities presumably led to schizophrenic symptoms.

Thus, the more refined twin studies provide support for genetic explanations but still leave many unanswered questions. Because of the limitations in twin studies, researchers have turned to the powerful design of the adoption study, which provides a "natural experiment" in which genetic and environmental factors can be independently assessed, because the child is separated from the biological parents.

Adoption Studies In the typical adoption study, researchers track the incidence of schizophrenia in children who are raised by nonschizophrenic parents but whose biological parents have schizophrenia. In cases in which the child is separated from the parents early in life, the confounding role of family environment is removed. Cross-fostering is another and rarer form of adoption study involving the less likely circumstance of a child whose biological parents have no disorder but who is adopted by a parent who has a schizophrenic spectrum disorder.

Researchers in Denmark used both types of adoption paradigms in a series of adoption studies begun in the 1960s (Kety, Rosenthal, Wender, & Schulsinger, 1968). Because the Danish government keeps comprehensive birth, adoption, and health records, this country was ideal for the study. The relatively homogeneous and stable population of Denmark provided further advantages for conducting this kind of research. The most important finding to emerge from these studies was that the rates of schizophrenia were higher in the biological relatives of the adoptees who had schizophrenia than in the relatives of the adoptees who did not have schizophrenia.

Further clues to solving the genetics-environment puzzle come from the results of cross-fostering adoption studies. Recall that a cross-fostering study involves identifying children whose biological parents did not have schizophrenia but whose rearing parents did. The researchers conducting the schizophrenia cross-fostering studies sought such individuals, again, from the Danish adoption register. By scanning the records from all of Denmark, Paul Wender and his co-workers (Wender et al., 1974) were able to find 38 individuals who were cross-fostered and compared them with nonschizophrenic and schizophrenic adoptees. The rate of schizophrenia and related disorders in the cross-fostered group was almost the same as the rate in the control adoptees. The researchers concluded from this finding that the family environment was far less significant than biological predispositions in making an individual vulnerable to developing schizophrenia.

However, environmental factors interact with genetic predispositions. Interactive models of genetic and environmental influences have received growing support from studies with more refined methodologies than the original Danish adoption studies. The largest of these studies was carried out by a team of researchers led by Pekka Tienari in Finland (Tienari, 1991; Tienari et al., 1987, 1989). Tienari and his colleagues undertook the massive task of tracking down the childbirth records of almost 20,000 women who had been diagnosed as having schizophrenia or paranoid psychosis, spanning almost a 20-year period and including the entire country of Finland. From this very large population, the researchers chose a sample of 361 women who had given their children up for legal adoption within the first four years of the child's life. The latest findings reported from this study (Wahlberg et al., 1997) revealed that the people with a high genetic predisposition growing up in homes with disturbed communication patterns (considered an environmental risk factor) had a much higher rate of thought disturbance than would be expected. By contrast, disturbed family communication styles seemed to have a more negative effect on the people with no biological risk of schizophrenia. The existence of such gene-environment interactions suggests that both sets of factors must be considered when evaluating an individual's risk of developing schizophrenia and related disorders.

High-Risk Design A third approach to studying the relative contributions of genetics and environmental factors to schizophrenia is the **high-risk design.** In this type of research, investigators follow the lives of children who are at risk for developing schizophrenia because they have a biological parent with the disorder. Children with one schizophrenic parent have a 12 percent risk over their lifetime of becoming schizophrenic, in contrast to a rate of approximately 1 percent in the general population (Keith et al., 1991). If both parents have schizophrenia, the lifetime risk to the offspring jumps dramatically, to rates of between 35 and 46 percent (Erlenmeyer-Kimling et al.,

1982). The children of people with schizophrenia, then, are important to study because of their statistically greater chance of developing the disorder.

By studying high-risk children prior to an age when they would be expected to show signs of schizophrenia, researchers hope to discover what distinguishes the subgroup of those who actually develop schizophrenia from those who lead lives free of symptoms. Researchers have also looked at other kinds of comparison groups, such as the children of people with other forms of psychiatric disorders, children who show behavioral signs of disturbance even though their parents are normal, and normal control groups of children.

Research on high-risk children has revealed that they show more signs of disturbance, compared with control groups of children, particularly along the schizophrenia spectrum of disorders (Tyrka et al., 1995). However, the results are far from definitive, because these high-risk children are also more prone to developing other Axis I disorders, not just schizophrenia (Erlenmeyer-Kimling et al., 1991; Mirsky et al., 1995). Even among these children who would seem most likely to develop schizophrenia, many never do. Some factor or factors must be involved that protect these vulnerable individuals from progressing to the point of showing overt signs of psychosis (Weintraub, 1987). Whether these protective factors are biological or experiential is a question that currently has no definitive answer.

Studies of Biological Markers

Another approach within the genetic model is the attempt by researchers to develop a mathematical model that would explain how the disorder passes from generation to generation. It is clear that schizophrenia does not follow a simple Mendelian model of dominant and recessive inheritance. Instead, it is more likely that schizophrenia has a complex pattern of transmission. The multifactorial polygenic threshold model (Gottesman, 1991), described in Chapter 4, proposes that several genes with varying influence are involved in the transmission of schizophrenia. The vulnerability for schizophrenia is actually a continuum from low to high, depending on the combination of genes that the individual inherits. The symptoms of schizophrenia are produced when the accumulation of genetic and environmental factors exceeds a certain threshold value.

Researchers trying to understand the specific mechanisms involved in such a complex model of genetic transmission have found it helpful to study biological markers, which are measurable characteristics whose family patterns parallel the pattern of schizophrenia inheritance. Investigators attempting to identify biological markers have experimented with a variety of psychophysiological measures thought to reflect some of the attentional deficits observed in people with schizophrenia. After decades of refining theory and technique, researchers have identified a relatively small number of possible markers that have promise for eventually indicating which individuals have an inherited vulnerability for the disorder.

Two measures stand out as particularly important in the search for biological markers: sustained attention and **smooth pursuit eye movements.** Laboratory measures of sustained attention (the Continuous Performance Test) involve having the person being tested make a response when a certain target stim-

Studying attentional defects in people with schizophrenia, a researcher records the time it takes to react to stimuli presented on the screen.

ulus is displayed. This target stimulus is presented along with other stimuli at unpredictable intervals. For instance, the researcher may instruct the person to push a button whenever the letter *A* appears from among a series of letters presented individually for very brief periods of time (on the order of milliseconds). This is a tedious task that requires constant vigilance by the participant in order to receive a high score. The researcher can also make the task more complex by adding other demands, such as requiring that the person push the button only if the letter *A* is preceded by the letter *Q*. Typically, people with schizophrenia do very poorly on these tasks, especially when the demands of the task are increased, so that the individual's cognitive capacities are stretched to their limits (Asarnow, Granholm, & Sherman, 1991; Nuechterlain et al., 1992). More to the point, the biological relatives of people with schizophrenia also show deficits on the more complex version of the Continuous Performance Test (Asarnow, Steffy, MacCrimmon, & Cleghorn, 1977; Rosenberg et al., 1997).

Researchers measure the second biological marker, disturbance in smooth pursuit eye movements, by having participants visually follow a target, such as a small point of light on a dark background, and closely monitoring their eye movements with recording devices. In contrast to normal individuals, people with schizophrenia show irregular pursuit of a moving target, along with many interruptions by extraneous eye movements. First-degree relatives of people with schizophrenia also show this abnormality in the smooth pursuit function, which is called eye tracking dysfunction.

Following the initial report of the finding of eye movement dysfunction (Holzman et al., 1974), researchers have found support for the concept of a complex genetic model underlying the inheritance of schizophrenia (Clementz, Grove, Iacono, & Sweeney, 1992; Iacono et al., 1992). According to this model, a genetic predisposition is inherited through the combined effect of several genes. This predisposition is thought to be a form of disease process that can affect different parts of the central nervous system (Holzman, 1992; Holzman & Matthysse, 1990).

A third behavioral abnormality that can serve as a biological marker is a defect in the ability to filter, or "tune out," auditory signals, a function known as **sensory gating**. This deficit is demonstrated by exposing individuals in the laboratory to repeated presentation of an auditory stimulus and measuring evoked brain potentials. People with schizophrenia do not show the sensory gating effect, meaning that they are more likely to have difficulty filtering out irrelevant distractions from the outside world. There is some evidence that this dysfunction is genetically based, as it is observed both in people with schizophrenia and in their relatives (Adler et al., 1998).

Genetic mapping has been extensively applied in schizophrenia research. Several "schizophrenia genes" have been identified through this procedure, but so far none have been definitively named. A variety of chromosomes have been identified as potential sites of schizophrenia since the search for this gene began. These include chromosomes 5 (Bassett, 1989; Sherrington et al., 1988), 2 (Aschauer et al., 1993), 21 (Zatz et al., 1991), 6 (Wang et al., 1995), 13 (Lin et al., 1997), and 22 (Chandy et al., 1998).

The Unique Case of the Genain Quadruplets

Drawing on many of the concepts, research findings, and theoretical models involved in biological explanations of schizophrenia is one investigation that stands alone in the annals of psychiatric literature—the long-term follow-up study of the Genain quadruplets. These four women, born in the early 1930s, shared an identical genetic makeup, and each woman developed symptoms of schizophrenia, starting in her twenties. The disorder was to remain with these women for their entire adult lives, although, as they entered later adulthood, their symptoms changed in severity. Extensive information is available about their family history and life events in adulthood. Analyses of these data suggested many intriguing new hypotheses about the dynamic interplay among the influences of family inheritance, early childhood experiences, and the unpredictable course of chronic psychological disturbance over the years of adulthood.

The pseudonym "Genain" is actually a coined word that stands for "dreadful genes," and the first names of the quadruplets are pseudonyms derived from the first letters in names of the research institute that sponsored much of the investigation, the National Institute of Mental Health (NIMH). The four women were named, accordingly, Nora, Iris, Myra, and Hester, in order of birth, with Nora being the "first-born" and Hester being the "youngest." Nora was also the first to be hospitalized for schizophrenia (at the age of 21), followed by Iris, 7 months later. The remaining two sisters were diagnosed as having schizophrenia when they all entered the NIMH for study in 1955. Prior to that time, Hester had shown clear symptoms of a psychotic disorder, but Myra had no psychotic symptoms until this hospitalization. Myra was also the only one to marry, and she bore two sons. All four sisters lived for the majority of their adult years in their mother's home, when they were not institutionalized in a state hospital.

The Genain quadruplets provided researchers with a unique opportunity to study the role of genetics in the development of schizophrenia. Would you be able to tell from this photograph which of the sisters developed the most severe psychotic symptoms in adulthood?

What makes the study of these women so interesting is the fact that, although they were concordant with regard to the existence of schizophrenia, the degree of severity of the disorder and its course over the decades of the study differed among them. Such differences have provided ample room for speculation about the relative contributions of genetics and life experiences as causes of the disorder.

In the original report of the study (Rosenthal, 1963), the divergence in diagnosis among the four women was explained in terms of different patterns of life stresses. For example, Hester was generally regarded as the least competent sister and, worse, was labeled a "sex maniac" and a "moron" by her parents. Iris, although physically more comparable to Nora and Myra, was paired with Hester, and their parents treated these two as the less capable pair throughout their childhood and adolescence. In their teens, both were, in fact, submitted to a surgical procedure on their genitals by the family physician, who thought they needed a cure for their excessive masturbation. Their parents gave Nora and Myra a great deal of favorable attention. Despite the fact that the two pairs were treated so differently, Mrs. Genain insisted that she always treated the four sisters "identically." Not only did she send contradictory and confusing messages, but her pressure for conformity became a dynamic that impeded the growth of the healthier sisters. Myra, for example, had never shown evidence of psychotic symptoms prior to her hospitalization for the study at NIMH. Was she inappropriately cast into the mold of the schizophrenia diagnosis by her own wish to conform, or by the staff's intention to treat her equally with her sisters? Or was she truly schizophrenic, and her symptoms for some reason lay dormant for another 20 years? These differing life stress factors might have pushed the sisters into differing degrees of disturbance.

Other stresses, however, were similar for all four sisters. One was the extreme interest generated by their uniqueness, causing them and their hometown to be the focus of media attention and publicity, despite Mrs. Genain's considerable efforts to keep her daughters out of the public limelight. Unfortunately, in the process of trying to protect her daughters, Mrs. Genain may have pushed them into their own fantasy worlds and out of touch with reality. Mrs. Genain's goal was to allow her daughters to lead normal lives, but the outcome was just the opposite. The stresses of such influences as the pressure to conform, the attention of the media, and their mother's desire to protect them might have interacted with the differences created by the "pairings" into the more and less competent twosomes.

In the 1981 follow-up, researchers tested the sisters extensively over a 3½-month period—with and without medication—on eye movement and continuous performance tests; CT scans; PET scans; dopamine activity; and other measures of brain function, personality, and intelligence. As a group, the four performed as would be expected on some of the tests, and their scores were very similar, reflecting their identical genetic endowment. One important exception was the CT scans, which showed no signs of ventricular enlargement in any of the four women. Across many of the tests, though, the sisters differed in their relative degree of impairment. The most dramatic difference was in their response to being taken off the antipsychotic medications that they had all been taking. Myra and Iris deteriorated less than the other two sisters, and they were eventually able to leave the hospital medication-free. In this regard, then, Myra and Iris became the better functioning pair, a switch from the earlier pairing of Nora and Myra.

Once again the question arises: why, given that they had the same genetic endowment, would the foursome show any differences in schizophrenic symptoms, much less shifts over the course of adulthood in the relative degree of impairment? The answer, according to the investigators, lies in the interactive effects of environmental stress and brain abnormalities that predispose an individual to developing the attentional and other processing deficits that can trigger symptoms of schizophrenia. Nora and Hester, the first and last born, were more likely to have suffered brain damage during delivery; Iris and Hester received the most negative treatment as children and teenagers. The order of relative impairment, then, corresponds to the interaction of these factors (see Table 10.2). Myra, according to this reasoning, was the most advantaged, because she was low on both factors; Hester, in contrast, was high on both factors and, therefore, had more severe symptoms. With genetics a constant factor, then, differences in the expression of schizophrenic symptoms may be accounted for by a combination of biological and psychological forces (Mirsky & Quinn, 1988). It is important to be cautious about placing too much emphasis on the role of Mrs. Genain's behavior as a cause of schizophrenia in her daughters.

Table 10.2

Contributions of Stress and Brain Damage in the Genain Quadruplets

Brain Damage	Environmental Stress	
	Low	High
Low	Myra	Iris
High	Nora	Hester

What makes the Genain study so important is not only the control over genetic factors that it provides, but also the fact that these variant patterns were discovered only after an extensive period of follow-up. These results could not have been detected by one-time assessments. This is an important fact to keep in mind when reading the literature on schizophrenia, much of which is based on short-term assessments.

Biological Stressors and Vulnerability

Although we tend to think of stress as a psychological event, there are many events that happen within the body, especially during development, that can be experienced as assaults with long-lasting consequences. Scientists are particularly interested in dramatic events during the prenatal period and delivery that may influence the development of schizophrenia among people who have a genetic vulnerability. These events include the exposure of pregnant women to harmful environmental conditions or the experience of birth complications. For example, the women who lived through the invasion of the Netherlands by Germany during World War II were more likely to bear children who later developed schizophrenia. Male offspring were particularly at risk (van Os & Selten, 1998). Other researchers examined the pregnancy and birth records of adults diagnosed with schizophrenia and found higher rates of problems during pregnancy, delivery, and the period immediately after birth (Ohman & Hultman, 1998). Presumably, these complications result in brain abnormalities that increase the likelihood of schizophrenia.

However, it is important to realize that birth complications, without an underlying vulnerability, are unlikely to cause schizophrenia. This is where the diathesis-stress model becomes relevant. According to the diathesis-stress model, individuals may inherit a vulnerability to schizophrenia, which is expressed when the individual is exposed to stressors from the environment. This underlying vulnerability has been called "schizotypy" by psychologist Paul Meehl (Meehl, 1962, 1990). The concept of a diathesis, or inherited, vulnerability to schizophrenia is one that underlies much of the current thinking regarding the causes of this complex disorder.

Psychological Perspective

There is no credible theory that proposes that schizophrenia develops exclusively as the result of psychological phenomena, such as life experiences, developmental difficulties, interpersonal problems, or emotional conflicts. However, the psychological theorists have offered some valuable insights into the ways in which the symptoms of this condition affect the lives of people with schizophrenia and the ways in which psychological principles can be applied in treatment. The most widely accepted psychological approach to understanding schizophrenia comes from the behavioral theories, which were first proposed in the 1960s as a radical alternative to the biological explanations of the disorder. At that time, the behavioral theorists were impressed by evidence from early experiments, showing that people with symptoms of schizophrenia could, through proper reinforcements, behave in socially appropriate ways. If the schizophrenic behaviors could be unlearned, these theorists wondered whether the same behaviors could have been acquired through a learning process.

What type of learning process could account for the acquisition of behaviors that stray so far from the norm? These theorists proposed that individuals first acquire the symptoms of schizophrenia through a failure to learn how to direct their attention to important cues in social interactions. Presumably, this faulty learning process begins during childhood. The child's lack of attentiveness might result from the experience of punishment by other people; retreating to an inner world of thoughts and fantasies becomes more rewarding for the child. The child has no incentive to pull away from this idiosyncratic universe, because the reality of the outside world is so unpleasant. Eventually, other children, parents, and teachers come to label this child "odd" or "eccentric" (Ullman & Krasner, 1975). This **labeling** may eventually lead to the individual's being called "schizophrenic"—and a vicious cycle begins. According to this theory, once labeled, the individual acts in ways that conform to this label (Scheff, 1966).

Following the behavioral line of argument further, these theorists propose that individuals hospitalized and labeled as schizophrenic can be drawn further into a pattern of maladaptive behaviors. Disturbed behaviors might be inadvertently reinforced in psychiatric hospitals. For example, nursing staff might let a disturbed individual sit quietly and hallucinate in a corner but would react negatively to the individual's assertiveness in requesting more attention. If staff members fail to reinforce socially appropriate behavior, the clients have no incentive to act in ways that others would perceive as normal. Further, to the extent that the atmosphere in many psychiatric hospitals lacks adequate stimulation, the clients have nothing to distract them from their idiosyncratic and disturbed ways of thinking. They may also receive rewards for maintaining the sick role, described in Chapter 7 as secondary gain. According to the behavioral perspective, all of these circumstances lead to a situation that maintains and exacerbates the symptoms of schizophrenia.

Sociocultural Perspective

Researchers working within the family systems perspective focus on the "system" of roles, interactions, and patterns of communication in the family environment in which the person with schizophrenia grew up. In studies on modes of communication and behavior within families with a schizophrenic member, researchers attempt to document deviant patterns of communication and inappropriate ways that parents interact with their children. These disturbances in family relationships are thought to lead to the development of defective emotional responsiveness and cognitive distortions fundamental to the psychological symptoms of schizophrenia.

Contemporary researchers have approached the issue by trying to predict outcome or recovery in adults hospitalized for schizophrenia. Instead of regarding a disturbed family as the cause of schizophrenia, these researchers view the family as a potential source of stress in the environment of the person who is trying to recover from a schizophrenic episode. The stress created by family members is reflected in the index of **expressed emotion (EE),** which provides a measure of the degree to which family members speak in ways that reflect criticism, hostile feelings, and emotional overinvolvement or overconcern. People living in families high in EE are more likely to suffer a relapse than are people who live in low-EE families (Brown, Birley, & Wing, 1972; Kavanagh, 1992; Leff, 1977; Leff & Vaughn, 1981; Vaughn & Leff, 1976; Vaughn et al., 1984). More recent refinements of the EE model regard this factor not simply as the trigger for schizophrenic symptoms but also as a response to unusual, disruptive, or poorly socialized behavior on the part of the schizophrenic individual (Rosenfarb, Goldstein, Mintz, & Nuechterlein, 1995; Weisman, Nuechterlein, Goldstein, & Snyder, 1998). Indeed, researchers are finding that EE seems to rise and fall along with the degree of burden represented by the disturbed child's presence in the home (Scazufca & Kuipers, 1998).

Moving beyond the family environment, broader social factors, such as social class and income, have also been studied in relationship to schizophrenia. A summary of this research is contained in the How People Differ box. The social causation and downward social drift hypotheses of schizophrenia provide systematic explanations of the possibility that social structure can be the source of environmental stressors that trigger symptoms in vulnerable individuals.

Many people with schizophrenia have difficulty readjusting to their families after a period of hospitalization. According to the theory of expressed emotion, returning to a family that is highly critical increases the chances that a relapse of the disorder will occur.

Schizophrenia and Social Class

In perhaps the first epidemiological study of mental illness to be conducted in the United States, Hollingshead and Redlich (1958) observed that schizophrenia was far more prevalent in the lowest socioeconomic classes, and numerous investigators since that time have supported the connection between lower social class and higher rates of schizophrenia (Gottesman, 1991). Over the years, this observation has been the source of a great deal of speculation about the role of social factors in either causing schizophrenia or influencing its course. Two principal explanations have been proposed: (1) the social causation hypothesis and (2) the downward social drift hypothesis.

According to the social causation hypothesis, membership in lower socioeconomic strata may actually cause schizophrenia. Members of the lowest classes of society experience numerous economic hardships and are often denied access to many of society's benefits, including high-quality education, health care, and employment. Because many are also members of ethnic or racial minorities, they may experience discrimination. These factors create a highly stressful environment, which might be conducive

to the development of schizophrenia. It is important to note that the social causation hypothesis need not contradict the diathesis-stress model; rather, the stresses of poverty and socioeconomic disadvantage may elicit schizophrenic symptoms at higher rates than in less disadvantaged social settings.

The other perspective, the downward social drift hypothesis, downplays the effects of socioeconomic stressors in the development of schizophrenia. Presumably, schizophrenia develops at equal rates across a variety of social, cultural, and economic backgrounds, but, once people develop the disorder, their economic standing declines precipitously. The debilitating symptoms of schizophrenia prevent individuals from pursuing economic success and preclude their living in more affluent areas. This perspective, therefore, downplays the potential stressors of poverty and lower social status in favor of a more directly biological approach to the causes of schizophrenia. The symptoms of the disorder are what account for the declining economic and social fortunes of people diagnosed with schizophrenia.

Each of these hypotheses seems a compelling explanation for the connection between social class and schizophrenia, but researchers have conducted relatively few studies to investigate these possibilities. Studies conducted in the 1960s indicated that individuals with schizophrenia tended to congregate in the lowest strata of society, even when their family backgrounds indicated histories of economic success (Turner & Wagonfeld, 1963). In a more recent investigation (Dohrenwend et al., 1992), patterns of schizophrenia were compared in two groups of Israelis:

(1) long-time European immigrants and (2) recent African and Middle Eastern immigrants. The former group represented a relatively stable and economically advantaged social group, whereas the latter consisted of relatively disadvantaged individuals. Again, the results supported the downward social drift perspective. Schizophrenia was more prevalent among the disadvantaged group of newer immigrants. The most able of the disadvantaged group achieved economic success despite hardships, whereas the most troubled of the advantaged group of older immigrants witnessed a decline in their economic success.

Overall, there is far too little research to resolve the contrasting viewpoints of the social causation and downward social drift hypotheses. Tentative evidence exists to support the downward social drift hypothesis that individuals with schizophrenia are unable to achieve economic and social success due to the severity of their symptoms; however, if we return to the diathesis-stress model of causation, poverty and social disadvantage would seem powerful stressors capable of eliciting schizophrenic symptoms. Interestingly, these perspectives may clarify the distribution of schizophrenia within a society, but broader epidemiological studies have not indicated a clear relationship between the prevalence of schizophrenia and the level of economic development across societies (Edgerton & Cohen, 1994; Susser & Wanderling, 1994). We are left to conclude that the relationship of schizophrenia to socioeconomic status may extend beyond these two competing perspectives to include broader factors, such as societal values and beliefs about mental illness, among others.

Treatment of Schizophrenia

The vulnerability model we have just discussed implies that schizophrenia has no single cause. Although a particular theory may appear to be dominant, treatment must be based on a multifaceted approach that incorporates various theoretical components. Current comprehensive models of care include biological treatments, psychological interventions primarily in the form of behavioral techniques, and sociocultural interventions that focus on milieu therapy and family involvement.

Biological Treatments

In the 1950s, effective medication was introduced for treating the symptoms of schizophrenia. This breakthrough had a massive impact on the mental health system, as you recall from our discussion in Chapter 1, helping to spur on the deinstitutionalization movement. The fact that medication could control the most debilitating symptoms of psychosis, at least to some extent, meant that hundreds of thousands of people could be treated on an outpatient basis, rather than be confined and under constant supervision.

Prior to the 1950s, somatic interventions involved treatments intended to alter brain functioning, including ECT. The most extreme somatic intervention was the prefrontal lobotomy. Although this procedure helped reduce aggressive behaviors in people who experienced hallucinations and delusions, lobotomies also had many unfavorable outcomes for the individual, including a significant loss of motivation, creativity, and cognitive function. With the advent of antipsychotic medication in the 1950s, the procedure was all but abandoned. Similarly, medications have replaced the use of ECT in treating schizophrenia.

There are several categories of antipsychotic medication, also called major tranquilizers or **neuroleptics** (derived from the Greek words meaning "to seize the nerve"). In addition to their sedating qualities, neuroleptics reduce the frequency and severity of psychotic symptoms. The various neuroleptics differ in the dosage needed to achieve therapeutic effects, ranging from low-potency medications that require large dosages to high-potency medications that require comparatively smaller dosages. The low-potency class includes such medications as chlorpromazine (Thorazine) and thioridazine (Mellaril); middle-potency medications include trifluoperazine (Stelazine) and thiothixene (Navane); high-potency medications include haloperidol (Haldol) and fluphenazine (Prolixin). A physician would be more likely to prescribe a low-potency medication for a highly agitated patient, because low-potency medications tend to be more sedating than the high-potency ones. The high-potency medications may be preferable for a patient who is less agitated, but they do carry the risk of more serious side effects.

These traditionally prescribed antipsychotic medications have their effects through the blocking of dopamine receptors. In other words, these medications contain chemical substances that become attached to the sites on the neurons that would ordinarily respond to the neurotransmitter dopamine. This action has two behavioral results, one therapeutic and the other unintended and troublesome. The therapeutic result is reduced frequency and intensity of psychotic symptoms, as the dopamine receptors are deactivated in the sections of the brain that affect thoughts and feelings. On the negative side are consequences that can greatly interfere with the individual's movements and endocrine function. People taking such medications may suddenly experience such symptoms as uncontrollable shaking, muscle tightening, and involuntary eye movements. These side effects occur when dopamine accumulates because it is not being taken up by neurons whose receptor sites have been blocked by the medication. As the dopamine level rises, the neurons in the other areas of the brain that control motor movements are thrown into dysregulation. Interestingly, physicians treat people with Parkinson's disease, a nervous disease that is caused by an insufficiency of dopamine, with a medication that enhances dopamine activity. Thus, a commonly reported side effect of this anti-Parkinsonian medication is psychotic-like behavior and thinking.

One of the most troubling effects from the long-term use of neuroleptics is an irreversible neurological disorder called tardive dyskinesia, which affects 10 to 20 percent of people who take some of the neuroleptics for a year or more. People with tardive dyskinesia experience uncontrollable movements in

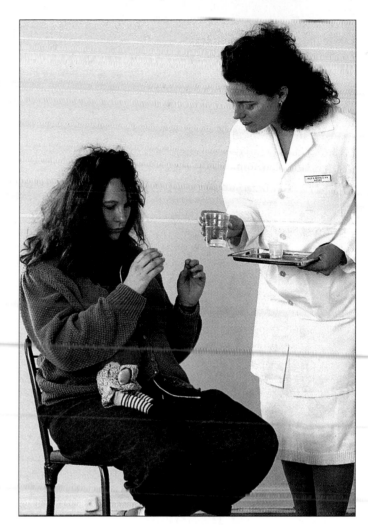

Sometimes a person with schizophrenia becomes so impaired that hospitalization is necessary.

various parts of their bodies, including the mouth, tongue, lips, fingers, arms, legs, and trunk. As you can imagine, these involuntary movements can seriously impair the person's ability to walk, breathe, eat, and talk, to say nothing of how embarrassing it is to be seen in this state.

Disturbed by the worrisome side effects of these traditional antipsychotic medications, as well as their ineffectiveness in treating negative symptoms, psychopharmacological researchers set out to develop new medications. In recent years, new medications, called "atypical antipsychotics" have been more widely prescribed, because they have fewer side effects and greater therapeutic effectiveness in the treatment of negative symptoms and cognitive deficits. Clozapine (Clozaril) is a serotonin blocker that also works on other neurotransmitter systems but that has a different biochemical mode of action from the neuroleptics. Clozapine has been enthusiastically welcomed by the 10 to 20 percent of people with schizophrenia whose symptoms have been unaffected by other antipsychotic medications, and it has been impressively effective, with fewer side effects than older medications (Wilson & Claussen, 1995). Unfortunately, taking clozapine poses a very serious health risk. A very small number of individuals taking clozapine have developed agranulocytosis, in which the bone marrow stops producing white blood cells, leaving the individual vulnerable to infection; thus, clozapine can be the indirect cause of death. Because of this alarming possibility, the prescription of this medication has been limited to a small group of people for whom other medications have been unsuccessful. Those taking clozapine must be closely monitored for any signs of agranulocytosis. Because of the serious health risks, clinicians have turned to newer atypical antipsychotics, such as risperidone (Risperdal), olanzapine (Zyprexa), and quetiapine (Seroquel), which have therapeutic effects similar to those of clozapine, but without the risk of agranulocytosis.

Although antipsychotic medications alleviate the symptoms of schizophrenia, it is important to keep in mind that these medications do not cure the disorder. Even though more recently introduced medications are effective in treating some of the negative symptoms, it is a rare individual who resumes normal functioning simply as the result of taking medicine.

One dilemma that health care providers face when recommending antipsychotic medication is whether or not people with schizophrenia should be maintained on full doses of these medications when they are not experiencing the overt positive symptoms of the disorder. Some clinicians recommend to certain clients that they reduce or stop medication during extended periods of good functioning, as long as clients can be closely monitored for the reappearance of symptoms. Obviously, the clinician's decision to interrupt medication should only be done following a careful evaluation of the client's symptoms and history (Nuechterlein, Gitlin, & Subotnik, 1995).

Psychological Treatments

The most common psychological interventions for people with schizophrenia are those derived from the behavioral perspective, in which it is assumed that much of the difficulty that many people with schizophrenia face is due to their having acquired bizarre and maladaptive behavior patterns. These treatments focus on the individual's symptoms that interfere with social adjustment and functioning. For example, consider Aimee, a woman whose paranoid delusions have caused her to respond to other people in ways that alienate them. She turns away when others start a conversation with her, acting in a cold and distant manner that discourages them from getting to know her. Her therapist might help Aimee develop the more socially appropriate behaviors of responding pleasantly to others and even, perhaps, initiating conversations herself. Aimee might also be a member of a therapy group comprising individuals with similar difficulties. The therapist would work with the group as a whole to encourage each member to develop more appropriate interpersonal behaviors.

In a token economy (Ayllon & Azrin, 1965), most often used in institutional settings, individuals are rewarded with plastic chips called "tokens" for acting in socially appropriate ways (see Table 10.3). They either do not earn tokens or must forfeit them when their behavior is inappropriate. The individual can use the tokens to acquire special privileges or opportunities. The expectation is that, over time, the new behaviors will become habitual and not dependent on being reinforced by tokens.

Table 10.3

Example of a Token Economy Used in Treating a Person with Schizophrenia

Earn tokens for the following behaviors:
- Eat with proper utensils
- Brush hair in the morning
- Keep clothing on during the day
- Answer when spoken to
- Participate in therapeutic activities

Lose tokens for the following behaviors:
- Shout at other people
- Take off clothes in public
- Eat with hands
- Refuse to participate in therapeutic activities

Consider the case of Cynthia, a woman with schizophrenia who is hospitalized and who has very poor personal hygiene and grooming. Her therapist might use a token economy system to encourage Cynthia to develop appropriate hygiene. For each privilege that she wishes to "purchase," she must cash in a fixed number of tokens. She may need 10 tokens to go on a weekend pass or 2 tokens to go to the hospital snack shop. Taking a daily shower may earn her 2 tokens, and combing her hair may be worth 1 token. The incentive to have these privileges would presumably be strong enough to motivate Cynthia to engage in appropriate grooming behaviors. Eventually, these behaviors become established and are reinforcing in their own right, so that the tokens are no longer necessary. Additionally, the attention and praise Cynthia receives when she earns each token can add to the reinforcement value of the tokens themselves. She learns to value such positive attention, making it more likely that she will work to maintain her grooming skills.

Social skills training is another behavioral intervention that involves reinforcing appropriate behaviors, especially those involved in interpersonal situations (Liberman, Massel, Mosk, & Wong, 1985). People with schizophrenia often speak or act in ways that others regard as abnormal. In social skills training, an individual's inappropriate behaviors are identified and targeted, and reinforcement becomes dependent on the individual's acting in more socially acceptable ways. For example, a disturbed individual may speak loudly or with an unusual tone, move in peculiar ways, stare at others, or fail to maintain an appropriate distance when speaking to people. In social skills training, the therapist provides feedback to the individual about the inappropriateness of each of these behaviors. This may take place in the context of role-playing exercises, direct instruction, or a group setting in which participants are encouraged to comment openly on each other's behaviors. With the feedback of others, the individual learns to behave in more appropriate ways until such behavior becomes virtually automatic (Bellack, Morrison, & Mueser, 1989). Social skills training can be especially helpful when teaching schizophrenic individuals ways to manage negative symptoms, such as their failure to show affect in social situations or to interact appropriately with others (Dobson, McDougall, Busheikin, & Aldous, 1995).

Clinicians may also incorporate cognitive-behavioral techniques in helping the client to detect the early signs of a relapse, to take a more positive approach to evaluating the ability to cope with daily problems, and to develop a broader range of ways to handle emotional distress and anxiety (Wasylenki, 1992). Disordered thinking processes and even delusions, as we discussed in the Research Focus box, may be reduced through cognitive-behavioral interventions (Alford & Beck, 1994).

In an innovative approach to psychotherapy with schizophrenic individuals, one group of researchers developed an intervention called "personal therapy," in which clinicians tailor psychotherapy to strengthen interpersonal skills and control social stress (Hogarty et al., 1997). Personal therapy rests on the assumption that stress-related emotions aggravate positive symptoms, such as delusions and hallucinations, as well as negative symptoms, such as social withdrawal and apathy. Within this framework, clinicians help clients study personal reactions to stress and develop coping strategies that facilitate relaxation in social contexts. Hogarty and his colleagues found that personal therapy was impressive for individuals living with their families in reducing the likelihood of relapse over a 3-year period. However, among those living independently of family, the individuals who participated in personal therapy had more psychotic relapses than did the individuals in a group receiving only supportive therapy. Research findings such as these point to the importance of therapeutic endeavors that involve those closest to the person with schizophrenia.

Sociocultural Treatments

From what you have read about schizophrenia, you can understand the way in which this disorder greatly involves other people in the life of the individual. Other people are certainly affected by the disturbing symptoms of a person with this condition, just as the person with schizophrenia is profoundly affected by others. Central to an integrative treatment is a therapeutic approach that includes a focus on interactions and relationships.

Milieu therapy is a model that involves social processes as a tool for changing the individual's behavior. In this approach, all staff and clients in a treatment setting work as a therapeutic community to promote positive functioning in the clients. Members of the community participate in group activities ranging from occupational therapy to training classes. The staff encourages clients to work with and spend time with other residents, even when leaving on passes. The entire community is involved in decision making, sometimes involving an executive council with elected members from units of the treatment setting. Every staff person, whether a therapist, nurse, or paraprofessional, takes part in the overall mission of providing an environment that supports positive change and appropriate social behaviors. The underlying idea of milieu therapy is that the pressure to conform to conventional social norms of behavior discourages the individual with schizophrenia from expressing

problematic symptoms. The "normalizing" effects of such an environment are intended to help the individual make a smoother and more effective transition to life outside the therapeutic community.

Some techniques, such as social skills training, are incorporated into an approach that involves the client's family. In one project (Falloon et al., 1985), researchers trained family members to use a structured problem-solving method in which they collectively defined a problem, considered various solutions, and agreed on a detailed solution plan. Families needing to improve interpersonal communication received training in communication skills. When conflict, anxiety, or depression were evident in any family member, the researchers provided specific behavioral strategies. The researchers then compared people who received in-home training with a group who were treated in a clinic and received individual psychotherapy to help them learn coping skills for living in the outside community. After 9 months of treatment, the family-managed individuals showed markedly different patterns of functioning, compared with those in the other group; they had fewer relapses, less intense symptoms, and fewer hospitalizations. Most impressive was that the family-managed individuals were able to maintain their gains through the second year of the study. By the end of the study, the researchers claimed that half of those in the family-managed group showed no psychiatric symptoms, whereas the individually treated people still showed high rates of disturbance.

Considerable information is now available for clinicians, families, and clients to draw on in their efforts to grope with this mysterious and devastating illness (Torrey, 1995). Treatment programs that combine medication with psychosocial interventions appear to have the most promise for maximizing the day-to-day functioning of individuals with this disorder. These programs include residential or community facilities that provide training in coping with the stress of the disorder and its symptoms, psycho education for families, and rehabilitation through training in occupational and social skills (Carpenter & Buchanan, 1994).

The coordination of services is especially important in programs geared toward helping people with schizophrenia. One approach to integrating various services is Assertive Community Treatment (ACT), in which a team of professionals from psychiatry, psychology, nursing, and social work reach out to clients in their homes and workplaces. A team of a dozen or so professionals work together to help approximately 100 clients comply with medical recommendations, manage their finances, obtain adequate health care, and deal with crises when they arise. This approach involves bringing care to the clients, rather than waiting for them to come to a facility for help, a journey that may be too overwhelming for seriously impaired people. Although approaches such as ACT are expensive, the benefits are impressive (Herinckx, Kinney, Clarke, & Paulson, 1997).

■ Schizophrenia: The Perspectives Revisited

Schizophrenia is a disorder that has mystified people for centuries, although only within the past 100 years has the disorder had a name. As researchers attempt to gain a scientific understanding of the disorder, clinicians, family members, and individuals who have schizophrenia seek ways to cope on a daily basis with its many widespread effects.

As we begin the twenty-first century, relatively few conclusions about the causes of schizophrenia are evident. One fact does stand out, however; people do not develop schizophrenia solely as the result of troubled childhoods. Biology clearly plays a central role, although the precise nature and extent of this role remain unclear. We do know that differences exist in the brain structure and functioning of people with schizophrenia, as compared with those of others. We also know that there is a strong likelihood that people with schizophrenia have relatives with this disorder, and, the closer the relative, the greater the rate of concordance. Scientists have delineated specific biological markers that have assisted them in their efforts to understand which factors and genes are implicated in the acquisition of this disorder.

Even though few would contest the central role of biological factors in determining schizophrenia, biology cannot tell the whole story. Events happen in the life of the person predisposed to schizophrenia that trigger the disorder. Twin studies show us that environmental factors must play a role; otherwise, identical twins would have a 100 percent concordance rate for this disorder. However, it is not yet known what factors in life make one more vulnerable to schizophrenia. Numerous studies of early life relationships have failed to pinpoint a causal connection between faulty parenting and the development of this disorder. What does seem clear is that certain stresses might trigger the disorder, leading to a cycle of disturbance. The difficulty of raising a child with schizophrenia can lead to tension in the parents, and this increased familial tension can exacerbate the child's disturbance.

Although current understanding of the causes of schizophrenia remains incomplete, scientists continue to look for ways to alleviate its symptoms. The consensus is that an integrative intervention that includes medication, psychological treatment, and social support provides the best context for helping people with schizophrenia (Kopelowicz & Liberman, 1998). Beginning with the biological approach, there is compelling evidence for the important role of medication in alleviating the distressing symptoms of this disorder. At the same time, it is important to keep in mind that medication does not cure the disorder but only treats the symptoms.

Just as biology is an insufficient explanation for the disorder, medication is an incomplete intervention for treating people with schizophrenia. Individualized treatment plans range from tightly structured, institutionally affiliated programs to periodic psychotherapy that is provided when needed. Generally, those who are incapacitated by the disorder require comprehensive and permanent treatment and support. But many people with schizophrenia function adequately in the world and need active intervention only on occasion, when psychotic symptoms flare up.

Despite the inadequacy of current knowledge about this disorder, the tremendous gains made during the past decade are certainly cause for optimism. New research techniques have provided scientists with access to the human brain, where many of the secrets of this perplexing disorder lie. Refinements in genetic research have also provided hope that scientists soon will learn why some relatives develop schizophrenia, while others do not. In light of the speed of recent advances, it is possible that, within a decade, we will look back to the 1990s with disbelief about our limited knowledge.

RETURN TO THE CASE

David Marshall

David's History

In part because they were so upset about David, Mr. and Mrs. Marshall found it difficult to remember many details about his early years. In response to my initial questions about his childhood, the Marshalls responded that he was a "normal kid." However, with further probing, they recalled that he was a "very quiet boy who kept most things to himself." David's subdued style stood in sharp contrast to the liveliness of his brother, Michael, who was a year older. When I asked about the family environment during David's early years, Mr. and Mrs. Marshall admitted that their marital relationship had been fairly "stormy" during those years and that they had come close to divorce when David was about 2 years old. With the help of marriage counseling, they worked things out over the course of a year.

In recalling David's childhood personality, Mrs. Marshall pointed out an interesting contrast with his adolescent years, in that he was an exceptionally neat and clean child. She remembered how angry he became if for some reason he was unable to take his 7 P.M. bath. By the time he was in his late teens, however, David's finicky habits had changed entirely. He did not wash for several days at a time, and he finally did so only at the insistence of his mother, who practically had to drag him into the shower. Mrs. Marshall said that she never would have believed that her formerly clean son would one day have greasy hair, carelessly pulled into a pony tail, unwashed for weeks at a time.

RETURN TO THE CASE

David Marshall (continued)

The Marshalls told me of their dismay and horror as they witnessed the almost total incapacitation of a once healthy young man. They spoke of the impact on their own lives, as they had come to worry about the safety of having such a disturbed young man living with them. I asked them to elaborate regarding this concern, and Mr. Marshall told me about David's nightly rituals in his room. With his door shut and locked, David each night lit two dozen candles as part of a "communication exercise with Zoroaster." Any use of fire by a man so disturbed was worrisome to his parents; the proximity of flames to the many spray cans in David's room increased their alarm even further.

Moving on to a discussion of family history, the Marshalls told me that the only relevant bit of information that came to mind was the fact that Mrs. Marshall's sister had a long history of psychological problems and had been hospitalized three times because she had "crazy beliefs, heard voices, and acted very strange."

Assessment

In light of David's severe disturbance, psychological testing was not viable. My assessment of David was, therefore, limited to a 00 minute mental status examination, in which his delusions and hallucinations were remarkable. Regardless of the question being asked, most of David's responses focused on his beliefs about Zoroaster and the aliens. His disorientation was apparent in his responses indicating that his name was "Brodo," that the date was the "36th of Fruen" in the "year of the next heaven, 9912," and that he was being held in a prison by the enemies of Zoroaster. After giving these answers, David laughed in a sinister way and then waved his arms high over his head in a spraying motion, both behaviors to which his mother had referred. He then stopped, as if he had heard something, and looked at his watch. The time was 11 A.M. Muttering to himself, "It's too early," he seemed to go off into a reverie. At that point, I concluded that David was hearing voices. When I asked him if this was the case, he said it was not a voice but a message telling him what he must do next to proceed on his mission. Further questioning at this point revealed David's beliefs about his secret mission and the daily messages he had been receiving from the television set. I asked David to carry out some simple calculations, which he did adequately, and to copy some simple geometric figures. In the process of doing so, he wrote elaborate equations all over the piece of paper and drew pictures of what he called "hollow soft forms." He asked me if I knew the difference between these and "hollow hard forms," which he illustrated on another sheet of paper. These drawings consisted of squiggles and letter-like symbols that apparently contained a great deal of meaning to David but that made no sense to others. Despite my best efforts to communicate with David in a logical and clear manner, he did not tell me anything about himself other than to talk about his delusions.

Diagnosis

As I evaluated David's personal history and current symptoms, all signs pointed to a diagnosis of schizophrenia. In terms of personal history, David was in the age group during which schizophrenia most commonly surfaces, and he had a biological relative with a disorder suggestive of schizophrenia. Of course, these two facts were not sufficient to conclude that David had schizophrenia. The course and symptoms of his disorder provided the most telling evidence.

David was a young man with a progressively worsening course of functioning. He had deteriorated markedly from his high-school years in his academic performance, personal habits, and interpersonal relations. During the years preceding his hospitalization, David had become increasingly symptomatic.

David's symptoms were those of a person with psychosis. He had delusions, hallucinations, loosening of associations, and bizarre behaviors. He was impaired in most areas of everyday functioning, living a life of social isolation, behaving in a bizarre and idiosyncratic manner, and failing to take care of himself, even in regard to personal hygiene.

As for the particular kind of schizophrenia David had, the most tenable diagnosis was undifferentiated type. I assigned this diagnosis because David was not catatonic or prominently paranoid in his delusions, nor was his symptom presentation prominently disorganized.

Axis I:	Schizophrenia, Undifferentiated Type
Axis II:	Deferred
Axis III:	No physical disorders or conditions

RETURN TO THE CASE

David Marshall (continued)

Axis IV: Problems related to the social
           environment (adjustment
           difficulties)
           Occupational problems
           (unemployed)

Axis V: Current Global Assessment of
           Functioning: 30
           Highest Global Assessment of
           Functioning (past year): 45

Case Formulation

There was little question that David Marshall had
schizophrenia, but I wondered what had caused
this tragic set of symptoms to unfold in a young
man who, as a child, was nothing other than a
quiet and reserved boy, and I wondered what had
taken place biologically and psychologically that
had caused the transition from shyness to schizophrenia over the course of his adolescent years. I
thought of the important biological fact that
David's aunt, in all likelihood, had schizophrenia.
The significance of this one fact, of course, lies in
the current understanding of the critically important role that genetics plays in the etiology of this
disorder. At the same time, experts know that biological predisposition is generally regarded as insufficient in determining whether or not a person
will develop schizophrenia. Consequently, I turned
to David's personal history for clues.

Throughout his early life, David was reticent
and withdrawn, compared with his active and outgoing brother. On the one hand, David's behavior
made him a target of his parents' scrutiny as they
attempted to find out what he was feeling and
thinking. On the other hand, David's parents
clearly devoted most of their attention to his older
brother, communicating to David the message
that they really were less concerned with his well-
being. I also wondered about the impact on David
of the discord between his parents during the
early years of his life.

Treatment Plan

The plan that I implemented for David took into
account the need for decisive intervention over the
short term and continued treatment for the years
ahead. I realized that, even when his psychotic
symptoms were under control, he would have
residual problems requiring monitoring and treatment. David's parents concurred with me that his
overt psychotic symptoms needed to be brought
under control and that this could best be accom-

plished by medication, but they worried whether
David would take the medication voluntarily.
Much to their surprise, David did agree to give it
a try. His decision to comply led me to wonder
whether David, on some level, had come to recognize the seriousness of his problem and had become more willing to accept help.

I recommended that David remain in the hospital for 3 months, during which time he could be
stabilized on his medication and the two of us could
develop a working relationship. Ideally, we would
continue to meet on an outpatient basis following
his discharge. Our therapeutic work would center
on several tasks. First, I wanted to help David develop an understanding of his disorder, as well as
impress on him the importance of maintaining an
ongoing relationship with a mental health professional. Second, I wanted to help him develop coping
strategies to use in his everyday life. He needed to
learn how to care for himself and to work on beginning to lead a more normal life.

During the initial weeks of David's hospitalization, the antipsychotic medication began to reduce the severity of his symptoms. As he became
more lucid, he was able to carry on conversations
without the intrusion of ideas about Zoroaster and
a secret mission of saving the world. David told
me of the despair he experienced about his symptoms and how incapable he felt of ever getting
anywhere in his life. Gradually, David interacted
more with other patients on the unit, though his
preference was clearly to stay in his room alone,
listening to rock music. At first, this preference for
being alone caused his parents some distress, and
they wondered whether he was really getting better or not. However, I felt less concerned, because
his behavior seemed markedly different from his
actions prior to his hospitalization. David clearly
cherished his privacy, and being alone did not necessarily mean that he was lost in a delusional
world.

After David had stabilized and his symptoms
were under control, he and I talked about discharge from the hospital. I recommended to David
that, instead of returning home, he should reside in
a halfway house. He rejected this idea outright, on
the grounds that such facilities do not afford much
privacy. We arrived at a compromise that he would
return home but attend a day treatment program
for at least 6 months. In such a program, David's
daily activities would be supervised, and he would
have an opportunity to socialize and take part in
vocational training. I agreed to continue seeing
him in weekly psychotherapy sessions.

RETURN TO THE CASE

David Marshall (continued)

Outcome of the Case

Following David's discharge from the hospital, he moved back home and followed my recommendation that he participate in the hospital's day treatment program, where he thrived with the support of the treatment staff. As I might have predicted, he remained a withdrawn young man who could feel content sitting alone in a corner and thinking. To the relief of his parents, David agreed to continue taking his medication, despite the fact that he complained about minor hand tremors.

After 12 months in the day treatment program, the treatment staff decided that David was ready for a trial run in a real job. He was placed in a position at a library, where he shelved books. He liked this job, because it involved so little contact with the public, and there was an orderliness about it which he found comforting. After a few months, David's supervisor noted his excellent performance and promoted him to a job at the circulation desk, which involved more contact with the public. This proved to be a mistake. The stress of exposure to many people over the course of the day was too much for David to handle, and within 2 weeks he had relapsed into a full-blown psychotic episode.

After a short hospital stay, in which he was restabilized on his medications, David returned to the day treatment program, where he remained for another 6 months. By this time, there was an opening in a group home, and David was finally able to move out of his parents' house. He now lives in this setting and has gone back to his former job at the library.

I have continued to see David over these past few years, but at present we meet only once a month, which seems most comfortable for David. Although we have worked together for more than 4 years, I have never gotten a clear message from David that he values our work or that he even cares about coming to psychotherapy. Nevertheless, it has become part of his life routine, and I hold on to the belief that our work together has played a role in his remaining relatively healthy for this long period. ■

Sarah Tobin, PhD

Summary

- Schizophrenia is a disorder with a range of symptoms involving disturbances in content of thought, form of thought, perception, affect, sense of self, motivation, behavior, and interpersonal functioning. Essential to the diagnosis is a marked disturbance lasting at least 6 months. During this 6-month period is an active phase of symptoms, such as delusions, hallucinations, disorganized speech, disturbed behavior, and negative symptoms. The active phase is often preceded by a prodromal phase and followed by a residual phase. The prodromal phase is characterized by maladaptive behaviors, such as social withdrawal, inability to work productively, eccentricity, poor grooming, inappropriate emotionality, peculiar thought and speech, unusual beliefs, odd perceptual experiences, and decreased energy and initiative. The residual phase involves continuing indications of disturbance similar to the behaviors of the prodromal phase.

- Several types of schizophrenia have been delineated. Catatonic type is characterized by bizarre motor behaviors, while disorganized type consists of symptoms including disorganized speech, disturbed behavior, and flat or inappropriate affect. People with schizophrenia, paranoid type, are preoccupied with one or more bizarre delusions or have auditory hallucinations related to a theme of being persecuted or harassed, but without disorganized speech or disturbed behavior. The diagnosis of undifferentiated type is used when a person shows a complex of schizophrenic symptoms but does not meet the criteria for paranoid, catatonic, or disorganized type. The term residual type applies to people who have been diagnosed with schizophrenia and show lingering signs of the disorder other than psychotic symptoms.

- In addition to the types, schizophrenia is characterized along dimensions. Building on the distinction between positive symptoms (e.g., hallucinations) and negative symptoms (e.g., lack of motivation), some experts suggest that there are two categories of schizophrenia, sometimes called Type I (positive) and Type II (negative). This dimension is considered important in predicting the long-term outcome of schizophrenia (negative symptoms associated with worse prognosis) and the choice of medication. The process-reactive dimension differentiates a disorder that appears gradually over time from that provoked by a precipitant.

- There are several disorders with symptoms like those of schizophrenia, including brief psychotic disorder, schizophreniform disorder, schizoaffective disorder, delusional disorders, and shared psychotic disorder. Theories about the cause of schizophrenia focus on the interaction between biology and experience, with particular attention to the notion of vulnerability. Presumably, individuals have a biologically determined predisposition to developing schizophrenia, but the disorder develops only when certain environmental conditions are in place. Biological researchers have focused on abnormalities of brain structure and function, genetic predispositions, biological markers, and biological stressors. The most common psychological interventions for people with schizophrenia are those derived from the behavioral perspective, in which it is assumed that much of the difficulty that many people with schizophrenia face is due to their having acquired bizarre and maladaptive behavior patterns. Researchers working within the family systems perspective focus on the "system" of roles, interactions, and patterns of communication in the family environment in which the person with schizophrenia grew up. Current comprehensive models of care include biological treatments, psychological interventions primarily in the form of behavioral techniques, and sociocultural interventions that focus on milieu therapy and family involvement.

Key Terms

See Glossary for definitions.

Active phase 311
Affective flattening 312
Alogia 312
Anhedonia 312
Avolition 312
Brief psychotic disorder 319
Cortical atrophy 325
Delusional disorders 322
Dementia praecox 310
Dopamine hypothesis 326

Expressed emotion (EE) 331
High-risk design 327
Labeling 331
Negative symptoms 312
Neuroleptics 333
Positive symptoms 312
Premorbid functioning 317
Process 316
Prodromal phase 311
Reactive 317
Residual phase 311

Schizoaffective disorder 321
Schizophrenia 310
Schizophrenia, catatonic type 313
Schizophrenia, disorganized type 313
Schizophrenia, paranoid type 313
Schizophrenia, residual type 314
Schizophrenia, undifferentiated type 313
Schizophreniform disorder 320
Sensory gating 329
Shared psychotic disorder 323
Smooth pursuit eye movements 328

Internet Resource

To get more information on the material covered in this chapter, visit our web site at **http://www.mhhe.com/halgin.** There you will find more information, resources, and links to topics of interest.

CASE REPORT: JASON NEWMAN

From the moment I entered the waiting room to greet 8-year-old Jason Newman and his parents, I could tell that my intake session would be a challenge. Jason's father, Marvin, was kneeling on the floor, trying to sponge up several gallons of water leaking from the water cooler that Jason had just knocked over. His mother, Janet, stood nearby and, with audible exasperation, scolded Jason for his carelessness. With a mixture of tearfulness and rage, Mrs. Newman sternly lashed out at Jason with the words "Why can't you be more careful?! Get over there and help your father clean up the mess you just made!" Instead of paying any attention to her, however, Jason was intensely committed to playing a game on his handheld Nintendo Gameboy. He made popping noises with his mouth, interspersed with cheers about his video accomplishments. Feeling like an intruder in a tense family scene, I awkwardly introduced myself. Even before responding to my introduction, Mrs. Newman crisply commented, "I'm glad you arrived when you did, so that you can see firsthand the kind of frustrations we face with Jason a dozen times every day!" I tried to offer calming and reassuring words, but I realized how upsetting such experiences must be for the entire family, including Jason.

As soon as we began the interview, Jason's parents eagerly proceeded to tell me the ways in which Jason had been creating havoc for most of his life. Neighbors had complained about his behavior for years, each of his classroom teachers had urged the Newmans to get help for him, and most of their relatives had explicitly conveyed their concern about Jason's behavior during family gatherings.

Mrs. Newman's voice was tense as she described her years of struggling with Jason's problems. She explained that, although he had been a quiet child during his infancy, this began to change around Jason's first birthday. As soon as he began walking, Jason became a "terror." When describing a day at home with Jason, Mrs. Newman said she often felt as though she were locked up with an unmanned motorcycle that roared through the house, wrecking everything in its path. Although I had heard many descriptions of hyperactive children, the words Janet Newman chose had tremendous power, leaving me with the sense that this was an exhausted and exasperated parent.

Mrs. Newman frequently used the term hyper in describing her son. Jason was a fidgeter, always squirming in his seat, frequently jumping up and running around, regardless of whether they were in church, at a movie, or at dinner at home. Jason was a constant source of aggravation to his playmates, because he caused trouble in any game they were playing. Even in the simplest of games, such as basketball, Jason broke the rules, stole the ball from other children, refused to wait his turn, or intentionally provoked others to the point that all the children on the playground yelled at him and told him to go home.

Mrs. Newman had lost count of the number of special teacher conferences to which she had been summoned. In every meeting, the story was the same: Jason did not pay attention in school; he disrupted virtually every classroom activity; he threw things at other children; he played tricks on the teachers; and he talked out loud even during quiet reading time. Each of Jason's teachers had observed that Jason was bright, but they could not get him to do his assignments, either for classroom activities or homework. Even when Jason did complete his homework, he usually lost it on his way to school, along with his books and pencils. The teachers had developed several intervention plans that included behavioral strategies, but the effectiveness of these attempts was limited. As Mr. Newman admitted, "We never followed through with the plan when Jason was home, so I guess that's why he hasn't changed very much."

The Newmans then explained what finally prompted them to seek professional help for Jason. His behavior had gotten so out of control that he was risking the safety of others. At school one day during the previous week, Jason was caught setting fires. Taking a box of wooden matches he had brought from home, Jason went into the boys' lavatory, ignited a roll of toilet paper and some paper towels, and threw a lit match into the wastebasket. The smoke detector set off the school fire alarm, and everyone was evacuated. This was the final straw for the school principal, who called the Newmans and made it clear that Jason could not return to school until a professional treatment plan was in place.

After talking with the Newmans, I asked Jason to meet with me for 15 minutes alone. This was a difficult session, but it gave me the opportunity to interact with Jason in a way that would reduce distractions and interruptions. He answered some of my questions, ignored others, and often abruptly changed the topic. I did get the sense that Jason was upset about his lack of friends. He told me that his teachers were "boring" and that he would rather stay home and practice basketball, because he wanted to play professional basketball when he grew up. After our talk, I could understand the ambivalence that clearly characterized his own mother's response to him. He was an attractive child with some very endearing qualities. At the same time, he engaged in many annoying behaviors that made even brief interactions with him feel exhausting.

Sarah Tobin, PhD

11

Development-Related Disorders

Chapter Outline

The disorders discussed in this chapter are conceptually related, because they first appear at birth or during youth. Because they strike so early, disorders that begin in childhood are of great concern to the adults who have a role in the child's life. Imagine what it would be like if, as a parent, you faced problems like Jason's on a daily basis. You would probably feel a great deal of personal distress as you struggled to deal with his needs. The emotional burden of having a disturbed child can be great for those who are close to the child, and the pain that the atypical child experiences can last throughout life. Some cases of disturbance are so serious that even the best efforts to bring these children into the mainstream of society have limited positive impact. During the past several decades, children have increasingly become a focus of mental health research, and there is now the promise of successful treatments for many people with development-related disorders that formerly created lifelong difficulties.

Most children are stubborn at times, but chronically difficult behavior becomes a source of distress and a burden to parents.

Introductory Issues

As you are reading about the conditions described in this chapter, you may wonder at times why mental retardation and learning disabilities, for example, are considered psychological disorders. Some would contend that it is inappropriate to include these conditions in a list of "disorders." Along related lines, some so-called disorders may actually represent developmental aberrations, rather than psychiatric abnormalities. For example, you will read about a disorder called oppositional defiant disorder, which

---

Mental Retardation

MINI-CASE

Juanita is a 5-year-old girl with Down syndrome. Her mother was 43 when she and her husband decided to start their family. Because of her age, Juanita's mother was advised to have prenatal testing for any abnormalities in the chromosomal makeup of the developing fetus. Juanita's parents were shocked and distressed when they learned the test results. When Juanita was born, her parents were prepared for what to expect in terms of the child's appearance, behavior, and possible medical problems. Fortunately, Juanita needed no special medical attention. Very early in Juanita's life, her parents consulted with educational specialists, who recommended an enrichment program designed to maximize cognitive functioning. From the age of 6 months, Juanita attended a program each morning in which the staff made intensive efforts to facilitate her motor and intellectual development. Now that she is school-age, Juanita will enter kindergarten at the local public school, where efforts will be made to bring her into the mainstream of education. Fortunately, Juanita lives in a school district in which the administrators recognize the importance of providing resources for pupils like Juanita, so that they will have the opportunity to learn and grow as normally as possible.

■ If you were an educator, what recommendations would you make regarding Juanita's involvement in the classroom?

■ How would you respond to critics of mainstreaming, who might complain that Juanita is taking a disproportionate amount of school resources?

DIAGNOSTIC FEATURES

● With an onset prior to age 18, people with mental retardation have subaverage intellectual functioning, as demonstrated by such measures as IQ, which is approximately 70 or below.

● They have concurrent deficits or impairments in adaptive functioning in at least two of the following areas: communication, self-care, home living, social/interpersonal skills, use of community resources, self-direction, functional academic skills, work, leisure, health, and safety.

● Degree of severity is either mild, moderate, severe, or profound.

Table 11.1

Classification of Mental Retardation by IQ Scores and Behavioral Competencies

Degree of Retardation	IQ Range	Behavioral Competencies	
		Preschool (0–5)	School Age (6–19)
Mild	50/55–70	Can develop social and communication skills; minimal retardation in sensory-motor area; often not distinguished until later ages	Can learn academic skills up to sixth grade level; can be guided toward social conformity.
Moderate	35/40–50/55	Can talk or learn to communicate; poor social awareness; fair motor skills; profits from self-help skill training; requires some supervision	Can profit from training in social and occupational skills; unlikely to progress beyond second-grade level; some independence in familiar places possible.
Severe	20/25–35/40	Poor motor development and minimal language skill; generally cannot profit from training in self-help; little communication	Can learn to talk or communicate; can be trained in elemental self-help skills; profits from systematic habit training.
Profound	Under 20 or 25	Gross retardation, with minimal capacity for functioning in sensory-motor areas; requires intense care	Some motor development present; may respond to very limited range of training in self-help.

involves a pattern of disruptive and uncooperative behavior. You may question if it is right to give a psychiatric diagnosis to a boy who frequently loses his temper, argues with his parents, refuses to obey rules, acts in annoying ways, swears, and lies. However, it is important to keep in mind that these are conditions that result in maladjustment or experiences of distress. Consequently, it makes sense that these conditions are included in the *DSM-IV* for many of the same reasons that other disorders are included.

Mental Retardation

Mental retardation, a condition present from childhood, is characterized by significantly below average general intellectual functioning (an IQ of 70 or below). Approximately 1 percent of the population has mental retardation, and it is more common in males. Mental retardation is a broad term that encompasses several gradations of intellectual functioning and adaptive behavior, which are reflected in the categorization system developed by the American Association of Mental Deficiency and incorporated into the psychiatric nomenclature.

Characteristics of Mental Retardation

In addition to intellectual deficits, people with mental retardation have significant impairments in various abilities involved in adapting to everyday life. For example, they may lack social skills and judgment, have difficulty communicating, or be unable to care for themselves. Many mentally retarded individuals depend on others for their personal care and well-being. Table 11.1 summarizes the common social and academic capabilities at each level of retardation.

Theories and Treatment of Mental Retardation

Mental retardation may result from an inherited condition or from an event or illness that takes place during the course of development at any point from conception through adolescence.

Inherited Causes

Some forms of mental retardation are genetically transmitted from the parents to the child at the time of conception. For example, infants with phenylketonuria (PKU) are born with an inability to utilize phenylalanine, an amino acid essential to the manufacturing of proteins. Phenylalanine builds up in the body's tissues and blood, leading to severe neural damage. Tay-Sachs disease is a metabolic disorder caused by the absence of a vital enzyme (hexosamindase A, or hex-A), which leads to the accumulation of lipid in nerve cells, leading to neural degeneration and early death, usually before the age of 5. Tay-Sachs disease is most commonly found in descendants of Eastern European (Ashkenazi) Jews. Fragile X syndrome, which derives its name from the fact that it is transmitted through the "Fragile X gene (FMR1)" on the X chromosome, is associated with severe forms of retardation, particularly in males.

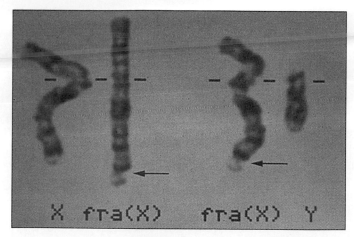

This is a micrograph of two X chromosomes of a female (left) and an X and a Y chromosome of a male (right). The two arrows point to the region known as a fragile site. Note that the indentation at the bottom of each looks as if it is ready to break.

Other forms of inherited disorders are the result of a chromosomal aberration during conception. **Down syndrome** is the most well known of these forms of mental retardation (named after the English physician who first described the disorder). As we pointed out in Chapter 4, Down syndrome is caused by an extra twenty-first chromosome. People with Down syndrome have a characteristic facial structure and one or more physical disabilities. All individuals with Down syndrome have mental retardation, generally ranging from mild to moderate. Compared with other children, their motor, cognitive, and social skills develop at a slower rate. Early in the twentieth century, people with Down syndrome were fated to live in institutions and rarely lived past the age of 9 years. Improvements in therapeutic and educational interventions, such as better medical treatment and the integration of children into schools and communities, have contributed to increases in life expectancy. Currently, most people with Down syndrome live into their fifties. However, the health of those living to this age is usually poor, and nearly all develop brain changes resembling those of Alzheimer's disease (see Chapter 12).

Environmental Causes

Environmental hazards are a second cause of mental retardation. These include exposure to certain drugs or toxic chemicals, maternal malnutrition, and infections in the mother during critical phases of fetal development. For example, researchers have determined that mothers who contract rubella ("German measles") during the first 3 months of pregnancy are likely to have a child with mental retardation. Problems during the baby's delivery that can cause mental retardation include infections, anoxia (loss of oxygen, leading to brain damage), and injury to the brain. Premature birth can also be associated with mental retardation. After birth and all during childhood, mental retardation can result from diseases, head injuries caused by accidents or child abuse, and exposure to toxic substances, such as lead or carbon monoxide.

Fetal alcohol syndrome (FAS) is a set of physical and mental birth defects that results from a mother's alcohol consumption during pregnancy. FAS is considered by some to be the leading cause of mental retardation, affecting approximately 1 of every 1,000 live births (Sampson et al., 1997). The condition is of particular concern among certain high-risk groups, such as African Americans, Native Americans, and Canadian Indians (U.S. Department of Health and Human Services, 1993).

At birth, infants with fetal alcohol syndrome are smaller in weight and length, and these deficiencies persist into childhood. Their IQ is usually in the mildly retarded range, although some are severely retarded. Many have a characteristic set of facial abnormalities involving the eyes, nose, jaw, and middle region of the face. Their internal organs may also be affected, particularly the cardiovascular system. Motor and cognitive deficits are also associated with the syndrome, including a lack of coordination, an inability to concentrate, and impairments in speech and hearing. Furthermore, they may be unable to form friendships, and they can become socially withdrawn and isolated.

There appears to be a direct connection between the amount of alcohol ingested by the mother and the degree of physical and behavioral problems in the child (Olson et al., 1997). It is not clear just how much alcohol is needed to cause this condition, though researchers have determined that drinking even relatively moderate amounts of alcohol during pregnancy can result in lower birth weight and can place the newborn at risk of dying (Hoyert, 1996; Jacobson, Jacobson, Sokol, & Ager, 1998).

In addition to alcohol, other substances, such as cocaine, cause irreparable damage to the developing fetus (Plessinger & Woods, 1998). Prenatal cocaine exposure causes a number of effects similar to those of alcohol, including smaller overall size and head circumference (Eyler et al., 1998) and complications during delivery (Rizk, Atterbury, & Groome, 1996). There is growing

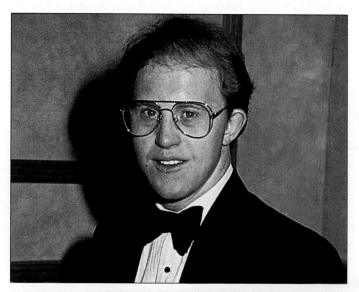

Chris Burke, who played the character Corky for four years on the ABC television series, Life Goes On, has Down Syndrome. His success as an actor and spokesperson has helped dispel myths about this condition and thwart prejudice toward people with Down Syndrome.

evidence that cocaine harms the developing nervous system and can lead to behavioral problems and lower intelligence test scores (Richardson, 1998).

As you can see, the developing human is vulnerable to toxic influences and requires adequate nutrition and nurturance for normal development to take place. In addition, many other factors can impair normal development during childhood and can play a role in causing mental retardation. Poor nutrition in the early years, particularly the first year of life, can cause mental retardation, leading to long-term deficits in cognitive and behavioral functions. Inadequate prenatal care or grossly inattentive parenting also can contribute to **failure to thrive,** a condition in which the child fails to grow physically and cognitively at a normal rate.

Treatment

Although there is no cure for mental retardation, early intervention can enrich the intellectual and physical development of people with this condition. Some people with mental retardation can learn the skills needed to live in a productive way in society. With educative interventions early in life, they can develop better motor abilities, coordination, language usage, and social skills. Through the process of **mainstreaming,** in which people with cognitive and physical disabilities are integrated with nondisabled individuals, they participate in ordinary school classrooms, where they are provided with assistance geared to their particular needs.

Behavioral interventions are the most useful in producing motor, language, social, and cognitive gains. Parents can participate in this process by rewarding a child for appropriate behaviors and by responding negatively to inappropriate behaviors. Family-based interventions provide parents with a context within which to discuss family problems and issues related to the family member who has mental retardation. Such interventions can provide an important source of support.

To see how a combined behavioral-family approach might work, consider the case of Lucy's parents, who are reluctant to take her out of the house, even to go grocery shopping. When they do, she pulls things off the shelves, cries when food items are taken away from her, and sits in the aisle, refusing to get up. A behavioral approach to treating the problem would involve training the parents to respond immediately to undesirable behaviors with verbal reprimands and to provide positive reinforcement for desirable ones. They might be instructed to yell forcefully when Lucy sits in the aisle and to touch and praise her when she acts appropriately.

Because of increased public awareness, more attention is being given to preventing the physical disorders that lead to mental retardation. The most straightforward form of prevention is the early detection of PKU by testing the baby for this disorder immediately after delivery. If the baby tests positive, steps are taken to correct the disorder by means of a special diet. The other genetic causes of mental retardation, however, cannot be reversed.

In contrast to genetically caused mental retardation, many environmentally caused forms of mental retardation can be prevented. In recent years, attempts have been made to teach people ways to improve conditions of prenatal development and to make the birth process safer. For example, alcoholic beverage containers and cigarette packages now have warning labels about the relationship between congenital disabilities and drinking alcohol or smoking during pregnancy. Community education programs within specific populations can be influential in changing alcohol-related behaviors among pregnant women in particular high-risk groups (Hankin, 1994). Counseling pregnant women who abuse or are dependent on alcohol or other substances can also help limit the damage to the developing fetus. Important technological advances have brought about improved conditions for childbirth, such as more effective measures for preventing oxygen deprivation during the birth process. Parents are also being alerted to the importance of protecting children from head injuries; for example, using bicycle helmets, children's car seats, and automobile seatbelts can prevent potentially debilitating traumas to the brain.

■ Autistic Disorder

In this section, we will turn our attention to conditions that seem to permeate every facet of a child's existence. Because of the encompassing nature of these conditions, they are referred to as **pervasive developmental disorders** and are characterized by severe impairment in several areas of development (e.g., social interaction or communication skills) or the presence of extremely odd behavior, interests, and activities. We will focus on the most common of these conditions, **autistic disorder,** which is characterized by a massive impairment in an individual's ability to communicate and relate emotionally to others.

Although we will not dwell on the other pervasive developmental disorders, you should be familiar with some of the conditions that have received considerable scientific attention. In **Rett's disorder,** which occurs only in females, the child develops normally through the first 5 months of life; however, between the age of 5 months and 4 years, some changes indicative of neurological and cognitive impairments occur. The growth of the child's head slows; this is accompanied by a loss of hand skills, followed by odd hand movements (e.g., hand-wringing), a loss of social engagement with others, poorly coordinated walking and bodily movements, psychomotor retardation, and severely impaired language. A child with **childhood disintegrative disorder** develops normally for the first 2 years but, before the age of 10, starts to lose language and motor skills as well as other adaptive functions, including bowel and bladder control. Serious deterioration also becomes evident in the child's social interaction and communication, which is accompanied by repetitive and stereotyped patterns of behavior, interests, and activities. Children with **Asperger's disorder** maintain adequate cognitive and language development but become severely impaired in social interaction. In addition, they develop restricted, repetitive, and stereotyped patterns of behavior, interests, and activities.

Characteristics of Autistic Disorder

Before the age of 3, usually in infancy, individuals with autistic disorder show oddities in several spheres that other people easily detect. From the early days of an infant's life, the parents

Mary Newport and her husband, Jerry, have Asperger's disorder, a condition characterized by a number of symptoms. People with this disorder often interact in unusual ways with others, possibly showing odd facial expressions, unusual posturing or gesturing, or inappropriate eye-to-eye gaze. Further, their interests, activities, and behaviors are often rigid and repetitive.

may be aware that the child seems somehow different, sometimes erroneously believing that the unresponsive child is deaf. Clinicians assign the diagnosis of autistic disorder based on symptoms that fall into three groups: impairment in social interaction; impairment in communication; and oddities of behavior, interests, and activities.

Individuals with autistic disorder show impaired social interaction in several ways. Their nonverbal behaviors convey a sense of emotional distancing, which is evidenced by avoiding eye contact, making odd facial expressions, posturing, and using gestures as a way of controlling interactions. Unlike most children, who are inclined to play with other children, children with autistic disorder refrain from peer relationships. Further, they seem to lack the ability to share thoughts, feelings, or interests with others. Their world is characterized by a preference for isolation, in which they lack an awareness of others, possibly even being oblivious to their own parents and siblings. As infants, they resist the cuddling or tickling of a parent. Unlike nonautistic babies, who smile when they are happy or in response to an adult's laughter, the autistic child remains aloof and unresponsive. To the extent that they do interact with people, they lack emotion and sensitivity.

Communication for the individual with autistic disorder is abnormal in several ways, both verbally and nonverbally. Many with the disorder either are unable to speak or show serious delays in language acquisition. Those who do speak are unlikely to initiate a conversation or remain involved in one. The language they use and the style of their speech make them sound very strange, because the tone, pitch, rate, and rhythm are unusual. For example, they may speak in a monotone voice and end sentences with a question-like rise; grammar may be of the sort that one would expect from a much younger child; and they may repeat words or phrases. They may confuse pronouns, such as *I* and *you*, saying, "You am hungry," for instance. Their speech is often characterized by **echolalia,** or the repetition of words or phrases that they hear. In response to the question "What is your name?" the person might say, "Your name, your name, your name." In less severe cases, the person with autistic disorder may be able to use speech normally but be unable to maintain a normal conversational exchange, instead speaking incessantly in a monologue. Even in inner communication, usually evidenced in the make-believe play of most children, the child with autistic disorder lacks the ability to engage in play that is age-appropriate.

Several behavioral oddities are characteristic of individuals with autistic disorder. They may be intensely preoccupied with one or more fixed interests, possibly to the exclusion of just about anything else. They may be particularly interested in the parts of objects, such as the buttons on sweaters, or moving objects, such as the rotating blade of an electric fan. They usually adhere to rituals and rigid daily routines, and they may become very disturbed at the slightest change. For example, when opening a can of soda, a boy with autistic disorder may insist that the tab be at a particular position and, if it is not, refuse to drink the soda. Bodily movements are often bizarre and include repetitive mannerisms. They may shake their arms, spin around repetitively, rock back and forth, or engage in harmful, self-damaging behavior, such as head-banging. Regressive behaviors are very common, such as temper tantrums, childish expressions of anger, and the soiling of clothes by defecating or urinating.

The unusual characteristics of autistic disorder become more prominent as the infant grows into the toddler and school-age years, and this disorder continues throughout the individual's life, taking one of a number of forms varying in symptoms and severity. Mental retardation is common, affecting three fourths of those with autistic disorder. The majority suffer long-lasting impairments that interfere with their ability to live independently as adults (Nordin & Gillberg, 1998).

In an unusual variant of this disorder, called autistic savant syndrome, the individual possesses, in addition to severe limitations, an extraordinary skill, such as the ability to perform extremely complicated numerical operations (for example, correctly naming the day of the week on which a date thousands of years away would fall) (Treffert, 1988). Some autistic savants have exceptional musical talents, such as the remarkable case

This 7-year-old boy with autistic disorder is seen with his aide who is giving him assistance with classroom activities.

of one who, at the age of 6 months, could hum complex operatic arias (Treffert, 1989). In fact, the autistic savant syndrome typically appears at an early age, when the young child with autistic disorder appears to have exceptional musical skills or the ability to solve extremely challenging puzzles, usually involving math calculations (Koegel, Valdez Menchaca, & Koegel, 1994). The autistic savant syndrome was dramatized in the movie *Rainman,* in which the central character had an astounding mathematical ability, as well as an incredible knowledge of baseball trivia.

Theories and Treatment of Autistic Disorder

The theory that autistic disorder is biologically caused is supported by evidence pointing to patterns of familial inheritance. In one large twin study, the concordance rate among monozygotic twins was 92 percent (Bailey et al., 1995). Furthermore, relatives in families having more than one person affected by autistic disorder show a higher rate of social and communication deficits (Piven et al., 1997). There is also emerging evidence of abnormalities on chromosome 15 that may play a role in the genetic transmission of autistic disorder (Cook et al., 1998).

Other biological evidence comes from studies of brain size and structure among people with autistic disorder. Among children with this disorder, there are abnormalities in blood flow patterns through the frontal lobes of the brain, suggesting a maturational delay (Zilbovicius et al., 1995). MRI scans among adults show that men with autistic disorder have greater brain volume and greater ventricular volume (Piven et al., 1995) but a smaller corpus callosum (Piven, Bailey, Ranson, & Arndt, 1997).

Although it is evident that neurological differences exist between normal people and people with autistic disorder, the basis for these differences and their implications are not clear. Some researchers suggest that there is a continuum or spectrum of autistic disorders, with different causes and distinct patterns of symptoms and neurological deficits. According to this view,

Asperger's disorder is regarded as a variant of so-called high-functioning autism (Ghaziuddin, Leininger, & Tsai, 1995; Kurita, 1997; Ramberg et al., 1996). Other researchers have attempted to differentiate groups of individuals with autistic disorder on the basis of performance on intelligence tests (Ehlers et al., 1997).

The earliest psychological explanations of autistic disorder focused on psychodynamic processes as being at the root of the disturbance in the child's attachment to the parents (Bettelheim, 1967; Kanner, 1943). The term *refrigerator mother* was used to describe the cold and detached type of parenting theorized to cause autistic disorder. In the 1970s, psychologists shifted to a more cognitive explanation of autistic disorder, regarding it as a disorder of language, attention, and perception (Rutter, 1984). Many theorists still believe that people develop autistic disorder because they lack an innate ability to form emotional bonds with others, beginning with their parents. This lack of an ability to form emotional attachment leads the individual to develop serious flaws in the ability to relate socially to others. Another possibility is that individuals with autism lack the ability to understand the mental states of other people (Yirmiya, Solomonica-Levi, Shulman, & Pilowsky, 1996), a cognitive deficit related to abnormalities in the prefrontal cortex (Happe et al., 1996).

According to the behavioral perspective, the primary issue is not what causes autistic disorder but how to reduce the parents' frustration as well as the emotional distance between the child and caregivers that the child's symptoms create. A cycle becomes established, in which the caregivers find it difficult to interact positively with the child, who recoils from their touch and their attempts to establish emotional warmth. It is also possible that the child's self-injurious behaviors are reinforced by attention from adults or by the escape such behaviors provide from situations the child finds even more aversive.

Public legislation in 1975 set a federal mandate for children with serious developmental disorders to be integrated into regular classrooms in the public schools.

Autistic Disorder

MINI-CASE

Brian is a 6-year-old child being treated at a residential school for mentally disabled children. As an infant, Brian did not respond well to his parents' efforts to play with and hold him. His mother noticed that his whole body seemed to stiffen when she picked him up out of his crib. No matter how much she tried, she could not entice Brian to smile. When she tried to play games by tickling his toes or touching his nose, he averted his eyes and looked out the window. Not until Brian was 18 months old did his mother first realize that his behavior reflected more than just a quiet temperament—that he, in fact, was developing abnormally. Brian never did develop an attachment to people; instead, he clung to a small piece of wood he carried with him everywhere. His mother often found Brian rocking his body in a corner, clinging to this piece of wood. Brian's language, though, finally indicated serious disturbance. At an age when most children start to put together short sentences, Brian was still babbling incoherently. His babbling did not sound like that of a normal infant. He said the same syllable over and over again—usually the last syllable of something that had just been said to him—in a high-pitched, monotone voice. Perhaps the most bizarre feature of Brian's "speech" was that it was not directed at the listener. Brian seemed to be communicating in a world of his own.

■ Which of Brian's behaviors would lead you to regard him as having autistic disorder?

■ What are the prospects that Brian will be able to benefit from therapy aimed at helping him relate normally to other people?

DIAGNOSTIC FEATURES

● With onset prior to age 3, individuals with this disorder experience serious delays or abnormal functioning in social interaction, communicative language, or play; furthermore, they show at least six symptoms from the following three groups:

● Qualitative impairment in social interaction manifested by at least two of the following:

  ● Impairment in the use of several nonverbal behaviors, such as facial expression, body postures, and eye contact

  ● Failure to develop appropriate peer relationships

  ● Lack of spontaneous sharing of enjoyment, interests, or achievements with others

  ● Lack of social or emotional reciprocity

● Qualitative impairments in communication as manifested by at least one of the following:

  ● Delay in or lack of spoken language development

  ● Impairment in the ability to initiate or sustain a conversation

  ● Stereotyped and repetitive use of language or idiosyncratic language

  ● Lack of spontaneous make-believe play or social imitative play

● Restricted repetitive and stereotyped patterns of behavior, interests, and activities manifested by at least one of the following:

  ● Preoccupation with stereotyped or restricted patterns of interest

  ● Inflexible adherence to nonfunctional routines or rituals

  ● Stereotyped and repetitive motor mannerisms (e.g. hand flapping or complex body movements)

  ● Preoccupation with parts of objects

Although the treatment of autistic disorder, with its severe and broad range of deficits, can appear to have little promise, clinicians are making inroads into ways that the behavior of these children can be successfully changed through medication and behavioral treatment programs. Medications that alter serotonin activity, such as fenfluramine, are used to alleviate some symptoms of this disorder, such as hyperactivity; unfortunately, no medication has been shown to ameliorate the profound symptoms of this pervasive developmental disorder. When medication is recommended, clinicians generally integrate it with behavioral interventions that focus on communication skills and other areas of social functioning. The underlying premise is that, when the child can communicate his or her needs more effectively, some of the disruptive and self-stimulatory behaviors will decrease (Koegel, Koegel, Hurley, & Frea, 1992). If children with autistic disorder are given reinforcement for appropriate behaviors, such as asking for help or feedback, they are less likely to engage in self-injurious or aggressive behaviors. In this type of treatment, clinicians find it more useful to focus on changing pivotal behaviors, with the goal of bringing about improvements in other behaviors, rather than focusing on changing isolated behavioral disturbances (Koegel et al., 1994). The therapist may also help the child develop new learning skills that will give him or her some experiences of success in problem solving; for example, the therapist might teach the child to break down a large problem, such as getting dressed, into smaller tasks that the child can accomplish. This is an important aspect of treatment, because the child with autistic disorder, when frustrated, is likely to regress to problem behaviors, such as rocking and head banging (Rutter, 1985). Clinicians also focus on the need to motivate the child to communicate more effectively. The "Natural Language Treatment Program" (Koegel, O'Dell, & Koegel, 1987) is designed to teach language skills by using stimuli and social and tangible reinforcers that are found within the child's natural environment.

Other behavioral strategies that clinicians use to treat people with autistic disorder are self-control procedures, such as self-monitoring of language, relaxation training, and covert conditioning. As simple as it seems, it also may be possible to help children with autistic disorder perform behavioral sequences by following picture cues on cards (Pierce & Schreibman, 1994). The most well-known—and, in some ways, radical—interventions were developed by psychologist Ivar Lovaas (Lovaas, 1977, 1981, 1987), whose behavioral treatments are intended to eliminate all odd behaviors, including those that involve self-harm. Clinicians teach children with autistic disorder appropriate eye contact and responsiveness to instructions as necessary preconditions for other therapeutic and educational interventions. This program targets undesirable behaviors and then reduces them through the operant conditioning methods of positive reinforcement, extinction, negative reinforcement, and, in some cases, punishment. More recently, clinicians have developed programs in which the principles and techniques of Lovaas' method can be applied in the home with impressive success (Sheinkopf & Siegel, 1998). This finding has particular importance, because the investigators were able to demonstrate that the techniques that Lovaas and his colleagues demonstrated as effective in the controlled conditions of the laboratory could also be effective in the child's home (Kazdin & Weisz, 1998).

To illustrate the way in which behavioral principles can be applied, consider the case of Dexter, a young boy who is aggressive toward other people and engages in disruptive behaviors, such as shouting. The therapist might ignore Dexter (extinction), thereby withdrawing the attention that has presumably reinforced his engaging in these behaviors. At the same time, the therapist gives Dexter positive reinforcement for engaging in desirable behaviors, such as interacting with other children and playing appropriately with toys. If extinction does not produce results, the therapist may remove Dexter from the play area and send him to a "time-out" room. For more resistant and dangerous behaviors, such as head-banging, the therapist may give verbal punishment (a loud "no") or, even more extreme, a slap on the thigh. The important point about this kind of treatment is that the consequence of the child's behavior occurs very soon after the behavior is performed. Shaping is another operant principle that is used in this therapy; it involves positive reinforcement for behaviors that increasingly approximate the desirable target behaviors. A child who cannot sit still in a chair must be rewarded first for sitting before the therapist can move on to more complex interactive skills.

An important fact to realize is that, for these behavioral programs to be effective, they must be carried out intensively for a long period of time, beginning early in the child's life (less than 4 years of age). In a long-term follow up of a research project begun in 1970, Lovaas (1987) reported that a high rate of success was achieved only after years of 40-hour-per-week treatment. Almost one half of the children treated with this intensive program went on to achieve normal intellectual and educational functioning by the time they reached first grade. This success rate is particularly striking in light of the fact that only 2 percent of the control group (who were treated for 10 hours or less per week) showed improvement.

Experts in this field have formulated interventions involving peer relationships, based on the belief that children with autistic disorder can derive some very important benefits from appropriate interactions with other children. In this approach, nondisabled or mildly disabled children are taught how to interact with autistic children. This situation approximates a more normal type of social environment, in which children typically serve a powerful role in modifying a peer's behavior. In contrast to interventions in which adults provide the reinforcement, peer-mediated interventions have the advantage of allowing children to carry on with their ordinary activities without adult interruption (Haring & Breen, 1992; Newsom & Rincover, 1989).

One behavioral technique that is the subject of considerable controversy involves aversive conditioning using stimuli that produce pain (see the Critical Issue box). In this method, the individual with autistic disorder experiences very harsh consequences for behaving in dangerous ways. These consequences go beyond slapping and include, for example, applying electric shock and hosing with cold water. The justification for these measures rests on the premise that the child will encounter greater harm by continuing to engage in self-damaging behaviors than would be incurred by the relatively brief application of a painful stimulus.

Given the complexity and seriousness of autistic disorder, its treatment requires a comprehensive program of intervention. This program must involve work with the family, peers, and the schools, as well as the individual with the disorder. In addition, institutional placement may be required, at least until the more dangerous behaviors are brought under control.

Learning, Communication, and Motor Skills Disorders

Perhaps you know someone who has a "block" about math. Even doing simple calculations causes this person to feel frustrated. Or you may have a classmate who has trouble reading and needs assistance with course assignments. In extreme forms, these problems may reflect a specific developmental disorder, which is a delay or deficit in an area of functioning, such as academic skills, language and speech, or motor coordination.

You may be wondering why a person's difficulty with math or reading is regarded as a psychological disorder. This is actually a very controversial issue. Some clinicians feel it is inappropriate to include learning difficulties in a classification system designed for the diagnosis of psychological disorders. However, the rationale for including these conditions is that they are often associated with emotional distress, and they may

Children with learning disorders find the classroom a frustrating place when they are unable to follow directions or to understand what they are reading.

seriously interfere with the person's everyday life and social relationships. For example, an eighth-grader who is having difficulty completing his homework assignments because of a reading disorder will probably feel ashamed and anxious. Over time, these emotions will have a cumulative impact on the individual's self-esteem and sense of well-being.

Learning Disorders

A **learning disorder** is a delay or deficit in an academic skill that is evident when an individual's achievement on standardized tests is substantially below what would be expected for others of comparable age, education, and level of intelligence. These disorders, which cause significant impairment in functioning, are estimated to affect 2 to 10 percent of Americans, and approximately 5 percent of public school children are currently diagnosed (American Psychiatric Association, 1994). Learning disorders are evident in three areas, each associated with a given academic skill: mathematics, writing, and reading.

The individual with **mathematics disorder** has difficulty with mathematical tasks and concepts. Impairment may be evident in linguistic skills (for example, understanding mathematical terms, symbols, or concepts), perceptual skills (such as reading arithmetic signs), attention skills (for example, copying numbers correctly), and mathematical skills (for example, learning multiplication tables). A school-age child with this disorder may have problems in these areas. An adult with this disorder might be unable to balance a checkbook because of difficulty performing simple mathematical calculations. In a **disorder of written expression,** the individual's writing is

characterized by poor spelling, grammatical or punctuation errors, and disorganization of paragraphs, which creates serious problems for children in many academic subjects. For adults, this disorder can be very embarrassing, perhaps limiting the person's range of job opportunities. **Reading disorder,** commonly called **dyslexia,** is a learning disorder in which the individual omits, distorts, or substitutes words when reading and reads in a slow, halting fashion. This inability to read inhibits the child's progress in a variety of school subjects. As with the disorder of written expression, adults with dyslexia face embarrassment and restrictions in the type of employment for which they may qualify. Although rates of reading disorder are comparable between males and females, the overwhelming majority of those actually assessed and diagnosed with this disorder are males. In all likelihood, this is because males are more commonly referred for assessments because of disruptive classroom behavior (American Psychiatric Association, 1994).

Adolescence is the peak time during which behavioral and emotional problems associated with learning disorders are particularly evident. As many as 40 percent of those with learning disorders drop out of school before finishing high school. Even outside the school context, however, many people with learning disorders have low self-esteem and feelings of incompetence and shame. On the other hand, a learning disorder does not necessarily sentence a person to a life of failure; in fact, some extremely famous people overcame a childhood learning disorder, including Albert Einstein, Thomas Edison, Woodrow Wilson, Nelson Rockefeller, Winston Churchill, Charles Darwin, General George Patton, and John F. Kennedy (see Table 11.2).

Communication Disorders

If you have ever tried to communicate an idea that others couldn't understand or have been so inarticulate that even your speech was incomprehensible, you have an idea about the experiences of people with disturbances in speech and language. What is difficult to imagine, however, is the emotional pain and frustration that people with communication disorders confront on a daily basis. **Communication disorders** are conditions characterized by impairment in the expression or understanding of language.

The long-term effects of communication disorders can be serious. For example, one study found that 44 percent of children with speech and language disorders had psychiatric diagnoses such as anxiety disorder. When researchers followed up on the children in this study 4 to 5 years after they were first evaluated, the incidence of psychiatric problems had risen to 60 percent. The problems the researchers identified in the follow-up included mood disorders and several disorders of childhood that you will read about shortly, including those involving attention deficits and conduct problems (Baker & Cantwell, 1987). Communication disorders are relatively common, with estimates ranging as high as 5 percent of all children having one of these conditions.

Expressive language disorder is a developmental disorder characterized by obvious problems of verbal expression. Children with this disorder do not have the ability to express themselves in ways appropriate to their age group. This may be evident in a language style that includes using limited and faulty vocabulary, speaking in short sentences with simplified

The Pros and Cons of Aversive Treatment for Autistic Disorder

In recent years, the methods for controlling the self-injurious behaviors of people with autistic disorder have caused considerable controversy. These treatments are used with individuals who bang their heads, bite themselves, pull their hair, and harm themselves in other ways. The most controversial form of these treatments is aversive therapy, which consists of severe punishments, including spanking, pinching, and the application of "white noise," electric shock, and cold showers. The most extreme aversive treatment involves the use of a "restrained time-out station." In this station, which is approximately the size of a telephone booth, the individuals are restrained for a 15-minute period, during which they receive aversive stimuli consisting of a stream of water vapor sprayed into their faces. During this process, their legs are bound together and shackled to a counter, their heads are covered with a helmet, and thick foam is placed over their eyes, all to prevent escape and injury during the treatment. The individuals' hands, also bound to a counter, are placed close to a button they can press to stop the stream of water vapor.

This procedure may sound totally inhumane to you, and many people have fought hard to prohibit such treatments and to ensure humane treatment for individuals with autistic disorder and others who may be unable to make informed decisions about their treatment. Clinicians and researchers in the field of autism treatment are equally strong advocates of the use of aversives (Linscheid et al., 1990). Those who responsibly use aversive treatments have reported considerable reductions in their clients' self-destructive behaviors, as well as deep personal satisfaction about helping their clients make important gains in their functioning (Harris, Handleman, Gill, & Fong, 1991). However, the strongest proponents of aversive treatment are family members who see the dramatic improvements in their relatives. Parents tell stories in which a child with autistic disorder has gone from dozens of self-injurious tantrums each day down to only a few of such outbursts as a result of this intervention. You may have read or heard about legal cases in which groups of parents have gone to court to keep states from closing schools using aversive treatments.

Although aversive treatments can dramatically alter the lives of people with autistic disorder who engage in serious self-destructive behavior, they are rightfully considered treatments of last resort. Comprehensive programs of contingency management and skills training that combine reinforcement and milder forms of punishment are often effective treatment alternatives, and they carry less potential for harm and misapplication. While aversives should never be embraced as a treatment of choice for individuals with autistic disorder, neither should life-saving interventions be discarded until more satisfactory treatments can be found.

Table 11.2

Famous People Who Had Problems in School

Winston Churchill (1874–1965)	Described as a "dull youth" by his father, who thought he would not be able to make a living, this legendary British statesman was also seen as hyperactive in childhood. Although Churchill enjoyed history and literature, he refused to study Latin, Greek, or math, and he repeatedly failed his school exams.
Charles Darwin (1809–1882)	When he was a child, his father told Darwin that he cared for nothing but "shooting, dogs, and rat-catching." Darwin failed in his medical studies and marked time in college until he took the trip on the *H.M.S. Beagle* that changed his life.
Thomas Edison (1874–1931)	In school, Edison's performance was so poor that his headmaster warned that he "would never make a success of anything." His mother helped him learn to read, and he soon began inventing.
Albert Einstein (1879–1955)	Einstein's parents feared that he was retarded because of his delayed speech and language development. His school performance on all subjects except mathematics was dismal, and he failed his college entrance exams. While in the process of developing his relativity theory, he had trouble holding down a job.
Henry Ford (1863–1947)	A poor reader in school, Ford always preferred working with machines. He achieved early prowess in fixing tools and building waterwheels and steam engines.
Isaac Newton (1642–1727)	Described as an "idler" and "mechanical dabbler," Newton proved to be so inefficient that he could not run the family farm. A poor student, he suddenly came to life after a fight with a bully motivated him to advance himself.

grammatical structures, omitting critical words or phrases, and putting words together in peculiar order. A person with this disorder may, for example, always use the present tense, referring to activities of the previous day by saying, "I have a good time yesterday." For some children, expressive language disorders are developmental conditions in which speaking abilities occur at a later age than normal, and progress more slowly than average. Others acquire this disorder, perhaps as a result of a medical illness or a neurological problem resulting from a head trauma.

Children with **mixed receptive-expressive language disorder** have difficulty in both expressing and understanding certain kinds of words or phrases, such as directions, or, in more severe forms, basic vocabulary or entire sentences. Even simple directions, such as "take the third door on the right," might confuse an individual with this disorder. When speaking, children with this disorder show some of the same communication problems as children with expressive language disorder. Mixed receptive-expressive language disorder can also be either developmental or acquired.

The expressive difficulties of some people are characterized not by their ability to understand or express language but by difficulties specific to speech. A person with **phonological disorder** substitutes, omits, or incorrectly articulates speech sounds. For example, a child may use a *t* sound for words containing the letter *k,* saying *tiss* rather than *kiss.* People often regard the mispronunciations of children as cute; however, these childhood speech patterns are likely to cause academic problems as the child grows older and may evoke ridicule from peers.

Stuttering involves a disturbance in the normal fluency and patterning of speech that is characterized by such verbalizations as sound repetitions and prolongations, broken words, the blocking out of sounds, word substitutions to avoid problematic words, and words expressed with an excess of tension.

Motor Skills Disorders

The primary form of motor skills disorder is **developmental coordination disorder**, which is characterized by marked impairment in the development of motor coordination. Children with this disorder encounter problems in academic achievement and daily living because of their severe lack of coordination, unassociated with another developmental disability (for example, cerebral palsy). In the early stages of life, children with developmental coordination disorder have trouble crawling, walking, and sitting. As they develop, other age-related tasks are also below average. They may be unable to tie shoelaces, play ball, complete a puzzle, or even write legibly. This disorder is also relatively common, with as many as 6 percent of children between the ages of 5 and 11 meeting the diagnostic criteria (American Psychiatric Association, 1994).

Theories and Treatment of Learning, Communication, and Motor Skills Disorders

The most widely accepted explanation of the learning, communication, and motor skills disorders involves neurological abnormalities (Brown & Aylward, 1987). Experts believe that

damage to various brain sites responsible for the affected functions has occurred during fetal development or during the birth process, or as a result of a neurological condition caused by a physical trauma or medical disorder.

One possible cause of certain kinds of developmental disorders is that the brain areas involved in vision, speech, and language comprehension cannot integrate information. For example, a child whose ability to remember sequences of letters or words is impaired and may have difficulties in comprehending speech. An 8-year-old child should be able to remember the following sentences: "Joe asked his mother to take him to see the cows in the barn. Luis carved a handsome statue out of wood with his sharp knife." However, an 8-year-old child with auditory memory problems would most likely confuse the sequence of events and forget most of the details. Impairment in the central nervous system that results in deficits in cognitive processing can result in serious social and emotional disturbance (Rourke, 1988).

The school environment is usually the primary site of treatment for specific developmental disorders. A treatment plan is designed by an interdisciplinary team consisting of various professionals, such as a school psychologist, a special education teacher, the classroom teacher, a speech language therapist, and possibly a neurologist. Typically, children with these disorders require more structure, fewer distractions, and the presentation of new material that uses more than one sensory modality at a time. For example, the instructor may teach math concepts by using oral presentation combined with hands-on manipulation of objects. Perhaps most important is building on the child's strengths, so that he or she can feel a sense of accomplishment and increased self-esteem (Aylward, Brown, Lewis, & Sabage, 1987).

Attention-Deficit and Disruptive Behavior Disorders

Think back to your days in grade school and try to recall classmates whom your teachers and peers regarded as constant nuisances. Perhaps they were so restless that they could not stay seated, or perhaps they were always getting into fights and causing trouble. Quite possibly these youths had one of the behavior disorders that we will discuss in this section. Children with these disorders commonly act in ways that are so disruptive and provocative that caretakers and peers respond with anger, impatience, punishment, or avoidance.

Attention-Deficit/Hyperactivity Disorder (ADHD)

Attention-deficit/hyperactivity disorder (ADHD) is a disorder involving inattentiveness and hyperactivity-impulsivity. Each of these two components of the disorder is defined in terms of several behavioral criteria. Inattentiveness is characterized by such behaviors as carelessness, forgetfulness in daily activities, and other attentional problems. Inattentive children commonly lose their belongings, are easily distracted, cannot follow through on instructions, and have difficulty organizing tasks. The hyperac-

Attention-Deficit/Hyperactivity Disorder

MINI-CASE

Joshua's mother has just had a conference with her son's teacher, who related that Joshua, age 7, has been extremely restless and distractible in class. Every few minutes, he is out of his desk, exploring something on a bookshelf or looking out the window. When in his seat, he kicks his feet back and forth, drums his fingers on the table, shifts around, and generally keeps up a constant high level of movement. He may ask to go to the bathroom three times in an hour. He speaks very quickly, and his ideas are poorly organized. During recess, Joshua is aggressive and violates many of the playground rules. Joshua's mother corroborated the teacher's description of Joshua with similar stories about his behavior at home. Although Joshua is of normal intelligence, he is unable to sustain concentrated attention on any one activity for more than a few minutes.

■ What features of Joshua's behavior suggest that he has ADHD?

■ What are some of the advantages of recommending that Joshua take Ritalin?

DIAGNOSTIC FEATURES

● With an onset of serious symptoms before the age of 7 that cause impairment in at least two settings, individuals with this condition show either a pattern of inattention or hyperactivity-impulsivity.

● Inattention is characterized by a pattern consisting of at least six of the following symptoms, which have persisted for at least 6 months: (1) makes careless mistakes or fails to attend to details; (2) has difficulty sustaining attention; (3) doesn't listen when spoken to; (4) doesn't follow through on instructions or responsibilities; (5) has difficulty organizing activities; (6) avoids tasks requiring sustained mental effort; (7) loses items necessary for tasks; (8) is easily distracted; (9) is often forgetful.

● Hyperactivity-impulsivity is characterized by at least six of the following symptoms, which have persisted for at least 6 months and which fall in the subgroup of hyperactivity or the subgroup of impulsivity.

● Hyperactivity is characterized by symptoms including (1) often fidgets or squirms; (2) often leaves seat inappropriately; (3) often runs about or climbs excessively when it is inappropriate; (4) often has difficulty playing or engaging in leisure activities; (5) is often "on the go" or acts as if "driven by a motor"; (6) often talks excessively.

● Impulsivity is characterized by symptoms including (1) often blurts out answers before questions have been completed; (2) often has difficulty awaiting turn; (3) often interrupts or intrudes.

● Types include (1) combined type, (2) predominantly inattentive type, and (3) predominantly hyperactive-impulsive type.

tive-impulsive component is further divided into the subtypes of hyperactivity and impulsivity. Hyperactivity is characterized by fidgeting, restlessness, running about inappropriately, difficulty in playing quietly, and talking excessively. Impulsivity is evident in individuals who blurt out answers, cannot wait their turn, and interrupt or intrude on others. Children can be diagnosed as having ADHD with a predominant characteristic of inattentiveness, hyperactivity-impulsivity, or a combination of the two.

The recognition that a child has ADHD usually occurs fairly early in the child's life. Prior to school age, children with ADHD are usually regarded as "difficult" by their parents, relatives, and friends, who are responding to the child's impulsivity and hyperactivity. Barkley and Edwards (1998) contend that, by age 5 to 8 years, "between 45 and 70% of children with ADHD have begun to show significant problems with defiance, resistance to parental authority, hostility toward others, and quick-temperedness" (p. 227).

ADHD typically persists throughout childhood into adolescence and, in some cases, even into adulthood. The long-term picture for children with ADHD can be complicated, with many developing other psychological disorders over time, such as mood and anxiety disorders (Biederman et al., 1996). One of the most disturbing experiences of some young people with ADHD involves the intense interpersonal problems that they experience; in fact, researchers have found that these "socially disabled" individuals are especially at risk of developing long-term psychological problems (Greene et al., 1997). Whereas some individuals develop psychological disorders in adolescence and adulthood, others get caught up in a pattern of problems with the law and substance abuse (Mannuzza et al., 1998). Even the children who outgrow ADHD enter their adolescent or adult years with a history of childhood difficulties that leave lasting marks on personality, self-esteem, and interpersonal relationships.

High energy levels can cause hyperactive children to behave in ways that seem out of control.

Conduct Disorder

You have probably read or heard stories about teenage gang wars, juvenile delinquency, criminal behavior, and drug use. Many of the youths involved in these criminal activities have **conduct disorder,** a condition characterized by the repetitive and persistent violation of the rights of other people.

Individuals with conduct disorder violate the rights of others and society's norms or laws. Their delinquent behaviors include stealing, truancy, running away from home, lying, firesetting, breaking and entering, physical cruelty to people and animals, sexual assault, and mugging. These individuals, many of whom also abuse drugs or alcohol, may act alone or in groups. When caught, they deny their guilt, shift blame onto others, and lack remorse about the consequences of their actions.

Clinicians differentiate between conduct disorder with childhood onset (prior to the age of 10) and conduct disorder with adolescent onset. Conduct disorder is one of the most frequently diagnosed disorders in outpatient and inpatient treatment programs for children: estimates range from 6 to 16 percent of male youths and 2 to 9 percent of females under the age of 18 (American Psychiatric Association, 1994). There are differing degrees of conduct disorder, with more serious cases in-

Conduct Disorder

Mini-Case

Bert, a 16-year-old high-school dropout, took pride in his ability to burglarize homes and to shoplift without getting caught. He bragged about his special skill in breaking into places and about his collection of computers and expensive stereo and video equipment. He was skilled at finding buyers for many of the items he stole, and he liked to brag about all his money by flashing big bills in his friends' faces. Bert lived with his mother, who spent most of her days and evenings at a local bar, not particularly interested in what he was doing. She was not even aware of the fact that he spent most of his time on the streets, trying to entice his peers to "rock" with him, which involved throwing rocks at animals, store windows, and cars. If property destruction was not their aim, they taunted people by laughing at passersby and calling out hurtful names. Recently, Bert has decided to move to a more sophisticated kind of crime. Rather than breaking and entering, he has begun to talk his way into the homes of unsuspecting victims. He goes from door to door, neatly dressed and pleasant in his interactions, offering to do odd jobs around the house. After conning his way in, Bert "cases" the house and walks off with valuables, such as jewelry, that are unlikely to be missed right away.

■ What characteristics of Bert's case point to a diagnosis of conduct disorder?

■ Do you think that, if Bert is apprehended, his case should be handled by the legal system or the mental health system?

Diagnostic Features

● Individuals with this disorder show a repetitive and persistent pattern of behavior in which they violate social norms or the rights of others, as evidenced by at least three of the following:

● Aggression to people and animals, including (1) often bullies, threatens, or intimidates; (2) often initiates physical fights; (3) has used a weapon; (4) has been physically cruel to people; (5) has been physically cruel to animals; (6) has stolen while confronting a victim; (7) has forced someone into sexual activity

● Destruction of property, including (1) has set fires to cause serious damage; (2) has destroyed others' property

● Deceitfulness or theft, including (1) has broken into a house, building, or car; (2) often "cons" others by lying in order to obtain goods or favors; (3) has stolen, as in shoplifting or forgery

● Serious violations of rules, including (1) stays out at night, despite parental prohibitions, beginning before age 13; (2) has run away from home overnight at least twice; (3) is often truant from school, beginning before age 13

volving arrest and stable delinquent behavior (Russo, Loeber, Lahey, & Keenan, 1994). Mild cases of conduct disorder involve pranks, insignificant lying, or group mischief. The persistence of conduct disorder over time in early to midadolescence is remarkably high. As shown in a four year longitudinal study, almost 90 percent of the boys diagnosed with conduct disorder when first studied continued to meet the criteria for conduct disorder at least once during the subsequent three years (Lahey et al., 1995).

To find out what eventually happens to children with conduct disorder, prominent researcher Lee Robins (1966), in a now classic study, followed into adulthood children who were seen at a child guidance clinic. Over the 30-year course of the study, the aggressive and antisocial children were more likely to have serious problems as adults than were the children with anxiety disorders. Furthermore, the more severe the antisocial behavior during childhood, the more likely it was that the individuals encountered serious problems in adulthood. These problems were most likely to be marital difficulties, reduced occupational and economic opportunities, impoverished social relationships, heavy alcohol use, and poor physical health. Only one in six of the original sample was completely free of psychological disorder in adulthood; more than one quarter had antisocial personality disorder. Subsequent studies have confirmed this pessimistic outlook, pointing to the remarkable stability of antisocial behavior over time and from generation to generation (Loeber, 1982; Robins, Tipp, & Pryzbeck, 1991; Storm-Mathisen & Vaglum, 1994; Zoccolillo, Pickles, Quinton, & Rutter, 1992).

Oppositional Defiant Disorder

Most children go through periods of negativism and mild defiance, particularly in adolescence, and most parents complain of occasional hostility or argumentativeness in their children; however, what if such behaviors are present most of the time? Children and adolescents with **oppositional defiant disorder** show a pattern of negative, hostile, and defiant behavior that results in significant family or school problems. This disorder is much more extreme than the typical childhood or adolescent rebelliousness, and it is more than a "phase." Youths with this disorder repeatedly lose their temper, argue, refuse to do what they are told, and deliberately annoy other people. They are touchy, resentful, belligerent, spiteful, and self-righteous. Rather than seeing themselves as the cause of their problems, they blame other people or insist that they are a victim of circumstances. Some young people who behave in this way are more oppositional with their parents than with outsiders, but most have problems in every sphere. To the extent that their behavior interferes with their school performance and social relationships, they lose the respect of teachers and the friendship of peers. These losses can lead them to feel inadequate and depressed.

Oppositional defiant disorder typically becomes evident between the ages of 8 and 12. Preadolescent boys are more likely to develop this disorder than are girls of the same age, but after puberty it tends to be equally common in males and females. In some cases, oppositional defiant disorder progresses to conduct disorder; in fact, most children with conduct

---

Oppositional Defiant Disorder

MINI-CASE

Mindy, at age 13, has changed in the past year from a relatively reserved and socially isolated young teenager to what her father now calls "a little tramp." Apart from her behavior, which includes staying out late at night, visiting the college dormitories in town and cutting most of her classes during the day, Mindy's looks suggest those of a much older and street-wise adolescent. Mindy dyed her hair orange, wears heavy makeup, and dresses in provocative clothes. The more her parents tell Mindy to behave and dress like a "normal" girl, the more Mindy seems driven to defy them. The expression of her anger toward her parents has reached such a level that they have lost sleep at night, fearing that Mindy might run away with one of the motorcyclists whom she has recently befriended.

■ What would make you think that Mindy has oppositional defiant disorder, rather than conduct disorder?

■ What kind of intervention might redirect Mindy from her oppositional behavior pattern?

DIAGNOSTIC FEATURES

● Individuals with this condition experience significant impairment because of their pattern of negative, hostile, and defiant behavior. This pattern lasts at least 6 months, during which they show four or more of the following criteria. They:

● Often lose temper;

● Often argue with adults;

● Often actively defy or refuse to comply with adults' requests or rules;

● Often deliberately annoy others;

● Often blame others for their mistakes or misbehavior;

● Are easily annoyed by others;

● Are often angry and resentful;

● Are often spiteful or vindictive.

disorder have histories of oppositional defiance. However, not all children with oppositional defiant disorder progress to the more serious disruptive behaviors associated with conduct disorder (Loeber, 1991).

Theories and Treatment of ADHD and Disruptive Behavior Disorders

The search for what causes some children to develop ADHD and disruptive behavior disorders is complicated by many factors, the most central of which involves the difficulty of separating environmental from biological influences on development. In our discussion of theories and treatment, we will focus on ADHD, because this condition has received the greatest amount of research attention.

Theories

The attentional deficit and hyperactivity associated with ADHD suggest that these problems may involve an abnormality of brain development that includes cognitive functions. In fact, ADHD was formerly called minimal brain dysfunction. Although this label is no longer in use, researchers continue to speak about subtle neuropsychological deficits that are the hallmark of children with ADHD (Nigg, Hinshaw, Carte, & Treuting, 1998). The fact that ADHD has a strong genetic component is well established, as indicated by family and twin studies (Sherman, McGue, & Iacono, 1997). With this plausible genetic etiology, investigators have tried to find possible links between genetic abnormalities and deficits in the biochemistry of the brain. For example, they have found altered patterns of glucose metabolism among adults with a history of childhood-onset ADHD, with lower activity in the frontal cortex, the part of the brain involved in controlling attention and motor activity (Zametkin & Rapoport, 1987). Neuropsychological evidence, in conjunction with data regarding the performance on laboratory tasks of people with ADHD, leads experts to suggest that a fundamental difficulty in inhibiting distracting and irrelevant behaviors may be the ultimate problem in this disorder (Hinshaw, 1987; Iaboni, Douglas, & Baker, 1995).

Various factors in addition to genetics are suggested as contributing to the neurological deficit underlying ADHD, such as birth complications, acquired brain damage, exposure to toxic substances, and infectious diseases. Researchers also suspect that there may be subtypes of ADHD, depending on whether it occurs with other disorders, such as mood or anxiety disorders, learning disabilities, or conduct or oppositional defiant disorder. Each of these subtypes may have a different pattern of family inheritance, risk factors, neurobiology, and responses to medications (Faraone, Biederman, Jetton, & Tsuang, 1997).

In trying to explain the relationship between biological abnormalities and behavioral problems in ADHD, Barkley (1998) focuses on impaired behavioral inhibition and self-control. This impairment is evidenced in four realms of functioning: (1) nonverbal working memory, (2) the internalization of self-directed speech, (3) the self-regulation of mood, motivation, and level of arousal, and (4) reconstitution—the ability to break down observed behaviors into component parts that can be recombined into new behaviors directed toward a goal. Consider how each of these impairments is expressed in a child's behavior. Problems with working memory cause the child to have difficulty keeping track of time or remembering such things as deadlines and commitments. Having an impaired internalization of self-directed speech means that these children fail to keep their thoughts to themselves or engage in private self-questioning or self-guidance; rather, they tend to talk too much and lack a sense of rule-governed behavior. Their impaired self-regulation of mood and motivation causes them to display all their emotions outwardly without censorship, while being unable to self-regulate their drive and motivation. An impaired ability to reconstitute results in a limited capacity to solve problems, because they are unable to analyze behaviors and synthesize new behaviors.

In addition to biological and psychological factors, sociocultural influences also play a role in the aggravation of the ADHD symptom picture. Many children with ADHD have grown up in a disturbed family environment (Biederman et al., 1995) and have had failure experiences in school, conditions that could contribute to attentional deficits and behavioral problems. On the other hand, the disruptive behavior of this disorder may contribute to these family and school problems. Raising a child with ADHD is more difficult than raising a non-ADHD child, and this stress on the family could lead to family disturbances. Similarly, the child's experiences of failure in school may be the result, rather than the cause, of attentional disturbances.

Treatment

Treatment of ADHD typically includes medications, which are effective in helping a large proportion of children with ADHD. Oddly, the medications that help these children calm down are stimulants, a discovery that was made accidentally when benzedrine, a stimulant, was prescribed to treat the headaches of children who had behavior problems. Methylphenidate (Ritalin), the most commonly prescribed stimulant for the treatment of ADHD, successfully improves the child's attentional control, impulse control, ability to work on a task without interruption, and academic productivity (Barkley & Edwards, 1998; Mayes et al., 1994). Teachers and parents report that, when hyperactive children are on stimulants, they are less disruptive and noisy; even their handwriting seems to improve.

No one knows exactly why methylphenidate works the way it does for children with ADHD, yet its effects are so dramatic that researchers have focused on the neurophysiological mechanisms of its action in hyperactive children. A number of hypotheses have emerged from this research, most involving catecholamine neurotransmitters, but these remain unconfirmed (Ernst & Zametkin, 1995). Some people are understandably concerned about the side effects associated with stimulant use. For example, some children on the medication have trouble sleeping and have a reduced appetite. More serious side effects involve the development of uncontrollable bodily twitches and verbalizations, as well as temporary growth suppression. Adults with ADHD treated with methylphenidate run the additional risk of becoming addicted to the drug, which has a long history as an abuse substance (Shaffer, 1994).

Adults with Attention-Deficit/Hyperactivity Disorder

Attention-deficit/hyperactivity disorder can cause serious social and learning problems for children, but until recently researchers believed that most children and adolescents grew out of their ADHD symptoms as they entered adulthood. Experts have since suggested that this may not always be the case. A proportion of children and adolescents diagnosed with ADHD may continue to struggle with the disorder well into their adult years. Although disagreement exists regarding how widespread and significant ADHD is for adults, the disorder is no longer applied exclusively to children and adolescents (American Psychiatric Association, 1994).

Researchers have taken two approaches to estimating the prevalence of ADHD among adults, and both routes have yielded some discrepant results. In the first, researchers followed children diagnosed with ADHD into adulthood. In some studies, as many as 30 to 50 percent of the children with ADHD continued to meet criteria for the disorder as adults (Biederman et al., 1993). A second approach, based on epidemiological data, involved extrapolation from the estimated 3.3 percent prevalence for childhood and adolescent ADHD. Other estimates would, of course, yield higher prevalence rates. Some researchers have attempted to explain the different rates of ADHD reported for adults by suggesting that some adults may not meet the full diagnostic criteria yet continue to exhibit some symptoms of the disorder. Again, research results are inconclusive and somewhat contradictory.

As students and consumers of psychological research, you are probably left in a quandary similar to that experienced by researchers and clinicians. Adults with a diagnosis of ADHD experience serious impairments in a variety of life situations, yet there is little agreement about the scope of this problem. Some people argue that adult ADHD is an unrecognized problem of serious magnitude, while others suggest that it may be the latest fad in diagnosis, offering an easy explanation for complicated life problems.

Put yourself in the place of parents trying to decide whether to follow the recommendation of putting a hyperactive child on medications that have worrisome side effects. In agreeing to go along with such a recommendation, parents are hoping that the benefits of the child's improved attentional control and decreased hyperactive behavior will make such a choice worthwhile. Experts in this field (Barkley & Edwards, 1998) believe that the benefits clearly outweigh the costs, in

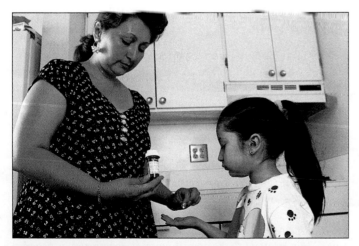

Parents face a difficult decision about whether or not to medicate a hyperactive child. Medication helps alleviate the symptoms of hyperactivity, but it may have undesirable side effects.

that children who feel more in control of themselves tend to be happier, to be more academically successful, and to behave in more socially appropriate ways. Further, they are more likely to have positive interactions with their parents, because the medications make it more likely that they will behave themselves. Unfortunately, ensuring that children will take this medication, even when it can be so helpful, is difficult. Reported rates of nonadherence to the medication range from 20 percent to as high as 70 percent, reflecting a variety of issues. For example, parents may be concerned about side effects, or they may feel that taking such medications will stigmatize their child. Perhaps the child's inherent oppositional nature makes the administration of the medication a very unpleasant interaction (Stine, 1994).

The behavioral approach is also widely used to understand and treat ADHD. Behavioral techniques are based on the assumption that hyperactivity is a learned behavior that can be unlearned through appropriate methods of reinforcement, by the teaching of self-control, and by changes in the environment. A therapist working with a child might use self-reinforcement to encourage the child to regulate such behaviors as settling into a task, delaying gratification, maintaining self-motivation, and monitoring progress toward goals. Implicit in the behavioral approach is the notion that the family must learn to use behavioral methods and be directly involved in helping the child reduce disruptive behaviors. Coordinating these efforts with comparable intervention by classroom teachers improves the odds for helping the child gain better self-control. Again, no one method is necessarily going to provide all the solutions; a multifaceted treatment approach involving medication, educational interventions, behavior modification, social skills training, and counseling is likely to produce the most successful outcomes.

Some of the interventions used for treating young people with ADHD are also applied when working with individuals with oppositional defiant disorder or conduct disorder, although conduct disorder commonly provides even greater challenges. The reason for this is that the home environment of many conduct-disordered children is characterized by severe problems, such as alcoholism and abuse. The children and adolescents themselves are often involved in serious drug abuse, while the stage is being set for their subsequent development of antisocial personality disorder (Myers, Stewart, & Brown, 1998).

A combination of behavioral, cognitive, and social learning approaches appears to be the most useful strategy in working with youths with disruptive behavior disorders. The goal of treatment is to help the child learn appropriate behaviors, such as cooperation and self-control, and to unlearn problem behaviors, such as aggression, stealing, and lying. Therapy focuses on reinforcement, behavioral contracting, modeling, and relaxation training and may take place in the context of peer therapy groups and parent training (Herbert, 1987). Unfortunately, intervention with youths who have disruptive behavior disorders is often initiated during adolescence, a developmental stage that some experts in this field consider to be too late. Behavioral interventions that begin during the earlier years of development are usually more promising (McMahon & Wells, 1989).

Separation Anxiety Disorder

Every child experiences anxiety. If you think back to your own childhood, you can probably remember times when you felt nervous or fearful. Perhaps you felt apprehensive on the first day of school or extremely shy when you first met a new playmate. These are common childhood reactions. For some children, though, anxiety becomes a very powerful and disruptive force. They cannot leave home without panicking, they cling to their parents, they are mute with strangers, or they worry obsessively about being hurt. In most cases, anxiety in children is diagnosed according to the same criteria as in adults (see Chapter 7). One anxiety disorder, separation anxiety disorder, is diagnosed only in children.

Characteristics of Separation Anxiety Disorder

Children with **separation anxiety disorder** have intense and inappropriate anxiety concerning separation from home or caregivers. To understand the nature of this disorder, let's take a look at the role of separation anxiety in normal childhood development. From the moment of birth, any infant's cries usually evoke caregiving behavior in adults. As infants develop in the first year of life, they are able to communicate their needs to caregivers in new ways, as they learn to reach, crawl, grasp, and use verbal ut-

terances. At the same time, children begin to develop a psychological attachment to their parents and become distressed when their parents are not present (Ainsworth, 1989). Although most children maintain a strong attachment to their parents, they become less distressed at separation at around the age of 18 months (Emde, Gaensbauer, & Harmon, 1976). However, a small percentage of children do not overcome the experience of separation anxiety but go on to develop symptoms of separation anxiety disorder. For example, Jennie wavers briefly and then skips happily into the classroom of her day care center when her father drops her off in the morning. In contrast, Emily is terrified when her parents leave her for any period of time.

Children like Emily experience severe reactions when confronted with the prospect of being apart from their parents. They become upset and often physically ill when facing a normal separation, such as when a parent leaves for work or when they go to a relative's house for a visit. Some may refuse to sleep overnight at a friend's house or to go to camp or school. When separated, they fear that something terrible will happen to their parents or to themselves—for example, that they will be kidnapped. When separated from their caretaker, they are likely to complain of physical maladies, such as headaches or stomachaches. Even going to sleep may represent a traumatic separation. They may insist that a parent stay with them until they fall asleep or may plead to sleep in their parents' bed because of nightmares involving separation. When not with an attachment figure, they become panicky, miserable, homesick, socially withdrawn, and sad. They are also demanding, intrusive, and in need of constant attention. Sometimes they cling so closely to a parent that they will not let the parent out of their sight.

This disorder usually becomes evident by the time a child is of school age, and it often follows a troubling life event, such as the death of a relative or a cherished pet, a move to a new locale, or a change in schools. It persists for years, although there may be extended periods when the child's separation anxiety diminishes, and it is equally common in boys and girls.

Theories and Treatment of Separation Anxiety Disorder

As you know, anxiety is an experience that involves both physical and psychological reactions. Recalling our discussion from Chapter 6, in which we explored anxiety disorders in adults, it is important to consider both of these factors in trying to explain and treat anxiety disorders in children. When looking at the biological component of anxiety, investigators have turned to such sources of information as familial patterns and responsiveness to antianxiety medication. As is the case in other areas of research, familial patterns provide information about the possible role of genetics.

Children who experience separation anxiety disorder in childhood are at a higher risk of developing panic disorder as adults, but, relevant to the contribution of genetics, they are also more likely to have a family history of panic disorder (Battaglia et al., 1995). This finding also suggests that there is a continua-

Separation Anxiety Disorder

MINI-CASE

Six weeks have gone by since the beginning of the school year, and 8-year-old Kira has not yet attended a full day of school. Each morning, she pleads with her mother to let her stay home, some days complaining of stomachaches and other days saying she feels so weak she fears she will faint on her walk to school. Kira's parents are perplexed by her behavior, because she did well in school during second grade and had a circle of good friends. On the few days that she has ventured to school, Kira has insisted that the school nurse call home to report her health problem of the day. While at home, Kira becomes alarmed if her mother leaves on an errand and insists that she be allowed to go along. Even sleep time is disturbed; Kira frequently wanders into her parents' bedroom in the middle of the night, complaining of nightmares involving her parents being killed. Concern about Kira's problems has prompted her mother to ask the school guidance counselor to help develop a plan of intervention for Kira and the family.

■ How do Kira's symptoms of separation anxiety disorder compare with those of an adult with agoraphobia or panic disorder with agoraphobia?

■ What kind of intervention do you think might help Kira and her parents get through this very difficult period?

DIAGNOSTIC FEATURES

● With onset prior to age 18, individuals with this condition experience developmentally inappropriate and excessive anxiety for at least 4 weeks concerning separation from home or from people to whom they are attached, as evidenced by at least three of the following:

  ● Recurrent excessive distress when they anticipate separation from home or important attachment figures

  ● Worry that harm may befall important attachment figures or that they will lose these people

  ● Worry that a bad event, such as being kidnapped, will cause a separation from a major attachment figure

  ● Reluctance or refusal to go to places, such as school, because of fear of separation

  ● Fear or reluctance to be alone or without attachment figures

  ● Reluctance or refusal to go to sleep without being near an attachment figure

  ● Repeated nightmares involving separation

  ● Repeated complaints of physical symptoms when separation is anticipated

tion into adulthood of the child's experience of anxiety, although it takes a different form. Presumably, these two disorders are different manifestations of the same problem.

Although biological research suggests a genetic component to anxiety disorders of childhood, learning also plays an important role. Children, like adults, respond to threatening situations with feelings of edginess, fear, and discomfort. It is possible that temperamental differences rooted in biology cause some children to experience heightened reactivity in these kinds of situations. From the psychodynamic and family systems perspectives, anxiety disorders are seen as the result of children's being held back and failing to learn how to negotiate the normal developmental tasks of separating from parents.

The clinician's primary task is to help the child gain control over anxiety-provoking situations. As with most childhood disorders, behavioral treatments have been demonstrated to be particularly effective. Behavioral techniques used for treating fears and anxieties in children include systematic desensitization, prolonged exposure, and modeling. Contingency management and self-management are also useful in teaching the child to react more positively and competently to a fear-provoking situation. These various behavioral techniques may be applied either individually or in combinations. For example, a child with separation anxiety disorder

may learn relaxation techniques along with cognitive strategies for thinking more positively about separation. When the disorder seems to have a link to problems within the family system, such as stress in the marital relationship, behavioral techniques may be combined with family interventions (Hamilton, 1994). Although traditional antianxiety medications are generally not effective (Graae, Milner, Rizzotto, & Klein, 1994), fluoxetine may reduce anxiety symptoms in children (Birmaher et al., 1994).

Regardless of the specific modality, at some point parents become involved in the child's treatment. Family therapists, in particular, give the greatest emphasis to the parents' role in helping the anxious child, but therapists from all perspectives recommend that treatment involve the family.

■ Other Disorders That Originate in Childhood

There is a set of relatively rare and unusual disorders that are limited to the childhood years. For the most part, these disappear by adulthood, but the symptoms may linger and have a profound impact on the individual's psychological well-being and social functioning.

Childhood Eating Disorders

Children with **pica,** a condition commonly associated with mental retardation, eat inedible substances, such as paint, string, hair, animal droppings, and paper. By contrast, in **feeding disorder of infancy or early childhood,** the individual persistently fails to eat, leading to a loss of weight and failure to gain weight. Another form of eating disorder is **rumination disorder,** in which the infant or child regurgitates and rechews food after it has been swallowed. Each of these eating disorders lasts at least 1 month and is not associated with transient stomach distress.

Tic Disorders

A **tic** is a rapid, recurring involuntary movement or vocalization. There are several kinds of tic disorders involving bodily movements or vocalizations. Examples of motor tics include eye blinking, facial twitches, and shoulder shrugging. Vocal tics include coughing, grunting, snorting, the uttering of obscenities (called **coprolalia**), and tongue clicking.

The tic disorder you are most likely to hear about is **Tourette's disorder,** a combination of chronic movement and vocal tics that is much more commonly reported in males. For most, the disorder begins gradually, usually with a single tic, such as eye blinking, which over time grows into more complex behaviors. People with Tourette's disorder usually make uncontrollable movements of the head and sometimes parts of the upper body. In some cases, individuals engage in complex bodily movements involving touching, squatting, twirling, or retracing steps. At the same time, they utter vocalizations that sound very

Baseball outfielder Jim Eisenreich, who has Tourette's disorder, has played for several major league baseball teams. After a long struggle with this condition, he obtained treatment and has become a model for young children with Tourette's. He receives them in the dugout wherever he plays. He gives talks around the country about having Tourette's, he has made a public service announcement shown on the air, he has played in fund-raising golf and bowling tournaments, and he participated in a video for children called "Handling It Like a Winner."

odd to others; for example, an individual may have a complex tic behavior in which he rolls his head around his neck while making sniffing and barking noises. In only a small percentage of cases do people with Tourette's disorder utter obscenities. This is not a passing condition but, rather, one that is usually lifelong, with onset in childhood or adolescence. Young people with this disorder commonly have other psychological symptoms as well, the most common of which are obsessive-compulsive symptoms, speech difficulties, and attentional problems (Zohar et al., 1997).

Elimination Disorders

Children with elimination disorders have not become "toilet-trained," long past the time when they were physiologically capable of maintaining continence and using the toilet properly. In **encopresis,** the child, who is at least 4 years old, repeatedly has bowel movements either in clothes or in another inappropriate place. Children with **enuresis** urinate in clothes or in bed after the age when they are expected to be continent; this is not an infrequent event but, rather, one that takes place at least twice a week for a minimum of 3 consecutive months in children who are at least 5 years old.

Reactive Attachment Disorder

Reactive attachment disorder of infancy or childhood is a severe disturbance in the individual's ability to relate to others. Some children with this disorder do not initiate social interactions or respond when it is appropriate; they may act extremely inhibited and avoidant. Other children show a very different symptom picture, in that they do not discriminate in their sociability but show inappropriate familiarity with strangers. This disturbed style of interpersonal relating arises from pathological caregiving; perhaps the parent or caregiver disregarded the child's emotional or physical needs during the early years of development. Alternatively, there might be so many changes in primary caregivers during early development that the child fails to develop stable attachments.

Stereotypic Movement Disorder

People with **stereotypic movement disorder** engage in repetitive, seemingly driven behaviors, such as waving, body rocking, head-banging, self-biting, and picking at their bodies. These behaviors interfere with normal functioning and sometimes cause bodily injury.

Selective Mutism

In **selective mutism,** the individual consciously refuses to talk in certain situations, usually when there is an expectation for interaction, such as at school. The condition is evident for an extended period of time, at least 1 month, and interferes significantly with normal functioning. Children with this disorder may speak spontaneously in some situations but refuse to speak in other settings.

Development-Related Disorders: The Perspectives Revisited

Now that you have read about the various forms of childhood disorders, you can appreciate our opening comments about the complexities involved in diagnosing and treating children. Perhaps you have also gained some insight into how painful it is for parents and teachers to see a child experience such problems. You can also understand the dilemmas faced by the adults in a child's life about the best course of action to follow in making treatment decisions.

In some ways, the disorders of childhood are like a microcosm of all abnormal psychology. In fact, there is considerable debate among researchers and clinicians about whether separate diagnostic categories should exist for children in the areas of schizophrenia and depression. The question of overlap between childhood and adult forms of psychological disorder is one that is likely to remain unresolved for some time, as researchers continue to explore whether these really are separate entities.

Questions might also be raised about the origin of a child's referral for psychological evaluation or treatment. A parent's reporting of a child's "symptoms" may be a cry for help from an overburdened parent of a normal but difficult child, or it may be the reflection of a disturbance that lies outside the child and instead within the parent, the family, the school, or the larger social milieu. Nevertheless, when children experience these symptoms, they are real, painful, and a legitimate cause of concern. If they are not treated seriously, the problems can accompany the child into adulthood, causing many years of prolonged unhappiness. Because of the relationship between early life difficulties and later adjustments, researchers are actively pursuing a number of intriguing leads for understanding and intervening in the disorders of childhood. Fortunately, therapeutic interventions, particularly involving behavioral methods, can have positive and significant effects on reducing many childhood symptoms (Weisz et al., 1994).

RETURN TO THE CASE

Jason Newman

Jason's History

At the second intake session, I first met with Jason and his parents, and then later I discussed Jason's history alone with Mr. and Mrs. Newman. I also spent some time alone with Jason. At first, Mr. Newman expressed reservations about going into detail, because I had told the Newmans in the initial meetings, before having a grasp of Jason's problem, that I may not continue as the clinician following the intake. I explained that I could take the case if family therapy would be sufficient; however, I would recommend another therapist if Jason's needs would be better served by a specialist in child treatment, but, in response to Mrs. Newman's urgings, he agreed. They proceeded to share with me the pain and distress of the past 7 years.

Although only 8 years old, Jason had for most of his life been unable to control his behavior. He had antagonized every important person in his life, time and time again. The older of two children, Jason had a 7-year-old sister, Anna, who showed none of the disturbance that was so much a part of Jason.

Jason's father was 34 years old; he owned and managed a small but successful local card store, where 32-year-old Mrs. Newman worked as a part-time salesperson while the children were in school. The Newmans had been married for 10 years, and they had been relatively happy prior to the onset of Jason's problems. For the past 7 years, however, the tension between Mr. and Mrs. Newman had intensified greatly. From what I could tell, it seemed as though Mr. Newman had denied the seriousness of Jason's problems, usually minimizing the troubles by making such comments as "He's just a typical boy." Alternatively, Mr. Newman blamed teachers for not having enough structure in the classroom.

As Jason's problems grew, Mr. Newman spent less and less time at home, contending that it was necessary to devote his energy to the family business. Thus, Mrs. Newman often felt isolated. She tried to turn to her friends, but over time she began to sense that they did not want to maintain the relationship, because they also found it difficult to interact with Jason. Mrs. Newman told me how she prayed every day that Jason would become normal. She knew he was an intelligent and attractive child but that acquaintances had come to detest him and teachers to dread him.

Assessment

Because Jason had recently taken an IQ test in school, it was not necessary to repeat intelligence testing. The report from the school psychologist indicated that Jason's IQ, as assessed with the WISC-III, placed him in the above-average range of intelligence for both verbal and performance IQ. I felt that it would be helpful to have some quantitative data about Jason's behavioral problems, however, so I asked his parents to complete a child behavior checklist and provided them with some other scales to be completed by Jason's teachers. Both assessment instruments confirmed the picture that Mr. and Mrs. Newman had conveyed in our discussions. Jason's scores were those found in hyperactive children. For example, on the Conners scale, Jason received scores that were more than a full standard deviation above the mean of the subscales of Learning Problems and Impulsivity-Hyperactivity, as well as the Hyperactivity Index.

RETURN TO THE CASE

Jason Newman (continued)

Diagnosis

There was little question in my mind that Jason met the criteria for attention-deficit/hyperactivity disorder. His current behaviors and his long history of behavioral disturbance made such a conclusion fairly obvious. No one involved with Jason was surprised with this diagnosis—including parents, teachers, and mental health professionals.

Axis I:	Attention-Deficit/Hyperactivity Disorder, Combined Type
Axis II:	None
Axis III:	No physical disorders or conditions
Axis IV:	Problems with primary support group (family tension) Educational problems
Axis V:	Current Global Assessment of Functioning: 55 Highest Global Assessment of Functioning (past year): 55

Case Formulation

Although in all likelihood biological factors played an important role in Jason's problem, there was certainly more to the picture. Jason's disruptive behavior was serving a function, both at home and in school. Perhaps, somewhat unconsciously, Jason was trying to seek attention. Feeling unable to control his own behavior or thoughts, Jason became increasingly hurt by his lack of friends, but, at the same time, he felt incapable of modifying his behavior in positive directions. His failure to obtain the nurturance that he craved led Jason to an escalation of his behavior, which culminated in the dangerous fire-setting at school.

Jason's problem was not one limited to his behavior alone; it had become a family and school problem and required intervention in both contexts.

Treatment Plan

Focusing first on Jason, I recommended that he participate in individual therapy with Dr. Clara Hill, a child psychiatrist highly regarded for her expertise in treating hyperactive children. My recommendation was based on two assumptions. First, I believed that Jason would benefit from medication. Second, I felt that Jason would respond positively to the idea that he would have his own private therapist, who would spend time alone with him each week. Regarding Mr. and Mrs. Newman, I suggested that they meet with Dr. Hill's colleague, a psychologist named Dr. Albert Kennedy, who would develop a contingency management program that could be implemented both at home and in school. Dr. Kennedy had ample experience with hyperactive children, and he was respected by the local school administrators and teachers for the interventions he had developed for other children. Dr. Kennedy would also meet with Mr. and Mrs. Newman on a regular basis to help them through the process and to give them an opportunity to work on their own relationship, focusing on the ways in which Jason's problem had so deeply affected both of them.

Outcome of the Case

Two years have passed since I first evaluated Jason, and the news so far has been promising. Jason started taking Ritalin shortly after seeing Dr. Hill, and the changes in his behavior were dramatic and quick. He settled down both at school and at home in ways that caused everyone who knew him to sigh with relief. Of course, he did not turn from urchin to angel overnight. In fact, he continued to be provocative and somewhat disruptive at times, but rarely to the extreme of his pretreatment days. Mr. and Mrs. Newman learned from Dr. Kennedy the importance both of being swift with repercussions for inappropriate behavior and of rewarding positive changes. Through meetings with the Newmans and consultations with school staff, Dr. Kennedy developed a comprehensive intervention program that was consistent and clear. Dr. Hill informed me that, after 6 months of weekly sessions with Jason, she reduced the frequency to bimonthly and then monthly meetings. At the point of each reduction in frequency, Jason's disruptive behaviors flared up temporarily, but in time he settled back into his new routine.

I was glad to learn of Jason's progress and felt confident that his prognosis could now be considered improved. It is difficult to know, however, what scars will remain with this boy from the turbulent years that preceded his treatment. I am hopeful that Jason's positive personality traits will serve as resources to help him continue to grow, unburdened by the hurts of his childhood years. ■

Sarah Tobin, PhD

Summary

- The category of development-related disorders is comprised of several sets of disorders that first appear at birth or during youth. Mental retardation is characterized by significantly below average general intellectual functioning, indicated by an IQ of 70 or below. In addition to intellectual deficits, people with mental retardation have significant impairments in various abilities, such as social skills, judgment, communication, and capacity for self-care. Mental retardation can result from an inherited condition or from an event or illness that takes place during development. Although there is no cure, early intervention can enrich the intellectual and physical development of people with this condition.

- Pervasive developmental disorders are characterized by severe impairment in several areas of development (e.g., social interaction or communication skills) or the presence of extremely odd behavior, interests, and activities. The most common of these conditions is autistic disorder, which is characterized by massive impairment in an individual's ability to communicate and relate emotionally to others. The theory that autistic disorder is biologically caused is supported by evidence pointing to patterns of familial inheritance, as well as studies of brain size and structure. Although psychological theories cannot explain the causes of autistic disorder, these approaches are valuable in regard to interventions, particularly those aimed at providing parents and teachers with the tools needed for modifying the maladaptive behaviors of autistic individuals.

- Another set of development-related disorders is comprised of conditions characterized by problems with learning, communication, or motor skills. A learning disorder is a delay or deficit in an academic skill that is evident when an individual's achievement on standardized tests is substantially below what would be expected for others of comparable age, education, and level of intelligence. Communication disorders are conditions characterized by impairment in the expression or understanding of language. The primary form of motor skills disorder is developmental coordination disorder, a condition characterized by marked impairment in the development of motor coordination. Most developmental disorders in these categories are viewed as neurologically based, with various causes, such as damage during fetal development, birth, or as the result of physical trauma or a medical disorder. The school setting is the most likely context for intervening with children who have these conditions.

- Attention-deficit/hyperactivity disorder (ADHD) involves inattentiveness and hyperactivity-impulsivity. Inattentiveness is characterized by behaviors such as carelessness, forgetfulness in daily activities, and other attentional problems. The hyperactive-impulsive component is further divided into the subtypes of hyperactivity and impulsivity. Hyperactivity is characterized by fidgeting, restlessness, inappropriate running about, difficulty in playing quietly, and excessively talking. Impulsivity is evident in individuals who blurt out answers, cannot wait their turn, and interrupt or intrude on others. Other conditions that involve children's disruptive behavior include conduct disorder and oppositional defiant disorder. Young people with conduct disorder repeatedly and persistently violate the rights of others, while those with oppositional defiant disorder show a pattern of negativistic, hostile, and defiant behavior, which results in family or school problems. Extensive research has focused on the causes and interventions for ADHD, with special attention given to neurological abnormality, possibly associated with genetic factors. Neurological abnormality presumably results in impaired behavioral inhibition and self-control. Over time, the child experiences a number of failure experiences and family disturbances, which aggravate personal difficulties. Treatment, especially for children with ADHD, typically includes medications, the most common of which is methylphenidate. Psychological techniques, especially those based on behavioral principles, are also regarded as important aspects of interventions aimed at helping individuals with ADHD gain control over their behavior and attention.

- Several other psychological disorders have received extensive attention by researchers and clinicians. Separation anxiety disorder involves the experience of intense and inappropriate anxiety concerning separation from home or caregivers. Childhood eating disorders include such conditions as pica, feeding disorder of infancy or early childhood, and rumination disorder. Tic disorders, such as Tourette's disorder, involve bodily movements or vocalizations. Elimination disorders, such as encopresis and enuresis, are characterized by a failure to maintain continence at an age-appropriate stage. Reactive attachment disorder is a severe disturbance in the individual's ability to relate to others. Individuals with stereotypic movement disorders engage in repetitive, seemingly driven bodily movements. Those with selective mutism refuse to talk in certain situations, such as at school.

Key Terms

See Glossary for Definitions.

Asperger's disorder 347
Attention-deficit/hyperactivity disorder
   (ADHD) 354
Autistic disorder 347
Childhood disintegrative disorder 347
Communication disorders 352
Conduct disorder 356
Coprolalia 362
Developmental coordination disorder 354
Disorder of written expression 352
Down syndrome 346
Dyslexia 352
Echolalin 348
Encopresis 362

Enuresis 362
Expressive language disorder 352
Failure to thrive 347
Feeding disorder of infancy or early
   childhood 362
Fetal alcohol syndrome (FAS) 346
Learning disorder 352
Mainstreaming 347
Mathematics disorder 352
Mental retardation 345
Mixed receptive-expressive language
   disorder 354
Oppositional defiant disorder 357
Pervasive developmental disorders 347

Phonological disorder 354
Pica 362
Reactive attachment disorder of infancy
   or childhood 362
Reading disorder 352
Rett's disorder 347
Rumination disorder 362
Selective mutism 362
Separation anxiety disorder 360
Stereotypic movement disorder 362
Stuttering 354
Tic 362
Tourette's disorder 362

Internet Resource

To get more information on the material covered in this chapter, visit our web site at **http://www.mhhe.com/halgin**. There you will find more information, resources, and links to topics of interest.

CASE REPORT: IRENE HELLER

As I prepared to leave my office to meet Irene Heller, the receptionist called on the intercom to tell me that this new client was "causing a stir in the waiting room." Irene was reportedly yelling at her son that he had no business taking her to the clinic. When I entered the waiting room, however, there was no turmoil but, rather, the site of a serene-looking grey-haired woman sitting next to a man in his mid-forties.

It seemed a sad irony that it was on her sixty-seventh birthday that Irene Heller was brought to the mental health clinic by her son Jonathan. As I went to meet her, my eyes were drawn immediately to the corsage she had pinned to her jacket; amid the small bouquet emerged a sign reading "Happy Birthday." Realizing that my attention was drawn to the flowers, Irene commented, "Aren't they a beautiful expression of my son's thoughtfulness?"

After some small talk, I suggested that we proceed to my office. Everything seemed relatively routine until Irene asked me if I was the same Sarah Tobin who had stolen her bicycle when she was 8 years old. Since we were in the middle of the hallway, I was perplexed about how to respond. The question was absurd in several ways, not the least of which was the fact that I was nearly two decades younger than Mrs. Heller. My initial response was to suggest that we wait until we reached my office to discuss her concerns, but Mrs. Heller didn't give me the opportunity to complete my sentence. Rather, she angrily threw her purse on the floor and shouted, "I will not move another step until you acknowledge what you did to me!" At that point, her son pleaded with his mother to cooperate. In a soothing voice, he tried to reassure her by saying, "Mother, this is Dr. Tobin. She is a psychologist who wants to help us find ways to make you feel better. Let's go to her office and tell her what has been going on." Fortunately, Irene agreed and began walking toward my office. On entering, she noticed my diploma hanging on the wall. In a matter-of-fact manner, she quickly translated the five lines of Latin as if she were a fluent speaker of the language. At that point, Jonathan interjected by mentioning that Mrs. Heller had, in recent years, taken up the study of Latin and Greek as a pastime. He then went on to explain that her ability to retain classical Greek and Latin vocabulary and grammar was remarkable, despite the fact that she couldn't recall her address and phone number or the names of her grandchildren.

As Jonathan attempted to tell me the sad story of Irene's debilitating condition, she launched into a monologue, trying to convince me that nothing was wrong with her. Fortunately, she agreed to permit Jonathan to continue to explain his version of events before interrupting again. According to Jonathan, his mother had changed over the past few years from an intellectually alert, vibrant, and active woman who loved teaching into a forgetful, easily distracted, unhappy individual. Her memory problems had become so serious that Jonathan worried about her safety. Would she remember to lock her door at night, to turn off the gas stove, or to take her medicine? He knew that, despite regular phone calls from him and from her friends, Irene was unable to stay on top of things. In fact, she was often unable to recall what a person had said just moments earlier, much less attend to her personal needs.

Jonathan explained that he had noticed alarming changes in his mother during the previous several months. Recently, Jonathan had been expecting his mother to visit his family in their new home. When she failed to show up at the appointed time, he telephoned her and she indignantly responded that he was trying to trick her. Apparently, Irene had gone to his former residence, ostensibly oblivious to the fact that he had moved nearly 2 months ago. Despite his insistence that he had reminded her of his new address just the day before, Irene claimed to have no recollection and insisted that he must be trying to free himself from any obligations to her. The following day, Irene called Jonathan as if nothing unusual had taken place between the two of them. Clearly, she had forgotten all the turmoil that had taken place less than 24 hours ago.

Jonathan went on to describe other situations in which Irene's loss of memory was accompanied by increasingly disruptive and uncharacteristic behaviors. For example, one day the manager of a local department store called Jonathan to complain that Irene was roaming aimlessly through the store, muttering the phrase "a stitch in time, a stitch in time." When the manager asked if he could be of help, Irene began to yell obscenities at him and tried to assault him. As the manager attempted to take her to the office, she screamed, "Murderer! Take your hands off me!" In anguish and embarrassment, Jonathan rushed to the store to find his mother sobbing quietly in a corner of the office. Although occasional peculiar events involving his mother had occurred during the year, none was this extreme, Jonathan had downplayed each one until it became obvious that Irene needed professional attention.

When I asked Irene about her understanding of what Jonathan was talking about, she acknowledged that she had become "a bit forgetful." To Jonathan's surprise, as well as mine, Irene then said, "Perhaps it would be a good idea for someone to help me, so that I don't do something dangerous." I was relieved to hear Irene say this, because her comment gave me reason to feel confident that she would go along with my recommendation that we conduct a comprehensive assessment of her condition.

Sarah Tobin, PhD

12

Cognitive Disorders

What would you think if someone in your life were to begin acting in the ways that Irene Heller did? Like Jonathan, you might first assume that she had an emotional problem, possibly related to an upsetting event in her life. Few people consider that a person's behavioral difficulties might be caused by brain damage or a disease that affects the nervous system, yet, as you will learn in this chapter, there are many ways in which neurological disorders can cause people to experience major changes in their intellectual functioning, mood, and perceptions. You will also see that a variety of physical conditions can cause cognitive impairments through damage to the central nervous system.

The Nature of Cognitive Disorders

Cognitive functions include the processing of thoughts, the capacity of memory, and the ability to be attentive. In the disorders we will discuss in this chapter, cognitive impairment is the central characteristic. This kind of impairment arises from various causes, including brain trauma, disease, or exposure to toxic substances (possibly including drugs). In *DSM-IV* the formal name for the group of disorders characterized by this set of symptoms is "delirium, dementia, amnestic and other cognitive disorders." For the sake of brevity, we will use the term *cognitive disorders* as a comprehensive label.

It may not be obvious that physical abnormalities can cause a set of presumably psychological symptoms, such as hallucinations and delusions. In fact, various physically based syndromes mimic schizophrenia, mood disorders, and personality disorders. People can develop delusions, hallucinations, mood disturbances, and extreme personality changes due to abnormalities in the body resulting from disease, reactions to medication, and exposure to toxic substances. People with disorders involving the brain are frequently found to be suffering from depression either due to the disabling effects of the illness or as a result of physiological changes that underlie both the physical and psychological abnormalities (McNamara, 1991). As you will see in Chapter 13, drugs and alcohol can also cause a person to think, feel, and act in ways that mimic serious psychological disturbances.

Differentiating symptoms that are associated with a psychological disorder from those arising in response to a physical disorder can be very difficult. Fortunately, this process has been facilitated by advances in neuropsychological assessment and the development of new technologies to assess brain structure and function (see Chapter 3). However, even in an age of sophisticated diagnostic technology, determining whether a person's psychological problems are attributable to physical factors can sometimes be very difficult. Consider the case of Flora, a 59-year-old woman who had been hospitalized many times for what appeared to be bipolar disorder. Her symptoms included suicide attempts, extreme belligerence toward her family, and grandiose beliefs about herself. Only after several psychiatric hospitalizations did an astute clinician determine that Flora's symptoms were caused by an endocrine disorder. After only a few weeks of treatment, Flora's medical condition improved, and her "psychiatric" symptoms diminished.

Another physical disorder with symptoms that appear to be psychological is **epilepsy**, a neurological condition that involves recurring bodily seizures with associated changes in EEG patterns. Because people with epilepsy may act in ways that strike others as being odd, or even psychotic, they may mistakenly be regarded as having a psychological disorder. Epilepsy has been misunderstood for centuries, and many people with this condition have experienced discrimination because of society's lack of understanding about epilepsy.

Epilepsy is classified into two groups according to the extent of brain involvement in the seizure: one type involves generalized seizures, and the other involves partial, or focal, seizures. People with generalized convulsive seizures may have what are called grand-mal seizures, during which they lose consciousness, stop breathing for a brief period, and undergo uncontrollable bodily jerking. Following the seizure, they feel drowsy and confused. Another form of generalized seizure consists of petit-mal seizures, in which the individual experiences a temporary loss of consciousness, possibly accompanied by rhythmic movements of the lips, mouth, head, and eyelids, but does not undergo the full-body spasms that occur with grand-mal seizures.

In contrast to generalized seizures, partial, or focal, seizures involve abnormal EEG patterns that are localized in a cortical or subcortical region of one cerebral hemisphere. Of particular interest to our discussion are seizures that arise from the temporal lobe or nearby limbic areas, because these seizures result in symptoms that have the appearance of psychological disturbances. For example, people with this condition, called temporal lobe epilepsy, may experience a number of symptoms, such as increased fear, mood swings, inappropriate affect, bursts of anger, illusions or hallucinations, altered thought processes, and bizarre behavior. A small percentage of people with temporal lobe epilepsy undergo a disturbing period of psychotic-like behavior following a seizure that can last from a few moments to as long as a few days.

As you can see, careful and precise diagnosis is necessary so that the clinician does not overlook an organic condition, such as epilepsy or endocrine disease, and treat an individual with such a disorder for an emotional disturbance.

Delirium

You have probably heard the term *delirious* used many times, possibly to describe someone who is in a state of uncontrolled excitement. Or perhaps you have personally experienced delirium in a different form while in the grips of a high fever or following an injury. You may have awakened from your sleep, not knowing where you were or what time it was. Family members may have been perplexed by your inability to respond to them in conversation. Perhaps you had some strange thoughts or perceptions that you later realized were hallucinations. If you have ever had such an experience, you know first-hand how a bodily disturbance can result in an altered state of consciousness accompanied by bizarre symptoms.

Delirium is a temporary state in which individuals experience a clouding of consciousness, in which they are unaware of what is happening around them and are unable to focus or pay attention. In addition, they experience cognitive changes, in which

A person in a state of delirium experiences numerous cognitive, emotional, and behavioral disturbances. Elderly hospital patients are particularly prone to delirium.

their memory is foggy and they are disoriented. A person in a state of delirium may forget what he or she had eaten for lunch only an hour earlier or be unaware of the day of the week, or even the season of the year. The speech of individuals experiencing delirium may be rambling or incoherent as they shift from one topic to another. These individuals may also experience delusions, illusions, or hallucinations, as well as emotional disturbances, such as anxiety, euphoria, or irritability. As you can imagine, such symptoms can be very frightening, both for the person who is experiencing them and for anyone who is observing. Not surprisingly, delirious individuals may do things that are physically dangerous, such as walking into traffic or falling down stairs. Health professionals are therefore concerned about the possibility that the delirious medical patient will get out of bed, unaware of being connected to medical equipment, such as a respiratory tube or urinary catheter.

Delirium is caused by a change in the brain's metabolism and usually reflects something abnormal occurring in the body. A variety of factors can cause delirium, including substance intoxication or withdrawal, head injury, high fever, and vitamin deficiency. People of any age can experience delirium, but it is more common among medically or psychiatrically hospitalized older adult patients (Johnson et al., 1990; Ritchie, Steiner, & Abrahamowicz, 1996). The higher incidence among older people is due to the fact that they are more prone to falls and are more likely to have undergone surgery, experiences that can provoke a state of delirium. Medications used to alleviate a patient's discomfort, such as benzodiazepines, can also bring on delirium (Marcantonio et al., 1994), so physicians treating these individuals realize that it is important to pay very close attention to the unintended effects of these medications (Singh, Gupta, & Singh, 1995).

Although delirium has no typical course, it follows some general trends. Delirium typically has a rapid onset, developing over a period of a few days at most, and its duration is brief. Rarely does delirium last for more than a month. Some individuals do show a slower, more subtle manifestation of symptoms, however. Over the course of a day, a delirious individual may

experience a variety of emotional disturbances, such as anxiety, fear, depression, irritability, euphoria, restlessness, difficulty in thinking clearly, and hypersensitivity to auditory and visual stimuli. As the delirium continues, these symptoms can fluctuate considerably by time of day, diminishing in the morning and worsening during the nights, when sleep may be disturbed by vivid dreams or nightmares (Levkoff et al., 1994). Testing does not usually reveal distinct neurological deficits in a person with delirium, but abnormal bodily movements, such as tremor or shaking, are often evident. Signs of autonomic nervous system disturbance are often present, such as tachycardia (rapid heartbeat), sweating, flushed face, dilated pupils, and elevated blood pressure. The individual either naturally recovers, is effectively treated, develops a progressive neurological deficit, or dies from the underlying physical condition.

Amnestic Disorders

As you have learned from our discussion of dissociative amnesia in Chapter 7, psychological factors can cause memory loss. There are biological causes for loss of memory as well; such conditions are referred to as **amnestic disorders.** People with amnestic disorders are unable to recall previously learned information or to register new memories. This inability to incorporate recent events into memory or to recall important information can be very disturbing, because the individual loses a sense of personal identity. The individual may try to cover up the social problems caused by memory loss through denial or confabulation, the fabrication of facts or events to fill a memory void. However, these tactics cannot compensate for the feeling of a lack of connectedness with one's own daily and past experiences.

The *DSM-IV* includes two major categories of amnestic disorders: those due to a general medical condition and those that are substance induced. Amnestic disorders due to medical conditions may be chronic (lasting a month or more) or transient. They can result from a wide variety of medical problems, such as head trauma, loss of oxygen, or herpes simplex. When drugs or medications cause serious memory impairment, the condition is referred to as **substance-induced persisting amnestic disorder.** This condition may be caused by an array of substances, including medications, illicit drugs, or environmental toxins, such as lead, mercury, insecticides, and industrial solvents. The most common cause of amnestic disorder is chronic alcohol use, as you will see in Chapter 13. Note the use of the word *persisting* in the diagnosis to distinguish this condition from the passing effects of substance intoxication or substance withdrawal. When assigning this diagnosis, the clinician indicates the problematic substance (for example, "barbiturate-induced persisting amnestic disorder").

Regardless of the specific reason for the amnesia, memory loss is the result of damage to the subcortical regions of the brain responsible for consolidating and retrieving memories. For some people, especially chronic abusers of alcohol, amnestic disorder persists for life, and impairment is quite severe, possibly requiring custodial care. For others, such as those whose condition results from medications, full recovery is possible.

Delirium

MINI-CASE

Jack is a 23 year-old carpenter whose co-workers brought him to the emergency room when he collapsed at work with a fever that seemed to be burning up his body. Although Jack was not ostensibly injured, it was obvious to Jack's co-workers that something was wrong. When they asked whether he was hurt, Jack repeatedly responded with the nonsensical answer, "The hammer's no good." Jack's co-workers were startled and perplexed by his bizarre suggestions that they were trying to steal his tools and by his various other paranoid-sounding remarks. Grabbing at things in the air, Jack insisted that objects were being thrown at him. Jack couldn't remember the names of anyone at the site; in fact, he was unsure of where he was. Initially, he resisted his co-workers' attempts to take him to the hospital because of his concern that they had formed a plot to harm him.

■ How would a clinician assess possible causes of Jack's delirium?

■ If you were one of Jack's co-workers, how would you react to his changes in behavior?

DIAGNOSTIC FEATURES

● People in this state experience a disturbance of consciousness with a reduced ability to focus, sustain, or shift their attention that develops over a short period of time (hours to days) and fluctuates during the day.

● They experience a change in cognition (e.g., memory problems, disorientation, language disturbance), or they develop a perceptual disturbance not better accounted for by dementia.

● The delirium is specified as being due to either a medical condition, substance intoxication, substance withdrawal, or multiple causes.

■ Dementia

The word *dementia* comes from the Latin words *de* (meaning "away from") and *mens* (meaning "mind"). **Dementia** is a form of cognitive impairment involving generalized progressive deficits in a person's memory and learning of new information, ability to communicate, judgment, and motor coordination. In addition to experiencing cognitive changes, people with dementia undergo changes in their personality and emotional state. As you might guess, such disturbances have a profound impact on a person's ability to work and interact normally with other people.

The main cause of dementia is profuse and progressive brain damage. Other physical conditions that can cause this dementia include vascular (circulatory) diseases, AIDS, head trauma, psychoactive substances, and various neurological disorders that we will discuss later in this chapter. Dementias are found in people of all ages, including children, but the most well known is Alzheimer's disease, which we will discuss in detail shortly.

Characteristics of Dementia

The symptoms of dementia may begin with mild forgetfulness, only slightly noticeable and annoying. However, if the underlying brain disorder that causes the dementia cannot be treated, the person's symptoms will become increasingly obvious and distressing. As the condition of people with dementia worsens, so does their capacity for caring for themselves, for staying in touch with what is going on around them, and for living a normal life.

Memory Loss

The first sign of dementia is slight memory impairment. In fact, a common but insensitive joke made by many people whose memory occasionally falters is that they must have Alzheimer's disease. However, the memory impairment of people with dementia is no laughing matter. As the disease progresses, they are able to remember less and less, until eventually they are incapable of retaining any new information. As time goes on, they become unable to remember even the basic facts about themselves and their lives.

Aphasia, Apraxia, and Agnosia

The term **aphasia** refers to a loss of the ability to use language. Aphasia is caused by damage to the brain's speech and language area, and this damage influences the production and understanding of language. Two forms of aphasia are Wernicke's aphasia and Broca's aphasia, both named after the people who discovered them. In **Wernicke's aphasia,** the individual is able to produce words but has lost the ability to comprehend them, so that these verbalizations have no meaning. In contrast to the person with Wernicke's aphasia, the person with **Broca's aphasia** has a disturbance of language production, but comprehension abilities are intact. In other words, the individual knows the rules of sentence construction and can grasp the meaning of language, but he or she is unable to produce complete sentences; verbal production is reduced to the fundamental communication of content with all modifiers left out.

Amnestic Disorder

MINI-CASE

Harvey is a 57-year-old music teacher in a public high school. While bicycling to work one day, he was struck by a car and was rushed to the emergency room. In addition to receiving a broken leg, Harvey suffered a head injury and was unable to remember anything that had happened during the preceding 2 weeks. Furthermore, he had no idea how old he was, where he was born, or whether he was married. This inability to remember his personal past was a source of great distress to Harvey. By contrast, Harvey had no trouble remembering the ambulance ride to the hospital or the name of the emergency room physician who first examined him. Following a 3-day hospital stay, Harvey was transferred to a rehabilitation facility for 3 months, where memory therapy helped him learn mnemonic strategies for recalling important information.

- What symptoms point to a diagnosis of amnestic disorder due to head trauma?

- At what point would Harvey's diagnosis be labeled "chronic"?

DIAGNOSTIC FEATURES

- People with this condition develop memory impairment evidenced by an inability to recall previously learned information or by an impaired ability to learn new information.

- The memory disturbance causes significant impairment and represents a decline from a previous level of functioning.

- The memory disturbance does not occur exclusively during the course of delirium or dementia.

- The condition is specified as being due to a medical condition, the use of a substance, or uncertain cause.

A person with **apraxia** has lost the ability to carry out coordinated bodily movements that he or she could previously perform without difficulty. This impairment is not due to physical weakness or decreased muscle tone but, rather, to brain deterioration. **Agnosia** is the inability to recognize familiar objects or experiences, despite the ability to perceive their basic elements.

Disturbance in Executive Functioning

Executive functioning includes cognitive abilities, such as abstract thinking, planning, organizing, and carrying out behaviors. Executive dysfunction is evident in many everyday activities. Consider the case of Max. The relatively simple task of boiling a pan of water becomes a frustrating event each day, because Max fails to turn on the burner. When the phone rings, he does not know which end of the phone to speak into. When asked to write down a phone number, he confuses the digits. In addition to obvious behavioral manifestations of executive dysfunction, the individual's abstract thinking is impaired. For example, when asked "In what way are a watermelon and a honeydew alike?" Max responded, "I'm not sure, but I guess it's because water and dew are both wet."

Alzheimer's Disease (Dementia of the Alzheimer's Type)

Many people fear that, as they get older, they will lose control of their mental functioning. However, this fear is largely unfounded, because only a very small percentage of older adults develop the form of dementia known as Alzheimer's disease, or

dementia of the Alzheimer's type. The term *senile* is sometimes mistakenly used to refer to this disorder, or more generally to the process of growing old. This is an unfortunate misnomer, as it implies that the aging process involves an inevitable loss of cognitive functions. The odds are actually low that a person will develop Alzheimer's disease later in life, but, for those who do, the disorder has tragic consequences.

DIAGNOSTIC FEATURES OF DEMENTIA OF THE ALZHEIMER'S TYPE

- People with this disorder develop multiple cognitive deficits manifested by memory impairment, and at least one of the following cognitive disturbances: (a) language disturbance; (b) impaired ability to carry out motor activities; (c) failure to recognize or identify objects; (d) disturbance in executive functioning, such as planning, organizing, or abstracting.

- The course is characterized by gradual onset and continuing cognitive decline.

- The cognitive deficits cause significant impairment and represent a decline from the previous level of functioning.

- The deficits are not due to other disorders, medical conditions, or substance use and do not occur exclusively during the course of a delirium.

The diagnosis of dementia involves a thorough physical and psychological assessment to evaluate such symptoms as aphasia, apraxia, and memory loss.

Alzheimer's disease was first reported in 1907 by a German psychiatrist and neuropathologist, Alois Alzheimer (1864–1915), who documented the case of a 51-year-old woman complaining of poor memory and disorientation to time and place (Alzheimer, 1907/1987). Eventually, the woman became depressed and began to hallucinate. She showed the classic cognitive symptoms of dementia, including loss of language and lack of recognition of familiar objects, as well as an inability to perform voluntary movements. Alzheimer was unable to explain this process of deterioration until after the woman died, when an autopsy revealed that most of the tissue in this woman's cerebral cortex had degenerated. On examining the brain tissue under a microscope, Alzheimer also found that individual neurons had degenerated and had formed abnormal clumps of neural tissue. A recent discovery of brain slides from this woman confirmed that the changes seen in her brain were similar to those typically found in current cases of the disease (Enserink, 1998). Although there is still no explanation for what causes the process of brain deterioration that forms the core of this disease, the term *Alzheimer's disease* has come to be associated with this severe cerebral atrophy, as well as the characteristic microscopic changes in brain tissue.

Several subtypes of Alzheimer's disease are identified by the prominent feature of the clinical presentation. When clinicians diagnose Alzheimer's disease, they specify one of the following subtypes: (1) with delirium, (2) with delusions, (3) with depressed mood, or (4) uncomplicated (for cases in which none of these other characteristics apply).

The prevalence of Alzheimer's disease is widely but inaccurately reported in the popular press as amounting to 12 percent of the population over the age of 65 and 50 percent of those over the age of 85. These figures are intended to document the seriousness of this disorder, but recent efforts at more precise prevalence estimates are somewhat less alarming. Based on death rates, statistics from other countries, and a critical analysis of the original sample on which U.S. estimates are based (people over the age of 65 living in East Boston), it is more reasonable to suggest that the prevalence is closer to 1 percent for ages 65–74, 7 percent for those aged 75–84, and 25 percent of those 85 or older (Whitbourne, in press).

Alzheimer's disease progresses in stages marked by the deterioration of cognitive functioning, along with changes in personality and interpersonal relationships. As you can see from Table 12.1, the behavioral symptoms of dementia due to Alzheimer's disease are memory loss, disorientation, decline of judgment, deterioration of social skills, and extreme flatness or changeability of affect. Other psychological symptoms include agitation, wandering, hallucinations, delusions, aggressiveness, insomnia, demandingness, and an inability to adapt to new routines or surroundings.

These symptoms evolve over time, but their rate of progress varies from person to person and according to the stage of the disease, with the most rapid deterioration occuring during the middle phase (Stern et al., 1994). The progression from early to late dementia in people with Alzheimer's usually occurs over a 5- to 10-year period, ending in death through the development of complicating diseases, such as pneumonia.

Dementia Caused by Other Conditions

Clinicians attempting to diagnose Alzheimer's disease are faced with the difficult task of determining whether the cognitive impairment shown by the individual is caused by other

Elderly people are often victims of the stereotype that they are prone to developing dementia. However, most elderly people are in good physical and psychological health and are able to enjoy productive lives.

Table 12.1

Stages of Alzheimer's Disease

Stage	Cognitive Deficits	Personality Changes
Forgetfulness	Forgetting names and where one has placed things	Appropriate concern with mild forgetfulness of familiar objects, but no objective deficits in work or social situations
Early confusional	Getting lost when going to familiar place; colleagues and family notice forgetfulness of names and words; poor reading comprehension; inability to concentrate	Denial of memory problems but anxiety accompanies symptoms of forgetfulness and confusion
Late confusional	Decreased knowledge of current events; forgetting of one's personal history; decreased ability to travel or handle finances	Very obvious use of denial regarding memory problems; flattening of affect and withdrawal from challenging situations
Early dementia	Cannot recall some important features of current life, such as address or telephone number and names of grandchildren; inability to recall some personal facts, such as the name of one's high school; some disorientation with regard to time or date	No assistance needed for toileting or eating but possible difficulty choosing proper clothing
Middle dementia	May occasionally forget name of spouse; largely unaware of all recent events and experiences and many events of life; unaware of surroundings or the season of year but can distinguish familiar from unfamiliar people in their environment	Totally dependent on spouse or caregiver for survival; many personality and emotional changes occur, including becoming delusional, obsessive, and anxious; fails to follow through on intentions due to forgetfulness of these intentions
Late dementia	Loss of all verbal abilities; incontinent of urine and requires assistance in toileting and feeding; loses basic psychomotor skills, including ability to walk	Complete deterioration of personality and social skills, as individual is almost totally unresponsive to all but the simplest form of communication

Source: Adapted from Reisberg, 1983.

physical disorders producing similar symptoms. In addition, depression may produce cognitive impairment in older people causing them to appear as though they have Alzheimer's disease when in fact they have a treatable psychological disorder.

Physical Conditions

Dementia can result from a variety of physical conditions, including infectious diseases such as neurosyphilis, encephalitis, tuberculosis meningitis, or localized infections in the brain. People who experience kidney failure may have symptoms of dementia as a result of the toxic accumulation of substances that the kidneys cannot cleanse from the blood. People with certain kinds of brain tumors also experience cognitive impairments and other symptoms of dementia.

Dementia can also result from anoxia (oxygen deprivation to the brain), which may occur during surgery under general anesthesia or may result from carbon monoxide poisoning. Anoxia can have severe effects on many brain functions, because neurons quickly die if they are deprived of oxygen. Because neurons in the brain do not replace themselves, the loss of a significant number of neurons can lead to concrete thinking and permanent impairments in such functions as new learning ability, attention, concentration, and tracking. The emotional ef-

fects of brain damage due to anoxia can include affective dulling and disinhibition, as well as depression. The person's ability to plan, initiate, and carry out activities can be drastically reduced.

Even the substances that a person ingests, such as drugs, and exposure to environmental toxins, such as industrial chemicals, intense fumes from house paint, styrene used in plastics manufacturing, and petroleum-distilled fuels, can cause brain damage and result in a condition called **substance-induced persisting dementia.**

Severe nutritional deficiencies can also cause dementia. People who are severely undernourished are prone to develop a deficiency of folate, a critical nutrient; this can lead to progressive cerebral atrophy. If the deficiency is not counteracted by dietary improvements, the individual can become depressed and show various cognitive impairments, such as poor memory and abstract reasoning. Many chronic heavy users of alcohol develop a thiamine deficiency, which leads to an organic disorder known as Korsakoff's syndrome, which we will discuss in Chapter 13.

Sometimes dementia associated with physical disorders and toxic reactions can be reversed if the person receives prompt and appropriate medical treatment. However, if no intervention for a treatable dementia takes place in the early

how People Differ

Discrimination Against People with AIDS

Despite advances in our understanding of AIDS and the human immunodeficiency virus (HIV) that causes the disease, many people continue to hold inaccurate beliefs about the virus and the disease. Some fail to recognize that the virus cannot be transmitted through casual contact. Others view the disease as a form of punishment for actions they view as sinful or wrong. Each of these beliefs expresses certain fears about HIV and feelings of vulnerability in the face of a frightening disease (Croteau, Nero, & Prosser, 1993). Because of such misunderstanding, people who have AIDS are often the victims of painful discrimination (Herek & Capitanio, 1994). Unlike people who develop dementia as a result of such diseases as Alzheimer's, individuals with dementia associated with AIDS often encounter painful discrimination. Other people may be less willing to be tolerant, empathetic, or understanding.

Discrimination against people with AIDS extends beyond discomfort with a serious illness and reflects widespread societal prejudice against groups of people, such as gays and lesbians or members of various ethnic minorities, who have been affected by AIDS in record numbers. Misplaced fears of HIV, AIDS, and various subgroups of people are manifested in many discriminatory practices. Some people who have AIDS have been denied adequate health care, housing, and employment; on a more personal level, they have been shunned by family members and other loved ones. Even for individuals who do not experience direct discrimination, knowledge of widespread bias can be an unwelcome stressor.

Efforts to end discrimination against people with AIDS fall into two broad categories: legal proceedings and education. Since the passage of the Americans with Disabilities Act (ADA), HIV and AIDS are considered medical disabilities eligible for legal protection from discrimination. Although no legal avenue can ensure that discrimination will not occur, the ADA sets a standard and expectation for nondiscrimination.

Educational efforts, particularly those targeted at specific prejudicial beliefs, can also help reduce discrimination. Clinicians and other educators recognize that discrimination may spring from a variety of sources because of the many fears and misconceptions about HIV/AIDS. They face the challenge of disseminating accurate information about the transmission of the virus, as well as facts about the groups being discriminated against. Similarly, they strive to reduce prejudice and fear by advocating openness to developing relationships with people infected with HIV. People usually find it more difficult to view HIV-positive individuals as fearsome and very different from themselves once they have made a personal connection (Penner & Fritzsche, 1993)

---

stages, the brain damage becomes irreversible. The more widespread the structural damage to the brain, the lower the chances the person with dementia will ever regain lost functions.

Often clinicians can pinpoint that the cause of dementia is one of several medical diseases or conditions that affect neurological functioning. For example, dementia due to head trauma is a condition in which an individual has sustained an injury to the brain, such as in an automobile accident. People who have traumatic brain injury typically develop amnesia and persisting memory problems. Various other common symptoms include sensory and motor deficits, language disturbance, attentional problems, irritability, anxiety, emotional upheaval, increased aggression, and other personality changes.

In recent years, particular attention has focused on the fact that many people with AIDS develop dementia; in fact, subtle deterioration in cognitive functioning is sometimes the first clue that a person has AIDS. As the disease progresses, cognitive deterioration usually becomes more obvious, leading to a diagnosis of dementia due to AIDS. People with this form of dementia are likely to become forgetful and unable to concentrate or solve problems. Movement disturbances include such symptoms as tremor, imbalance, and loss of coordination. Psychological symptoms may include delusions and hallucinations. Over time, the loss of control over emotions, behavior, and thought becomes so pervasive that many individuals become deeply depressed, apathetic, and socially withdrawn. Complicating the psychological and physical difficulties experienced by people with AIDS is the societal discrimination they encounter (see How People Differ feature box).

Pick's disease is a relatively rare progressive degenerative disease that affects the frontal and temporal lobes of the cerebral cortex. It is caused by the accumulation in neurons of unusual protein deposits called Pick bodies. In addition to having memory problems, people with this disorder become socially disinhibited, acting either inappropriately and impulsively or apathetic and unmotivated. In contrast to the sequence of changes shown by people with Alzheimer's disease, people with Pick's disease undergo personality alterations before they begin to have memory problems. For example, they may experience deterioration in social skills, language abnormalities, flat emotionality, and a loss of inhibition.

Parkinson's disease involves neuronal degeneration of the basal ganglia, the subcortical structures that control motor movements. Deterioration of diffuse areas of the cerebral cortex may occur. Dementia does not occur in all people with Parkinson's disease, but rates are estimated as high as 60 percent, mostly involving those who are older and at a more advanced stage of the disease. Parkinson's disease is usually progressive, with the most striking feature of the disorder being various motor disturbances. At rest, the person's hands, ankles, or head may shake involuntarily. The person's muscles become rigid, and it is difficult for him or her to initiate movement, a symptom referred to as **akinesia.** A general slowing of motor activity, known as **bradykinesia,** also occurs, as does a loss of fine motor coordination. For example, some people with Parkinson's disease walk with a slowed, shuffling gait; they have difficulty starting to walk and, once started, have difficulty stopping. In addition to these motor abnormalities, they show signs of cognitive deterioration, such as slowed scanning on visual recognition tasks, diminished conceptual flexibility, and slowing on motor response tests. The individual's face also appears expressionless and speech becomes stilted, losing its normal rhythmic quality. They have difficulty producing words on tests that demand verbal fluency. However, many cognitive functions, such as attention, concentration, and immediate memory remain intact.

Lewy body dementia, first identified in 1961, is very similar to Alzheimer's disease, with progressive loss of memory, language, calculation, and reasoning, as well as other higher mental functions. However, the progress of the illness may be more rapid than seen in Alzheimer's disease. Lewy bodies are tiny, spherical structures consisting of deposits of protein found in dying nerve cells, found in damaged regions deep within the brains of people with Parkinson's disease. Lewy body dementia is diagnosed when Lewy bodies are found more diffusely dispersed throughout the brain. It is not clear whether the condition called Lewy body dementia is a distinct illness or a variant of either Alzheimer's or Parkinson's disease, although some claim that this is the second most common form of dementia (Kalra, Bergeron, & Lang, 1996). To make matters more confusing, there is also a Lewy body variant of Alzheimer's disease (Hansen, 1997). Obviously, more information is needed on this important but somewhat mysterious condition.

Yet another form of dementia specifically involves the frontal lobes of the brain, and therefore is known as **frontal lobe dementia.** Rather than a decline in memory, as is seen in Alzheimer's disease, frontal lobe dementia is reflected in personality changes, such as apathy, lack of inhibition, obsessiveness, and loss of judgment. Eventually, the individual becomes neglectful of personal habits and loses the ability to communicate. The onset of frontal lobe dementia is slow and insidious, usually beginning in the sixties. On autopsy, the brain shows atrophy in the frontal and temporal cortex, but there are no amyloid plaques or arterial damage. Some evidence supports the notion that this form of dementia is linked to a gene located on chromosome 17 (Froelich et al., 1997).

Although primarily a disease involving loss of motor control, **Huntington's disease** is a degenerative neurological disorder that can also affect personality and cognitive functioning. Huntington's disease is a genetic disease involving an

At the age of 37 Michael J. Fox disclosed his 6-year struggle with Parkinson's disease and the fact that he had undergone surgery to control the symptoms of the disorder.

abnormality on chromosome 4 that causes a protein, now known as huntington, to accumulate and reach toxic levels (Singhrao et al., 1998). The symptoms first appear during adulthood, usually in people in their forties but sometimes as early the age of 20. The disease involves the death of neurons in subcortical motor control structures, as well as decreases in the neurotransmitters GABA, acetylcholine, and substance P.

A number of disturbances are associated with Huntington's disease, ranging from altered cognitive functioning to social and personality changes. The disease is associated with mood disturbances, changes in personality, irritability and explosiveness, suicidality, changes in sexuality, and a range of specific cognitive deficits. Because of these symptoms, the disorder may be incorrectly diagnosed as schizophrenia or a mood disorder, even if the individual has no history suggestive of these disorders. People with Huntington's disease can also appear apathetic because of their decreased ability to plan, initiate, or carry out complex activities. Their uncontrolled motor movement interferes with sustained performance of any behavior, even maintaining an upright posture, and eventually most people with Huntington's disease become bedridden.

Creutzfeldt-Jakob disease is a rare neurological disease thought to be caused by an infectious agent that results in abnormal protein accumulations in the brain. Initial symptoms include fatigue, appetite disturbance, sleep problems, and concentration difficulties. As the disease progresses, the individual shows increasing signs of dementia and eventually dies. Underlying these symptoms is widespread damage known as spongiform encephalopathy, meaning that large holes develop in brain tissue. The disease appears to be transmitted to humans from cattle who have been fed the body parts of dead farm animals infected with the disease (particularly sheep, in whom the disease is known as scrapies). In 1996, an epidemic in England of "mad cow disease," along with reported cases of the disease in humans, led to a ban against British beef.

Another possible cause of dementia is cardiovascular disease affecting the supply of blood to the brain. Such a condition is called **vascular dementia.** Dementia can follow a stroke, in which case it is called acute onset vascular dementia, but the most common form of vascular dementia is multi-infarct dementia or MID, caused by transient attacks in which blood flow to the brain is interrupted by a clogged or burst artery. The damage to the artery deprives the surrounding neurons of blood and oxygen, which causes the neurons to die. Although each infarct is too small to be noticed at first, over time the progressive damage caused by the infarcts leads the individual to lose cognitive abilities.

Vascular dementia resembles the dementia due to Alzheimer's disease in some ways. People with vascular dementia experience memory impairment, as well as one of the following: (1) aphasia, (2) apraxia, (3) agnosia, or (4) disturbance in executive functioning. However, there are some significant differences between these two forms of dementia. People with vascular dementia show a particular set of physical abnormalities, such as walking difficulties and weakness in the arms and legs. Furthermore, people with vascular dementia show a pattern of cognitive functioning that is distinctly different from that found in people with Alzheimer's. In the typical clinical picture of vascular dementia, certain cognitive functions remain intact and others show significant loss, a pattern called patchy deterioration. Another unique feature of vascular dementia is that it shows a stepwise deterioration in cognitive functioning: a function that was relatively unimpaired is suddenly lost or severely deteriorates. This is in contrast to the gradual pattern of deterioration in Alzheimer's disease. Like Alzheimer's disease, however, there is no treatment to reverse the cognitive losses in MID.

Depression

Adding to the complexity of separating the causes of dementia in disorders other than Alzheimer's is the fact that depression can lead to symptoms that mimic those apparent in the early stages of Alzheimer's disease. These cognitive changes constitute a condition known as **pseudodementia,** or false dementia (Caine, 1981). Depression may also co-exist with Alzheimer's disease, particularly during the early to middle phases, when the individual is still cognitively intact enough to be aware of the onset of the disorder and to foresee the deterioration that lies ahead. Depression also occurs in conjunction with other illnesses that cause dementia, including Parkinson's disease and vascular dementia (Kim & Rovner, 1994).

Clinicians treating a person with cognitive impairment who is also depressed have the difficult task of trying to determine if the depression is caused by Alzheimer's disease or whether the cognitive impairment is caused by depression. Distinguishing between pseudodementia and Alzheimer's disease is important, because depression can be successfully treated. Several indicators can help the clinician differentiate depression from dementia. For example, depressed individuals are more keenly aware of their impaired cognition and frequently complain about their faulty memory. In contrast, the individual with Alzheimer's usually tries to hide or minimize the extent of impairment or explain it away when the loss cannot be con-

Caring for an elderly friend or relative can be emotionally difficult, especially when that person is depressed.

cealed. As the disorder progresses, people with Alzheimer's disease lose awareness of the extent of their cognitive deficits and may even report improvement as they lose their capacity for critical self-awareness. The order of symptom development also differs between Alzheimer's disease and depression. In depressed elderly people, mood changes precede memory loss; the reverse is true for people with Alzheimer's disease.

Clinicians can also distinguish pseudodementia by the nature of the individual's symptoms, which follow the classic pattern seen in people with major depressive disorders. The person with depression is anxious, has difficulty sleeping, shows disturbed appetite patterns, and experiences suicidal thoughts, low self-esteem, guilt, and lack of motivation. People with dementia, in contrast, experience unsociability, uncooperativeness, hostility, emotional instability, confusion, disorientation, and reduced alertness. People with pseudodementia also are likely to have a history of prior depressive episodes that may have been undiagnosed. Their memory problems and other cognitive complaints have a very abrupt onset, compared with those of people with dementia, who experience a more slowly developing downward course (Wells, 1979). Another clue that can help clinicians distinguish between Alzheimer's and pseudodementia may be found by exploring the individual's recent past to determine whether a stressful event has occurred that may have precipitated the onset of depression. Sensitive tests of memory may also enable the clinician to distinguish pseudodementia from Alzheimer's disease. People with pseudodementia are likely not to respond when they are unsure of the correct answer; by contrast, individuals with Alzheimer's adopt a fairly liberal criterion for making responses and, as a result, give many incorrect answers (Gainotti & Marra, 1994).

Diagnosis of Alzheimer's Disease

Because of the importance of early diagnosis to rule out treatable dementias, researchers and clinicians have devoted significant energy and attention to the development of behavioral

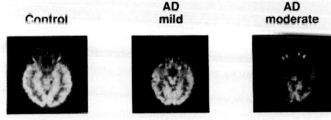

Control **AD mild** **AD moderate**

The temporal lobe in Alzheimer's disease. Pictured here are PET scans of the brains of a normal control subject, an individual in the early stages of Alzheimer's disease (AD mild), and one in the later stages of the disease (AD moderate). Darker areas reflect lower brain activity. The brain of the normal control shows normal levels of activity; the AD mild brain shows decreased activity in the temporal lobe; the brain of the individual with more advanced Alzheimer's shows a more severe decrease in brain activity.

tests for diagnosing Alzheimer's disease in its initial stages. An erroneous diagnosis would be a fatal mistake if the person had a dementia that would have been reversible if the proper treatment had been applied when the symptoms first became evident. Similarly, if the individual had a disorder with a nonorganic basis, a crucial opportunity to intervene would have been missed. Unfortunately, the early symptoms of Alzheimer's do not provide a sufficient basis for diagnosis. A definitive diagnosis of Alzheimer's disease can be made only in an autopsy by studying microscopic changes in brain tissue, leaving clinicians with the only option of conducting diagnosis by exclusion. However, in the later stages of the disease, there are diagnostic guidelines that can be applied and are claimed to have 85 to 90 percent accuracy. These guidelines were developed in 1984 by a joint commission of the National Institute of Neurological and Communicative Disorders and Stroke and the Alzheimer's Disease and Related Diseases Association and are therefore referred to as the NINCDS/ADRDA Guidelines (McKhann et al., 1984). The diagnosis of Alzheimer's disease based on the NINCDS/ADRDA criteria involves thorough medical and neuropsychological screenings. Even with these very stringent and complete guidelines, however, the diagnosis they lead to is at best one of "probable" Alzheimer's disease, reflecting the fact that the only certain diagnosis can be obtained through autopsy.

Brain imaging techniques are increasingly being used for diagnosing Alzheimer's disease. Although such measures have been regarded as assisting in the process of diagnosis by exclusion, evidence is accumulating to support the use of brain scans (CAT and MRI) to provide more positive indicators of the disease as well. For example, such measures detect atrophy in the hippocampus, the first area to be affected by the disease (Jack et al., 1998; Krasuski et al., 1998). Neuron loss in this area seems to be a good prediction of the development of the disease within a 4-year period (de Leon et al., 1997). Later in the disease, brain scans can reveal the presence of more marked abnormalities characteristic of the disease, such as areas of widespread atrophy and enlarged cerebral ventricles. PET scans and EEGs are also being used increasingly to augment clinically based diagnoses (Maas et al., 1997; Strijers et al., 1997; Swanwick, Rowan, Coen, & O'Mahony, 1996). Biological markers are providing another

tool to be used in the diagnostic process. The presence of a certain allele of one of the genes thought to be responsible for Alzheimer's disease may assist in determining who is at risk for developing the disorder years before symptoms emerge (Julin et al., 1998).

The most commonly used method for diagnosing Alzheimer's disease is a specialized form of the mental status examination known as the Mini-Mental State Examination (Folstein, Folstein, & McHugh, 1975) (see Table 12.2). People with Alzheimer's disease respond in particular ways to several of the items on this instrument; they tend to be circumstantial, repeat themselves, and lack richness of detail when describing objects, people, and events.

Theories and Treatment of Alzheimer's Disease

All theories regarding the cause of Alzheimer's disease focus on biological abnormalities involving the nervous system. Other theoretical perspectives, however, can offer insight into the impact of the disease on the individual's life and relationships with others.

Biological Perspective

Two major types of changes occur in the brains of people with Alzheimer's disease. The first is the formation of **neurofibrillary tangles,** in which the cellular material within the cell bodies of neurons becomes replaced by densely packed, twisted microfibrils, or tiny strands, of protein. Neurofibrillary tangles are made up of one form of a protein called **tau,** which normally helps maintain the internal support structure of the axons. The collapse of the

In diagnosing a person thought to have Alzheimer's disease, clinicians use a variety of approaches, including psychological testing. A primary focus of such testing includes an evaluation of the individual's cognitive functions, with particular attention to memory.

Dan McCoy/Rainbow

Table 12.2

Mini-Mental State Examination

Questions to assess orientation	What's the (year) (season) (date) (day) (month)?
	Where are we (state) (county) (town) (hospital) (floor)?
Assessment of memory for new information	Name three objects: 1 second to say each.
	Then ask the patient all three after you have said them.
	Give 1 point for each correct answer.
	Then repeat them until he or she learns all three.
	Count trials and record.
Attention and calculation	Serial 7s (subtracting 7 from 100 serially)
	1 point for each correct answer
	Stop after five answers.
	Alternatively spell *world* backwards.
Memory recall	Ask for the three objects repeated above.
	Give 1 point for each correct answer.
Language	Name a pencil, and watch.
	Repeat the following: "No ifs, ands, or buts."
	Follow a three-stage command: "Take a paper in your right hand, fold it in half, and put it on the floor."
	Read and obey the following: CLOSE YOUR EYES.
	Write a sentence.
Copy design	Two intersecting pentagons
Assessment of level of consciousness	Alert
	Drowsy
	Stupor
	Coma

Source: Folstein et al., 1975.

transport system within the neuron leads to altered communication between neurons and, ultimately, perhaps to the neuron's death. Neurofibrillary tangles develop early in the disease and may become quite widespread before the individual shows any behavioral symptoms.

The second change that occurs in the brains of people with Alzheimer's disease is the development of **amyloid plaques,** which are clusters of dead or dying neurons mixed with fragments of protein molecules. They are called "amyloid" because their core is composed of a substance called beta-amyloid. There are several types of beta-amyloid; the one linked with Alzheimer's disease is referred to as "beta-amyloid-42." Beta-amyloid is formed as an abnormal byproduct of the formation of a protein found in the normal brain, referred to as amyloid precursor protein (APP). Apart from the fact that beta-amyloid forms insoluble plaques, the substance itself is toxic to neurons.

Until the late 1980s, biological theories focused on changes in levels of neurotransmitters or in structures that were thought to account for the degeneration of the brain and behavioral losses associated with Alzheimer's. The most prominent of these

theories proposed that the primary disturbances involved in Alzheimer's disease are in the acetylcholine neurotransmitter system, which is involved in the processes of learning and memory (Coyle, Price, & DeLong, 1983). According to this view, people with Alzheimer's disease have insufficient amounts of **choline acetyltransferase (CAT),** which is essential for the synthesis of acetylcholine. Particularly important in this account of Alzheimer's disease is the fact that many of the biochemical and structural changes found in the brains of people with this disorder are in the hippocampus, a structure in the limbic system involved in memory and the learning of new information. Changes in this area of the brain are presumed to play a major role in the cognitive deficits associated with Alzheimer's disease.

Although there are various theories being tested to understand the causes of Alzheimer's disease, the most probable is that an underlying defect in the genetic programming of neural activity triggers whatever changes may take place within the brain as a result of degenerative processes (Wisniewski, Wegiel, & Kotula, 1996). The genetic theory was given impetus from the discovery that a form of the disease called early-onset familial

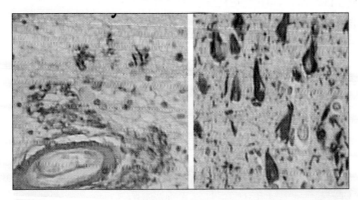

The major microscopic signs of Alzheimer's disease include ß-amyloid deposits shown on the left and neurofibrillary tangles shown on the right.

Alzheimer's disease, which begins at the unusually young age of 40 to 50 years, occurs with higher than expected prevalence in certain families. Another gene appears to be involved in a form of late-onset familial Alzheimer's disease that starts at the more expected age of 60 or 65 years. These genes are postulated to lead to excess amounts of beta-amyloid protein.

Aided by the discovery of familial patterns of early onset Alzheimer's disease along with the burgeoning technology of genetic engineering, researchers have identified several genes that may hold the key to understanding the cause of the disease. The ApoE gene has three common forms, ∈2, ∈3, and ∈4. Each one produces a corresponding form of apolipoprotein E (Apo E) called "E2," "E3," and "E4." The presence of the ∈4 allele sets up the mechanism for production of the E4 form of Apo E, which is thought to damage the microtubules within the neuron, which probably play an essential role in the activity of the cell. Ordinarily, Apo E2 and Apo E3 protect the tau protein, which helps stabilize the microtubules. The theory is that, if the tau protein is unprotected by Apo E2 and Apo E3, the microtubules will degenerate, eventually leading to the destruction of the neuron. (See Table 12.3.)

The attention of Alzheimer's researchers was originally directed to chromosome 21 when it was discovered that people with Down syndrome, who have three rather than the normal two of chromosome 21, have a 100 percent chance of developing Alzheimer's disease. People with Down syndrome have high levels of APP, which in turn leads to high levels of beta-amyloid. The suspicion about chromosome 21 arose only relatively recently, because it was only within the past few decades that people with Down syndrome lived past their thirties, long enough to develop Alzheimer's disease. On autopsy, the brains of people with Down syndrome are found to be virtually indistinguishable from those of people who suffered from Alzheimer's disease.

Most early-onset familial Alzheimer's disease cases are associated with defects in the so-called presenilin genes (PS1 and PS2), which, as the name implies, are thought to be involved in causing the brain to "age" prematurely. The mean age of onset in families with mutations in the PS1 gene is 45 years (ranging from 32 to 56 years) and 52 years for people with PS2 gene mutations (40 to 85 years). The pattern of inheritance for the presenilin genes is autosomal dominant, meaning that, if one parent carries the allele that is associated with the disease, the offspring has a 50 percent chance of developing the disorder. Alzheimer's researchers are attempting to determine how

Table 12.3

Genes associated with Alzheimer's Disease

Name of Gene	Chromosome	Proposed Action	Risk Factors
ApoE gene	19	ApoE is a protein that carries blood cholesterol throughout the body, but it also binds to beta-amyloid; therefore, it is thought to play a role in plaque formation.	The "E4" allele is found in about 40 percent of all people with late-onset familial Alzheimer's disease. People who inherit one ApoE4 allele are twice as likely to develop the disease, and people who inherit two have a risk that is 8–10 times that of the normal population.
APP gene	21	It is theorized to control the production of the protein that generates beta-amyloid.	It is believed to be responsible for 2 to 3 percent of all published cases of familial Alzheimer's disease and a slightly higher proportion (5 to 7 percent) of early-onset cases.
Presenilin genes (PS1 and PS2)	14 (PS1) 1 (PS2)	It is proposed that these genes lead APP to increase its production of beta-amyloid.	The PS1 gene is thought to account for up to 50 to 80 percent of reported cases. The PS2 gene accounts for a much smaller percentage of early-onset familial Alzheimer's disease cases.

Source: Folstein et al., 1975.

presenilin genes 1 and 2 interact with APP, beta-amyloid, plaques, and tangles. In one study, people with early-onset Alzheimer's disease and presenilin 1 and 2 mutations had more of a longer form of beta-amyloid in their brains than did those with the sporadic form of AD (Tanzi et al., 1996). This finding suggests that mutations in the presenilins may cause amyloid to be produced at abnormally high levels in the disease.

Environmental Perspective

As compelling as the genetic theory is, it accounts for only 40 percent of late-onset Alzheimer's disease and 50 percent of the early-onset form of the disease. Furthermore, it is known that there is less than perfect correspondence between monozygotic twins in the development of the disease (Gatz et al., 1997). Mechanisms other than genetics are apparently needed to explain the so-called sporadic (nonfamilial) form of the disease. Support for the notion that there are environmental contributors to Alzheimer's disease comes from an unusual study of more than 3,700 Japanese-born men who spent their adult years in Honolulu. When these men were studied in the years 1991–1993 (at the ages of 71–93 years), they had a rate of Alzheimer's disease of 5.4 percent, comparable with that seen among men of similar age in American and European populations. However, among a similar group of men living in Japan, the rate of Alzheimer's disease was only 1.5 percent, a finding that reflects the lower prevalence of the disorder in Japan. Something about the American diet or culture must have increased the risk of the disease among the Japanese-American men (White et al., 1996).

Another unusual study provides a somewhat different perspective on possible environmental contributions to Alzheimer's disease. The "Nun Study" is an ongoing investigation of a sample of nearly 700 members of the School Sisters of Notre Dame, a religious order chosen as the focus of research because members of this group have had lower rates of Alzheimer's disease than would be expected on the basis of their age. In trying to understand what facets of their lifestyle might account for this lowered risk for Alzheimer's, researchers have focused on the fact that many of the nuns have advanced academic degrees and have led intellectually challenging lives well into their eighties. Apparently, their mental activity has served as a protective factor against the disease (Snowdon, 1997).

Medical Treatment of Alzheimer's Disease

Clearly, the ultimate goal of the intense research on Alzheimer's disease is to find effective treatment, if not a cure. There is a great deal of optimism in the scientific community that this treatment, when it is found, will also benefit those who suffer from other degenerative diseases of the brain (Hardy & Gwinn-Hardy, 1998). As the search for the cause of Alzheimer's disease proceeds, researchers are attempting to find medications that will alleviate its symptoms.

Two medications are approved by the U.S. Food and Drug Administration for use in the treatment of Alzheimer's disease symptoms. These medications, which target the neurotransmitter acetylcholine, are THA, or tetrahydroaminoacridine (also

In trying to understand the lower risk of Alzheimer's disease among nuns, researchers have focused on the hypothesis that the higher than average level of mental activity common among sisters may serve as a protective factor against developing this disorder.

called tacrine and given the brand name Cognex) and donepezil hydrochloride (Aricept). Both fall in the category of anticholinesterase medications, because they work by inhibiting the action of acetylcholinesterase (also called cholinesterase), the enzyme that normally destroys acetylcholine after its release into the synaptic cleft. Because they inhibit the action of acetylcholinesterase, these medications slow the breakdown of acetylcholine; therefore, higher levels remain in the brain. Unfortunately, both medications have side effects. Tacrine can produce toxic effects in the liver, and the required doses are too high for some people. Aricept is as effective as tacrine in targeting cognitive symptoms, although it has gastrointestinal side effects related to the effects of acetylcholinesterase inhibitors (diarrhea and nausea). However, its required dose is lower, and it does not interfere with liver function (Barner & Gray, 1998; Rogers & Friedhoff, 1998). Both medications have the advantage that they give the patient a period of relief from the disturbing cognitive symptoms that occur in the early stages of the disease. While these are the only approved medications on the market, there are other acetylcholinesterase agents (citicoline, arecoline, and ENA 713, also called Exelon), as well as medications that work on other neurotransmitters.

Surprisingly, estrogen replacement therapy (ERT), normally used to alleviate the symptoms of hormonal changes in older women, is beginning to hold promise as an intervention for delaying cognitive deterioration in women with Alzheimer's disease (Kawas et al., 1997). A third category of medications targets the so-called free radicals, which are molecules formed when beta-amyloid breaks into fragments; free radicals are thought to damage neurons in the surrounding brain tissue. Antioxidants are agents that can disarm free radicals and, therefore, may be another treatment for Alzheimer's disease. One of these medications is seligiline (l-deprenyl or Eldepryl), which seemed to be effective as a short-term treatment, but it has not shown much benefit over the long term (Freedman et al., 1998). Vitamin E is another antioxidant being tried as a treatment of this disorder. Finally, the fortuitous discovery that

President Ronald Reagan in 1989, before he was diagnosed with Alzheimer's disease in 1994.

patients with arthritis being treated with ibuprofen seemed to be protected from Alzheimer's disease led to the recommendation that this drug be used in the treatment of Alzheimer's disease. In addition to ibuprofen (Advil, Motrin), other nonsteroidal anti-inflammatory drugs such as naproxen sodium (Aleve), and indomethacin (Indocin), are thought to offer some protection against the disease (Stewart, Kawas, Corrada, & Metter, 1997). Another anti-inflammatory agent called prednisone is also being tested as a treatment to slow the progression of Alzheimer's disease (Aisen & Pasinetti, 1998).

Behavioral Management of Symptoms

As biomedical researchers continue their search for treatments to cure or alleviate the symptoms, behavioral psychologists are developing strategies to maximize the daily functioning of people with Alzheimer's disease. These efforts are often targeted at the **caregivers,** who are the people (usually family members) primarily responsible for caring for the person with the disease. Caregivers often suffer adverse effects from the constant demands placed on them, effects known as **caregiver burden.** However, caregivers can be taught behavioral strategies that can promote the patient's independence and reduce his or her distressing behaviors. Support groups can also provide a forum in which caregivers learn ways to manage the emotional stress associated with their role.

Behavioral strategies aimed at increasing the patient's independence include giving prompts, cues, and guidance in the steps involved in self-maintenance. For example, the patient can be encouraged to relearn the steps involved in getting dressed and then be positively rewarded with praise and attention for having completed those steps. Modeling can be used, so that the client relearns previous skills through imitation. Finally, time management can be helpful in that, if the caregiver is taught to follow a strict daily schedule, the client is more likely to be able to fall into a regular routine of everyday activities. All of these methods benefit both the client and the caregiver. The client regains some measure of independence, and the caregiver's burden is reduced to the extent that the client can engage in self-care tasks.

Behavioral strategies can also eliminate, or at least reduce the frequency of, wandering and aggression in an Alzheimer's patient. One possible approach, which is not always practical, involves extinction. The caregiver ignores certain disruptive behaviors, with the intention of eliminating the reinforcement that has helped maintain them. However, extinction is not practical for behaviors that may lead to harm in the client, such as wandering if it involves leaving the house and walking into the street. One possibility is to give the client positive reinforcement for staying within certain boundaries. However, this may not be sufficient, and, at that point, protective barriers need to be installed. Another possible approach is for the caregiver to identify situations that are particularly problematic for the patient, such as in the bathtub or at the table. Behavioral methods can then be used in these circumstances. For example, if the problem occurs while eating, it may be that the patient can be encouraged to relearn how to use a knife and fork, rather than needing to be fed. Again, such an intervention can reduce caregiver burden, as well as increase the patient's functional skills.

These behavioral interventions can be implemented through individual therapy or in a support group. The support group facilitator can teach these methods to participants. Furthermore, caregivers can share strategies among themselves based on their own experiences. The emotional support that caregivers can provide for each other can be just as valuable as the actual instruction they receive.

You can see, then, that although the prospect of Alzheimer's is frightening and painful for all individuals involved, a number of interventions are available. Until a cure for the disorder is found, however, clinicians must be content to see their gains

Caregivers can be trained to provide therapeutic reinforcement.

Caring for a Person with Alzheimer's Disease

Although experts on Alzheimer's disease have not yet discovered its causes, they have made impressive advances in understanding its social impact and, particularly, its emotional toll on the family. At the same time, investigators are suggesting strategies that can help reduce caregiver burden.

As pointed out in the text, caregiver burden is a major concern among gerontological researchers working in the area of Alzheimer's disease. Research in this area began in the mid-1980s, with the publication of key studies identifying the severe demands placed on Alzheimer's caregivers (Chenoweth & Spencer, 1986; George & Gwyther, 1986; Pearlin, Mullan, Semple, & Skaff, 1990; Zarit, Todd, & Zarit, 1986). (See Table 12.4.) Since the problem was first identified, hundreds of publications have documented the devastating impact on spouses and adult children of individuals with Alzheimer's disease. Most recently, attention has focused on how the caregiving experience varies according to one's ethnicity and culture. The problems are exacerbated, for example, among Latino families, due to the fact that they are at higher risk for earlier and more debilitating chronic illnesses (Aranda & Knight, 1997).

Researchers have suggested that caregivers may need to use a variety of coping strategies to ward off depression (Williamson & Schulz, 1993). Active coping strategies may be particularly well suited for situations in which the caregiver can have some direct effect. Thus, caregivers who are feeling depressed about memory loss in their loved ones may feel better once they have taken practical steps to help the family member remain as independent as possible. In situations that are not subject to change, such as sadness at witnessing the decline of a loved one, acceptance may be a more effective coping strategy.

Surprisingly, some caregivers experience unexpected positive aspects in taking care of a loved one (Schulz, Visintainer, & Williamson, 1990; Talkington-Boyer & Snyder, 1994). Over time, individuals may gain expertise as caregivers and feel some sense of improvement in well-being even as they cope with the very difficult challenges faced by their role as caregivers (Kling, Seltzer, & Ryff, 1997). Some find comfort in the response of a relative to caregiving efforts; others find some gratification in the support from other family members and friends (Kinney & Stephens, 1989). The presence of role rewards from caregiving may actually help these individuals feel better (Stephens, Franks, & Townsend, 1994). Some caregivers may also interpret their burden in spiritual terms, regarding their role as consistent with the teachings of their religion. Prayer, spiritual reading materials, and a message of forgiveness may be important resources to which caregivers turn (Kaye & Robinson, 1994).

Research interest in the experience of caregiving has burgeoned, leading to the development of programs aimed at helping reduce caregiver burden. Researchers have demonstrated that caregivers can benefit from both brief psychodynamic cognitive-behavioral therapies for depression (Gallagher-Thompson & Steffen, 1994) and interventions that help them develop more effective coping strategies (McNaughton, Patterson, Smith, & Grant, 1995). Various services are available within the community, including diagnostic and medical assessment programs, counseling, support groups, financial planning assistance, and home care services. Telephone information and referral services have been developed that provide emotional support, along with useful knowledge about

Table 12.4

Examples of Caregiver Burden

The following items from the Screen for Caregiver Burden illustrate the kinds of concerns that caregivers experience. The prevalence of each concern among a representative sample of caregivers is indicated across from each item:

Item	Prevalence (%)
My spouse continues to drive when he/she shouldn't.	43
I have little control over my spouse's behavior.	87
I have to do too many jobs/chores (feeding, shopping, paying bills) that my spouse used to do.	67
I am upset that I cannot communicate with my spouse.	73
I feel so alone—as if I have the world on my shoulders.	43
I have to cover up for my spouse's mistakes.	60
I am totally responsible for keeping our household in order.	70

From P.P. Vitaliano, et al., "The Screen for Caregiver Burden" in *The Gerontologist,* 1991, 31:76–83. Copyright © The Gerontological Society of America, Washington DC. Reprinted by permission.

Alzheimer's (Coyne, Potnexa, & Broken Nose, 1994). Many institutions that care for elderly persons offer day care services, so that caregivers can work outside the home. Long-term facilities may also offer respite services, allowing caregivers to leave their relatives in the care of the institution for a period of several days to a few weeks while the caregivers take needed breaks or vacations. These programs, which involve short stays or daily care within the institution, can make the ultimate transition to institutional living easier for Alzheimer's patients and for those who care for them. Finally, the World Wide Web is increasingly being used as an intervention for caregivers; electronic bulletin boards and information services provide quick responses and can be conveniently accessed by those who have the resources to be able to maintain home computers.

Some older people are able to take advantage of computer networks that provide information and support for relatives of Alzheimer's patients.

measured less as progress toward a cure and more as success in prolonging the period of maximum functioning for the individual and the individual's family.

Cognitive Disorders: The Perspectives Revisited

The cognitive impairments associated with the disorders discussed in this chapter are, by definition, best understood from a biological perspective. However, the biological perspective has not yet produced a viable treatment for one of the most devastating of these disorders, Alzheimer's disease. Until a cure is found, individuals and their families whose lives are touched by the disease must be willing to try a variety of approaches to alleviate the suf-

fering caused by Alzheimer's. Many research programs are currently underway to explore strategies for reducing the stress placed on caregivers. Some of these approaches involve innovative, high-technology methods, such as computer networks; others take the more traditional approach of providing emotional support to individuals with Alzheimer's disease and their families. The application of cognitive-behavioral and other methods of therapy to helping people cope with Alzheimer's is another useful approach. It seems that the bottom line in all this research on understanding and treating those affected by Alzheimer's disease is that it is not necessary for psychologists to wait until biomedical researchers discover a cure. Much can be done to improve the quality of life for people with Alzheimer's and to maintain their functioning and their dignity as long as possible.

RETURN TO THE CASE

Irene Heller

Irene's History

In order to put together a picture of Irene Heller's life history, I had to rely on her as well as Jonathan for details. For parts of the story, she was coherent and accurate in her recall. For other parts, however, she left out pieces of information, which Jonathan had to fill in. Fortunately, Jonathan had collected a considerable amount of information about his mother from relatives and her friends. When he joined in telling the story, his voice was filled with sadness.

Irene grew up in a poor family in a small mining town in the Appalachians. Despite the family's poverty, she attended a state university and on graduation was offered a fellowship to pursue a doctorate in mathematics, an unusual opportunity for a woman in the 1930s. However, Irene declined the fellowship, because she met and fell in love with Jonathan's father and they decided to get married. The couple had three sons in short succession. After the birth of their third child, Irene's husband became caught up in gambling and drinking, eventually leaving his wife and moving across the country, never to be heard from again.

Over the years, Irene managed to get by, struggling as a poorly paid teacher. All three boys did well academically, going on to college and successful careers, one in New York City and the other two in the same city as Irene. By the time she retired from teaching, she had gained enormous respect from the people in her community, from her fellow teachers, and from the many students she helped in her role as teacher and advisor. She had accumulated a large enough pension to allow her to fulfill her life's dream of being able to travel, pursue her interests in gardening and needlework, and "just plain relax." However, her deterioration over the course of the past year had made those plans impossible.

Jonathan repeatedly noted that the onset of his mother's problems seemed to coincide with her retirement. He had come to recognize that her problems were far more serious than adjustment difficulties, but he couldn't help wondering whether the major life change had triggered something that was waiting to happen. When I asked Jonathan to be more specific about his mother's problems, he discussed her memory difficulties, her poor judgment, and her inappropriate behaviors.

Assessment

Irene agreed to take a battery of tests, and I referred her to Dr. Furcolo, the staff neuropsychologist. Dr. Furcolo's report indicated that Irene had moderate cognitive deficits, including the inaccurate naming of objects, poor performance on tests of abstract reasoning and verbal fluency, disorientation as to time and place, and impairment of recent memory. Her intellectual abilities were relatively intact on scales of well-learned abilities measured in a familiar format and on scales of immediate memory recall not requiring any encoding processes. In contrast, she performed poorly on intelligence test scales involving unfamiliar, abstract, speed-dependent tasks that strained her capacity for attention and learning. Irene showed no signs of a psychotic disorder, nor did she suffer from specific symptoms of depression. Her symptoms appeared to have had a gradual onset and to have progressed over at least a 2-year period. Irene's annoyance when she described her symptoms reinforced my impression, and Dr. Furcolo's, that her irritability was related to frustration over her declining mental faculties.

In a case such as Irene's, in which there is a strong likelihood of a medical problem, a comprehensive medical workup is necessary, including laboratory tests and brain imaging. Irene agreed to my recommendation that she be admitted to the hospital for 3 days of testing. The test results showed that her endocrine and metabolic functioning were normal, and there was no evidence of excessive alcohol or substance use. Irene's EKG, blood pressure, cerebral angiography (X ray of cerebral blood vessels), and measure of cerebral blood flow showed no evidence of cardiovascular or cerebrovascular abnormalities. The CT scan revealed some atrophy and enlargement of ventricles, but there was no evidence of focal lesions or trauma. Her EEG pattern showed some evidence of slowing but no evidence of focal abnormalities.

Diagnosis

I assumed that Irene was experiencing more than just emotional problems related to her retirement. The medical workup and the nature of her symptoms pointed to a physically based disorder involving dementia; specifically, all signs pointed to a diagnosis of dementia of the Alzheimer type.

RETURN TO THE CASE

Irene Heller (continued)

Axis I.	Dementia of the Alzheimer Type
Axis II:	Deferred
Axis III:	Alzheimer's disease
Axis IV:	Problems related to the social environment (living alone in unsupervised housing)
Axis V:	Current Global Assessment of Functioning: 28
	Highest Global Assessment of Functioning (past year): 60

Case Formulation

I formed the diagnosis of dementia of the Alzheimer type for this 67-year-old retired school-teacher after extensive medical and neuropsychological testing and observation on an inpatient unit by an interdisciplinary team of professionals. Irene had had symptoms of dementia for an undetermined period of time, possibly as long as 2 years, when she apparently first noted long-term memory loss and difficulty registering new information into short-term memory. Although Irene's retirement occurred around the time her symptoms first appeared, it is not likely that the retirement caused the onset of the disorder. It did not appear that retirement in and of itself presented a stress to Irene, who was looking forward to spending her time in travel and other leisure pursuits.

Treatment Planning

Irene's dementia was sufficiently advanced so that a return to her home without any supervision or assistance was out of the question. I consulted with Mary Lyon, the hospital's social worker, about the options that were available locally for Irene. Ms. Lyon recommended that Irene move into an apartment complex that provided supervised living arrangements for elderly people. The income from the sale of her house, plus her retirement pension, would give her the financial resources to live in a reasonably large and comfortable apartment without the responsibilities of owning a home. In addition to helping with Irene's residential arrangements, Ms. Lyon consulted with Irene, Jonathan, and me about treatment options. We all agreed that a multidisciplinary treatment team was needed, including a psychologist, a social worker, and a counselor from the local Council on Aging. In particular, Irene needed help with developing methods of self-care and independent living.

Outcome of the Case

More than 3 years have passed since my consultation with Irene and her son. Sadly but predictably, matters have not improved in Irene's life. She initially moved into a supervised apartment and attended a day program at a local nursing home, but her deterioration was rapid and unyielding. After only 6 months, Irene had to move into a nursing home, because she repeatedly endangered herself by carelessly disposing of matches and by wandering out of her apartment at night and getting lost.

In a recent note I received from Jonathan, he explained how impaired his mother had become. Although she had some good days in which they could converse satisfactorily, on most days she seemed unaware that he was her son. Jonathan ended his note with the expression of a faint hope that science might find some of the answers to this tragic disease. ■

Sarah Tobin, PhD

Summary

- Cognitive disorders (formally called "delirium, dementia, amnestic and other cognitive disorders") are those in which the central characteristic is cognitive impairment that results from such causes as brain trauma, disease, or exposure to toxic substances.

- Delirium is a temporary state in which individuals experience a clouding of consciousness in which they are unaware of what is happening and are unable to focus or pay attention. They experience cognitive changes in which their memory is foggy and they are disoriented, and they may have various other symptoms, such as rambling speech, delusions, hallucinations, and emotional disturbances. Delirium, which is caused by a change in the metabolism of the brain, can result from various factors, including substance intoxication or withdrawal, head injury, high fever, and vitamin deficiency. The onset is generally rapid and the duration brief.

- Amnestic disorders are conditions in which people are unable to recall previously learned information or to register new memories. These disorders are due either to the use of substances or to such medical conditions as head trauma, loss of oxygen, and herpes simplex.

- Dementia is a form of cognitive impairment involving generalized progressive deficits in a person's memory and learning of new information, ability to communicate, judgment, and motor coordination. In addition to experiencing cognitive changes, individuals with this condition undergo changes in their personality and emotional state. Dementia results from profuse and progressive brain damage associated with physical conditions, such as vascular diseases, AIDS, head trauma, psychoactive substances, and various neurological disorders. The most well-known form of dementia is Alzheimer's disease, a condition associated with severe cerebral atrophy as well as characteristic microscopic changes in the brain. Alzheimer's disease is specified according to subtypes: (1) with delirium, (2) with delusions, (3) with depressed mood, or (4) uncomplicated. The diagnosis of Alzheimer's is challenging for several reasons. Some conditions, such as vascular dementia, have symptoms similar to those of Alzheimer's. Other conditions, such as depression, can lead to symptoms that mimic those in the early stages of Alzheimer's. All theories regarding the cause of Alzheimer's disease focus on biological abnormalities involving the nervous system—specifically, two types of brain changes. The first is the formation of neurofibrillary tangles, in which the cellular material within the cell bodies of neurons becomes replaced by densely packed, twisted microfibrils, or tiny strands, of protein. The second change involves the development of amyloid plaques, which are clusters of dead or dying neurons mixed with fragments of protein molecules. In addition to biological explanations, researchers have also focused on environmental contributors to Alzheimer's, as well as the role of certain behaviors in preventing the development of the disease. Although there is no cure for this disease, researchers are attempting to find medications, such as anticholinesterase agents, that alleviate its symptoms. At the same time, experts have focused their attention on refining behavioral techniques for managing symptoms and have given particular attention to strategies for alleviating caregiver burden.

Key Terms

See Glossary for definitions.

Agnosia 373
Akinesia 377
Amnestic disorders 371
Amyloid plaques 380
Aphasia 372
Apraxia 373
Bradykinesia 377
Broca's aphasia 372
Caregiver burden 383
Caregivers 383

Choline acetyltransferase (CAT) 380
Creutzfeldt-Jakob disease 377
Delirium 370
Dementia 372
Epilepsy 370
Executive functioning 373
Frontal lobe dementia 377
Huntington's disease 377
Lewy body dementia 377
Neurofibrillary tangles 379

Parkinson's disease 377
Pick's disease 376
Pseudodementia 378
Substance-induced persisting amnestic disorder 371
Substance-induced persisting dementia 375
Tau 379
Vascular dementia 378
Wernicke's aphasia 372

Internet Resource

To get more information on the material covered in this chapter, visit our web site at **http://www.mhhe.com/halgin**. There you will find more information, resources, and links to topics of interest.

CASE REPORT: CARL WADSWORTH

One morning, our receptionist gave me a message to call Dr. Elaine Golden, the director of residency training in the medical school, and I called her back as soon as I found a free moment that afternoon. Dr. Golden told me that she was looking for a psychotherapist to treat one of the physicians in the surgical residency program. It was not unusual for physicians in training to be referred for treatment of depression or anxiety, but neither of those was a problem for 31-year-old Dr. Carl Wadsworth. I sensed even in the tone of Elaine's voice that the case of Carl Wadsworth was unusual, an impression that was confirmed when Elaine emphasized the importance of keeping the case absolutely confidential. Before Elaine proceeded to tell me the details, however, I felt that it would be important for me to remind her about the standards of confidentiality, as well as the exceptions to these standards. I explained that I would, of course, keep the case confidential, unless there was serious reason to believe that a client was in danger of harming himself or another person, or was involved in the abuse of a child, an elder, or a person with a disability. Elaine assured me that none of these issues pertained to the case of Carl Wadsworth. Rather, her concern pertained more to the reputation of this young doctor and that of the medical school. As it turned out, Carl Wadsworth was addicted to cocaine. Not only was he using the substance on a daily basis, but he had begun to sell drugs to fellow medical residents and medical students in order to pay for his own habit.

After hearing Elaine share this disturbing information about a physician-in-training, I asked her point blank, "Why aren't you throwing this guy out of the program?" Elaine responded nondefensively, "I've thought seriously about that possibility. However, I think we have a case of a young man who can be salvaged from his self-destructive behavior." She went on to explain, "Carl is a gifted physician, who has, sadly, become caught in a trap, from which he is pleading for help to be released. Sarah, I think that you can help him."

Elaine explained that Carl had called her at home late the previous night, with his wife, Anne, sitting by his side. With a trembling voice, he had begun the phone discussion with the startling words, "Dr. Golden, I desperately need your help. I'm a junkie." As Elaine told me this story, I thought about how fortunate Carl was to have a relationship with such a caring and concerned mentor. Elaine listened carefully to Carl's story and arranged to see him the next morning. In that appointment she told Carl that it was imperative that he contact me that day to set up an appointment, which he did. That afternoon, I received a call from Carl, who urgently pleaded that I see him as soon as possible. We agreed to meet the next morning.

When I first met Carl Wadsworth, I was struck by the fact that he seemed so young and unsure of himself. Rather than wearing his hospital uniform, or any clothing suggestive of his profession, Carl wore a college sweatshirt and matching sweatpants. My guess was that he would have felt embarrassed sitting in the waiting room of the mental health clinic in medical attire. Carl's face was gaunt and haggard, suggesting that he was run down, perhaps to the point of exhaustion. My suspicions were confirmed. After introducing himself, he apologized for his ostensible weariness, explaining that he hadn't slept much in recent days. After entering my office, Carl proceeded to tell me the painful story of his seduction by cocaine and the eventual hold it took over his whole life. He acknowledged that the problem had become so serious that he risked destroying his family and ruining his career. These realizations became startlingly apparent to him when Anne, pregnant with their second child, told Carl that she would divorce him if he did not obtain professional help.

Carl explained that, when he first began using cocaine 1 year ago, he fully believed that he could control his use and maintain it as a harmless pastime. Predictably, though, Carl began to rely on the drug more and more heavily. Money problems began to accumulate, and, rather than attribute these to the expense of his cocaine habit, he blamed them on his inadequate salary. It became necessary to draw on the family bank account to pay the household bills. Carl soon began to spend more and more time away from home. Telling Anne that he was at work, he spent hours each day seeking ways to pick up extra cash. At the hospital, his work had become sloppy, and Elaine had let him know that he was at risk of being dismissed from the hospital. His patients complained to the nursing staff about his abrupt and insensitive manner.

As we talked about the changes in Carl's professional behavior, I could see that he was becoming increasingly distraught, and, when I asked him about his family life, he fought to hold back tears. He explained that he loved his wife and daughter very much but that he found himself losing control in his interactions with them. He had become irritable and impatient with them and occasionally so angry that he had come close to physical violence.

When Carl first came to see me, he was in serious trouble. He was accurate in his perception that his personal life and his career were on the line and that he needed help immediately.

Sarah Tobin, PhD

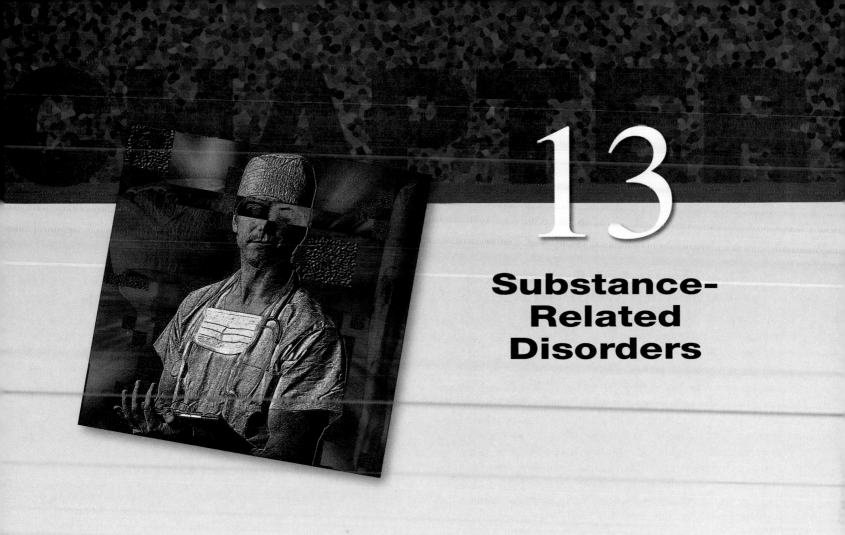

13

Substance-Related Disorders

We live in a society in which the use of mind-altering substances has become a central part of the culture. Leafing through any popular magazine, you are certain to see advertisements with successful, attractive people using cigarettes. Watching a sporting event on television, you will surely see commercials with fun-loving, happy people consuming alcohol. These legal drugs represent only a small fraction of the substances that Americans ingest each day. As you will see, both legal and illegal drugs affect all sectors of the population, including well-educated and professional people such as Carl.

The Nature of Substance Abuse and Dependence

A **substance** is a chemical that alters a person's mood or behavior when it is smoked, injected, drunk, inhaled, or swallowed in pill form. Although most of our discussion will focus on drugs of abuse, it is important to realize that people often use medications and toxic chemicals to induce altered psychological states. Because substances are so much a part of everyday life, most people take them for granted. A glass of wine at dinner, a cup of coffee in the morning, a beer or two at a party, a sleeping pill at night—none of these may seem particularly unusual or troublesome. Although most people are able to regulate their use of such substances, many drugs pose high risks. Findings from the National Comorbidity Study have revealed that Americans between the ages of 15 and 54 are more affected by dependence on psychoactive substances than by any other psychiatric disturbance (Anthony, Warner, & Kessler, 1994). More than half of all Americans (51 percent) have used an illegal drug or a prescription drug for nonmedical purposes during the course of their lives (Warner et al., 1995), and over one quarter (26.6 percent) of the U.S. population have seriously abused or become dependent on drugs during their lifetime (Kessler et al., 1994). Within the U.S. population, economically disadvantaged people are at particularly high risk for having problems with drugs (SAMHSA, 1997).

For many people, addictive behavior involves the use of more than one substance.

Many people die each year because of their own dangerous use of drugs, and many others die as the result of accidents or homicides committed by substance-abusing individuals. Although the number of alcohol-related fatalities decreased during the 1990s, the statistics are still quite disturbing—38.6 percent, or 16,189, of all traffic fatalities in 1997 were attributed to alcohol. Young people are particularly at risk. Among the adolescents between the ages of 16 and 20 involved in fatal crashes in 1997, 14.3 percent were driving while intoxicated. The intoxication rate among fatally injured drivers was even higher for those in their early twenties (26.3 percent of those 21 to 24 years old) (National Highway Traffic Safety Administration, 1997).

Behaviors Associated with Substance-Related Disorders

In this section, we will discuss the ways in which substances affect human behavior. Although each substance has specific effects, which depend on its chemical composition and its effects on the brain or body, you will find it helpful to have an overview of how substances in general affect behavior.

Substance-Induced Disorders

The phrases "driving under the influence (DUI)" and "driving while intoxicated (DWI)" are commonly used in legal reports about motor vehicle violations or accidents. In order to appreciate the seriousness of such an accusation, it is important to understand what is meant by intoxication. **Substance intoxication** is the temporary maladaptive experience of behavioral or psychological changes due to the accumulation of a substance in the body. Let's take a closer look at this definition. A condition of substance intoxication is a transient phenomenon that is limited to the period that the substance is biologically potent in the body. The behavior of an intoxicated person is maladaptive, which means that his or her functioning is impaired significantly. In the case of alcohol intoxication, the individual experiences impaired judgment and attention, slurred speech, abnormal eye movements, slowed reflexes, unsteady walking, and changeable moods. By contrast, the person who becomes intoxicated following the ingestion of amphetamines experiences accelerated bodily functioning, as well as perspiration or chills. Even people who drink a great amount of a caffeinated beverage can experience troubling bodily sensations, such as nervousness, twitching, insomnia, and agitation.

In addition to the effects that follow the ingestion of substances, psychological and physical changes also occur when some substances are discontinued, a reaction that is referred to as **substance withdrawal.** A person in a state of substance withdrawal experiences significant distress or impairment at home, at work, or in other important life contexts. Withdrawal takes different forms, according to the actual substance involved. For example, nicotine withdrawal commonly includes anxiety and irritability. People taking substances with higher potency can undergo such severe psychological and physical withdrawal symptoms that they need medical care. A phenomenon called **tolerance** is related to substance withdrawal. This occurs when an individual requires larger and larger amounts of the substance in order to achieve its desired effects or when the person feels less of its effects after using the same amount of the substance. For example, a man may find that he now needs to drink two six-packs of beer in order to achieve the same state of relaxation that was previously attained with a single six-pack. You will see as you read this chapter that tolerance can develop in different ways—in some instances, tolerance is caused by changes in the body's metabolism of the drug; in others, it results from the way the drug affects the nervous system.

As you will see later in the chapter, when we discuss specific substances, the extent of substance intoxication and the distress associated with substance withdrawal are influenced by the way in which individuals take a specific drug into the body, how rapidly acting the substance is, and how lasting the effect of the drug is. Drugs that are efficiently absorbed into the bloodstream due to intravenous injection or smoking are likely to lead to a more intense kind of intoxication than are drugs taken in pill form. Drugs that have an immediate impact on the person are more seductive than those that take longer to take effect. Further, drugs that have a powerful, but short-lived, effect are more likely to lead to patterns of abuse, because the person craves to repeat the experience time and again within a short time frame.

In addition to the diagnostic categories of substance intoxication and substance withdrawal, there are several other substance-induced disorders that have symptoms that are quite similar to the psychological disorders we discussed in previous chapters. For example, there are several cognitive disorders (Chapter 12) related to substances, such as substance-induced delirium, substance-induced persisting dementia, and substance-induced persisting amnestic disorder. In addition to these cognitive disorders, the *DSM-IV* lists the following substance-induced conditions: psychotic disorder, mood disorder, anxiety disorder, sexual dysfunction, and sleep disorder. Therefore, clinicians conducting their initial assessment of clients realize that it is important to consider the possibility that the symptoms might be the result of substance use. For example, the clinician considers whether manic symptoms are due to bipolar disorder or amphetamines, or whether bizarre symptoms are due to psychosis or hallucinogenic drugs.

Substance Use Disorders

When does a person's use of substances become abuse? When does a person's need for substances reach the point of dependency and become an addiction? These are questions that researchers and clinicians have struggled with for decades. Currently, **substance abuse** is defined as the maladaptive pattern of substance use occurring within a 12-month period that leads to significant impairment or distress evidenced by one or more of the following: (1) failure to meet obligations, (2) use of substances in physically hazardous situations, (3) legal problems, or (4) interpersonal problems.

People who abuse substances find that their lives are affected in many ways. They neglect obligations at work, and their commitments to home and family start to erode. In addition to letting their work and family life slide, they may begin to take risks that are personally dangerous and put others in jeopardy, such as driving or operating powerful machinery while intoxicated. Legal problems arise for many people who abuse substances, because their behavior puts them into positions in which they violate the law. In addition to arrests for driving while intoxicated, they may face charges of disorderly conduct or assaultive behavior. Last, and most common, the life of the substance-abusing person is often characterized by interpersonal problems. During episodes of intoxication, they may become argumentative and possibly violent with close ones. Even when the substance-abusing person is sober, his or her relationships are commonly strained and unhappy.

The main feature of abuse, then, is a pattern of behavior in which the individual continues to use substances, even when it is clear that such behavior entails significant risks or creates problems in living. For example, a college professor may insist on having three martinis at lunch, despite the fact that this interferes with her ability to teach her afternoon seminar. Her behavior is characterized as abuse, because her drinking interferes with her work responsibilities. By contrast, her sister, who occasionally has a glass of wine with dinner, would not be regarded as abusing alcohol, because there is no evidence of impairment.

The notion of substance abuse carries with it no implication that the individual is addicted to the substance. Continuing with the example of the three-martini professor, the question is to what extent she "needs" to have those drinks in order to get through the day. If she has reached the point at which she relies on this form of drinking, she would be considered dependent on alcohol. **Substance dependence** is a maladaptive pattern of substance use manifested by a cluster of cognitive, behavioral, and physiological symptoms during a 12-month period and caused by the continued use of a substance.

Experts also strive to understand the roles that psychological and physiological factors play in determining dependence on or tolerance to a substance. Physiological dependence is determined when an individual shows signs of either tolerance or withdrawal. As you will see later in this chapter, clinicians treating people with substance problems must understand these physiological patterns, especially when monitoring the symptoms of withdrawal or when recommending somatic interventions, such as medication.

■ Alcohol

We begin our discussion of disorders by focusing on alcohol, a substance that has received increased attention in recent years because of the tremendous personal and societal costs associated with the abuse of this mind-altering drug.

Patterns of Use and Abuse

Although the amount of alcohol consumed per person in the United States has steadily decreased since reaching a peak in 1980 (see Figure 13.1), many people use alcohol on a regular basis. More than half of all Americans over the age of 12 admit that they had had at least one drink in the month prior to being surveyed (SAMSHA, 1997). Approximately 5 percent are considered heavy drinkers, meaning that they consume five or more drinks on the same occasion on at least five days in the month. Among high school seniors, 82 percent report having had a drink, and 64 percent report having been drunk at some point in their lives (Johnston, O'Malley, & Bachman, in preparation).

According to the National Comorbidity Study, one in seven Americans (14 percent) has a history of alcohol abuse or dependence (Anthony et al., 1994). These estimates vary by sex, with one fifth of the men in the United States (20.1 percent) having a lifetime prevalence of alcohol abuse and/or dependence, which is more than twice the rate for women (8.2 percent). Among women, however, there are variations in prevalence by age, with higher rates reported for adolescent females than for any other age group of women (Kandel et al., 1997).

Effects of Alcohol Use

One of the reasons people consume alcohol is to achieve an altered mood and state of awareness. Before examining the long-term effects of chronic alcohol use, we will look first at its immediate effects on the user and the mechanisms thought to be responsible for these effects.

Immediate Effects

In small amounts, alcohol has sedating effects, leading to feelings of warmth, comfort, and relaxation. In larger amounts, alcohol may lead the drinker to feel more outgoing, self-confident, and uninhibited. Some people stop drinking when they have achieved the positive mood they were seeking from alcohol. If an individual continues to drink beyond that point, though, the effects of alcohol as a **depressant** drug become more apparent, as feelings of sleepiness, uncoordination, dysphoria, and irritability set in. Excessive drinking affects a person's vital func-

The unpredictability and dysfunctional behavior of an alcoholic parent or spouse create tension and insecurity for all family members.

tions and can be fatal. The mixture of alcohol with other drugs is referred to as **potentiation,** meaning that the effect of two drugs taken together is greater than the effect of either substance alone. For example, combining alcohol, which is a depressant, with another depressant would exaggerate the effects on the body and possibly would be fatal.

The rate at which alcohol is absorbed into the bloodstream depends in part on the concentration of alcohol in the particular beverage, the amount of alcohol consumed, the rate at which it is consumed, and the amount of food present in the

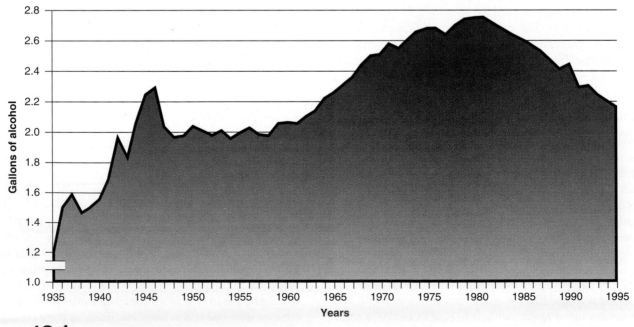

Figure 13.1

Total per capita alcohol consumption, United States, 1935–1995

Table 13.1

Alcohol Impairment Chart

Men: Approximate Blood Alcohol Percentage

Drinks*	Body Weight in Pounds								Effect on Person
	100	120	140	160	180	200	220	240	
0	.00	.00	.00	.00	.00	.00	.00	.00	Only safe driving limit.
1	.04	.03	.03	.02	.02	.02	.02	.02	Impairment begins.
2	.08	.06	.05	.05	.04	.04	.03	.03	
3	.11	.09	.08	.07	.06	.06	.05	.05	
4	.15	.12	.11	.09	.08	.08	.07	.06	Driving skills significantly affected.
5	.19	.16	.13	.12	.11	.09	.09	.08	Possible criminal penalties.
6	.23	.19	.16	.14	.13	.11	.10	.09	
7	.26	.22	.19	.16	.15	.13	.12	.11	
8	.30	.25	.21	.19	.17	.15	.14	.13	Legally intoxicated.
9	.34	.28	.24	.21	.19	.17	.15	.14	Criminal penalties imposed.
10	.38	.31	.27	.23	.21	.19	.17	.16	

Women: Approximate Blood Alcohol Percentage

Drinks*	Body Weight in Pounds									Effect on Person
	90	100	120	140	160	180	200	220	240	
0	.00	.00	.00	.00	.00	.00	.00	.00	.00	Only safe driving limit.
1	.05	.05	.04	.03	.03	.03	.02	.02	.02	Impairment begins.
2	.10	.09	.08	.07	.06	.05	.05	.04	.04	
3	.15	.14	.11	.11	.09	.08	.07	.06	.06	Driving skills significantly affected.
4	.20	.18	.15	.13	.11	.10	.09	.08	.08	Possible criminal penalties.
5	.25	.23	.19	.16	.14	.13	.11	.10	.09	
6	.30	.27	.23	.19	.17	.15	.14	.12	.11	
7	.35	.32	.27	.23	.20	.18	.16	.14	.13	
8	.40	.36	.30	.26	.23	.20	.18	.17	.15	Legally intoxicated.
9	.45	.41	.34	.29	.26	.23	.20	.19	.17	Criminal penalties imposed.
10	.51	.45	.38	.32	.28	.25	.23	.21	.19	

Subtract .01% for each 40 minutes of drinking.

*One drink is equal to 1¼ oz. of 80 proof liquor, 12 oz. of beer, or 4 oz. of table wine.

stomach. The rate of alcohol absorption also depends on individual characteristics, including gender and a person's metabolic rate, or the rate at which the body converts nutrients to energy (in this case, the "nutrient" is alcohol). The rate at which alcohol is metabolized determines how long the person will continue to experience the effects of alcohol. The average person metabolizes alcohol at a rate of one third of an ounce of 100 percent alcohol per hour, which is equivalent to an ounce of whiskey per hour. A guide to blood alcohol levels is shown in Table 13.1.

Following a bout of extensive intake of alcohol, a person is likely to experience an abstinence syndrome, what everyone knows as a "hangover." The symptoms of hangover include nausea and vomiting, tremors, extreme thirst, headache, tiredness, irritability, depression, and dizziness. The extent of a person's hangover depends on how much alcohol he or she has consumed and over what period of time. Metabolic rate also affects the duration of a person's hangover. Contrary to whatever advice one hears about homemade remedies, there is no cure for a hangover, other than to wait for the body to recover.

Long-Term Effects

In part, the reason for alcohol's harmful long-term effects may be attributed to the factor of tolerance. The more a person consumes, the more alcohol that person needs to achieve the desired impact. Heavy drinkers tend to increase their intake of alcohol over time, thereby increasing the likelihood of bodily damage. As we will see later, scientists are attempting to understand the biochemical changes associated with long-term heavy alcohol use as a way of comprehending the factors leading to tolerance and dependence.

Alcohol affects almost every organ system in the body, either directly or indirectly. Long-term use of alcohol can lead to permanent brain damage, with symptoms of dementia, blackouts, seizures, hallucinations, and damage to the peripheral parts of the nervous system. Two forms of dementia are associated with long-term, heavy alcohol use: Wernicke's disease and Korsakoff's syndrome. **Wernicke's disease**, as discussed in Chapter 12, is an acute condition involving delirium, eye movement disturbances, difficulties in movement and balance, and deterioration of the peripheral nerves to the hands and feet. The cause of Wernicke's disease is not alcohol itself, but a thiamine (Vitamin B) deficiency due to the deleterious effects of alcohol on the metabolism of nutrients, as well as an overall pattern of poor nutrition. Adequate thiamine intake can reverse Wernicke's disease. People who develop Wernicke's disease are likely to develop **Korsakoff's syndrome**, a permanent form of dementia in which the individual develops retrograde and anterograde amnesia, leading to an inability to remember recent events or to learn new information. It is thought that both disorders represent the same underlying disease process, with Wernicke's being the acute form and Korsakoff's being the chronic form of the disorder. The chances of recovering from Korsakoff's syndrome are less than one in four, and about one quarter of those who have this disorder require permanent institutionalization.

Death from long-term, heavy alcohol use is often associated with liver disease. Most chronic alcohol users develop fatty liver, a condition characterized by abnormal changes in the blood vessels in the liver. This condition develops in 90 to 100 percent of heavy drinkers and may be a precursor to cirrhosis, a degenerative disease that results in progressive and irreversible liver damage. Cirrhosis is one of the primary factors associated with death due to chronic alcohol use. Although the rate of death from this disease has diminished over the past 20 years, it remains the tenth leading cause of death in the United States (Peters, Kochanek, & Murphy, 1998). Heavy alcohol consumption also causes a number of harmful changes in the gastrointestinal system, including inflammation of the esophagus, stomach lining, and pancreas, and a slowing down of smooth muscle contractions throughout the gastrointestinal tract. These conditions can interfere with the process of digestion and can lead to serious nutritional imbalances, including thiamine deficiency, as mentioned earlier, and even malnutrition. A diet that is deficient in zinc may lead to a decrease in the activity of **alcohol dehydrogenase (ADH),** a zinc-containing enzyme in the stomach. ADH breaks down a portion of the alcohol into fatty acids, carbon dioxide, and water before it enters the bloodstream. As a result of lowered ADH activity, a greater portion of the alcohol enters the bloodstream without first being broken down, increasing

The aftermath of a fatal accident. Alcohol is estimated to be involved in about half of all traffic fatalities.

its effect throughout the body. Women appear to be more vulnerable to the effects of alcohol because of their lower amounts of ADH, leading to the dispersion of greater amounts of undigested alcohol throughout the body's tissues. As a result, women reach higher blood alcohol concentrations for a given amount of alcohol consumption, and they are more susceptible to liver disease caused by excessive alcohol intake.

The list of damaging effects of alcohol is long. Chronic alcohol consumption lowers a person's bone strength and puts the individual at risk for developing chronic muscle injury due to atrophy and a bone-weakening disease called osteoporosis. Alcohol can increase a person's risk of developing various forms of cancer, a risk that grows if the individual also smokes cigarettes. A reduction in the functioning of the immune system, which helps fight off cancer as well as infectious diseases, appears to play a role in the deteriorative process. Because of the effects of alcohol on the immune system, people infected with HIV who drink heavily are more likely to accelerate the progression of AIDS. Finally, the abrupt withdrawal of alcohol after chronic usage can result in such symptoms as severe hangover, sleep disturbances, profound anxiety, tremulousness, sympathetic hyperactivity, psychosis, seizures, and even death.

Theories of Alcohol Dependence

Researchers in the field of alcohol dependence were among the first in abnormal psychology to recognize the need for a biopsychosocial model to explain why some people develop alcoholism (Zucker & Gomberg, 1986). This model, as applied to alcohol dependence, emphasizes genetic vulnerability in interaction with influences from the home and peer environments.

Biological Perspective

Researchers are making major advances in understanding the important role that biology plays in determining whether a person becomes dependent on alcohol. Pointing to the influence of genetics, it is a well-established finding that the risk of alcohol dependence runs in families. Siblings of alcohol-dependent individuals have a three to eight times greater risk of becoming dependent themselves. Based on research with twins, the heritability of alcohol dependence is estimated to be 50 to 60 percent, meaning that at least half of the tendency to develop alcohol dependence is due to genetic factors (Reich et al., 1998).

Given the inherited component of alcohol dependence, it seems likely that biological markers could be identified that would help indicate a person's predisposition to the disorder. One potential marker is the individual's subjective reaction to alcohol, or how much alcohol is needed to produce the feeling of being under the influence of the substance. Researchers have found that genetically predisposed people who have less of a subjective reaction following the intake of alcohol in a laboratory seem to be at higher risk of becoming dependent themselves (Schuckit & Smith, 1997). Another possible biological marker is the event-related brain potential (ERP), the positive voltage charge that occurs 300–500 milliseconds after exposure to a stimulus. An abnormal ERP response is an inherited characteristic linked to a high genetic risk for alcohol dependence (Begleiter et al., 1998).

Although there is strong evidence that predisposition to alcohol dependence has a genetic basis, there is much that is not known, such as the number of genes, their locations, and the way in which they lead to vulnerability. It is hoped that the process of genetic mapping will identify genetic markers of alcohol susceptibility that can be linked to behavioral responses to alcohol (Buck, 1995). Most research activity now focuses on a gene called *Gad-1*, which regulates the production of gamma aminobutyric acid (GABA), a derivative of a fatty acid that acts as an inhibitory neurotransmitter in the central nervous system. GABA receptors are highly sensitive to sedatives, such as diazepam (Valium), another central nervous system depressant. They also play a role in the symptoms of alcohol withdrawal, which are associated with physical dependence on alcohol. In trying to locate the Gad-1 gene, researchers work with inbred strains of mice, which are given injections of alcohol and then observed after the alcohol has worn off and they are showing signs of alcohol withdrawal, such as convulsions. Through a process of genetic mapping and selective breeding, researchers have identified three markers on chromosomes 1, 4, and 11 that seem closely linked to withdrawal susceptibility (Buck, Metten, Belknap, & Crabbe, 1997). Two of these sites are on chromosomes with many GABA receptor genes that are also associated with withdrawal from other depressants.

Psychological Perspective

Proponents of the behavioral perspective view alcohol dependence as resulting from a process in which classical conditioning plays a role in the development of cravings (O'Brien, Childress, Ehrman, & Robbins, 1998). However, theorists and researchers realize that alcohol dependence must be due to a broader range of factors. One model that is gaining considerable support is the **expectancy model,** which has evolved from cognitive-behavioral and social learning perspectives (Dimeff & Marlatt, 1998). According to this model, people with alcohol dependence develop problematic beliefs about alcohol relatively early in life through a combination of reinforcement and observational learning.

According to the expectancy model of alcohol dependence, people who are trying to remain abstinent may struggle when faced with situations that cause them to question their ability to control their drinking.

Concepts central to the expectancy model are self-efficacy and coping. Self-efficacy, as you will recall from Chapter 4, refers to an individual's perception that he or she has the ability to meet the challenges of a difficult situation. The concept of coping, as used in the cognitive-behavioral model, refers to the strategies that an individual uses to reduce the perception of a threat or danger. According to the expectancy model, these cognitive factors, along with the individual's ideas or expectations about the effects of alcohol, presumably play a role in determining whether or not an individual will relapse to problem drinking. A sample of an assessment inventory based on the model is shown in Table 13.2.

The expectancy model describes a series of reactions that occurs when an alcohol-dependent individual attempts to remain abstinent. Consider the contrasting cases of Marlene, who has been successful in remaining abstinent, and Edward, who has been unsuccessful. Both Marlene and Edward encounter high-risk situations, such as parties at which other people are consuming alcohol. Marlene is able to abstain from drinking at the party, because she has learned how to cope with such situations, and she feels capable of carrying through with her intention not to drink alcohol. Each successful episode of abstinence reinforces her sense of self-efficacy, causing her to feel more capable of abstaining in subsequent situations. Unlike Marlene, some individuals, such as Edward, lack a satisfactory coping response. The actual consumption of alcohol is not what leads to a relapse but, rather, the individual's interpretation of the act of drinking as a sign of loss of self-control. Thus, when Edward enters a high-risk situation, he feels incapable of staying away from alcohol because of his low sense of self-efficacy. A compelling expectation that alcohol will have a positive mood-altering effect adds to his low sense of self-efficacy and leads him to take the first drink. The positive sensations the alcohol produces further undermine Edward's resolve, but cognitive factors enter at this point in the process as well. Having violated the self-imposed rule of remaining abstinent, he now is subject to the **abstinence violation effect,** a sense of loss of

Table 13.2

Sample Items from Expectancy-Based Assessment Measures

The Inventory of Drinking Situations is used to determine which situations represent a high risk for the alcohol dependent individual. Each item is rated on the following 4-point scale: "I DRANK HEAVILY—Never, Rarely, Frequently, Almost Always." The items on the Situational Confidence Questionnaire (Annis, 1984) are the same but are rated according to the scale of "I WOULD BE ABLE TO RESIST THE URGE TO DRINK HEAVILY," with percentages ranging from Not at All Confident (0 percent) to Very Confident (100 percent).

Determinants	Item	Scale
Intrapersonal	When I felt that I had let myself down	Negative emotional state
	When I had trouble sleeping	Negative physical state
	When I felt confident and relaxed	Positive emotional state
	When I convinced myself that I was a new person now and could take a few drinks	Testing personal control
	When I remembered how good it tasted	Urges and temptations
Interpersonal	When other people treated me unfairly	Social rejection
	When pressure built up at work because of the demands of my superior	Work problems
	When I felt uneasy in the presence of someone	Tension
	When I had an argument with a friend	Family/friends problems
	When I was out with friends and they stopped by for a drink	Social pressure to drink
	When I was out with friends "on the town" and wanted to increase my enjoyment	Social drinking
	When I wanted to heighten my sexual enjoyment	Intimacy

control over one's behavior that has an overwhelming and demoralizing effect (see Figure 13.2). Thus, Edward's self-efficacy is further eroded, initiating a downward spiral, which eventually ends in renewed alcohol dependence.

Sociocultural Perspective

Researchers and theorists working within the sociocultural perspective regard stressors within the family, community, and culture as factors that, when combined with genetic vulnerability, lead the individual to develop alcohol dependence. The sociocultural perspective was given support in a landmark longitudinal study conducted in the early 1980s. Researchers followed individuals from childhood or adolescence to adulthood, the time when most individuals who become alcohol dependent make the transition from social or occasional alcohol use to dependence (Zucker & Gomberg, 1986). Those most likely to become alcohol dependent in adulthood had a history of childhood antisocial behavior, including aggressive and sadistic behavior, trouble with the law, rebelliousness, lower achievement in school, completion of fewer years of school, and a higher truancy rate. These individuals also showed a variety of behaviors possibly indicative of early neural dysfunction, including nervousness and fretfulness as infants, hyperactivity as children, and poor physical coordination. It was thought that these characteristics reflect a genetically based vulnerability, which, when combined with environmental stresses, leads to the development of alcohol dependence. More recent studies

have continued to support the role of family environment as influenced by larger sociocultural factors. In a 4-year study of more than 400 adolescents, researchers found higher rates of alcohol use among children from families with lower socioeconomic and income levels. Family composition also played a role in the development of alcohol abuse, with the children from stepfamilies at higher risk for using alcohol (Duncan, Duncan, & Hops, 1998).

Another approach within the sociocultural perspective focuses on the offspring of parents who are dependent on alcohol. According to this perspective, adult children of alcoholics (ACOAs) are at a heightened risk for developing difficulties in their relationships with others (Woititz, 1983) and are at a higher risk for becoming dependent on alcohol. For example, because of their chaotic and unpredictable home life during childhood, these people go through life finding it difficult to know what "normal" is. They are unable to have fun, and they have difficulty establishing intimate relationships. Further, according to this view, they tend to feel different from other people, act impulsively, lie, and desperately seek approval and attention. The increasing recognition given to the problems shared by children of alcoholics has helped many people gain self-understanding. Although this is a compelling argument, it is important to recognize that the research support for the ACOA perspective is mixed. Research focusing on personality characteristics that differentiate ACOAs from non-ACOAs does not support such a broad-based set of distinctions (Mintz,

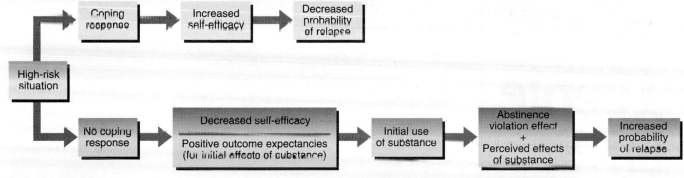

Figure 13.2

A cognitive-behavioral model of the relapse process

Kashubeck, & Tracy, 1995). There is a risk of overidentifying with the list of ACOA-related traits, because they are so general that at least some of them can apply to virtually anyone (Logue, Sher, & Frensch, 1992).

Critics may raise questions about the legitimacy of general characterizations of the family members of alcoholics, but there is no question that alcohol-related disorders create emotional stress for individuals and families. In addition, there is a wider social cost. Besides the damaging effects of substances on the fabric of society, there are the exorbitant financial costs associated with medical treatment for alcohol-related conditions, lost work time, the loss of human life, and the treatment of children with fetal alcohol syndrome. In one recent year, the societal cost of alcohol abuse and dependence was estimated to be $148 billion (NIDA, 1998).

Treatment of Alcohol Dependence

The search for the effective treatment of alcohol dependence has been a difficult and challenging process. Alcohol use is so much a part of Western culture that many people who abuse or are dependent on alcohol do not realize that their behavior is problematic. There are no legal sanctions against the use of alcohol other than a minimum drinking age; in fact, endorsements of drinking as a socially acceptable behavior frequently appear in advertising. Little consideration is given to the down side of alcohol consumption—namely, that it can involve a serious disorder. Nor is much attention given to the fact that alcohol-related disorders are treatable.

Most alcohol-dependent individuals do not seek treatment voluntarily. Of the millions of Americans who abuse or are dependent on alcohol, less than 10 percent receive treatment. Most people with alcohol problems have a remarkable capacity for denial, insisting to themselves and to others that their alcohol consumption is not really a problem (Massella, 1991).

Biological Treatment

The biological treatment of alcohol dependence consists of medications used for a variety of alcohol-related problems. Some medications are used to control symptoms of co-existing conditions; for example, benzodiazepines can manage the symptoms

of withdrawal and prevent the development of **delirium tremens,** a physical condition consisting of autonomic nervous system dysfunction, confusion, and possibly seizures. Other antianxiety medications, and antidepressants, may help reduce the individual's dependence on alcohol by alleviating the symptoms of anxiety and depression, which can foster the need for alcohol.

There are other medications for treating alcohol dependence, and they are designed to counter the presumed brain changes associated with drinking. These medications stimulate various neurotransmitter systems that produce biochemical changes in the brain. The GABA system is one logical target, because it is implicated in both the short- and long-term changes in the brain associated with alcohol intake. Agents that interact with GABA receptors in the brain reduce alcohol intoxication and consumption in laboratory animals. Although the results of interventions with humans given acamprosate, a medication that acts on the GABA system, are encouraging (Sass, Soyka, Mann, & Zieglgansberger, 1996), not all individuals respond to this treatment (Chick, 1995). Favorable outcomes have been achieved with citalopram, a medication that inhibits the uptake of serotonin, thus raising the available level of serotonin in the nervous system (Tiihonen et al., 1996). Buspirone, a medication used in treating anxiety disorders, also appears to reduce alcohol consumption in dependent individuals through its effects on serotonin uptake. Medications that decrease the amount of effective dopamine in the brain also seem to have promise as a way to reduce alcohol dependence and consumption.

Naltrexone, marketed as ReVia, is a medication that has been used for more than a decade to treat opioid addictions and is now regarded as an effective treatment for alcohol dependence. The way in which naltrexone works is not well understood, but researchers do know that it blocks the pleasurable effects of opioids that a person ingests, as well as the body's own opioids. (It is thought that, when alcohol is consumed, the brain releases its own opioids.) As a result, a person taking naltrexone who then drinks alcohol will find the experience much less reinforcing and is therefore more likely to abstain, presumably making a more comprehensive intervention, such as psychotherapy, more viable (Volpicelli et al., 1995).

Another category of medications used to treat alcohol dependence consists of those that are intended to produce a strongly aversive physiological reaction when a person drinks. This method relies on an aversive conditioning process, in

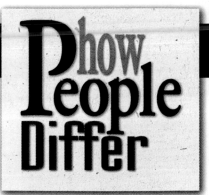

The Influence of Race and Culture on Alcoholism

Researchers have discovered that the symptoms of alcoholism are consistent across a variety of cultures and ethnic groups (Helzer, Burnam, & McEvoy, 1991), but their work has also demonstrated differences in prevalence and possible precipitants to alcohol dependence. Perhaps no one will ever develop an exhaustive list of the myriad factors that influence drinking behavior, but an examination of current perspectives on cultural and racial differences in alcohol abuse and dependence sheds light on how social settings and expectations influence the development of the disorder.

Alcohol use is common throughout the world, yet different societies view drinking in very different ways. For example, in some American societies, such as the Amish and certain conservative religious orders, alcohol use is strictly discouraged or prohibited. On the other hand, in many European societies, alcohol is integrated into the daily diet and is a standard accompaniment to meals. In some Asian societies, it is acceptable for men to consume large quantities of alcohol, often in the company of work colleagues. In those societies, drinking by women is strongly discouraged.

Differences in social views of alcohol consumption highlight the interplay of culture and symptomatology. In one study, for example, African American and Caucasian men developed alcoholism at similar rates, yet the African American men experienced significantly more alcohol-related problems, including health and interpersonal problems (Herd, 1994). As a group, the African American men were less tolerant of drinking outside of social settings—for instance, when driving or with young children. For others, their religious affiliation provided an ethical stance against intoxication. At the same time, many of the African American men included in the study had come from disadvantaged, urban environments. Disadvantages in health care, employment, and education, combined with a higher police presence relative to affluent neighborhoods, might have contributed to the relatively higher frequency of alcohol-related problems. Interestingly, similar cultural and social deprivations seem to contribute to the high rates of alcoholism in Russia and other countries of the former Soviet bloc (Anderson & Hibbs, 1992).

Cross-cultural studies have demonstrated lower rates of alcoholism in some Asian countries, such as Taiwan and Korea, relative to Western nations (Helzer et al., 1990). Although heavy drinking by men may become problematic when sanctioned in certain work settings, drinking by women and drinking outside of social situations are often discouraged. Furthermore, some members of Asian cultures seem vulnerable to the buildup of potentially toxic by-products of alcohol, making intoxication a potentially unpleasant experience.

Women may differ from men in their patterns of alcohol use and dependence. While men may drink to excess to suppress painful emotions, women seem more likely to drink to escape painful interpersonal situations (Hodgins, el-Guebaly, & Armstrong, 1995). In traditional, male-dominated societies, strong prohibitions may prevent women from drinking to the point of intoxication, accounting for the low rates of alcoholism among Hispanic and Asian women (Canino, 1994; Helzer et al., 1990).

These are just a few of the possible explanations for the variability in patterns of alcohol use and alcoholism throughout the world. Despite this variability, it is important to remember that alcohol dependence is a problem worldwide and that each individual who becomes dependent may have reached that point for a variety of reasons, including biological predisposition, psychological distress, and cultural influences.

---

which the unpleasant reaction to alcohol provoked by the medication causes the individual to form a negative association to alcohol intake, providing a strong incentive for not drinking. The medication used in this form of treatment is **disulfiram,** known popularly as Antabuse. Disulfiram inhibits **aldehyde dehydrogenase (ALDH),** an enzyme that, along with ADH, is responsible for metabolizing alcohol. When ALDH is inhibited, the level of blood acetaldehyde, a toxic substance, rises, and within 30 minutes the individual experiences a severe physical reaction lasting for as long as 1 hour. Depending on the amount of alcohol in the body, this reaction includes a headache, hot and flushed face, chest pain, weakness, sweating, thirst, blurred vision, confusion, rapid heart rate and palpitations, a drop in blood pressure, difficulty breathing, nausea, and vomiting. Although relatively effective in curbing the craving for alcohol, most experts recommend that this be combined with psychosocial interventions (Tinsley, Finlayson, & Morse, 1998). Another treatment strategy is to combine acamprosate with disulfiram in an attempt to improve effectiveness (Besson et al., 1998). The use of disulfiram is not without risks, however. Because of the intensity of the physical reaction it provokes, disulfiram must be used with caution for individuals with cirrhosis, a disorder that is common among chronic alcohol users (Saxon, Sloan, Reoux, & Haver, 1998).

Before leaving the topic of pharmacological treatments for alcohol dependence, it is important to point out that such treatments are controversial. Criticism roots on what some perceive as an irony—using one form of substance to eliminate the abuse of another. Furthermore, these treatments have yet to prove their effectiveness over the long term in the treatment of individuals with alcohol dependence (Schuckit, 1996).

Psychological Treatment

Although disulfiram is a biological intervention, you can see that it relies heavily on the behavioral principles of aversive conditioning. It is not an ideal aversive stimulus, however, because its effects are not immediate. Other behavioral methods use an aversive conditioning model in which something unpleasant, such as a mild electric shock, occurs in direct association with alcohol consumption during a treatment session. Again, although this approach appears to have obvious merit and has been used for more than 50 years, most experts do not regard its effectiveness rate to be high enough to counter the objections about its safety (Cannon, Baker, Gino, & Nathan, 1988).

In the **cue exposure method**, another behavioral approach, the individual is given a priming dose of alcohol, which initiates the craving for more alcohol. At that point, the individual is urged to refuse further alcohol. Each successive treatment constitutes an extinction trial intended to reduce craving. This method shows promise as a means of reducing problem drinking in people who do not meet the criteria for alcohol dependence (Sitharthan, Sitharthan, Hough, & Kavanagh, 1997). However, among individuals hospitalized for alcohol dependence, the exposure to alcohol cues can have an effect opposite to the intended outcome, leading to an increased craving for alcohol (Stasiewicz et al., 1997).

An alternative to approaches aimed at replacing positive associations to alcohol with aversive ones is **relapse prevention therapy,** a treatment method developed by University of Washington psychologist G. Alan Marlatt and his colleagues. This method is based on the expectancy model (Dimeff & Marlatt, 1998). Built into the model is the assumption that alcohol-dependent individuals invariably are faced with the temptation to have a drink and at some point fail to follow through with the desire to abstain. What happens at that point is crucial. According to the notion of the abstinence violation effect, if the lapse is seen as a sign of weakness, or a character flaw, this will damage the individual's sense of self-efficacy so severely that the possibility of future abstinence seems out of the question. If, instead, the individual can learn to interpret the drinking episode as a single incident that was unfortunate but not a permanent failing, the individual's self-efficacy can remain intact and a relapse can be prevented.

In relapse prevention, the individual learns decision-making abilities that make it possible for him or her to analyze a high-risk situation and determine which coping skills would work best to prevent a relapse. Skill training can also help individuals learn how to express and receive positive and negative feelings, how to initiate contact, and how to reply to criticism. For example, consider the case of a woman named Sheila, who knows that going to a party will put her in a high-risk situation. For years, Sheila believed that she needed alcohol in such situations so that she could "loosen up," thereby appearing more likable and lively. Now that she is trying to maintain abstinence, she can make alternative plans prior to going to a party that will prepare her with coping skills, such as staying away from the bar and asking a friend to keep her glass full with a nonalcoholic beverage. Cognitive restructuring would help Sheila interpret high-risk situations more productively. If she believes that it is necessary to have alcohol to be popular and lively, she can learn to reframe this belief, so she can see that people like her even if she is not high on alcohol. Maintenance is an important part of the treatment approach as well; therefore, Marlatt emphasizes the need for continued therapeutic contacts, social support from friends and family, and changes in lifestyle to find alternate sources of gratification. Sheila needs to keep in periodic contact with her therapist, to find new friends and seek help from her family, and to find other ways to socialize, such as joining a health club. Skill training and the development of alternate coping methods can also be combined with behavioral techniques, such as cue exposure (Marlatt, 1990).

The goal of relapse prevention cannot be achieved in one step; rather, it requires a graded program that exposes the individual to high-risk situations in greater and greater increments. At each step, the therapist encourages the individual to draw inferences from successful behavior that will reinforce feelings of self-efficacy. The relapse prevention model is growing in popularity. Furthermore, the effectiveness of interventions involving self-control can be improved when stress management principles are incorporated into the program and when clients are given help in improving supportive relationships with others outside the therapeutic setting (Hodgson, 1994).

Alcoholics Anonymous

While biologists and psychologists continue to explore treatment approaches based on scientific models of alcohol dependence, one intervention model, whose roots are in spirituality rather than science, continues to be used on a widespread basis: Alcoholics Anonymous, or AA. This movement was founded in 1935 by Bill W., a Wall Street stockbroker, and Dr. Bob, a surgeon from Akron, Ohio, and from these humble beginnings AA has grown to worldwide proportions. More than 2 million members participate in approximately 98,000 AA groups throughout the world (http://www.alcoholicsanonymous.org/en24doc4.html). Along with an increase in the number of AA participants have been a general acceptance and recognition of the value of this approach, and it is now a component of most treatment programs in the United States.

The standard recovery program in AA involves a strong commitment to participate in AA-related activities, with the most important component being the AA meeting. Every AA meeting begins with an introduction of members, who state their first names, followed by the statement "I am an alcoholic." This ritual is the basis for the name of the program, Alcoholics Anonymous, meaning that members never consider themselves not to be alcoholics and that they are not required to divulge their identities. During the meeting, one or more members share their experiences about how they developed drinking problems, the suffering their drinking caused, the personal debasement they may have

Meetings are central to the Alcoholics Anonymous movement. Members describe their experiences with alcohol dependence, hoping to inspire others to resist the omnipresent temptations of the addiction.

felt when they lied and cheated, and how they "hit bottom" and began to turn around their drinking patterns and their lives. The 12 steps to recovery form the heart of AA's philosophy. This emphasis on honesty, confrontation, and storytelling is seen as the essential element of the 12-step program. The popularity and massive development of AA have led to many variants on the basic theme, with specialized groups for nonsmokers, single-gender groups, and members of alternative lifestyles, for example (Johnson & Chappel, 1994). (See Table 13.3.)

The second component of AA is the constant availability of another member, called a sponsor, who can provide support during times of crisis, when the urge to drink becomes overpowering. Round-the-clock hot lines staffed by AA volunteers also help make such assistance continuously available. Third, the spiritual element is a major factor within the AA movement, in that members admit that they are powerless over alcohol and turn over their lives to a power greater than themselves. The AA experience differs considerably from person to person, with some people deriving benefit from attendance at meetings, and others from adherence to the spiritual principles (Caldwell & Cutler, 1998).

The fundamental approach that AA fosters with regard to understanding alcohol dependence is that alcoholism is a disease that prevents those who have it from controlling their drinking (Yalisove, 1998). If the alcoholic does succumb to temptation and goes on a drinking binge, this is attributed within the AA model not to a moral failing but to a biological process. A second tenet of AA is that alcoholics are never cured; they are "recovering." The goal of AA treatment is total abstinence. According to the AA philosophy, one drink is enough to send the individual back into a state of alcohol dependence.

An offshoot of AA was formed in the early 1950s for relatives and friends of people with alcohol dependence. Called Al-Anon, to distinguish it from AA, this program provides support for people who are close to alcoholics and need help to cope with the problems alcoholism creates in their lives. A later

Substance Dependence

MINI-CASE (ALCOHOL DEPENDENCE)

Rhona is a 55-year-old homemaker married to a successful builder. Every afternoon, she makes herself the first of a series of daiquiris. On many evenings, she has passed out on the couch by the time her husband arrives home from work. Rhona lost her driver's license a year ago after being arrested three times on charges of driving while intoxicated. Although Rhona's family has urged her to obtain treatment for her disorder, she denies that she has a problem because she can "control" her drinking. The mother of three grown children, Rhona began to drink around the age of 45, when her youngest child left for college. Prior to this time, Rhona kept herself extremely busy through her children's extracurricular activities. When she found herself alone every afternoon, she took solace in having an early cocktail. Over a period of several years, the "cocktail" developed into a series of five or six strong drinks. Rhona's oldest daughter has lately begun to insist that something be done for her mother. She does not want to see Rhona develop the fatal alcohol-related illness that caused the premature death of her grandmother.

■ Why would Rhona's pattern of alcohol use be regarded as dependence rather than abuse?

■ What factors in her life may be contributing to Rhona's use of alcohol?

DIAGNOSTIC FEATURES

● During a 12-month period, people with substance dependence show at least three of the following:

● Tolerance

● Withdrawal

● Use of the substance in larger amounts or over a longer period than intended

● Persistent desire or unsuccessful efforts to cut down or control substance use

● Extensive time devoted to activities involved in obtaining, using, or recovering from substance use

● A giving up of or reduction in important activities because of substance use

● Continued use despite knowledge of a substance-caused physical or psychological problem

Table 13.3

Is AA for You?

Answer "yes" or "no" to the following questions.

1. **Have you ever decided to stop drinking for a week or so, but lasted for only a couple of days?**
   Most of us in AA made all kinds of promises to ourselves and to our families. We could not keep them. Then we came to AA. AA said: "Just try not to drink today." (If you do not drink today, you cannot get drunk today.)

2. **Do you wish people would mind their own business about your drinking—stop telling you what to do?**
   In AA we do not *tell* anyone to do anything. We just talk about our own drinking, the trouble we got into, and how we stopped. We will be glad to help you, if you want us to.

3. **Have you ever switched from one kind of drink to another in the hope that this would keep you from getting drunk?**
   We tried all kinds of ways. We made our drinks weak. Or just drank beer. Or we did not drink cocktails. Or drank only on weekends. You name it, we tried it. But, if we drank *anything* with alcohol in it, we usually got drunk eventually.

4. **Have you had to have an eye-opener on awakening during the past year?**
   Do you need a drink to get started, or to stop shaking? This is a pretty sure sign that you are not drinking "socially."

5. **Do you envy people who can drink without getting into trouble?**
   At one time or another, most of us have wondered why we were not like most people, who really can take it or leave it.

6. **Have you had problems connected with drinking during the past year?**
   Be honest! Doctors say that, if you have a problem with alcohol and keep on drinking, it will get worse—never better. Eventually, you will die, or end up in an institution for the rest of your life. The only hope is to stop drinking.

7. **Has your drinking caused trouble at home?**
   Before we came into AA, most of us said that it was the people or problems at home that made us drink. We could not see that our drinking just made everything worse. It never solved problems anywhere or anytime.

8. **Do you ever try to get "extra" drinks at a party because you do not get enough?**
   Most of us used to have a "few" before we started out if we thought it was going to be that kind of party. And, if drinks were not served fast enough, we would go someplace else to get more.

9. **Do you tell yourself you can stop drinking any time you want to, even though you keep getting drunk when you don't mean to?**
   Many of us kidded ourselves into thinking that we drank because we wanted to. After we came into AA, we found out that, once we started to drink, we couldn't stop.

10. **Have you missed days of work or school because of drinking?**
    Many of us admit now that we "called in sick" lots of times when the truth was that we were hung-over or on a drunk.

11. **Do you have "blackouts"?**
    A "blackout" is when we have been drinking hours or days which we cannot remember. When we came to AA, we found out that this is a pretty sure sign of alcoholic drinking.

12. **Have you ever felt that your life would be better if you did not drink?**
    Many of us started to drink because drinking made life seem better, at least for a while. By the time we got into AA, we felt trapped. We were drinking to live and living to drink. We were sick and tired of being sick and tired.

What's Your Score?

Did you answer "yes" four or more times? If so, you are probably in trouble with alcohol. Why do we say this? Because thousands of people in AA have said so for many years. They found out the truth about themselves—the hard way. But, again, only *you* can decide whether you think AA is for you. Try to keep an open mind on the subject. If the answer is yes, we will be glad to show you how we stopped drinking ourselves. Just call. AA does not promise to solve your life's problems. But we can show you how we are learning to live without drinking "one day at a time." We stay away from that "first drink." If there is no first one, there cannot be a tenth one. And, when we got rid of alcohol, we found that life became much more manageable.

ALCOHOLICS ANONYMOUS® is a fellowship of men and women who share their experience, strength and hope with each other that they may solve their common problem and help others to recover from alcoholism.
- The only requirement for membership is a desire to stop drinking. There are no dues or fees for AA membership; we are self-supporting through our own contributions.
- AA is not allied with any sect, denomination, politics, organization or institution; does not wish to engage in any controversy; neither endorses nor opposes any causes.
- Our primary purpose is to stay sober and help other alcoholics to achieve sobriety.

movement, called Alateen, is specifically designed for teenagers whose lives have been affected by alcoholism in the family. As we mentioned earlier, there are also groups for adult children of alcoholics, which focus on the psychological problems that result from growing up in a family with an alcoholic parent. There are currently 30,000 Al-Anon and Alateen groups existing in 112 countries (http://www.al-anon.alateen.org/helppro.html).

Millions of people credit AA for their sobriety; in addition, proponents of AA cite glowing outcome figures, which, if correct, would make it the most successful approach to treating alcohol dependence. According to AA, the average length of abstinence is slightly over 4 years; 29 percent have been abstinent for more than 5 years, 38 percent from 1 to 5 years, and 33 percent for less than a year. One survey conducted in Finland and based on "anniversary announcements" of sobriety in the AA newsletters reported that, among those reaching 5-year sobriety anniversaries, 90 percent continued as sober members for at least another year (Makela, 1994).

What lessons can researchers and clinicians learn from AA? We can see from the elements involved in this program that AA has much in common with a cognitive-behavioral approach. AA encourages the alcohol-dependent individual to avoid self-blame for failures and to develop alternative coping skills, features shared with the expectancy model that may also enhance the outcome of AA (Morgenstern et al., 1997). Similarly, AA encourages the individual to use coping skills that rely on seeking help from outside the self rather than from within. Both approaches, however, share the element of recommending continued contact with the treatment provider. They also include an emphasis on social support, one of the most striking elements in the AA model. All alcohol treatment programs, however, share the major limitation of appealing to and being effective with only those who are motivated to change. Without that motivation, neither medication nor the most elaborate psychological treatment strategy will have a lasting impact.

■ Substances Other Than Alcohol

Various substances other than alcohol have the potential for abuse and dependence. In the following sections, we will review the major categories of substances and examine their effects on behavior and their mechanisms of action. Many of these drugs share features, however, in that they alter the neurons in an area of the brain involved in the regulation of pleasure or reward.

Dopamine is one of the major neurotransmitters involved in this pleasure pathway. The functions associated with dopamine in addition to the sensation of pleasure include motor movement, awareness, judgment, and motivation. A circuit of dopamine-producing neurons located at the top of the brainstem in an area called the ventral tegmental area (VTA) plays a particularly important role in regulating the sensation of pleasure (see Figure 13.3).

These neurons relay messages about pleasure to neurons in a structure within the limbic system called the nucleus accumbens. They also project to the frontal cortex. This entire circuit is known as the mesolimbic dopamine system. It is thought to play a role in survival, in that the sensation of pleasure associated with such activities as eating and sexual arousal helps ensure that organisms engage in activities that maintain life and perpetuate the species.

Psychoactive drugs seem to activate the mesolimbic dopamine system. Substances such as heroin and LSD mimic the effects of a natural neurotransmitter on the neurons in the brain's pleasure center. Others, such as PCP, block the synaptic receptors and, consequently, interfere with normal transmission. Such drugs as cocaine interfere with the molecules responsible for ensuring that dopamine is absorbed from the synapse back to the neurons that released them. Drugs such as methamphetamine stimulate the excess release of neurotransmitters, resulting in heightened stimulation and arousal. Thus, many drugs with abuse potential become addictive by virtue of their actions on the dopamine system in the mesolimbic pathway, even though each drug may operate according to a different mechanism.

Over a prolonged period of time, the constant use of one of these substances produces permanent changes in the brain. If the substance is not present in the individual's nervous system, the neurons change their functioning. For example, in the case of cocaine, dopamine accumulates in the synapses because cocaine blocks the reabsorption of dopamine by the presynaptic neurons. As the dopamine accumulates, the neurons with dopamine receptors decrease the number of receptors they produce, a process called "down regulation." If the individual stops taking cocaine, dopamine levels eventually return to normal, but now there are fewer dopamine receptors available to be stimulated. The individual experiences this state as a craving for higher levels of dopamine, leading to a desire for more cocaine. Another change that occurs in the brain is the destruction of neurons as a result of long-term or heavy substance use.

In attempting to understand the role of biology in drug dependence, researchers have searched for genes that control levels of dopamine, the neurotransmitter thought to play a primary role in the brain's response to drugs. For various reasons, researchers must rely on evidence from animal models. One approach involves removing a specific gene in mice and observing the results (these mice are appropriately called "knockout" mice). Such a manipulation was performed on the gene for a protein called Nurr1. When this happened, the mice failed to generate neurons containing dopamine in the midbrain area involved in the brain's pleasure circuit. One effect of such a manipulation was that the mice continued to have reduced dopamine levels into adulthood (Zetterstrom et al., 1997). If this result is generalized to humans, it would mean that such an abnormality may cause a craving for drugs to counteract the dopamine deficiency. A second approach involves studying the response to drugs among inbred mice with identical genetic makeups. Using this strategy, researchers have found differences among these mice strains in their responses to drugs, with some strains refusing most drugs and others showing preferences for many drugs of abuse (Crabbe, Gallagher, Cross, & Belknap, 1998; Grisel et al., 1997).

Among humans, the situation is obviously far more complicated. However, some progress has been made by comparing the DNA of people who abuse drugs with the DNA of people who do not. This method has resulted in the identification of a gene that

THE BRAIN

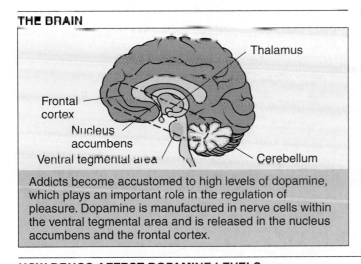

Thalamus

Frontal cortex

Nucleus accumbens

Ventral tegmental area

Cerebellum

Addicts become accustomed to high levels of dopamine, which plays an important role in the regulation of pleasure. Dopamine is manufactured in nerve cells within the ventral tegmental area and is released in the nucleus accumbens and the frontal cortex.

DOPAMINE'S NORMAL ACTION

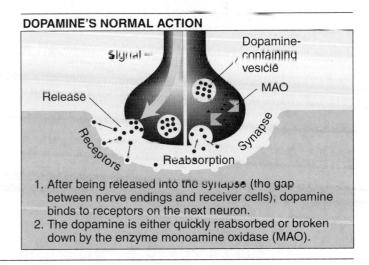

Signal

Dopamine-containing vesicle

MAO

Release

Receptors

Synapse

Reabsorption

1. After being released into the synapse (the gap between nerve endings and receiver cells), dopamine binds to receptors on the next neuron.
2. The dopamine is either quickly reabsorbed or broken down by the enzyme monoamine oxidase (MAO).

HOW DRUGS AFFECT DOPAMINE LEVELS

Cocaine

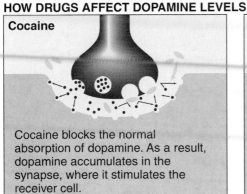

Cocaine blocks the normal absorption of dopamine. As a result, dopamine accumulates in the synapse, where it stimulates the receiver cell.

Amphetamines

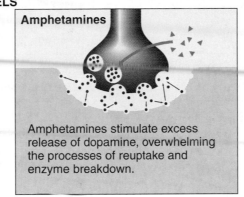

Amphetamines stimulate excess release of dopamine, overwhelming the processes of reuptake and enzyme breakdown.

Cigarettes

Nicotine

MAO

Blocker

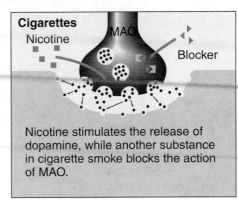

Nicotine stimulates the release of dopamine, while another substance in cigarette smoke blocks the action of MAO.

Figure 13.3

Normal action of dopamine. Dopamine is released into the synapse and binds to receptors on the postsynaptic neuron. The dopamine is either reabsorbed or broken down by monoamine oxidase (MAO).

leads to the production of the COMT enzyme (catechol-o-methyl-transferase). This enzyme, found throughout the body, is involved in breaking down and inactivating dopamine. The version of the gene that produces higher levels of COMT is found more often in individuals who are drug abusers (Vandenbergh et al., 1997). In another approach, researchers investigated the role of subjective responses to drugs. In an unusual study of subjective responses to marijuana in identical twins and fraternal twins, researchers found that identical twin pairs were more likely than fraternal twin pairs to have similar reactions to the drug, a finding that supports the notion that there is a genetic component involved in the ways people experience the effects of drugs (Lyons et al., 1997).

Clearly, more research on humans is needed to understand the contribution of genetic factors to drug abuse and dependence. Furthermore, in humans, as compared with mice, learning and environmental factors are important contributors that add to whatever genetic vulnerabilities may exist. For example, in one comprehensive long-term study of more than 650 teenagers, the use of alcohol, cigarettes, and marijuana was tracked. Various factors were found to be powerful influences associated with increased substance use; these factors included the failure of parents to monitor their children, conflict between parents and children, academic failure, and the influential behavior of their peers (Duncan, Duncan, Biglan, & Ary, 1998).

As we will see later, current treatment programs rely heavily on psychosocial factors (in conjunction with medical treatments), but, in the future, treatment based on insights gained from genetic research may also hold important potential for curbing the cravings that initially predispose an individual to a life of drug dependence (Crawley et al., 1997).

Stimulants

You have perhaps on occasion wished you could be more alert and energetic. You may have sought a "pick-me-up," such as a cup of coffee. Caffeine is just one substance in a category of drugs called **stimulants**—substances that have an activating effect on the nervous system. The stimulants associated with psychological disorders are amphetamines, cocaine, and caffeine. These differ in their chemical structure, their specific physical and psychological effects, and their potential danger to the user. In the following sections, we will discuss the major stimulant drugs.

Amphetamines

Amphetamines are stimulants, or "uppers," that cause a range of effects, depending on the amount, method, and duration of use, as well as the specific form of the drug that is taken. In

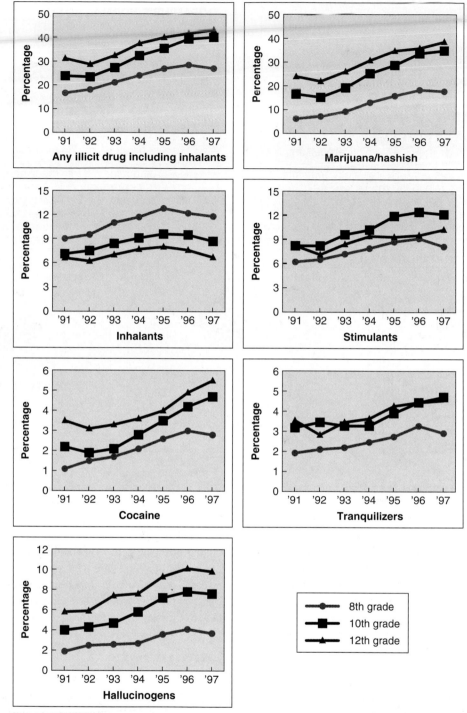

Figure 13.4

Trends in annual prevalence of lifetime use of illicit drugs for eighth- tenth- and twelfth-graders.

Source: Monitoring the Future Study (www.isr.umich.edu/scr/mtf).

moderate amounts taken orally, amphetamines and related drugs cause euphoria, increased confidence, talkativeness, and energy. When taken intravenously, amphetamines have more powerful effects. Immediately after injection, the user feels a surge, or "rush," of extremely pleasurable sensations that some describe as similar to orgasm. A smokeable methamphetamine called "ice" (because of its crystalline appearance) is a highly addictive and toxic amphetamine.

One reason that amphetamines become a problem for users is that people quickly build up tolerance. For example, people who use them for dieting find that, after a certain period (as brief as 4 to 6 weeks), they must use higher doses to maintain the same appetite suppressant effect. At that point, they have become dependent on the drug's mood-altering results. Tolerance to amphetamines also extends to psychological effects. In order to achieve the same "high," long-term

Amphetamine Dependence

MINI-CASE

Catherine is a 23-year-old salesperson who tried for 3 years to lose weight. Her physician prescribed amphetamines but cautioned her about the possibility that she might become dependent on them. She did begin to lose weight, but she also discovered that she liked the extra energy and good feelings caused by the diet pills. When Catherine returned to her doctor after having lost the desired weight, she asked him for a refill of her prescription to help her maintain her new figure. When he refused, Catherine asked around among her friends until she found the name of a physician who was willing to accommodate her wishes for ongoing refills of the prescription. Over the course of a year, Catherine has developed a number of psychological problems, including depression, paranoid thinking, and irritability. Despite the fact that she realizes that something is wrong, she feels driven to continue using the drug.

■ Why would Catherine be regarded as dependent on amphetamines?

■ What kind of personality traits would you expect to find in a person who has such limited control over both eating behavior and substance dependence?

DIAGNOSTIC FEATURES

● During a 12-month period, people with amphetamine dependence show at least three of the following:

 ● Tolerance

 ● Withdrawal

 ● Use of amphetamines in larger amounts or over a longer period than intended

 ● Persistent desire or unsuccessful efforts to cut down or control amphetamine use

 ● Extensive time devoted to activities involved in obtaining, using, or recovering from amphetamine use

 ● A giving up of or reduction in important activities because of amphetamine use

 ● Continued use despite knowledge of a amphetamine-caused physical or psychological problem

---

users must take greater doses of the drug. A debate exists about whether amphetamines cause physical dependence, but most researchers agree that these drugs are psychologically addictive.

Although an overdose of amphetamines rarely results in death, many medical problems can occur, such as stroke, heart irregularity, kidney failure, temporary paralysis, circulatory collapse, seizures, and even coma. Some users develop psychotic symptoms, including delusions, hallucinations, or profound mood disturbance. Paranoid delusions may develop, as well as tactile hallucinations, such as feeling that bugs are crawling on the skin. People in this state may have little control over their behavior; feeling terrified or out of control, they may act in violent or self-destructive ways.

When people discontinue amphetamines after heavy usage, they exhibit withdrawal symptoms, called "crashing," that include profound depression, extreme hunger, craving for the drug, exhaustion, and disturbed sleep. These symptoms can last for 2 weeks or more, and some residual problems may last for a year.

The route to amphetamine dependence can occur in one of two ways: through medical abuse or through street abuse. In medical abuse, the individual begins taking amphetamines for a medical reason, such as to reduce weight or to treat fatigue, increasing the dose as tolerance develops and obtaining the drug by seeking multiple or refillable prescriptions. Efforts to stop taking the drug result in an increase of the symptoms it was intended to reduce, leading the individual to increase dosages to harmful levels. Because of these worrisome effects, ethical physicians are reluctant to prescribe these medications. Street abusers take amphetamines deliberately to alter their state of consciousness, perhaps in alternation with depressants. An even more dangerous mode of amphetamine use involves taking the drug in "runs" of continuous ingestion for 2 to 4 days, a pattern that often results in withdrawal and psychosis.

Cocaine

Cocaine became the drug of choice for recreational users during the 1980s and spread to every segment of the population. The widespread availability of **crack cocaine,** a crystallized, inexpensive form of street cocaine that is usually smoked, has added to the problem.

Cocaine has a fascinating history that dates back thousands of years. In the United States, its popular use can be traced to the late 1800s, when it was marketed as a cure for everything from fatigue to malaria. A major pharmaceutical company, Parke-Davis, sold tablets, sprays, and cigarettes that contained cocaine. Coca-Cola was developed in the 1880s, and its stimulating mixture of cocaine and caffeine made it a popular beverage. The cocaine was eliminated from Coca-Cola in 1905.

In the early 1900s, as the use of cocaine continued to spread, authorities in medicine and government began to question the medicinal value of the drug and the harm it could cause. Reports of addiction, death, and associated crime circulated throughout the United States, resulting in legislation prohibiting the interstate shipment of cocaine-containing products. Government controls continued to tighten on the distribution of cocaine for medicinal purposes until it was banned. The drug then became so expensive and difficult to obtain that its use sharply declined for several decades.

Many contend that the widespread availability of crack cocaine is at the root of many contemporary social problems.

During the 1960s and 1970s, a resurgence of cocaine use occurred, because the drug became inaccurately perceived once again as relatively harmless. When crack cocaine became available in the 1980s, a new set of social problems developed that continues today. A significant proportion of the population struggles with cocaine dependence. According to the National Household Survey (SAMSHA, 1997), approximately 1.7 million Americans 12 years and older (.8 percent of the population) are cocaine users, meaning that they use cocaine at least once per month. Of these cocaine users, about 668,000 of these use crack. The highest rate of cocaine use is among the 18 to 25 age group (2 percent of this age group). No longer is cocaine viewed as an innocuous recreational drug; rather, cocaine is now implicated in various social problems, such as increased crime committed by drug-dependent individuals and or the neglect and abuse of children by parents who are incapacitated. It is estimated that about half a million "crack" babies are born prematurely to crack-addicted mothers.

Compared with amphetamines, the stimulating effects of cocaine last for a shorter period of time but are much more intense. Users experience the strongest effects within the first 10 minutes after administration, and these effects quickly subside. In moderate doses, cocaine leads to feelings of euphoria, sexual excitement, potency, energy, and talkativeness. At higher doses, users may experience psychotic symptoms; for example, they may become delusional, hallucinate, and feel confused, suspicious, and agitated. Their paranoid delusions tend to include suspicions that the police or drug dealers are about to apprehend them or that others who are nearby plan to attack them and steal their cocaine. They may have illusory experiences, perhaps misinterpreting an unexplained noise or misperceiving an object in ways that coincide with their delusional thinking. They may also hallucinate that bugs or foreign objects are on their skin and try desperately to scratch off these objects. Violence is a common part of the scenario; these people may become dangerously out of control and lash out at others, including those who are closest to them.

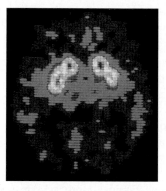 

Following the prolonged use of cocaine, nerve endings deaden in the brain's system of pleasure regulation. A brain scan (right) provides a graphic image of the drop in the number of functioning dopamine receptors.

Table 13.4

Sample Items from the Cocaine Abuse Assessment Profile: Addiction/Dependency Self-Test

Each item receives a "yes" or "no" answer; a "yes" counts toward a positive cocaine abuse score.

1. Do you tend to use whatever supplies of cocaine you have on hand, even though you try to save some for another time?
2. Do you go on cocaine binges for 24 hours or longer?
3. Do you need to be high on cocaine in order to have a good time?
4. Does the sight, thought, or mention of cocaine trigger urges and cravings for the drug?
5. Do you feel guilty and ashamed of using cocaine and like yourself less for doing it?
6. Have your values and priorities been distorted by cocaine use?
7. Do you tend to spend time with certain people or go to certain places because you know that cocaine will be available?
8. Do you hide your cocaine use from "straight" friends or family because you're afraid of their reactions?
9. Have you become less involved in your job or career due to cocaine use?
10. Do you worry about whether you are capable of living a normal and satisfying life without cocaine?

Studying Crack Babies

In recent years, the media have brought attention to many disturbing consequences of substance abuse. The tragic effects of alcohol on developing fetuses are now well known, and every alcoholic beverage container includes a caution directed to pregnant women. What about other substances? Perhaps you have read about or have seen horrifying stories of newborn babies who are addicted to cocaine, sometimes referred to as "crack babies." Health professionals have documented that the overwhelming majority of infants with prolonged exposure to cocaine during the mother's pregnancy show symptoms of withdrawal that last for the first week of life (Dicker & Leighton, 1994). It is understandable that society is very alarmed by the image of babies being born with addictions.

The study of addicted newborns presents many research challenges, the most significant of which is the fact that isolating the effects of cocaine on the developing fetus is so difficult. Consider some of the findings. Infants who were exposed to cocaine and other drugs prior to birth have a stunted body length, smaller head size, and lower birth weight than other infants (Bateman, Ng, Hansen, & Heagarty, 1993; Griffith & Chasnoff, 1994; Harsham, Keller, & Disbrow, 1994). Pregnancies are significantly briefer among addicted women, compared with those not using substances. How are we to interpret such reports, in light of the fact that many pregnant women who are addicted to cocaine also use alcohol, marijuana, and tobacco? Which of these substances, or combination of substances, might be causing the congenital disabilities?

Richardson and Day (1994) collected detailed information from pregnant women each trimester on their use of cocaine and other substances, such as alcohol, tobacco, and marijuana. They found that, when exposure to other substances is controlled, cocaine does not seem to cause deformity or interfere with infant growth. Other researchers assert that cocaine causes harm to the fetus only when taken at relatively high doses (Dicker & Leighton, 1994; Hutchings, 1993). There are other confounding variables in this kind of research, such as the health risks to the developing fetus due to inadequate prenatal care.

Because of the many confounding variables in studying addicted women, some researchers have focused their attention on animal data. For example, Azmitia and his colleagues (Azmitia, Kramer, & Whitaker-Azmitia, 1994) have studied the effects of cocaine on pregnant rats and their pups. They found that rats that had been injected with cocaine gave birth to pups with brains that were 20 percent smaller and bodies that were 25 percent lighter than those in the control group. The effects of cocaine on the rat fetus were certainly dramatic, but can we conclude that there would be comparable negative effects on developing human fetuses?

Although some might be pessimistic about the long-term outlook of babies who are born to addicted mothers, not all infants exposed to drugs face the same poor prognosis. Researchers have demonstrated that early intervention with mother and child is crucial (Van Bremen & Chasnoff, 1994). Especially when individual, professional attention is provided in the home environment and the school context, these children can develop in ways comparable to other children (Kne, Wright-Shaw, & Hicks, 1994). Obviously important is the environment in which the child grows. An addicted mother will be limited in her ability to provide a nurturing and healthy home for her growing child (Mirin, 1994).

The abuse of substances in our society continues to be a major social problem that requires the expert attention of professionals in the fields of public health and mental health. In addition to societal efforts to curb abuse, especially among pregnant women, increased attention must be given to studying the impact of every toxic substance on prenatal development. Further attention must be given to developing interventions for the children who have been put at risk.

Needless to say, the psychotic-like states that result from cocaine use are distressing and even terrifying. When the effects of cocaine wear off, the user "comes down," or "crashes," experiencing a depressed mood, sleep disturbance, agitation, craving, and fatigue. Chronic heavy users experience these symptoms intensely for up to 3 or 4 days, and for a month afterward they may still feel some effects of withdrawal.

In addition to the powerful, addictive effects of cocaine, this substance poses a significant danger to a person's vital functions of breathing and blood circulation. The risks associated with cocaine are the result of the drug's actions as a local anesthetic and as a stimulant to the central nervous system and sympathetic nervous system. Cocaine simultaneously increases the sympathetic nervous system stimulation to the heart and anesthetizes the heart muscle, so that it is less able to contract and pump blood. During a binge, the individual seeks an ever greater high by taking in more and more cocaine, leading to higher and higher blood levels of the drug. At such levels, the pumping of the heart becomes impaired, and it becomes unable to contract to force blood into the arteries. Also, high blood levels of cocaine have a paradoxical effect on the way it is eliminated from the blood. Rather than being eliminated in higher

Caffeine Intoxication

MINI-CASE

Carla is a 19-year-old college sophomore who felt compelled to excel at every endeavor and to become involved in as many activities as time and energy would permit. As her commitments increased and her studies became more burdensome, Carla became more and more reliant on coffee, soda, and over-the-counter stimulants to reduce her need for sleep. During final examination week, Carla overdid it. For 3 days straight, she consumed approximately 10 cups of coffee a day, along with a box of "No-Doz." In addition to her bodily symptoms of restlessness, twitching muscles, flushed face, stomach disturbance, and heart irregularities, Carla began to ramble when she spoke. At first, Carla thought she was having a heart attack, or possibly an anxiety attack associated with her final exams. At her roommate's insistence, Carla went to the health service, where the treating physician recognized her condition as caffeine intoxication.

- How do you think Carla's state of worry about exams contributed to her intense reaction to caffeine?

- What physical symptoms helped Carla's physician realize that she was in a state of caffeine intoxication?

DIAGNOSTIC FEATURES

- This condition, which follows recent consumption in excess of 250 mg of caffeine (more than two or three cups of brewed coffee), causes significant impairment or distress, as evidenced by at least five of the following:

- Restlessness

- Nervousness

- Excitement

- Insomnia

- Flushed face

- Frequent urination

- Gastrointestinal disturbance

- Muscle twitching

- Rambling speech

- Rapid or irregular heart rate

- Periods of inexhaustibility

- Psychomotor agitation

---

amounts, as you might expect, the elimination rate actually is reduced, further contributing to a rise in cocaine blood levels. Other calamitous changes in the heart also occur during a binge: oxygen can be cut off to the heart muscle, further impairing its ability to contract, and changes in the heart's electrophysiological functioning lead to irregular rhythms. Cocaine may also produce the effect of kindling, through which the user develops convulsions, because the brain's threshold for seizures has been lowered by repeated exposure to cocaine.

Caffeine-Related Disorders

Caffeine is a drug that has been used or at least tried by virtually everyone. In fact, most Americans ingest caffeine daily, either in coffee, tea, chocolate candy, or caffeinated soft drinks. It is also an ingredient in many prescription and nonprescription medications, including headache remedies and diet pills.

Although people may not think of caffeine as a substance of abuse, it is in the category of psychoactive drugs. Caffeine's effect on mood and alertness occur through its activation of the sympathetic nervous system. Even half a cup of coffee can bring about slight improvements in mood, alertness, and clarity of thought; however, as the amount of caffeine ingested on one occasion increases (up to three to four cups of coffee), more symptoms of anxiety and irritability similar to those seen in amphetamine use begin to appear. After four to six cups of coffee, an individual can develop symptoms that resemble those of a

panic attack and may experience overstimulation, anxiety, dizziness, ringing in the ears, feelings of unreality, visual hallucinations, and confusion. People who are susceptible to panic attacks may experience these symptoms even after consuming relatively small amounts of caffeine.

Unlike other substance-related disorders, it is uncommon for people to consult clinicians because of problems associated with caffeine intake. However, sometimes people seek help because they are experiencing some disturbing symptoms, not realizing the possibility that caffeine might cause them. The diagnosis of caffeine intoxication is assigned when the individual is distressed or functionally impaired and experiences a set of at least five symptoms following caffeine ingestion. These symptoms include restlessness, nervousness, excitement, insomnia, flushed face, frequent urination, stomach disturbance, muscle twitching, rambling thoughts, heartbeat irregularity, periods of inexhaustible energy, and psychomotor agitation. In some cases, caffeine can cause symptoms similar to those of anxiety disorders and sleep disorders. When this occurs, the clinician assigns the diagnosis of caffeine-induced anxiety disorder or caffeine-induced sleep disorder.

You might think that only large quantities of caffeine at one time can bring on physical symptoms, but, in fact, the regular consumption of two to three cups a day can cause the symptoms of intoxication. A person who drinks up to six cups of coffee a day on a regular basis may develop delirium. Over the course of years of such heavy consumption, the individual may develop such medical conditions as high blood pressure, rapid and irregular heartbeat, increased respiration rate, and peptic ulcers.

If we know caffeine has so many negative physical and psychological effects, why do people consume it regularly? Part of the reason that many people continue to consume caffeine is that they experience unpleasant withdrawal symptoms when they stop, such as headache, decreased arousal, fatigue, anxiety, nausea, muscle tension, and irritability (Hughes et al., 1992).

Cannabis-Related Disorders

Marijuana (also called "grass," "pot," and "weed") is the most widely used illegal drug in the country. Close to one third of all Americans over the age of 12 have tried marijuana (Substance Abuse and Mental Health Services Administration, 1994); of these, more than one fifth have used it more than 100 times.

Two factors seem to be of central importance in accounting for the relative popularity of marijuana. First, only 40 percent of the Americans surveyed by the National Institute of Drug Abuse regard trying marijuana as harmful—a far smaller number than those who perceive cocaine use to be risky. Among high school seniors, marijuana has the lowest perceived risk of all illegal drugs. Second, marijuana is the most widely available illegal drug, and it is perceived as easily available, as indicated by the fact that 90 percent of high school seniors regard this drug as relatively easy to obtain (Johnson, O'Malley, & Bachman, in preparation).

Marijuana has been used for more than 4,000 years in many cultures throughout the world. The active drug in marijuana, delta-9-tetrahydrocannabinol (THC), comes from cannabis sativa, a tall, leafy, green plant that thrives in warm climates. The more sunlight the plant receives, the higher the percentage of active THC it produces. Marijuana comes from the dried leaves of the plant, and hashish, containing a more potent form of THC, comes from the resins of the plant's flowers. The marijuana or hashish that reaches the street is never pure THC; other substances, such as tobacco, are always mixed in with it. Synthetic forms of THC are used for medicinal purposes, such as treating asthma and glaucoma and reducing nausea in cancer patients undergoing chemotherapy.

The most common way to take marijuana is to smoke it, but it can also be eaten or injected intravenously. When a person smokes marijuana, the peak blood levels are reached in about 10 minutes, but the subjective effects of the drug do not become apparent for another 20 to 30 minutes. The effects of intoxication last for 2 to 3 hours, but the metabolites of THC may remain in the body for 8 or more days.

People take marijuana in order to alter their perceptions of their environment and their bodily sensations. The desired effects include relaxation, a heightened sense of sensuality and sexuality, and an increased awareness of internal and external stimuli. However, a number of maladaptive behavioral and psychological changes may occur, including impaired coordination, increased anxiety, the sensation of slowed time, impaired

Some young people feel that they can achieve social acceptance by agreeing with those who pressure them to try drugs. Researchers have found that marijuana users are much more likely to abuse other substances as well.

judgment, and social withdrawal. Other disturbing conditions, including delirium, cannabis-induced anxiety disorder, and cannabis-induced psychotic disorder, may also develop. Bodily changes associated with marijuana use include watery eyes, increased appetite, dry mouth, and faster heart rate. The quality and intensity of the experience depend on the purity and form of the drug, on how much is ingested, and on what the user's expectations are about the drug's effects.

Most of the acute effects of cannabis intoxication are reversible, but, when marijuana is taken over long periods, abuse is likely to lead to dependence and to have a number of adverse effects on a person's bodily functioning and psychological stability. Nasal and respiratory problems, such as those encountered by tobacco smokers, can develop, including chronic sinus inflammation, bronchial constriction, breathing difficulty, and loss of lung capacity. After years of heavy marijuana use, as with all forms of smoking, the risk of cancer and cardiovascular disease increases. Marijuana can also have negative effects on immunological and reproductive functioning. Men who use the drug regularly have a lower sperm count and are more likely to produce defective sperm, and women may experience delayed ovulation.

There is considerable controversy over the psychological effects of long-term use, but, in one carefully controlled study, the findings were fairly clear. Among college students who were considered "heavy" users (smoking marijuana approximately 29 out of 30 days), a variety of abnormalities were apparent in neuropsychological testing conducted 24 hours after their last drug use. Compared with the "light" users (who smoked 1 day of the past 30), the heavy users showed cognitive deficits in the areas of attention, memory, and learning (Pope & Yurgelun-Todd, 1996). The heavy users found it more difficult to sustain and shift attention, and they were less able to store information into memory. These findings are in agreement with those of others on adults showing deficits in mathematical skills, verbal expression, and memory retrieval (Block & Ghoneim, 1993).

Cannabis (Marijuana) Dependence

MINI-CASE

Gary, a 22-year-old man, has lived with his parents since dropping out of college 3 years ago, midway through his freshman year. Gary was an average student in high school and, although popular, was not involved in many extracurricular activities. When he entered college, Gary became interested in the enticing opportunities for new experiences, and he began to smoke marijuana casually with his roommates. However, unlike his roommates, who limited their smoking to parties, Gary found that a nightly "hit" helped him relax. He started to rationalize that it also helped him study, because his thinking was more creative. As his first semester went by, he gradually lost interest in his studies, preferring to stay in his room and listen to music while getting high. He realized that it was easy to support his habit by selling marijuana to other people in the dorm. Although he convinced himself that he was not really a dealer, Gary became one of the primary suppliers of marijuana on campus. When he received his first-semester grades, he did not feel particularly discouraged about the fact that he had flunked out. Rather, he felt that he could benefit from having more time to himself. He moved home and became friendly with some local teenagers who frequented a nearby park and shared drugs there. Gary's parents have all but given up on him, having become deeply discouraged by his laziness and unproductivity. They know that he is using drugs, but they feel helpless in their efforts to get him to seek professional help. They have learned that it is better to avoid discussing the matter with Gary, because vehement arguments always ensue.

- In what ways was Gary's development of a problem with cannabis influenced by the college environment?

- What advice would you give Gary's parents to help them cope with the situation?

DIAGNOSTIC FEATURES

- During a 12-month period, people with cannabis dependence show at least three of the following:

- Tolerance

- Withdrawal

- Use of cannabis in larger amounts or over a longer period than intended

- Persistent desire or unsuccessful efforts to cut down or control cannabis use

- Extensive time devoted to activities involved in obtaining, using, or recovering from cannabis use

- A giving up of or reduction in important activities because of cannabis use

- Continued use despite knowledge of a cannabis-caused physical or psychological problem

Hallucinogen-Related Disorders

Hallucinogens are drugs that cause abnormal perceptual experiences in the form of illusions or hallucinations, which are usually visual. Hallucinogen intoxication causes maladaptive behavioral and psychological changes, such as anxiety, depression, ideas of reference, the fear of losing one's mind, paranoid thinking, and generally impaired functioning. Also prominent are perceptual changes, such as the intensification of perceptions, feelings of depersonalization, hallucinations, and illusions. Physiological responses include dilation of the pupils, increased heart rate, sweating, heart palpitations, blurred vision, tremors, and uncoordination. For some individuals, the reaction is especially severe and may cause hallucinogen-induced disorders, including delirium, psychotic disorder, mood disorder, and anxiety disorder.

Hallucinogens come in a number of forms, both naturally occurring and synthetic. The most frequently used hallucinogens are lysergic acid diethylamide (LSD), psilocybin (found in hallu-cinogenic mushrooms), dimethyltryptamine (DMT), mescaline (peyote), dimethoxymethylamphetamine (DOM or STP, which stands for "serenity, tranquility, and peace"), methylene dioxymethamphetamine (MDMA), and phencyclidine (PCP).

LSD was discovered in a pharmaceutical laboratory in the late 1930s, when a scientist named Albert Hofmann was working with a fungus that was accidentally absorbed into his skin, causing him to have an hallucinogenic experience. A few days after this experience, he thought he would take a small amount to study the effects. This "small" amount was actually many times larger than what is now known to be a sufficient dose to trigger hallucinations, and Hofmann experienced intense and frightening effects. For example, he reported thinking that he was losing his mind, that he was outside his own body, and that time was standing still. Everything around him seemed distorted, and he became terrified of what he saw—experiences now known to be typical effects of LSD ingestion. As reports of

LSD is often eaten in the form of drug-impregnated paper known as "blotter acid."

sive and irrational, even violent. Unlike LSD, PCP can precipitate a temporary psychotic state, with symptoms that are virtually indistinguishable from those of schizophrenia. Through a combination of effects on the autonomic nervous system, PCP can also produce severely toxic, life-threatening effects, including coma, convulsions, and high blood pressure, progressing to severe brain damage with psychotic symptoms. Very disturbing cases have been reported of PCP users becoming so disoriented that they died as a result of accidental falls, drowning, or self inflicted injuries.

Some people who use hallucinogens develop a condition called hallucinogen persisting perception disorder, in which they experience flashbacks or spontaneous hallucinations, delusions, or disturbances in mood similar to the changes that took place while they were intoxicated with the drug. Their perceptual experiences may include sights of geometric figures, flashes of color, halos around objects, and false perceptions of movement. Some people report that they can induce these experiences voluntarily, while others find that they occur spontaneously, possibly when they are stressed, are weary, are using another drug, or even entering a darkened room. These experiences can occur as long as 5 years after ingestion of the hallucinogen.

Heroin- and Opioid-Related Disorders

Opioids are drugs that include naturally occurring substances and semisynthetic and synthetic drugs. Morphine and opium are naturally occurring opioids derived from the opium poppy. Semisynthetic opioids, such as heroin, are produced by slight chemical alterations in the basic poppy drug. Heroin is the most abused of the opioids, and the most highly addictive. Most heroin sold on the street is in the form of powder that is mixed, or "cut," with other

this powerful drug spread through the scientific community, researchers wondered whether LSD could be used to understand the symptoms of schizophrenia, which the drug seemed to mimic. This gave rise to a new theory of schizophrenia, but researchers later determined that the LSD actions are quite different from those occurring in people with schizophrenia. Another theory was that LSD could break down the individual's ego defenses and thus make psychotherapy more effective. This theory was also abandoned, however. In the 1960s, LSD became the central component of a nationwide drug "culture" started by two former Harvard professors, Timothy Leary and Richard Alpert (Alpert now calls himself Baba Ram Dass). Many of the "flower children" of the 1960s celebrated the effects of LSD in art, music, and theater.

LSD is an extremely potent drug. After ingesting LSD, which is usually taken orally, the user experiences hallucinogen intoxication with dizziness, weakness, and various physiological changes that lead to euphoria and hallucinations. This experience can last from 4 to 12 hours, with the "high" depending on such factors as the dose, the individual's expectations, the user's prior drug experiences, the setting, and the person's psychiatric history. During the period of LSD intoxication (or "trip"), individuals risk engaging in bizarre, and even dangerous, behaviors. They may injure themselves, have an accident, or attempt to "fly" from a high place, for example.

Other hallucinogens differ from LSD in various ways, although they all stimulate visual and sometimes auditory hallucinations. Psilocybin (hallucinogenic mushrooms), in low doses, also produces relaxation and feelings of euphoria. PCP, also called "angel dust," "rocket fuel," and "purple," has very unpredictable effects when smoked. In low doses, it acts as a depressant, and the user feels effects similar to alcohol intoxication. Larger doses cause distorted perceptions of the self and the environment, sometimes causing users to become aggres-

The fatal drug overdose of comedian Chris Farley at the height of his career renewed public awareness of the danger involved in using drugs such as heroin.

Hallucinogen Dependence

MINI-CASE (LSD)

Candace is a 45-year-old artist who has used LSD for a number of years, because she feels that doing so enhances her paintings and makes them more visually exciting. Although she claims to know how much LSD she can handle, she is occasionally caught off guard and experiences disturbing side effects. She begins sweating, has blurred vision, is uncoordinated, and shakes all over. She commonly becomes paranoid and anxious, and she may act in strange ways, such as running out of her studio and into the street, ranting incoherently. On more than one occasion, she has been picked up by the police and taken to an emergency room, where she was given antipsychotic medication.

■ What aspect of Candace's use of LSD points to a diagnosis of hallucinogen dependence?

■ What hazards does Candace face from her long-term use of LSD?

DIAGNOSTIC FEATURES

● During a 12-month period, people with hallucinogen dependence show at least three of the following:

● Tolerance

● Withdrawal

● Use of hallucinogens in larger amounts or over a longer period than intended

● Persistent desire or unsuccessful efforts to cut down or control hallucinogen use

● Extensive time devoted to activities involved in obtaining, using, or recovering from hallucinogen use

● A giving up of or reduction in important activities because of hallucinogen use

● Continued use despite knowledge of a hallucinogen-caused physical or psychological problem

drugs or other powdered substances. Although most users inject heroin directly into their bloodstream, increasingly users are sniffing or snorting the drug. There are also synthetic opioids, including methadone, codeine, and other manufactured drugs that have morphine-like effects. **Methadone** is prescribed to heroin-dependent individuals to help them get control over their addiction with a safer and more controlled reaction. Codeine is a commonly prescribed pain killer and cough suppressant.

In one recent survey, it was found that more than 2.4 million people in the United States used heroin at some time in their lives, and more than 200,000 people admitted to using heroin within the 30 days prior to the survey (SAMSHA, 1997). There has been a disturbing trend of increasing new heroin use since the early 1990s, with 141,000 new heroin users in 1995 alone; in that year, most of the new users were under the age of 26. Teenagers, however, showed the greatest increase in use, with four times the number of first-time users in 1995 than in the 1980s. One of the most disturbing features of these statistics on heroin use is the fact that drug overdoses are common. Users are often unaware of how strong the drug is, and they may inadvertently take too large a dose, leading to fatal or near-fatal effects. An indication of how common such overdoses are comes from the Drug Abuse Warning Network (DAWN), a data source of drug-related hospital emergency department episodes from 21 metropolitan areas in the country. In 1996, approximately 14 percent of all drug-related episodes involved heroin, a number that has increased greatly even since the late 1980s. The cities of Newark, San Francisco, Los Angeles, and Boston had the highest number of heroin-related admissions for drug treatment. In the cities of New York and Seattle, heroin-related treatment admissions were second only to cocaine.

Following its injection or inhalation, heroin reaches the brain, where it is converted to morphine and binds to opioid receptors. Its effects are perceived by the user as a "rush," a feeling that varies according to the amount of drug taken in and the speed with which it binds to opioid receptors. Along with pleasurable feelings, however, the user also experiences a set of undesirable side effects, including warm flushing of the skin, dry mouth, a heavy feeling in the extremities, nausea, vomiting, and severe itching. Following these initial effects, there are residual psychological and physiological changes, including drowsiness, a clouding of cognitive functions, and a slowing of cardiac and respiratory functions, which can be fatal.

There are many undesirable long-term effects of heroin use, not the least of which is heroin dependence. People who suffer from heroin dependence compulsively seek the substance, as their life purpose becomes totally fixated on seeking and using the drug. In part, these behavioral effects result from changes in their brains, as their bodies adapt to the presence of the drug, and go through withdrawal if the drug supply is cut off. Withdrawal can occur anywhere from 6 to 24 hours after the last administration of heroin. The symptoms of withdrawal include restlessness, muscle and bone pain, insomnia, diarrhea, vomiting, cold flashes with goose bumps ("cold turkey"), and leg movements. These symptoms typically peak between 24 and 48 hours after the last dose and diminish after 7 days. However, for some people, withdrawal is a process that persists for many months. Oddly enough, addicted individuals may choose to go through withdrawal in an effort to reduce their tolerance for the drug, so that they can again experience the intense rush they feel when their bodies are deprived of it.

There are a number of additional long-term psychological and physical effects of heroin use. As with some of the other disorders discussed in this chapter, long-term heroin use can also induce other serious conditions, including delirium, psychotic disorder, mood disorder, sexual dysfunction, and sleep disorder. There are also serious physical effects, including scarred or collapsed veins, bacterial infections of blood vessels and heart valves, skin infections, and liver or kidney disease. The individual's poor health condition and heroin's negative effects on respiratory functioning can cause lung complications, including pneumonia and tuberculosis. In addition, the additives mixed into heroin include insoluble substances that can clog the major arteries in the body. Arthritis and other rheumatologic problems may occur as the result of immune reactions to these substances. Some of the most serious effects of heroin use come about as the result of sharing needles among heroin users. These effects include infections from hepatitis, HIV, and other viruses passed through the blood. The sexual partners and children of heroin users then become susceptible to these diseases (NIDA, 1997).

Sedative-, Hypnotic-, and Anxiolytic-Related Disorders

Sedatives, hypnotics, and anxiolytics (antianxiety medications) include a wide range of substances that induce relaxation, sleep, tranquility, and reduced awareness of the environment. They are brain depressants. All have medical value and are manufactured by pharmaceutical companies; therefore, they are not illegal. However, because these drugs have high potential for abuse, much tighter federal controls have been placed on them since the 1970s. The term **sedative** refers

What begins as a seemingly harmless use of barbiturates to induce sleep can quickly become a serious problem of dependence and abuse.

to a drug that has a calming effect on the central nervous system, and the term **hypnotic** refers to sleep-inducing qualities. Anxiolytics are antianxiety agents that induce a calmer mental state in the user.

Intoxication resulting from the use of these drugs involves maladaptive behavioral or psychological changes, such as inappropriate sexual or aggressive behavior, unstable mood, impaired judgment, and generally impaired functioning. Other changes include symptoms such as slurred speech, incoordination, unsteady walking, impaired attention and memory, and stupor or possibly coma. Withdrawal symptoms may include trembling, insomnia, nausea, sweating, psychomotor agitation,

---

Opioid Dependence

MINI-CASE (HEROIN)

Jimmy is a 38-year-old homeless man who has been addicted to heroin for the past 10 years. He began to use the drug at the suggestion of a friend who told him it would help relieve the pressure Jimmy was feeling from his unhappy marriage and financial problems. In a short period of time, he became dependent on the drug and got involved in a theft ring in order to support his habit. Ultimately, he lost his home and moved to a shelter, where he was assigned to a methadone treatment program.

■ What are the health risks associated with Jimmy's heroin use?

■ What do you think the prognosis is for Jimmy's recovery?

DIAGNOSTIC FEATURES

● During a 12-month period, people with heroin dependence show at least three of the following:

● Tolerance

● Withdrawal

● Use of heroin in larger amounts or over a longer period than intended

● Persistent desire or unsuccessful efforts to cut down or control heroin use

● Extensive time devoted to activities involved in obtaining, using, or recovering from heroin use

● A giving up of or reduction in important activities because of heroin use

● Continued use despite knowledge of a heroin-caused physical or psychological problem

Table 13.5

Commonly Abused Drugs

Substance	Examples of Proprietary or Street Names	Medical Uses	Route of Administration	DEA Schedule*	Period of Detection
Stimulants					
Amphetamine	Biphetamine, dexedrine; **black beauties, crosses, hearts**	Attention-deficit/ hyperactivity disorder (ADHD), obesity, narcolepsy	Injected, oral, smoked, sniffed	II	1–2 days
Cocaine	**Coke, crack, flake, rocks, snow**	Local anesthetic, vasoconstrictor	Injected, smoked, sniffed	II	1–4 days
Methamphetamine	Desoxyn; **crank, crystal, glass, ice, speed**	ADHD, obesity, narcolepsy	Injected, oral, smoked, sniffed	II	1–2 days
Methylphenidate	Ritalin	ADHD, narcolepsy	Injected, oral	II	1–2 days
Nicotine	Habitrol patch, Nicorette gum, Nicotrol spray, Prostep patch; **cigars, cigarettes, smokeless tobacco, snuff, spit tobacco**	Treatment for nicotine dependence	Smoked, sniffed, oral, transdermal	Not scheduled	1–2 days
Hallucinogens and Other Compounds					
LSD	**Acid, microdot**	None	Oral	I	8 hours
Mescaline	**Buttons, cactus, mesc, peyote**	None	Oral	I	2–3 days
Phencyclidine and similar drugs	PCP; **angel dust, boat, hog, love boat**	Anesthetic (veterinary)	Injected, oral, smoked	I, II	2–8 days
Psilocybin	**Magic mushroom, purple passion, shrooms**	None	Oral	I	8 hours
Amphetamine variants	DOB, DOM, MDA, MDMA; **Adam, ecstasy, STP, XTC**	None	Oral	I	1–2 days
Marijuana	**Blunt, grass, herb, pot, reefer, sinsemilla, smoke, weed**	No approved use, but recommended by some for nausea reduction in cancer patients, glaucoma	Oral, smoked	I	1 day–5 weeks
Hashish	**Hash**	None	Oral, smoked	I	1 day–5 weeks
Tetrahydrocannabinol	Marinol, THC	Antiemetic	Oral, smoked	I, II	1 day–5 weeks

Table 13.5 *(continued)*

Steroids

Anabolic steroids	Testosterone (T/E ratio), Stanazolol, Nandrolene	Hormone replacement therapy	Oral, injected	III	Oral: up to 3 weeks (for testosterone and others); injected: up to 3 months (Nandrolene up to 9 months)

Opioids and Morphine Derivatives

Codeine	Tylenol w/codeine, Robitussin A-C, Empirin w/codeine, Fiorinal w/codeine	Analgesic, antitussive	Injected, oral	II, III, IV	1–2 days
Heroin	Diacetylmorphine; **horse, smack**	None	Injected, smoked, sniffed	I	1–2 days
Methadone	Amidone, Dolophine, Methadose	Analgesic, treatment for opiate dependence	Injected, oral	II	1 day–1 week
Morphine	Roxanol, Duramorph	Analgesic	Injected, oral, smoked	II, III	1–2 days
Opium	Laudanum, Paregoric; **Dover's powder**	Analgesic, antidiarrheal	Oral, smoked	II, III, V	1–2 days

Depressants

Alcohol	Beer, wine, liquor	Antidote for methanol poisoning	Oral	Not Scheduled	6–10 hours
Barbiturates	Amytal, Nembutal, Seconal, Phenobarbital; **barbs**	Anesthetic, anticonvulsant, hypnotic, sedative	Injected, oral	II, III, IV	2–10 days
Benzodiazepines	Activan, Halcion, Librium, Rohypnol, Valium; **roofies, tranks, xanax**	Antianxiety, anticonvulsant, hypnotic, sedative	Injected, oral	IV	1–6 weeks
Methaqualone	**Quaalude, ludes**	None	Oral	I	2 weeks

*Drug Enforcement Administration (DEA) Schedule I and II drugs have a high potential for abuse. They require greater storage security and have a quota on manufacture, among other restrictions. Schedule I drugs are available for research only and have no approved medical use. Schedule II drugs are available only through prescription, cannot have refills, and require a form for ordering. Schedule III and IV drugs are available with prescription, may have five refills in 6 months, and may be ordered orally. Most Schedule V drugs are available over-the-counter.

anxiety, transient illusions or hallucinations, and possibly even grand mal seizures. In severe cases, the use of this group of drugs can result in a range of induced disorders, such as mood, anxiety, sleep, and psychotic disorders.

Barbiturates

Barbiturates are widely prescribed medications that serve important medical functions as anesthetics and anticonvulsants.

They were also once widely used to induce sleep, although such prescriptions are now unusual, due to public awareness about the dangers of these drugs. People who use these substances recreationally are seeking a dulling of consciousness similar to the effects of alcohol use. In low doses, these drugs give the individual both a feeling of calm and sedation and a sense of increased outgoingness, talkativeness, and euphoria. In higher doses, barbiturates induce sleep.

Barbiturate users find that they quickly become tolerant to these drugs and need larger and larger doses to achieve the desired effects, not realizing the hazards of such abuse, such as the risk of respiratory failure. Many users increase the risk of death by combining these drugs with alcohol, which potentiates the effects of barbiturates.

The barbiturates most frequently abused are ones whose effects persist for several hours, including secobarbital (Seconal), pentobarbitol (Nembutal), amobarbital (Amytal), butabarbitol (Butisol), and combinations of these substances, amobarbital and tuinal. (The street names for these drugs are "blue heavens," "blue devils," "blue angels," "goofballs," and "rainbows.") The sedative effects of barbiturates are due to their action on the GABA and benzodiazepine receptors in the brain.

Barbiturate-like Substances

When the nonbarbiturate sedative-hypnotics were introduced in the 1970s, it was thought that they would be nonaddictive and safe substitutes for the barbiturates. They were originally intended to resolve some of the barbiturates' side effects, such as sleep disturbances and the feelings of morning-after "hangovers" (Schuckit, 1989). However, it was soon found that the nonbarbiturates have equally addicting effects. They have since been withdrawn from medical use because of their high abuse potential and because nonaddictive substitutes are now available.

One frequently used drug in the category of barbiturate-like substances is methaqualone, once marketed as Quaalude and popularly called "lude." Users of methaqualone report that the "high" they experience is more pleasant than that achieved from barbiturate use, because there is less of a "knock-out" effect. The feeling that users desire is total dissociation from their physical and mental selves, loss of inhibitions, and greater euphoria during sexual encounters. This last effect is an illusion, because in reality the user's sexual performance is impaired. Tolerance and dependence develop in ways similar to that for barbiturate use.

Another group of nonbarbiturate medications, sold over-the-counter, are used to induce sleep. The most common brands are NyTol and Sominex. These are actually antihistamines, whose efficacy in inducing sleep is variable from person to person.

Anxiolytics

The antianxiety medications include diazepam (Valium), clonazepam (Clonopin), chlordiazepoxide (Librium), flurazepam (Dalmane), and temazepam (Restoril). These medications are used specifically to treat anxiety, although they do have other medical uses. They are the most widely prescribed of all medicines. Only in recent years has the extent of the legal abuse of antianxiety medications become evident. At one time, prescriptions for these medications were open-ended; that is, physicians prescribed them without limits on the length of time they could be taken, in the belief that tolerance and dependence did not develop. We now know that these drugs have the potential for both responses (Lader, 1994). In the years since these problems were recognized, the federal government has placed tighter controls on these substances.

Abusers of antianxiety medications seek the sense of calm and relaxation that these substances produce; over time, some people increase their intake and become dependent. People who use them for more than a year usually have withdrawal symptoms when they stop. These symptoms include restlessness, irritability, insomnia, muscle tension, and occasionally other bodily sensations, such as weakness, visual problems, and various aches and pains. They may have troubling nightmares and become hypersensitive to light and sound.

Other Drugs of Abuse

So far in this chapter, we have discussed the more commonly used substances, but other substances cause serious psychological problems for millions of people and are tremendously costly for society. For example, although people do not become intoxicated from smoking or chewing nicotine products, many are physiologically dependent on this substance. As the confirmed health risks of nicotine use become known, many people have tried to give up the habit, but they find themselves tormented by a craving for nicotine, as well as such symptoms as depression, insomnia, irritability, anxiety, restlessness, decreased heart rate, weight gain, and concentration difficulty.

In addition to nicotine, other legal and easily available products are associated with substance-related disorders. Inhalants have received increasing attention in recent years, because some people intentionally use such products as gasoline, glue, paint, and other chemical substances to create altered psychological states, such as euphoria. Deeply breathing the fumes from these substances, abusers develop maladaptive behavioral and psychological changes. Symptoms include dizziness, uncoordination, slurred speech, tremor, blurred vision, and stupor. Tolerance develops fairly quickly.

The use of anabolic steroids to enhance strength and musculature, particularly among athletes, has become an international concern that is generally brought to the attention of the public every time the Olympic games are held. More than 1 million Americans admit to having used anabolic steroids, and more than 300,000 people continue to use them each year (Substance Abuse and Mental Health Services Administration, 1995). The most likely user is a teenage boy who wants to improve his appearance. Using anabolic steroids along with engaging in intensive physical workouts does accelerate the growth of muscles, but at a great psychological and physical cost. Abusers tend to be irritable, aggressive, and moody, while their bodies develop a wide array of problems, ranging from kidney and liver diseases to deterioration of the reproductive system. When young people take steroids, they also tend to abuse other drugs. For example, among ninth-graders, many anabolic steroid users also abuse marijuana, cocaine, smokeless tobacco, and injectable drugs (DuRant et al., 1995).

Another substance that people sometimes abuse is nitrous oxide, or laughing gas, which many dentists use to help patients relax in preparation for a dental procedure. This substance induces a state that is characterized by feelings of lightheadedness and a sensation of floating that lasts for a few minutes. Although extensive research has not been conducted on the consequences of nitrous oxide use, there is concern about the abuse of nitrite inhalants (aerosols and anesthetics), more commonly known as "poppers." These inhalants create a mild euphoria, a change in the perception of time, feelings of relaxation, and intensification of sexual feelings. They are considered dangerous, however, because they are thought to irritate the respiratory system and impair immune functioning.

By this point in the chapter, you have probably come to realize that there is no end to the list of substances that people are likely to use in their efforts to alter consciousness. The *DSM-IV* even includes catnip as a substance to which some individuals turn in their efforts to produce experiences that are likened to intoxication with marijuana or LSD.

Treatment for Substance Abuse and Dependence

As the high cost of drug dependence to society and individuals became more and more apparent in the 1980s and 1990s, researchers searched for effective treatment methods. The Drug Abuse Treatment Outcome Study (DATOS) was begun in the mid-1990s in order to evaluate the effectiveness of four common drug treatment approaches. Researchers followed more than 10,000 patients in almost 100 programs in 11 cities over a 3-year period. In contrast to the more generally discouraging estimates of drug treatment effectiveness available prior to this study, evidence has been accumulating from DATOS that some of the more commonly used methods can have very positive outcomes, including significant reductions in drug associated illegal acts and HIV risk (Camacho, Bartholomew, Joe, & Simpson, 1997; Simpson, Joe, & Brown, 1997).

The four major categories of drug treatment studied by DATOS included outpatient methadone programs, long-term residential programs, outpatient drug free programs, and short-term inpatient programs. In outpatient methadone programs, clients are given methadone to reduce cravings for heroin and block its effects. They also receive counseling and vocational skills development to help them rebuild their lives. In long-term residential programs, clients are given continual drug-free treatment in a residential community they share with counselors and fellow recovering addicts (sometimes called a therapeutic community). In outpatient drug-free programs, a wide range of psychosocial approaches are used, including 12-step programs. Finally, in short-term inpatient programs, clients are stabilized medically and then are encouraged to remain abstinent through taking steps to change their lifestyle.

The methods used in these treatment formats rely on one or more components of biological treatment combined with psychotherapy and efforts to provide clients with social supports and improvements in their occupational and family functioning.

Biological Treatment

In biological treatments, clients are given substances that block or reduce the craving for drugs. One of the oldest forms of treatment for heroin dependence is the provision of methadone which, as we described earlier, is a synthetic opioid. Methadone blocks the effects of heroin and eliminates withdrawal symptoms. When correctly prescribed, methadone is neither intoxicating nor sedating, and it does not interfere with everyday activities. The symptoms of withdrawal are suppressed for 1 to 3 days, and the craving associated with heroin dependence is relieved. Furthermore, should the individual take heroin when on methadone treatment, the "rush" is greatly reduced. Although methadone can be taken safely for 10 years or longer, ideally, this form of treatment is combined with behavioral therapy or supportive treatment. A side benefit of methadone treatment is a reduction in illnesses associated with heroin use. Unfortunately, individuals taking methadone become physically dependent on it and cannot easily discontinue use.

Another pharmaceutical approach involves the provision of LAAM (levo-alpha-acetyl-methadol), which, like methadone, is a synthetic opioid that can be used to treat heroin addiction. However, LAAM has longer-lasting effect, and needs to be administered only three times per week, rather than daily. Naltrexone is another medication used in treating heroin dependence; rather than simply reducing craving, it actually blocks the effects of opioids. A person taking naltrexone cannot experience the pleasurable effects of heroin and, therefore, would be less likely to seek it. A third pharmacological intervention (although not approved by the FDA) is buprenorphine. This medication is similar to methadone, but it has a far lower potential of inducing physical dependence. An individual can discontinue buprenorphine without experiencing the withdrawal symptoms associated with methadone discontinuation.

Behavioral and Cognitive Therapies

A number of effective behavioral treatments are available for the treatment of drug dependence. One of these is contingency management, in which the client earns "points" for producing negative drug tests. These points can then be traded for desired items or participation in activities. Cognitive-behavioral therapy involves providing clients with interventions that modify their thoughts, expectancies, and behaviors associated with drug use. This treatment can also include training in coping stategies. Relapse prevention strategies similar to those in alcohol treatment programs can also be used.

Many experts recommend combining behavioral treatment with biological interventions. Psychosocial services, such as vocational counseling, psychotherapy, and family therapy are important adjuncts to increase the effectiveness of methadone treatment (NIDA, 1997a). In addition to the method of intervention itself, however, a major factor predicting the success of treatment is the client's motivation to remain in treatment. DATOS researchers found that a period of 3 months in treatment is needed to prevent relapse (Simpson, Joe, Dansereau, & Chatham, 1997). Not surprisingly, clients who are highly motivated to change are more likely to participate for this amount of time (Joe, Simpson, & Broome, 1998). Adding to the likelihood of continuing involvement in the treatment program is the quality of the therapeutic relationship between the client and the counselor (Simpson, Joe, Rowan-Szal, & Greener, 1997). Other pretreatment conditions further influence the treatment outcome; researchers in the DATOS project found that individuals with poor family relations, whose psychosocial functioning is poor, tended to have higher motivation for treatment and, hence, better outcomes (Griffith, Knight, Joe, & Simpson, 1998).

■ Substance Abuse and Dependence: The Perspectives Revisited

The biopsychosocial model is extremely useful for understanding substance dependence and approaches to treatment. Scientists have made remarkable leaps in the past decade in understanding how people come to abuse substances, as well as the most effective interventions for treating those with substance problems. Unfortunately, treatment programs for people with substance problems have encountered serious obstacles in recent years. The

National Institute of Drug Abuse reports that, during the 1990s, there was a drop in services provided to substance-dependent individuals. Managed care has played a role in this process, reducing the number of covered days in treatment from 28 to 14 or fewer—far less time than the 3 months that researchers recommended as the minimum. Most people in short-term inpatient programs report that they feel they are not getting the psychological support they need (NIDA, 1997).

In the years ahead, society will continue to deal with the tremendous costs of substance abuse. The emotional havoc experienced by millions of people who have suffered privately with addictions will continue to expand from within the person to the social contexts in which Americans work and live. Dramatic social initiatives will be needed to respond to the powerful biological, psychological, and sociocultural forces involved in the development and maintenance of abuse and dependence.

RETURN TO THE CASE

Carl Wadsworth

Carl's History

After meeting with Carl for an initial intake session, I asked him to return 2 days later, so that I could take some additional history. When Carl returned for our second meeting, he seemed relieved and said that acknowledging the fact that he had a problem was tremendously comforting to him. I explained to Carl that I wanted to get a clearer picture of his life history, and he proceeded to tell the story that would later help me understand how he had gotten to this point of desperation.

An only child, Carl grew up in a small Midwestern town, where his father was a well-loved and respected "family doctor." Carl's father had himself been the son of a physician, and Carl's parents generally assumed throughout his childhood that he would carry on the family tradition. This meant that Carl had to devote himself entirely to his schoolwork, because math and science did not come easily to him. In college, he became desperate about his studies and repeatedly sought help from his classmates. After he entered medical school, this pattern of dependence continued, and he found one or two older students to help him through his exams, lab work, and hospital duties because they felt sorry for him. Even though Carl felt guilty about his reliance on others, he contended that it was necessary, because his parents would be crushed if he failed. In his third year of medical school, Carl met Anne, a nurse at the medical school, and they married after a few months of dating. Shortly after their marriage, Anne became pregnant, and they mutually agreed that she would stay home and care for their baby after the birth.

Assessment

The only psychological test I administered to Carl was the MMPI-2. The diagnostic picture seemed fairly clear to me, but I usually find it helpful to have the quantitative data that the MMPI-2 provides to formulate my treatment recommendations. Carl's profile was that of a man struggling with dependency issues and having a propensity for acting out, particularly when confronted with difficult or demanding situations. I was not surprised to see that Carl scored very high on indicators of addiction proneness.

Diagnosis

Carl's Axis I diagnosis was clear. Carl was using large amounts of cocaine, he had begun to undermine successful life pursuits in his attempt to satisfy his cravings, cocaine use was interfering with his work and family life, and he had become more and more withdrawn from others as he compulsively pursued satisfaction for his cravings. As apparent as the diagnosis of cocaine dependence was, this single diagnostic label could not tell the whole story. It was apparent to me that Carl also had a personality disorder, a style of functioning that led him to define himself according to the wishes of his parents and to deal with difficult problems by becoming pathologically dependent on others.

Axis I: Cocaine Dependence
Axis II: Dependent Personality Disorder
Axis III: Deferred
Axis IV: Problems with primary support
          group (marital tensions)
          Occupational problems

RETURN TO THE CASE

Carl Wadsworth (continued)

Axis V: Current Global Assessment of Functioning: 50. Serious impairment.
Highest Global Assessment of Functioning (past year): 70

Case Formulation

What would lead a young man to risk such a promising career and potentially happy family life just to get high on cocaine? Obviously, there is no simple explanation for why Carl could have become so compulsively involved in a world of drugs. Looking back to Carl's youth, I saw a boy growing up in a family in which intense pressure to become a doctor not only determined his career choice but also set the stage for him to become reliant on others to reach his goal. It was as if Carl had absorbed a message from his father that a medical career was the only acceptable option and that his failure to achieve such a goal would result in rejection. Desperate to avoid this, Carl resorted to any means necessary to succeed, rationalizing that his dependence on others was necessary for the good of other people. As the pressures of medical training mounted and his own feelings of inadequacy grew, Carl sought out someone on whom to rely. His marriage to Anne probably was more of an expression of his need for a caretaker than an expression of love and mutuality. As time went by, Anne could not save Carl from his own feelings of low self-esteem, so he felt compelled to find something that would make him feel better about himself. Unfortunately, that something was cocaine, an insidious substance that would delude Carl into believing that he was happy, competent, and successful.

Treatment Plan

Carl Wadsworth had both immediate and long-term treatment needs. First and foremost, his cocaine dependence required aggressive intervention. I knew that Carl would not receive my recommendation enthusiastically, but I felt that a 4-week inpatient stay would be necessary in order for him to receive the multidisciplinary attention that a severe substance-abuse problem requires. The long-term plan would involve intensive psychotherapy, probably lasting at least a year following his discharge from the substance-abuse treatment program. As I expected, Carl raised a number of concerns about the interruption of his medical training, the disruption of his family life, and one other concern that was at the heart of his objections—what would other people think? In response, I impressed on Carl the seriousness and urgency of his problem. I also convinced

him that this was a good time for him to begin to work on being more honest with other people. Initially, Carl took offense at this observation, but he soon began to see my point. Furthermore, I pointed out to Carl that he needed to come to grips with the issues in his life that had led him to become involved in using drugs, and he needed to develop autonomy and an improved sense of self-esteem. Perhaps he could begin to set his own goals in life; perhaps he could tap his own inner resources to achieve those goals; and perhaps he could develop new cognitive strategies that would result in his feeling better about himself. All this would require intensive confrontational psychotherapy.

Outcome of the Case

Carl did follow through on my recommendations, although initially it seemed to me that his compliance was dictated by a fear of being expelled from residency training. On entering the treatment center, Carl was not completely prepared for the rigor and vigilance shown by the staff in preventing the patients from gaining access to drugs. He made unsuccessful attempts to obtain cocaine, and other patients and staff harshly confronted this behavior. The harshness of the confrontation apparently awakened Carl to the depth of his problem; this proved to be a major turning point in Carl's recovery.

By the time of his discharge, Carl had shown a good deal of psychological growth and was prepared to move to the next step of treatment: intensive psychotherapy. Carl was referred to a psychologist who specializes in treating professionals with substance-abuse problems. A part of Carl's treatment involved participation in weekly meetings of a local group of physicians who had similar problems with substance abuse. The changes in Carl over the course of a year were dramatic. By the time his second child was born, Carl's priorities had evolved to a point at which he was able to recognize how central his wife and children were in his life. At work, he consciously devoted his efforts to resuming a bedside manner with patients that he had, a few years earlier, engendered a great deal of respect from others. Carl began to think in more constructive ways, looking for solutions to life's problems, rather than escape, and feeling that he had the personal competence to work toward these solutions.

As I recall the case of Carl Wadsworth, I think of a man who was on the verge of self-destruction. Had he not encountered an understanding supervisor who responded to his crisis with firm insistence that he get help, I fear that Carl's fate would have been tragic. ∎

Sarah Tobin, PhD

Summary

- A substance is a chemical that alters a person's mood or behavior when smoked, injected, drunk, inhaled, or swallowed in pill form. Substance intoxication is the temporary maladaptive experience of behavioral or psychological changes that are due to the accumulation of a substance in the body. When some substances are discontinued, people may experience symptoms of substance withdrawal that involve a set of physical and psychological disturbances. To counteract withdrawal symptoms, people are inclined to use more of the substance, causing them to develop tolerance. Substance abuse is a maladaptive pattern of substance use that leads to significant impairment or distress.

- Approximately one in seven Americans has a history of alcohol abuse or dependence. The short-term effects of alcohol use are appealing to many people because of the sedating qualities of this substance, although side effects, such as hangovers, are distressing. The long-term effects of heavy use are worrisome and involve serious harm to many organs of the body, possibly resulting in medical problems and dementia. Researchers in the field of alcohol dependence were among the first to propose the biopsychosocial model to explain the development of a psychological disorder. In the realm of biological contributors, researchers have focused on the role of genetics in light of the fact that dependence runs in families. This line of research has focused on markers and genetic mapping. Psychological theories focus on concepts derived from behavioral theory, as well as cognitive-behavioral and social learning perspectives. For example, according to the widely accepted expectancy model, people with alcohol dependence develop problematic beliefs about alcohol early in life through reinforcement and observational learning. Researchers and theorists working within the sociocultural perspective regard stressors within the family, community, and culture as factors that lead the person to develop alcohol dependence.

- Treatment for alcohol problems may be derived in varying degrees from each of three perspectives. In biological terms, medications may be used to control symptoms of withdrawal, to control symptoms associated with co-existing conditions, or to provoke nausea following alcohol ingestion. Various psychological interventions are used, some of which are based on behavioral and cognitive-behavioral techniques. Alcoholics Anonymous is a 12-step recovery program built on the premise that alcoholism is a disease.

- Stimulants have an activating effect on the nervous system. Amphetamines in moderate amounts cause euphoria, increased confidence, talkativeness, and energy. In higher doses, the user has more intense reactions and, over time, can become addicted and develop psychotic symptoms. Cocaine users experience stimulating effects for a shorter period of time that are nevertheless quite intense. In moderate doses, cocaine leads to euphoria, sexual excitement, potency, energy, and talkativeness. At higher doses, psychotic symptoms may develop. In addition to the disturbing psychological symptoms, serious medical problems can arise from the use of cocaine. Although not typically regarded as an abused substance, high levels of caffeine can cause a number of psychological and physical problems. Cannabis, or marijuana, causes altered perception and bodily sensations, as well as maladaptive behavioral and psychological reactions. Most of the acute effects of cannabis intoxication are reversible, but a long period of abuse is likely to lead to dependence and to have adverse psychological and physical effects. Hallucinogens cause abnormal perceptual experiences in the form of illusions and hallucinations. Opioids include naturally occurring substances (e.g., morphine and opium) as well as semisynthetic (e.g., heroin) and synthetic (e.g., methadone) drugs. Opioid users experience a rush, involving a range of psychological reactions as well as intense bodily sensations, some of which reflect life-threatening symptoms, particularly during episodes of withdrawal. Sedatives, hypnotics, and anxiolytics are substances that induce relaxation, sleep, tranquility, and reduced awareness.

- Various treatment programs for people with substance-related disorders have emerged within the biopsychosocial perspective. Biological treatment may involve the prescription of substances that block or reduce craving. Behavioral treatment involves such techniques as contingency management, while cognitive-behavioral techniques are used to help clients modify their thoughts, expectancies, and behaviors associated with drug use.

Key Terms

See Glossary for definitions.

Abstinence violation effect 397
Acohol dehydrogenase (ADH) 396
Aldehyde dehydrogenase (ALDH) 400
Crack cocaine 407
Cue exposure method 401
Delirium tremens 399
Depressant 394
Disulfiram 400

Expectancy model 397
Hallucinogens 412
Hypnotic 415
Korsakoff's syndrome 396
Methadone 414
Potentiation 394
Relapse prevention therapy 401
Sedative 415

Stimulants 405
Substance 392
Substance abuse 393
Substance dependence 393
Substance intoxication 392
Substance withdrawal 392
Tolerance 393
Wernicke's disease 396

Internet Resource

To get more information on the material covered in this chapter, visit our web site at **www.mhhe.com/halgin.**
There you will find more information, resources, and links to topics of interest.

CASE REPORT: ROSA NOMIREZ

Stories such as the one of 19-year-old Rosa had become all too familiar at the clinic, with the spreading epidemic of eating disorders among girls and young women. It was not Rosa who first contacted me, nor was it one of her family members. Rather, Rosa's varsity tennis coach, Joannie Lyons, called me that October morning to speak to me about one of her freshman players, who seemed to be "withering away."

Coach Lyons acknowledged that she didn't really know that much about Rosa, because of Rosa's preference for remaining very private about her life. What she did know was what she had observed during the 5 weeks Rosa had been on campus, participating on the tennis team. In that brief period of time, Rosa had lost nearly 20 pounds and was now down to a weight of 87 pounds. Coach Lyons explained to me that, when she expressed her concern about the weight loss in mid-September, Rosa downplayed the issue by saying that she had been having some problems adjusting to the campus food.

Two weeks later, Rosa's weight continued to dwindle. When Coach Lyons once again asked about her weight loss, Rosa minimized the issue and insisted that she was just trying to lose a few more pounds, so that she would look better in her tennis uniform. The coach didn't buy this story but confronted Rosa with a stern statement of alarm. She went a step further and suspended Rosa from the team until she had undergone a complete physical examination. This brought the problem to a crisis point for Rosa, which led to a tearful admission that she had been starving herself and forcing herself to exercise several extra hours each day. When she did eat, she occasionally induced vomiting. After I heard this disturbing story, I urged Coach Lyons to have Rosa contact me immediately.

Several days went by before I received Rosa's voice-mail message. As I listened to her faint voice, I found it difficult to understand what she was saying. After listening three times, I was able to discern the words "Coach Lyons suspended me, but it's not my fault. She wants me to see you soon." I didn't feel particularly comforted by what seemed like Rosa's ambivalent attitude about obtaining help. Having dealt with numerous eating-disordered clients in the past, I was prepared for a struggle, and that is initially what I encountered.

When Rosa came in for her first appointment, I was taken by the fact that she was dressed in baggy pants and an oversized sweatshirt, which concealed her bodily profile. Her face seemed gaunt, but not dramatically different from what I've seen among contemporary college women. It was clear to me that the task of getting things going would rest on my shoulders, since Rosa volunteered very little. In response to my questioning about her eating, Rosa initially responded with irritation in her voice. She claimed that she had "merely been trying to lose a few pounds," because she hated looking "overweight." She claimed that she was trying to shed all her "baby fat," so that she would "feel better" about herself. The thought of going back to being a "117-pound hippo" was terrifying, and she was prepared to do everything she could to stay slim. With a challenging look and tone of voice, she asked, "Is there really anything wrong with wanting to be attractive? What's the big deal?" When I asked her about her admitting a problem to Coach Lyons, she downplayed the interaction, claiming that she was simply trying to get the coach off her back.

I wasn't sure how to respond to Rosa in light of the depth of her denial and the rigidity of her resistance to accepting professional help. I chose to refrain from a confrontation with Rosa; instead, I asked if I might review the medical report of her physical examination. Reluctantly, she handed me Dr. Kennedy's report, which I reviewed quickly. Although I was inclined to react strongly about the dramatic contents of the report, I remained calm and asked Rosa what she thought about Dr. Kennedy's recommendation that, if she were to lose another 5 pounds, medical hospitalization would be necessary. For nearly a minute, Rosa stared at me. In the silence of that minute, much was communicated. The quiet was punctuated by tears that began to flow down Rosa's face, accompanied by the strained words "I'm scared."

Once the barrier of Rosa's resistance had been penetrated, she was prepared to tell me her story. We spent another 2 hours together that afternoon, during which Rosa told me about the emotional battle that had been going on in her thoughts and the havoc that had been taking place in her body. Apparently, in the months prior to coming to college, Rosa's anxiety had escalated to such a point that she was worrying each day. Although many athletic scholarship offers came her way, she also felt an inner pressure that began to frighten her. She explained that choosing a college was extremely difficult for her. Throughout her senior year, she had been told that she was a "star." What seemed so flattering at first came to feel distressing and worrisome. Would she be able to live up to the high expectations of others?

As the start of college came close, Rosa began to "worry about everything." She feared that she would struggle with academic demands as well as athletic pressures. Over the course of those months, she also began to see her body in distorted ways. Rather than seeing the muscular development of a premier athlete, she saw bulges that she equated with obesity. Distorted thoughts about her competence became intertwined with distorted images of her body.

Following this intense 2-hour session, my initial doubts about Rosa's receptivity to psychotherapy faded. I came to realize that Rosa was opening the door to her emotions, and it was important for me to take advantage of this special opportunity to help Rosa get her life back on track.

Sarah Tobin, PhD

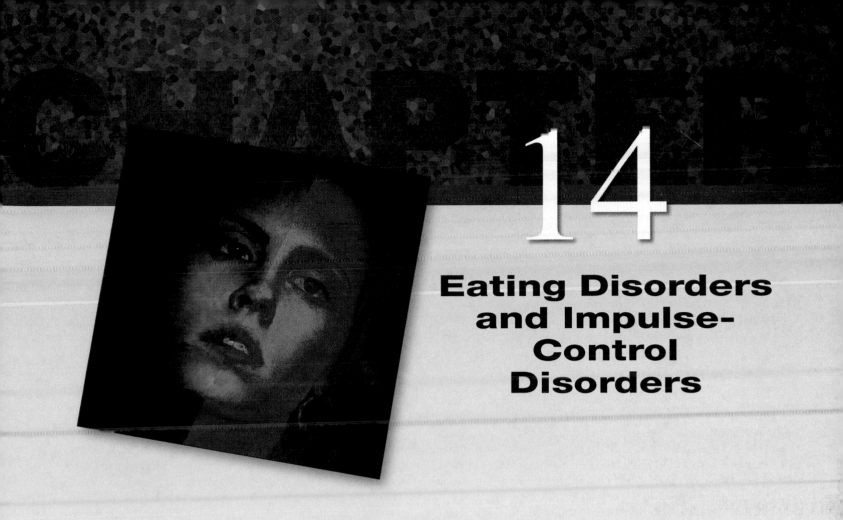

14

Eating Disorders and Impulse-Control Disorders

Chapter Outline

The story of Rosa Nomirez is disturbing and provocative. Why would a young woman with so much going for her place her physical health in such jeopardy? What thoughts might have been going through the mind of this talented athlete that resulted in such gross distortions about herself? How did things reach such a dangerous point that, on a daily basis, she found herself unable to control a condition that was overtaking her mind and body? In this chapter, we will cover various conditions that involve a loss of self-control. In the first section, we will discuss conditions in which the loss of control results in disorders characterized by conflicts about food, eating, exercise, and body image. In the second section of the chapter, we will discuss the conditions in which the loss of control is experienced in a variety of other ways, all of which are characterized by behaviors that are in response to seemingly irresistible impulses. Let's turn our attention first to eating disorders.

Eating Disorders

The psychological meaning of food extends far beyond its nutritive powers. It is common for people to devote many hours and much effort to choosing, preparing, and serving food. In addition to physical dependence on food, humans have strong emotional associations with food. Hungry people feel irritable and unhappy; by contrast, a good meal can cause people to feel contented and nurtured.

For some people, food takes on inordinate significance, and they find themselves enslaved to bizarre and unhealthy rituals that revolve around the process of eating. People with eating disorders struggle to control their disturbed attitudes and behaviors regarding food, and, to the distress of those who are close to them, many put their lives at risk. We will look at two disorders associated with eating: anorexia nervosa and bulimia nervosa. Although they are distinct disorders, they have important similarities. Consequently, we will combine our discussion of the theories and treatment of these disorders.

Characteristics of Anorexia Nervosa

Although many people in Western society diet to lose weight at some point in their lives, people with the eating disorder anorexia nervosa carry the wish to be thin to an extreme, developing an intense fear of becoming fat that leads them to diet to the point of emaciation. (Table 14.1 contains sample items that assess an individual's concern about gaining weight.) Four symptoms characterize anorexia nervosa. First, people with **anorexia nervosa** refuse or are unable to maintain normal weight, which is defined as weight less than 85 percent of that expected for a person of that height and body frame. Second, people with anorexia nervosa have an intense fear of gaining weight or becoming fat, even though they may be grossly underweight. Third, they have a distorted perception of the weight or shape of their body, possibly denying the seriousness of abnormally low body weight. Some misperceive themselves as being overweight, whereas others focus on a specific body part,

Table 14.1

Items from the Goldfarb Fear of Fat Scale

_____ My biggest fear is of becoming fat.

_____ I am afraid to gain even a little weight.

_____ Becoming fat would be the worst thing that could happen to me.

_____ If I eat even a little, I may lose control and not stop eating.

_____ Staying hungry is the only way I can guard against losing control and becoming fat.

such as buttocks or thighs, as being fat. In either case, these body perceptions deeply affect their self-evaluation. Fourth, postpubescent females with anorexia nervosa experience amenorrhea, the absence of at least three consecutive menstrual cycles.

Some anorexic individuals (restricting type) engage in various behaviors geared toward weight loss, such as abusing laxatives or diet pills and becoming compulsive exercisers. Others (binge eating/purging type) overeat and then force themselves to **purge,** or rid themselves of whatever they have just eaten. The starvation associated with anorexia nervosa causes a number of physical abnormalities, such as menstrual disturbance, dry and cracking skin, slowed heartbeat, reduced gastrointestinal activity, and muscular weakness. As the self-starvation continues, the bodily signs of physical disturbance become more evident. For example, some people with this disorder begin to grow fine, downy hair on the trunk of the body, and for some a yellowing of the skin occurs. Those who induce vomiting commonly experience abnormalities of the salivary glands, dental enamel erosion, and scarring of hand skin from contact with teeth. The extreme results of self-starvation are catastrophic and include anemia, impaired kidney functioning, heart problems, and bone deterioration. Death is alarmingly common; in fact, among the most severe cases that require hospitalization, 1 of every 10 dies as a result of starvation, medical complications, or suicide (Crisp, Callender, Halek, & Hsu, 1992; Keller et al., 1995).

The word *anorexia* literally means "without appetite," a somewhat misleading term in light of the fact that loss of appetite is not the key feature of this disorder, at least not initially. On the contrary, people with this disorder are very interested in eating and having normal appetites, although they have difficulty reading their hunger cues. Some anorexic individuals go to great lengths to prepare high-calorie meals and baked goods for other people, taking great delight in handling the food as they prepare it. Others develop compulsive rituals involving food. For example, they may hide food around the house, eat meals in a ritualistic fashion, and take many hours to eat a small portion of food. Aware of how unusual such behaviors will seem to others, they go to extremes to conceal their eccentric eating habits.

is the fact that one in five of the women with eating disorders during their college years continued to struggle with the problem a decade later. Among men the picture was different. Ten years after college, more than half the men reported having gained at least 10 pounds; with their weight gain came body weight concerns, a desire to lose weight, and increased dieting behavior. Data from such studies highlight the prominence of issues pertaining to eating and body image in American society.

Characteristics of Bulimia Nervosa

People with the eating disorder known as **bulimia nervosa** alternate between the extremes of eating large amounts of food in a short time, then compensating for the added calories by vomiting or other extreme actions. Episodes of overeating are known as **binges** and are characterized by (1) eating an amount of food within a 2-hour period that is much greater than most people would eat under similar circumstances and (2) feeling a lack of control over what or how much is being eaten. People with bulimia nervosa also engage in inappropriate behaviors that are

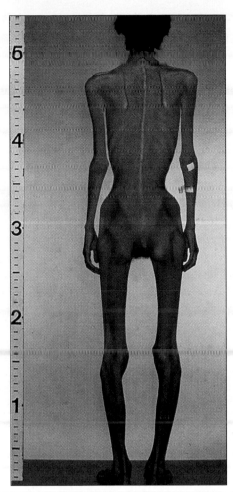

Some individuals with anorexia nervosa engage in such extreme starvation behavior that they put themselves at risk of death.

Body image disturbance is a core feature of anorexia nervosa. As anorexics look in the mirror, they see an obese person, rather than the skin and bones so evident to everyone else. In fact, family members of people with this disorder experience a great deal of frustration, because they are unable to convince them that they are actually horrendously thin.

Estimates of the prevalence of this disorder range from a low of .5 percent to a high of 3.7 percent in women, depending on whether diagnostic criteria are narrowly or broadly defined. Apart from differences in the basis for these estimates, it is also likely that there is a spectrum of anorexic syndromes in women. Along this spectrum, certain forms of the disorder show familial patterns of inheritance, as well as comorbidity with major depression and bulimia nervosa (Walters & Kendler, 1995).

Although these statistics indicate that the problem of eating disorders is a serious one, research on the long-term duration of eating disorders offers some hope. Heatherton and his colleagues (Heatherton et al., 1997) conducted a 10-year longitudinal study of the eating attitudes and behaviors of 509 women and 206 men. They found that eating-disordered behavior among the women declined substantially over that period, with rates dropping by more than half. Maturing into adulthood and escaping from intense social pressures that emphasize thinness among college women seem to make the difference. On the darker side, however,

A person with bulimia would think nothing of sitting down to eat a collection of high-fat, high-carbohydrate foods. Following a binge on such food, a bulimic is likely to purge by vomiting.

Anorexia Nervosa

MINI-CASE

Lorraine is an 18-year-old first-year college student who, since leaving home to go to school, has been losing weight steadily. Initially, Lorraine wanted to lose a few pounds, thinking this would make her look sexier. She stopped eating at the cafeteria, because they served too many starchy foods, choosing instead to prepare her own low-calorie meals. Within 2 months, she became obsessed with dieting and exercise and with a fear that she might gain weight and become fat. She stopped menstruating, and her weight dropped from 110 to 80 pounds. Regardless of the repeated expressions of concern by her friends that she appeared emaciated, Lorraine insisted that she was fat. When Lorraine went home for Thanksgiving break, her parents were so alarmed that they insisted she go for professional help.

- What behaviors of Lorraine's are symptoms of anorexia nervosa?

- What role do you think the stresses of college adjustment played in Lorraine's development of this eating disorder?

DIAGNOSTIC FEATURES

- People with anorexia nervosa fall into two groups (restricting type and binge eating/purging type) with the following characteristics:

  - They refuse to maintain body weight at or above minimally normal weight for their age and height.

  - They have an intense fear of gaining weight or becoming fat, even though they are underweight.

  - They experience a disturbance in the way they experience body weight, or their self-evaluation is unduly influenced by body weight or shape, or they deny the seriousness of their deficient weight.

  - Females who are beyond puberty miss at least three consecutive menstrual cycles.

intended to prevent weight gain. Those with the **purging type** try to force out of their bodies what they have just eaten; to do this, they induce vomiting, administer an enema, or take laxatives or diuretics. Those with the **nonpurging type** try to compensate for what they eat by fasting or engaging in excessive exercise. In both cases, these individuals get caught up in a vicious cycle of binging, followed by desperate attempts to cleanse themselves of the foods that were so gratifying during the eating episode. Following the purging, hunger returns and the cycle begins again.

Many people find it difficult to imagine what would motivate a person to engage in behaviors that are usually regarded as disgusting. Again, it is important to keep in mind that this is a disorder in which a person feels out of control. Resisting the urge to binge seems impossible. The individual derives satisfaction from relieving the ensuing feelings of discomfort. Most people with bulimia nervosa prefer to use vomiting in order to gain this relief. Over time, the vomiting behavior may become a goal in itself, because for many of these individuals it begins to provide an odd sort of pleasure. Experienced individuals can induce vomiting at will.

Although some people have both anorexia nervosa and bulimia nervosa, two critical features distinguish these disorders. The first is body image. People with anorexia nervosa have very distorted perceptions of their body size. Even when close to a chronic state of starvation, anorexics see themselves as overweight. By contrast, the individual with bulimia nervosa has an accurate body-perception, but still worries about gaining weight. The second difference is the amount of weight that the individual has lost. People with anorexia nervosa weigh significantly below the norm for height and build, whereas many people with bulimia nervosa have weight that is average or above average.

Many medical complications commonly develop in individuals with bulimia nervosa. The most serious of these problems are the life-threatening complications associated with purging. For example, the medication ipecac syrup, which is used to induce vomiting in people who have swallowed a poisonous substance, has severe toxic effects when taken regularly and in large doses by people with eating disorders. These effects occur throughout the gastrointestinal, cardiovascular, and nervous systems. Dental decay, which results from recurrent vomiting, is common, as cavities develop and teeth take on a ragged appearance. The salivary glands become enlarged, and skin calluses develop on hands that brush against teeth in the vomiting process. In females, menstrual irregularity is common. Toxic effects can also result from the laxatives, diuretics, and diet pills that bulimics use to induce weight loss. Some with bulimia nervosa also engage in harmful behaviors, such as using enemas, regurgitating and then rechewing their food, or overusing saunas in efforts to lose weight. In addition to the effects of dehydration caused by binging and purging, the bulimic individual runs the risk of permanent gastrointestinal damage, fluid retention in the hands and feet, and destruction of the heart muscle or collapse of the heart valves.

Although diagnosable cases of bulimia nervosa are relatively uncommon (1 to 2 percent of high school and college women and .2 percent of college men), a disturbingly large percentage of young people have some symptoms of this disorder (5 to 15 percent of adolescent girls and young adult women) (Carlat & Camargo, 1991; Herzog, Keller, Lavori, & Sacks, 1991). Stice and his colleagues (Stice, Killen, Hayward, & Taylor, 1998) have conducted research on the age of onset for binge

Bulimia Nervosa

MINI-CASE

Cynthia is a 26-year-old dance teacher. Cynthia has struggled with her weight since adolescence. A particular problem for Cynthia has been her love of high-calorie carbohydrates. She regularly binges on a variety of sweets and then forces herself to vomit. Over the years, Cynthia has developed a number of physical problems from the frequent cycles of binging and purging. She recently went to her physician, complaining of severe stomach cramps that had bothered her for several weeks.

■ What physical symptoms in addition to stomach cramps might signal to Cynthia's physician that she has bulimia nervosa?

■ How does Cynthia's disorder differ from Lorraine's anorexia nervosa?

DIAGNOSTIC FEATURES

● People with bulimia nervosa fall into two groups (purging type or nonpurging type) with the following characteristics:

● They engage in recurrent episodes of binge eating that are characterized by (1) eating an amount of food in a 2-hour period that is substantially larger than what most people would eat and (2) experiencing a lack of control over eating during these episodes.

● They engage in recurrent compensatory behavior aimed at preventing weight gain (e.g., self-induced vomiting, fasting, excessive exercise, or misuse of laxative, diuretics, or enemas).

● The binge eating and compensatory behaviors both occur on average at least twice a week for 3 months.

● Their self-evaluation is unduly influenced by body weight and shape.

---

eating and purging among girls. They found that the age of highest risk for the development of binge behavior is around 16, while it is nearly 2 years later, around age 18, that purging is most likely to develop. These researchers believe that it takes approximately that long for teens who get caught up in dieting/binge eating behavior to abandon dieting in favor of more extreme weight loss measures, such as vomiting.

Compared to the attention given to the study of eating disorders in girls and women, relatively little research has taken place involving males, yet investigations have turned up some interesting findings. Among a group of 135 males hospitalized at Massachusetts General Hospital between 1980 and 1994, 62 (46 percent) had bulimia nervosa, 30 (22 percent) anorexia nervosa, and the remaining 43 (32 percent) an unspecified eating disorder. Researchers uncovered interesting data about sexual orientation among these patients, with 42 percent of the bulimic individuals identifying themselves as either homosexual or bisexual, and 58 percent of the anorexic patients considering themselves asexual. As is the case with eating-disordered girls and women, many of the males also had co-existing psychological disorders, such as major depressive disorder (54 percent), substance abuse (37 percent), and personality disorder (26 percent) (Carlat, Camargo, & Herzog, 1997).

Theories and Treatment of Eating Disorders

Food is important to us for biological, psychological, and sociocultural reasons. In explanations of the development of eating disorders, each of these factors is seen as playing an important role. Clearly, this is an area within the field of abnormal psychology to which a biopsychosocial perspective aptly applies.

Theories

Proponents of the biological perspective view eating disorders as resulting from biochemical abnormalities with possible genetic links. Researchers have observed that eating disorders tend to run in families and that mood disorders are far more common in families of people with eating disorders (Strober, 1991). Recalling our discussion of the strong genetic influences in the acquisition of mood disorders, you can understand why investigators have pursued the possibility that the two disorders might be somehow intertwined and passed along from one generation to the next.

Evidence is also accumulating that suggests that people with eating disorders have abnormalities in the norepinephrine and serotonin neurotransmitter systems. Serotonin, in particular, seems to play a role in the regulation of feelings of hunger or satiety. A deficiency of serotonin appears to be related to feelings of hunger (leading to binging), and an excess is related to feelings of fullness (leading to anorexia).

Working on the premise that lowered brain serotonin neurotransmission contributes to bulimia nervosa, one group of researchers used a dietary mixture to impair serotonin activity in subjects known to be at risk for developing bulimic symptoms (Smith, Fairburn, & Cowen, 1999). Ten healthy women who had recovered from bulimia nervosa were administered an amino acid mixture lacking tryptophan, a serotonin precursor. Compared with 12 healthy women with no psychiatric history, those with a history of bulimia experienced a lowering of mood, increased concerns about body image, and subjective loss of control of eating after taking the tryptophan-free mixture. These investigators concluded that chronic depletion of tryptophan associated with persistent dieting can lead to the development of eating disorders in vulnerable individuals.

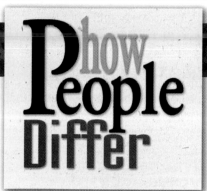

Does Modern Society Cause Eating Disorders?

In recent decades, widely accepted standards of beauty have continued to evolve toward an ever thinner ideal. At the same time, eating disorders have become alarmingly prevalent among the adolescents and women. It is no longer unusual for teenagers, and even younger girls, to worry about their weight and restrict their eating in pursuit of a slimmer figure (French & Jeffery, 1994; Rolls, Federoff, & Guthrie, 1991). Although eating disorders are not exclusive to Western culture, their occurrence is fairly rare in non-Western and nonindustrialized societies. Several examples illustrate the magnitude of these differences. In contrast to the relatively high rates of anorexia nervosa in the United States, only one participant out of more than 7,000 Chinese residents of Hong Kong meets the criteria for a diagnosis of anorexia nervosa (Sing, 1994). Within the United States, eating disorders are far less prevalent among African American women than among Caucasian women (Root, 1990), and a similar pattern holds true for specific symptoms, such as restrictive dieting and body image distortion (Lawrence & Thelen, 1995).

The infrequency of eating disorders in non-Western cultures has led some researchers to suggest that anorexia and bulimia nervosa are culturally bound syndromes attributable to an obsession with thinness as the sole standard for feminine beauty (King, 1993; Raphael & Lacey, 1992). Numerous studies have documented the changing ideals of beauty in the United States, noting that rates of dieting increase with trends toward thinness. Perhaps due to accompanying health improvements, the average body mass and height of women have increased over the past several decades, making the pursuit of the idealized figure more and more difficult to attain (Rolls et al., 1991). Interestingly, as women from other cultures adopt Western standards of beauty, restrictive dieting and eating disorders become more prevalent, lending further support to the role of society in causing these problems.

Surely we cannot attribute all eating disorders to the damaging effects of cultural standards for beauty, yet disordered eating is clearly influenced by broad social standards of how women, and to a lesser extent men, should appear. Women and men with certain personality characteristics, such as perfectionism, obsessiveness, and a sense of personal ineffectiveness, may be more likely to adhere to rigid societal standards for beauty. Other individuals may, by virtue of biological predispositions and problems in their psychosocial development, be more likely to develop disordered patterns of eating. Psychological and biological explanations, however, remain limited without careful consideration of widespread cultural demands for thinness.

As we know, norepinephrine and serotonin deficiencies are also theorized to underlie mood and compulsive disorders. Furthermore, there is a high occurrence of these disorders in people who also have bulimia or anorexia nervosa (Mitchell, Specker, & deZwaan, 1991). Therefore, it seems natural to suggest that a similar biochemical abnormality may be responsible for eating disorders. Further support for this proposal comes from the observations that people with mood disorders often experience a change in appetite, that disorders of the endocrine system often involve changes in mood, and that people with bulimia nervosa are especially prone to depression (Kaye, Weltzin, Hsu, & Bulik, 1991).

From the psychological perspective, eating disorders are seen as developing in young people who suffer a great deal of inner turmoil and pain and become obsessed with bodily issues, often turning to food for feelings of comfort and nurturance. Individuals with eating disorders tend to have difficulty understanding and labeling their emotions, and over time they learn that eating can provide a means for dealing with unpleasant and unclear emotional states (Leon, Fulkerson, Perry, & Early-Zald, 1995). In trying to understand the development of an eating-disordered response to inner pain, researchers have been particularly interested in the fact that some women with bulimia nervosa have a history of being abused sexually or physically during childhood (Andrews, Valentine, & Valentine, 1995). Researchers continue to study connections between the experiences of being hurt during childhood and self-inflicted bodily harm later in life.

For individuals with bulimia nervosa, a food ritual can provide immediate distraction and relief from distress. Researchers have found that even food that does not taste very good can provide comfort for the frantic individual who feels desperate for relief from inner turmoil (Polivy, Herman, & McFarlane, 1994). But why resort to binging and purging in an attempt to gain relief from distress? To answer questions such as these, some researchers have focused on the fact that many individuals who engage in bulimic behaviors are highly suggestible people, who are easily hypnotized, and who are high in the capacity for dissociation (Covino et al., 1994). Perhaps bulimic behaviors serve as self-hypnotic experiences that alter consciousness and ease inner pain and turmoil.

Cognitive factors are also considered relevant within the psychological perspective as an explanation of eating disorders. According to cognitive theories, over time people with eating disorders become trapped in their pathological patterns because

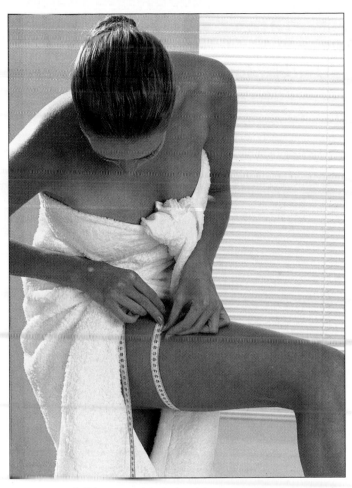

Many women in Western society feel unduly pressured to attain standards of thinness, and they obsess about their appearance.

of a resistance to change that commonly characterizes their thought processes (Mizes & Christiano, 1995). They avoid problems rather than resolve them; they resort to wishful thinking rather than realistic appraisal; and they tend not to seek social support, even when they are in serious trouble (Troop, Holbrey, Trowler, & Treasure, 1994).

The pursuit of emotional comfort through eating may also be seen as a desperate expression of the individual's unresolved feelings of dependency on his or her parents (Bornstein & Greenberg, 1991). Such feelings may lead the individual to become tormented by feelings of guilt at the prospect of separating emotionally from the parents (Friedman, 1985). A great deal of attention has been given to the striking correlation between early struggles with eating disorders and the subsequent development of borderline personality disorder (Kennedy, McVey, & Katz, 1990)—a connection that suggests that these individuals have some fundamental difficulties in the development of identity that go back to early relationships with parents—in some cases, connected to the experience of abuse (Waller, 1994).

Our discussion of the individual's conflict over separation from the family is an appropriate lead-in to a consideration of family theories within the sociocultural perspective. A traditional view of family systems theorists has been that some girls develop anorexia nervosa in an effort to assert their independence from an overly involved family (Minuchin, Rosman, & Baker, 1978). According to this view, girls who feel that their families are standing in the way of their becoming autonomous develop abnormal eating patterns as a way to become separated from their parents. Other disturbances in the family may also contribute to the development of eating disorders, including a family that is chaotic, incapable of resolving conflict, unaffectionate, and unempathic to the child's needs (Strober & Humphrey, 1987). These families tend to lack a close-knit style of relating and to take an avoidant approach when confronted with conflict (Dare, Le-Grange, Eisler, & Rutherford, 1994).

From a broader sociocultural perspective, a primary influence on the development of eating disorders is society's attitudes toward eating and diet. Society's idealization of thinness leads many adolescent girls to equate beauty with a slim figure. As an adolescent girl matures, she reads magazines, talks to her friends, and watches television and movies, repeatedly confronting the glamorization of thinness. All of this is happening during a period of development in which individuals become preoccupied with the way they are perceived by others, a concept called the "social self" (Striegel-Moore, Silberstein, & Rodin, 1993). Those who feel inadequate about their appearance develop a social self that focuses inordinately on inadequacies of their body. This relationship between body image dissatisfaction and social anxiety presumably serves as the basis from which eating disorders emerge.

Each of the two major forms of eating disorder develops, then, as the result of a complex interaction among biological, psychological, and sociological factors. In the case of anorexia nervosa, it seems that biological factors, dieting, and psychosocial influences come together and set the stage for developing this disorder. Once the stage is set, the individual becomes trapped in a cycle of physiological changes that leads to the desire for more dieting and weight loss. For those with bulimia nervosa, physiological influences also play a prominent role in the maintenance of binging and purging behaviors. The extreme behaviors of excessive food intake followed by purging provoke neurochemical changes that cause the individual to become addicted to these abnormal eating patterns (Heebink & Halmi, 1994).

Treatment

Given the multiple perspectives on the causes of eating disorders, it follows that effective treatment usually requires a combination of approaches. Medications, particularly those affecting serotonin, are sometimes prescribed for people with eating disorders. Medications such as fluoxetine (Prozac) have been found to be effective in treating the symptoms of bulimia nervosa, but the effect of these medications for anorexic symptoms has been questioned. In one study of 31 women with anorexia nervosa being treated on an inpatient unit over a 7-week period, fluoxetine was not significantly beneficial (Attia, Haiman, Walsh, & Flater, 1998). In other research, however, involving people who were assessed a year after being discharged from inpatient treatment, fluoxetine was more effective than a placebo in helping them maintain weight and fend off depression, anxiety, obsessions, and compulsions (Kaye et al., 1997). Researchers will continue to investigate the short-term and long-term benefits of such medications for people with anorexia nervosa. The picture for bulimia nervosa is less fuzzy, in that compelling research evidence points out the effectiveness of serotonin-related medications in alleviating bulimic symptoms (Jimerson et al., 1997).

Regardless of the potential effectiveness of medications, it is clear from a biopsychosocial perspective that psychotherapy is necessary in treating people with eating disorders. Christopher Fairburn and his colleagues at Oxford University compared three interventions for people with bulimia nervosa: cognitive-behavioral therapy, behavioral therapy, and focal interpersonal therapy in which emphasis was placed on current interpersonal problems rather than the eating disorder. At the 1-year follow-up, 86 percent of the clients treated with behavioral therapy techniques still had bulimia nervosa, compared with only 37 percent of those treated with cognitive-behavioral therapy and 28 percent of those treated with focal interpersonal therapy (Fairburn, 1997). Similar findings regarding the efficacy of both cognitive-behavioral therapy and interpersonal therapy have been reported by Stewart Agras and his colleagues at Stanford University (Agras & Apple, 1998).

The techniques of cognitive-behavioral therapy for the treatment of eating disorders are fairly straightforward. As proposed by Fairburn (1997), the treatment involves 12 elements for each disorder (see Table 14.2). Building on a good therapeutic relationship, the clinician teaches the client self-monitoring techniques, an understanding of the cognitive model, the importance of weekly weighing and regular eating patterns, and other techniques designed to bring about healthy eating habits. The client learns self-control strategies, problem solving techniques, cognitive restructuring, and ways to prevent relapse.

Interpersonal therapy uses techniques similar to those used for treating depression. In this approach, no specific attempt is made to change the eating behavior of the person with an eating disorder; instead, therapy focuses on helping the client cope with stress in interpersonal situations and with feelings of low self-esteem. The client learns to recognize emotions as triggers of disordered eating, particularly binge eating. Further, negative emotions are often provoked by troubled interpersonal behaviors. Presumably, interpersonal therapy reduces the emotional triggers that provoke binge eating (Agras & Apple, 1998). Group therapy can also be helpful in the treatment of eating disorders. In cognitive-behavioral groups, clients learn to reformulate the way they think about eating and are given practical help in changing their eating behaviors. As is true with other types of groups, the participants provide support and help to each other.

Within the sociocultural perspective, interventions incorporating a family component are used for clients with eating disorders who are still in their teens and whose condition has been relatively brief in duration (Eisler et al., 1997). Although there has been debate among family therapists about whether this intervention should include all family members, a review of research points to the conclusion that involvement of the parents and the teen is sufficient to bring about positive change (Wilson & Fairburn, 1998).

Table 14.2

Elements of Cognitive-Behavioral Therapy for Bulimia Nervosa

1. Development of a good therapeutic relationship
2. Self-monitoring
3. Education about the cognitive model of the maintenance of bulimia nervosa and the need for both behavioral and cognitive change
4. Establishment of regular weekly weighing
5. Education about body weight regulation, the adverse effects of dieting, and the consequences of purging
6. Prescription of a regular pattern of eating (three meals a day plus planned snacks)
7. Self-control strategies (e.g., stimulus control techniques)
8. Problem solving
9. Modification of rigid dieting (e.g., consumption of previously avoided foods)
10. Cognitive restructuring for overcoming concerns about eating and body shape and weight
11. Exposure methods for increasing acceptance of body weight and shape
12. Relapse prevention training

Source: Fairburn, 1997.

In conclusion, eating disorders are conditions in which there is a complex interaction of biological, psychological, and sociocultural factors. Unlike some disorders we have discussed, in which biology seems to set the stage for the disorder, eating disorders seem more likely to arise as a result of interpersonal and intrapersonal conflict. Interpersonal influences, most notably within the family system and the peer network, evoke intense concerns about body image and attractiveness. Distorted self-perception and disturbed thinking compound the problem, and in time bodily changes become part of the overall picture. Biopsychosocial intervention approaches bring together techniques from all three spheres. In the biological sphere, the treatment may involve medication, but not necessarily. What is necessary, however, is a medical component that focuses on healthy bodily functioning and eating behaviors. The most effective psychological techniques are those emphasizing distorted thinking and perception. The sociocultural component may include family or group therapy. Aggressive intervention, especially at an early stage of eating-disordered behavior, can change the course of these potentially devastating disorders.

Impulse-Control Disorders

We will turn our attention now to a set of disorders in which people repeatedly lose control of behavior in response to irresistible impulses. Most people have had experiences involving impulses to do something they later regretted. Some people yell at drivers who cut them off in traffic; others yell angrily at people who are annoying them. These are relatively common responses, although they can be disturbing or even dangerous at times. However, imagine behaviors that are repeatedly taken to an extreme, which a person feels unable to control. In this section, we will discuss disorders that are characterized by a seeming inability to resist the urge to engage in certain unacceptable and harmful behaviors. These disorders involve disturbances in the ability to regulate an **impulse**—an urge to take an action. People with **impulse-control disorders** repeatedly engage in behaviors that are potentially harmful, feeling unable to stop themselves and experiencing a sense of desperation if they are thwarted from carrying out their impulsive behavior. Impulsive behavior in and of itself is not necessarily harmful; in fact, we all act impulsively on occasion. Usually our impulsive acts have no ill effects, but in some instances they may involve risk. Consider the following example. While walking through a clothing store, Yolanda decides on the spur of the moment to charge an expensive sweater that is beyond her budget; she may regret her decision later, but few serious consequences will result. Were Yolanda to use all her financial resources to buy an expensive sports car, the consequences would be considerably more serious. This pattern of "compulsive buying" (McElroy et al., 1994; Schlosser, Black, Repertinger, & Freet, 1994), although not a diagnosis in the *DSM-IV*, gives you a sense of what the impulse-control disorders are like.

Impulse-control disorders have three essential features. First, people with these disorders are unable to refrain from acting on impulses that are harmful to themselves or others. Some people attempt to fight their impulses, and others give in when they feel the urge to act. The act can be either spontaneous or planned. Second, before they act on their impulses, people with these disorders feel pressured to act, experiencing tension and anxiety that can be relieved only by following through on their impulses. Some people with these disorders experience a feeling of arousal that they liken to sexual excitement. Third, on acting on their impulses, they experience a sense of pleasure or gratification, also likened to the release of sexual tension (American Psychiatric Association, 1994).

Individuals with impulse-control disorders are not usually conflicted at the moment of choosing to engage in the behavior, because they are not inclined to proceed through a rational decision-making process. Conflict, regret, and remorse, if they do occur, happen afterward.

Kleptomania

You may have heard the term *kleptomaniac* used to describe a person who shoplifts or takes things from other people's houses. People with the impulse-control disorder called **kleptomania** are driven by a persistent urge to steal, although their theft is not motivated by a wish to own the object or by the monetary value of the item they have stolen.

Characteristics of Kleptomania

There is a common misconception that people with kleptomania are driven by the wish to acquire possessions; in fact, that is not the case. It is not the idea of having the object that is appealing but, rather, the excitement of engaging in the act of

---

Kleptomania

MINI-CASE

Gloria is a 45-year-old well-dressed and attractive executive with a comfortable salary and a busy lifestyle. For the past few years, she has been under considerable stress and has worked long hours as the result of reorganizations in her company. As a teenager, Gloria occasionally took small, inexpensive items, such as hair barrettes and nail polish, from the drug store, even though she could afford to pay for them. Lately, Gloria has started shoplifting again. This time, her behavior has an intensity that she cannot control. During her lunch hour, Gloria often visits one of the large department stores near her office building, walks around until she finds something that catches her eye, and then slips it into her purse or pocket. Although she has sworn to herself that she will never steal again, every few days she finds the tension so great that she cannot stay out of the stores.

- What characteristics differentiate Gloria's behavior from that of an ordinary shoplifter?

- What events in Gloria's life could have triggered her recent bout of kleptomania?

DIAGNOSTIC FEATURES

- People with this condition have irresistible, recurrent urges to steal, not out of anger or vengeance, nor in response to a delusion or hallucination, nor to obtain objects for personal use or monetary value.

- They experience an increasing sense of tension immediately prior to the theft.

- They feel pleasure, gratification, or relief at the time they are committing the theft.

People with kleptomania are less interested in what they steal than in the act of stealing itself.

stealing the object. In the process of stealing, they sense a release of tension that feels gratifying, as they experience a temporary thrill. Despite the transient positive sensation, the urge to steal feels unpleasant, unwanted, intrusive, and senseless. People with kleptomania steal just about anything, although the most common objects are food, clothes, jewelry, cosmetics, compact discs, toys, pens and paper, and money. Most people with kleptomania steal from a store or workplace, but for some the behavior is limited to stealing from a particular person, perhaps someone for whom they have intense feelings of attraction or jealousy. Keep in mind that it is not the intrinsic value of these objects that motivates the person with kleptomania to steal but, rather, the urge to release tension. In fact, most people with kleptomania are perplexed about what to do with their acquired items. Some hoard the objects, as in the case of a woman whose closet was overflowing with thousands of inexpensive plastic combs and brushes that she took over the course of several years. Others give away or even throw away the items. This lack of interest in the stolen items is the main feature that differentiates a typical shoplifter or burglar from a person with kleptomania.

Theories and Treatment of Kleptomania

Although kleptomania is a fascinating psychological disorder, researchers have given it relatively little attention, perhaps because relatively few cases come to professional attention, except for those referred to forensic psychologists. Clinicians usually become aware that a person has kleptomania only when he or she is in treatment for another psychological problem, such as an anxiety disorder, psychoactive substance abuse, an eating disorder, or a mood disorder. The fact that most people with kleptomania who are seen in a clinical context also have another psychological disorder (Sarasalo, Bergman, & Toth, 1996) raises an interesting question. Is kleptomanic behavior a symptom of another disorder, possibly biologically caused? With this possibility in mind, some researchers have speculated that a serotonin deficiency might underlie kleptomania. This idea is supported by the fact that the medication fluoxetine (Prozac), which increases the availability of serotonin in the nervous system, reduces kleptomanic behavior (McElroy et al., 1991).

In addition to using pharmacological interventions, clinicians also employ behavioral treatments to help individuals control their urge to steal. In covert sensitization, the client is instructed to conjure up aversive images (vomit, for example) when the compulsion to steal emerges. Alternatively, the clinician may instruct the client to use thought-stopping techniques, in which dramatic internal cries to resist thinking about the stealing behavior prevent the person from following through on the urge.

Pathological Gambling

Gambling is a common activity. Even if you do not consider yourself a "gambler," you have probably bought a raffle ticket, scratched off the disk on a game card in a cereal package, sent a card in the mail to a sweepstakes contest, bet on your home team, or wagered a dollar with a friend that your answer to a test question was correct. Perhaps you have been to a gambling casino and have played the slot machines or have sat at the blackjack table for an hour or two. If you have had any of these experiences, you know how thrilling it can be to see your bet pay off. People who are troubled by **pathological gambling** have an urge to gamble that is much stronger than that of the average person, and they often end up spending their entire lives in pursuit of big wins. Table 14.3 contains some questions that are helpful in determining whether a person's gambling behavior is a cause for concern.

Many pathological gamblers get started through rather harmless ventures, such as a neighborhood poker game. Most people gamble recreationally with no ill effects; by contrast, pathological gamblers get caught up in a cycle they are unable to control.

Table 14.3

Questions to Assess Pathological Gambling

Gamblers Anonymous offers the following questions to any one who may have a gambling problem. These questions are provided to help the individual decide if he or she is a compulsive gambler and wants to stop gambling.

1. Did you ever lose time from work or school due to gambling?

2. Has gambling ever made your home life unhappy?

3. Did gambling affect your reputation?

4. Have you ever felt remorse after gambling?

5. Did you ever gamble to get money with which to pay debts or otherwise solve financial difficulties?

6. Did gambling cause a decrease in your ambition or efficiency?

7. After losing did you feel you must return as soon as possible and win back your losses?

8. After a win did you have a strong urge to return and win more?

9. Did you often gamble until your last dollar was gone?

10. Did you ever borrow to finance your gambling?

11. Have you ever sold anything to finance gambling?

12. Were you reluctant to use "gambling money" for normal expenditures?

13. Did gambling make you careless of the welfare of your family?

14. Did you ever gamble longer than you had planned?

15. Have you ever gambled to escape worry or trouble?

16. Have you ever committed, or considered committing, an illegal act to finance gambling?

17. Did gambling cause you to have difficulty in sleeping?

18. Do arguments, disappointments, or frustrations create within you an urge to gamble?

19. Did you ever have an urge to celebrate any good fortune by a few hours of gambling?

20. Have you ever considered self-destruction as a result of your gambling?

Most compulsive gamblers will answer yes to at least seven of these questions.

Source: Gamblers Anonymous at http://www.gamblersanonymous.org/20questions.html.

Characteristics of Pathological Gambling

During the late 1980s, the sports world was shaken by the story that one of the leading baseball figures of all time, Pete Rose, had been betting thousands of dollars a day on baseball games. Admitting his guilt, Rose publicly acknowledged that he was unable to control his gambling, despite his realization that this would lead to his banishment from baseball. Pete Rose's problem brought attention to a disorder with which few Americans were familiar.

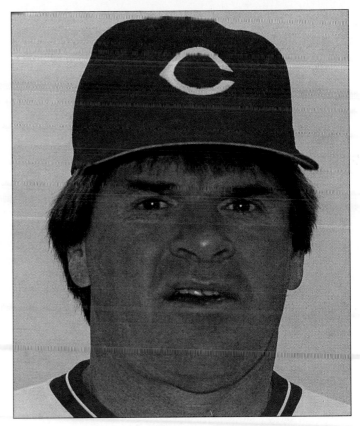

When Pete Rose was discovered to be a pathological gambler, Americans were shocked that a national hero would ruin his reputation with what appeared to be senseless behavior.

During this same time period, federal laws were changed in ways that would increase the availability of high-stakes gambling to many Americans. For example, the Indian Gaming Regulatory Act of 1988 permitted the establishment of casino gambling on Native American lands. Towns and cities around the nation built casinos and placed gambling boats in nearby waters, attracting people to legal gambling who had never in their lives entered a gambling establishment. State lotteries became very popular during the 1980s, as did off-track betting. Pathological gambling is becoming a serious problem in U.S. society, affecting millions of Americans, and some experts believe that the increasing incidence of pathological gambling is directly related to the tremendous growth of legalized gambling enterprises. It is estimated that the lifetime prevalence of this disorder is slightly less than 1 percent. Pathological gamblers are more likely than nongamblers to be male, non-White, unmarried, and at risk for other disorders, including antisocial personality disorder, alcohol dependence, and nicotine dependence (Cunningham-Williams, Cottler, Compton, & Spitznagel, 1998).

Pathological gambling is a more serious condition than the occasional buying of a lottery ticket or involvement in an office betting pool. Pathological gamblers are preoccupied with gambling to such an extent that it is difficult for them to get the idea of betting out of their mind. Repeated efforts to control their gambling are usually unsuccessful; during these attempts, they are likely to be restless and irritable. They become caught up in a pattern of "chasing," in which they return to betting following a loss in an effort to make back what they have lost.

Pathological Gambling

MINI-CASE

Wayne is a 22-year-old auto mechanic, a father of two, married to a factory worker. Two years ago, he went to the local race track with a friend, who showed him how to bet on horses. To his surprise, Wayne made some good bets and came home with a $50 profit. Buoyed by his success, he made repeated trips to the track and, in time, began taking days off from work to bet on the races. On one of these occasions, Wayne won $5,000. This made him feel extremely proud of his betting expertise and convinced him that he had special skills at picking the right horse. Even though he was losing many of his bets, he now felt certain that his winnings would more than compensate. He had a feeling of self-confidence that, for once in his life, he was a success. To keep up his image, Wayne started to make larger and larger bets on long-shots that failed to pay off. As his losses accumulated into the tens of thousands of dollars, he grew panicky and felt driven to bet even more.

■ What factors do you think were the primary contributors to Wayne's moving from being a recreational gambler to becoming a pathological gambler?

■ What pleasure, if any, do you think Wayne experienced in gambling once he began to lose?

DIAGNOSTIC FEATURES

● People with this disorder engage in persistent and recurrent maladaptive gambling characterized by at least five of the following:

 ● They are preoccupied with gambling.

 ● They need to gamble increasing amounts of money to achieve the desired level of excitement.

 ● They are repeatedly unsuccessful in their attempts to control or stop gambling.

 ● They are restless or irritable when they try to cut down or stop.

 ● They gamble in an effort to escape problems or relieve unpleasant emotions.

 ● After losing money, they often return to gambling in an effort to gain back what they have lost.

 ● They lie to family members, therapists, or other people in order to conceal the extent of their gambling.

 ● They commit illegal acts, such as forgery, fraud, or theft, to finance their gambling.

 ● They jeopardize or lose a significant relationship, job, or educational or career opportunity because of gambling.

 ● They rely on others for money to help out with desperate financial problems caused by their gambling.

Although U.S. society presents many opportunities for gambling, not everyone who gambles becomes a pathological gambler. How does such a seemingly harmless pastime develop into a compulsive, self-destructive pattern? According to the late psychiatrist Robert L. Custer (1982), who in the 1970s established the first clinic for the treatment of pathological gambling in the United States, gambling progresses through a series of stages. In the first stage, the individual is simply a recreational gambler who enjoys gambling as a social activity. Movement into the next stage, which is the beginning of a pathological gambling pattern, occurs when the individual begins to win. At this point, the gambler gains an identity as a "winner," and, the more often that success is encountered in gambling, the more this identity becomes reinforced. If at this point the gambler encounters a **big win,** a gain of large amounts of money in one bet, he or she is propelled into a pattern of addiction that inevitably becomes almost impossible to break. This event is so reinforcing, both financially and psychologically, that the individual is obsessed with the need to re-experience it. In the doomed search for another big win, a cycle becomes established in which the pathological gambler has periodic wins that maintain an unreasonable optimism; however, these gains never erase the debt, because, for every win experienced, continued gambling leads to

heavier losses. In time, the gambler's physical, psychological, and financial resources are depleted, and the person considers drastic action, such as committing suicide, running away, or embarking on a life of crime.

Theories and Treatment of Pathological Gambling

We have just seen the stages that lead from recreational to pathological gambling. These stages seem to involve some of the same factors that play a role in alcohol and drug addiction, in that the individual continually seeks pleasure from a behavior that, although leading to trouble, possesses strong reward potential. Interestingly, a biopsychosocial perspective is also becoming viewed as an appropriate model to use in understanding the causes of this disorder.

From a biological perspective, the gambler's perpetual pursuit of the big win can be seen as similar to the alcohol-dependent person's search for stimulation and pleasurable feelings through alcohol use, though there are some differences between the two in that the spending of money does not have the same intrinsically rewarding quality as the taking of a psychoactive substance. However, researchers are finding that people with pathological gambling have abnormalities in

CRITICAL ISSUE

Legalized Gambling

Gambling has become an important part of our society and economy. Many local and state governments have turned to gambling, in the form of lotteries and casinos, to supplement tight budgets, and many areas in the midst of economic hardship now look to legalized gambling to raise them toward prosperity. In some areas of the country, Native American tribes have discovered a rich source of revenue in casino gambling. In fact, Americans spend several hundred billion dollars each year on gambling (Volberg, 1994).

The vast majority of people will gamble at least once in their lives. Most people who go to casinos or purchase lottery tickets view their activities as forms of recreation (Abbott & Cramer, 1993). However, some do not stop at recreational betting but go on to become pathological gamblers. As legalized gambling proliferates, many people worry that the incidence of pathological gambling will rise, bringing with it a host of problems for the individual, the family, and society in general.

Prevalence rates for pathological gambling vary considerably from state to state but may go as high as 2 to 3 percent (Ladouceur, Dube, & Bujold, 1994). The highest rates of pathological gambling seem to occur in states where gambling has been legal for many years. Since pathological gamblers tend to gamble frequently and often experience serious financial losses, it seems that the availability of legalized gambling leads to a gradual and consistent increase in pathological gambling over time. Experts worry about losses in job productivity and increases in criminal behavior. Some suggest that the apparent economic benefits of gambling may be illusory once these hidden costs are considered.

Few people argue that there is no danger in gambling, yet many point out that the responsibility for compulsive gambling rests with the individual. Paralleling arguments against gun control is the belief of gambling advocates that we cannot protect people from all dangers. They contend that gambling provides economic benefits and recreation for many, and they assert that, just because some people cannot limit their gambling, accessibility need not be limited for everyone else.

An increase in any activity that engenders compulsive behavior will probably lead a greater number of people to develop that behavior, and legalized gambling is no exception. However, experts are not yet sure about the relationship between legalized gambling and the widespread development of the serious psychological disorder of pathological gambling.

---

the dopamine system of the brain that resemble those of people who abuse substances (Bergh, Eklund, Sodersten, & Nordin, 1997). Individuals with these disorders may share a "reward deficiency system" that leads them to seek excess stimulation, be it through drugs, food, or gambling (Blum et al., 1996). Such a deficiency may have a genetic basis, as indicated by studies on pathological gamblers who possess an abnormality in the gene that regulates the production of dopamine receptors (Comings et al., 1996).

In addition to a biological vulnerability to addiction, another factor that contributes to a person's likelihood of becoming a pathological gambler is the experience of gambling during childhood and adolescence. For example, in one subgroup of pathological gamblers, 36 percent of the subjects stated that they had begun wagering before the age of 15 (Volberg, 1994). Some researchers suggest that individuals with certain personality characteristics may have a predisposition to developing the disorder. In particular, a high level of the trait of impulsivity (Steel & Blaszczynski, 1998) or a combination of high levels of impulsivity and psychopathy are thought to predispose individuals to seek the excitement provided by involvement in gambling (Blaszczynski, Steel & McConaghy, 1997).

Sociocultural factors are also involved in the acquisition and maintenance of pathological gambling. As we mentioned earlier, the 1980s saw an increased availability of legalized gambling through state lotteries, off-track betting, and casinos, a trend that shows no signs of subsiding. Individuals with a vulnerability to this disorder are therefore more likely to be in situations in which they will be unable to resist the urge to gamble.

Persuading pathological gamblers to enter treatment is challenging because of their tendency to deny the seriousness of their problem. Only a small percentage of pathological gamblers seek help for their problem, as most tend to deny the seriousness of their disorder. Therefore, for any intervention to work, clinicians must first deal with the gambler's resistance to treatment.

In keeping with the biopsychosocial model of understanding the disorders, treatment methods that combine elements of the various perspectives seem to have the greatest chance of success. Although abnormalities in the dopaminergic system are suggested to relate to the cause of the disorder, clinical trials are pointing to the effectiveness of serotonin reuptake inhibitors (such as clomipramine and fluvoxamine) as biological interventions (DeCaria et al., 1996). As the evidence on these interventions continues to be gathered, clinicians are also finding success in the use of behavioral and cognitive-behavioral

As many states have turned to legalized betting as a way to generate revenues, more people than ever have become part of the gambling culture.

methods of treatment (Lopez Viets & Miller, 1997). Such interventions may include correcting the gambler's inaccurate perceptions of gambling, providing training in problem solving and social skills, and incorporating elements of the relapse prevention model (Sylvain, Ladouceur, & Boisvert, 1997). In addition to traditional psychotherapy approaches, many pathological gamblers benefit from the confrontation and support that peers provide in such programs as Gamblers Anonymous.

Pyromania

The sight of fire is fascinating to many people. If a building is on fire, most passersby stop and watch while it is brought under control. Candles and fireplaces are commonly regarded as backdrops to a romantic or an intimate evening. For the very small percentage of the population who have the impulse-control disorder called pyromania, fascination with fire goes beyond this normal degree of interest and becomes a compulsive and dangerous urge to set fires deliberately.

Characteristics of Pyromania

As is true for all people with impulse-control disorders, people with **pyromania** cannot restrain themselves from acting on strong and compelling urges; in this case, the urges involve the intense desire to prepare, set, and watch fires. Before the fire, these people become tense and aroused; on setting the fire, they experience intense feelings of pleasure, gratification, or relief. Even when not actively involved in firesetting, they are fascinated with, interested in, and curious about fire and anything to do with it. For example, they may have police scanners that alert them to ongoing fires, so that they can rush out immediately to watch the fire. Some even find ways to become involved with firefighting, so that they can be more personally involved in the excitement of witnessing a raging fire close up. The behavior of

the person with pyromania differs from that of an arsonist, who starts fires for an ulterior motive, such as financial gain, political dissent, vengeance, or the concealment of a crime. Unfortunately, the research evidence in this field is based largely on findings with chronic firesetters and individuals incarcerated for the crime of arson (Barnett, Richter, Sigmund, & Spitzer, 1997). The potential significance of this disorder is indicated by statistics showing that arson is the second leading cause of fire-related deaths in the United States (Anonymous, 1997).

As with pathological gambling, pyromania is more common in males, with most showing the first signs of a pathological interest in fire during childhood and early adolescence (Hanson, MacKay-Soroka, Staley, & Poulton, 1994).

Theories and Treatment of Pyromania

Most individuals with pyromania have one or more other problems or disorders, and in most cases the disorder is rooted in childhood problems and firesetting behavior. Firesetting children have a compelling attraction to and curiosity about fire, which develops as a result of their observation and modeling of

The lure of a fire proves to be so fascinating for the pyromaniac that the urge to start fires is irresistible.

Pyromania

MINI-CASE

Floyd, a 32-year-old man, developed an intense fascination with fires and firefighting equipment as a child. By the time he reached adolescence, he had begun to set abandoned buildings on fire, because he found the experience to be exhilarating and sexually exciting. After graduating from high school, he applied to be a firefighter for the city, but he was denied a position because his psychological profile showed that he had difficulty controlling destructive impulses. He moved to a small town, where he knew he could join the volunteer fire brigade without any questions. However, since such a small town had few fires, Floyd deliberately began to set fires himself. At first, no one noticed anything unusual about the increase in the number of fires that had occurred since Floyd joined the department. After watching Floyd's reaction to the fires, though, the fire chief began to suspect that it was Floyd who was setting the fires.

■ What behaviors shown by Floyd during a fire might have led the fire chief to suspect that Floyd had pyromania?

■ Why would Floyd not be considered an arsonist?

DIAGNOSTIC FEATURES

● People with this condition show evidence of the following characteristics:

● They deliberately and repeatedly set fires.

● They experience a sense of tension or affective arousal before the firesetting.

● They are fascinated with, interested in, curious about, or attracted to fire and things associated with fire.

● They feel pleasure, gratification, or relief when setting fires or when watching or participating in the events following a fire.

● Their firesetting is not done for ulterior motives, such as monetary gain, an expression of political ideology, the concealment of criminal activity, or an expression of anger or vengeance.

---

adult firesetting behavior. They have access to firestarting materials, lack remorse over firesetting, and feel motivated to start fires out of curiosity and a view of the act as fun. Furthermore, their parents are ineffective or uninterested in disciplining their children for this behavior (Kolko & Kazdin, 1994). These children also tend to be highly aggressive, have higher levels of psychopathology, and are deficient in social skills (Kolko & Kazdin, 1991; Moore, Thompson-Pope, & Whited, 1996). Emotional neglect and abuse are additional factors found within the homes of these children (Showers & Pickrell, 1987).

As adults, individuals who engage in firesetting behavior continue to show other disturbances, including a history of psychoactive substance abuse and extreme difficulties in interpersonal relationships (Puri, Baxter, & Cordess, 1995). Suicidality, antisocial personality disorder, thought disorder, chronic depression, and mental retardation are additional characteristics found in samples of adult arsonists (Rasanen, Hakko, & Vaisanen, 1995b; Repo, Virkkunen, Rawlings, & Linnoila, 1997a; Repo, Virkkunen, Rawlings, & Linnoila, 1997b; Stewart, 1993). Furthermore, pointing perhaps to the role of sociocultural factors, individuals with a history of firesetting have low levels of education and employment (Rasanen, Hakko, & Vaisanen, 1995a). Biological factors are also beginning to be addressed, and abnormally low levels of serotonin have been identified in individuals with a long history of firesetting (Virkkunen, Eggert, Rawlings, & Linnoila, 1996).

Given the evidence that chronic firesetting has its roots in childhood, treatment programs aimed at youths would seem to have the most potential for success. Thus, programs developed for children and adolescents in psychiatric hospitals focus on prevention by incorporating didactic techniques regarding fire safety, as well as interventions that focus on self-esteem (DeSalvatore & Hornstein, 1991). Outreach and community prevention are additional strategies that are recommended to reduce the likelihood of a child becoming a firesetter (Maciak, Moore, Leviton, & Guinan, 1998; Webb, Sakheim, Towns-Miranda, & Wagner, 1990).

A variety of therapeutic methods have also been used with youths and adults, including therapy based on behavioral, cognitive, psychodynamic, and family approaches in individual and group modalities (Kolko, Watson, & Faust, 1991; Raines & Foy, 1994; Soltys, 1992). It is also recommended that clinicians focus on some of the other problems found in chronic firesetters, such as low self-esteem, depression, communication problems, and inability to control anger (Stewart, 1993).

Sexual Impulsivity

People with **sexual impulsivity** are unable to control their sexual behavior, and they feel driven to engage in frequent and indiscriminate sexual activity. Although this condition is not an official *DSM-IV* diagnosis, the symptoms and behaviors of people with sexual impulsivity are quite similar to those associated with impulse-control disorders. During the past two decades, clinicians have seen increasing numbers of clients looking for help to contain uncontrollable sexuality, perhaps in response to media discussions of the condition, resulting from the publication of such books as *Out of the Shadows: Understanding Sexual Addiction* (Carnes, 1983) and *Secret Life: An Autobiography,* by award-winning poet Michael Ryan (1995).

Characteristics of Sexual Impulsivity

People with the disorder of sexual impulsivity are preoccupied with sex, feeling uncontrollably driven to seek out sexual encounters, which they later regret. This drive is similar to that reported in other impulse-control disorders, involving a state in which the individual is transfixed by the need for sex. People with sexual impulsivity feel that they cannot control the number of their sexual encounters, or even the contexts in which they are likely to initiate sexual behavior. Terms such as "sexual addiction," "sexual compulsivity," and "sexual dependency" are also used to characterize this disorder, indicating the pervasive effects that the drive for sexuality has on the lives of these individuals. There is concern among professionals that the research base is not sufficiently established to consider this behavior as a form of psychopathology (Gold & Heffner, 1998; Rinehart & McCabe, 1997). However, those who support the existence of this disorder maintain that a literature is building across professions to support the existence of the disorder as a valid entity (Carnes, 1996).

As is true in other impulse-control disorders, the uncontrollable behavior of people with sexual impulsivity interferes with their ability to carry out normal social and occupational responsibilities and can place their social status in jeopardy (Gordon, Fargason, & Kramer, 1995). They feel a great deal of distress about their behavior; following sexual encounters, they are likely to feel dejected, hopeless, and ashamed. Although a few are consumed by the constant need to masturbate, most seek out partners, usually people they do not know or care to know following the anonymous sexual encounter. In extreme cases, sexual impulsivity may extend into very serious deviant and violent behavior, including "lust" murders and serial killing (Blanchard, 1995).

One of the first detailed investigations of sexual impulsivity, which was conducted with a male homosexual and bisexual sample, provides an indication of the extreme nature of this disorder (Quadland, 1985). In this group, individuals with sexual impulsivity averaged more than 29 partners per month and more than 2,000 sexual encounters over their lifetimes. They frequently sought sex in public settings and used alcohol or drugs with sex, and they typically had a history of few long-term relationships. Although the disorder is more common in men, women also have this condition, although it is expressed in different ways; women tend to be more passive in their openness to sexual encounters, while men are more likely to be intrusive, possibly exploitive, in their pursuits (Ross, 1996).

Individuals with sexual impulsivity commonly suffer with a co-existing condition, such as depression or substance abuse (Black, Kehrberg, Flumerfelt, & Schlosser, 1997). Some people with this condition experience dissociative symptoms linked to their sexual impulsivity. They describe going into an altered state of consciousness, sometimes referred to as a "Doctor Jekyll/Mr. Hyde" effect (Griffin-Shelley, Benjamin, & Benjamin, 1995).

A singles bar provides the "perfect" opportunity for someone with sexual impulsivity to seek a sexual encounter with no strings attached.

Theories and Treatment of Sexual Impulsivity

A disorder as potentially dangerous as sexual impulsivity calls for a comprehensive approach to understanding and treatment. As in other disorders we have seen in this chapter, a biopsychosocial model provides an excellent starting point for such an integrated approach (Goodman, 1998). Those working within the biological perspective suggest that sexual impulsivity is comparable to the other addictions, with a similar biochemical basis (Sunderwirth, Milkman, & Jenks, 1996). However, in trying to understand the origins of sexual impulsivity, researchers have focused primarily on the roots of the disorder within the early life experiences of the individual. Exposure to an abusive family environment is one of the key factors thought to predispose an individual toward this behavior (Carnes & Delmonico, 1996). In adulthood, this relationship between violence and sexuality may persist as the perpetrator uses sex as a hostile activity directed toward the partner (Irons, 1996).

Treatment for sexual impulsivity involves a combination of components derived from the insight-oriented, behavioral, and family systems approaches. Insight-oriented therapy focuses on bringing to the surface the individual's underlying conflicts that motivate the behavior. These conflicts include resolving nonsexual problems through sexual means, needing reassurance, and feeling insecure about one's sex role (Weissberg & Levay, 1986). Behavioral techniques include aversive covert conditioning (McConaghy, Armstrong, & Blaszczynski, 1985), imaginal desensitization (McConaghy, Blaszczysnki, & Frankova, 1991), and behavioral contracting (Schwartz & Brasted, 1985). If sexual impulsivity is associated with other psychological disorders, such as mood disorder or obsessive-compulsive disorder, treatment of these associated conditions with medications may also be warranted (Sealy, 1995). Family or couples therapy is also an important component of therapy for clients whose excessive sexual behavior occurs in the context of long-term close relationships. The early involvement of partners and children in this process is seen as crucial to the success of the intervention (Matheny, 1998).

Sexual Impulsivity

MINI-CASE

Raj is a 24-year-old clerk who lives alone in an apartment in a large city. A loner since high school, Raj nevertheless is intensely preoccupied with the pursuit of sex. At work, he constantly thinks about each person he meets as a potential sexual partner. Repeatedly on his mind are plans to find new places where he can have sex. On a typical day, Raj goes to a pornographic movie theater during his lunch hour, where he seeks to have oral sexual activities with as many different men as he can find. On his way home from work, he often stops at a highway rest area, where he once again seeks anonymous sex partners. During the weekend, he frequents singles bars, where he usually succeeds in picking up women. Although he continues to involve himself in these sexual activities, Raj is quite distressed by his behavior. Guilt and negative feelings about himself cause him to feel depressed, and even suicidal at times. However, his behavior seems to him to be beyond his control. Although he has thought of obtaining professional help, he is too embarrassed to admit his problem to anyone.

■ How does Raj's sexual impulsivity differ from the behavior of a person with a paraphilia?

■ In what ways are Raj's symptoms similar to those of people with other impulse-control disorders?

DIAGNOSTIC FEATURES

● People with this condition are unable to control their sexual behavior, and they feel driven to engage in frequent and indiscriminate sexual activity.

● They experience an increasing sense of tension prior to engaging in a sexual act.

● They feel a great deal of distress about their behavior and, following sexual encounters, are likely to feel dejected, hopeless, and ashamed.

● Their compulsive pursuit of sexual encounters interferes with their ability to carry out normal social and occupational responsibilities.

Trichotillomania

The urge to pull out one's hair, which becomes a compulsion in people with the rare disorder called **trichotillomania,** may seem bizarre and far removed from the realm of everyday human behavior. In American culture, for example, many people, especially women, are self-conscious about body hair and go to some trouble to remove it. However, for some people, the act of hair-pulling develops a compulsive quality, causing them to become so preoccupied with pulling out their hair that they are oblivious to the fact that they may actually be marring their appearance. Estimates of prevalence are generally in the range of 1 to 2 percent of the population (American Psychiatric Association, 1994), although some figures are as high as 5 percent (Graber & Arndt, 1993), particularly among female adolescents and young adults. For some, the condition is relatively transient, while for others it lasts for decades.

Characteristics of Trichotillomania

Like people with other impulse-control disorders, the person with trichotillomania experiences an increasing sense of tension immediately prior to pulling out the hair or when trying to resist the urge to pull. The experience of hair-pulling results in feelings of relief, pleasure, or gratification. People with trichotillomania are upset by their uncontrollable behavior and may find that their social, occupational, or other areas of func-

tioning are impaired because of this disorder. They feel unable to stop this behavior, even when the pulling results in bald patches and lost eyebrows, eyelashes, armpit hair, and pubic hair. In extreme cases, some individuals swallow the hair after they have pulled it out, risking the danger that it will solidify in the stomach or intestines (a condition referred to as a trichobezoar or "Rapunzel syndrome").

Trichotillomania often goes undetected, because those suffering from the irresistible urge to pull out their own hair usually deny their behavior.

Trichotillomania

MINI-CASE

For most of her childhood and adolescence, 15-year-old Janet lived a fairly isolated existence, with no close friends. Although Janet never discussed her unhappiness with anyone, she often felt very depressed and hopeless. As a young child, Janet lay in bed on many nights, secretly tugging at her hair. Over time, this behavior increased to the point at which she plucked the hair, strand by strand, from her scalp. Typically, she pulled out a hair, examined it, bit it, and either threw it away or swallowed it. Because her hair was thick and curly, her hair loss was not initially evident, and Janet kept it carefully combed to conceal the bald spots. One of her teachers noticed that Janet was pulling her hair in class, and, in looking more closely, she saw these patches on Janet's head. She referred Janet to the school psychologist, who called Janet's mother and recommended professional help.

- What connection might there be between Janet's unhappiness and her hair-pulling behavior?

- What clues help differentiate Janet's disorder from a medically caused loss of hair?

DIAGNOSTIC FEATURES

- People with this condition show evidence of the following characteristics:

  - They recurrently pull out hair, which causes considerable hair loss.

  - They experience an increasing sense of tension immediately before pulling out hair or when they try to resist hair-pulling behavior.

  - They feel pleasure, gratification, or relief when pulling out hair.

  - Their behavior causes significant distress or impairment.

People with this disorder are secretive about what they are doing and tend to engage in hair-pulling only when alone. For some, the interest goes beyond their own bodily hair and may involve pulling the hair from another person, or even from pets, dolls, and materials, such as carpets and sweaters. Even when clear physical evidence suggests intentional hair-pulling, people with this disorder tend to deny that they are engaging in the behavior. They may even conceal the damage they have done by wearing hats or rearranging their hair to cover bald spots. In cases involving children and adolescents, parents may become alarmed at the mysterious hair loss and take the child to a dermatologist or pediatrician with a concern about a medical problem. On examination, the health professional may notice many short, broken hairs around the bald areas on the skin, indicating that the hairs have been plucked. In other cases, it is not a dermatological concern that brings clinical attention but, rather, another psychological problem, such as depression, anxiety, or an eating disorder.

Trichotillomania often co-exists with other disorders, including depression, anxiety disorder, substance abuse, or an eating disorder (Hanna, 1997). These conditions may bring the individual into treatment, at which point the hair-pulling compulsion may be disclosed.

Theories and Treatment of Trichotillomania

Trichotillomania is an intriguing disorder that is not well understood; however, each of the major perspectives offers some insights. From a biological perspective, trichotillomania is seen as sharing some characteristics with obsessive-compulsive

disorder (Christenson & Crow, 1996). Supporting this notion are the observations that, in both disorders, behavior is driven by anxiety or tension, and people with both disorders respond to medication.

A biological perspective for understanding trichotillomania is given support by several investigations of brain structure and function. Subtle differences within the frontal lobes of the brains of people with the disorder have been found when compared with those of normal controls (Grachev, 1997). Abnormalities have also been found in the basal ganglia, subcortical structures involved in motor control, which are involved in the production of the symptoms of obsessive-compulsive disorder (O'Sullivan et al., 1997). Although it is difficult for researchers to delineate the specific relationship between brain abnormalities and the symptoms of trichotillomania, investigators have noted particular deficits on neuropsychological tests that support the inference of brain involvement in causing this disorder (Stanley, Hannay, & Breckenridge, 1997).

Behavioral theorists regard the disorder as a complex interaction among environmental cues, hair-pulling, and the consequences of pulling (Mansueto, Stemberger, Thomas, & Golomb, 1997). Specifically, individuals with this disorder learn to associate hair-pulling behavior with relief from tension (Stanley, Borden, Mouton, & Breckenridge, 1995). Thus, a young woman who experiences a sense of relief from the anxiety of studying may experience transient relief when she tugs on her hair. Over time, she may return to the hair-pulling behavior in an effort to regain the sense of relief she experienced the last time.

Finally, within the sociocultural perspective, trichotillomania is seen as originating in disturbed parent-child relationships. An upset child who feels neglected, abandoned, or emotionally overburdened may resort to this behavior in an attempt to gain attention or to derive a disturbed form of gratification (Krishnan, Davidson, & Guajardo, 1985).

Various pharmacological treatments are being tested to determine which is most effective in reducing the symptoms of this perplexing disorder. These medications include paroxetine (Paxil) (Block, West, & Baharoglu, 1998), velafaxine (Effexor) (Ninan et al., 1998), fluvoxamine (Luvox) (Stanley et al., 1997), sertraline (Zoloft) (Bradford & Gratzer, 1995), and citalopram (Celexa) (Stein, Bouwer, & Maud, 1997).

Although the disorder may have a biological component, learning also appears to play a role, and the most effective treatments over the long term combine medication with behavioral therapy (Keuthen et al., 1998). One successful behavioral treatment for people with trichotillomania is habit reversal, in which the individual is trained to be more aware of the behavior and then is taught a new response to compete with hair-pulling (Rapp et al., 1998). For example, the individual may be taught to brush her hair instead of pulling it (Stoylen, 1996). Based on the assumption that the individual has become desensitized to pain, this process may be enhanced by providing the individual with a cream to apply to the scalp that increases the amount of pain felt during hair-pulling (Ristvedt & Christenson, 1996). As effective as this treatment can be, it is nevertheless helpful to combine it with social support (Rapp et al., 1998).

Intermittent Explosive Disorder

All people lose their tempers on occasion, but most are able to let off steam without causing any harm. In contrast, people with **intermittent explosive disorder** feel a recurrent inability to resist assaultive or destructive acts of aggression.

Characteristics of Intermittent Explosive Disorder

The behaviors found in people with intermittent explosive disorder are occasional bouts of extreme rage, in which they become assaultive or destructive without serious provocation. During these episodes, these people can cause serious physical harm to themselves, other people, and property. While in the midst of an episode, they feel as if they are under a spell, and some have even used terms that suggest that it is like a seizure state. Just prior to the outburst, they may feel an impending sense that something is about to happen, an experience that has been compared to the aura, or anticipatory state, that people with epilepsy experience prior to a seizure. Between episodes, they may be somewhat impulsive or aggressive by nature, but not to such a degree that their behavior is harmful. Because of their outbursts, most individuals with this disorder have difficulties at work and at home. They may lose their jobs, and their partners may become intolerant. This rare disorder is more common among men, some of whom are imprisoned for their destructive or assaultive behavior. Women with this disorder are more likely to be sent to a mental health facility for treatment. This disorder is often associated with other clinical disorders, particularly mood disorders, which are estimated to occur in over 90 percent of individuals with the diagnosis. Other comorbid conditions include substance use disorders and anxiety disorders, which are found in nearly half of the individuals diagnosed with intermittent explosive disorder (McElroy et al., 1998).

Theories and Treatment of Intermittent Explosive Disorder

Many features of intermittent explosive disorder suggest that a complex interaction of biological and environmental factors lead an individual to develop an inability to control aggressive outbursts (Kavoussi, Armstead, & Coccaro, 1997). In terms of specific biological factors, alterations in the serotonergic system are suggested

---

Intermittent Explosive Disorder

MINI-CASE

Ed, a 28-year-old high-school teacher, has unprovoked, violent outbursts of aggressive and assaultive behavior. During these episodes, Ed throws whatever objects he can get his hands on and yells profanities. He soon calms down, though, and feels intense regret for whatever damage he has caused, explaining that he didn't know what came over him. In the most recent episode, he threw a coffeepot at another teacher in the faculty lounge, inflicting serious injury. After the ambulance took the injured man to the hospital, Ed's supervisor called the police.

■ What differentiates Ed, who has intermittent explosive disorder, from a person with antisocial personality disorder?

■ For what medical conditions should Ed be tested?

DIAGNOSTIC FEATURES

● People with this condition show evidence of the following characteristics:

● During several separate episodes, they are unable to resist aggressive impulses, which result in serious acts of assault or destruction.

● Their level of aggressiveness during these episodes is grossly out of proportion to any precipitating stressors.

● Their aggressive episodes are not associated with another mental or physical disorder.

A sudden eruption of rage causes people with intermittent explosive disorder to lose control over what they say and do.

Eating Disorders and Impulse-Control Disorders: The Perspectives Revisited

In this chapter, we have discussed several disorders that involve people's struggles to control strong urges to act in ways that are destructive or detrimental to their existence. Some of these disorders represent behaviors that, in moderation, are not problematic. Nothing is wrong with dieting, gambling, or having sexual interests. It is also normal to lose one's temper on occasion. However, when these behaviors are carried to an extreme, they can become a source of distress to the individual and to others. In contrast, firestarting and stealing are outside the realm of what society regards as acceptable behavior, because these actions violate the rights of others and are against the law. Regardless of the degree of acceptability of the behavior, the main issue in understanding these disorders is that the individual feels powerless to control the impulse to act.

A number of the disorders we have covered in this chapter cause considerable harm to other people in addition to the client. Even if the client does not recognize a need for treatment, interventions may be mandated by legal authorities or may be insisted on by family members. Unfortunately, the nature of these disorders makes it particularly difficult for these individuals to seek help and, even when they do, to seize control over their behavior.

In their attempt to explain impulse-control disorders, experts have proposed that these conditions fall on an "affective spectrum" that includes mood disorders, obsessive-compulsive disorder, substance abuse disorders, eating disorders, and anxiety disorders (McElroy et al., 1992). All these conditions share certain symptoms, hypothesized biological mechanisms, and treatments. As researchers continue to explore these links, we can look forward to improved understanding of these mysterious and disabling psychological phenomena.

as providing a possible vulnerability to the disorder (Stein, Hollander, & Liebowitz, 1993). The use of alcohol further complicates the picture. People who engage in impulsive violent behavior while intoxicated have abnormally low rates of serotonin turnover in the brain (Virkkunen, Goldman, Nielsen, & Linnoila, 1995).

In terms of psychological factors, learning theorists would point to the concepts of operant conditioning to explain the behavior of people who explode occasionally. In such circumstances, they probably provoke intense reactions, possibly of fear and submission, in people around them, leading to a powerful form of reinforcement. This conceptualization can be carried into the realm of sociocultural theory as well, as we consider the influence on family systems and intimate relationships when a person's behavior is so threatening and violent.

Based on the findings of serotonergic abnormalities among people with this disorder, clinicians advocate the use of medications in treatment. However, it is recognized that psychotherapeutic methods must be combined with somatic approaches. For example, people with this disorder can be taught to monitor their levels of anger and find verbal rather than physical outlets (Lion, 1992).

RETURN TO THE CASE

Rosa Nomirez

Rosa's History

I had been relieved at the end of our intake session when Rosa agreed to initiate psychotherapy. She approached our first psychotherapy session with a style that was considerably different from that which she showed during her first meeting with me. She seemed more open, as well as more eager to deal with the issues that had been troubling her. As

soon as we sat down, Rosa launched into telling me about her life.

Rosa began to tell me about her 19 years of life, which were filled with countless experiences of success. She explained that she felt she had been "blessed with good fortune," causing her to feel at times as though she was "living under a lucky star." She was the only child of a middle-class Puerto Rican family that resided in a wealthy suburb of San Juan. Both of Rosa's,

RETURN TO THE CASE

Rosa Nomirez (continued)

parents were successful business executives who had risen to positions of prominence in the banking field. She spoke of them with deep affection, while alluding to the intense levels of pressure they placed on her to succeed.

Rosa realized that the pressure she felt from her parents began to emerge even prior to her birth. Even though she was an only-child, she knew that she was the second-born in the family, with her birth taking place 2 years after the tragic death of her brother, Juan, on his fifth birthday. Juan had died in a freak accident when the bike he had just received for his birthday careened down a hillside and slammed into a tree. Although Rosa's parents never spoke of the accident, and rarely mentioned Juan's name, her Uncle Rico shared with Rosa the details of the event and the emotional devastation that followed for her parents.

According to Rico, Rosa's parents had mourned the death of Juan for a year, after which they decided to try to have another child. This time, however, they promised that they "would be more careful." Rico had told Rosa about the overprotectiveness of her parents. From the day that Rosa was carried into the home for the first time, she was treated like a fragile work of art. Rarely was she left unattended, even for a few moments. When her parents were at work, she was left in the hands of her grandmother, who doted over her with solicitous affection.

Rosa was sent to the finest schools, and she excelled in academics as well as athletics. From an early age, she was nurtured to be a tennis pro, with private lessons beginning in early childhood. Rosa's parents' expectations for her were very high. If she did poorly in a competitive tennis match, more tennis lessons were added to her weekly schedule. If she received any grade less than an A in school, her parents lectured her about the importance of her studies and took away some privileges until she attained perfect grades.

As Rosa told me about her parents' childrearing practices, I inquired about her feelings growing up in a family with such high expectations. To my surprise, Rosa did not speak negatively about these experiences. Rather, she stated, "I felt so fortunate to know, on a daily basis, how much my parents loved me." She stated that she never resented their demands but shared their values to make her life the best it could possibly be. She explained that she has always loved her parents deeply and, in fact, missed them intensely since coming to college, feeling "desperately homesick."

When we turned our attention to Rosa's eating disorder, I could perceive a tensing of her body. It was obvious that she was reluctant to talk about how this horrendous problem had developed, but she realized that it was important for me to know the history, so that I could help her. In beginning to tell me about the roots of her eating disorder, Rosa began with the emphatic statement, "I want you to understand that this problem had nothing to do with my parents. They never said a word about my weight or my appearance." Although I thought it odd that she would begin with that disclaimer, I decided to leave the parental issue aside and to proceed to a direct questioning about when and how Rosa had gotten caught up in this self-destructive behavior.

Rosa recalled the day she associates with the development of her eating problem. In the fall of her senior year, she was being contacted by college tennis coaches who had heard about her remarkable athletic skills. She was told by more than a dozen colleges that she would be awarded a 4-year scholarship, based on her athletic and academic accomplishments. Rather than feel jubilant, Rosa suddenly felt intense self-consciousness. One December night, following a dinnertime discussion about which college Rosa was intending to choose, she rushed from the table in tears to an upstairs bathroom and vomited. Feeling a sense of relief, Rosa then went to her bedroom and fell asleep.

In the weeks and months that followed, Rosa outwardly seemed fine. She had made a choice about college and had resumed her successful endeavors in school and tennis. However, as Rosa explained, the facade masked inner turmoil. Self-doubts tormented her, and she worried most of the time about whether she would be able to fulfill the high expectations everyone seemed to have for her. As high school graduation approached, she realized that she would be the class valedictorian. As commencement day approached, Rosa was increasingly getting caught up in a cycle of self-starvation and excessive exercise. She had convinced herself that these behaviors were temporary and that she would "return to normal" right after graduation. The summer months flew by, and she left for college at the end of August. Rosa hoped and prayed that she could board the plane in San Juan and leave her "sick" behaviors on the island, beginning college with a healthy sense of herself and optimism about her future. When her tennis coach confronted her about the problem, Rosa realized, however, that she had carried with her a "suitcase of worries" that was killing her.

RETURN TO THE CASE

Rosa Nomirez (continued)

Assessment

Although the diagnosis of Rosa's problem seemed straightforward, I recommended that she complete the MMPI-2, to shed some more light on her personality. As expected, Rosa's profile was that of a young woman who was markedly defensive and striving to present herself in a favorable light. Even though Rosa's defensiveness was evident, so also was a profile characterized as perfectionistic, hypersensitive, and depressive—features commonly found in individuals with eating disorders.

Besides the data from the clinical interview and the MMPI-2, I also had Dr. Kennedy's medical report, which highlighted a number of health problems commonly associated with eating disorders. Rosa had lost nearly 20 percent of her body weight in the past several months. She had stopped menstruating and showed signs of anemia, dehydration, and electrolyte disturbance. Dr. Kennedy's medical conclusions were stated in frank and stern language. He recommended regular medical monitoring by university health personnel and stated that he considered hospitalization imperative if there was not an immediate improvement in Rosa's eating behavior.

Diagnosis

The psychological as well as the medical symptoms shown by Rosa pointed directly to an eating disorder. Although some clients with obsessive concerns about weight and compulsive behaviors pertaining to eating meet the criteria for obsessive-compulsive disorder, Rosa's clinical picture was focused exclusively on body image issues. She had not been engaging in binge eating, thus ruling out a diagnosis of bulimia nervosa. Rather, Rosa's condition met all the criteria for anorexia nervosa. She had been refusing to maintain appropriate body weight; she had an intense fear of gaining weight, even though dramatically underweight; she had a disturbed perception of her body weight and figure, while denying the seriousness of her dangerously low weight; and she had not menstruated in several months. Characteristics involving self-starvation and excessive exercise supported a subclassification of "restricting type."

Axis I: Anorexia Nervosa, Restricting Type
Axis II: No evidence of personality disorder
Axis III: Anemia, dehydration, electrolyte disturbance, amenorrhea
Axis IV: Educational problems, problems related to social environment (homesickness), and athletic pressures
Axis V: Current Global Assessment of Functioning: 60
          Highest Global Assessment of Functioning (past year): 90

Case Formulation

Rosa's history reads like a textbook case of a young woman at risk for developing an eating disorder. Constantly striving for perfection in every facet of her life, Rosa came to define herself in terms of the highest standards in each of her endeavors. She internalized her parents' high expectations and accepted nothing less than perfection in academic and athletic pursuits. As pressures mounted, and the expectations of others continued to intensify, Rosa reached a point at which her defenses began to break down. Being told that she was a "star" was gratifying at first, but Rosa began to worry that she would be unable to fulfill the dreams that so many people had for her. As her self-doubts increased, her distortions about her intelligence, personality, and attractiveness also increased. In a desperate attempt to make things right, she began to starve herself in a misguided attempt to appear more attractive to others and, in turn, possibly to feel better about herself.

Treatment Plan

When treating clients with serious eating disorders, I have learned over the years to attend first and foremost to their medical status. Even with the best of psychotherapeutic intervention, the health dangers require professional medical monitoring and intervention. I was relieved to know that Rosa was willing to cooperate with Dr. Kennedy's recommendations, the first of which was an emergency consultation with the staff nutritionist, Shelley Hatch, who put together a nutritional plan for Rosa. Ms. Hatch realized, just as well as I, that there was considerable risk that Rosa might pay lip service to complying with the nutritional plan, while secretly engaging in some of the self-destructive behaviors that had become so deeply entrenched. Ms. Hatch joined forces with me in conveying the dangerousness of Rosa's health condition, and the fact that hospitalization would be necessary if Rosa failed to regain some weight. Further, Rosa was expected to go for a medical check-up with Dr. Kennedy three times during the first week, then gradually move to less frequent appointments.

RETURN TO THE CASE

Rosa Nomirez (continued)

The medical and nutritional interventions were absolutely necessary in Rosa's case, but she would certainly need more. I recommended that she see me weekly in psychotherapy and that she participate in a group for eating-disordered women that met on campus. Rosa agreed to the weekly individual psychotherapy sessions but vehemently resisted the notion of participating in group therapy. Despite my strong recommendation, she made it clear that she would feel exposed and ashamed sharing her problems with other people, even those with the very same concerns. She reminded me of a cultural factor that I should have been more sensitive to: in Puerto Rican culture, seeking professional psychological help for problems carries a great stigma. It was difficult enough for her to admit to herself and to health professionals that she had problems; to tell her peers would be catastrophic. I respected the intensity of her feelings about the group and backed off with that idea. At the same time, however, I emphasized the importance of her compliance with the intervention plan involving regular psychotherapy sessions in addition to the health interventions. She agreed.

As soon as we began our regular sessions, Rosa seemed to plunge right into the issues. In fact, I recall being startled by her insight into the development of her problems. Rosa realized that her emotional difficulties did not have their roots in her adolescence but, rather, dated back to the early years of her life. Rosa began the second session with the profound statement, "I had to be perfect to erase the pain my parents felt following Juan's death." She proceeded to explain that, following Juan's bicycle accident, he remained a powerful presence in the family, even though he was rarely discussed. In her childhood, Rosa found herself wishing that she could find ways to make her parents happy and to help them put the tragedy behind them. She recalled wonderful memories of gratification when they celebrated her athletic and academic accomplishments, as well as memories of inner pain when they expressed any disappointments. As she approached adulthood, her striving for perfection intensified. She wanted to attend a prestigious college, and wanted to be as beautiful as possible. In a matter of months, many of these issues became confused, and Rosa was responding in unhealthy and desperate attempts to cope.

Much of my work with Rosa involved cognitive techniques, in which I tried to help her develop more accurate views of herself, the world, and her future potential. At the same time, I realized that it was important for her to have a good understanding of her family dynamics and the ways in which early life experiences influenced the development of her eating disorder. Our work did not involve "blaming" her parents, as Rosa feared that it might. Rather, she came to understand the ways in which their pain, and their needs, played a role in her pathological pursuit of perfection.

Outcome of the Case

Much to my relief, Rosa did comply with the medical and nutritional regimen proposed by Dr. Kennedy and Ms. Hatch. In fact, during the early weeks of treatment, Rosa was not only eating balanced meals but she also was allowing herself to indulge in an occasional milkshake, with the goal of returning to the target weight she had set. She was also working with her coach to establish an exercise program that made sense for conditioning purposes but was not excessive.

With the health components of the treatment plan working so smoothly, Rosa was in the right frame of mind to make optimal use of psychotherapy. I continued to see Rosa weekly for 6 months, during which she made major advances in self-understanding as well as behavior change. She came to realize that, not only did she not have to be perfect, but relentless striving for perfection would lead her to misery. She came to realize that she couldn't win every tennis match, nor did she need to. She realized that she needn't be devastated if she did not attain a 4.0 grade point average each semester. And she realized that her body did not have to look like that of a fashion model. Central to Rosa's growth was her gentle confrontation with her parents when she returned home between semesters. In a loving way, she found the words to express her appreciation for all they had given her, while at the same time conveying her need to have the pressure lessened at this point in her life. Rosa told me that, at first, they seemed defensive but seemed to "wake up" when she told them about the serious health problems she had developed a few months earlier due to her disordered eating. This discussion seemed to be a turning point for Rosa, enabling her to move from the confining demands imposed by her parents to a point at which she could set goals and expectations for herself.

Rosa developed a close working alliance with me during those 6 months. At the end of February, when I suggested that we consider terminating, she seemed genuinely sad at first, yet she recognized the importance of taking the work she had

RETURN TO THE CASE

Rosa Nomirez (continued)

been doing in psychotherapy into her own hands. She felt confident that she could stay healthy, and she promised to contact me should she find herself slipping back into unhealthy behaviors. In fact, in mid-April, the pressures of the tennis season seemed a bit overwhelming for Rosa, and she found herself having some of the same obsessions. After a few days of skipping meals, she realized that she was in danger, so she called me for an appointment. In that 50-minute session, Rosa did virtually all the talking. She explained what was going on in her thoughts and in her behavior, and she laid out a treatment plan for herself. Feeling confident that she could take care of this issue before it worsened, she left the session in good spir-

its, stating that there was no need for further meetings at that time. I trusted her judgment.

The next time I heard from Rosa was the following September, in a note telling me how well things were going. The tennis team had lost the championship game in May, but, rather than fret about it, Rosa explained that she had found a way to leave it behind her and have a great summer at home, working in a day care center with children in poverty worse than any challenge she had ever faced. That was the last time Rosa ever contacted me, although I did see occasional stories in the campus newspaper about the ups and downs of the tennis team. In each of the accompanying photos, Rosa looked healthy and happy. ■

Sarah Tobin, PhD

Summary

- People with anorexia nervosa experience four kinds of symptoms. They (1) refuse or are unable to maintain normal weight, (2) have an intense fear of gaining weight or becoming fat, even though they may be grossly underweight, (3) have a distorted perception of the weight or shape of their body, and (4) experience amenorrhea, if postpubertal. People with bulimia nervosa alternate between the extremes of eating large amounts of food in a short time (binges) and then compensating for the added calories by vomiting or performing other extreme actions. Those with the purging type try to force out of their bodies what they have just eaten, while those with the nonpurging type try to compensate for what they eat by fasting or exercising excessively. Very serious physical and medical problems can arise in association with these disorders. Attempts to understand and treat eating disorders emerge within biological, psychological, and sociocultural perspectives. Biochemical abnormalities in the norepinephrine and serotonin neurotransmitter systems, perhaps with a genetic basis, are thought to be involved in eating disorders. The psychological perspective views eating disorders as developing in people who suffer a great deal of inner turmoil and pain, and who become obsessed with body issues, often turning to food for comfort and nurturance. According to cognitive theories, over time people with eating disorders become trapped in their pathological patterns because of resistance to change. Within the sociocultural perspective, eating disorders have been explained in terms of family systems theories and, more broadly, in terms of society's attitudes toward eating and diet. Treatment of eating disorders requires a combination of

approaches. While medications, particularly those affecting serotonin, are sometimes prescribed, it is also clear that psychotherapy is necessary, particularly those using cognitive-behavioral and interpersonal techniques. Family therapy, particularly when the client is a teen, can also be an important component of an intervention plan.

- People with impulse-control disorders repeatedly engage in behaviors that are potentially harmful, feeling unable to stop themselves and experiencing a sense of desperation if they are thwarted from carrying out their impulsive behavior. People with kleptomania are driven by a persistent urge to steal, not because they wish to have the stolen objects but because they experience a thrill while engaging in the act of stealing. In addition to recommending medication, such as fluoxetine, clinicians commonly treat people with kleptomania with behavioral treatments, such as covert sensitization, to help them control the urge to steal.

- People with pathological gambling have an intense urge to gamble, causing them to become preoccupied with such risk-taking behaviors. From a biological perspective, the gambler's perpetual pursuit of the big win can be seen as a drive for stimulation and pleasurable feelings. Certain personality characteristics, such as impulsivity and psychopathy, also seem to predispose people to developing this condition. Sociocultural factors, such as the spread of legalized gambling, may aggravate the tendency of some vulnerable individuals to become immersed in such behavior. Treatment methods that combine various approaches seem most effective. Medications, such as selective serotonin reuptake inhibitors, have been shown to be helpful with some clients, as have behavioral and cognitive-behavioral techniques. Many pathological gamblers also benefit from participation in peer groups, such as Gamblers Anonymous.

- People with pyromania are driven by the intense desire to prepare, set, and watch fires. This disorder seems to be rooted in childhood problems and firesetting behavior. In adulthood, people with pyromania typically have various dysfunctional characteristics, such as problems with substance abuse as well as relationship difficulties. Some treatment programs focus on children showing early signs of developing this disorder. With adults, various approaches are used, with the aim of focusing on the client's broader psychological problems, such as low self-esteem, depression, communication problems, and inability to control anger.

- People with sexual impulsivity are unable to control their sexual behavior and feel driven to engage in frequent and indiscriminate sexual activity, which they later regret. Individuals with this condition commonly suffer with a co-existing condition, such as depression, phobic disorder, or substance abuse, and some experience dissociative symptoms. Although this condition can be understood as related to a biochemical disturbance, most experts focus on early life experiences. Treatment usually combines components derived from insight-oriented, behavioral, and family systems approaches.

- People with trichotillomania have an irresistible urge to pull out their hair. This condition, which shares some features with obsessive-compulsive disorder, responds to some of the same medications prescribed to people with OCD. Furthermore, certain brain abnormalities have been implicated. Behavioral theorists regard the disorder as resulting from the reinforcement associated with tension relief following random hair pulling. Sociocultural theorists focus on the development of this condition within the context of disturbed parent-child relationships, in which an upset child resorts to this kind of behavior in an attempt to gain attention. Various medications for treating this disorder are being tested, although clinicians would usually recommend that treatment include behavioral therapy, such as habit reversal.

- People with intermittent explosive disorder feel a recurrent inability to resist assaultive or destructive acts of aggression. Theorists propose that an interaction of biological and environmental factors lead to this condition. In terms of biology, serotonin seems to be implicated. In terms of psychological and sociocultural factors, theorists focus on the reinforcing qualities of emotional outbursts, as well as the effects of such behaviors on family systems and intimate relationships. Treatment may involve the prescription of medication, although psychotherapeutic methods would also be included in the intervention.

Key Terms

See Glossary for definitions.

Anorexia nervosa 426
Big win 436
Binges 427
Bulimia nervosa 427
Impulse 433

Impulse-control disorders 433
Intermittent explosive disorder 443
Kleptomania 433
Nonpurging type 428
Pathological gambling 434

Purge 426
Purging type 428
Pyromania 438
Sexual impulsivity 439
Trichotillomania 441

Internet Resource

To get more information on the material covered in this chapter, visit our web site at **http://www.mhhe.com/halgin**. There you will find more information, resources, and links to topics of interest.

CASE REPORT: MARK CHEN

It had been more than 10 years since I treated Mark Chen. At the time, he had been an undergraduate student, who came to see me in his senior year for serious depression. In fact, he had been so depressed that he had to be hospitalized for 2 weeks and treated with electroconvulsive therapy. I hadn't heard from him since that time and occasionally wondered how he might be doing. One unusually warm January afternoon, I received a phone call from Mark's wife, Tanya, urgently asking for my assistance. Apparently, Mark was experiencing a recurrence of his depression with intensity so great that Tanya feared he might kill himself. Tanya recalled that Mark had seen me a decade earlier and explained that she didn't know where to turn. Her emotion-packed words alerted me to the frightening situation she was facing: "Dr. Tobin, he's been sitting home for the past 2 days, holding a knife to his wrist. What should I do?"

I asked Tanya whether she felt she would be able to persuade Mark to go with her to the emergency room, where I could conduct an evaluation. As I held the phone, I could hear Tanya murmuring to Mark, but I heard no response. She spoke louder to him and soon began to cry with impassioned pleas for him to answer. Still no response.

Given the seriousness of the situation, I discussed with Tanya ways that she might get Mark to the hospital. Since she was alone and he was immobilized, she didn't think it would be possible for her to take him without assistance. I suggested she call an ambulance service, and I gave her the name of a local company with expertise in dealing with individuals in psychiatric crisis. I also suggested that she contact a relative or friend to come to her apartment and help her deal with the situation. She followed both recommendations, first summoning an ambulance and then calling her best friend, Anita, who was able to provide her with support in this troubling situation.

Two hours after we ended our phone contact, I received a call from the emergency room with a request that I come down to do an evaluation on Mark Chen. Knowing that I was walking into a stressful situation, I braced myself for the likelihood that I might have to make some difficult decisions about hospitalizing Mark.

When I entered the consulting room, I came upon Tanya and a man I didn't recognize. Admittedly, 10 years had passed since my brief treatment of Mark Chen. But how could this man be only 32 years old? Perhaps it was his unshaven face, his unkempt hair, and his weary look that made him seem so much older. I extended my hand to greet Mark, but my words fell on seemingly deaf ears. Sitting in the chair like a lump of flesh, Mark was immobile. He uttered no words and made absolutely no movements. Then, suddenly, he grabbed the pen from the nearby desk and gouged at his wrist. With a split-second reaction, I pulled the pen from his hand and in a strong but calming voice said, "Mark, you are in the hospital. I am Dr. Sarah Tobin. Remember, I treated you 10 years ago when you were in college. You need help again, and Tanya and I are trying to help you. Please cooperate with us. You mustn't hurt yourself."

The decisions that I dreaded were now before me. Mark was clearly in danger of hurting himself. Ideally, he would be able to recognize the depth of his depression and comply with my recommendation that he sign himself into the hospital. Realistically, however, Mark did not seem to comprehend a word I was saying. I placed the Informed Consent form before him, but he stared blankly at the paper with absolutely no responsiveness. There was no other choice for me but to commit Mark to the hospital. The process of taking away a person's voluntary control over personal choices is one of the most unpleasant aspects of the work of a mental health professional. Every time I face the task of committing a person to the hospital, I am temporarily paralyzed by questions about how I would feel if I were in that person's place. Would I be enraged? Would I be frightened? Would I feel relieved?

I discussed the dilemma with Tanya and asked her how she felt participating in committing Mark to the hospital. Choking on her own emotion, she found it difficult to speak in a way that I could understand. She did nod her agreement, however, so I proceeded to complete the legal forms documenting the need to take this decision out of Mark's hands.

The next decision I faced pertained to the nature of the initial intervention for Mark's profound depression. Mark had not eaten in days and had gotten only a minimal amount of sleep. Furthermore, Tanya reported with some embarrassment, Mark had urinated and defecated in his clothing, almost unaware of what was happening. With a symptom picture as serious as Mark's, we did not have the luxury of waiting for antidepressant medications to take effect. Mark's condition called for electroconvulsive therapy, a treatment that had been tremendously helpful for Mark 10 years earlier. When I raised this suggestion with Tanya, she seemed initially irritated, stating, "Isn't there a less dangerous treatment you can use?" After I reassured Tanya about the safety of ECT, as well as the urgency of Mark's condition, she agreed to sign the forms granting permission for this treatment. Once again, we were facing the troubling task of deciding on a course of action for a person deemed incapable of making such important choices for himself.

After all the necessary forms were completed, I summoned psychiatric aides to bring a wheelchair to escort Mark Chen to the treatment unit. A hospital wristband was placed on Mark, indicating that he should remain under 24-hour watch and that all "dangerous objects" should be kept out of his reach. As Mark was wheeled out of the consulting room, I tried to reassure Tanya that I believed he would show improvement within a few days and that these difficult choices were necessary and wise.

Sarah Tobin, PhD

15

Ethical and Legal Issues

T he case of Mark Chen is indeed provocative. You might find it disturbing to confront the fact that profoundly important choices about hospitalization and treatment are sometimes made by people other than the client. In some instances, these decisions are made by strangers, such as police officers or emergency room physicians, who have little or no information about the person other than the behavior they are observing. However, even staunch protectors of personal freedom and individual rights realize that, in certain situations, people are incapable of acting in their own best interest; in some cases, they are so impaired that their lives or the safety of others is at risk. In this chapter, we will discuss the ways in which the work of mental health professionals is affected by and informed by ethical and legal issues.

■ Ethical Issues

When most people think about psychological interventions, they focus on the helping nature of the therapeutic relationship. From the chapters you have read so far, you might conclude that psychotherapy is usually a voluntary process in which a person willingly seeks help and therapy proceeds in a straightforward manner. We will now turn our attention to some of the complexities associated with the delivery of professional services. These complexities relate to the responsibilities of mental health professionals, the ethical issues in the provision of mental health care, the legal issues pertaining to the rights of clients in treatment, and the responsibilities of a society to ensure the protection of its citizens. These issues have emerged in the context of broader social and historical changes in the mental health system, such as deinstitutionalization, increased attention to potential abuses in psychotherapy, and heightened publicity regarding medical malpractice.

Roles and Responsibilities of Clinicians

As you are reading this final chapter of the text, think back to our discussion in Chapter 2 about the work and responsibilities of clinicians. In that chapter, we spoke of the clinician as an expert in human relations with a range of responsibilities for assessing and helping people with psychological problems. Throughout the book, you have read about the cases of Dr. Tobin, as well as many other clinical examples involving the work of clinicians with their clients. By now, you have developed an appreciation for how demanding and difficult this work must be. Adding to the challenges involved in diagnosis and treatment, clinicians also contend with a number of difficult issues pertaining to professional and ethical practice. In the sections that follow, we will examine some of the concerns that mental health professionals face in their efforts to maintain the highest standards of practice.

Therapist Competence

It would be naive to think that possessing a doctorate in clinical psychology or a degree in medicine is a guarantee that a professional is capable of treating every client requesting services. Mental health professionals are guided by standards that specify that they possess the skills needed to treat people who approach them for professional services. In other words, they should have the intellectual competence to assess, conceptualize, and treat clients whom they accept into treatment. Furthermore, they need to be emotionally capable of managing the clinical issues that emerge in treatment.

Consider how inappropriate it would be for a clinician without any training or experience in the treatment of people with severe eating disorders to advertise that he is opening a specialty practice in treating women with anorexia nervosa. Obviously, he would be practicing in a field in which he lacks the competence to treat people with specialized treatment needs, and his behavior would be unethical. In a case such as this, the absurdity is evident. However, there are other cases in which the clinician may have the training and experience, but not the emotional competence, to deal with certain kinds of clinical issues. An example of this is the case of a profoundly depressed clinician who is treating clients also suffering from severe mood disturbance. Although this clinician's training may be sufficient, the active nature of the clinician's own psychological disorder could impede his or her ability to be a wise and constructive consultant in the life of a client suffering with the same problem.

Mental health professionals are expected to conduct regular self-scrutiny, in which they make an effort to objectively evaluate their competence to carry out their work. When faced with prospective clients whose needs are beyond the clinician's competence, a referral should be made, or the clinician should obtain appropriate supervision. Self-assessment of emotional competence is a bit more difficult, in that it can be difficult to recognize the depth or extent of one's own problems. Astute clinicians regularly seek out the advice of senior or peer consultants to help them make such evaluations.

Informed Consent

Assuming that the clinician has the intellectual and emotional competence to treat, the next set of issues pertains to obligations within the treatment context. Although it would be unusual to have a legalistic contract for therapy, experts in the field recommend some form of a therapeutic understanding. In other words, clinicians should provide clients with the information they will need to make decisions about therapy. According to Koocher and Keith-Spiegel (1998), there are several key elements in the sound therapeutic contract. At the outset of therapy, clinicians should discuss the goals of treatment, the process of therapy, the client's rights, the therapist's responsibilities, the treatment risks, the techniques that will be used, financial issues, and the limits of confidentiality. When these matters have been discussed, the client gives **informed consent**, an indication that he or she has participated in setting the treatment goals, understands and agrees to the treatment plan, and knows the clinician's credentials (Koocher, 1994). Generally, clients are given a written statement containing this information. In cases in which a risk is involved in treatment, such as when medication or electroconvulsive therapy is recommended, the client should understand the possible short-term and long-term side effects. The clinician has a responsibility to ensure that the client is made aware of these issues, is given answers to these questions, and is given the opportunity to refuse treatment.

This process has some complications. Psychotherapy is an imprecise procedure, and it is not always possible to predict its course, risks, or benefits. The clinician's job, however, is to give a best estimate at the onset of therapy and to provide further information as therapy proceeds. Most people are able to discuss these matters with the clinician and to make an informed choice. However, what happens when prospective clients are unable to understand the issues in order to make informed consent? This is the case with people who are out of touch with reality, people who are mentally retarded, and children. In these cases, the clinician must work with the individual's family or other legally appointed guardians, as Dr. Tobin did in her dealings with Mark Chen. Because he was so depressed and catatonic, she found it necessary to turn to Mark's wife to obtain consent for the administration of electroconvulsive therapy. The clinician must make every effort to ensure that the client's rights are protected.

Confidentiality

Part of the informed consent process involves informing the client that what takes place in therapy is private. **Confidentiality**, long regarded as a sacred part of the clinician-client relationship, refers to the principle that the therapist must safeguard disclosures in therapy as private. Why is confidentiality so important? In order for clients to feel comfortable disclosing intimate details, they need to have the assurance that the clinician will protect this information. For example, if a man tells his therapist that he is having an extramarital affair, he would do so with the understanding that the therapist would not divulge this information to others. In fact, safeguards against the disclosure of confidential information exist within the laws of most states.

The content of therapy is legally considered **privileged communication**. In other words, the clinician may not disclose any information about the client in a court of law without the client's expressed permission. This issue would arise in a court proceeding; for example, a therapist might be summoned to appear in a divorce case and be asked to divulge information about a client's sexual dysfunction that had been discussed in therapy. Because the content of therapy is "privileged communication," the therapist must have the client's permission before discussing any information that had emerged in therapy. In the context of the courts, privileged communication differs from the general notion that the public is entitled to relevant evidence pertaining to a case (Smith-Bell & Winslade, 1994). However, there are certain kinds of cases in which the court is entitled to information shared within the therapy context. For example, in certain kinds of child custody cases, a judge may deem that therapy information is crucial in order to protect the welfare of the child. Other exceptions to privilege involve cases in which a defendant is using mental disability as a defense in a criminal trial; in this kind of case, the court would likely rule that the defendant has waived the psychologist-client privilege as it relates to the defendant's mental state at the time of the alleged crime. Along similar lines, an exception to privilege applies in a case in which a psychologist is appointed by a court to determine whether the defendant is competent to stand trial; obviously, the psychologist would be expected to share findings from such an evaluation with the court. However, the psychologist would not necessarily have blanket

Before being admitted to a psychiatric hospital, this client is asked to give informed consent indicating that he understands the nature of the treatment he will receive.

permission to share all that was communicated during the evaluation; the psychologist cannot disclose any statements by the defendant regarding the offense, unless the individual gives explicit permission (Brant, 1998).

As you can see, the work of a mental health professional involves many challenges in cases in which there is a legal aspect. For the most part, the legal system is committed to protecting the sanctity of private communication between a mental health professional and a client who has turned to that professional for help. In some instances, however, the client's rights must be overlooked for the good of society and the welfare of other people, such as children, who might be at risk of harm.

There are some important exceptions to the principle of confidentiality, such as cases involving abuse. Every state requires some form of **mandated reporting** by professionals when they learn first hand of cases involving child abuse or neglect. Abuse, which may be physical or sexual, is defined as an act by a caretaker that causes serious physical or emotional injury. Neglect is characterized as the intentional withholding of food, clothing, shelter, or medical care (Brant, 1998). In recent years, many states have expanded mandated reporting statutes to include a wider range of vulnerable people, such as those who are handicapped or developmentally disabled as well as impaired elders who cannot otherwise protect themselves (Smith-Bell & Winslade, 1994).

Clinicians as well as teachers and other health professionals are required by law to notify the appropriate authorities about cases in which vulnerable individuals are being abused or neglected. The purpose of mandated reporting is to protect victims from continuing abuse and neglect, to initiate steps toward clinical intervention with the abused individual, and to deter, punish, and rehabilitate abusers.

Another exception to the principle of confidentiality involves instances in which the clinician learns that a client is planning to hurt another person. In such cases, the clinician has a **duty to warn**. This means that the clinician is required to inform the intended victim that the client plans to harm him or her. Duty to warn laws have their origins in a famous case that took place in 1969 in California. The "Tarasoff" case (*Tarasoff v. Regents of the University of California et al.,* 1976) involved a young woman named Tatiana Tarasoff, who was a student at the University of California at Berkeley. She was shot and fatally stabbed by a man named Prosenjit Poddar, whom she had dated the previous year and with whom she had broken off relations. Her parents successfully sued the university following her murder on the grounds that she was not properly warned about the fact that Poddar, who was a client at the counseling center, intended to kill her. The psychologist who treated the murderer had become alarmed when Poddar told him that he was going to go after Tarasoff and kill her. The psychologist informed the police, who then interviewed Poddar. After assurances from Poddar, the police let him go. The court ruled that the psychologist had not gone far enough in preventing Tarasoff's murder. He should have told her that Poddar was intent on killing her. It took several years for this case to proceed through the legal system, and its ramifications continue to be felt by psychotherapists who struggle to differentiate between their clients' serious threats and random fantasies. In trying to make these distinctions, clinicians recurrently weigh the client's right of confidentiality against concern for the rights of other people.

When you hear about a clinician's duty to warn, you may feel that it is a logical precaution worth taking. After all, if another person's life is at stake, you would think that a clinician would certainly want to do everything to let that person know. However, the situation is more complicated than it seems. In fact, some experts assert that the Tarasoff decision produced negative clinical effects (La Fond, 1994). In dealing with potentially dangerous clients, clinicians are more likely to initiate commitment proceedings so as to protect possible victims. This means that some people will be institutionalized who might not present an actual threat. Another drawback to duty to warn is that clinicians steer away from difficult topics pertaining to the issue of possible harm to others. Without even being aware of it, clinicians may find that they avoid asking a client about possible dangerous behavior, because they do not want to be burdened by the legal responsibilities to take action. Complicating the matter even further is the imprecise nature of predicting dangerousness, which we will discuss later in the chapter.

Relationships with Clients

As you were reading the case studies in this book, you probably noticed that, in addition to speaking about the client, Dr. Tobin also spoke about herself in terms of her emotional reactions to her clients. In a few instances, she spoke about how difficult and exasperating her work with some clients can be. The therapeutic relationship is, by definition, intense and intimate. Because of the charged nature of this relationship, clinicians know that they must proceed with utmost vigilance in their

 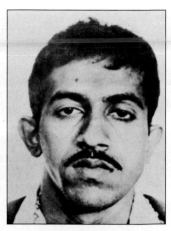

Tatiana Tarasoff, a junior at the University of California, was stabbed to death on the doorstep of her home by Prosenjit Poddar, who had told his therapist that he intended to kill her.

interactions with clients. Clear roles and boundaries are essential in order for the client to feel safe and trusting, and for the clinician to maintain objectivity and effectiveness. When boundaries are violated within a therapeutic relationship, the consequences can be catastrophic for clients.

The most extreme form of violation of the therapeutic relationship involves sexual intimacy with clients, which is explicitly forbidden in the ethical codes of the mental health professions. Other forms of involvement with clients can fall into gray areas, however. While clinicians are urged to maintain neutrality and distance in their dealings with clients, these efforts are at times complicated, as is the case for clinicians working in small towns. What should the only psychologist in town do when it turns out that a prospective new client is also her son's sixth-grade teacher or baseball coach? Ethical codes in the mental health professions urge clinicians to avoid developing such dual relationships and to look for alternatives, if at all possible. Certain kinds of relationships with clients would always be considered inappropriate. In addition to sexual or romantic involvements, it would be inappropriate for clinicians to become involved in business relationships with clients, because the boundaries, and thus the clinician's objectivity, would be blurred (Koocher & Keith-Spiegel, 1998).

The Business of Psychotherapy

As we have discussed the mental health field throughout this book, we have focused on the helping aspects of the profession. It is the opportunity to touch positively the lives of those in need that draws people to such a career. It is only a matter of time, however, before idealistic helpers find that they depend for their livelihood on a complex health care system characterized by intense pressures to control costs.

Although some clients are able to pay for their therapy, most are reliant on a third party payor, such as a public assistance program or an insurance policy. In terms of health insurance, during the 1990s major changes in the American health care system took place involving the introduction and expansion of managed health care programs. In principle, such institutions as health maintenance organizations and managed care mental health systems made sense, because they emerged from efforts to contain costs in order to keep insurance premiums affordable. As managed health care has expanded, however, many clinicians have found that they struggle with recurring ethical dilemmas, as they try to "balance the needs and best interests of their clients with an array of rewards, sanctions, and other inducements" (Koocher & Keith-Spiegel, 1998, p. 251). In some cases, clinicians are given financial incentives to limit care. When the case involves psychiatric hospitalization, an expensive proposition, pressures may be placed on the clinician to make the inpatient stay unreasonably brief, possibly placing the client at risk.

In order to adhere to the highest standards of ethical practice, good clinicians are alert to the financial pressures that affect their work. The American health care system will continue to evolve in to the new century, and unexpected ethical challenges are likely to emerge in response to technological changes in society and in the delivery of mental health services (DeLeon, Vandenbos, Sammons, & Frank, 1998). As these changes take place, good clinicians will continue to strive to adhere to the principles that hold the good of their clients and of society above their own needs and wishes.

Former heavyweight boxing champion Mike Tyson leaves Massachusetts General Hospital in September 1998 following a psychological evaluation ordered by the Nevada Athletic Commission, as a result of his biting his opponent's ear during a boxing match.

Special Roles for Clinicians

In addition to their work as psychotherapists, clinicians are sometimes called on for special roles, each with its own set of ethical challenges. Among these special roles are the instances in which a clinician is an expert witness in court, becomes involved in a child custody case, or evaluates people with dementia.

The role of expert witness has a number of challenges, in that the clinician is called on to provide specialized information not commonly known by people outside the mental health profession. For example, a psychologist may be asked to conduct a specialized examination of a defendant or to critique the assessment findings of another professional. In such instances, the psychologist is expected to be an unbiased professional who is helping the court understand technical information pertinent to court deliberations. The process becomes ethically challenging, however, due to the fact that one of the parties involved in the legal proceeding is paying for the psychologist's services and opinions. In such contexts, the ethical clinician strives to be thoughtful, cautious, nondefensive, and scientifically rigorous (Koocher & Keith-Spiegel, 1998).

Even more complicated than the role of expert witness is the task of conducting evaluations in child protection cases. Such evaluations are deemed necessary in situations in which there are concerns about the child's welfare. For example, if there has been evidence or charges involving abuse, a mental health professional may be called on to make recommendations about the child's care. A clinician may be appointed as an agent of the court or a child protection agency, or may be hired by one of the parents. In some instances, the clinician is appointed as a **guardian ad litem**, a person appointed by the court to represent or make decisions for a person (e.g., minor or incapacitated adult) who is legally incapable of doing so in a civil legal proceeding.

As evaluators in child protection cases, clinicians may be asked to address such concerns as the extent to which the child's psychological well-being is being affected, the nature of the therapeutic interventions that are warranted, the psychological effect of a child being given over to one or both parents, and the psychological effect on the child if separated from the parents (Committee on Professional Practice and Standards Board of Professional Affairs, 1998). Table 15.1 specifies the guidelines that psychologists are expected to follow when conducting such evaluations. As you can see, clinicians willing to take on such responsibilities find themselves in positions where they must manage various kinds of pressure. Because their professional efforts have such tremendous consequences on the lives of those involved, they know that they must proceed with the utmost caution and diligence.

Clinicians may also be called on to conduct evaluations of people suffering with various symptoms reflective of cognitive decline. Such evaluations are most commonly conducted by psychologists, because, among the mental health professionals, they have the unique training and experience to administer neuropsychological tests that assess memory and cognitive functioning in order to differentiate normal changes from symptoms of serious deterioration. As is the case with evaluations involving child protection cases, guidelines have been published to alert psychologists to the special issues involved in the evaluation of cognitive decline. Those guidelines are listed in Table 15.2 (APA Presidential Task Force on Dementia, 1998).

Commitment of Clients

The case of Mark Chen at the beginning of this chapter highlights one of the most disturbing aspects of the work of mental health professionals—making a decision to involuntarily detain an individual in a psychiatric hospital. Imagine how you might feel and what you might do if a loved one told you that he is so despondent that he is going to kill himself? Obviously, you would be very alarmed and would want to do anything possible to stop him from hurting or killing himself. In order to deal with situations such as this, all states have laws designed to protect

Table 15.1

Guidelines for Psychological Evaluations in Child Protection Matters

1. The primary purpose of the evaluation is to provide relevant, professionally sound results or opinions in matters where a child's health and welfare may have been and/or may in the future be harmed.

2. In child protection cases, the child's interest and well-being are paramount.

3. The evaluation addresses the particular psychological and developmental needs of the child and/or parent(s) that are relevant to child protection issues, such as physical abuse, sexual abuse, neglect, and/or serious emotional harm.

4. The role of the psychologist conducting evaluations is that of a professional expert who strives to maintain an unbiased, objective stance.

5. The serious consequences of psychological assessment in child protection matters place a heavy burden on psychologists.

6. Psychologists gain specialized competence.

7. Psychologists are aware of personal and societal biases and engage in nondiscriminatory practice.

8. Psychologists avoid multiple relationships.

9. Based on the nature of the referral questions, the scope of the evaluation is determined by the evaluator.

10. Psychologists performing psychological evaluations in child protection matters obtain appropriate informed consent from all adult participants and, as appropriate, inform the child participant. Psychologists need to be particularly sensitive to consent issues.

11. Psychologists inform participants about the disclosure of information and the limits of confidentiality.

12. Psychologists use multiple methods of data gathering.

13. Psychologists neither overinterpret nor inappropriately interpret clinical or assessment data.

14. Psychologists conducting a psychological evaluation in child protection matters provide an opinion regarding the psychological functioning of an individual only after conducting an evaluation of the individual adequate to support their statements or conclusions.

15. Recommendations, if offered, are based on whether the child's health and welfare have been and/or may be seriously harmed.

16. Psychologists clarify financial arrangements.

17. Psychologists maintain appropriate records.

mentally ill individuals from harming themselves or other people. **Commitment** is an emergency procedure for the involuntary hospitalization of a person who, if not hospitalized, is deemed to be likely to create harm for self or other people as a result of mental illness (Brant, 1998).

The concept of commitment stems from the legal principle that the state has the authority to protect those who are unable to protect themselves; in the law, this authority is referred to as **parens patriae.** This responsibility is vested in various professionals, such as psychologists, physicians, and nurse specialists, who are authorized to sign an application for a time-limited commitment (usually 10 days); if a health professional is not accessible, a police officer may file commitment papers. In this application, the professional states why the failure to hospitalize the individual would result in the likelihood of serious harm due to mental illness. In some instances, application is made to a district court judge, perhaps by a family member; after hearing the reasons for commitment, the judge may issue a warrant to apprehend the mentally ill person in order for that individual to be assessed by a qualified professional. Once the individual is hospitalized, subsequent applications and hearings may be necessary to extend the period of commitment.

As you think about the concept of involuntary commitment, it is probably clear to you that it is a very complex issue. Does one person have the right to interfere with another's decisions or freedom of action? If your friend wants to kill himself, what right have you or anyone else to stop him? Consider the question of dangerousness. Your friend's threats are very serious, but what if his risk is less obvious? Perhaps he has stopped eating for the past few days, or perhaps he has been drinking and driving. Would these behaviors be considered dangerous enough to warrant his involuntary hospitalization?

Clinicians and legal experts have struggled with questions regarding involuntary commitment for the past two decades, and standards have alternated between being overly restrictive and overly liberal. For example, when commitment procedures have been very stringent, it was difficult to keep all but the most extremely disturbed individuals in the hospital. More recently, the trend has been toward less strict requirements for commitment, as public officials have reinterpreted commitment laws to make it easier to place seriously disturbed individuals in hospitals (La Fond & Durham, 1992). This trend has resulted in part from the fact that communities lack the resources to provide appropriate aftercare for hospitalized patients. Professionals are concerned about releasing

Table 15.2

Guidelines for the Evaluation of Dementia and Age-Related Cognitive Decline

1. Psychologists performing evaluations of dementia and age-related cognitive decline should be familiar with the prevailing diagnostic nomenclature and specific diagnostic criteria.

2. Psychologists attempt to obtain informed consent.

3. Psychologists gain specialized competence.

4. Psychologists seek and provide appropriate consultation.

5. Psychologists are aware of personal and societal biases and engage in nondiscriminatory practice.

6. Psychologists conduct a clinical interview as part of the evaluation.

7. Psychologists are aware that standardized psychological and neuropsychological tests are important tools in the assessment of dementia and age-related cognitive decline.

8. When measuring cognitive changes in individuals, psychologists attempt to estimate premorbid abilities.

9. Psychologists are sensitive to the limitations and sources of variability and error in psychometric performance.

10. Psychologists recognize that providing constructive feedback, support, and education, as well as maintaining a therapeutic alliance, can be important parts of the evaluation process.

Source: APA Presidential Task Force on the Assessment of Age-Consistent Memory Decline and Dementia. (1998).

patients into the community when the facilities within that community are deficient, so they are more inclined to seek justification for keeping the patient in the hospital (Turkheimer & Parry, 1994).

The move to relax the criteria for involuntary commitment was also a response to the increase in the numbers of mentally ill homeless people living on the streets of large cities. There are about half a million homeless people in the United States, and about one quarter to one third of these are psychiatrically disturbed (Cohen & Thompson, 1992). In fact, the pendulum has now swung in the opposite direction, with increasing numbers of homeless people being involuntarily hospitalized to provide them with shelter.

Questions regarding commitment involve evaluations of dangerousness by professionals who do commitment evaluations. Forensic psychologists are often called on to assess dangerousness, usually in the context of predicting whether a person will be dangerous in the future. As you might imagine, this is often a difficult determination to make. Most psychologists agree that the best prediction of future dangerousness is the level of dangerousness shown by the person in the past. An individual who has murdered several times is more likely to harm someone in the future than is an individual with no homicidal history. Even when the probability of dangerousness is high, however, there is still room for error in the prediction of future behavior. The consequences of erroneous predictions are, of course, very significant. The supposedly dangerous individual might be institutionalized unnecessarily, or the person deemed nondangerous might go on to commit serious harm.

Right to Treatment

The admission to psychiatric hospitals, whether voluntary or involuntary, is only the beginning of the story for people entering these facilities. Once admitted, the client enters a world that is unfamiliar to most people. They may feel frightened; if hospitalized against their will, they may feel outraged. Such reactions are understandable, and health professionals try to ensure that clients are given appropriate care and that they understand their legal rights. We have already discussed the importance of obtaining informed consent, when possible, prior to beginning treatment to ensure that clients understand the nature of treatment, the options available, and the client's rights.

Perhaps the most important legal right of the person entering a psychiatric hospital is the right to treatment. It may seem odd that laws are needed to ensure that patients in hospitals be provided with treatment, but, as you read the legal history of

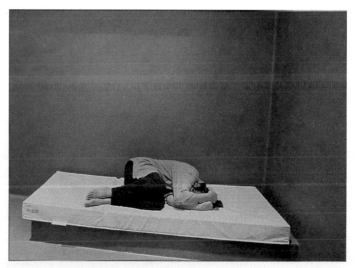

If a psychiatric patient is seen as potentially dangerous, the patient may be contained in a seclusion room. In such instances, a member of the clinical staff must write in the medical record the rationale for the seclusion as well as the duration.

Homeless and Mentally Ill—the Right to Refuse Treatment

Since the beginning of the deinstitutionalization movement in the 1970s, the number of people involuntarily committed to psychiatric hospitals has decreased dramatically. The trend toward community-based treatment for individuals with severe mental illness, and particularly those diagnosed with schizophrenia, has provided many with higher-quality and less restrictive treatment, yet many others who might have languished in hospitals years ago now find themselves homeless.

There is evidence that individuals with schizophrenia who are homeless experience more severe symptoms than those who are not homeless. Opler and his colleagues (Opler et al., 1994) compared the symptoms of homeless and nonhomeless schizophrenic men in New York City. Those who were homeless experienced more hallucinations, and they were more troubled by persecutory delusions, emotional problems, and impulsive behavior. They also had greater problems with alcohol and drug abuse and were more likely to be noncompliant with their medications.

Medication noncompliance has been cited as one reason for widespread homelessness among people with schizophrenia. Among outpatients being treated with antipsychotic medications to control their hallucinations and delusions, 40 percent or more refuse medication or fail to take it as prescribed. Because of their legal right to refuse unwanted treatment, most clients are free to refuse medication and other forms of treatment, even in instances in which their symptoms would probably improve. Treatment can be legally mandated only in rare instances when clients pose a serious threat to their own safety or the safety of someone else or when they cannot understand the consequences of their decision to refuse treatment or medication (Cournos, 1989; Marcos & Cohen, 1986). In recent years, many people have advocated committing homeless mentally ill persons to hospitals, where they could receive medication and treatment for their illnesses. They argue that theirs is a humane solution to homelessness caused by an untreated illness; their opponents suggest it is a return to the dark days before deinstitutionalization.

The dilemma of involuntary medication came to national attention in the late 1980s with the case of Joyce Brown, a homeless woman from New York City. Ms. Brown, a 40-year-old African American woman, had lived on the streets of Manhattan for a year and a half; the police took her to a psychiatric ward of Bellevue Hospital under a new law that allowed the involuntary hospitalization and treatment of mentally ill homeless people. She was described as disheveled, hostile, and verbally abusive while living on the street, and authorities suggested that she was delusional and required hospitalization. To many, her behavior while living on the street seemed bizarre and disorganized, yet, before the judge, she seemed coherent and rational as she claimed that her seemingly strange behavior was necessary for her to survive in a potentially dangerous city. Ms. Brown contested her hospitalization and, after a series of court appearances, was finally released. Her notoriety brought her a speaking engagement at Harvard Law School, but only weeks later she returned to her street corner (Cournos, 1989).

Joyce Brown's case illustrates the importance accorded the right to refuse treatment by our legal system, even when that decision might lead to increased symptoms of schizophrenia and impairment in the person's ability to live a safe and secure life. This apparently bleak choice between institutionalization and homelessness might be better understood through research into why clients who are schizophrenic refuse medication, despite the sometimes dire consequences. Their decision is often attributed to medication that does not completely eliminate symptoms and causes unpleasant side effects or to a lack of understanding of its importance. However, without more research, we are left to wonder about less extreme ways to solve this problem.

these statutes, you will understand why they are necessary. The right to treatment emerged as the outcome of a landmark legal case, *Wyatt v. Stickney* (1971, 1972). In this case, a patient named Ricky Wyatt instituted a class action suit against the commissioner of mental health for the state of Alabama, Dr. Stickney, in response to the horrifying conditions in psychiatric and mental retardation facilities. These institutions failed to provide even a minimum of treatment and, indeed, were so inhumane that they were actually detrimental to the patient's mental health. At the time, the court relied on a principle put forth by a legal scholar (Birnbaum, 1960), invoking the constitutional right to due process in making the ruling against Alabama. In other words, the court ruled that people cannot be committed to an institution that is supposed to help them unless they can be guaranteed that they will be helped. Otherwise, their commitment constitutes the equivalent of imprisonment without a trial. Along these lines, patients have the right to a "humane" environment, including privacy, appropriate clothing, opportunities for social interaction, mail, telephone and visitation privileges, comfortable furnishings, physical exercise, and adequate diet. Another related right is that of liberty and safety (*Youngberg v. Romeo,* 1982), a right that includes the right to move about the ward and to be protected from violent patients. Seclusion and mechanical restraints cannot be used unless medically indicated and, when used, can be used only for a limited amount of time and only for appropriate purposes (La Fond, 1994).

An alternative to involuntary institutionalization is outpatient commitment, in which the patient is not forced to reside within the institution but lives in the community. Outpatient commitment is particularly appropriate in mandating that patients take prescribed medications and keep mental health appointments to prevent their psychological condition from deteriorating to a point at which hospitalization would otherwise be necessary. Support for the idea of outpatient commitment dwindled with the budget cuts for community services in the 1980s, but access to outpatient treatment was given support in connection with the Americans with Disabilities Act of 1990 (Perlin, 1994). According to this act, individuals with disabilities cannot be discriminated against and are entitled to be brought into the mainstream of society (House Committee on Energy and Commerce, 1990). People with psychiatric disorders are, therefore, entitled to be treated in the community, rather than relegated to institutions. In order to fulfill the conditions of this act, the government is obligated to provide funding for community-based treatment.

Refusal of Treatment

One client right that has engendered considerable controversy is the right to refuse unwanted treatment. It is accepted in our society that competent adults have the right to either accept or decline medical treatment. If a physician tells a woman that she has breast cancer that warrants immediate surgery, the patient has the right to accept or ignore the recommendation. It would be unfathomable that the court would become involved in taking away this woman's right to determine her own health choices. In the realm of psychiatry, the issue is more complicated, however, primarily because some psychologically disturbed individuals are cognitively incapable of deciding what is best for them. This was the case with Mark Chen, whose case you read at the beginning of the chapter. Because Mark's mental status was characterized by intense depression with catatonic features, his wife was called on to grant permission for this dramatic procedure. On the other hand, had Mark been cognitively alert and responsive, he would have had the right to make this decision and would have had the legal right to decline Dr. Tobin's recommendation. This right is based on the principle that a competent person has the right to control interventions involving his or her body (Kapp, 1994).

The case involving the prescription of psychoactive medications is a bit more complex, however, because medications are not generally regarded as being as risky as ECT or psychosurgery. Nevertheless, many states have enacted laws that give the client the right to refuse unwanted medications. But what happens when a client's disorder is putting the individual or others at great risk? In these cases, the clinician must obtain

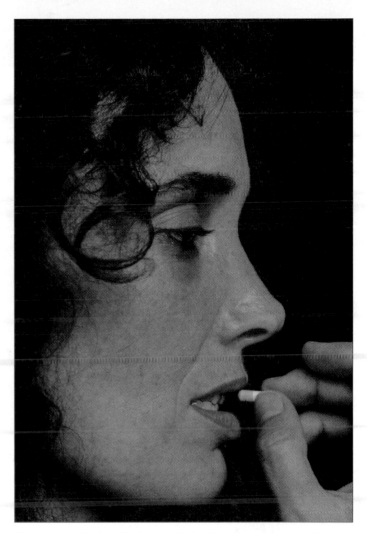

Although psychiatric patients have the legal right to refuse prescribed medication, a clinician may obtain a court order to administer medication to a severely disturbed individual who is deemed to be in dire need of this form of intervention.

a written order from a court of law, documenting the need for medication. This procedure is based on landmark cases (*Rennie v. Klein,* 1979; *Rogers v. Okin,* 1979) that assert the right of clients to refuse psychoactive medications.

In recent years, increasing legal attention has been given to the regulation of treatments that are considered harsh and controversial. Recall our discussion in Chapter 11 about the use of aversive treatments for people with autistic disorder. The treatments, such as the application of aversive noise or unpleasant shock, would be regarded as extreme by most people and, therefore, would be refused by people capable of making an informed choice. However, some clients are incapable of making informed decisions about such interventions. Consequently, many states have enacted legal protections for clients being treated with aversive and avoidance conditioning; a court applies a doctrine called "substituted judgment" for people deemed incompetent of making such treatment decisions themselves. Substituted judgment is a subjective analysis of what the client would decide if he or she were cognitively capable of making the decision (Brant, 1998). A judge might be faced with the very difficult case of trying to imagine whether he or she would willingly approve the administration of aversive shock as a treatment designed to extinguish life-threatening head-banging behavior. As in so many of the issues we have discussed so far, the issues are complicated and ambiguous. Efforts are continually being made, by the legal and mental health professions, to balance the issue of human freedoms with the issue of caring for those incapable of caring for themselves.

Clients also have the right to be placed in what is called the **least restrictive alternative** to treatment in an institution. This evolved from several legal cases brought to trial on behalf of mental patients in various states. One U.S. Supreme Court ruling in particular received national attention. This case (*O'Connor v. Donaldson,* 1975) involved several issues relevant to the commitment and treatment of mental patients, including the right to refuse treatment and the right to a humane environment. Donaldson was committed at the age of 49 to a mental hospital in Chattahoochee, Florida, on the basis of his father's contention that Donaldson was dangerous. However, Donaldson never exhibited signs of threatening behavior. His disorder, which was diagnosed as paranoid schizophrenia, went into remission soon after his commitment. Nevertheless, Donaldson was kept in the hospital for nearly two decades, during which time he was denied many fundamental privileges, such as the right to send and receive mail. Donaldson's successful lawsuit, along with several less well-known cases, paved the way for major changes in the mental health system. Society was forced to recognize that the presence of mental illness in a person is not sufficient reason for confinement to a mental hospital.

■ Forensic Issues in Psychological Treatment

During the past decade, several legal cases received remarkable attention from the media, because they involved difficult questions about the psychological functioning of people who had carried out horrific acts of violence. Consider the case of Jeffrey Dahmer, a meek-sounding Milwaukee candy factory worker, who brutally murdered 17 boys and young men, engaged in sexual acts with corpses, and ate the flesh of those he had sacrificed. Would any sane person have carried out such outrageous acts? Did Dahmer understand the nature of his acts? Was he competent to stand trial? Questions such as these, which perplexed the public as well as the courts, fall within the field of forensic psychology. In this rapidly growing field, professionals with backgrounds in law and mental health tackle a variety of questions regarding the relationship between criminal behavior and psychological disturbance.

Insanity Defense

Contrary to popular belief, insanity is not a psychological term but, rather, a legal term that refers to the individual's lack of moral responsibility for committing criminal acts. The **insanity defense** refers to the argument presented by a lawyer acting on behalf of the client that, because of the existence of a mental disorder, the client should not be held legally responsible for criminal actions. The insanity defense has a long history dating back to the 1800s. To understand the basis of the insanity defense, it is important to know the assumptions on which criminal law is based—that people have free choice in their actions and that, if they break the law, they must be held responsible. People who are "insane," however, are considered to lack freedom of choice over controlling their behavior, as well as the mental competence to distinguish right from wrong. The insanity defense originated as an attempt to protect people with mental disorders from being punished for harmful behavior resulting from their disturbed psychological state.

The insanity defense emerged from various legal precedents and the legal profession's attempts at clarification (Caplan, 1984). In 1843, the M'Naghten Rule was handed down in a disturbing case involving a Scottish woodcutter named Daniel M'Naghten. Under the delusional belief that he was being commanded by God, M'Naghten killed an official of the English government. When he went to trial, the argument was presented that he should not be held responsible for the murder, because his mental disorder prevented him from knowing the difference between right and wrong. He believed that he was following the commands of a higher power and, therefore, saw nothing wrong in his behavior. This is why the M'Naghten rule is often referred to as the "right-wrong test."

The M'Naghten Rule was criticized, because it did not address the question of the individual's capacity to control harmful behavior. About 30 years later, the irresistible impulse test went a step further to add the notion that some disturbed behaviors may result from people's inability to inhibit actions they feel compelled to carry out. They may "know" that an act is wrong but be unable to stop themselves from acting on their impulses. You can imagine how difficult it is to make the determination of irresistible impulse. It may not be possible to establish that the defendant's criminal behavior resulted from an inability to distinguish right from wrong or an inability to control impulses.

Other changes in the mid-twentieth century broadened the scope of the insanity defense. The first, known as the Durham Rule, emerged from a court decision in 1954, asserting that a person is not criminally responsible if the "unlawful act was the product of mental disease or defect." This rule is significant, because it allows for the insanity defense to be used in cases involving many forms of mental disorders. Its intent was to protect individuals with disturbed psychological functioning due to any of a variety of conditions, including personality disorders. As you can imagine, this rule, although well-intentioned, created tremendous legal difficulties, because it put the burden on mental health experts to prove whether or not a defendant is mentally disturbed, even when there is not overt psychosis.

In an attempt to develop uniform standards for the insanity defense, the American Law Institute (ALI) published guidelines in 1962 (Sec. 4.01) that take a middle position between the pre-Durham Rule codes and the liberal standing taken by the Durham Rule. According to the ALI, people are not responsible for criminal behavior if their mental disorder prevents them from "appreciating" the wrongfulness of their behavior (a variation of

The case of John Hinckley, who in 1981 tried to assassinate President Ronald Reagan, raised public concern over possible misuse of the insanity defense. Hinckley, who was declared insane by the courts, was not imprisoned; instead, he was committed to treatment at St. Elizabeth's Hospital in Washington, DC, where he still resides.

the M'Naghten right-wrong rule) or from exerting the necessary willpower to control their acts (the irresistible impulse rule). The important term here is *appreciating*. In other words, knowing what is right and wrong is not equivalent to "understanding" that one's behavior is wrong (Gutheil & Appelbaum, 1982). An important feature of the ALI code is the exclusion from the insanity defense of people whose only maladaptive behavior is repeated criminal or otherwise antisocial conduct. The ALI guideline is considered a more viable standard of insanity than the Durham Rule, because it takes the question of guilt or innocence away from mental health experts and places it in the hands of the jury, who can then make a determination based on the evidence related to the crime itself. Despite this improvement, the ALI guidelines remain problematic.

In the years following the publication of the ALI standards, the insanity defense became much more widely used up to the point of the case of John Hinckley, a young man who attempted to assassinate President Reagan soon after his inauguration in 1981. At the time, Hinckley was obsessed with actress Jodie Foster. Hinckley believed that, if he killed the president, Jodie Foster would be so impressed that she would fall in love with him and marry him. He even thought that they would live in the White House someday. When the case went to trial, the jury confronted a very difficult question—was John Hinckley's behavior that of an "insane" person or that of a cold-blooded assassin? They ruled that he was insane, and he was sent to a mental hospital rather than a prison. This case brought to the nation's attention the rarely used but controversial insanity plea as it had been broadened through the Durham and ALI standards. The public was particularly outraged about the possibility that an assassin could get away with murder on the grounds of having a mental disorder.

To tighten the standards of the insanity defense, Congress passed the Insanity Defense Reform Act of 1984 (Shapiro, 1986). This act was an attempt to clear up the ambiguity inherent in the ALI standards regarding the severity and nature of an accused person's mental disorder. In order for people to be designated as insane according to the Reform Act, they must meet criteria of severe disturbance. In other words, people with personality disorders would probably not be considered insane according to the new law. This law also changed the nature of the legal arguments used to establish the insanity defense. Instead of the prosecuting attorney having the responsibility of proving that the defendant was sane, the defense must show that the defendant was insane. This means that the defense must provide a stronger case to convince the jury that the defendant should not go to jail. Prior to this law, the defense needed only to provide "reasonable doubt" regarding the prosecution's argument that the defendant was sane.

The upshot of these changes in insanity guidelines is that it is now harder for a defendant to be acquitted on the basis of the insanity plea. This is a federal law that applies in federal cases, and individual states vary in the nature of the insanity defense used in criminal proceedings at the state level. Some states have moved toward separating the question of guilt from that of mental disorder by allowing the plea of "guilty, but mentally ill" (Simon & Aaronson, 1988). The defendant is not then exonerated from the crime but is given special consideration by virtue of having a mental disorder. Another important feature of the Reform Act was developed in response to criticisms that "insane" people were often released from mental hospitals after a much shorter period of time than they would have spent in a jail. With the Reform Act, people who are guilty, but mentally ill, are treated in a psychiatric institution. Should their psychological condition improve, they would then be moved to a prison for the duration of the "sentence."

From the photo in his 1977 high school yearbook, would you suspect that Jeffrey L. Dahmer would become an infamous serial murderer? The July 1991 picture shows Dahmer in Milwaukee County Circuit Court, where he was found guilty of killing and sexually mutilating at least 15 young men.

The Prediction of Violent Behavior

John Hinckley's attempted assassination of President Reagan and Mark David Chapman's murder of John Lennon brought a troubling question to the attention of the public. How possible is it to predict dangerousness among psychologically disordered individuals? Virtually every day the news includes stories about brutal murders, commonly committed by people with ostensible psychological disorders. When such terrible events occur, many people wonder why the murder couldn't have been predicted based on the personality and history of the perpetrator. Didn't people know that the murderer was dangerous? Couldn't somebody have seen the murder coming and done something to stop it? If the individual had a history of psychiatric treatment, couldn't the person's therapist have predicted the violence and done something to avert it?

Such questioning has been raised not only by the public but also by experts in both criminal justice and mental health fields. Even a decade before Hinckley and Chapman received such notoriety, researchers were struggling with the thorny issue of the prediction of dangerousness. During the 1970s, psychiatrists and psychologists were severely criticized as being nearly inept in this task, a conclusion that was based on a handful of studies contending that psychiatrists and psychologists were wrong at least twice as often as they were accurate when attempting such predictions. If, indeed, the professionals were so imprecise on this very crucial task, some very troubling questions might follow. One prominent researcher in this field, John Monahan (1981, 1984), asked professionals in both the mental health system and the criminal justice system to consider the question of how imprisoned offenders could be designated as "safe" enough to be released, if these professionals were so incapable of making an accurate prediction about the future likelihood of these individuals' acting in violent ways.

During the early 1980s, notions about violence prediction evolved considerably, due to more precise research methods using actuarial statistics. Violent behavior prior to admission to a psychiatric unit was found to be the best predictor of violence after admission (Janofsky, Spears, & Neubauer, 1988). However, even this one predictor, significant though it was, could not tell the whole story due to the high proportion of "false negatives." In other words, not all individuals with histories of pre-admission violence were subsequently violent. Again, the lack of precise predictors of dangerousness among psychologically disturbed individuals left researchers as well as experts in the fields of mental health and criminal justice looking for improved methods of prediction.

One group of Norwegian researchers (Blomhoff, Seim, & Friis, 1990) undertook a study in which they attempted to refine predictors of dangerousness among psychiatrically hospitalized patients by comparing 25 patients who committed acts of violence while psychiatrically hospitalized with 34 patients on the same ward who were not violent during their stay in the hospital. These researchers confirmed the notion that the best single predictor of violence is a history of previous violence. Further, they found that violent behavior is much more likely among individuals with a history of violence in their families of origin, as well as with personal histories of drug abuse.

In addition to the variables of history of violence, violent family background, and history of drug abuse, other predictors have emerged as significant: being

---

In the decade following these reforms, controversy surrounding the insanity plea resurfaced, and once again the U.S. judicial system struggled with some of the thorny legal issues raised in the case of John Hinckley. Partly because of the storm of criticism following the Hinckley case, however, a very different route was taken in 1992. This time, the case involved a 31-year-old man, Jeffrey Dahmer, mentioned earlier. Dahmer confessed to murdering and dismembering 17 boys and young men and explained that he was driven to kill out of a compulsion to have sex with dead bodies. The trial took place in Milwaukee for the 15 murders that Dahmer claimed to have committed in Wisconsin. Dahmer's defense attorney argued that Dahmer's bizarre acts could only be those of someone who was insane.

The effects of the Reform Act could be seen in the outcome of the Dahmer case (Glynn, 1992). Unlike Hinckley, who was sent to a psychiatric hospital for treatment, Dahmer was sent to

prison in February 1992, with a sentence of 15 consecutive life terms. A sixteenth life term was added later for his first murder, that of an Ohio hitchhiker in 1978. His plea of "guilty but insane" was rejected by the jury, who believed him to be responsible for his crimes and able to appreciate the wrongfulness of his conduct. At numerous points during the trial, questions were raised about the exact nature of his disorder. In the end, it was decided that he was not psychotic but, rather, had a sexual disorder; however, this was not considered sufficient grounds for absolving him of responsibility. Two years after his imprisonment, publicity surrounding the publication of *A Father's Story* by his father, Lionel Dahmer, drew national attention once again to Dahmer's mental state and psychological problems throughout his life. The sadistic murders he committed were apparently responses to tormenting thoughts and urges linking sex and mutilation. The final chapter of this tragic story was the brutal slaying of Dahmer him-

(continued)

male, moving frequently, being unemployed, having low intelligence, growing up in a violent subculture, having weapons available, and having victims available (Beck, 1987). However, even with all of these factors present, would a professional evaluating such an individual have enough information to predict with certainty that this person will, in fact, go out and harm someone? Unfortunately not. Again, there is the issue of the problem of false negatives. A number of men with such histories do not go on to act in violent ways, thus leaving professionals reluctant to point the accusatory finger of prediction. Furthermore, not all men who commit violent acts have identifiable risk factors in their backgrounds, making it even more difficult for psychologists to know how much weight to give any of those factors.

Although success in predicting violence from psychological factors has been limited, assessments of dangerousness and violence potential continue to play an important role in court proceedings in this country. Some researchers have suggested that the proper role for psychologists might be to assess the risk for violent action by a particular person rather than to make a specific prediction based on behavior in general (Litwack, Kirschner, & Wack, 1993). They

have argued that the strategies psychologists used in the past have been too broad and that certain predictors or risk factors might not apply to all types of violence. For example, the type of information used to assess the likelihood of an individual's committing an act of sexual abuse against a child might be very different from the information that would be used to predict a murder or an armed robbery. Psychologists also need to pay more attention to actuarial statistics and base rates for the frequency of certain violent acts in society as a whole and to the influence of the social environment in encouraging or discouraging violence. If we follow the suggestions of Litwack and his colleagues, the role of the psychologist is to make an informed assessment of risk; that is, how likely is it that a given individual will engage in a particular type of violence? It then becomes the job of the public and the legal system to determine what degree of risk is acceptable.

Because of the seriousness of the problem of the inaccuracy of dangerousness prediction, much more research must be carried out before society can feel confident about the judgments of professionals on this issue. Monahan (1993) advises that the risk of failure to predict violence can be significantly reduced by adhering to guidelines that take into account previous legal cases.

First, the clinician should be educated in knowing what risk factors to look for in assessing a client's potential harm to others, such as a history of violence and the base rate of specific types of violent crimes. Second, the clinician should attempt to gather relevant information, such as records of past treatment and arrests. Using this information, the clinician should be able to take the third step, which is to apply a prediction model that takes into account both the demographic characteristics of the client and the features of the client's disorder. Having determined the risk of violence, the clinician must ensure that this information is communicated to others, including documentation of the risk assessment in a client's records. Preventative actions can then be implemented, such as institutionalization, warning the victim, and increasing the contact with the client in the community. Consulting a colleague, or getting a second opinion, is another preventative step the clinician can take. Following through on the client's care after treatment has ended must also be undertaken, as many dangerous acts are committed after the client has stopped seeing a therapist and begins to deteriorate psychologically. The documentation of these steps is also essential for protecting the clinician from legal action should these protective actions fail.

self at the age of 34 by another Wisconsin prison inmate in November 1994. Although Dahmer had been heavily guarded, a lapse in security one night allowed a seriously disturbed fellow prisoner to attack and beat him to death.

Other highly publicized cases since Dahmer's have brought out other subtleties in the insanity defense as it is currently construed. In both cases, the accused confessed that they had committed murder but claimed that they had been driven to these drastic actions as a result of abuse by their "victims." Lyle and Erik Menendez, two young men in California, admitted to the premeditated murder of their parents in response, they claimed, to years of sexual and emotional abuse. Erik, 23 years old, and Lyle, 26, were accused of having shot their parents, Jose and Kitty Menendez, as the couple watched television and ate ice cream in their Beverly Hills mansion in late August 1989. Both brothers admitted to the killings but claimed they had acted in self-defense. Their

defense attorneys presented the argument of "imperfect self-defense," asserting that they acted out of the mistaken belief that their parents were about to kill them, a belief that stemmed from a lifelong history of physical, emotional, and sexual abuse. According to defense attorneys, 12 years of abuse led Erik, at the age of 18, to be tormented by feelings of powerlessness, hopelessness, helplessness, and fear. These feelings led him to believe that his parents, with their violent tendencies, could and would kill the sons to keep the molestation secret. The defense claimed that, on the night of the killings, a family argument was the stimulus for Erik to enter an altered state. Without conscious thought, he retrieved his shotgun, loaded it, and burst in on his parents. The prosecution claimed that the brothers' actions were motivated by their wish to collect a $14 million inheritance. Supporting this argument was the fact that Lyle spent $15,000 a few days after the shootings on expensive jewelry for himself and his brother.

Another dramatic example, specifically focused on the irresistible impulse defense, was the highly publicized case of Lorena Bobbitt, a Virginia woman who committed the unthinkable act of cutting off her husband's penis. Her defense attorneys used the irresistible impulse defense for Lorena Bobbitt, claiming that she was temporarily insane as the result of years of physical and psychological abuse by her husband, John Wayne Bobbitt. At the time that she committed the act, she reported having gone to the refrigerator for a glass of water when she spotted a large kitchen knife. She claimed that at that point she became overcome with what she called "pictures," or mental images, of having been abused by him. According to Lorena Bobbitt, she remembered nothing of what happened until after the incident. While fleeing in her car, she discovered she was holding the knife in one hand and the dismembered body part in the other. During the 8-day trial, the defense and prosecution debated her psychological state during the episode and whether the act was intentional and premeditated. The jury concluded that she was temporarily insane and acquitted her of all charges of malicious and unlawful wounding. As mandated by Virginia law, the judge in the case committed Lorena Bobbitt to a state psychiatric hospital to determine whether or not she posed a danger to herself or others. After the 45-day period, she was released.

In the Menendez and Bobbitt cases, a history of having been abused was seen by juries as providing an important context for understanding the assault. Years of abuse were seen as provoking a state in which the defendants were not responsible for their actions, even those with horrendous consequences. Both cases stimulated considerable controversy, because once again they threw into the public eye the issue of excusing a person from being responsible for his or her acts due to psychological factors.

Adding to the complex debate about the insanity defense was the perplexing case of Theodore Kaczynski, more commonly known as the Unabomber. After being apprehended by federal authorities from his wilderness cabin in Montana, Kaczynski admitted that he had killed three people and had maimed many others with package bombs in a solitary 18-year campaign aimed at bringing down the technological system. From his history and extensive clinical evaluation, fairly compelling evidence pointed toward a diagnosis of schizophrenia, paranoid type. Rather than follow the advice of his attorneys to consider using an insanity defense, however, Kaczynski was outspoken in his rejection of such efforts. He did not consider himself to be psychologically disturbed, nor did he consider his acts to be those of an insane person. Many of those involved in the trial sighed with relief when Kaczynski agreed to plead guilty. By doing so, a thorny judicial debate was avoided. What did emerge from this trial, however, was the realization among forensic experts that more precision is needed in determining the competency of a person who is on trial for bizarre acts, such as those committed by Kaczynski.

Competency to Stand Trial

The case of Theodore Kaczynski involved a man whose history and behavior at the time of the trial raised many questions about the extent to which he was competent to participate in legal proceedings with an informed understanding of what was taking place in

After many years of eluding capture, Theodore Kaczynski, commonly known as the Unabomber, was apprehended by law enforcement officers working on a tip from his brother who recognized Theodore Kaczynski's disordered style of thought in the anonymous manifesto published by *The New York Times* and *The Washington Post*.

the trial and to participate in his own defense. The determination of **competency to stand trial** pertains to the question of whether a defendant is aware of and able to participate in criminal proceedings against him or her. In other words, a person should not be tried, convicted, sentenced, or punished while, as a result of mental illness, he or she is not able to understand the legal proceedings or assist in his or her own defense (Brant, 1998). To make this determination, the judge calls on a psychologist or psychiatrist to conduct an examination of the defendant and to testify about the defendant's competency. This decision is never taken lightly; in fact, a finding of incompetency must be based on a preponderance of the evidence; in other words, both the quantity and the quality of the evidence clearly point to a conclusion that the defendant is suffering from mental illness or defect and that the defendant is unable to understand or participate in the court proceedings (Brant, 1998). The job of the mental health expert is to evaluate the defendant's cognitive capacity, emotional stamina, and ongoing symptoms. For example, if a man is hallucinating and evidently delusional, he will probably have a very difficult time participating in the court proceedings. In other cases, however, defendants whose crime was committed while they were in a disturbed mental state may appear "normal" when interviewed about the crime. The forensic expert must determine, though, whether the stress of the criminal trial would precipitate a psychotic episode.

In efforts to increase the precision of competency assessments, forensic experts have developed standardized instruments to be used in such evaluations. One such instrument is the MacArthur Structured Assessment of the Competencies of Criminal Defendants (MacSAC-CD) (Bonnie et al., 1997; Hoge et al., 1997a, 1997b). The MacSAC-CD was developed to replace imprecise assessment techniques that have been common for years. Rather than rely on the defendant's answers to such questions as "Where does the judge sit in the courtroom?" the MacSAC-CD tries to measure the extent to which the defendant is able to understand more cognitively complex information. For example, the defendant may be told a story about two men, Fred and Reggie, who get into a barroom fight during a game of pool. Fred hits Reggie so hard with a pool stick that Reggie falls, injuring his head and nearly dying. The tester then describes the legal system and the roles of a lawyer, prosecutor, and judge; then the tester asks the defendant questions in order to assess his or her understanding of the legal process. Instruments such as the MacSAC-CD have considerable appeal, because they establish national norms that can be used in court evaluations throughout the country.

As you can see from our discussion of forensic issues, there is a whole body of knowledge and practice regarding mental disorders that has very little to do with psychology per se. Mental health professionals are playing an increasingly important role in the legal system and, at the same time, are finding that they must familiarize themselves with a whole array of forensic issues. Clearly, the areas of intersection between psychology and the law will continue to grow as society looks for interventions that are humane, ethical, and effective.

Courts often rely on the testimony of psychologists for guidance in determining issues of insanity or competency.

RETURN TO THE CASE

Mark Chen

Mark's History

Gathering information about Mark's life history was challenging, due to the fact that he was too emotionally incapacitated to tell me the story himself. I had to rely on the clinical record from his hospitalization a decade ago, as well as the information provided by his wife. Prior to meeting with Tanya the afternoon of Mark's admission, I obtained Mark's chart from the Medical Records Department and quickly read it in order to refresh my memory of that previous treatment. Then, when I met with Tanya, I was able to ask questions about Mark's life and experiences during the 10 intervening years.

Mark was born in San Francisco, the only son of parents who had immigrated to the United States from Taiwan a year prior to his birth. Although they spoke very little English, they chose to give their son a Western-sounding name in the hope that he would be perceived as American. Both parents worked in the garment industry, in circumstances that were harsh. Mark's mother operated a sewing machine, and his father was a technician responsible for maintaining industrial equipment in the factory. Although the Chens had little affection for their jobs, they felt fortunate to obtain work permits in positions with benefits, such as life insurance. Little did they realize how important those benefits would prove to be. Just before Mark's fifth birthday, Mr. Chen was killed in a gruesome machine accident at work.

Alone and emotionally devastated, Mrs. Chen wanted to pack up her belongings and take Mark back to Taiwan, feeling that her dream of a better life in the States had been an unrealistic fantasy. Although she had once intended to gain American citizenship, this goal suddenly seemed pointless. With the support of caring relatives, Mrs. Chen reconsidered and remained in San Francisco. She quit her job in the factory and began working as a maid in a luxury hotel.

Mark was educated in public schools, where he was regarded as a model student. His mother was able to manage the household with the earnings from her job and the interest from the $50,000 life insurance money. The road was not an easy one for her, however, in that she began to suffer from recurring episodes of depression in her late twenties. Fortunately, she had access to good health care and found a physician who prescribed effective antidepressant medication. Although Mrs. Chen's doctor had urged her to see a clinical psychologist or psychiatrist, Mrs. Chen refused, because she would feel too ashamed. In fact, Mrs. Chen didn't like the idea of taking medication, either. Periodically, she stopped taking her meds and, within a month or two, became depressed, stopped going to work, and felt incapable of caring for Mark. Fortunately, she had a sister who lived nearby, who swung into action each time, to make sure that Mrs. Chen was taken for help and Mark was adequately cared for.

Even though Mark's life had been filled with much emotional stress, including the untimely

RETURN TO THE CASE

Mark Chen (continued)

death of his father and the depressive episodes of his mother, he seemed to manage. He occasionally became moody and felt a bit sorry for himself, but those feelings subsided in a few days. He excelled in his high-school classes and won a full scholarship to the university, where he chose to pursue a degree in management.

By the time Mark had reached his senior year, he had found that there was an emotional storm raging within him that caused him to experience periods of despair and hopelessness. His customary optimism and good cheer suddenly gave way to expressions of pessimism and gloom. There were ups and downs during his freshman and sophomore years, but life seemed to feel great for Mark during his junior year. He had begun dating Tanya and had found a great sense of peace and security in that relationship. They decided to live together during their senior year, with the expectation that they would consider marriage later on. Mark's mother disapproved of this plan but decided to go along with it, believing that his positive state of mental health was probably due to his happy relationship with Tanya.

During Mark's senior year, he took a turn for the worse during the final exam period at the end of the first semester. Feeling stressed and overwhelmed, he slipped into a depression far more intense than he had ever experienced, or ever observed in his mother. When it became apparent that Mark's symptoms could not be managed on an outpatient basis, he agreed to enter the hospital and agreed to the administration of ECT.

Mark recovered quickly from that depression and went on to marry Tanya and obtain a well-paying job as an account executive. He continued to take antidepressant medication for several years, then decided to try life without meds. He realized that his thinking was remarkably similar to his mother's unwise decision about medication but, nevertheless, felt that he wanted to try this path himself. Several years went by, during which Mark was psychologically healthy. Other than the customary mood swings of life, he experienced no worrisome signs of a mood disorder. All that changed the week before he was brought in for this hospitalization.

When I asked Tanya in the admission interview about any recent stressors in their lives, she responded, "No, not at all. Things have been going great. In fact, we have both been so happy in recent weeks since learning that I'm pregnant." When Tanya spoke those words, she was not even imagining the possibility that good news can also cause stress. Some people with a history of severe emotional disturbance respond in ways far different from what others might expect.

Assessment

Assessing a client in such a severe state of depression is obviously difficult. Not only were traditional psychological tests out of the question, but it was even impossible to engage Mark in an interview. My assessment would have to rest on behavioral observations and the reports of other people. Mark's immobilization reflected a depth of depression that was so great that his body seemed to have shut down in a self-protective maneuver.

Although I could see that Mark was immobilized, I could not conclude with certainty that he was depressed. Drugs can cause a person to be immobilized. So can certain medical conditions. Consequently, I had to rely on Tanya's report about Mark's behavior during the past several days. I asked her directly whether it was possible that Mark had used any drugs, to which she responded with an emphatic "no." Explaining that they were both "health fanatics," she assured me that he did not, and would not, put anything into his body other than prescription medication—even those he didn't like to take. She had been with him for the entire period during which he had become symptomatic, and was certain that nothing had happened to Mark out of the ordinary. The only spark for Mark's depression seemed to be the good news about their impending parenthood.

Diagnosis

Based on Mark's symptom picture and history, it was safe to conclude that he was suffering from a mood disturbance. I had ruled out drugs as the cause for his state of stupor, and there was no evidence of a medical condition that could explain what he was experiencing. (Of course, a complete medical examination would still be conducted by a hospital physician.) Had I not had so much information about Mark's psychiatric and family history, I would have considered several diagnostic possibilities. However, the fact that he had a previous episode of major depression, and that his mother also had a history of depression, the conclusion seemed clear that Mark's symptom picture was that of a person with major depressive disorder. His bodily immobility pointed to further

RETURN TO THE CASE

Mark Chen (continued)

specificity—namely, that his condition involved catatonic features.

Axis I: Major Depressive Disorder, Recurrent, with Catatonic Features
Axis II: No personality disorder
Axis III: None
Axis IV: Familial stressor—recent news of his wife's pregnancy (planned)
Axis V: Current Global Assessment of Functioning: 20
Highest Global Assessment of Functioning (past year): 95

Case Formulation

Mark's history, in both biological and psychological terms, contained several aspects that would predispose a person to a mood disorder. The fact that his mother suffered from recurrent depression was an important clue regarding the potential role of genetics in causing Mark's depression. In addition to a possible biological predisposition, some of Mark's life experiences could also have influenced the development of his mood disorder. The death of his father when Mark was only 5 years old apparently evoked a powerful emotional reaction within the family that would have an impact on Mark for the rest of his life. As Mark grew older, he found it difficult to manage intense stress. His personal difficulty managing stress was compounded by the fact that he felt that it would be culturally unacceptable to seek professional help to deal with his emotional problems. As a college student facing seemingly insurmountable pressures, Mark fell into a deep depression requiring an extreme intervention. Although he found ways to cope following his recovery from the first depressive episode, he lacked sufficient coping resources to thwart a recurrence of his depression. Even though a decade had passed between episodes, a new stressor—anxiety about becoming a parent—sent him into a state of emotional havoc. This occurrence was especially salient for Mark, in light of his unresolved feelings of loss about the premature death of his father during Mark's childhood.

Treatment Plan

My intervention plan for Mark required special attention to issues of immediate management before turning my attention to longer-term treatment planning. Mark needed a dramatic intervention to help him recover from the depth of immobilizing depression that had overtaken him. His inability to take care of himself and his self-injurious behavior justified the recommendation of electroconvulsive therapy. It was fortunate that his wife was willing to sign forms giving permission for the multiple administrations recommended by the medical professionals.

Following Mark's emergence from his incapacitating state, a course of antidepressant medication and psychotherapy would be recommended. In individual treatment, Mark could attempt to understand the factors in his life that might have sparked the current mood episode, while paying special attention to cognitive strategies he could develop to reduce the likelihood of subsequent episodes.

Outcome of the Case

In textbook fashion, Mark's response to the course of six ECT treatments involved a seemingly miraculous recovery. In fact, after only three treatments, Mark was saying that he was feeling great. His thinking had become clearer, and his catatonic-like behaviors had subsided. Although he expressed some reservations about completing the full course of ECT, he went along with the recommendation of the treatment team. He also agreed to begin a regimen of antidepressant medication and to continue working with me in individual psychotherapy.

One of the first issues I felt it important to address in our therapy was Mark's feelings about having been committed to the hospital and administered ECT without his making an informed choice about these decisions. Mark's response in this discussion consisted of a perplexing mixture of gratitude and anger. He acknowledged that he felt markedly better, and that he was deeply thankful to me and to his wife for our willingness to make the hospitalization and treatment choice for him. At the same time, however, he said, "I don't ever want to be in this position again, of having someone else take control over such important decisions." I could see his point and could empathize with the emotionality of his reaction, but I also felt a bit defensive. Rather than getting into a lecture justifying these choices, I suggested that we move our focus to the task of helping Mark develop strategies to minimize the likelihood of a recurrence of incapacitating depression.

I saw Mark weekly for 8 months, and all seemed to be going well. Matters took a turn for the worse, however, shortly after Tanya delivered their baby. Although their new son was healthy and normal, Mark once again found that deep emotions

RETURN TO THE CASE

Mark Chen (continued)

were being stirred up in response to the increasing demands of being a new parent. A week after his wife and son came home from the hospital, Mark found that he was becoming unexplainably sad and tearful each day. His symptoms were evident in one of our sessions, and we talked about what he was going through. We increased the frequency of our sessions to twice weekly for the next few weeks, and Mark's psychiatrist also raised the dosage of his medication. Mark responded quite positively to these added efforts and gradually returned to a normal mood. We resumed weekly meetings, which we continued for another year. We then reduced the frequency of sessions to monthly meetings, and more recently to twice yearly. Mark has remained stabilized on a relatively low dose of antidepressant medication. Although all has seemed fine for the past several years, Mark and his wife both realize the importance of their vigilance for any signs of deepening depression. Mark knows that he is vulnerable to a recurrence, but, if action can be taken quickly, the development of disturbing symptoms surrounding his previous hospitalizations might be avoidable. ■

Sarah Tobin, PhD

Summary

- Clinicians have various roles and responsibilities. They are expected to have the intellectual competence to assess, conceptualize, and treat clients whom they accept into treatment, in addition to being emotionally capable of managing the clinical issues that emerge. When beginning work with clients, they should obtain the client's informed consent to ensure that the client understands the goals of treatment, the process of therapy, the client's rights, the therapist's responsibilities, the treatment risks, the techniques that will be used, financial issues, and the limits of confidentiality.

- Confidentiality is the principle that the therapist must safeguard disclosures in therapy as private. With only a few exceptions, the content of therapy is considered privileged communication; that is, the clinician may not disclose any information about the client in a court without the client's expressed permission. Exceptions to the principle of confidentiality include instances involving mandated reporting and duty to warn. Mental health professionals are mandated by law to report information involving the abuse or neglect of a child or people who are unable to protect themselves. The duty to warn involves the clinician's responsibility to take action to inform a possible victim of a client's intention to do harm to that person.

- In their relationships with clients, clinicians are expected to adhere to the highest standards of ethical and professional conduct. They are to avoid inappropriate relationships, such as sexual intimacy with clients, and are expected to maintain neutrality and distance in their dealings with clients. In overseeing the business aspects of psychotherapy practice, mental health professionals face various challenges, particularly when operating within managed health care delivery systems. Sometimes clinicians are called on for special roles that present unique ethical challenges (e.g., expert witness, child custody evaluations, and evaluations of people with dementia).

- Clinicians are sometimes involved in the process of commitment, an emergency procedure for the involuntary hospitalization of a person who, if not hospitalized, is deemed to be likely to create harm for self or other people as a result of mental illness. Clients who are hospitalized have the right to treatment—the right to a humane environment with appropriate amenities, in addition to liberty and safety. Clients also have the right to refuse unwanted treatment, unless a court deems that the client is at risk of harming self or others without needed intervention. Clients also have the right to be placed in the least restrictive alternative to treatment in an institution.

- The major forensic issues that pertain to the field of mental health involve the insanity defense and the competency to stand trial. The insanity defense is the argument presented by a lawyer acting on behalf of the client that, because of the existence of a mental disorder, the client should not be held legally responsible for criminal actions. Various controversies have emerged during the past two decades regarding the insanity defense, as courts have struggled with issues of assessing a defendant's responsibility in well-publicized cases involving violent assault and murder. The determination of competency to stand trial pertains to the question of whether a defendant is aware of and able to participate in criminal proceedings against him or her.

Key Terms

See Glossary for definitions.

Commitment 456
Competency to stand trial 464
Confidentiality 453

Duty to warn 454
Guardian ad litem 455
Informed consent 452
Insanity defense 460

Least restrictive alternative 460
Mandated reporting 453
Parens patriae 456
Privileged communication 453

Internet Resource

To get more information on the material covered in this chapter, visit our web site at **http://www.mhhe.com/halgin.** There you will find more information, resources, and links to topics of interest.

Glossary

A

Abstinence violation effect A sense of loss of control over one's behavior that has an overwhelming and demoralizing effect. 397

Active phase A period in the course of schizophrenia in which psychotic symptoms are present. 311

Acute stress disorder An anxiety disorder that develops after a traumatic event with symptoms such as depersonalization, numbing, dissociative amnesia, intense anxiety, hypervigilance, and impairment of everyday functioning. People with this disorder may reexperience the event and desperately avoid reminders of the trauma. These symptoms arise within the month following the trauma and last from 2 days to 4 weeks. 190

Adjustment disorder A diagnostic category used for a reaction that is more extreme than would normally be expected under the circumstances. 43

Adoption study A method of comparing genetic versus environmental contributions to a disorder by tracking the incidence of disorders in children whose biological parents have diagnosed psychological disorders but whose rearing parents do not. 25

Adult antisocial behavior Illegal or immoral behavior such as stealing, lying, or cheating. 142

Affect An individual's outward expression of emotion. 69

Affective flattening A symptom of schizophrenia in which an individual seems unresponsive and which is reflected in relatively motionless body language and facial reactions, as well as minimal eye contact. 312

Agnosia The inability to recognize familiar objects or experiences, despite the ability to perceive their basic elements. 373

Agoraphobia Intense anxiety about being trapped or stranded in a situation without help if a panic attack occurs. 173

Akinesia A motor disturbance in which a person's muscles become rigid and movement is difficult to initiate. 377

Alcohol dehydrogenase (ADH) A zinc-containing enzyme that breaks down alcohol into fatty acids, carbon dioxide, and water before it enters the bloodstream. 396

Aldehyde dehydrogenase (ALDH) An enzyme that is involved in metabolizing alcohol. 400

Alogia Speechlessness or a notable lack of spontaneity or responsiveness in conversation. 312

Alters The alternative personalities that develop in an individual with dissociative identity disorder. 226

Amnestic disorders Cognitive disorders involving the inability to recall previously learned information or to register new memories. 371

Amyloid plaques A characteristic of Alzheimer's disease in which clusters of dead or dying neurons become mixed together with fragments of protein molecules. 380

Anal stage A period of psychosexual development in which the toddler's pleasure focuses on anal stimulation from holding onto and expelling feces. 103

Analog observation A form of behavioral assessment that takes place in a setting or context specifically designed for observing the target behavior. 87

Anhedonia A loss of interest in or ability to experience pleasure from activities that most people find appealing. 312

Anorexia nervosa An eating disorder characterized by an inability to maintain normal weight, an intense fear of gaining weight, and distorted body perception. 426

Antecedents Events preceding a specified behavior. 86

Antisocial personality disorder A personality disorder characterized by a lack of regard for society's moral or legal standards. 141

Anxiety A future-oriented and global response, involving both cognitive and emotional components, in which an individual is inordinately apprehensive, tense, and uneasy about the prospect of something terrible happening. 172

Anxiety disorders Disorders characterized by intense, irrational, and incapacitating apprehension. 172

Aphasia A loss of the ability to use language. 372

Apraxia A loss of the ability to carry out coordinated bodily movements that the individual could previously perform without difficulty. 373

Asperger's disorder A pervasive developmental disorder in which a child maintains adequate cognitive and language development but becomes severely impaired in social interaction. Children with this disorder also develop restricted,

repetitive, and stereotyped patterns of behavior, interests, and activities. 347

Assessment The evaluation of a person in terms of the psychological, physical, and social factors that have the most influence on the individual's functioning. 64

Assigned (biological) sex The sex of the individual that is recorded on the birth certificate. 255

Asylum Literally a place of refuge or safety, the term was originally used to describe a psychiatric facility and later came to have negative connotations. 11

Attachment style The way a person relates to a caregiver figure. 107

Attention-deficit/hyperactivity disorder (ADHD) A behavior disorder of childhood involving problems with inattentiveness, hyperactivity, and impulsivity. 354

Attributions Explanations that people make of the things that happen to them. 290

Auditory hallucination An hallucination that involves hearing sounds, often voices or even entire conversations. 72

Autistic disorder A pervasive developmental disorder involving massive impairment in an individual's ability to communicate and relate emotionally to others. 347

Automatic thoughts Ideas so deeply entrenched that the individual is not even aware that they lead to feelings of unhappiness and discouragement. 118

Aversions Responses of discomfort or dislike to a particular object or situation. 177

Aversive conditioning A form of conditioning in which a painful stimulus is paired with an initially neutral stimulus. 116

Avoidant personality disorder A personality disorder whose most prominent feature is that the individual desires, but is fearful of, any involvement with other people and is terrified at the prospect of being publicly embarrassed. 157

Avolition A lack of initiative, either not wanting to take any action or lacking the energy and will to take action. 312

Axis A class of information in DSM-IV regarding an aspect of the individual's functioning. 42

B

Base rate The frequency with which a disorder occurs in the general population. 38

Baseline The period in which a participant is observed prior to being given treatment,

470

the purpose being to document the frequency of the target behavior. 24

Behavioral assessment A form of measurement based on objective recording of the individual's behavior. 86

Behavioral checklists and inventories Behavioral assessment devices in which the client checks off or rates whether or not certain events or experiences have transpired. 87

Behavioral interviewing A specialized form of interviewing in which the clinician asks for information on the behavior under consideration as well as what preceded and followed that behavior 86.

Behavioral medicine An interdisciplinary approach to medical conditions affected by psychological factors that is rooted in learning theory. 224

Behavioral observation A behavioral method of assessment in which the clinician observes the individual and records the frequency of specific behaviors along with any relevant situational factors. 87

Behavioral perspective A theoretical perspective in which it is assumed that abnormality is caused by faulty learning experiences. 115

Behavioral self-report A method of behavioral assessment in which the individual provides information about the frequency of particular behaviors. 86

Benzodiazepines Medications that slow down central nervous system reactions that are thought to contribute to anxiety. 176

Big win A gain of large amounts of money in one bet, which propels the pathological gambler into a pattern of uncontrollable gambling. 436

Binges The ingestion of large amounts of food during a short period of time, even after reaching a point of feeling full, and a lack of control over what or how much is eaten. 427

Biofeedback A procedure in which people learn to monitor and control their autonomic responses, such as blood pressure, heart rate, skin conductance, and muscular tension. 130

Biological markers Measurable characteristics or traits whose patterns parallel the inheritance of a disorder or other characteristic. 25

Biological perspective A theoretical perspective in which it is assumed that disturbances in emotions, behavior, and cognitive processes are caused by abnormalities in the functioning of the body. 122

Biopsychosocial A model in which the interaction of biological, psychological, and sociocultural factors is seen as influencing the development of the individual. 7

Bipolar disorder A mood disorder involving manic episodes—intense and very disruptive experiences of heightened mood, possibly alternating with major depressive episodes. 281

Bipolar I disorder The diagnosis used to describe a clinical course in which the individual experiences one or more manic episodes with the possibility, though not the necessity, of having experienced one or more major depressive episodes. 283

Bipolar II disorder The diagnosis used to describe a clinical course in which the individual experiences one or more major depressive episodes and at least one hypomanic episode. 283

Blood pressure The resistance offered by the arteries to the flow of blood as it is pumped from the heart. 88

Borderline personality disorder A personality disorder characterized by a pervasive pattern of poor impulse control and instability in mood, interpersonal relationships, and self-image. 145

Bradykinesia A motor disturbance involving a general slowing of motor activity. 377

Brief psychotic disorder A disorder characterized by the sudden onset of psychotic symptoms that are limited to a period of less than a month. 319

Broca's aphasia A form of aphasia that involves a disturbance in language production but intact comprehension abilities. 372

Bulimia nervosa An eating disorder involving the alternation between the extremes of eating large amounts of food in a short time, and then compensating for the added calories either by vomiting or other extreme actions to avoid gaining weight. 427

C

Caregiver burden The adverse effects on caregivers from the constant demands placed on them by their role. 383

Caregivers The people (usually family members) primarily responsible for caring for a person with a chronic disease, such as Alzheimer's disease. 383

Case study method An intensive study of a single person described in detail. 24

Catatonia Extreme motor disturbances in a psychotic disorder not attributable to physiological causes. 68

Catecholamine hypothesis An hypothesis that asserts that a relative shortage of norepinephrine (a catecholamine) causes depression, and an overabundance of norepinephrine causes mania. 287

Childhood disintegrative disorder A pervasive developmental disorder in which the child develops normally for the first 2 years and then starts to lose language, social, and motor skills, as well as other adaptive functions, including bowel and bladder control. 347

Choline acetyltransferase (CAT) An enzyme that is essential for the synthesis of acetylcholine. 380

Chromosomes Structures found in each cell of the body that contain the genes and exist in a pair, with one chromosome contributed from each parent at conception. 127

Classical conditioning The learning of a connection between an originally neutral stimulus and a naturally evoking stimulus that produces an automatic reflexive reaction. 115

Client A person seeking psychological treatment. 36

Client-centered An approach based on the belief held by Rogers that people are innately good and that the potential for self-improvement lies within the individual. 108

Clinical psychologist A mental health professional with training in the behavioral sciences who provides direct service to clients. 37

Cognitive distortions Errors that depressed people make in the way they draw conclusions from their experiences. 291

Cognitive restructuring One of the fundamental techniques of cognitive-behavioral therapy in which clients learn to reframe negative ideas into more positive ones. 121

Cognitive triad A negative view of the self, the world, and the future. 291

Cognitive-behavioral perspective A theoretical perspective in which it is assumed that abnormality is caused by maladaptive thought processes that result in dysfunctional behavior. 115

Command hallucination An hallucination in which the individual hears an instruction to take an action. 72

Commitment Legal procedure designed to protect individuals from doing harm to themselves or others through involuntary institutionalization or other forms of mental health treatment. 456

Community mental health center (CMHC) Outpatient clinic that provides psychological services on a sliding fee scale to serve individuals who live within a certain geographic area. 55

Comorbid Multiple diagnostic conditions that occur simultaneously within the same individual. 37

Competency to stand trial A prediction by a mental health expert of the defendant's cognitive and emotional stability during the period of the trial. 464

Complex traits Characteristics that reflect an inheritance pattern that does not follow the simple rules of dominant and recessive genes. 128

Compulsion A repetitive and seemingly purposeful behavior performed in response to uncontrollable urges or according to a ritualistic or stereotyped set of rules. 68, 185

Computed axial tomography (CAT or CT scan) A series of X-rays taken from various angles around the body which are integrated by a computer to produce a composite picture. 89

Concordance rate Agreement ratios between people diagnosed as having a particular disorder and their relatives. 25

Conditioned fear reactions Acquired associations between an internal or external cue and feelings of intense anxiety. 175

Conditioned response An acquired response to a stimulus that was previously neutral. 116

Conditioned stimulus A previously neutral stimulus that, after repeated pairings with the unconditioned stimulus, elicits a conditioned response. 115

Conduct disorder A development-related disorder that involves repeated violations of the rights of others and society's norms and laws; the childhood precursor of antisocial personality disorder in adulthood. 355

Confidentiality The principle that disclosures in therapy must be safeguarded by the therapist as private. 453

Consequences Events following a specified behavior. 86

Content of thought Ideas that fill a client's mind. 68

Contingency management A form of behavioral therapy that involves the principle of rewarding a client for desired behaviors and not providing rewards for undesired behaviors. 120

Continuous amnesia Inability to recall past events from a particular date up to and including the present time. 231

Control group The group of participants that does not receive the "treatment" thought to influence the behavior under study. 21

Conversion disorder A somatoform disorder involving the translation of unacceptable drives or troubling conflicts into physical symptoms. 206

Coping The process through which people reduce stress. 220

Coprolalia The involuntary uttering of obscenities. 362

Correlation An association, or co-relation, between two variables, that can range in value from +1.0 to −1.0. 22

Cortical atrophy A wasting away of tissue in the cerebral cortex of the brain. 325

Cortisol A hormone involved in the mobilization of the body's resources in times of stress. 288

Counterconditioning The process of replacing an undesired response to a stimulus with an acceptable response. 120

Covert conditioning A behavioral intervention in which the therapist instructs the client to imagine a highly negative experience when engaging in an undesirable behavior. 248

Crack cocaine A crystallized form of cocaine that is usually smoked. 407

Creutzfeldt-Jakob disease A neurological disease transmitted from animals to humans that leads to dementia and death resulting from abnormal protein accumulations in the brain. 377

Crossfostering study A method of comparing genetic versus environmental contributions to a disorder by tracking the incidence of disorders in children who are adopted by parents with psychological disorders but whose biological parents are psychologically healthy. 25

Cue exposure methods A behavioral approach to alcohol treatment in which the individual is given a priming dose of alcohol, which initiates the craving for more alcohol; the person is then urged to refuse further alcohol. 401

Culture-bound syndromes Recurrent patterns of abnormal behavior or experience that are limited to specific societies or cultural areas. 50

Cyclothymic disorder A mood disorder that, compared with bipolar disorder, involves a less intense vacillation between states of euphoria and dysphoria. 282

Day treatment program A structured program in a community treatment facility that provides activities similar to those provided in a psychiatric hospital. 55

Decision tree A strategy used for diagnosis, consisting of yes/no questions that guide clinicians in ruling in or out psychological disorders. 48

Defense mechanisms Tactics that keep unacceptable thoughts, instincts, and feelings out of conscious awareness and thus protect the ego against anxiety. 99

Deinstitutionalization movement The release of psychiatric patients into community treatment sites as a result of dramatic changes in public policy. 17

Delirium A temporary state in which individuals experience a clouding of consciousness in which they are unaware of what is happening around them and are unable to focus or pay attention. 370

Delirium tremens A physical condition consisting of autonomic nervous system dysfunction, confusion, and possible seizures associated with alcohol withdrawal. 399

Delusional disorder A disorder marked by a single striking psychotic symptom—an organized system of nonbizarre false beliefs. 322

Delusions Deeply entrenched false beliefs not consistent with the client's intelligence or cultural background. 69

Demand characteristics The expectations of participants in an experiment about what is going to happen to them or the proper way to respond. 22

Dementia A form of cognitive impairment involving generalized progressive deficits in a person's memory and learning of new information, ability to communicate, judgment, and motor coordination. 372

Dementia praecox The term coined by Kraepelin to describe what is currently known as schizophrenia. According to

Kraepelin, this condition involves a degeneration of the brain that begins at a young age and ultimately leads to a disintegration of the entire personality. 310

Denial/intrusion phase A period following a traumatic event during which the person alternates between denial, the experience of forgetting the event or pretending it did not occur, and intrusion, the experience of disruptive thoughts and feelings about the event. 192

Deoxyribonucleic acid (DNA) A molecule containing a sequence of nucleotides that forms the structure of the chromosome. 127

Dependent personality disorder A personality disorder whose main characteristic is that the individual is extremely passive and tends to cling to other people, to the point of being unable to make any decisions or to take independent action. 158

Dependent variable The variable whose value is the outcome of the experimenter's manipulation of the independent variable. 21

Depersonalization An altered experience of the self, ranging from feeling that one's body is not connected to one's mind to the feeling that one is not real. 73

Depersonalization disorder A dissociative disorder in which the individual experiences recurrent and persistent episodes of depersonalization. 233

Depressant A psychoactive substance that causes the depression of central nervous system activity. 394

Developmental coordination disorder A condition characterized by marked impairment in the development of motor coordination. 354

Deviation IQ An index of intelligence derived from comparing the individual's score on an intelligence test with the mean score for that individual's reference group. 76

Dexamethasone suppression test (DST) A method of testing neuroendocrine functioning by injecting the individual with dexamethasone, which in normal individuals results in the suppression of cortisol. 288

Diagnostic and Statistical Manual of Mental Disorders (DSM) A book published by the American Psychiatric Association that contains standard terms and definitions of psychological disorders. 38

Diathesis-stress model The proposal that people are born with a predisposition (or "diathesis") that places them at risk for developing a psychological disorder if exposed to certain extremely stressful life experiences. 8, 129

Discrimination In learning theory, the process through which learning becomes increasingly specific to a given situation. 48, 116

Disorder of written expression A learning disorder in which the individual's writing is characterized by poor spelling, grammatical or punctuation errors, and disorganization of paragraphs. 352

Dissociative amnesia An inability to remember important personal details and experiences; is usually associated with traumatic or very stressful events. 231

Dissociative fugue A dissociative disorder in which a person, confused about personal identity, suddenly and unexpectedly travels to another place and is unable to recall past history or identity. 232

Dissociative identity disorder A dissociative disorder, formerly called multiple personality disorder, in which an individual develops more than one self or personality. 228

Disulfiram Known popularly as Antabuse, a medication used in the treatment of alcoholism that inhibits aldehyde dehydrogenase (ALDH) and causes severe physical reactions when combined with alcohol. 400

Dizygotic twins Nonidentical, or fraternal, twins who are genetically alike only to the same degree as other siblings. 25

Double-blind technique An experimental procedure in which neither the person giving the treatment nor the person receiving the treatment knows whether the participant is in the experimental or control group. 22

Down syndrome A form of mental retardation caused by abnormal chromosomal formation during conception. 346

Dream analysis A method used in psychoanalysis in which the client relates the events of a dream to the clinician and free associates these events. 105

Duty to warn The clinician's responsibility to notify a potential victim of a client's harmful intent toward that individual. 454

Dysfunctional attitudes Personal rules or values people hold that interfere with adequate adjustment. 118

Dyslexia A learning disorder in which the individual omits, distorts, or substitutes words when reading and reads in a slow, halting fashion. 352

Dyspareunia A sexual dysfunction affecting both males and females that involves recurrent or persistent genital pain before, during, or after sexual intercourse. 265

Dysphoria The emotion of sadness. 278

Dysphoric mood Unpleasant feelings, such as sadness or irritability. 71

Dysthymic disorder A mood disorder involving chronic depression of less intensity than major depressive disorders. 278

E

Ego In psychoanalytic theory, the structure of personality that gives the individual the mental powers of judgment, memory, perception, and decision making, enabling the individual to adapt to the realities of the external world. 99

Electrocardiogram (ECG) A measure of the electrical impulses that pass through the heart. 88

Electrodermal response Minor electrical changes in the skin that result from sweating; also called galvanic skin response (GSR). 88

Electroencephalogram (EEG) A measure of changes in the electrical activity of the brain. 88

Electromyography (EMG) A measurement of electrical activity of the muscles. 88

Emotion-focused coping A type of coping in which a person does not change anything about the situation itself, but instead tries to improve feelings about the situation. 220

Encopresis An elimination disorder in which the child is incontinent of feces and has bowel movements either in clothes or in another inappropriate place. 362

Enuresis An elimination disorder in which the child is incontinent of urine and urinates in clothes or in bed after the age when the child is expected to be continent. 362

Environmental assessment scales Measures of key environmental dimensions hypothesized to influence behavior. 88

Epilepsy A neurological condition that involves recurring bodily seizures with associated changes in EEG patterns. 370

Episode A time-limited period during which specific symptoms of a disorder are present. 278

Euphoria The emotion of elation. 278

Euphoric mood A feeling state that is more cheerful and elated than average, possibly even ecstatic. 71

Executive functioning Cognitive abilities such as abstract thinking, planning, organizing, and carrying out of behaviors. 070

Exhibitionism A paraphilia in which a person has intense sexual urges and arousing fantasies involving the exposure of genitals to a stranger. 247

Existential A theoretical position in psychology that emphasizes the importance of fully appreciating each moment as it occurs. 108

Expectancy model An approach to alcohol dependence that focuses on cognitive-behavioral and social learning perspectives. According to this view, people acquire the belief that alcohol will reduce stress; will make them feel more competent socially, physically, and sexually; and will give them feelings of pleasure. 397

Experimental group The group of participants that receives the "treatment" thought to influence the behavior under study. 21

Experimental method A research method that involves altering or changing the conditions to which participants are exposed (independent variable) and observing the effects of this manipulation on the participants' behavior (dependent variable). 21

Expressed emotion (EE) An index of the degree to which family members speak in ways that reflect criticism, hostile feelings, and emotional overinvolvement or overconcern with regard to the schizophrenic individual. 331

Expressive language disorder A communication disorder characterized by having a limited and faulty vocabulary, speaking in short sentences with simplified grammatical structures, omitting critical words or phrases, or putting words together in peculiar order. 352

Extinction The cessation of behavior in the absence of reinforcement. 117

F

Factitious disorder A disorder in which people fake symptoms or disorders not for the purpose of any particular gain, but because of an inner need to maintain a sick role. 214

Factitious disorder by proxy (or Munchausen's syndrome by proxy) A condition in which a person induces physical symptoms in another person who is under that person's care. 216

Failure to thrive A condition in which the child does not grow physically and cognitively at a normal rate due to poor prenatal care or grossly inadequate and inattentive parenting. 347

Family dynamics The pattern of interactions among the members of a family. 112

Family history Information gathered in a psychological assessment regarding the sequence of major events in the lives of the client's relatives, including those who are closest to the client as well as more distantly related family members. 65

Family perspective A theoretical perspective in which it is assumed that abnormality is caused by disturbances in the pattern of interactions and relationships within the family. 112

Family therapy Psychological treatment in which the therapist works with several or all members of the family. 55

Fear An innate, almost biologically based alarm response to a dangerous or life-threatening situation. 172

Feeding disorder of infancy or early childhood A disorder involving the persistent failure to eat, leading to a loss of weight or failure to gain weight. 362

Female orgasmic disorder A sexual dysfunction in which a woman experiences problems in having an orgasm during sexual activity. 262

Female sexual arousal disorder A sexual dysfunction characterized by a persistent or recurrent inability to attain or maintain the normal physiological and psychological arousal responses during sexual activity. 262

Fetal alcohol syndrome (FAS) A condition associated with mental retardation in a child whose mother consumed large amounts of alcohol on a regular basis while pregnant. 346

Fetish A strong, recurrent sexual attraction to a nonliving object. 248

Fetishism A paraphilia in which the individual is preoccupied with an object and depends on this object rather than sexual intimacy with a partner for achieving sexual gratification. 248

Fixation Arrested development at a particular stage of psychosexual development attributable to excessive or inadequate gratification at that stage. 103

Flooding A behavioral technique in which the client is immersed in the sensation of anxiety by being exposed to the feared situation in its entirety. 180

Free association A method used in psychoanalysis in which the client speaks freely, saying whatever comes to mind. 105

Frontal lobe dementia A form of dementia that involves the frontal lobes of the brain. 377

Frotteur A person with the paraphilia of frotteurism. 250

Frotteurism A paraphilia in which the individual has intense sexual urges and sexually arousing fantasies of rubbing against or fondling an unsuspecting stranger. 250

Functional Magnetic Resonance Imaging A variant of the traditional MRI, which makes it possible to construct a picture of activity in the brain. 89

G

Galvanic skin response (GSR) See **Electrodermal response**. 88

Gender identity The individual's self-perception as a male or female. 255

Gender identity disorder A condition in which there is a discrepancy between an individual's assigned sex and gender identity, involving a strong and persistent identification with the other gender. 255

Gender role The behaviors and attitudes a person has that are indicative of maleness or femaleness in one's society. 255

Gene The basic unit of heredity. 127

Generalization The expansion of learning from the original situation to one that is similar. 116

Generalized amnesia Inability to remember anything from one's past life. 231

Generalized anxiety disorder An anxiety disorder characterized by anxiety that is not associated with a particular object, situation, or event but seems to be a constant feature of a person's day-to-day existence. 183

Genetic mapping The attempt by biological researchers to identify the structure of a gene and the characteristics it controls. 25

Genital stage A period of psychosexual development coinciding with the resurfacing of sexual energy just prior to puberty. 103

Genitality The ability to express sexual feelings in a mature way and in appropriate contexts, reached when the individual is able to "work and love" (in Freud's words). 104

Genome The complete set of instructions for "building" all the cells that make up an organism. 127

Global Assessment of Functioning (GAF) Scale Axis V of the *DSM-IV*, a scale that rates the individual's overall level of psychological health. 46

Graduated exposure A procedure in which clients gradually expose themselves to increasingly greater anxiety-provoking situations. 180

Grandiosity An exaggerated view of oneself as possessing special and extremely favorable personal qualities and abilities. 152

Group therapy Psychological treatment in which the therapist facilitates discussion among several clients who talk together about their problems. 55

Guardian ad litem A person appointed by the court to represent or make decisions for a person (e.g., a minor or an incapacitated adult) who is legally incapable of doing so in a civil legal proceeding. 455

Gustatory hallucination An hallucination involving the false sensation of taste, usually unpleasant. 72

H

Halfway house A community treatment facility designed for deinstitutionalized clients leaving a hospital who are not yet ready for independent living. 55

Hallucination A false perception not corresponding to the objective stimuli present in the environment. 71

Hallucinogens Psychoactive substances that cause abnormal perceptual experiences in the form of illusions or hallucinations, usually visual in nature. 412

Heritability The proportion of the offspring's phenotype that is due to genetic causes. 129

Hierarchy of needs According to Maslow, the order in which human needs must be fulfilled. 109

High-risk design A research method in which investigators follow the lives of children who are considered to be at risk for developing schizophrenia because they have a biological parent with the disorder. 327

Hippocampus A limbic system structure responsible for the consolidation of short-term memory into long-term memory. 125

Histrionic personality disorder A personality disorder characterized by exaggerated emotional reactions, approaching theatricality, in everyday behavior. 151

Host The central personality of an individual with dissociative identity disorder. 226

Humanistic An approach to personality and psychological disorder that regards people as motivated by the need to

understand themselves and the world and to derive greater enrichment from their experiences by fulfilling their unique individual potential. 107

Huntington's disease A hereditary condition causing dementia that involves a widespread deterioration of the subcortical brain structures and parts of the frontal cortex that control motor movements. 377

Hyperactivity A motor pattern involving abnormally energized physical activity, often characterized by quick movements and fast talking. 68

Hypnotherapy: A method of therapy in which hypnosis is used for various purposes, such as helping a person recall repressed memories. 230

Hypnotism The process of inducing a trance state. 16

Hypoactive sexual desire disorder A sexual dysfunction in which the individual has an abnormally low level of interest in sexual activity. 261

Hypochondriasis: A somatoform disorder characterized by the misinterpretation of normal bodily functions as signs of serious illness. 212

Hypomanic episode A period of elated mood not as extreme as a manic episode. 282

Hypothalamus A small structure in the brain that coordinates the activities of the central nervous system with systems involved in the control of emotion, motivation, and bodily regulation. 125

Hypothesis formation process The stage of research in which the researcher generates ideas about a cause-effect relationship between the behaviors under study. 19

Hysteria A disorder in which psychological problems become expressed in physical form. 16

Hysterical neurosis A term used by Freud to describe conversion disorder, implying that it is a reaction to anxiety. 207

I

Id In psychoanalytic theory, the structure of personality that contains the sexual and aggressive instincts. 98

Identity One's self-concept or sense of who one is. 147

Identity confusion A lack of clear sense of who one is, ranging from confusion about one's role in the world to actual delusional thinking. 73

Imaginal flooding A behavioral technique in which the client is immersed through imagination in the feared situation. 180

Impulse An urge to act. 433

Impulse-control disorders Psychological disorders in which people repeatedly engage in behaviors that are potentially harmful, feeling unable to stop themselves and experiencing a sense of desperation if their attempts to carry out the behaviors are thwarted. 433

In vivo observation   A form of behavioral assessment in which the individual is observed in the natural context in which the target behavior occurs. 87

Inappropriate affect   The extent to which a person's emotional expressiveness fails to correspond to the content of what is being discussed. 69

Incidence   The frequency of new cases within a given time period. 23

Independent variable   The variable whose level is adjusted or controlled by the experimenter. 21

Individual psychotherapy   Psychological treatment in which the therapist works on a one-to-one basis with the client. 55

Indolamine hypothesis   A hypothesis that proposes that a deficiency of serotonin causes depression. 287

Informed consent   The process, often in the form of a written statement, in which a client participates in setting treatment goals, understands and agrees to the treatment plan, and knows the credentials of the clinician. 452

Insanity defense   The argument, presented by a lawyer acting on behalf of the client, that, because of the existence of a mental disorder, the client should not be held legally responsible for criminal actions. 460

Insight   A sense of understanding and awareness about oneself and one's world. 73

Intelligence quotient   A method of quantifying performance on an intelligence test, originally calculated according to the ratio of a person's tested age to that person's chronological age, and changed in the 1960 revision of the Stanford-Binet to the deviation IQ. 76

Intensity of affect   Strength of emotional expression. 69

Intermittent explosive disorder   An impulse-control disorder involving an inability to hold back urges to express strong angry feelings and associated violent behaviors. 443

Irrational beliefs   Views about the self and the world that are unrealistic, extreme, and illogical. 118

J

Judgment   The intellectual process in which an individual considers and weighs options in order to make a decision. 73

K

Kleptomania   An impulse-control disorder that involves the persistent urge to steal. 433

Korsakoff's syndrome   A permanent form of dementia associated with long-term alcohol use in which the individual develops retrograde and anterograde amnesia, leading to an inability to remember recent events or learn new information. 396

L

Labeling   A social process in which an individual is designated as having a certain disease or disorder; once given this label, the individual acts in ways that conform to the label. 331

La belle indifference   Lack of concern by some people with a conversion disorder over what might otherwise be construed as very disturbing physical problems. 207

Lactate   A chemical in the blood whose production is stimulated by physical exertion; it is found at higher levels in people with panic disorder. 175

Lactate theory   A theory of panic disorder proposing that the intense anxiety experienced during a panic attack results from an increase of lactate in the blood. 175

Latency   In psychoanalytic theory, a period of psychosexual development during which the child interacts with peers and imitates the behavior of parents and other adults of the same biological sex as the child. 103

Latent   A state in which a disorder is present and capable of becoming evident but is not yet obvious or active. 156

Learned helplessness model   A behavioral approach to depression that proposes that depressed people have come to view themselves as incapable of having an effect on their environment. 290

Learning disorder   A delay or deficit in an academic skill that is evident when an individual's achievement on standardized tests is substantially below what would be expected for others of comparable age, education, and level of intelligence. 352

Least restrictive alternative   A treatment setting that provides the fewest constraints on the client's freedom. 460

Lewy body dementia   A form of dementia similar to Alzheimer's disease with progressive loss of memory, language, calculation, and reasoning, as well as other higher mental functions. 377

Libido   An instinctual pressure for gratification of sexual and aggressive desires. 99

Limbic system   A set of loosely connected structures that form a ring within the center portion of the brain and that provide the neurological basis for the interaction between "rational" and "irrational" human behaviors. 125

Localized amnesia   Inability to remember all events that occurred in a specific time period. 231

Lovemap   The representation of an individual's sexual fantasies and preferred practices. 254

M

Magical thinking   A peculiarity of thinking in which an individual makes a connection between two objects or events that other people would see as unrelated. 69

Magnetic resonance imaging (MRI)   The use of radiowaves rather than X-rays to construct a picture of the living brain based on the water content of various tissues. 89

Mainstreaming   A governmental policy to integrate fully into society people with cognitive and physical disabilities. 347

Major depressive disorder   A mood disorder in which the individual experiences acute, but time-limited, episodes of depressive symptoms. 278

Major depressive episode   A period in which the individual experiences intense psychological and physical symptoms related to a dysphoric mood. 278

Male erectile disorder   A sexual dysfunction marked by a recurrent partial or complete failure to attain or maintain an erection during sexual activity. 262

Male orgasmic disorder   A sexual dysfunction in which a man experiences problems having an orgasm during sexual activity; Also known as inhibited male orgasm. 264

Malingering   The fabrication of physical or psychological symptoms for some ulterior motive. 213

Mandated reporting   The legal requirement that professionals notify appropriate authorities about cases in which children and certain other groups of vulnerable individuals are being abused. 453

Manic episode   A period of euphoric mood with symptoms involving abnormally heightened levels of thinking, behavior, and emotionality. 281

Masochism   The seeking of pleasure from being subjected to pain. 251

Mathematics disorder   A learning disorder in which the individual has difficulty with mathematical tasks and concepts. 352

Medical model   The view that abnormal behaviors result from physical problems and should be treated medically. 15

Melancholic features   A specifier for a depressive episode in which the individual loses interest in most activities, awakens much earlier than usual in the morning, has significant loss of appetite, and possibly experiences psychomotor agitation or retardation and excessive or inappropriate guilt feelings. 279

Mental retardation   A condition, present from childhood, characterized by significantly below-average general intellectual functioning (an IQ of 70 or below). 345

Mental status   A term used by clinicians to describe what the client thinks about and how the client thinks, talks, and acts. 66

Mental status examination   A method of objectively assessing a client's behavior and functioning in a number of spheres, with particular attention to the symptoms associated with psychological disturbance. 67

Mesmerism   Derived from the name Mesmer; a process of bringing about a state of heightened suggestibility through the words and actions of a charismatic individual. 16

Methadone A synthetic opioid that produces a safer and more controlled reaction than heroin and that is used in treating heroin addiction. 414

Milieu therapy A treatment approach, used in an inpatient psychiatric facility, in which all facets of the milieu, or environment, are components of the treatment. 55, 114

Mixed episode A period of at least a week during which the symptoms of both a manic episode and a major depressive episode occur in rapidly alternating fashion. 281

Mixed receptive/expressive language disorder A communication disorder in which the individual has difficulty understanding and expressing certain kinds of words or phrases, such as directions, or, in more severe forms, basic vocabulary or entire sentences. 354

Mobility of affect The ease and speed with which people move from one kind of feeling or level of emotional intensity to another. 69

Modality The form in which psychotherapy is offered. 55

Modeling Acquiring new behavior by imitating that of another person. 117

Monozygotic twins Identical twins, who share the same genetic inheritance. 25

Mood A person's experience of emotion. 70

Moral treatment The philosophy popular in the mid-19th century that people can, with the proper care, develop self-control over their own disturbed behaviors. 13

Motor behavior How a person moves; may refer to fine movements such as handling small objects or the large movements involved in walking. 68

Multiaxial system A multidimensional classification and diagnostic system that summarizes a variety of relevant information about an individual's physical and psychological functioning. 42

Multi-factorial polygenic threshold The position that several genes with varying influence are involved in the transmission of a disorder or characteristic. 129

Multiple baseline approach In behavioral research, the observation of different dependent variables in a person over the course of treatment, or observing the behavior as it occurs under different conditions. 25

Munchausen's syndrome: An extreme form of factitious disorder in which the individual goes to great lengths to maintain a sick role. 215

Mutation An alteration that develops in genes when DNA reproduces itself. 127

N

Narcissistic personality disorder A personality disorder primarily characterized by an unrealistic, inflated sense of self-importance and a lack of sensitivity to the needs of other people. 152

Negative reinforcement The removal of aversive conditions when certain behaviors are performed. 117

Negative symptoms The symptoms of schizophrenia, including affective flattening, alogia, avolition, and anhedonia, that involve functioning below the level of normal behavior. 312

Neurofibrillary tangles A characteristic of Alzheimer's disease in which the material within the cell bodies of neurons becomes filled with densely packed, twisted protein microfibrils, or tiny strands. 379

Neuroleptics A category of medications used to reduce the frequency and intensity of psychotic symptoms; also called major tranquilizers. 333

Neuron The nerve cell; the basic unit of structure and function within the nervous system. 123

Neuropsychological assessment A process of gathering information about a client's brain functioning on the basis of performance on psychological tests. 90

Neurosis Behavior that involves symptoms that are distressing to an individual and that the person recognizes as unacceptable; unofficially used to characterize psychological disorders considered to be less severe than psychosis. 42

Neurotransmitter A chemical substance released from the transmitting neuron into the synaptic cleft, where it drifts across the synapse and is absorbed by the receiving neuron. 124

Nonpurging type A form of bulimia nervosa in which individuals compensate for what they eat by fasting or engaging in excessive exercise. 428

Normal mood (euthymic mood) A feeling state that is neither unduly happy nor sad but shows day-to-day variations within a relatively limited range considered to be appropriate. 71

O

Object relations One's unconscious representations of important people in one's life. 105

Observation process The stage of research in which the researcher watches and records the behavior of interest. 19

Obsession An unwanted thought, word, phrase, or image that persistently and repeatedly comes into a person's mind and causes distress. 68, 185

Obsessive-compulsive disorder An anxiety disorder characterized by recurrent obsessions or compulsions that are inordinately time-consuming or that cause significant distress or impairment. 160, 185

Olfactory hallucination An hallucination involving the perception of a smell. 72

Operant conditioning A learning process in which an individual acquires behaviors through reinforcement. 116

Oppositional defiant disorder A disruptive behavior disorder of childhood that is characterized by undue hostility, stubbornness, strong temper, belligerence, spitefulness, and self-righteousness. 356

Orgasmic reconditioning A behavioral intervention geared toward a relearning process in which the individual associates sexual gratification with appropriate stimuli. 250

Orientation A person's awareness of time, place, and identity. 68

Outcry phase The first reaction to a traumatic event, in which the individual reacts with alarm accompanied by a strong emotion. 192

Overvalued idea A thought that has an odd and absurd quality but is not usually bizarre or deeply entrenched. 69

P

Pain disorder A somatoform disorder in which the only symptom is pain that has no physiological basis. 209

Panic attack A period of intense fear and physical discomfort accompanied by the feeling that one is being overwhelmed and is about to lose control. 172

Panic control therapy (PCT) Treatment that consists of cognitive restructuring, exposure to bodily cues associated with panic attacks, and breathing retraining. 176

Panic disorder An anxiety disorder in which an individual has panic attacks on a recurrent basis or has constant apprehension and worry about the possibility of recurring attacks. 172

Paranoid personality disorder A personality disorder whose outstanding feature is that the individual is extremely suspicious of others and is always on guard against potential danger or harm. 154

Paraphilias A disorder in which an individual has recurrent, intense sexually arousing fantasies, sexual urges, or behaviors involving (1) nonhuman objects, (2) children or other nonconsenting persons, or (3) the suffering or humiliation of self or partner. 243

Parasuicide A suicidal gesture to get attention from loved ones, family, or professionals. 147

Parasympathetic nervous system The part of the autonomic nervous system that carries out the maintenance functions of the body when it is at rest, directing most of the body's activities to producing and storing energy so that it can be used when the body is in action. 126

Parens patriae The state's authority to protect those who are unable to protect themselves. 456

Parkinson's disease A disease that can cause dementia and that involves the degeneration of neurons in the subcortical structures that control motor movements. 377

Partialism A paraphilia in which the person is interested solely in sexual gratification from a specific body part, such as feet. 249

Participant modeling A form of therapy in which the therapist first shows the client a desired behavior and then guides the client through the behavioral change. 121

Pathological gambling An impulse-control disorder involving the persistent urge to gamble. 434

Patient Consistent with the medical model, a term used to refer to someone who receives treatment. 36

Peak experiences In Maslow's theory, feelings of tremendous inner happiness and of being totally in harmony with oneself and the world. 109

Pedophilia A paraphilia in which an adult's sexual urges are directed toward children. 244

Penetrance The extent to which a genotype is expressed in the individual's phenotype. 129

Percentile score The percentage of those who obtain scores below a certain number on a test. 74

Personal history Information gathered in a psychological assessment regarding important events and relationships in areas of the client's life, such as school performance, peer relationships, employment, and health. 65

Personality disorder Ingrained patterns of relating to other people, situations, and events with a rigid and maladaptive pattern of inner experience and behavior, dating back to adolescence or early adulthood. 140

Personality trait An enduring pattern of perceiving, relating to, and thinking about the environment and others. 140

Person-centered theory The humanistic theory that focuses on the uniqueness of each individual, the importance of allowing each individual to achieve maximum fulfillment of potential, and the need for the individual to confront honestly the reality of his or her experiences in the world. 108

Pervasive developmental disorders Conditions that begin in childhood and have a major impact on social and cognitive functioning; involve serious deficits in social interaction and communication skills, as well as odd behavior, interests, and activities. 347

Phallic stage A period of psychosexual development in which the genital area of the body is the focus of the child's sexual feelings. 103

Phenotype The expression of the genetic program in the individual's physical and psychological attributes. 127

Phonological disorder A communication disorder in which the individual misarticulates, substitutes, or omits speech sounds. 354

Pick's disease A relatively rare degenerative disease that affects the frontal and temporal lobes of the cerebral cortex and that can cause dementia. 376

Pituitary gland A major gland in the endocrine system, located in the brain and under the control of the hypothalamus; sometimes called the "master" gland. 126

Placebo condition The condition used in experimental research in which people are given an inert substance or treatment that is similar in all other ways to the experimental treatment. 21

Pleasure principle In psychoanalytic theory, a motivating force oriented toward the immediate and total gratification of sensual needs and desires. 98

Polygenic A model of inheritance in which more than one gene participates in the process of determining a given characteristic. 128

Population The entire group of individuals sharing a particular characteristic. 20

Positive reinforcement Providing reward when certain behaviors are performed. 117

Positive symptoms The symptoms of schizophrenia, including delusions, hallucinations, disturbed speech, and disturbed behavior, that are exaggerations or distortions of normal thoughts, emotions, and behavior. 312

Positron emission tomography (PET) scan A measure of brain activity in which a small amount of radioactive sugar is injected into an individual's bloodstream, following which a computer measures the varying levels of radiation in different parts of the brain and yields a multicolored image. 89

Post-traumatic stress disorder (PTSD) An anxiety disorder in which the individual experiences several distressing symptoms for more than a month following a traumatic event, such as a reexperiencing of the traumatic event, an avoidance of reminders of the trauma, a numbing of general responsiveness, and increased arousal. 190

Potentiation The combination of the effects of two or more psychoactive substances such that the total effect is greater than the effect of either substance alone. 394

Prefrontal area The area at the very front of the cerebral cortex responsible for abstract planning and judgment. 125

Premature ejaculation A sexual dysfunction in which a man reaches orgasm well before he wishes to, perhaps even prior to penetration. 264

Premorbid functioning The period prior to the onset of the individual's symptoms. 317

Prevalence The number of people who have ever had a disorder at a given time or over a specified period. 24

Primary gain The relief from anxiety or responsibility due to the development of physical or psychological symptoms. 217

Primary process thinking In psychoanalytic theory, loosely associated, idiosyncratic, and distorted cognitive representation of the world. 99

Primary reinforcers Rewards that satisfy a biological need, making them intrinsically rewarding. 117

Principal diagnosis The disorder that is considered to be the primary reason the individual seeks professional help. 49

Privileged communication Information provided by a client to a clinician that cannot be disclosed in a court of law without the client's expressed permission. 453

Probability The odds or likelihood that an event will happen. 19

Probands In genetic research, people who have the symptoms of a particular disorder. 286

Problem-focused coping Coping in which the individual takes action to reduce stress by changing whatever it is about the situation that makes it stressful. 220

Process schizophrenia The gradual appearance of schizophrenia over time; contrasts with *reactive schizophrenia*. 316

Prodromal phase A period in the course of schizophrenia, prior to the active phase of symptoms, during which the individual shows progressive deterioration in social and interpersonal functioning. 311

Prognosis A client's likelihood of recovering from a disorder. 46

Projective test A technique in which the test-taker is presented with an ambiguous item or task and is asked to respond by providing his or her own meaning or perception. 83

Pseudodementia Literally, false dementia, or a set of symptoms caused by depression that mimic those apparent in the early stages of Alzheimer's. 378

Psychiatrist A medical doctor (MD) with advanced training in treating people with psychological disorders. 37

Psychoanalysis A theory and system of practice that relies heavily on the concepts of the unconscious mind, inhibited sexual impulses, early development, and the use of the "free association" technique and dream analysis. 16

Psychoanalytic model An approach that seeks explanations of abnormal behavior in the workings of unconscious psychological processes. 15

Psychodynamic perspective The theoretical orientation in psychology that emphasizes unconscious determinants of behavior. 98

Psychodynamics The processes of interaction among personality structures that lie beneath the surface of observable behavior. 98

Psychological factors affecting medical condition Situations in which psychological or behavior factors have an adverse effect on a medical condition. 218

Psychological testing A broad range of measurement techniques, all of which involve having people provide scorable information about their psychological functioning. 38

Psychometrics Literally, "measurement of the mind," reflecting the goal of finding the most suitable tests for psychological variables under study. 74

Psychomotor agitation A motor pattern involving an obvious level of personal discomfort in which the individual appears to be restless and stirred up. 68

Psychomotor retardation A motor pattern involving abnormally slow movements and lethargy. 68

Psychoneuroimmunology The study of connections among psychological stress, nervous system functioning, and the immune system. 222

Psychopathy A personality type characterized by a cluster of traits that constitutes the core of what is now called antisocial personality disorder. 141

Psychosexual stages According to psychoanalytic theory, the normal sequence of development through which each individual passes between infancy and adulthood. 99

Psychosis Behavior involving loss of contact with reality. 42

Psychotherapy The treatment of abnormal behavior through psychological techniques. 16

Punishment The application of an aversive stimulus. 117

Purge To eliminate food through unnatural methods, such as vomiting or the excessive use of laxatives. 426

Purging type A form of bulimia nervosa in which individuals force out of their bodies what they have just eaten. 428

Pyromania An impulse-control disorder involving the persistent and compelling urge to start fires. 438

Q

Quasi-experimental design A design that is like an experimental design but lacks the key ingredient of random assignment to groups. 22

R

Range of affect The extent and variety of an individual's emotional expression. 70

Rapid cyclers Individuals with bipolar disorder who have four to eight mood episodes within the course of a year. 284

Reactive attachment disorder of infancy or childhood A disorder involving a severe disturbance in the ability to relate to others in which the individual is unresponsive to people, is apathetic, and prefers to be alone rather than to interact with friends or family. 362

Reactive schizophrenia The development of schizophrenia in response to a precipitant that provokes the onset of symptoms; contrasts with *process schizophrenia*. 317

Reactivity Change in a person's behavior in response to knowledge that he or she is being observed. 87

Reading disorder (dyslexia) A learning disorder in which the individual omits, distorts, or substitutes words when reading and reads in a slow and halting fashion. 352

Reality principle In psychoanalyic theory, motivational force that leads the individual to confront the constraints of the external world. 99

Reinforcement The "strengthening" of a behavior. 117

Relapse prevention therapy A treatment method based on the expectancy model, in which individuals are encouraged not to view lapses from abstinence as signs of certain failure. 401

Relaxation training A behavioral technique used in the treatment of anxiety disorders that involves progressive and systematic patterns of muscle tensing and relaxing. 176

Reliability The consistency of measurements or diagnoses. 38, 74

Representativeness The extent to which a sample adequately reflects the characteristics of the population from which it is drawn. 21

Residual phase A period in the course of schizophrenia, following the active phase, in which there are continuing indications of disturbance, evidenced by the same kinds of behaviors that characterize the prodromal phase. 311

Resistance The unconscious blocking of anxiety-provoking thoughts or feelings. 106

Reticular formation A diffuse collection of ascending and descending pathways that controls the level and direction of arousal of brain activity through the excitation of certain pathways and the inhibition of others. 124

Rett's disorder A pervasive developmental disorder, occurring only in females, in which the child develops normally until between 5 months and 4 years of age and then begins to show a number of neurological and cognitive impairments, including a deceleration of head growth, stereotyped movements of the hand, a lack of bodily coordination, language impairments, and social withdrawal. 347

Rumination disorder An eating disorder in which the infant or child regurgitates food after it has been swallowed and then either spits it out or reswallows it. 362

S

Sadomasochist A person who derives sexual pleasure from both inflicting and receiving pain. 251

Sample A selection of individuals from a larger group. 20

Schizoaffective disorder A psychotic disorder involving the experience of a major depressive episode, a manic episode, or a mixed episode while also meeting the diagnostic criteria for schizophrenia. 321

Schizoid personality disorder A personality disorder primarily characterized by an indifference to social relationships, as well as a very limited range of emotional experience and expression. 155

Schizophrenia A disorder with a range of symptoms involving disturbances in content of thought, form of thought, perception, affect, sense of self, motivation, behavior, and interpersonal functioning. 310

Schizophrenia, catatonic type A type of schizophrenia characterized by a variety of bodily movement abnormalities. 313

Schizophrenia, disorganized type A type of schizophrenia characterized by a combination of symptoms, including disorganized speech and behavior and flat or inappropriate affect. Even delusions and hallucinations lack a coherent theme. 313

Schizophrenia, paranoid type A type of schizophrenia characterized by preoccupation with one or more bizarre delusions or with auditory hallucinations that are related to a particular theme of being persecuted or harassed. 313

Schizophrenia, residual type A type of schizophrenia in which people who have previously been diagnosed as having schizophrenia may no longer have prominent psychotic symptoms but still show some lingering signs of the disorder, such as emotional dullness, social withdrawal, eccentric behavior, or illogical thinking. 314

Schizophrenia, undifferentiated type A type of schizophrenia characterized by a complex of schizophrenic symptoms, such as delusions, hallucinations, incoherence, or disorganized behavior, that does not meet the criteria for other types of schizophrenia. 313

Schizophrenia spectrum disorders A term used by some researchers to characterize a continuum of disorders, including schizophrenia, schizoid personality disorder, and schizotypal personality disorder. 155

Schizophreniform disorder A disorder characterized by psychotic symptoms that are essentially the same as those found in schizophrenia, except for the duration and chronic nature of the symptoms; specifically, symptoms usually last from 1 to 6 months. 320

Schizotypal personality disorder A personality disorder that primarily involves peculiarities and eccentricities of thought, behavior, appearance, and interpersonal style. People with this disorder may have peculiar ideas, such as magical thinking and beliefs in psychic phenomena. 156

Seasonal pattern A specifier for a depressive episode in which the individual has varying symptoms according to time of year, with symptoms usually developing during the same months every year. 279

Secondary gain: The sympathy and attention that a sick person receives from other people. 217

Secondary process thinking   In psychoanalytic theory, the kind of thinking involved in logical and rational problem solving. 98

Secondary reinforcers   Rewards that derive their value from association with primary reinforcers. 117

Sedative   A psychoactive substance that has a calming effect on the central nervous system. 415

Selective amnesia   Inability to remember some, but not all, events that occurred in a specified time period. 231

Selective mutism   A disorder originating in childhood in which the individual consciously refuses to talk, sometimes accompanying this refusal by oppositional or avoidant behavior. 362

Selective serotonin reuptake inhibitors (SSRI)   Medications that block the reuptake of serotonin at the synapse, enabling more of this neurotransmitter to be available at the receptor sites. 130

Self-actualization   In humanistic theory, the maximum realization of the individual's potential for psychological growth. 109

Self-efficacy   The individual's perception of competence in various life situations. 118

Self-monitoring   A self-report technique in which the client keeps a record of the frequency of specified behaviors. 87

Self-report clinical inventory   A psychological test with standardized questions having fixed response categories that the test-taker completes independently, self-reporting the extent to which the responses are accurate characterizations. 77

Sensate focus   A method of treatment xfor sexual dysfunctions that involves the partners' taking turns stimulating each other in nonsexual but affectionate ways at first, then gradually progressing over a period of time toward genital stimulation. 268

Sensory gating   The ability to filter sensory input. 329

Separation anxiety disorder   A childhood disorder characterized by intense and inappropriate anxiety, lasting at least 4 weeks, concerning separation from home or caregivers. 360

Sexual aversion disorder   A sexual dysfunction characterized by an active dislike of intercourse or related sexual activities. 261

Sexual dysfunction   An abnormality in an individual's sexual responsiveness and reactions. 258

Sexual impulsivity   An impulse-control disorder in which people feel uncontrollably driven to seek out sexual encounters and to engage in frequent and indiscriminate sexual activity. 439

Sexual masochism   A paraphilia marked by an attraction to achieving sexual gratification by having painful stimulation applied to one's own body. 251

Sexual orientation   The degree to which a person is erotically attracted to members of the same or opposite sex. 255

Sexual sadism   A paraphilia in which sexual gratification is derived from activities that harm, or from urges to harm, another person. 251

Shaping   A learning technique in which reinforcement is provided for behaviors that increasingly resemble a desired outcome. 117

Shared psychotic disorder   A psychotic disorder in which one or more people develop a delusional system as a result of a close relationship with a psychotic person who is delusional. 323

Single Photon Emission Computed Tomography (SPECT) procedure   A variant of the PET scan that permits a longer and more detailed imaging analysis. 89

Single-subject design   An experimental procedure in which one person at a time is studied in both the experimental and control conditions. 24

Situationally bound (cued) panic attack   A panic attack that is triggered by anticipation of or exposure to a specific situation or cue. 172

Situationally predisposed panic attack   A panic attack that is usually but not invariably triggered by exposure to a situational cue. 173

Smooth pursuit eye movements   A biological marker that is measured by having a person visually follow a target; people with schizophrenia and their relatives have been found to show irregular pursuit of a moving target with many interruptions by extraneous eye movements. 328

Social cognition   The factors that influence the way people perceive themselves and other people and form judgments about the causes of behavior. 118

Social learning   A theoretical perspective that focuses on how people develop personality and psychological disorders through their relationships with others and through observation of other people. 118

Social phobia   An anxiety disorder characterized by irrational and unabating fear that one's behavior will be scrutinized by others, causing the individual to feel embarrassed and humiliated. 181

Sociocultural perspective   The theoretical perspective that emphasizes the ways that individuals are influenced by people, social institutions, and social forces in the world around them. 112

Somatic hallucination   An hallucination involving the false perception of bodily sensation. 72

Somatization disorder   A somatoform disorder in which multiple and recurrent bodily symptoms, which lack a physiological basis, are the expression of psychological issues. 207

Somatoform disorders   A variety of conditions in which psychological conflicts become translated into physical problems or complaints. 206

Specific phobia   An irrational and unabating fear of a particular object, activity, or situation. 177

Spectatoring   The experience in which the individual feels unduly self-conscious during sexual activity, as if evaluating and monitoring his or her performance during the sexual encounter. 261

Splitting   A defense, common in people with borderline personality disorder, in which individuals perceive others, or themselves, as being all good or all bad, usually resulting in disturbed interpersonal relationships. 147

Squeeze technique   A method of treatment for premature ejaculation in which the partner stimulates the man's penis during foreplay and squeezes it when he indicates he is approaching orgasm. 268

Standardized   Uniform procedures used for both test administration and scoring. 74

Stereotypic movement disorder   A disorder in which the individual voluntarily repeats nonfunctional behaviors, such as rocking or head-banging, that can be damaging to his or her physical well-being. 362

Stimulant   A psychoactive substance that has an activating effect on the central nervous system. 405

Stimulus discrimination   Differentiation between two stimuli that possess similar but essentially different characteristics. 116

Stop-start procedure   A method of treatment for premature ejaculation in which the man or his partner stimulates him to sexual excitement, and, as he approaches the point of orgasmic inevitability, stimulation is stopped. When this procedure is repeated over time, the man can develop greater control over his orgasmic response. 268

Stress   The unpleasant emotional reaction that a person has when an event is perceived by an individual as threatening. 219

Stress inoculation training   Stress reduction method that helps people prepare for difficult situations that have occurred in the past and are likely to occur again in the future. 225

Stressor   An event that disrupts the individual's life, also called a **stressful life event.** 219

Structured interview   A standardized series of assessment questions, with a predetermined wording and order. 65

Stuttering   A communication disorder that involves a disturbance in the normal fluency and patterning of speech that is characterized by such verbalizations as sound repetitions or prolongations, broken words, the blocking out of sounds, word substitutions to avoid problematic words, or words expressed with an excess of tension. 354

Subcortical structures Parts of the brain that operate much of the time as relay stations to prepare information for processing in the cerebral cortex and to carry out the instructions for action that the cerebral cortex gives to the muscles and glands. 124

Substance A chemical that alters a person's mood or behavior when it is smoked, injected, drunk, inhaled, or swallowed in pill form. 392

Substance abuse The pattern of maladaptive substance use that leads to significant impairment or distress. 393

Substance dependence A maladaptive pattern of substance use manifested by a cluster of cognitive, behavioral, and physiological symptoms during a 12-month period and caused by the continued use of a substance. 393

Substance intoxication The temporary maladaptive experience of behavioral or psychological changes that are due to the accumulation of a substance in the body. 392

Substance withdrawal Psychological and physical changes that occur when some substances are discontinued. 392

Substance-induced persisting amnestic disorder An amnestic disorder caused by drugs or environmental toxins. 371

Substance-induced persisting dementia A form of dementia caused by the ingestion of substances, such as drugs, or exposure to toxins. 375

Suicidal intent The level of commitment to taking one's own life. 300

Suicidal lethality The dangerousness of a suicidal person's intended method of dying. 300

Superego In psychoanalytic theory, the structure of personality that includes the conscience and the ego ideal; it incorporates societal prohibitions and exerts control over the seeking of instinctual gratification. 99

Survey method A research tool, used to gather information from a sample of people considered representative of a particular population, in which participants are asked to answer questions about the topic of concern. 23

Sympathetic nervous system The part of the autonomic nervous system primarily responsible for mobilizing the body's stored resources when these resources are needed for activities that require energy. 126

Syndrome A collection of symptoms that form a definable pattern. 41

Systematic desensitization A variant of counterconditioning that involves presenting the client with progressively more anxiety-provoking images while in a relaxed state. 120

T

Target behavior A behavior of interest or concern in an assessment. 87

Tau A protein that normally helps maintain the internal support structure of the axons. 379

Theoretical perspective An orientation to understanding the causes of human behavior and the treatment of abnormality. 98

Thinking style and language A term used in a mental status exam to indicate how a person thinks. This includes information on the client's vocabulary use and sentence structure. 69

Thought stopping A cognitive-behavioral method in which the client learns to stop having anxiety-provoking thoughts. 180

Tic A rapid, recurring, involuntary movement or vocalization. 362

Token economy A form of contingency management in which a client who performs desired activities earns chips or tokens that can later be exchanged for tangible benefits. 121

Tolerance The extent to which the individual requires larger and larger amounts of a substance in order to achieve its desired effects, or the extent to which the individual feels less of its effects after using the same amount of the substance. 393

Tourette's disorder A tic disorder involving a combination of chronic movement and vocal tics. 362

Transference The carrying over toward the therapist of the feelings the client had toward parents or other significant people in the client's life. 105

Transsexualism A term sometimes used to refer to gender identity disorder, specifically pertaining to individuals choosing to undergo sex reassignment surgery. 255

Transvestic fetishism A paraphilia in which a man has an uncontrollable craving to dress in women's clothing in order to derive sexual gratification. 252

Traumatic experience A disastrous or an extremely painful event that has severe psychological and physiological effects. 190

Trephining The drilling of a hole in the skull, presumably as a way of treating psychological disorders during prehistoric times. 9

Trichotillomania An impulse-control disorder involving the compulsive, persistent urge to pull out one's own hair. 441

U

Unconditioned response A reflexive response that occurs naturally in the presence of the unconditioned stimulus without having been learned. 116

Unconditioned stimulus The stimulus that naturally produces a response without having been learned. 115

Unexpected (uncued) panic attack A panic attack that occurs in the absence of a specific situation or cue. 172

Unstructured interview A series of open-ended questions aimed at determining the client's reasons for being in treatment, symptoms, health status, family background, and life history. 64

V

Vaginismus A sexual dysfunction that involves recurrent or persistent involuntary spasms of the musculature of the outer part of the vagina. 265

Validity The extent to which a test, diagnosis, or rating accurately and distinctly characterizes a person's psychological status. 38, 74

Variable A dimension along which people, things, or events differ. 21

Vascular dementia A form of dementia resulting from a vascular disease that causes deprivation of the blood supply to the brain. 378

Vicarious reinforcement A form of learning in which a new behavior is acquired through the process of watching someone else receive reinforcement for the same behavior. 118

Visual hallucination An hallucination involving the false visual perception of objects or persons. 72

Voyeur A person with the paraphilia of voyeurism. 253

Voyeurism A paraphilia in which the individual has a compulsion to derive sexual gratification from observing the nudity or sexual activity of others. 253

W

Wernicke's aphasia A form of aphasia in which the individual is able to produce language but has lost the ability to comprehend, so that these verbal productions have no meaning. 372

Wernicke's disease An acute condition—associated with long-term, heavy alcohol use—involving delirium, eye movement disturbances, difficulties in movement and balance, and deterioration of the peripheral nerves to the hands and feet. 396

Working through A phase of psychoanalytic treatment in which the clinician helps the client achieve a healthier resolution of issues than had occurred in the client's early childhood environment. 106

References

A

Abbott, D. A., & Cramer, S. L. (1993). Gambling attitudes and participation: A Midwestern survey. *Journal of Gambling Studies, 9,* 247–263.

Abraham, K. (1911/1968). Notes on the psychoanalytic investigation and treatment of manic-depressive insanity and allied conditions. In K. Abraham (Ed.), *Selected papers of Karl Abraham.* New York: Basic Books.

Abramowitz, J. S. (1997). Effectiveness of psychological and pharmacological treatments for obsessive-compulsive disorder: A quantitative review. *Journal of Consulting and Clinical Psychology, 65,* 44–52.

Abramson, L. Y., Seligman, M. E. P., & Teasdale, J. D. (1978). Learned helplessness in humans: Critique and reformulation. *Journal of Abnormal Psychology, 87,* 49–74.

Adebimpe, V. R. (1994). Race, racism, and epidemiological surveys. *Hospital and Community Psychiatry, 45,* 27–31.

Adler, A. (1931/1958). *What life should mean to you.* New York: Capricorn.

Adler, L. E., Olincy, A., Waldo, M., Harris, J. G., Griffith, J., Stevens, K., Flach, K., Nagamoto, H., Bickford, P., Leonard, S., & Freedman, R. (1998). Schizophrenia, sensory gating, and nicotinic receptors. *Schizophrenia Bulletin, 24,* 189–202.

Agras, W. S., & Apple, R. F. (1998). Sally and her eating disorder: A case of bulimia nervosa. In R. P. Halgin & S. K. Whitbourne (Eds.), *A casebook in abnormal psychology: From the files of experts* (pp. 268–283). New York: Oxford University Press.

Ainsworth, M. D. S. (1989). Attachments beyond infancy. *American Psychologist, 44,* 709–716.

Ainsworth, M. D. S., Blehar, M., Waters, E., & Wall, S. (1978). *Patterns of attachment.* Hillsdale, NJ: Erlbaum.

Aisen, P. S., & Pasinetti, G. M. (1998). Glucocorticoids in Alzheimer's disease. The story so far. *Drugs and Aging, 12,* 1–9.

Akhtar, S. (1996). Further exploration of gender differences in personality disorders. *American Journal of Psychiatry, 153,* 846–847.

Alden, L. E., & Capreol, M. J. (1993). Avoidant personality disorder: Interpersonal problems as predictors of treatment response. *Behavior Therapy, 24,* 357–376.

Alexander, P. C. (1992). Application of attachment theory to the study of sexual abuse. *Journal of Consulting and Clinical Psychology, 60,* 185–195.

Alford, B. A., & Beck, A. T. (1994). Cognitive therapy of delusional beliefs. *Behaviour Research and Therapy, 32,* 369–380.

Alloy, L. B., & Abramson, L. Y. (1979). Judgement of contingency in depressed and nondepressed students: Sadder but wiser? *Journal of Experimental Psychology: General, 108,* 441–485.

Alpert, J., Brown, L., Ceci, S., Courtois, C., Loftus, E., & Ornstein, P. (1996). *Working group on investigation of memories of childhood abuse: Final Report.* Washington DC: American Psychological Association.

Althof, S. E., & Seftel, A. D. (1995). The evaluation and treatment of erectile dysfunction. *Psychiatric Clinics of North America,* 171–192.

Alzheimer, A. (1907/1987). About a peculiar disease of the cerebral cortex. *Alzheimer's Disease and Associated Disorders, 1,* 7–8.

American Psychiatric Association. (1994) *DSM–IV Diagnostic and Statistical Manual.* Washington, DC: American Psychiatric Association.

Anastasi, A., & Urbina, S. (1996). *Psychological testing* (7th ed.). New York: Macmillan.

Anderson, R. N., Kochanek, K. D., & Murphy, S. L. (Eds.). (1997). *Report of final mortality statistics, 1995.* (Vol. 45 [11, Suppl. 2]). Hyattsville, MD: National Center for Health Statistics.

Anderson, S. C., & Hibbs, V. K. (1992). Alcoholism in the Soviet Union. *Social Work, 35,* 441–453.

Andreasen, N. C. (1987). Creativity and mental illness: Prevalence rates in writers and their first-degree relatives. *American Journal of Psychiatry, 144,* 1288–1292.

Andreasen, N. C. (1987). The diagnosis of schizophrenia. *Schizophrenia Bulletin, 13,* 9–22.

Andreasen, N. C. (1998). Jeff: A difficult case of schizophrenia. In R. P. Halgin & S. K. Whitbourne (Eds.), *A casebook in abnormal psychology: From the files of experts* (pp. 198–209). New York: Oxford University Press.

Andrews, B., Valentine, E. R., & Valentine, J. D. (1995). Depression and eating disorders following abuse in childhood in two generations of women. *British Journal of Clinical Psychology, 34,* 37–52.

Annis, H. M. (1984). *Inventory of Drinking Situations.* Toronto: Addition Research Foundation.

Anonymous. (1997). Urgan community intervention to prevent Halloween arson–Detroit, Michigan, 1985-1996. *MMWR Morbidity & Mortality Weekly Report, 46,* 299–304.

Anthony, J. C., & Petronis, K. R. (1991). Panic attacks and suicide attempts. *Archives of General Psychiatry, 48,* 1114.

Anthony, J. C., Warner, L. A., & Kessler, R. C. (1994). Comparative epidemiology of dependence on tobacco, alcohol, controlled substances, and inhalants: Basic findings from the National Comorbidity Survey. *Experimental and Clinical Psychopharmacology, 2,* 244–268.

APA Presidential Task Force on the Assessment of Age-Consistent Memory Decline and Dementia. (1998). *Guidelines for the evaluation of dementia and age-related cognitive decline.* Washington, DC: American Psychological Association.

Aranda, M. P., & Knight, B. G. (1997). The influence of ethnicity and culture on the caregiver stress and coping process: A socio-cultural review and analysis. *Gerontologist, 37,* 342–354.

Arango, V., Underwood, M. D., & Mann, J. J. (1992). Alterations in monoamine receptors in the brain of suicide victims. *Journal of Clinical Psychopharmacology, 12,* 8S–12S.

Arend, R., Gove, F. L., & Sroufe, L. (1979). Continuity of individual adaptation from infancy to kindergarten: A predictive study of ego-resiliency and curiosity in preschoolers. *Child Development, 50,* 950–959.

Armfield, J. M., & Mattiske, J. K. (1996). Vulnerability representation: The role of perceived dangerousness, uncontrollability, unpredictability and disgustingness in spider fear. *Behaviour Research & Therapy, 34,* 899–909.

Arndt, S., Andreasen, N. C., Flaum, M., Miller, D., & Nopoulos, P. (1995). A longitudinal study of symptom dimensions in schizophrenia. Prediction and patterns of change. *Archives of General Psychiatry, 52,* 352–360.

Asarnow, R. F., Granholm, E., & Sherman, T. (1991). Span of apprehension in schizophrenia. In S. R. Steinhauer, J. H. Gruzelier, & J. Zubin (Eds.), *Handbook of schizophrenia: Vol. 5. Neuropsychology, psychophysiology and information processing* (pp. 335–370). Amsterdam: Elseview.

481

Asarnow, R. F., Steffy, R. A., MacCrimmon, D. J., & Cleghorn, J. M. (1977). An attentional assessment of foster children at risk for schizophrenia. *Journal of Abnormal Psychology, 86,* 267–275.

Aschauer, H. N., Fischer, G., Isenberg, K. E., Meszaros, K., Willinger, U., Todd, R. D., Beran, H., Strobl, R., Lang, M., Fuchs, K. (1993). No proof of linkage between schizophrenia-related disorders including schizophrenia and chromosome 2q21 region. Special Issue: Genetic epidemiology of psychiatric disorders. *European Archives of Psychiatry and Clinical Neuroscience, 243,* 193–198.

Asher, R. (1951). Munchausen's syndrome. *Lancet, 1,* 339–341.

Asmundson, G. J., Larsen, D. K., & Stein, M. B. (1998). Panic disorder and vestibular disturbance: An overview of empirical findings and clinical implications. *Journal of Psychosomatic Research, 44,* 107–120.

Asscheman, H., & Gooren, L. J. (1992). Hormone treatment in transsexuals. *Journal of Psychology and Human Sexuality, 5,* 39–54.

Astin, M. C., Ogland-Hand, S. M., Coleman, E. M., & Foy, D. W. (1995). Post-traumatic stress disorder and childhood abuse in battered women: Comparisons with maritally distressed women. *Journal of Consulting and Clinical Psychology, 63,* 308–312.

Attia, E., Haiman, C., Walsh, B. T., & Flater, S. R. (1998). Does fluoxetine augment the inpatient treatment of anorexia nervosa? *American Journal of Psychiatry, 155,* 548–551.

Ayllon, T., & Azrin, N. H. (1965). The measurement and reinforcement of behavior of psychotics. *Journal of Experimental Analysis of Behavior, 8,* 351–383.

Aylward, E. H., Brown, F. R., III, Lewis, M. E. B., & Sabage, C. R. (1987). Planning for treatment of learning disabilities and associated primary handicapping conditions. In I. F. R. Brown & E. H. Aylward (Eds.), *Diagnosis and management of learning disabilities: An interdisciplinary approach* (pp. 127–146). Boston: College Hill Press.

Azmitia, E., Kramer, K., & Whitaker-Azmitia, P. (1994). In vitro release of 5-hydroxytryptamine from fetal and maternal brain by drugs of abuse. *Developmental Brain Research, 78,* 142–146.

B

Baer, L., Rauch, S. L., Ballantine, T., Martuza, R., Cosgrove, R., Cassem, E., Giriunas, I., Manzo, P. A., Dimino, C., & Jenike, M. A. (1995). Cingulotomy for intractable obsessive-compulsive disorder. *Archives of General Psychiatry, 52,* 384–392.

Bagley, C., Wood, M., & Young, L. (1994). Victim to abuser: Mental health and behavioral sequels of child sexual abuse in a community survey of young adult males. *Child Abuse & Neglect, 18,* 683–697.

Bailey, A., Le Couteur, A., Gottesman, I., Bolton, P., Simonoff, E., Yuzda, E., & Rutter, M. (1995). Autism as a strongly genetic disorder: Evidence from a British twin study. *Psychological Medicine, 25,* 63–77.

Bailey, J. M., & Kucker, K. J. (1995). Childhood sex-typed behavior and sexual orientation: A conceptual analysis and quantitative review. *Developmental Psychology, 31,* 43–45.

Baker, G. A., Hanley, J. R., Jackson, H. F., Kimmance, S., & Slade, P. (1993). Detecting the faking of amnesia: Performance differences between simulators and patients with memory impairment. *Journal of Clinical and Experimental Neuropsychology, 15,* 668–684.

Baker, J. D., Capron, E. W., & Azorlosa, J. (1996). Family environment characteristics of persons with histrionic and dependent personality disorders. *Journal of Personality Disorders, 10,* 82–87.

Baker, L., & Cantwell, D. P. (1987). A prospective psychiatric follow up of children with speech/language disorders. *Journal of the American Academy of Child and Adolescent Psychiatry, 36,* 546–553.

Baker, R. A. (1990). *They call it hypnosis.* Buffalo: Prometheus Books.

Bandura, A. (1971). Psychotherapy based upon modeling principles. In A. E. Bergin & S. L. Garfield (Eds.), *Handbook of psychotherapy and behavior change* (pp. 653–708). New York: Wiley.

Bandura, A. (1986). *Social foundations of thought and action: A social cognitive theory.* Englewood Cliffs, NJ: Prentice Hall.

Bandura, A. (1991). Human agency: The rhetoric and the reality. *American Psychologist, 46,* 157–162.

Bandura, A. (1997). *Self-efficacy: The exercise of control.* New York: W. H. Freeman.

Barbaree, H., & Seto, M. C. (1997). Pedophilia: Assessment and treatment. In D. R. Laws & W. T. O'Donohue (Eds.), *Sexual deviance: Theory, assessment, and treatment* (pp. 175–193). New York: Guilford Press.

Barber, J. P. (1994). Efficacy of short-term dynamic psychotherapy: Past, present, and future. *Journal of Psychotherapy Practice and Research, 3,* 108–121.

Barefoot, J. C., Siegler, I. C., Nowling, J. B., Peterson, B. L., Haney, T. L., & Williams, R. B., Jr. (1987). Suspiciousness, health, and mortality: A follow-up study of 500 older adults. *Psychosomatic Medicine, 49,* 450–457.

Barkley, R. A. (1998). Attention-deficit hyperactivity disorder. *Scientific American, 279,* 66–71.

Barkley, R. A., & Edwards, G. (1998). Paul: An instructive case of attention-deficit/hyperactivity disorder. In R. P. Halgin & S. K. Whitbourne (Eds.), *A casebook in abnormal psychology: From the files of experts* (pp. 212–235). New York: Oxford University Press.

Barlow, D. H. (1980). Causes of sexual dysfunction: The role of anxiety and cognitive interference. *Journal of Consulting and Clinical Psychology, 54,* 140–148.

Barlow, D. H. (1988). *Anxiety and its disorders: The nature and treatment of anxiety and panic.* New York: Guilford Press.

Barlow, D. H. (1990). Long-term outcome for patients with panic disorder treated with cognitive-behavioral therapy. *Journal of Clinical Psychiatry, 51,* 17–23.

Barlow, D. H., & Brown, T. A. (1998). Eric: A case example of panic disorder with agoraphobia. In R. P. Halgin & S. K. Whitbourne (Eds.), *A casebook of abnormal psychology: From the files of experts* (pp. 38–57). New York: Oxford University Press.

Barlow, D. H., Brown, T. A., & Craske, M. G. (1994). Definitions of panic attacks and panic disorder in DSM-IV: Implications for research. *Journal of Abnormal Psychology, 103,* 553–564.

Barlow, D. H., Craske, M. G., Cerny, J. A., & Klosko, J. S. (1989). Behavioral treatment of panic disorder. *Behavior Therapy, 20,* 261–282.

Barlow, D. H., Esler, J. L., & Vitali, A. E. (1998). Psychosocial treatments for panic disorders, phobias, and generalized anxiety disorder. In P. E. Nathan & J. M. Gorman (Eds.), *A guide to treatments that work* (pp. 288–318). New York: Oxford University Press.

Barner, E. L., & Gray, S. L. (1998). Donepezil use in Alzheimer's disease. *Annals of Pharmacotherapy, 32,* 70–77.

Barnett, W., Richter, P., Sigmund, D., & Spitzer, M. (1997). Recidivism and concomitant criminality in pathological firesetters. *Journal of Forensic Sciences, 42,* 879–883.

Barondes, S. H. (1994). Thinking about Prozac. *Science, 263,* 1102–1103.

Barrett-Lennard, G. T. (1962). Dimensions of therapist response as causal factors in therapeutic change. *Psychological Monographs, 76.*

Barsky, A. J. (1996). Hypochondriasis: Medical management and psychiatric treatment. *Psychosomatics, 37,* 48–56.

Barsky, A. J., Brener, J., Coeytaux, R. R., & Cleary, P. D. (1995). Accurate awareness of heartbeat in hypochondriacal and non-hypochondriacal patients. *Journal of Psychosomatic Research, 39,* 489–497.

Barsky, A. J., Cleary, P. D., Sarnie, M. K., & Ruskin, J. N. (1994). Panic disorder, palpitations, and the awareness of cardiac activity. *Journal of Nervous and Mental Disease, 182,* 63–71.

Bartholomew, K. (1997). Adult attachment processes: Individual and couple perspectives. *British Journal of Medical Psychology, 70,* 249–263.

Bartholomew, K., & Horowitz, L. M. (1991). Attachment styles among young adults: A test of a four-category model. *Journal of Personality and Social Psychology, 61,* 226–244.

Bartol, C. R. (1991). Predictive validation of the MMPI for small-town police officers who fail. *Professional Psychology: Research and Practice, 22,* 127–132.

Bassett, A. S. (1989). Chromosome 5 and schizophrenia: Implications for genetic linkage studies. *Schizophrenia Bulletin, 15,* 393–402.

Bateman, D., Ng, S., Hansen, C., & Heagarty, M. (1993). The effects of intrauterine cocaine exposure in newborns. *American Journal of Public Health, 83,* 190.

Battaglia, M., Bertella, S., Politi, E., Bernardeschi, L., Perna, G., Gabriele, A., & Bellodi, L. (1995). Age at onset of panic disorder: Influence of familial liability to the disease and of childhood separation anxiety disorder. *American Journal of Psychiatry, 152,* 1362–1364.

Baucom, D. H., Shoham, V., Mueser, K. T., Daiuto, A. D., & Stickle, T. R. (1998). Empirically supported couple and family interventions for marital distress and adult mental health problelms. *Journal of Consulting and Clinical Psychology, 66,* 53–88.

Bauer, M. S., Calabrese, J. R., Dunner, D. L., Post, R., Whybrow, P. C., Gyulai, L., Tay, L. K., Younkin, S. R., Bynum, D., & Lavori, P. (1994). Multisite data reanalysis of the validity of rapid cycling as a course modifier for bipolar disorder in DSM-IV. *American Journal of Psychiatry, 151,* 506–515.

Bech, P., & Angst, J. (1996). Quality of life in anxiety and social phobia. *International Clinical Psychopharmacology, 3,* 97–100.

Beck, A. T. (1967). *Depression: Clinical, experimental, and theoretical aspects.* New York: Harper & Row.

Beck, A. T., Emery, G., & Greenberg, R. L. (1985). *Anxiety disorders and phobias: A cognitive perspective.* New York: Basic Books.

Beck, A. T., Freeman, A., & Associates. (1990). *Cognitive therapy of personality disorders.* New York: Guilford Press.

Beck, A. T., Rush, A. J., Shaw, B. F., & Emery, G. (1979). *Cognitive therapy of depression: A treatment manual.* New York: Guilford Press.

Beck, A. T., Steer, R. A., & Brown, G. K. (1996). *Beck Depression Inventory-II.* San Antonio, TX: Psychological Corporation.

Beck, A. T., Steer, R. A., Kovacs, M., & Garrison, B. (1985). Hopelessness and eventual suicide: A 10-year prospective study of patients hospitalized with suicidal ideation. *American Journal of Psychiatry, 142,* 559–563.

Beck, A. T., & Weishaar, M. (1989). Cognitive therapy. In A. Freeman, K. M. Simon, L. E. Beutler, & H. Arkowitz (Eds.), *Comprehensive handbook of cognitive therapy* (pp. 21–36). New York: Plenum Press.

Beck, J. C. (1987). The potentially violent patient: Legal duties, clinical practice, and risk management. *Psychiatric Annals, 17,* 695–699.

Beere, D. (1995). Loss of "background": A perceptual theory of dissociation. *Dissociation: Progress in the Dissociative Disorders, 8,* 165–174.

Begleiter, H., Porjooz, B., Reich, T., Edenberg, H. J., Goate, A., Blangero, J., Almasy, L., Foroud, T., Van Eerdewegh, P., Polich, J., Rohrbaugh, J., Kuperman, S., Bauer, L. O., O'Connor, S. J., Chorlian, D. B., Li, T. K., Conneally, P. M., Hesselbrock, V., Rice, J. P., Schuckit, M. A., Cloninger, R., Nurnberger, J., Jr., Crowe, R., & Bloom, F. E. (1998). Quantitative trait loci analysis of human event-related brain potentials: P3 voltage. *Electroencephalography & Clinical Neurophysiology, 108,* 244–250.

Bellack, A. S., Morrison, R. L., & Mueser, K. T. (1989). Social problem solving in schizophrenia. *Schizophrenia Bulletin, 15,* 101–116.

Bemporad, J. R. (1985). Long-term analytic treatment of depression. In E. E. Beckham & W. R. Leber (Eds.), *Handbook of depression: Treatment, assessment, and research* (pp. 82–89). Homewood, IL: Dorsey Press.

Bender, L. (1938). A visual motor Gestalt test and its clinical use (Research Monograph No. 3). New York: American Orthopsychiatric Association.

Benton, A. L. (1974). *The Visual Retention Test: Clinical and experimental applications* (4th ed.). New York: Psychological Corporation.

Berelowitz, M., & Tarnopolsky, S. (1993). The validity of borderline personality disorder: An updated review of recent research. In P. Tyrer & G. Stein (Eds.), *Personality disorder reviewed* (pp. 90–112). London: Gaskell.

Bergh, C., Eklund, T., Sodersten, P., & Nordin, C. (1997). Altered dopamine function in pathological gambling. *Psychological Medicine, 27,* 473–475.

Bergin, A. E., & Strupp, H. H. (1972). *Changing frontiers in the science of psychotherapy.* New York: Aldine-Atherton.

Berlin, F. S. (1998). Hal, driven by an invisible force: A case of pedophilia. In R. P. Halgin & S. K. Whitbourne (Eds.), *A casebook in abnormal psychology: From the files of experts* (pp. 114–126). New York: Oxford University Press.

Berrettini, W. H., Ferraro, T. N., Goldin, L. R., Detera-Wadleigh, S. D., Choi, H., Muniec, D., Guroff, J. J., Kazuba, D. M., Nurnberger, J. I., Jr., Hsieh, W. T., Hoehe, M. R., & Gershon, E. S. (1997). A linkage study of bipolar illness. *Archives of General Psychiatry, 54,* 27–35.

Berrettini, W. H., Ferraro, T. N., Goldin, L. R., Weeks, D. E., Detera-Wadleigh, S. D., Nurnberger, J. I., Jr., & Gershon, E. S. (1994). Chromosome 18 DNA markers and manic-depressive illness: Evidence for a susceptibility gene. *Proceedings of the National Academy of Sciences, 91,* 5918–5921.

Besson, J., Aeby, F., Kasas, A., Lehert, P., & Potgieter, A. (1998). Combined efficacy of acamprosate and disulfiram in the treatment of alcoholism: A controlled study. *Alcoholism, Clinical & Experimental Research, 22,* 573–579.

Bettelheim, B. (1967). *The empty fortress.* New York: Free Press.

Beutler, L. E., Consoli, A. J., & Williams, R. E. (1995). Integrative and eclectic therapies in practice. In B. Bongar & L. E. Beutler (Eds.), *Comprehensive textbook of psychotherapy: Theory and practice* (pp. 274–292). New York: Oxford University Press.

Biederman, J., Faraone, S., Milberger, S., Guite, J., Mick, E., Chen, L., Mennin, D., Marrs, A., Ouellette, C., Moore, P., Spencer, T., Norman, D., Wilens, T., Kraus, I., & Perrin, J. (1996). A prospective 4-year follow-up study of attention-deficit hyperactivity and related disorders. *Archives of General Psychiatry, 53,* 437–446.

Biederman, J., Faraone, S. V., Mick, E., Spencer, T., Wilens, T., Kiely, K., Guite, J. Ablon, J. S., Reed, E., & Warburton, R. (1995). High risk for attention deficit hyperactivity disorder among children of parents with childhood onset of the disorder: A pilot study. *American Journal of Psychiatry, 152,* 431–435.

Biederman, J., Faraone, S. V., Spencer, T., Wilens, T., Norman, D., Lapey, K. A., Mick, E., Lehman, B. K., & Doyle, A. (1993). Patterns of psychiatric comorbidity, cognition, and psychosocial functioning in adults with attention deficit hyperactivity disorder. *American Journal of Psychiatry, 150,* 1792–1798.

Bieling, P. J., & Alden, L. E. (1997). The consequences of perfectionism for patients with social phobia. *British Journal of Clinical Psychology, 36,* 387–395.

Binder, J. L., Strupp, H. H., & Henry, W. P. (1995). Psychodynamic therapies in practice: Time-limited dynamic therapy. In B. Bongar & L. E. Beutler (Eds.), *Comprehensive textbook of psychotherapy: Theory and practice* (pp. 48–63). New York: Oxford University Press.

Binder, R. L., McNiel, D. E., & Goldstone, R. L. (1996). Is adaptive coping possible for adult survivors of childhood sexual abuse? *Psychiatric Services, 47,* 186–188.

Binzer, M., Andersen, P. M., & Kullgren, G. (1997). Clinical characteristics of patients with motor disability due to conversion disorder: A prospective control group study. *Journal of Neurology, Neurosurgery & Psychiatry, 63,* 83–88.

Biringen, Z. (1994). Attachment theory and research: Application to clinical practice. *American Journal of Orthopsychiatry, 64,* 404–420.

Birmaher, B., Waterman, G. S., Ryan, N., Cully, M., Balach, L., Ingram, J., & Brodsky, M. (1994). Fluoxetine for childhood anxiety disorders. *Journal of the American Academy of Child and Adolescent Psychiatry, 33,* 993–999.

Birnbaum, M. (1960). The right to treatment. *American Bar Association Journal, 46,* 499–503.

Black, D. W., Kehrberg, L. L. D., Flumerfelt, D. L., Schlosser, S. S. (1997). Characteristics of 36 subjects reporting compulsive sexual behavior. *American Journal of Psychiatry, 154,* 243–249.

Blanchard, E. B., Hickling, E. J., Taylor, A. E., Loos, W. R., Forneris, C. A., & Jaccard, J. (1996a). Who develops PTSD from motor vehicle accidents? *Behaviour Research and Therapy, 34,* 1–10.

Blanchard, E. B., Zucker, K. J., Cohen-Kettenis, P. T., Gooren, L. J. G., & Bailey, J. M. (1996b). Birth order and sibling sex ratio in two samples of Dutch gender-dysphoric homosexual males. *Archives of Sexual Behavior, 25,* 495–514.

Blanchard, G. T. (1995). Sexually addicted lust murderers. *Sexual Addiction and Compulsivity, 2,* 62–71.

Blanchard, R. (1989). The concept of autogynephilia and the typology of male gender dysphoria. *Journal of Nervous and Mental Disease, 177,* 616–623.

Blanchard, R. (1992). Nonmonotonic relation of autogynephilia and heterosexual attraction. *Journal of Abnormal Psychology, 101,* 271–276.

Blanchard, R., & Bogaert, A. F. (1996). Homosexuality in men and number of older brothers. *American Journal of Psychiatry, 153,* 27–31.

Blaszczynski, A., Steel, Z., & McConaghy, N. (1997). Impulsivity in pathological gambling: The antisocial impulsivist. *Addiction, 92,* 75–87.

Blatt, S. J., & Felsen, I. (1993). Different kinds of folks may need different kinds of strokes: The effect of patients' characteristics on therapeutic process and outcome. *Psychotherapy Research, 3,* 245–259.

Blazer, D., Hughes, D. C., & George, L. K. (1987). The epidemiology of depression in an elderly community population. *The Gerontologist, 27,* 281–287.

Bleich, A., Koslowsky, M., Dolev, A., & Lerer, B. (1997). Post-traumatic stress disorder and depression. An analysis of comorbidity. *British Journal of Psychiatry, 170,* 479–482.

Bleuler, E. (1911). *Dementia praeco oder gruppe der schizophrenien. (Dementia praecox or the group of schizophrenias).* Leipzig: F. Deuticke.

Bliss, E. L. (1980). Multiple personalities: A report of 14 cases with implications for schizophrenia and hysteria. *Archives of General Psychiatry, 37,* 1388–1397.

Block, C., West, S. A., & Baharoglu, B. (1998). Paroxetine treatment of trichotillomania in an adolescent. *Journal of Child & Adolescent Psychopharmacology, 8,* 69–71.

Block, R. I., & Ghoneim, M. M. (1993). Effects of chronic marijuana use on human cognition. *Psychopharmacology, 110,* 219–228.

Blomhoff, S., Seim, S., & Friis, S. (1990). Can prediction of violence among psychiatric inpatients be improved? *Hospital and Community Psychiatry, 41,* 771–775.

Blos, P. (1967). The second individuation of adolescence. *The Psychoanalytic Study of the Child, 22,* 162–186.

Blum, K., Sheridan, P. J., Wood, R. C., Braverman, E. R., Chen, T. J., Cull, J. G., & Comings, D. E. (1996). The D2 dopamine receptor gene as a determinant of reward deficiency syndrome. *Journal of the Royal Society of Medicine, 89,* 396–400.

Bonnie, R. J., Hoge, S. K., Monahan, J., Poythress, N., Eisenberg, M., & Feucht-Haviar, T. (1997). The MacArthur Adjudicative Competence Study: A comparison of criteria for assessing the competence of criminal defendants. *Journal of the American Academy of Psychiatry and the Law, 25,* 249–259.

Boor, M. (1982). The multiple personality epidemic: Additional cases and inferences regarding diagnosis, etiology, dynamics, and treatment. *Journal of Nervous and Mental Disease, 170,* 302–304.

Bornstein, R. F. (1998). Reconceptualizing personality disorder diagnosis in the DSM-V; The discriminant validity challenge. *Clinical Psychology: Science and Practice, 5,* 333–343.

Bornstein, R. F., & Greenberg, R. P. (1991). Dependency and eating disorders in female psychiatric patients. *Journal of Nervous and Mental Disease, 179,* 148–152.

Bornstein, R. F., & Masling, J. M. (1994). *Empirical perspectives on object relations theory.* Washington, DC: American Psychological Association.

Bouchard, T. J., Jr., Lykken, D. T., McGue, M., Segal, N. L., & Tellegen, A. (1990). Sources of human psychological differences: The Minnesota study of twins reared apart. *Science, 250,* 223–228.

Bourin, M., Baker, G. B., & Bradwejn, J. (1998). Neurobiology of panic disorder. *Journal of Psychosomatic Research, 44,* 163–180.

Bouwer, C., & Stein, D. J. (1997). Association of panic disorder with a history of traumatic suffocation. *American Journal of Psychiatry, 154,* 1566–1570.

Bowlby, J. (1980). *Attachment and loss: Volume III: Loss: Sadness and depression.* New York: Basic Books.

Boyer, J. L., & Guthrie, L. (1985). Assessment and treatment of the suicidal patient. In E. E. Beckham & W. R. Leber (Eds.), *Handbook of depression: Treatment, assessment, and research* (pp. 606–633). Homewood, IL: Dorsey Press.

Bradford, J. M., & Gratzer, T. G. (1995). A treatment for impulse control disorders and paraphilia: A case report. *Canadian Journal of Psychiatry, 40,* 4–5.

Bradley, S. J., & Zucker, K. J. (1997). Gender identity disorder: A review of the past 10 years. *Journal of the Academy of Child and Adolescent Psychiatry, 36,* 872–880.

Brant, J. (1998). *Law and mental health professionals: Massachusetts.* Washington, DC: American Psychological Association.

Bremner, J. D., Krystal, J. H., Charney, D. S., & Southwick, S. M. (1996). Neural mechanisms in dissociative amnesia for childhood abuse: Relevance to the current controversy surrounding the "false memory syndrome." *American Journal of Psychiatry, 153,* 71–82.

Brent, D. A., Perper, J., Moritz, G., Allman, C., Friend, A., Schweers, J., Roth, C., Balach, L., & Harrington, K. (1992). Psychiatric effects of exposure to suicide among the friends and acquaintances of adolescent suicide victims. *Journal of the American Academy of Child and Adolescent Psychiatry, 31,* 629–639.

Brent, D. A., Perper, J. A., Moritz, G., Allman, C., Schweers, J., Roth, C., Balach, L., Canobbio, R., & Liotus, L. (1993). Psychiatric sequelae to the loss of an adolescent peer to suicide. *Journal of the American Academy of Child and Adolescent Psychiatry, 32,* 509–517.

Brent, D. A., Perper, J. A., Moritz, G., Baugher, M., & Allman, C. (1993). Suicide in adolescents with no apparent psychopathology. *Journal of the American Academy of Child and Adolescent Psychiatry, 32,* 494–500.

Breslau, N., Davis, G. C., Andreski, P., Peterson, E. L., & Schultz, L. R. (1997). Sex differences in post-traumatic stress disorder. *Archives of General Psychiatry, 54,* 1044–1048.

Breslow, N., Evans, L., & Langley, J. (1985). On the prevalence and roles of females in the sadomasochistic subculture: Report of an empirical study. *Archives of Sexual Behavior, 14,* 303–317.

Breuer, A., & Freud, S. (1892/1982). *Studies in hysteria* (J. Strachey, A. Freud, Trans.) New York: Basic Books.

Brick, S. S., & Chu, J. A. (1991). The simulation of multiple personalities: A case report. *Psychotherapy, 28,* 267–272.

Briggs, L., & Joyce, P. R. (1997). What determines post-traumatic stress disorder symptomatology for survivors of childhood sexual abuse? *Child Abuse & Neglect, 21,* 575–582.

Bright, R. A., & Everitt, D. E. (1992). B-blockers and depression: Evidence against an association. *Journal of the American Medical Association, 267,* 1783–1787.

Brodsky, B. S., Cloitre, M., & Dulit, R. A. (1995). Relationship of dissociation to self-mutilation and childhood abuse in borderline personality disorder. *American Journal of Psychiatry, 152,* 1788–1792.

Brown, A. (1995). Treatment for rapid cyclers. *Psychopharmacology Update, 6,* 1–5.

Brown, F. R., III, & Aylward, E. H. (1987). *Diagnosis and management of learning disabilities: An interdisciplinary approach.* Boston: College Hill Press.

Brown, G. W., Birley, J. L. T., & Wing, J. K. (1972). Influence of family life on the course of schizophrenic disorders: A replication. *British Journal of Psychiatry, 121,* 241–258.

Brown, L., Sherbenou, R. J., & Johnsen, S. K. (1997). *Test of Nonverbal Intelligence-3 (TONI-3).* Minneapolis: American Guidance Service.

Brown, T. A., Barlow, D. H., & Liebowitz, M. R. (1994). The empirical basis of generalized anxiety disorder. *American Journal of Psychiatry, 151,* 1272–1280.

Buchanan, R. W., Breier, A., Kirkpatrick, B., Ball, P., & Carpenter, W. T., Jr. (1998). Positive and negative symptom response to clozapine in schizophrenic patients with and without the deficit syndrome. *American Journal of Psychiatry, 155,* 751–760.

Budman, S. H. (1996). Introduction to special section on group and managed care. *International Journal of Group Psychotherapy, 46,* 293–295.

Buchsbaum, M. S. (1990). The frontal lobes, basal ganglia, and temporal lobes as sites for schizophrenia. *Schizophrenia Bulletin, 16,* 379–389.

Buck, K. J. (1995). Strategies for mapping and identifying quantitative trait loci specifying behavioral responses to alcohol. *Alcohol: Clinical and Experimental Research, 19,* 795–801.

Buck, K. J., Metten, P., Belknap, J. K., & Crabbe, J. C. (1997). Quantitative trait loci involved in genetic predisposition to acute alcohol withdrawal in mice. *Journal of Neuroscience, 17,* 3946–3955.

Bukstein, O. G., Brent, D. A., Perper, J. A., Moritz, G., Baugher, M., Schweers, J., Roth, C., & Balach, L. (1993). Risk factors for completed suicide among adolescents with a lifetime history of substance abuse: A case-control study. *Acta Psychiatrica Scandinavica, 88,* 403–408.

Butler, G., Fennell, M., Robson, P., & Gelder, M. (1991). Comparison of behavior therapy and cognitive behavior therapy in the treatment of generalized anxiety disorder. *Journal of Consulting and Clinical Psychology, 59,* 167–175.

Butler, L. D., Duran, R. E., Jasiukaitis, P., Koopman, C., & Spiegel, D. (1996). Hypnotizability and traumatic experience: A diathesis-stress model of dissociative symptomatology. *American Journal of Psychiatry, 153,* 42–63.

C

Cadoret, R. J., Winokur, G., Langbehn, D., Troughton, E., Yates, W. R., & Stewart, M. A. (1996). Depression spectrum disease, I: The role of gene-environment interaction. *American Journal of Psychiatry, 153,* 892–899.

Cadoret, R. J., Yates, W. R., Troughton, E., Woodworth, G., & Stewart, M. A. (1995). Genetic-environmental interaction in the genesis of aggressivity and conduct disorders. *Archives of General Psychiatry, 52,* 916–924.

Caine, E. D. (1981). Pseudodementia. *Archives of General Psychiatry, 38,* 1359–1364.

Caldwell, P. E., & Cutter, H. S. (1998). Alcoholics Anonymous affiliation during early recovery. *Journal of Substance Abuse Treatment, 15,* 221–228.

Calev, A., Nigal, D., Shapira, B., Tubi, N., Chazan, S., Beh-Yehuda, Y., Kugelmass, S., & Leher, B. (1991). Early and long-term effects of electroconvulsive therapy and depression on memory and other cognitive functions. *Journal of Nervous and Mental Disease, 179,* 526–533.

Camacho, L. M., Bartholomew, N. G., Joe, G. W., & Simpson, D. D. (1997). Maintenance of HIV risk reduction among injection opioid users: A 12 month post-treatment follow-up. *Drug & Alcohol Dependence, 47,* 11–18.

Canino, G. (1994). Alcohol use and misuse among Hispanic women: Selected factors, processes, and studies. *International Journal of the Addictions, 29,* 1083–1100.

Cannon, D. S., Baker, T. B., Gino, A., & Nathan, P. E. (1988). Alcohol aversion and abstinence. In T. D. Baker & D. Cannon (Eds.), *Assessment and treatment of addictive disorders* (pp. 205–237). New York: Praeger Press.

Cannon, T. D., Kaprio, J., Lonnqvist, J., Huttunen, M., & Koskenvuo, M. (1998). The genetic epidemiology of schizophrenia in a Finnish twin cohort. A population-based modeling study. *Archives of General Psychiatry, 55,* 67–74.

Caplan, L. (1984). *The insanity defense and the trial of John W. Hinckley, Jr.* Boston: David R. Godin.

Cardena, E., & Spiegel, D. (1996). Diagnostic issues, criteria, and comorbidity of dissociative disorders. In L. K. Michelson & W. J. Ray (Eds.), *Handbook of dissociation: Theoretical, empirical, and clinical perspectives* (pp. 227–250). New York: Plenum Press.

Carlat, D. J., Camargo, C. A. (1991). Review of bulimia nervosa in males. *American Journal of Psychiatry, 148,* 831–843.

Carlat, D. J., & Camargo, C. A., Jr., & Herzog, D. B. (1997). Eating disorders in males: A report on 135 patients. *American Journal of Psychiatry, 154,* 1127–1132.

Carlson, C. R., & Hoyle, R. H. (1993). Efficacy of abbreviated progressive muscle relaxation training: A quantitative review of behavioral medicine research. *Journal of Consulting and Clinical Psychology, 61,* 1059–1067.

Carlson, G. A., Fennig, S., & Bromet, E. J. (1994). The confusion between bipolar disorder and schizophrenia in youth: Where does it stand in the 1990s? *Journal of the American Academy of Child and Adolescent Psychiatry, 33,* 453–460.

Carlsson, A. (1988). The current status of the dopamine hypothesis of schizophrenia. *Neuropsychopharmacology, 1,* 179–186.

Carmelli, D., & Swan, G. E. (1996). The relationship of Type A behavior and its components to all-cause mortality in an elderly subgroup of men from the Western Collaborative Group Study. *Journal of Psychosomatic Research, 40,* 475–483.

Carnes, P. (1983). *Out of the shadows: Understanding sexual addiction.* Minneapolis: Compcare.

Carnes, P. J. (1996). Addiction or compulsion: Politics or illness? *Sexual Addiction and Compulsivity, 3,* 127–150.

Carnes, P. J., & Delmonico, D. L. (1996). Childhood abuse and multiple addictions: Research findings in a sample of self-identified sexual addicts. *Sexual Addiction and Compulsivity, 3,* 258–268.

Carpenter, W. T. (1987). Approaches to knowledge and understanding of schizophrenia. *Schizophrenia Bulletin, 13,* 1–7.

Carpenter, W. T., & Buchanan, R. W. (1994). Schizophrenia. *New England Journal of Medicine, 330,* 681–690.

Carr, R. E. (1998). Panic disorder and asthma: Causes, effects and research implications. *Journal of Psychosomatic Research, 44,* 43–52.

Caspi, A., Moffitt, T. E., Newman, D. L., & Silva, P. A. (1996). Behavioral observations at age 3 years predict adult psychiatric disorders. Longitudinal evidence from a birth cohort. *Archives of General Psychiatry, 53,* 1033–1039.

Centers for Disease Prevention and Control. (1993). Fetal alcohol syndrome United States, 1979–1992. *Morbidity and Mortality Weekly Reports, 42,* 339–341.

Chadwick, P. D. J., & Lowe, C. F. (1994). A cognitive approach to measuring and modifying delusions. *Behaviour Research and Therapy, 32,* 355–367.

Chambless, D. L., & Goldstein, A. J. (1982). *Agoraphobia: Multiple perspectives on theory and treatment.* New York: Wiley.

Chandy, K. G., Fantino, E., Wittekindt, O., Kalman, K., Tong, L.-L., Ho, T.-H., Gutman, G. A., Crocq, M.-A., Ganguli, R., Nimgaonkar, V., Morris-Rosendahl, D. J., & Gargus, J. J. (1998). Isolation of a novel potassium channel gene hSKCa3 containing a polymorphic CAG repeat: A candidate for schizophrenia and bipolar disorder? *Molecular Psychiatry, 3,* 32–37.

Chatterjee, S., Sunitha, T. A., Velayudhan, A., & Khanna, S. (1997). An investigation into the psychobiology of social phobia: Personality domains and serotonergic function. *Acta Psychiatrica Scandinavica, 95,* 544–550.

Chenoweth, B., & Spencer, B. (1986). Dementia: The experience of family caregivers. *Gerontologist, 30,* 267–272.

Chick, J. (1995). Acamprosate as an aid in the treatment of alcoholism. *Alcohol and Alcoholism, 30,* 785–787.

Chodoff, P. (1963). Late effects of the concentration camp syndrome. *Archives of General Psychiatry, 8,* 323–333.

Chodorow, N. (1978). *The reproduction of mothering.* Berkeley: University of California Press.

Christensen, G. A., Mackenzie, T. B., & Mitchell, J. E. (1991). Characteristics of 60 adult chronic hair pullers. *American Journal of Psychiatry, 148,* 365–370.

Christenson, G. A., & Crow, S. J. (1996). The characterization and treatment of trichotillomania. *Journal of Clinical Psychiatry, 8,* 42–47.

Christianson, S. A., & Engelberg, E. (1997). Remembering and forgetting traumatic experiences: A matter of survival. In M. A. Conway (Ed.), *Recovered memories and false memories. Debates in psychology.* (pp. 230–250). Oxford, U.K.: Oxford University Press.

Clark, D. A., Beck, A. T., & Beck, J. S. (1994). Symptom differences in major depression, dysthymia, panic disorder, and generalized anxiety disorder. *American Journal of Psychiatry, 151,* 205–209.

Clark, D. A., Steer, R. A., & Beck, A. T. (1994). Common and specific dimensions of self-reported anxiety and depression: Implications for the cognitive and tripartite models. *Journal of Abnormal Behavior, 103,* 645–654.

Clark, D. B. (1989). Performance-related medical and psychological disorders in instrumental musicians. *Annals of Behavioral Medicine, 11,* 28–34.

Clark, D. B., & Agras, W. S. (1991). The assessment and treatment of performance anxiety in musicians. *American Journal of Psychiatry, 148,* 598–605.

Clark, D. M., Salkovskis, P. M., Ost, L. G., Breitholtz, E., Koehler, K. A., Westling, B. E., Jeavons, A., & Gelder, M. (1997). Misinterpretation of body sensations in panic disorder. *Journal of Consulting and Clinical Psychology, 65,* 203–213.

Classen, C., Koopman, C., & Spiegel, D. (1993). Trauma and dissociation. *Bulletin of the Menninger Clinic, 57,* 178–194.

Cleckley, H. M. (1976). *The mask of sanity* (5th ed.). St. Louis: Mosby.

Clementz, B. A., Grove, W. M., Iacono, W. G., & Sweeney, J. A. (1992). Smooth-pursuit eye movement dysfunction and liability for schizophrenia: Implications for genetic modeling. *Journal of Abnormal Psychology, 101,* 117–129.

Coccaro, E. F., & Kavoussi, R. J. (1997). Fluoxetine and impulsive aggressive behavior in personality-disordered subjects. *Archives of General Psychiatry, 54,* 1081–1088.

Coffey, B. J., Miguel, E. C., Biederman, J., Baer, L., Rauch, S. L., O'Sullivan, R. L., Savage, C. R., Phillips, K., Borgman, A., Green-Leibovitz, M. I., Moore, E., Park, K. S., & Jenike, M. A. (1998). Tourette's disorder with and without obsessive-compulsive disorder in adults: Are they different? *Journal of Nervous and Mental Disease, 186,* 201–206.

Cohen, C. I., & Thompson, K. S. (1992). Homeless mentally ill or mentally ill homeless? *American Journal of Psychiatry, 149,* 816–823.

Cohen, S., Frank, E., Doyle, W. J., Skoner, D. P., Rabin, B. S., & Gwaltney, J. M. J. (1998). Types of stressors that increase susceptibility to the common cold in healthy adults. *Health Psychology, 17,* 214–223.

Cohen, S., & Herbert, T. B. (1996). Health psychology: Psychological factors and physical disease from the perspective of human psychoneuroimmunology. *Annual Review of Psychology, 47,* 113–142.

Cohen, S., & Williamson, G. M. (1991). Stress and infectious disease in humans. *Psychological Bulletin, 109,* 5–24.

Cohen-Kettenis, P. T., & Gooren, L. J. (1992). The influence of hormone treatment on psychological functioning of transsexuals. Special issue: Gender dysphoria: Interdisciplinary approaches in clinical management. *Journal of Psychology and Human Sexuality, 5,* 55–67.

Cohen-Kettenis, P. T., & van Goozen, S. H. M. (1997). Sex reassignment of adolescent transsexuals: A follow-up study. *Journal of the American Academy of Child and Adolescent Psychiatry, 36,* 263–271.

Collaer, M. L., & Hines, M. (1995). Human behavioral sex differences: A role for gonadal hormones during early development? *Psychological Bulletin, 118,* 55–107.

Comings, D. E., Rosenthal, R. J., Lesieur, H. R., Rugle, L. J., Muhleman, D., Chiu, C., Dietz, G., & Gade, R. (1996). A study of the dopamine D2 receptor gene in pathological gambling. *Pharmacogenetics, 6,* 223–234.

Committee on Professional Practice and Standards Board of Professional Affairs. (1998). *Guidelines for psychological evaluations in child protection matters.* Washington, DC: American Psychological Association.

Compas, B. E., Haaga, D. A., Keefe, F. J., Leitenberg, H., & Williams, D. A. (1998). Sampling of empirically supported psychological treatments from health psychology: Smoking, chronic pain, cancer, and bulimia nervosa. *Journal of Consulting and Clinical Psychology, 66,* 89–112.

Constantino, G., Malgady, R. G., & Rogler, L. H. (1988). *TEMAS (Tell-Me-A-Story) Manual.* Los Angeles: Western Psychology Services.

Cook, E. H., Jr., Courchesne, R. Y., Cox, N. J., Lord, C., Gonen, D., Guter, S. J., Lincoln, A., Nix, K., Haas, R., Leventhal, B. L., & Courchesne, E. (1998). Linkage-disequilibrium mapping of autistic disorder, with 15q11–13 markers. *American Journal of Human Genetics, 62,* 1077–1803.

Coons, P. M. (1980). Multiple personality: Diagnostic considerations. *Journal of Clinical Psychiatry, 41,* 330–336.

Coons, P. M., Bowman, E. S., Pellow, T. A., & Schneider, P. (1989). Post-traumatic aspects of the treatment of victims of sexual abuse and incest. *Psychiatric Clinics of North America, 12,* 325–335.

Cooper, R. S., Rotimi, C. N., & Ward, R. (1999). The puzzle of hypertension in African-Americans. *Scientific American.*

Coplan, J. D., Goetz, R., Klein, D. F., Papp, L. A., Fyer, A. J., Liebowitz, M. R., Davies, S. O., & Gorman, J. M. (1998). Plasma cortisol concentrations preceding lactate-induced panic. Psychological, biochemical, and physiological correlates. *Archives of General Psychiatry, 55,* 130–136.

Coppen, A. (1994). Depression as a lethal disease: Prevention strategies. 146th Annual Meeting of the American Psychiatric Association: Depression: New subtypes and therapeutic challenges (1993, San Francisco, California). *Journal of Clinical Psychiatry, 55,* 37–45.

Corey-Bloom, J., Jernigan, T., Archibald, S., Harris, M. J., & Jeste, D. V. (1995). Quantitative magnetic resonance imaging of the brain in late-life schizophrenia. *American Journal of Psychiatry, 152,* 447–449.

Cornelius, J. R., Salloum, I. M., Mezzich, J., Cornelius, M. D., Fabrega, H., Ehler, J. G., Ulrich, R. F., Thase, M. E., & Mann, J. J. (1995). Disproportionate suicidality in patients with comorbid major depression and alcoholism. *American Journal of Psychiatry, 152,* 358–364.

Coryell, W. (1998). The treatment of psychotic depression. *Journal of Clinical Psychiatry, 1,* 22–27.

Coryell, W., Endicott, J., & Keller, M. (1992). Rapidly cycling affective disorder: Demographics, diagnosis, family history, and course. *Archives of General Psychiatry, 49,* 126–131.

Coryell, W., Winokur, G., Shea, T., Maser, J. D., Endicott, J., & Akiskal, H. S. (1994). The long-term stability of depressive subtypes. *American Journal of Psychiatry, 151,* 199–204.

Costa, P. T., Jr., & McCrae, R. R. (1992). *NEO-PI-R manual.* Odessa, FL: Psychological Assessment Resources.

Costa, P. T., Jr., & VandenBos, G. R. (Eds.). (1996). *Psychological aspects of serious illness: Chronic conditions, fatal diseases, and clinical care.* Washington, DC: American Psychological Association.

Cote, H., & Wilchensky, M. (1996). The use of sexoanalysis for patients with gender identity disorder. *The Canadian Journal of Human Sexuality, 5,* 261–270.

Couprie, W., Wijdicks, E. F. M., Rooijmans, H. G. M., & van Gijn, J. (1995). Outcome in conversion disorder: A follow-up study. *Journal of Neurology, Neurosurgery and Psychiatry, 58,* 750–752.

Cournos, F. (1989). Involuntary medication and the case of Joyce Brown. *Hospital and Community Psychiatry, 40,* 736–740.

Covino, N. A., Jimerson, D. C., Wolfe, B. E., Franko, D. L., & Frankel, F. H. (1994). Hypnotizability, dissociation, and bulimia nervosa. *Journal of Abnormal Psychology, 103,* 455–459.

Cowley, D. S., & Arana, G. W. (1990). The diagnostic utility of lactate sensitivity in panic disorder. *Archives of General Psychiatry, 47,* 277–284.

Coyle, J. T., Price, D. L., DeLong, M. R. (1983). Alzheimer's disease: A disorder of cortical cholinergic innervation. *Science, 219,* 1184–1190.

Coyne, A. C., Potnexa, M., & Broken Nose, M. (1994). Caregiving and dementia: The impact of telephone helpline services. *The American Journal of Alzheimer's Care and Related Disorders and Research,* 1–7.

Crabbe, J. C., Gallaher, E. J., Cross, S. J., & Belknap, J. K. (1998). Genetic determinants of sensitivity to diazepam in inbred mice. *Behavioral Neuroscience, 112,* 668–677.

Craighead, L. W., Craighead, W. E., Kazdin, A. E., & Mahoney, M. J. (1994). Cognitive and behavioral perspectives: An introduction. In L. W. Craighead, W. E. Craighead, A. E. Kazdin, & M. J. Mahoney (Eds.), *Cognitive and behavioral interventions: An empirical approach to mental health problems* (pp. 1–14). Boston: Allyn & Bacon.

Craighead, W. E., Craighead, L. W., & Ilardi, S. S. (1998). Psychosocial treatments for major depressive disorder. In P. E. Nathan & J. M. Gorman (Eds.), *A guide to treatments that work.* New York: Oxford University Press.

Craighead, W. E., Miklowitz, D. J., Vajk, F. C., & Frank, E. (1998). Psychosocial treatments for bipolar disorder. In P. E. Nathan & J. M. Gorman (Eds.), *A guide to treatments that work* (pp. 240–248). New York: Oxford University Press.

Craske, M. G., Glover, D., & DeCola, J. (1995). Predicted versus unpredicted panic attacks: Acute vs. general distress. *Journal of Abnormal Psychology, 104,* 214–223.

Crawley, J. N., Belknap, J. K., Collins, A., Crabbe, J. C., Frankel, W., Henderson, N., Hitzemann, R. J., Maxson, S. C., Miner,

L. L., Silva, A. J., Wehner, J. M., Wynshaw-Boris, A., & Paylor, R. (1997). Behavioral phenotypes of inbred mouse strains: Implications and recommendations for molecular studies. *Psychopharmacology, 132,* 107–124.

Crisp, A. H., Callender, J. S., Halek, C., & Hsu, L. K. G. (1992). Long-term mortality in anorexia nervosa: A 20-year follow-up of the St. George's and Aberdeen cohorts. *British Journal of Psychiatry, 161,* 104–107.

Crits-Cristoph, P. (1992). The efficacy of brief dynamic psychotherapy: A meta-analysis. *American Journal of Psychiatry, 149,* 151–158.

Cronbach, L. J. (1990). *Essentials of psychological testing* (5th ed.). New York: Harper & Row.

Croteau, J. M., Nero, C. I., & Prosser, D. J. (1993). Social and cultural sensitivity in group-specific HIV and AIDS programming. *Journal of Counseling and Development, 71,* 290–296.

Crow, T. J. (1985). The two-syndrome concept: Origins and current status. *Schizophrenia Bulletin, 11,* 433–443.

Crow, T. J. (1990). Temporal lobe asymmetries as the key to the etiology of schizophrenia. *Schizophrenia Bulletin, 16,* 433–443.

Csernansky, J. G., & Bardgett, M. E. (1998). Limbic-cortical neuronal damage and the pathophysiology of schizophrenia. *Schizophrenia Bulletin, 24,* 231–248.

Csernansky, J. G., & Newcomer, J. W. (1994). Are there neurochemical indicators of risk for schizophrenia? *Schizophrenia Bulletin, 20,* 75–88.

Culbertson, F. M. (1997). Depression and gender. *American Psychologist, 52,* 25–31.

Cunningham-Williams, R. M., Cottler, L. B., Comton, W. M., III, & Spitznagel, E. L. (1998). Taking chances: Problem gamblers and mental health disorders—Results from the St. Louis Epidemiologic Catchment Area Study. *American Journal of Public Health, 88,* 1092–1096.

Curran, D. K. (1987). *Adolescent suicidal behavior.* Washington, DC: Hemisphere.

Custer, R. L. (1982). An overview of compulsive gambling. In S. Kieffer (Ed.), *Addictive disorders update.* New York: Human Sciences Press.

D

Daniel, L. E., Park, L., Jefferson, J., & Greist, J. (1997). Treating post-traumatic stress disorder in female adult victims of childhood incest. *Family Therapy, 23,* 1–9.

Dannenbaum, S. E., & Lanyon, R. I. (1993). The use of subtle items in detecting deception. *Journal of Personality Assessment, 61,* 501–510.

Dantzler, A., & Salzman, C. (1995). Treatment of bipolar depression. *Psychiatric Services, 46,* 229–230.

Dare, O., Le-Grange, D., Eisler, I., & Rutherford, J. (1994). Redefining the psychosomatic family. Family process of 26 eating disorder families. *International Journal of Eating Disorders, 16,* 211–226.

Davidson, J. R. T., & Foa, E. B. (1991). Diagnostic issues in post-traumatic stress disorder: Considerations for the DSM-IV. *Journal of Abnormal Psychology, 100,* 346–355.

Davidson, J. R. T., Ford, S. M., Smith, R. D., & Potts, N. L. S. (1991). Long term treatment of social phobia with clonazepam. *Journal of Clinical Psychiatry, 53,* 16–20.

Davis, K. L., Buchsbaum, M. S., Shihabuddin, L., Spiegel-Cohen, J., Metzger, M., Frecska, E., Keefe, R. S., & Powchik, P. (1998). Ventricular enlargement in poor-outcome schizophrenia. *Biological Psychiatry, 43,* 783–793.

Davis, S. F., Pierce, M. C., Yandell, L. R., Arnow, P. S., & Loree, A. (1995). Cheating in college and the Type A personality: A reevaluation. *College Student Journal, 29,* 493–497.

Davison, G. C. (1968). Elimination of a sadistic fantasy by a client-controlled counter-conditioning technique: A case study. *Journal of Abnormal Psychology, 73,* 84–90.

Day, R., & Wong, S. (1996). Anomalous perceptual asymmetries for negative emotional stimuli in the psychopath. *Journal of Abnormal Psychology, 105,* 648–652.

DeCaria, C. M., Hollander, E., Grossman, R., Wong, C. M., Mosovich, S. A., & Cherkasky, S. (1996). Diagnosis, neurobiology, and treatment of pathological gambling. *Journal of Clinical Psychiatry, 8,* 80–83.

Deckel, A. W., Hesselbrock, V., & Bauer, L. (1996). Antisocial personality disorder, childhood delinquency, and frontal brain functioning: EEG and neuropsychological findings. *Journal of Clinical Psychology, 52,* 639–650.

De Leo, D., Carollo, G., & Buono, M. D. (1995). Lower suicide rates associated with a tele-help/tele-check service for the elderly at home. *American Journal of Psychiatry, 152,* 632–634.

de Leon, M. J., Convit, A., DeSanti, S., Bobinski, M., George, A. E., Wisniewski, H. M., Rusinek, H., Carroll, R., & Saint Louis, L. A. (1997). Contribution of structural neuroimaging to the early diagnosis of Alzheimer's disease. *International Psychogeriatrics, 1,* 183–190.

DeLeon, P. H., Vandenbos, G. R., Sammons, M. T., & Frank, R. G. (1998). Changing health care environment in the United States: Steadily evolving into the twenty-first century. In A. N. Weins (Ed.), *Comprehensive clinical psychology: Volume 2: Professional Issues* (pp. 393–409). Oxford, U.K.: Elsevier.

DeLisi, L. E., Hoff, A. L., Schwartz, J. E., Shields, G. W., Halthore, S. N., Gupta, S. M., Henn, F. A., & Anand, A. (1991). Brain morphology in first-episode schizophrenic-like psychotic patients: A quantitative magnetic resonance imaging study. *Biological Psychiatry, 29,* 159–175.

DeLongis, A., Folkman, S., & Lazarus, R. S. (1988). The impact of daily stress on health and mood: Psychological and social resources as mediators. *Journal of Personality and Social Psychology, 54,* 486–495.

Demopulos, C., Fava, M., McLean, N. E., Alpert, J. E., Nierenberg, A. A., & Rosenbaum, J. F. (1996). Hypochondriacal concerns in depressed outpatients. *Psychosomatic Medicine, 58,* 314–320.

Derogatis, L. R. (1994). *Manual for the Symptom Check List-90 Revised (SCL-90-R).* Minneapolis: National Computer Systems.

DeRubeis, R. J., & Crits-Cristoph, P. (1998). Empirically supported individual and group psychological treatments for adult mental disorders. *Journal of Consulting and Clinical Psychology, 66,* 17–52.

DeSalvatore, G., & Hornstein, R. (1991). Juvenile firesetting: Assessment and treatment in psychiatric hospitalization and residential placement. *Child and Youth Care Forum, 20,* 103–114.

de Silva, P. (1993). Post-traumatic stress disorder: Cross-cultural aspects. *International Review of Psychiatry, 5,* 217–229.

de Silva, P. (1993). Fetishism and sexual dysfunction: Clinical presentation and management. *Sexual and Marital Therapy, 8,* 147–155.

Deutsch, A. (1949). *The mentally ill in America.* (2nd ed.). New York: Columbia University Press.

Devinsky, O., Putnam, F., Grafman, J., Bromfield, E., & Theodore, W. H. (1989). Dissociative states and epilepsy. *Neurology, 39,* 835–840.

Diaferia, G., Bianchi, I., Bianchi, M. L., Cavedini, P., Erzegovesi, S., & Bellodi, L. (1997). Relationship between obsessive-compulsive personality disorder and obsessive-compulsive disorder. *Comprehensive Psychiatry, 38,* 38–42.

Dick, C. L., Bland, R. C., & Newman, S. C. (1994). Panic disorder. *Acta Psychiatrica Scandinavica, 89,* 45–53.

Dicker, M., & Leighton, E. A. (1994). Trends in the U.S. prevalence of drug-using parturient women and drug-affected newborns, 1979 through 1990. *American Journal of Public Health, 84,* 1433–1438.

Dimeff, L. A., & Marlatt, G. A. (1998). Preventing relapse and maintaining change in addictive behaviors. *Clinical Psychology: Science and Practice, 5,* 513–525.

Dinardo, P. A., Brown, T. A., & Barlow, D. H. (1994). *Anxiety interview schedule for DSM-IV (DIS-IV).* Albany, NY: Graywind.

Dinnerstein, D. (1976). *The mermaid and the Minotaur: Sexual arrangements and human malaise.* New York: Harper.

Dixon, W. A., Heppner, P. P., & Rudd, M. D. (1994). Problem-solving appraisal, hopelessness, and suicide ideation: Evidence for a mediational model. *Journal of Counseling Psychiatry, 41,* 91–98.

Dobson, D. J., McDougall, G., Busheikin, J., & Aldous, J. (1995). Effects of social skills training and social milieu treatment on symptoms of schizophrenia. *Psychiatric Services, 46,* 376–380.

Dohrenwend, B. P., Levav, P. E., Schwartz, S., Naveh, G., Link, B. G., Skodol, A. E., & Stueve, A. (1992). Socioeconomic status and psychiatric disorders: The causation-selection issue. *Science, 255,* 946–952.

Dreher, H. (1996). Is there a systematic way to diagnose and treat somatization disorder? *Advances, 12,* 50–57.

Dubovsky, S. L. (1994). Challenges in conceptualizing psychotic mood disorders. *Bulletin of the Menninger Clinic, 58,* 197–214.

Duncan, S. C., Duncan, T. E., Biglan, A., & Ary, D. V. (1998). Contributions of the social context to the development of adolescent substance use: A multivariate latent growth modeling approach. *Drug and Alcohol Dependence, 50,* 57–71.

Duncan, T. E., Duncan, S., & Hops, H. (1998). Latent variable modeling of longitudinal and multilevel alcohol use data. *Journal of Studies on Alcohol, 59,* 399–408.

DuRant, R. H., Rickert, V. I., Ashworth, C. W., Newman, C., & Slavens, G. (1995). Use of multiple drugs among adolescents who use anabolic steroids. *New England Journal of Medicine, 328,* 922–926.

Durkheim, E. (1897/1952). *Suicide: A study in sociology* (J. A. Spaulding, C. Simpson, Trans.). London: Routledge and Kegan Paul.

Dutton, D. G., & Painter, S. (1993). The battered woman syndrome: Effects of severity and intermittency of abuse. *American Journal of Orthopsychiatry, 63,* 614–622.

E

Eaker, E. D. (1998). Psychosocial risk factors for coronary heart disease in women. *Cardiology Clinics, 16,* 103–111.

Eastman, C. I., Young, M. A., Fogg, L. F., Liu, L., & Meaden, P. M. (1998). Bright light treatment of winter depression: A placebo-controlled trial. *Archives of General Psychiatry, 55,* 883–889.

Eaton, W. W., Kessler, R. C., Wittchen, H. U., & Magee, W. J. (1994). Panic and panic disorder in the United States. *American Journal of Psychiatry, 151,* 413–420.

Eaton, W. W., Sigal, J. J., & Weinfeld, M. (1982). Impairment in Holocaust survivors after 33 years: Data from an unbiased community sample. *American Journal of Psychiatry, 139,* 773–777.

Eaton, W. W., Thara, R., Federman, B., Melton, B., & Liang, K. (1995). Structure and course of positive and negative symptoms in schizophrenia. *Archives of General Psychiatry, 52,* 127–134.

Edgerton, R. B., & Cohen, A. (1994). Culture and schizophrenia: The DOSMD challenge. *British Journal of Psychiatry, 164,* 222–231.

Egeland, J. A., Gerhard, D. A., Pauls, D. L., Sussex, J. N., Kidd, K. K., Allen, C. R., Hostetter, A. M., & Housman, D. E. (1987). Bipolar affective disorders linked to DNA markers on chromosome 11. *Nature, 325,* 783–787.

Ehlers, A., Mayou, R. A., & Bryant, B. (1998). Psychological predictors of chronic post-traumatic stress disorder after motor vehicle accidents. *Journal of Abnormal Psychology, 107,* 509–519.

Ehlers, S., Nyden, A., Gillberg, C., Sandberg, A. D., Dahlgren, S. O., Hjelmquist, E., & Oden, A. (1997). Asperger syndrome, autism and attention disorders: A comparative study of the cognitive profiles of 120 children. *Journal of Child Psychology and Psychiatry & Allied Disciplines, 38,* 207–217.

Eisler, I., Dare, C., Russell, G. F., Szmukler, G., le Grange, D., & Dodge, E. (1997). Family and individual therapy in anorexia nervosa. A 5-year follow-up. *Archives of General Psychiatry, 54,* 1025–1030.

El-khatib, H. E., & Dickey, T. O. (1995). Sertraline for body dysmorphic disorder. *Journal of the American Academy of Child and Adolescent Psychiatry, 34,* 1404–1405.

Elkin, I., Shea, M. T., Watkins, J. T., Imber, S. D., Sotsky, S. M., Collins, J. F., Glass, D. R., Pilkonis, P. A., Leber, W. R., Docherty, J. P., Fiester, S. J, & Parloff, M. B. (1989). National Institute of Mental Health treatment of depression collaborative research program: General effectiveness of treatments. *Archives of General Psychiatry, 46,* 971–982.

Ellason, J. W., & Ross, C. A. (1997). Two-year follow-up of inpatients with dissociative identity disorder. *American Journal of Psychiatry, 154,* 832–839.

Ellason, J. W., Ross, C. A., & Fuchs, D. L. (1996). Lifetime Axis I and II comorbidity and childhood trauma history in dissociative identity disorder. *Psychiatry: Interpersonal & Biological Processes, 59,* 255–266.

Ellis, A. (1998). Flora: A case of severe depression and treatment with rational emotive behavior therapy. In R. P. Halgin & S. K. Whitbourne (Eds.), *A casebook in abnormal psychology: From the files of experts* (pp. 166–181). New York: Oxford University Press.

Emde, R. N., Gaensbauer, R. J., & Harmon, R. J. (1976). *Emotional expressions in infancy: A biobehavioral study.* New York: International Universities Press.

Emmelkamp, P. M. G. (1982). *Phobic and obsessive-compulsive disorders.* New York: Plenum Press.

Emmelkamp, P. M. G. (1994). Behavior therapy with adults. in A. E. Bergin & S. L. Garfield (Eds.), *Handbook of psychotherapy and behavior change* (pp. 379–427). New York: Wiley.

Enserink, M. (1998). First Alzheimer's disease confirmed. *Science, 279,* 2037.

Ensink, K., Robertson, B. A., Zissis, C., & Leger, P. (1997). Post-traumatic stress disorder in children exposed to violence. *South African Medical Journal, 87,* 1526–1530.

Erdelyi, M. H. (1985). *Psychoanalysis: Freud's cognitive psychology.* New York: Freeman.

Erikson, E. H. (1963). *Childhood and society.* (2nd ed.). New York: Norton.

Erlenmeyer-Kimling, L., Cornblatt, B., Friedman, D., Marcuse, Y., Rutschmann, J., Simmens, S., & Devi, S. (1982). Neurological, electrophysiological, and attentional deviations in children at risk for schizophrenia. In F. A. Henn & H. A. Nasrallah (Eds.), *Schizophenia as a brain disease* (pp. 61–98). New York: Oxford University Press.

Erlenmeyer-Kimling, L., Rock, D., Squires-Wheeler, E., Roberts, S., & Yang, J. (1991). Early life precursors of psychiatric outcomes in adulthood in subjects at risk for schizophrenia or affective disorders. *Psychiatry Research, 39,* 239–256.

Ernst, M., & Zametkin, A. J. (1995). The interface of genetics, neuroimaging, and neurochemistry in attention deficit-hyperactivity disorder. In F. Bloom & D. Kupfer (Eds.), *Psychopharmacology: The fourth generation of progress* (pp. 1643–1652). New York: Raven.

Evans, D. L., Leserman, J., Perkins, D. O., Stern, R. A., Murphy, C., Zheng, B., Gettes, D., Longmate, J. A., Silva, S. G., van der Horst, C. M., Hall, C. D., Folds, J. D., Golden, R. N., & Petitto, J. M. (1997). Severe life stress as a predictor of early disease progression in HIV infection. *American Journal of Psychiatry, 154,* 630–634.

Eyler, F. D., Behnke, M., Conlon, M., Woods, N. S., & Wobie, K. (1998). Birth outcome from a prospective, matched study of prenatal crack/cocaine use: I. Interactive and dose effects on health and growth. *Pediatrics, 101,* 229–237.

Eysenck, H. J. (1952). The effects of psychotherapy: An evaluation. *Journal of Consulting Psychology, 16,* 319–324.

Eysenck, H. J. (1967). *The biological basis of personality.* Springfield, IL: Charles C Thomas Press.

Eysenck, H. J. (1991). *Smoking, personality and stress: Psychosocial factors in the prevention of cancer and coronary heart disease.* New York: Springer-Verlag.

Eysenck, H. J. (1994). Neuroticism and the illusion of mental health. *American Psychologist, 49,* 971–972.

F

Fairburn, C. G. (1997). Eating disorders. In D. M. Clark & C. G. Fairburn (Eds.), *The science and practice of cognitive behaviour therapy.* Oxford, U.K.: Oxford University Press.

Falloon, I. R., Boyd, J. L., McGill, C. W., Williamson, M., Razani, J., Moss, H. B., Gilderman, A. M., & Simpson, G. M. (1985). Family management in the prevention of morbidity of schizophrenia. *Archives of General Psychiatry, 42,* 887–896.

Famularo, R., Fenton, T., Augustyn, M., & Zuckerman, B. (1996). Persistence of pediatric post-traumatic stress disorder after two years. *Child Abuse and Neglect, 20,* 1245–1248.

Faraone, S. V., Biederman, J., Jetton, J. G., & Tsuang, M. T. (1997). Attention deficit and conduct disorder: Longitudinal evidence for a familial subtype. *Psychological Medicine, 27,* 291–300.

Farber, I. E. (1975). Sane and insane constructions and misconstructions. *Journal of Abnormal Psychology, 84,* 589–620.

Fava, M., & Rosenbaum, J. F. (1991). Suicidality and fluoxetine: Is there a relationship? *Journal of Clinical Psychiatry, 52,* 108–111.

Figueroa, E., & Silk, K. R. (1997). Biological implications of childhood sexual abuse in borderline personality disorder. *Journal of Personality Disorders, 11,* 71–92.

Figueroa, R. A., & Sassenrath, J. M. (1989). A longitudinal study of the predictive validity of the System of Multicultural Assessment (SOMPA). *Psychology in the Schools, 26,* 5–19.

Fine, C. G. (1996). A cognitively based treatment model for DSM–IV dissociative identity disorder. In L. K. Michelson & W. J. Ray (Eds.), *Handbook of dissociation: Theoretical, empirical, and clinical perspectives* (pp. 401–411). New York: Plenum Press.

First, M. B., Spitzer, R. L., Gibbon, M. & Williams, J. B. W. (1997). *SCID-I/P (for DSM-IV) Patient Edition Structured Clinical Interview for DSM-IV Axis I Disorders, Research Version, Patient/Non-patient Edition. (SCID-I/P).* New York: Biometrics Research, New York State Psychiatric Institute.

Firstman, R., & Talan, J. (1997). *The death of innocents.* New York: Bantam.

Fisher, S., & Greenberg, R. P. (1977). *The scientific credibility of Freud's theory and therapy.* New York: Basic Books.

Fitts, S. N., Gibson, P., Redding, C. A., & Deiter, P. J. (1989). Body dysmorphic disorder: Implications for its validity as a DSM-III-R clinical syndrome. *Psychological Reports, 64,* 655–658.

Flakierska-Praquin, N., Lindstrom, M., & Gillberg, C. (1997). School phobia with separation anxiety disorder: A comparative 20- to 29-year follow-up study of 35 school refusers. *Comprehensive Psychiatry, 38,* 17–22.

Flint, A. J., Koszycki, D., Vaccarino, F. J., Cadieux, A., Boulenger, J. P., & Bradwejn, J. (1998). Effect of aging on cholecystokinin induced panic. *American Journal of Psychiatry, 155,* 283–285.

Foa, E. B., Steketee, G., & Rothbaum, B. O. (1989). Behavioral/cognitive conceptualizations of post-traumatic stress disorder. *Behavior Therapy, 20,* 155–176.

Foa, E. B., Steketee, G. S., & Ozarow, B. J. (1985). Behavior therapy with obsessive-compulsives: From theory to treatment. In M. Mavissakalian, S. M. Turner, & L. Michelson (Eds.), *Obsessive-compulsive disorder: Psychological and pharmacological treatment* (pp. 49–129). New York: Plenum Press.

Folkman, S., Lazarus, R. S., Gruen, R. J., & DeLongis, A. (1986). Appraisal, coping, health status, and psychological symptoms. *Journal of Personality and Social Psychology, 50,* 571–579.

Folstein, M. F., Folstein, S. E., & McHugh, P. R. (1975). Mini-Mental State: A practical method for grading the cognitive state of patients for the clinician. *Journal of Psychiatric Research, 12,* 189–198.

Ford, C. V. (1995). Dimensions of somatization and hypochondriasis. *Neurologic Clinics, 13,* 241–253.

Ford, C. V., & Folks, D. G. (1985). Conversion disorders: An overview. *Psychosomatics, 26,* 371–383.

Forsyth, J. P., & Chorpita, B. F. (1997). Unearthing the nonassociative origins of fears and phobias: A rejoinder. *Journal of Behavior Therapy & Experimental Psychiatry, 28,* 297–305.

Foster, S. L., Bell-Dolan, D. J., & Burge, D. A. (1988). Behavioral observation. In A. S. Bellack & M. Hersen (Eds.), *Behavioral assessment: A practical handbook* (3rd ed., pp. 119–160). New York: Pergamon.

Frank, E., Kupfer, D. J., Perel, J. M., Cornes, C., Jarrett, D. B., Mallinger, A. G., Thase, M. E., McEachran, A. B., & Grochociniski, V. J. (1990). Three-year outcomes for maintenance therapies in recurrent depression. *Archives of General Psychiatry, 48,* 1053–1059.

Frank, E., Kupfer, D. J., Wagner, E. F., McEachran, A. B., & Cornes, C. (1991). Efficacy of interpersonal psychotherapy as a maintenance treatment of recurrent depression: Contributing factors. *Archives of General Psychiatry, 48,* 1053–1059.

Frankel, F. H. (1996). Dissociation: The clinical realities. *American Journal of Psychiatry, 153,* 64–70.

Frankl, V. (1963). *Man's search for meaning.* New York: Simon & Schuster.

Franklin, M. E., & Foa, E. B. (1998). Cognitive-behavioral treatments for obsessive-compulsive disorder. In P. E. Nathan & J. M. Gorman (Eds.), *A guide to treatments that work* (pp. 339–357). New York: Oxford University Press.

Franzek, E., & Beckmann, H. (1998). Different genetic background of schizophrenia spectrum psychoses: A twin study. *American Journal of Psychiatry, 155,* 76–83.

Frederick, R. I. (1998). *Validity indicator profile.* Minnetonka, MN: National Computer System.

Fredrikson, M., Annas, P., & Wik, G. (1997). Parental history, aversive exposure and the development of snake and spider phobia in women. *Behaviour Research and Therapy, 35,* 23–28.

Freedman, M., Rewilak, D., Xerri, T., Cohen, S., Gordon, A. S., Shandling, M., & Logan, A. G. (1998). L-deprenyl in Alzheimer's disease: Cognitive and behavioral effects. *Neurology, 50,* 660–668.

Freeman, A., Pretzer, J., Fleming, B., & Simon, K. M. (1990). *Clinical applications of cognitive therapy.* New York: Plenum Press.

Freeman, L. N., Shaffer, D., & Smith, H. (1996). Neglected victims of homicide: The needs of young siblings of murder victims. *American Journal of Orthopsychiatry, 66,* 337–345.

French, S. A., & Jeffery, R. W. (1994). Consequences of dieting to lose weight: Effects on physical and mental health. *Health Psychology, 13,* 195–212.

Freud, S. (1900). The interpretation of dreams. In J. Strachey (Ed.), *The standard edition of the complete psychological works of Sigmund Freud* (Vols. 4 and 5). London: Hogarth.

Freud, S. (1905). Three essays on the theory of sexuality. In J. Strachey (Ed.), *The standard edition of the complete psychological works of Sigmund Freud* (Vol. 7). London: Hogarth.

Freud, S. (1911). Formulations of the two principles of mental functioning. In J. Strachey (Ed.), *The standard edition of the complete psychological works of Sigmund Freud* (Vol. 12). London: Hogarth.

Freud, S. (1913). Totem and taboo. In J. Strachey (Ed.), *The standard edition of the complete psychological works of Sigmund Freud* (Vol. 13). London: Hogarth.

Freud, S. (1913-14/1963). Further recommendations in the technique of psychoanalysis. In S. Freud (Ed.), *Therapy and technique.* New York: Collier.

Freud, S. (1917). Mourning and melancholia. In J. Strachey (Ed.), *The standard edition of the complete psychological works of Sigmund Freud* (Vol. 14, pp. 151–169). London: Hogarth.

Freud, S. (1923). The ego and the id. In J. Strachey (Ed.), *The standard edition of the complete psychological works of Sigmund Freud* (Vol. 19). London: Hogarth.

Freud, S. (1925). An autobiographical study. In J. Strachey (Ed.), *The standard edition of the complete psychological works of Sigmund Freud* (Vol. 20). London: Hogarth.

Freund, K., Seto, M., & Kuban, M. (1997). Frotteurism: the theory of courtship disorder. In D. R. Laws & W. T. O'Donohue (Eds.), *Sexual deviance: Theory, assessment, and treatment* (pp. 111–130). New York: Guilford Press.

Friedman, M. (1985). Survivor guilt in the pathogenesis of anorexia nervosa. *Psychiatry, 48,* 25–39.

Friedman, M., Breall, W. S., Goodwin, M. L., Sparagon, B. J., Ghandour, G., & Fleischmann, N. (1996). Effect of Type A behavioral counseling on frequency of episodes of silent myocardial ischemia in coronary patients. *American Heart Journal, 132,* 933–937.

Froelich, S., Basun, H., Forsell, C., Lilius, L., Axelman, K., Andreadis, A., & Lannfelt, L. (1997). Mapping of a disease locus for familial rapidly progressive frontotemporal dementia to chromosome 17q12-21. *American Journal of Medical Genetics, 74,* 380–385.

Frost, R. O., Krause, M. S., & Steketee, G. (1996). Hoarding and obsessive-compulsive symptoms. *Behavior Modification, 20,* 116–132.

Frumkin, R. M. (1997). Significant neglected sociocultural and physical factors affecting intelligence. *American Psychologist, 52,* 76–77.

Fulton, M., & Winokur, G. (1993). A comparative study of paranoid and schizoid personality disorder. *American Journal of Psychiatry, 150,* 1363–1367.

G

Gainotti, G., & Marra, C. (1994). Some aspects of memory disorders clearly distinguish dementia of the Alzheimer's type from depressive pseudo-dementia. *Journal of Clinical and Experimental Neuropsychology, 16,* 65–78.

Gallagher-Thompson, D., & Steffen, A. M. (1994). Comparative effects of cognitive-behavioral and brief psychodynamic psychotherapies for depressed family caregivers. *Journal of Consulting and Clinical Psychology, 62,* 543–549.

Garmezy, N. (1970). Process and reactive schizophrenia: Some conceptions and issues. *Schizophrenia Bulletin, 2,* 30–67.

Gatz, M., Pedersen, N. L., Berg, S., Johansson, B., Johansson, K., Mortimer, J. A., Posner, S. F., Viitanen, M., Winblad, B., & Ahlbom, A. (1997). Heritability for Alzheimer's disease: The study of dementia in Swedish twins. *Journals of Gerontology. Series A, Biological Sciences and Medical Sciences, 52,* M117–125.

Gay, P. (1988). *Freud: A life for our time.* New York: Norton.

Gelerneter, C. S., Uhde, T. W., Cimbolic, P., Arnkoff, D. B., Vitone, B. J., Tancer, M. E., & Bartko, J. J. (1991). Cognitive-behavioral and pharmacological treatments of social phobia: A controlled study. *Archives of General Psychiatry, 48,* 938–945.

Geller, D., Biederman, J., Jones, J., Park, K., Schwartz, S., Shapiro, S., & Coffey, B. (1998). Is juvenile obsessive-compulsive disorder a developmental subtype of the disorder? A review of the pediatric literature. *Journal of the American Academy of Child & Adolescent Psychiatry, 37,* 420–427.

Gentry, W. D. (1984). *Handbook of behavioral medicine.* New York: Guilford Press.

George, L. K., & Gwyther, L. P. (1986). Caregiver well-being: A multidimensional examination of family caregivers of demented adults. *Gerontologist, 26,* 253–259.

Gershon, E. S. (1983). The genetics of affective disorders. In L. Grinspoon (Ed.), *Psychiatry update* (pp. 434–457). Washington, DC: American Psychiatry Press.

Ghaziuddin, M., Leininger, L., & Tsai, L. (1995). Brief report: Thought disorder in Asperger syndrome: Comparison with high-functioning autism. *Journal of Autism and Developmental Disorder, 25,* 311–317.

Gitlin, M. J. (1990). *The psychotherapist's guide to psychopharmacology.* New York: Free Press.

Glassman, A. (1969). Indoleamines and affective disorder. *Psychosomatic Medicine, 31,* 107–114.

Glassman, J. N. S., Magulac, M., & Darko, D. F. (1987). Folie à famille: Shared paranoid disorder in a Vietnam veteran and his family. *American Journal of Psychiatry, 144,* 658–660.

Glynn, S. M. (1992). If Dahmer's not crazy, who is? *The National Law Journal, 14,* 13–25.

Goenjian, A. K., Najarian, L. M., Pynoos, R. S., Steinberg, A. M., Manoukian, G., Tavosian, A., & Fairbanks, L. A. (1994). Post-traumatic stress disorder in elderly and younger adults after the 1988 earthquake in Armenia. *American Journal of Psychiatry, 151,* 895–901.

Goisman, R. M., Warshaw, M. G., Peterson, L. G., Rogers, M. P., Cuneo, P., Hunt, M. F., Tomlin-Albanese, J. M., Kazim, A., Gollan, J. K., & Epstein-Kaye, T. (1994). Panic, agoraphobia, and panic disorder with agoraphobia: Data from a multicenter anxiety disorders study. *Journal of Nervous and Mental Disease, 182,* 72–79.

Gold, S. N., & Heffner, C. L. (1998). Sexual addiction: Many conceptions, minimal data. *Clinical Psychology Review, 18,* 367–381.

Goldberg, J. F., & Harrow, M. (1994). Kindling in bipolar disorders: A longitudinal follow-up study. *Biological Psychiatry, 35,* 70–72.

Goldberg, J. F., Harrow, M., & Grossman, L. S. (1995). Course and outcome in bipolar affective disorder: A longitudinal follow-up study. *American Journal of Psychiatry, 152,* 379–384.

Golden, C. J., Purisch, A. D., & Hammeke, T. A. (1985). *Luria-Nebraska neuropsychological battery: Forms I and II.* Los Angeles: Western Psychological Corporation.

Goldfarb, L. (1985). The Goldfarb Fear of Fat Scale. *Journal of Personality Assessment, 49,* 329–332.

Goldman, S. J., D'Angelo, E. J., & DeMaso, D. R. (1993). Psychopathology in the families of children and adolescents with borderline personality disorder. *American Journal of Psychiatry, 150,* 1832–1835.

Goldstein, R., Powers, S. I., McCusker, J., & Lewis, B. F. (1996). Lack of remorse in antisocial personality disorder among drug abusers in residential treatment. *Journal of Personality Disorders, 10,* 321–334.

Goleman, D. (1995, October). Early violence leaves its marks on the brain. *New York Times,* pp. C–1, C–10.

Golomb, M., Fava, M., Abraham, M., & Rosenbaum, J. F. (1995). Gender differences in personality disorders. *American Journal of Psychiatry, 152,* 579–582.

Goodman, A. (1998). *Sexual addiction: An integrated approach.* Madison, CT: International Universities Press.

Goodman, W. K., Price, L. H., Rasmussen, S. A., Mazure, C., Delgado, P., Heninger, G. R., & Charney, D. S. (1989a). The Yale-Brown Obsessive Compulsive Scale. II. Validity. *Archives of General Psychiatry, 46,* 1012–1016.

Goodman, W. K., Price, L. H., Rasmussen, S. A., Mazure, C., Fleischmann, R. L., Hill, C. L., Heninger, G. R., & Charney, D. S. (1989b). The Yale-Brown Obsessive Compulsive Scale. I. Development, use, and reliability. *Archives of General Psychiatry, 46,* 1006–1011.

Gordon, L. J., III, Fargason, P. J., & Kramer, J. J. (1995). Sexual behaviors of patients in a residential chemical dependency program: Comparison of sexually compulsive physicians and nonphysicians with non-sexually compulsive physicians and nonphysicians. *Sexual Addiction and Compulsivity, 2,* 233–255.

Gorman, J. M., & Liebowitz, M. R. (1986). Panic and anxiety disorders. In A. M. Cooper, A. J. Frances, & M. H. Sacks (Eds.), *The personality disorders and neuroses* (pp. 325–337). New York: Basic Books.

Gottesman, I. I. (1991). *Schizophrenia genesis: The origins of madness.* New York: Freeman.

Gottesman, I. I., & Shields, J. (1982). *Schizophrenia: The epigenetic puzzle.* Cambridge: Cambridge University Press.

Gould, S. J. (1981). *The mismeasure of man.* New York: Norton.

Graae, F., Milner, J., Rizzotto, L., & Klein, R. G., (1994). Clonazepam in childhood anxiety disorder. *Journal of the American Academy of Child and Adolescent Psychiatry, 33,* 372–376.

Graber, J., & Arndt, W. B. (1993). Trichotillomania. *Comprehensive Psychiatry, 34,* 340–346.

Grachev, I. D. (1997). MRI-based morphometric topographic parcellation of human neocortex in trichotillomania. *Psychiatry and Clinical Neurosciences, 51,* 315–321.

Greaves, G. B. (1980). Multiple personality: 165 years after Mary Reynolds. *Journal of Nervous and Mental Disease, 168,* 577–596.

Green, B. L., Grace, M. C., Lindy, J. D., Gleser, G. C., & Leonard, A. (1990). Risk factors for PTSD and other diagnoses in a general sample of Vietnam veterans. *American Journal of Psychiatry, 147,* 729–733.

Greenberg, B. D., George, M. S., Martin, J. D., Benjamin, J., Schlaepfer, T. E., Altemus, M., Wassermann, E. M., Post, R. M., & Murphy, D. L. (1997). Effect of prefrontal repetitive transcranial magnetic stimulation in obsessive-compulsive disorder: A preliminary study. *American Journal of Psychiatry, 154,* 867–869.

Greenberg, J. R., & Mitchell, S. A. (1983). *Object relations in psychoanalytic theory.* Cambridge, MA: Harvard University Press.

Greenberg, R. P., Bornstein, R. F., Zborowski, M. J., Fisher, S., & Greenberg, M. D. (1994). A meta-analysis of fluoxetine outcomes in the treatment of depression. *The Journal of Nervous and Mental Disease, 182,* 547–551.

Greene, R. W., Biederman, J., Faraone, S. V., Sienna, M., & Garcia-Jetton, J. (1997). Adolescent outcome of boys with attention-deficit/hyperactivity disorder and social disability: Results from a 4-year longitudinal follow-up study. *Journal of Consulting and Clinical Psychology, 65,* 758–767.

Greist, J. H. (1990). Treating the anxiety: Therapeutic options in obsessive-compulsive disorder. *Journal of Clinical Psychiatry, 51,* 29–34.

Greist, J. H., Jefferson, J. W., Kobak, K. A., Katzelnick, D. J., & Serlin, R. C. (1995). Efficacy and tolerability of serotonin transport inhibitors in obsessive-compulsive disorder. *Archives of General Psychiatry, 52,* 53–60.

Grenyer, B. F., & Luborsky, L. (1996). Dynamic change in psychotherapy: Mastery of interpersonal conflicts. *Journal of Consulting and Clinical Psychology, 64,* 411–416.

Griffin-Shelley, E., Benjamin, L., & Benjamin, R. (1995). Sex addiction and dissociation. *Sexual Addiction and Compulsivity, 2,* 295–306.

Griffith, D., & Chasnoff, I. (1994). Three-year outcome of children exposed prenatally to drugs. *Journal of the American Academy of Child and Adolescent Psychiatry, 33,* 20–27.

Griffith, J. D., Knight, D. K., Joe, G. W., & Simpson, D. D. (1998). Implications of family and peer relations for treatment engagement and follow-up outcomes: An integrative model. *Psychology of Addictive Behaviors, 12,* 113–126.

Grilo, C. M., Becker, D. F., Fehon, D. C., Walker, M. L., Edell, W. S., & McGlashan, T. H. (1996). Gender differences in personality disorders in psychiatrically hospitalized adolescents. *American Journal of Psychiatry, 153,* 1089–1091.

Grisel, J. E., Belknap, J. K., O'Toole, L. A., Helms, M. L., Wenger, C. D., & Crabbe, J. C. (1997). Quantitative trait loci affecting methamphetamine responses in BXD recombinant inbred mouse strains. *Journal of Neuroscience, 17,* 745–754.

Grossman, L. S., Harrow, M., Goldberg, J. F., & Fichtner, C. G. (1991). Outcome of schizoaffective disorder at two long-term follow-ups: Comparisons with outcome of schizophrenia and affective disorders. *American Journal of Psychiatry, 148,* 1359–1365.

Groth-Marnat, G. (1997). *Handbook of psychological assessment* (3rd ed.). New York: Wiley.

Gunderson, J. G. (1984). *Borderline personality disorders.* Washington, DC: American Psychiatric Press.

Gunderson, J. G. (1989). Borderline personality disorders. in American Psychiatric Association Task Force on Treatments of Psychiatric Disorders (Eds.), *Treatments of psychiatric disorders* (Vol. 3, pp. 2749–2759). Washington, DC: American Psychiatric Association.

Gunderson, J. G., Ronningstam, E., & Smith, L. E. (1991). Narcissistic personality disorder: A review of data on DSM-III-R descriptions. *Journal of Personality Disorders, 5,* 167–177.

Gur, R. E., Cowell, P., Turetsky, B. I., Gallacher, F., Cannon, T., Bilker, W., & Gur, R. C. (1998). A follow-up magnetic resonance imaging study of schizophrenia: Relationship of neuroanatomical changes to clinical and neurobehavioral measures. *Archives of General Psychiatry, 55,* 145–152.

Gureje, O., Ustun, T. B., & Simon, G. E. (1997). The syndrome of hypochondriasis: A cross-national study in primary care. *Psychological Medicine, 27,* 1001–1010.

Gutheil, T. G., & Appelbaum, P. S. (1982). *Clinical handbook of psychiatry and the law.* New York: McGraw-Hill.

Guzder, J., Paris, J., Zelkowitz, P., & Marchessault, K. (1996). Risk factors for borderline personality in children. *Journal of the American Academy of Child and Adolescent Psychiatry, 35,* 26–33.

Guziec, J., Lazarus, A., & Harding, J. J. (1994). Case of a 29-year-old nurse with factitious disorder: The utility of psychiatric intervention on a general medical floor. *General Hospital Psychiatry, 16,* 47–53.

H

Haenen, M. A., Schmidt, A. J. M., Kroeze, S., & van den Hout, M. A. (1996). Hypochondriasis and symptom reporting—The effect of attention versus distraction. *Psychotherapy and Psychosomatics, 65,* 43–48.

Halgin, R. P., & Vivona, J. M. (1995). Adult survivors of childhood sexual abuse: Diagnostic and treatment challenges. In R. S. Feldman (Ed.), *The psychology of adversity*. Amherst: University of Massachusetts Press.

Hall, G. C. N., Shondrick, D. D., & Hirschman, R. (1993). Conceptually derived treatments for sexual aggressors. *Professional Psychology: Research and Practice, 24,* 2–69.

Halstead, W. C. (1947). *Brain and intelligence: A quantitative study of the frontal lobes.* Chicago: University of Chicago Press.

Hamilton, B. (1994). A systematic approach to a family and school problem: A case study in separation anxiety disorder. *Family Therapy, 21,* 149–152.

Hankin, J. R. (1994). FAS prevention strategies: Passive and active measures. *Alcohol Health and Research World, 18,* 62–66.

Hanna, G. L. (1997). Trichotillomania and related disorders in children and adolescents. *Child Psychiatry and Human Development, 27,* 255–268.

Hanna, G. L., Himle, J. A., Curtis, G. C., Koram, D. Q., Weele, J. V., Leventhal, B. L., & Cook, E. H., Jr. (1998). Serotonin transporter and seasonal variation in blood serotonin in families with obsessive-compulsive disorder. *Neuropsychopharmacology, 18,* 102–111.

Hansen, L. A. (1997). The Lewy body variant of Alzheimer's disease. *Journal of Neural Transmission. Supplementum, 51,* 83–93.

Hanson, M., MacKay-Soroka, S., Staley, S., & Poulton, L. (1994). Delinquent firesetters: A comparative study of delinquency and firesetting histories. *Canadian Journal of Psychiatry, 39,* 230–232.

Happe, F., Ehlers, S., Fletcher, P., Frith, U., Johansson, M., Gillberg, C., Dolan, R., Frackowiak, R., & Frith, C. (1996). "Theory of mind" in the brain. Evidence from a PET scan study of Asperger syndrome. *Neuroreport, 8,* 197–201.

Hardy, J., & Gwinn-Hardy, K. (1998). Genetic classification of primary neurodegenerative disease. *Science, 282,* 1075–1083.

Hare, R. D. (1991). *The Hare Psychopathy Checklist-Revised.* Toronto: Multi-Health Systems.

Hare, R. D. (1993). *Without conscience: The disturbing world of the psychopaths among us.* New York: Simon & Schuster.

Hare, R. D. (1997). *Hare Psychopathy Checklist-Revised (PCL-R).* Odessa, FL: Personality Assessment Resources.

Hare, R. D., McPherson, L. M., & Forth, A. E. (1988). Male psychopaths and their criminal careers. *Journal of Consulting and Clinical Psychology, 56,* 710–714.

Haring, T. G., & Breen, C. G. (1992). A peer mediated social network intervention to enhance the social integration of persons with moderate and severe disabilities. *Journal of Applied Behavior Analysis, 25,* 319–334.

Harpur, T. J., & Hare, R. D. (1994). Assessment of psychopathy as a function of age. *Journal of Abnormal Psychology, 103,* 604–609.

Harris, S. L., Handleman, J. S., Gill, M. J., & Fong, P. L. (1991). Does punishment hurt? The impact of aversives on the clinician. *Research in Developmental Disabilities, 12,* 17–24.

Harsham, J., Keller, J. H., & Disbrow, D. (1994). Growth patterns of infants exposed to cocaine and other drugs in utero. *Journal of the American Dietetic Association, 94,* 999–1007.

Hartung, C. M., & Widiger, T. A. (1998). Gender differences in the diagnosis of mental disorders: Conclusions and controversies of the DSM-IV. *Psychological Bulletin, 123,* 260–278.

Haslam, N., & Beck, A. T. (1994). Subtyping major depression: A taxometric analysis. *Journal of Abnormal Psychology, 103,* 686–692.

Hatfield, E., & Rapson, R. (1994). Love and attachment processes. In M. Lewis & J. M. Haviland (Eds.), *Handbook of emotions* (pp. 595–604). New York: Guilford Press.

Hathaway, S. R., & McKinley, J. C. (1989). *The Minnesota Multiphasic Personality Inventory-2.* Minneapolis: University of Minnesota Press.

Haugland, G., Siegel, C., Hopper, K., & Alexander, M. J. (1997). Mental illness among homeless individuals in a suburban county. *Psychiatric Services, 48,* 504–509.

Hays, R. D., Wells, K. B., Sherbourne, C. D., Rogers, W., & Spritzer, K. (1995). Functioning and well-being outcomes of patients with depression compared with chronic general medical illnesses. *Archives of General Psychiatry, 52,* 11–19.

Haywood, T. W., & Grossman, L. S. (1994). Denial of deviant sexual arousal and psychopathology in child molesters. *Behavior Therapy, 25,* 327–340.

Haywood, T. W., Kravitz, H. M., Wasyliw, O. E., Goldberg, J., & Cavanaugh, J. L., Jr. (1996). Cycle of abuse and psychopathology in cleric and noncleric molesters of children and adolescents. *Child Abuse and Neglect, 20,* 1233–1243.

Hazan, C., & Shaver, P. R. (1994). Attachment as an organizational framework for research on close relationships. *Psychological Inquiry, 5,* 1–22.

Heard, H. L., & Linehan, M. M. (1994). Dialectical behavior therapy: An integrative approach to the treatment of borderline personality disorder. *Journal of Psychotherapy Integration, 4,* 55–82.

Heatherton, T. F., Mahamedi, F., Striepe, M., Field, A. E., & Keel, P. (1997). A 10-year longitudinal study of body weight, dieting, and eating disorder symptoms. *Journal of Abnormal Psychology, 106,* 117–125.

Heebink, D. M., & Halmi, K. A. (1994). Eating disorders. In J. M. Oldham & M. B. Riba (Eds.), *Review of psychiatry* (pp. 227–252). Washington, DC: American Psychiatric Press.

Heim, C., Owens, M. J., Plotsky, P. M., & Nemeroff, C. B. (1997). Persistent changes in corticotropin-releasing factor systems due to early life stress: Relationship to the pathophysiology of major depression and post-traumatic stress disorder. *Psychopharmacology Bulletin, 33,* 185–192.

Heiman, J. R., & LoPiccolo, J. (1988). *Becoming orgasmic: A sexual and personal growth program for women.* New York: Prentice Hall.

Heimann, S. W. (1997). SSRI for body dysmorphic disorder. *Journal of the American Academy of Child and Adolescent Psychiatry, 36,* 868.

Heimberg, R. G., & Barlow, D. H. (1988). Psychosocial treatments for social phobia. *Psychosomatics, 29,* 27–37.

Heldring, M. (1998). Fighting for health care on the hill: A tale of a senator, a psychologist, and the American people. *Professional Psychology: Research and Practice, 29,* 3–4.

Helzer, J. E., Burnam, A., & McEvoy, L. T. (1991). Alcohol abuse and dependence. In L. N. Robins & D. A. Regier (Eds.), *Psychiatric disorders in America* (pp. 81–115). New York: Free Press.

Helzer, J. E., Canino, G. J., Yeh, E. K. Bland, R. C., Lee, C. K., Hwu, H. G., & Newman, S. (1990). Alcoholism–North America and Asia. A comparison of population surveys with the Diagnostic Interview Schedule. *Archives of General Psychiatry, 47,* 313–319.

Herbert, M. (1987). *Conduct disorders of childhood and adolescence* (2nd ed.). Chichester, U.K.: Wiley.

Herd, D. (1994). Predicting drinking problems among black and white men: Results from a national survey. *Journal of Studies on Alcohol, 55,* 61–71.

Herek, G. M., & Capitanio, J. P. (1994). Conspiracies, contagion, and compassion: Trust and public reactions to AIDS. *AIDS Education and Prevention, 6,* 365–375.

Herinckx, H. A., Kinney, R. F., Clarke, G. N., & Paulson, R. I. (1997). Assertive community treatment versus usual care in engaging and retaining clients with severe mental illness. *Psychiatric Services, 48,* 1297–1306.

Herman, J., Perry, J. C., & van der Kolk, B. A. (1989). Childhood trauma in borderline personality disorder. *American Journal of Psychiatry, 145,* 490–495.

Hermann, R. C., Dorwart, R. A., Hoover, C. W., & Brody, J. (1995). Variation in ECT use in the United States. *American Journal of Psychiatry, 152,* 869–875.

Herrnstein, R. J., & Murray, C. (1994). *The bell curve.* New York: Free Press.

Herzberg, F., Mausner, B., & Snydernan, B. B. (1959). *The motivation to work.* New York: Wiley.

Herzog, D. B., Keller, M. B., Lavori, P. W., & Sacks, N. R. (1991). The course and outcome of bulimia nervosa. *Journal of Clinical Psychiatry, 52,* 4–8.

Hinshaw, S. P. (1987). On the distinction between attentional deficits/hyperactivity and conduct problems/aggression in child psychopathology. *Psychological Bulletin, 101,* 443–463.

Hiroto, D. S. (1974). Locus of control and learned helplessness. *Journal of Experimental Psychology, 102,* 187–193.

Hiroto, D. S., & Seligman, M. E. P. (1975). Generality of learned helplessness in man. *Journal of Personality and Social Psychology, 31,* 311–327.

Hoberman, H. M., & Lewinsohn, P. M. (1985). The behavioral treatment of depression. In E. E. Beckham & W. R. Lever (Eds.), *Handbook of depression: Treatment, assessment, and research* (pp. 39–81). Homewood, IL: Dorsey Press.

Hobfall, S. E., Spielberger, C. D., Breznitz, S., Figley, C., Folkman, S., Lepper-Green, G., Meichenbaum, D., Milgram, N. A., Sandler, I., Sarason, & van der Kolk, B. (1991). War-related stress: Addressing the stress of war and other traumatic events. *American Psychologist, 46,* 848–855.

Hodgins, D. C., el-Guebaly, N., & Armstrong, S. (1995). Prospective and retrospective reports of mood states before relapse to substance abuse. *Journal of Consulting and Clinical Psychology, 63,* 400–407.

Hodgson, R. (1994). Treatment of alcohol problems. *Addiction, 89,* 1529–1534.

Hoehn, T., Braune, S., Scheibe, G., & Albus, M. (1997). Physiological, biochemical and subjective parameters in anxiety patients with panic disorder during stress exposure as compared with healthy controls. *European Archives of Psychiatry and Clinical Neuroscience, 247,* 264–274.

Hoehn-Saric, R., Mcleod, D. R., & Hipsley, P. (1995). Is hyperarousal essential to obsessive-compulsive disorder? Diminished physiologic flexibility, but not hyperarousal, characterizes patients with obsessive-compulsive disorder. *Archives of General Psychiatry, 52,* 688–693.

Hoek, H. W., Susser, E., Buck, K. A., Lumey, L. H., Lin, S. P., & Gorman, J. M. (1996). Schizoid personality disorder after prenatal exposure to famine. *American Journal of Psychiatry, 153,* 1637–1639.

Hoffart, A., Thornes, K., Hedley, L. M., & Strand, J. (1994). DSM-III-R Axis I and II disorders in agoraphobic patients with and without panic disorder. *Acta Psychiatrica Scandinavica, 89,* 186–191.

Hoffman, J. A. (1984). Psychological separation of late adolescents from their parents. *Journal of Counseling Psychology, 31,* 170–178.

Hogarty, G. E., Greenwald, D., Ulrich, R. F., Kornblith, S. J., DiBarry, A. L., Cooley, S., Carter, M., & Flesher, S. (1997). Three-year trials of personal therapy among schizophrenia patients living with or independent of family, II: Effects on adjustment of patients. *American Journal of Psychiatry, 154,* 1514–1524.

Hoge, S. K., Poythress, N., Bonnie, R. J., Monahan, J., Eisenberg, M., & Feucht-Haviar, T. (1997). The MacArthur Adjudicative Competence Study: Development and validation of a research instrument. *Law and Human Behavior, 21,* 141–179.

Hoge, S. K., Poythress, N., Bonnie, R. J., Monahan, J., Eisenberg, M., & Feucht-Haviar, T. (1997). The MacArthur Adjudicative Competence Study: Diagnosis, psychopathology, and competence-related abilities. *Behavioral Sciences and the Law, 15,* 329–345.

Hoglend, P. (1993). Personality disorders and long-term outcome after brief dynamic psychotherapy. *Journal of Personality Disorders, 7,* 168–181.

Holden, R., Pakula, I., & Mooney, P. (1997). A neuroimmunological model of antisocial and borderline personality disorders. *Human Psychopharmacology, 12,* 291–308.

Hollander, E. (1993). Obsessive-compulsive spectrum disorders: An overview. *Psychiatric Annals, 23,* 355–358.

Hollender, M. H. (1997). Genital exhibitionism in men and women. In L. B. Schlesinger & E. Revitch (Eds.), *Sexual dynamics of anti-social behavior* (2nd ed.). Springfield, IL: Charles C Thomas.

Hollingshead, A. B., & Redlich, F. C. (1958). *Social class and mental illness: A community study.* New York: Wiley.

Holmes, T. H., & Rahe, R. H. (1967). The social readjustment rating scale. *Journal of Psychosomatic Research, 11,* 213–218.

Holzman, P. S. (1992). Behavioral markers for schizophrenia useful for genetic studies. *Journal of Psychiatric Research, 26,* 427–445.

Holzman, P. S., & Matthysse, S. (1990). The genetics of schizophrenia: A review. *Psychological Science, 1,* 279–286.

Holzman, P. S., Proctor, L. R., Levy, D. L., Yasillo, N. J., Meltzer, H. Y., & Hurt, S. W. (1974). Eye-tracking dysfunctions in schizophrenic patients and their relatives. *Archives of General Psychiatry, 31,* 143–151.

Horger, B. A., & Roth, R. H. (1996). The role of mesoprefrontal dopamine neurons in stress. *Critical Reviews in Neurobiology, 10,* 395–418.

Horney, K. (1950). *Our inner conflicts.* New York: Norton.

Horowitz, M. J. (1986). Stress response syndromes: A review of post-traumatic and adjustment disorders. *Hospital and Community Psychiatry, 37,* 241–249.

House Committee on Energy and Commerce, H.R. Rep. No 485 (1990), 101st Cong., 101st., 2d Sess., pt. 4.

Houston, B. K., Babyak, M. A., Chesney, M. A., Black, G., & Ragland, D. R. (1997). Social dominance and 22-year all-cause mortality in men. *Psychosomatic Medicine, 59,* 5–12.

Hoyert, D. L. (1996). Medical and life style risk factors affecting fetal mortality, 1989–90. National Center for Health Statistics. *Vital Health Statistics, 20.*

Hrdina, P. D., Demeter, E., Vu, T. B., Sotonyi, P., & Palkovits, M. (1993). 5-HT uptake sites and 5-HT-sub-2 receptors in brain of antidepressant-free suicide victims/depressives: Increase in 5-HT-sub-2 sites in cortex and amygdala. *Brain Research, 614,* 37–44.

Hughes, J. R., Oliveto, A. H., Helzer, J. E., Higgins, S. T., & Bickel, W. K. (1992). Should caffeine abuse, dependence, or withdrawal be added to DSM-IV and ICD-10? *American Journal of Psychiatry, 149,* 33–40.

Hutchings, D. (1993). The puzzle of cocaine's effects following maternal use during pregnancy: Are there recognizable differences? *Neurotoxicology and Teratology, 15,* 281–286.

Hyams, K. C., Wignall, F. S., & Roswell, R. (1996). War syndromes and their evaluation: From the U.S. Civil War to the Persian Gulf War. *Annals of Internal Medicine, 125,* 398–405.

Hyman, I. E., Jr., & Loftus, E. F. (1997). Some people recover memories of childhood trauma that never really happened. In P. S. Appelbaum & L. A. Uyehara (Eds.), *Trauma and memory: Clinical and legal controversies* (pp. 3–24). New York: Oxford University Press.

I

Iaboni, F., Douglas, V. I., & Baker, A. G. (1995). Effects of reward and response costs on inhibition in ADHD children. *Journal of Abnormal Psychology, 104,* 232–240.

Iacono, W. G., Moreau, M., Beiser, M., Fleming, J. A. E., & Lin, T. Y. (1992). Smooth-pursuit eye tracking in first-episode psychotic patients and their relatives. *Journal of Abnormal Psychology, 101,* 104–116.

Insel, R. R., Ninan, P. T., Aloi, J., Jimerson, D. C., Skolnick, P., & Paul, S. M. (1984). A benzodiazepine receptor mediated model of anxiety. *Archives of General Psychiatry, 41,* 741–750.

Irons, R. R. (1996). Comorbidity between violence and addictive disease. *Sexual Addiction and Compulsivity, 3,* 85–96.

Isometsä, E. T., Heikkinen, M. E., Marttunen, M. J., Henriksson, M. M., Aro, H. M., & Lönnqvist, J. K. (1995). The last appointment before: Is suicide intent communicated? *American Journal of Psychiatry, 152,* 919–922.

J

Jack, C. R., Jr., Petersen, R. C., Xu, Y. C., O'Brien, P. C., Waring, S. C., Tangalos, E. G., Smith, G. E., Ivnik, R. J., Thibodeau, S. N., & Kokmen, E. (1998). Hippocampal atrophy and apolipoprotein E genotype are independently associated with Alzheimer's disease. *Annals of Neurology, 43,* 303–310.

Jacobs, G. D., Benson, H., & Friedman, R. (1996). Perceived benefits in a behavioral-medicine insomnia program: A clinical report. *American Journal of Medicine, 100,* 212–216.

Jacobson, J. L., Jacobson, S. W., Sokol, R. J., & Ager, J. W., Jr. (1998). Relation of maternal age and pattern of pregnancy drinking to functionally significant cognitive deficit in infancy. *Alcoholism, Clinical & Experimental Research, 22,* 345–351.

Jacobson, N. S., Dobson, K. S., Fruzetti, A. E., Schmaling, K. B., & Salusky, S. (1991). Marital therapy as a treatment for depression. *Journal of Consulting and Clinical Psychology, 59,* 547–557.

Janoff-Bulman, R. (1992). *Shattered assumptions: Towards a new psychology of trauma.* New York: Free Press.

Janofsky, J. S., Spears, S., & Neubauer, D. N. (1988). Psychiatrists' accuracy in predicting violent behavior on an inpatient unit. *Hospital and Community Psychiatry, 39,* 1090–1094.

Janszky, I., Szedmak, S., Istok, R., & Kopp, M. (1997). Possible role of sweating in the pathophysiology of panic attacks. *International Journal of Psychophysiology, 27,* 249–252.

Jenike, M. A., Baer, L., Ballantine, T., Martuz, R. L., Tynes, S., Giriunas, I., Buttolph, L., & Cassem, H. N. (1991). Cingulotomy for refractive obsessive-compulsive disorder. *Archives of General Psychiatry, 48,* 548–555.

Jenike, M. A., Baer, L., & Minichiello, W. E. (1986). *Obsessive-compulsive disorders.* Littleton, MA: PSG.

Jenkins, C. D. (1995). An integrated behavioral medicine approach to improving care of patients with diabetes mellitus. *Behavioral Medicine, 21,* 53–65.

Jensen, A. R. (1987). Differential psychology: Towards consensus. In S. Modgil & C. Modgil (Eds.), *Arthur Jensen: Consensus and controversy* (pp. 353–399). New York: Falmer Press.

Jimerson, D. C., Wolfe, B. E., Metzger, E. D., Finkelstein, D. M., Cooper, T. B., & Levine, J. M. (1997). Decreased serotonin function in bulimia nervosa. *Archives of General Psychiatry, 54,* 529–534.

Joe, G. W., Simpson, D. D., & Broome, K. M. (1998). Effects of readiness for drug abuse treatment on client retention and assessment of process. *Addiction, 93,* 1177–1190.

Johnson, J. C., Gottlieb, G. L., Sullivan, E., Wanich, C., Kinosian, B., Forciea, M. A., Sims, R., & Hogue, C. (1990). Using DSM-III criteria to diagnose delirium in elderly general medical patients. *Journal of Gerontology: Medical Sciences, 45,* M113–119.

Johnson, J. C., Weissman, M. M., & Klerman, G. L. (1990). Panic disorder, comorbidity, and suicide attempts. *Archives of General Psychiatry, 47,* 805–808.

Johnson, N. P., & Chappel, J. N. (1994). Using AA and other 12-step programs more effectively. *Journal of Substance Abuse Treatment, 11,* 137–142.

Johnston, L. D., O'Malley, P. M., & Bachman, J. G. (in preparation). *National survey results on drug use from the Monitoring the Future study, 1975–1998. Volume I: Secondary school students.* (NIH Publication No.). Rockville, MD: National Institute on Drug Abuse.

Jones, E. (1953). *The life and work of Sigmund Freud: The formative years and the great discoveries.* New York: Basic Books.

Jones, M. K., & Menzies, R. G. (1997). The cognitive mediation of obsessive-compulsive handwashing. *Behaviour Research and Therapy, 35,* 843–850.

Jones, V. F., Badgett, J. T., Minella, J. L., & Schuschke, L. A. (1993). The role of the male caretaker in Munchausen syndrome by proxy. *Clinical Pediatrics, 32,* 245–247.

Jordan, B. K., Schlenger, W. E., Fairbank, J. A., & Caddell, J. M. (1996). Prevalence of psychiatric disorders among incarcerated women. II. Convicted felons entering prison. *Archives of General Psychiatry, 53,* 513–519.

Julin, P., Almkvist, O., Basun, H., Lannfelt, L., Svensson, L., Winblad, B., & Wahlund, L. O. (1998). Brain volumes and regional cerebral blood flow in carriers of the Swedish Alzheimer amyloid protein mutation. *Alzheimer's Disease and Associated Disorders, 12,* 49–53.

Jung, C. G. (1916). General aspects of dream psychology. In H. Read, M. Fordham, & G. Alder (Eds.), *The collected works of C. G. Jung.* (Vol. 8, pp. 237–280). Princeton, NJ: Princeton University Press.

Jung, C. G. (1961). *Memories, dreams, reflections.* New York: Pantheon.

K

Kahn, M. (1991). *Between therapist and client: The new relationship.* New York: W. H. Freeman.

Kalra, S., Bergeron, C., & Lang, A. E. (1996). Lewy body disease and dementia. A review. *Archives of Internal Medicine, 156,* 487–493.

Kandel, D., Chen, K., Warner, L. A., Kessler, R. C., & Grant, B. (1997). Prevalence and demographic correlates of symptoms of last year dependence on alcohol, nicotine, marijuana and cocaine in the U.S. population. *Drug and Alcohol Dependence, 44,* 11–29.

Kanner, L. (1943). Autistic disturbances of affective contact. *Nervous Child, 2,* 217–250.

Kaplan, H. S. (1979). *Disorders of sexual desire: The new sex therapy* (Vol. 2). New York: Brunner/Mazel.

Kaplan, H. S. (1983). *The evaluation of sexual disorders: Psychological and medical aspects.* New York: Brunner/Mazel.

Kaplan, H. S. (1986). Psychosexual dysfunctions. In A. M. Cooper, A. J. Frances, & M. H. Sacks (Eds.), *The personality disorders and neuroses* (pp. 467–479). New York: Basic Books.

Kaplan, H. S. (1998). Ernie: A complicated case of premature ejaculation. In R. P. Halgin & S. K. Whitbourne (Eds.), *A casebook in abnormal psychology: From the files of experts* (pp. 128–142). New York: Oxford University Press.

Kapp, M. B. (1994). Treatment and refusal rights in mental health: Therapeutic justice and clinical accommodation. *American Journal of Orthopsychiatry, 64,* 223–234.

Kardiner, A., & Spiegel, H. (1947). *War stress and neurotic illness* (2nd ed.) New York: P. E. Hoeber.

Karon, B. P. (1995). Provision of psychotherapy under managed health care: A growing crisis and national nightmare. *Professional Psychology: Research and Practice, 26,* 5–9.

Katon, W., Von Korff, M., Lin, E., Walker, E., Simon, G. E., Bush T., Robinson, P., & Russo, J. (1995). Collaborative management to achieve treatment guidelines. *Journal of the American Medical Association, 273,* 1026–1031.

Katschnig, H., & Amering, M. (1994). The long-term course of panic disorder. In B. E. Wolfe & J. D. Maer (Eds.), *Treatment of panic disorder. A consensus development conference.* Washington, DC: American Psychiatric Press.

Katzelnick, D. J., Kobak, K. A., Greist, J. H., Jefferson, J. W., Mantle, J. M., & Serlin, R. C. (1995). Sertraline for social phobia: A double-blind, placebo-controlled crossover study. *American Journal of Psychiatry, 152,* 1368–1371.

Kavanagh, D. J. (1992). Recent developments in expressed emotion and schizophrenia. *British Journal of Psychiatry, 160,* 601–620.

Kavoussi, R., Armstead, P., & Coccaro, E. (1997). The neurobiology of impulsive aggression. *Psychiatric Clinics of North America, 20,* 395–403.

Kawas, C., Resnick, S., Morrison, A., Brookmeyer, R., Corrada, M., Zonderman, A., Bacal, C., Lingle, D. D., & Metter, E. (1997). A prospective study of estrogen replacement therapy and the risk of developing Alzheimer's disease: The Baltimore Longitudinal Study of Aging. *Neurology, 48,* 1517–1521.

Kaye, J., & Robinson, K. M. (1994). Spirituality among caregivers. *Image: Journal of Nursing Scholarship, 26,* 218–221.

Kaye, M. B., Weltzin, T. E., Hsu, L. K. G., Sokol, M. S., McConana, C., & Piotnicov, K. H. (1997, May 17–22). *Relapse prevention with fluoxetine in anorexia nervosa: A double-blind placebo-controlled study. (Abstract).* Paper presented at the 150th Annual Meeting of the American Psychiatric Association, San Diego.

Kaye, W. H., Weltzin, T. E., Hsu, L. K. G., & Bulik, C. M. (1991). An open trial of fluoxetine in patients with anorexia nervosa. *Journal of Clinical Psychiatry, 52,* 464–471.

Kazdin, A. E., & Weisz, J. R. (1998). Identifying and developing empirically supported child and adolescent treatments. *Journal of Consulting and Clinical Psychology, 66,* 19–36.

Keck, P. E., & McElroy, S. L. (1998). Pharmacologic treatment of bipolar disorders. In P. E. Nathan & J. M. Gorman (Eds.), *A guide to treatments that work* (pp. 249–269). New York: Oxford University Press.

Keefe, R. S., Silverman, J. M., Mohs, R. C., Siever, L. J., Harvey, P. D., Friedman, L., Roitman, S. E., DuPre, R. L., Smith, C. J., Schmeidler, J., & Davis, L. L. (1997). Eye tracking, attention, and schizotypal symptoms in nonpsychotic relatives of patients with schizophrenia. *Archives of General Psychiatry, 54,* 169–176.

Kehrer, C. A., & Linehan, M. M. (1996). Interpersonal and emotional problem solving skills and parasuicide among women with borderline personality disorder. *Journal of Personality Disorders, 10,* 153–163.

Keith, S. J., Regier, D. A., & Rae, D. S. (1991). Schizophrenic disorders. In L. N. Robins & D. A. Regier (Eds.), *Psychiatric disorders in America* (pp. 33–52).

Keller, M. B., Herzog, D. B., Lavori, P. W., Bradburn, I. S., & Mahoney, E. M. (1995). A prospective study of outcome in bulimia nervosa and the long-term effects of three psychological treatments. *Archives of General Psychiatry, 52,* 304–312.

Keller, M. B., Klein, D. N., Hirschfield, R. M. A., Kocsis, J. H., McCullough, J. P., Miller, I., First, M. B., Holzer, C. P. I., Keitner, G. I., Marin, D. B., & Shea, T. (1995). Results of the DSM-IV mood disorders field trial. *American Journal of Psychiatry, 152,* 843–849.

Keller, M. B., Lavori, P. W., Wunder, J., Beardslee, W. R., Schwartz, C. E., & Roth, J. (1992). Chronic course of anxiety disorders in children and adolescents. *Journal of the American Academy of Child and Adolescent Psychiatry, 31,* 595–599.

Kemperman, I., Russ, M. J., & Shearin, E. (1997). Self-injurious behavior and mood regulation in borderline patients. *Journal of Personality Disorders, 11,* 146–157.

Kendler, K. S., Davis, C. G., & Kessler, R. C. (1997). The familial aggregation of common psychiatric and substance use disorders in the National Comorbidity Survey: A family history study. *British Journal of Psychiatry, 170,* 541–548.

Kendler, K. S., & Diehl, S. R. (1993). The genetics of schizophrenia: A current, genetic-epidemiologic perspective. *Schizophrenia Bulletin, 19,* 261–285.

Kendler, K. S., Kessler, R. C., Walters, E. E., MacLean, C., Neale, M. C., Heath, A. C., & Eaves, L. J. (1995). Stressful life events, genetic liability, and onset of an episode of major depression in women. *American Journal of Psychiatry, 152,* 833–842.

Kendler, K. S., Neale, M. C., Kessler, R. C., Heath, A. C. & Eaves, L. J. (1993). A longitudinal twin study of 1-year prevalence of major depression in women. *Archives of General Psychiatry, 50,* 843–852.

Kendler, K. S., Neale, M. C., & Walsh, D. (1995). Evaluating the spectrum concept of schizophrenia in the Roscommon Family Study. *American Journal of Psychiatry, 152,* 749–754.

Kennedy, B. L., & Schwab, J. J. (1997). Utilization of medical specialists by anxiety disorder patients. *Psychosomatics, 38,* 109–112.

Kennedy, S. H., McVey, G., & Katz, R. (1990). Personality disorders in anorexia nervosa and bulimia nervosa. *Journal of Psychiatric Research, 24,* 259–269.

Kernberg, O. F. (1967). Borderline personality organization. *Journal of the American Psychoanalytic Association, 15,* 641–685.

Kernberg, O. F. (1984). *Severe personality disorders: Psychotherapeutic strategies.* New Haven, CT: Yale University Press.

Kernberg, O. F., Selzer, M. A., Koenigsberg, H. W., Carr, A. C., & Applebaum, A. H. (1989). *Psychodynamic psychotherapy of borderline patients.* New York: Basic Books.

Kerr, G., & Goss, J. (1996). The effects of a stress management program on injuries and stress levels. *Journal of Applied Sport Psychology, 8,* 109–117.

Kessler, R. C. (1997). The prevalence of psychiatric comorbidity. In S. Wetzler & W. C. Sanderson (Eds.), *Treatment strategies for patients with psychiatric comorbidity* (pp. 23–48). New York: Wiley.

Kessler, R. C., McGonagle, K. A., Zhao, S., Nelson, C. B., Hughes, M., Eshleman, S., Wittchen, H., & Kendler, K. S. (1994). Lifetime and 12-month prevalence of DSM-III-R psychiatric disorders in the United States: Results from the National Comorbidity Survey. *Archives of General Psychiatry, 51,* 8–19.

Kessler, R. C., Sonnega, A., Bromet, E., Hughes, M., & Nelson, C. B. (1995). Post-traumatic stress disorder in the National Comorbidity Survey. *Archives of General Psychiatry, 52,* 1048–1060.

Kessler, R. C., Stein, M. B., & Berglund, P. (1998). Social phobia subtypes in the National Comorbidity Survey. *American Journal of Psychiatry, 155,* 613–619.

Kety, S. S., Rosenthal, D., Wender, P. H., & Schulsinger, F. (1968). The types and prevalence of mental illness in the biological and adoptive families of adopted schizophrenics. In D. Rosenthal & S. S. Kety (Eds.), *The transmission of schizophrenia* (pp. 345–362). New York: Pergamon.

Keuthen, N. J., O'Sullivan, R. L., Goodchild, P., Rodriguez, D., Jenike, M. A., & Baer, L. (1998). Retrospective review of treatment outcome for 63 patients with trichotillomania. *American Journal of Psychiatry, 155,* 560–561.

Kilpatrick, K. L., & Williams, L. M. (1997). Post-traumatic stress disorder in child witnesses to domestic violence. *American Journal of Orthopsychiatry, 67,* 639–644.

Kim, E., & Rovner, B. W. (1994). Depression in dementia. *Psychiatric Annals, 24,* 173–177.

King, M. B. (1993). Cultural aspects of eating disorders. *International Review of Psychiatry, 5,* 205–216.

Kingdon, D., Turkington, D., & John, C. (1994). Cognitive behaviour therapy of schizophrenia: The amenability of delusions and hallucinations to reasoning. *British Journal of Psychiatry, 164,* 581–587.

Kinney, J. M., & Stephens, M. A. P. (1989). Hassles and uplifts of giving care to a family member with dementia. *Psychology and Aging, 4,* 402–408.

Kinsey, A. C., Pomeroy, W. B., & Martin, C. E. (1948). *Sexual behavior in the human male.* Philadelphia: Saunders.

Kinsey, A. C., Pomeroy, W. B., Martin, C. E., & Gebhard, P. H. (1953). *Sexual behavior in the human female.* Philadelphia: Saunders.

Kirk, S. A., & Kutchins, H. (1992). *The selling of DSM: The rhetoric of science in psychiatry.* New York: A. de Gruyter.

Kirkpatrick, B., & Buchanan, R. W. (1990). The neural basis of the deficit syndrome of schizophrenia. *The Journal of Nervous and Mental Disease, 178,* 545–553.

Kirmayer, L. J., Robbins, J. M., & Paris, J. (1994). Somatoform disorders: Personality and the social matrix of somatic distress. *Journal of Abnormal Psychology, 103,* 125–136.

Klein, D. F. (1981). Anxiety reconceptualized. In D. F. Klein & J. Raskin (Eds.), *Anxiety: New research and changing concepts* (pp. 235–263). New York: Raven Press.

Klein, D. F. (1993). False suffocation alarms, spontaneous panics, and related conditions: An integrative hypothesis. *Archives of General Psychiatry, 50,* 306–317.

Klein, D. F., & Hurowitz, G. I. (1998). Irene: A case of bipolar disorder. In R. P. Halgin S. K. Whitbourne (Eds.), *A casebook in abnormal psychology: From the files of experts.* New York: Oxford University Press.

References

Klein, D. F., & Ross, D. C. (1993). Reanalysis of the National Institute on Mental Health Treatment of Depression Collaborative Research Program general effectiveness report. *Neuropsychopharmacology, 8,* 241–251.

Klein, D. N., Norden, K. A., Ferro, T., Leader, J. B., Kasch, K. L., Klein, L. M., Schwartz, J. E., & Aronson, T. A. (1998). Thirty-month naturalistic follow-up study of early-onset dysthymic disorder: Course, diagnostic stability, and prediction of outcome. *Journal of Abnormal Psychology, 107,* 338–348.

Klein, I., & Janoff-Bulman, R. (1996). Trauma history and personal narratives: Some clues to coping among survivors of child abuse. *Child Abuse and Neglect, 20,* 45–54.

Klein, M. (1964). *Contributions to psychoanalysis.* New York: McGraw-Hill.

Kleinknecht, R. A., Dinnel, D. L., Kleinknecht, E. E., Hiruma, N., & Harada, N. (1997). Cultural factors in social anxiety: A comparison of social phobia symptoms and Taijin Kyofusho. *Journal of Anxiety Disorders, 11,* 157–177.

Klerman, G. L. (1987). Clinical epidemiology of suicide. *Journal of Clinical Psychiatry, 48,* 33–38.

Klerman, G. L., Weissman, M. M., Rounsaville, B. J., & Chevron, E. S. (1984). *Interpersonal psychotherapy of depression.* New York: Basic Books.

Kling, K. C., Seltzer, M. M., & Ryff, C. D. (1997). Distinctive late-life challenges: Implications for coping and well-being. *Psychology and Aging, 12,* 288–295.

Klosko, J. S., Barlow, D. H., Tassinari, R., & Cerny, J. A. (1990). A comparison of alprazolam and behavior therapy in treatment of panic disorder. *Journal of Consulting and Clinical Psychology, 58,* 77–84.

Kluft, R. P. (1984a). Aspects of the treatment of multiple personality disorder. *Psychiatric Annals, 14,* 51–55.

Kluft, R. P. (1984b). An introduction to multiple personality disorder. *Psychiatric Annals, 14,* 19–24.

Kluft, R. P. (1986). High functioning multiple personality disorders. *Journal of Nervous and Mental Disease, 174,* 722–726.

Kluft, R. P. (1987a). First-rank symptoms as a diagnostic clue to multiple personality disorder. *American Journal of Psychiatry, 144,* 293–298.

Kluft, R. P. (1987b). The simulation and dissimulation of multiple personality disorder. *American Journal of Clinical Hypnosis, 30,* 104–118.

Kluft, R. P. (1989). Playing for time: Temporizing techniques in the treatment of multiple personality disorder. *American Journal of Clinical Hypnosis, 32,* 90–98.

Kluft, R. P. (1997). The argument for the reality of delayed recall of trauma. In L. A. U. M. R. E. Paul S. Appelbaum (Ed.), *Trauma and memory: Clinical and legal controversies* (pp. 25–57). New York: Oxford University Press.

Kluft, R. P. (1998). Joe: A case of dissociative identity disorder. In R. P. Halgin & S. K. Whitbourne (Eds.), *A casebook in abnormal psychology: From the files of experts* (pp. 90–112). New York: Oxford University Press.

Kne, T., Shaw, M. W., Garfield, E. F., & Hicks, J. (1994). A program to address the needs of drug-exposed children. *Journal of School Health, 64,* 251–253.

Knight, R. (1953). Borderline states. *Bulletin of the Menninger Clinic, 17,* 1–12.

Koegel, L. K., Koegel, R. L., Hurley, C., & Frea, W. D. (1992). Improving pragmatic skills and disruptive behavior in children with autism through self-management. *Journal of Applied Behavior Analysis, 25,* 341–354.

Koegel, L. K., Valdez-Menchaca, M. C., & Koegel, R. L. (1994). Autism: Social communication difficulties and related behaviors. In V. B. V. Hasselt & M. Hersen (Eds.), *Advanced abnormal psychology* (pp. 165–187). New York: Plenum Press.

Koegel, R. L., O'Dell, M. C., & Koegel, L. K. (1987). A natural language paradigm for teaching non-verbal autistic children. *Journal of Autism and Developmental Disorders, 9,* 383–397.

Kohut, H. (1966). Forms and transformations of narcissism. *Journal of the American Psychoanalytic Association, 14,* 243–272.

Kohut, H. (1971). *The analysis of the self.* New York: International Universities Press.

Kohut, H. (1984). *How does analysis cure.* New York: International Universities Press.

Kolko, D. J., & Kazdin, A. E. (1991). Aggression and psychopathology in matchplaying and firesetting children: A replication and extension. *Journal of Clinical Child Psychology, 20,* 191–201.

Kolko, D. J., & Kazdin, A. E. (1994). Children's descriptions of their firesetting incidents: Characteristics and relationship to recidivism. *Journal of the American Academy of Child and Adolescent Psychiatry, 33,* 114–122.

Kolko, D. J., Watson, S., & Faust, J. (1991). Fire safety/prevention skills training to reduce involvement with fire in young psychiatric inpatients: Preliminary findings. *Behavior Therapy, 22,* 269–284.

Konner, M. (1994, October 2). Out of darkness. *New York Times Sunday Magazine,* 70–73.

Koocher, G. P. (1994). The commerce of professional psychology and the new ethics code. *Professional Psychology: Research and Practice, 25,* 355–361.

Koocher, G. P., & Keith-Spiegel, P. (1998). *Ethics in psychology: Professional standards and cases.* New York: Oxford University Press.

Kopelowicz, A., & Liberman, R. P. (1998). Psychosocial treatments for schizophrenia. In P. E. Nathan & J. M. Gorman (Eds.), *A guide to treatments that work* (pp. 190–211). New York: Oxford University Press.

Korpi, E. R., Kleinman, J. E., & Wyatt, R. J. (1988). GABA concentrations in forebrain areas of suicide victims. *Biological Psychiatry, 23,* 109–114.

Koski, L. R., & Shaver, P. R. (1997). Attachment and relationship satisfaction across the lifespan. In R. J. Sternberg & M. Hojjat (Eds.), *Satisfaction in close relationships* (pp. 26–55). New York, NY: The Guilford Press.

Krafft-Ebing, R. V. (1886/1950). *Psychopathia sexualis.* New York: Pioneer.

Kramer, P. D. (1993). *Listening to Prozac: A psychiatrist explores antidepressant drugs and the remaking of the self.* New York: Viking.

Krasuski, J. S., Alexander, G. E. Horwitz, B., Daly, E. M., Murphy, D. G., Rapoport, S. I., & Schapiro, M. B. (1998). Volumes of medial temporal lobe structures in patients with Alzheimer's disease and mild cognitive impairment (and in healthy controls). *Biological Psychiatry, 43,* 60–68.

Kremen, W. S., Seidman, L. S., Pepple, J. R., Lyons, M. J., Tsuang, M. T., & Faraone, S. V. (1994). Neuropsychological risk indicators for schizophrenia: A review of family studies. *Schizophrenia Bulletin, 20,* 103–119.

Krishnan, K. R. R., Davidson, J. R. T., & Guajardo, C. (1985). Trichotillomania—A review. *Comprehensive Psychiatry, 26,* 123–128.

Kropp, P., Gerber, W. D., Keinath-Specht, A., Kopal, T., & Niederberger, U. (1997). Behavioral treatment in migraine. Cognitive-behavioral therapy and blood-volume-pulse biofeedback: A cross-over study with a two-year follow-up. *Functional Neurology, 12,* 17–24.

Krupnick, J. L., Elkin, I., Collins, J., & Simmens, S. (1994). Therapeutic alliance and clinical outcomes in the NIMH Treatment of Depression Collaborative Research Program: Preliminary findings. *Psychotherapy, 31,* 28–35.

Kubany, E. S. (1994). A cognitive model of guilt typology in combat-related PTSD. *Journal of Traumatic Stress, 7,* 3–19.

Kuhl, V. (1994). The managed care revolution: Implications for humanistic psychotherapy. *Journal of Humanistic Psychology, 34,* 62–81.

Kuiper, B., & Cohen-Kettenis, P. (1988). Sex reassignment surgery: A study of 141 Dutch transsexuals. *Archives of Sexual Behavior, 17,* 439–457.

Kurita, H. (1997). A comparative study of Asperger syndrome with high-functioning atypical autism. *Psychiatry and Clinical Neurosciences, 51,* 67–70.

Kurtz, R. R., & Grummon, D. L. (1972). Different approaches to the measurement of therapist empathy and their relationship to therapy outcomes. *Journal of Consulting and Clinical Psychology, 39,* 106–115.

Kusumakar, V., Yatham, L. N., Haslam, D. R., Parikh, S. V., Matte, R., Silverstone, P. H., & Sharma, V. (1997). Treatment of mania, mixed state, and rapid cycling. *Canadian Journal of Psychiatry, 42,* 79S–85S.

Kutchins, H., & Kirk, S. A. (1997). DSM: *The psychiatric bible and the creation of mental disorders.* New York: Free Press.

L

Lader, M. (1994). Anxiolytic drugs: Dependence, addiction and abuse. *European Neuropsychopharmacology, 4,* 5–91.

Ladouceur, R., Dube, D., & Bujold, A. (1994). Prevalence of pathological gambling and related problems among college students in the Quebec metropolitan area. *Canadian Journal of Psychiatry, 29,* 289–293.

La Fond, J. Q. (1994). Law and the delivery of involuntary mental health services. *American Journal of Orthopsychiatry, 64,* 209–222.

La Fond, J. Q., & Durham, J. L. (1992). *Back to the asylum: The future of mental health law in the United States.* New York: Oxford University Press.

Lahey, B. B., Loeber, R., Hart, E. L., Frick, P. J., Applegate, B., Zhang, Q., Green, S. M., & Russo, M. F. (1995). Four-year longitudinal study of conduct disorder in boys: Patterns and predictors of persistence. *Journal of Abnormal Psychology, 104,* 83–93.

Laing, R. D. (1959). *The divided self.* New York: Penguin.

Laing, R. D., (1964). Is schizophrenia a disease? *International Journal of Social Psychiatry, 10,* 184–193.

Laird, L. K. (1995). Luvox joins growing list of approved obsessive-compulsive treatment. *Psychopharmacology Update, 6,* 1–2.

Lantz, P. M., House, J. S., Lepkowski, J. M., Williams, D. R., Mero, R. P., & Chen, J. (1998). Socioeconomic factors, health behaviors, and mortality: Results from a nationally representative prospective study of U.S. adults. *Journal of the American Medical Association, 279,* 1703–1708.

Lanyon, R. I. (1986). Theory and treatment of child molestation. *Journal of Consulting and Clinical Psychology, 54,* 176–182.

Laporte, L., & Guttman, H. (1996). Traumatic childhood experiences as risk factors for borderline and other personality disorders. *Journal of Personality Disorders, 10,* 247–259.

Lauer, J., Black, D. W., & Keen, P. (1993). Multiple personality disorder and borderline personality disorder: Distinct entities of variations on a common theme? *Annals of Clinical Psychiatry, 5,* 129–134.

Laumann, E. O., Gagnon, J. H., Michael, R. T., & Michaels, S. (1994). *The social organization of sexuality.* Chicago: University of Chicago Press.

Laumann, E. O., Paik, A., & Rosen, R. C. (1999). Sexual dysfunction in the United States. *Journal of the American Medical Association, 281,* 537–544.

Lavik, N. J., Hauff, E., Skrondal, A., & Solberg, O. (1996). Mental disorder among refugees and the impact of persecution and exile: Some findings from an out-patient population. *British Journal of Psychiatry, 169,* 726–732.

Lawrence, C. M., & Thelen, M. H. (1995). Body image, dieting, and self-concept: Their relation in African-American and Caucasian children. *Journal of Clinical Child Psychology, 24,* 41–48.

Lazarus, A. A. (1968). Learning theory and the treatment of depression. *Behaviour Research and Therapy, 6,* 83–89.

Lazarus, R. S., & Folkman, S. (1984). *Stress, appraisal, and coping.* New York: Springer.

Leavitt, F. (1997). False attribution of suggestibility to explain recovered memory of childhood sexual abuse following extended amnesia. *Child Abuse and Neglect, 21,* 265–272.

Lecci, L., Karoly, P., Ruehlman, L. S., & Lanyon, R. I. (1996). Goal-relevant dimensions of hypochondriacal tendencies and their relation to symptom manifestation and psychological distress. *Journal of Abnormal Psychology, 105,* 42–52.

Leckman, J. F., Grice, D. E., Boardman, J., Zhang, H., Vitale, A., Bondi, C., Alsobrook, J., Peterson, B. S., Cohen, D. J., Rasmussen, S. A., Goodman, W. K., McDougle, C. J., & Pauls, D. L. (1997). Symptoms of obsessive-compulsive disorder. *American Journal of Psychiatry, 154,* 911–917.

Lecrubier, Y., & Weiller, E. (1997). Comorbidities in social phobia. *International Clinical Psychopharmacology, 12,* S17–21.

Lee, H. S., Song, D. H., Kim, C. H., & Choi, H. K. (1996). An open clinical trial of fluoxetine in the treatment of premature ejaculation. *Journal of Clinical Psychopharmacology, 16,* 379–382.

Lee, K. A., Vaillant, G. E., Torrey, W. C., & Elder, G. H. (1995). A 50-year prospective study of the psychological sequelae of World War II combat. *American Journal of Psychiatry, 152,* 516–522.

Leff, J. (1977). International variations in the diagnosis of psychiatric illness. *British Journal of Psychiatry, 131,* 329–338.

Leff, J., & Vaughn, C. (1981). The role of maintenance therapy and relatives' expressed emotion in relapse of schizophrenia: A two-year follow-up. *British Journal of Psychiatry, 139,* 102–104.

Leibenluft, E., Moul, D. E., Schwartz, P. J., Madder, P. A., & Wehr, T. A. (1993). A clinical trial of sleep deprivation in combination with antidepressant medication. *Psychiatry Research, 46,* 213–227.

Lenzenweger, M. F., Loranger, A. W., Korfine, L., & Neff, C. (1997). Detecting personality disorders in a nonclinical population. Application of a 2-stage procedure for case identification. *Archives of General Psychiatry, 54,* 345–351.

Leon, G. R., Fulkerson, J. A., Perry, C. L., & Early-Zald, M. B. (1995). Prospective analysis of personality and behavioral vulnerabilities and gender influences in the later development of disordered eating. *Journal of Abnormal Psychology, 104,* 140–149.

Lerner, M., & Remen, R. N. (1987). Tradecraft of the Commonweal Cancer Help Program. *Advances, 4,* 11–25.

Leserman, J., Petitto, J. M., Perkins, D. O., Folds, J. D., Golden, R. N., & Evans, D. L. (1997). Severe stress, depressive symptoms, and changes in lymphocyte subsets in human immunodeficiency virus-infected men. A 2-year follow-up study. *Archives of General Psychiatry, 54,* 279–285.

Lester, D. (1993). The effectiveness of suicide prevention centers. *Suicide and Life Threatening Behavior, 23,* 263–267.

Levant, R. (1998). Assessing and treating normative male alexythymia. In G. P. Koocher, J. C. Norcross, & S. S. Hill (Eds.), *Psychologists' desk reference* (pp. 330–333). New York: Oxford University Press.

Levenson, J. L., & Bemis, C. (1991). The role of psychological factors in cancer onset and progression. *Psychosomatics, 32,* 124–132.

Levkoff, S. E., Liptzin, B., Evans, D. A., & Cleary, P. D. (1994). Progression and resolution of delirium in elderly patients hospitalized for acute care. *American Journal of Geriatric Psychiatry, 2,* 230–238.

Lewinsohn, P. M., & Shaw, D. (1969). Feedback about interpersonal behavior as an agent of behavior change: A case study in the treatment of depression. *Psychotherapy and Psychosomatics, 17,* 82–88.

Lewis, D. O., Yeager, C. A., Swica, Y., Pincus, J. H., & Lewis, M. (1997). Objective documentation of child abuse and dissociation in 12 murderers with dissociative identity disorder. *American Journal of Psychiatry, 154,* 1703–1710.

Lewy, A. J., Bauer, V. K., Cutler, N. L., Sack, R. L., Ahmed, S., Thomas, K. H., Blood, M. L., & Latham Jackson, J. M. (1998). Morning vs. evening light treatment of patients with winter depression. *Archives of General Psychiatry, 55,* 890–896.

Liberman, R. P., Massel, H. K., Mosk, M. D., & Wong, S. E. (1985). Social skills training for chronic mental patients. *Hospital and Community Psychiatry, 36,* 396–403.

Liddle, P. F., Friston, K. J., Frith, C. D., Hirsch, S. R., Jones, T., & Frackowiak, R. S. (1992). Patterns of cerebral blood flow in schizophrenia. *British Journal of Psychiatry, 160,* 179–186.

Lidz, T. (1946). Nightmares and combat neuroses. *Psychiatry, 9,* 37–49.

Liebowitz, M. R., Fyer, A. J., Gorman, J. M., Dillon, D., Appleby, I. L., Levy, G., Anderson, S., Levitt, M., Palij, M., Davies, S. O., & Klein, D. F. (1984). Lactate provocation of panic attacks: I. Clinical behavioral findings. *Archives of General Psychiatry, 31,* 764–770.

Lima, B. R., Pai, S., Santacruz, H., & Lozano, J. (1991). Psychiatric disorders among poor victims following a major disaster: Armero, Colombia. *Journal of Nervous and Mental Disease, 179,* 420–427.

References

Lin, A. S., Chen, C. H., Hwu, H. G., Lin, H. N., & Chen, J. A. (1998). Psychopathological dimensions in schizophrenia: A correlational approach to items of the SANS and SAPS. *Psychiatry Research, 77,* 121–130.

Lin, M. W., Sham, P., Hwu, H. G., Collier, D., Murray, R., & Powell, J. F. (1997). Suggestive evidence for linkage of schizophrenia to markers on chromosome 13 in Caucasian but not Oriental populations. *Human Genetics, 99,* 417–420.

Linehan, M. M. (1993a). *Cognitive-behavioral treatment of borderline personality disorder.* New York: Guilford Press.

Linehan, M. M. (1993b). *Skills training manual for treating borderline personality disorder.* New York: Guilford Press.

Linscheid, T. R., Iwata, B. A., Ricketts, R. W., Williams, D. E., & Griffin, J. C. (1990). Clinical evaluation of the self-injurious behavior inhibiting system (SIBIS). *Journal of Applied Behavior Analysis, 23,* 53–78.

Lion, J. R. (1992). The intermittent explosive disorder. *Psychiatric Annals, 22,* 64–66.

Liotti, L. (1994). *Cognitive therapies in action: Evolving innovative practice.* San Francisco: Jossey Bass.

Lipowski, Z. J. (1988). Somatization: The concept and its clinical application. *American Journal of Psychiatry, 145,* 1358–1368.

Litwack, T. R., Kirschner, S. M., & Wack, R. C. (1993). The assessment of dangerousness and prediction of violence: Recent research and future prospects. *Psychiatric Quarterly, 64,* 245–273.

Livesley, W. J., Schroeder, M. L., & Jackson, D. N. (1990). Dependent personality disorder and attachment problems. *Journal of Personality Disorders, 4,* 131–140.

Livesley, W. J., Schroeder, M. L., Jackson, D. N., & Jang, K. L. (1994). Categorical distinctions in the study of personality disorder: Implications for classification. *Journal of Abnormal Psychology, 103,* 6–17.

Lochman, J. E., & Dodge, K. A. (1994). Social-cognitive processes of severely violent, moderately aggressive, and nonaggressive boys. *Journal of Consulting and Clinical Psychology, 62,* 366–374.

Loeber, R. (1982). The stability of antisocial and delinquent child behavior: A review. *Child Development, 53,* 1431–1446.

Loeber, R. (1991). Adolescent behavior: More enduring than changeable? *Journal of the American Academy of Child and Adolescent Psychiatry, 30,* 393–397.

Loewenstein, R. J. (1990). Somatoform disorders in victims of incest and child abuse. In P. K. Richard (Ed.), *Incest-related syndromes of adult psychopathology* (pp. 75–111). Washington, DC: American Psychiatric Press.

Loftus, E. F. (1993a). Psychologists in the eyewitness world. *American Psychologist, 48,* 550–552.

Loftus, E. F. (1993b). The reality of repressed memories. *American Psychologist, 48,* 518–537.

Logue, M. B., Sher, K. J., & Frensch, P. A. (1992). Purported characteristics of adult children of alcoholics: A possible "Barnum" effect. *Professional Psychology: Research and Practice, 23,* 226–232.

Lonigan, C. J., Shannon, M. P., Taylor, C. M., Finch, A. J., Sallee, F. R. (1994). Children exposed to disaster: II. Risk factors for the development of post-traumatic symptomatology. *Journal of the American Academy of Child and Adolescent Psychiatry, 33,* 94–105.

Lopez Viets, V. C., & Miller, W. R. (1997). Treatment approaches for pathological gamblers. *Clinical Psychology Review, 17,* 689–702.

LoPiccolo, J., & Stock, W. E. (1986). Treatment of sexual dysfunction. *Journal of Consulting and Clinical Psychology, 54,* 158–167.

Loranger, A. W., Sartorius, N., Andreoli, A., Berger, P., Buchheim, P., Channabasavanna, S. M., Coid, B., Dahl, A., Diekstra, R. F. W., Ferguson, B., Jacobsberg, L. B., Mombour, W., Pull, C., Ono, Y., & Regier, D. A. (1994). The International Personality Disorder Examination. *Archives of General Psychiatry, 51,* 215–224.

Lovaas, O. I. (1977). *The autistic child: Language development through behavior modification.* New York: Irvington.

Lovaas, O. I. (1981). *Teaching developmentally disabled children.* Baltimore: University Park Press.

Lovaas, O. I. (1987). Behavior treatment and normal educational and intellectual functioning in young autistic children. *Journal of Consulting and Clinical Psychology, 55,* 3–9.

Luborsky, L. (1984). *Principles of psychoanalytic psychotherapy: A manual for supportive-expressive treatment.* New York: Basic Books.

Luntz, B. K., & Widom, C. S. (1994). Antisocial personality disorder in abused and neglected children grown up. *American Journal of Psychiatry, 151,* 670–674.

Lussier, R. G., Steiner, J., Grey, A., & Hansen, C. (1997). Prevalence of dissociative disorders in an acute care day hospital population. *Psychiatric Services, 48,* 244–246.

Lykken, D. I. (1957). A study of anxiety in the sociopathic personality. *Journal of Abnormal and Social Psychology, 55,* 6–10.

Lykken, D. T. (1995). *The antisocial personalities.* Hillsdale, NJ: Erlbaum.

Lykken, D. T. (1997). Incompetent parenting: Its causes and cures. *Child Psychiatry and Human Development, 27,* 129–137.

Lynam, D. R. (1997). Pursuing the psychopath: Capturing the fledgling psychopath in a nomological net. *Journal of Abnormal Psychology, 106,* 425–438.

Lyons, M. J., Toomey, R., Meyer, J. M., Green, A. I., Eisen, S. A., Goldberg, J., True, W. R., & Tsuang, M. T. (1997). How do genes influence marijuana use? The role of subjective effects. *Addiction, 92,* 409–417.

Lyons, M. J., True, W. R., Eisen, S. A., Goldberg, J., Meyer, J. M., Faraone, S. V., Eaves, L. J. & Tsuang, M. T. (1995). Differential heritability of adult and juvenile antisocial traits. *Archives of General Psychiatry, 52,* 906–915.

M

Maas, L. C., Harris, G. J., Satlin, A., English, C. D., Lewis, R. F., & Renshaw, P. F. (1997). Regional cerebral blood volume measured by dynamic susceptibility contrast MR imaging in Alzheimer's disease: A principal components analysis. *Journal of Magnetic Resonance Imaging, 7,* 215–219.

MacDonald, M. (1981). *Mystical bedlam: Madness, anxiety, and healing in seventeenth-century England.* New York: Cambridge University Press.

Maciak, B. J., Moore, M. T., Leviton, L. C., & Guinan, M. E. (1998). Preventing Halloween arson in an urban setting: A model for multisectoral planning and community participation. *Health Education & Behavior, 25,* 194–211.

Macksoud, M. S., & Aber, J. L. (1996). The war experiences and psychosocial development of children in Lebanon. *Child Development, 67,* 70–88.

Magnavita, N., Narda, R., Sani, L., Carbone, A., De Lorenzo, G., & Sacco, A. (1997). Type A behaviour pattern and traffic accidents. *British Journal of Medical Psychology, 70,* 103–107.

Maher, W. B., & Maher, B. A. (1985). Psychopathology: I. From ancient times to the eighteenth century. In G. A. Kimble & K. Schlesinger (Eds.), *Topics in the history of psychology* (Vol. 2, pp. 251–294). Hillsdale, NJ: Lawrence Erlbaum.

Mahler, M. (1971). A study of the separation-individuation process and its possible application to borderline phenomena in the psychoanalytic situation. *Psychoanalytic Study of the Child, 26,* 403–424.

Mahler, M., Bergman, A., & Pine, F. (1975). *The psychological birth of the infant: Symbiosis and individuation.* New York: Basic Books.

Mahler, M., & Gosliner, B. (1955). On symbiotic child psychosis: Genetic, dynamic and restitutive aspects. *Psychoanalytic Study of the Child, 10,* 195–212.

Mahler, M. S., & McDevitt, J. B. (1982). Thoughts on the emergence of the sense of self, with particular emphasis on the body self. *Journal of the American Psychoanalytic Association, 30,* 827–848.

Maier, S. F., & Seligman, M. E. P. (1976). Learned helplessness: Theory and evidence. *Journal of Experiment Psychology: General, 105,* 3–46.

Makela, K. (1994). Rates of attrition among the membership of Alcoholics Anonymous in Finland. *Journal of Studies on Alcohol, 55,* 91–95.

Malan, D. H. (1979). *Individual psychotherapy and the science of psychodynamics.* Boston: Butterworth.

Maldonado, J. R., Butler, L. D., & Spiegel, D. (1998). Treatments for dissociative disorders. In P. E. Nathan & J. M. Gorman (Eds.), *A guide to treatments that work* (pp. 423–446). New York: Oxford University Press.

Maletzky, B. M. (1997). Exhibitionism: Assessment and treatment. In R. D. Laws & W. T. O'Donohue (Eds.), *Sexual deviance: Theory, assessment, and treatment* (pp. 40–74). New York: Guilford Press.

Maletzky, B. M. (1998). The paraphilias: Research and treatment. In P. E. Nathan & J. M. Gorman (Eds.), *A guide to treatments that work* (pp. 472–500). New York: Oxford University Press.

Malgady, R. G., Constantino, G., & Rogler, L. H. (1984). Development of a thematic apperception test (TEMAS) for urban hispanic children. *Journal of Consulting and Clinical Psychology, 52,* 986–996.

Malmberg, A., Lewis, G., David, A., & Allebeck, P. (1998). Premorbid adjustment and personality in people with schizophrenia. *British Journal of Psychiatry, 172,* 308–313.

Mannuzza, S., Klein, R. G., Bessler, A., Malloy, P., & LaPadula, M. (1998). Adult psychiatric status of hyperactive boys grown up. *American Journal of Psychiatry, 155,* 493–498.

Mansueto, C. S., Stemberger, R. M., Thomas, A. M., & Golomb, R. G. (1997). Trichotillomania: A comprehensive behavioral model. *Clinical Psychology Review, 17,* 567–577.

Marazziti, D., Rotondo, A., Martini, C., Giannaccini, G., Lucacchini, A., Pancioli-Guadagnucci, M. L., Diamond, B. I., Borison, R., & Cassano, G. B. (1994). Changes in peripheral benzodiazepine receptors in patients with panic disorder and obsessive-compulsive disorder. *Neuropsychobiology, 29,* 8–11.

Marcantonio, E. R., Juarez, G., Goldman, L., Mangione, C. M., Ludwig, L. E., Lind, L., Katz, N., Cook, E. F., Orav, E. J., Lee, T. H. (1994). The relationship of postoperative delirium with psychoactive medications. *Journal of the American Medical Association, 272,* 1518–1522.

Marcos, L. R., & Cohen, N. L. (1986). Taking the suspected mentally ill off the streets to public general hospitals. *The New England Journal of Medicine, 315,* 1158–1161.

Margraf, J., Ehlers, A., & Roth, W. T. (1986). Biological models of panic disorder—A review. *Behavior Research and Therapy, 24,* 553–567.

Marino-Junior, R., & Cosgrove, G. R. (1997). Neurosurgical treatment of neuropsychiatric illness. *Psychiatric Clinics of North America, 20,* 933–943.

Markovitz, P. J., Calabrese, J. R., Schulz, S. C., & Meltzer, H. Y. (1991). Fluoxetine in the treatment of borderline and schizotypal personality disorders. *American Journal of Psychiatry, 148,* 1064–1067.

Marks, I. M. (1988). Blood-injury phobia: A review. *American Journal of Psychiatry, 145,* 1207–1213.

Marlatt, G. A. (1990). Cue exposure and relapse prevention in the treatment of addictive behaviors. *Addictive Behaviors, 15,* 395–399.

Marmar, C. R., Weiss, D. S., Schlenger-William, E., Fairbank, J. A., Jordan, B. K., Kulka, R. A., & Hough, R. L. (1994). Peritraumatic dissociation and post-traumatic stress in male Vietnam theater veterans. *American Journal of Psychiatry, 151,* 902–907.

Martin, R. L. (1992). Diagnostic issues for conversion disorder. *Hospital and Community Psychiatry, 43,* 771–773.

Martin, R. L., & Yutzy, S. H. (1996). Somatoform disorders. In R. E. Hales & S. C. Yudofsky (Eds.), *The American Psychiatric Press synopsis of psychiatry* (pp. 547–572). Washington, DC: American Psychiatric Press.

Marttunen, M. J., Aro, H. M., & Lonnqvist, J. K. (1993). Precipitant stressors in adolescent suicide. *Journal of the American Academy of Child and Adolescent Psychiatry, 32,* 1178–1183.

Masellis, M., Basile, V., Meltzer, H. Y., Lieberman, J. A., Sevy, S., Macciardi, F. M., Cola, P., Howard, A., Badri, F., Nothen, M. M., Kalow, W., & Kennedy, J. L. (1998). Serotonin subtype 2 receptor genes and clinical response to clozapine in schizophrenia patients. *Neuropsychopharmacology, 19,* 123–132.

Masling, J. (Ed.). (1983). Empirical studies of psychoanalytical theories (Vol. 1). Hillsdale, HJ: Analytic Press.

Maslow, A. (1954/1970). *Motivation and personality.* New York: Harper & Row.

Maslow, A. (1971). *The farther reaches of human nature.* New York: Viking.

Maslow, A. H. (1962). *Toward a psychology of being.* Princeton, NJ: Van Nostrand.

Massella, J. D. (1991). Intervention: Breaking the addiction cycle. In D. C. Daley & M. S. Raskin (Eds.), *Treating the chemically dependent and their families.* Newbury Park, CA: Sage Publications.

Masters, W. H., & Johnson, V. E. (1966). *Human sexual response.* Boston: Little, Brown.

Masters, W. H., & Johnson, V. E. (1970). *Human sexual inadequacy.* Boston: Little, Brown.

Masters, W. H., Johnson, V. E., & Kolodny, R. C. (1982). *Human sexuality.* Boston: Little, Brown.

Masterson, J. F. (1981). *The narcissistic and borderline disorders: An integrated developmental approach.* New York: Brunner/Mazel.

Masterson, J. F., & Klein, R. (1989). *Psychotherapy of the disorders of the self.* New York: Brunner/Mazel.

Matheny, J. C. H. (1998). Strategies for assessment and early treatment with sexually addicted families. *Sexual Addiction and Compulsivity, 5,* 27–48.

Maxmen, J. S., & War, N. G. (1995). *Psychotropic drugs fast facts* (2nd ed.). New York: Norton.

May, R. (1983). *The discovery of being: Writings in existential psychology.* New York: Norton.

Mayes, S. D., Crites, D. L., Bixler, E. O., Humphrey, F. J., & Mattison, R. E. (1994). Methylphenidate and ADHD: Influence of age, IQ and neurodevelopmental status. *Developmental Medicine and Child Neurology, 36,* 1099–1107.

McCabe, M. P. (1992). A program for the treatment of inhibited sexual desire in males. *Psychotherapy, 29,* 288–296.

McCarroll, J. E., Ursano, R. J., & Fullerton, C. S. (1993). Symptoms of post-traumatic stress disorder following recovery of war dead. *American Journal of Psychiatry, 150,* 1875–1877.

McCarroll, J. E., Ursano, R. J., & Fullerton, C. S. (1995) Symptoms of PTSD following recovery of war dead: 13–15 month follow-up. *American Journal of Psychiatry, 152,* 939–941.

McClearn, G. E., Vogler, G. P., & Plomin, R. (1996). Genetics and behavioral medicine. *Behavioral Medicine, 22,* 93–102.

McConaghy, N., Armstrong, M. S., & Blaszczynski, A. (1985). Expectancy, covert sensitization and imaginal desensitization in compulsive sexuality. *Acta Psychiatrica Scandinavica, 72,* 176–187.

McConaghy, N., Blaszczynski, A., & Frankova, A. (1991). Comparison of imaginal desensitization with other behavioural treatments of pathological gambling: A two- to nine-year follow-up. *British Journal of Psychiatry, 159,* 390–393.

McCullough-Vaillant, L. (1994). The next step in short-term dynamic psychotherapy: A clarification of objectives and techniques in an anxiety-regulating model. *Psychotherapy, 31,* 642–654.

McDaniel, J. S., Musselman, D. L., Porter, M. R., Reed, D. A., & Nemeroff, C. B. (1995). Depression in patients with cancer. Diagnosis, biology, and treatment. *Archives of General Psychiatry, 52,* 89–99.

McElroy, S. L., Hudson, J. I., Pope, H. G., Jr., Keck, P. E., Jr., & Aizley, H. G. (1992). The DSM-III-R impulse control disorders not elsewhere classified: Clinical characteristics and relationship to other psychiatric disorders. *American Journal of Psychiatry, 149,* 318–327.

McElroy, S. L., Keck, P. E., Pope, H. G., Smith, J. M. R., & Strakowski, S. M. (1994). Compulsive buying: A report of 20 cases. *Journal of Clinical Psychiatry, 55,* 242–248.

McElroy, S. L., Pope, H. G., Jr., Hudson, J. I., Keck, P. E., Jr., & White, K. L. (1991). Kleptomania: A report of 20 cases. *American Journal of Psychiatry, 148,* 652–657.

McElroy, S. L., Soutullo, C. A., Beckman, D. A., Taylor, P., Jr., & Keck, P. E., Jr. (1998). DSM-IV intermittent explosive disorder: A report of 27 cases. *Journal of Clinical Psychiatry, 59,* 203–210.

McGlashan, T. H. (1983). The borderline syndromes: II. Is it a variant of schizophrenia or affective disorder? *Archives of General Psychiatry, 40,* 1319–1323.

McGlashan, T. H., & Fenton, W. S. (1991). Classical subtypes for schizophrenia: Literature review for DSM-IV. *Schizophrenia Bulletin, 17,* 609–632.

McGlashan, T. H., & Williams, P. V. (1990). Predicting outcome in schizoaffective psychosis. *Journal of Nervous and Mental Disease, 178,* 518–520.

McGue, M., & Christensen, K. (1997). Genetic and environmental contributions to depression symptomatology: Evidence from Danish twins 75 years of age and older. *Journal of Abnormal Psychology, 106,* 439–448.

McGue, M., & Gottesman, I. I. (1989). Genetic linkage in schizophrenia: Perspectives from genetic epidemiology. *Schizophrenia Bulletin, 15,* 453–464.

McGue, M., Hirsch, B., & Lykken, D. T. (1993). Age and the self-perception of ability: A twin study analysis. *Psychology and Aging, 8,* 72–80.

McKay, D., Todaro, J., Neziroglu, F., & Campisi, T. (1997). Body dysmorphic disorder: A preliminary evaluation of treatment and maintenance using exposure with response prevention. *Behaviour Research and Therapy, 35,* 67–70.

McKhann, G., Drachman, D., Folstein, M., Katzman, R., Price, D., & Stadlan, E. M. (1984). Clinical diagnosis of Alzheimer's disease: Report of the NINCDS-ADRDA Work Group under the auspices of Department of Health and Human Services Task Force on Alzheimer's Disease. *Neurology, 34,* 939–944.

McLeod, C. C., Budd, M. A., & McClelland, D. C. (1997). Treatment of somatization in primary care. *General Hospital Psychiatry, 19,* 251–258.

McMahon, F. J., Hopkins, P. J., Xu, J., McInnis, M. G., Shaw, S., Cardon, L., Simpson, S. G., MacKinnon, D. F., Stine, O. C., Sherrington, R., Meyers, D. A., & DePaulo, J. R. (1997). Linkage of bipolar affective disorder to chromosome 18 markers in a new pedigree series. *American Journal of Human Genetics, 61,* 1397–1404.

McMahon, F. J., Stine, O. C., Chase, G. A., Meyers, D. A., Simpson, S. G., & DePaulo, J. R. J. (1994). Influence of clinical subtype, sex, and lineality on age at onset of major affective disorder in a family sample. *American Journal of Psychiatry, 151,* 210–215.

McMahon, R. J., & Wells, K. C. (1989). Conduct disorders. In E. J. Mash & R. A. Barkley (Eds.), *Treatment of childhood disorders* (pp. 73–132). New York: Guilford Press.

McNally, R. J. (1987). Preparedness and phobias: A review. *Psychological Bulletin, 101,* 283–303.

McNally, R. J. (1994). Choking phobia: A review of the literature. *Comprehensive Psychiatry, 35,* 83–89.

McNally, R. J., & Steketee, G. S. (1985). Etiology and maintenance of severe animal phobias. *Behavioral Research and Therapy, 23,* 431–435.

McNamara, M. E. (1991). Psychological factors affecting neurological conditions: Depression and stroke, multiple sclerosis, Parkinson's disease, and epilepsy. *Psychosomatics, 32,* 255–267.

McNaughton, M. E., Patterson, T. L., Smith, T. L., & Grant, I. (1995). The relationship among stress, depression, locus of control, irrational beliefs, social support, and health in Alzheimer's disease caregivers. *Journal of Nervous and Mental Disease, 183,* 78–85.

Meana, J. J., Barturen, F., Martin, I., & Garcia-Sevilla, J. A. (1993). Evidence of increased non-adrenoreceptor (-sup-3H)idazoxan binding sites in the frontal cortex of depressed suicide victims. *Biological Psychiatry, 34,* 498–501.

Meehl, P. E. (1962). Schizotaxia, schizotypy, schizophrenia. *American Psychologist, 17,* 827–828.

Meehl, P. E. (1990). Toward an integrated theory of schizotaxia, schizotypy, and schizophrenia. *Journal of Personality Disorders, 4,* 1–99.

Meichenbaum, D. (1985). *Stress inoculation training.* New York: Pergamon Press.

Meichenbaum, D. (1993). Changing conceptions of cognitive behavior modification: Retrospect and prospect. *Journal of Consulting and Clinical Psychology, 61,* 202–204.

Meichenbaum, D. (1998). Sheila and Karen: Two cases of post-traumatic stress. In R. P. Halgin & S. K. Whitbourne (Eds.), *A casebook in abnormal psychology: From the files of experts* (pp. 72–87). New York: Oxford University Press.

Melnick, M. (1997). Methodological errors in the prediction of ability. *American Psychologist, 52,* 72.

Mendlewicz, J., & Rainer, J. D. (1977). Adoption study supporting genetic transmission in manic-depressive illness. *Nature, 268,* 327–329.

Mercer, J. R. (1979). *The System of Multicultural Pluralistic Assessment: Conceptual and technical manual.* New York: Psychological Corporation.

Merckelbach, H., & Muris, P. (1997). The etiology of childhood spider phobia. *Behaviour Research and Therapy, 35,* 1031–1034.

Merskey, H. (1992). The manufacture of personalities: The production of multiple personality disorder. *British Journal of Psychiatry, 160,* 327–340.

Metalsky, G. I., Halberstadt, L. J., & Abramson, L. Y. (1987). Vulnerability to depressive mood reactions: Toward a more powerful test of the diathesis-stress and causal mediation components of the reformulated theory of depression. *Journal of Personality and Social Psychology, 52,* 386–393.

Meyer, A. (1957). *Psychobiology: A science of man.* Springfield, IL: Charles C Thomas Press.

Miller, B. C. (1995). Characteristics of effective day treatment programming for persons with borderline personality disorder. *Psychiatric Services, 46,* 605–608.

Miller, N. E., & Banuazizi, A. L. I. (1968). Instrumental learning by curarized rats of a specific visceral response, intestinal or cardiac. *Journal of Comparative and Physiological Psychology, 65,* 1–7.

Miller, N. E., & Dworkin, B. R. (1977). Effects of learning on visceral functions: Biofeedback. *New England Journal of Medicine, 296,* 1274–1278.

Miller, S. B., Dolgoy, L., Friese, M., & Sita, A. (1996). Dimensions of hostility and cardiovascular response to interpersonal stress. *Journal of Psychosomatic Research, 41,* 81–95.

Miller, T. Q., Smith, T. W., Turner, C. W., Guijarro, M. L., & Hallet, A. J. (1996). A meta-analytic review of research on hostility and physical health. *Psychological Bulletin, 119,* 322–348.

Millon, T. (1991). Classification in psychopathology: Rationale, alternatives, and standards. *Journal of Abnormal Psychology, 100,* 245–261.

Millon, T. (1993). *Manual for the Millon Adolescent Clinical Inventory.* Minneapolis: National Computer Systems.

Millon, T. (1994). *Manual for the Millon Clinical Multiaxial Inventory-III.* Minneapolis: National Computer Systems.

Millon, T. (1998). Ann: My first case of borderline personality disorder. In R. P. Halgin & S. K. Whitbourne (Eds.), *A casebook in abnormal psychology: From the files of experts* (pp. 8–22). New York: Oxford University Press

Millon, T. (1998b). DSM narcissistic personality disorder: Historical reflections and future directions. In E. F. Ronningstam (Ed.), *Disorders of narcissism: Diagnostic, clinical, and empirical implications* (pp. 75–101). Washington, DC: American Psychiatric Press.

Millon, T., & Davis, R. D. (1996). *Disorders of personality: DSM-IV and beyond* (2nd ed.). New York: John Wiley & Sons.

Millon, T., & Davis, R. D. (1997). The MCMI-III: Present and future directions. *Journal of Personality Assessment, 68,* 69–85.

Mintz, L. B., Kashubeck, S., & Tracy, L. S. (1995). Relations among parental alcoholism, eating disorders, and substance abuse in nonclinical college women: Additional evidence against the uniformity myth. *Journal of Counseling Psychology, 42,* 65–70.

Minuchin, S., Rosman, B. L., & Baker, L. (1978). *Psychosomatic families: Anorexia nervosa in context.* Cambridge, MA: Harvard University Press.

Mirin, S. M. (1994). *Substance abuse and psychopathology.* Washington, DC: American Psychiatric Press.

Mirsky, A. F., Kugelmass, S., Ingraham, L. J., Frenkel, E., & Nathan, M. (1995). Overview and summary: Twenty-five-year follow-up of high-risk children. *Schizophrenia Bulletin, 21,* 227–239.

Mirsky, A. F., & Quinn, O. W. (1988). The Genain quadruplets. *Schizophrenia Bulletin, 14,* 595–612.

Mitchell, J. (1974). *Psychoanalysis and feminism.* New York: Pantheon.

Mitchell, J. E., Specker, S. M., & deZwaan, M. (1991). Comorbidity and medical complications of bulimia nervosa. *Journal of Clinical Psychiatry, 52,* 13–20.

Mizes, J. S., & Christiano, B. A. (1995). Assessment of cognitive variables relevant to cognitive behavioral perspectives on anorexia nervosa and bulimia nervosa. *Behaviour Research and Therapy, 33,* 95–105.

Mohr, D. O., & Beutler, L. E. (1990). Erectile dysfunction: A review of diagnostic and treatment procedures. *Clinical Psychology Review, 10,* 123–150.

Moldin, S. O., & Gottesman, II. (1997). At issue: Genes, experience, and chance in schizophrenia-positioning for the 21st century. *Schizophrenia Bulletin, 23,* 547–561.

Monahan, J. (1981). *The clinical prediction of violent behavior.* Washington, DC: U.S. Government Printing Office.

Monahan, J. (1984). The prediction of violent behavior: Toward a second generation of theory and policy. *American Journal of Psychiatry, 141,* 10–15.

Monahan, J. (1993). Limiting therapist exposure to Tarasoff liability. *American Psychologist, 48,* 242–250.

Money, J. (1984). Paraphilias: Phenomenology and classification. *American Journal of Psychotherapy, 38,* 164–179.

Money, J., & Ehrhardt, A. (1973/1996). *Man and woman, boy and girl.* Northvale, NJ: Jason Aronson.

Montejo-Gonzales, A. L., Llorca, G., Izquierdo, J. A., Ledesma, A., Bousono, M., Calcedo, A., Carrasco, J. L., Ciudad, J., Daniel, E., De la Gandara, J., Derecho, J., Franco, M., Gomez, M. J., Macias, J. A., Martin, T., Perez, V., Sanchez, J. M., Sanchez, S., & Vicens, E. (1997). SSRI-induced sexual dysfunction: Fluoxetine, paroxetine, sertraline, and fluvoxamine in a prospective, multicenter, and descriptive clinical study of 344 patients. *Journal of Sex and Marital Therapy, 23,* 176–194.

Moore, J. M., Jr., Thompson-Pope, S. K., & Whited, R. M. (1996). MMPI-A profiles of adolescent boys with a history of firesetting. *Journal of Personality Assessment, 67,* 116–126.

Moos, R. H., Cronkite, R. C., & Moos, B. S. (1998). Family and extrafamily resources and the 10-year course of treated depression. *Journal of Abnormal Psychology, 107,* 450–460.

Moos, R. H., & Moos, B. S. (1986). *Family Environment Scale Manual* (2nd ed.). Palo Alto, CA: Consulting Psychologists Press.

Morgan, C. D., & Murray, H. A. (1935). A method for investigating fantasies: The Thematic Apperception test. *American Medical Association Archives of Neurology and Psychiatry, 34,* 289–306.

Morgenstern, J., Labouvie, E., McCrady, B. S., Kahler, C. W., & Frey, R. M. (1997). Affiliation with Alcoholics Anonymous after treatment: A study of its therapeutic effects and mechanisms of action. *Journal of Consulting and Clinical Psychology, 65,* 768–777.

Morgenstern, J., Langenbucher, J., Labouvie, E., & Miller, K. J. (1997). The comorbidity of alcoholism and personality disorders in a clinical population: Prevalence rates and relation to alcohol typology variables. *Journal of Abnormal Psychology, 106,* 74–84.

Morris, A., Baker, B., Devins, G. M., & Shapiro, C. M. (1997). Prevalence of panic disorder in cardiac outpatients. *Canadian Journal of Psychiatry, 42,* 185–190.

Mrazek, F. J. (1984). Sexual abuse of children. In B. Lahey & A. E. Kazdin (Eds.), *Advances in child clinical psychology* (Vol. 6, pp. 199–215). New York: Plenum Press.

Mueser, K. T., & Liberman, R. P. (1995). Behavior therapy in practice. In B. Bongar & L. E. Beutler (Eds.), *Comprehensive textbook of psychotherapy: Theory and practice* (pp. 84–110). New York: Oxford University Press.

Mukherjee, S., Sackeim, H. A., & Schnur, D. B. (1994). Electroconvulsive therapy of acute manic episodes: A review of 50 years' experience. *American Journal of Psychiatry, 151,* 169–176.

Munich, R. L. (1993). Conceptual issues in the psychoanalytic psychotherapy of patients with borderline personality disorder. In W. H. Sledge & A. Tasman (Eds.), *Clinical challenges in psychiatry* (pp. 61–88). Washington, DC: American Psychiatric Press.

Murphy, M. J., DeBernardo, C. R., & Shoemaker, W. E. (1998). Impact of managed care on independent practice and professional ethics: A survey of independent practitioners. *Professional Psychology: Research and Practice, 29,* 43–51.

Murray, H. A. (1938). *Explorations in personality.* New York: Oxford University Press.

Murray, H. A. (1943). *Thematic Apperception Test manual.* Cambridge, MA: Harvard University Press.

Myers, M. G., Stewart, D. G., & Brown, S. A. (1998). Progression from conduct disorder to antisocial personality disorder following treatment for adolescent substance abuse. *American Journal of Psychiatry, 155,* 479–485.

N

Naglieri, J. A. (1997). IQ: Knowns and unknowns: Hits and misses. *American Psychologist, 52,* 75–76.

Nagy, L. M., Morgan, C. A., Southwick, S. M., & Charney, D. S. (1993). Open prospective trial of fluoxetine for post-traumatic stress disorder. *Journal of Clinical Psychopharmacology, 13,* 107–113.

Najavits, L. M., Weiss, R. D., & Shaw, S. R. (1997). The link between substance abuse and post-traumatic stress disorder in women. A research review. *American Journal on Addictions, 6,* 273–283.

Narrow, W. E., Regier, D. A., Rae, D. S., Manderscheid, R. W., & Locke, B. Z. (1993). Use of services by persons with mental and addictive disorders: Findings from the National Institute of Mental Health Epidemiologic Catchment Area Program. *Archives of General Psychiatry, 50,* 95–107.

Nash, M. R., Hulsey, T. L., Sexton, M. C., Harralson, T. L., & Lambert, W. (1993). Long-term sequelae of childhood sexual abuse: Perceived family environment psychopathology, and dissociation. *Journal of Consulting and Clinical Psychology, 61,* 276–283.

Nassberger, L., & Traskman-Bendz, L. (1993). Increased soluble interleukin-2 receptor concentrations in suicide attempters. *Acta Psychiatrica Scandinavica, 88,* 48–52.

Nathan, P. E. (1998). Practice guidelines: Not yet ideal. *American Psychologist, 53,* 290–299.

National Highway Traffic Safety Administration. (1997). *Traffic safety facts, 1996: Alcohol.* Washington, DC: U.S. Department of Transportation, National Highway Traffic Safety Administration, National Center for Statistics and Analysis, Research, and Development.

National Institutes of Health. (1985). *Electroconvulsive therapy. NIH Consensus Statement* (5[11]: 1–23). Bethesda, MD.

Neisser, U. (1997). Never a dull moment. *American Psychologist, 52,* 79–81.

Nelson, E., & Rice, J. (1997). Stability of diagnosis of obsessive-compulsive disorder in the Epidemiologic Catchment Area study. *American Journal of Psychiatry, 154,* 826–831.

Nelson, J. C., & Davis, J. M. (1997). DST studies in psychotic depression: A meta-analysis. *American Journal of Psychiatry, 154,* 1497–1503.

Newman, J. P., Schmitt, W. A., & Voss, W. D. (1997). The impact of motivationally neutral cues on psychopathic individuals: Assessing the generality of the response modulation hypothesis. *Journal of Abnormal Psychology, 106,* 563–575.

Newsom, C., & Rincover, A. (1989). Autism. In E. J. Mash & R. A. Barkley (Eds.), *Treatment of childhood disorders* (pp. 286–346). New York: Guilford Press.

Neziroglu, F. A., & Yaryura-Tobias, J. A. (1993). Exposure, response prevention, and cognitive therapy in the treatment of body dysmorphic disorder. *Behavior Therapy, 24,* 431–438.

Nicholas, L. M., Tancer, M. E., Silva, S. G., Underwood, L. E., & Stabler, B. (1997). Short stature, growth hormone deficiency, and social anxiety. *Psychosomatic Medicine, 59,* 372–375.

NIDA. (1997) *NIDA research report—Heroin abuse and addiction* (NIH Publication No. 97–4165). Rockville, MD.

NIDA. (1998). *The economic costs of alcohol and drug abuse in the United States, 1992* (98–3478). Rockville, MD: National Institute on Drug Abuse.

Niederehe, G., & Schneider, L. S. (1998). Treatments for depression and anxiety in the aged. In P. E. Nathan & J. M. Gorman (Eds.), *A guide to treatments that work* (pp. 270–287). New York: Oxford University Press.

Nigg, J. T., Hinshaw, S. P., Carte, E. T., & Treuting, J. J. (1998). Neuropsychological correlates of childhood attention-deficit/hyperactivity disorder: Explainable by comorbid disruptive behavior or reading problems? *Journal of Abnormal Psychology, 107,* 468–480.

Nigg, J. T., Lohr, N. E., Westen, D., Gold, L. J., & Silk, K. R. (1992). Malevolent object representations in borderline personality disorder and major depression. *Journal of Abnormal Psychology, 101,* 61–67.

Ninan, P. T., Knight, B., Kirk, L., Rothbaum, B. O., Kelsey, J., & Nemeroff, C. B. (1998). A controlled trial of venlafaxine in trichotillomania: Interim phase I results. *Psychopharmacology Bulletin, 34,* 221–224.

Nolen-Hoeksema, S., Parker, L., & Larson, J. (1994). Ruminative coping with depressed mood following loss. *Journal of Personality and Social Psychology, 67,* 92–104.

Norcross, J. (1992). *Handbook of eclectic psychotherapy.* New York: Brunner/Mazel.

Nordin, V., & Gillberg, C. (1998). The long-term course of autistic disorders: Update on follow-up studies. *Acta Psychiatrica Scandinavica, 97,* 99–108.

North, C. S., Smith, E. M., & Spitznagel, E. L. (1994). Post-traumatic stress disorder in survivors of a mass shooting. *American Journal of Psychiatry, 151,* 82–88.

Nuechterlein, K. H., Dawson, M. E., Gitlin, M., Ventura, J., Goldstein, M. J., Snyder, K. S., Yee, C. M., & Mintz, J. (1992). Developmental processes in schizophrenic disorders: Longitudinal studies of vulnerability and stress. *Schizophrenia Bulletin, 18,* 387–425.

Nuechterlein, K. H., Gitlin, M. J., & Subotnik, K. L. (1995). The early course of schizophrenia and long-term maintenance neuroleptic therapy. *Archives of General Psychiatry, 52,* 203–205.

Nunes, E. V., Frank, K. A., & Kornfeld, D. S. (1987). Psychologic treatment for the Type A behavior pattern and for coronary heart disease: A meta-analysis of the literature. *Psychosomatic Medicine, 48,* 159–173.

O

O'Brien, C. P., Childress, A. R., Ehrman, R., & Robbins, S. J. (1998). Conditioning factors in drug abuse: Can they explain compulsion? *Journal of Psychopharmacology, 12,* 15–22.

O'Connor, T. G., McGuire, S., Reiss, D., Hetherington, E. M., & Plomin, R. (1998). Co-occurrence of depressive symptoms and antisocial behavior in adolescence: A common genetic liability. *Journal of Abnormal Psychology, 107,* 27–37.

O'Connor v. Donaldson. (1975). 95 S. Ct. 2486.

Ogles, B. M., Lambert, M. J., & Sawyer, J. D. (1995). Clinical significance of the National Institute of Mental Health Treatment of Depression Collaborative Research Program data. *Journal of Consulting and Clinical Psychology, 64,* 321–326.

O'Halloran, R. L., & Dietz, P. E. (1993). Autoerotic fatalities with power hydraulics. *Journal of Forensic Sciences, 38,* 359–364.

Ohman, A., & Hultman, C. M. (1998). Electrodermal activity and obstetric complications in schizophrenia. *Journal of Abnormal Psychology, 107,* 228–237.

Okin, R. L. (1995). Testing the limits of deinstitutionalization. *Psychiatric Services, 46,* 73–78.

Okin, R. L., Borus, J. F., & Baer, L. (1995). Long-term outcome of state hospital patients discharged into structured community residential settings. *Psychiatric Services, 46,* 73–78.

O'Leary, K. D., & Beach, S. R. H. (1990). Marital therapy: A viable treatment for depression and marital discord. *American Journal of Psychiatry, 147,* 183–186.

Ollendisk, T. H., Mattis, S. G., & King, N. J. (1994). Panic in children and adolescents: A review. *Journal of Child Psychology and Psychiatry and Allied Disciplines, 35,* 113–134.

Olson, H. C., Streissguth, A. P., Sampson, P. D., Barr, H. M., Bookstein, F. L., & Thiede, K. (1997). Association of prenatal alcohol exposure with behavioral and learning problems in early adolescence. *Journal of the American Academy of Child and Adolescent Psychiatry, 36,* 1187–1194.

Opler, L. A., Caton, C. L. M., Shrout, P., Dominguez, B., & Kass, F. I. (1994). Symptom profiles and homelessness in schizophrenia. *Journal of Nervous and Mental Disease, 182,* 174–178.

Orne, M. T., Dinges, D. F., & Orne, E. C. (1984). On the differential diagnosis of multiple personality in the forensic context. *International Journal of Clinical and Experimental Hypnosis, 32,* 118–169.

Ost, L. G. (1987). Age of onset in different phobias. *Journal of Abnormal Psychology, 96,* 223–229.

Ost, L. G., Jerremalm, A., & Johansson, J. (1984). Individual response patterns and the effects of different behavioral methods on the treatment of social phobia. *Behaviour Research and Therapy, 22,* 697–708.

O'Sullivan, R. L., Rauch, S. L., Breiter, H. C., Grachev, I. D., Baer, L., Kennedy, D. N., Keuthen, N. J., Savage, C. R., Manzo, P. A., Caviness, V. S., & Jenike, M. A. (1997). Reduced basal ganglia volumes in trichotillomania measured via morphometric magnetic resonance imaging. *Biological Psychiatry, 42,* 39–45.

P

Pandey, G. N., Pandey, S. C., Dwivedi, Y., Sharma, R. P., Janicak, P. G., & Davis, J. M. (1995). Platelet serotonin-2A receptors: A potential biological marker for suicidal behavior. *American Journal of Psychiatry, 152,* 850–855.

Papp, L. A., Coplan, J., & Gorman, J. M. (1994). Anxiety disorders, In J. M. Oldham & M. B. Riba (Eds.), *Review of psychiatric disorders.* Washington, DC: American Psychiatric Press.

Papp, L. A., Martinez, J. M., Klein, D. F., Coplan, J. D., Norman, R. G., Cole, R., de Jesus, M. J., Ross, D., Goetz, R., & Gorman, J. M. (1997). Respiratory psychophysiology of panic disorder: Three respiratory challenges in 98 subjects. *American Journal of Psychiatry, 154,* 1557–1565.

Paris, J. (1997a). Antisocial and borderline personality disorders: Two separate diagnoses or two aspects of the same psychopathology? *Comprehensive Psychiatry, 38,* 237–242.

Paris, J. (1997b). Childhood trauma as an etiological factor in the personality disorders. *Journal of Personality Disorders, 11,* 34–49.

Park, L., Jefferson, J., & Greist, J. (1997). Obsessive-compulsive disorder: Treatment options. *CNS Drugs, 7,* 187–202.

Parker, P. E. (1993). A case report of Munchausen syndrome with mixed psychological features. *Psychosomatics, 34,* 360–364.

Patrick, C. J., Bradley, M. M. & Lang, P. J. (1993). Emotion in the criminal psychopath: Startle reflex modulation. *Journal of Abnormal Psychology, 102,* 82–92.

Patrick, C. J., Cuthbert, B. N., & Lang, P. J. (1994). Emotion in the criminal psychopath: Four image processing. *Journal of Abnormal Psychology, 103,* 523–534.

Pearlin, L. I., Mullan, J. T., Semple, S. J., & Skaff, M. M. (1990). Caregiving and the stress process: An overview of concepts and their measures. *Gerontologist, 30,* 583–591.

Pennebaker, J. W. (1997a). *Opening up: The healing power of expressing emotions* (rev. ed.). New York: Guilford Press.

Pennebaker, J. W. (1997b). Writing about emotional experiences as a therapeutic process. *Psychological Science, 8,* 162–166.

Pennebaker, J. W., Colder, M., & Sharp, L. K. (1990). Accelerating the coping process. *Journal of Personality and Social Psychology, 58,* 528–537.

Penner, L. A., & Fritzsche, B. A. (1993). Magic Johnson and reactions to people with AIDS: A natural experiment. *Journal of Personality and Social Psychology, 58,* 528–537.

Perlin, M. L. (1994). Law and the delivery of mental health services in the community. *American Journal of Orthopsychiatry, 64,* 194–208.

Peters, K. D., Kochanek, K. D., & Murphy, S. L. (1998). Deaths: Final data for 1996. *National Vital Statistics Reports, Vol. 47,* No. 9.

Peterson, C., & Seligman, M. E. P. (1984). Causal explanations as a risk factor for depression: Theory and evidence. *Psychological Review, 91,* 347–374.

Phelps, R., Eisman, E. J., & Kohout, J. (1998). Psychological practice and managed care: Results of the CAPP Practitioner Survey. *Professional Psychology: Research and Practice, 29,* 31–36.

Phillips, K. A. (1996). Body dysmorphic disorder: Diagnosis and treatment of imagined ugliness. *Journal of Clinical Psychiatry, 57,* 61–65.

Phillips, K. A., & Diaz, S. F. (1997). Gender differences in body dysmorphic disorder. *Journal of Nervous and Mental Disease, 185,* 570–577.

Phillips, K. A., McElroy, S. L., Keck, P. E., & Pope, H. G. (1993). Body dysmorphic disorder: 30 cases of imagined ugliness. *American Journal of Psychiatry, 150,* 302–308.

Phillips, K. A., Nierenberg, A. A., Brendel, G., & Fava, M. (1996). Prevalence and clinical features of body dysmorphic disorder in atypical major depression. *Journal of Nervous and Mental Disease, 184,* 125–129.

Phillips, K. A., & Taub, S. L. (1995). Skin picking as a symptom of body dysmorphic disorder. *Psychopharmacology Bulletin, 31,* 279–288.

Pickar, D., Breier, A., Hsiao, J. K., Doran, A. R., Wolkowitz, O. M., Pato, C. N., Konicki, P. E., & Potter, W. Z. (1990). Cerebrospinal fluid and plasma monoamine metabolites and their relation to psychosis. *Archives of General Psychiatry, 47,* 641–648.

Pierce, K. L., & Schreibman, L. (1994). Teaching daily living skills to children with autism in unsupervised settings through pictorial self-management. *Journal of Applied Behavior Analysis, 27,* 471–481.

Pine, D. S., Cohen, P., Gurley, D., Brook, J., & Ma, Y. (1998). The risk for early-adulthood anxiety and depressive disorders in adolescents with anxiety and depressive disorders. *Archives of General Psychiatry, 55,* 56–64.

Pini, S., Cassano, G. B., Simonini, E., Savino, M., Russo, A., & Montgomery, S. A. (1997). Prevalence of anxiety disorders comorbidity in bipolar depression, unipolar depression and dysthymia. *Journal of Affective Disorders, 42,* 145–153.

Pitts, F. N., Jr., & McClure, J. N., Jr. (1967). Lactate metabolism in anxiety neurosis. *New England Journal of Medicine, 277,* 1329–1336.

Piven, J., Arndt, S., Bailey, J., Havercamp, S., Andreasen, N. C., & Palmer, P. (1995). An MRI study of brain size in autism. *American Journal of Psychiatry, 152,* 1145–1149.

Piven, J., Bailey, J., Ranson, B. J., & Arndt, S. (1997). An MRI study of the corpus callosum in autism. *American Journal of Psychiatry, 154,* 1051–1056.

Piven, J., Palmer, P., Jacobi, D., Childress, D., & Arndt, S. (1997). Broader autism phenotype: Evidence from a family history study of multiple-incidence autism families. *American Journal of Psychiatry, 154,* 185–190.

Plessinger, M. A., & Woods, J. R., Jr. (1998). Cocaine in pregnancy. Recent data on maternal and fetal risks. *Obstetrics and Gynecology Clinics of North America, 25,* 99–118.

Polivy, J., Herman, C. P., & McFarlane, T. (1994). Effects of anxiety on eating: Does palatability moderate distress-induced overeating in dieters? *Journal of Abnormal Psychology, 103,* 393–396.

Polkinghorne, D. E. (1992). Research methodology in humanistic psychology. Special Issue: The humanistic movement in psychology: History, celebration and prospectus. *Humanistic Psychologist, 20,* 218–242.

Pope, H. G., Jr., & Yurgelun-Todd, D. (1996). The residual cognitive effects of heavy marijuana use in college students. *Journal of the American Medical Association, 275,* 521–527.

Pope, K. S., & Tabachnick, B. G. (1995). Recovered memories of abuse among therapy patients: A national survey. *Ethics and Behavior, 5,* 237–248.

Prentky, R. A. (1997). Arousal reduction in sexual offenders: A review of antiandrogen interventions. *Sexual Abuse: Journal of Research and Treatment, 9,* 335–347.

Prentky, R. A., Knight, R., & Lee, A. F. (1997a). Risk factors associated with recidivism among extrafamilial child molesters. *Journal of Consulting and Clinical Psychology, 65,* 141–149.

Prentky, R. A., Knight, R. A., Sims-Knight, J. E., Straus, H., Rokous, F., & Cerce, D. (1989). Developmental antecedents of sexual aggression. *Development and Psychopathology, 1,* 153–169.

Prentky, R. A., Lee, A. F., Knight, R., & Cerce, D. (1997b). Recidivism rates among child molesters and rapists: A methodological analysis. *Law and Human Behavior, 21,* 635–659.

Prescott, C. A., & Gottesman, I. I. (1993). Genetically mediated vulnerability to schizophrenia. *Psychiatric Clinics of North America, 16,* 245–267.

Prochaska, J. O. (1982). *Systems of psychotherapy: A transtheoretical analysis.* Pacific Grove, CA: Brooks/Cole.

Prochaska, J. O., & DiClemente, C. C. (1983). Stages of processes of self-change of smoking: Toward an integrative model of change. *Journal of Consulting and Clinical Psychology, 51,* 390–395.

Proulx, J., Pellerin, B., Paradis, Y., McKibben, A., Aubut, J., & Ouimet, M. (1997). Static and dynamic predictors of recidivism in sexual aggressors. *Sexual Abuse: Journal of Research and Treatment, 9,* 7–27.

Purcell, R., Maruff, P., Kyrios, M., & Pantelis, C. (1998). Cognitive deficits in obsessive-compulsive disorder on tests of frontal-striatal function. *Biological Psychiatry, 43,* 348–357.

Puri, B. K., Baxter, R., & Cordess, C. C. (1995). Characteristics of fire-setters. A study and proposed multiaxial psychiatric classification. *British Journal of Psychiatry, 166,* 393–396.

Putnam, F. W., Guroff, J. J., Silberman, E. K., Barban, L., & Post, R. M. (1986). The clinical phenomenology of multiple personality disorder: Review of 100 recent cases. *Journal of Clinical Psychiatry, 47,* 285–293.

Q

Quadland, M. O. (1985). Compulsive sexual behavior: Definition of a problem and approach to treatment. *Journal of Sex and Marital Therapy, 11,* 121–132.

R

Rachman, S. (1966). Sexual fetishism: An experimental analog. *Psychological Record, 16,* 293–296.

Rachman, S., & Hodgson, R. J. (1968). Experimentally induced "sexual fetishism" replication and development. *Psychological Record, 18,* 25–27.

Raines, J. C., & Foy, C. W. (1994). Extinguishing the fires within: Treating juvenile firesetters. *Families in Society, 75,* 595–606.

Rakic, Z., Starcevic, V., Maric, J., & Kelin, K. (1996). The outcome of sex reassignment surgery in Belgrade: 32 patients of both sexes. *Archives of Sexual Behavior, 25,* 515–525.

Ramberg, C., Ehlers, S., Nyden, A., Johansson, M., & Gillberg, C. (1996). Language and pragmatic functions in school-age children on the autism spectrum. *European Journal of Disorders of Communication, 31,* 387–413.

Ramsay, R., Gorst-Unsworth, C., & Turner, S. W. (1993). Psychiatric morbidity in survivors of organised state violence including torture: A retrospective series. *British Journal of Psychiatry, 162,* 55–59.

Rapaport, J. L. (1990). The waking nightmare: An overview of obsessive-compulsive disorder. *Journal of Clinical Psychiatry, 51,* 25–28.

Raphael, F. J., & Lacey, J. H. (1992). Sociocultural aspects of eating disorders. *Annals of Medicine, 24,* 293–296.

Rapoport, J., & Inoff-Germain, G. (1997). Medical and surgical treatment of obsessive-compulsive disorder. *Neurological Clinics, 15,* 421–428.

Rapp, J. T., Miltenerger, R. G., Long, E. S., Elliott, A. J., & Lumley, V. A. (1998). Simplified habit reversal treatment for chronic hair pulling in three adolescents: A clinical replication with direct observation. *Journal of Applied Behavior Analysis, 31,* 299–302.

Rasanen, P., Hakko, H., & Vaisanen, E. (1995a). Arson trend increasing–A real challenge to psychiatry. *Journal of Forensic Sciences, 40,* 976–979.

Rasanen, P., Hakko, H., & Vaisanen, E. (1995b). The mental state of arsonists as determined by forensic psychiatric examinations. *Bulletin of the American Academy of Psychiatry and the Law, 23,* 547–553.

Rauch, S., Baer, L., & Jenike, M. A. (1996). Treatment-resistant obsessive-compulsive disorder: Practical strategies for management. In M. Pollack, M. Otto, & J. Rosenbaum (Eds.), *Challenges in clinical practice: Pharmocologic and psychosocial strategies* (pp. 201–218). New York: Guilford Press.

Rauch, S. L., & Jenike, M. A. (1998). Pharmacologic treatment of obsessive-compulsive disorder. In P. E. Nathan & J. M. Gorman (Eds.), *A guide to treatments that work* (pp. 358–376). New York: Oxford University Press.

Rauch, S. L., Savage, C. R., Alpert, N. M., Dougherty, D., Kendrick, A., Curran, T., Brown, H. D., Manzo, P., Fischman, A. J., & Jenike, M. A. (1997). Probing striatal function in obsessive-compulsive disorder: A PET study of implicit sequence learning. *Journal of Neuropsychiatry and Clinical Neurosciences, 9,* 568–573.

Rauch, S. L., van der Kolk, B. A., Fisler, R. E., Alpert, N. M., Orr, S. P., Savage, C. R., Fischman, A. J., Jenike, M. A., & Pitman, R. K. (1996). A symptom provocation study of post-traumatic stress disorder using positron emission tomography and script-driven imagery. *Archives of General Psychiatry, 53,* 380–387.

Reed, T. E. (1997). The genetic hypothesis: It was not tested but it could have been. *American Psychologist, 52,* 77–78.

Reich, J. H., & Green, A. J. (1991). Effect of personality disorders on outcome of treatment. *Journal of Nervous and Mental Disease, 170,* 74–82.

Reich, T., Edenberg, H. J., Goate, A., Williams, J. T., Rice, J. P., Van Eerdewegh, P., Foroud, T., Hesselbrock, V., Schuckit, M. A., Bucholz, K., Poresz, B., Li, T. K., Conneally, P. M., Nurnberger, J. I., Jr., Tischfield, J. A., Crowe, R. R., Cloninger, C. R., Wu, W., Shears, S., Carr, K., Crose, C., Willig, C., & Begleiter, H. (1998). Genome-wide search for genes affecting the risk for alcohol dependence. *American Journal of Medical Genetics, 81,* 207–215.

Reidy, D. E. (1994). The mental health system as an agent of stigma. *Resources: Workforce Issues in Mental Health Systems, 6,* 3–10.

Reisberg, B. (1983). Clinical presentation, diagnosis, and symptomatology of age-associated cognitive decline and Alzheimer's disease. In B. Reisberg (Ed.), *Alzheimer's disease* (pp. 173–187). New York: Free Press.

Renner, M. J., & Mackin, R. S. (1998). A life stress instrument for classroom use. *Teaching of Psychology, 25,* 46–48.

Rennie v. Klein. 462 F. Supp. 1131 (1979).

Repo, E., Virkkunen, M., Rawlings, R., & Linnoila, M. (1997a). Criminal and psychiatric histories of Finnish arsonists. *Acta Psychiatrica Scandinavica, 95,* 318–323.

Repo, E., Virkkunen, M., Rawlings, R., & Linnoila, M. (1997b). Suicidal behavior among Finnish fire setters. *European Archives of Psychiatry and Clinical Neuroscience, 247,* 33–307.

Resnick, H. S., Kilpatrick, D. G., Dansky, B. S., Saunders, B. E., & Best, C. L. (1993). Prevalence of civilian trauma and post-traumatic stress disorder in a representative national sample of women. *Journal of Consulting and Clinical Psychology, 61,* 984–991.

Rhoads, J. M. (1989). Exhibitionism and voyeurism. In T. S. Karasu (Ed.), *Treatment of psychiatric disorders* (Vol. 1, pp. 670–673). Washington, DC: American Psychiatric Association.

Rice, J., Reich, T., Andreasen, N. C., Endicott, J., Van Eerdewegh, M., Fishman, R., Herschfeld, R. M. A., & Klerman, G. L. (1987). The familial transmission of bipolar illness. *Archives of General Psychiatry, 44,* 441–447.

Richardson, G., & Day, N. (1994). Detrimental effects of prenatal cocaine exposure: Illusion or reality? *Journal of the American Academy of Child and Adolescent Psychiatry, 33,* 28–34.

Richardson, G. A. (1998). Prenatal cocaine exposure. A longitudinal study of development. *Annals of the New York Academy of Sciences, 846,* 144–152.

Rinehart, N. J., & McCabe, M. P. (1997). Hypersexuality: Psychopathology or normal variant of sexuality? *Sexual and Marital Therapy, 12,* 45–60.

Ristvedt, S. L., & Christenson, G. A. (1996). The use of pharmacologic pain sensitization in the treatment of repetitive hair-pulling. *Behaviour Research and Therapy, 34,* 647–658.

Ritchie, J., Steiner, W., & Abrahamowicz, M. (1996). Incidence of and risk factors for delirium among psychiatric inpatients. *Psychiatric Services, 47,* 727–730.

Rizk, B., Atterbury, J. L., & Groome, L. J. (1996). Reproductive risks of cocaine. *Human Reproduction Update, 2,* 43–55.

Robins, L. N., (1966). *Deviant children grow up: A sociological and psychiatric study of sociopathic personality.* Baltimore: Williams & Wilkins.

Robins, L. N., & Regier, D. A. (1991). *Psychiatric disorders in America.* New York: Free Press.

Robins, L. N., Helzer, J. E., Weissman, M. M., Orvaschel, H., Gruenberg, E., Burke, J. D., & Regier, D. A. (1984). Lifetime prevalence of specific psychiatric disorders in three sites. *Archives of General Psychiatry, 41,* 949–958.

Robins, L. N., & Regier, D. A. (1991). *Psychiatric disorders in America.* New York: Free Press.

Robins, L. N., Tipp, J., & Pryzbeck, T. (1991). Antisocial personality. In L. N. Robins & D. A. Regier (Eds.), *Psychiatric disorders in America* (pp. 224–271). New York: Free Press.

Robinson, S., Rapaport, B. S. M., & Rapaport, J. (1994). The present state of people who survived the Holocaust as children. *Acta Psychiatrica Scandinavica, 89,* 242–245.

Rogers, C. R. (1951). *Client-centered therapy: Its current practice implications and theory.* Boston: Houghton Mifflin.

Rogers, C. R. (1959). A theory of therapy, personality, and interpersonal relationships as developed in the client-centered framework. In S. Koch (Ed.), *Psychology: A study of a science* (Vol. 3, pp. 184–256). New York: McGraw-Hill.

Rogers, C. R., & Dymond, R. F. (Eds.) (1954). *Psychotherapy and behavior change.* Chicago: University of Chicago Press.

Rogers, R. (Ed.). (1997). *Clinical assessment of feigned mental illness.* New York: Guilford Press.

Rogers, S. L., & Friedhoff, L. T. (1998). Long-term efficacy and safety of donepezil in the treatment of Alzheimer's disease. An interim analysis of the results of a U.S. multicentre open-label extension study. *European Neuropsychopharmacology, 8,* 67–75.

Rogers v. Okin. 478 F. Supp. 1342 (D Mass) 1979.

Roitman, S. E., Cornblatt, B. A., Bergman, A., Obuchowski, M., Mitropoulou, V., Keefe, R. S., Silverman, J. M., & Siever, L. J. (1997). Attentional functioning in schizotypal personality disorder. *American Journal of Psychiatry, 154,* 655-660.

Rolls, B. J., Federoff, I. C., & Guthrie, J. F. (1991). Gender differences in eating behavior and body weight regulation. *Health Psychology, 10,* 133–142.

Ronningstam, E., Gunderson, J., & Lyons, M. (1995). Changes in pathological narcissism. *American Journal of Psychiatry, 152,* 253–257.

Root, M. P. (1990). Disordered eating in women of color. *Sex Roles, 22,* 525–536.

Rosen, J. C., Reiter, J., & Orosan, P. (1995). Cognitive-behavioral body image therapy for body dysmorphic disorder. *Journal of Consulting and Clinical Psychology, 63,* 263–269.

Rosenbaum, M. (1980). The role of the term schizophrenia in the decline of diagnoses of multiple personality. *Archives of General Psychiatry, 37,* 1383–1385.

Rosenberg, D. R., Dick, E. L., O'Hearn, K. M., & Sweeney, J. A. (1997). Response-inhibition deficits in obsessive-compulsive disorder: An indicator of dysfunction in frontostriatal circuits. *Journal of Psychiatry & Neuroscience, 22,* 29–38.

Rosenberg, D. R., Sweeney, J. A., Squires-Wheeler, E., Keshavan, M. S., Cornblatt, B. A., & Erlenmeyer-Kimling, L. (1997). Eye-tracking dysfunction in offspring from the New York High-Risk Project: Diagnostic specificity and the role of attention. *Psychiatry Research, 66,* 121–130.

Rosenfarb, I. S., Goldstein, M. J., Mintz, J., & Nuechterlein, K. H. (1995). Expressed emotion and subclinical psychopathology observed within the transactions between schizophrenic patients and their family members. *Journal of Abnormal Psychology, 104,* 259–267.

Rosenhan, D. L. (1973). On being sane in insane places. *Science, 179.* 250–258.

Rosenthal, D. (1963). *The Genain quadruplets: A case study and theoretical analysis of heredity and environment in schizophrenia.* New York: Basic Books.

Roskies, E., Seraganian, P., Oseasohn, R., Smilga, C., Martin, N., & Hanley, J. A. (1989). Treatment of psychological stress responses in healthy Type A men. In R. W. J. Neufeld (Ed.), *Advances in the investigation of psychological stress* (pp. 284–304). New York: Wiley.

Rosler, A., & Witztum, E. (1998). Treatment of men with paraphilia with a long-acting analogue of gonadotropin-releasing hormone. *New England Journal of Medicine, 338,* 416–422.

Ross, C. A. (1989). *Multiple personality disorder: Diagnosis, clinical features, and treatment.* New York: Wiley.

Ross, C. A. (1997a). Cognitive therapy of dissociative identity disorder. In P. S. Appelbaum, L. A, Uyehara, & M. R. Elin (Eds.), *Trauma and memory: Clinical and legal controversies* (pp. 360–377). New York: Oxford University Press.

Ross, C. A. (1997b). *Dissociative identity disorder: Diagnosis, clinical features, and treatment of multiple personality* (2nd ed.). New York: John Wiley & Sons.

Ross, C. A., Miller, S. D., Bjornson, L., Reagor, P., Fraser, G. A., & Anderson, G. (1991). Abuse histories in 102 cases of multiple personality disorder. *Canadian Journal of Psychiatry, 36,* 97–101.

Ross, C. A., Miller, S. D., Reagor, P., Bjornson, L., Fraser, G. A., & Anderson, G. (1990). Structured interview data on 102 cases of multiple personality disorder from four centers. *American Journal of Psychiatry, 147,* 596–601.

Ross, C. J. (1996). A qualitative study of sexually addicted women. *Sexual Addiction and Compulsivity, 3,* 43–53.

Roth, T., Roehrs, T. A., & Rosenthal, L. (1994). Normative and pathological aspects of daytime sleepiness. In J. M. Oldham & M. B. Riba (Eds.), *Review of Psychiatry* (Vol. 13, pp. 707–728). Washington, DC: American Psychiatric Press.

Rothbaum, P. A., Bernstein, D.M., Haller, O., Phelps, R., & Kohout, J. (1998). New Jersey psychologists' report on managed mental health care. *Professional Psychology: Research and Practice, 29,* 37–42.

Rounsaville, B. J., O'Malley, S., Foley, S., & Weisman, M. M. (1988). Role of manual-guided training in the conduct and efficacy of interpersonal psychotherapy for depression. *Journal of Consulting and Clinical Psychology, 50,* 681–688.

Rourke, B. P. (1988). Socioemotional disturbances of learning disabled children. *Journal of Consulting and Clinical Psychology, 56,* 801–810.

Roy, A., Segal, N. L., & Sarchiapone, M. (1995). Attempted suicide among living co-twins of twin suicide victims. *American Journal of Psychiatry, 152,* 1075–1076.

Rubin, P., Holm, S., Friberg, L., Videbech, P., Andersen, H. S., Bendsen, B. B., Stromso, N., Larsen, J. K., Lassen, N. A., & Hemmingsen, R. (1991). Altered modulation of prefrontal and subcortical brain activity in newly diagnosed schizophrenia and schizophreniform disorder. *Archives of General Psychiatry, 48,* 987–995.

Rudd, M. D., Rajab, M. H., & Dahm, P. F. (1994). Problem-solving appraisal in suicide ideators and attempters, *American Journal of Orthopsychiatry, 64,* 136–149.

Rupp, A., & Keith, S. J. (1993). The costs of schizophrenia: Assessing the burden. *Psychiatric Clinics of North America, 16,* 413–423.

Ruschena, D., Mullen, P. E., Burgess, P., Cordner, S. M., Barry-Walsh, J., Drummer, O. H., Palmer, S., Browne, C., & Wallace, C. (1998). Sudden death in psychiatric patients, *British Journal of Psychiatry, 172,* 331–336.

Rushton, J. P. (1995). *Race, evolution, and behavior.* New Brunswick, NJ: Transaction.

Rushton, J. P. (1997). Race, IQ, and the APA Report on The Bell Curve. *American Psychologist, 52,* 69–70.

Russ, M. J., Shearin, E. N., Clarkin, J. F., & Harrison, K. (1993). Subtypes of self-injurious patients with borderline personality disorder. *American Journal of Psychiatry, 150,* 1869-1871.

Russo, M. F., Loeber, R., Lahey, B. B., & Keenan, K. (1994). Oppositional defiant and conduct disorders: Validation of the DSM-III-R and an alternative diagnostic option. *Journal of Clinical Child Psychiatry, 23,* 56–68.

Rutter, M. (1984). Psychopathology and development: II. Childhood experiences and personality development. *Australian and New Zealand Journal of Psychiatry, 18,* 314–327.

Rutter, M. (1985). The treatment of autistic children. *Journal of Child Psychology and Psychiatry, 26,* 193–214.

Ryan, M. (1995). *Secret life: An autobiography.* New York: Pantheon.

S

Sabo, A. N. (1997). Etiological significance of associations between childhood trauma and borderline personality disorder: Conceptual and clinical implications. *Journal of Personality Disorders, 11,* 50–70.

Sacco, W. P., & Beck, A. T. (1985). Cognitive therapy of depression. In E. E. Beckham & W. R. Leber (Eds.), *Handbook of depression: Treatment, assessment, and research* (pp. 3–38). Homewood, IL: Dorsey Press.

Sachdev, P., & Hay, P. (1996). Site and size of lesion and psychosurgical outcome in obsessive-compulsive disorder: A magnetic resonance imaging study. *Biological Psychiatry, 38,* 739–742.

Sachdev, P., Sachdev, J. (1997). Sixty years of psychosurgery: Its present status and its future. *Australian and New Zealand Journal of Psychiatry, 31,* 457–464.

Safran, J. D. (1990). Towards a refinement of cognitive therapy in light of interpersonal theory: I. Theory. *Clinical Psychology Review, 10,* 87–105.

Saletu, B., Anderer, P., Brandstatter, N., Frey, R., Grunberger, J. G., Klosch, G., Mandl, M., Wetter, T., & Zietlhofer, J. (1994). Insomnia in generalized anxiety disorder: Polysomnographic, psychometric and clinical investigations before, during and after therapy with a long- versus a short-half-life benzodiazephine (quazepam versus triazolam). *Neuropsychobiology, 29,* 69–90.

Salkovskis, P. M., & Westbrook, D. (1989). Behavior therapy and obsessional ruminations: Can failure be turned into success? *Behavior Research and Therapy, 24,* 597–602.

Salkovskis, P. M., Westbrook, D., Davis, J., Jeavons, A., & Gledhill, A. (1997). Effects of neutralizing on intrusive thoughts: An experiment investigating the etiology of obsessive-compulsive disorder. *Behaviour Research & Therapy, 35,* 211–219.

Salmon, P., & Calderbank, S. (1996). The relationship of childhood physical and sexual abuse to adult illness behavior. *Journal of Psychosomatic Research, 40,* 329–336.

Salzman, J. P., Salzman, C., & Wolfson, A. N. (1997). Relationship of childhood abuse and maternal attachment to the development of borderline personality disorder. In M. C. Zanarini (Ed.), *Role of sexual abuse in the etiology of borderline personality disorder. Progress in psychiatry, No. 49* (pp. 71–91). Washington, DC: American Psychiatric Press.

Sampson, P. D., Streissguth, A. P., Bookstein, F. L., Little, R. E., Clarren, S. K., Dehaene, P., Hanson, J. W., & Graham, J. M., Jr. (1997). Incidence of fetal alcohol syndrome and prevalence of alcohol-related neurodevelopmental disorder. *Teratology, 56,* 317–326.

Sanderson, W. C., & Barlow, D. H. (1990). A description of patients diagnosed with DSM-III-R generalized anxiety disorder. *Journal of Nervous and Mental Disease, 178,* 588–591.

Sarasalo, E., Bergman, B., & Toth, J. (1996). Personality traits and psychiatric and somatic morbidity among kleptomaniacs. *Acta Psychiatrica Scandinavica, 94,* 358–364.

Sass, H., Soyka, M., Mann, K., & Zieglgansbeger, W. (1996). Relapse prevention by acamprosate. Results from a placebo-controlled study on alcohol dependence. *Archives of General Psychiatry, 53,* 673–680.

Sasson, Y., Zohar, J., Chopra, M., Lustig, M., Iancu, I., & Hendler, T. (1997). Epidemiology of obsessive-compulsive disorder: A world view. *Journal of Clinical Psychiatry, 12,* 7–10.

Saudino, K. J., Pedersen, N. L., Lichtenstein, P., McClearn, G. E., & Plomin, R. (1997). Can personality explain genetic influences on life events? *Journal of Personality and Social Psychology, 72,* 196–206.

Saxon, A. J., Sloan, K. L., Reoux, J., & Haver, V. M. (1998). Disulfiram use in patients with abnormal liver function test results. *Journal of Clinical Psychiatry, 59,* 313–316.

Sayers, J. (1991). *Mothers of psychoanalysis.* New York: Norton.

Scarr, S. (1992). Developmental theories for the 1990s: Development and individual differences. *Child Development, 63,* 1–19.

Scazufca, M., & Kuipers, E. (1998). Stability of expressed emotion in relatives of those with schizophrenia and its relationship with burden of care and perception of patients' social functioning. *Psychological Medicine, 28,* 453–461.

Schacter, D. L., Norman, K. A., & Koutstaal, W. (1997). The recovered memories debate: A cognitive neuroscience perspective. In M. A. Conway (Ed.), *Recovered memories and false memories. Debates in psychology.* Oxford, U.K.: Oxford University Press.

Scheff, T. J. (1966). *Being mentally ill: A sociological theory.* Chicago: Aldine.

Scheflin, A. W., & Brown, D. (1996). Repressed memory or dissociative amnesia: What the science says. *Journal of Psychiatry & Law, 24,* 143–188.

Schildkraut, J. J. (1965). The catecholamine hypothesis of affective disorders: A review of supporting evidence. *American Journal of Psychiatry, 122,* 509–522.

Schildkraut, J. J., Hirshfeld, A. J., & Murphy, J. M. (1994). Mind and mood in modern art: II. Depressive disorders, spirituality, and early deaths in the abstract expressionist artists of the New York School. *American Journal of Psychiatry, 151,* 482–488.

Schlosser, S., Black, D. W., Repertinger, S., & Freet, D. (1994). Compulsive buying: Demography, phenomenology, and comorbidity in 46 subjects. *General Hospital Psychiatry, 16,* 205–212.

Schmidt, N. B., Lerew, D. R., & Trakowski, J. H. (1997). Body vigilance in panic disorder: Evaluating attention to bodily perturbations. *Journal of Consulting and Clinical Psychology, 65,* 214–220.

Schneider, K. (1959). *Clinical psychopathology.* New York: Grune & Stratton.

Schreiber, F. R. (1973). *Sybil.* Chicago: Henry Regnery.

Schuckit, M. A. (1989). *Drug and alcohol abuse: A clinical guide to diagnosis and treatment.* New York: Plenum Medical Book.

Schuckit, M. A., & Smith, T. L. (1996). Recent developments in the pharmacotherapy of alcohol dependence. *Journal of Consulting and Clinical Psychology, 64,* 669–676.

Schuckit, M. A., & Smith, T. L. (1997). Assessing the risk for alcoholism among sons of alcoholics. *Journal of Studies on Alcohol, 58,* 141–145.

Schulkin, J. (1994). Melancholic depression and the hormones of adversity: A role for the amygdala. *Current Directions in Psychological Science, 3,* 41–44.

Schulz, R., Visintainer, P., & Williamson, G. M. (1990). Psychiatric and physical morbidity effects of caregiving. *Journal of Gerontology: Psychological Sciences, 45,* 181–191.

Schwartz, M. F. (1994). The Masters and Johnson treatment program for sex offenders: Intimacy, empathy and trauma resolution. *Sexual Addiction and Compulsivity, 1,* 261–277.

Schwartz, M. F., & Brasted, W. S. (1985). Sexual addiction. *Medical Aspects of Human Sexuality, 19,* 106–107.

Scroppo, J. C., Drob, S. L., Weinberger, J. L., & Eagle, P. (1998). Identifying dissociative identity disorder: A self-report and projective study. *Journal of Abnormal Psychology, 107,* 272–284.

Sealy, J. R. (1995). Psychopharmacologic intervention in addictive sexual behavior. *Sexual Addiction and Compulsivity, 2,* 257–276.

Segraves, R. T., & Althof, S. (1998). Psychotherapy and pharmacotherapy of sexual dysfunctions. In P. E. Nathan & J. M. Gorman (Eds.), *A guide to treatments that work* (pp. 447–471). New York: Oxford University Press.

Seligman, M. E. P. (1971). Phobias and preparedness. *Behavior Therapy, 2,* 307–320.

Seligman, M. E. P. (1995). The effectiveness of psychotherapy: The *Consumer Reports* study. *American Psychologist, 50,* 965–975.

Semans, J. H. (1956). Premature ejaculation: A new approach. *Southern Medical Journal, 49,* 353–361.

Serban, G. (1992). Multiple personality: An issue for forensic psychiatry. *American Journal of Psychotherapy, 46,* 269–280.

Serin, R. C., Malcolm, P. B., Khanna, A., & Barbaree, H. E. (1994). Psychopathy and deviant sexual arousal in incarcerated sexual offenders. *Journal of Interpersonal Violence, 9,* 3–11.

Shader, R. I., & Scharfman, E. L. (1989). Depersonalization disorder. In T. B. Karasu (Ed.), *Treatments of psychiatric disorders* (pp. 2217–2222). Washington, DC: American Psychiatric Press.

Shadish, W. R., Matt, G. E., Navarro, A. M., Siegle, G., Crits-Christoph, P., Hazelrigg, M. D., Jorm, A. F., Lyons, L. C., Nietzel, M. T., Prout, H. T., Robinson, L., Smith, M. L., Svartberg, M., & Weiss, B. (1997). Evidence that therapy works in clinically representative conditions. *Journal of Consulting & Clinical Psychology, 65,* 355–65.

Shaffer, D. (1994). Attention deficit hyperactivity disorder in adults. *American Journal of Psychiatry, 151,* 633–638.

Shafran, R. (1997). The manipulation of responsibility in obsessive-compulsive disorder. *British Journal of Clinical Psychology, 36,* 397–407.

Shalev, A. Y., Freedman, S., Peri, T., Brandes, D., Sahar, T., Orr, S. P., & Pitman, R. K. (1998). Prospective study of post-traumatic stress disorder and depression following trauma. *American Journal of Psychiatry, 155,* 630–637.

Shalev, A. Y., Peri, T., Canetti, L., & Schreiber, S. (1996). Predictors of PTSD in injured trauma survivors: A prospective study. *American Journal of Psychiatry, 153,* 219–225.

Shapiro, D. (1965). *Neurotic styles.* New York: Basic Books.

Shapiro, D. (1986). The insanity defense reform act of 1984. *Bulletin of the American Academy of Forensic Psychology, 1,* 1–6.

Sharf, R. S. (1996). *Theories of psychotherapy and counseling: Concepts and cases.* Pacific Grove, CA: Brooks/Cole.

Shearin, E. N., & Linehan, M. M. (1994). Dialectical behavior therapy for borderline personality disorder: Theoretical and empirical foundations. Scandanavian Symposium: Borderline conditions (1993, Copenhagen, Denmark). *Acta Psychiatrica Scandinavica, 89,* 61–68.

Sheinkopf, S. J., & Siegel, B. (1998). Home-based behavioral treatment of young children with autism. *Journal of Autism and Developmental Disorders, 28,* 15–23.

Sheldon, A. E., & West, M. (1990). Attachment pathology and low social skills in avoidant personality disorder: An exploratory study. *Canadian Journal of Psychiatry, 35,* 596–599.

Sherman, D. K., McGue, M. K., & Iacono, W. G. (1997). Twin concordance for attention deficit hyperactivity disorder: A comparison of teachers' and mothers' reports. *American Journal of Psychiatry, 154,* 532–535.

Sherrington, R., Brynjolfsson, J., Petursson, H., Potter, M., Dudleston, K., Barraclough, B., Wasmuth, J., Dobbs, M., & Gurling, H. (1988). Location of the susceptibility locus for schizophrenia on chromosome 5. *Nature, 336,* 164–167.

Shneidman, E. S. (1984). Aphorisms of suicide and some implications for psychotherapy. *American Journal of Psychotherapy, 38,* 319–328.

Shostrom, E. L. (1974). *Manual for personality orientation inventory.* San Diego: EdITS/Educational & Industrial Testing Service.

Showers, J., & Pickrell, E. (1987). Child firesetters: A study of three populations. *Hospital and Community Psychiatry, 38,* 495–501.

Schulman, B. (1985). Cognitive therapy and the individual psychology of Alfred Adler. In M. J. Mahoney & A. Freeman (Eds.), *Cognition and psychotherapy* (pp. 243–258). New York: Plenum Press.

Shulman, I. D., Cox, B. J., Swinson, R. P., Kuch, K., & Reichman, J. T. (1994). Precipitating events, locations and reactions associated with initial unexpected panic attacks. *Behaviour Research and Therapy, 32,* 17–20.

Siegman, A. W. (1994). From Type A to hostility to anger: Reflections on the history of coronary-prone behavior. In A. W. Siegman & T. W. Smith (Eds.), *Anger, hostility, and the heart* (pp. 1–21). Hillsdale, NJ: Erlbaum.

Sifneos, P. E. (1979). *Short-term dynamic psychotherapy, evaluation, and technique.* New York: Plenum Press.

Sifneos, P. E. (1981). Short-term anxiety provoking psychotherapy: Its history, technique, outcome, and instruction. In S. H. Budman (Ed.), *Form of brief therapy* (pp. 45–81). New York: Guilford Press.

Silk, K. R., Lee, S., Hill, E. M., & Lohr, N. E. (1995). Borderline personality disorder symptoms and severity of sexual abuse. *American Journal of Psychiatry, 152,* 1059–1064.

Silva, C., McFarlane, J., Soeken, K., Parker, B., & Reel, S. (1997). Symptoms of post-traumatic stress disorder in abused women in a primary care setting. *Journal of Women's Health, 6,* 543–552.

Silverstein, J. L. (1996). Exhibitionism as countershame. *Sexual Addiction and Compulsivity, 3,* 33–42.

Simon, R. J., & Aaronson, E. E. (1988). *The insanity defense: A critical assessment of law and policy in the post-Hinckley era.* New York: Praeger.

Simons, A. D., Gordon, J. S., Monroe, S. M., & Thase, M. E. (1995). Toward an integration of psychologic, social, and biologic factors in depression: Effects on outcome and course of cognitive therapy. *Journal of Consulting and Clinical Psychology, 63,* 369–377.

Simpson, D. D., Joe, G. W., & Brown, B. S. (1997). Treatment retention and follow-up outcomes in the Drug Abuse Treatment Outcome Study (DATOS). *Psychology of Addictive Behaviors, 11,* 294–307.

Simpson, D. D., Joe, G. W., Dansereau, D. F., & Chatham, L. R. (1997). Strategies for improving methadone treatment process and outcomes. *Journal of Drug Issues, 27,* 239–260.

Simpson, D. D., Joe, G. W., Rowan-Szal, G. A., & Greener, J. M. (1997). Drug abuse treatment process components that improve retention. *Journal of Substance Abuse Treatment, 14,* 565–572.

Simpson, M. (1989). Multiple personality disorder. *British Journal of Psychiatry, 155,* 565.

Sing, L. (1994). The Diagnostic Interview Schedule and anorexia nervosa in Hong Kong. *Archives of General Psychiatry, 51,* 251–252.

Singh, R. K., Gupta, A. K., & Singh, B. (1995). Acute organic brain syndrome after fluoxetine treatment. *American Journal of Psychiatry, 152,* 295–296.

Singhrao, S. K., Thomas, P., Wood, J. D., MacMillan, J. C., Neal, J. W., Harper, P. S., & Jones, A. L. (1998). Huntington protein colocalizes with lesions of neurodegenerative diseases: An investigation in Huntington's, Alzheimer's, and Pick's diseases. *Experimental Neurology, 150,* 213–222.

Sitharthan, T., Sitharthan, G., Hough, M. J., & Kavanagh, D. J. (1997). Cue exposure in moderation drinking: A comparison with cognitive-behavior therapy. *Journal of Consulting & Clinical Psychology, 65,* 878–882.

Skinner, B. F. (1953). *Science and human behavior.* New York: Free Press.

Slovenko, R. (1993). The multiple personality and the criminal law. *Medicine and Law, 12,* 329–340.

Smith, G. R., Jr. (1990). *Somatization disorder in the medical setting.* (Vol. DHHS Pub. No. [ADM]90-1631). Washington, DC: National Institute of Mental Health, Superintendent of Documents, U.S. Government Printing Office.

Smith, K. A., Fairburn, C. G., & Cowen, P. J. (1999). Symptomatic relapse in bulimia nervosa following acute tryptophan depletion. *Archives of General Psychiatry, 56,* 171–176.

Smith, T. W. (1996). *American sexual behavior: Trends, socio-demographic differences, and risk behavior* (GSS Topical Report No. 25). Chicago: National Opinion Research Center, University of Chicago.

Smith-Bell, M., & Winslade, W. J. (1994). Privacy, confidentiality, and privilege in psychotherapeutic relationships. *American Journal of Orthopsychiatry, 64,* 180–193.

Snaith, P., Tarsh, M. J., & Reid, R. W. (1993). Sex reassignment surgery: A study of 141 Dutch transsexuals. *British Journal of Psychiatry, 162,* 681–685.

Snowdon, D. A. (1997). Aging and Alzheimer's disease: Lessons from the Nun Study. *Gerontologist, 37,* 150–156.

Sobin, C., Prudic, J., Devanand, D. P., Nobler, M. S., & Sackeim, H. A. (1996). Who responds to electroconvulsive therapy? A comparison of effective and ineffective forms of treatment. *British Journal of Psychiatry, 169,* 322–329.

Sokolov, S. T. H., Kutcher, S. P., & Joffe, R. T. (1994). Basal thyroid iindices in adolescent depression and bipolar disorder. *Journal of the American Academy of Child and Adolescent Psychiatry, 33,* 469–475.

Soloff, P. H., Cornelius, J., George, A., Nathan, S., Perel, J. M., & Ulrich, R. F. (1993). Efficacy of phenelzine and haloperidol in borderline personality disorder. *Archives of General Psychiatry, 50,* 377–395.

Soltys, S. M. (1992). Pyromania and firesetting behaviors. *Psychiatric Annals, 22,* 79–83.

Southall, D. P., Plunkett, M. C., Banks, M. W., Falkov, A. F., & Samuels, M. P. (1997). Covert video recordings of life-threatening child abuse: Lessons for child protection. *Pediatrics, 100,* 735–760.

Southwick, S. M., Krystal, J. H., Bremner, J. D., Morgan, C. A., III, Nicolaou, A. L., Nagy, L. M., Johnson, D. R., Heninger, G. R., & Charney, D. S. (1997). Noradrenergic and serotonergic function in post-traumatic stress disorder. *Archives of General Psychiatry, 54,* 749–758.

Southwick, S. M., & Yehuda, R. (1993). The interaction between pharmacotherapy and psychotherapy in the treatment of post-traumatic stress disorder. *American Journal of Psychotherapy, 47,* 404–410.

Southwick, S. M., & Yehuda, R., Giller, E. L. (1995). Psychological dimensions of depression in borderline personality disorder. *American Journal of Psychiatry, 152,* 789–791.

Spaner, D., Bland, R. C., & Newman, S. C. (1994). Major depressive disorder. *Acta Psychiatrica Scandinavica, 89,* 7–15.

Spangler, D. L., Simons, A. D., Monroe, S. M., & Thase, M. E. (1996). Gender differences in cognitive diathesis-stress domain match: Implications for differential pathways to depression. *Journal of Abnormal Psychology, 105,* 53–657.

Spanos, N. P. (1996). *Multiple identities and false memories: A sociocognitive perspective.* Washington, DC: American Psychological Association.

Sparr, L., & Pankratz, L. D. (1983). Factitious post-traumatic stress disorder. *American Journal of Psychiatry, 140,* 1016–1019.

Spearman, C. (1904). General Intelligence: Objectively determined and measured. *American Journal of Psychology, 15,* 201–292.

Spence, S. A., Hirsch, S. R., Brooks, D. J., & Grasby, P. M. (1998). Prefrontal cortex activity in people with schizophrenia and control subjects. Evidence from positron emission tomography for remission of "hypofrontality" with recovery from acute schizophrenia. *British Journal of Psychiatry, 172,* 164–167.

Spence, S. H. (1997). Structure of anxiety symptoms among children: A confirmatory factor-analytic study. *Journal of Abnormal Psychology, 106,* 280–297.

Sperling, M. B., Berman, W. H., & Fagen, G. (1992). Classification of adult attachment: An integrative taxonomy from attachment and psychoanalytic theories. Midwinter Meeting of the Society for Personality Assessment (1991, New Orleans, Louisiana). *Journal of Personality Assessment, 59,* 239–247.

Sperling, M. B., Sharp, J. L., & Fishler, P. H. (1991). On the nature of attachment in a borderline population: A preliminary investigation. *Psychological Reports, 68,* 543–546.

Spiegel, D., & Cardena, E. (1991). Disintegrated experience: The dissociative disorders revisited. *Journal of Abnormal Psychology, 100,* 366–378.

Spiro, A., Schnurr, P. P., & Aldwin, C. M. (1994). Combat-related post-traumatic stress disorder symptoms in older men. *Psychology and Aging, 9,* 17–26.

Spitz, H. H. (1997). Some questions about the results of the Abecedarian Early Intervention Project cited by the APA Task Force on Intelligence. *American Psychologist, 52,* 72.

Spitzer, R. L. (1975). On pseudoscience in science, logic in remission, and psychiatric diagnosis: A critique of D. L. Rosenhan's "On Being Sane in Insane Places." *Journal of Abnormal Psychology, 84,* 442–452.

Sroufe, L. A., Fox, N. E., & Pancake, V. R. (1983). Attachment and dependency in developmental perspective. *Child Development, 54,* 1615–1627.

Stabenau, J. R., & Pollin, W. (1993). Heredity and environment in schizophrenia, revisited: The contribution of twin and high-risk studies. *Journal of Nervous and Mental Disease, 181,* 290–297.

Stabler, B., Tancer, M. E., Ranc, J., & Underwood, L. E. (1996). Evidence for social phobia and other psychiatric disorders in adults who were growth hormone deficient during childhood. *Anxiety, 2,* 86–89.

Standard & Poor's Industry Surveys, October, 1995, Vol. 1 A–L.

Stanley, M. A., Borden, J. W., Mouton, S. G., & Breckenridge, J. K. (1995). Nonclinical hair-pulling: Affective correlates and comparison with clinical samples. *Behaviour Research and Therapy, 33,* 179–186.

Stanley, M. A., Breckenridge, J. K., Swann, A. C., Freeman, E. B., & Reich, L. (1997). Fluvoxamine treatment of trichotillomania. *Journal of Clinical Psychopharmacology, 17,* 278–283.

Stanley, M. A., Hannay, H. J., & Breckenridge, J. K. (1997). The neuropsychology of trichotillomania. *Journal of Anxiety Disorders, 11,* 473–488.

Stanley, M. A., & Turner, S. M. (1995). Current status of pharmacological and behavioral treatment of obsessive-compulsive disorder. *Behavior Therapy, 26,* 163–186.

Starcevic, V., & Bogojevic, G. (1997). Comorbidity of panic disorder with agoraphobia and specific phobia: Relationship with the subtypes of specific phobia. *Comprehensive Psychiatry, 38,* 315–320.

Stasiewicz, P. R., Gulliver, S. B., Bradizza, C. M., Rohsenow, D. J., Torrisi, R., & Monti, P. M. (1997). Exposure to negative emotional cues and alcohol cue reactivity with alcoholics: A preliminary investigation. *Behaviour Research and Therapy, 35,* 1143–1149.

Steel, Z., & Blaszczynski, A. (1998). Impulsivity, personality disorders and pathological gambling severity. *Addiction, 93,* 895–905.

Stein, D. J., Bouwer, C., & Maud, C. M. (1997). Use of the selective serotonin reuptake inhibitor citalopram in treatment of trichotillomania. *European Archives of Psychiatry & Clinical Neuroscience, 247,* 234–236.

Stein, D. J., Hollander, E., & Liebowitz, M. R. (1993). Neurobiology of impulsivity and the impulse control disorders. *Journal of Neuropsychiatry & Clinical Neurosciences, 5,* 9–17.

Stein, M. B., Forde, D. R., Anderson, G., & Walker, J. R. (1997). Obsessive compulsive disorder in the community: An epidemiologic survey with clinical reappraisal. *American Journal of Psychiatry, 154,* 1120–1126.

Stein, M. B., Koverola, C., Hanna, C., Torchia, M. G., & McClarty, B. (1997). Hippocampal volume in women victimized by childhood sexual abuse. *Psychological Medicine, 27,* 951–959.

Stein, M. B., Walker, J. R., & Forde, D. R. (1996). Public-speaking fears in a community sample. Prevalence, impact on functioning, and diagnostic classification. *Archives of General Psychiatry, 53,* 169–174.

Steinberg, M. (1991). The spectrum of depersonalization: Assessment and treatment. *Annual Review of Psychiatry, 10,* 223–247.

Steinberg, M. (1993). *Structured Clinical Interview for DSM-IV Dissociative Disorders (SCID-D).* Washington, DC: American Psychiatric Press.

Steinberg, M., Bancroft, J., & Buchanan, J. (1993). Multiple personality disorder in criminal law. *Bulletin of the American Academy of Psychiatry and the Law, 21,* 345–356.

Steinberg, M., & Hall, P. (1997). The SCID-D diagnostic interview and treatment planning in dissociative disorders. *Bulletin of the Menninger Clinic, 61,* 108–120.

Steiner, W. (1991). Fluoxetine-induced mania in a patient with obsessive-compulsive disorder. *American Journal of Psychiatry, 148,* 1403–1404.

Steketee, G. (1994). Behavioral assessment and treatment planning with obsessive-compulsive disorder: A review emphasizing clinical application. *Behavior Therapy, 25,* 613–633.

Steketee, G. (1998). Judy: A compelling case of obsessive-compulsive disorder. In R. P. Halgin & S. K. Whitbourne (Eds.), *A casebook in abnormal psychology: From the files of experts* (pp. 58–71). New York: Oxford University Press.

Stephens, M. A. P., Franks, M. M., & Townsend, A. L. (1994). Stress and rewards in women's multiple roles: The case of women in the middle. *Psychology and Aging, 9,* 45–52.

Stephenson, W. (1953). *The study of behavior: Q technique and its methodology.* Chicago: University Chicago Press.

Stern, A. (1938). Psychoanalytic investigation of therapy in the borderline group of neuroses. *Psychoanalytic Quarterly, 7,* 467–489.

Stern, R. G., Mohs, R. C., Davidson, M., Schmeidler, J., Silverman, J., Kramer-Ginsberg, E., Searcey, T., Bierer, L., & Davis, K. L. (1994). A longitudinal study of Alzheimer's disease: Measurement, rate, and predictors of cognitive deterioration. *American Journal of Psychiatry, 151,* 390–396.

Stewart, L. A. (1993). Profile of female firesetters: Implications for treatment. *British Journal of Psychiatry, 163,* 248–256.

Stewart, W. F., Kawas, C., Corrada, M., & Metter, E. J. (1997). Risk of Alzheimer's disease and duration of NSAID use. *Neurology, 48,* 626–632.

Stice, E., Killen, J. D., Hayward, C., & Taylor, C. B. (1998). Age of onset for binge eating and purging during late adolescence: A 4-year survival analysis. *Journal of Abnormal Psychology, 107,* 671–675.

Stiebel, V. G. (1995). Maintenance electroconvulsive therapy for chronically mentally ill patients: A case series. *Psychiatric Services, 46,* 265–268.

Stine, J. J. (1994). Psychosocial and psychodynamic issues affecting noncompliance with psychostimulant treatment. *Journal of Child and Adolescent Psychopharmacology, 4,* 75–86.

Stokes, P. E. (1993). Fluoxetine: A five-year review. *Clinical Therapeutics, 15,* 216–243.

Stone, A. (1990). *The fate of borderline patients: Successful outcome and psychiatric practice.* New York: Guilford Press.

Storm-Mathisen, A., & Vaglum, P. (1994). Conduct disorder patients 20 years later: A personal follow-up study. *Acta Psychiatrica Scandinavica, 89,* 415–420.

Stoylen, I. J. (1996). Treatment of trichotillomania by habit reversal. *Scandinavian Journal of Behaviour Therapy, 25,* 149–153.

Street, L. L., & Barlow, D. H. (1994). Anxiety disorders. In L. W. Craighead, W. E. Craighead, A. E. Kazdin, & M. J. Mahoney (Eds.), *Cognitive and behavioral interventions: An empirical approach to mental health problems* (pp. 71–87). Boston: Allyn & Bacon.

Stretch, R. H., Marlowe, D. H., Wright, K. M., Bliese, P. D., Knudson, K. H., & Hoover, C. H. (1996). Post-traumatic stress disorder symptoms among Gulf War veterans. *Military Medicine, 161,* 407–410.

Striegel-Moore, R. H., Silberstein, L. R., & Rodin, J. (1993). The social self in bulimia nervosa: Public self-consciousness, social anxiety, and perceived fraudulence. *Journal of Abnormal Psychology, 102,* 297–303.

Strijers, R. L., Scheltens, P., Jonkman, E. J., de Rijke, W., Hooijer, C., & Jonker, C. (1997). Diagnosing Alzheimer's disease in community-dwelling elderly: A comparison of EEG and MRI. *Dementia and Geriatric Cognitive Disorders, 8,* 198–202.

Strober, M. (1991). Family-genetic studies of eating disorders. *Journal of Clinical Psychiatry, 52,* 9–12.

Strober, M., & Humphrey, L. L. (1987). Familial contributions to the etiology and course of anorexia nervosa and bulimia. *Journal of Consulting and Clinical Psychology, 55,* 654–659.

Strohle, A., Kellner, M., Yassouridis, A., Holsboer, F., & Wiedemann, K. (1998). Effect of flumazenil in lactate-sensitive patients with panic disorder. *American Journal of Psychiatry, 155,* 610–612.

Strupp, H. H., & Bonder, J. L. (1984). *Psychotherapy in a new key: A guide to time-limited dynamic psychotherapy.* New York: Basic Books.

Substance Abuse and Mental Health Services Administration (1995). *National household survey on drug abuse: Population estimates 1994.* U.S. Department of Health and Human Services.

Sullivan, H. S. (1953a). *Conceptions of modern psychiatry.* New York: Norton.

Sullivan, H. S. (1953b). *The interpersonal theory of psychiatry.* New York: Norton.

Suls, J., & Sanders, G. S. (1988). Type A behavior as a general risk factor for physical disorder. *Journal of Behavioral Medicine, 11,* 201–226.

Summers, F. (1994). *Object relations theory and psychopathology: A comprehensive text.* Hillsdale, NJ: Analytic Press.

Sunderwirth, S., Milkman, H., & Jenks, N. (1996). Neurochemistry and sexual addiction. *Sexual Addiction and Compulsivity, 3,* 22–32.

Susser, E., & Wanderling, J. (1994). Epidemiology of nonaffective acute remitting psychosis vs. schizophrenia. *Archives of General Psychiatry, 51,* 294–301.

Sutker, P. B., Uddo, M., Brailey, K., & Allain, A. N. (1993). War-zone trauma and stress-related symptoms in Operation Desert Shield/Storm (ODS) returnees. *Journal of Social Issues, 49,* 33–50.

Swaffer, T., & Hollin, C. R. (1995). Adolescent firesetting: Why do they say they do it? *Journal of Adolescence, 18,* 619–623.

Swanwick, G. R. J., Rowan, M., Coen, R. F., & O'Mahony, D. (1996). Clinical application of electrophysiological markers in the differential diagnosis of depression and very mild Alzheimer's disease. *Journal of Neurology, Neurosurgery and Psychiatry, 60,* 82–86.

Swartz, M., Landerman, R., George, L. K., Blazer, D. G., & Escobar, J. (1991). Somatization disorder. In L. N. Robins & D. A. Regier (Eds.), *Psychiatric disorders in America: The epidemiologic catchment area study* (pp. 220–257). New York: Free Press.

Sylvain, C., Ladouceur, R., & Boisvert, J. M. (1997). Cognitive and behavioral treatment of pathological gambling: A controlled study. *Journal of Consulting & Clinical Psychology, 65,* 727–732.

Szasz, G., Stevenson, R. W. D., Lee, L., & Sanders, H. D. (1987). Induction of penile erection by intracavernosal injection: A double-blind comparison of phenoxybenzamine versus papaverine-phentolamine versus saline. *Archives of Sexual Behavior, 16,* 371–378.

Szasz, T. (1961). *The myth of mental illness.* New York: Harper & Row.

T

Talkington-Boyer, S., & Snyder, D. K. (1994). Assessing impact on family caregivers to Alzheimer's disease patients. *American Journal of Family Therapy, 22,* 57–66.

Tallis, F. (1997). The neuropsychology of obsessive-compulsive disorder: A review and consideration of clinical implications. *British Journal of Clinical Psychology, 36,* 3–20.

Tanzi, R. E., Kovacs, D. M., Kim, T.-W., Moir, R. D., Guenette, S. Y., & Wasco, W. (1996). The presenilin genes and their role in early-onset familial Alzheimer's disease. *Alzheimer's Disease Review, 1,* 91–98.

Tarasoff v. Regents of the University of California et al., Cal. Rep., 14, 551 Pg., 2d, 334 (1976).

Taylor, S., Kuch, K., Koch, W. J., Crockett, D. J., & Passey, G. (1998). The structure of post-traumatic stress syndrome. *Journal of Abnormal Psychology, 107,* 154–160.

Taylor, S. E., Repetti, R. L., & Seeman, T. (1997). Health psychology: What is an unhealthy environment and how does it get under the skin? *Annual Review of Psychology, 48,* 411–447.

Teicher, M. H., Glod, C., & Cole, J. O. (1990). Emergence of intense suicide preoccupation during fluoxetine treatment. *American Journal of Psychiatry, 147,* 207–210.

Terr, L. C. (1991). Childhood traumas: An outline and overview. *American Journal of Psychiatry, 148,* 10–20.

Thaker, G. K., Cassady, S., Adami, H., Moran, M., & Ross, D. E. (1996). Eye movements in spectrum personality disorders: Comparison of community subjects and relatives of schizophrenic patients. *American Journal of Psychiatry, 153,* 362–368.

Thase, M. E., & Kupfer, D. J. (1996). Recent developments in the pharmacotherapy of mood disorders. *Journal of Consulting and Clinical Psychology, 64,* 646–659.

Thase, M. E., Reynolds, C. F., Frank, E., & Simons, A. D. (1994). Response to cognitive-behavioral therapy in chronic depression. *Journal of Psychotherapy Practice and Research, 3,* 204–214.

Thigpen, C. H., & Cleckley, H. M. (1957). *The three faces of Eve.* New York: McGraw-Hill.

Thomas, A. M., & LoPiccolo, J. (1994). Sexual functioning in persons with diabetes: Issues in research, treatment, and education. *Clinical Psychology Review, 14,* 61–85.

Thorndike, R. L., Hagen, E. P. & Sattler, J. M. (1986a). *Guide for administering and scoring the Fourth Edition Stanford-Binet Intelligence Scale.* Chicago: Riverside.

Thorndike, R. L., Hagen, E. P. & Sattler, J. M. (1986b). *Technical manual for the Stanford-Binet: Fourth Edition.* Chicago: Riverside.

Tienari, P. (1991). Interaction between genetic vulnerability and family environment: The Finnish adoptive family study of schizophrenia. *Acta Psychiatrica Scandinavica, 84,* 460–465.

Tienari, P., Lahti, I., Sorri, A., Naarala, M., Moring, J., & Wahlberg, K. (1989). The Finnish Adoptive Family Study of Schizophrenia: Possible joint effects of genetic vulnerability and family environment. *British Journal of Psychiatry, 155,* 29–32.

Tienari, P., Sorri, A., Lahti, I., Naarala, M., Wahlberg, K. E., Moring, J., Pohjola, J., & Wynne, L. C. (1987). Genetic and psychosocial factors in schizophrenia: The Finnish Adoptive Family Study. *Schizophrenia Bulletin, 13,* 477–484.

Tiihonen, J., Katila, H., Pekkonen, E., Jaaskelainen, I. P., Huotilainen, M., Aronen, H. J., Ilmoniemi, R. J., Rasanen, P., Virtanen, J., Salli, E., & Karhu, J. (1998). Reversal of cerebral asymmetry in schizophrenia measured with magnetoencephalography. *Schizophrenia Research, 30,* 209–219.

Tiihonen, J., Ryynänen, O.-P., Kauhanen, J., Hakola, H. P. A., & Salaspuro, M. (1996). Citalopram in the treatment of alcoholism: A double-blind placebo-controlled study. *Pharmacopsychiatry, 29,* 27–29.

Timmons, M. J., Chandler-Holtz, D., & Semple, W. E. (1996). Post-traumatic stress symptoms in mothers following children's reports of sexual abuse: An exploratory study. *American Journal of Orthopsychiatry, 66,* 463–467.

Tinsley, J. A., Finlayson, R. E., & Morse, R. M. (1998). Developments in the treatment of alcoholism. *Mayo Clinic Proceedings, 73,* 857–863.

Tolin, D. F., Lohr, J. M., Sawchuk, C. N., & Lee, T. C. (1997). Disgust and disgust sensitivity in blood-injection-injury and spider phobia. *Behaviour Research & Therapy, 35,* 949–953.

Tomac, T. A., Rummans, T. A., Pileggi, T. S., & Li, H. (1997). Safety and efficacy of electroconvulsive therapy in patients over age 85. *American Journal of Geriatric Psychiatry, 5,* 126–130.

Tomasson, K., Kent, D., & Coryell, W. (1991). Somatization and conversion disorders: Comorbidity and demographics at presentation. *Acta Psychiatrica Scandinavica, 84,* 288–293.

Torgerson, S. (1985). Relationship of schizotypal personality disorder to schizophrenia: Genetics. *Schizophrenia Bulletin, 11,* 554–563.

Torgerson, S. (1986). Genetic factors in moderately severe and mild affective disorders. *Archives of General Psychiatry, 43,* 222–226.

Torrey, E. F. (1995). *Surviving schizophrenia: A manual for families, consumers, and providers* (3rd ed.). New York: Free Press.

Trask, P. C., & Sigmon, S. T. (1997). Munchausen syndrome: A review and new conceptualization. *Clinical Psychology-Science and Practice, 4,* 346–358.

Treffert, D. (1989). *Extraordinary people: Understanding "idiot savants."* New York: Harper & Row.

Treffert, D. A. (1988). The idiot savant: A review of the syndrome. *American Journal of Psychiatry, 145,* 563–572.

Troop, N. A., Holbrey, A., Trowler, R., & Treasure, J. L. (1994). Ways of coping in women with eating disorders. *Journal of Nervous and Mental Disease, 182,* 535–540.

Tross, S., Herndon, J., 2nd, Korzun, A., Kornblith, A. B., Cella, D. F., Holland, J. F., Raich, P., Johnson, A., Kiang, D. T., Perloff, M., Norton, L., Wood, W., & Holland, J. C. (1996). Psychological symptons and disease-free and overall survival in women with stage II breast cancer. Cancer and Leukemia Group B. *Journal of the National Cancer Institute, 88,* 661–667.

Truax, C. B., & Carkhuff, R. (1967). *Toward effective counseling and psychotherapy: Training and practice.* Chicago: Aldine.

True, W. R., Rice, J., Eisen, S. A., Heath, A. C., Goldberg, J., Lyons, M. J., & Nowak, J. (1993). A twin study of genetic and environmental contributions to liability for post-traumatic stress symptoms. *Archives of General Psychiatry, 50,* 257–264.

Trzepacz, P. T., & Baker, R. W. (1993). *The psychiatric mental status examination.* New York: Oxford University Press.

Tuma, A. H., & Maser, J. (Eds.). (1985). *Anxiety and the anxiety disorders.* Hillsdale, NJ: Erlbaum.

Turk, D. C. (1994). Perspectives on chronic pain: The role of psychological factors. *Current Directions in Psychological Science, 3,* 45–48.

Turkheimer, E., & Parry, C. D. H. (1994). Why the gap? Practice and policy in civil commitment hearings. *American Psychologist, 47,* 646–655.

Turner, R. J., & Wagonfeld, M. O. (1963). Occupational mobility and schizophrenia. *American Sociological Review, 32,* 104–113.

Turnquist, K. (1993). Second-trimester markers of fetal size in schizophrenia. *American Journal of Psychiatry, 150,* 1571–1572.

Tyrka, A. R., Cannon, T. D., Haslam, N., Mednick, S. A., Schulsinger, F., Schulsinger, H., & Parnas, J. (1995). The latent structure of schizotypy: I. Premorbid indicators of a taxon of individuals at risk for schizophrenia-spectrum disorders. *Journal of Abnormal Psychology, 104,* 173–183.

U

Uhde, T. W., Tancer, M. E., Black, B., & Brown, T. M. (1991) Phenomenology and neurobiology of social phobia: Comparison with panic disorder. *Journal of Clinical Psychiatry, 52,* 31–40.

Ullman, L. P., & Krasner, L. (1975). *A psychological approach to abnormal behavior* (2nd ed.). Englewood Cliffs, NJ: Prentice-Hall.

U.S. Department of Commerce (1989). *Statistical Abstracts of the United States* (109th ed.). Washington, DC: U.S. Government Printing Office.

V

Vaillant, G. E. (1994). Ego mechanisms of defense and personality psychopathology. *Journal of Abnormal Psychology, 103,* 44–50.

VanBremen, J. R., & Chasnoff, I. J. (1994). Policy issues for integrating parenting interventions and addition treatment for women. *National Association for Perinatal Addiction Research and Education, 14,* 254–274.

Vandenbergh, D. J., Rodriguez, L. A., Miller, I. T., Uhl, G. R., & Lachman, H. M. (1997). High-activity catechol-O-methyltransferase allele is more prevalent in polysubstance abusers. *American Journal of Medical Genetics, 74,* 439–442.

van der Hart, O., Boon, S., & Heijtmajer Jansen, O. (1997). Ritual abuse in European countries: A clinician's perspective. In A. F. George (Ed.), *The dilemma of ritual abuse: Cautions and guides for therapists. Clinical practice, No. 41* (pp. 137–163). Washington, DC: American Psychiatric Press.

van der Kolk, B. A. (1997). The psycho-biology of post-traumatic stress disorder. *Journal of Clinical Psychiatry, 58,* 16–24.

VanManen, K. J., & Whitbourne, S. K. (1997). Psychosocial development and life experiences in adulthood: A 22-year sequential study. *Psychology and Aging, 12,* 239–246.

van Os, J., & Selten, J. P. (1998). Prenatal exposure to maternal stress and subsequent schizophrenia. The May 1940 invasion of The Netherlands. *British Journal of Psychiatry, 172,* 324–326.

Vaughn, C. E., & Leff, J. P. (1976). The influence of family and social factors on the course of psychiatric illness: A comparison of schizophrenic with depressed neurotic patients. *British Journal of Psychiatry, 129,* 125–137.

Vaughn, C. E., Snyder, K. S., Jones, S., Freeman, W. B., & Falloon, I. R. (1984). Family factors in schizophrenic relapse. *Archives of General Psychiatry, 41,* 1169–1177.

Veale, D., Boocock, A., Gournay, K., & Dryden, W. (1996). Body dysmorphic disorder: A survey of fifty cases. *British Journal of Psychiatry, 169,* 196–201.

Velden, M. (1997). The heritability of intelligence: Neither known nor unknown. *American Psychologist, 52,* 72–73.

Verrier, R. L., & Mittleman, M. A. (1996). Life-threatening cardiovascular consequences of anger in patients with coronary heart disease. *Cardiology Clinics, 14,* 289–307.

Viola, J. M., Hicks, R., & Porter, T. (1993). Gulf War veterans with PTSD. *Military Medicine, 158,* A4.

Virkkunen, M., Eggert, M., Rawlings, R., & Linnoila, M. (1996). A prospective follow-up study of alcoholic violent offenders and firesetters. *Archives of General Psychiatry, 53,* 523–529.

Virkkunen, M., Goldman, D., Nielsen, D. A., & Linnoila, M. (1995). Low brain serotonin turnover rate (low CSF 5-HIAA) and impulsive violence. *Journal of Psychiatry and Neuroscience, 20,* 271–275.

Volberg, R. A. (1994). The prevalence and demographics of pathological gamblers: Implications for public health. *American Journal of Public Health, 84,* 237–241.

Volpicelli, J. R., Watson, N. T., King, A. C., Sherman, C. E., & O'Brien, C. P. (1995). Effect of naltrexone on alcohol "high" in alcoholics. *American Journal of Psychiatry, 152,* 613–615.

W

Wachtel, P. L. (1977). *Psychoanalysis and behavior therapy: Toward an integration.* New York: Basic Books.

Wachtel, P. L. (1997). *Psychoanalysis, behavior therapy, and the relational world.* Washington, DC: American Psychological Association.

Wagner, A., & Linehan, M. (1997). Biosocial perspective on the relationship of childhood sexual abuse, suicidal behavior, and borderline personality disorder. In M. Zanarini (Ed.), *Role of sexual abuse in the etiology of borderline personality disorder. Progress in psychiatry, No. 49* (pp. 203–244). Washington, DC: American Psychiatric Press.

Wagner, A. W., & Linehan, M. M. (1994). Relationship between childhood sexual abuse and topography of parasuicide among women with borderline personality disorder. *Journal of Personality Disorders, 8,* 1–9.

Wahlberg, K. E., Wynne, L. C., Oja, H., Keskitalo, P., Pykäläinen, L., Lahti, I., Moring, J., Naarala, M., Sorri, A., Seitamaa, M., Laksy, K., Kolassa, J., & Tienari, P. (1997). Gene-environment interaction in vulnerability to schizophrenia: Findings from the Finnish Adoptive Family Study of Schizophrenia. *American Journal of Psychiatry, 154,* 355–362.

Wallace, S. T., & Alden, L. E. (1997). Social phobia and positive social events: The price of success. *Journal of Abnormal Psychology, 106,* 416–424.

Waller, G. (1994). Childhood sexual abuse and borderline personality disorder in the eating disorders. *Child Abuse and Neglect, 10,* 97–101.

Walsh, J. J., Eysenck, M. W., Wilding, J., & Valentine, J. (1994). Type A, neuroticism, and physiological functioning (actual and reported). *Personality and Individual Differences, 16,* 959–965.

Walters, E. E., & Kendler, K. S. (1995). Anorexia nervosa and anorexic-like syndromes in a population-based female twin sample. *American Journal of Psychiatry, 152,* 64–71.

Wandersman, A., & Nation, M. (1998). Urban neighborhoods and mental health: Psychological contributions to understanding toxicity, resilience, and interventions. *American Psychologist, 53,* 647–656.

Wang, S., Sun, C. E., Walczak, C. A., Ziegle, J. S., Kipps, B. R., Goldin, L. R., & Diehl, S. R. (1995). Evidence for a susceptibility locus for schizophrenia on chromosome 6pter-p22. *Nature Genetics, 10,* 41–46.

Warner, L. A., Koester, R. C., Hughes, M., Anthony, J. C., & Nelson, C. B. (1995). Prevalence and correlates of drug use and dependence in the United States. Results from the National Comorbidity Survey. *Archives of General Psychiatry, 52,* 219–229.

Warren, S. L., Huston, L., Egeland, B., & Sroufe, L. A. (1997). Child and adolescent anxiety disorders and early attachment. *Journal of the American Academy of Child and Adolescent Psychiatry, 36,* 637–644.

Wasylenki, D. A. (1992). Psychotherapy of schizophrenia revisited. *Hospital and Community Psychiatry, 43,* 123–127.

Waters, E., Wippman, J., & Sroufe, L. A. (1979). Attachment, positive effect, and competence in the peer group: Two studies in construct validation. *Child Development, 50,* 821–829.

Watkins, C. E., Campbell, V. L., Nieberding, R., & Hallmark, R. (1995). Contemporary practice of psychological assessment by clinical psychologists. *Professional Psychology: Research and Practice, 26,* 54–60.

Watkins, J. G. (1984). The Bianchi (L. A. Hillside Strangler) case: Sociopath or multiple personality? *International Journal of Clinical Experimental Hypnosis, 32,* 67–101.

Webb, N. B., Sakheim, G. A., Towns-Miranda, L., & Wagner, C. R. (1990). Collaborative treatment of juvenile firesetters: Assessment and outreach. *American Journal of Orthopsychiatry, 60,* 305–310.

Wechsler, D. (1989). *Wechsler Preschool and Primary Scale of Intelligence-Revised.* San Antonio, TX: Psychological Corporation.

Wechsler, D. (1991). *Wechsler Intelligence Scale for Children-Third Edition.* San Antonio, TX: Psychological Corporation.

Wechsler, D. (1997). *Wechsler Adult Intelligence Scale-Third Edition.* San Antonio, TX: Psychological Corporation.

Weine, S. M., Becker, D. F., McGlashan, T. H., Laub, D., Lazrove, S., Vojvoda, D., Hyman, L. (1995). Psychiatric consequences of "ethnic cleansing": Clinical assessments and trauma testimonies of newly resettled Bosnian refugees. *American Journal of Psychiatry, 152,* 536–542.

Weintraub, S. (1987). Risk factors in schizophrenia: The Stony Brook high-risk project. *Schizophrenia Bulletin, 13,* 439–450.

Weisenberg, M. (1998). Cognitive aspects of pain and pain control. *International Journal of Clinical and Experimental Hypnosis, 46,* 44–61.

Weisman, A. G., Nuechterlein, K. H., Goldstein, M. J., & Snyder, K. S. (1998). Expressed emotion, attributions, and schizophrenia symptom dimensions. *Journal of Abnormal Psychology, 107,* 355–359.

Weissberg, J. H., & Levay, A. N. (1986). Compulsive sexual behavior. *Medical Aspects of Human Sexuality, 20,* 129–130.

Weissman, M. M. (1990). The hidden patient: Unrecognized panic disorder. *Journal of Clinical Psychiatry, 51, 5–8.*

Weissman, M. M. (1993). The epidemiology of personality disorders: A 1990 update. *Journal of Personality Disorders, 7* (Supplement, Spring), 44–62.

Weissman, M. M., Bland, R. C., Canino, G. J., Faravelli, C., Greenwald, S., Hwu, H. G., Joyce, P. R., Karam, E. G., Lee, C. K., Lellouch, J., Lepine, J. P., Newman, S. C., Oakley-Browne, M. A., Rubio-Stipec, M., Wells, J. E., Wickramaratne, P. J., Wittchen, H. U., & Yeh, E. K. (1997). The cross-national epidemiology of panic disorder. *Archives of General Psychiatry, 54,* 305–309.

Weissman, M. M., Bland, R. C., Canino, G. J., Greenwald, S., Lee, C. K., Newman, S. C., Rubio-Stipec, M., & Wickramaratne, P. J. (1996). The cross-national epidemiology of social phobia: A preliminary report. *International Clinical Psychopharmacology, 3,* 9–14.

Weissman, M. M., Klerman, G. L., Markowitz, J. S., Ouellette, R., & Phil, M. (1989). Suicidal ideation and suicide attempts in panic disorder and attacks. *New England Journal of Medicine, 321,* 1209–1214.

Weissman, M. M., & Markowitz, J. C. (1994). Interpersonal psychotherapy: Current status. *Archives of General Psychiatry, 51* (Suppl.), 599–606.

Weisz, J. R., Weiss, B., Han, S. S., Granger, D. A., & Morton, T. (1994). Effects of psychotherapy with children and adolescents revisited: A meta-analysis of treatment outcome studies. *Psychological Bulletin, 117,* 450–468.

Wells, C. E. (1979). Pseudodementia. *American Journal of Psychiatry, 136,* 895–900.

Wender, P. H., Kety, S. S., Rosenthal, D., Shulsinger, F., Ortmann, J., & Lunde, I. (1986). Psychiatric disorders in the biological and adoptive families of adopted individuals with affective disorders. *Archives of General Psychiatry, 43,* 923–939.

Wender, P. H., Rosenthal, D., Kety, S. S., Schulsinger, F., & Welner, J. (1974). Cross-fostering: A research strategy for clarifying the role of genetic and experimental factors in the etiology of schizophrenia. *Archives of General Psychiatry, 30,* 121–128.

West, L., Mercer, S. O., & Altheimer, E. (1993). Operation Desert Storm: The response of a social work outreach team. *Social Work in Health Care, 19,* 81–98.

West, M., & Sheldon, A. E. R. (1988). Classification of pathological attachment patterns in adults. *Journal of Personality Disorders, 2,* 153–159.

Westen, D., & Cohen, R. P. (1993). The self in borderline personality disorder: A psychodynamic perspective. In Z. V. Segal & S. J. Blatt (Eds.), *The self in emotional distress: Cognitive and psychodynamic perspectives* (pp. 334–368). New York: Guilford Press.

Westen, D. (1991a). Clinical assessment of object relations using the TAT. *Journal of Personality Assessment, 56,* 56–74.

Westen, D. (1991b). Social cognition and object relations. *Psychological Bulletin, 109,* 429–455.

Westen, D., Lohr, N. E., Silk, K., & Kerber, K. (1991). *Measuring object relations and social cognition using the TAT: Scoring manual* (Vol. 2). Ann Arbor: University of Michigan.

Whitbourne, S. K. (in press). *The psychology of adult development and aging.* New York: Wiley.

Whitbourne, S. K., Zuschlag, M. K., Elliot, L. B., & Waterman, A. S. (1992). Psychosocial development in adulthood: A 22-year sequential study. *Journal of Personality and Social Psychology, 63,* 260–271.

White, L., Petrovitch, H., Ross, G. W., Masaki, K. H., Abbott, R. D., Teng, E. L., Rodriguez, B. L., Blanchette, P. L., Havlik, R. J., Wergowske, G., Chiu, D., Foley, D. J., Murdaugh, C., & Curb, J. D. (1996). Prevalence of dementia in older Japanese-American men in Hawaii: The Honolulu-Asia Aging Study. *Journal of the American Medical Association, 276,* 955–960.

Whiteman, M. C., Fowkes, F. G., Deary, I. J., & Lee, A. J. (1997). Hostility, cigarette smoking and alcohol consumption in the general population. *Social Science and Medicine, 44,* 1089–1096.

Wible, C. G., Shenton, M. E., Hokama, H., Kikinis, R., Jolesz, F. A., Metcalf, D., & McCarley, R. W. (1995). Prefrontal cortex and schizophrenia. A quantitative magnetic resonance imaging study. *Archives of General Psychiatry, 52,* 279–288.

Widiger, T. A. (1998). Murray: A challenging case of antisocial personality disorder. In R. P. Halgin & S. K. Whitbourne (Eds.), *A casebook in abnormal psychology: From the files of experts* (pp. 24–36). New York: Oxford University Press.

Widiger, T. A., & Corbitt, E. M. (1995). Are personality disorders well-classified in DSM-IV? In W. J. Livesley (Ed.), *The DSM-IV personality disorders* (pp. 103–126). New York: Guilford Press.

Widiger, T. A., & Shea, T. (1991). Differentiation of Axis I and Axis II disorders. *Journal of Abnormal Psychology, 100,* 399–406.

Wilbur, C. B., & Kluft, R. P. (1989). Multiple personality disorder. In T. B. Karasu (Ed.), *Treatment of psychiatric disorders* (pp. 2197–2216). Washington, DC: American Psychiatric Association.

Wilhelm, S., McNally, R. J., Baer, L., & Florin, I. (1997). Autobiographical memory in obsessive-compulsive disorder. *British Journal of Clinical Psychology, 36,* 21–31.

Williamson, G. M., & Schulz, R. (1993). Coping with specific stressors in Alzheimer's disease caregiving. *Gerontologist, 33,* 747–755.

Wilson, G. T., & Fairburn, C. G. (1998). Treatments for eating disorders. In P. E. Nathan & J. M. Gorman (Eds.), *A guide to treatments that work* (pp. 501–530). New York: Oxford University Press.

Wilson, W. H., & Claussen, A. M. (1995). 18-month outcome of Clozapine treatment for 100 patients in a state psychiatric hospital. *Psychiatric Services, 46,* 386–389.

Winnicott, D. W. (1971). *Playing and reality.* Middlesex, England: Penguin.

Winokur, G., Black, D. W., & Nasrallah, A. (1988). Depressions secondary to other psychiatric disorders and medical illnesses. *American Journal of Psychiatry, 145,* 233–237.

Winokur, G., Coryell, W., Akiskal, H. S., Endicott, J., Keller, M., & Mueller, T. (1994). Manic-depressive (bipolar) disorder: The course in light of a prospective ten-year follow-up of 131 patients. *Acta Psychiatrica Scandinavica, 89,* 102–110.

Winokur, G., Coryell, W., Keller, M., Endicott, J., & Leon, A. (1995). A family study of manic-depressive (bipolar I) disease. *Archives of General Psychiatry, 52,* 367–373.

Winston, A., Laikin, M., Pollack, J., Samstag, L. W., McCullough, L., & Muran, J. C. (1994). Short-term psychotherapy of personality disorders. *American Journal of Psychiatry, 151,* 190–194.

Winston, A., Pollack, J., McCullough, L., Flegenheimber, W., Kestenbaum, R., & Trujillo, M. (1991). Brief psychotherapy of personality disorders. *Journal of Nervous and Mental Disease, 179,* 188–193.

Wisniewski, H. M., Wegiel, J., & Kotula, L. (1996). Some neuropathological aspects of Alzheimer's disease and its relevance to other disciplines. *Neuropathology and Applied Neurobiology, 22,* 3–11.

Wittchen, H. U., & Beloch, E. (1996). The impact of social phobia on quality of life. *International Clinical Psychopharmacology, 3,* 15–23.

Wittchen, H. U., Kessler, R. C., Zhao, S., & Abelson, J. (1995). Reliability and clinical validity of UM-CIDI DSM-III-R generalized anxiety disorder. *Journal of Psychiatric Research, 29,* 95–110.

Wittchen, H. U., Zhao, S., Kessler, R. C., & Eaton, W. W. (1994). DSM-III-R generalized anxiety disorder in the National Comorbidity Survey. *Archives of General Psychiatry, 51,* 355–364.

Woititz, J. G. (1983). *Adult children of alcoholics.* Deerfield Beach, FL: Health Communications.

Wolkin, A., Rusinek, H., Vaid, G., Arena, L., Lafargue, T., Sanfilipo, M., Loneragan, C., Lautin, A., & Rotrosen, J. (1998). Structural magnetic resonance image averaging in schizophrenia. *American Journal of Psychiatry, 155,* 1064–1073.

Wolpe, J. (1958). *Psychotherapy by reciprocal inhibition.* Stanford: Stanford University Press.

Wolpe, J. (1973). *The practice of behavior therapy.* Elmsford, NY: Pergamon.

Wolpe, J., & Lang, J. (1977). *Manual for the Fear Survey Schedule.* San Diego: EdITS.

Woo, T.-U., Whitehead, R. E., Melchitsky, D. S., & Lewis, D. A. (1998). A subclass of prefrontal gamma-aminobutyric acid axon terminals are selectively altered in schizophrenia. *Proceedings of the National Academy of Sciences, 95,* 5341–5346.

Woodruff-Borden, J., Stanley, M. A., Lister, S. C., & Tabacchi, M. R. (1997). Nonclinical panic and suicidality: Prevalence and psychopathology. *Behaviour Research and Therapy, 35,* 109–116.

World Health Organization. (1997). *Composite International Diagnostic Interview (CID).*

Wyatt v. Stickney, 325 F. Supp. 781 (M.D. Ala. 1971); 344 F. Supp. (M.D. Ala. 1972).

Y

Yalisove, D. (1998). The origins and evolution of the disease concept of treatment. *Journal of Studies on Alcohol, 59,* 469–476.

Yalom, I. D. (1995). *The theory and practice of group psychotherapy* (4th ed.). New York: Basic Books.

Yee, A. H. (1997). Evading the controversy. *American Psychologist, 52,* 70–71.

Yirmiya, N., Solomonica-Levi, D., Shulman, C., & Pilowsky, T. (1996). Theory of mind abilities in individuals with autism, Down syndrome, and mental retardation of unknown etiology: The role of age and intelligence. *Journal of Child Psychology and Psychiatry and Allied Disciplines, 37,* 1003–1014.

Yonkers, K. A., Zlotnick, C., Allsworth, J., Warshaw, M., Shea, T., & Keller, M. B. (1998). Is the course of panic disorder the same in women and men? *American Journal of Psychiatry, 155,* 596–602.

Youngberg v. Romeo, 457 U.S. 307 (1982).

Z

Zametkin, A. J., & Rapoport, J. L. (1987). Neurobiology of attention deficit disorder with hyperactivity: Where have we come in 50 years? *Journal of the American Academy of Child and Adolescent Psychiatry, 26,* 676–686.

Zanarini, M. C., & Frankenburg, F. R. (1997). Pathways to the development of borderline personality disorder. *Journal of Personality Disorders, 11,* 93–104.

Zanarini, M.C., Williams, A. A., Lewis, R. E., Reich, R. B., Vera, S. C., Marino, M. F., Levin, A., Yong, L., & Frankenburg, F. R. (1997). Reported pathological childhood experiences associated with the development of borderline personality disorder. *American Journal of Psychiatry, 154,* 1101–1106.

Zarit, S.H., Todd, P. A., & Zarit, J. M. (1986). Subjective burden of husbands and wives as caregivers: A longitudinal study. *Gerontologist, 26,* 260–266.

Zatz, M., Melo, M. S., Passos-Bueno, M. R., Valada-Filho, H., Vieira-Filho, A. H. G., Vainzof, M., Rapaport, D., & Gentil-Filho, V. (1991). Association of schizophrenia and Becker dystrophy (BMD): A susceptibility locus for schizophrenia at Xp21 or an effect of the dystrophin gene on the brain? *American Journal of Human Genetics, 49,* 364.

Zatzick, D. F., Weiss, D. S., Marmar, C. R., Metzler, T. J., Wells, K., Golding, J. M., Stewart, A., Schlenger, W. E., & Browner, W. S. (1997). Post-traumatic stress disorder and functioning and quality of life outcomes in female Vietnam veterans. *Military Medicine, 162,* 661–665.

Zetterstrom, R. H., Solomin, L., Jansson, L., Hoffer, B. J., Olson, L., & Perlmann, T. (1997). Dopamine neuron agenesis in Nurr1-deficient mice. *Science, 276,* 248–250.

Zilbovicius, M., Garreau, B., Samson, Y., Remy, P., Barthelemy, C., Syrota, A., & Lelord, G. (1995). Delayed maturation of the frontal cortex in childhood autism. *American Journal of Psychiatry, 152,* 248–252.

Zimmerman, M. (1994). Diagnosing personality disorders: A review of issues and research methods. *Archives of General Psychiatry, 51,* 225–245.

Zinbarg, R. E., & Barlow, D. H. (1996). Structure of anxiety and the anxiety disorders: A hierarchical model. *Journal of Abnormal Psychology, 105,* 181–193.

Zoccolillo, M., Pickles, A., Quinton, D., & Rutter, M. (1992). The outcome of childhood conduct disorder: Implications for defining antisocial personality disorder and conduct disorder. *Psychological Medicine, 22,* 971–986.

Zohar, A. H., & Bruno, R. (1997). Normative and pathological obsessive-compulsive behavior and ideation in childhood: A question of timing. *Journal of Child Psychology and Psychiatry & Allied Disciplines, 38,* 993–999.

Zohar, A. H., Pauls, D. L., Ratzoni, G., Apter, A., Dycian, A., Binder, M., King, R., Lockman, J. F., Kron, S., & Cohen, D. J. (1997). Obsessive-compulsive disorder with and without tics in an epidemiological sample of adolescents. *American Journal of Psychiatry, 154,* 274–276.

Zubin, J., & Spring, B. (1977). Vulnerability—A new view of schizophrenia. *Journal of Abnormal Psychology, 86,* 103–126.

Zuschlag, M. K., & Whitbourne, S. K. (1994). Psychosocial development in three generations of college students. *Journal of Youth and Adolescence, 23,* 567–577.

Zucker, R. A., & Gomberg, E. S. L. (1986). Etiology of alcoholism reconsidered: The case for biopsychosocial process. *American Psychologist, 41,* 783–793.

Credits

Line Art

Chapter 1

Figure 1.4 From J. S. Bailey, N. M. Hutchinson, & H. A. Murphy, *Journal of Applied Behavior Analysis, 16*: 33. Copyright © 1983. Used by permission of the Journal of Applied Behavior Analysis, and the author.

Chapter 3

Table 3.2 From *Composite International Diagnostic Interview.* Copyright © 1997. Used by permission of World Health Organization.

Chapter 4

Table 4.2 Hazan, C. & Shaver P. R., "Attachment as an organizational framework for research on close relationships," *Psychological Inquiry, 5,* 1994, pp. 1-22. Copyright © 1994. Used by permission of Lawrence Erlbaum Associates, Inc., and the author.
Table 4.3 A. Jones and R. Crandall, "Validation of a short index of self-actualization," in *Personality and Social Psychology Bulletin, 12*: 63-73. Copyright © 1986. Used by permission of Sage Publications, Inc.
Table 4.5 Adapted from A. Ellis, "The impossibility of achieving consistently good mental health," *American Psychologist, 42,* 1987, pp. 364-375. Copyright © 1987 by the American Psychological Association. Adapted by permission. **Figure 4.1** From CHILDHOOD AND SOCIETY by Erik H. Erikson. Copyright 1950, © 1963 by W. W. Norton & Company, Inc., renewed © 1978, 1991 by Erik H. Erikson. Reprinted by permission of W. W. Norton & Company, Inc. **Figure 4.3** Adapted from A. T. Beck, A. J. Rush, B. F. Shaw, and G. Emery, *Cognitive therapy of depression.* Copyright © 1979. Used by permission of The Guilford Press.
Figure 4.4 Adapted from A. Ellis, "The impossibility of achieving consistently good mental health," *American Psychologist, 42,* 1987, pp. 364-375. Copyright © 1987 by the American Psychological Association. Adapted with permission.

Chapter 6

Table 6.1 A. H. Tuma & J. Maser (eds.), *Anxiety and the anxiety disorders.* Copyright © 1985. Used by permission of Lawrence Erlbaum Associates, Inc.
Table 6.4 A stylized version of W. K. Goodman, L. H. Price, S. A. Rasmussen, C. Mazure, P. Delgado, G. R. Heninger, & D. S. Charney, "The Yale-Brown Obsessive Compulsive Scale. I. Validity," *Archives of General Psychiatry, 46,* 1989a, pp. 1012-1016 used by permission of W. K. Goodman. Copies of the original Yale-Brown Obsessive Compulsive Scale can be obtained from Dr. Wayne Goodman, University of Florida, College of Medicine, Gainesville, FL 32610.
Figure 6.1 D. H. Barlow, "Long-term outcome for patients with panic disorder treated with cognitive-behavioral therapy," *Journal of Clinical Psychiatry, 51* (12, Suppl. A), pp. 17-23, 1990. Copyright 1990, Physicians Postgraduate Press. Reprinted by permission. **Figure 6.2** D. H. Barlow, "Long-term outcome for patients with panic disorder treated with cognitive-behavioral therapy," *Journal of Clinical Psychiatry, 51* (12, Suppl. A), pp. 17-23, 1990. Copyright 1990,

Physicians Postgraduate Press. Reprinted by permission. **Figure 6.3** From W. C. Sanderson and D. H. Barlow, "A description of patients diagnosed with DSM-III-R generalized anxiety disorder," *Journal of Nervous and Mental Disease, 178,* pp. 588-591. Copyright © 1990. Used by permission of Lippincott Williams & Wilkins.

Chapter 9

Table 9.2 From D. Neville and S. Barnes, "The Suicidal Phone Call," *Journal of Psychosocial Nursing and Mental Health Services, 23*: 14-18. Copyright © 1985. Used by permission of Slack, Inc.

Chapter 10

Figure 10.1 From: SCHIZOPHRENIC GENESIS by Gottesman © 1991 by Irving I. Gottesman. Used with permission by W. H. Freeman and Company.

Chapter 11

Table 11.1 FE. J. Mash & L. G. Terdal (eds.), *Behavioral assessment of childhood disorders,* 2/e, pp. 317-354. Copyright © 1988. Used by permission of The Guilford Press.

Chapter 12

Table 12.1 Reprinted with the permission of The Free Press, a Division of Simon & Schuster, Inc. from ALZHEIMER'S DISEASE: The Standard Reference edited by Barry Reisberg, M.D. Copyright © 1983 by Barry Reisberg, M.D. **Table 12.4** Republished with permission of the Gerontological Society of America, 1030 15th Street, NW, Suite 250, Washington, DC 20005. The Screen for Caregiver Burden (Table), P. P. Vitaliano et al., *The Gerontologist,* 1991, Vol. 31. Reproduced by permission of the publisher via Copyright Clearance Center, Inc.

Chapter 13

Figure 13.2 From G. A. Marlatt & J. R. Gordon, *Relapse prevention: Maintenance strategies in addictive behavior change.* Copyright © 1985. Used by permission of The Guilford Press. **Table 13.2** From H. M. Annis, *Inventory of Drinking Situations: Short Form.* Copyright © 1984. Used by permission of Centre for Addiction and Mental Health.

Chapter 14

Table 14.1 From L. Goldfarb, "The Goldfarb Fear of Fat Scale," *Journal of Personality Assessment, 49,* 1985, pp. 329-332. Copyright © 1985. Used by permission of Lawrence Erlbaum Associates, Inc., and the author.

Chapter 15

Table 15.1 Adapted from Committee on Professional Practice and Standards Board of Professional Affairs, *Guidelines for Psychological Evaluations in Child Protection Matters,* 1998. Copyright © 1998 by the American Psychological Association. Adapted with permission. **Table 15.2** Adapted from APA Presidential Task Force on the Assessment of Age-Consistent Memory Decline and Dementia, *Guidelines for the Evaluation of Dementia and Age-Related Cognitive Decline,* 1998. Copyright © 1998 by the American Psychological Association. Adapted with permission.

Photos

Chapter 1

CO 1 + TOC 1, © Michael Newman/PhotoEdit; p. 4, © PhotoEdit; p. 5, © Michael Newman/PhotoEdit; p. 6, © Bruce Wellman/Stock, Boston; p. 9, Published by permission of the National Museum of Denmark; p. 11, © Scala/Art Resource N.Y.; p. 12 top, Corbis/Bettmann; p. 12 bottom, © 1997 North Wind Picture Archive; p. 13, Stock Montage; p. 14 top, National Library of Medicine; p. 14 bottom, The Granger Collection; p. 15 bottom, The Granger Collection; p. 15 top, Wellcome Institute Library, London; p. 16, Corbis/Bettmann; p. 17, © Mark Greenberg and J. Ross Baughman/Envision; p. 18, © Ken Whitmore/Tony Stone Images; p. 21, Picture of Bio-Light, Courtesy of ENVIRO-MED, Vancouver, WA; p. 28, © Charles Votaw Photography.

Chapter 2

CO 2 + TOC 2, © Eric R. Berndt/Unicorn Stock Photos; p. 36, © B.W. Hoffmann/Unicorn Stock Photos; p. 40, Courtesy of Robert Spitzer; p. 41, © Peter Cade/Tony Stone Images; p. 46, © DJD Photography; p. 50, © PhotoEdit; p. 51, © Zigy Kaluzny/Tony Stone Images; p. 54, © Mary Kate Denny/PhotoEdit; p. 55, Courtesy McLean Hospital/Photo by Aerial Photos International, Inc.; p. 56 left, © D & I MacDonald/Unicorn Stock Photos; p. 56 top, © Michael Newman/PhotoEdit.

Chapter 3

CO 3 + TOC 3, © Roy Marsch/The Stock Market; p. 64, © Richard T. Nowitz/Photo Researchers, Inc.; p. 67, © Michael Newman/PhotoEdit; p. 69, © Bill Bachman/Photo Researchers; p. 74 top, © Steve Skjold; p. 74 bottom, © Paul Conklin/PhotoEdit; p. 76, © Corbis Media; p. 84, © Rorschach Psychodiagnostic; p. 86, Reprinted by permission of the publisher from Henry A. Murray, THEMATIC APPERCEPTION TEST, Cambridge, Mass.: Harvard University Press, Copyright © 1943 by the President and Fellows of Harvard College, © 1971 by Henry A. Murray; p. 87, © Richard Phelps Frieman/Photo Researchers, Inc.; p. 89 left, © Krishna Nayak/Supercomputer Computations Research Institute, Florida State University, Copyright 1995; p. 89 right, © Scott Camazine/Photo Researchers, Inc.; p. 90, © Simon Fraser/Department of Neuroradiology/Newcastle General Hospital/SPL/Photo Researchers, Inc.; p. 91 top, © Marcus E. Raichle, MD, Washington University School of Medicine; p. 91 bottom, © Will and Deni McIntyre/Photo Researchers.

Chapter 4

CO 4 + TOC 4, Corel Photo CD; p. 98, Freud Museum, London; p. 99, © James Newberry; p. 103, Digital Image © Corbis Media/Laura Dwight; p. 105 left, Digital Image © ChromoSohm Inc./Corbis; p. 105 right, Hulton-Deutsch Collection/Corbis Media; p. 107 bottom, © Ewing Galloway; p. 107 top, Johns Hopkins University; p. 109 top left, Digital Image © Corbis Media/Laura

Collection/Corbis Media; **p. 107 bottom,** © Ewing Galloway; **p. 107 top,** Johns Hopkins University; **p. 109 top left,** Digital Image © Corbis Media/Laura Dwight; **p. 109,** A. Lincoln, Stock Montage; **p. 109,** H. Tubman, Corbis/Bettmann; **p. 109,** M.L. King, © Ernst Haas/ Tony Stone Images; **p. 109,** Mother Theresa, Corbis/ Bettmann; **p. 113,** © Jeff Greenberg/Index Stock Imagery; **p. 115,** © Merritt Vincent/PhotoEdit; **p. 116,** © Christopher Johnson/ Stock Boston; **p. 118,** © Elizabeth Crews/The Image Works; **p. 121,** © James Newberry; **p. 123,** CNRI/SPL/ Photo Researchers; **p. 125,** © James King-Holmes/ SPL/Photo Researchers, Inc.; **p. 130,** © Will and Deni McIntyre/Photo Researchers.

Chapter 5

CO 5 + TOC 5, © Frank Siteman/Index Stock Imagery; **p. 141,** Corbis-Bettmann; **p. 142,** © Ronald Lopez/Unicorn Stock Photos; **p. 144,** Warner Brothers/Shooting Star © All Rights Reserved; **p. 145,** © A. Ramey/PhotoEdit; **p. 147,** Paramount/Shooting Star © All Rights Reserved; **p. 149,** Superstock; **p. 150,** © Judy Allen; **p. 151,** © R. P. Kingston/Index Stock Imagery; **p. 152,** © Pam Hasegawa; **p. 157 top,** © Sylvain Grandadam/Photo Researchers; **p. 157 bottom,** Innervisions; **p. 159,** © James Newberry.

Chapter 6

CO 6 + TOC 6, Corel Photo CD; **p. 172,** © Alex Webb/Magnum; **p. 173,** © Ted Russell/The Image Bank/Texas; **p. 175,** © Dennis Barnes; **p. 177,** © Neal and Molly Jansen; **p. 179,** © Pablo Corral V/Corbis Media; **p. 183,** © Eric R. Berndt/Unicorn Stock Photos; **p. 186,** Shooting Star; **p. 187,** Archives of General Psychiatry, Vol. 44, pages 211-218, copyright 1987, Dr. Lewis Baxter, American Medical Association; **p. 193 top,** AP/Wide World Photos; **p. 193 bottom,** © Jim Hays/Unicorn Stock Photo; **p. 195,** © Jeremy Davies, Dreamworks/ Shooting Star © All Rights Reserved.

Chapter 7

CO 7 + TOC 7, © Richard Abarno/The Stock Market; **p. 206,** © David Madison/Tony Stone Images; **p. 207,** © Sigmund Freud Copyrights/Mary Evans Picture Library; **p. 210,** © DJD Photography; **p. 212,** © James Newberry; **p. 216,** © Michael J. Okoniewski; **p. 217,** © Myrleen Ferguson Cate/ PhotoEdit; **p. 220 top,** © DJD Photography; **p. 220 bottom,** © D. L. Baldwin/Photo Network; **p. 224,** © Dan McCoy/Rainbow; **p. 225,** © David Frazier PhotoLibrary CD; **p. 226,** Adapted with permission of Allyn & Bacon from D. Meichenbaum *Stress noculation.* Copyright © 1985; **p. 227,** Post-Crescent/ Gamma Liaison; **p. 229,** © Ann Woelfle Bater/Unicorn Stock Photos; **p. 231 top,** Innervisions; **p. 231 bottom,** Digital Image © ChromoSohm Inc./Corbis; **p. 234,** © Martin/ Custom Medical Stock Photo.

Chapter 8

CO 8 + TOC 8, © Elizabeth Holmes/Omni Photo Communications; **p. 242,** © Charles Votraw Photography; **p. 244,** © DJD Photography; **p. 248,** © Harry Wilkes/Stock Boston; **p. 250,** © Robert Brenner/PhotoEdit; **p. 251,** © David Young-Wolff/PhotoEdit; **p. 252,** Innervisions; **p. 255,** Corbis/ Bettmann; **p. 259 left,** © Patrick Watson/Image Works; **p. 259 right,** © Patrick Watson/Image Works; **p. 265,** © David Young Wolff/PhotoEdit; **p. 260,** © Chuck Mason/International Stock.

Chapter 9

CO 9 + TOC 9, Corel Photo CD; **p. 278,** © SPL/ Photo Researchers, Inc.; **p. 280,** © Deneve Feigh Bunde/ Unicorn Stock Photos; **p. 281,** © Jeff Greenberg/ Unicorn Stock Photos; **p. 282,** © Culver Pictures; **p. 283 top,** Stedelijk Museum, Amsterdam, Holland/ Superstock; **p. 283 bottom,** Innervisions; **p. 286,** © Sobel/Klonksy/The Image Bank, Texas; **p. 287,** © Miwako Ikeda/International Stock; **p. 288,** © Bill Aron/PhotoEdit; **p. 290,** © F. Reischl/Unicorn Stock Photos; **p. 294,** © Will & Deni McIntyre/Photo Researchers; **p. 295 bottom,** © Eric Carle/Stock Boston; **p. 295 top,** © Michael Newman/ PhotoEdit; **p. 296,** © Michael Newman/ PhotoEdit; **p. 297,** AP/Wide World Photos, Inc.; **p. 300 top,** © Mary Kate Denny/PhotoEdit; **p. 300 bottom,** © Joel Gordon; **p. 301,** © R. Hutchings/ Photo Researchers.

Chapter 10

CO 10 + TOC 10, © Greg Greer/Unicorn Stock Photos; **p. 310,** Orlando Sentinel; **p. 312,** © Judy Allen; **p. 313 bottom,** © Grunnitus/Monkmeyer; **p. 313 top,** © Neal and Molly Jansen; **p. 315,** © Nik Kleinberg/Stock Boston; **p. 317 left,** © Nelson/Custom Medical Stock Photo; **p. 317 right,** © Dan McCoy/Rainbow; **p. 319,** © MacDonald Photography/Unicorn Stock Photos; **p. 323,** © DJD Photography; **p. 324,** © Judy Allen; **p. 328,** © Dan McCoy/Rainbow; **p. 329,** Courtesy of Monte S. Buchsbaum, M.D.; **p. 331,** © Judy Allen; **p. 333,** © Michael Newman/PhotoEdit.

Chapter 11

CO 11 + TOC 11, Digital Stock Photo CD; **p. 344,** © Camilla Smith/Rainbow; **p. 346 top,** Micrographs printed with permission: The National Fragile X Foundation, Denver, CO; **p. 346 bottom,** B. King/ Gamma Liaison; **p. 348,** Los Angeles Times Syndicate; **p. 349 top,** © Ellen B. Senisi/Photo Researchers; **p. 349 bottom,** © Paul Conklin/ Uniphoto; **p. 352,** © Bob Daemmrich; **p. 355,** © Al Cook; **p. 359,** © Michael Newman/ PhotoEdit; **p. 362,** AP/Wide World Photos.

Chapter 12

CO 12 + TOC 12, © Noblo Stock/International Stock; **p. 371,** © Mark Richards/PhotoEdit; **p. 374 top,** © John Griffin/The Image Works; **p. 374 bottom,** © Kay Ghernush/The Image Bank, Texas; **p. 377,** AP/Wide World Photos; **p. 378,** © Christopher Brown/Stock Boston; **p. 379 top,** Courtesy of Dr. William Jagust, Lawrence Berkeley Laboratory and University of California, Davis; **p. 379 bottom,** © Dan McCoy/Rainbow; **p. 381,** Courtesy of Dr. John Hardy and Dr. Dennis Dickson, "Science" Vol. 282, Nov. 6, 1998, p. 1076; **p. 382,** School Sisters of Notre Dame; **p. 383 top,** Courtesy Ronald Reagan Library; **p. 383 bottom,** © Kindra Clineff/Index Stock Imagery; **p. 385,** © Schmid-Langsfeld/The Image Bank, Texas.

Chapter 13

CO 13 + TOC 13, © Frank Pedrick/The Image Works; **p. 392,** © Dan McCoy; William McCoy/ Rainbow/PNI; **p. 394,** © Bachmann/Photo Network; **p. 396,** © Robert W. Ginn/Unicorn Stock Photos; **p. 397,** © Innervisions; **p. 402,** © Mary Kate Denny/PhotoEdit; **p. 408 top,** © Billy E. Barnes/ Transparencies, Inc.; **p. 408 bottom,** Courtesy Brookhaven National Laboratory; **p. 411,** © Mark M. Walker/Index Stock Imagery; **p. 413 top,** Drug Enforcement Agency; **p. 413 bottom,** Gamma Liasion.

Chapter 14

CO 14 + TOC 14, © Paul Sisul/Tony Stone Images; **p. 427 top,** © 1990 Custom Medical Stock Photo. All Rights Reserved; **p. 427 bottom,** © Esbin-Anderson/Omni-Photo Communications, Inc.; **p. 431,** © Superstock; **p. 434 top,** © Eric Berndt/ Unicorn Stock Photos; **p. 434 bottom,** AP/Wide World Photos; **p. 435,** © Robert Brenner/PhotoEdit; **p. 435,** From www.gamblersanonymous.org/20 questions.html Reprinted by permission of Gamblers Anonymous; **p. 438 top,** © Brad Bower/Stock, Boston; **p. 438 bottom,** © Miro Vintoniv/Stock, Boston; **p. 440,** © Walter Bibikow/The Image Bank, Chicago; **p. 441,** © Judy Allen; **p. 444,** © James Stirling/The Image Bank/PNI.

Chapter 15

CO 15 + TOC 15, Photo Disc; **p. 453,** © Walter Bibikow/The Image Bank, Texas; **p. 454 left,** AP/Wide World Photos, Inc.; **p. 454 right,** AP/Wide World Photos, Inc.; **p. 455,** AP/Wide World Photos; **p. 457,** © G & M David DeLossy/The Image Bank, Chicago; **p. 459,** © Gianfranco Gorgoni/Contact Press Images/PNI; **p. 461,** © Trippett/Sipa Press; **p. 462 both,** AP/Wide World Photos; **p. 464,** © Gregory Rec/Gamma Liaison; **p. 465,** © Dennis MacDonald/Unicorn Stock Photos.

Name Index

Note: Page numbers in *italics* indicate figures; page numbers followed by *t* indicate tables.

Subject Index

Note: Page numbers in *italics* indicate illustrations; page numbers followed by *t* indicate tables.

HUMAN BODY
REVEALED

Written by
DR. SUE DAVIDSON
AND BEN MORGAN

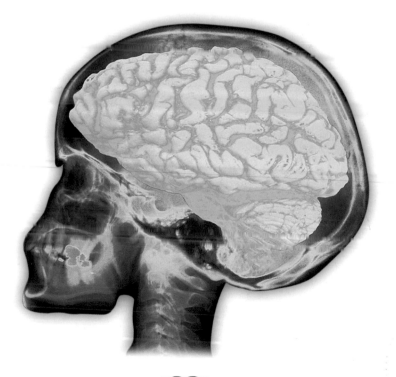

DK Publishing

LONDON, NEW YORK, MUNICH,
MELBOURNE, and DELHI

SENIOR EDITOR CAREY SCOTT
SENIOR ART EDITOR JOANNE CONNOR
PHOTOSHOP ILLUSTRATOR LEE GIBBONS
DESIGN ASSISTANT JOANNE LITTLE
CATEGORY PUBLISHER SUE GRABHAM
ART DIRECTOR GILLIAN ALLAN
PICTURE RESEARCHER SEAN HUNTER
JACKET DESIGNER CHRIS DREW
JACKET EDITOR BETH APPLE
DTP DESIGNER JILL BUNYAN
PRODUCTION CONTROLLER DULCIE ROWE

First American edition, 2002

02 03 04 05 10 9 8 7 6 5 4 3 2 1

Published in the United States by
DK Publishing, Inc.
375 Hudson Street
New York, NY 10014

DK Publishing offers special discounts for bulk purchases for sales
promotions or premiums. Specific, large-quantity needs can be met with
special editions, including personalized covers, excerpts of existing guides,
and corporate imprints. For more information, contact Special Markets
Department, DK Publishing, Inc., 375 Hudson Street, New York, NY 10014
Fax: 212-689-5254.

A Cataloging-in-Publication record is available from
the Library of Congress

ISBN 0-7894-8882-5

Color reproduction by
Colourscan, Singapore
Printed in China by
Leo Paper Products

See our complete
product line at
www.dk.com

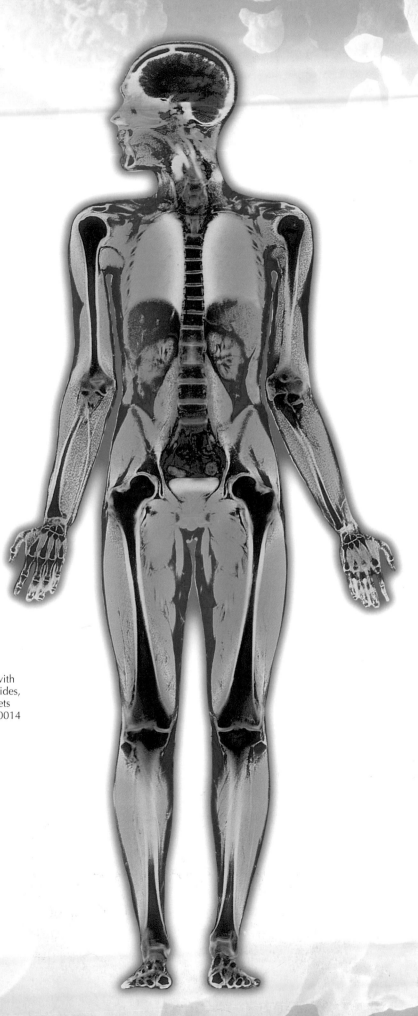